Peterson's® Two-Year Colleges 2021

About Peterson's®

Peterson's® has been your trusted educational publisher for over 50 years. It's a milestone we're quite proud of, as we continue to offer the most accurate, dependable, high-quality educational content in the field, providing you with everything you need to succeed. No matter where you are on your academic or professional path, you can rely on Peterson's for its books, online information, expert test-prep tools, the most up-to-date education exploration data, and the highest quality career success resources—everything you need to achieve your education goals. For our complete line of products, visit **www.petersons.com**.

For more information about Peterson's range of educational products, contact Peterson's, 4380 S. Syracuse Street, Suite 200, Denver, CO 80237, or find us online at **www.petersons.com**.

Previous editions published as *Peterson's Annual Guide to Undergraduate Study* © 1970, 1971, 1972, 1973, 1974, 1975, 1976, 1977, 1978, 1979, 1980, 1981, 1982 and as *Peterson's Two-Year Colleges* © 1983, 1984, 1985, 1986, 1987, 1988, 1989, 1990, 1991, 1992, 1993, 1994, 1995, 1996, 1997, 1998, 1999, 2000, 2001, 2002, 2003, 2004, 2005, 2006, 2007, 2008, 2009, 2010, 2011, 2012, 2013, 2014, 2015, 2016, 2017, 2018, 2019

ISSN 0894-9328
ISBN: 978-0-7689-4404-4

Printed in the United States of America

10 9 8 7 6 5 4 3 2 1 21 20

Fifty-first Edition

Contents

A Note from the Peterson's® Editors

For more than 50 years, Peterson's has given students and parents the most comprehensive, up-to-date information on undergraduate institutions in the United States. Peterson's researches the data published in *Peterson's Two-Year Colleges* each year. The information is furnished by the colleges and is accurate at the time of publishing.

This guide also features advice and tips on the college search and selection process, such as how to decide if a two-year college is right for you, how to approach transferring to another college, and what's in store for adults returning to college. If you seem to be getting more, not less, anxious about choosing and getting into the right college, *Peterson's Two-Year Colleges* provides just the right help, giving you the information you need to make important college decisions and ace the admission process.

Opportunities abound for students, and this guide can help you find what you want in a number of ways:

"What You Need to Know About Two-Year Colleges" outlines the basic features and advantages of two-year colleges. "Surviving Standardized Tests" gives an overview of the common examinations students take prior to attending college. "Who's Paying for This? Financial Aid Basics" provides guidelines for financing your college education. "Frequently Asked Questions About Transferring" takes a look at the two-year college scene from the perspective of a student who is looking toward the day when he or she may pursue additional education at a four-year institution. "Returning to School: Advice for Adult Students" is an analysis of the pros and cons (mostly pros) of returning to college after already having begun a professional career. "Coming to America: Tips for International Students Considering Study in the U.S." is an article written particularly for students overseas who are considering a U.S. college education. "Community Colleges and the Green Economy" offers information on some exciting "green" programs at community colleges throughout the United States, as well as two insightful essays by Mary F. T. Spilde, President, Lane Community College and Tom Sutton, Director of Wind Energy and Technical Services, Kalamazoo Valley Community College. Finally, "How to Use This Guide" gives details on the data in this guide: what terms mean and why they're here.

- If you already have specifics in mind, such as a particular institution or major, turn to the easy-to-use **Two-Year Colleges At-a-Glance Chart** or **Indexes.** You can look up a particular feature—location and programs offered—or use the alphabetical index and immediately find the colleges that meet your criteria.
- For information about particular colleges, turn to the **Profiles of Two-Year Colleges** section. Here, our comprehensive college profiles are arranged alphabetically by state. They provide a complete picture of need-to-know information about every accredited two-year college—from admission to graduation, including expenses, financial aid, majors, and campus safety. All the information you need to apply is placed together at the conclusion of each college **Profile.** Display ads, which appear near some of the institutions' profiles, have been provided and paid for by those colleges or universities that wished to supplement their profile data with additional information about their institution.
- In addition, two-page narrative descriptions, which appear in the **Featured Two-Year Colleges** section, are paid for and written by college officials and offer great detail about each college. They are edited to provide a consistent format across entries for your ease of comparison.

Peterson's publishes a full line of books—education exploration, test prep, financial aid, and career preparation. Peterson's publications can be found at high school guidance offices, college libraries and career centers, and your local bookstore and library. Peterson's books are also available at www.petersonsbooks.com.

We welcome any comments or suggestions you may have about this publication. Your feedback will help us make educational dreams possible for you—and others like you.

Colleges will be pleased to know that Peterson's helped you in your selection. Admissions staff members are more than happy to answer questions, address specific problems and help in any way they can. The editors at Peterson's wish you great success in your college search.

The College Admissions Process: An Overview

What You Need to Know About Two-Year Colleges

David R. Pierce

Two-year colleges—better known as community colleges—are often called "the people's colleges." With their open-door policies (admission is open to individuals with a high school diploma or its equivalent), community colleges provide access to higher education for millions of Americans who might otherwise be excluded from higher education. Community college students are diverse and of all ages, races, and economic backgrounds. While many community college students enroll full-time, an equally large number attend on a part-time basis so they can fulfill employment and family commitments as they advance their education.

Community colleges can also be referred to as either technical or junior colleges, and they may either be under public or independent control. What unites two-year colleges is that they are regionally accredited, postsecondary institutions, whose highest credential awarded is the associate degree. With few exceptions, community colleges offer a comprehensive curriculum, which includes transfer, technical, and continuing education programs.

IMPORTANT FACTORS IN A COMMUNITY COLLEGE EDUCATION

The student who attends a community college can count on receiving high-quality instruction in a supportive learning community. This setting frees the student to pursue his or her own goals, nurture special talents, explore new fields of learning, and develop the capacity for lifelong learning.

From the student's perspective, four characteristics capture the essence of community colleges:

1. They are community-based institutions that work in close partnership with high schools, community groups, and employers in extending high-quality programs at convenient times and places.
2. Community colleges are cost effective. Annual tuition and fees at public community colleges average approximately half those at public four-year colleges and less than 15 percent of private four-year institutions. In addition, since most community colleges are generally close to their students' homes, these students can also save a significant amount of money on the room, board, and transportation expenses traditionally associated with a college education.
3. Community colleges provide a caring environment, with faculty members who are expert instructors, known for excellent teaching and meeting students at the point of their individual needs, regardless of age, sex, race, current job status, or previous academic preparation. Community colleges join a strong curriculum with a broad range of counseling and career services that are intended to assist students in making the most of their educational opportunities.
4. Many offer comprehensive programs, including transfer curricula in such liberal arts programs as chemistry, psychology, and business management, that lead directly to a baccalaureate degree and career programs that prepare students for employment or assist those already employed in upgrading their skills. For those students who need to strengthen their academic skills, community colleges also offer a wide range of developmental programs in mathematics, languages, and learning skills, designed to prepare the student for success in college studies.

GETTING TO KNOW YOUR TWO-YEAR COLLEGE

The first step in determining the quality of a community college is to check the status of its accreditation. Once you have established that a community college is appropriately accredited, find out as much as you can about the programs and services it has to offer. Much of that information can be found in materials the college provides. However, the best way to learn about a college is to visit in person.

During a campus visit, be prepared to ask a lot of questions. Talk to students, faculty members, administrators, and counselors about the college and its programs, particularly those in which you have a special interest. Ask about available certificates and associate degrees. Don't be shy. Do what you can to dig below the surface. Ask college officials about the transfer rate to four-year colleges. If a college emphasizes student services, find out what particular assistance is offered, such as educational or career guidance. Colleges are eager to provide you with the information you need to make informed decisions.

COMMUNITY COLLEGES CAN SAVE YOU MONEY

If you are able to live at home while you attend college, you will certainly save money on room and board, but it does cost something to commute. Many two-year colleges offer you instruction in your own home through online learning programs or through home study courses that can save both time and money. Look into all the options, and be sure to add up all the costs of attending various colleges before deciding which is best for you.

FINANCIAL AID

Many students who attend community colleges are eligible for a range of federal financial aid programs, state aid, and on-campus jobs. Your high school counselor or the financial aid officer at a community college will also be able to help you. It is in your interest to apply for financial aid months in advance of the date you intend to start your college program, so find out early what assistance is available to you. While many community colleges are able to help students who make a last-minute decision to attend college, either through short-term loans or emergency grants, if you are considering entering college and think you might need financial aid, it is best to find out as much as you can as early as you can.

WORKING AND GOING TO SCHOOL

Many two-year college students maintain full-time or part-time employment while they earn their degrees. Over the years, a steadily growing number of students have chosen to attend community colleges while they fulfill family and employment responsibilities. To enable these students to balance the demands of home, work, and school, most community colleges offer classes at night and on weekends.

For the full-time student, the usual length of time it takes to obtain an associate degree is two years. However, your length of study will depend on the course load you take: the fewer credits you earn each term, the longer it will take you to earn a degree. To assist you in moving more quickly toward earning your degree, many community colleges now award credit through examination or for equivalent knowledge gained through relevant life experiences. Be certain to find out the credit options that are available to you at the college in which you are interested. You may discover that it will take less time to earn a degree than you first thought.

PREPARATION FOR TRANSFER

Studies have repeatedly shown that students who first attend a community college and then transfer to a four-year college or university do at least as well academically as the students who entered the four-year institutions as freshmen. Most community colleges have agreements with nearby four-year institutions to make transfer of credits easier. If you are thinking of transferring, be sure to meet with a counselor or faculty adviser before choosing your courses. You will want to map out a course of study with transfer in mind. Make sure you also find out the credit-transfer requirements of the four-year institution you might want to attend.

ATTENDING A TWO-YEAR COLLEGE IN ANOTHER REGION

Although many community colleges serve a specific county or district, they are committed (to the extent of their ability) to the goal of equal educational opportunity without regard to economic status, race, creed, color, sex, or national origin. Independent two-year colleges recruit from a much broader geographical area—throughout the United States and, increasingly, around the world.

Although some community colleges do provide on-campus housing for their students, most do not. However, even if on-campus housing is not available, most colleges do have housing referral services.

NEW CAREER OPPORTUNITIES

Community colleges realize that many entering students are not sure about the field in which they want to focus their studies or the career they would like to pursue. Often, students discover fields and careers they never knew existed. Community colleges have the resources to help students identify areas of career interest and to set challenging occupational goals.

Once a career goal is set, you can be confident that a community college will provide job-relevant, technical education. About half of the students who take courses for credit at community colleges do so to prepare for employment or to acquire or upgrade skills for their current job. Especially helpful in charting a career path is the assistance of a counselor or a faculty adviser, who can discuss job opportunities in your chosen field and help you map out your course of study.

In addition, since community colleges have close ties to their communities, they are in constant contact with leaders in business, industry, organized labor, and public life. Community colleges work with these individuals and their organizations to prepare students for direct entry into the world of work. For example, some community colleges have established partnerships with local businesses and industries to provide specialized training programs. Some also provide the academic portion of apprenticeship training, while others offer extensive job-shadowing and cooperative education opportunities. Be sure to examine all of the career-preparation opportunities offered by the community colleges in which you are interested.

David R. Pierce is the former President of the American Association of Community Colleges.

Surviving Standardized Tests

WHAT ARE STANDARDIZED TESTS?

Colleges and universities in the United States use tests to help evaluate applicants' readiness for admission or to place them in appropriate courses. The tests that are most frequently used by colleges are the ACT® of American College Testing, Inc., and the College Board's SAT®. In addition, the Educational Testing Service (ETS) offers the TOEFL® test, which evaluates the English-language proficiency of nonnative speakers. The tests are offered at designated testing centers located at high schools and colleges throughout the United States and U.S. territories and at testing centers in various countries throughout the world.

Upon request, special accommodations for students with documented visual, hearing, physical, or learning disabilities are available. Examples of special accommodations include tests in Braille or large print and such aids as a reader, recorder, magnifying glass, or sign language interpreter. Additional testing time may be allowed in some instances. Contact the appropriate testing program or your guidance counselor for details on how to request special accommodations.

THE ACT®

The ACT® is a standardized college entrance examination that measures knowledge and skills in English, mathematics, reading comprehension, and science reasoning and the application of these skills to future academic tasks. The ACT® consists of four multiple-choice tests.

Test 1: English

- 75 questions, 45 minutes
- Usage and mechanics
- Rhetorical skills

Test 2: Mathematics

- 60 questions, 60 minutes
- Pre-algebra
- Elementary algebra
- Intermediate algebra
- Coordinate geometry
- Plane geometry
- Trigonometry

Test 3: Reading

- 40 questions, 35 minutes
- Prose fiction
- Humanities
- Social studies
- Natural sciences

Test 4: Science

- 40 questions, 35 minutes
- Data representation
- Research summary
- Conflicting viewpoints

Each section is scored from 1 to 36 and is scaled for slight variations in difficulty. Students are not penalized for incorrect responses. The composite score is the average of the four scaled scores. The ACT® Plus Writing includes the four multiple-choice tests and a writing test, which measures writing skills emphasized in high school English classes and in entry-level college composition courses.

To prepare for the ACT®, ask your guidance counselor for a free guidebook, "Preparing for the ACT®," or download it at www.act.org/content/dam/act/unsecured/documents/Preparing-for-the-ACT.pdf. Besides providing general test-preparation information and additional test-taking strategies, this guidebook provides full-length practice tests, including a Writing test, information about the optional Writing Test, strategies to prepare for the tests, and what to expect on test day.

DON'T FORGET TO . . .

- ❑ Take the SAT® or ACT® before application deadlines.
- ❑ Note that test registration deadlines precede test dates by about six weeks.
- ❑ Register to take the TOEFL® test if English is not your native language and you are planning on studying at a North American college.
- ❑ Contact the College Board or American College Testing, Inc., in advance if you need special accommodations when taking tests.

THE SAT®

The redesigned SAT®, which saw its first test-takers in the spring of 2016, has these sections: Evidence-Based Reading and Writing, Math, and the Essay. It is based on 1,600 points—the top scores for the Math section and the Evidence-Based Reading and Writing section will be 800, and the Essay score is reported separately.

Evidence-based Reading Test

- 52 questions; 65 minutes
- Passages in U.S. and world literature, history/social studies, and science
- Paired passages
- Lower and higher text complexities
- Words in context, command of evidence, and analysis

Writing and Language Test

- 44 questions; 35 minutes
- Passages in careers, history/social studies, humanities, and science
- Argument, informative/explanatory, and nonfiction narrative passages

- Words in context, grammar, expression of ideas, and analysis

Mathematics Test

- One no-calculator section (25 minutes)
- One calculator section (55 minutes)
- Content includes algebra, problem solving and data analysis, advanced math, area and volume calculations, trigonometric functions, and lines, triangles, and circles using theorems.

Essay (Optional)

- 50 minutes
- Argument passage written for a general audience
- Analysis of argument in passage using text evidence
- Score: 3–12 (Reading: 1–4 scale, Analysis: 1–4 scale, Writing: 1–4 scale)

According to the College Board's website, the "Eight Key Changes" are the following:

- **Relevant Words in Context:** Students need to interpret the meaning of words based on the context of the passage in which they appear. The focus is on "relevant" words—not obscure ones.
- **Command of Evidence:** In addition to demonstrating writing skills, students need to show that they're able to interpret, synthesize, and use evidence found in a wide range of sources.
- **Essay Analyzing a Source:** Students read a passage and explain how the author builds an argument, supporting support their claims with actual data from the passage.
- **Math Focused on Three Key Areas:** Problem Solving and Data Analysis (using ratios, percentages, and proportional reasoning to solve problems in science, social science, and career contexts), the Heart of Algebra (mastery of linear equations and systems), and Passport to Advanced Math (more complex equations and the manipulation they require).
- **Problems Grounded in Real-World Contexts:** All of the questions are grounded in the real world, directly related to work performed in college.
- **Analysis in Science and in Social Studies:** Students need to apply reading, writing, language, and math skills to answer questions in contexts of science, history, and social studies.
- **Founding Documents and Great Global Conversation:** Students will find an excerpt from one of the Founding Documents—such as the Declaration of Independence, the Constitution, and the Bill of Rights—or a text from the "Great Global Conversation" about freedom, justice, and human dignity.
- **No Penalty for Wrong Answers:** Students earn points for the questions they answer correctly.

Check out the College Board's website at https://collegreadiness.collegeboard.org for the most up-to-date information.

Top 10 Ways Not to Take the Test

1. Cramming the night before the test.
2. Not becoming familiar with the directions before you take the test.
3. Not becoming familiar with the format of the test before you take it.
4. Not knowing how the test is graded.
5. Spending too much time on any one question.
6. Second-guessing yourself.
7. Not checking spelling, grammar, and sentence structure in essays.
8. Writing a one-paragraph essay.
9. Forgetting to take a deep breath—
10. and finally—Don't lose it!

SAT SUBJECT TESTS™

Subject Tests are required by some institutions for admission and/or placement in freshman-level courses. Each Subject Test measures one's knowledge of a specific subject and the ability to apply that knowledge. Students should check with each institution for its specific requirements. In general, students are required to take three Subject Tests (one English, one mathematics, and one of their choice).

Subject Tests are given in the following areas: biology, chemistry, Chinese, French, German, Italian, Japanese, Korean, Latin, literature, mathematics, modern Hebrew, physics, Spanish, U.S. history, and world history. These tests are one hour long and are primarily multiple-choice tests. Three Subject Tests may be taken on one test date.

Scored like the current SAT®, students gain a point for each correct answer and lose a fraction of a point for each incorrect answer. The raw scores are then converted to scaled scores that range from 200 to 800.

THE TOEFL® INTERNET-BASED TEST (IBT)

The Test of English as a Foreign Language Internet-Based Test (TOEFL® iBT) is designed to help assess a student's grasp of English if it is not the student's first language. Performance on the TOEFL® test may help interpret scores on the critical reading sections of the SAT®. The test consists of four integrated sections: speaking, listening, reading, and writing. The TOEFL® iBT emphasizes integrated skills. The paper-based versions of the TOEFL® will continue to be administered in certain countries where the Internet-based version has not yet been introduced. For further information, visit www.toefl.org.

WHAT OTHER TESTS SHOULD I KNOW ABOUT?

The AP® Program

This program allows high school students to try college-level work and build valuable skills and study habits in the process. Subject matter is explored in more depth in AP courses than in other high school classes. A qualifying score on an AP test—which varies from school to school—can earn you college credit or advanced placement. Getting qualifying grades on enough exams can even earn you a full year's credit and sophomore standing at more than 1,500 higher-education institutions. There are more than thirty AP courses across multiple subject areas, including art history, biology, and computer science. Speak to your guidance counselor for information about your school's offerings.

College-Level Examination Program (CLEP®)

The CLEP enables students to earn college credit for what they already know, whether it was learned in school, through independent study, or through other experiences outside of the classroom. More than 2,900 colleges and universities now award credit for qualifying scores on one or more of the 33 CLEP exams. The exams, which are 90 minutes in length and are primarily multiple choice, are administered at participating colleges and universities. For more information, check out the website at www.collegeboard.com/clep.

WHAT CAN I DO TO PREPARE FOR THESE TESTS?

Know what to expect. Get familiar with how the tests are structured, how much time is allowed, and the directions for each type of question. Get plenty of rest the night before the test and eat breakfast that morning.

There are a variety of products, from books to software to videos, available to help you prepare for most standardized tests. Find the learning style that suits you best. As for which products to buy, there are two major categories— those created by the test-makers and those created by private companies. The best approach is to talk to someone who has been through the process and find out which product or products he or she recommends.

Some students report significant increases in scores after participating in coaching programs. Longer-term programs (40 hours) seem to raise scores more than short-term programs (20 hours), but beyond 40 hours, score gains are minor. Math scores appear to benefit more from coaching than critical reading scores.

Resources

There is a variety of ways to prepare for standardized tests—find a method that fits your schedule and your budget. But you should definitely prepare. Far too many students walk into these tests cold, either because they find standardized tests frightening or annoying or they just haven't found the time to study. The key is that these exams are standardized. That means these tests are largely the same from administration to administration; they always test the same concepts. They have to, or else you couldn't compare the scores of people who took the tests on different dates. The numbers or words may change, but the underlying content doesn't.

So how do you prepare? At the very least, you should review relevant material, such as math formulas and commonly used vocabulary words, and know the directions for each question type or test section. You should take at least one practice test and review your mistakes so you don't make them again on the test day. Beyond that, you know best how much preparation you need. You'll also find lots of material in libraries or bookstores to help you: books and software from the test- makers and from other publishers (including Peterson's) or live courses that range from national test-preparation companies to teachers at your high school who offer classes.

Who's Paying for This? Financial Aid Basics

A college education can be expensive costing more than $150,000 for four years at some of the higher priced private colleges and universities. Even at the lower-cost state colleges and universities, the cost of a four-year education can approach $60,000. Determining how you and your family will come up with the necessary funds to pay for your education requires planning, perseverance, and learning as much as you can about the options that are available to you. But before you get discouraged, College Board statistics show that 53 percent of full-time students attend four-year public and private colleges with tuition and fees less than $9,000, while 20 percent attend colleges that have tuition and fees more than $36,000. College costs tend to be less in the western states and higher in New England.

Paying for college should not be looked at as a four-year financial commitment. For many families, paying the total cost of a student's college education out of current income and savings is usually not realistic. For families that have planned ahead and have financial savings established for higher education, the burden is a lot easier. But for most, meeting the cost of college requires the pooling of current income and assets and investing in longer-term loan options. These family resources, together with financial assistance from state, federal, and institutional sources, enable millions of students each year to attend the institution of their choice.

FINANCIAL AID PROGRAMS

There are three types of financial aid:

1. Gift-aid—Scholarships and grants are funds that do not have to be repaid.
2. Loans—Loans must be repaid, usually after graduation; the amount you have to pay back is the total you've borrowed plus any accrued interest. This is considered a source of self-help aid.
3. Student employment—Student employment is a job arranged for you by the financial aid office. This is another source of self-help aid.

The federal government has four major grant programs—the Federal Pell Grant, the Federal Supplemental Educational Opportunity Grant, Academic Competitiveness Grants (ACG), and National SMART (Science and Mathematics Access to Retain Talent) grants. ACG and SMART grants are limited to students who qualify for a Pell Grant and are awarded to a select group of students. Overall, these grants are targeted to low-to-moderate income families with significant financial need. The federal government also sponsors a student employment program called the Federal Work-Study Program, which offers jobs both on and off campus, and several loan programs, including those for students and for parents of undergraduate students.

There are two types of student loan programs: subsidized and unsubsidized. The subsidized Federal Direct Loan and the Federal Perkins Loan are need-based, government-subsidized loans. Students who borrow through these programs do not have to pay interest on the loan until after they graduate or leave school. The unsubsidized Federal Direct Loan and the Federal Direct PLUS Loan Program are not based on need, and borrowers are responsible for the interest while the student is in school. These loans are administered by different methods. Once you choose your college, the financial aid office will guide you through this process.

After you've submitted your financial aid application and you've been accepted for admission, each college will send you a letter describing your financial aid award. Most award letters show estimated college costs, how much you and your family are expected to contribute, and the amount and types of aid you have been awarded. Most students are awarded aid from a combination of sources and programs. Hence, your award is often called a financial aid "package."

SOURCES OF FINANCIAL AID

Millions of students and families apply for financial aid each year. Financial aid from all sources exceeds $143 billion per year. The largest single source of aid is the federal government, which will award more than $100 billion this year.

The next largest source of financial aid is found in the college and university community. Most of this aid is awarded to students who have a demonstrated need based on the Federal Methodology. Some institutions use a different formula, the Institutional Methodology (IM), to award their own funds in conjunction with other forms of aid. Institutional aid may be either need-based or non-need based. Aid that is not based on need is usually awarded for a student's academic performance (merit awards), specific talents or abilities, or to attract the type of students a college seeks to enroll.

Another source of financial aid is from state government. All states offer grant and/or scholarship aid, most of which is need-based. However, more and more states are offering substantial merit-based aid programs. Most state programs award aid only to students attending college in their home state.

Other sources of financial aid include:

- Private agencies
- Foundations
- Corporations
- Clubs
- Fraternal and service organizations

- Civic associations
- Unions
- Religious groups that award grants, scholarships, and low-interest loans
- Employers that provide tuition reimbursement benefits for employees and their children

More information about these different sources of aid is available from high school guidance offices, public libraries, college financial aid offices, directly from the sponsoring organizations, and online at www.petersons.com/college-search/scholarship-search.aspx.

HOW NEED-BASED FINANCIAL AID IS AWARDED

When you apply for aid, your family's financial situation is analyzed using a government-approved formula called the Federal Methodology. This formula looks at five items:

1. Demographic information of the family
2. Income of the parents
3. Assets of the parents
4. Income of the student
5. Assets of the student

This analysis determines the amount you and your family are expected to contribute toward your college expenses, called your Expected Family Contribution, or EFC. If the EFC is equal to or more than the cost of attendance at a particular college, then you do not demonstrate financial need. However, even if you don't have financial need, you may still qualify for aid, as there are grants, scholarships, and loan programs that are not need-based.

If the cost of your education is greater than your EFC, then you do demonstrate financial need and qualify for assistance. The amount of your financial need that can be met varies from school to school. Some are able to meet your full need, while others can only cover a certain percentage of need. Here's the formula:

Cost of Attendance
– Expected Family Contribution
= Financial Need

The EFC remains constant, but your need will vary according to the costs of attendance at a particular college. In general, the higher the tuition and fees at a particular college, the higher the cost of attendance will be. Expenses for books and supplies, room and board, transportation, and other miscellaneous items are included in the overall cost of attendance. It is important to remember that you do not have to be low-income to qualify for financial aid. Many middle and upper-middle income families qualify for need-based financial aid.

APPLYING FOR FINANCIAL AID

Every student must complete the Free Application for Federal Student Aid (FAFSA®) to be considered for financial aid. The FAFSA is available from your high school guidance office, many public libraries, colleges in your area, or directly from the U.S. Department of Education.

Students are encouraged to apply for federal student aid on the Web. The electronic version of the FAFSA can be accessed at http://www.fafsa.ed.gov.

The NEW Federal Student Aid ID

In order for a student to complete the online FAFSA, he or she will need a Federal Student Aid (FSA) ID. You can get this online at https://fsaid.ed.gov/npas/index.htm. Since May 2015, the FSA ID has replaced the previously used PIN system. Parents of dependent students also need to obtain their own FSA ID in order to sign their child's FAFSA electronically online.

The FSA ID can be used to access several federal aid-related websites, including FAFSA.gov and StudentLoans.gov. It consists of a username and password and can be used to electronically sign Federal Student Aid documents, access your personal records, and make binding legal obligations. The FSA ID is beneficial in several ways:

- It removes your personal identifiable information (PII), such as your Social Security number, from your log-in credentials.
- It creates a more secure and efficient way to verify your information when you log in to access to your federal student aid information online.
- It gives you the ability to easily update your personal information.
- It allows you to easily retrieve your username and password by requesting a secure code be sent to your e-mail address or by answering challenge questions.

It's relatively simple to create an FSA ID and should only take a few minutes. In addition, you will have an opportunity to link your current Federal Student Aid PIN (if you already have one) to your FSA ID. The final step is to confirm your e-mail address. You will receive a secure code to the e-mail address you provided when you set up your FSA ID. Once you retrieve the code from your e-mail account and enter it—to confirm your e-mail address is valid—you will be able to use this e-mail address instead of your username to log in to any of the federal aid-related websites, making the log-in process EVEN simpler for you and your parents.

When you initially create your FSA ID, your information will need to be verified with the Social Security Administration. This process can take anywhere from one to three days. For that reason, it's a good idea to take care of setting up your FSA ID as early as possible, so it will be all set when you are ready to begin completing your FAFSA.

IMPORTANT NOTE: Since your FSA ID provides access to your personal information and is used to sign online documents, it's imperative that you protect this ID. Don't share it with *anyone* or write it down in an insecure location—you could place yourself at great risk for identify theft.

If Every College You're Applying to for Fall 2020 Requires the FAFSA

. . . then it's pretty simple: Complete the FAFSA after October 1, 2019, being certain to send it in before any college-imposed deadlines. (Students will now be permitted to send in the

2020-21 FAFSA before January 1, 2019.) Students (and parents, as appropriate) are required to report income for an earlier tax year, so for the 2020-21 school year, you would report 2018 income information.

After you send in your FAFSA, you'll receive a Student Aid Report (SAR) that includes all of the information you reported and shows your EFC. If you provided an e-mail address, the SAR is sent to you electronically; otherwise, you will receive a SAR or SAR Acknowledgment in the mail, which lists your FAFSA information but may require you to make any corrections on the FAFSA website. Be sure to review the SAR, checking to see if the information you reported is accurately represented. If you used estimated numbers to complete the FAFSA, you may have to resubmit the SAR with any corrections to the data. The college(s) you have designated on the FAFSA will receive the information you reported and will use that data to make their decision.

The CSS/Financial Aid PROFILE®

To award their own funds, some colleges require an additional application, the CSS/Financial Aid PROFILE® form. The PROFILE asks supplemental questions that some colleges and awarding agencies feel provide a more accurate assessment of the family's ability to pay for college. It is up to the college to decide whether it will use only the FAFSA or both the FAFSA and the PROFILE. PROFILE applications are available from the high school guidance office and on the Web. Both the paper application and the website list those colleges and programs that require the PROFILE application.

If a College Requires the PROFILE

Step 1: Register for the CSS/Financial Aid PROFILE in the fall of your senior year in high school. You can apply for the PROFILE online at http://profileonline.collegeboard.com/prf/index.jsp. Registration information with a list of the colleges that require the PROFILE is available in most high school guidance offices. There is a fee for using the Financial Aid PROFILE application ($25 for the first college, which includes the $9 application fee, and $16 for each additional college). You must pay for the service by credit card when you register. If you do not have a credit card, you will be billed. A limited number of fee waivers are automatically granted to first-time applicants based on the financial information provided on the PROFILE.

Step 2: Fill out your customized CSS/Financial Aid PROFILE. Once you register, your application will be immediately available online and will have questions that all students must complete, questions which must be completed by the student's parents (unless the student is independent and the colleges or programs selected do not require parental information), and *may* have supplemental questions needed by one or more of your schools or programs. If required, those will be found in Section Q of the application.

In addition to the PROFILE application you complete online, you may also be required to complete a Business/ Farm Supplement via traditional paper format. Completion of this form is not a part of the online process. If this form is required, instructions on how to download and print the supplemental form are provided. If your biological or adoptive parents are separated or divorced and your colleges and programs require it, your noncustodial parent may be asked to complete the Noncustodial PROFILE.

Once you complete and submit your PROFILE application, it will be processed and sent directly to your requested colleges and programs.

IF YOU DON'T QUALIFY FOR NEED-BASED AID

If you are not eligible for need-based aid, you can still find ways to lessen your burden.

Here are some suggestions:

- Search for merit scholarships. You can start at the initial stages of your application process. College merit awards are increasingly important as more and more colleges award these to students they especially want to attract. As a result, applying to a college at which your qualifications put you at the top of the entering class may give you a larger merit award. Another source of aid to look for is private scholarships that are given for special skills and talents. Additional information can be found at www.finaid.org.
- Seek employment during the summer and the academic year. The student employment office at your college can help you locate a school-year job. Many colleges and local businesses have vacancies remaining after they have hired students who are receiving Federal Work-Study Program financial aid.
- Borrow through the unsubsidized Federal Direct Loan program. This is generally available to all students. The terms and conditions are similar to the subsidized loans. The biggest difference is that the borrower is responsible for the interest while still in college, although the government permits students to delay paying the interest right away and add the accrued interest to the total amount owed. You must file the FAFSA to be considered.
- After you've secured what you can through scholarships, working, and borrowing, you and your parents will be expected to meet your share of the college bill (the Expected Family Contribution). Many colleges offer monthly payment plans that spread the cost over the academic year. If the monthly payments are too high, parents can borrow through the Federal Direct PLUS Loan Program, through one of the many private education loan programs available, or through home equity loans and lines of credit. Families seeking assistance in financing college expenses should inquire at the financial aid office about what programs are available at the college. Some families seek the advice of professional financial advisers and tax consultants.

Frequently Asked Questions About Transferring

Muriel M. Shishkoff

Among the students attending two-year colleges are a large number who began their higher education knowing they would eventually transfer to a four-year school to obtain their bachelor's degree. There are many reasons why students go this route. Upon graduating from high school, some simply do not have definite career goals. Although they don't want to put their education on hold, they prefer not to pay exorbitant amounts in tuition while trying to "find themselves." As the cost of a university education escalates—even in public institutions—the option of spending the freshman and sophomore years at a two-year college looks attractive to many students. Others attend a two-year college because they are unable to meet the initial entrance standards—a specified grade point average (GPA), standardized test scores, or knowledge of specific academic subjects—required by the four-year school of their choice. Many such students praise the community college system for giving them the chance to be, academically speaking, "born again." In addition, students from other countries often find that they can adapt more easily to language and cultural changes at a two-year school before transferring to a larger, more diverse four-year college.

If your plan is to attend a two-year college with the ultimate goal of transferring to a four-year school, you will be pleased to know that the increased importance of the community college route to a bachelor's degree is recognized by all segments of higher education. As a result, many two-year schools have revised their course outlines and established new courses in order to comply with the programs and curricular offerings of the universities. Institutional improvements to make transferring easier have also proliferated at both the two-and four-year levels. The generous transfer policies of the Pennsylvania, New York, and Florida state university systems, among others, reflect this attitude; these systems accept all credits from students who have graduated from accredited community colleges.

If you are interested in moving from a two-year college to a four-year school, the sooner you make up your mind that you are going to make the switch, the better position you will be to transfer successfully (that is, without having wasted valuable time and credits). The ideal point at which to make such a decision is **before** you register for classes at your two-year school; a counselor can help you plan your course work with an eye toward fulfilling the requirements needed for your major course of study.

Naturally, it is not always possible to plan your transferring strategy that far in advance, but keep in mind that the key to a successful transfer is **preparation,** and preparation takes time—time to think through your objectives and time to plan the right classes to take.

As students face the prospect of transferring from a two-year to a four-year school, many thoughts and concerns about this complicated and often frustrating process race through their minds. Here are answers to the questions that are most frequently asked by transferring students.

Q Does every college and university accept transfer students?

A Most four-year institutions accept transfer students, but some do so more enthusiastically than others. Graduating from a community college is an advantage at, for example, Arizona State University and the University of Massachusetts Boston; both accept more community college transfer students than traditional freshmen. At the University at Albany, SUNY, graduates of two-year transfer programs within the State University of New York System are given priority for upper-division (i.e., junior-and senior-level) vacancies.

Schools offering undergraduate work at the upper division only are especially receptive to transfer applications. On the other hand, some schools accept only a few transfer students; others refuse entrance to sophomores or those in their final year. Princeton University requires an "excellent academic record and particularly compelling reasons to transfer." Check the catalogs of several colleges for their transfer requirements before you make your final choice.

Q Do students who go directly from high school to a four-year college do better academically than transfer students from community colleges?

A On the contrary: some institutions report that transfers from two-year schools who persevere until graduation do *better* than those who started as freshmen in a four-year college.

Q Why is it so important that my two-year college be accredited?

A Four-year colleges and universities accept transfer credits only from schools formally recognized by a regional, national, or professional educational agency. This accreditation signifies that an institution or program of study meets or exceeds a minimum level of educational quality necessary for meeting stated educational objectives.

Q After enrolling at a four-year school, may I still make up necessary courses at a community college?

A Some institutions restrict credit after transfer to their own facilities. Others allow students to take a limited number of transfer courses after matriculation, depending on the subject matter. A few provide opportunities for cross-registration or dual enrollment, which means taking classes on more than one campus.

Q What do I need to do to transfer?

A First, send for your high school and college transcripts. Having chosen the school you wish to transfer to, check its admission requirements against your transcripts. If you find that you are admissible, file an application as early as possible before the deadline. Part of the process will be asking your former schools to send official transcripts to the admission office, i.e., not the copies you used in determining your admissibility.

Plan your transfer program with the head of your new department as soon as you have decided to transfer. Determine the recommended general education pattern and necessary preparation for your major. At your present school, take the courses you will need to meet transfer requirements for the new school.

Q What qualifies me for admission as a transfer student?

A Admission requirements for most four-year institutions vary. Depending on the reputation or popularity of the school and program you wish to enter, requirements may be quite selective and competitive. Usually, you will need to show satisfactory test scores, an academic record up to a certain standard, and completion of specific subject matter.

Transfer students can be eligible to enter a four-year school in a number of ways: by having been eligible for admission directly upon graduation from high school, by making up shortcomings in grades (or in subject matter not covered in high school) at a community college, or by satisfactory completion of necessary courses or credit hours at another postsecondary institution. Ordinarily, students coming from a community college or from another four-year institution must meet or exceed the receiving institution's standards for freshmen and show appropriate college-level course work taken since high school. Students who did not graduate from high school can present proof of proficiency through results on the the GED® Test, the HiSET® Exam, or another state-approved high school equivalency test.

Q Are exceptions ever made for students who don't meet all the requirements for transfer?

A Extenuating circumstances, such as disability, low family income, refugee or veteran status, or athletic talent, may permit the special enrollment of students who would not otherwise be eligible but who demonstrate the potential for academic success. Consult the appropriate office—the Educational Opportunity Program, the disabled students' office, the athletic department, or the academic dean—to see whether an exception can be made in your case.

Q How far in advance do I need to apply for transfer?

A Some schools have a rolling admission policy, which means that they process transfer applications as they are received, all year long. With other schools, you must apply during the priority filing period, which can be up to a year before you wish to enter. Check the date with the admission office at your prospective campus.

Q Is it possible to transfer courses from several different institutions?

A Institutions ordinarily accept the courses that they consider transferable, regardless of the number of accredited schools involved. However, there is the danger of exceeding the maximum number of credit hours that can be transferred from all other schools or earned through credit by examination, extension courses, or correspondence courses. The limit placed on transfer credits varies from school to school, so read the catalog carefully to avoid taking courses you won't be able to use. To avoid duplicating courses, keep attendance at different campuses to a minimum.

Q What is involved in transferring from a semester system to a quarter or trimester system?

A In the semester system, the academic calendar is divided into two equal parts. The quarter system is more aptly named trimester, since the academic calendar is divided into three equal terms (not counting a summer session). To convert semester units into quarter units or credit hours, simply multiply the semester units by one and a half. Conversely, multiply quarter units by two thirds to come up with semester units. If you are used to a semester system of fifteen- to sixteen-week courses, the ten-week courses of the quarter system may seem to fly by.

Q Why might a course be approved for transfer credit by one four-year school but not by another?

A The beauty of postsecondary education in the United States lies in its variety. Entrance policies and graduation requirements are designed to reflect and serve each institution's mission. Because institutional policies vary so widely, schools may interpret the subject matter of a course from quite different points of view. Given that the granting of transfer credit indicates that a course is viewed as being, in effect, parallel to one offered by the receiving institution, it is easy to see how this might be the case at one university and not another.

Q Must I take a foreign language to transfer?

A Foreign language proficiency is often required for admission to a four-year institution; such proficiency also often figures in certain majors or in the general education pattern. Often, two or three years of a single language in high school will do the trick. Find out if scores received on Advanced Placement (AP®) examinations, placement examinations given by the foreign language department, or SAT Subject Tests™ will be accepted in lieu of college course work.

Q Will the school to which I'm transferring accept pass/no pass, pass/fail, or credit/no credit grades in lieu of letter grades?

A Usually, a limit is placed on the number of these courses you can transfer, and there may be other restrictions as well. If you want to use other-than-letter grades for the fulfillment of general education requirements or lower-division (freshman and sophomore) preparation for the major, check with the receiving institution.

Q Which is more important for transfer—my grade point average or my course completion pattern?

A Some schools believe that your past grades indicate academic potential and overshadow prior preparation for a specific degree program. Others require completion of certain introductory courses before transfer to prepare you for upper-division work in your major. In any case, appropriate course selection will cut down the time to graduation and increase your chances of making a successful transfer.

Q What happens to my credits if I change majors?

A If you change majors after admission, your transferable course credit should remain fairly intact. However, because you may need extra or different preparation for your new major, some of the courses you've taken may now be useful only as electives. The need for additional lower-level preparation may mean you're staying longer at your new school than you originally planned. On the other hand, you may already have taken courses that count toward your new major as part of the university's general education pattern.

Excerpted (and updated) from *Transferring Made Easy: A Guide to Changing Colleges Successfully,* by Muriel M. Shishkoff, © 1991 by Muriel M. Shishkoff (published by Peterson's).

Returning to School: Advice for Adult Students

Sandra Cook, Ph.D.
Associate Vice President for Enrollment Management, San Diego State University

Many adults think for a long time about returning to school without taking any action. One purpose of this article is to help the "thinkers" finally make some decisions by examining what is keeping them from action. Another purpose is to describe not only some of the difficulties and obstacles that adult students may face when returning to school but also tactics for coping with them.

If you have been thinking about going back to college, and believing that you are the only person your age contemplating college, you should know that approximately 7 million adult students are currently enrolled in higher education institutions. This number represents 50 percent of total higher education enrollments. The majority of adult students are enrolled at two-year colleges.

There are many reasons why adult students choose to attend a two-year college. Studies have shown that the three most important criteria that adult students consider when choosing a college are location, cost, and availability of the major or program desired. Most two-year colleges are public institutions that serve a geographic district, making them readily accessible to the community. Costs at most two-year colleges are far less than at other types of higher education institutions. For many students who plan to pursue a bachelor's degree, completing their first two years of college at a community college is an affordable means to that end. If you are interested in an academic program that will transfer to a four-year institution, most two-year colleges offer the "general education" courses that compose most freshman and sophomore years. If you are interested in a vocational or technical program, two-year colleges excel in providing this type of training.

SETTING THE STAGE

There are three different "stages" in the process of adults returning to school. The first stage is uncertainty. Do I really want to go back to school? What will my friends or family think? Can I compete with those 18-year-old whiz kids? Am I too old? The second stage is choice. Once the decision to return has been made, you must choose where you will attend. There are many criteria to use in making this decision. The third stage is support. You have just added another role to your already-too-busy life. There are, however, strategies that will help you accomplish your goals—perhaps not without struggle, but with grace and humor nonetheless. Let's look at each of these stages.

UNCERTAINTY

Why are you thinking about returning to school? Is it to

- fulfill a dream that had to be delayed?
- become more educationally well-rounded?
- fill an intellectual void in your life?

These reasons focus on personal growth.

If you are returning to school to

- meet people and make friends
- attain and enjoy higher social status and prestige among friends, relatives, and associates
- understand/study a cultural heritage
- have a medium in which to exchange ideas

You are interested in social and cultural opportunities.

If you are like most adult students, you want to

- qualify for a new occupation
- enter or reenter the job market
- increase earnings potential
- qualify for a more challenging position in the same field of work

You are seeking career growth.

Understanding the reasons why you want to go back to school is an important step in setting your educational goals and will help you to establish some criteria for selecting a college. However, don't delay your decision because you have not been able to clearly define your motives. Many times, these aren't clear until you have already begun the process, and they may change as you move through your college experience.

Assuming you agree that additional education will benefit you, what is it that keeps you from returning to school? You may have a litany of excuses running through your mind:

- I don't have time.
- I can't afford it.
- I'm too old to learn.
- My friends will think I'm crazy.

- I'll be older than the teachers and other students.
- My family can't survive without me to take care of them every minute.
- I'll be X years old when I finish.
- I'm afraid.
- I don't know what to expect.

And that is just what these are—excuses. You can make school, like anything else in your life, a priority or not. If you really want to return, you can. The more you understand your motivation for returning to school and the more you understand what excuses are keeping you from taking action, the easier your task will be.

If you think you don't have time: The best way to decide how attending class and studying can fit into your schedule is to keep track of what you do with your time each day for several weeks. Completing a standard time-management grid (each day is plotted out by the half hour) is helpful for visualizing how your time is spent. For each 3-credit-hour class you take, you will need to find 3 hours for class plus 6 to 9 hours for reading-studying-library time. This study time should be spaced evenly throughout the week, not loaded up on one day. It is not possible to learn or retain the material that way. When you examine your grid, see where there are activities that could be replaced with school and study time. You may decide to give up your bowling league or some time in front of the TV. Try not to give up sleeping, and don't cut out every moment of free time. Here are some suggestions that have come from adults who have returned to school:

- Enroll in a time-management workshop. It helps you rethink how you use your time.
- Don't think you have to take more than one course at a time. You may eventually want to work up to taking more, but consider starting with one. (It is more than you are taking now!)
- If you have a family, start assigning to them those household chores that you usually do—and don't redo what they do.
- Use your lunch hour or commuting time for reading.

If you think you cannot afford it: As mentioned earlier, two-year colleges are extremely affordable. If you cannot afford the tuition, look into the various financial aid options. Most federal and state funds are available to full- and part-time students. Loans are also available. While many people prefer not to accumulate a debt for school, these same people will think nothing of taking out a loan to buy a car. After five or six years, which is the better investment? Adult students who work should look into whether their company has a tuition-reimbursement policy. There are also private scholarships, available through foundations, service organizations, and clubs, that are focused on adult learners. Your public library, the Web, and a college financial aid adviser are three excellent sources for reference materials regarding financial aid.

If you think you are too old to learn: This is pure myth. A number of studies have shown that adult learners perform as well as, or better than, traditional-age students.

If you are afraid your friends will think you're crazy: Who cares? Maybe they will, maybe they won't. Usually, they will admire your courage and be just a little jealous of your ambition (although they'll never tell you that). Follow your dreams, not theirs.

If you are concerned because the teachers or students will be younger than you: Don't be. The age differences that may be apparent in other settings evaporate in the classroom. If anything, an adult in the classroom strikes fear into the hearts of some 18-year-olds because adults have been known to be prepared, ask questions, be truly motivated, and be there to learn!

If you think your family will have a difficult time surviving while you are in school: If you have done everything for them up to now, they might struggle. Consider this an opportunity to help them become independent and self-sufficient. Your family can only make you feel guilty if you let them. You are not abandoning them; you are becoming an educational role model. When you are happy and working toward your goals, everyone benefits. Admittedly, it sometimes takes time for them to realize this. For single parents, there are schools that offer support groups, child care, and cooperative babysitting.

If you're appalled at the thought of being X years old when you graduate in Y years: How old will you be in Y years if you don't go back to school?

If you are afraid or don't know what to expect: Know that these are natural feelings when one encounters any new situation. Adult students find that their fears usually dissipate once they begin classes. Fear of trying is usually the biggest roadblock to the reentry process.

No doubt you have dreamed up a few more reasons for not making the decision to return to school. Keep in mind that what you are doing is making up excuses, and you are using these excuses to release you from the obligation to make a decision about your life. The thought of returning to college can be scary. Anytime anyone ventures into unknown territory, there is a risk, but taking risks is a necessary component of personal and professional growth. It is your life, and you alone are responsible for making the decisions that determine its course. Education is an investment in your future.

CHOICE

Once you have decided to go back to school, your next task is to decide where to go. If your educational goals are well defined (e.g., you want to pursue a degree in order to change careers), then your task is a bit easier. But even if your educational goals are still evolving, do not defer your return. Many students who enter higher education with a specific major in mind change that major at least once.

Most students who attend a public two-year college choose the community college in the district in which they live. This is generally the closest and least expensive option if the school offers the programs you want. If you are planning to begin your education at a two-year college and then transfer to a four-year school, there are distinct advantages to choosing your four-year school early. Many community and four-year colleges have "articulation" agreements that designate what credits from the two-year school will transfer to the four-year college and how. Some four-year institutions accept an associate degree as equivalent to the freshman and sophomore years, regardless of the courses you have taken. Some four-year schools accept two-year college work only on a course-by-course basis. If you can identify which school you will transfer to, you can know in advance exactly how your two-year credits will apply, preventing an unexpected loss of credit or time.

Each institution of higher education is distinctive. Your goal in choosing a college is to come up with the best student-institution fit—matching your needs with the offerings and characteristics of the school. The first step in choosing a college is to determine what criteria are most important to you in attaining your educational goals. Location, cost, and program availability are the three main factors that influence an adult student's college choice. In considering location, don't forget that some colleges have conveniently located branch campuses. In considering cost, remember to explore your financial aid options before ruling out an institution because of its tuition. Program availability should include not only the major in which you are interested, but also whether or not classes in that major are available when you can take them.

Some additional considerations beyond location, cost, and programs are:

- Does the school have a commitment to adult students and offer appropriate services, such as child care, tutoring, and advising?
- Are classes offered at times when you can take them?
- Are there academic options for adults, such as credit for life or work experience, credit by examination (including CLEP), credit for military service, or accelerated programs?
- Is the faculty sensitive to the needs of adult learners?

Once you determine which criteria are vital in your choice of an institution, you can begin to narrow your choices. There are myriad ways for you to locate the information you desire. Many newspapers publish a "School Guide" several times a year in which colleges and universities advertise to an adult student market. In addition, schools themselves publish catalogs, class schedules, and promotional materials that contain much of the information you need, and they are yours for the asking. Many colleges sponsor information sessions and open houses that allow you to visit the campus and ask questions. An appointment with an adviser is a good way to assess the fit between you and the institution. Be sure to bring your questions with you to your interview.

SUPPORT

Once you have made the decision to return to school and have chosen the institution that best meets your needs, take some additional steps to ensure your success during your crucial first semester. Take advantage of institutional support and build some social support systems of your own. Here are some ways of doing just that:

- Plan to participate in any orientation programs. These serve the threefold purpose of providing you with a great deal of important information, familiarizing you with the campus and its facilities, and giving you the opportunity to meet and begin networking with other students.
- Take steps to deal with any academic weaknesses. Take mathematics and writing placement tests if you have reason to believe you may need some extra help in these areas. It is not uncommon for adult students to need a math refresher course or a program to help alleviate math anxiety. Ignoring a weakness won't make it go away.
- Look into adult reentry programs. Many institutions offer adults workshops focusing on ways to improve study skills, textbook reading, test-taking, and time-management skills.
- Build new support networks by joining an adult student organization, making a point of meeting other adult students through workshops, or actively seeking out a "study buddy" in each class—that invaluable friend who shares and understands your experience.
- Incorporate your new status as "student" into your family life. Doing your homework with your children at a designated "homework time" is a valuable family activity and reinforces the importance of education.
- Make sure you take a reasonable course load in your first semester. It is far better to have some extra time on your hands and to succeed magnificently than to spend the entire semester on the brink of a breakdown. Also, whenever possible, try to focus your first courses not only on requirements, but also on areas of personal interest.
- Faculty members, advisers, and student affairs personnel are there to help you during difficult times—let them assist you as often as necessary.

After completing your first semester, you will probably look back in wonder at why you thought going back to school was so imposing. Certainly, it's not without its occasional exasperations. But, as with life, keeping things in perspective and maintaining your sense of humor make the difference between just coping and succeeding brilliantly.

Coming to America: Tips for International Students Considering Study in the U.S.

Introduction: Why Study in the United States?

Are you thinking about going to a college or university in the United States? If you're looking at this book, you probably are! All around the world, students like you, pursuing higher education, are considering that possibility. They envision themselves on modern, high-tech campuses in well-known cities, surrounded by American students, taking classes and having fun. A degree from a U.S. school would certainly lead to success and fortune, either back in your home country or perhaps even in the United States, wouldn't it?

It can be done—but becoming a student at a college or university in the U.S. requires academic talent, planning, time, effort, and money. While there may be only a small number of institutions of higher learning in your country, there are more than 2,900 four-year colleges and universities in the United States. Choosing one, being accepted, and then traveling and becoming a student in America is a big undertaking.

If this is your dream, here is some helpful information and expert tips from professionals who work with international students at colleges and universities throughout the United States.

Timing and Planning

The journey to a college or university in the U.S. often starts years in advance. Most international students choose to study in the U.S. because of the high quality of academics. Your family may also have a lot of input on this decision, too.

"We always tell students they should be looking in the sophomore year, visiting in the junior year, and applying in the senior year," says Father Francis E. Chambers, OSA, D.Min., Associate Director of International Admission at Villanova University. He stresses that prospective students need to be taking challenging courses in the years leading up to college. "We want to see academic rigor. Most admission decisions are based on the first six semesters—senior year is too late."

Heidi Gregori-Gahan, Assistant Provost for International Programs at the University of Southern Indiana agrees that it's important to start early. "Plan ahead and do your homework. There is so much to choose from—so many schools, programs, degrees, and experiences. It can be overwhelming."

While students in some countries may pay an agent to help them get into a school in the United States, Gregori-Gahan often directs potential international students to EducationUSA (http://educationusa.state.gov), a U.S. State Department network of over 400 international student advising centers in more than 170 countries. "They are there to provide unbiased information about studying in the United States and help you understand the process and what you need to do."

Two to three years of advance planning is also recommended by Daphne Durham, who has been an international student adviser at Harvard, Suffolk University, Valdosta State University, and the University of Georgia. She points out that the academic schedule in other countries is often different than that of the United States, so you need to synchronize your calendar accordingly.

You will have to take several tests in order to gain admission to a U.S. school, so it's important to know when those tests are given in your country, then register and take them so your scores will be available when you apply. Even if you have taken English in school, you will probably have to take The Test of English as a Foreign Language (TOEFL®), but some schools also accept the International English Language Testing Sytem (IELTS). You will probably also have to take the SAT® or ACT® tests, which are achievement or aptitude tests, and are usually required of all students applying for admission, not just international students.

"Make sure you understand how the international admissions process works at the school or schools you want to attend," says Durham. "What test scores are needed and when? Does the school have a fixed calendar or rolling admissions?" Those are just some of the many factors that can impact your application and could make a difference in when you are able to start school.

"Every university is unique in what's required and what they need to do. Even navigating each school's different website can be challenging," explains Gregori-Gahan.

Searching for Schools

This book contains information on thousands of four-year colleges and universities, and it will be a valuable resource for you in your search and application process. But with so many options, how do you decide which school you should attend?

"Where I find a big difference with international students is if their parents don't recognize the school, they don't apply to the school," says Fr. Chambers. "They could be overlooking a lot of great schools. They have to look outside the box."

The school Gregori-Gahan represents is in Evansville, Indiana, and it probably isn't familiar to students abroad. "Not many people have heard of anything beyond New York and California and maybe Florida. I like to tell students that this is 'real America.' But happy international students on our campus have recruited others to come here."

She points out that Internet technology has made a huge difference in the search process for international students. Websites full of information, live chat, webinars, virtual tours, and admission interviews via Skype have made it easier for potential students to connect with U.S. institutions, get more information, and be better able to visualize the campus.

One thing than will help narrow your search for a school is knowing specifically what you want to study. You need to know what the course of study is called in the United States, what it means, and what is required in order to study that subject. You also need to consider your future plans. What are your goals and objectives? What do you plan to do after earning your degree?

"If you're going to overcome the hurdles and get to a U.S. school, you have to have a directed path chosen," says Durham.

The other thing that could help your search process is finding a school that is a good fit.

Fit Is Important

You want your clothing and shoes to fit you properly and be comfortable, so a place where you will spend four or more years of your life studying should also be comfortable and appropriate for you. So how can you determine if a particular school is a good fit?

"We really recommend international students visit first. Yes, there are websites and virtual tours, but there's still nothing that beats an in-person visit," says Fr. Chambers. He estimates that 50 to 60 percent of Villanova's international students visited the campus before enrolling.

"It can be hard to get a sense of a place—you're so far away and you're probably not going to set foot on campus until you arrive," says Gregori-Gahan. "There is a high potential for culture shock."

You need to ask yourself what is important to you in a campus environment, then do some homework to ensure that the schools you are considering meet those needs. Here are some things to consider when it comes to fit:

- **Location:** Is it important for you to be in a well-known city or is a part of the United States that is unfamiliar a possibility? "Look at geographic areas, but also cost of living," recommends Durham. "Be sure to factor in transportation costs also, especially if you plan to return to your home country regularly."
- **Student population:** Some small schools have just 1,000 students while larger ones may have 30,000 students or more.
- **Familiar faces:** Is it important for you to be at a school with others from your home nation or region?
- **Climate:** Some students want a climate similar to where they live now, but others are open and curious about seasons and weather conditions they may not have ever experienced. "We do have four seasons here," says Gregori-Gahan. "Sometimes students who come here from tropical regions are concerned about the winters. The first snow is so exciting, but after that, students may not be aware of how cold it really is."
- **Amenities:** Do you want to find your own housing or choose a school where the majority of students live on campus? Is there public transportation available or is it necessary to walk or have a bicycle or car? Does the school or community have access to things that are important to you culturally and meet the traditions you want to follow?
- **Campus size:** Some campuses are tightly compacted into a few city blocks, but others cover hundreds of acres of land. "International students are amazed by how green and spacious our campus is, with blooming flowers, trees, and lots of grass," says Gregori-Gahan.
- **Academic offerings:** Does this school offer the program you want to study? Can you complete it in four years or perhaps sooner? What sort of internship and career services are available?
- **Finances:** Can you afford to attend this school? Is there any sort of financial assistance available for international students?
- **Support services:** Durham suggests students look carefully at each school's offerings for international students. "Does the school have online guidance for getting your visa? Is ESL tutoring available? Does the school offer host family or community friend programs?" She also suggests you look for campus support groups for students from your country or region.

Looking at the listings and reading the in-depth descriptions in this book can help you search for a school that is a good fit for you.

Government Requirements

The one thing that every international student must have in order to study in the United States is a student visa. Having accurate advice and following all the necessary steps regarding the visa process is essential to being able to enter this country and start school.

As you schedule your tests and application deadlines, you must also consider how long it will take to get your visa. This varies depending on where you live; in some countries, extensive background checks are required. The subject you plan to study can also impact your visa status; it does help to have a major rather than be undeclared. The U.S. State Department website, http://travel.state.gov/content/visas/english/study-exchange.html, can give you an idea of how long it will take.

In addition to the visa, you will also need a Form I-20, which is a U.S. government immigration form. You must have that form when you get to the United States.

"It's very different from being a tourist. You need to be prepared to meet with an immigration officer and be interviewed about your college," explains Durham. "Where you are going, why you are going, where the school is located, what you are studying, and so on."

You also need to keep in mind that there are reporting requirements once you are a student in the U.S. Every semester, your adviser has to report to the government to confirm that you are enrolled in and attending school in order for you to stay in the United States.

Finances

Part of the visa process includes having the funds to pay for the cost of your schooling and support yourself. Finances are a huge hurdle in the process of becoming a college student in the United States.

"It's crucial. So many foreign systems offer 'free' higher education to students. How is your family going to handle the ongoing expense of attending college for four years or longer in the United States?" Durham reiterates that planning ahead is key because there are so many details. Student loans require a U.S.-based cosigner. Each school has its own financial aid deadlines. You have to factor in your own government's requirements, such currency exchange and fund transfers.

The notion that abundant funds are available to assist international students is not true. Sometimes state schools may offer diversity waivers or there may be special scholarship opportunities for international students. But attending school in the U.S. is still a costly venture.

"We do offer financial aid to international students, but they still have to be able to handle a large portion of the costs. Full-need scholarships are not likely," explained Fr. Chambers. "Sometimes students think that once they get here, it will all work out and the funds will be there. But the scenario for the first year has to be repeated each year they are on campus.

Once You Arrive...

You've taken your tests, researched schools, found a good fit, applied, got accepted, arranged the financing, gotten your visa and I-20, and made it to the campus in the United States. Now what?

You can expect the school where you have enrolled to be welcoming and helpful, but within reason. If you arrive on a weekend, or at a time outside of the time when international students are scheduled to arrive, the assistance you need may not be available to you.

Every school offers different levels of assistance to international students. For instance, Villanova offers a full-service office that can assist students with everything from visas, to employment, to finding a place for students to stay over breaks.

Fr. Chambers attends the international student orientation session to greet the students he's worked with through the recruitment and application process. "But I rarely see an international student after that. I think that bodes well for them being integrated into the entire university."

"Those of us who work with international students are really working to help them adjust," says Gregori-Gahan. "International students get here well before school starts so they can get over jet lag. We have orientation sessions and pair them with peer advisers who help them navigate the first few days, and we assure them that we are there for them."

Students should be open to their new setting, but they should be prepared that things may not be at all how they had envisioned during their planning and searching process. "While you may think you'll meet lots of Americans, don't underestimate the importance of community with your traditional home culture and people," says Durham.

Don't Make These Mistakes

The journey to college attendance in the United States is a long one, with many steps. The experts warn about mistakes to avoid along the way.

"Not reading through everything thoroughly and not understanding what the program of study really is and what will it cost. You have to be really clear on the important details," says Gregori-Gahan.

"Every school does things differently," cautions Fr. Chambers. "International students must be aware of that as they are applying."

Durham stresses that going to school in the United States is too big a decision to leave to someone else. "Students need to know about their school—they have to be in charge of their application."

"It involves a lot of work to be successful and happy and not surprised by too many things," Gregori-Gahan says.

Hopefully now, you are more informed and better prepared to pursue your dream of studying at a college or university in the United States.

Community Colleges and the Green Economy

Community colleges are a focal point for state and national efforts to create a green economy and workforce. As the United States transforms its economy into a "green" one, community colleges are leading the way—filling the need for both educated technicians whose skills can cross industry lines as well as those technicians who are able to learn new skills as technologies evolve.

President Obama extolled community colleges as "the unsung heroes of America's education system," essential to our country's success in the "global competition to lead in the growth of industries of the twenty-first century." With the support of state governments, and, more importantly, local and international business partners, America's community colleges are rising to meet the demands of the new green economy. Community colleges are training individuals to work in fields such as renewable energy, energy efficiency, wind energy, green building, and sustainability. The programs are as diverse as the campuses housing them.

Here is a quick look at just some of the exciting "green" programs available at community colleges throughout the United States.

At Mesalands Community College in Tucumcari, New Mexico, the North American Wind Research and Training Center provides state-of-the-art facilities for research and training qualified technicians in wind energy technology to help meet the need for an estimated 170,000 new positions in the industry by 2030. The Center includes a facility for applied research in collaboration with Sandia National Laboratories—the first-ever such partnership between a national laboratory and a community college. It also provides associate degree training for wind energy technicians, meeting the fast-growing demand for "windsmiths" in the western part of the country—jobs that pay $45,000–$60,000 per year. For more information, visit http://www.mesalands.edu.

Cape Cod Community College (CCCC) in Massachusetts has become one of the nation's leading colleges in promoting and integrating sustainability and green practices throughout all campus operations and technical training programs. Ten years ago, Cape Wind Associates, Cape Cod's first wind farm, provided $50,000 to jumpstart CCCC's wind technician program—considered a state model for community-based clean energy workforce development and education. In addition, hundreds of CCCC students have earned associate degrees in environmental technology and environmental studies, as well as certificate programs in coastal zone management, environmental site assessment, solar thermal technology, and more. Visit http://www.capecod.edu/web/natsci/env/programs for more information.

At Oakland Community College in Michigan, more than 350 students are enrolled in the college's Renewable Energies and Sustainable Living program and its related courses. Students gain field experience refurbishing public buildings with renewable materials, performing energy audits for the government, and working with small businesses and hospitals to reduce waste and pollution. To learn more, visit http://www.oaklandcc.edu/est/.

Portland Community College (PCC) in Portland, Oregon, offers associate degree and certificate options in Renewable Energy Systems (RES) training, preparing technicians for solar power, wind power, fuel cell, and other renewable energy fields. Students can earn an Associate in Applied Science (A.A.S.) degree or a One-Year Certificate in EET: Renewable Energy Systems. PCC's Microelectronic Technology Department offers an A.A.S. degree and a Certificate of Completion (COC) in Solar Voltaic Manufacturing Technology. The COC provides an orientation in solar manufacturing for those who have no prior education or experience in the field, which enables students to obtain entry-level jobs in this industry and eventually complete their A.A.S. degree.

Central Carolina Community College (CCCC) in Pittsboro, North Carolina, has been leading the way in "green" programs for more than a decade. It offered a sustainable agriculture class at its Chatham campus in 1996 and soon became the first community college in the nation to offer an Associate in Applied Science degree in sustainable agriculture and the first in North Carolina to offer an associate degree in biofuels. In addition, it was the first North Carolina community college to offer a North American Board of Certified Energy Practitioners (NABCEP)–approved solar PV panel installation course as part of its green building/renewable energy program. CCC also offers an associate degree in sustainable technology, a Natural Chef culinary arts program, an ecotourism certificate, and certificates in other green programs. For more information about Central Carolina Community College's green programs, visit http://www.cccc.edu/green.

At Metropolitan Community College in Omaha, Nebraska, the Continuing Education Department in partnership with ProTrain is offering green/renewable energy/sustainability online training courses. The courses are designed to provide students with the workforce skills necessary for many in-demand green-collar occupations. Green/Renewable Energy courses include Building Energy Efficient Level, Fundamentals of Solar Hot Water Heating, Green Building Sales (or Technical) Professional, and more. Sustainability Green Supply Chain Training courses include Alternative Energy Operations, Carbon Strategies, Green Building for Contractors, and Sustainability 101. Visit www.theknowledgebase.org/metropolitan/.

At Cascadia Community College in Bothell, Washington, thanks to a grant from Puget Sound Energy (PSE), students in the Energy Informatics class designed a kiosk screen that shows the energy usage and solar generation at the local 21 Acres Center for Local Food and Sustainable Living. The PSE grant supports the classroom materials for renewable energy education and the Web-based monitoring software that allows students and interested community members to track how much energy is being generated as the weather changes. For more information, visit http://www.cascadia.edu/Default.aspx.

At Grand Rapids Community College, the federally funded Pathways to Prosperity program has successfully prepared low-income residents for jobs in fields such as renewable energy. More than 200 people have completed the program, which began in 2010 thanks to a $4-million grant from the Department of Labor, and found jobs in industries ranging from energy-efficient building construction to alternative energy and sustainable manufacturing. For additional information, check out http://cms.grcc.edu/workforce-training/pathways-prosperity.

Established in 2008, the Green Institute at Heartland Community College in Normal, Illinois, supports a wide range of campus initiatives, educational programs, and community activities that are related to sustainability, energy conservation, renewable energy, recycling, retro-commissioning, and other environmental technologies. For more information, visit http://www.heartland.edu/greenInstitute/.

Most of California's 112 community colleges offer some type of green-tech classes. These include photovoltaic panel installation and repair, green construction practices, and biotechnology courses leading to careers in agriculture, medicine, and environmental forensics. Visit http://www.californiacommunitycolleges.cccco.edu/ProgramstoWatch/MoreProgramstoWatch/GreenTechnology.aspx.

Linn-Benton Community College (LBCC) in Albany, Oregon, is now offering training for the Oregon Green Technology Certificate. Oregon Green Tech is a federally funded program that is designed to prepare entry-level workers with foundational skills for a variety of industries associated with or in support of green jobs. Students learn skills in green occupations that include green energy production; manufacturing, construction, installation, monitoring, and repair of equipment for solar, wind, wave, and bio-energy; building retro-fitting; process recycling; hazardous materials removal work; and more. LBCC is one of ten Oregon community colleges to provide training for the Green Technology Certificate, offered through the Oregon Consortium and Oregon Workforce Alliance. Visit http://www.linnbenton.edu for additional information.

The Santa Fe Community College Sustainable Technology Center in New Mexico offers several green jobs training programs along with various noncredit courses. It also provides credit programs from certificates in green building systems, environmental technology training, and solar energy training as well as an Associate in Applied Science (A.A.S.) degree in environmental technology. For more information, go online to http://www.sfcc.edu/sustainable_technologies_center.

In Colorado, Red Rocks Community College (RRCC) offers degree and certificate programs in renewable energy (solar photovoltaic, solar thermal, and wind energy technology), energy and industrial maintenance, energy operations and process technology, environmental technology, water quality management, and energy audit. RRCC has made a commitment to the national challenge of creating and sustaining a green workforce and instructs students about the issues of energy, environmental stewardship, and renewable resources across the college curriculum. For more information, visit http://www.rrcc.edu/green/.

At GateWay Community College in Phoenix, Arizona, graduates of the Environmental Science program now work for the U.S. Geological Survey (USGS), the Arizona Department of Environmental Quality (ADEQ), the Occupational Safety and Health Administration (OSHA), and municipalities across the state and region, as well as private consultants and environmental organizations. For additional information, check out http://www.gatewaycc.edu/environment.

During the past 4.5 years, 17 Illinois community colleges and their partners have created 35 certificate and degree programs to prepare students for careers in green industry sectors. Over 185 courses were created and piloted, online and on-site, in communities across Illinois. The courses were created using open-source materials, with the intent to be shared with other colleges and universities through the Department of Labor's Trade Adjustment Assistance Community College and Career Training (TAACCCT) Grant Program repository.

Next you'll find two essays about other green community college programs. The first essay was written by the president of Lane Community College in Eugene, Oregon, about the role Lane and other community colleges are playing in creating a workforce for the green economy. Then, read a first-hand account of the new Wind Turbine Training Program at Kalamazoo Valley Community College in Kalamazoo, Michigan—a program that has more applicants than spaces and one whose students are being hired BEFORE they even graduate. It's clear that there are exciting "green" programs at community colleges throughout the United States.

The Role of Community Colleges in Creating a Workforce for the Green Economy

by Mary F.T. Spilde, President
Lane Community College

Community colleges are expected to play a leadership role in educating and training the workforce for the green economy. Due to close connections with local and regional labor markets, colleges assure a steady supply of skilled workers by developing and adapting programs to respond to the needs of business and industry. Further, instead of waiting for employers to create job openings, many colleges are actively engaged in local economic development to help educate potential employers to grow their green business opportunities and to participate in the creation of the green economy.

As the green movement emerges there has been confusion about what constitutes a green job. It is now clear that many of the green jobs span several economic sectors such as renewable energy, construction, manufacturing, transportation and agriculture. It is predicted that there will be many middle skill jobs requiring more than a high school diploma but less than a bachelor's degree. This is precisely the unique role that community colleges play. Community colleges develop training programs, including pre-apprenticeship, that ladder the curriculum to take lower skilled workers through a relevant and sequenced course of study that provides a clear pathway to career track jobs. As noted in *Going Green: The Vital Role of Community Colleges in Building a Sustainable Future and Green Workforce* by the National Council for Workforce Education and the Academy for Educational Development, community colleges are strategically positioned to work with employers to redefine skills and competencies needed by the green workforce and to create the framework for new and expanded green career pathways.

While there will be new occupations such as solar and wind technologists, the majority of the jobs will be in the energy management sector—retrofitting the built environment. For example, President Obama called for retrofitting more than 75 percent of federal buildings and more than 2 million homes to make them more energy-efficient. The second major area for growth will be the "greening" of existing jobs as they evolve to incorporate green practices. Both will require new knowledge, skills and abilities. For community colleges, this means developing new programs that meet newly created industry standards and adapting existing programs and courses to integrate green skills. The key is to create a new talent pool of environmentally conscious, highly skilled workers.

These two areas show remarkable promise for education and training leading to high wage/high demand jobs:

- Efficiency and energy management: There is a need for auditors and energy efficiency experts to retrofit existing buildings. Consider how much built environment we have in this country, and it's not difficult to see that this is where the vast amount of jobs are now and will be in the future.
- Greening of existing jobs: There are few currently available jobs that environmental sustainability will not impact. Whether it is jobs in construction, such as plumbers, electricians, heating and cooling technicians, painters, and building supervisors, or chefs, farmers, custodians, architects, automotive technicians and interior designers, all will need to understand how to lessen their impact on the environment.

Lane Community College offers a variety of degree and certificate programs to prepare students to enter the energy efficiency fields. Lane has offered an Energy Management program since the late 1980s—before it was hip to be green! Students in this program learn to apply basic principles of physics and analysis techniques to the description and measurement of energy in today's building systems, with the goal of evaluating and recommending alternative energy solutions that will result in greater energy efficiency and energy cost savings. Students gain a working understanding of energy systems in today's built environment and the tools to analyze and quantify energy efficiency efforts. The program began with an emphasis in residential energy efficiency/solar energy systems and has evolved to include commercial energy efficiency and renewable energy system installation technology.

The Renewable Energy Technician program is offered as a second-year option within the Energy Management program. Course work prepares students for employment designing and installing solar electric and domestic hot water systems. Renewable Energy students, along with Energy Management students, take a first-year curriculum in commercial energy efficiency giving them a solid background that includes residential energy efficiency, HVAC systems, lighting, and physics and math. In the second year, Renewable Energy students diverge from the Energy Management curriculum and take course work that starts with two courses in electricity fundamentals and one course in energy economics. In the following terms, students learn to design, install, and develop a thorough understanding of photovoltaics and domestic hot water systems.

Recent additions to Lane's offerings are Sustainability Coordinator and Water Conservation Technician degrees. Both programs were added to meet workforce demand.

Lane graduates find employment in a wide variety of disciplines and may work as facility managers, energy auditors, energy program coordinators, or control system specialists, for such diverse employers as engineering firms, public and private utilities, energy equipment companies, and departments of energy and as sustainability leaders within public and private sector organizations.

Lane Community College also provides continuing education for working professionals. The Sustainable Building Advisor (SBA) Certificate Program is a nine-month, specialized training program for working professionals. Graduate are able to advise employers or clients on strategies and tools for implementing sustainable building practices. Benefits from participating in the SBA program often include saving long-term building operating costs; improving the environmental, social, and economic viability of the region; and reducing environmental impacts and owner liability—not to mention the chance to improve one's job skills in a rapidly growing field.

The Building Operators Certificate is a professional development program created by The Northwest Energy Efficiency Council. It is offered through the Northwest Energy Education

Institute at Lane. The certificate is designed for operations and maintenance staff working in public or private commercial buildings. It certifies individuals in energy and resource-efficient operation of building systems at two levels: Level I–Building System Maintenance and Level II–Equipment Troubleshooting and Maintenance.

Lane Community College constantly scans the environment to assess workforce needs and develop programs that provide highly skilled employees. Lane, like most colleges, publishes information in its catalog on workforce demand and wages so that students can make informed decisions about program choice.

Green jobs will be a large part of a healthy economy. Opportunities will abound for those who take advantage of programs with a proven record of connecting with employers and successfully educating students to meet high skills standards.

Establishing a World-Class Wind Turbine Technician Academy

by Thomas Sutton, Director of Wind Energy and Technical Services
Kalamazoo Valley Community College

When Kalamazoo Valley Community College (KVCC) decided it wanted to become involved in the training of utility-grade technicians for wind-energy jobs, early on the choice was made to avoid another "me too" training course.

Our program here in Southwest Michigan, 30 miles from Lake Michigan, had to meet industry needs and industry standards.

It was also obvious from the start that the utility-grade or large wind industry had not yet adopted any uniform training standards in the United States.

Of course, these would come, but why should the college wait when European standards were solidly established and working well in Germany, France, Denmark and Great Britain?

As a result, in 2009, KVCC launched its Wind Turbine Technician Academy, the first of its kind in the United States. The noncredit academy runs 8 hours a day, five days a week, for twenty-four weeks of intense training in electricity, mechanics, wind dynamics, safety, and climbing. The college developed this program rather quickly—in eight months—to fast-track individuals into this emerging field.

KVCC based its program on the training standards forged by the Bildungszentrum fur Erneuerebare Energien (BZEE)—the Renewable Energy Education Center. Located in Husum, Germany, the BZEE was created and supported by major wind-turbine manufacturers, component makers, and enterprises that provide operation and maintenance services.

As wind-energy production increased throughout Europe, the need for high-quality, industry-driven, international standards emerged. The BZEE has become the leading trainer for wind-turbine technicians across Europe and now in Asia.

With the exception of one college in Canada, the standards were not yet available in North America. When Kalamazoo Valley realized it could be the first college or university in the United States to offer this training program—that was enough motivation to move forward.

For the College to become certified by the BZEE, it needed to hire and send an electrical instructor and a mechanical instructor to Germany for six weeks of "train the trainer." The instructors not only had to excel in their respective fields, they also needed to be able to climb the skyscraper towers supporting megawatt-class turbines—a unique combination of skills to possess. Truly, individuals who fit this job description don't walk through the door everyday—but we found them! Amazingly, we found a top mechanical instructor who was a part-time fireman and comfortable with tall ladder rescues and a skilled electrical instructor who used to teach rappelling off the Rockies to the Marine Corps.

In addition to employing new instructors, the College needed a working utility-grade nacelle that could fit in its training lab that would be located in the KVCC Michigan Technical Education Center. So one of the instructors traveled to Denmark and purchased a 300-kilowatt turbine.

Once their own training was behind them and the turbine was on its way from the North Sea, the instructors quickly turned to crafting the curriculum necessary for our graduates to earn both an academy certificate from KVCC and a certification from the BZEE.

Promoting the innovative program to qualified potential students across the country was the next step. News releases were published throughout Michigan, and they were also picked up on the Internet. Rather quickly, KVCC found itself with more than 500 requests for applications for a program built for 16 students.

Acceptance into the academy includes a medical release, a climbing test, reading and math tests, relevant work experience, and, finally, an interview. Students in the academy's pioneer class, which graduated in spring 2010, ranged in age from their late teens to early 50s. They hailed from throughout Michigan, Indiana, Ohio, and Illinois as well as from Puerto Rico and Great Britain.

The students brought with them degrees in marketing, law, business, science, and architecture, as well as entrepreneurial experiences in several businesses, knowledge of other languages, military service, extensive travel, and electrical, computer, artistic, and technical/mechanical skills.

Kalamazoo Valley's academy has provided some high-value work experiences for the students in the form of two collaborations with industry that has allowed them to maintain and/or repair actual utility-grade turbines, including those at the 2.5 megawatt size. This hands-on experience will add to the attractiveness of the graduates in the market place. Potential employers were recently invited to an open house where they could see the lab and meet members of this pioneer class.

The College's Turbine Technician Academy has also attracted a federal grant for $550,000 to expand its program through additional equipment purchases. The plan is to erect our own climbing tower. Climbing is a vital part of any valid program, and yet wind farms cannot afford to shut turbines down just for climb-training. The funds were put to use engineering, fabricating, and erecting a wind training tower that incorporated all of the necessary components to teach competency-based work at heights safety training.

When the students are asked what best distinguishes the Kalamazoo Valley program, their answers point to the experienced instructors and the working lab, which is constantly changing to offer the best training experiences. Students also consistently report that the hands-on field experience operating and maintaining the five large turbines during the course has set them apart at companies where they work.

Industry continues to tell us that community colleges need to offer fast-track training programs of this caliber if the nation is to reach the U.S. Department of Energy's goal of 20 percent renewable energy by 2030. This would require more than 1,500 new technicians each year.

The Wind Turbine Technician Academy continues the process improvements as directed by industry input. The academy not only holds the BZEE certification, it is also one of the few American Wind Energy Association (AWEA) Seal of Approval schools in the nation.

With that in mind, KVCC plans to host several BZEE orientation programs for other community colleges in order to encourage them to consider adopting the European training standards and start their own programs.

Meanwhile, applications are continuing to stream in from across the country for the next Wind Turbine Technician Academy program at Kalamazoo Valley Community College. For more information about the program, visit **http://www.kvccgrovescenter.com/career/wtta.**

How to Use This Guide

Peterson's *Two-Year Colleges 2021* contains a wealth of information for anyone interested in colleges offering associate degrees. This section details the criteria that institutions must meet to be included in this guide and provides information about research procedures used by Peterson's.

QUICK-REFERENCE CHART

The **Two-Year Colleges At-a-Glance Chart** is a geographically arranged table that lists colleges by name and city within the state, or country in which they are located. Areas listed include the United States, Canada, and other countries; the institutions are included because they are accredited by recognized U.S. accrediting bodies (see **Criteria for Inclusion** section).

The At-a-Glance chart contains basic information that enables you to compare institutions quickly according to broad characteristics such as degrees awarded, enrollment, application requirements, financial aid availability, and numbers of sports and majors offered. A dagger (†) after the institution's name indicates that an institution has an entry in the **Featured Two-Year Colleges** section.

Column 1: Degrees Awarded

C= *college transfer associate degree:* the degree awarded after a "university-parallel" program, equivalent to the first two years of a bachclor's degree.

T= *terminal associate degree:* the degree resulting from a one- to three-year program providing training for a specific occupation.

B= *bachelor's degree (baccalaureate):* the degree resulting from a liberal arts, science, professional, or preprofessional program normally lasting four years, although in some cases an accelerated program can be completed in three years.

M= *master's degree:* the first graduate (postbaccalaureate) degree in the liberal arts and sciences and certain professional fields, usually requiring one to two years of full-time study.

D= *doctoral degree* (research/scholarship, professional practice, or other)

Column 2: Institutional Control

Private institutions are designated as one of the following:

Ind = *independent* (nonprofit)

I-R = *independent-religious:* nonprofit; sponsored by or affiliated with a particular religious group or having a nondenominational or interdenominational religious orientation.

Prop = *proprietary* (profit-making)

Public institutions are designated by the source of funding, as follows:

Fed = *federal*

St = *state*

Comm = *commonwealth* (Puerto Rico)

Terr = *territory* (U.S. territories)

Cou = *county*

Dist = *district:* an administrative unit of public education, often having boundaries different from units of local government.

City = *city*

St-L = *state and local:* local may refer to county, district, or city.

St-R = *state-related:* funded primarily by the state but administratively autonomous.

Column 3: Student Body

M= *men only* (100% of student body)

PM = *coed, primarily men*

W= *women only* (100% of student body)

PW = *coed, primarily women*

M/W = *coeducational*

Column 4: Undergraduate Enrollment

The figure shown represents the number of full-time and part-time students enrolled in undergraduate degree programs as of fall 2019.

Columns 5–7: Enrollment Percentages

Figures are shown for the percentages of the fall 2019 undergraduate enrollment made up of students attending part-time (column 5) and students 25 years of age or older (column 6). Also listed is the percentage of students in the last graduating class who completed a college-transfer associate program and went directly on to four-year colleges (column 7).

For columns 8 through 15, the following letter codes are used: Y = yes; N = no; R = recommended; S = for some.

Columns 8–10: Admission Policies

The information in these columns shows whether the college has an open admission policy (column 8) whereby virtually all applicants are accepted without regard to standardized test scores, grade average, or class rank; whether a high school equivalency certificate is accepted in place of a high school diploma for admission consideration (column 9); and whether a high school transcript (column 10) is required as part of the application process. In column 10, the combination of the codes R and S indicates that a high school transcript is recommended for all applicants (R) or required for some (S).

Columns 11–12: Financial Aid

These columns show which colleges offer the following types of financial aid: need-based aid (column 11) and part-time jobs (column 12), including those offered through the federal government's Federal Work-Study program.

Columns 13–15: Services and Facilities

These columns show which colleges offer the following: career counseling (column 13) on either an individual or group basis, job placement services (column 14) for individual students, and college-owned or -operated housing facilities (column 16) for noncommuting students.

Column 16: Sports

This figure indicates the number of sports that a college offers at the intramural and/or intercollegiate levels.

Column 17: Majors

This figure indicates the number of major fields of study in which a college offers degree programs.

PROFILES OF TWO-YEAR COLLEGES AND SPECIAL MESSAGES

The **Profiles of Two-Year Colleges** contain basic data in capsule form for quick review and comparison. The following outline of the **Profile** format shows the section headings and the items that each section covers. Any item that does not apply to a particular college or for which no information was supplied is omitted from that college's **Profile.**

Bulleted Highlights

The bulleted highlights section features important information, for quick reference and comparison. The number of possible bulleted highlights that an ideal **Profile** would have if all questions were answered in a timely manner follow. However, not every institution provides all of the information necessary to fill out every bulleted line. In such instances, the line will not appear.

First Bullet

Institutional control: Private institutions are designated as independent (nonprofit), proprietary (profit-making), or independent, with a specific religious denomination or affiliation. Nondenominational or interdenominational religious orientation is possible and would be indicated.

Public institutions are designated by the source of funding. Designations include federal, state, province, commonwealth (Puerto Rico), territory (U.S. territories), county, district (an administrative unit of public education, often having boundaries different from units of local government), city, state and local (local may refer to county, district, or city), or state-related (funded primarily by the state but administratively autonomous).

Religious affiliation is also noted here.

Institutional type: Each institution is classified as one of the following:

> ***Primarily two-year college:*** Awards baccalaureate degrees, but the vast majority of students are enrolled in two-year programs.
>
> ***Four-year college:*** Awards baccalaureate degrees; may also award associate degrees; does not award graduate (postbaccalaureate) degrees.
>
> ***Upper-level institution:*** Awards baccalaureate degrees, but entering students must have at least two years of previous college-level credit; may also offer graduate degrees.
>
> ***Comprehensive institution:*** Awards baccalaureate degrees; may also award associate degrees; offers graduate degree programs, primarily at the master's, specialist's, or professional level, although one or two doctoral programs may be offered.
>
> ***University:*** Offers four years of undergraduate work plus graduate degrees through the doctorate in more than two academic or professional fields.

Founding date: If the year an institution was chartered differs from the year when instruction actually began, the earlier date is given.

System or administrative affiliation: Any coordinate institutions or system affiliations are indicated. An institution that has separate colleges or campuses for men and women but shares facilities and courses is termed a coordinate institution. A formal administrative grouping of institutions, either private or public, of which the college is a part, or the name of a single institution with which the college is administratively affiliated, is a system.

Second Bullet

Setting: Schools are designated as urban (located within a major city), suburban (a residential area within commuting distance of a major city), small-town (a small but compactly settled area not within commuting distance of a major city), or rural (a remote and sparsely populated area). The phrase *easy access to...* indicates that the campus is within an hour's drive of the nearest major metropolitan area that has a population greater than 500,000.

Third Bullet

Endowment: The total dollar value of funds and/or property donated to the institution or the multicampus educational system of which the institution is a part.

Fourth Bullet

Student body: An institution is coed (coeducational—admits men and women), primarily (80 percent or more) women, primarily men, women only, or men only.

Undergraduate students: Represents the number of full-time and part-time students enrolled in undergraduate degree programs as of fall 2019. The percentage of full-time undergraduates and the percentages of men and women are given.

Category Overviews

Undergraduates

For fall 2019, the number of full- and part-time undergraduate students is listed. This list provides the number of states and U.S. territories, including the District of Columbia and Puerto Rico (or for Canadian institutions, provinces and territories), and other countries from which undergraduates come. Percentages of undergraduates who are part-time or full-time students; transfers in; live on campus; out-of-state; Black or African American, non-Hispanic/Latino; Hispanic/Latino; Asian, non-Hispanic/Latino; Native Hawaiian or other Pacific Islander, non-Hispanic/Latino; American Indian or Alaska Native, non-Hispanic/Latino are given.

Retention: The percentage of freshmen (or, for upper-level institutions, entering students) who returned the following year for the fall term.

Freshmen

Admission: Figures are given for the number of students who applied for fall 2019 admission, the number of those who were admitted, and the number who enrolled. Freshman statistics include the average high school GPA; the percentage of freshmen who took the SAT® and received critical reading, writing, and math scores above 500, above 600, and above 700; as well as the percentage of freshmen taking the ACT® who received a composite score of 18 or higher.

Faculty

Total: The total number of faculty members; the percentage of full-time faculty members as of fall 2019; and the percentage of full-time faculty members who hold doctoral/first professional/ terminal degrees.

Student-faculty ratio: The school's estimate of the ratio of matriculated undergraduate students to faculty members teaching undergraduate courses.

Majors

This section lists the major fields of study offered by the college.

Academics

Calendar: Most colleges indicate one of the following: 4-1-4, 4-4-1, or a similar arrangement (two terms of equal length plus an abbreviated winter or spring term, with the numbers referring to months); semesters; trimesters; quarters; 3-3 (three courses for each of three terms); modular (the academic year is divided into small blocks of time; courses of varying lengths are assembled according to individual programs); or standard year (for most Canadian institutions).

Degrees: This names the full range of levels of certificates, diplomas, and degrees, including prebaccalaureate, graduate, and professional, that are offered by this institution:

Associate degree: Normally requires at least two but fewer than four years of full-time college work or its equivalent.

Bachelor's degree (baccalaureate): Requires at least four years but not more than five years of full-time college-level work or its equivalent. This includes all bachelor's degrees in which the normal four years of work are completed in three years and bachelor's degrees conferred in a five-year cooperative (work-study plan) program. A cooperative plan provides for alternate class attendance and employment in business, industry, or government. This allows students to combine actual work experience with their college studies.

Master's degree: Requires the successful completion of a program of study of at least the full-time equivalent of one but not more than two years of work beyond the bachelor's degree.

Doctoral degree (doctorate; research/scholarship, professional, or other): The highest degree in graduate study. The doctoral degree classification includes Doctor of Education, Doctor of Juridical Science, Doctor of Public Health, Doctor of Philosophy, Doctor of Podiatry, Doctor of Veterinary Medicine, and many more.

Post-master's certificate: Requires completion of an organized program of study of 24 credit hours beyond the master's degree but does not meet the requirements of academic degrees at the doctoral level.

Special study options: Details are next given here on study options available at each college:

Accelerated degree program: Students may earn a bachelor's degree in three academic years.

Academic remediation for entering students: Instructional courses designed for students deficient in the general competencies necessary for a regular postsecondary curriculum and educational setting.

Adult/continuing education programs: Courses offered for nontraditional students who are currently working or are returning to formal education.

Advanced placement: Credit toward a degree awarded for acceptable scores on College Board Advanced Placement (AP®) tests.

Cooperative (co-op) education programs: Formal arrangements with off-campus employers allowing students to combine work and study in order to gain degree-related experience, usually extending the time required to complete a degree.

Distance learning: For-credit courses that can be accessed off-campus via cable television, the Internet, satellite, DVD, correspondence course, or other media.

Double major: A program of study in which a student concurrently completes the requirements of two majors.

English as a second language (ESL): A course of study designed specifically for students whose native language is not English.

External degree programs: A program of study in which students earn credits toward a degree through a combination of independent study, college courses, proficiency examinations, and personal experience. External degree programs require minimal or no classroom attendance.

Freshmen honors college: A separate academic program for talented freshmen.

Honors programs: Any special program for very able students offering the opportunity for educational enrichment, independent study, acceleration, or some combination of these.

Independent study: Academic work, usually undertaken outside the regular classroom structure, chosen or designed by the student with departmental approval and instructor supervision.

Internships: Any short-term, supervised work experience usually related to a student's major field, for which the student earns academic credit. The work can be full-or part-time, on or off-campus, paid or unpaid.

Off-campus study: A formal arrangement with one or more domestic institutions under which students may take courses at the other institution(s) for credit.

Part-time degree program: Students may earn a degree through part-time enrollment in regular session (daytime) classes or evening, weekend, or summer classes.

Self-designed major: Program of study based on individual interests, designed by the student with the assistance of an adviser.

Services for LD students: Special help for learning-disabled students with resolvable difficulties, such as dyslexia.

Study abroad: An arrangement by which a student completes part of the academic program studying in another country. A college may operate a campus abroad or it may have a cooperative agreement with other U.S. institutions or institutions in other countries.

Summer session for credit: Summer courses through which students may make up degree work or accelerate their program.

Tutorials: Undergraduates can arrange for special in-depth academic assignments (not for remediation) working with faculty members one-on-one or in small groups.

ROTC: Army, Naval, or Air Force Reserve Officers' Training Corps programs offered either on campus, at a branch campus [designated by a (b)], or at a cooperating host institution [designated by (c)].

Unusual degree programs: Nontraditional programs such as a 3-2 degree program, in which three years of liberal arts study is followed by two years of study in a professional field at another institution (or in a professional division of the same institution), resulting in two bachelor's degrees or a bachelor's and a master's degree.

Library

The name of the college's main library, plus the number of other libraries on campus will appear followed by: *Books:* number of physical and digital/electronic books; *Serial titles:* number of physical and digital/electronic serial titles; and the number of *Databases*. Also included here (if provided by the school) are the number of "Weekly public service hours" and study area information—the number of hours and days of the week open and if students can reserve study rooms.

Student Life

Housing options: The institution's policy about whether students are permitted to live off-campus or are required to live on campus for a specified period; whether freshmen-only, coed, single-sex, cooperative, and disabled student housing options are available; whether campus housing is leased by the school and/or provided by a third party; whether freshman applicants are given priority for college housing. The phrase *college housing not available* indicates that no college-owned or -operated housing facilities are provided for undergraduates and that noncommuting students must arrange for their own accommodations.

Activities and organizations: Lists information on drama-theater groups, choral groups, marching bands, student-run campus newspapers, student-run radio stations, and social organizations (sororities, fraternities, eating clubs, etc.) and how many are represented on campus.

Campus security: Campus safety measures including 24-hour emergency response devices (telephones and alarms) and patrols by trained security personnel, student patrols, late-night transport-escort service, and controlled dormitory access (key, security card, etc.).

Student services: Information provided indicates services offered to students by the college, such as legal services, health clinics, personal-psychological counseling, and women's centers.

Athletics

Membership in one or more of the following athletic associations is indicated by initials.

NCAA: National Collegiate Athletic Association

NAIA: National Association of Intercollegiate Athletics

NCCAA: National Christian College Athletic Association

NJCAA: National Junior College Athletic Association

USCAA: United States Collegiate Athletic Association

CIS: Canadian Interuniversity Sports

The overall NCAA division in which all or most intercollegiate teams compete is designated by a roman numeral I, II, or III. All teams that do not compete in this division are listed as exceptions.

Sports offered by the college are divided into two groups: intercollegiate (**M** or **W** following the name of each sport indicates that it is offered for men or women or **M/W** if the sport is offered for both men and women) and intramural. An **s** in parentheses following an **M, W or M/W** for an intercollegiate sport indicates that athletic scholarships (or grants-in-aid) are offered for men and/or women in that sport, and a c indicates a club team as opposed to a varsity team.

Standardized Tests

The most commonly required standardized tests are the ACT®, SAT®, and SAT Subject Tests™. These and other standardized tests may be used for selective admission, as a basis for counseling or course placement, or for both purposes. This section notes if a test is used for admission or placement and whether it is required, required for some, or recommended.

In addition to the ACT and SAT, the following standardized entrance and placement examinations are referred to by their initials:

ABLE: Adult Basic Learning Examination

ACT ASSET: ACT Assessment of Skills for Successful Entry and Transfer

ACT PEP: ACT Proficiency Examination Program

CAT: California Achievement Tests

CELT: Comprehensive English Language Test

CPAt: Career Programs Assessment

CPT: Computerized Placement Test

DAT: Differential Aptitude Test

LSAT: Law School Admission Test

MAPS: Multiple Assessment Program Service

MCAT: Medical College Admission Test

MMPI: Minnesota Multiphasic Personality Inventory

OAT: Optometry Admission Test

PAA: Prueba de Aptitude Académica (Spanish-language version of the SAT)

PCAT: Pharmacy College Admission Test

PSAT/NMSQT: Preliminary SAT National Merit Scholarship Qualifying Test

SCAT: Scholastic College Aptitude Test

SRA: Scientific Research Association (administers verbal, arithmetical, and achievement tests)

TABE: Test of Adult Basic Education

TASP: Texas Academic Skills Program

TOEFL: Test of English as a Foreign Language (for international students whose native language is not English)

WPCT: Washington Pre-College Test

Costs

Costs are given for the 2019-20 academic year or for the 2018-19 academic year if 2019-20 figures were not yet available. Annual expenses may be expressed as a comprehensive fee (including full-time tuition, mandatory fees, and college room and board) or as separate figures for full-time tuition, fees, room and board, or room only. For public institutions where tuition differs according to residence, separate figures are given for area or state residents and for nonresidents. Part-time tuition is expressed in terms of a per-unit rate (per credit, per semester hour, etc.) as specified by the institution.

The tuition structure at some institutions is complex in that freshmen and sophomores may be charged a different rate from that for juniors and seniors, a professional or vocational division may have a different fee structure from the liberal arts division of the same institution, or part-time tuition may be prorated on a sliding scale according to the number of credit hours taken. Tuition and fees may vary according to academic program, campus/location, class time (day, evening, weekend), course/credit load, course level, degree level, reciprocity agreements, and student level. Room and board charges are reported as an average for one academic year and may vary according to the board plan selected, campus/location, type of housing facility, or student level. If no college-owned or college-operated housing facilities are offered, the phrase *college housing not available* will appear in the Housing section of the Student Life paragraph.

Tuition payment plans that may be offered to undergraduates include tuition prepayment, installment payments, and deferred payment. A tuition prepayment plan gives a student the option of locking in the current tuition rate for the entire term of enrollment by paying the full amount in advance rather than year by year. Colleges that offer such a prepayment plan may also help the student to arrange financing.

The availability of full or partial undergraduate tuition waivers to minority students, children of alumni, employees or their children, adult students, and senior citizens may be listed.

Financial Aid

The number of Federal Work Study and/or part-time jobs and average earnings are listed. Financial aid deadlines are given as well.

Applying

Application and admission options include the following:

Early admission: Highly qualified students may matriculate before graduating from high school.

Early action plan: An admission plan that allows students to apply and be notified of an admission decision well in advance of the regular notification dates. If accepted, the candidate is not committed to enroll; students may reply to the offer under the college's regular reply policy.

Early decision plan: A plan that permits students to apply and be notified of an admission decision (and financial aid offer, if applicable) well in advance of the regular notification date. Applicants agree to accept an offer of admission and to withdraw their applications from other colleges. Candidates who are not accepted under early decision are automatically considered with the regular applicant pool, without prejudice.

Deferred entrance: The practice of permitting accepted students to postpone enrollment, usually for a period of one academic term or year.

Application fee: The fee required with an application is noted. This is typically nonrefundable, although under certain specified conditions it may be waived or returned.

Requirements: Other application requirements are grouped into three categories: required for all, required for some, and recommended. They may include an essay, standardized test scores, a high school transcript, a minimum high school grade point average (expressed as a number on a scale of 0 to 4.0, where 4.0 equals A, 3.0 equals B, etc.), letters of recommendation, an interview on campus or with local alumni, and, for certain types of schools or programs, special requirements such as a musical audition or an art portfolio.

Application deadlines and notification dates: Admission application deadlines and dates for notification of acceptance or rejection are given either as specific dates or as **rolling** and **continuous.** Rolling means that applications are processed as they are received, and qualified students are accepted as long as there are openings. Continuous means that applicants are notified of acceptance or rejection as applications are processed up until the date indicated or the actual beginning of classes. The application deadline and the notification date for transfers are given if they differ from the dates for freshmen. Early decision and early action application deadlines and notification dates are also indicated when relevant.

Admissions Contact

The name, title, and phone number of the person to contact for application information are given at the end of the Profile. The admission office address is listed in most cases. Toll-free phone numbers may also be included. The admission office fax number and e-mail address, if available, are listed, provided the school wanted them printed for use by prospective students. Finally, the URL of the institution's Web site is provided.

Additional Information

When applicable, each college that has a **Featured Two-Year College Close-Up** in the guide will have a cross-reference appended to the Profile, referring you directly to the page number of that **Featured Two-Year College Close-Up.**

Institutional Changes Since *Peterson's® Two-Year Colleges 2020*

Here you will find an alphabetical listing of institutions that have recently closed, merged with other institutions, or changed their name or status.

FEATURED TWO-YEAR COLLEGES

These narrative descriptions provide an inside look at certain colleges, shifting the focus to a variety of other factors that should also be considered. The descriptions provide a wealth of information that is crucial in the college decision-making equation—such as tuition, financial aid, academic programs, and life on campus. Prepared exclusively by college officials, the descriptions are designed to help give students a better sense of the individuality of each institution, in terms that include campus environment, student activities, and lifestyle. Such quality-of-life intangibles can be the deciding factors in the college selection process. The absence of any college or university does not constitute an editorial decision on the part of Peterson's. In essence, these descriptions are an open forum for colleges, on a voluntary basis, to communicate their particular message to prospective students. The colleges included have paid a fee to Peterson's to provide this information. The Close-Ups in the **Featured Two-Year Colleges** section are edited to provide a generally consistent format across entries for your ease of comparison.

INDEXES

Associate Degree Programs at Two- and Four-Year Colleges

These indexes present hundreds of undergraduate fields of study that are currently offered most widely according to the colleges' responses on *Peterson's Annual Survey of Undergraduate Institutions*. The majors appear in alphabetical order, each followed by an alphabetical list of the schools that offer an associate-level program in that field. Liberal Arts and Studies indicates a general program with no specified major. The terms used for the majors are those of the U.S. Department of Education Classification of Instructional Programs (CIPs). Many institutions, however, use different terms. Readers should refer to the **Featured Two-Year Colleges** two-page descriptions in this book for the school's exact terminology. In addition, although the term "major" is used in this guide, some colleges may use other terms, such as "concentration," "program of study," or "field."

DATA COLLECTION PROCEDURES

The data contained in the **Profiles** of Two-Year Colleges and **Indexes** were researched in winter and spring 2019 through *Peterson's Annual Survey of Undergraduate Institutions*. Questionnaires were sent to the more than 1,700 colleges that meet the outlined inclusion criteria. All data included in this edition have been submitted by officials (usually admission and financial aid officers, registrars, or institutional research personnel) at the colleges themselves. All usable information received in time for publication has been included. The omission of any particular item from the **Profiles** of Two-Year Colleges and **Indexes** listing signifies either that the item is not applicable to that institution or that data were not available. Because of the comprehensive editorial review that takes place in our offices and because all material comes directly from college officials, Peterson's has every reason to believe that the information presented in this guide is accurate at the time of printing. However, students should check with a specific college or university at the time of application to verify such figures as tuition and fees, which may have changed since the publication of this volume.

CRITERIA FOR INCLUSION IN THIS BOOK

Peterson's Two-Year Colleges 2021 covers accredited institutions in the United States, U.S. territories, and other countries that award the associate degree as their most popular undergraduate offering (a few also offer bachelor's, master's, or doctoral degrees). The term two-year college is the commonly used designation for institutions that grant the associate degree, since two years is the normal duration of the traditional associate degree program. However, some programs may be completed in one year, others require three years, and, of course, part-time programs may take a considerably longer period. Therefore, "two-year college" should be understood as a conventional term that accurately describes most of the institutions included in this guide but which should not be taken literally in all cases. Also included are some non-degree-granting institutions, usually branch campuses of a multicampus system, which offer the equivalent of the first two years of a bachelor's degree, transferable to a bachelor's degree–granting institution.

To be included in this guide, an institution must have full accreditation or be a candidate for accreditation (preaccreditation) status by an institutional or specialized accrediting body recognized by the U.S. Department of Education or the Council for Higher Education Accreditation (CHEA). Institutional accrediting bodies, which review each institution as a whole, include the six regional associations of schools and colleges (Middle States, New England, North Central, Northwest, Southern, and Western), each of which is responsible for a specified portion of the United States and its territories. Other institutional accrediting bodies are national in scope and accredit specific kinds of institutions (e.g., Bible colleges, independent colleges, and rabbinical and Talmudic schools). Program registration by the New York State Board of Regents is considered to be the equivalent of institutional accreditation, since the board requires that all programs offered by an institution meet its standards before recognition is granted. This guide also includes institutions outside the United States that are accredited by these U.S. accrediting bodies. There are recognized specialized or professional accrediting bodies in more than forty different fields, each of which is authorized to accredit institutions or specific programs in its particular field. For specialized institutions that offer programs in one field only, we designate this to be the equivalent of institutional accreditation. A full explanation of the accrediting process and complete information on recognized, institutional (regional and national), and specialized accrediting bodies can be found online at **www.ed.gov/admins/finaid/accred/index.html**.

Institutional Changes Since *Peterson's®* *Two-Year Colleges 2020*

The American Academy of Dramatic Arts (Los Angeles, CA): *name changed to The American Academy of Dramatic Arts*

American Academy of Dramatic Arts (New York, NY): *name changed to The American Academy of Dramatic Arts*

American National University (Charlottesville, VA): *closed.*

American National University (Danville, KY): *closed.*

American National University (Florence, KY): *closed.*

American National University (Harrisonburg, VA): *closed.*

American National University (Kettering, OH): *closed.*

American National University (Lexington, KY): *closed.*

American National University (Lynchburg, VA): *closed.*

American National University (Richmond, KY): *closed.*

American National University (Youngstown, OH): *closed.*

Antioch University (Midwest Yellow Springs, OH): *closed.*

Antonelli College (Cincinnati, OH): *closed.*

Antonelli College (Hattiesburg, MS): *closed.*

Antonelli College (Jackson, MS): *closed.*

Bethel College (Mishawaka, IN): *name changed to Bethel University*

Central Community College (Columbus, NE): *closed.*

Central Community College (Grand Island, NE): *closed.*

Central Community College (Hastings, NE): *closed.*

College America (Colorado Springs, CO): *closed*

Delaware Technical and Community College System (Dover, DE) *closed*

Florida Keys Community College (Key West, FL): *name changed to The College of the Florida Keys*

MacMurray College (Jacksonville, IL): *closed.*

Metro Business College (Jefferson City, MO): *closed.*

Metro Business College (Rolla, MO): *closed.*

Metro Business College (Cape Girardeau, MO): *closed.*

Nebraska Christian College of Hope International University (Papillion, NE): *closed.*

Notre Dame de Namur University (Belmont, CA): *closed.*

North Florida Community College (Madison, FL): *name changed to North Florida College*

Rochester College (Detroit, MI): *name changed to Rochester University*

Quick-Reference Chart

Two-Year Colleges At-a-Glance

This chart includes the names and locations of accredited two-year colleges in the United States, Canada, and other countries and shows institutions' responses to the *Peterson's Annual Survey of Undergraduate Institutions*. If an institution submitted incomplete data, one or more columns opposite the institution's name is blank. A dagger after the school name indicates that the institution has one or more entries in the *Featured Two-Year Colleges* section. If a school does not appear, it did not report any of the information.

Y—Yes; N—No; R—Recommended; S—For Some

Institution	Location	Degrees Awarded: College Transfer Associate (C), Terminal Associate (T), Bachelor's (B), Master's (M), Doctoral (D)	Institutional Control: Independent, Independent-Religious, Proprietary, Federal, State, Commonwealth, Territory, County, District, City, State and Local, State-Related	Student Body: Men, Primarily Men, Women, Primarily Women, Coed	Undergraduate Enrollment	Percent Attending Part-Time	Percent 25 Years of Age or Older	Percent of Grads Going on to Four-Year Colleges	Open Admissions	High School Equivalency Certificate Accepted	High School Transcript Required	Need-Based Aid Available	Part-Time Jobs Available	Career Counseling Available	Job Placement Services Available	College Housing Available	Number of Sports Offered	Number of Majors Offered
UNITED STATES																		
Alabama																		
Bevill State Community College	Jasper	C,T	St	M/W	3,872	59	25	19	Y	Y		Y	Y	Y	Y	Y		14
Coastal Alabama Community College	Bay Minette	C,T	St	M/W	3,323	36												
H. Councill Trenholm State Community College	Montgomery	C	St	M/W	1,845													
Lawson State Community College	Birmingham	C,T	St	M/W	3,031	41												
Lurleen B. Wallace Community College	Andalusia	C,T	St	M/W	1,767	51	22		Y	Y	S	Y	Y	Y		Y	3	11
Marion Military Institute	Marion	C	St	M/W	408		1		N	Y	Y	Y	Y	Y		Y	14	2
Northwest-Shoals Community College	Muscle Shoals	C	St	M/W	3,512	63	19	53	Y	Y	Y	Y	Y	Y		N		19
Alaska																		
University of Alaska Anchorage, Kenai Peninsula College	Soldotna	C,T,B	St	M/W	2,142	67			Y	Y	Y	Y	Y			N		9
Arizona																		
Carrington College – Mesa	Mesa	T	Prop	M/W	599	6												
Carrington College – Phoenix East	Phoenix	T	Prop	M/W	261	32												
Carrington College – Phoenix North	Phoenix	T	Prop	M/W	653													
Chandler-Gilbert Community College	Chandler	C,T	St-L	M/W	15,585	72	12		Y			Y	Y	Y	Y	N	6	93
Cochise County Community College District	Sierra Vista	C,T	St-L	M/W	3,918	61												
Coconino Community College	Flagstaff	C,T	St	M/W	3,608	69												
Din&,e College	Tsaile	C,T	Fed	M/W	1,657	51												
Eastern Arizona College	Thatcher	C,T	St-L	M/W	6,027	71	46	10	Y		R	Y	Y	Y	Y	Y	13	60
Mohave Community College	Kingman	C	St	M/W	4,071	80												
Rio Salado College	Tempe	C,T	St-L	M/W	20,865													
Tohono O'odham Community College	Sells	C,T	Pub	M/W	431	68	58	52	Y	Y	Y			Y		Y	1	13
Arkansas																		
Arkansas State University Mid-South	West Memphis	C,T	St	M/W	1,423	75												
Arkansas State University – Newport	Newport	C,T	St	M/W	2,270	54												
Black River Technical College	Pocahontas	C,T	St	M/W	1,472	44	43		Y	Y	S	Y		Y	Y	Y		14
Cossatot Community College of the University of Arkansas	De Queen	C,T	St	M/W	1,575													
North Arkansas College	Harrison	C,T	St-L	M/W	2,429	39												
Ozarka College	Melbourne	C,T	St	M/W	1,123													
South Arkansas Community College	El Dorado	C,T	St	M/W	1,412	62	43		Y	Y	Y	Y	Y	Y	Y	N	1	20
University of Arkansas Community College at Morrilton	Morrilton	C,T	St	M/W	1,902	46												
University of Arkansas – Pulaski Technical College	North Little Rock	C,T	St	M/W	10,255	53												
California																		
Allan Hancock College	Santa Maria	C,T	Dist	M/W	10,387	71												
Barstow Community College	Barstow	C,T	Dist	M/W	4,791													
Cabrillo College	Aptos	C,T	Dist	M/W	11,321													
Carrington College – Pleasant Hill	Pleasant Hill	T	Prop	M/W	437	18												
Carrington College – Sacramento	Sacramento	T	Prop	M/W	1,186	21												
Carrington College – San Jose	San Jose	T	Prop	M/W	715	9												
Carrington College – San Leandro	San Leandro	T	Prop	M/W	416	4												
Chaffey College	Rancho Cucamonga	C,T	Dist	M/W	21,399													
Citrus College	Glendora	C	Dist	M/W	18,672	47			Y	Y	Y	Y	Y	Y	Y	N	10	59
City College of San Francisco	San Francisco	C,T	Dist	M/W	32,950													
Coastline Community College	Fountain Valley	C	Dist	M/W	11,431	78												
College of Alameda	Alameda	C,T	Dist	M/W	7,302													
College of Marin	Kentfield	C,T	Dist	M/W	5,026	73												
College of the Canyons	Santa Clarita	C,T	Dist	M/W	19,865	68												
College of the Redwoods	Eureka	C,T	Dist	M/W	4,572													
College of the Sequoias	Visalia	C,T	Dist	M/W	13,449	62												
College of the Siskiyous	Weed	C,T	Dist	M/W	3,045													
Compton College	Compton	C,T	Dist	M/W	7,900													
Copper Mountain College	Joshua Tree	C,T	Dist	M/W	2,500	32												
Cosumnes River College	Sacramento	C,T	Dist	M/W	14,545													
Cuyamaca College	El Cajon	C,T	Dist	M/W	7,706	79												
De Anza College	Cupertino	C,T	Dist	M/W	18,882	50	56		Y			Y	Y	Y	Y	N	13	77
East Los Angeles College	Monterey Park	C,T	Dist	M/W	31,749	75												
Feather River College	Quincy	C,T,B	Dist	M/W	1,990	77	52	33	Y			Y	Y	Y	Y	Y	9	26
FIDM/Fashion Institute of Design & Merchandising, Orange County Campus	Irvine	C,T	Prop	PW	71	6												
FIDM/Fashion Institute of Design & Merchandising, San Diego Campus	San Diego	C,T	Prop	PW	66	8												
Foothill College	Los Altos Hills	C,T	Dist	M/W	15,765	67												
Fullerton College	Fullerton	C,T	Dist	M/W	17,176	72	24		Y			Y	Y	Y	Y	N	13	75
Glendale Career College	Glendale	C,T	Prop	M/W	600													
Imperial Valley College	Imperial	C,T	Dist	M/W	10,592													
Los Angeles City College	Los Angeles	C,T	Dist	M/W	14,937	78			Y		R		Y	Y	Y	Y	3	51
Los Angeles Mission College	Sylmar	C,T	Dist	M/W	10,128	81	33		Y			Y	Y	Y		N		24
MiraCosta College	Oceanside	C,T,B	Dist	M/W	14,687	66	32		Y			Y	Y				2	40

This chart includes the names and locations of accredited two-year colleges in the United States, Canada, and other countries and shows institutions' responses to the *Peterson's Annual Survey of Undergraduate Institutions.* If an institution submitted incomplete data, one or more columns opposite the institution's name is blank. A dagger after the school name indicates that the institution has one or more entries in the *Featured Two-Year Colleges* section. If a school does not appear, it did not report any of the information.

Y—Yes; N—No; R—Recommended; S—For Some

Institution	Location	Degrees Awarded: College Transfer Associate (C), Terminal Associate (T), Bachelor's (B), Master's (M), Doctoral (D)	Institutional Control: Independent (Ind), Independent-Religious (I-R), Proprietary (Prop), Federal, State, Commonwealth, Territory, County, District, City, State and Local, State-Related	Student Body: Men, Primarily Men, Women, Primarily Women, Coed	Undergraduate Enrollment	Percent Attending Part-Time	Percent 25 Years of Age or Older	Percent of Grads Going on to Four-Year Colleges	Open Admissions	High School Equivalency Certificate Accepted	High School Transcript Required	Need-Based Aid Available	Part-Time Jobs Available	Career Counseling Available	Job Placement Services Available	College Housing Available	Number of Sports Offered	Number of Majors Offered
Mt. San Antonio College	Walnut	C,T	Dist	M/W	4,753	39		14	Y		S	Y	Y	Y	Y	Y	14	81
Mt. San Jacinto College	San Jacinto	C,T	Dist	M/W	14,170	64												
Napa Valley College	Napa	C,T	Dist	M/W	6,908	72												
Ohlone College	Fremont	C,T	Dist	M/W	11,318	72												
San Joaquin Delta College	Stockton	C,T	Dist	M/W	18,102		31		Y			Y	Y	Y	Y	N	18	57
Santa Barbara City College	Santa Barbara	T	Dist	M/W	18,092	56												
Santa Rosa Junior College	Santa Rosa	C,T	Dist	M/W	18,984													
Shasta College	Redding	C,T	Dist	M/W	10,240	58												
Sierra College	Rocklin	C,T	Dist	M/W	18,796	66	35		Y			Y	Y	Y	Y	Y	13	60
Theatre of Arts	Hollywood	B	Prop	M/W					Y		Y			Y	Y	Y		
Ventura College	Ventura	C,T	Dist	M/W	12,750													
Colorado																		
Aims Community College	Greeley	C,T	Dist	M/W	6,099	64												
Arapahoe Community College	Littleton	C,T,B	St	M/W	10,963	81	28		Y			Y	Y	Y	Y	N		33
Bel – Rea Institute of Animal Technology	Denver	T	Prop	M/W	275				Y	Y	Y	Y		Y		Y		1
Colorado Northwestern Community College	Rangely	C,T	St	M/W	1,154	58												
Community College of Aurora	Aurora	C,T	St	M/W	7,982	77												
Community College of Denver	Denver	C,T	St	M/W	8,232	70			Y			Y	Y	Y	Y	N	23	21
Front Range Community College	Westminster	C,T,B	St	M/W	18,880	74	34		Y			Y	Y	Y	Y	N		34
IBMC College	Fort Collins	T	Prop	M/W	1,020		63		Y	Y	Y	Y	Y	Y	Y	N		7
Lamar Community College	Lamar	C,T	St	M/W	811	47												
Northeastern Junior College	Sterling	C,T	St	M/W	1,392	43	24		Y		R	Y	Y	Y	Y	Y	8	44
Pueblo Community College	Pueblo	C,T,B	St	M/W	5,617	68												
Connecticut																		
Asnuntuck Community College	Enfield	C,T	St	M/W	1,945	66												
Capital Community College	Hartford	C,T	St	M/W	3,315													
Gateway Community College	New Haven	C,T	St	M/W	8,201	68												
Housatonic Community College	Bridgeport	C,T	St	M/W	5,138	66	41		Y	Y	Y	Y	Y	Y	Y			12
Manchester Community College	Manchester	C,T	St	M/W	5,511	67	32		Y	Y	Y		Y			N	4	31
Middlesex Community College	Middletown	C,T	St	M/W	2,424	65	39	80	Y	Y	Y	Y	Y	Y	Y	N		26
Naugatuck Valley Community College	Waterbury	C,T	St	M/W	6,378	66												
Delaware																		
Delaware College of Art and Design	Wilmington	C	Ind	M/W	210	9												
Delaware Technical & Community College, Terry Campus	Dover	C,T	St	M/W	2,955	57												
Florida																		
City College	Altamonte Springs	T,B	Ind	PW	217													
City College	Fort Lauderdale	T,B	Ind	M/W	677													
City College	Gainesville	T,B	Ind	M/W	426													
City College	Miami	T,B	Ind	M/W	416													
College of Central Florida	Ocala	C,T,B	St-L	M/W	6,820	56												
Daytona State College	Daytona Beach	C,B	St	M/W	13,430	59	40		Y	Y	Y	Y	Y	Y	Y	N	9	45
Eastern Florida State College	Cocoa	C,T,B	St	M/W	16,711	65												
Florida SouthWestern State College	Fort Myers	C,T,B	St-L	M/W	16,672	62	22		Y	Y	Y	Y	Y			Y	5	41
Gulf Coast State College	Panama City	C,T,B	St	M/W	4,797	66	33		Y	Y	Y	Y	Y	Y	Y	N	4	43
Hillsborough Community College	Tampa	C,T	St	M/W	22,404	54	33		Y	Y	Y	Y	Y	Y		Y	5	43
Miami Dade College	Miami	C,T,B	St-L	M/W	56,001	58	28		Y	Y	Y	Y	Y	Y	Y	N	4	193
Pensacola State College	Pensacola	C,B	St	M/W	7,771	56	70	61	Y	Y	Y	Y	Y	Y	Y	Y	10	106
Seminole State College of Florida	Sanford	C,T,B	St-L	M/W	17,706	65												
Southeastern College – West Palm Beach	West Palm Beach	T	Prop	M/W	558	52	70		Y	Y	Y	Y	Y	Y	Y	N		9
Georgia																		
Andrew College	Cuthbert	C	I-R	M/W	293													
Atlanta Metropolitan State College	Atlanta	C,T	St	M/W	2,241													
East Georgia State College	Swainsboro	C,T,B	St	M/W	3,001	23												
Georgia Highlands College	Rome	C,T,B	St	M/W	6,184	53												
Hawaii																		
Hawaii Tokai International College	Kapolei	C,T	Ind	M/W	64			84	N	Y	Y	Y				Y		1
Honolulu Community College	Honolulu	C,T	St	M/W	4,368	63												
Kapiolani Community College	Honolulu	C,T	St	M/W	6,899													
Kauai Community College	Lihue	C	St	M/W	1,486													
Leeward Community College	Pearl City	C,T	St	M/W	7,942	58												
Idaho																		
Carrington College – Boise	Boise	T	Prop	M/W	440	12												
College of Eastern Idaho	Idaho Falls	C,T	St	M/W	1,595	66	33		Y	Y	Y	Y	Y	Y	Y	N		16
College of Southern Idaho	Twin Falls	T	St-L	M/W	6,906	72												
College of Western Idaho	Nampa	C,T	St	M/W	9,204													
North Idaho College	Coeur d'Alene	C,T	St-L	M/W	5,723	40			N		S	Y	Y	Y	Y	Y	18	67
Illinois																		
Black Hawk College	Moline	C,T	St-L	M/W	4,472	65	27	67	Y		R	Y	Y	Y	Y	N	6	28
Carl Sandburg College	Galesburg	C,T	St-L	M/W	1,944													
City Colleges of Chicago, Harold Washington College	Chicago	C,T	St-L	M/W	8,464													
City Colleges of Chicago, Harry S. Truman College	Chicago	C,T	St-L	M/W	13,174													
City Colleges of Chicago, Kennedy-King College	Chicago	C,T	St-L	M/W	2,818	44												
City Colleges of Chicago, Malcolm X College	Chicago	C,T	St-L	M/W	6,031	58												
City Colleges of Chicago, Wilbur Wright College	Chicago	C,T	St-L	M/W	6,826	68												

This chart includes the names and locations of accredited two-year colleges in the United States, Canada, and other countries and shows institutions' responses to the *Peterson's Annual Survey of Undergraduate Institutions*. If an institution submitted incomplete data, one or more columns opposite the institution's name is blank. A dagger after the school name indicates that the institution has one or more entries in the *Featured Two-Year Colleges* section. If a school does not appear, it did not report any of the information.

Y—Yes; N—No; R—Recommended; S—For Some

		Degrees Awarded College Transfer Associate (C), Terminal Associate (T), Bachelor's (B), Master's (M), Doctoral (D)	**Institutional Control** Independent, Independent-Religious, Proprietary, Federal, State, Commonwealth, Territory, County, District, City, State and Local, State-Related	**Student Body** Men, Primarily Men, Women, Primarily Women, Coed	Undergraduate Enrollment	Percent Attending Part-Time	Percent 25 Years of Age or Older	Percent of Grads Going on to Four-Year Colleges	Open Admissions	High School Equivalency Certificate Accepted	High School Transcript Required	Need-Based Aid Available	Part-Time Jobs Available	Career Counseling Available	Job Placement Services Available	College Housing Available	Number of Sports Offered	Number of Majors Offered
College of DuPage	Glen Ellyn	C,T	St-L	M/W	23,903	67			Y		.	Y	Y	Y	Y	N	12	83
College of Lake County	Grayslake	C,T	Dist	M/W	17,577	72												
Danville Area Community College	Danville	C,T	St-L	M/W	2,279	61	24	51	Y	Y	Y	Y	Y	Y	Y	N	5	31
Fox College	Bedford Park	T	Priv	M/W	443					Y						N		6
Harper College	Palatine	C,T	St-L	M/W	13,477	66	30		Y		Y	Y	Y	Y		N	12	65
Heartland Community College	Normal	C,T	St-L	M/W	4,722	62												
Kankakee Community College	Kankakee	C,T	St-L	M/W	3,306	63												
Kaskaskia College	Centralia	C,T	St-L	M/W	3,248	60	20		Y	Y	Y	Y	Y	Y	Y	N	8	41
Kishwaukee College	Malta	C,T	St-L	M/W	3,775	57	26		Y		R,S	Y	Y	Y		Y	8	29
McHenry County College	Crystal Lake	C,T	St-L	M/W	7,031	69	27		Y		R	Y	Y	Y	Y	N	6	26
Morton College	Cicero	C,T	St-L	M/W	4,439	74	28		Y	Y	Y	Y	Y	Y	Y	N	6	28
Northwestern College – Chicago Campus	Chicago		Prop	M/W	1,082	56	61		N	Y		Y	Y	Y	Y	N		10
Oakton Community College	Des Plaines	C,T	Dist	M/W	7,652		34		Y	Y	R	Y	Y	Y		N	10	29
Rend Lake College	Ina	C,T	St	M/W	2,287	51	23		Y	Y	Y	Y	Y	Y	Y	N	5	32
Rock Valley College	Rockford	C	Dist	M/W	6,092	55	25		Y		Y	Y	Y	Y	Y	N	6	31
Shawnee Community College	Ullin	C,T	St-L	M/W	1,083	41	20		Y	Y	Y	Y	Y	Y	Y	N	3	19
South Suburban College	South Holland	C,T	St-L	M/W	4,073	74	52		Y	Y	Y	Y	Y	Y		N	5	23
Waubonsee Community College	Sugar Grove	C,T	Dist	M/W	10,721	68												
Indiana																		
Vincennes University	Vincennes	C,B	St	M/W	17,239	45	30		Y	Y	Y	Y	Y			Y	7	88
Iowa																		
Des Moines Area Community College	Ankeny	C,T	St-L	M/W	23,258	74	24		Y		S	Y	Y	Y	Y	Y	8	50
Hawkeye Community College	Waterloo	C,T	St-L	M/W	5,112	59	27		Y	Y	Y	Y	Y	Y	Y	N	11	38
Iowa Central Community College	Fort Dodge	C,T	St-L	M/W	5,237	51	13		Y	Y	R,S	Y	Y	Y	Y	Y	18	49
Northeast Iowa Community College	Calmar	C,T	St-L	M/W	4,408	74	32		Y		R	Y	Y	Y	Y	N	8	29
Northwest Iowa Community College	Sheldon	C,T	St	M/W	1,747													
St. Luke's College	Sioux City	C,T,B	Ind	M/W	235	48	51	60	N	Y	Y	Y	Y	Y	Y	N		4
Southeastern Community College	West Burlington	C	St-L	M/W	2,844	54												
Southwestern Community College	Creston	C,T	St	M/W	1,581	57	29		Y	Y	Y	Y	Y	Y	Y	Y	8	16
Western Iowa Tech Community College	Sioux City	C,T	St	M/W	5,976	70	37		Y	Y	R	Y	Y	Y		Y	8	51
Kansas																		
Cloud County Community College	Concordia	C,T	St-L	M/W	1,873	57												
Donnelly College	Kansas City	C,T,B	I-R	M/W	303	46	50		Y	Y	R	Y	Y	Y	Y	N	1	8
Garden City Community College	Garden City	C,T	Cou	M/W	1,997	46												
Hesston College	Hesston	C,T,B	I-R	M/W	378	9	15		Y	Y	Y	Y	Y	Y		Y	9	12
Hutchinson Community College	Hutchinson	C,T	St-L	M/W	5,574	63	25	80	Y	Y	Y	Y	Y	Y		Y	12	56
Kentucky																		
American National University – Louisville	Louisville	T,B	Prop	M/W	233													
American National University – Pikeville	Pikeville	T	Prop	M/W														
Daymar College	Bowling Green	C	Prop	PW	499													
Gateway Community and Technical College	Florence	C,T	St	M/W	4,719	73	11		Y	Y	Y			Y		N		26
Henderson Community College	Henderson	C,T	St	M/W	1,586	68												
Hopkinsville Community College	Hopkinsville	C,T	St	M/W	3,120	60			Y	Y	R	Y	Y	Y	Y	N	5	14
Maysville Community and Technical College	Maysville	C,T	St	M/W	3,889	65			Y	Y	Y	Y	Y	Y	Y	N		17
Owensboro Community and Technical College	Owensboro	C,T	St	M/W	4,004	59	37		Y	Y	Y	Y	Y	Y	Y	N		26
Somerset Community College	Somerset	C,T	St	M/W	5,657	61	43		Y	Y	Y	Y	Y	Y		N		22
West Kentucky Community and Technical College	Paducah	C,T	St	M/W	4,985	59	25		Y	Y	Y	Y	Y	Y	Y	N	1	26
Louisiana																		
Baton Rouge Community College	Baton Rouge	C,T	St	M/W	8,242													
Bossier Parish Community College	Bossier City	C	St	M/W	6,229	47	41		Y			Y	Y	Y	Y	N	10	35
Delgado Community College	New Orleans	C,T	St	M/W	18,698	58												
Nunez Community College	Chalmette	C,T	St	M/W	2,599	62												
Southern University at Shreveport	Shreveport	C,T	St	M/W	2,651	43												
Sowela Technical Community College	Lake Charles	C,T	St	M/W	3,459	48												
Maine																		
Central Maine Community College	Auburn	C,T	St	M/W	3,218	63	36		N	Y	Y	Y	Y	Y	Y	Y	7	32
Southern Maine Community College	South Portland	C,T	St	M/W	8,491	60			Y	Y	Y	Y	Y	Y		Y	5	36
Maryland																		
Baltimore City Community College	Baltimore	C,T	St	M/W	6,953													
Chesapeake College	Wye Mills	C,T	St-L	M/W	2,184	74	25		Y	Y	Y	Y	Y	Y		N	5	25
College of Southern Maryland	La Plata	C,T	St-L	M/W	8,411	63												
Community College of Baltimore County	Baltimore	C,T	Cou	M/W	18,830	73			Y	Y	Y			Y		N	9	59
Hagerstown Community College	Hagerstown	C,T	St-L	M/W	3,848	72	34		Y		S	Y	Y	Y	Y	N	8	31
Harford Community College	Bel Air	C,T	St-L	M/W	6,100	64												
Montgomery College	Rockville	C	St-L	M/W	21,132	66	29		Y		R	Y	Y	Y	Y	N	12	44
Prince George's Community College	Largo	C,T	Cou	M/W	11,861	75												
Wor-Wic Community College	Salisbury	C,T	St-L	M/W	2,894	75	42		Y		R		Y	Y		N		20
Massachusetts																		
Benjamin Franklin Institute of Technology	Boston	C,T,B	Ind	M/W	597	22	25		Y	Y	Y		Y	Y	Y	N	3	16
Bristol Community College	Fall River	C,T	St	M/W	7,637		38			Y	Y	Y	Y	Y	Y	N	5	61
Bunker Hill Community College	Boston	C	St	M/W	12,657	67												
Cape Cod Community College	West Barnstable	C,T	St	M/W	3,221													
Massachusetts Bay Community College	Wellesley Hills	C,T	St	M/W	4,368	66												
Mount Wachusett Community College	Gardner	C,T	St	M/W	3,674	67	47		Y	Y	Y	Y	Y	Y	Y	N	8	41

This chart includes the names and locations of accredited two-year colleges in the United States, Canada, and other countries and shows institutions' responses to the *Peterson's Annual Survey of Undergraduate Institutions*. If an institution submitted incomplete data, one or more columns opposite the institution's name is blank. A dagger after the school name indicates that the institution has one or more entries in the *Featured Two-Year Colleges* section. If a school does not appear, it did not report any of the information.

Y—Yes; N—No; R—Recommended; S—For Some

Institution	Location	Degrees Awarded: College Transfer Associate (C), Terminal Associate (T), Bachelor's (B), Master's (M), Doctoral (D)	Institutional Control: Independent (Ind), Independent-Religious, Proprietary, Federal, State, Commonwealth, Territory, County, District, City, State and Local, State-Related	Student Body: Men, Primarily Men, Women, Primarily Women, Coed	Undergraduate Enrollment	Percent Attending Part-Time	Percent 25 Years of Age or Older	Percent of Grads Going on to Four-Year Colleges	Open Admissions	High School Equivalency Certificate Accepted	High School Transcript Required	Need-Based Aid Available	Part-Time Jobs Available	Career Counseling Available	Job Placement Services Available	College Housing Available	Number of Sports Offered	Number of Majors Offered
Northern Essex Community College	Haverhill	C,T	St	M/W	4,932	68	33		Y	Y	Y	Y	Y	Y	Y	N	11	57
Quinsigamond Community College	Worcester	C,T	St	M/W	7,293	66	38		Y	Y	Y	Y	Y	Y	Y	N	7	58
Springfield Technical Community College	Springfield	C,T	St	M/W	5,066	57	37		Y	Y	Y	Y	Y	Y	Y	N	3	50
Michigan																		
Bay de Noc Community College	Escanaba	C,T	Cou	M/W	1,820	61	12		Y	Y	R	Y	Y			Y	4	27
Bay Mills Community College	Brimley	C	Dist	M/W	620													
Delta College	University Center	C,T	Dist	M/W	7,819	65	31		Y		R	Y	Y	Y	Y	N	6	61
Glen Oaks Community College	Centreville	C,T	St-L	M/W	1,221	57												
Grand Rapids Community College	Grand Rapids	C,T	Dist	M/W	13,252	70	29		Y	Y	Y	Y	Y	Y		N	6	35
Kirtland Community College	Roscommon	C,T	Dist	M/W	1,460	69	36		Y	Y	Y	Y	Y	Y	Y	N	3	21
Monroe County Community College	Monroe	C,T	Cou	M/W	3,144	70												
Muskegon Community College	Muskegon	C,T	St-L	M/W	4,506	67												
Schoolcraft College	Livonia	C,T,B	Dist	M/W	9,230	76	30		Y	Y	R,S	Y	Y	Y	Y	N	6	44
Southwestern Michigan College	Dowagiac	C,T	St-L	M/W	2,141	57	22		Y	Y	Y	Y	Y			Y	7	22
Wayne County Community College District	Detroit	C,T	St-L	M/W	14,957	87												
Minnesota																		
Alexandria Technical and Community College	Alexandria	C,T	St	M/W	2,481	56	24		Y	Y	S	Y	Y	Y		N	4	25
Anoka-Ramsey Community College	Coon Rapids	C,T	St	M/W	8,808	62			Y	Y	S	Y	Y	Y		N	11	34
Anoka Technical College	Anoka	C,T	St	M/W	1,527	53			Y	Y	Y	Y	Y	Y	Y	N		22
Central Lakes College	Brainerd	C,T	St	M/W	4,357	63	21		Y	Y	Y	Y	Y	Y	Y	N	7	30
Century College	White Bear Lake	C,T	St	M/W	8,653	60	37		Y	Y	Y	Y	Y	Y		N	12	53
Dakota County Technical College	Rosemount	C,T	St	M/W	3,672	54												
Dunwoody College of Technology	Minneapolis	T,B	Ind	PM	1,358	18	49		N	Y	Y	Y	Y	Y	Y	Y		28
Inver Hills Community College	Inver Grove Heights	C,T	St	M/W	6,342	61												
Lake Superior College	Duluth	C,T	St	M/W	4,690	61												
Mesabi Range College	Virginia	C,T	St	M/W	1,165	48	23		Y	Y	Y	Y	Y	Y	Y	Y	6	16
Minnesota State College–Southeast Technical	Winona	C,T	St	M/W	1,814	61												
Minnesota State Community and Technical College	Fergus Falls	C,T	St	M/W	2,429	84	34	68	Y	Y		Y	Y	Y	Y	Y		70
Minnesota State Community and Technical College – Detroit Lakes	Detroit Lakes	C,T	St	M/W	755	59	26				Y					N		21
Minnesota State Community and Technical College – Moorhead	Moorhead	C	St	M/W	2,276	50	26				Y					Y	6	37
Minnesota State Community and Technical College – Wadena	Wadena	C,T	St	M/W	548	39	26				Y							11
Normandale Community College	Bloomington	C,T	St	M/W	14,993													
Northland Community and Technical College	Thief River Falls	C,T	St	M/W	3,156	60	32		Y	Y	Y	Y	Y	Y		N	7	33
Ridgewater College	Willmar	C,T	St	M/W					Y	Y	Y	Y	Y			N	5	50
Saint Paul College – A Community & Technical College	St. Paul	C,T	St-R	M/W	5,928	59												
Mississippi																		
Coahoma Community College	Clarksdale	C,T	St-L	M/W	2,216	11												
East Central Community College	Decatur	C,T	St-L	M/W	2,281													
Meridian Community College	Meridian	C,T	St-L	M/W	3,402	33	33		Y	Y	Y	Y	Y	Y	Y	Y	10	27
Mississippi Delta Community College	Moorhead	C,T	Dist	M/W	1,944	14			N	Y	Y	Y	Y	Y		Y	4	44
Northeast Mississippi Community College	Booneville	C,T	St	M/W	3,512													
Missouri																		
Cottey College	Nevada	C,B	Ind	W	265	2												
Crowder College	Neosho	C,T	St-L	M/W	4,401	57	26		Y	Y	Y	Y	Y	Y	Y	Y	4	46
East Central College	Union	C,T	Dist	M/W	2,629	54												
Metropolitan Community College – Kansas City	Kansas City	C,T	St-L	M/W	19,234	60												
Missouri State University – West Plains	West Plains	C,T	St	M/W	1,869	57												
Ozarks Technical Community College	Springfield	C,T	Dist	M/W	13,260	56												
Pinnacle Career Institute	Kansas City	C	Prop	M/W	221													
Pinnacle Career Institute – North Kansas City	Kansas City	T	Prop	M/W	5													
St. Charles Community College	Cottleville	C,T	St	M/W	6,363	49	24		Y	Y	S	Y	Y	Y	Y	Y	8	30
St. Louis Community College	St. Louis	C,T	Pub	M/W	18,157	64												
State Technical College of Missouri	Linn	T	St	PM	1,724	17	10			Y	Y	Y	Y	Y	Y	Y	7	25
Montana																		
Dawson Community College	Glendive	C,T	St-L	M/W	339	58	18		Y	Y	Y	Y	Y			Y	8	13
Great Falls College Montana State University	Great Falls	C,T	St	M/W	1,315	60	47		Y	Y	Y	Y	Y	Y		N		15
Nebraska																		
Metropolitan Community College	Omaha	C,T	St-L	M/W	17,003	58												
Nebraska Indian Community College	Macy	C,T	Fed	M/W	180	74												
Nevada																		
College of Southern Nevada	Las Vegas	C,B	St	M/W														
Truckee Meadows Community College	Reno	C,T,B	St	M/W	11,316	73	35	44	Y			Y	Y	Y		N	1	54
Western Nevada College	Carson City	C,T,B	St	M/W	3,702	67	42	70	Y	Y	R,S		Y	Y		N	1	19
New Jersey																		
Assumption College for Sisters	Denville	C	I-R	W	53													
Bergen Community College	Paramus	C,T	Cou	M/W	16,469													
Brookdale Community College	Lincroft	C,T	Cou	M/W	11,856													
Camden County College	Blackwood	C,T	St-L	M/W	9,735	57			Y	Y	S	Y	Y	Y	Y	N	8	46
County College of Morris	Randolph	C,T	Cou	M/W	7,949	52												
Eastern International College	Belleville	C,T,B	Prop	M/W														
Essex County College	Newark	C,T	Cou	M/W	11,979	45												

This chart includes the names and locations of accredited two-year colleges in the United States, Canada, and other countries and shows institutions' responses to the *Peterson's Annual Survey of Undergraduate Institutions*. If an institution submitted incomplete data, one or more columns opposite the institution's name is blank. A dagger after the school name indicates that the institution has one or more entries in the *Featured Two-Year Colleges* section. If a school does not appear, it did not report any of the information.

Y—Yes; N—No; R—Recommended; S—For Some

		Degrees Awarded: College Transfer Associate (C), Terminal Associate (T), Bachelor's (B), Master's (M), Doctoral (D)	Institutional Control: County, District, City, State and Local, State-Related; Federal, State, Commonwealth, Territory; Independent, Independent-Religious, Proprietary	Student Body: Men, Primarily Men, Women, Primarily Women, Coed	Undergraduate Enrollment	Percent Attending Part-Time	Percent 25 Years of Age or Older	Percent of Grads Going on to Four-Year Colleges	Open Admissions	High School Equivalency Certificate Accepted	High School Transcript Required	Need-Based Aid Available	Part-Time Jobs Available	Career Counseling Available	Job Placement Services Available	College Housing Available	Number of Sports Offered	Number of Majors Offered
Mercer County Community College	Trenton	C,T	St-L	M/W	7,979	61												
Middlesex County College	Edison	C,T	Cou	M/W	11,673				Y	Y	Y	Y	Y	Y	Y	N	7	40
Passaic County Community College	Paterson	C,T	Cou	M/W	6,480													
Raritan Valley Community College	Branchburg	C,T	St-L	M/W	7,793	62	27	65	Y		Y	Y	Y	Y		N	7	52
Union County College	Cranford	C,T	St-L	M/W	9,181	54	40		Y	Y	Y	Y	Y	Y	Y	N	10	35
New Mexico																		
Carrington College – Albuquerque	Albuquerque	T	Prop	M/W	434	8												
Central New Mexico Community College	Albuquerque	C,T	St	M/W	23,717	72												
Clovis Community College	Clovis	C,T	St	M/W	4,175	76												
Do&nna Ana Community College	Las Cruces	C,T	St-L	M/W	8,891	55												
Eastern New Mexico University – Roswell	Roswell	C,T	St	M/W	4,347													
New Mexico State University – Grants	Grants	C,T	St	M/W	11,687	17												
San Juan College	Farmington	C,T	St	M/W	6,741	65	54		Y	Y	Y	Y	Y	Y	Y	N	2	49
New York																		
Adirondack Community College	Queensbury	C,T	St-L	M/W	3,468	45	24		Y	Y		Y	Y	Y	Y	Y	8	22
American Academy McAllister Institute of Funeral Service	New York	T	Ind	M/W	460	86	75		Y	Y	Y	Y		Y		N		1
Borough of Manhattan Community College of the City University of New York	New York	C,T	St-L	M/W	25,500	30	25		Y	Y	Y	Y	Y	Y	Y		4	44
Bronx Community College of the City University of New York	Bronx	C,T	St-L	M/W	11,368	42												
Cayuga County Community College	Auburn	C,T	St-L	M/W	3,669	63	31	35	Y		Y	Y	Y	Y	Y	N	8	35
The College of Westchester	White Plains	C,T,B	Prop	M/W	906	20	46		N	Y	Y	Y	Y	Y	Y	N		10
Columbia-Greene Community College	Hudson	C,T	St-L	M/W	1,461	64	37		Y	Y	Y	Y	Y	Y	Y	N	3	16
Dutchess Community College	Poughkeepsie	C,T	St-L	M/W	8,691	60	13		Y	Y	Y	Y	Y	Y		Y	6	31
Elim Bible Institute and College	Lima	C	I-R	M/W	106	19	31			Y	Y					Y		1
Finger Lakes Community College	Canandaigua	C,T	St-L	M/W	3,716	37												
Fiorello H. LaGuardia Community College of the City University of New York	Long Island City	C,T	St-L	M/W	18,285	44	30	62	Y	Y	Y	Y	Y	Y	Y	N	5	43
Fulton-Montgomery Community College	Johnstown	C,T	St-L	M/W	2,833	34												
Jamestown Community College	Jamestown	C,T	St-L	M/W	4,467	56	27	50	Y	Y	Y	Y	Y	Y		Y	10	31
Nassau Community College	Garden City	C,T	St-L	M/W	15,168	37			Y	Y	Y	Y	Y	Y	Y	N	17	53
Niagara County Community College	Sanborn	C,T	St-L	M/W	4,997	45			Y	Y	Y	Y	Y				2	42
Onondaga Community College	Syracuse	C,T	St-L	M/W	9,834	52												
Queensborough Community College of the City University of New York	Bayside	C,T	St-L	M/W	14,035	40	25	74	Y	Y	Y	Y	Y	Y	Y	N	11	35
Rockland Community College	Suffern	C,T	St-L	M/W	7,434	44												
Schenectady County Community College	Schenectady	C,T	St-L	M/W	6,634	67												
State University of New York College of Technology at Alfred	Alfred	C,T,B	St	M/W	3,780	8	13	27	N	Y	Y	Y	Y	Y	Y	Y	19	67
Sullivan County Community College	Loch Sheldrake	C,T	St-L	M/W	1,538	49												
Westchester Community College	Valhalla	C,T	St-L	M/W					Y	Y	Y	Y	Y	Y	Y	N	11	50
North Carolina																		
Alamance Community College	Graham	C,T	St	M/W	4,233	39	48		Y	Y	Y	Y	Y	Y	Y	N		28
Asheville-Buncombe Technical Community College	Asheville	C,T	St	M/W					Y	Y	S	Y	Y	Y	Y	N		42
Brunswick Community College	Supply	C,T	St	M/W	2,725													
Carolinas College of Health Sciences	Charlotte	T	Pub	M/W	433	89												
Carteret Community College	Morehead City	C,T	St	M/W	1,363	58												
Central Piedmont Community College	Charlotte	C,T	St-L	M/W	19,364	61												
Cleveland Community College	Shelby	C,T	St	M/W	2,536	73			Y	Y	Y	Y	Y	Y	Y	N	2	21
College of The Albemarle	Elizabeth City	C,T	St	M/W	2,572	69	21		Y	Y	Y	Y	Y	Y	Y	N	13	27
Craven Community College	New Bern	C,T	St	M/W	2,961	69			Y	Y	Y	Y	Y	Y	Y	N		36
Davidson County Community College	Lexington	C,T	St-L	M/W	4,101													
Fayetteville Technical Community College	Fayetteville	C,T	St	M/W	12,021	61	49	12	Y	Y	Y	Y	Y	Y	Y	N	6	47
Gaston College	Dallas	C,T	St-L	M/W	5,362													
Halifax Community College	Weldon	C,T	St-L	M/W	1,087	59	27		Y	Y	Y	Y	Y			N		21
Haywood Community College	Clyde	C,T	St-L	M/W	1,632	63	34	44	Y	Y	Y	Y	Y	Y	Y	Y		31
James Sprunt Community College	Kenansville	C,T	St	M/W	1,266	68	21		Y	Y	Y	Y	Y	Y		N	2	21
Johnston Community College	Smithfield	C,T	St	M/W	4,152	63												
Lenoir Community College	Kinston	C,T	St	M/W	2,526	66	29	31	Y	Y	Y	Y	Y	Y	Y	Y	3	39
Mayland Community College	Spruce Pine	C,T	St-L	M/W	1,472		39		Y	Y	Y	Y	Y	Y	Y	N		13
Mitchell Community College	Statesville	C,T	St	M/W	3,164	69												
Piedmont Community College	Roxboro	C,T	St	M/W	1,414	72			Y	Y	S	Y	Y	Y		N		22
Pitt Community College	Winterville	C,T	St-L	M/W	8,902	48												
Richmond Community College	Hamlet	C,T	St	M/W	2,586	62	31		Y	Y	Y	Y	Y	Y	Y	N		21
Southwestern Community College	Sylva	C	St	M/W	2,324	69			Y		Y	Y	Y	Y		N		30
Vance-Granville Community College	Henderson	C,T	St	M/W	4,057	58												
North Dakota																		
Cankdeska Cikana Community College	Fort Totten	C,T	Fed	M/W	251	37												
Dakota College at Bottineau	Bottineau	C,T	St	M/W	996													
Lake Region State College	Devils Lake	C,T	St	M/W	1,982	74	20		Y	Y	S	Y	Y	Y		Y	5	14
North Dakota State College of Science	Wahpeton	C,T	St	M/W	2,977	49	8		Y	Y	Y	Y	Y	Y	Y	Y	6	38
Ohio																		
Bowling Green State University – Firelands College	Huron	C,T,B	St	M/W	1,970	52												
Central Ohio Technical College	Newark	T	St	M/W	3,468	81	19		Y	Y	S	Y	Y	Y	Y		10	25
Cincinnati State Technical and Community College	Cincinnati	C,T	St	M/W	9,630	70												
Daymar College	Columbus	T	Prop	M/W	67													

This chart includes the names and locations of accredited two-year colleges in the United States, Canada, and other countries and shows institutions' responses to the *Peterson's Annual Survey of Undergraduate Institutions*. If an institution submitted incomplete data, one or more columns opposite the institution's name is blank. A dagger after the school name indicates that the institution has one or more entries in the *Featured Two-Year Colleges* section. If a school does not appear, it did not report any of the information.

Y—Yes; N—No; R—Recommended; S—For Some

Institution	Location	**Degrees Awarded** College Transfer Associate (C), Terminal Associate (T), Bachelor's (B), Master's (M), Doctoral (D)	**Institutional Control** Independent, Independent-Religious, Proprietary, Federal, State, Commonwealth, Territory, County, District, City, State and Local, State-Related	**Student Body** Men, Primarily Men, Women, Primarily Women, Coed	Undergraduate Enrollment	Percent Attending Part-Time	Percent 25 Years of Age or Older	Percent of Grads Going on to Four-Year Colleges	Open Admissions	High School Equivalency Certificate Accepted	High School Transcript Required	Need-Based Aid Available	Part-Time Jobs Available	Career Counseling Available	Job Placement Services Available	College Housing Available	Number of Sports Offered	Number of Majors Offered
Eastern Gateway Community College	Steubenville	C,T	St-L	M/W	25,648	78	77		Y	Y	S	Y	Y	Y	Y	N	2	21
Edison State Community College	Piqua	C,T	St	M/W	3,248	77	43		Y	Y			Y	Y	Y	N	4	47
James A. Rhodes State College	Lima	C,T	St	M/W	3,883	60												
Kent State University at Ashtabula	Ashtabula	C,T,B	St	M/W	2,026	49												
Kent State University at East Liverpool	East Liverpool	C,T,B	St	M/W	1,120	49												
Kent State University at Salem	Salem	C,B	St	M/W	1,697	40												
Kent State University at Trumbull	Warren	C,B	St	M/W	2,277	35												
Kent State University at Tuscarawas	New Philadelphia	C,B	St	M/W	2,168	37	25		Y	Y	Y	Y	Y	Y	Y	N	8	21
Lakeland Community College	Kirtland	C,T	St-L	M/W	6,524	72	43		Y	Y	Y	Y	Y	Y	Y	N	5	39
Northwest State Community College	Archbold	C,T	St	M/W	2,857	81	42	13	Y	Y	Y	Y	Y	Y	Y	N	5	51
Ohio Business College	Sandusky	C	Prop	M/W	265	36												
Ohio Business College	Sheffield Village	T	Prop	M/W	199													
Ohio Technical College	Cleveland	T	Prop	M/W	944		21		Y	Y	Y	Y		Y	Y			8
Owens Community College	Toledo	C,T	St	M/W	12,572	66												
Stark State College	North Canton	C,T	St-R	M/W	11,833	74	45		Y	Y	Y	Y	Y	Y	Y	N		28
The University of Akron Wayne College	Orrville	C,T,B	St	M/W	2,353	53												
University of Cincinnati Clermont College	Batavia	C,T,B	St	M/W	26,932	14												
Zane State College	Zanesville	C,T	St-L	M/W	2,275													
Oklahoma																		
Carl Albert State College	Poteau	C,T	St	M/W	2,194	40												
Eastern Oklahoma State College	Wilburton	C,T	St	M/W	1,772													
Oklahoma State University Institute of Technology	Okmulgee	C,T,B	St	M/W	2,309	37	25		Y	Y	Y	Y	Y	Y	Y	Y	7	24
Seminole State College	Seminole	C,T	St	M/W	1,531	46	25		Y		R	Y	Y	Y		Y	7	27
Tulsa Community College	Tulsa	C,T	St	M/W	6,588	27												
Oregon																		
Central Oregon Community College	Bend	C,T	Dist	M/W	4,871	53			Y	Y		Y	Y	Y		Y	12	84
Chemeketa Community College	Salem	C,T	St-L	M/W	12,371	50												
Clackamas Community College	Oregon City	C,T	Dist	M/W	6,270	62	39		Y			Y	Y	Y	Y	Y	8	39
Clatsop Community College	Astoria	C,T	Cou	M/W	1,071	58												
Columbia Gorge Community College	The Dalles	C,T	St	M/W	1,245	56												
Linn-Benton Community College	Albany	C,T	St-L	M/W	5,617	54												
Portland Community College	Portland	C,T	St-L	M/W	20,000		52		Y			Y	Y	Y	Y	N	18	49
Sumner College	Portland	T	Prop	PW	261													
Treasure Valley Community College	Ontario	C,T	St-L	M/W	1,866	57												
Pennsylvania																		
Bucks County Community College	Newtown	C,T	Cou	M/W	7,480	64	28	59	Y	Y	Y	Y	Y	Y	Y	N	11	57
Community College of Allegheny County	Pittsburgh	C,T	Cou	M/W	16,031	68				Y	R	Y	Y	Y	Y	N	7	82
Community College of Beaver County	Monaca	C,T	St	M/W	2,779													
Community College of Philadelphia	Philadelphia	C,T	St-L	M/W	30,194													
Delaware County Community College	Media	C,T	St-L	M/W	13,248	60												
Douglas Education Center	Monessen	T	Prop	M/W	334													
Harrisburg Area Community College	Harrisburg	C,T	St-L	M/W	17,422	72	41		Y		S		Y	Y		N	4	61
Lackawanna College	Scranton	C,T,B	Ind	M/W	1,991	33	32		Y	Y	Y	Y	Y	Y	Y	Y	11	42
Lehigh Carbon Community College	Schnecksville	C,T	St-L	M/W	6,953	64												
Luzerne County Community College	Nanticoke	C,T	Cou	M/W	4,920	60			Y	Y	R	Y	Y	Y	Y	N	6	67
Manor College	Jenkintown	C,T,B	I-R	M/W	740	35												
Montgomery County Community College	Blue Bell	C,T	Cou	M/W	10,309	69	30	56	Y	Y	Y	Y	Y	Y		Y	5	62
Northampton Community College	Bethlehem	C,T	St-L	M/W	9,769	56	34		Y	Y	S	Y	Y	Y	Y	Y	10	65
Penn State DuBois	DuBois	C,T,B	St-R	M/W	563	22	12		N	Y	Y	Y	Y			N	7	127
Penn State Fayette, The Eberly Campus	Lemont Furnace	C,T,B	St-R	M/W	589	11	11		N	Y	Y	Y	Y			N	11	124
Penn State Mont Alto	Mont Alto	C,T,B	St-R	M/W	730	20	13		N	Y	Y	Y	Y			Y	10	120
Pittsburgh Career Institute	Pittsburgh	T	Prop	M/W	136													
University of Pittsburgh at Titusville	Titusville	C,T	St-R	M/W	225	17												
Westmoreland County Community College	Youngwood	C,T	Cou	M/W	4,645	63	37		Y	Y	Y	Y	Y	Y	Y	N	8	52
South Carolina																		
Central Carolina Technical College	Sumter	C,T	St	M/W	4,522	64												
Clinton College	Rock Hill	T	I-R	M/W	148													
Denmark Technical College	Denmark	C,T	St	M/W	1,043	37												
Greenville Technical College	Greenville	C,T	St	M/W	11,745	59			Y	Y		Y	Y	Y		Y	7	34
Midlands Technical College	Columbia	C,T	St-L	M/W	10,946	54												
Spartanburg Methodist College	Spartanburg	C,T	I-R	M/W	790	1												
Trident Technical College	Charleston	C,T	St-L	M/W	12,351	63	35		Y	Y	S	Y	Y	Y	Y	N		39
University of South Carolina Lancaster	Lancaster	C,T,B	St	M/W	1,593	50	13		Y	Y	Y	Y	Y	Y	Y	N	3	4
University of South Carolina Union	Union	C,B	St	M/W	905	46												
Williamsburg Technical College	Kingstree	C,T	St	M/W	732	73	25		Y	Y	Y	Y	Y	Y	Y	N		5
South Dakota																		
Lake Area Technical Institute	Watertown	T	St	M/W	2,228	32	15		Y	Y	Y	Y	Y	Y	Y	N	6	29
Mitchell Technical Institute	Mitchell	T	St	M/W	1,198	30												
Western Dakota Technical Institute	Rapid City	T	St	M/W	1,214	50	47		Y	Y	Y	Y	Y	Y	Y	N		23
Tennessee																		
Chattanooga State Community College	Chattanooga	C,T	St	M/W	10,438	54												
Cleveland State Community College	Cleveland	C,T	St	M/W	3,370	47	24	16	Y	Y	Y	Y	Y	Y	Y	N	10	22
Daymar College	Clarksville	C,T,B	Prop	M/W	532	28												
Daymar College	Murfreesboro	C,B	Prop	M/W														
Daymar College	Nashville	C,T	Prop	M/W	286													

This chart includes the names and locations of accredited two-year colleges in the United States, Canada, and other countries and shows institutions' responses to the *Peterson's Annual Survey of Undergraduate Institutions.* If an institution submitted incomplete data, one or more columns opposite the institution's name is blank. A dagger after the school name indicates that the institution has one or more entries in the *Featured Two-Year Colleges* section. If a school does not appear, it did not report any of the information.

Y—Yes; N—No; R—Recommended; S—For Some

Institution	Location	Degrees Awarded: College Transfer Associate (C), Terminal Associate (T), Bachelor's (B), Master's (M), Doctoral (D)	Institutional Control: Independent, Independent-Religious, Proprietary, Federal, State, Commonwealth, Territory, County, District, City, State and Local, State-Related	Student Body: Men, Primarily Men, Women, Primarily Women, Coed	Undergraduate Enrollment	Percent Attending Part-Time	Percent 25 Years of Age or Older	Percent of Grads Going on to Four-Year Colleges	Open Admissions	High School Equivalency Certificate Accepted	High School Transcript Required	Need-Based Aid Available	Part-Time Jobs Available	Career Counseling Available	Job Placement Services Available	College Housing Available	Number of Sports Offered	Number of Majors Offered
Dyersburg State Community College	Dyersburg	C,T	St	M/W	2,816	56	31		Y	Y	Y	Y	Y	Y	Y	N	8	19
Motlow State Community College	Lynchburg	C,T	St	M/W	6,991	51	23		Y	Y	Y	Y		Y	Y	N	4	11
Northeast State Community College	Blountville	C,T	St	M/W	6,085	47	28		Y	Y	Y	Y	Y					18
Pellissippi State Community College	Knoxville	C,T	St	M/W	8,837													
Southwest Tennessee Community College	Memphis	C,T	St	M/W	10,167	59												
Volunteer State Community College	Gallatin	C,T	St	M/W	9,144	48	28		Y	Y	Y	Y	Y	Y		N	3	19
Walters State Community College	Morristown	C,T	St	M/W	6,280	48	29		Y	Y	Y	Y	Y	Y	Y	N	5	20
Texas																		
Alvin Community College	Alvin	C,T	St-L	M/W	5,573	77	26		Y		S	Y	Y	Y	Y	N	2	55
Amarillo College	Amarillo	C,T	St-L	M/W			36		Y		Y	Y	Y	Y	Y	N	5	83
Austin Community College District	Austin	C,T,B	St-L	M/W	41,056	78	37		Y	Y	Y	Y	Y	Y		N	4	109
Blinn College	Brenham	C,T	St-L	M/W	19,476	54	11		Y	Y	Y	Y	Y	Y	Y	Y	11	49
Brazosport College	Lake Jackson	C,T,B	St-L	M/W	3,893													
Central Texas College	Killeen	C,T	St-L	M/W	16,073	73												
Cisco College	Cisco	C,T	St-L	M/W	4,022	60												
Coastal Bend College	Beeville	C,T	Cou	M/W	3,776	64												
College of the Mainland	Texas City	C,T	St-L	M/W	4,188	73												
Collin County Community College District	McKinney	C,T,B	St-L	M/W	35,144	69	94		Y			Y	Y	Y	Y	Y	4	53
Del Mar College	Corpus Christi	C,T	St-L	M/W	11,833	77												
Eastfield College	Mesquite	C,T	St-L	M/W	12,403	76												
Galveston College	Galveston	C,T,B	St-L	M/W	2,306	68	39		Y	Y	S	Y	Y	Y		Y	7	49
Houston Community College	Houston	C,T	St-L	M/W	56,151	71	41		Y		S	Y	Y	Y	Y	N		77
Lamar Institute of Technology	Beaumont	T	St	M/W	3,265	58												
Lone Star College – CyFair	Cypress	C,T	St-L	M/W	21,636	69												
Lone Star College – Kingwood	Kingwood	C,T	St-L	M/W	12,287	69												
Lone Star College – Montgomery	Conroe	C,T	St-L	M/W	14,411	69												
Lone Star College – North Harris	Houston	C,T	St-L	M/W	16,290	71												
Lone Star College – Tomball	Tomball	C,T	St-L	M/W	9,013	70												
McLennan Community College	Waco	C,T	Cou	M/W	8,705	68	32		Y	Y	Y	Y	Y	Y	Y	N	5	26
Navarro College	Corsicana	C,T	St-L	M/W	8,173	64	18		Y	Y	Y	Y	Y	Y	Y	Y	8	46
Palo Alto College	San Antonio	C,T	Dist	M/W	8,376	82												
Paris Junior College	Paris	C,T	St-L	M/W	4,858	66	21		Y	Y	Y	Y	Y	Y		Y	9	65
San Jacinto College	Pasadena	C	St-L	M/W	32,452	72	27	15	Y	Y	Y			Y	Y	N	6	79
South Plains College	Levelland	C,T	St-L	M/W	9,053	49												
Southwest Texas Junior College	Uvalde	C,T	St-L	M/W	7,049				Y	Y	Y	Y	Y	Y	Y	Y	9	25
Tarrant County College District	Fort Worth	C,T	Cou	M/W	51,100	73			Y			Y	Y	Y	Y	N	6	42
Texarkana College	Texarkana	C,T	St-L	M/W	4,239	64												
Trinity Valley Community College	Athens	C,T	St-L	M/W	4,449	56												
Tyler Junior College	Tyler	C,T,B	St-L	M/W	10,106	40												
Weatherford College	Weatherford	C,T,B	St-L	M/W	5,637		23		Y	Y	R	Y	Y	Y	Y	Y	5	19
Utah																		
Nightingale College	Ogden	C,B	Prop	M/W	527													
Salt Lake Community College	Salt Lake City	C,T	St	M/W	29,620	74												
Snow College	Ephraim	C,T	St	M/W	5,574	42												
Vermont																		
New England Culinary Institute	Montpelier	C,B	Prop	M/W	300	14												
Virginia																		
American National University – Danville	Danville	T,B	Prop	M/W														
Blue Ridge Community College	Weyers Cave	C,T	St	M/W	4,099													
Dabney S. Lancaster Community College	Clifton Forge	C,T	St	M/W	1,186	64												
Danville Community College	Danville	C,T	St	M/W	4,387													
John Tyler Community College	Chester	C,T	St	M/W	10,144	76												
Piedmont Virginia Community College	Charlottesville	C,T	St	M/W	5,358	79			Y		S	Y	Y	Y	Y	N	8	21
Tidewater Community College	Norfolk	C,T	St	M/W	20,941	65												
Virginia Western Community College	Roanoke	C,T	St	M/W	7,271	72												
Washington																		
Bellevue College	Bellevue	C,T,B	St	M/W	4,155	56												
Bellingham Technical College	Bellingham	C,T	St	M/W	2,864		61		Y		S	Y	Y	Y	Y	N		25
Carrington College – Spokane	Spokane	T	Prop	M/W	407													
Cascadia College	Bothell	C,T,B	St	M/W	2,759	45	19		Y							N	3	4
Clover Park Technical College	Lakewood	T	St	M/W	9,829													
Edmonds Community College	Lynnwood	C,T	St-L	M/W	8,435	57												
North Seattle College	Seattle	C,T	St	M/W	6,303	69												
Northwest School of Wooden Boatbuilding	Port Hadlock	T	Ind	M/W			75			Y	Y			Y		N		1
Olympic College	Bremerton	C,T,B	St	M/W	7,253													
Renton Technical College	Renton	C,T,B	St	M/W	3,546	65												
West Virginia																		
Blue Ridge Community and Technical College	Martinsburg	C,T	St	M/W	6,532	84	73		Y	Y	Y			Y	Y	N		24
Eastern West Virginia Community and Technical College	Moorefield	C,T	St	M/W	639													
Pierpont Community & Technical College	Fairmont	C,T	St	M/W	1,938	40												
Potomac State College of West Virginia University	Keyser	C,T,B	St	M/W	1,340	24												
Wisconsin																		
Fox Valley Technical College	Appleton	T	St-L	M/W	12,239	83	43		Y		S	Y	Y	Y	Y	N		60
Milwaukee Area Technical College	Milwaukee	C,T	Dist	M/W	20,215	65												

This chart includes the names and locations of accredited two-year colleges in the United States, Canada, and other countries and shows institutions' responses to the *Peterson's Annual Survey of Undergraduate Institutions.* If an institution submitted incomplete data, one or more columns opposite the institution's name is blank. A dagger after the school name indicates that the institution has one or more entries in the *Featured Two-Year Colleges* section. If a school does not appear, it did not report any of the information.

Y—Yes; N—No; R—Recommended; S—For Some

Institution	Location	**Degrees Awarded** College Transfer Associate (C), Terminal Associate (T), Bachelor's (B), Master's (M), Doctoral (D)	**Institutional Control** Independent, Independent-Religious, Proprietary, Federal, State, Commonwealth, Territory, County, District, City, State and Local, State-Related	**Student Body** Men, Primarily Men, Women, Primarily Women, Coed	Undergraduate Enrollment	Percent Attending Part-Time	Percent 25 Years of Age or Older	Percent of Grads Going on to Four-Year Colleges	Open Admissions	High School Equivalency Certificate Accepted	High School Transcript Required	Need-Based Aid Available	Part-Time Jobs Available	Career Counseling Available	Job Placement Services Available	College Housing Available	Number of Sports Offered	Number of Majors Offered
Northeast Wisconsin Technical College	Green Bay	T	St-L	M/W	8,105		47			Y		Y	Y	Y	Y		3	73
Southwest Wisconsin Technical College	Fennimore	T	St-L	M/W	2,640	73	41		Y		Y	Y	Y	Y	Y	Y	3	19
Wyoming																		
Casper College	Casper	C,T	St-L	M/W	3,626	52												
Laramie County Community College	Cheyenne	C,T	Dist	M/W	4,284	63	39			Y	S	Y				Y	1	
Western Wyoming Community College	Rock Springs	C,T	St-L	M/W	3,183	66												

Profiles of Two-Year Colleges

NOTICE: Certain portions of or information contained in this book have been submitted and paid for by the educational institution identified, and such institutions take full responsibility for the accuracy, timeliness, completeness and functionality of such content. Such portions or information include (i) each display ad in the "Profiles" section from pages 53 through 318 that comprises a half or full page of information covering a single educational institution, and (ii) each two-page description in the "Featured Two-Year Colleges" section from pages 322 through 327.

U.S. AND U.S. TERRITORIES

ALABAMA

Bevill State Community College
Jasper, Alabama

- **State-supported** 2-year, founded 1969, part of Alabama Community College System
- **Rural** 245-acre campus with easy access to Birmingham
- **Coed,** 3,872 undergraduate students, 41% full-time, 59% women, 41% men

Undergraduates 1,583 full-time, 2,289 part-time. Students come from 10 states and territories; 2% are from out of state; 7% transferred in. *Retention:* 59% of full-time freshmen returned.
Freshmen *Admission:* 820 enrolled.
Majors Administrative assistant and secretarial science; child-care and support services management; computer and information sciences; electrician; emergency medical technology (EMT paramedic); general studies; heating, ventilation, air conditioning and refrigeration engineering technology; industrial mechanics and maintenance technology; instrumentation technology; liberal arts and sciences/liberal studies; manufacturing engineering technology; registered nursing/registered nurse; tool and die technology; vehicle maintenance and repair technologies.
Academics *Calendar:* semesters. *Degree:* certificates and associate. *Special study options:* academic remediation for entering students, adult/continuing education programs, advanced placement credit, cooperative education, distance learning, honors programs, off-campus study, part-time degree program, services for LD students, summer session for credit.
Library Main Library plus 5 others. Weekly public service hours: 56.
Student Life *Housing Options:* coed. Campus housing is university owned. *Activities and Organizations:* drama/theater group, choral group, Student Government Association, Campus Ministries, Circle K, Outdoorsmen Club, Sigma Kappa Delta.
Costs (2019–20) *Tuition:* state resident $3930 full-time, $131 per credit hour part-time; nonresident $7860 full-time, $262 per credit hour part-time. Full-time tuition and fees vary according to course load and program. Part-time tuition and fees vary according to course load and program. *Required fees:* $900 full-time, $29 per credit hour part-time. *Room and board:* room only: $1300. Room and board charges vary according to location. *Payment plan:* installment. *Waivers:* employees or children of employees.
Financial Aid Of all full-time matriculated undergraduates who enrolled in 2016, 2,711 applied for aid, 2,568 were judged to have need, 45 had their need fully met. 41 Federal Work-Study jobs (averaging $3494). In 2016, 62 non-need-based awards were made. *Average percent of need met:* 42%. *Average financial aid package:* $5291. *Average need-based gift aid:* $6235. *Average non-need-based aid:* $1937.
Applying *Options:* electronic application, early admission. *Application deadlines:* rolling (freshmen), rolling (transfers). *Notification:* continuous (freshmen), continuous (transfers).
Freshman Application Contact Ms. Melissa Stowe, Dean of Students, Bevill State Community College, 1411 Indiana Avenue, Jasper, AL 35501. *Phone:* 205-387-0511 Ext. 5813. *E-mail:* melissa.stowe@bscc.edu. *Website:* http://www.bscc.edu/.

Bishop State Community College
Mobile, Alabama

Freshman Application Contact Bishop State Community College, 351 North Broad Street, Mobile, AL 36603-5898. *Phone:* 251-405-7000. *Toll-free phone:* 800-523-7235. *Website:* http://www.bishop.edu/.

Calhoun Community College
Decatur, Alabama

Freshman Application Contact Admissions Office, Calhoun Community College, PO Box 2216, Decatur, AL 35609-2216. *Phone:* 256-306-2593. *Toll-free phone:* 800-626-3628. *Fax:* 256-306-2941. *E-mail:* admissions@calhoun.edu. *Website:* http://www.calhoun.edu/.

Central Alabama Community College
Alexander City, Alabama

Freshman Application Contact Ms. Donna Whaley, Central Alabama Community College, 1675 Cherokee Road, Alexander City, AL 35011-0699. *Phone:* 256-234-6346 Ext. 6232. *Toll-free phone:* 800-634-2657. *Website:* http://www.cacc.edu/.

Chattahoochee Valley Community College
Phenix City, Alabama

Freshman Application Contact Chattahoochee Valley Community College, 2602 College Drive, Phenix City, AL 36869-7928. *Phone:* 334-291-4929. *Website:* http://www.cv.edu/.

Coastal Alabama Community College
Bay Minette, Alabama

- **State-supported** 2-year, founded 1965, part of Alabama Community College System
- **Small-town** 105-acre campus
- **Coed**

Undergraduates 2,139 full-time, 1,184 part-time. 3% are from out of state; 9% live on campus.
Faculty *Student/faculty ratio:* 15:1.
Academics *Calendar:* semesters. *Degree:* certificates and associate. *Special study options:* academic remediation for entering students, adult/continuing education programs, advanced placement credit, cooperative education, honors programs, internships, part-time degree program, services for LD students.
Library Austin R. Meadows Library plus 3 others. *Books:* 66,811 (physical); *Serial titles:* 2,924 (physical); *Databases:* 67. Weekly public service hours: 40.
Student Life *Campus security:* 24-hour emergency response devices and patrols, controlled dormitory access.
Athletics Member NJCAA.
Applying *Options:* early admission, deferred entrance. *Required:* high school transcript.
Freshman Application Contact Ms. Carmelita Mikkelsen, Director of Admissions and High School Relations, Coastal Alabama Community College, 1900 Highway 31 South, Bay Minette, AL 36507. *Phone:* 251-580-2213. *Toll-free phone:* 800-381-3722. *Fax:* 251-580-2285. *E-mail:* cmikkelsen@faulknerstate.edu. *Website:* http://www.coastalalabama.edu/.

Community College of the Air Force
Maxwell Gunter Air Force Base, Alabama

Freshman Application Contact Ms. Gwendolyn Ford, Chief of Admissions Flight, Community College of the Air Force, 100 South Turner Boulevard, Maxwell Air Force Base, Maxwell - Gunter AFB, AL 36114-3011. *Phone:* 334-649-5081. *Fax:* 334-649-5015. *E-mail:* gwendolyn.ford@us.af.mil. *Website:* http://www.airuniversity.af.mil/Barnes/CCAF/.

Enterprise State Community College
Enterprise, Alabama

Director of Admissions Mr. Gary Deas, Associate Dean of Students/Registrar, Enterprise State Community College, 600 Plaza Drive, Enterprise, AL 36330. *Phone:* 334-347-2623 Ext. 2233. *E-mail:* gdeas@eocc.edu. *Website:* http://www.escc.edu/.

Fortis College
Mobile, Alabama

Admissions Office Contact Fortis College, 7033 Airport Boulevard, Mobile, AL 36608. *Toll-free phone:* 855-4-FORTIS. *Website:* http://www.fortis.edu/.

Fortis College
Montgomery, Alabama

Admissions Office Contact Fortis College, 3470 Eastdale Circle, Montgomery, AL 36117. *Toll-free phone:* 855-4-FORTIS. *Website:* http://www.fortis.edu/.

Fortis College
Montgomery, Alabama

Admissions Office Contact Fortis College, 3736 Atlanta Highway, Montgomery, AL 36109. *Toll-free phone:* 855-4-FORTIS. *Website:* http://www.fortis.edu/.

Fortis Institute

Birmingham, Alabama

Admissions Office Contact Fortis Institute, 100 London Parkway, Suite 150, Birmingham, AL 35211. *Toll-free phone:* 855-4-FORTIS. *Website:* http://www.fortis.edu/.

Gadsden State Community College

Gadsden, Alabama

Freshman Application Contact Mrs. Jennie Dobson, Admissions and Records, Gadsden State Community College, PO Box 227, 1001 George Wallace Drive, Gadsden, AL 35902-0227. *Phone:* 256-549-8210. *Toll-free phone:* 800-226-5563. *Fax:* 256-549-8205. *E-mail:* info@gadsdenstate.edu. *Website:* http://www.gadsdenstate.edu/.

George Corley Wallace State Community College

Selma, Alabama

Director of Admissions Ms. Sunette Newman, Registrar, George Corley Wallace State Community College, PO Box 2530, Selma, AL 36702. *Phone:* 334-876-9305. *Website:* http://www.wccs.edu/.

H. Councill Trenholm State Community College

Montgomery, Alabama

- **State-supported** 2-year, founded 1966, part of Alabama Community College System
- **Urban** 83-acre campus with easy access to Montgomery
- **Coed**
- 31% of applicants were admitted

Undergraduates Students come from 2 states and territories; 69% Black or African American, non-Hispanic/Latino; 2% Hispanic/Latino; 1% Asian, non-Hispanic/Latino; 0.1% American Indian or Alaska Native, non-Hispanic/Latino; 0.2% Two or more races, non-Hispanic/Latino; 0.2% Race/ethnicity unknown; 0.1% international. *Retention:* 60% of full-time freshmen returned.
Faculty *Student/faculty ratio:* 15:1.
Academics *Calendar:* semesters. *Degree:* certificates, diplomas, and associate. *Special study options:* academic remediation for entering students, adult/continuing education programs, advanced placement credit, cooperative education, distance learning, English as a second language, external degree program, independent study, internships, part-time degree program, services for LD students, summer session for credit.
Library Trenholm State Learning Resources plus 2 others. *Books:* 10,315 (physical), 36,943 (digital/electronic); *Serial titles:* 91 (physical), 59 (digital/electronic); *Databases:* 18. Weekly public service hours: 108.
Student Life *Campus security:* 24-hour patrols.
Standardized Tests *Required for some:* SAT or ACT (for admission).
Costs (2019–20) *Tuition:* state resident $3144 full-time, $131 per credit hour part-time; nonresident $6288 full-time, $262 per credit hour part-time. *Required fees:* $624 full-time, $26 per credit hour part-time.
Financial Aid Of all full-time matriculated undergraduates who enrolled in 2018, 1,627 applied for aid, 1,627 were judged to have need, 1,627 had their need fully met. 20 Federal Work-Study jobs (averaging $1811). *Average percent of need met:* 88. *Average financial aid package:* $5380. *Average need-based gift aid:* $5380.
Applying *Options:* electronic application, early admission. *Required:* high school transcript.
Freshman Application Contact Dr. Tennie McBryde, Director of Admissions/Records, H. Councill Trenholm State Community College, Montgomery, AL 36108. *Phone:* 334-420-4306. *Toll-free phone:* 866-753-4544. *Fax:* 334-420-4201. *E-mail:* tmcbryde@trenholmstate.edu. *Website:* http://www.trenholmstate.edu/.

Jefferson State Community College

Birmingham, Alabama

Freshman Application Contact Mrs. Lillian Owens, Director of Admissions and Retention, Jefferson State Community College, 2601 Carson Road, Birmingham, AL 35215-3098. *Phone:* 205-853-1200 Ext. 7990. *Toll-free phone:* 800-239-5900. *Fax:* 205-856-6070. *E-mail:* lowens@jeffstateonline.com. *Website:* http://www.jeffersonstate.edu/.

J. F. Drake State Community and Technical College

Huntsville, Alabama

Freshman Application Contact Mrs. Kristin Treadway, Assistant Director of Admissions, J. F. Drake State Community and Technical College, Huntsville, AL 35811. *Phone:* 256-551-3111. *Toll-free phone:* 888-413-7253. *E-mail:* kristin.treadway@drakestate.edu. *Website:* http://www.drakestate.edu/.

J F Ingram State Technical College

Deatsville, Alabama

Admissions Office Contact J F Ingram State Technical College, 5375 Ingram Rd, Deatsville, AL 36022. *Website:* http://www.istc.edu/.

Lawson State Community College

Birmingham, Alabama

- **State-supported** 2-year, founded 1949, part of Alabama Community College System
- **Urban** 30-acre campus
- **Coed**

Undergraduates 1,791 full-time, 1,240 part-time. Students come from 14 states and territories; 1 other country; 1% are from out of state; 79% Black or African American, non-Hispanic/Latino; 1% Hispanic/Latino; 0.2% Asian, non-Hispanic/Latino; 0.3% Native Hawaiian or other Pacific Islander, non-Hispanic/Latino; 0.1% American Indian or Alaska Native, non-Hispanic/Latino; 0.7% Two or more races, non-Hispanic/Latino; 7% Race/ethnicity unknown; 0.2% international; 7% transferred in; 1% live on campus. *Retention:* 41% of full-time freshmen returned.
Faculty *Student/faculty ratio:* 17:1.
Academics *Calendar:* semesters. *Degree:* certificates and associate. *Special study options:* academic remediation for entering students, adult/continuing education programs, advanced placement credit, cooperative education, distance learning, honors programs, internships, part-time degree program, services for LD students, summer session for credit.
Library Lawson State Library.
Student Life *Campus security:* 24-hour emergency response devices and patrols, controlled dormitory access.
Athletics Member NJCAA.
Financial Aid Of all full-time matriculated undergraduates who enrolled in 2018, 91 Federal Work-Study jobs (averaging $3000).
Applying *Options:* electronic application. *Required:* high school transcript.
Freshman Application Contact Mr. Jeff Shelley, Director of Admissions and Records, Lawson State Community College, 3060 Wilson Road, SW, Birmingham, AL 35221-1798. *Phone:* 205-929-6361. *Fax:* 205-923-7106. *E-mail:* jshelley@lawsonstate.edu. *Website:* http://www.lawsonstate.edu/.

Lurleen B. Wallace Community College

Andalusia, Alabama

- **State-supported** 2-year, founded 2003, part of Alabama Community College System
- **Small-town** 200-acre campus
- **Coed,** 1,767 undergraduate students, 49% full-time, 56% women, 44% men

Undergraduates 866 full-time, 901 part-time. Students come from 13 states and territories; 5 other countries; 3% are from out of state; 25% Black or African American, non-Hispanic/Latino; 2% Hispanic/Latino; 0.3% Asian, non-Hispanic/Latino; 0.5% American Indian or Alaska Native, non-Hispanic/Latino; 3% Two or more races, non-Hispanic/Latino; 0.3% Race/ethnicity unknown; 0.1% international; 6% transferred in; 5% live on campus.
Freshmen *Admission:* 440 enrolled.
Faculty *Total:* 105, 53% full-time. *Student/faculty ratio:* 17:1.
Majors Administrative assistant and secretarial science; child-care and support services management; computer and information sciences; diagnostic medical sonography and ultrasound technology; diesel mechanics technology; emergency medical technology (EMT paramedic); forest technology; general studies; industrial electronics technology; liberal arts and sciences/liberal studies; registered nursing/registered nurse.
Academics *Calendar:* semesters. *Degree:* certificates and associate. *Special study options:* academic remediation for entering students, cooperative education, distance learning, honors programs, independent study, part-time degree program, summer session for credit.
Library Lurleen B. Wallace Library plus 3 others. *Books:* 37,670 (physical), 44,963 (digital/electronic); *Serial titles:* 34 (physical); *Databases:* 57. Students can reserve study rooms.

Student Life *Housing Options:* Campus housing is university owned. *Activities and Organizations:* drama/theater group, choral group, Student Government Association, Student Ambassadors, Campus Civitan, Christian Student Ministries, Saints Angels. *Campus security:* cameras. *Student services:* personal/psychological counseling.
Athletics Member NJCAA. *Intercollegiate sports:* baseball M(s), basketball M(s)/W(s), softball W(s).
Costs (2019–20) *Tuition:* state resident $3930 full-time, $131 per credit hour part-time; nonresident $7860 full-time, $262 per credit hour part-time. Full-time tuition and fees vary according to course load. Part-time tuition and fees vary according to course load. *Required fees:* $870 full-time, $29 per credit hour part-time. *Room and board:* $5550. *Payment plan:* installment. *Waivers:* senior citizens and employees or children of employees.
Applying *Options:* electronic application. *Required for some:* high school transcript. *Application deadlines:* rolling (freshmen), rolling (out-of-state freshmen), rolling (transfers).
Freshman Application Contact Lurleen B. Wallace Community College, PO Box 1418, Andalusia, AL 36420-1418. *Phone:* 334-881-2273.
Website: http://www.lbwcc.edu/.

Marion Military Institute

Marion, Alabama

- **State-supported** 2-year, founded 1842, part of Alabama Community College System
- **Rural** 130-acre campus with easy access to Birmingham
- **Coed,** 409 undergraduate students, 100% full-time, 27% women, 73% men

Undergraduates 407 full-time, 2 part-time. Students come from 45 states and territories; 51% are from out of state; 20% Black or African American, non-Hispanic/Latino; 7% Hispanic/Latino; 3% Asian, non-Hispanic/Latino; 0.7% Native Hawaiian or other Pacific Islander, non-Hispanic/Latino; 1% American Indian or Alaska Native, non-Hispanic/Latino; 4% Two or more races, non-Hispanic/Latino; 5% transferred in; 100% live on campus. *Retention:* 41% of full-time freshmen returned.
Freshmen *Admission:* 1,064 applied, 613 admitted, 269 enrolled.
Faculty *Total:* 28, 71% full-time. *Student/faculty ratio:* 15:1.
Majors General studies; liberal arts and sciences/liberal studies.
Academics *Calendar:* semesters. *Degree:* associate. *Special study options:* academic remediation for entering students, English as a second language, honors programs, services for LD students, study abroad. *ROTC:* Army (b), Air Force (c).
Library Baer Memorial Library. Weekly public service hours: 65; study areas open 24 hours, 5–7 days a week.
Student Life *Housing:* on-campus residence required through sophomore year. *Options:* coed. Campus housing is university owned. Freshman campus housing is guaranteed. *Activities and Organizations:* drama/theater group, choral group, marching band, Honor Guard, White Knights Precision Drill Team, Swamp Fox, Marching Band, Scuba Tigers. *Campus security:* 24-hour patrols. *Student services:* health clinic, personal/psychological counseling, veterans affairs office.
Athletics Member NJCAA. *Intercollegiate sports:* baseball M(s), basketball M(s), cross-country running M(s)/W(s), golf M(s)/W(s), softball W(s), tennis M(s)/W(s). *Intramural sports:* baseball M/W, basketball M/W, football M/W, riflery M/W, sand volleyball M/W, soccer M/W, softball M/W, swimming and diving M/W, table tennis M/W, ultimate Frisbee M/W, volleyball M/W, water polo M/W.
Standardized Tests *Required:* SAT or ACT (for admission).
Costs (2020–21) *One-time required fee:* $2470. *Tuition:* state resident $6000 full-time; nonresident $12,000 full-time. *Required fees:* $948 full-time. *Room and board:* $4950. *Waivers:* employees or children of employees.
Financial Aid Of all full-time matriculated undergraduates who enrolled in 2018, 382 applied for aid, 97 were judged to have need. 39 Federal Work-Study jobs (averaging $566).
Applying *Options:* electronic application, deferred entrance. *Application fee:* $30. *Required:* high school transcript, minimum 2.0 GPA. *Application deadlines:* rolling (freshmen), rolling (transfers). *Notification:* continuous (freshmen), continuous (transfers).
Freshman Application Contact Mrs. Brittany Crawford, Director of Admissions, Marion Military Institute, 1101 Washington Street, Marion, AL 36756. *Phone:* 800-664-1842. *Toll-free phone:* 800-664-1842. *Fax:* 334-683-2383. *E-mail:* bcrawford@marionmilitary.edu.
Website: http://www.marionmilitary.edu/.

Northeast Alabama Community College

Rainsville, Alabama

Freshman Application Contact Northeast Alabama Community College, PO Box 159, Rainsville, AL 35986-0159. *Phone:* 256-228-6001 Ext. 2325.
Website: http://www.nacc.edu/.

Northwest-Shoals Community College

Muscle Shoals, Alabama

- **State-supported** 2-year, founded 1963, part of Alabama Community College System
- **Small-town** 210-acre campus
- **Endowment** $743,320
- **Coed,** 3,512 undergraduate students, 37% full-time, 61% women, 39% men

Undergraduates 1,288 full-time, 2,224 part-time. Students come from 4 states and territories; 3 other countries; 1% are from out of state; 10% Black or African American, non-Hispanic/Latino; 7% Hispanic/Latino; 0.7% Asian, non-Hispanic/Latino; 0.1% Native Hawaiian or other Pacific Islander, non-Hispanic/Latino; 0.8% American Indian or Alaska Native, non-Hispanic/Latino; 4% Two or more races, non-Hispanic/Latino; 2% Race/ethnicity unknown; 0.8% international; 6% transferred in.
Freshmen *Admission:* 1,689 applied, 1,689 admitted, 748 enrolled. *Average high school GPA:* 3.3.
Faculty *Total:* 185, 43% full-time, 5% with terminal degrees. *Student/faculty ratio:* 17:1.
Majors Accounting technology and bookkeeping; administrative assistant and secretarial science; child-care and support services management; child development; computer and information sciences; criminal justice/police science; diagnostic medical sonography and ultrasound technology; drafting and design technology; emergency medical technology (EMT paramedic); environmental engineering technology; general studies; industrial electronics technology; industrial mechanics and maintenance technology; liberal arts and sciences/liberal studies; medical/clinical assistant; multi/interdisciplinary studies related; radiologic technology/science; registered nursing/registered nurse; salon/beauty salon management.
Academics *Calendar:* semesters. *Degree:* certificates and associate. *Special study options:* academic remediation for entering students, accelerated degree program, adult/continuing education programs, advanced placement credit, cooperative education, distance learning, double majors, honors programs, independent study, internships, off-campus study, part-time degree program, services for LD students, summer session for credit.
Library Larry W. McCoy Learning Resource Center. *Books:* 63,303 (physical), 38,115 (digital/electronic); *Databases:* 2. Weekly public service hours: 62.
Student Life *Housing:* college housing not available. *Activities and Organizations:* choral group, Student Government Association, Science Club, Phi Theta Kappa, Baptist Campus Ministry, Northwest-Shoals Singers. *Campus security:* 24-hour emergency response devices.
Costs (2020–21) *Tuition:* state resident $3990 full-time, $133 per credit hour part-time; nonresident $7980 full-time, $266 per credit hour part-time. Full-time tuition and fees vary according to course load. Part-time tuition and fees vary according to course load. *Required fees:* $841 full-time, $27 per credit hour part-time. *Waivers:* senior citizens and employees or children of employees.
Financial Aid Of all full-time matriculated undergraduates who enrolled in 2018, 42 Federal Work-Study jobs (averaging $1496). *Financial aid deadline:* 6/1.
Applying *Options:* electronic application. *Required:* high school transcript. *Application deadlines:* rolling (freshmen), rolling (transfers). *Notification:* continuous (transfers).
Freshman Application Contact Mrs. Tracy Raby, Director of Admissions/Registrar, Northwest-Shoals Community College, PO Box 2545, Muscle Shoals, AL 35662. *Phone:* 256-331-5462. *Fax:* 256-331-5366. *E-mail:* tracy@nwscc.edu.
Website: http://www.nwscc.edu/.

Reid State Technical College

Evergreen, Alabama

Freshman Application Contact Ms. Mandy Godwin, Assistant to the Registrar, Reid State Technical College, Evergreen, AL 36401-0588. *Phone:* 251-578-1313 Ext. 148. *E-mail:* mwilson@rstc.edu. *Website:* http://www.rstc.edu/.

Remington College–Mobile Campus
Mobile, Alabama

Freshman Application Contact Remington College–Mobile Campus, 828 Downtowner Loop West, Mobile, AL 36609. *Phone:* 251-343-8200. *Toll-free phone:* 800-323-8122. *Website:* http://www.remingtoncollege.edu/.

Shelton State Community College
Tuscaloosa, Alabama

Freshman Application Contact Ms. Sharon Chastine, Secretary to the Associate Dean of Student Services Enrollment, Shelton State Community College, 9500 Old Greensboro Road, Tuscaloosa, AL 35405. *Phone:* 205-391-2309. *Fax:* 205-391-3910. *E-mail:* schastine@sheltonstate.edu. *Website:* http://www.sheltonstate.edu/.

Snead State Community College
Boaz, Alabama

Freshman Application Contact Mr. Jason Cannon, Vice President Student Services, Snead State Community College, PO Box 734, Boaz, AL 35957-0734. *Phone:* 256-840-4150. *Fax:* 256-593-7180. *E-mail:* jcannon@snead.edu. *Website:* http://www.snead.edu/.

Southern Union State Community College
Wadley, Alabama

Freshman Application Contact Admissions Office, Southern Union State Community College, PO Box 1000, Roberts Street, Wadley, AL 36276. *Phone:* 256-395-5157. *E-mail:* info@suscc.edu. *Website:* http://www.suscc.edu/.

Wallace Community College
Dothan, Alabama

Freshman Application Contact Mr. Keith Saulsberry, Director, Enrollment Services/Registrar, Wallace Community College, 1141 Wallace Drive, Dothan, AL 36303. *Phone:* 334-983-3521 Ext. 2470. *Toll-free phone:* 800-543-2426. *Fax:* 334-983-3600. *E-mail:* ksaulsberry@wallace.edu. *Website:* http://www.wallace.edu/.

Wallace State Community College
Hanceville, Alabama

Director of Admissions Ms. Jennifer Hill, Director of Admissions, Wallace State Community College, PO Box 2000, 801 Main Street, Hanceville, AL 35077-2000. *Phone:* 256-352-8278. *Toll-free phone:* 866-350-9722. *Website:* http://www.wallacestate.edu/.

ALASKA

Alaska Career College
Anchorage, Alaska

Freshman Application Contact Alaska Career College, 1415 East Tudor Road, Anchorage, AK 99507. *Website:* http://www.alaskacareercollege.edu/.

Alaska Christian College
Soldotna, Alaska

Admissions Office Contact Alaska Christian College, 35109 Royal Place, Soldotna, AK 99669. *Website:* http://www.alaskacc.edu/.

Charter College
Anchorage, Alaska

Director of Admissions Ms. Lily Sirianni, Vice President, Charter College, 2221 East Northern Lights Boulevard, Suite 120, Anchorage, AK 99508. *Phone:* 907-277-1000. *Toll-free phone:* 888-200-9942. *Website:* http://www.chartercollege.edu/.

Ilisagvik College
Barrow, Alaska

Freshman Application Contact Tennessee Judkins, Recruiter, Ilisagvik College, PO Box 749, Barrow, AK 99723. *Phone:* 907-852-1772. *Toll-free phone:* 800-478-7337. *Fax:* 907-852-1789. *E-mail:* tennessee.judkins@ilisagvik.edu. *Website:* http://www.ilisagvik.edu/.

University of Alaska Anchorage, Kenai Peninsula College
Soldotna, Alaska

- **State-supported** primarily 2-year, founded 1964, part of University of Alaska
- **Rural** 360-acre campus
- **Coed,** 2,142 undergraduate students, 33% full-time, 64% women, 36% men

Undergraduates 702 full-time, 1,440 part-time. Students come from 40 states and territories; 4 other countries; 2% Black or African American, non-Hispanic/Latino; 6% Hispanic/Latino; 4% Asian, non-Hispanic/Latino; 2% Native Hawaiian or other Pacific Islander, non-Hispanic/Latino; 6% American Indian or Alaska Native, non-Hispanic/Latino; 9% Two or more races, non-Hispanic/Latino; 16% Race/ethnicity unknown; 1% international.
Faculty *Total:* 117, 28% full-time. *Student/faculty ratio:* 18:1.
Majors Business administration and management; early childhood education; emergency medical technology (EMT paramedic); general studies; human services; instrumentation technology; petroleum technology; practical nursing, vocational nursing and nursing assistants related; psychology.
Academics *Calendar:* semesters. *Degrees:* certificates, associate, and bachelor's. *Special study options:* academic remediation for entering students, adult/continuing education programs, advanced placement credit, cooperative education, distance learning, double majors, English as a second language, independent study, internships, part-time degree program, services for LD students.
Library Kenai Peninsula College Library.
Student Life *Housing:* college housing not available. *Campus security:* 24-hour emergency response devices. *Student services:* health clinic, personal/psychological counseling, veterans affairs office.
Costs (2020–21) *Tuition:* state resident $5616 full-time, $234 per credit hour part-time; nonresident $5616 full-time, $234 per credit hour part-time. *Required fees:* $828 full-time. *Waivers:* senior citizens and employees or children of employees.
Applying *Options:* electronic application. *Application fee:* $40. *Required:* high school transcript. *Application deadlines:* rolling (freshmen), rolling (out-of-state freshmen), rolling (transfers). *Notification:* continuous (freshmen), continuous (out-of-state freshmen), continuous (transfers).
Freshman Application Contact Ms. Ginger Rose, Admission and Student Records Coordinator, University of Alaska Anchorage, Kenai Peninsula College, 156 College Road, Soldotna, AK 99669. *Phone:* 907-262-0311. *Toll-free phone:* 877-262-0330. *E-mail:* glrose@alaska.edu. *Website:* http://www.kpc.alaska.edu/.

University of Alaska Anchorage, Kodiak College
Kodiak, Alaska

Freshman Application Contact University of Alaska Anchorage, Kodiak College, 117 Benny Benson Drive, Kodiak, AK 99615-6643. *Phone:* 907-486-1235. *Toll-free phone:* 800-486-7660. *Website:* http://www.koc.alaska.edu/.

University of Alaska Anchorage, Matanuska-Susitna College
Palmer, Alaska

Freshman Application Contact Ms. Sandra Gravley, Student Services Director, University of Alaska Anchorage, Matanuska-Susitna College, PO Box 2889, Palmer, AK 99645-2889. *Phone:* 907-745-9712. *Fax:* 907-745-9747. *E-mail:* info@matsu.alaska.edu. *Website:* http://www.matsu.alaska.edu/.

University of Alaska, Prince William Sound College
Valdez, Alaska

Freshman Application Contact Dr. Denise Runge, Academic Affairs, University of Alaska, Prince William Sound College, PO Box 97, Valdez, AK

99686-0097. *Phone:* 907-834-1600. *Toll-free phone:* 800-478-8800. *Fax:* 907-834-1691. *E-mail:* drunge@pwscc.edu. *Website:* http://www.pwsc.alaska.edu/.

University of Alaska Southeast, Ketchikan Campus

Ketchikan, Alaska

Freshman Application Contact Admissions Office, University of Alaska Southeast, Ketchikan Campus, 2600 7th Avenue, Ketchikan, AK 99901-5798. *Phone:* 907-225-6177. *Toll-free phone:* 888-550-6177. *Fax:* 907-225-3895. *E-mail:* ketch.info@uas.alaska.edu. *Website:* http://www.ketch.alaska.edu/.

University of Alaska Southeast, Sitka Campus

Sitka, Alaska

Freshman Application Contact Ms. Teal Gordon, Admissions Representative, University of Alaska Southeast, Sitka Campus, UAS Sitka, 1332 Seward Avenue, Sitka, AK 99835. *Phone:* 907-747-7726. *Toll-free phone:* 800-478-6653. *Fax:* 907-747-7731. *E-mail:* ktgordon@uas.alaska.edu. *Website:* http://www.uas.alaska.edu/sitka/.

AMERICAN SAMOA

American Samoa Community College

Pago Pago, American Samoa

Freshman Application Contact Elizabeth Leuma, Admissions Officer, American Samoa Community College, PO Box 2609, Pago Pago 96799, American Samoa. *Phone:* 684-699-9155 Ext. 411. *Fax:* 684-699-1083. *Website:* http://www.amsamoa.edu/.

ARIZONA

Arizona College

Glendale, Arizona

Freshman Application Contact Admissions Department, Arizona College, 4425 West Olive Avenue, Suite 300, Glendale, AZ 85302-3843. *Phone:* 602-222-9300. *E-mail:* lhicks@arizonacollege.edu. *Website:* http://www.arizonacollege.edu/.

Arizona Western College

Yuma, Arizona

Freshman Application Contact Nicole D. Harral, Director of Admissions/Registrar, Arizona Western College, PO Box 929, Yuma, AZ 85366. *Phone:* 928-344-7600. *Toll-free phone:* 888-293-0392. *Fax:* 928-344-7543. *E-mail:* nicole.harral@azwestern.edu. *Website:* http://www.azwestern.edu/.

Carrington College–Mesa

Mesa, Arizona

- **Proprietary** 2-year, founded 1977, part of Carrington Colleges Group, Inc.
- **Suburban** campus
- **Coed**

Undergraduates 565 full-time, 34 part-time. 2% are from out of state; 14% transferred in. *Retention:* 61% of full-time freshmen returned.
Faculty *Student/faculty ratio:* 26:1.
Academics *Degree:* certificates and associate.
Applying *Required:* essay or personal statement, high school transcript, interview.
Freshman Application Contact Carrington College–Mesa, 1001 West Southern Avenue, Suite 130, Mesa, AZ 85210. *Website:* http://www.carrington.edu/.

Carrington College–Phoenix East

Phoenix, Arizona

- **Proprietary** 2-year, part of Carrington Colleges Group, Inc.
- **Urban** campus
- **Coed**

Undergraduates 178 full-time, 83 part-time. 1% are from out of state; 8% Black or African American, non-Hispanic/Latino; 37% Hispanic/Latino; 6% Asian, non-Hispanic/Latino; 0.4% Native Hawaiian or other Pacific Islander, non-Hispanic/Latino; 3% American Indian or Alaska Native, non-Hispanic/Latino; 2% Two or more races, non-Hispanic/Latino; 6% Race/ethnicity unknown; 19% transferred in. *Retention:* 39% of full time freshmen returned.
Faculty *Student/faculty ratio:* 8:1.
Academics *Degree:* certificates and associate.
Applying *Required:* essay or personal statement, high school transcript, interview.
Freshman Application Contact Carrington College–Phoenix East, 2149 West Dunlap Avenue, Suite 100, Phoenix, AZ 85021. *Website:* http://www.carrington.edu/.

Carrington College–Phoenix North

Phoenix, Arizona

- **Proprietary** 2-year, founded 1976, part of Carrington Colleges Group, Inc.
- **Urban** campus
- **Coed**

Undergraduates 653 full-time. 3% are from out of state; 7% Black or African American, non-Hispanic/Latino; 57% Hispanic/Latino; 0.9% Asian, non-Hispanic/Latino; 0.6% Native Hawaiian or other Pacific Islander, non-Hispanic/Latino; 7% American Indian or Alaska Native, non-Hispanic/Latino; 1% Two or more races, non-Hispanic/Latino; 2% Race/ethnicity unknown; 15% transferred in. *Retention:* 68% of full-time freshmen returned.
Faculty *Student/faculty ratio:* 39:1.
Academics *Degree:* certificates and associate.
Applying *Required:* essay or personal statement, high school transcript, interview.
Freshman Application Contact Carrington College–Phoenix North, 8503 North 27th Avenue, Phoenix, AZ 85051. *Website:* http://www.carrington.edu/.

Central Arizona College

Coolidge, Arizona

Freshman Application Contact Dr. James Moore, Dean of Records and Admissions, Central Arizona College, 8470 North Overfield Road, Coolidge, AZ 85128. *Phone:* 520-494-5261. *Toll-free phone:* 800-237-9814. *Fax:* 520-426-5083. *E-mail:* james.moore@centralaz.edu. *Website:* http://www.centralaz.edu/.

Chandler-Gilbert Community College

Chandler, Arizona

- **State and locally supported** 2-year, founded 1985, part of Maricopa County Community College District System
- **Suburban** 188-acre campus with easy access to Phoenix
- **Coed,** 15,585 undergraduate students, 28% full-time, 52% women, 48% men

Undergraduates 4,353 full-time, 11,232 part-time. Students come from 15 states and territories; 36 other countries; 3% are from out of state; 4% Black or African American, non-Hispanic/Latino; 26% Hispanic/Latino; 6% Asian, non-Hispanic/Latino; 0.2% Native Hawaiian or other Pacific Islander, non-Hispanic/Latino; 2% American Indian or Alaska Native, non-Hispanic/Latino; 4% Two or more races, non-Hispanic/Latino; 5% Race/ethnicity unknown.
Freshmen *Admission:* 1,272 enrolled.
Faculty *Total:* 568, 25% full-time. *Student/faculty ratio:* 28:1.
Majors Accounting; accounting technology and bookkeeping; administrative assistant and secretarial science; aircraft powerplant technology; airframe mechanics and aircraft maintenance technology; airline pilot and flight crew; American Indian/Native American studies; anthropology; astronomy; biochemistry; biology/biological sciences; business administration and management; business administration, management and operations related; business/commerce; business, management, and marketing related; chemistry; commercial and advertising art; commercial photography; communication and media related; computer and information sciences; computer and information sciences and support services related; computer and information systems security; computer installation and repair technology; computer programming; computer programming (vendor/product certification); computer science;

computer systems analysis; computer systems networking and telecommunications; creative writing; criminal justice/police science; criminal justice/safety; dance; data entry/microcomputer applications; data modeling/warehousing and database administration; dietetic technology; dietitian assistant; digital communication and media/multimedia; dramatic/theater arts; economics; electrical and power transmission installation; electromechanical technology; elementary education; engineering technology; family and community services; fine/studio arts; food science; forensic science and technology; funeral service and mortuary science; general studies; geography; geology/earth science; history; human nutrition; information technology; insurance; kindergarten/preschool education; kinesiology and exercise science; liberal arts and sciences and humanities related; liberal arts and sciences/liberal studies; licensed practical/vocational nurse training; lineworker; literature; marketing research; massage therapy; mathematics; mechanic and repair technologies related; mental health counseling; meteorology; musical theater; music management; music performance; music related; network and system administration; organizational behavior; organizational leadership; philosophy; photography; physical fitness technician; physical sciences; physics; political science and government; pre-engineering; psychology; registered nursing/registered nurse; religious studies; retail management; secondary education; social work; sociology; Spanish; sustainability studies; visual and performing arts; web page, digital/multimedia and information resources design.
Academics *Calendar:* semesters. *Degree:* certificates, diplomas, and associate. *Special study options:* academic remediation for entering students, advanced placement credit, English as a second language, freshman honors college, honors programs, independent study, part-time degree program, services for LD students, study abroad, summer session for credit.
Library Chandler-Gilbert Community College Library.
Student Life *Housing:* college housing not available. *Activities and Organizations:* student-run radio station, choral group. *Campus security:* 24-hour emergency response devices and patrols, late-night transport/escort service. *Student services:* personal/psychological counseling, veterans affairs office.
Athletics Member NJCAA. *Intercollegiate sports:* baseball M, basketball M/W, golf M/W, soccer M/W, softball W, volleyball W.
Costs (2020–21) *Tuition:* area resident $2040 full-time; state resident $9624 full-time; nonresident $7824 full-time. *Required fees:* $30 full-time. *Payment plan:* installment. *Waivers:* employees or children of employees.
Applying *Options:* electronic application.
Freshman Application Contact Alex Gadberry, Coordinator of Student Recruitment, Chandler-Gilbert Community College, 2626 East Pecos Road, Chandler, AZ 85225-2479. *Phone:* 480-726-4228. *E-mail:* alexander.gadberry@cgc.edu. *Website:* http://www.cgc.maricopa.edu/.

Cochise County Community College District

Sierra Vista, Arizona

- **State and locally supported** 2-year, founded 1962
- **Rural** 732-acre campus with easy access to Tucson
- **Coed**

Undergraduates 1,519 full-time, 2,399 part-time. Students come from 17 states and territories; 2 other countries; 8% are from out of state; 5% Black or African American, non-Hispanic/Latino; 45% Hispanic/Latino; 2% Asian, non-Hispanic/Latino; 0.6% Native Hawaiian or other Pacific Islander, non-Hispanic/Latino; 0.5% American Indian or Alaska Native, non-Hispanic/Latino; 5% Two or more races, non-Hispanic/Latino; 1% Race/ethnicity unknown; 1% international; 3% transferred in; 2% live on campus. *Retention:* 63% of full-time freshmen returned.
Faculty *Student/faculty ratio:* 16:1.
Academics *Calendar:* semesters. *Degrees:* certificates and associate (profile includes campuses in Douglas and Sierra Vista, AZ). *Special study options:* academic remediation for entering students, adult/continuing education programs, advanced placement credit, cooperative education, distance learning, English as a second language, honors programs, independent study, internships, part-time degree program, services for LD students, summer session for credit.
Library Andrea Cracchiolo plus 1 other. *Books:* 55,145 (physical), 40,945 (digital/electronic); *Serial titles:* 22 (physical), 7,401 (digital/electronic); *Databases:* 16. Weekly public service hours: 45.
Student Life *Campus security:* 24-hour emergency response devices and patrols, late-night transport/escort service.
Athletics Member NJCAA.
Costs (2019–20) *Tuition:* state resident $2640 full-time, $88 per credit hour part-time; nonresident $7800 full-time, $260 per credit hour part-time. Full-time tuition and fees vary according to course load, program, and reciprocity agreements. Part-time tuition and fees vary according to course load, program, and reciprocity agreements. *Room and board:* $7362; room only: $2400. Room and board charges vary according to housing facility.
Financial Aid Of all full-time matriculated undergraduates who enrolled in 2014, 1,300 applied for aid, 1,121 were judged to have need. 72 Federal Work-Study jobs (averaging $5437). In 2014, 22. *Average financial aid package:* $5876. *Average need-based loan:* $3658. *Average need-based gift aid:* $3730. *Average non-need-based aid:* $1666. *Financial aid deadline:* 6/15.
Applying *Options:* electronic application, deferred entrance. *Required for some:* high school transcript. *Recommended:* high school transcript.
Freshman Application Contact Ms. Debbie Quick, Director of Admissions and Records, Cochise County Community College District, 901 North Colombo Avenue, Sierra Vista, AZ 85635-2317. *Phone:* 520-515-3640. *Toll-free phone:* 800-593-9567. *Fax:* 520-515-5452. *E-mail:* quickd@cochise.edu. *Website:* http://www.cochise.edu/.

Coconino Community College

Flagstaff, Arizona

- **State-supported** 2-year, founded 1991
- **Small-town** 5-acre campus
- **Endowment** $322,526
- **Coed**

Undergraduates 1,134 full-time, 2,474 part-time. 1% Black or African American, non-Hispanic/Latino; 18% Hispanic/Latino; 1% Asian, non-Hispanic/Latino; 0.2% Native Hawaiian or other Pacific Islander, non-Hispanic/Latino; 18% American Indian or Alaska Native, non-Hispanic/Latino; 4% Two or more races, non-Hispanic/Latino; 2% Race/ethnicity unknown; 22% transferred in. *Retention:* 57% of full-time freshmen returned.
Faculty *Student/faculty ratio:* 25:1.
Academics *Calendar:* semesters. *Degree:* certificates and associate. *Special study options:* academic remediation for entering students, adult/continuing education programs, distance learning, honors programs, independent study, internships, part-time degree program, study abroad, summer session for credit. *ROTC:* Air Force (b).
Library Information Resources and Library Services.
Student Life *Campus security:* 24-hour emergency response devices, student patrols, late-night transport/escort service, security patrols during hours of operation, electronic access throughout the campuses with security cards.
Applying *Options:* electronic application.
Freshman Application Contact Veronica Hipolito, Director of Student Services, Coconino Community College, 2800 South Lone Tree Road, Flagstaff, AZ 86001. *Phone:* 928-226-4334 Ext. 4334. *Toll-free phone:* 800-350-7122. *Fax:* 928-226-4114. *E-mail:* veronica.hipolito@coconino.edu. *Website:* http://www.coconino.edu/.

CollegeAmerica–Flagstaff

Flagstaff, Arizona

Freshman Application Contact CollegeAmerica–Flagstaff, 399 South Malpais Lane, Flagstaff, AZ 86001. *Phone:* 928-213-6060 Ext. 1402. *Toll-free phone:* 800-622-2894. *Website:* http://www.collegeamerica.edu/.

CollegeAmerica–Phoenix

Phoenix, Arizona

Admissions Office Contact CollegeAmerica–Phoenix, 9801 North Metro Parkway East, Phoenix, AZ 85051. *Toll-free phone:* 800-622-2894. *Website:* http://www.collegeamerica.edu/.

Diné College

Tsaile, Arizona

- **Federally supported** 2-year, founded 1968
- **Rural** 1200-acre campus
- **Coed**

Undergraduates 815 full-time, 842 part-time.
Academics *Calendar:* semesters. *Degree:* certificates and associate. *Special study options:* academic remediation for entering students, adult/continuing education programs, off-campus study, part-time degree program, services for LD students, summer session for credit.
Library Tsaile-Navajo Community College Library plus 1 other.
Student Life *Campus security:* 24-hour emergency response devices and patrols, student patrols, late-night transport/escort service.
Athletics Member NJCAA.
Financial Aid Of all full-time matriculated undergraduates who enrolled in 2018, 898 applied for aid, 898 were judged to have need. 19 Federal Work-Study jobs (averaging $1381). 10 state and other part-time jobs (averaging

$1753). *Average financial aid package:* $2435. *Average need-based gift aid:* $729.

Applying *Options:* early admission. *Application fee:* $20. *Required:* high school transcript, Certificate of Indian Blood form for Native American Students.

Freshman Application Contact Mrs. Louise Litzin, Registrar, Diné College, PO Box 67, Tsaile, AZ 86556. *Phone:* 928-724-6633. *Toll-free phone:* 877-988-DINE. *Fax:* 928-724-3349. *E-mail:* louise@dinecollege.edu. *Website:* http://www.dinecollege.edu/.

Eastern Arizona College

Thatcher, Arizona

- **State and locally supported** 2-year, founded 1888, part of Arizona State Community College System
- **Small-town** 557-acre campus
- **Endowment** $7.9 million
- **Coed,** 6,027 undergraduate students, 29% full-time, 56% women, 44% men

Undergraduates 1,762 full-time, 4,265 part-time. Students come from 18 states and territories; 17 other countries; 2% are from out of state; 3% Black or African American, non-Hispanic/Latino; 22% Hispanic/Latino; 0.7% Asian, non-Hispanic/Latino; 0.5% Native Hawaiian or other Pacific Islander, non-Hispanic/Latino; 6% American Indian or Alaska Native, non-Hispanic/Latino; 2% Two or more races, non-Hispanic/Latino; 3% Race/ethnicity unknown; 0.7% international; 4% transferred in; 2% live on campus.

Freshmen *Admission:* 3,288 applied, 3,288 admitted, 1,195 enrolled.

Faculty *Total:* 336, 28% full-time, 12% with terminal degrees. *Student/faculty ratio:* 18:1.

Majors Administrative assistant and secretarial science; anthropology; art; automobile/automotive mechanics technology; biology/biological sciences; business administration and management; business/commerce; business, management, and marketing related; business operations support and secretarial services related; business teacher education; chemistry; civil engineering technology; commercial and advertising art; cosmetology; criminal justice/law enforcement administration; criminal justice/police science; diesel mechanics technology; drafting and design technology; dramatic/theater arts; early childhood education; elementary education; emergency medical technology (EMT paramedic); environmental biology; fine/studio arts; fire science/firefighting; foreign languages and literatures; forestry; general studies; geology/earth science; graphic design; health and physical education/fitness; heating, air conditioning, ventilation and refrigeration maintenance technology; history; industrial electronics technology; industrial mechanics and maintenance technology; information science/studies; liberal arts and sciences/liberal studies; machine shop technology; mathematics; mining technology; multi/interdisciplinary studies related; music; pharmacy technician; photographic and film/video technology; physics; political science and government; pre-chiropractic; premedical studies; pre-optometry; pre-pharmacy studies; pre-physical therapy; psychology; registered nursing/registered nurse; secondary education; small business administration; sociology; speech communication and rhetoric; welding technology; wildlife biology; writing.

Academics *Calendar:* semesters. *Degree:* certificates and associate. *Special study options:* academic remediation for entering students, adult/continuing education programs, advanced placement credit, cooperative education, distance learning, double majors, external degree program, independent study, internships, off-campus study, part-time degree program, services for LD students, student-designed majors, study abroad, summer session for credit.

Library Alumni Library. *Books:* 16,229 (physical), 252,789 (digital/electronic); *Serial titles:* 47 (physical), 117,957 (digital/electronic); *Databases:* 85. Weekly public service hours: 80; students can reserve study rooms.

Student Life *Housing Options:* men-only, women-only. Campus housing is university owned. *Activities and Organizations:* drama/theater group, choral group, marching band, Latter-Day Saints Student Association, ASEAC (Associated Students Eastern Arizona College, Multicultural Council, Phi Theta Kappa, Student Nursing Club. *Campus security:* 24-hour emergency response devices, late-night transport/escort service, 20-hour patrols by trained security personnel. *Student services:* personal/psychological counseling.

Athletics Member NJCAA. *Intercollegiate sports:* baseball M(s), basketball M(s)/W(s), golf M(s)/W(s), softball W(s), tennis W(s), volleyball W(s). *Intramural sports:* basketball M/W, cheerleading M/W, football M/W, racquetball M/W, soccer M/W, swimming and diving M/W, table tennis M/W, ultimate Frisbee M/W, volleyball M/W.

Costs (2020–21) *Tuition:* area resident $2700 full-time, $90 per credit hour part-time; state resident $2700 full-time, $90 per credit hour part-time; nonresident $11,400 full-time, $380 per credit hour part-time. Full-time tuition and fees vary according to course load. *Room and board:* $6926; room only: $3182. Room and board charges vary according to board plan and housing facility. *Payment plan:* installment. *Waivers:* senior citizens and employees or children of employees.

Financial Aid Of all full-time matriculated undergraduates who enrolled in 2016, 1,105 applied for aid, 994 were judged to have need, 45 had their need fully met. In 2016, 99 non-need-based awards were made. *Average percent of need met:* 42%. *Average financial aid package:* $6372. *Average need-based gift aid:* $6122. *Average non-need-based aid:* $2635.

Applying *Options:* electronic application, early admission, deferred entrance. *Recommended:* high school transcript. *Application deadlines:* rolling (freshmen), rolling (out-of-state freshmen), rolling (transfers), rolling (early action). *Early decision deadline:* rolling (for plan 1), rolling (for plan 2). *Notification:* continuous (freshmen), continuous (out-of-state freshmen), continuous (transfers), rolling (early decision plan 1), rolling (early decision plan 2), rolling (early action).

Freshman Application Contact Suzette Udall, Records Assistant, Eastern Arizona College, 615 North Stadium Avenue, Thatcher, AZ 85552-0769. *Phone:* 928-428-8904. *Toll-free phone:* 800-678-3808. *Fax:* 928-428-3729. *E-mail:* admissions@eac.edu.
Website: http://www.eac.edu/.

Estrella Mountain Community College

Avondale, Arizona

Freshman Application Contact Estrella Mountain Community College, 3000 North Dysart Road, Avondale, AZ 85392. *Phone:* 623-935-8812. *Website:* http://www.estrellamountain.edu/.

Fortis College

Phoenix, Arizona

Admissions Office Contact Fortis College, 555 North 18th Street, Suite 110, Phoenix, AZ 85006. *Toll-free phone:* 855-4-FORTIS. *Website:* http://www.fortis.edu/.

GateWay Community College

Phoenix, Arizona

Freshman Application Contact Director of Admissions and Records, GateWay Community College, 108 North 40th Street, Phoenix, AZ 85034. *Phone:* 602-286-8200. *Fax:* 602-286-8200. *E-mail:* enroll@gatewaycc.edu. *Website:* http://www.gatewaycc.edu/.

Glendale Community College

Glendale, Arizona

Freshman Application Contact Ms. Mary Blackwell, Dean of Enrollment Services, Glendale Community College, 6000 West Olive Avenue, Glendale, AZ 85302. *Phone:* 623-435-3305. *Fax:* 623-845-3303. *E-mail:* admissions.recruitment@gccaz.edu. *Website:* http://www.gccaz.edu/.

Mesa Community College

Mesa, Arizona

Freshman Application Contact Carmen Newland, Dean, Enrollment Services, Mesa Community College, 1833 West Southern Avenue, Mesa, AZ 85202-4866. *Phone:* 480-461-7600. *Toll-free phone:* 866-532-4983. *Fax:* 480-844-3117. *E-mail:* admissionsandrecords@mesacc.edu. *Website:* http://www.mesacc.edu/.

Mohave Community College

Kingman, Arizona

- **State-supported** 2-year, founded 1971
- **Small-town** 160-acre campus
- **Coed**

Undergraduates 809 full-time, 3,262 part-time. Students come from 19 states and territories; 5% are from out of state; 1% Black or African American, non-Hispanic/Latino; 25% Hispanic/Latino; 2% Asian, non-Hispanic/Latino; 0.4% Native Hawaiian or other Pacific Islander, non-Hispanic/Latino; 2% American Indian or Alaska Native, non-Hispanic/Latino; 3% Two or more races, non-Hispanic/Latino; 0.8% Race/ethnicity unknown; 0.7% international.

Faculty *Student/faculty ratio:* 13:1.

Academics *Calendar:* semesters. *Degree:* certificates, diplomas, and associate. *Special study options:* academic remediation for entering students, adult/continuing education programs, cooperative education, distance learning, English as a second language, independent study, part-time degree program, summer session for credit.

Library Mohave Community College Library.
Student Life *Campus security:* late-night transport/escort service.
Applying *Options:* electronic application, early admission, deferred entrance.
Freshman Application Contact Ana Masterson, Chief Student Services Officer, Mohave Community College, 1971 Jagerson Avenue, Kingman, AZ 86409. *Phone:* 928-757-0803. *Toll-free phone:* 888-664-2832. *Fax:* 928-757-0808. *E-mail:* amasterson@mohave.edu. *Website:* http://www.mohave.edu/.

Northland Pioneer College
Holbrook, Arizona

Freshman Application Contact Ms. Suzette Willis, Coordinator of Admissions, Northland Pioneer College, PO Box 610, Holbrook, AZ 86025. *Phone:* 928-536-6271. *Toll-free phone:* 800-266-7845. *Fax:* 928-536-6212. *Website:* http://www.npc.edu/.

Paradise Valley Community College
Phoenix, Arizona

Freshman Application Contact Paradise Valley Community College, 18401 North 32nd Street, Phoenix, AZ 85032-1200. *Phone:* 602-787-7020. *Website:* http://www.pvc.maricopa.edu/.

The Paralegal Institute at Brighton College
Scottsdale, Arizona

Freshman Application Contact Patricia Yancy, Director of Admissions, The Paralegal Institute at Brighton College, 2933 West Indian School Road, Drawer 11408, Phoenix, AZ 85061-1408. *Phone:* 602-212-0501. *Toll-free phone:* 800-354-1254. *Fax:* 602-212-0502. *E-mail:* paralegalinst@mindspring.com. *Website:* http://www.theparalegalinstitute.edu/.

Penn Foster College
Scottsdale, Arizona

Freshman Application Contact Admissions, Penn Foster College, 14300 North Northsight Boulevard, Suite 120, Scottsdale, AZ 85260. *Phone:* 888-427-1000. *Toll-free phone:* 800-471-3232. *Website:* http://www.pennfostercollege.edu/.

Phoenix College
Phoenix, Arizona

Freshman Application Contact Ms. Brenda Stark, Director of Admissions, Registration, and Records, Phoenix College, 1202 West Thomas Road, Phoenix, AZ 85013. *Phone:* 602-285-7503. *Fax:* 602-285-7813. *E-mail:* kathy.french@pcmail.maricopa.edu. *Website:* http://www.phoenixcollege.edu/.

Pima Community College
Tucson, Arizona

Freshman Application Contact Terra Benson, Director of Admissions and Registrar, Pima Community College, 4905B East Broadway Boulevard, Tucson, AZ 85709-1120. *Phone:* 520-206-4640. *Fax:* 520-206-4790. *E-mail:* tbenson@pima.edu. *Website:* http://www.pima.edu/.

Pima Medical Institute - East Valley
Mesa, Arizona

Freshman Application Contact Pima Medical Institute - East Valley, 2160 South Power Road, Mesa, AZ 85209. *Phone:* 480-898-9898. *Toll-free phone:* 800-477-PIMA. *Website:* http://www.pmi.edu/.

Pima Medical Institute - Mesa
Mesa, Arizona

Freshman Application Contact Admissions Office, Pima Medical Institute - Mesa, 957 South Dobson Road, Mesa, AZ 85202. *Phone:* 480-644-0267 Ext. 225. *Toll-free phone:* 800-477-PIMA. *Website:* http://www.pmi.edu/.

Pima Medical Institute - Phoenix
Phoenix, Arizona

Admissions Office Contact Pima Medical Institute - Phoenix, 13610 North Black Canyon Highway, Phoenix, AZ 85029. *Website:* http://www.pmi.edu/.

Pima Medical Institute - Tucson
Tucson, Arizona

Freshman Application Contact Admissions Office, Pima Medical Institute - Tucson, 3350 East Grant Road, Tucson, AZ 85716. *Phone:* 520-326-1600 Ext. 5112. *Toll-free phone:* 800-477-PIMA. *Website:* http://www.pmi.edu/.

The Refrigeration School
Phoenix, Arizona

Freshman Application Contact Mr. John Palumbo, Regional Director of Admissions, The Refrigeration School, 4210 East Washington Street. *Phone:* 602-275-7133. *Toll-free phone:* 888-943-4822. *Fax:* 602-267-4811. *E-mail:* info@rsiaz.edu. *Website:* http://www.refrigerationschool.com/.

Rio Salado College
Tempe, Arizona

- **State and locally supported** 2-year, founded 1978, part of Maricopa County Community College District System
- **Urban** campus
- **Coed**

Undergraduates Students come from 38 other countries; 4% are from out of state. *Retention:* 34% of full-time freshmen returned.
Faculty *Student/faculty ratio:* 13:1.
Academics *Calendar:* semesters. *Degree:* certificates and associate. *Special study options:* academic remediation for entering students, accelerated degree program, adult/continuing education programs, advanced placement credit, cooperative education, distance learning, double majors, English as a second language, external degree program, honors programs, independent study, internships, part-time degree program, services for LD students, summer session for credit.
Library Rio Salado Library and Information Center.
Student Life *Campus security:* 24-hour emergency response devices, late-night transport/escort service.
Costs (2019–20) *Tuition:* state resident $2040 full-time, $85 per credit hour part-time; nonresident $5500 full-time, $250 per credit hour part-time. Full-time tuition and fees vary according to course load and reciprocity agreements. Part-time tuition and fees vary according to course load and reciprocity agreements. *Required fees:* $30 full-time, $15 per term part-time. *Payment plans:* installment, deferred payment.
Applying *Options:* electronic application, early admission, deferred entrance.
Freshman Application Contact Laurel Redman, Director of Admissions, Records and Registration, Rio Salado College, 2323 West 14th Street, Tempe 85281. *Phone:* 480-517-8563. *Toll-free phone:* 800-729-1197. *Fax:* 480-517-8199. *Website:* http://www.riosalado.edu/.

Scottsdale Community College
Scottsdale, Arizona

Freshman Application Contact Ms. Laura Krueger, Director of Admissions and Records, Scottsdale Community College, 9000 East Chaparral Road, Scottsdale, AZ 85256. *Phone:* 480-423-6133. *Fax:* 480-423-6200. *E-mail:* laura.krueger@scottsdalecc.edu. *Website:* http://www.scottsdalecc.edu/.

Sessions College for Professional Design
Tempe, Arizona

Freshman Application Contact Ms. Mhelanie Hernandez, Director of Admissions, Sessions College for Professional Design, 350 South Mill Avenue, Suite B-104, Tempe, AZ 85281. *Phone:* 480-212-1704. *Toll-free phone:* 800-258-4115. *E-mail:* admissions@sessions.edu. *Website:* http://www.sessions.edu/.

South Mountain Community College
Phoenix, Arizona

Director of Admissions Dean of Enrollment Services, South Mountain Community College, 7050 South Twenty-fourth Street, Phoenix, AZ 85040. *Phone:* 602-243-8120. *Website:* http://www.southmountaincc.edu/.

Southwest Institute of Healing Arts
Tempe, Arizona

Director of Admissions Katie Yearous, Student Advisor, Southwest Institute of Healing Arts, 1100 East Apache Boulevard, Tempe, AZ 85281. *Phone:* 480-994-9244. *Toll-free phone:* 888-504-9106. *E-mail:* joannl@swiha.net. *Website:* http://www.swiha.org/.

Tohono O'odham Community College
Sells, Arizona

- **Public** 2-year, founded 1998
- **Rural** 42-acre campus
- **Endowment** $362,851
- **Coed,** 431 undergraduate students, 32% full-time, 59% women, 41% men

Undergraduates 136 full-time, 295 part-time. Students come from 7 states and territories; 5% are from out of state; 3% Black or African American, non-Hispanic/Latino; 2% Hispanic/Latino; 86% American Indian or Alaska Native, non-Hispanic/Latino; 1% Two or more races, non-Hispanic/Latino; 7% transferred in; 10% live on campus. *Retention:* 36% of full-time freshmen returned.

Freshmen *Admission:* 97 enrolled.

Faculty *Total:* 62, 29% full-time, 27% with terminal degrees. *Student/faculty ratio:* 7:1.

Majors Biology/biological sciences; business administration and management; carpentry; early childhood education; electrician; elementary education; fine/studio arts; health services/allied health/health sciences; interdisciplinary studies; liberal arts and sciences/liberal studies; painting and wall covering; plumbing technology; social sciences.

Academics *Calendar:* semesters. *Degree:* certificates, diplomas, and associate. *Special study options:* academic remediation for entering students, adult/continuing education programs, cooperative education, double majors, part-time degree program, services for LD students, summer session for credit.

Library Tohono O'odham Community College Library plus 1 other. *Books:* 10,734 (physical); *Serial titles:* 208 (physical); *Databases:* 69. Weekly public service hours: 44.

Student Life *Housing Options:* coed, men-only, women-only. Campus housing is university owned. *Activities and Organizations:* Student Senate, AISES, Archery Club. *Campus security:* 24-hour patrols. *Student services:* personal/psychological counseling.

Athletics Member NJCAA. *Intercollegiate sports:* basketball M(s)/W(s).

Costs (2020–21) *Tuition:* area resident $466 full-time, $34 per credit hour part-time; state resident $466 full-time, $34 per credit hour part-time; nonresident $466 full-time, $34 per credit hour part-time. *Required fees:* $110 full-time, $55 per term part-time.

Financial Aid Of all full-time matriculated undergraduates who enrolled in 2019, 133 applied for aid, 89 were judged to have need, 89 had their need fully met. In 2019, 10 non-need-based awards were made. *Average percent of need met:* 100%. *Average financial aid package:* $2827. *Average need-based gift aid:* $2827. *Average non-need-based aid:* $1604.

Applying *Options:* electronic application. *Required:* high school transcript. *Application deadlines:* rolling (freshmen), rolling (transfers). *Notification:* continuous (freshmen), continuous (transfers), rolling (early decision).

Freshman Application Contact Gloria Benevidez, Student Support Specialist, Tohono O'odham Community College, PO Box 3129, Sells, AZ 85634. *Phone:* 520-383-8401. *E-mail:* gbenevidez@tocc.edu. *Website:* http://www.tocc.edu/.

Universal Technical Institute
Avondale, Arizona

Freshman Application Contact Director of Admission, Universal Technical Institute, 10695 West Pierce Street, Avondale, AZ 85323. *Phone:* 623-245-4600. *Toll-free phone:* 800-510-5072. *Fax:* 623-245-4601. *Website:* http://www.uti.edu/.

Yavapai College
Prescott, Arizona

Freshman Application Contact Mrs. Sheila Jarrell, Admissions, Registration, and Records Manager, Yavapai College, 1100 East Sheldon Street, Prescott, AZ 86301-3297. *Phone:* 928-776-2107. *Toll-free phone:* 800-922-6787. *Fax:* 928-776-2151. *E-mail:* registration@yc.edu. *Website:* http://www.yc.edu/.

ARKANSAS

Arkansas Northeastern College
Blytheville, Arkansas

Freshman Application Contact Arkansas Northeastern College, PO Box 1109, Blytheville, AR 72316. *Phone:* 870-762-1020. *Fax:* 870-763-1654. *Website:* http://www.anc.edu/.

Arkansas State University–Beebe
Beebe, Arkansas

Freshman Application Contact Mr. Ronald Hudson, Coordinator of Student Recruitment, Arkansas State University–Beebe, PO Box 1000, Beebe, AR 72012. *Phone:* 501-882-8860. *Toll-free phone:* 800-632-9985. *E-mail:* rdhudson@asub.edu. *Website:* http://www.asub.edu/.

Arkansas State University Mid-South
West Memphis, Arkansas

- **State-supported** 2-year, founded 1993, part of Arkansas State University System
- **Suburban** 80-acre campus with easy access to Memphis
- **Endowment** $967,261
- **Coed**

Undergraduates 356 full-time, 1,067 part-time. Students come from 5 states and territories; 2 other countries; 1% are from out of state; 56% Black or African American, non-Hispanic/Latino; 4% Hispanic/Latino; 0.7% Asian, non-Hispanic/Latino; 0.1% Native Hawaiian or other Pacific Islander, non-Hispanic/Latino; 0.6% American Indian or Alaska Native, non-Hispanic/Latino; 3% Two or more races, non-Hispanic/Latino; 0.7% international; 3% transferred in. *Retention:* 40% of full-time freshmen returned.

Faculty *Student/faculty ratio:* 14:1.

Academics *Calendar:* semesters. *Degree:* certificates and associate. *Special study options:* academic remediation for entering students, adult/continuing education programs, advanced placement credit, distance learning, independent study, internships, part-time degree program, services for LD students, summer session for credit.

Library Sandra C. Goldsby Library.

Student Life *Campus security:* 24-hour emergency response devices, security during class hours.

Athletics Member NJCAA.

Standardized Tests *Required:* SAT, ACT or ACT Compass (for admission).

Costs (2019–20) *Tuition:* area resident $92 full-time, $92 per credit hour part-time; state resident $112 full-time, $112 per credit hour part-time; nonresident $152 full-time, $152 per credit hour part-time. *Required fees:* $514 full-time, $22 per credit hour part-time, $5 per term part-time.

Financial Aid Of all full-time matriculated undergraduates who enrolled in 2018, 39 Federal Work-Study jobs (averaging $1676).

Applying *Options:* early admission.

Freshman Application Contact Leslie D Anderson, Registrar, Arkansas State University Mid-South, 2000 West Broadway, West Memphis, AR 72301. *Phone:* 870-733-6732. *Toll-free phone:* 866-733-6722. *Fax:* 870-733-6710. *E-mail:* landerson@asumidsouth.edu. *Website:* http://www.asumidsouth.edu/.

Arkansas State University–Mountain Home
Mountain Home, Arkansas

Freshman Application Contact Ms. Delba Parrish, Admissions Coordinator, Arkansas State University–Mountain Home, 1600 South College Street, Mountain Home, AR 72653. *Phone:* 870-508-6180. *Fax:* 870-508-6287. *E-mail:* dparrish@asumh.edu. *Website:* http://www.asumh.edu/.

Arkansas State University–Newport
Newport, Arkansas

- **State-supported** 2-year, founded 1989, part of Arkansas State University System
- **Rural** 189-acre campus
- **Endowment** $2.0 million
- **Coed**

Undergraduates 1,039 full-time, 1,231 part-time. Students come from 8 states and territories; 1 other country; 5% are from out of state; 14% Black or African American, non-Hispanic/Latino; 3% Hispanic/Latino; 0.6% Asian, non-

Hispanic/Latino; 0.5% American Indian or Alaska Native, non-Hispanic/Latino; 1% Two or more races, non-Hispanic/Latino; 4% Race/ethnicity unknown; 0.2% international; 4% transferred in.
Faculty *Student/faculty ratio:* 17:1.
Academics *Calendar:* semesters. *Degree:* certificates, diplomas, and associate. *Special study options:* academic remediation for entering students, adult/continuing education programs, advanced placement credit, cooperative education, distance learning, double majors, external degree program, independent study, internships, off-campus study, part-time degree program, services for LD students, summer session for credit.
Library Harryette M. Hodges and Kaneaster Hodges, Sr. Library plus 2 others. *Books:* 11,653 (physical), 27 (digital/electronic); *Databases:* 6. Weekly public service hours: 40.
Student Life *Campus security:* text-based alert system; campus police 8-5 on-site.
Standardized Tests *Required:* SAT or ACT or ACT Compass (for admission). *Recommended:* SAT or ACT (for admission), SAT and SAT Subject Tests or ACT (for admission), SAT Subject Tests (for admission).
Financial Aid Of all full-time matriculated undergraduates who enrolled in 2018, 19 Federal Work-Study jobs (averaging $4500).
Applying *Options:* electronic application. *Required:* high school transcript.
Director of Admissions Candace L. Gross, Dean of Enrollment Services, Arkansas State University–Newport, 7648 Victory Boulevard, Newport, AR 72112. *Phone:* 870-512-7800. *Toll-free phone:* 800-976-1676. *Fax:* 870-512-7825. *E-mail:* candace_gross@asun.edu. *Website:* http://www.asun.edu/.

Baptist Health College Little Rock
Little Rock, Arkansas

Admissions Office Contact Baptist Health College Little Rock, 11900 Colonel Glenn Road, Suite 100, Little Rock, AR 72210-2820. *Website:* http://www.bhclr.edu/.

Black River Technical College
Pocahontas, Arkansas

- **State-supported** 2-year, founded 1972
- **Small-town** 55-acre campus
- **Coed,** 1,472 undergraduate students, 56% full-time, 66% women, 34% men

Undergraduates 825 full-time, 647 part-time. Students come from 3 states and territories; 3% Black or African American, non-Hispanic/Latino; 3% Hispanic/Latino; 0.3% Asian, non-Hispanic/Latino; 0.3% Native Hawaiian or other Pacific Islander, non-Hispanic/Latino; 0.3% American Indian or Alaska Native, non-Hispanic/Latino; 2% Two or more races, non-Hispanic/Latino; 0.7% Race/ethnicity unknown; 8% transferred in.
Freshmen *Admission:* 354 enrolled.
Faculty *Student/faculty ratio:* 13:1.
Majors Administrative assistant and secretarial science; aircraft powerplant technology; criminal justice/law enforcement administration; criminal justice/police science; dietetics; early childhood education; emergency medical technology (EMT paramedic); fire science/firefighting; forensic science and technology; industrial mechanics and maintenance technology; liberal arts and sciences/liberal studies; middle school education; multi/interdisciplinary studies related; registered nursing/registered nurse.
Academics *Calendar:* semesters. *Degree:* certificates and associate. *Special study options:* academic remediation for entering students, cooperative education, honors programs, internships, part-time degree program, services for LD students, student-designed majors, summer session for credit.
Library Black River Technical College Library.
Student Life *Campus security:* night patrol.
Standardized Tests *Required for some:* ACT, ACT ASSET, or SAT.
Costs (2020–21) *Tuition:* area resident $15,635 full-time, $14,497 per year part-time; state resident $15,635 full-time, $14,497 per year part-time; nonresident $17,867 full-time, $16,357 per year part-time. *Required fees:* $1440 full-time, $48 per credit hour part-time. *Room and board:* $5326. *Payment plans:* installment, deferred payment. *Waivers:* senior citizens and employees or children of employees.
Applying *Required for some:* high school transcript, interview. *Application deadlines:* rolling (freshmen), rolling (transfers).
Freshman Application Contact Mary Anderson, Admissions, Black River Technical College, 1410 Highway 304 East, Pocahontas, AR 72455. *Phone:* 870-248-4000 Ext. 4011.
Website: http://www.blackrivertech.edu/.

Bryan University
Rogers, Arkansas

Admissions Office Contact Bryan University, 3704 West Walnut Street, Rogers, AR 72756. *Website:* http://www.bryanu.edu/.

College of the Ouachitas
Malvern, Arkansas

Freshman Application Contact Janet Hunt, Student Success Coordinator, College of the Ouachitas, One College Circle, Malvern, AR 72104. *Phone:* 501-337-5000 Ext. 1194. *Toll-free phone:* 800-337-0266. *Fax:* 501-337-9382. *E-mail:* jhunt@coto.edu. *Website:* http://www.coto.edu/.

Cossatot Community College of the University of Arkansas
De Queen, Arkansas

- **State-supported** 2-year, founded 1991, part of University of Arkansas System
- **Rural** 30-acre campus
- **Endowment** $76,785
- **Coed**

Undergraduates Students come from 8 states and territories; 1 other country; 2% are from out of state; 11% Black or African American, non-Hispanic/Latino; 18% Hispanic/Latino; 0.9% Asian, non-Hispanic/Latino; 0.3% Native Hawaiian or other Pacific Islander, non-Hispanic/Latino; 3% American Indian or Alaska Native, non-Hispanic/Latino.
Faculty *Student/faculty ratio:* 15:1.
Academics *Calendar:* semesters. *Degree:* certificates and associate. *Special study options:* academic remediation for entering students, accelerated degree program, advanced placement credit, cooperative education, distance learning, double majors, honors programs, independent study, internships, off-campus study, part-time degree program, services for LD students, summer session for credit.
Library The Educational Resource Center.
Student Life *Campus security:* daytime campus police force, evening patrol by city police force.
Financial Aid Of all full-time matriculated undergraduates who enrolled in 2018, 14 Federal Work-Study jobs (averaging $2700).
Applying *Options:* electronic application. *Recommended:* high school transcript.
Freshman Application Contact Mrs. Tommi Cobb, Admissions Coordinator, Cossatot Community College of the University of Arkansas, 183 College Drive, DeQueen, AR 71832. *Phone:* 870-584-4471 Ext. 1158. *Toll-free phone:* 800-844-4471. *Fax:* 870-642-5088. *E-mail:* tcobb@cccua.edu. *Website:* http://www.cccua.edu/.

East Arkansas Community College
Forrest City, Arkansas

Freshman Application Contact Ms. Sharon Collier, Director of Enrollment Management/Institutional Research, East Arkansas Community College, 1700 Newcastle Road, Forrest City, AR 72335-2204. *Phone:* 870-633-4480. *Toll-free phone:* 877-797-3222. *Fax:* 870-633-3840. *E-mail:* dadams@eacc.edu. *Website:* http://www.eacc.edu/.

Jefferson Regional Medical Center School of Nursing
Pine Bluff, Arkansas

Admissions Office Contact Jefferson Regional Medical Center School of Nursing, 1600 West 40th Avenue, Pine Bluff, AR 71603. *Website:* http://www.jrmc.org/school-of-nursing/.

National Park College
Hot Springs, Arkansas

Freshman Application Contact National Park College, 101 College Drive, Hot Springs, AR 71913. *Phone:* 501-760-4202. *Website:* http://www.np.edu/.

North Arkansas College

Harrison, Arkansas

- **State and locally supported** 2-year, founded 1974
- **Small-town** 40-acre campus
- **Coed**
- 100% of applicants were admitted

Undergraduates 1,491 full-time, 938 part-time. Students come from 1 other country; 7% are from out of state; 6% transferred in. *Retention:* 54% of full-time freshmen returned.
Faculty *Student/faculty ratio:* 14:1.
Academics *Calendar:* semesters. *Degree:* certificates and associate. *Special study options:* academic remediation for entering students, adult/continuing education programs, advanced placement credit, distance learning, freshman honors college, honors programs, independent study, internships, part-time degree program, services for LD students, summer session for credit.
Library North Arkansas College Library plus 1 other.
Student Life *Campus security:* 24-hour emergency response devices.
Athletics Member NJCAA.
Applying *Options:* deferred entrance. *Required for some:* high school transcript.
Freshman Application Contact Mrs. Charla Jennings, Director of Admissions, North Arkansas College, 1515 Pioneer Drive, Harrison, AR 72601. *Phone:* 870-391-3221. *Toll-free phone:* 800-679-6622. *Fax:* 870-391-3339. *E-mail:* charlam@northark.edu. *Website:* http://www.northark.edu/.

NorthWest Arkansas Community College

Bentonville, Arkansas

Freshman Application Contact NorthWest Arkansas Community College, One College Drive, Bentonville, AR 72712. *Phone:* 479-636-9222. *Toll-free phone:* 800-995-6922. *Fax:* 479-619-4116. *E-mail:* admissions@nwacc.edu. *Website:* http://www.nwacc.edu/.

Ozarka College

Melbourne, Arkansas

- **State-supported** 2-year, founded 1973
- **Rural** 40-acre campus
- **Coed**

Undergraduates 8% are from out of state. *Retention:* 79% of full-time freshmen returned.
Faculty *Student/faculty ratio:* 14:1.
Academics *Calendar:* semesters. *Degree:* certificates and associate. *Special study options:* academic remediation for entering students, advanced placement credit, distance learning, external degree program, internships, services for LD students, summer session for credit.
Library Ozarka College Library.
Student Life *Campus security:* security patrols after business hours.
Applying *Options:* electronic application, deferred entrance. *Required:* high school transcript. *Required for some:* essay or personal statement, interview. *Recommended:* minimum 2.0 GPA.
Freshman Application Contact Ms. Dylan Mowery, Director of Admissions, Ozarka College, PO Box 10, Melbourne, AR 72556. *Phone:* 870-368-7371 Ext. 2013. *Toll-free phone:* 800-821-4335. *E-mail:* dmmowery@ozarka.edu. *Website:* http://www.ozarka.edu/.

Phillips Community College of the University of Arkansas

Helena, Arkansas

Director of Admissions Mr. Lynn Boone, Registrar, Phillips Community College of the University of Arkansas, PO Box 785, Helena, AR 72342-0785. *Phone:* 870-338-6474. *Website:* http://www.pccua.edu/.

Remington College–Little Rock Campus

Little Rock, Arkansas

Director of Admissions Brian Maggio, Director of Recruitment, Remington College–Little Rock Campus, 10600 Colonel Glenn Road, Suite 100, Little Rock, AR 72204. *Phone:* 501-312-0007. *Toll-free phone:* 800-323-8122. *Fax:* 501-225-3819. *E-mail:* brian.maggio@remingtoncollege.edu. *Website:* http://www.remingtoncollege.edu/.

Shorter College

North Little Rock, Arkansas

Director of Admissions Mr. Keith Hunter, Director of Admissions, Shorter College, 604 Locust Street, North Little Rock, AR 72114-4885. *Phone:* 501-374-6305. *Website:* http://www.shortercollege.edu/.

South Arkansas Community College

El Dorado, Arkansas

- **State-supported** 2-year, founded 1975, part of Arkansas Division of Higher Education
- **Small-town** campus
- **Coed,** 1,412 undergraduate students, 38% full-time, 70% women, 30% men

Undergraduates 534 full-time, 878 part-time. Students come from 3 states and territories; 13% are from out of state; 37% Black or African American, non-Hispanic/Latino; 6% Hispanic/Latino; 0.6% Asian, non-Hispanic/Latino; 0.1% Native Hawaiian or other Pacific Islander, non-Hispanic/Latino; 0.4% American Indian or Alaska Native, non-Hispanic/Latino; 0.6% Two or more races, non-Hispanic/Latino; 1% Race/ethnicity unknown; 11% transferred in. *Retention:* 54% of full-time freshmen returned.
Freshmen *Admission:* 241 applied, 241 admitted, 241 enrolled. *Average high school GPA:* 2.9.
Faculty *Total:* 97, 53% full-time. *Student/faculty ratio:* 14:1.
Majors Administrative assistant and secretarial science; business/commerce; business, management, and marketing related; chemical technology; cinematography and film/video production; clinical/medical laboratory technology; criminal justice/police science; early childhood education; education (multiple levels); emergency medical technology (EMT paramedic); general studies; industrial technology; management information systems; medical radiologic technology; multi/interdisciplinary studies related; occupational therapist assistant; physical therapy technology; registered nursing/registered nurse; surgical technology; web page, digital/multimedia and information resources design.
Academics *Calendar:* semesters. *Degree:* certificates and associate. *Special study options:* academic remediation for entering students, adult/continuing education programs, advanced placement credit, distance learning, internships, part-time degree program, services for LD students, summer session for credit.
Library South Arkansas Community College Library.
Student Life *Housing:* college housing not available. *Campus security:* security guard. *Student services:* personal/psychological counseling.
Athletics Member NJCAA. *Intercollegiate sports:* basketball M/W.
Costs (2019–20) *Tuition:* area resident $2520 full-time, $84 per credit hour part-time; state resident $3104 full-time, $97 per credit hour part-time; nonresident $5160 full-time, $172 per credit hour part-time. Full-time tuition and fees vary according to course load and program. Part-time tuition and fees vary according to course load and program. *Required fees:* $840 full-time, $26 per credit hour part-time, $30 per term part-time. *Waivers:* senior citizens and employees or children of employees.
Applying *Options:* electronic application, early admission, deferred entrance. *Required:* high school transcript. *Application deadlines:* rolling (freshmen), rolling (out-of-state freshmen), rolling (transfers). *Notification:* continuous (freshmen), continuous (out-of-state freshmen), continuous (transfers).
Freshman Application Contact Mr. Dean Inman, Director of Enrollment Services, South Arkansas Community College, PO Box 7010, El Dorado, AR 71731-7010. *Phone:* 870-864-7142. *Toll-free phone:* 800-955-2289. *Fax:* 870-864-7137. *E-mail:* dinman@southark.edu. *Website:* http://www.southark.edu/.

Southeast Arkansas College

Pine Bluff, Arkansas

Admissions Office Contact Southeast Arkansas College, 1900 Hazel Street, Pine Bluff, AR 71603. *Toll-free phone:* 888-SEARK TC (in-state); 888-SEARC TC (out-of-state). *Website:* http://www.seark.edu/.

Southern Arkansas University Tech

Camden, Arkansas

Freshman Application Contact Mrs. Lisa Smith, Admissions Analyst, Southern Arkansas University Tech, PO Box 3499, Camden, AR 71711-1599. *Phone:* 870-574-4558. *Fax:* 870-574-4442. *E-mail:* lsmith@sautech.edu. *Website:* http://www.sautech.edu/.

University of Arkansas Community College at Batesville

Batesville, Arkansas

Freshman Application Contact Ms. Amy Foree, Enrollment Specialist, University of Arkansas Community College at Batesville, PO Box 3350, Batesville, AR 72503. *Phone:* 870-612-2113. *Toll-free phone:* 800-508-7878. *Fax:* 870-612-2129. *E-mail:* amy.foree@uaccb.edu. *Website:* http://www.uaccb.edu/.

University of Arkansas Community College at Hope

Hope, Arkansas

Freshman Application Contact University of Arkansas Community College at Hope, PO Box 140, Hope, AR 71802. *Phone:* 870-772-8174. *Website:* http://www.uacch.edu/.

University of Arkansas Community College at Morrilton

Morrilton, Arkansas

- **State-supported** 2-year, founded 1961, part of University of Arkansas System
- **Rural** 89-acre campus
- **Coed**

Undergraduates 1,033 full-time, 869 part-time. Students come from 4 states and territories; 3 other countries; 8% Black or African American, non-Hispanic/Latino; 8% Hispanic/Latino; 0.7% Asian, non-Hispanic/Latino; 0.1% Native Hawaiian or other Pacific Islander, non-Hispanic/Latino; 0.3% American Indian or Alaska Native, non-Hispanic/Latino; 6% Two or more races, non-Hispanic/Latino; 0.6% Race/ethnicity unknown; 2% international; 9% transferred in.
Faculty *Student/faculty ratio:* 22:1.
Academics *Calendar:* semesters. *Degree:* certificates and associate. *Special study options:* academic remediation for entering students, advanced placement credit, cooperative education, distance learning, double majors, independent study, internships, part-time degree program, services for LD students, summer session for credit.
Library E. Allen Gordon Library. *Books:* 27,196 (physical), 177,896 (digital/electronic); *Serial titles:* 81 (physical); *Databases:* 35. Weekly public service hours: 66; students can reserve study rooms.
Student Life *Campus security:* 24-hour emergency response devices, late-night transport/escort service.
Standardized Tests *Recommended:* SAT or ACT (for admission), ACT Compass, ACCUPLACER.
Costs (2019–20) *Tuition:* area resident $2760 full-time, $92 per credit hour part-time; state resident $3060 full-time, $102 per credit hour part-time; nonresident $3900 full-time, $130 per credit hour part-time. Full-time tuition and fees vary according to course load and program. Part-time tuition and fees vary according to course load and program. *Required fees:* $1260 full-time, $42 per credit hour part-time.
Financial Aid Of all full-time matriculated undergraduates who enrolled in 2015, 1,178 applied for aid, 1,028 were judged to have need, 31 had their need fully met. In 2015, 45. *Average percent of need met:* 44. *Average financial aid package:* $6082. *Average need-based loan:* $1686. *Average need-based gift aid:* $3161. *Average non-need-based aid:* $1033.
Applying *Options:* electronic application, early admission, deferred entrance. *Required:* high school transcript. *Required for some:* immunization records, prior college transcript(s).
Freshman Application Contact Ms. Lindsey Grier, Administrative Specialist, University of Arkansas Community College at Morrilton, 1537 University Boulevard, Morrilton, AR 72110. *Phone:* 501-977-2053. *Toll-free phone:* 800-264-1094. *Fax:* 501-977-2123. *E-mail:* grierlindsey@uaccm.edu. *Website:* http://www.uaccm.edu/.

University of Arkansas–Pulaski Technical College

North Little Rock, Arkansas

- **State-supported** 2-year, founded 1945
- **Urban** 40-acre campus with easy access to Little Rock
- **Coed**

Undergraduates 4,856 full-time, 5,399 part-time. Students come from 5 states and territories; 0.5% are from out of state; 1% transferred in.
Faculty *Student/faculty ratio:* 25:1.
Academics *Calendar:* semesters. *Degree:* certificates and associate. *Special study options:* academic remediation for entering students, advanced placement credit, distance learning, part-time degree program, services for LD students, summer session for credit.
Library Ottenheimer Library.
Student Life *Campus security:* certified law enforcement personnel 7 am to 11 pm.
Applying *Options:* electronic application. *Required:* high school transcript.
Freshman Application Contact Mr. Clark Atkins, Director of Admissions, University of Arkansas–Pulaski Technical College, 3000 West Scenic Drive, North Little Rock, AR 72118. *Phone:* 501-812-2734. *Fax:* 501-812-2316. *E-mail:* catkins@pulaskitech.edu. *Website:* http://www.pulaskitech.edu/.

University of Arkansas Rich Mountain

Mena, Arkansas

Freshman Application Contact Wendy McDaniel, Director of Admissions, University of Arkansas Rich Mountain, 1100 College Drive, Mena, AR 71953. *Phone:* 479-394-7622 Ext. 1440. *E-mail:* wmcdaniel@uarichmountain.edu. *Website:* http://www.uarichmountain.edu/.

CALIFORNIA

Advanced College - South Gate

South Gate, California

Admissions Office Contact Advanced College - South Gate, 13180 Paramount Boulevard, South Gate, CA 90280. *Website:* http://www.advancedcollege.edu/.

Advanced College - Stockton

Stockton, California

Admissions Office Contact Advanced College - Stockton, 8838 North West Lane, Stockton, CA 95120. *Website:* http://www.advancedcollege.edu/.

Advanced Training Associates

El Cajon, California

Admissions Office Contact Advanced Training Associates, 1810 Gillespie Way, Suite 104, El Cajon, CA 92020. *Toll-free phone:* 800-720-2125. *Website:* http://www.advancedtraining.edu/.

Allan Hancock College

Santa Maria, California

- **District-supported** 2-year, founded 1920
- **Small-town** 120-acre campus
- **Endowment** $1.1 million
- **Coed**

Undergraduates 2,996 full-time, 7,391 part-time. Students come from 27 states and territories; 12 other countries; 1% are from out of state; 6% transferred in. *Retention:* 72% of full-time freshmen returned.
Faculty *Student/faculty ratio:* 22:1.
Academics *Calendar:* semesters. *Degree:* certificates and associate. *Special study options:* adult/continuing education programs, advanced placement credit, cooperative education, distance learning, English as a second language, part-time degree program, services for LD students, study abroad, summer session for credit.
Library Learning Resources Center.
Student Life *Campus security:* 24-hour emergency response devices and patrols, student patrols, late-night transport/escort service.
Financial Aid Of all full-time matriculated undergraduates who enrolled in 2018, 250 Federal Work-Study jobs (averaging $3000).
Applying *Options:* electronic application.
Freshman Application Contact Ms. Adela Esquivel Swinson, Director of Admissions and Records, Allan Hancock College, 800 South College Drive, Santa Maria, CA 93454-6399. *Phone:* 805-922-6966 Ext. 3272. *Toll-free phone:* 866-342-5242. *Fax:* 805-922-3477. *Website:* http://www.hancockcollege.edu/.

The American Academy of Dramatic Arts–Los Angeles

Los Angeles, California

Freshman Application Contact Steven Hong, Director of Admissions, The American Academy of Dramatic Arts–Los Angeles, 1336 North La Brea Avenue, Los Angeles, CA 90028. *Phone:* 323-464-2777 Ext. 103. *Toll-free phone:* 800-222-2867. *E-mail:* shong@aada.edu. *Website:* http://www.aada.edu/.

American Career College - Los Angeles

Los Angeles, California

Director of Admissions Tamra Adams, Director of Admissions, American Career College - Los Angeles, 4021 Rosewood Avenue, Los Angeles, CA 90004. *Phone:* 323-668-7555. *Toll-free phone:* 877-832-0790. *E-mail:* info@americancareer.com. *Website:* http://americancareercollege.edu/.

American Career College - Ontario

Ontario, California

Director of Admissions Juan Tellez, Director of Admissions, American Career College - Ontario, 3130 East Sedona Court, Ontario, CA 91764. *Phone:* 951-739-0788. *Toll-free phone:* 877-832-0790. *E-mail:* info@amerciancareer.com. *Website:* http://americancareercollege.edu/.

American Career College - Orange County

Anaheim, California

Director of Admissions Susan Pailet, Senior Executive Director of Admission, American Career College - Orange County, 1200 North Magnolia Avenue, Anaheim, CA 92801. *Phone:* 714-952-9066. *Toll-free phone:* 877-832-0790. *E-mail:* info@americancareer.com. *Website:* http://americancareercollege.edu/.

American Medical Sciences Center

Glendale, California

Admissions Office Contact American Medical Sciences Center, 225 West Broadway, Suite 115, Glendale, CA 91204-5108. *Website:* http://www.amsc.edu/.

American River College

Sacramento, California

Freshman Application Contact American River College, 4700 College Oak Drive, Sacramento, CA 95841-4286. *Phone:* 916-484-8171. *Website:* http://www.arc.losrios.edu/.

Antelope Valley College

Lancaster, California

Freshman Application Contact Welcome Center, Antelope Valley College, 3041 West Avenue K, SSV Building, Lancaster, CA 93536. *Phone:* 661-722-6300 Ext. 6331. *Website:* http://www.avc.edu/.

Bakersfield College

Bakersfield, California

Freshman Application Contact Bakersfield College, 1801 Panorama Drive, Bakersfield, CA 93305-1299. *Phone:* 661-395-4301. *Website:* http://www.bakersfieldcollege.edu/.

Barstow Community College

Barstow, California

- **District-supported** 2-year, founded 1959, part of California Community College System
- **Small-town** 50-acre campus
- **Coed**

Faculty *Student/faculty ratio:* 35:1.
Academics *Calendar:* semesters. *Degree:* certificates and associate. *Special study options:* academic remediation for entering students, adult/continuing education programs, cooperative education, English as a second language, external degree program, part-time degree program, services for LD students, student-designed majors, summer session for credit.
Library Thomas Kimball Library.
Student Life *Campus security:* evening security personnel.
Applying *Options:* early admission, deferred entrance. *Recommended:* high school transcript.
Freshman Application Contact Barstow Community College, 2700 Barstow Road, Barstow, CA 92311-6699. *Phone:* 760-252-2411 Ext. 7236. *Website:* http://www.barstow.edu/.

Berkeley City College

Berkeley, California

Freshman Application Contact Dr. May Kuang-chi Chen, Vice President of Student Services, Berkeley City College, 2050 Center Street, Berkeley, CA 94704. *Phone:* 510-981-2820. *Fax:* 510-841-7333. *E-mail:* mrivas@peralta.edu. *Website:* http://www.berkeleycitycollege.edu/.

Beverly Hills Design Institute

Beverly Hills, California

Freshman Application Contact Beverly Hills Design Institute, 8484 Wilshire Boulevard, Suite 730, Beverly Hills, CA 90211. *Phone:* 310-360-8888. *Website:* http://www.bhdi.edu/.

Bryan College

El Cajon, California

Freshman Application Contact Bryan College, 2065 North Marshall Avenue, El Cajon, CA 92020. *Phone:* 916-649-2400. *Toll-free phone:* 866-649-2400. *Website:* http://www.bryancollege.edu/.

Bryan University

Los Angeles, California

Admissions Office Contact Bryan University, 3580 Wilshire Boulevard, Los Angeles, CA 90010. *Website:* http://losangeles.bryanuniversity.edu/.

Butte College

Oroville, California

Freshman Application Contact Mr. Brad Zuniga, Director of Recruitment, Outreach and New Student Orientation, Butte College, 3536 Butte Campus Drive, Oroville, CA 95965-8399. *Phone:* 530-895-2948. *Website:* http://www.butte.edu/.

Cabrillo College

Aptos, California

- **District-supported** 2-year, founded 1959, part of California Community College System
- **Small-town** 120-acre campus with easy access to San Jose
- **Coed**

Undergraduates *Retention:* 72% of full-time freshmen returned.
Faculty *Student/faculty ratio:* 21:1.
Academics *Calendar:* semesters. *Degree:* certificates and associate. *Special study options:* academic remediation for entering students, adult/continuing education programs, advanced placement credit, cooperative education, distance learning, double majors, English as a second language, honors programs, independent study, internships, part-time degree program, services for LD students, study abroad, summer session for credit.
Library Cabrillo College Library.
Student Life *Campus security:* 24-hour emergency response devices and patrols, late-night transport/escort service.
Financial Aid Of all full-time matriculated undergraduates who enrolled in 2018, 50 Federal Work-Study jobs (averaging $4000).
Applying *Options:* early admission. *Required for some:* high school transcript.
Freshman Application Contact Tama Bolton, Director of Admissions and Records, Cabrillo College, 6500 Soquel Drive, Aptos, CA 95003-3194. *Phone:* 831-477-3548. *Fax:* 831-479-5782. *E-mail:* tabolton@cabrillo.edu. *Website:* http://www.cabrillo.edu/.

California Institute of Arts & Technology

San Diego, California

Admissions Office Contact California Institute of Arts & Technology, 2820 Camino Del Rio South, Suite 100, San Diego, CA 92108. *Website:* http://www.ciat.edu/.

Cambridge Junior College

Yuba City, California

Freshman Application Contact Admissions Office, Cambridge Junior College, 990-A Klamath Lane, Yuba City, CA 95993. *Phone:* 530-674-9199. *Fax:* 530-671-7319. *Website:* http://www.cambridge.edu/.

Cañada College

Redwood City, California

Freshman Application Contact Cañada College, 4200 Farm Hill Boulevard, Redwood City, CA 94061-1099. *Phone:* 650-306-3125. *Website:* http://www.canadacollege.edu/.

Carrington College–Citrus Heights

Citrus Heights, California

Freshman Application Contact Carrington College–Citrus Heights, 7301 Greenback Lane, Suite A, Citrus Heights, CA 95621. *Website:* http://www.carrington.edu/.

Carrington College–Pleasant Hill

Pleasant Hill, California

- **Proprietary** 2-year, founded 1997, part of Carrington Colleges Group, Inc.
- **Coed**

Undergraduates 357 full-time, 80 part-time. 1% are from out of state; 11% Black or African American, non-Hispanic/Latino; 32% Hispanic/Latino; 16% Asian, non-Hispanic/Latino; 3% Native Hawaiian or other Pacific Islander, non-Hispanic/Latino; 0.5% American Indian or Alaska Native, non-Hispanic/Latino; 2% Two or more races, non-Hispanic/Latino; 3% Race/ethnicity unknown; 0.7% international; 24% transferred in.
Faculty *Student/faculty ratio:* 21:1.
Academics *Degree:* certificates and associate.
Applying *Required:* essay or personal statement, high school transcript, interview.
Freshman Application Contact Carrington College–Pleasant Hill, 380 Civic Drive, Suite 300, Pleasant Hill, CA 94523. *Website:* http://www.carrington.edu/.

Carrington College–Pomona

Pomona, California

Freshman Application Contact Carrington College–Pomona, 901 Corporate Center Drive, Suite 300, Pomona, CA 91768. *Toll-free phone:* 877-206-2106. *Website:* http://www.carrington.edu/.

Carrington College–Sacramento

Sacramento, California

- **Proprietary** 2-year, founded 1967, part of Carrington Colleges Group, Inc.
- **Coed**

Undergraduates 935 full-time, 251 part-time. 11% are from out of state; 9% Black or African American, non-Hispanic/Latino; 31% Hispanic/Latino; 12% Asian, non-Hispanic/Latino; 2% Native Hawaiian or other Pacific Islander, non-Hispanic/Latino; 1% American Indian or Alaska Native, non-Hispanic/Latino; 3% Two or more races, non-Hispanic/Latino; 5% Race/ethnicity unknown; 0.3% international; 11% transferred in.
Faculty *Student/faculty ratio:* 15:1.
Academics *Degree:* certificates and associate.
Applying *Required:* essay or personal statement, high school transcript, interview.
Freshman Application Contact Carrington College–Sacramento, 8909 Folsom Boulevard, Sacramento, CA 95826. *Website:* http://www.carrington.edu/.

Carrington College–San Jose

San Jose, California

- **Proprietary** 2-year, founded 1999, part of Carrington Colleges Group, Inc.
- **Coed**

Undergraduates 654 full-time, 61 part-time. 2% Black or African American, non-Hispanic/Latino; 54% Hispanic/Latino; 16% Asian, non-Hispanic/Latino; 3% Native Hawaiian or other Pacific Islander, non-Hispanic/Latino; 4% Two or more races, non-Hispanic/Latino; 0.7% Race/ethnicity unknown; 0.8% international; 13% transferred in.
Faculty *Student/faculty ratio:* 24:1.
Academics *Degree:* certificates and associate.
Applying *Required:* essay or personal statement, high school transcript, interview.
Freshman Application Contact Carrington College–San Jose, 5883 Rue Ferrari, Suite 125, San Jose, CA 95138. *Website:* http://www.carrington.edu/.

Carrington College–San Leandro

San Leandro, California

- **Proprietary** 2-year, founded 1986, part of Carrington Colleges Group, Inc.
- **Coed**

Undergraduates 398 full-time, 18 part-time. 26% are from out of state; 19% Black or African American, non-Hispanic/Latino; 51% Hispanic/Latino; 9% Asian, non-Hispanic/Latino; 2% Native Hawaiian or other Pacific Islander, non-Hispanic/Latino; 0.5% American Indian or Alaska Native, non-Hispanic/Latino; 2% Two or more races, non-Hispanic/Latino; 0.7% Race/ethnicity unknown; 0.5% international; 16% transferred in. *Retention:* 65% of full-time freshmen returned.
Faculty *Student/faculty ratio:* 27:1.
Academics *Degree:* certificates and associate.
Applying *Required:* essay or personal statement, high school transcript, interview.
Freshman Application Contact Carrington College–San Leandro, 15555 East 14th Street, Suite 500, San Leandro, CA 94578. *Website:* http://www.carrington.edu/.

Carrington College–Stockton

Stockton, California

Freshman Application Contact Carrington College–Stockton, 1313 West Robinhood Drive, Suite B, Stockton, CA 95207. *Website:* http://www.carrington.edu/.

Casa Loma College–Van Nuys

Los Angeles, California

Admissions Office Contact Casa Loma College–Van Nuys, 6725 Kester Avenue, Los Angeles, CA 91405. *Website:* http://www.casalomacollege.edu/.

CBD College

Los Angeles, California

Admissions Office Contact CBD College, 3699 Wilshire Boulevard, 4th Floor, Los Angeles, CA 90010. *Website:* http://www.cbd.edu/.

Cerritos College

Norwalk, California

Freshman Application Contact Cerritos College, 11110 Alondra Boulevard, Norwalk, CA 90650-6298. *Phone:* 562-860-2451 Ext. 2102. *Website:* http://www.cerritos.edu/.

Cerro Coso Community College

Ridgecrest, California

Freshman Application Contact Mrs. Heather Ootash, Counseling/Matriculation Coordinator, Cerro Coso Community College, 3000 College Heights Boulevard, Ridgecrest, CA 93555. *Phone:* 760-384-6291. *Fax:* 760-375-4776. *E-mail:* hostash@cerrocoso.edu. *Website:* http://www.cerrocoso.edu/.

Chabot College
Hayward, California

Director of Admissions Paulette Lino, Director of Admissions and Records, Chabot College, 25555 Hesperian Boulevard, Hayward, CA 94545-5001. *Phone:* 510-723-6700. *Website:* http://www.chabotcollege.edu/.

Chaffey College
Rancho Cucamonga, California

- **District-supported** 2-year, founded 1883, part of California Community College System
- **Suburban** 200-acre campus with easy access to Los Angeles
- **Coed**

Faculty *Student/faculty ratio:* 24:1.
Academics *Calendar:* semesters. *Degree:* certificates and associate. *Special study options:* academic remediation for entering students, adult/continuing education programs, advanced placement credit, cooperative education, English as a second language, honors programs, internships, part-time degree program, services for LD students, study abroad, summer session for credit. *ROTC:* Army (c).
Library Chaffey College Library.
Student Life *Campus security:* 24-hour emergency response devices, late-night transport/escort service.
Financial Aid Of all full-time matriculated undergraduates who enrolled in 2018, 700 Federal Work-Study jobs (averaging $3000).
Applying *Options:* early admission.
Freshman Application Contact Erlinda Martinez, Coordinator of Admissions, Chaffey College, 5885 Haven Avenue, Rancho Cucamonga, CA 91737-3002. *Phone:* 909-652-6610. *E-mail:* erlinda.martinez@chaffey.edu. *Website:* http://www.chaffey.edu/.

Citrus College
Glendora, California

- **District-supported** 2-year, founded 1915, part of California Community College System
- **Small-town** 104-acre campus with easy access to Los Angeles
- **Coed,** 18,672 undergraduate students, 53% full-time, 55% women, 45% men

Undergraduates 9,852 full-time, 8,820 part-time. 4% Black or African American, non-Hispanic/Latino; 64% Hispanic/Latino; 9% Asian, non-Hispanic/Latino; 0.1% Native Hawaiian or other Pacific Islander, non-Hispanic/Latino; 0.1% American Indian or Alaska Native, non-Hispanic/Latino; 3% Two or more races, non-Hispanic/Latino; 0.9% Race/ethnicity unknown; 3% international.
Freshmen *Admission:* 11,388 applied, 11,388 admitted.
Faculty *Total:* 509, 30% full-time. *Student/faculty ratio:* 30:1.
Majors Administrative assistant and secretarial science; art; automobile/automotive mechanics technology; behavioral sciences; biological and physical sciences; biology/biological sciences; business administration and management; business/commerce; child development; computer and information sciences related; computer graphics; computer science; construction trades related; cosmetology; criminal justice/law enforcement administration; criminal justice/police science; dance; dance related; data processing and data processing technology; dental assisting; diesel mechanics technology; drafting and design technology; dramatic/theater arts; electrical, electronic and communications engineering technology; engineering; engineering technology; English; English language and literature related; French; German; health and physical education/fitness; history; hydrology and water resources science; Japanese; journalism; liberal arts and sciences/liberal studies; library and archives assisting; library and information science; licensed practical/vocational nurse training; mathematics; mechanical engineering/mechanical technology; modern languages; music; natural sciences; photography; physical education teaching and coaching; physical sciences; psychology; public administration; real estate; recording arts technology; registered nursing/registered nurse; security and loss prevention; social sciences; sociology; Spanish; speech communication and rhetoric; visual and performing arts; water quality and wastewater treatment management and recycling technology.
Academics *Calendar:* semesters. *Degree:* certificates, diplomas, and associate. *Special study options:* academic remediation for entering students, advanced placement credit, cooperative education, distance learning, double majors, English as a second language, honors programs, part-time degree program, services for LD students, study abroad, summer session for credit.
Library Hayden Library. Students can reserve study rooms.
Student Life *Housing:* college housing not available. *Activities and Organizations:* drama/theater group, student-run newspaper, choral group, Student Government, Alpha Gamma Sigma (AGS), Veterans Network, International Friendship Club, Citrus Business Association (CBA). *Campus security:* 24-hour patrols, student patrols, late-night transport/escort service. *Student services:* health clinic, personal/psychological counseling, legal services, veterans affairs office.
Athletics *Intercollegiate sports:* baseball M, basketball M/W, cross-country running M/W, football M, golf M/W, soccer M/W, softball W, swimming and diving M/W, volleyball W, water polo M/W.
Financial Aid Of all full-time matriculated undergraduates who enrolled in 2018, 141 Federal Work-Study jobs (averaging $5500).
Applying *Options:* electronic application, early decision. *Required:* high school transcript. *Application deadline:* rolling (freshmen).
Freshman Application Contact Admissions and Records, Citrus College, Glendora, CA 91741-1899. *Phone:* 626-914-8511. *Fax:* 626-914-8613. *E-mail:* admissions@citruscollege.edu.
Website: http://www.citruscollege.edu/.

City College of San Francisco
San Francisco, California

- **District-supported** 2-year, founded 1935, part of California Community College System
- **Urban** 56-acre campus
- **Coed**

Faculty *Student/faculty ratio:* 23:1.
Academics *Calendar:* semesters. *Degree:* certificates, diplomas, and associate. *Special study options:* academic remediation for entering students, adult/continuing education programs, advanced placement credit, English as a second language, internships, off-campus study, part-time degree program, services for LD students, study abroad, summer session for credit.
Library Louise and Claude Rosenberg, Jr. Library plus 2 others.
Student Life *Campus security:* 24-hour emergency response devices and patrols, late-night transport/escort service.
Financial Aid ***Financial aid deadline:*** 6/11.
Applying *Options:* early admission.
Freshman Application Contact Ms. Mary Lou Leyba-Frank, Dean of Admissions and Records, City College of San Francisco, 50 Phelan Avenue, San Francisco, CA 94112-1821. *Phone:* 415-239-3291. *Fax:* 415-239-3936. *E-mail:* mleyba@ccsf.edu. *Website:* http://www.ccsf.edu/.

Clovis Community College
Fresno, California

Admissions Office Contact Clovis Community College, 10309 North Willow Avenue, Fresno, CA 93730. *Website:* http://www.cloviscollege.edu/.

Coastline Community College
Fountain Valley, California

- **District-supported** 2-year, founded 1976, part of Coast Community College District System
- **Urban** campus with easy access to Orange County
- **Coed**

Undergraduates 2,488 full-time, 8,943 part-time. 12% Black or African American, non-Hispanic/Latino; 28% Hispanic/Latino; 22% Asian, non-Hispanic/Latino; 0.5% Native Hawaiian or other Pacific Islander, non-Hispanic/Latino; 0.8% American Indian or Alaska Native, non-Hispanic/Latino; 4% Two or more races, non-Hispanic/Latino; 2% Race/ethnicity unknown.
Faculty *Student/faculty ratio:* 32:1.
Academics *Calendar:* semesters. *Degree:* certificates and associate. *Special study options:* academic remediation for entering students, accelerated degree program, adult/continuing education programs, advanced placement credit, cooperative education, distance learning, double majors, English as a second language, external degree program, honors programs, independent study, internships, off-campus study, part-time degree program, services for LD students, study abroad, summer session for credit.
Library Coastline Virtual Library plus 1 other.
Student Life *Campus security:* 24-hour emergency response devices.
Financial Aid Of all full-time matriculated undergraduates who enrolled in 2015, 12,392 applied for aid, 11,568 were judged to have need, 12 had their need fully met. *Average percent of need met:* 15. *Average financial aid package:* $3819. *Average need-based loan:* $3290. *Average need-based gift aid:* $3714. *Average indebtedness upon graduation:* $10,514. *Financial aid deadline:* 8/15.
Applying *Options:* electronic application, early admission. *Recommended:* high school transcript.
Freshman Application Contact Jennifer McDonald, Director of Admissions and Records, Coastline Community College, 11460 Warner Avenue, Fountain Valley, CA 92708. *Phone:* 714-241-6163. *Website:* http://www.coastline.edu/.

College of Alameda
Alameda, California

- **District-supported** 2-year, founded 1970, part of Peralta Community College District System
- **Urban** 62-acre campus with easy access to San Francisco
- **Coed**

Faculty *Student/faculty ratio:* 32:1.
Academics *Calendar:* semesters. *Degree:* certificates and associate. *Special study options:* academic remediation for entering students, adult/continuing education programs, cooperative education, off-campus study, part-time degree program, services for LD students, summer session for credit.
Library Learning Resources Center.
Financial Aid Of all full-time matriculated undergraduates who enrolled in 2018, 90 Federal Work-Study jobs (averaging $2500).
Freshman Application Contact College of Alameda, 555 Ralph Appezzato Memorial Parkway, Alameda, CA 94501-2109. *Phone:* 510-748-2204. *Website:* http://alameda.peralta.edu/.

College of Marin
Kentfield, California

- **District-supported** 2-year, founded 1926, part of California Community College System
- **Suburban** 410-acre campus with easy access to San Francisco
- **Coed**

Undergraduates 1,345 full-time, 3,681 part-time. 3% Black or African American, non-Hispanic/Latino; 31% Hispanic/Latino; 8% Asian, non-Hispanic/Latino; 0.3% Native Hawaiian or other Pacific Islander, non-Hispanic/Latino; 0.2% American Indian or Alaska Native, non-Hispanic/Latino; 6% Two or more races, non-Hispanic/Latino; 1% Race/ethnicity unknown; 1% international.
Academics *Calendar:* semesters. *Degree:* certificates and associate. *Special study options:* academic remediation for entering students, advanced placement credit, cooperative education, distance learning, double majors, English as a second language, part-time degree program, services for LD students, summer session for credit.
Library Main Library plus 1 other.
Student Life *Campus security:* 24-hour emergency response devices and patrols, security cameras.
Costs (2019–20) *Tuition:* state resident $1380 full-time, $46 per credit part-time; nonresident $9210 full-time, $307 per credit part-time. *Required fees:* $110 full-time.
Applying *Options:* electronic application.
Admissions Office Contact College of Marin, 835 College Avenue, Kentfield, CA 94904. *Website:* http://www.marin.edu/.

College of San Mateo
San Mateo, California

Director of Admissions Mr. Henry Villareal, Dean of Admissions and Records, College of San Mateo, 1700 West Hillsdale Boulevard, San Mateo, CA 94402-3784. *Phone:* 650-574-6590. *E-mail:* csmadmission@smccd.edu. *Website:* http://www.collegeofsanmateo.edu/.

College of the Canyons
Santa Clarita, California

- **District-supported** 2-year, founded 1969, part of California Community College System
- **Suburban** 224-acre campus with easy access to Los Angeles
- **Coed**

Undergraduates 6,445 full-time, 13,420 part-time. Students come from 49 other countries; 3% are from out of state; 5% Black or African American, non-Hispanic/Latino; 47% Hispanic/Latino; 10% Asian, non-Hispanic/Latino; 0.3% Native Hawaiian or other Pacific Islander, non-Hispanic/Latino; 0.2% American Indian or Alaska Native, non-Hispanic/Latino; 2% Two or more races, non-Hispanic/Latino; 3% Race/ethnicity unknown; 0.9% international; 41% transferred in.
Faculty *Student/faculty ratio:* 17:1.
Academics *Calendar:* semesters. *Degree:* certificates and associate. *Special study options:* academic remediation for entering students, accelerated degree program, adult/continuing education programs, advanced placement credit, cooperative education, distance learning, double majors, English as a second language, honors programs, internships, part-time degree program, services for LD students, study abroad, summer session for credit.
Library College of the Canyons Library. *Books:* 59,059 (physical), 138,941 (digital/electronic); *Serial titles:* 58 (physical), 2 (digital/electronic); *Databases:* 53. Weekly public service hours: 116; students can reserve study rooms.
Student Life *Campus security:* 24-hour emergency response devices, late-night transport/escort service.
Costs (2019–20) *Tuition:* area resident $1104 full-time, $46 per credit part-time; state resident $1104 full-time, $46 per credit part-time; nonresident $7752 full-time, $323 per credit part-time. Full-time tuition and fees vary according to course load. Part-time tuition and fees vary according to course load. *Required fees:* $52 full-time.
Applying *Options:* electronic application. *Recommended:* high school transcript.
Freshman Application Contact Dr. Jasmine Ruys, Dean, Enrollment Services, College of the Canyons, 26455 Rockwell Canyon Road, Santa Clarita, CA 91355. *Phone:* 661-362-3280. *Fax:* 661-254-7996. *E-mail:* jasmine.ruys@canyons.edu. *Website:* http://www.canyons.edu/.

College of the Desert
Palm Desert, California

Freshman Application Contact College of the Desert, 43-500 Monterey Avenue, Palm Desert, CA 92260-9305. *Phone:* 760-776-7441 Ext. 7441. *Website:* http://www.collegeofthedesert.edu/.

College of the Redwoods
Eureka, California

- **District-supported** 2-year, founded 1964, part of California Community College System
- **Small-town** 322-acre campus
- **Coed**

Undergraduates 5% are from out of state. *Retention:* 55% of full-time freshmen returned.
Faculty *Student/faculty ratio:* 18:1.
Academics *Calendar:* semesters. *Degree:* certificates and associate. *Special study options:* academic remediation for entering students, adult/continuing education programs, advanced placement credit, cooperative education, distance learning, English as a second language, honors programs, off-campus study, part-time degree program, services for LD students, summer session for credit.
Library College of the Redwoods Library.
Student Life *Campus security:* 24-hour emergency response devices and patrols, late-night transport/escort service.
Financial Aid Of all full-time matriculated undergraduates who enrolled in 2018, 50 Federal Work-Study jobs (averaging $4000). 20 state and other part-time jobs (averaging $4000).
Applying *Options:* early admission.
Freshman Application Contact Director of Enrollment Management, College of the Redwoods, 7351 Tompkins Hill Road, Eureka, CA 95501-9300. *Phone:* 707-476-4100. *Toll-free phone:* 800-641-0400. *Fax:* 707-476-4400. *Website:* http://www.redwoods.edu/.

College of the Sequoias
Visalia, California

- **District-supported** 2-year, founded 1925, part of California Community College System
- **Small-town** 215-acre campus with easy access to Fresno
- **Endowment** $3.0 million
- **Coed**

Undergraduates 5,147 full-time, 8,302 part-time. Students come from 15 states and territories; 6 other countries; 0.1% are from out of state; 53% transferred in.
Faculty *Student/faculty ratio:* 27:1.
Academics *Calendar:* semesters. *Degree:* certificates and associate. *Special study options:* academic remediation for entering students, accelerated degree program, adult/continuing education programs, advanced placement credit, cooperative education, distance learning, double majors, English as a second language, freshman honors college, honors programs, internships, off-campus study, part-time degree program, services for LD students, study abroad, summer session for credit. *ROTC:* Air Force (c).
Library College of the Sequoias Library.
Student Life *Campus security:* 24-hour emergency response devices and patrols, student patrols, late-night transport/escort service, 18-hour patrols by trained security personnel.
Athletics Member NJCAA.
Applying *Required:* high school transcript.
Freshman Application Contact Ms. Lisa Hott, Director for Admissions, College of the Sequoias, 915 South Mooney Boulevard, Visalia, CA 93277-

2234. *Phone:* 559-737-4844. *Fax:* 559-737-4820. *Website:* http://www.cos.edu/.

College of the Siskiyous
Weed, California

- **District-supported** 2-year, founded 1957, part of California Community College System
- **Rural** 260-acre campus
- **Coed**

Faculty *Student/faculty ratio:* 20:1.
Academics *Calendar:* semesters. *Degree:* certificates and associate. *Special study options:* academic remediation for entering students, adult/continuing education programs, advanced placement credit, cooperative education, distance learning, double majors, English as a second language, honors programs, independent study, internships, part-time degree program, services for LD students, student-designed majors, summer session for credit.
Library College of the Siskiyous Library.
Student Life *Campus security:* 24-hour emergency response devices, controlled dormitory access.
Applying *Options:* early admission, deferred entrance.
Freshman Application Contact Recruitment and Admissions, College of the Siskiyous, 800 College Avenue, Weed, CA 96094-2899. *Phone:* 530-938-5555. *Toll-free phone:* 888-397-4339. *E-mail:* admissions-weed@siskyous.edu. *Website:* http://www.siskiyous.edu/.

Columbia College
Sonora, California

Freshman Application Contact Admissions Office, Columbia College, 11600 Columbia College Drive, Sonora, CA 95370. *Phone:* 209-588-5231. *Fax:* 209-588-5337. *E-mail:* ccadmissions@yosemite.edu. *Website:* http://www.gocolumbia.edu/.

Community Christian College
Redlands, California

Freshman Application Contact Mr. Enrique D. Melendez, Assistant Director of Admissions, Community Christian College, 251 Tennessee Street, Redlands, CA 92373. *Phone:* 909-222-9556. *Fax:* 909-335-9101. *E-mail:* emelendez@cccollege.edu. *Website:* http://www.cccollege.edu/.

Compton College
Compton, California

- **District-supported** 2-year, founded 1927, part of California Community College System
- **Urban** 83-acre campus with easy access to Los Angeles
- **Coed**

Undergraduates Students come from 4 states and territories; 25 other countries; 25% Black or African American, non-Hispanic/Latino; 60% Hispanic/Latino; 7% Asian, non-Hispanic/Latino; 0.5% Native Hawaiian or other Pacific Islander, non-Hispanic/Latino; 0.1% American Indian or Alaska Native, non-Hispanic/Latino; 3% Two or more races, non-Hispanic/Latino; 4% Race/ethnicity unknown.
Academics *Calendar:* semesters. *Degree:* associate. *Special study options:* academic remediation for entering students, adult/continuing education programs, advanced placement credit, English as a second language, honors programs, part-time degree program, services for LD students, summer session for credit.
Library Compton Community College Library.
Student Life *Campus security:* 24-hour patrols.
Financial Aid Of all full-time matriculated undergraduates who enrolled in 2018, 300 Federal Work-Study jobs (averaging $3000).
Applying *Options:* early admission.
Director of Admissions Ms. Stephanie Atkinson-Alston, Interim Associate Dean, Admissions and Records, Compton College, 1111 East Artesia Boulevard, Compton, CA 90221-5393. *Phone:* 310-900-1600 Ext. 2047. *Website:* http://www.compton.edu/.

Concorde Career College
Garden Grove, California

Freshman Application Contact Chris Becker, Director, Concorde Career College, 12951 South Euclid Street, Suite 101, Garden Grove, CA 92840. *Phone:* 714-703-1900. *Fax:* 714-530-4737. *E-mail:* cbecker@concorde.edu. *Website:* http://www.concorde.edu/.

Concorde Career College
North Hollywood, California

Freshman Application Contact Madeline Volker, Director, Concorde Career College, 12412 Victory Boulevard, North Hollywood, CA 91606. *Phone:* 818-766-8151. *Fax:* 818-766-1587. *E-mail:* mvolker@concorde.edu. *Website:* http://www.concorde.edu/.

Concorde Career College
San Bernardino, California

Admissions Office Contact Concorde Career College, 201 East Airport Drive, San Bernardino, CA 92408. *Website:* http://www.concorde.edu/.

Concorde Career College
San Diego, California

Admissions Office Contact Concorde Career College, 4393 Imperial Avenue, Suite 100, San Diego, CA 92113. *Website:* http://www.concorde.edu/.

Contra Costa College
San Pablo, California

Freshman Application Contact Admissions and Records Office, Contra Costa College, San Pablo, CA 94806. *Phone:* 510-235-7800 Ext. 7500. *Fax:* 510-412-0769. *E-mail:* ar@contracosta.edu. *Website:* http://www.contracosta.cdu/.

Copper Mountain College
Joshua Tree, California

- **District-supported** 2-year, founded 1966
- **Rural** 26-acre campus
- **Endowment** $102,297
- **Coed**
- 90% of applicants were admitted

Undergraduates 1,712 full-time, 788 part-time. 7% Black or African American, non-Hispanic/Latino; 13% Hispanic/Latino; 4% Asian, non-Hispanic/Latino; 2% American Indian or Alaska Native, non-Hispanic/Latino; 7% Race/ethnicity unknown. *Retention:* 65% of full-time freshmen returned.
Faculty *Student/faculty ratio:* 14:1.
Academics *Calendar:* semesters. *Degree:* certificates and associate. *Special study options:* academic remediation for entering students, advanced placement credit, distance learning, English as a second language, honors programs, independent study, internships, off-campus study, services for LD students, summer session for credit.
Library Greenleaf Library.
Student Life *Campus security:* 24-hour emergency response devices.
Applying *Options:* electronic application.
Freshman Application Contact Greg Brown, Executive Vice President for Academic and Student Affairs, Copper Mountain College, 6162 Rotary Way, Joshua Tree, CA 92252. *Phone:* 760-366-3791. *Toll-free phone:* 866-366-3791. *Fax:* 760-366-5257. *E-mail:* gbrown@cmccd.edu. *Website:* http://www.cmccd.edu/.

Cosumnes River College
Sacramento, California

- **District-supported** 2-year, founded 1970, part of Los Rios Community College District System
- **Suburban** 180-acre campus with easy access to Sacramento
- **Coed**

Undergraduates 14,545 full-time.
Faculty *Student/faculty ratio:* 34:1.
Academics *Calendar:* semesters. *Degree:* certificates and associate. *Special study options:* academic remediation for entering students, accelerated degree program, adult/continuing education programs, advanced placement credit, cooperative education, distance learning, double majors, English as a second language, freshman honors college, honors programs, independent study, internships, off-campus study, part-time degree program, services for LD students, study abroad, summer session for credit.
Library Cosumnes River College Library plus 1 other.
Student Life *Campus security:* 24-hour emergency response devices and patrols, student patrols, late-night transport/escort service.
Financial Aid Of all full-time matriculated undergraduates who enrolled in 2018, 139 Federal Work-Study jobs (averaging $2000).

Applying *Options:* electronic application, early admission.
Freshman Application Contact Admissions and Records, Cosumnes River College, 8401 Center Parkway, Sacramento, CA 95823-5799. *Phone:* 916-691-7411. *Website:* http://www.crc.losrios.edu/.

Crafton Hills College
Yucaipa, California

Director of Admissions Larry Aycock, Admissions and Records Coordinator, Crafton Hills College, 11711 Sand Canyon Road, Yucaipa, CA 92399-1799. *Phone:* 909-389-3663. *E-mail:* laycock@craftonhills.edu. *Website:* http://www.craftonhills.edu/.

Cuesta College
San Luis Obispo, California

Freshman Application Contact Cuesta College, PO Box 8106, San Luis Obispo, CA 93403-8106. *Phone:* 805-546-3130 Ext. 2262. *Website:* http://www.cuesta.edu/.

Cuyamaca College
El Cajon, California

- **District-supported** 2-year, founded 1978, part of Grossmont-Cuyamaca Community College District
- **Suburban** 165-acre campus with easy access to San Diego
- **Coed**

Undergraduates 1,636 full-time, 6,070 part-time. Students come from 8 other countries.
Academics *Calendar:* semesters. *Degree:* certificates, diplomas, and associate. *Special study options:* academic remediation for entering students, adult/continuing education programs, advanced placement credit, cooperative education, distance learning, double majors, English as a second language, honors programs, internships, off-campus study, part-time degree program, services for LD students, student-designed majors, study abroad, summer session for credit. *ROTC:* Army (c), Air Force (c).
Library Library plus 1 other.
Student Life *Campus security:* 24-hour emergency response devices and patrols, late-night transport/escort service.
Financial Aid Of all full-time matriculated undergraduates who enrolled in 2018, 42 Federal Work-Study jobs (averaging $2700). 51 state and other part-time jobs (averaging $1100).
Applying *Options:* electronic application, early admission.
Freshman Application Contact Ms. Susan Topham, Dean of Admissions and Records, Cuyamaca College, 900 Rancho San Diego Parkway, El Cajon, CA 92019-4304. *Phone:* 619-660-4302. *Fax:* 619-660-4575. *E-mail:* susan.topham@gcccd.edu. *Website:* http://www.cuyamaca.edu/.

Cypress College
Cypress, California

Freshman Application Contact Admissions Office, Cypress College, 9200 Valley View, Cypress, CA 90630-5897. *Phone:* 714-484-7346. *Fax:* 714-484-7446. *E-mail:* admissions@cypresscollege.edu. *Website:* http://www.cypresscollege.edu/.

De Anza College
Cupertino, California

- **District-supported** 2-year, founded 1967, part of California Community College System
- **Suburban** 112-acre campus with easy access to San Francisco, San Jose
- **Coed,** 18,882 undergraduate students, 50% full-time, 50% women, 50% men

Undergraduates 9,418 full-time, 9,464 part-time. 4% Black or African American, non-Hispanic/Latino; 27% Hispanic/Latino; 26% Asian, non-Hispanic/Latino; 0.6% Native Hawaiian or other Pacific Islander, non-Hispanic/Latino; 0.2% American Indian or Alaska Native, non-Hispanic/Latino; 2% Race/ethnicity unknown; 17% international; 0.8% transferred in. *Retention:* 61% of full-time freshmen returned.
Freshmen *Admission:* 206 enrolled.
Faculty *Total:* 725, 37% full-time. *Student/faculty ratio:* 26:1.
Majors Accounting; administrative assistant and secretarial science; art; art history, criticism and conservation; automobile/automotive mechanics technology; behavioral sciences; biology/biological sciences; business administration and management; business automation/technology/data entry; business machine repair; ceramic arts and ceramics; child development; clinical laboratory science/medical technology; commercial and advertising art; communication; computer graphics; computer numerically controlled (CNC) machinist technology; computer programming; computer science; computer technology/computer systems technology; construction engineering technology; corrections; criminal justice/law enforcement administration; criminal justice/police science; criminal justice/safety; developmental and child psychology; drafting/design engineering technologies related; dramatic/theater arts; drawing; economics; energy management and systems technology; engineering; engineering technology; English; environmental studies; film/cinema/video studies; graphic design; high performance and custom engine technology; history; humanities; industrial technology; information science/studies; intercultural/multicultural and diversity studies; international relations and affairs; journalism; kinesiology and exercise science; legal assistant/paralegal; liberal arts and sciences/liberal studies; licensed practical/vocational nurse training; machine tool technology; marketing/marketing management; mass communication/media; mathematics; medical/clinical assistant; music; network and system administration; nursing practice; office management; philosophy; photography; physical education teaching and coaching; physical therapy; physics; political science and government; pre-engineering; printmaking; professional, technical, business, and scientific writing; psychology; purchasing, procurement/acquisitions and contracts management; radio and television; real estate; registered nursing/registered nurse; rhetoric and composition; sculpture; social sciences; sociology; Spanish.
Academics *Calendar:* quarters. *Degree:* certificates, diplomas, and associate. *Special study options:* academic remediation for entering students, adult/continuing education programs, distance learning, English as a second language, honors programs, independent study, internships, part-time degree program, services for LD students, student-designed majors, study abroad, summer session for credit. *ROTC:* Army (c), Air Force (c).
Library A. Robert DeHart Learning Center. Study areas open 24 hours, 5–7 days a week; students can reserve study rooms.
Student Life *Housing:* college housing not available. *Activities and Organizations:* drama/theater group, student-run newspaper, choral group, Student Nurses Association, Phi Theta Kappa, Automotive Club, Vietnamese Club, Filipino Club. *Campus security:* 24-hour emergency response devices, student patrols, late-night transport/escort service. *Student services:* health clinic, personal/psychological counseling, legal services, veterans affairs office.
Athletics Member NCAA. All Division II. *Intercollegiate sports:* baseball M, basketball M/W, cross-country running M/W, football M, golf M/W, soccer M/W, softball W, swimming and diving M/W, tennis M/W, track and field M/W, volleyball M/W, water polo M. *Intramural sports:* badminton M/W, basketball M, soccer M/W, swimming and diving M/W, volleyball M/W.
Costs (2020–21) *Tuition:* state resident $372 full-time; nonresident $2496 full-time, $177 per unit part-time. *Required fees:* $165 full-time, $31 per credit part-time, $55 per term part-time. *Payment plan:* installment. *Waivers:* minority students and adult students.
Applying *Options:* electronic application. *Application deadlines:* rolling (freshmen), rolling (out-of-state freshmen), rolling (transfers). *Notification:* continuous (freshmen), continuous (out-of-state freshmen), continuous (transfers).
Freshman Application Contact De Anza College, 21250 Stevens Creek Boulevard, Cupertino, CA 95014-5793. *Phone:* 408-864-5300. *Website:* http://www.deanza.fhda.edu/.

Deep Springs College
Deep Springs, California

Freshman Application Contact Jack Davis, Chair, Applications Committee, Deep Springs College, HC 72, Box 45001, Dyer, NV 89010-9803. *Phone:* 760-872-2000. *Fax:* 760-874-0314. *E-mail:* apcom@deepsprings.edu. *Website:* http://www.deepsprings.edu/.

Diablo Valley College
Pleasant Hill, California

Freshman Application Contact Ileana Dorn, Director of Admissions and Records, Diablo Valley College, Pleasant Hill, CA 94523-1529. *Phone:* 925-685-1230 Ext. 2330. *Fax:* 925-609-8085. *E-mail:* idorn@dvc.edu. *Website:* http://www.dvc.edu/.

East Los Angeles College
Monterey Park, California

- **District-supported** 2-year, founded 1945, part of Los Angeles Community College District System
- **Urban** 84-acre campus with easy access to Los Angeles
- **Coed**

Undergraduates 8,063 full-time, 23,686 part-time. Students come from 17 states and territories; 0.1% are from out of state; 11% transferred in.
Academics *Calendar:* semesters. *Degree:* certificates and associate. *Special study options:* academic remediation for entering students, accelerated degree program, adult/continuing education programs, advanced placement credit, cooperative education, distance learning, double majors, English as a second language, freshman honors college, honors programs, independent study, internships, off-campus study, part-time degree program, services for LD students, student-designed majors, study abroad, summer session for credit.
Library ELAC Helen Miller Bailey Library plus 2 others.
Student Life *Campus security:* 24-hour emergency response devices and patrols, late-night transport/escort service, Los Angeles County Sheriff Substation.
Standardized Tests *Required:* international students require TOEFL score of 450, CBT score 133, iBT score 45 or higher (for admission).
Financial Aid Of all full-time matriculated undergraduates who enrolled in 2018, 189 Federal Work-Study jobs (averaging $3000).
Applying *Options:* electronic application, early admission. *Recommended:* high school transcript.
Freshman Application Contact Mr. Jeremy Allred, Associate Dean of Admissions, East Los Angeles College, 1301 Avenida Cesar Chavez, Monterey Park, CA 91754. *Phone:* 323-265-8801. *Fax:* 323-265-8688. *E-mail:* allredjp@elac.edu. *Website:* http://www.elac.edu/.

East San Gabriel Valley Regional Occupational Program & Technical Center
West Covina, California

Admissions Office Contact East San Gabriel Valley Regional Occupational Program & Technical Center, 1501 West Del Norte Avenue, West Covina, CA 91790. *Website:* http://www.esgvrop.org/.

El Camino College
Torrance, California

Director of Admissions Mr. William Mulrooney, Director of Admissions, El Camino College, 16007 Crenshaw Boulevard, Torrance, CA 90506-0001. *Phone:* 310-660-3418. *Toll-free phone:* 866-ELCAMINO. *Fax:* 310-660-6779. *E-mail:* wmulrooney@elcamino.edu. *Website:* http://www.elcamino.edu/.

Empire College
Santa Rosa, California

Freshman Application Contact Ms. Dahnja Barker, Admissions Officer, Empire College, 3035 Cleveland Avenue, Santa Rosa, CA 95403. *Phone:* 707-546-4000. *Toll-free phone:* 877-395-8535. *Website:* http://www.empcol.edu/.

Evergreen Valley College
San Jose, California

Freshman Application Contact Evergreen Valley College, 3095 Yerba Buena Road, San Jose, CA 95135-1598. *Phone:* 408-270-6423. *Website:* http://www.evc.edu/.

Feather River College
Quincy, California

- **District-supported** primarily 2-year, founded 1968, part of California Community College System
- **Rural** 420-acre campus
- **Endowment** $48,205
- **Coed,** 1,990 undergraduate students, 23% full-time, 52% women, 48% men

Undergraduates 460 full-time, 1,530 part-time. 9% are from out of state; 15% Black or African American, non-Hispanic/Latino; 23% Hispanic/Latino; 3% Asian, non-Hispanic/Latino; 2% Native Hawaiian or other Pacific Islander, non-Hispanic/Latino; 3% American Indian or Alaska Native, non-Hispanic/Latino; 0.2% Two or more races, non-Hispanic/Latino; 4% Race/ethnicity unknown; 0.5% international; 10% transferred in; 20% live on campus. *Retention:* 100% of full-time freshmen returned.
Freshmen *Admission:* 304 applied, 304 admitted, 302 enrolled.
Faculty *Total:* 107, 24% full-time, 10% with terminal degrees. *Student/faculty ratio:* 19:1.
Majors Agriculture; anthropology; biology/biological sciences; business/commerce; child-care provision; computer programming; cooking and related culinary arts; corrections and criminal justice related; English; environmental studies; health and physical education/fitness; history; horse husbandry/equine science and management; humanities; kinesiology and exercise science; liberal arts and sciences/liberal studies; licensed practical/vocational nurse training; mathematics; natural resources/conservation; parks, recreation and leisure; physical sciences; political science and government; social sciences; sociology; visual and performing arts; wildlife, fish and wildlands science and management.
Academics *Calendar:* semesters plus summer and winter terms. *Degrees:* certificates, diplomas, associate, and bachelor's. *Special study options:* academic remediation for entering students, adult/continuing education programs, advanced placement credit, cooperative education, distance learning, double majors, English as a second language, independent study, part-time degree program, services for LD students, summer session for credit.
Library Feather River College Library. *Databases:* 35. Weekly public service hours: 61; students can reserve study rooms.
Student Life *Housing Options:* coed. Campus housing is university owned. *Activities and Organizations:* drama/theater group, choral group, Student Environmental Association, Horse Show Team, Prisoner and Student Social Justice Journalism Club, International, Cultural & Diversity Club, Black Student Union. *Campus security:* student patrols, part-time private security company patrols. *Student services:* health clinic, personal/psychological counseling.
Athletics *Intercollegiate sports:* baseball M, basketball M/W, cross-country running W, equestrian sports M(s)/W(s), football M, sand volleyball W, soccer M/W, softball W, track and field W, volleyball W.
Costs (2019–20) *Tuition:* area resident $1461 full-time, $46 per credit part-time; state resident $1461 full-time, $46 per credit part-time; nonresident $9441 full-time, $312 per credit part-time. Full-time tuition and fees vary according to course load. Part-time tuition and fees vary according to course load. *Required fees:* $81 full-time, $2 per credit part-time, $18 per term part-time. *Room and board:* room only: $5350. Room and board charges vary according to housing facility. *Payment plan:* installment.
Financial Aid Of all full-time matriculated undergraduates who enrolled in 2018, 444 applied for aid, 384 were judged to have need, 3 had their need fully met.
Applying *Options:* electronic application, deferred entrance.
Freshman Application Contact Gretchen Baumgartner, Feather River College, 570 Golden Eagle Avenue, Quincy, CA 95971. *Phone:* 530-2830202 Ext. 285. *Toll-free phone:* 800-442-9799. *E-mail:* gbaumgartner@frc.edu. *Website:* http://www.frc.edu/.

FIDM/Fashion Institute of Design & Merchandising, Orange County Campus
Irvine, California

- **Proprietary** 2-year, founded 1981, part of FIDM/Fashion Institute of Design & Merchandising
- **Urban** campus with easy access to Los Angeles
- **Coed, primarily women**

Undergraduates 67 full-time, 4 part-time. Students come from 11 states and territories; 5 other countries; 2% are from out of state; 25% transferred in. *Retention:* 67% of full-time freshmen returned.
Faculty *Student/faculty ratio:* 18:1.
Academics *Calendar:* quarters. *Degree:* associate. *Special study options:* academic remediation for entering students, accelerated degree program, adult/continuing education programs, advanced placement credit, cooperative education, distance learning, English as a second language, independent study, internships, part-time degree program, services for LD students, study abroad, summer session for credit.
Library FIDM Orange County Campus Library. Students can reserve study rooms.
Student Life *Campus security:* 24-hour emergency response devices, late-night transport/escort service, security guard escort.
Standardized Tests *Recommended:* SAT or ACT (for admission).
Applying *Options:* electronic application, deferred entrance. *Application fee:* $25. *Required:* essay or personal statement, high school transcript, minimum 2.5 GPA, 3 letters of recommendation, interview, entrance project.
Freshman Application Contact Mr. Michael Mirabella, Admissions, FIDM/Fashion Institute of Design & Merchandising, Orange County Campus,

919 So Grand Avenue, Los Angeles, CA 90015. *Phone:* 213-624-1200. *Toll-free phone:* 888-974-3436. *Website:* http://www.fidm.edu/.

FIDM/Fashion Institute of Design & Merchandising, San Diego Campus
San Diego, California

- **Proprietary** 2-year, founded 1985, part of FIDM/Fashion Institute of Design & Merchandising
- **Urban** campus with easy access to San Diego
- **Coed, primarily women**

Undergraduates 61 full-time, 5 part-time. Students come from 17 states and territories; 4 other countries; 22% are from out of state; 26% transferred in. *Retention:* 74% of full-time freshmen returned.
Faculty *Student/faculty ratio:* 21:1.
Academics *Calendar:* quarters. *Degree:* associate. *Special study options:* academic remediation for entering students, accelerated degree program, adult/continuing education programs, advanced placement credit, cooperative education, distance learning, English as a second language, independent study, internships, part-time degree program, services for LD students, study abroad, summer session for credit.
Library FIDM San Diego Campus Library. Students can reserve study rooms.
Student Life *Campus security:* 24-hour emergency response devices and patrols.
Standardized Tests *Recommended:* SAT or ACT (for admission).
Applying *Options:* electronic application, deferred entrance. *Application fee:* $25. *Required:* essay or personal statement, high school transcript, minimum 2.5 GPA, 3 letters of recommendation, interview, major-determined project.
Freshman Application Contact Ms. Denise Baca, Campus Director, FIDM/Fashion Institute of Design & Merchandising, San Diego Campus, 350 Tenth Avenue, San Diego, CA 92101. *Phone:* 619-235-2049. *Toll-free phone:* 800-243-3436. *E-mail:* dbaca@fidm.edu. *Website:* http://www.fidm.edu/.

Folsom Lake College
Folsom, California

Freshman Application Contact Admissions Office, Folsom Lake College, 10 College Parkway, Folsom, CA 95630. *Phone:* 916-608-6500. *Website:* http://www.flc.losrios.edu/.

Foothill College
Los Altos Hills, California

- **District-supported** 2-year, founded 1958, part of Foothill-DeAnza Community College District
- **Suburban** 122-acre campus with easy access to San Jose
- **Endowment** $15.0 million
- **Coed**

Undergraduates 5,191 full-time, 10,574 part-time. Students come from 16 states and territories; 109 other countries; 1% are from out of state; 4% Black or African American, non-Hispanic/Latino; 19% Hispanic/Latino; 26% Asian, non-Hispanic/Latino; 0.9% Native Hawaiian or other Pacific Islander, non-Hispanic/Latino; 0.4% American Indian or Alaska Native, non-Hispanic/Latino; 4% Two or more races, non-Hispanic/Latino; 1% Race/ethnicity unknown; 6% international.
Academics *Calendar:* quarters. *Degree:* certificates and associate. *Special study options:* academic remediation for entering students, accelerated degree program, adult/continuing education programs, advanced placement credit, cooperative education, distance learning, English as a second language, honors programs, independent study, internships, off-campus study, part-time degree program, services for LD students, student-designed majors, study abroad, summer session for credit. *ROTC:* Army (c), Air Force (c).
Library Hubert H. Semans Library.
Student Life *Campus security:* 24-hour emergency response devices and patrols, late-night transport/escort service.
Athletics Member NJCAA.
Financial Aid Of all full-time matriculated undergraduates who enrolled in 2017, 46 Federal Work-Study jobs (averaging $4000).
Applying *Options:* electronic application. *Recommended:* high school transcript.
Freshman Application Contact Ms. Shawna Aced, Registrar, Foothill College, Admissions and Records, 12345 El Monte Road, Los Altos Hills, CA 94022. *Phone:* 650-949-7771. *E-mail:* acedshawna@hda.edu. *Website:* http://www.foothill.edu/.

Fremont College
Cerritos, California

Freshman Application Contact Natasha Dawson, Director of Admissions, Fremont College, 18000 Studebaker Road, Suite 900A, Cerritos, CA 90703. *Phone:* 562-809-5100. *Toll-free phone:* 800-373-6668. *Fax:* 562-809-5100. *E-mail:* info@fremont.edu. *Website:* http://www.fremont.edu/.

Fresno City College
Fresno, California

Freshman Application Contact Office Assistant, Fresno City College, 1101 East University Avenue, Fresno, CA 93741-0002. *Phone:* 559-442-4600 Ext. 8604. *Fax:* 559-237-4232. *E-mail:* fcc.admissions@fresnocitycollege.edu. *Website:* http://www.fresnocitycollege.edu/.

Fullerton College
Fullerton, California

- **District-supported** 2-year, founded 1913, part of California Community College System
- **Suburban** 79-acre campus with easy access to Los Angeles
- **Coed,** 23,107 undergraduate students, 25% full-time, 52% women, 47% men

Undergraduates 5,805 full-time, 16,897 part-time. Students come from 20 states and territories; 1% are from out of state; 4% Black or African American, non-Hispanic/Latino; 62% Hispanic/Latino; 15% Asian, non-Hispanic/Latino; 0.4% American Indian or Alaska Native, non-Hispanic/Latino; 3% Race/ethnicity unknown. *Retention:* 64% of full-time freshmen returned.
Freshmen *Admission:* 3,326 enrolled.
Faculty *Total:* 908, 35% full-time. *Student/faculty ratio:* 25:1.
Majors Accounting technology and bookkeeping; administrative assistant and secretarial science; anthropology; apparel and textile marketing management; apparel and textiles; applied horticulture/horticulture operations; architectural technology; area studies related; art; astronomy; automobile/automotive mechanics technology; biological and physical sciences; biology/biological sciences; biomedical technology; building/construction site management; building/home/construction inspection; business administration and management; carpentry; chemical technology; chemistry; child-care provision; computer science; construction trades related; cosmetology; criminal justice/police science; dance; drafting and design technology; dramatic/theater arts; economics; electrical/electronics equipment installation and repair; engineering; English; environmental studies; ethnic, cultural minority, gender, and group studies related; fashion/apparel design; foods, nutrition, and wellness; foreign languages and literatures; geography; geology/earth science; graphic and printing equipment operation/production; graphic design; hazardous materials management and waste technology; health and physical education/fitness; health/medical preparatory programs related; history; humanities; information technology; interior design; international business/trade/commerce; journalism; landscaping and groundskeeping; legal administrative assistant/secretary; legal assistant/paralegal; liberal arts and sciences/liberal studies; mass communication/media; mathematics; mechanical engineering/mechanical technology; microbiology; music; parks, recreation and leisure; philosophy; physics; plant nursery management; political science and government; psychology; radio and television; real estate; recording arts technology; religious studies; sales, distribution, and marketing operations; small business administration; sociology; speech communication and rhetoric; sport and fitness administration/management; technology/industrial arts teacher education.
Academics *Calendar:* semesters. *Degree:* certificates, diplomas, and associate. *Special study options:* academic remediation for entering students, adult/continuing education programs, advanced placement credit, cooperative education, English as a second language, honors programs, part-time degree program, services for LD students, study abroad, summer session for credit. *ROTC:* Army (c), Navy (c), Air Force (c).
Library William T. Boyce Library. Students can reserve study rooms.
Student Life *Housing:* college housing not available. *Activities and Organizations:* drama/theater group, student-run newspaper, radio station. *Campus security:* 24-hour patrols, late-night transport/escort service. *Student services:* health clinic, personal/psychological counseling, women's center, legal services, veterans affairs office.
Athletics *Intercollegiate sports:* badminton W, baseball M, basketball M/W, cross-country running M/W, football M, golf W, soccer M/W, softball W, swimming and diving M/W, tennis M/W, track and field M/W, volleyball W, water polo M/W.
Costs (2020–21) *Tuition:* area resident $1142 full-time; state resident $1142 full-time; nonresident $7118 full-time. Full-time tuition and fees vary according to course load. Part-time tuition and fees vary according to course load. *Required fees:* $38 full-time.

Financial Aid Of all full-time matriculated undergraduates who enrolled in 2018, 767 Federal Work-Study jobs (averaging $4.0 million). *Average indebtedness upon graduation:* $5237. *Financial aid deadline:* 6/30.
Applying *Options:* electronic application, early admission. *Application deadlines:* rolling (freshmen), rolling (transfers).
Freshman Application Contact Fullerton College, 321 East Chapman Avenue, Fullerton, CA 92832-2095. *Phone:* 714-992-7076.
Website: http://www.fullcoll.edu/.

Gavilan College
Gilroy, California

Freshman Application Contact Gavilan College, 5055 Santa Teresa Boulevard, Gilroy, CA 95020-9599. *Phone:* 408-848-4754. *Website:* http://www.gavilan.edu/.

Glendale Career College
Glendale, California

- **Proprietary** 2-year
- **Coed**

Undergraduates *Retention:* 85% of full-time freshmen returned.
Faculty *Student/faculty ratio:* 15:1.
Academics *Degree:* certificates, diplomas, and associate.
Admissions Office Contact Glendale Career College, 240 North Brand Boulevard, Lower Level, Glendale, CA 91203. *Website:* http://www.glendalecareer.com/.

Glendale Community College
Glendale, California

Freshman Application Contact Ms. Sharon Combs, Dean, Admissions, and Records, Glendale Community College, 1500 North Verdugo Road, Glendale, CA 91208. *Phone:* 818-240-1000 Ext. 5910. *E-mail:* scombs@glendale.edu. *Website:* http://www.glendale.edu/.

Golden West College
Huntington Beach, California

Freshman Application Contact Golden West College, PO Box 2748, 15744 Golden West Street, Huntington Beach, CA 92647-2748. *Phone:* 714-892-7711 Ext. 58965. *Website:* http://www.goldenwestcollege.edu/.

Grossmont College
El Cajon, California

Freshman Application Contact Admissions Office, Grossmont College, 8800 Grossmont College Drive, El Cajon, CA 92020-1799. *Phone:* 619-644-7186. *Website:* http://www.grossmont.edu/.

Gurnick Academy of Medical Arts
San Mateo, California

Freshman Application Contact Gurnick Academy of Medical Arts, 2121 South El Camino Real, Building C 2000, San Mateo, CA 94403. *Website:* http://www.gurnick.edu/.

Hartnell College
Salinas, California

Director of Admissions Director of Admissions, Hartnell College, 411 Central Avenue, Salinas, CA 93901. *Phone:* 831-755-6711. *Fax:* 831-759-6014. *Website:* http://www.hartnell.edu/.

Healthcare Career College
Paramount, California

Admissions Office Contact Healthcare Career College, 8527 Alondra Boulevard, #174, Paramount, CA 90723. *Website:* http://www.healthcarecareercollege.edu/.

Imperial Valley College
Imperial, California

- **District-supported** 2-year, founded 1922, part of California Community College System
- **Rural** 160-acre campus
- **Coed**
- 100% of applicants were admitted

Undergraduates 1% Black or African American, non-Hispanic/Latino; 91% Hispanic/Latino; 0.6% Asian, non-Hispanic/Latino; 0.1% American Indian or Alaska Native, non-Hispanic/Latino; 0.4% Two or more races, non-Hispanic/Latino; 3% Race/ethnicity unknown.
Faculty *Student/faculty ratio:* 28:1.
Academics *Calendar:* semesters. *Degree:* certificates and associate. *Special study options:* academic remediation for entering students, accelerated degree program, adult/continuing education programs, advanced placement credit, distance learning, double majors, English as a second language, part-time degree program, services for LD students, student-designed majors, summer session for credit.
Library Spencer Library. *Databases:* 45. Weekly public service hours: 57; students can reserve study rooms.
Student Life *Campus security:* student patrols, emergency phone poles on campus.
Athletics Member NJCAA.
Applying *Options:* electronic application. *Required for some:* high school transcript. *Recommended:* high school transcript.
Freshman Application Contact Imperial Valley College, 380 East Aten Road, PO Box 158, Imperial, CA 92251-0158. *Phone:* 760-355-6244. *Website:* http://www.imperial.edu/.

Institute of Technology
Clovis, California

Admissions Office Contact Institute of Technology, 564 West Herndon Avenue, Clovis, CA 93612. *Website:* http://www.iot.edu/.

International Sports Sciences Association
Carpinteria, California

Admissions Office Contact International Sports Sciences Association, 1015 Mark Avenue, Carpinteria, CA 93013. *Website:* http://www.college.issaonline.edu/.

Irvine Valley College
Irvine, California

Director of Admissions Mr. John Edwards, Director of Admissions, Records, and Enrollment Services, Irvine Valley College, 5500 Irvine Center Drive, Irvine, CA 92618. *Phone:* 949-451-5416. *Website:* http://www.ivc.edu/.

Lake Tahoe Community College
South Lake Tahoe, California

Freshman Application Contact Office of Admissions and Records, Lake Tahoe Community College, One College Drive, South Lake Tahoe, CA 96150. *Phone:* 530-541-4660 Ext. 211. *Fax:* 530-541-7852. *E-mail:* admissions@ltcc.edu. *Website:* http://www.ltcc.edu/.

Laney College
Oakland, California

Freshman Application Contact Mrs. Barbara Simmons, District Admissions Officer, Laney College, 900 Fallon Street, Oakland, CA 94607-4893. *Phone:* 510-466-7369. *Website:* http://www.laney.edu/.

Las Positas College
Livermore, California

Director of Admissions Mrs. Sylvia R. Rodriguez, Director of Admissions and Records, Las Positas College, 3000 Campus Hill Drive, Livermore, CA 94551. *Phone:* 925-373-4942. *Website:* http://www.laspositascollege.edu/.

Lassen Community College
Susanville, California

Freshman Application Contact Mr. Chris J. Alberico, Registrar, Lassen Community College, Highway 139, PO Box 3000, Susanville, CA 96130. *Phone:* 530-257-6181. *Website:* http://www.lassencollege.edu/.

Laurus College
San Luis Obispo, California

Admissions Office Contact Laurus College, 81 Higuera Street, Suite 110, San Luis Obispo, CA 93401. *Website:* http://www.lauruscollege.edu/.

Learnet Academy
Los Angeles, California

Admissions Office Contact Learnet Academy, 3251 West 6th Street, 2nd Floor, Los Angeles, CA 90020. *Website:* http://www.learnet.edu/.

Long Beach City College
Long Beach, California

Director of Admissions Mr. Ross Miyashiro, Dean of Admissions and Records, Long Beach City College, 4901 East Carson Street, Long Beach, CA 90808-1780. *Phone:* 562-938-4130. *Website:* http://www.lbcc.edu/.

Los Angeles City College
Los Angeles, California

- **District-supported** 2-year, founded 1929, part of Los Angeles Community College District (LACCD)
- **Urban** 42-acre campus
- **Coed,** 14,937 undergraduate students, 22% full-time, 58% women, 42% men

Undergraduates 3,264 full-time, 11,673 part-time. 7% Black or African American, non-Hispanic/Latino; 55% Hispanic/Latino; 8% Asian, non-Hispanic/Latino; 0.2% Native Hawaiian or other Pacific Islander, non-Hispanic/Latino; 0.3% American Indian or Alaska Native, non-Hispanic/Latino; 2% Two or more races, non-Hispanic/Latino; 8% Race/ethnicity unknown; 2% international. *Retention:* 65% of full-time freshmen returned.

Freshmen *Admission:* 1,535 enrolled.

Faculty *Total:* 450, 41% full-time. *Student/faculty ratio:* 34:1.

Majors Accounting; accounting technology and bookkeeping; administrative assistant and secretarial science; art; banking and financial support services; biological and physical sciences; business administration and management; chemistry; child development; Chinese; cinematography and film/video production; computer and information sciences and support services related; computer and information sciences related; computer engineering technology; computer science; criminal justice/law enforcement administration; criminal justice/police science; dental laboratory technology; dietetics; dietetic technology; dramatic/theater arts; electrical/electronics equipment installation and repair; engineering; English; finance; French; graphic design; humanities; human services; industrial radiologic technology; information technology; Japanese; journalism; Korean; legal administrative assistant/secretary; legal assistant/paralegal; liberal arts and sciences/liberal studies; marketing/marketing management; mathematics; medical administrative assistant and medical secretary; music; photographic and film/video technology; physics; political science and government; radio and television; radiologic technology/science; real estate; registered nursing/registered nurse; Spanish; speech communication and rhetoric; substance abuse/addiction counseling.

Academics *Calendar:* semesters. *Degree:* certificates, diplomas, and associate. *Special study options:* academic remediation for entering students, accelerated degree program, adult/continuing education programs, advanced placement credit, cooperative education, distance learning, double majors, English as a second language, freshman honors college, honors programs, internships, part-time degree program, services for LD students, study abroad, summer session for credit. *ROTC:* Army (c), Navy (c), Air Force (c).

Library Martin Luther King Jr. Library. *Books:* 155,239 (physical), 19,195 (digital/electronic); *Serial titles:* 88 (physical); *Databases:* 38. Weekly public service hours: 69.

Student Life *Activities and Organizations:* drama/theater group, student-run newspaper, choral group. *Campus security:* 24-hour emergency response devices and patrols, student patrols, late-night transport/escort service. *Student services:* health clinic, personal/psychological counseling, veterans affairs office.

Athletics *Intramural sports:* basketball M/W, soccer M/W, softball M/W.

Costs (2020–21) *Tuition:* area resident $46 full-time, $46 per unit part-time; state resident $1220 full-time, $46 per unit part-time; nonresident $7464 full-time, $297 per unit part-time. *Required fees:* $24 full-time, $12 per term part-time. *Room and board:* $15,804.

Applying *Options:* electronic application. *Recommended:* high school transcript. *Application deadlines:* 9/5 (freshmen), 9/5 (transfers). *Notification:* continuous until 9/5 (freshmen), continuous until 9/5 (transfers).

Freshman Application Contact Los Angeles City College, 855 North Vermont Avenue, Los Angeles, CA 90029-3590. *Phone:* 323-953-4000 Ext. 2011.
Website: http://www.lacitycollege.edu/.

Los Angeles County College of Nursing and Allied Health
Los Angeles, California

Freshman Application Contact Admissions Office, Los Angeles County College of Nursing and Allied Health, 1237 North Mission Road, Los Angeles, CA 90033. *Phone:* 323-226-4911. *Website:* http://www.dhs.lacounty.gov/wps/portal/dhs/conah/.

Los Angeles Harbor College
Wilmington, California

Freshman Application Contact Los Angeles Harbor College, 1111 Figueroa Place, Wilmington, CA 90744-2397. *Phone:* 310-233-4091. *Website:* http://www.lahc.edu/.

Los Angeles Mission College
Sylmar, California

- **District-supported** 2-year, founded 1974, part of Los Angeles Community College District System, California Community Colleges
- **Urban** 33-acre campus with easy access to Los Angeles
- **Coed,** 10,128 undergraduate students, 19% full-time, 61% women, 39% men

Undergraduates 1,896 full-time, 8,232 part-time. 0.2% are from out of state; 3% Black or African American, non-Hispanic/Latino; 78% Hispanic/Latino; 2% Asian, non-Hispanic/Latino; 0.1% Native Hawaiian or other Pacific Islander, non-Hispanic/Latino; 0.2% American Indian or Alaska Native, non-Hispanic/Latino; 1% Two or more races, non-Hispanic/Latino; 5% Race/ethnicity unknown; 0.6% international; 13% transferred in. *Retention:* 67% of full-time freshmen returned.

Freshmen *Admission:* 1,220 enrolled.

Faculty *Total:* 350, 23% full-time.

Majors Accounting; administrative assistant and secretarial science; biology/biological sciences; business administration and management; computer programming; criminal justice/police science; culinary arts; developmental and child psychology; dramatic/theater arts; English; family and consumer economics related; finance; geography; history; humanities; liberal arts and sciences/liberal studies; mathematics; music; philosophy; physical sciences; psychology; social sciences; sociology; Spanish.

Academics *Calendar:* semesters. *Degree:* certificates and associate. *Special study options:* academic remediation for entering students, adult/continuing education programs, advanced placement credit, distance learning, double majors, English as a second language, honors programs, independent study, internships, off-campus study, part-time degree program, services for LD students, study abroad, summer session for credit.

Library Los Angeles Mission College Library.

Student Life *Housing:* college housing not available. *Activities and Organizations:* drama/theater group, choral group. *Campus security:* 24-hour emergency response devices and patrols, late-night transport/escort service. *Student services:* health clinic, personal/psychological counseling, veterans affairs office.

Costs (2019–20) *Tuition:* state resident $46 per unit part-time; nonresident $297 per unit part-time. Part-time tuition and fees vary according to course load. *Required fees:* $12 per term part-time.

Financial Aid Of all full-time matriculated undergraduates who enrolled in 2018, 57 Federal Work-Study jobs (averaging $3800).

Applying *Options:* early admission. *Application deadline:* rolling (freshmen). *Notification:* continuous (freshmen).

Freshman Application Contact Los Angeles Mission College, 13356 Eldridge Avenue, Sylmar, CA 91342-3245.
Website: http://www.lamission.edu/.

Los Angeles ORT College - Los Angeles

Los Angeles, California

Admissions Office Contact Los Angeles ORT College - Los Angeles, 6435 Wilshire Boulevard, Los Angeles, CA 90048. *Website:* http://www.laort.edu/.

Los Angeles Pierce College

Woodland Hills, California

Director of Admissions Ms. Shelley L. Gerstl, Dean of Admissions and Records, Los Angeles Pierce College, 6201 Winnetka Avenue, Woodland Hills, CA 91371-0001. *Phone:* 818-719-6448. *Website:* http://www.piercecollege.edu/.

Los Angeles Southwest College

Los Angeles, California

Director of Admissions Dan W. Walden, Dean of Academic Affairs, Los Angeles Southwest College, 1600 West Imperial Highway, Los Angeles, CA 90047-4810. *Phone:* 323-242-5511. *Website:* http://www.lasc.edu/.

Los Angeles Trade-Technical College

Los Angeles, California

Freshman Application Contact Los Angeles Trade-Technical College, 400 West Washington Boulevard, Los Angeles, CA 90015-4108. *Phone:* 213-763-7127. *Website:* http://www.lattc.edu/.

Los Angeles Valley College

Valley Glen, California

Freshman Application Contact Los Angeles Valley College, 5800 Fulton Avenue, Valley Glen, CA 91401. *Phone:* 818-947-5518. *Website:* http://www.lavc.edu/.

Los Medanos College

Pittsburg, California

Freshman Application Contact Ms. Gail Newman, Director of Admissions and Records, Los Medanos College, 2700 East Leland Road, Pittsburg, CA 94565-5197. *Phone:* 925-439-2181 Ext. 7500. *Website:* http://www.losmedanos.net/.

Mendocino College

Ukiah, California

Freshman Application Contact Mendocino College, 1000 Hensley Creek Road, Ukiah, CA 95482-0300. *Phone:* 707-468-3103. *Website:* http://www.mendocino.edu/.

Merced College

Merced, California

Admissions Office Contact Merced College, 3600 M Street, Merced, CA 95348-2898. *Website:* http://www.mccd.edu/.

Merritt College

Oakland, California

Freshman Application Contact Ms. Barbara Simmons, District Admissions Officer, Merritt College, 12500 Campus Drive, Oakland, CA 94619-3196. *Phone:* 510-466-7369. *E-mail:* hperdue@peralta.cc.ca.us. *Website:* http://www.merritt.edu/.

MiraCosta College

Oceanside, California

- **District-supported** primarily 2-year, founded 1934, part of California Community College System
- **Suburban** 131-acre campus with easy access to San Diego
- **Endowment** $14.1 million
- **Coed,** 14,687 undergraduate students, 34% full-time, 56% women, 44% men

Undergraduates 5,024 full-time, 9,663 part-time. 2% are from out of state; 3% Black or African American, non-Hispanic/Latino; 33% Hispanic/Latino; 6% Asian, non-Hispanic/Latino; 0.5% Native Hawaiian or other Pacific Islander, non-Hispanic/Latino; 0.3% American Indian or Alaska Native, non-Hispanic/Latino; 7% Two or more races, non-Hispanic/Latino; 2% Race/ethnicity unknown; 1% international.
Freshmen *Admission:* 2,768 enrolled.
Faculty *Total:* 634, 23% full-time. *Student/faculty ratio:* 23:1.
Majors Accounting technology and bookkeeping; administrative assistant and secretarial science; adult development and aging; architectural technology; art; biological and physical sciences; biology/biotechnology laboratory technician; biomedical technology; business administration and management; child-care and support services management; child-care provision; computer programming; computer science; computer systems networking and telecommunications; criminal justice/police science; dance; data entry/microcomputer applications; drafting and design technology; history; hospitality administration; liberal arts and sciences/liberal studies; licensed practical/vocational nurse training; mathematics; medical/clinical assistant; music; office management; photographic and film/video technology; plant nursery management; psychology; psychology related; real estate; recording arts technology; registered nursing/registered nurse; restaurant, culinary, and catering management; sales, distribution, and marketing operations; small business administration; sociology; surgical technology; theater design and technology; web/multimedia management and webmaster.
Academics *Calendar:* semesters. *Degrees:* certificates, diplomas, associate, and bachelor's. *Special study options:* academic remediation for entering students, accelerated degree program, adult/continuing education programs, advanced placement credit, cooperative education, distance learning, double majors, English as a second language, honors programs, independent study, internships, part-time degree program, services for LD students, student-designed majors, study abroad, summer session for credit.
Library MiraCosta College Library.
Student Life *Activities and Organizations:* drama/theater group, student-run newspaper, choral group, Inter Varsity Christian Fellowship, Accounting and Business Club, Backstage Players (Drama), Gay Straight Alliance, Puente Diversity Network. *Campus security:* 24-hour emergency response devices, student patrols, late-night transport/escort service, trained security personnel during class hours. *Student services:* health clinic, personal/psychological counseling, veterans affairs office.
Athletics *Intercollegiate sports:* basketball M/W, soccer M/W.
Costs (2019–20) *Tuition:* $46 per credit hour part-time; state resident $46 per credit hour part-time; nonresident $311 per credit hour part-time. Full-time tuition and fees vary according to course load and degree level. Part-time tuition and fees vary according to course load and degree level. *Required fees:* $48 per term part-time, $48 per term part-time. *Room and board:* Room and board charges vary according to housing facility. *Payment plans:* installment, deferred payment.
Applying *Options:* electronic application, early admission, deferred entrance. *Application deadlines:* rolling (freshmen), rolling (transfers).
Freshman Application Contact Jane Sparks, Interim Director of Admissions and Records, MiraCosta College, One Barnard Drive, Oceanside, CA 92057. *Phone:* 760-795-6620. *Toll-free phone:* 888-201-8480. *E-mail:* admissions@miracosta.edu.
Website: http://www.miracosta.edu/.

Mission College

Santa Clara, California

Admissions Office Contact Mission College, 3000 Mission College Boulevard, Santa Clara, CA 95054-1897. *Website:* http://www.missioncollege.edu/.

Modesto Junior College

Modesto, California

Freshman Application Contact Ms. Martha Robles, Dean of Student Services and Support, Modesto Junior College, 435 College Avenue, Modesto, CA 95350. *Phone:* 209-575-6470. *Fax:* 209-575-6859. *E-mail:* mjcadmissions@mail.yosemite.cc.ca.us. *Website:* http://www.mjc.edu/.

Monterey Peninsula College

Monterey, California

Director of Admissions Ms. Vera Coleman, Registrar, Monterey Peninsula College, 980 Fremont Street, Monterey, CA 93940-4799. *Phone:* 831-646-4007. *E-mail:* vcoleman@mpc.edu. *Website:* http://www.mpc.edu/.

Moorpark College
Moorpark, California

Freshman Application Contact Ms. Katherine Colborn, Registrar, Moorpark College, 7075 Campus Road, Moorpark, CA 93021-2899. *Phone:* 805-378-1415. *Website:* http://www.moorparkcollege.edu/.

Moreno Valley College
Moreno Valley, California

Freshman Application Contact Jamie Clifton, Director, Enrollment Services, Moreno Valley College, 16130 Lasselle Street, Moreno Valley, CA 92551. *Phone:* 951-571-6293. *E-mail:* admissions@mvc.edu. *Website:* http://www.mvc.edu/.

Mt. San Antonio College
Walnut, California

- **District-supported** 2-year, founded 1946, part of California Community College System
- **Suburban** 421-acre campus with easy access to Los Angeles
- **Coed,** 29,799 undergraduate students, 10% full-time, 8% women, 8% men

Undergraduates 2,878 full-time, 1,875 part-time. 4% Black or African American, non-Hispanic/Latino; 63% Hispanic/Latino; 18% Asian, non-Hispanic/Latino; 0.2% Native Hawaiian or other Pacific Islander, non-Hispanic/Latino; 0.2% American Indian or Alaska Native, non-Hispanic/Latino; 3% Two or more races, non-Hispanic/Latino; 0.2% Race/ethnicity unknown; 2% international. *Retention:* 80% of full-time freshmen returned.

Freshmen *Admission:* 4,753 enrolled.

Faculty *Total:* 1,304, 32% full-time. *Student/faculty ratio:* 24:1.

Majors Accounting; administrative assistant and secretarial science; advertising; agricultural business and management; agriculture; airframe mechanics and aircraft maintenance technology; airline pilot and flight crew; air traffic control; animal/livestock husbandry and production; animal sciences; apparel and textiles; applied horticulture/horticulture operations; architectural engineering technology; avionics maintenance technology; biological and physical sciences; building/construction finishing, management, and inspection related; business administration and management; business teacher education; child development; civil engineering technology; commercial and advertising art; computer and information sciences; computer engineering technology; computer graphics; computer science; corrections; criminal justice/police science; dairy science; data processing and data processing technology; drafting and design technology; drafting/design engineering technologies related; electrical, electronic and communications engineering technology; emergency medical technology (EMT paramedic); engineering technology; English language and literature related; environmental studies; family and consumer sciences/human sciences; fashion merchandising; finance; fire science/firefighting; forest technology; health and physical education/fitness; heating, air conditioning, ventilation and refrigeration maintenance technology; horse husbandry/equine science and management; horticultural science; hotel/motel administration; humanities; industrial and product design; industrial radiologic technology; interior design; journalism; kindergarten/preschool education; landscape architecture; legal administrative assistant/secretary; legal assistant/paralegal; machine tool technology; marketing/marketing management; materials science; mathematics; medical administrative assistant and medical secretary; mental health counseling; music; occupational safety and health technology; ornamental horticulture; parks, recreation and leisure; parks, recreation and leisure facilities management; photography; physical sciences related; pre-engineering; quality control technology; radio and television; real estate; registered nursing/registered nurse; respiratory care therapy; sign language interpretation and translation; social sciences; surveying technology; transportation and materials moving related; visual and performing arts; welding technology; wildlife, fish and wildlands science and management.

Academics *Calendar:* semesters. *Degree:* certificates, diplomas, and associate. *Special study options:* academic remediation for entering students, adult/continuing education programs, advanced placement credit, cooperative education, distance learning, double majors, English as a second language, honors programs, independent study, part-time degree program, services for LD students, study abroad, summer session for credit. *ROTC:* Army (b), Air Force (b).

Library Learning Resources Center. *Books:* 75,587 (physical), 82,336 (digital/electronic); *Databases:* 113. Students can reserve study rooms.

Student Life *Activities and Organizations:* drama/theater group, student-run radio station, choral group, Alpha Gamma Sigma, Muslim Student Association, Student Government, Asian Student Association, Kasama-Filipino Student Organization. *Campus security:* 24-hour emergency response devices and patrols, late-night transport/escort service. *Student services:* health clinic, personal/psychological counseling, women's center.

Athletics *Intercollegiate sports:* baseball M, basketball M/W, cheerleading M/W, cross-country running M/W, football M, golf M/W, sand volleyball W, soccer M/W, softball W, swimming and diving M/W, tennis M/W, track and field M/W, volleyball W, water polo M/W, wrestling M.

Costs (2020–21) *Tuition:* area resident $1288 full-time; state resident $1288 full-time; nonresident $9548 full-time. *Required fees:* $62 full-time. *Room and board:* $15,084.

Applying *Options:* electronic application, early admission, deferred entrance. *Required for some:* high school transcript. *Notification:* continuous (freshmen), continuous (transfers).

Freshman Application Contact Mt. San Antonio College, 1100 North Grand Avenue, Walnut, CA 91789-1399. *Website:* http://www.mtsac.edu/.

Mt. San Jacinto College
San Jacinto, California

- **District-supported** 2-year, founded 1963, part of California Community College System
- **Suburban** 180-acre campus with easy access to San Diego
- **Endowment** $1.6 million
- **Coed**

Undergraduates 5,105 full-time, 9,065 part-time. Students come from 4 states and territories; 8% Black or African American, non-Hispanic/Latino; 37% Hispanic/Latino; 5% Asian, non-Hispanic/Latino; 0.2% Native Hawaiian or other Pacific Islander, non-Hispanic/Latino; 0.4% American Indian or Alaska Native, non-Hispanic/Latino; 6% Two or more races, non-Hispanic/Latino; 0.6% Race/ethnicity unknown; 7% transferred in. *Retention:* 70% of full-time freshmen returned.

Faculty *Student/faculty ratio:* 27:1.

Academics *Calendar:* semesters. *Degree:* certificates, diplomas, and associate. *Special study options:* academic remediation for entering students, adult/continuing education programs, advanced placement credit, distance learning, double majors, English as a second language, honors programs, off-campus study, part-time degree program, services for LD students, study abroad, summer session for credit.

Library Milo P. Johnson Library plus 1 other.

Student Life *Campus security:* part-time trained security personnel.

Financial Aid Of all full-time matriculated undergraduates who enrolled in 2018, 109 Federal Work-Study jobs (averaging $1114). 125 state and other part-time jobs (averaging $1000).

Applying *Options:* early admission. *Recommended:* high school transcript.

Freshman Application Contact Mt. San Jacinto College, 1499 North State Street, San Jacinto, CA 92583-2399. *Phone:* 951-639-5212. *Website:* http://www.msjc.edu/.

MTI College
Sacramento, California

Freshman Application Contact Director of Admissions, MTI College, 5221 Madison Avenue, Sacramento, CA 95841. *Phone:* 916-339-1500. *Fax:* 916-339-0305. *Website:* http://www.mticollege.edu/.

Napa Valley College
Napa, California

- **District-supported** 2-year, founded 1942, part of California Community College System
- **Suburban** 188-acre campus with easy access to San Francisco
- **Coed**

Undergraduates 1,909 full-time, 4,999 part-time. *Retention:* 66% of full-time freshmen returned.

Faculty *Student/faculty ratio:* 22:1.

Academics *Calendar:* semesters. *Degree:* certificates and associate. *Special study options:* academic remediation for entering students, advanced placement credit, cooperative education, distance learning, English as a second language, part-time degree program, services for LD students, study abroad, summer session for credit.

Library Napa Valley College Library plus 1 other.

Student Life *Campus security:* late-night transport/escort service.

Athletics Member NJCAA.

Financial Aid Of all full-time matriculated undergraduates who enrolled in 2014, 50 Federal Work-Study jobs (averaging $2763). 63 state and other part-time jobs (averaging $2652).

Applying *Required for some:* high school transcript.
Director of Admissions Mr. Oscar De Haro, Vice President of Student Services, Napa Valley College, 2277 Napa-Vallejo Highway, Napa, CA 94558-6236. *Phone:* 707-253-3000. *Toll-free phone:* 800-826-1077. *E-mail:* odeharo@napavalley.edu. *Website:* http://www.napavalley.edu/.

National Career College
Panorama City, California

Admissions Office Contact National Career College, 14355 Roscoe Boulevard, Panorama City, CA 91402. *Website:* http://www.nccusa.edu/.

National Polytechnic College
Commerce, California

Admissions Office Contact National Polytechnic College, 6630 Telegraph Road, Commerce, CA 90040. *Website:* http://www.npcollege.edu/.

Norco College
Norco, California

Freshman Application Contact Mark DeAsis, Director, Enrollment Services, Norco College, 2001 Third Street, Norco, CA 92860. *E-mail:* admissionsnorco@norcocollege.edu. *Website:* http://www.norcocollege.edu/.

North-West College
West Covina, California

Admissions Office Contact North-West College, 2121 West Garvey Avenue, West Covina, CA 91790. *Toll-free phone:* 888-408-4211. *Website:* http://www.nw.edu/.

Ohlone College
Fremont, California

- **District-supported** 2-year, founded 1967, part of California Community College System
- **Suburban** 530-acre campus with easy access to San Jose
- **Coed**

Undergraduates 3,180 full-time, 8,138 part-time. Students come from 11 states and territories; 40 other countries; 0.2% are from out of state; 4% Black or African American, non-Hispanic/Latino; 18% Hispanic/Latino; 30% Asian, non-Hispanic/Latino; 0.7% Native Hawaiian or other Pacific Islander, non-Hispanic/Latino; 0.2% American Indian or Alaska Native, non-Hispanic/Latino; 5% Two or more races, non-Hispanic/Latino; 19% Race/ethnicity unknown; 3% international. *Retention:* 55% of full-time freshmen returned.
Faculty *Student/faculty ratio:* 27:1.
Academics *Calendar:* semesters. *Degrees:* certificates and associate (profile includes campuses in Fremont and Newark CA). *Special study options:* academic remediation for entering students, adult/continuing education programs, advanced placement credit, cooperative education, distance learning, double majors, English as a second language, external degree program, honors programs, internships, off-campus study, part-time degree program, services for LD students, student-designed majors, study abroad, summer session for credit. *ROTC:* Army (c), Air Force (c).
Library Ohlone College Library plus 1 other.
Student Life *Campus security:* 24-hour emergency response devices and patrols, late-night transport/escort service.
Financial Aid Of all full-time matriculated undergraduates who enrolled in 2018, 35 Federal Work-Study jobs (averaging $1800).
Applying *Options:* early admission. *Required for some:* high school transcript.
Freshman Application Contact Ohlone College, 43600 Mission Boulevard, Fremont, CA 94539-5884. *Phone:* 510-659-6107. *Website:* http://www.ohlone.edu/.

Orange Coast College
Costa Mesa, California

Admissions Office Contact Orange Coast College, 2701 Fairview Road, Costa Mesa, CA 92626. *Website:* http://www.orangecoastcollege.edu/.

Oxnard College
Oxnard, California

Freshman Application Contact Mr. Joel Diaz, Registrar, Oxnard College, 4000 South Rose Avenue, Oxnard, CA 93033-6699. *Phone:* 805-986-5843. *Fax:* 805-986-5943. *E-mail:* jdiaz@vcccd.edu. *Website:* http://www.oxnardcollege.edu/.

Palomar College
San Marcos, California

Freshman Application Contact Dr. Kendyl Magnuson, Senior Director of Enrollment Services, Palomar College, 1140 W Mission Road, San Marcos, CA 92069. *Phone:* 760-744-1150 Ext. 2171. *Fax:* 760-744-2932. *E-mail:* kmagnuson@palomar.edu. *Website:* http://www.palomar.edu/.

Palo Verde College
Blythe, California

Freshman Application Contact Diana Rodriguez, Vice President of Student Services, Palo Verde College, 1 College Drive, Blythe, CA 92225. *Phone:* 760-921-5428. *Fax:* 760-921-3608. *E-mail:* diana.rodriguez@paloverde.edu. *Website:* http://www.paloverde.edu/.

Pasadena City College
Pasadena, California

Admissions Office Contact Pasadena City College, 1570 East Colorado Boulevard, Pasadena, CA 91106-2041. *Website:* http://www.pasadena.edu/.

PCI College
Cerritos, California

Admissions Office Contact PCI College, 17215 Studebaker Road #310, Cerritos, CA 90703. *Website:* http://www.pci-ed.com/.

Pima Medical Institute - Chula Vista
Chula Vista, California

Freshman Application Contact Admissions Office, Pima Medical Institute - Chula Vista, 780 Bay Boulevard, Chula Vista, CA 91910. *Phone:* 619-425-3200. *Toll-free phone:* 800-477-PIMA. *Website:* http://www.pmi.edu/.

Platt College
Alhambra, California

Director of Admissions Mr. Detroit Whiteside, Director of Admissions, Platt College, 1000 South Fremont A9W, Alhambra, CA 91803. *Phone:* 323-258-8050. *Toll-free phone:* 888-866-6697 (in-state); 888-80-PLATT (out-of-state). *Website:* http://www.plattcollege.edu/.

Platt College
Anaheim, California

Admissions Office Contact Platt College, 1551 South Douglass Road, Anaheim, CA 92806. *Website:* http://www.plattcollege.edu/.

Platt College
Ontario, California

Director of Admissions Ms. Jennifer Abandonato, Director of Admissions, Platt College, 3700 Inland Empire Boulevard, Ontario, CA 91764. *Phone:* 909-941-9410. *Toll-free phone:* 888-80-PLATT. *Website:* http://www.plattcollege.edu/.

Porterville College
Porterville, California

Director of Admissions Ms. Judy Pope, Director of Admissions and Records/Registrar, Porterville College, 100 East College Avenue, Porterville, CA 93257-6058. *Phone:* 559-791-2222. *Website:* http://www.portervillecollege.edu/.

Professional Golfers Career College

Temecula, California

Freshman Application Contact Mr. Gary Gilleon, Professional Golfers Career College, 26109 Ynez Road, Temecula, CA 92591. *Phone:* 951-719-2994 Ext. 1021. *Toll-free phone:* 800-877-4380. *Fax:* 951-719-1643. *E-mail:* garygilleon@golfcollege.edu. *Website:* http://www.golfcollege.edu/.

Reedley College

Reedley, California

Freshman Application Contact Admissions and Records Office, Reedley College, 995 North Reed Avenue, Reedley, CA 93654. *Phone:* 559-638-0323. *Fax:* 559-637-2523. *Website:* http://www.reedleycollege.edu/.

Rio Hondo College

Whittier, California

Freshman Application Contact Rio Hondo College, 3600 Workman Mill Road, Whittier, CA 90601-1699. *Phone:* 562-692-0921 Ext. 3415. *Website:* http://www.riohondo.edu/.

Riverside City College

Riverside, California

Freshman Application Contact Joy Chambers, Dean of Enrollment Services, Riverside City College, Riverside, CA 92506. *Phone:* 951-222-8600. *Fax:* 951-222-8037. *E-mail:* admissionsriverside@rcc.edu. *Website:* http://www.rcc.edu/.

Sacramento City College

Sacramento, California

Director of Admissions Mr. Sam T. Sandusky, Dean, Student Services, Sacramento City College, 3835 Freeport Boulevard, Sacramento, CA 95822-1386. *Phone:* 916-558-2438. *Website:* http://www.scc.losrios.edu/.

Saddleback College

Mission Viejo, California

Freshman Application Contact Admissions Office, Saddleback College, 28000 Marguerite Parkway, Mission Viejo, CA 92692. *Phone:* 949-582-4555. *Fax:* 949-347-8315. *E-mail:* earaiza@saddleback.edu. *Website:* http://www.saddleback.edu/.

The Salvation Army College for Officer Training at Crestmont

Rancho Palos Verdes, California

Freshman Application Contact Capt. Brian Jones, Director of Curriculum, The Salvation Army College for Officer Training at Crestmont, 30840 Hawthorne Boulevard, Rancho Palos Verdes, CA 90275. *Phone:* 310-544-6442. *Fax:* 310-265-6520. *Website:* http://www.crestmont.edu/.

San Bernardino Valley College

San Bernardino, California

Director of Admissions Ms. Helena Johnson, Director of Admissions and Records, San Bernardino Valley College, 701 South Mount Vernon Avenue, San Bernardino, CA 92410-2748. *Phone:* 909-384-4401. *Website:* http://www.valleycollege.edu/.

San Diego City College

San Diego, California

Freshman Application Contact Ms. Lou Humphries, Registrar/Supervisor of Admissions, Records, Evaluations and Veterans, San Diego City College, 1313 Park Boulevard, San Diego, CA 92101-4787. *Phone:* 619-388-3474. *Fax:* 619-388-3505. *E-mail:* lhumphri@sdccd.edu. *Website:* http://www.sdcity.edu/.

San Diego Mesa College

San Diego, California

Freshman Application Contact Ms. Cheri Sawyer, Admissions Supervisor, San Diego Mesa College, 7250 Mesa College Drive, San Diego, CA 92111. *Phone:* 619-388-2686. *Fax:* 619-388-2960. *E-mail:* csawyer@sdccd.edu. *Website:* http://www.sdmesa.edu/.

San Diego Miramar College

San Diego, California

Freshman Application Contact Ms. Dana Stack, Admissions Supervisor, San Diego Miramar College, 10440 Black Mountain Road, San Diego, CA 92126-2999. *Phone:* 619-536-7854. *E-mail:* dstack@sdccd.edu. *Website:* http://www.sdmiramar.edu/.

San Joaquin Delta College

Stockton, California

- **District-supported** 2-year, founded 1935, part of California Community College System
- **Urban** 165-acre campus with easy access to Sacramento
- **Coed,** 18,102 undergraduate students

Undergraduates Students come from 20 states and territories; 0.2% are from out of state; 13% Black or African American, non-Hispanic/Latino; 44% Hispanic/Latino; 17% Asian, non-Hispanic/Latino; 0.5% Native Hawaiian or other Pacific Islander, non-Hispanic/Latino; 0.3% American Indian or Alaska Native, non-Hispanic/Latino; 5% Two or more races, non-Hispanic/Latino; 0.5% Race/ethnicity unknown; 0.3% international. *Retention:* 77% of full-time freshmen returned.

Faculty *Total:* 544, 41% full-time. *Student/faculty ratio:* 27:1.

Majors Accounting; agricultural business and management; agricultural mechanization; agriculture; animal sciences; anthropology; art; automobile/automotive mechanics technology; biology/biological sciences; broadcast journalism; business administration and management; chemistry; civil engineering technology; commercial and advertising art; comparative literature; computer science; construction engineering technology; corrections; criminal justice/police science; crop production; culinary arts; dance; dramatic/theater arts; economics; electrical, electronic and communications engineering technology; engineering; engineering related; engineering technology; English; family and consumer sciences/human sciences; fashion merchandising; fire science/firefighting; geology/earth science; heating, air conditioning, ventilation and refrigeration maintenance technology; history; humanities; journalism; liberal arts and sciences/liberal studies; licensed practical/vocational nurse training; machine tool technology; mathematics; mechanical engineering/mechanical technology; music; natural resources management and policy; natural sciences; ornamental horticulture; philosophy; photography; physical education teaching and coaching; physical sciences; political science and government; psychology; registered nursing/registered nurse; religious studies; rhetoric and composition; social sciences; sociology.

Academics *Calendar:* semesters. *Degree:* certificates and associate. *Special study options:* academic remediation for entering students, adult/continuing education programs, advanced placement credit, cooperative education, distance learning, English as a second language, honors programs, independent study, part-time degree program, services for LD students, summer session for credit.

Library Goleman Library plus 1 other.

Student Life *Housing:* college housing not available. *Activities and Organizations:* drama/theater group, student-run newspaper, radio and television station, choral group. *Campus security:* 24-hour emergency response devices and patrols, late-night transport/escort service. *Student services:* personal/psychological counseling, legal services, veterans affairs office.

Athletics Member NJCAA. *Intercollegiate sports:* baseball M, basketball M/W, cross-country running M/W, fencing M/W, football M, golf M/W, soccer M/W, softball W, swimming and diving M/W, tennis M/W, track and field M/W, volleyball W, water polo M/W, wrestling M. *Intramural sports:* badminton M/W, basketball M/W, bowling M/W, soccer M/W, swimming and diving M/W, tennis M/W, ultimate Frisbee M/W, volleyball M/W, weight lifting M/W.

Costs (2019–20) *Tuition:* state resident $1288 full-time, $644 per year part-time; nonresident $7420 full-time, $3710 per year part-time. Full-time tuition and fees vary according to course load. Part-time tuition and fees vary according to course load. *Payment plan:* installment. *Waivers:* employees or children of employees.

Financial Aid Of all full-time matriculated undergraduates who enrolled in 2018, 10,718 applied for aid, 9,634 were judged to have need, 79 had their need fully met. In 2018, 6 non-need-based awards were made. *Average percent of need met:* 30%. *Average financial aid package:* $6003. *Average*

need-based loan: $2477. *Average need-based gift aid:* $5823. *Average non-need-based aid:* $229. *Average indebtedness upon graduation:* $11,752.
Applying *Options:* electronic application, early admission. *Application deadlines:* rolling (freshmen), rolling (transfers). *Notification:* continuous (freshmen), continuous (transfers).
Freshman Application Contact Ms. Amy Courtright, Registrar, San Joaquin Delta College, 5151 Pacific Avenue, Stockton, CA 95207. *Phone:* 209-954-5151 Ext. 6182. *E-mail:* amy.courtright@deltacollege.edu.
Website: http://www.deltacollege.edu/.

San Joaquin Valley College
Hanford, California

Freshman Application Contact San Joaquin Valley College, 215 West 7th Street, Hanford, CA 93230. *Toll-free phone:* 866-544-7898. *Website:* http://www.sjvc.edu/campuses/central-california/hanford/.

San Joaquin Valley College
Hesperia, California

Freshman Application Contact San Joaquin Valley College, 9331 Mariposa Road, Hesperia, CA 92344. *Toll-free phone:* 866-544-7898. *Website:* http://www.sjvc.edu/campuses/southern-california/victor-valley/.

San Joaquin Valley College
Temecula, California

Freshman Application Contact Ms. Robyn Whiles, Enrollment Services Director, San Joaquin Valley College, 27270 Madison Avenue, Suite 103, Temecula, CA 92590. *Phone:* 559-651-2500. *Toll-free phone:* 866-544-7898. *E-mail:* admissions@sjvc.edu. *Website:* http://www.sjvc.edu/campuses/southern-california/temecula/.

San Joaquin Valley College
Visalia, California

Freshman Application Contact Susie Topjian, Enrollment Services Director, San Joaquin Valley College, 8400 West Mineral King Boulevard, Visalia, CA 93291. *Phone:* 559-651-2500. *Toll-free phone:* 866-544-7898. *Fax:* 559-734-9048. *E-mail:* admissions@sjvc.edu. *Website:* http://www.sjvc.edu/campuses/central-california/visalia/.

San Joaquin Valley College - Antelope Valley (Lancaster)
Lancaster, California

Freshman Application Contact San Joaquin Valley College - Antelope Valley (Lancaster), 42135 10th Street West, Suite 147, Lancaster, CA 93534. *Toll-free phone:* 866-544-7898. *Website:* http://www.sjvc.edu/campuses/southern-california/antelope-valley/.

San Joaquin Valley College - Bakersfield
Bakersfield, California

Freshman Application Contact Enrollment Services Director, San Joaquin Valley College - Bakersfield, 201 New Stine Road, Bakersfield, CA 93309. *Phone:* 661-834-0126. *Toll-free phone:* 866-544-7898. *Fax:* 661-834-8124. *E-mail:* admissions@sjvc.edu. *Website:* http://www.sjvc.edu/campuses/central-california/bakersfield.

San Joaquin Valley College - Fresno
Fresno, California

Freshman Application Contact Enrollment Services Director, San Joaquin Valley College - Fresno, 295 East Sierra Avenue, Fresno, CA 93710. *Phone:* 559-448-8282. *Toll-free phone:* 866-544-7898. *Fax:* 559-448-8250. *E-mail:* admissions@sjvc.edu. *Website:* http://www.sjvc.edu/campuses/central-california/fresno/.

San Joaquin Valley College–Fresno Aviation Campus
Fresno, California

Freshman Application Contact Enrollment Services Coordinator, San Joaquin Valley College–Fresno Aviation Campus, 4985 East Anderson Avenue, Fresno, CA 93727. *Phone:* 559-453-0123. *Toll-free phone:* 866-544-7898. *Fax:* 599-453-0133. *E-mail:* admissions@sjvc.edu. *Website:* http://www.sjvc.edu/campuses/central-california/fresno-aviation/.

San Joaquin Valley College Modesto (Salida)
Salida, California

Freshman Application Contact Enrollment Services Director, San Joaquin Valley College Modesto (Salida), 5380 Pirrone Road, Salida, CA 95368. *Phone:* 209-543-8800. *Toll-free phone:* 866-544-7898. *Fax:* 209-543-8320. *E-mail:* admissions@sjvc.edu. *Website:* http://www.sjvc.edu/campuses/northern-california/modesto/.

San Joaquin Valley College–Online
Visalia, California

Freshman Application Contact Enrollment Services Director, San Joaquin Valley College–Online, 8344 West Mineral King Avenue, Visalia, CA 93291. *Toll-free phone:* 866-544-7898. *E-mail:* admissions@sjvc.edu. *Website:* http://www.sjvc.edu/online-programs/.

San Joaquin Valley College - Ontario
Ontario, California

Freshman Application Contact Enrollment Services Director, San Joaquin Valley College - Ontario, 4580 Ontario Mills Parkway, Ontario, CA 91764. *Phone:* 909-948-7582. *Toll-free phone:* 866-544-7898. *Fax:* 909-948-3860. *E-mail:* admissions@sjvc.edu. *Website:* http://www.sjvc.edu/campuses/southern-california/ontario/.

San Joaquin Valley College - Rancho Cordova
Rancho Cordova, California

Freshman Application Contact Enrollment Services Director, San Joaquin Valley College - Rancho Cordova, 11050 Olson Drive, Suite 210, Rancho Cordova, CA 95670. *Phone:* 916-638-7582. *Toll-free phone:* 866-544-7898. *Fax:* 916-638-7553. *E-mail:* admissions@sjvc.edu. *Website:* http://www.sjvc.edu/campuses/northern-california/rancho-cordova/.

San Jose City College
San Jose, California

Freshman Application Contact Mr. Carlo Santos, Director of Admissions/Registrar, San Jose City College, 2100 Moorpark Avenue, San Jose, CA 95128-2799. *Phone:* 408-288-3707. *Fax:* 408-298-1935. *Website:* http://www.sjcc.edu/.

Santa Ana College
Santa Ana, California

Freshman Application Contact Mrs. Christie Steward, Admissions Clerk, Santa Ana College, 1530 West 17th Street, Santa Ana, CA 92706-3398. *Phone:* 714-564-6053. *Website:* http://www.sac.edu/.

Santa Barbara Business College
Bakersfield, California

Admissions Office Contact Santa Barbara Business College, 5300 California Avenue, Bakersfield, CA 93309. *Website:* http://www.sbbcollege.edu/.

Santa Barbara Business College
Santa Maria, California

Admissions Office Contact Santa Barbara Business College, 303 East Plaza Drive, Santa Maria, CA 93454. *Website:* http://www.sbbcollege.edu/.

Santa Barbara City College

Santa Barbara, California

- **District-supported** 2-year, founded 1908, part of California Community College System
- **Small-town** 65-acre campus
- **Endowment** $21.1 million
- **Coed**

Undergraduates 7,952 full-time, 10,140 part-time. Students come from 66 other countries; 6% are from out of state; 3% Black or African American, non-Hispanic/Latino; 29% Hispanic/Latino; 3% Asian, non-Hispanic/Latino; 1% Native Hawaiian or other Pacific Islander, non-Hispanic/Latino; 0.7% American Indian or Alaska Native, non-Hispanic/Latino; 4% Two or more races, non-Hispanic/Latino; 3% Race/ethnicity unknown; 10% international; 5% transferred in.
Faculty *Student/faculty ratio:* 27:1.
Academics *Calendar:* semesters. *Degree:* certificates and associate. *Special study options:* academic remediation for entering students, adult/continuing education programs, advanced placement credit, cooperative education, distance learning, double majors, English as a second language, honors programs, independent study, internships, part-time degree program, services for LD students, study abroad, summer session for credit. *ROTC:* Army (c).
Library Eli Luria Library.
Student Life *Campus security:* 24-hour emergency response devices and patrols, late-night transport/escort service.
Financial Aid Of all full-time matriculated undergraduates who enrolled in 2014, 179 Federal Work-Study jobs (averaging $4299).
Applying *Options:* electronic application, early admission. *Recommended:* high school transcript.
Freshman Application Contact Ms. Allison Curtis, Director of Admissions and Records, Santa Barbara City College, Santa Barbara, CA 93109. *Phone:* 805-965-0581 Ext. 2352. *Fax:* 805-962-0497. *E-mail:* admissions@sbcc.edu. *Website:* http://www.sbcc.edu/.

Santa Monica College

Santa Monica, California

Freshman Application Contact Santa Monica College, 1900 Pico Boulevard, Santa Monica, CA 90405-1628. *Phone:* 310-434-4774. *Website:* http://www.smc.edu/.

Santa Rosa Junior College

Santa Rosa, California

- **District-supported** 2-year, founded 1918, part of California Community College System
- **Urban** 100-acre campus with easy access to San Francisco
- **Endowment** $41.3 million
- **Coed**

Undergraduates Students come from 36 other countries; 3% are from out of state; 2% Black or African American, non-Hispanic/Latino; 34% Hispanic/Latino; 5% Asian, non-Hispanic/Latino; 0.3% Native Hawaiian or other Pacific Islander, non-Hispanic/Latino; 0.7% American Indian or Alaska Native, non-Hispanic/Latino; 4% Two or more races, non-Hispanic/Latino; 7% Race/ethnicity unknown.
Academics *Calendar:* semesters. *Degree:* certificates and associate. *Special study options:* academic remediation for entering students, adult/continuing education programs, advanced placement credit, cooperative education, distance learning, English as a second language, independent study, internships, off-campus study, part-time degree program, services for LD students, study abroad, summer session for credit.
Library Doyle Library plus 1 other. Students can reserve study rooms.
Student Life *Campus security:* 24-hour emergency response devices and patrols, student patrols.
Financial Aid Of all full-time matriculated undergraduates who enrolled in 2009, 135 Federal Work-Study jobs (averaging $2210). 43 state and other part-time jobs (averaging $7396).
Applying *Options:* electronic application, early admission.
Admissions Office Contact Santa Rosa Junior College, 1501 Mendocino Avenue, Santa Rosa, CA 95401-4395. *Website:* http://www.santarosa.edu/.

Santiago Canyon College

Orange, California

Freshman Application Contact Tuyen Nguyen, Admissions and Records, Santiago Canyon College, 8045 East Chapman Avenue, Orange, CA 92869. *Phone:* 714-628-4902. *Website:* http://www.sccollege.edu/.

Shasta College

Redding, California

- **District-supported** 2-year, founded 1948, part of California Community College System
- **Rural** 336-acre campus
- **Endowment** $1.3 million
- **Coed**

Undergraduates 4,336 full-time, 5,904 part-time. 2% are from out of state.
Academics *Calendar:* semesters. *Degree:* certificates and associate. *Special study options:* academic remediation for entering students, adult/continuing education programs, advanced placement credit, cooperative education, distance learning, double majors, English as a second language, honors programs, internships, part-time degree program, services for LD students, summer session for credit.
Library Shasta College Learning Resource Center.
Student Life *Campus security:* 24-hour emergency response devices, student patrols, late-night transport/escort service, 16-hour patrols by trained security personnel.
Financial Aid Of all full-time matriculated undergraduates who enrolled in 2013, 66 Federal Work-Study jobs (averaging $2448).
Applying *Options:* early admission. *Required:* high school transcript.
Director of Admissions Dr. Kevin O'Rorke, Dean of Enrollment Services, Shasta College, PO Box 496006, 11555 Old Oregon Trail, Redding, CA 96049-6006. *Phone:* 530-242-7669. *Website:* http://www.shastacollege.edu/.

Sierra College

Rocklin, California

- **District-supported** 2-year, founded 1936, part of California Community College System
- **Suburban** 327-acre campus with easy access to Sacramento
- **Coed,** 19,165 undergraduate students, 34% full-time, 54% women, 44% men

Undergraduates 6,477 full-time, 12,319 part-time. Students come from 22 states and territories; 8 other countries; 0.7% are from out of state; 4% Black or African American, non-Hispanic/Latino; 8% Hispanic/Latino; 9% Asian, non-Hispanic/Latino; 0.8% Native Hawaiian or other Pacific Islander, non-Hispanic/Latino; 1% American Indian or Alaska Native, non-Hispanic/Latino; 0.4% Race/ethnicity unknown; 0.5% international; 1% live on campus. *Retention:* 68% of full-time freshmen returned.
Freshmen *Admission:* 24,000 applied, 24,000 admitted, 3,914 enrolled.
Majors Accounting; administrative assistant and secretarial science; agriculture; American Sign Language (ASL); animal/livestock husbandry and production; apparel and textile manufacturing; apparel and textile marketing management; applied horticulture/horticulture operations; architectural drafting and CAD/CADD; art; automobile/automotive mechanics technology; biological and physical sciences; biology/biological sciences; business administration and management; business/commerce; cabinetmaking and millwork; chemistry; child development; commercial photography; computer and information sciences and support services related; computer installation and repair technology; computer programming; computer systems networking and telecommunications; construction trades; criminal justice/police science; data entry/microcomputer applications; digital communication and media/multimedia; electrical/electronics equipment installation and repair; engineering; English; equestrian studies; fire science/firefighting; forestry; general studies; geology/earth science; graphic design; hazardous materials management and waste technology; health and physical education/fitness; industrial electronics technology; information technology; liberal arts and sciences/liberal studies; licensed practical/vocational nurse training; manufacturing engineering technology; mathematics; mechanical drafting and CAD/CADD; music; network and system administration; parks, recreation and leisure; philosophy; physics; psychology; real estate; registered nursing/registered nurse; rhetoric and composition; sales, distribution, and marketing operations; small business administration; social sciences; visual and performing arts; web page, digital/multimedia and information resources design; women's studies.
Academics *Calendar:* semesters. *Degree:* certificates and associate. *Special study options:* academic remediation for entering students, accelerated degree program, advanced placement credit, distance learning, double majors, English as a second language, honors programs, independent study, internships, off-campus study, part-time degree program, services for LD students, study abroad, summer session for credit.
Library Leary Resource Center plus 1 other.
Student Life *Housing Options:* coed. Campus housing is university owned. *Activities and Organizations:* drama/theater group, student-run newspaper, choral group, Drama Club, Student Government, Art Club, Band, Aggie Club. *Campus security:* 24-hour emergency response devices and patrols, late-night

transport/escort service. *Student services:* health clinic, personal/psychological counseling.
Athletics *Intercollegiate sports:* baseball M, basketball M/W, football M, golf M, soccer W, softball W, swimming and diving M/W, tennis M/W, volleyball W, water polo M/W, wrestling M. *Intramural sports:* archery M/W, badminton M/W, basketball M/W, tennis M/W, volleyball M/W.
Applying *Options:* electronic application, early admission. *Application deadline:* rolling (freshmen). *Notification:* continuous (freshmen), continuous (transfers).
Freshman Application Contact Sierra College, 5100 Sierra College Boulevard, Rocklin, CA 95677. *Phone:* 916-660-7341.
Website: http://www.sierracollege.edu/.

Skyline College
San Bruno, California

Freshman Application Contact Terry Stats, Admissions Office, Skyline College, 3300 College Drive, San Bruno, CA 94066-1698. *Phone:* 650-738-4251. *E-mail:* stats@smccd.net. *Website:* http://skylinecollege.edu/.

Solano Community College
Fairfield, California

Freshman Application Contact Solano Community College, 4000 Suisun Valley Road, Fairfield, CA 94534. *Phone:* 707-864-7000 Ext. 4313. *Website:* http://www.solano.edu/.

South Coast College
Orange, California

Director of Admissions South Coast College, 2011 West Chapman Avenue, Orange, CA 92868. *Toll-free phone:* 877-568-6130. *Website:* http://www.southcoastcollege.edu/.

Southwestern College
Chula Vista, California

Freshman Application Contact Admissions, Southwestern College, 900 Otay Lakes Road, Chula Vista, CA 91910-7299. *Phone:* 619-421-6700 Ext. 5215. *Fax:* 619-482-6489. *Website:* http://www.swccd.edu/.

Spartan College of Aeronautics and Technology
Inglewood, California

Freshman Application Contact Admissions Office, Spartan College of Aeronautics and Technology, 8911 Aviation Boulevard, Inglewood, CA 90301. *Phone:* 866-451-0818. *Toll-free phone:* 800-879-0554. *Website:* http://www.spartan.edu/.

Taft College
Taft, California

Freshman Application Contact Nichole Cook, Admissions/Counseling Technician, Taft College, 29 Cougar Court, Taft, CA 93268. *Phone:* 661-763-7790. *Fax:* 661-763-7758. *E-mail:* ncook@taftcollege.edu. *Website:* http://www.taftcollege.edu/.

Theatre of Arts
Hollywood, California

- **Proprietary** primarily 2-year, part of Campus Hollywood
- **Urban** campus with easy access to Los Angeles
- **Coed**

Faculty *Total:* 17.
Academics *Degree:* bachelor's.
Library Jessica plus 1 other. Weekly public service hours: 40; study areas open 24 hours, 5–7 days a week.
Student Life *Housing Options:* Campus housing is university owned. *Activities and Organizations:* drama/theater group.
Costs (2020–21) *One-time required fee:* $75. *Comprehensive fee:* $76,376 includes full-time tuition ($39,996), mandatory fees ($19,800), and room and board ($16,580). No tuition increase for student's term of enrollment. *Room and board:* college room only: $11,164. Room and board charges vary according to housing facility. *Payment plans:* installment, deferred payment.
Applying *Options:* electronic application. *Required:* high school transcript, interview. *Application deadline:* 1/8 (freshmen).
Freshman Application Contact Theatre of Arts, 1536 North Highland Avenue, Hollywood, CA 90028. *Phone:* 323-3371064.
Website: http://www.toa.edu/.

Unitek College
Fremont, California

Admissions Office Contact Unitek College, 4670 Auto Mall Parkway, Fremont, CA 94538. *Website:* http://www.unitekcollege.edu/.

Valley College of Medical Careers
West Hills, California

Admissions Office Contact Valley College of Medical Careers, 8399 Topanga Canyon Boulevard, Suite 200, West Hills, CA 91304. *Website:* http://www.vcmc.edu/.

Ventura College
Ventura, California

- **District-supported** 2-year, founded 1925, part of California Community College System
- **Suburban** 103-acre campus with easy access to Los Angeles
- **Coed**

Undergraduates 11% are from out of state.
Faculty *Student/faculty ratio:* 26:1.
Academics *Calendar:* semesters. *Degree:* certificates, diplomas, and associate. *Special study options:* academic remediation for entering students, adult/continuing education programs, advanced placement credit, English as a second language, independent study, internships, part-time degree program, services for LD students, summer session for credit.
Library Ventura College Library.
Student Life *Campus security:* 24-hour emergency response devices and patrols, student patrols.
Financial Aid Of all full-time matriculated undergraduates who enrolled in 2018, 70 Federal Work-Study jobs.
Applying *Required:* high school transcript.
Freshman Application Contact Ms. Susan Bricker, Registrar, Ventura College, 4667 Telegraph Road, Ventura, CA 93003-3899. *Phone:* 805-654-6456. *Fax:* 805-654-6357. *E-mail:* sbricker@vcccd.net. *Website:* http://www.venturacollege.edu/.

Victor Valley College
Victorville, California

Freshman Application Contact Ms. Greta Moon, Interim Director of Admissions and Records, Victor Valley College, 18422 Bear Valley Road, Victorville, CA 92395. *Phone:* 760-245-4271. *Fax:* 760-843-7707. *E-mail:* moong@vvc.edu. *Website:* http://www.vvc.edu/.

West Coast Ultrasound Institute
Beverly Hills, California

Admissions Office Contact West Coast Ultrasound Institute, 291 S. La Cienega Boulevard, Suite 500, Beverly Hills, CA 90211. *Website:* http://wcui.edu/.

West Hills College - Coalinga
Coalinga, California

Freshman Application Contact Sandra Dagnino, West Hills College - Coalinga, 300 Cherry Lane, Coalinga, CA 93210-1399. *Phone:* 559-934-3203. *Toll-free phone:* 800-266-1114. *Fax:* 559-934-2830. *E-mail:* sandradagnino@westhillscollege.com. *Website:* http://www.westhillscollege.com/.

West Hills College - Lemoore
Lemoore, California

Admissions Office Contact West Hills College - Lemoore, 555 College Avenue, Lemoore, CA 93245. *Website:* http://www.westhillscollege.com/.

West Los Angeles College

Culver City, California

Director of Admissions Mr. Len Isaksen, Director of Admissions, West Los Angeles College, 9000 Overland Avenue, Culver City, CA 90230-3519. *Phone:* 310-287-4255. *Website:* http://www.lacolleges.net/.

West Valley College

Saratoga, California

Freshman Application Contact Ms. Barbara Ogilive, Supervisor, Admissions and Records, West Valley College, 14000 Fruitvale Avenue, Saratoga, CA 95070-5698. *Phone:* 408-741-4630. *E-mail:* barbara_ogilvie@westvalley.edu. *Website:* http://www.westvalley.edu/.

Woodland Community College

Woodland, California

Admissions Office Contact Woodland Community College, 2300 East Gibson Road, Woodland, CA 95776. *Website:* http://wcc.yccd.edu/.

Yuba College

Marysville, California

Director of Admissions Dr. David Farrell, Dean of Student Development, Yuba College, 2088 North Beale Road, Marysville, CA 95901-7699. *Phone:* 530-741-6705. *Website:* http://yc.yccd.edu/.

COLORADO

Aims Community College

Greeley, Colorado

- **District-supported** 2-year, founded 1967
- **Urban** 185-acre campus with easy access to Denver
- **Coed**

Undergraduates 2,205 full-time, 3,894 part-time. 2% are from out of state; 2% Black or African American, non-Hispanic/Latino; 39% Hispanic/Latino; 1% Asian, non-Hispanic/Latino; 0.2% Native Hawaiian or other Pacific Islander, non-Hispanic/Latino; 0.5% American Indian or Alaska Native, non-Hispanic/Latino; 3% Two or more races, non-Hispanic/Latino; 0.7% Race/ethnicity unknown; 3% transferred in; 100% live on campus. *Retention:* 70% of full-time freshmen returned.
Faculty *Student/faculty ratio:* 18:1.
Academics *Calendar:* semesters. *Degree:* certificates, diplomas, and associate. *Special study options:* academic remediation for entering students, adult/continuing education programs, advanced placement credit, cooperative education, English as a second language, external degree program, freshman honors college, honors programs, part-time degree program, student-designed majors, summer session for credit. *ROTC:* Air Force (c).
Library Aims Community College Library.
Student Life *Campus security:* 24-hour emergency response devices, day and evening patrols by trained security personnel.
Costs (2019–20) *Tuition:* area resident $2021 full-time; state resident $3172 full-time; nonresident $12,758 full-time. Full-time tuition and fees vary according to program. Part-time tuition and fees vary according to program. *Required fees:* $260 full-time.
Applying *Options:* early admission, deferred entrance.
Freshman Application Contact Ms. Susie Gallardo, Admissions Technician, Aims Community College, Box 69, 5401 West 20th Street, Greeley, CO 80632-0069. *Phone:* 970-330-8008 Ext. 6624. *E-mail:* wgreen@chiron.aims.edu. *Website:* http://www.aims.edu/.

Arapahoe Community College

Littleton, Colorado

- **State-supported** primarily 2-year, founded 1965, part of Colorado Community College and Occupational Education System
- **Suburban** 52-acre campus with easy access to Denver
- **Coed,** 10,963 undergraduate students, 19% full-time, 56% women, 44% men

Undergraduates 2,051 full-time, 8,912 part-time. Students come from 36 states and territories; 6% are from out of state; 3% Black or African American, non-Hispanic/Latino; 16% Hispanic/Latino; 4% Asian, non-Hispanic/Latino; 0.3% Native Hawaiian or other Pacific Islander, non-Hispanic/Latino; 0.6% American Indian or Alaska Native, non-Hispanic/Latino; 4% Two or more races, non-Hispanic/Latino; 5% Race/ethnicity unknown; 2% international; 6% transferred in.
Freshmen *Admission:* 1,956 applied, 1,956 admitted, 1,083 enrolled.
Faculty *Total:* 532, 19% full-time. *Student/faculty ratio:* 20:1.
Majors Accounting technology and bookkeeping; architectural engineering technology; automation engineer technology; automobile/automotive mechanics technology; building/construction site management; business administration and management; clinical/medical laboratory technology; commercial photography; computer and information sciences; computer and information systems security; computer programming (specific applications); computer systems networking and telecommunications; cosmetology; criminal justice/law enforcement administration; crisis/emergency/disaster management; emergency medical technology (EMT paramedic); funeral service and mortuary science; game and interactive media design; general studies; graphic design; health information/medical records technology; interior design; journalism; legal assistant/paralegal; liberal arts and sciences and humanities related; liberal arts and sciences/liberal studies; mechanical engineering/mechanical technology; music technology; physical therapy technology; registered nursing/registered nurse; retailing; science technologies related; telecommunications technology.
Academics *Calendar:* semesters. *Degrees:* certificates, diplomas, associate, and bachelor's. *Special study options:* academic remediation for entering students, accelerated degree program, adult/continuing education programs, advanced placement credit, cooperative education, distance learning, double majors, English as a second language, external degree program, independent study, internships, off-campus study, part-time degree program, services for LD students, study abroad, summer session for credit. *ROTC:* Army (c), Air Force (c).
Library ACC Library & Learning Commons plus 1 other. *Books:* 30,246 (physical), 372,182 (digital/electronic); *Serial titles:* 550 (physical), 191,651 (digital/electronic); *Databases:* 77. Weekly public service hours: 69; students can reserve study rooms.
Student Life *Housing:* college housing not available. *Activities and Organizations:* drama/theater group, student-run newspaper, choral group, National Society of Leadership and Success, Phi Theta Kappa, American Society of Interior Designers, History Club, STEM Club. *Campus security:* 24-hour emergency response devices and patrols, late-night transport/escort service. *Student services:* personal/psychological counseling, veterans affairs office.
Costs (2019–20) *Tuition:* state resident $4467 full-time, $149 per credit hour part-time; nonresident $18,327 full-time, $611 per credit hour part-time. Full-time tuition and fees vary according to degree level, program, and reciprocity agreements. Part-time tuition and fees vary according to degree level, program, and reciprocity agreements. *Required fees:* $347 full-time, $12 per credit hour part-time, $24 per term part-time. *Payment plan:* installment. *Waivers:* employees or children of employees.
Financial Aid Of all full-time matriculated undergraduates who enrolled in 2018, 1,101 applied for aid. 50 Federal Work-Study jobs (averaging $2642). 142 state and other part-time jobs (averaging $3138).
Applying *Options:* electronic application, early admission, deferred entrance. *Application deadlines:* rolling (freshmen), rolling (out-of-state freshmen), rolling (transfers). *Notification:* continuous (freshmen), continuous (out-of-state freshmen), continuous (transfers).
Freshman Application Contact Arapahoe Community College, 5900 South Santa Fe Drive, PO Box 9002, Littleton, CO 80160-9002. *Phone:* 303-797-5623.
Website: http://www.arapahoe.edu/.

Bel–Rea Institute of Animal Technology

Denver, Colorado

- **Proprietary** 2-year, founded 1971
- **Suburban** 6-acre campus with easy access to Denver
- **Coed,** 275 undergraduate students, 100% full-time, 93% women, 7% men

Undergraduates 275 full-time. Students come from 18 states and territories; 2 other countries; 40% are from out of state; 0.4% Black or African American, non-Hispanic/Latino; 10% Hispanic/Latino; 0.7% Asian, non-Hispanic/Latino; 0.4% Native Hawaiian or other Pacific Islander, non-Hispanic/Latino; 0.4% American Indian or Alaska Native, non-Hispanic/Latino; 11% Two or more races, non-Hispanic/Latino.
Freshmen *Admission:* 265 applied, 64 admitted, 52 enrolled.
Faculty *Total:* 18, 44% full-time, 11% with terminal degrees. *Student/faculty ratio:* 24:1.
Majors Veterinary/animal health technology.
Academics *Calendar:* quarters. *Degree:* associate. *Special study options:* academic remediation for entering students, internships, off-campus study, services for LD students, summer session for credit.

Library Bel-Rea Institute Library. *Books:* 3,005 (physical); *Serial titles:* 103 (physical), 6 (digital/electronic); *Databases:* 2. Weekly public service hours: 38.
Student Life *Campus security:* Emergency Text Notification. *Student services:* veterans affairs office.
Costs (2020–21) *Comprehensive fee:* $23,777 includes full-time tuition ($12,338) and room and board ($11,439). No tuition increase for student's term of enrollment. *Room and board:* college room only: $7182. *Payment plan:* installment.
Applying *Options:* electronic application. *Required:* high school transcript, minimum 2.4 GPA, Wunderlik test required for H.S. GPA under 2.4. *Application deadlines:* rolling (freshmen), rolling (transfers).
Freshman Application Contact Bel-Rea Institute of Animal Technology, 1681 South Dayton Street, Denver, CO 80247. *Phone:* 303-751-8700. *Toll-free phone:* 800-950-8001.
Website: http://www.belrea.edu/.

CollegeAmerica–Denver
Denver, Colorado

Freshman Application Contact Admissions Office, CollegeAmerica–Denver, 1385 South Colorado Boulevard, Denver, CO 80222. *Phone:* 303-300-8740 Ext. 7020. *Toll-free phone:* 800-622-2894. *Website:* http://www.collegeamerica.edu/.

CollegeAmerica–Fort Collins
Fort Collins, Colorado

Freshman Application Contact CollegeAmerica–Fort Collins, 4601 South Mason Street, Fort Collins, CO 80525. *Phone:* 970-223-6060 Ext. 8002. *Toll-free phone:* 800-622-2894. *Website:* http://www.collegeamerica.edu/.

Colorado Academy of Veterinary Technology
Colorado Springs, Colorado

Admissions Office Contact Colorado Academy of Veterinary Technology, 2766 Janitell Road, Colorado Springs, CO 80906. *Website:* http://www.cavt.edu/.

Colorado Northwestern Community College
Rangely, Colorado

- **State-supported** 2-year, founded 1962, part of Colorado Community College and Occupational Education System
- **Rural** 150-acre campus
- **Coed**

Undergraduates 484 full-time, 670 part-time. 21% are from out of state; 3% Black or African American, non-Hispanic/Latino; 13% Hispanic/Latino; 1% Asian, non-Hispanic/Latino; 0.3% Native Hawaiian or other Pacific Islander, non-Hispanic/Latino; 0.4% American Indian or Alaska Native, non-Hispanic/Latino; 3% Two or more races, non-Hispanic/Latino; 9% Race/ethnicity unknown; 2% international; 10% transferred in; 45% live on campus. *Retention:* 46% of full-time freshmen returned.
Faculty *Student/faculty ratio:* 13:1.
Academics *Calendar:* semesters. *Degree:* certificates and associate. *Special study options:* academic remediation for entering students, adult/continuing education programs, advanced placement credit, distance learning, double majors, independent study, internships, part-time degree program, services for LD students, student-designed majors, summer session for credit.
Library Colorado Northwestern Community College Library plus 1 other. *Books:* 19,000 (physical), 10,524 (digital/electronic); *Serial titles:* 137 (physical); *Databases:* 47. Students can reserve study rooms.
Student Life *Campus security:* student patrols, late-night transport/escort service, controlled dormitory access.
Athletics Member NJCAA.
Costs (2019–20) *Tuition:* area resident $4467 full-time; state resident $4467 full-time; nonresident $7446 full-time. Full-time tuition and fees vary according to course load, location, and program. Part-time tuition and fees vary according to course load, location, and program. *Required fees:* $380 full-time. *Room and board:* $7590; room only: $2800. Room and board charges vary according to board plan, housing facility, and location.
Financial Aid Of all full-time matriculated undergraduates who enrolled in 2018, 379 applied for aid, 301 were judged to have need, 65 had their need fully met. In 2018, 20. *Average percent of need met:* 58. *Average financial aid package:* $8485. *Average need-based loan:* $6274. *Average need-based gift aid:* $5935. *Average non-need-based aid:* $1755.
Applying *Options:* electronic application, early admission, deferred entrance. *Required:* high school transcript. *Required for some:* 3 letters of recommendation.
Director of Admissions John Anderson, Director of Enrollment Services/Registrar, Colorado Northwestern Community College, 500 Kennedy Drive, Rangely, CO 81648-3598. *Phone:* 970-675-3217. *Toll-free phone:* 800-562-1105. *Fax:* 970-675-3343. *E-mail:* John.Anderson@cncc.edu. *Website:* http://www.cncc.edu/.

Colorado School of Trades
Lakewood, Colorado

Freshman Application Contact Colorado School of Trades, 1575 Hoyt Street, Lakewood, CO 80215-2996. *Phone:* 303-233-4697 Ext. 44. *Toll-free phone:* 800-234-4594. *Website:* http://www.schooloftrades.edu/.

Community College of Aurora
Aurora, Colorado

- **State-supported** 2-year, founded 1983, part of Colorado Community College System
- **Suburban** campus with easy access to Denver
- **Coed**

Undergraduates 1,867 full-time, 6,115 part-time. Students come from 60 other countries; 2% are from out of state; 18% Black or African American, non-Hispanic/Latino; 30% Hispanic/Latino; 6% Asian, non-Hispanic/Latino; 0.4% Native Hawaiian or other Pacific Islander, non-Hispanic/Latino; 0.5% American Indian or Alaska Native, non-Hispanic/Latino; 5% Two or more races, non-Hispanic/Latino; 6% Race/ethnicity unknown; 4% international; 5% transferred in. *Retention:* 54% of full-time freshmen returned.
Faculty *Student/faculty ratio:* 20:1.
Academics *Calendar:* semesters. *Degree:* certificates and associate. *Special study options:* academic remediation for entering students, adult/continuing education programs, cooperative education, distance learning, English as a second language, external degree program, independent study, internships, off-campus study, part-time degree program, services for LD students, summer session for credit.
Library Community College of Aurora Learning Resource Center. *Books:* 3,374 (physical), 252,009 (digital/electronic); *Serial titles:* 11 (physical), 22,725 (digital/electronic); *Databases:* 84. Weekly public service hours: 63.
Student Life *Campus security:* late-night transport/escort service.
Costs (2019–20) *Tuition:* area resident $3825 full-time; state resident $3825 full-time, $149 per credit hour part-time; nonresident $14,913 full-time, $611 per credit hour part-time. *Required fees:* $251 full-time, $66 per credit hour part-time, $66 per credit hour part-time.
Applying *Required for some:* high school transcript.
Director of Admissions Kristen Cusack, Director, Admissions and Records, Community College of Aurora, 16000 East CentreTech Parkway, Aurora, CO 80011-9036. *Phone:* 303-360-4701. *Fax:* 303-361-7432. *E-mail:* kristen.cusack@ccaurora.edu. *Website:* http://www.ccaurora.edu/.

Community College of Denver
Denver, Colorado

- **State-supported** 2-year, founded 1970, part of Colorado Community College System
- **Urban** 124-acre campus with easy access to Denver
- **Coed,** 8,232 undergraduate students, 30% full-time, 59% women, 41% men
- 100% of applicants were admitted

Undergraduates 2,453 full-time, 5,779 part-time. 13% Black or African American, non-Hispanic/Latino; 34% Hispanic/Latino; 6% Asian, non-Hispanic/Latino; 0.1% Native Hawaiian or other Pacific Islander, non-Hispanic/Latino; 1% American Indian or Alaska Native, non-Hispanic/Latino; 4% Two or more races, non-Hispanic/Latino; 2% Race/ethnicity unknown; 6% international; 12% transferred in.
Freshmen *Admission:* 2,294 applied, 2,294 admitted, 1,493 enrolled.
Faculty *Total:* 407, 27% full-time. *Student/faculty ratio:* 20:1.
Majors Accounting technology and bookkeeping; administrative assistant and secretarial science; business administration and management; computer and information sciences; dental hygiene; drafting and design technology; electroneurodiagnostic/electroencephalographic technology; general studies; graphic design; human services; legal assistant/paralegal; liberal arts and sciences/liberal studies; licensed practical/vocational nurse training; machine shop technology; management information systems; office management; quality control and safety technologies related; radiologic technology/science;

science technologies related; veterinary/animal health technology; welding technology.

Academics *Calendar:* semesters. *Degree:* certificates and associate. *Special study options:* academic remediation for entering students, accelerated degree program, adult/continuing education programs, advanced placement credit, cooperative education, distance learning, double majors, English as a second language, external degree program, honors programs, independent study, internships, off-campus study, part-time degree program, services for LD students, summer session for credit. *ROTC:* Army (b).

Library Auraria Library. Students can reserve study rooms.

Student Life *Housing:* college housing not available. *Activities and Organizations:* choral group, Phi Theta Kappa, Black Student Alliance, La Mision, SAFI, Chinese Culture Club. *Campus security:* 24-hour emergency response devices and patrols, late-night transport/escort service. *Student services:* health clinic, personal/psychological counseling, veterans affairs office.

Athletics *Intramural sports:* archery M/W, badminton M/W, basketball M/W, bowling M/W, cross-country running M/W, equestrian sports M/W, fencing M/W, field hockey M/W, football M/W, golf M/W, gymnastics M/W, racquetball M/W, riflery M/W, rugby M/W, skiing (cross-country) M/W, skiing (downhill) M/W, soccer M/W, swimming and diving M/W, table tennis M/W, tennis M/W, track and field M/W, volleyball M/W, weight lifting M/W.

Costs (2020–21) *Tuition:* area resident $3765 full-time, $149 per credit hour part-time; state resident $3765 full-time, $149 per credit hour part-time; nonresident $14,845 full-time, $611 per credit hour part-time. Full-time tuition and fees vary according to course load, location, program, and reciprocity agreements. Part-time tuition and fees vary according to course load, location, program, and reciprocity agreements. *Required fees:* $985 full-time. *Waivers:* employees or children of employees.

Applying *Options:* early admission, deferred entrance.

Freshman Application Contact Andrew Garcia, Director of Admissions, Recruitment and Outreach, Community College of Denver, PO Box 173363, Campus Box 215, Denver, CO 80217-3363. *Phone:* 303-352-3079. *Fax:* 303-556-2431. *E-mail:* andrew.garcia@ccd.edu.
Website: http://www.ccd.edu/.

Concorde Career College
Aurora, Colorado

Admissions Office Contact Concorde Career College, 111 North Havana Street, Aurora, CO 80010. *Website:* http://www.concorde.edu/.

Front Range Community College
Westminster, Colorado

- **State-supported** primarily 2-year, founded 1968, part of Community Colleges of Colorado System
- **Suburban** 90-acre campus with easy access to Denver
- **Endowment** $625,313
- **Coed,** 18,880 undergraduate students, 26% full-time, 56% women, 44% men

Undergraduates 4,999 full-time, 13,881 part-time. Students come from 43 states and territories; 85 other countries; 2% are from out of state; 2% Black or African American, non-Hispanic/Latino; 19% Hispanic/Latino; 3% Asian, non-Hispanic/Latino; 0.2% Native Hawaiian or other Pacific Islander, non-Hispanic/Latino; 0.7% American Indian or Alaska Native, non-Hispanic/Latino; 4% Two or more races, non-Hispanic/Latino; 4% Race/ethnicity unknown; 3% international; 10% transferred in. *Retention:* 59% of full-time freshmen returned.

Freshmen *Admission:* 4,793 applied, 4,793 admitted, 2,265 enrolled.

Faculty *Total:* 1,247, 20% full-time. *Student/faculty ratio:* 17:1.

Majors Accounting technology and bookkeeping; animation, interactive technology, video graphics and special effects; applied horticulture/horticulture operations; architectural engineering technology; automation engineer technology; automobile/automotive mechanics technology; business administration and management; CAD/CADD drafting/design technology; computer and information sciences; computer systems networking and telecommunications; criminal justice/police science; early childhood education; electrical, electronic and communications engineering technology; energy management and systems technology; general studies; geographic information science and cartography; health information/medical records technology; heating, ventilation, air conditioning and refrigeration engineering technology; holistic health; hospitality administration; interior design; legal assistant/paralegal; liberal arts and sciences and humanities related; liberal arts and sciences/liberal studies; medical office assistant; organizational leadership; recording arts technology; registered nursing/registered nurse; science technologies related; sign language interpretation and translation; surgical technology; veterinary/animal health technology; welding technology; wildlife, fish and wildlands science and management.

Academics *Calendar:* semesters. *Degrees:* certificates, associate, and bachelor's. *Special study options:* academic remediation for entering students, advanced placement credit, cooperative education, distance learning, double majors, English as a second language, freshman honors college, honors programs, independent study, internships, off-campus study, part-time degree program, services for LD students, student-designed majors, study abroad, summer session for credit. *ROTC:* Army (c), Air Force (c).

Library College Hill Library plus 2 others. *Books:* 32,801 (physical), 546 (digital/electronic); *Databases:* 12. Weekly public service hours: 54; students can reserve study rooms.

Student Life *Housing:* college housing not available. *Activities and Organizations:* drama/theater group, student-run newspaper, Student Government Association, Student Colorado Registry of Interpreters for the Deaf, Students in Free Enterprise (SIFE), Gay-Straight Alliance, Recycling Club. *Campus security:* 24-hour emergency response devices and patrols, late-night transport/escort service. *Student services:* personal/psychological counseling, veterans affairs office.

Costs (2019–20) *Tuition:* state resident $4372 full-time, $149 per credit hour part-time; nonresident $10,996 full-time, $611 per credit hour part-time. Full-time tuition and fees vary according to program. Part-time tuition and fees vary according to program. *Required fees:* $412 full-time, $206 per term part-time. *Payment plan:* installment. *Waivers:* employees or children of employees.

Applying *Options:* electronic application, early admission, deferred entrance.

Freshman Application Contact Ms. Miori Gidley, Registrar, Front Range Community College, Westminster, CO 80031. *Phone:* 303-404-5000. *Fax:* 303-439-2614. *E-mail:* miori.gidley@frontrange.edu.
Website: http://www.frontrange.edu/.

IBMC College
Fort Collins, Colorado

- **Proprietary** 2-year, founded 1987
- **Suburban** campus with easy access to Denver
- **Coed,** 1,020 undergraduate students, 100% full-time, 85% women, 15% men
- 92% of applicants were admitted

Undergraduates 1,020 full-time. Students come from 16 states and territories; 4 other countries; 3% are from out of state; 1% Black or African American, non-Hispanic/Latino; 20% Hispanic/Latino; 0.5% Asian, non-Hispanic/Latino; 0.2% Native Hawaiian or other Pacific Islander, non-Hispanic/Latino; 0.6% American Indian or Alaska Native, non-Hispanic/Latino; 1% Two or more races, non-Hispanic/Latino. *Retention:* 69% of full-time freshmen returned.

Freshmen *Admission:* 1,064 applied, 977 admitted, 355 enrolled.

Faculty *Total:* 115, 40% full-time, 3% with terminal degrees. *Student/faculty ratio:* 8:1.

Majors Accounting technology and bookkeeping; business administration and management; dental assisting; legal assistant/paralegal; medical administrative assistant and medical secretary; medical/clinical assistant; office occupations and clerical services.

Academics *Calendar:* continuous. *Degree:* certificates, diplomas, and associate. *Special study options:* accelerated degree program, adult/continuing education programs, cooperative education, honors programs, internships, summer session for credit.

Library IBMC College plus 6 others. *Books:* 834 (physical), 124,000 (digital/electronic).

Student Life *Housing:* college housing not available. *Activities and Organizations:* Alpha Beta Kappa, Circle of Hope, Relay for Life, Peer Mentoring, Peer Tutor.

Costs (2020–21) *Tuition:* $14,400 full-time.

Applying *Options:* electronic application. *Required:* high school transcript, interview. *Application deadline:* rolling (freshmen).

Freshman Application Contact Mr. Kyle Yates, Admissions Representative, IBMC College, 3842 South Mason Street, Fort Collins, CO 80525. *Phone:* 970-223-2669. *Toll-free phone:* 800-495-2669. *E-mail:* kyates@ibmc.edu.
Website: http://www.ibmc.edu/.

IntelliTec College - Colorado Springs
Colorado Springs, Colorado

Director of Admissions Director of Admissions, IntelliTec College - Colorado Springs, 2315 East Pikes Peak Avenue, Colorado Springs, CO 80909. *Phone:* 719-632-7626. *Toll-free phone:* 800-748-2282. *Website:* http://www.intelliteccollege.edu/.

IntelliTec College - Grand Junction
Grand Junction, Colorado

Freshman Application Contact Admissions, IntelliTec College - Grand Junction, 772 Horizon Drive, Grand Junction, CO 81506. *Phone:* 970-245-8101. *Toll-free phone:* 800-748-2282. *Fax:* 970-243-8074. *Website:* http://www.intelliteccollege.edu/.

Lamar Community College
Lamar, Colorado

- **State-supported** 2-year, founded 1937, part of Colorado Community College and Occupational Education System
- **Small-town** 125-acre campus
- **Coed**

Undergraduates 433 full-time, 378 part-time. Students come from 29 states and territories; 9 other countries; 11% are from out of state; 9% Black or African American, non-Hispanic/Latino; 28% Hispanic/Latino; 0.2% Asian, non-Hispanic/Latino; 0.4% Native Hawaiian or other Pacific Islander, non-Hispanic/Latino; 1% American Indian or Alaska Native, non-Hispanic/Latino; 3% Two or more races, non-Hispanic/Latino; 2% Race/ethnicity unknown; 5% international; 7% transferred in; 20% live on campus. *Retention:* 54% of full-time freshmen returned.
Faculty *Student/faculty ratio:* 21:1.
Academics *Calendar:* semesters. *Degree:* certificates, diplomas, and associate. *Special study options:* academic remediation for entering students, adult/continuing education programs, advanced placement credit, cooperative education, distance learning, double majors, English as a second language, independent study, internships, part-time degree program, services for LD students, student-designed majors, summer session for credit.
Library Learning Resources Center. *Books:* 10,825 (physical); *Serial titles:* 23 (physical). Weekly public service hours: 53.
Student Life *Campus security:* 24-hour emergency response devices and patrols, student patrols, late-night transport/escort service, controlled dormitory access.
Athletics Member NJCAA.
Costs (2019–20) *Tuition:* state resident $3574 full-time, $148 per credit hour part-time; nonresident $5956 full-time, $248 per credit hour part-time. Full-time tuition and fees vary according to course load, program, and reciprocity agreements. Part-time tuition and fees vary according to course load, program, and reciprocity agreements. *Required fees:* $376 full-time, $376 per year part-time. *Room and board:* $4435; room only: $2150. Room and board charges vary according to housing facility.
Applying *Options:* electronic application, early admission.
Freshman Application Contact Director of Admissions, Lamar Community College, 2401 South Main Street, Lamar, CO 81052-3999. *Phone:* 719-336-1592. *Toll-free phone:* 800-968-6920. *E-mail:* admissions@lamarcc.edu. *Website:* http://www.lamarcc.edu/.

Lincoln College of Technology - Denver
Denver, Colorado

Freshman Application Contact Lincoln College of Technology - Denver, 11194 East 45th Avenue, Denver, CO 80239. *Phone:* 800-347-3232 Ext. 43032. *Toll-free phone:* 844-215-1513. *Website:* http://www.lincolntech.edu/.

Morgan Community College
Fort Morgan, Colorado

Freshman Application Contact Ms. Kim Maxwell, Morgan Community College, 920 Barlow Road, Fort Morgan, CO 80701-4399. *Phone:* 970-542-3111. *Toll-free phone:* 800-622-0216. *Fax:* 970-867-6608. *E-mail:* kim.maxwell@morgancc.edu. *Website:* http://www.morgancc.edu/.

Northeastern Junior College
Sterling, Colorado

- **State-supported** 2-year, founded 1941, part of Colorado Community College and Occupational Education System
- **Small-town** 65-acre campus
- **Coed,** 1,392 undergraduate students, 57% full-time, 55% women, 45% men

Undergraduates 790 full-time, 602 part-time. Students come from 23 states and territories; 21 other countries; 10% are from out of state; 4% Black or African American, non-Hispanic/Latino; 19% Hispanic/Latino; 0.9% Asian, non-Hispanic/Latino; 0.2% Native Hawaiian or other Pacific Islander, non-Hispanic/Latino; 0.5% American Indian or Alaska Native, non-Hispanic/Latino; 4% Two or more races, non-Hispanic/Latino; 2% Race/ethnicity unknown; 4% international; 5% transferred in; 35% live on campus.
Freshmen *Admission:* 1,314 applied, 1,314 admitted, 395 enrolled. *Average high school GPA:* 3.0.
Faculty *Total:* 92, 57% full-time. *Student/faculty ratio:* 15:1.
Majors Accounting; agricultural business and management; agricultural teacher education; agriculture; agronomy and crop science; animal sciences; anthropology; art; art history, criticism and conservation; automobile/automotive mechanics technology; biology/biological sciences; business administration and management; chemistry; child development; communication; cosmetology; criminal justice/police science; dramatic/theater arts; economics; elementary education; emergency medical technology (EMT paramedic); English; equestrian studies; farm and ranch management; fine/studio arts; geography; geology/earth science; history; journalism; liberal arts and sciences/liberal studies; licensed practical/vocational nurse training; marketing/marketing management; mathematics; music; natural sciences; philosophy; physical education teaching and coaching; physical sciences; political science and government; pre-engineering; psychology; registered nursing/registered nurse; social sciences; sociology.
Academics *Calendar:* semesters. *Degree:* certificates and associate. *Special study options:* academic remediation for entering students, accelerated degree program, adult/continuing education programs, advanced placement credit, cooperative education, distance learning, double majors, English as a second language, honors programs, internships, part-time degree program, services for LD students, summer session for credit.
Library Monahan Library. *Books:* 26,933 (physical), 105,876 (digital/electronic); *Serial titles:* 79 (physical), 40 (digital/electronic); *Databases:* 8. Weekly public service hours: 71.
Student Life *Housing:* on-campus residence required for freshman year. *Options:* coed, women-only. Campus housing is university owned. Freshman applicants given priority for college housing. *Activities and Organizations:* drama/theater group, choral group, Associated Student Government, Post Secondary Agriculture (PAS), Crossroads, NJC Ambassadors, Business Club. *Campus security:* 24-hour emergency response devices, late-night transport/escort service, controlled dormitory access, campus wide security cameras. *Student services:* health clinic, personal/psychological counseling.
Athletics Member NJCAA. *Intercollegiate sports:* baseball M(s), basketball M(s)/W(s), equestrian sports M(s)/W(s), golf M(s)/W(s), soccer M(s)/W(s), softball W(s), volleyball W(s), wrestling M(s). *Intramural sports:* basketball M/W, volleyball M/W.
Costs (2019–20) *Tuition:* state resident $4467 full-time, $149 per credit hour part-time; nonresident $6701 full-time, $223 per credit hour part-time. Full-time tuition and fees vary according to course load and reciprocity agreements. Part-time tuition and fees vary according to course load and reciprocity agreements. *Required fees:* $605 full-time, $24 per credit hour part-time, $14 per term part-time. *Room and board:* $7080; room only: $3058. Room and board charges vary according to board plan and housing facility. *Payment plan:* installment. *Waivers:* senior citizens and employees or children of employees.
Financial Aid Of all full-time matriculated undergraduates who enrolled in 2018, 37 Federal Work-Study jobs (averaging $1858). 91 state and other part-time jobs (averaging $1804).
Applying *Options:* electronic application. *Recommended:* high school transcript. *Application deadlines:* rolling (freshmen), rolling (transfers). *Notification:* continuous (freshmen), continuous (transfers).
Freshman Application Contact Adam Kunkel, Director of Admission, Northeastern Junior College, 100 College Avenue, Hays Student Center-Room 137, Sterling, CO 80751. *Phone:* 970-521-7000. *Toll-free phone:* 800-626-4637. *Fax:* 970-521-6715. *E-mail:* adam.kunkel@njc.edu. *Website:* http://www.njc.edu/.

Otero Junior College
La Junta, Colorado

Freshman Application Contact Mrs. Lauren Berg, Registrar, Otero Junior College, 1802 Colorado Avenue, La Junta, CO 81050. *Phone:* 719-384-6831. *Fax:* 719-384-6933. *E-mail:* lauren.berg@ojc.edu. *Website:* http://www.ojc.edu/.

Pikes Peak Community College
Colorado Springs, Colorado

Freshman Application Contact Pikes Peak Community College, 5675 South Academy Boulevard, Colorado Springs, CO 80906-5498. *Phone:* 719-540-7041. *Toll-free phone:* 866-411-7722. *Website:* http://www.ppcc.edu/.

Pima Medical Institute - Aurora

Aurora, Colorado

Admissions Office Contact Pima Medical Institute - Aurora, 13750 East Mississippi Avenue, Aurora, CO 80012. *Toll-free phone:* 800-477-PIMA. *Website:* http://www.pmi.edu/.

Pima Medical Institute - Colorado Springs

Colorado Springs, Colorado

Freshman Application Contact Pima Medical Institute - Colorado Springs, 5725 Mark Dabling Boulevard, Colorado Springs, CO 80919. *Phone:* 719-482-7462. *Toll-free phone:* 800-477-PIMA. *Website:* http://www.pmi.edu/.

Pima Medical Institute - Denver

Denver, Colorado

Freshman Application Contact Admissions Office, Pima Medical Institute - Denver, 7475 Dakin Street, Denver, CO 80221. *Phone:* 303-426-1800. *Toll-free phone:* 800-477-PIMA. *Website:* http://www.pmi.edu/.

Pueblo Community College

Pueblo, Colorado

- **State-supported** primarily 2-year, founded 1933, part of Colorado Community College System
- **Urban** 35-acre campus
- **Endowment** $1.1 million
- **Coed**

Undergraduates 1,770 full-time, 3,880 part-time. Students come from 23 states and territories; 0.8% are from out of state; 5% Black or African American, non-Hispanic/Latino; 32% Hispanic/Latino; 5% Asian, non-Hispanic/Latino; 0.2% Native Hawaiian or other Pacific Islander, non-Hispanic/Latino; 2% American Indian or Alaska Native, non-Hispanic/Latino; 3% Two or more races, non-Hispanic/Latino; 3% Race/ethnicity unknown; 0.6% international; 9% transferred in. *Retention:* 10% of full-time freshmen returned.
Faculty *Student/faculty ratio:* 16:1.
Academics *Calendar:* semesters. *Degrees:* certificates, associate, and bachelor's. *Special study options:* academic remediation for entering students, accelerated degree program, advanced placement credit, cooperative education, distance learning, double majors, English as a second language, honors programs, independent study, internships, part-time degree program, services for LD students, summer session for credit.
Library PCC Library. *Books:* 19,162 (physical), 33,004 (digital/electronic); *Serial titles:* 695 (physical), 7,707 (digital/electronic); *Databases:* 12. Weekly public service hours: 60.
Student Life *Campus security:* 24-hour emergency response devices and patrols, late-night transport/escort service.
Costs (2019–20) *Tuition:* state resident $4300 full-time, $180 per credit hour part-time; nonresident $15,060 full-time, $628 per credit hour part-time. *Required fees:* $750 full-time, $21 per credit hour part-time, $58 per term part-time.
Applying *Options:* electronic application, early admission, deferred entrance.
Freshman Application Contact Mrs. Barbara Benedict, Director of Admissions and Records, Pueblo Community College, 900 West Orman Avenue, Pueblo, CO 81004. *Phone:* 719-549-3039. *Toll-free phone:* 888-642-6017. *Fax:* 719-549-3012. *E-mail:* barbara.benedict@pueblocc.edu. *Website:* http://www.pueblocc.edu/.

Red Rocks Community College

Lakewood, Colorado

Freshman Application Contact Admissions Office, Red Rocks Community College, 13300 West 6th Avenue, Lakewood, CO 80228-1255. *Phone:* 303-914-6360. *Fax:* 303-914-6919. *E-mail:* admissions@rrcc.edu. *Website:* http://www.rrcc.edu/.

Spartan College of Aeronautics and Technology

Broomfield, Colorado

Freshman Application Contact Spartan College of Aeronautics and Technology, 10851 West 120th Avenue, Broomfield, CO 80021. *Phone:* 303-466-7383. *Toll-free phone:* 800-510-3216. *Website:* http://www.spartan.edu/.

Trinidad State Junior College

Trinidad, Colorado

Freshman Application Contact Bernadine DeGarbo, Student Services Administrative Assistant, Trinidad State Junior College, 600 Prospect Street, Trinidad, CO 81082. *Phone:* 719-846-5621. *Toll-free phone:* 800-621-8752. *Fax:* 719-846-5620. *E-mail:* bernadine.degarbo@trinidadstate.edu. *Website:* http://www.trinidadstate.edu/.

CONNECTICUT

Asnuntuck Community College

Enfield, Connecticut

- **State-supported** 2-year, founded 1972, part of Connecticut State Colleges & Universities (CSCU)
- **Suburban** 36-acre campus
- **Endowment** $137,046
- **Coed**

Undergraduates 652 full-time, 1,293 part-time. 8% are from out of state; 16% Black or African American, non-Hispanic/Latino; 13% Hispanic/Latino; 3% Asian, non-Hispanic/Latino; 0.3% American Indian or Alaska Native, non-Hispanic/Latino; 3% Two or more races, non-Hispanic/Latino; 2% Race/ethnicity unknown; 16% transferred in. *Retention:* 68% of full-time freshmen returned.
Faculty *Student/faculty ratio:* 17:1.
Academics *Calendar:* semesters. *Degree:* certificates and associate. *Special study options:* academic remediation for entering students, adult/continuing education programs, advanced placement credit, cooperative education, distance learning, double majors, English as a second language, independent study, internships, part-time degree program, services for LD students, student-designed majors, summer session for credit.
Library ACC Library plus 1 other.
Student Life *Campus security:* 24-hour emergency response devices, late-night transport/escort service.
Applying *Options:* deferred entrance. *Application fee:* $20. *Required:* high school transcript, interview.
Freshman Application Contact Jennifer Anilowski, Interim Director of Admissions, Asnuntuck Community College, 170 Elm Street, Enfield, CT 06082. *Phone:* 860-253-3090. *Fax:* 860-253-3014. *E-mail:* janilowski@asnuntuck.edu. *Website:* http://www.asnuntuck.edu/.

Capital Community College

Hartford, Connecticut

- **State-supported** 2-year, founded 1946, part of Connecticut State Colleges & Universities (CSCU)
- **Urban** 10-acre campus
- **Coed**

Undergraduates *Retention:* 51% of full-time freshmen returned.
Academics *Calendar:* semesters. *Degree:* certificates and associate. *Special study options:* academic remediation for entering students, accelerated degree program, adult/continuing education programs, advanced placement credit, distance learning, double majors, English as a second language, independent study, internships, part-time degree program, services for LD students, summer session for credit.
Library Arthur C. Banks, Jr. Library plus 1 other.
Student Life *Campus security:* late-night transport/escort service, security staff during hours of operation, emergency telephones 7 am - 11 pm.
Financial Aid Of all full-time matriculated undergraduates who enrolled in 2018, 87 Federal Work-Study jobs (averaging $3000). 160 state and other part-time jobs (averaging $3000).
Applying *Application fee:* $20. *Recommended:* high school transcript.
Freshman Application Contact Ms. Jackie Phillips, Director of the Welcome and Advising Center, Capital Community College, 950 Main Street, Hartford, CT 06103. *Phone:* 860-906-5078. *Toll-free phone:* 800-894-6126. *E-mail:* jphillips@ccc.commnet.edu. *Website:* http://www.ccc.commnet.edu/.

Gateway Community College

New Haven, Connecticut

- **State-supported** 2-year, founded 1992, part of Connecticut Community–Technical College System
- **Urban** 5-acre campus with easy access to New York City
- **Coed**

Undergraduates 2,590 full-time, 5,611 part-time. 20% Black or African American, non-Hispanic/Latino; 24% Hispanic/Latino; 4% Asian, non-Hispanic/Latino; 0.2% American Indian or Alaska Native, non-Hispanic/Latino; 4% Two or more races, non-Hispanic/Latino; 2% Race/ethnicity unknown; 0.5% international; 11% transferred in. *Retention:* 57% of full-time freshmen returned.
Faculty *Student/faculty ratio:* 17:1.
Academics *Calendar:* semesters. *Degree:* certificates and associate. *Special study options:* academic remediation for entering students, adult/continuing education programs, advanced placement credit, distance learning, English as a second language, external degree program, independent study, internships, off-campus study, part-time degree program, services for LD students, summer session for credit.
Library Gateway Community College Library plus 2 others.
Student Life *Campus security:* late-night transport/escort service.
Athletics Member NJCAA.
Financial Aid Of all full-time matriculated undergraduates who enrolled in 2016, 71 Federal Work-Study jobs (averaging $3024). 80 state and other part-time jobs (averaging $2139). *Average indebtedness upon graduation:* $2590.
Applying *Options:* early admission, deferred entrance. *Application fee:* $20. *Required:* high school transcript. *Required for some:* essay or personal statement, interview.
Freshman Application Contact Mr. Joseph Carberry, Director of Enrollment Management, Gateway Community College, 20 Church Street, New Haven, CT 06510. *Phone:* 203-285-2011. *Toll-free phone:* 800-390-7723. *Fax:* 203-285-2018. *E-mail:* jcarberry@gatewayct.edu. *Website:* http://www.gwcc.commnet.edu/.

Goodwin College

East Hartford, Connecticut

Freshman Application Contact Mr. Nicholas Lentino, Assistant Vice President for Admissions, Goodwin College, One Riverside Drive, East Hartford, CT 06118. *Phone:* 860-727-6765. *Toll-free phone:* 800-889-3282. *Fax:* 860-291-9550. *E-mail:* nlentino@goodwin.edu. *Website:* http://www.goodwin.edu/.

Housatonic Community College

Bridgeport, Connecticut

- **State-supported** 2-year, founded 1967, part of Connecticut State Colleges & Universities (CSCU)
- **Urban** 4-acre campus with easy access to New York City
- **Coed,** 5,138 undergraduate students, 34% full-time, 61% women, 39% men

Undergraduates 1,729 full-time, 3,409 part-time. 31% Black or African American, non-Hispanic/Latino; 33% Hispanic/Latino; 3% Asian, non-Hispanic/Latino; 0.1% Native Hawaiian or other Pacific Islander, non-Hispanic/Latino; 0.2% American Indian or Alaska Native, non-Hispanic/Latino; 2% Two or more races, non-Hispanic/Latino; 1% Race/ethnicity unknown; 0.7% international; 7% transferred in. *Retention:* 57% of full-time freshmen returned.
Freshmen *Admission:* 3,606 applied, 3,606 admitted, 1,070 enrolled.
Faculty *Total:* 378, 21% full-time. *Student/faculty ratio:* 16:1.
Majors Accounting; administrative assistant and secretarial science; art; avionics maintenance technology; business administration and management; commercial and advertising art; criminal justice/law enforcement administration; humanities; human services; liberal arts and sciences/liberal studies; mathematics; physical therapy.
Academics *Calendar:* semesters. *Degree:* certificates and associate. *Special study options:* academic remediation for entering students, adult/continuing education programs, advanced placement credit, cooperative education, distance learning, double majors, English as a second language, honors programs, independent study, internships, off-campus study, part-time degree program, services for LD students, summer session for credit.
Library Housatonic Community College Library. *Books:* 55,000 (physical), 45,290 (digital/electronic); *Serial titles:* 104 (physical); *Databases:* 99. Students can reserve study rooms.
Student Life *Activities and Organizations:* drama/theater group, student-run newspaper, Student Senate, Association of Latin American Students, Community Action Network, Drama Club, Phi Theta Kappa. *Campus security:* 24-hour emergency response devices, late-night transport/escort service. *Student services:* personal/psychological counseling, women's center, veterans affairs office.
Financial Aid Of all full-time matriculated undergraduates who enrolled in 2018, 70 Federal Work-Study jobs (averaging $2850).
Applying *Options:* electronic application, deferred entrance. *Application fee:* $20. *Required:* high school transcript. *Application deadlines:* rolling (freshmen), rolling (transfers). *Notification:* continuous (freshmen), continuous (transfers).
Freshman Application Contact Housatonic Community College, 900 Lafayette Boulevard, Bridgeport, CT 06604-4704.
Website: http://www.housatonic.edu/.

Manchester Community College

Manchester, Connecticut

- **State-supported** 2-year, founded 1963, part of Connecticut State Colleges & Universities (CSCU)
- **Small-town** campus
- **Coed,** 5,511 undergraduate students, 33% full-time, 55% women, 45% men

Undergraduates 1,824 full-time, 3,687 part-time. 19% Black or African American, non-Hispanic/Latino; 22% Hispanic/Latino; 6% Asian, non-Hispanic/Latino; 0.1% Native Hawaiian or other Pacific Islander, non-Hispanic/Latino; 0.2% American Indian or Alaska Native, non-Hispanic/Latino; 3% Two or more races, non-Hispanic/Latino; 3% Race/ethnicity unknown; 19% transferred in.
Freshmen *Admission:* 2,237 applied, 2,237 admitted, 1,276 enrolled.
Faculty *Total:* 301, 29% full-time. *Student/faculty ratio:* 19:1.
Majors Accounting; administrative assistant and secretarial science; business administration and management; clinical/medical laboratory technology; commercial and advertising art; criminal justice/law enforcement administration; dramatic/theater arts; engineering science; fine/studio arts; general studies; hotel/motel administration; human services; industrial engineering; industrial technology; information science/studies; journalism; kindergarten/preschool education; legal administrative assistant/secretary; legal assistant/paralegal; liberal arts and sciences/liberal studies; management information systems; marketing/marketing management; medical administrative assistant and medical secretary; music; occupational therapist assistant; physical therapy technology; respiratory care therapy; social work; speech communication and rhetoric; surgical technology; teacher assistant/aide.
Academics *Calendar:* semesters. *Degree:* certificates and associate. *Special study options:* adult/continuing education programs, part-time degree program.
Student Life *Housing:* college housing not available.
Athletics Member NJCAA. *Intercollegiate sports:* baseball M, basketball M/W, soccer M/W, softball W.
Costs (2019–20) *Tuition:* area resident $3912 full-time, $163 per credit hour part-time; state resident $3912 full-time, $163 per credit hour part-time; nonresident $11,736 full-time, $489 per credit hour part-time. *Required fees:* $482 full-time.
Applying *Options:* electronic application. *Application fee:* $20. *Required:* high school transcript.
Freshman Application Contact Manchester Community College, PO Box 1046, Manchester, CT 06045-1046.
Website: http://www.manchestercc.edu/.

Middlesex Community College

Middletown, Connecticut

- **State-supported** 2-year, founded 1966, part of Connecticut State Colleges & Universities (CSCU)
- **Suburban** 38-acre campus with easy access to Hartford
- **Endowment** $452,240
- **Coed,** 2,424 undergraduate students, 35% full-time, 57% women, 43% men

Undergraduates 848 full-time, 1,576 part-time. Students come from 6 states and territories; 5 other countries; 1% are from out of state; 10% Black or African American, non-Hispanic/Latino; 20% Hispanic/Latino; 3% Asian, non-Hispanic/Latino; 0.1% Native Hawaiian or other Pacific Islander, non-Hispanic/Latino; 0.2% American Indian or Alaska Native, non-Hispanic/Latino; 5% Two or more races, non-Hispanic/Latino; 1% Race/ethnicity unknown; 11% transferred in. *Retention:* 55% of full-time freshmen returned.
Freshmen *Admission:* 937 applied, 877 admitted, 472 enrolled.
Faculty *Total:* 182, 25% full-time, 20% with terminal degrees. *Student/faculty ratio:* 15:1.
Majors Accounting; administrative assistant and secretarial science; biological and physical sciences; biology/biotechnology laboratory technician; broadcast journalism; business administration and management; commercial

and advertising art; computer programming; criminal justice/police science; engineering science; engineering technology; environmental studies; fine/studio arts; human services; industrial radiologic technology; intermedia/multimedia; liberal arts and sciences/liberal studies; marketing/marketing management; mass communication/media; medical administrative assistant and medical secretary; medical radiologic technology; mental health counseling; ophthalmic laboratory technology; pre-engineering; substance abuse/addiction counseling; veterinary/animal health technology.
Academics *Calendar:* semesters. *Degree:* certificates and associate. *Special study options:* academic remediation for entering students, accelerated degree program, adult/continuing education programs, advanced placement credit, cooperative education, distance learning, double majors, English as a second language, honors programs, independent study, internships, off-campus study, part-time degree program, services for LD students, summer session for credit.
Library Jean Burr Smith Library.
Student Life *Housing:* college housing not available. *Activities and Organizations:* drama/theater group, student-run newspaper, Phi Theta Kappa, Human Services Association, Peace and Justice Club, Poetry Club, International Student Club. *Campus security:* 24-hour emergency response devices and patrols.
Costs (2019–20) *Tuition:* area resident $3984 full-time, $166 per credit hour part-time; state resident $3984 full-time, $166 per credit hour part-time; nonresident $11,952 full-time. Full-time tuition and fees vary according to course load, degree level, program, and reciprocity agreements. Part-time tuition and fees vary according to course load, degree level, program, and reciprocity agreements. *Required fees:* $492 full-time, $88 per credit hour part-time. *Payment plan:* installment. *Waivers:* employees or children of employees.
Financial Aid Of all full-time matriculated undergraduates who enrolled in 2018, 50 Federal Work-Study jobs (averaging $5000). 2 state and other part-time jobs (averaging $5000).
Applying *Options:* electronic application, early admission, deferred entrance. *Application fee:* $20. *Required:* high school transcript, G.E.D. or evidence of prior learning if no HS diploma. *Application deadlines:* rolling (freshmen), rolling (out-of-state freshmen), rolling (transfers).
Freshman Application Contact Lauren Katusha, Director of Admissions, Middlesex Community College, 100 Training Hill Road, Middletown, CT 06457. *Phone:* 860-9182161. *Fax:* 860-344-3055. *E-mail:* lkatusha@mxcc.commnet.edu.
Website: http://www.mxcc.commnet.edu/.

Naugatuck Valley Community College
Waterbury, Connecticut

- **State-supported** 2-year, founded 1992, part of Connecticut State Colleges & Universities (CSCU)
- **Urban** 110-acre campus
- **Coed**

Undergraduates 2,173 full-time, 4,205 part-time. Students come from 7 states and territories; 2 other countries; 0.3% are from out of state; 11% Black or African American, non-Hispanic/Latino; 30% Hispanic/Latino; 3% Asian, non-Hispanic/Latino; 0.1% Native Hawaiian or other Pacific Islander, non-Hispanic/Latino; 0.1% American Indian or Alaska Native, non-Hispanic/Latino; 4% Two or more races, non-Hispanic/Latino; 4% Race/ethnicity unknown; 0.3% international; 10% transferred in. *Retention:* 59% of full-time freshmen returned.
Faculty *Student/faculty ratio:* 17:1.
Academics *Calendar:* semesters. *Degree:* certificates and associate. *Special study options:* academic remediation for entering students, accelerated degree program, adult/continuing education programs, advanced placement credit, cooperative education, distance learning, English as a second language, external degree program, honors programs, independent study, internships, off-campus study, part-time degree program, services for LD students, summer session for credit.
Library Max R. Traurig Learning Resource Center. *Books:* 38,400 (physical); *Serial titles:* 108 (physical); *Databases:* 12. Weekly public service hours: 65; students can reserve study rooms.
Student Life *Campus security:* 24-hour emergency response devices and patrols, late-night transport/escort service, security escort service.
Standardized Tests *Required:* ACCUPLACER (for admission).
Financial Aid Of all full-time matriculated undergraduates who enrolled in 2018, 70 Federal Work-Study jobs (averaging $1942). 16 state and other part-time jobs (averaging $1660).
Applying *Options:* electronic application, deferred entrance. *Application fee:* $20. *Required:* high school transcript. *Required for some:* interview.
Freshman Application Contact Noel Rosamilio, Associate Dean of Enrollment Management, Naugatuck Valley Community College, Kinney Hall, K500, 750 Chase Parkway, Waterbury, CT 06708. *Phone:* 203-596-8780. *E-mail:* nrosamilio@nv.edu. *Website:* http://www.nvcc.commnet.edu/.

Northwestern Connecticut Community College
Winsted, Connecticut

Freshman Application Contact Admissions Office, Northwestern Connecticut Community College, Park Place East, Winsted, CT 06098-1798. *Phone:* 860-738-6330. *Fax:* 860-738-6437. *E-mail:* admissions@nwcc.commnet.edu. *Website:* http://www.nwcc.commnet.edu/.

Norwalk Community College
Norwalk, Connecticut

Freshman Application Contact Mr. Curtis Antrum, Admissions Counselor, Norwalk Community College, 188 Richards Avenue, Norwalk, CT 06854-1655. *Phone:* 203-857-7060. *Fax:* 203-857-3335. *E-mail:* admissions@ncc.commnet.edu. *Website:* http://www.ncc.commnet.edu/.

Quinebaug Valley Community College
Danielson, Connecticut

Freshman Application Contact Dr. Toni Moumouris, Director of Admissions, Quinebaug Valley Community College, 742 Upper Maple Street, Danielson, CT 06239. *Phone:* 860-774-1130 Ext. 318. *Fax:* 860-774-7768. *E-mail:* qu_isd@commnet.edu. *Website:* http://www.qvcc.edu/.

Three Rivers Community College
Norwich, Connecticut

Freshman Application Contact Admissions Office, Three Rivers Community College, CT. *Phone:* 860-215-9296. *E-mail:* admissions@trcc.commnet.edu. *Website:* http://www.threerivers.edu/.

Tunxis Community College
Farmington, Connecticut

Freshman Application Contact Ms. Tamika Davis, Director of Admissions, Tunxis Community College, 271 Scott Swamp Road, Farmington, CT 06032. *Phone:* 860-773-1494. *Fax:* 860-606-9501. *E-mail:* pmccluskey@tunxis.edu. *Website:* http://www.tunxis.edu/.

DELAWARE

Delaware College of Art and Design
Wilmington, Delaware

- **Independent** 2-year, founded 1997
- **Urban** 1-acre campus
- **Endowment** $65,295
- **Coed**

Undergraduates 192 full-time, 18 part-time. Students come from 9 states and territories; 45% are from out of state; 10% transferred in; 50% live on campus. *Retention:* 54% of full-time freshmen returned.
Faculty *Student/faculty ratio:* 9:1.
Academics *Calendar:* semesters. *Degree:* associate. *Special study options:* academic remediation for entering students, adult/continuing education programs, advanced placement credit, double majors, off-campus study, part-time degree program, services for LD students, study abroad, summer session for credit.
Library Information Resource Center plus 1 other.
Applying *Options:* electronic application, deferred entrance. *Application fee:* $25. *Required:* essay or personal statement, high school transcript, minimum 2.0 GPA, interview, portfolio.
Freshman Application Contact Ms. Allison Gullo, Delaware College of Art and Design, 600 North Market Street, Wilmington, DE 19801. *Phone:* 302-622-8867 Ext. 111. *Fax:* 302-622-8870. *E-mail:* agullo@dcad.edu. *Website:* http://www.dcad.edu/.

Delaware Technical & Community College, Jack F. Owens Campus
Georgetown, Delaware

Freshman Application Contact Ms. Claire McDonald, Admissions Counselor, Delaware Technical & Community College, Jack F. Owens

Campus, PO Box 610, Georgetown, DE 19947. *Phone:* 302-856-5400. *Fax:* 302-856-9461. *Website:* http://www.dtcc.edu/.

Delaware Technical & Community College, Stanton/George Campus

Wilmington, Delaware

Freshman Application Contact Ms. Rebecca Bailey, Admissions Coordinator, Wilmington, Delaware Technical & Community College, Stanton/George Campus, 333 Shipley Street, Wilmington, DE 19713. *Phone:* 302-571-5343. *Fax:* 302-577-2548. *Website:* http://www.dtcc.edu/.

Delaware Technical & Community College, Terry Campus

Dover, Delaware

- **State-supported** 2-year, founded 1972, part of Delaware Technical and Community College System
- **Small-town** campus
- **Coed**

Undergraduates 4,731 full-time, 9,464 part-time. 25% Black or African American, non-Hispanic/Latino; 11% Hispanic/Latino; 3% Asian, non-Hispanic/Latino; 0.1% Native Hawaiian or other Pacific Islander, non-Hispanic/Latino; 0.5% American Indian or Alaska Native, non-Hispanic/Latino; 3% Two or more races, non-Hispanic/Latino; 2% Race/ethnicity unknown; 1% international; 6% transferred in. *Retention:* 52% of full-time freshmen returned.
Academics *Calendar:* semesters. *Degree:* certificates, diplomas, and associate. *Special study options:* part-time degree program.
Student Life *Campus security:* 24-hour emergency response devices, late-night transport/escort service.
Athletics Member NJCAA.
Costs (2019–20) *Tuition:* area resident $153 full-time, $153 per credit hour part-time; state resident $153 full-time, $153 per credit hour part-time; nonresident $381 full-time, $381 per credit hour part-time. *Required fees:* $752 full-time. *Room and board:* $6000; room only: $4000.
Financial Aid Of all full-time matriculated undergraduates who enrolled in 2018, 50 Federal Work-Study jobs (averaging $1500).
Applying *Options:* electronic application, early admission, deferred entrance. *Application fee:* $10. *Required for some:* high school transcript.
Freshman Application Contact Mrs. Maria Harris, Admissions Officer, Delaware Technical & Community College, Terry Campus, 100 Campus Drive, Dover, DE 19904. *Phone:* 302-857-1020. *Fax:* 302-857-1296. *E-mail:* terry-info@dtcc.edu. *Website:* http://www.dtcc.edu/.

FLORIDA

Academy for Nursing and Health Occupations

West Palm Beach, Florida

Admissions Office Contact Academy for Nursing and Health Occupations, 5154 Okeechobee Boulevard, Suite 201, West Palm Beach, FL 33417. *Website:* http://www.anho.edu/.

Advance Science College

Hialeah, Florida

Admissions Office Contact Advance Science College, 3750 W. 12 Avenue, Hialeah, FL 33012. *Website:* http://www.asicollege.edu/.

Altierus Career College - Tampa

Tampa, Florida

Freshman Application Contact Altierus Career College - Tampa, 3319 West Hillsborough Avenue, Tampa, FL 33614. *Phone:* 813-879-6000 Ext. 129. *Website:* http://www.altierus.edu/.

American Medical Academy

Miami, Florida

Admissions Office Contact American Medical Academy, 12215 SW 112 Street, Miami, FL 33186-4830. *Website:* http://www.ama.edu/.

ATA Career Education

Spring Hill, Florida

Admissions Office Contact ATA Career Education, 7351 Spring Hill Drive, Suite 11, Spring Hill, FL 34606. *Website:* http://www.atafl.edu/.

Aviator College of Aeronautical Science & Technology

Fort Pierce, Florida

Admissions Office Contact Aviator College of Aeronautical Science & Technology, 3800 St. Lucie Boulevard, Fort Pierce, FL 34946. *Website:* http://aviator.edu/FlightSchool/.

Broward College

Fort Lauderdale, Florida

Freshman Application Contact Mr. Willie J. Alexander, Associate Vice President for Student Affairs/College Registrar, Broward College, 225 East Las Olas Boulevard, Fort Lauderdale, FL 33301. *Phone:* 954-201-7471. *Fax:* 954-201-7466. *E-mail:* walexand@broward.edu. *Website:* http://www.broward.edu/.

Cambridge College of Healthcare & Technology

Delray Beach, Florida

Admissions Office Contact Cambridge College of Healthcare & Technology, 5150 Linton Boulevard, Suite 340, Delray Beach, FL 33484. *Website:* http://www.cambridgehealth.edu/.

Chipola College

Marianna, Florida

Freshman Application Contact Mrs. Kathy L. Rehberg, Registrar, Chipola College, 3094 Indian Circle, Marianna, FL 32446-3065. *Phone:* 850-718-2233. *Fax:* 850-718-2287. *E-mail:* rehbergk@chipola.edu. *Website:* http://www.chipola.edu/.

City College

Altamonte Springs, Florida

- **Independent** primarily 2-year
- **Coed, primarily women**

Undergraduates 217 full-time. *Retention:* 47% of full-time freshmen returned.
Faculty *Student/faculty ratio:* 17:1.
Academics *Calendar:* semesters. *Degrees:* diplomas, associate, and bachelor's.
Standardized Tests *Required:* TABE (for admission).
Applying *Application fee:* $25. *Required:* high school transcript, interview.
Director of Admissions Ms. Kimberly Bowden, Director of Admissions, City College, 177 Montgomery Road, Altamonte Springs, FL 32714. *Phone:* 352-335-4000. *Fax:* 352-335-4303. *E-mail:* kbowden@citycollege.edu. *Website:* http://www.citycollege.edu/.

City College

Fort Lauderdale, Florida

- **Independent** primarily 2-year, founded 1984
- **Coed**
- 91% of applicants were admitted

Faculty *Student/faculty ratio:* 20:1.
Academics *Calendar:* semesters. *Degrees:* certificates, associate, and bachelor's.
Standardized Tests *Required:* TABE (for admission).
Applying *Application fee:* $40. *Required:* high school transcript, interview.
Freshman Application Contact City College, 2000 West Commercial Boulevard, Suite 200, Fort Lauderdale, FL 33309. *Phone:* 954-492-5353. *Toll-free phone:* 866-314-5681. *Website:* http://www.citycollege.edu/.

City College
Gainesville, Florida

- **Independent** primarily 2-year, founded 1986
- **Coed**
- 98% of applicants were admitted

Faculty *Student/faculty ratio:* 15:1.
Academics *Calendar:* semesters. *Degrees:* certificates, associate, and bachelor's.
Standardized Tests *Required:* TABE (for admission).
Applying *Application fee:* $40. *Required:* high school transcript, interview.
Freshman Application Contact Admissions Office, City College, 7001 Northwest 4th Boulevard, Gainesville, FL 32607. *Phone:* 352-335-4000. *Website:* http://www.citycollege.edu/.

City College
Hollywood, Florida

Admissions Office Contact City College, 6565 Taft Street, Hollywood, FL 33024. *Toll-free phone:* 866-314-5681. *Website:* http://www.citycollege.edu/.

City College
Miami, Florida

- **Independent** primarily 2-year, founded 1997
- **Coed**
- 62% of applicants were admitted

Faculty *Student/faculty ratio:* 22:1.
Academics *Calendar:* semesters. *Degrees:* certificates, associate, and bachelor's.
Standardized Tests *Required:* TABE (for admission).
Applying *Application fee:* $40. *Required:* high school transcript, interview.
Freshman Application Contact Admissions Office, City College, 9300 South Dadeland Boulevard, Suite PH, Miami, FL 33156. *Phone:* 305-666-9242. *Fax:* 305-666-9243. *Website:* http://www.citycollege.edu/.

College of Business and Technology–Cutler Bay Campus
Cutler Bay, Florida

Freshman Application Contact College of Business and Technology–Cutler Bay Campus, 19151 South Dixie Highway, Cutler Bay, FL 33157. *Phone:* 305-273-4499 Ext. 1100. *Website:* http://www.cbt.edu/.

College of Business and Technology–Flagler Campus
Miami, Florida

Freshman Application Contact College of Business and Technology–Flagler Campus, 8230 West Flagler Street, Miami, FL 33144. *Phone:* 305-273-4499 Ext. 1100. *Website:* http://www.cbt.edu/.

College of Business and Technology–Hialeah Campus
Hialeah, Florida

Freshman Application Contact College of Business and Technology–Hialeah Campus, 935 West 49 Street, Hialeah, FL 33012. *Phone:* 305-273-4499 Ext. 1100. *Website:* http://www.cbt.edu/.

College of Business and Technology–Main Campus
Miami, Florida

Freshman Application Contact College of Business and Technology–Main Campus, 8700 West Flagler Street, Suite 420, Miami, FL 33174. *Phone:* 305-273-4499 Ext. 1100. *Website:* http://www.cbt.edu/.

College of Business and Technology–Miami Gardens
Miami Gardens, Florida

Freshman Application Contact College of Business and Technology–Miami Gardens, 5190 NW 167 Street, Miami Gardens, FL 33014. *Phone:* 305-273-4499 Ext. 1100. *Website:* http://www.cbt.edu/.

College of Central Florida
Ocala, Florida

- **State and locally supported** primarily 2-year, founded 1957, part of Florida College System
- **Small-town** 139-acre campus
- **Endowment** $65.4 million
- **Coed**

Undergraduates 3,016 full-time, 3,804 part-time. 3% are from out of state; 14% Black or African American, non-Hispanic/Latino; 15% Hispanic/Latino; 2% Asian, non-Hispanic/Latino; 0.5% Native Hawaiian or other Pacific Islander, non-Hispanic/Latino; 0.4% American Indian or Alaska Native, non-Hispanic/Latino; 5% Two or more races, non-Hispanic/Latino; 1% Race/ethnicity unknown; 2% international; 6% transferred in.
Academics *Calendar:* semesters. *Degrees:* certificates, diplomas, associate, and bachelor's. *Special study options:* academic remediation for entering students, adult/continuing education programs, advanced placement credit, cooperative education, distance learning, English as a second language, freshman honors college, honors programs, independent study, internships, part-time degree program, services for LD students, summer session for credit.
Library Clifford B. Stearns Learning Resources Center. *Books:* 75,935 (physical), 43,910 (digital/electronic); *Databases:* 152. Students can reserve study rooms.
Student Life *Campus security:* 24-hour emergency response devices and patrols, student patrols, late-night transport/escort service.
Athletics Member NJCAA.
Costs (2019–20) *Tuition:* $113 per credit hour part-time; state resident $3388 full-time, $113 per credit part-time; nonresident $13,146 full-time, $438 per credit hour part-time. Full-time tuition and fees vary according to degree level. Part-time tuition and fees vary according to degree level.
Financial Aid Of all full-time matriculated undergraduates who enrolled in 2017, 1,184 applied for aid, 753 were judged to have need, 23 had their need fully met. In 2017, 38. *Average percent of need met:* 55. *Average financial aid package:* $1744. *Average need-based loan:* $2164. *Average need-based gift aid:* $1731. *Average non-need-based aid:* $889.
Applying *Options:* electronic application, early admission. *Application fee:* $30. *Required:* high school transcript.
Freshman Application Contact Mr. Alton Austin, Director of Enrollment Services/Registrar, College of Central Florida, 3001 SW College Road, Ocala, FL 34474. *Phone:* 352-237-2111 Ext. 1751. *Fax:* 352-873-5882. *E-mail:* austina@cf.edu. *Website:* http://www.cf.edu/.

The College of the Florida Keys
Key West, Florida

Freshman Application Contact The College of the Florida Keys, 5901 College Road, Key West, FL 33040-4397. *Phone:* 305-296-9081 Ext. 237. *Website:* http://www.fkcc.edu/.

Concorde Career Institute
Jacksonville, Florida

Admissions Office Contact Concorde Career Institute, 7259 Salisbury Road, Jacksonville, FL 32256. *Website:* http://www.concorde.edu/.

Concorde Career Institute
Miramar, Florida

Admissions Office Contact Concorde Career Institute, 10933 Marks Way, Miramar, FL 33025. *Website:* http://www.concorde.edu/.

Concorde Career Institute
Orlando, Florida

Admissions Office Contact Concorde Career Institute, 3444 McCrory Place, Orlando, FL 32803. *Website:* http://www.concorde.edu/.

Concorde Career Institute

Tampa, Florida

Admissions Office Contact Concorde Career Institute, 4202 West Spruce Street, Tampa, FL 33607. *Website:* http://www.concorde.edu/.

Daytona College

Ormond Beach, Florida

Admissions Office Contact Daytona College, 469 South Nova Road, Ormond Beach, FL 32174-8445. *Website:* http://www.daytonacollege.edu/.

Daytona State College

Daytona Beach, Florida

- **State-supported** primarily 2-year, founded 1957, part of Florida College System
- **Suburban** 100-acre campus with easy access to Orlando
- **Endowment** $14.1 million
- **Coed,** 13,430 undergraduate students, 41% full-time, 61% women, 39% men

Undergraduates 5,562 full-time, 7,868 part-time. Students come from 22 other countries; 2% are from out of state; 12% Black or African American, non-Hispanic/Latino; 17% Hispanic/Latino; 2% Asian, non-Hispanic/Latino; 0.2% Native Hawaiian or other Pacific Islander, non-Hispanic/Latino; 0.3% American Indian or Alaska Native, non-Hispanic/Latino; 4% Two or more races, non-Hispanic/Latino; 2% Race/ethnicity unknown; 0.2% international.
Freshmen *Admission:* 1,941 admitted, 1,941 enrolled.
Faculty *Total:* 885, 28% full-time, 16% with terminal degrees. *Student/faculty ratio:* 18:1.
Majors Accounting technology and bookkeeping; aeronautical/aerospace engineering technology; biology teacher education; business administration and management; business administration, management and operations related; chemistry teacher education; community health services counseling; computer engineering technology; computer programming; computer programming (specific applications); construction engineering technology; criminal justice/law enforcement administration; dental hygiene; digital communication and media/multimedia; drafting and design technology; early childhood education; electrical, electronic and communications engineering technology; elementary education; emergency medical technology (EMT paramedic); engineering technologies and engineering related; environmental science; fire prevention and safety technology; health information/medical records technology; hospitality administration; information technology; interior design; legal assistant/paralegal; liberal arts and sciences/liberal studies; mathematics teacher education; medical radiologic technology; music technology; network and system administration; occupational therapist assistant; office management; operations management; photographic and film/video technology; photography; physical therapy technology; physics teacher education; registered nursing/registered nurse; respiratory care therapy; restaurant, culinary, and catering management; science teacher education; special education; web page, digital/multimedia and information resources design.
Academics *Calendar:* semesters. *Degrees:* certificates, diplomas, associate, bachelor's, and postbachelor's certificates. *Special study options:* academic remediation for entering students, adult/continuing education programs, advanced placement credit, cooperative education, distance learning, English as a second language, external degree program, freshman honors college, honors programs, independent study, internships, off-campus study, part-time degree program, services for LD students, study abroad, summer session for credit. *ROTC:* Army (c), Air Force (c).
Library Daytona State College Library Services plus 1 other. *Books:* 36,740 (physical), 211,462 (digital/electronic); *Serial titles:* 164 (physical); *Databases:* 100. Weekly public service hours: 68; students can reserve study rooms.
Student Life *Housing:* college housing not available. *Activities and Organizations:* drama/theater group, student-run newspaper, choral group, Phi Theta Kappa International Honors Society, Student Government Association, Student Respiratory Therapy Club, Business Club, Student Paralegal Club, national fraternities, national sororities. *Campus security:* 24-hour emergency response devices and patrols, late-night transport/escort service, emergency alert system capable of delivering text messages, voice calls, and email messages to college email accounts. *Student services:* personal/psychological counseling, women's center, veterans affairs office.
Athletics Member NJCAA. *Intercollegiate sports:* baseball M(s), basketball M(s)/W(s), cross-country running M(s)/W(s), soccer M(s)/W(s), softball W(s), volleyball W(s). *Intramural sports:* basketball M/W, football M/W, golf W, soccer M/W, table tennis M/W, volleyball M/W.
Financial Aid Of all full-time matriculated undergraduates who enrolled in 2018, 2,803 applied for aid, 2,799 were judged to have need. 206 Federal Work-Study jobs (averaging $1876). 2 state and other part-time jobs (averaging $1862). In 2018, 81 non-need-based awards were made. *Average need-based loan:* $1555. *Average need-based gift aid:* $1755. *Average non-need-based aid:* $1028. *Average indebtedness upon graduation:* $2483.
Applying *Options:* electronic application, early admission, deferred entrance. *Required:* high school transcript. *Application deadlines:* rolling (freshmen), rolling (transfers). *Notification:* continuous (freshmen), continuous (transfers).
Freshman Application Contact Dr. Karen Sanders, Director of Admissions and Recruitment, Daytona State College, 1200 International Speedway Boulevard, Daytona Beach, FL 32114. *Phone:* 386-506-3050. *E-mail:* karen.sanders@daytonastate.edu.
Website: http://www.daytonastate.edu/.

Eastern Florida State College

Cocoa, Florida

- **State-supported** primarily 2-year, founded 1960, part of Florida Community College System
- **Suburban** 100-acre campus with easy access to Orlando
- **Coed**

Undergraduates 5,929 full-time, 10,782 part-time. Students come from 67 other countries; 11% Black or African American, non-Hispanic/Latino; 10% Hispanic/Latino; 2% Asian, non-Hispanic/Latino; 0.3% Native Hawaiian or other Pacific Islander, non-Hispanic/Latino; 0.6% American Indian or Alaska Native, non-Hispanic/Latino; 3% Two or more races, non-Hispanic/Latino; 1% Race/ethnicity unknown; 0.7% international.
Faculty *Student/faculty ratio:* 23:1.
Academics *Calendar:* semesters. *Degrees:* certificates, associate, and bachelor's. *Special study options:* academic remediation for entering students, accelerated degree program, adult/continuing education programs, advanced placement credit, cooperative education, distance learning, double majors, English as a second language, external degree program, honors programs, independent study, internships, part-time degree program, services for LD students, study abroad, summer session for credit. *ROTC:* Army (b), Air Force (b).
Library UCF Library.
Student Life *Campus security:* 24-hour emergency response devices and patrols.
Athletics Member NJCAA.
Financial Aid Of all full-time matriculated undergraduates who enrolled in 2018, 200 Federal Work-Study jobs (averaging $2244). 200 state and other part-time jobs (averaging $2000).
Applying *Options:* electronic application, early admission. *Application fee:* $30. *Required:* high school transcript.
Freshman Application Contact Ms. Stephanie Burnette, Registrar, Eastern Florida State College, 1519 Clearlake Road, Cocoa, FL 32922-6597. *Phone:* 321-433-7271. *Fax:* 321-433-7172. *E-mail:* cocoaadmissions@brevardcc.edu. *Website:* http://www.easternflorida.edu/.

Florida Career College

Boynton Beach, Florida

Admissions Office Contact Florida Career College, 1749 North Congress Avenue, Boynton Beach, FL 33426. *Website:* http://www.floridacareercollege.edu/.

Florida Career College

Hialeah, Florida

Admissions Office Contact Florida Career College, 3750 West 18th Avenue, Hialeah, FL 33012. *Toll-free phone:* 888-852-7272. *Website:* http://www.floridacareercollege.edu/.

Florida Career College

Jacksonville, Florida

Admissions Office Contact Florida Career College, 6600 Youngerman Circle, Jacksonville, FL 32244. *Website:* http://www.floridacareercollege.edu/.

Florida Career College

Lauderdale Lakes, Florida

Admissions Office Contact Florida Career College, 3383 North State Road 7, Lauderdale Lakes, FL 33319. *Website:* http://www.floridacareercollege.edu/.

Florida Career College

Margate, Florida

Admissions Office Contact Florida Career College, 3271 North State Road 7, Margate, FL 33063. *Website:* http://www.floridacareercollege.edu/.

Florida Career College

Miami, Florida

Director of Admissions Mr. David Knobel, President, Florida Career College, 1321 Southwest 107th Avenue, Suite 201B, Miami, FL 33174. *Phone:* 305-553-6065. *Toll-free phone:* 888-852-7272. *Website:* http://www.floridacareercollege.edu/.

Florida Career College

Orlando, Florida

Admissions Office Contact Florida Career College, 989 North Semoran Boulevard, Orlando, FL 32807. *Website:* http://www.floridacareercollege.edu/.

Florida Career College

Pembroke Pines, Florida

Admissions Office Contact Florida Career College, 7891 Pines Boulevard, Pembroke Pines, FL 33024. *Toll-free phone:* 888-852-7272. *Website:* http://www.floridacareercollege.edu/.

Florida Career College

Tampa, Florida

Admissions Office Contact Florida Career College, 9950 Princess Palm Avenue, Tampa, FL 33619. *Website:* http://www.floridacareercollege.edu/.

Florida Career College

West Palm Beach, Florida

Admissions Office Contact Florida Career College, 6058 Okeechobee Boulevard, West Palm Beach, FL 33417. *Toll-free phone:* 888-852-7272. *Website:* http://www.floridacareercollege.edu/.

Florida Gateway College

Lake City, Florida

Freshman Application Contact Admissions, Florida Gateway College, 149 SE College Place, Lake City, FL 32025-8703. *Phone:* 386-755-4236. *E-mail:* admissions@fgc.edu. *Website:* http://www.fgc.edu/.

The Florida School of Traditional Midwifery

Gainseville, Florida

Freshman Application Contact Admissions Office, The Florida School of Traditional Midwifery, 810 East University Avenue, 2nd Floor, Gainseville, FL 32601. *Phone:* 352-338-0766. *Fax:* 352-338-2013. *E-mail:* info@midwiferyschool.org. *Website:* http://www.midwiferyschool.org/.

Florida SouthWestern State College

Fort Myers, Florida

- **State and locally supported** primarily 2-year, founded 1962, part of Florida College System
- **Urban** 413-acre campus with easy access to Fort Myers / Cape Coral
- **Endowment** $19.0 million
- **Coed,** 16,672 undergraduate students, 38% full-time, 64% women, 36% men

Undergraduates 6,337 full-time, 10,335 part-time. Students come from 44 states and territories; 33 other countries; 2% are from out of state; 12% Black or African American, non-Hispanic/Latino; 34% Hispanic/Latino; 2% Asian, non-Hispanic/Latino; 0.2% Native Hawaiian or other Pacific Islander, non-Hispanic/Latino; 0.4% American Indian or Alaska Native, non-Hispanic/Latino; 2% Two or more races, non-Hispanic/Latino; 6% Race/ethnicity unknown; 2% international; 3% transferred in; 2% live on campus. *Retention:* 63% of full-time freshmen returned.

Freshmen *Admission:* 6,397 applied, 5,084 admitted, 2,809 enrolled. *Average high school GPA:* 2.9.

Faculty *Total:* 605, 36% full-time, 36% with terminal degrees. *Student/faculty ratio:* 28:1.

Majors Accounting technology and bookkeeping; architectural technology; biology/biotechnology laboratory technician; biology teacher education; business administration and management; business administration, management and operations related; cardiovascular technology; chemical technology; child-care provision; civil engineering technology; community health services counseling; computer programming; computer systems networking and telecommunications; criminal justice/law enforcement administration; dental hygiene; drafting and design technology; early childhood education; elementary education; emergency medical technology (EMT paramedic); English/language arts teacher education; fire prevention and safety technology; forensic science and technology; health information/medical records technology; homeland security, law enforcement, firefighting and protective services related; information technology; legal assistant/paralegal; liberal arts and sciences/liberal studies; management information systems; mathematics teacher education; medical radiologic technology; network and system administration; operations management; opticianry; physical therapy technology; registered nursing/registered nurse; respiratory care therapy; respiratory therapy technician; science teacher education; substance abuse/addiction counseling; turf and turfgrass management; web page, digital/multimedia and information resources design.

Academics *Calendar:* semesters. *Degrees:* certificates, associate, and bachelor's. *Special study options:* academic remediation for entering students, accelerated degree program, advanced placement credit, distance learning, double majors, English as a second language, honors programs, independent study, internships, off-campus study, part-time degree program, services for LD students, study abroad, summer session for credit.

Library Richard H. Rush Library. *Books:* 37,233 (physical), 35,669 (digital/electronic); *Databases:* 120. Weekly public service hours: 79.

Student Life *Housing Options:* coed. Campus housing is university owned. *Activities and Organizations:* drama/theater group, student-run newspaper, choral group. *Campus security:* 24-hour emergency response devices and patrols, late-night transport/escort service, controlled dormitory access, Rave Guardian app for students, faculty, and staff. *Student services:* personal/psychological counseling, veterans affairs office.

Athletics Member NJCAA. *Intercollegiate sports:* baseball M(s), basketball M(s)/W(s), softball W(s), volleyball W(s). *Intramural sports:* basketball M/W, soccer M/W, volleyball W.

Costs (2019–20) *Tuition:* state resident $2436 full-time, $81 per credit hour part-time; nonresident $9750 full-time, $325 per credit hour part-time. Full-time tuition and fees vary according to degree level. Part-time tuition and fees vary according to degree level. *Required fees:* $965 full-time, $32 per credit hour part-time. *Room and board:* $10,500; room only: $6000. *Payment plan:* installment. *Waivers:* employees or children of employees.

Financial Aid Of all full-time matriculated undergraduates who enrolled in 2014, 3,887 applied for aid, 3,311 were judged to have need, 68 had their need fully met. In 2014, 166 non-need-based awards were made. *Average percent of need met:* 47%. *Average financial aid package:* $6172. *Average need-based loan:* $3461. *Average need-based gift aid:* $5119. *Average non-need-based aid:* $2588.

Applying *Options:* electronic application, early admission, deferred entrance. *Application fee:* $30. *Required:* high school transcript. *Application deadlines:* 7/31 (freshmen), 7/31 (transfers). *Notification:* continuous (freshmen), continuous (transfers).

Freshman Application Contact FSW Admissions, Florida SouthWestern State College, 8099 College Parkway, Fort Myers, FL 33919. *Phone:* 239-489-9054. *Fax:* 239-489-9094. *E-mail:* admissions@fsw.edu. *Website:* http://www.fsw.edu/.

Florida State College at Jacksonville

Jacksonville, Florida

Freshman Application Contact Dr. Peter Biegel, Registrar, Florida State College at Jacksonville, 501 West State Street, Jacksonville, FL 32202. *Phone:* 904-632-5112. *Toll-free phone:* 888-873-1145. *E-mail:* pbiegel@fscj.edu. *Website:* http://www.fscj.edu/.

Florida Technical College

Orlando, Florida

Director of Admissions Ms. Jeanette E. Muschlitz, Director of Admissions, Florida Technical College, 12900 Challenger Parkway, Orlando, FL 32826. *Phone:* 407-678-5600. *Toll-free phone:* 888-574-2082. *Website:* http://www.ftccollege.edu/.

Fortis College
Cutler Bay, Florida

Admissions Office Contact Fortis College, 19600 South Dixie Highway, Suite B, Cutler Bay, FL 33157. *Toll-free phone:* 855-4-FORTIS. *Website:* http://www.fortis.edu/.

Fortis College
Orange Park, Florida

Admissions Office Contact Fortis College, 700 Blanding Boulevard, Suite 16, Orange Park, FL 32065. *Toll-free phone:* 855-4-FORTIS. *Website:* http://www.fortis.edu/.

Fortis Institute
Pensacola, Florida

Admissions Office Contact Fortis Institute, 4081 East Olive Road, Suite B, Pensacola, FL 32514. *Toll-free phone:* 855-4-FORTIS. *Website:* http://www.fortis.edu/.

Fortis Institute
Port St. Lucie, Florida

Admissions Office Contact Fortis Institute, 9022 South US Highway 1, Port St. Lucie, FL 34952. *Toll-free phone:* 855-4-FORTIS. *Website:* http://www.fortis.edu/.

Galen College of Nursing
St. Petersburg, Florida

Admissions Office Contact Galen College of Nursing, 11101 Roosevelt Boulevard North, St. Petersburg, FL 33716. *Toll-free phone:* 877-223-7040. *Website:* http://www.galencollege.edu/.

Gulf Coast State College
Panama City, Florida

- **State-supported** primarily 2-year, founded 1957, part of Florida College System
- **Urban** 80-acre campus
- **Coed,** 4,797 undergraduate students, 34% full-time, 63% women, 37% men

Undergraduates 1,625 full-time, 3,172 part-time. Students come from 15 states and territories; 3% are from out of state; 11% Black or African American, non-Hispanic/Latino; 7% Hispanic/Latino; 3% Asian, non-Hispanic/Latino; 0.1% Native Hawaiian or other Pacific Islander, non-Hispanic/Latino; 0.6% American Indian or Alaska Native, non-Hispanic/Latino; 4% Two or more races, non-Hispanic/Latino; 4% Race/ethnicity unknown; 0.6% international; 3% transferred in.
Freshmen *Admission:* 855 enrolled.
Faculty *Total:* 282, 47% full-time. *Student/faculty ratio:* 19:1.
Majors Accounting technology and bookkeeping; animation, interactive technology, video graphics and special effects; automation engineer technology; business administration and management; business administration, management and operations related; CAD/CADD drafting/design technology; child-care provision; civil engineering technology; communications technology; computer/information technology services administration related; computer programming; computer programming (vendor/product certification); computer systems networking and telecommunications; construction engineering technology; criminal justice/law enforcement administration; dental hygiene; diagnostic medical sonography and ultrasound technology; digital arts; digital communication and media/multimedia; early childhood education; electrical, electronic and communications engineering technology; emergency medical technology (EMT paramedic); engineering technology; fire prevention and safety technology; forensic science and technology; health services/allied health/health sciences; hospitality administration; liberal arts and sciences/liberal studies; management information systems; manufacturing engineering technology; medical administrative assistant and medical secretary; medical radiologic technology; music technology; network and system administration; nuclear medical technology; office management; physical therapy technology; registered nursing/registered nurse; respiratory care therapy; restaurant, culinary, and catering management; surgical technology; transportation/mobility management; web page, digital/multimedia and information resources design.
Academics *Calendar:* semesters. *Degrees:* certificates, associate, and bachelor's. *Special study options:* academic remediation for entering students, accelerated degree program, adult/continuing education programs, advanced placement credit, cooperative education, distance learning, double majors, English as a second language, external degree program, honors programs, independent study, off-campus study, part-time degree program, services for LD students, study abroad, summer session for credit.
Library Gulf Coast State College Library. *Books:* 29,718 (physical), 84,826 (digital/electronic); *Serial titles:* 44 (physical), 42,430 (digital/electronic); *Databases:* 133.
Student Life *Housing:* college housing not available. *Activities and Organizations:* drama/theater group, student-run newspaper, radio and television station, choral group, Student Government Association, TRiO Society, Visionaries Ink, Student Veteran's Association. *Campus security:* 24-hour patrols, late-night transport/escort service, patrols by trained security personnel during campus hours. *Student services:* personal/psychological counseling, veterans affairs office.
Athletics Member NJCAA. *Intercollegiate sports:* baseball M(s), basketball M(s)/W(s), softball W(s), volleyball W(s).
Costs (2019–20) *Tuition:* state resident $2370 full-time, $99 per credit hour part-time; nonresident $8633 full-time, $360 per credit hour part-time. Full-time tuition and fees vary according to degree level. Part-time tuition and fees vary according to degree level. *Required fees:* $620 full-time, $26 per credit hour part-time.
Financial Aid Of all full-time matriculated undergraduates who enrolled in 2018, 145 Federal Work-Study jobs (averaging $3200). 60 state and other part-time jobs (averaging $2600).
Applying *Options:* electronic application, early admission, deferred entrance. *Application fee:* $20. *Required:* high school transcript. *Application deadlines:* rolling (freshmen), rolling (transfers). *Notification:* continuous (freshmen).
Freshman Application Contact Ms. Shelby Antolchick, Application Process Specialist, Gulf Coast State College, 5230 West U.S. Highway 98, Panama City, FL 32401. *Phone:* 850-769-1551 Ext. 2936. *Fax:* 850-913-3308. *E-mail:* santolchi@gulfcoast.edu.
Website: http://www.gulfcoast.edu/.

Gwinnett Institute
Orlando, Florida

Admissions Office Contact Gwinnett Institute, 1900 North Alafaya Trail, Orlando, FL 32826. *Website:* http://www.gwinnettcollege.edu/locations/orlando/.

Health Career Institute
West Palm Beach, Florida

Admissions Office Contact Health Career Institute, 1764 North Congress Avenue, West Palm Beach, FL 33409. *Website:* http://www.hci.edu/.

Hillsborough Community College
Tampa, Florida

- **State-supported** 2-year, founded 1968, part of Florida College System
- **Urban** campus with easy access to Tampa, Clearwater, St. Petersburg
- **Coed,** 22,404 undergraduate students, 46% full-time, 58% women, 42% men

Undergraduates 10,377 full-time, 12,027 part-time. Students come from 28 states and territories; 88 other countries; 3% are from out of state; 18% Black or African American, non-Hispanic/Latino; 22% Hispanic/Latino; 3% Asian, non-Hispanic/Latino; 0.2% Native Hawaiian or other Pacific Islander, non-Hispanic/Latino; 0.3% American Indian or Alaska Native, non-Hispanic/Latino; 4% Two or more races, non-Hispanic/Latino; 3% Race/ethnicity unknown; 2% international; 9% transferred in.
Freshmen *Admission:* 5,231 enrolled.
Faculty *Total:* 1,115, 29% full-time, 19% with terminal degrees. *Student/faculty ratio:* 25:1.
Majors Accounting technology and bookkeeping; aquaculture; architectural engineering technology; architectural technology; biotechnology; business administration and management; cardiovascular technology; child-care and support services management; clinical research coordinator; community health services counseling; computer and information systems security; computer engineering technology; computer programming; computer programming (specific applications); criminal justice/law enforcement administration; dental hygiene; diagnostic medical sonography and ultrasound technology; dietetic technology; digital communication and media/multimedia; electrical, electronic and communications engineering technology; emergency medical technology (EMT paramedic); engineering technology; environmental science; fire prevention and safety technology; health services administration; hospitality administration; information technology; information technology project management; legal assistant/paralegal; liberal arts and sciences/liberal studies; medical radiologic technology; network and system administration; nuclear medical technology; office management; operations management;

opticianry; optometric technician; registered nursing/registered nurse; respiratory care therapy; restaurant, culinary, and catering management; restaurant/food services management; veterinary/animal health technology; web page, digital/multimedia and information resources design.
Academics *Calendar:* semesters. *Degrees:* certificates, associate, and postbachelor's certificates. *Special study options:* academic remediation for entering students, advanced placement credit, cooperative education, distance learning, English as a second language, honors programs, independent study, internships, off-campus study, part-time degree program, services for LD students, study abroad, summer session for credit. *ROTC:* Army (c), Air Force (c).
Library Dale Mabry Library plus 4 others. *Books:* 103,082 (physical), 47,229 (digital/electronic); *Serial titles:* 1,063 (physical), 37,610 (digital/electronic); *Databases:* 116.
Student Life *Housing Options:* coed. Campus housing is university owned. *Activities and Organizations:* drama/theater group, student-run newspaper, radio station, choral group. *Campus security:* campus escorts, jump starts and vehicle assistance, training in safety education and awareness, door and building locks/unlocks. *Student services:* personal/psychological counseling, veterans affairs office.
Athletics Member NJCAA. *Intercollegiate sports:* baseball M(s), basketball M(s)/W(s), softball W(s), tennis W(s), volleyball W(s).
Applying *Options:* electronic application, early admission. *Required:* high school transcript. *Application deadlines:* rolling (freshmen), rolling (transfers).
Freshman Application Contact Ms. Nevaler T. Davis, College Registrar, Hillsborough Community College, PO Box 31127, Tampa, FL 33631-3127. *Phone:* 813-259-6565. *E-mail:* ndavis5@hccfl.edu.
Website: http://www.hccfl.edu/.

Hope College of Arts and Sciences
Pompano Beach, Florida

Admissions Office Contact Hope College of Arts and Sciences, 1200 SW 3rd Street, Pompano Beach, FL 33069. *Website:* http://www.hcas.edu/.

Jones Technical Institute
Jacksonville, Florida

Admissions Office Contact Jones Technical Institute, 8813 Western Way, Jacksonville, FL 32256. *Website:* http://www.jtech.org/.

Lake-Sumter State College
Leesburg, Florida

Freshman Application Contact Ms. Bonnie Yanick, Enrollment Specialist, Lake-Sumter State College, 9501 U.S. Highway 441, Leesburg, FL 34788-8751. *Phone:* 352-365-3561. *Fax:* 352-365-3553. *E-mail:* admissinquiry@lscc.edu. *Website:* http://www.lssc.edu/.

Medical Prep Institute of Tampa Bay
Tampa, Florida

Admissions Office Contact Medical Prep Institute of Tampa Bay, 2304 East Busch Boulevard, Tampa, FL 33612. *Website:* http://www.medicalprepinstitute.org/.

Med-Life Institute
Kissimmee, Florida

Admissions Office Contact Med-Life Institute, 4727 West Irlo Bronson Memorial Highway, Kissimmee, FL 34746. *Website:* http://www.medlifeinstitute.com/.

Med-Life Institute
Lauderdale Lakes, Florida

Admissions Office Contact Med-Life Institute, 4000 North State Road 7, Lauderdale Lakes, FL 33319. *Website:* http://www.medlifeinstitute.com/.

Med-Life Institute
Naples, Florida

Admissions Office Contact Med-Life Institute, 4995 East Tamiami Trail, Naples, FL 34112. *Website:* http://www.medlifeinstitute.com/.

Meridian College
Sarasota, Florida

Admissions Office Contact Meridian College, 7020 Professional Parkway East, Sarasota, FL 34240. *Website:* http://www.meridian.edu/.

Miami Dade College
Miami, Florida

- **State and locally supported** primarily 2-year, founded 1960, part of Florida College System
- **Urban** campus
- **Endowment** $137.1 million
- **Coed,** 56,001 undergraduate students, 42% full-time, 57% women, 43% men

Undergraduates 23,589 full-time, 32,412 part-time. Students come from 37 states and territories; 165 other countries; 0.4% are from out of state; 14% Black or African American, non-Hispanic/Latino; 70% Hispanic/Latino; 1% Asian, non-Hispanic/Latino; 0.1% Native Hawaiian or other Pacific Islander, non-Hispanic/Latino; 0.1% American Indian or Alaska Native, non-Hispanic/Latino; 0.6% Two or more races, non-Hispanic/Latino; 2% Race/ethnicity unknown; 6% international; 0.1% transferred in.
Freshmen *Admission:* 44,910 applied, 44,910 admitted, 12,173 enrolled.
Faculty *Total:* 2,355, 30% full-time, 25% with terminal degrees. *Student/faculty ratio:* 26:1.
Majors Accounting technology and bookkeeping; aeronautics/aviation/aerospace science and technology; agriculture; airline pilot and flight crew; air traffic control; American studies; animation, interactive technology, video graphics and special effects; anthropology; architectural drafting and CAD/CADD; architectural engineering technology; architectural technology; art; Asian studies; audiology and speech-language pathology; automation engineer technology; aviation/airway management; banking and financial support services; behavioral sciences; biology/biological sciences; biology teacher education; biomedical technology; biotechnology; business administration and management; business administration, management and operations related; business automation/technology/data entry; CAD/CADD drafting/design technology; chemistry; chemistry teacher education; child-care provision; child development; cinematography and film/video production; civil engineering technology; clinical/medical laboratory technology; commercial and advertising art; community health services counseling; comparative literature; computer and information sciences; computer engineering technology; computer graphics; computer installation and repair technology; computer programming; computer programming (specific applications); computer programming (vendor/product certification); computer science; computer software technology; computer support specialist; computer systems networking and telecommunications; computer technology/computer systems technology; construction engineering technology; cooking and related culinary arts; corrections; corrections and criminal justice related; court reporting; criminal justice/law enforcement administration; criminal justice/police science; culinary arts; customer service support/call center/teleservice operation; dance; dental hygiene; diagnostic medical sonography and ultrasound technology; dietetics; dietetic technology; drafting and design technology; dramatic/theater arts; early childhood education; economics; education; education related; education (specific levels and methods) related; electrical and electronic engineering technologies related; electrical, electronic and communications engineering technology; electrician; elementary education; emergency medical technology (EMT paramedic); engineering; engineering related; engineering technology; English; entrepreneurship; environmental engineering technology; environmental science; finance; fire prevention and safety technology; fire science/firefighting; food science; forensic science and technology; forestry; French; funeral service and mortuary science; game and interactive media design; general studies; geology/earth science; German; health information/medical records administration; health information/medical records technology; health/medical preparatory programs related; health professions related; health services/allied health/health sciences; heating, air conditioning, ventilation and refrigeration maintenance technology; heating, ventilation, air conditioning and refrigeration engineering technology; histologic technician; histologic technology/histotechnologist; history; homeland security, law enforcement, firefighting and protective services related; horticultural science; hospitality administration; hotel/motel administration; humanities; human services; industrial technology; information science/studies; information technology; interior design; international relations and affairs; Italian; journalism; kindergarten/preschool education; landscaping and groundskeeping; Latin American studies; legal administrative assistant/secretary; legal assistant/paralegal; liberal arts and sciences/liberal studies; logistics, materials, and supply chain management; management information systems; manufacturing engineering technology; marketing/marketing management; massage therapy; mass communication/media; mathematics; mathematics teacher education;

medical/clinical assistant; medical radiologic technology; middle school education; music; music performance; music teacher education; music technology; natural sciences; network and system administration; nonprofit management; nuclear medical technology; office management; operations management; ophthalmic technology; opticianry; ornamental horticulture; parks, recreation and leisure; pharmacy technician; philosophy; phlebotomy technology; photographic and film/video technology; photography; physical education teaching and coaching; physical sciences; physical therapy technology; physician assistant; physics; physics teacher education; pipefitting and sprinkler fitting; plant nursery management; plumbing technology; political science and government; Portuguese; pre-engineering; psychology; public administration; radio and television; radio and television broadcasting technology; radiologic technology/science; real estate; recording arts technology; registered nursing/registered nurse; respiratory care therapy; respiratory therapy technician; restaurant, culinary, and catering management; restaurant/food services management; science teacher education; security and loss prevention; sheet metal technology; sign language interpretation and translation; social sciences; social work; sociology; Spanish; special education; special education–individuals with hearing impairments; substance abuse/addiction counseling; teacher assistant/aide; telecommunications technology; theater design and technology; tourism and travel services management; veterinary/animal health technology; web page, digital/multimedia and information resources design.

Academics *Calendar:* 16-16-6-6. *Degrees:* certificates, associate, bachelor's, and postbachelor's certificates. *Special study options:* academic remediation for entering students, accelerated degree program, adult/continuing education programs, advanced placement credit, cooperative education, distance learning, English as a second language, freshman honors college, honors programs, independent study, internships, off-campus study, part-time degree program, services for LD students, study abroad, summer session for credit. *ROTC:* Army (b), Air Force (c).

Library Miami Dade College Learning Resources plus 9 others. *Books:* 185,820 (physical), 60,221 (digital/electronic); *Serial titles:* 708 (physical), 46,482 (digital/electronic); *Databases:* 126. Weekly public service hours: 69; students can reserve study rooms.

Student Life *Housing:* college housing not available. *Activities and Organizations:* drama/theater group, student-run newspaper, radio and television station, choral group, Student Government Association, Phi Theta Kappa, Phi Beta Lambda (business), Future Educators of America Professional, Kappa Delta Pi Honor Society (education). *Campus security:* 24-hour emergency response devices and patrols, student patrols, late-night transport/escort service, Emergency Mass Notification System (EMNS), campus public address systems, LiveSafe mobile safety App for students/employees. *Student services:* health clinic, personal/psychological counseling, veterans affairs office.

Athletics Member NCAA, NJCAA. All NCAA Division I. *Intercollegiate sports:* baseball M(s), basketball M(s)/W(s), softball W(s), volleyball W(s).

Costs (2019–20) *One-time required fee:* $30. *Tuition:* state resident $1987 full-time, $83 per credit hour part-time; nonresident $7947 full-time, $331 per credit hour part-time. Full-time tuition and fees vary according to course load, degree level, and program. Part-time tuition and fees vary according to course load, degree level, and program. *Required fees:* $851 full-time, $35 per semester hour part-time. *Payment plan:* installment. *Waivers:* employees or children of employees.

Financial Aid Of all full-time matriculated undergraduates who enrolled in 2018, 800 Federal Work-Study jobs (averaging $5000). 125 state and other part-time jobs (averaging $5000).

Applying *Options:* electronic application, early admission. *Application fee:* $30. *Required:* high school transcript. *Application deadlines:* rolling (freshmen), rolling (transfers). *Notification:* continuous (freshmen), continuous (transfers).

Freshman Application Contact Ms. Elisabet Vizoso, Interim College Registrar, Miami Dade College, 11011 SW 104th Street, Miami, FL 33176. *Phone:* 305-237-2206. *Fax:* 305-237-2532. *E-mail:* evizoso@mdc.edu. *Website:* http://www.mdc.edu/.

North Florida College

Madison, Florida

Freshman Application Contact Mr. Bobby Scott, North Florida College, 325 Northwest Turner Davis Drive, Madison, FL 32340. *Phone:* 850-973-9450. *Toll-free phone:* 866-937-6322. *Fax:* 850-973-1697. *Website:* http://www.nfcc.edu/.

Northwest Florida State College

Niceville, Florida

Freshman Application Contact Ms. Karen Cooper, Director of Admissions, Northwest Florida State College, 100 College Boulevard, Niceville, FL 32578. *Phone:* 850-729-4901. *Fax:* 850-729-5206. *E-mail:* cooperk@nwfsc.edu. *Website:* http://www.nwfsc.edu/.

NRI Institute of Health Sciences

Royal Palm Beach, Florida

Admissions Office Contact NRI Institute of Health Sciences, 500 Royal Palm Beach Boulevard, Royal Palm Beach, FL 33411. *Website:* http://www.nriinstitute.edu/.

Pasco-Hernando State College

New Port Richey, Florida

Freshman Application Contact Ms. Estela Carrion, Director of Admissions and Student Records, Pasco-Hernando State College, 10230 Ridge Road, New Port Richey, FL 34654-5199. *Phone:* 727-816-3261. *Toll-free phone:* 877-TRY-PHSC. *Fax:* 727-816-3389. *E-mail:* carrioe@phsc.edu. *Website:* http://www.phsc.edu/.

Pensacola State College

Pensacola, Florida

- **State-supported** primarily 2-year, founded 1948, part of Florida College System
- **Urban** 130-acre campus with easy access to Mobile, Alabama
- **Endowment** $11.3 million
- **Coed,** 10,661 undergraduate students, 32% full-time, 46% women, 27% men

Undergraduates 3,410 full-time, 4,361 part-time. Students come from 25 states and territories; 5% are from out of state; 15% Black or African American, non-Hispanic/Latino; 7% Hispanic/Latino; 3% Asian, non-Hispanic/Latino; 0.4% Native Hawaiian or other Pacific Islander, non-Hispanic/Latino; 0.7% American Indian or Alaska Native, non-Hispanic/Latino; 6% Two or more races, non-Hispanic/Latino; 2% Race/ethnicity unknown; 0.4% international; 3% transferred in.

Freshmen *Admission:* 3,410 applied, 3,410 admitted, 1,376 enrolled. *Average high school GPA:* 2.5.

Faculty *Student/faculty ratio:* 19:1.

Majors Accounting; accounting technology and bookkeeping; administrative assistant and secretarial science; agricultural business and management; agriculture; architectural technology; art; art teacher education; biochemistry; biology/biological sciences; botany/plant biology; building/property maintenance; business administration and management; business administration, management and operations related; business/commerce; chemical technology; chemistry; child-care and support services management; child-care provision; civil engineering technology; commercial and advertising art; communications technology; computer and information sciences; computer and information sciences related; computer and information systems security; computer engineering; computer graphics; computer programming; computer programming (specific applications); computer programming (vendor/product certification); computer science; computer systems analysis; construction engineering technology; consumer services and advocacy; cooking and related culinary arts; criminal justice/law enforcement administration; cyber/computer forensics and counterterrorism; dental hygiene; diagnostic medical sonography and ultrasound technology; dietetics; drafting and design technology; dramatic/theater arts; early childhood education; education; education (specific levels and methods) related; electrical, electronic and communications engineering technology; elementary education; emergency medical technology (EMT paramedic); engineering; engineering technology; English; fire prevention and safety technology; food service systems administration; foods, nutrition, and wellness; forensic science and technology; geology/earth science; graphic design; hazardous materials management and waste technology; health/health-care administration; health information/medical records administration; health information/medical records technology; history; homeland security related; hospitality administration; hotel/motel administration; hotel, motel, and restaurant management; information science/studies; information technology; journalism; landscaping and groundskeeping; legal administrative assistant/secretary; legal assistant/paralegal; liberal arts and sciences/liberal studies; management information systems; management information systems and services related; management science; mathematics; medical radiologic technology; music; music teacher education; natural resources management and policy; nursing assistant/aide and patient care assistant/aide; nursing science; office management; operations management; ornamental horticulture; pharmacy technician; philosophy; photography; physical fitness technician; physical therapy technology; physics; pre-dentistry studies; pre-law studies; premedical studies; prenursing studies; pre-pharmacy studies; pre-veterinary studies; psychology; registered nursing/registered nurse; restaurant, culinary, and catering management; sociology; special education; telecommunications

technology; veterinary/animal health technology; web page, digital/multimedia and information resources design.
Academics *Calendar:* semesters. *Degrees:* certificates, diplomas, associate, and bachelor's. *Special study options:* academic remediation for entering students, adult/continuing education programs, advanced placement credit, cooperative education, distance learning, double majors, English as a second language, external degree program, honors programs, independent study, internships, part-time degree program, services for LD students, summer session for credit. *ROTC:* Army (b).
Library Edward M. Chadbourne Library plus 3 others. Students can reserve study rooms.
Student Life *Activities and Organizations:* drama/theater group, student-run newspaper, choral group, Student Government Association, Health Occupations Students of America (HOSA), SkillsUSA, African-American Student Association, Forestry Club. *Campus security:* 24-hour emergency response devices and patrols, late-night transport/escort service. *Student services:* personal/psychological counseling, veterans affairs office.
Athletics Member NJCAA. *Intercollegiate sports:* baseball M(s), basketball M(s)/W(s), softball W(s), volleyball W(s). *Intramural sports:* archery M/W, badminton M/W, basketball M/W, bowling M/W, racquetball M/W, soccer M/W, softball W, tennis M/W, volleyball M/W.
Costs (2020–21) *One-time required fee:* $30. *Tuition:* state resident $2572 full-time, $105 per credit hour part-time; nonresident $10,289 full-time, $420 per credit hour part-time. Full-time tuition and fees vary according to course level and degree level. Part-time tuition and fees vary according to course level and degree level. *Room and board:* $7650. *Payment plans:* installment, deferred payment. *Waivers:* employees or children of employees.
Financial Aid Of all full-time matriculated undergraduates who enrolled in 2018, 120 Federal Work-Study jobs (averaging $3000).
Applying *Options:* electronic application, early admission. *Application fee:* $30. *Required:* high school transcript. *Application deadlines:* 8/30 (freshmen), 8/30 (transfers). *Notification:* continuous until 8/30 (freshmen), continuous until 8/30 (transfers).
Freshman Application Contact Ms. Kathy Dutremble, Registrar, Pensacola State College, 1000 College Boulevard, Pensacola, FL 32504. *Phone:* 850-484-2076. *Fax:* 850-484-1020. *E-mail:* kdutremble@pensacolastate.edu. *Website:* http://www.pensacolastate.edu/.

Praxis Institute
Miami, Florida

Admissions Office Contact Praxis Institute, 1850 SW 8th Street, 4th Floor, Miami, FL 33135. *Website:* http://www.praxis.edu/.

Professional Hands Institute
Miami, Florida

Admissions Office Contact Professional Hands Institute, 10 NW 42 Avenue, Suite 200, Miami, FL 33126. *Website:* http://prohands.edu/.

Remington College–Heathrow Campus
Lake Mary, Florida

Admissions Office Contact Remington College–Heathrow Campus, 7131 Business Park Lane, Lake Mary, FL 32746. *Toll-free phone:* 800-323-8122. *Website:* http://www.remingtoncollege.edu/.

SABER College
Miami, Florida

Admissions Office Contact SABER College, 3990 W. Flagler Street, Suite 103, Miami, FL 33134. *Website:* http://www.sabercollege.edu/.

St. Johns River State College
Palatka, Florida

Director of Admissions Dean of Admissions and Records, St. Johns River State College, 5001 Saint Johns Avenue, Palatka, FL 32177-3897. *Phone:* 386-312-4032. *Fax:* 386-312-4289. *Website:* http://www.sjrstate.edu/.

Seminole State College of Florida
Sanford, Florida

- **State and locally supported** primarily 2-year, founded 1966, part of Florida College System
- **Small-town** 200-acre campus with easy access to Orlando
- **Endowment** $24.6 million
- **Coed**

Undergraduates 6,137 full-time, 11,569 part-time. Students come from 21 states and territories; 68 other countries; 3% are from out of state; 16% Black or African American, non-Hispanic/Latino; 24% Hispanic/Latino; 3% Asian, non-Hispanic/Latino; 0.3% Native Hawaiian or other Pacific Islander, non-Hispanic/Latino; 0.3% American Indian or Alaska Native, non-Hispanic/Latino; 3% Two or more races, non-Hispanic/Latino; 3% Race/ethnicity unknown; 2% international; 7% transferred in. *Retention:* 52% of full-time freshmen returned.
Faculty *Student/faculty ratio:* 26:1.
Academics *Calendar:* semesters. *Degrees:* certificates, diplomas, associate, bachelor's, and postbachelor's certificates. *Special study options:* academic remediation for entering students, accelerated degree program, adult/continuing education programs, advanced placement credit, cooperative education, distance learning, double majors, English as a second language, external degree program, honors programs, independent study, internships, part-time degree program, services for LD students, study abroad, summer session for credit. *ROTC:* Army (b).
Library Seminole State Library at Sanford Lake Mary plus 3 others. *Books:* 67,023 (physical), 145,374 (digital/electronic); *Serial titles:* 520 (physical), 18,003 (digital/electronic); *Databases:* 130. Weekly public service hours: 60; students can reserve study rooms.
Student Life *Campus security:* 24-hour emergency response devices and patrols, late-night transport/escort service.
Athletics Member NJCAA.
Applying *Options:* electronic application, early admission, deferred entrance. *Required:* high school transcript, minimum 2.0 GPA.
Admissions Office Contact Seminole State College of Florida, 100 Weldon Boulevard, Sanford, FL 32773-6199. *Website:* http://www.seminolestate.edu/.

Southeastern College–West Palm Beach
West Palm Beach, Florida

- **Proprietary** 2-year, founded 1988
- **Urban** campus
- **Coed,** 558 undergraduate students, 48% full-time, 83% women, 17% men

Undergraduates 269 full-time, 289 part-time. Students come from 6 states and territories; 2% are from out of state.
Freshmen *Admission:* 429 enrolled.
Majors Computer systems networking and telecommunications; diagnostic medical sonography and ultrasound technology; emergency medical technology (EMT paramedic); health professions related; information technology; licensed practical/vocational nurse training; medical/clinical assistant; pharmacy technician; registered nursing/registered nurse.
Academics *Degree:* certificates, diplomas, and associate. *Special study options:* accelerated degree program, adult/continuing education programs, advanced placement credit, cooperative education, distance learning, English as a second language, internships, off-campus study, part-time degree program, services for LD students, summer session for credit.
Library Southeastern College Library. *Books:* 1,728 (physical); *Serial titles:* 26 (physical); *Databases:* 5. Weekly public service hours: 50.
Student Life *Housing:* college housing not available. *Campus security:* 24-hour patrols, late-night transport/escort service.
Standardized Tests *Required:* Wonderlic Assessment, TEAS (for admission).
Costs (2020–21) *Tuition:* $19,724 full-time, $822 per credit hour part-time. Full-time tuition and fees vary according to course load and program. Part-time tuition and fees vary according to course load and program. *Required fees:* $910 full-time. *Payment plan:* installment. *Waivers:* employees or children of employees.
Financial Aid Of all full-time matriculated undergraduates who enrolled in 2018, 263 applied for aid, 263 were judged to have need, 263 had their need fully met. *Average percent of need met:* 81%.
Applying *Application fee:* $55. *Required:* high school transcript, interview. *Required for some:* essay or personal statement, letters of recommendation. *Application deadlines:* rolling (freshmen), rolling (transfers), rolling (early action). *Early decision deadline:* rolling (for plan 1), rolling (for plan 2). *Notification:* continuous (freshmen), continuous (transfers), rolling (early decision plan 1), rolling (early decision plan 2), rolling (early action).
Freshman Application Contact Admissions Office, Southeastern College–West Palm Beach, 1756 North Congress Avenue, West Palm Beach, FL 33409. *Website:* http://www.sec.edu/.

Southern Technical College

Orlando, Florida

Freshman Application Contact Mr. Robinson Elie, Director of Admissions, Southern Technical College, 1485 Florida Mall Avenue, Orlando, FL 32809. *Phone:* 407-438-6000. *Toll-free phone:* 877-347-5492. *E-mail:* relie@southerntech.edu. *Website:* http://www.southerntech.edu/.

Southern Technical College

Tampa, Florida

Director of Admissions Admissions, Southern Technical College, 3910 Riga Boulevard, Tampa, FL 33619. *Phone:* 813-630-4401. *Toll-free phone:* 877-347-5492. *Website:* http://www.southerntech.edu/locations/tampa/.

South Florida State College

Avon Park, Florida

Freshman Application Contact Ms. Brenda Desantiago, Admissions, South Florida State College, 600 West College Drive, Avon Park, FL 33825. *Phone:* 863-784-7416. *Website:* http://www.southflorida.edu/.

Tallahassee Community College

Tallahassee, Florida

Freshman Application Contact Student Success Center, Tallahassee Community College, 444 Appleyard Drive, Tallahassee, FL 32304-2895. *Phone:* 850-201-8555. *E-mail:* admissions@tcc.fl.edu. *Website:* http://www.tcc.fl.edu/.

Ultimate Medical Academy Clearwater

Clearwater, Florida

Freshman Application Contact Ultimate Medical Academy Clearwater, 1255 Cleveland Street, Clearwater, FL 33755. *Toll-free phone:* 888-205-2510. *Website:* http://www.ultimatemedical.edu/.

Ultimate Medical Academy Online

Tampa, Florida

Freshman Application Contact Online Admissions Department, Ultimate Medical Academy Online, 3101 West Dr. Martin Luther King Jr. Boulevard, Tampa, FL 33607. *Phone:* 888-209-8848. *Toll-free phone:* 888-205-2510. *E-mail:* onlineadmissions@ultimatemedical.edu. *Website:* http://www.ultimatemedical.edu/.

Universal Career School

Sweetwater, Florida

Admissions Office Contact Universal Career School, 10720 W. Flagler Street, Suite 21, Sweetwater, FL 33174. *Website:* http://www.ucs.edu/.

GEORGIA

Albany Technical College

Albany, Georgia

Freshman Application Contact Albany Technical College, 1704 South Slappey Boulevard, Albany, GA 31701. *Phone:* 229-430-3520. *Toll-free phone:* 877-261-3113. *Website:* http://www.albanytech.edu/.

Altierus Career College

Norcross, Georgia

Admissions Office Contact Altierus Career College, 1750 Beaver Ruin Road, Suite 500, Norcross, GA 30093. *Website:* http://www.altierus.edu/.

Andrew College

Cuthbert, Georgia

- **Independent United Methodist** 2-year, founded 1854
- **Rural** 40-acre campus
- **Coed**

Undergraduates Students come from 13 other countries; 24% are from out of state. *Retention:* 50% of full-time freshmen returned.
Faculty *Student/faculty ratio:* 9:1.
Academics *Calendar:* semesters. *Degree:* certificates and associate. *Special study options:* academic remediation for entering students, advanced placement credit, English as a second language, honors programs, part-time degree program, services for LD students, summer session for credit.
Library Pitts Library.
Student Life *Campus security:* 24-hour patrols, controlled dormitory access, campus police.
Athletics Member NJCAA.
Standardized Tests *Required:* SAT or ACT (for admission).
Applying *Options:* electronic application, early admission, deferred entrance. *Application fee:* $20. *Required:* high school transcript. *Required for some:* essay or personal statement, 1 letter of recommendation, interview. *Recommended:* minimum 2.0 GPA.
Freshman Application Contact Ms. Bridget Kurkowski, Director of Admission, Andrew College, 413 College Street, Cuthbert, GA 39840. *Phone:* 229-732-5986. *Toll-free phone:* 800-664-9250. *Fax:* 229-732-2176. *E-mail:* admissions@andrewcollege.edu. *Website:* http://www.andrewcollege.edu/.

Athens Technical College

Athens, Georgia

Freshman Application Contact Athens Technical College, 800 US Highway 29 North, Athens, GA 30601-1500. *Phone:* 706-355-5008. *Website:* http://www.athenstech.edu/.

Atlanta Metropolitan State College

Atlanta, Georgia

- **State-supported** 2-year, founded 1974, part of University System of Georgia
- **Urban** 68-acre campus
- **Coed**

Undergraduates 22% are from out of state. *Retention:* 56% of full-time freshmen returned.
Faculty *Student/faculty ratio:* 23:1.
Academics *Calendar:* semesters. *Degree:* associate. *Special study options:* academic remediation for entering students, adult/continuing education programs, cooperative education, distance learning, independent study, part-time degree program, services for LD students, study abroad, summer session for credit.
Library Atlanta Metropolitan College Library.
Student Life *Campus security:* 24-hour emergency response devices and patrols.
Athletics Member NJCAA.
Costs (2019–20) *Tuition:* state resident $2425 full-time, $101 per credit hour part-time; nonresident $9051 full-time, $377 per credit hour part-time. *Required fees:* $1080 full-time, $440 per credit hour part-time, $1080 per term part-time. *Room and board:* $6480.
Applying *Options:* electronic application. *Application fee:* $20. *Required:* high school transcript, certificate of immunization.
Freshman Application Contact Ms. Audrey Reid, Director, Office of Admissions, Atlanta Metropolitan State College, 1630 Metropolitan Parkway, SW, Atlanta, GA 30310-4498. *Phone:* 404-756-4004. *Fax:* 404-756-4407. *E-mail:* admissions@atlm.edu. *Website:* http://www.atlm.edu/.

Atlanta Technical College

Atlanta, Georgia

Freshman Application Contact Atlanta Technical College, 1560 Metropolitan Parkway, SW, Atlanta, GA 30310. *Phone:* 404-225-4455. *Website:* http://www.atlantatech.edu/.

Augusta Technical College

Augusta, Georgia

Freshman Application Contact Augusta Technical College, 3200 Augusta Tech Drive, Augusta, GA 30906. *Phone:* 706-771-4150. *Website:* http://www.augustatech.edu/.

Brown College of Court Reporting

Atlanta, Georgia

Admissions Office Contact Brown College of Court Reporting, 1900 Emery Street NW, Suite 200, Atlanta, GA 30318. *Website:* http://www.bccr.edu/.

Central Georgia Technical College

Warner Robins, Georgia

Freshman Application Contact Central Georgia Technical College, 80 Cohen Walker Drive, Warner Robins, GA 31088. *Phone:* 770-531-6332. *Toll-free phone:* 866-430-0135. *Website:* http://www.centralgatech.edu/.

Chattahoochee Technical College

Marietta, Georgia

Freshman Application Contact Chattahoochee Technical College, 980 South Cobb Drive, SE, Marietta, GA 30060. *Phone:* 770-757-3408. *Website:* http://www.chattahoocheetech.edu/.

Coastal Pines Technical College

Waycross, Georgia

Freshman Application Contact Coastal Pines Technical College, 1701 Carswell Avenue, Waycross, GA 31503. *Phone:* 912-338-5251. *Toll-free phone:* 877-ED-AT-OTC. *Website:* http://www.coastalpines.edu/.

Columbus Technical College

Columbus, Georgia

Freshman Application Contact Columbus Technical College, 928 Manchester Expressway, Columbus, GA 31904-6572. *Phone:* 706-649-1901. *Website:* http://www.columbustech.edu/.

East Georgia State College

Swainsboro, Georgia

- **State-supported** primarily 2-year, founded 1973, part of University System of Georgia
- **Rural** 207-acre campus
- **Coed**

Undergraduates 2,308 full-time, 693 part-time. Students come from 5 states and territories; 1 other country; 0.2% are from out of state; 44% Black or African American, non-Hispanic/Latino; 4% Hispanic/Latino; 0.9% Asian, non-Hispanic/Latino; 0.1% Native Hawaiian or other Pacific Islander, non-Hispanic/Latino; 0.2% American Indian or Alaska Native, non-Hispanic/Latino; 3% Two or more races, non-Hispanic/Latino; 0.9% Race/ethnicity unknown; 0.3% international; 9% transferred in; 12% live on campus. *Retention:* 1% of full-time freshmen returned.
Faculty *Student/faculty ratio:* 26:1.
Academics *Calendar:* semesters. *Degrees:* certificates, associate, and bachelor's. *Special study options:* academic remediation for entering students, adult/continuing education programs, advanced placement credit, distance learning, honors programs, independent study, off-campus study, part-time degree program, services for LD students, study abroad, summer session for credit.
Library East Georgia College Library. Students can reserve study rooms.
Student Life *Campus security:* 24-hour patrols, late-night transport/escort service, controlled dormitory access.
Athletics Member NJCAA.
Financial Aid Of all full-time matriculated undergraduates who enrolled in 2018, 43 Federal Work-Study jobs (averaging $1560).
Applying *Options:* early admission, deferred entrance. *Application fee:* $20. *Required:* high school transcript.
Freshman Application Contact East Georgia State College, 131 College Circle, Swainsboro, GA 30401-2699. *Phone:* 478-289-2112. *Website:* http://www.ega.edu/.

Fortis College

Smyrna, Georgia

Admissions Office Contact Fortis College, 2140 South Cobb Drive, Smyrna, GA 30080. *Toll-free phone:* 855-4-FORTIS. *Website:* http://www.fortis.edu/.

Georgia Highlands College

Rome, Georgia

- **State-supported** primarily 2-year, founded 1970, part of University System of Georgia
- **Suburban** 226-acre campus with easy access to Atlanta
- **Endowment** $40,227
- **Coed**

Undergraduates 2,885 full-time, 3,299 part-time. Students come from 23 states and territories; 1% are from out of state; 16% Black or African American, non-Hispanic/Latino; 15% Hispanic/Latino; 2% Asian, non-Hispanic/Latino; 0.1% Native Hawaiian or other Pacific Islander, non-Hispanic/Latino; 0.2% American Indian or Alaska Native, non-Hispanic/Latino; 4% Two or more races, non-Hispanic/Latino; 0.4% Race/ethnicity unknown; 6% transferred in. *Retention:* 67% of full-time freshmen returned.
Faculty *Student/faculty ratio:* 21:1.
Academics *Calendar:* semesters. *Degrees:* associate and bachelor's. *Special study options:* academic remediation for entering students, advanced placement credit, cooperative education, distance learning, double majors, honors programs, independent study, part-time degree program, services for LD students, study abroad, summer session for credit.
Library Georgia Highlands College Library–Floyd Campus plus 4 others. *Books:* 79,592 (physical), 178,561 (digital/electronic); *Serial titles:* 48 (physical), 4,380 (digital/electronic); *Databases:* 382. Weekly public service hours: 58; students can reserve study rooms.
Student Life *Campus security:* 24-hour emergency response devices and patrols, emergency phone/email alert system.
Athletics Member NJCAA.
Standardized Tests *Required for some:* COMPASS. *Recommended:* SAT or ACT (for admission).
Financial Aid Of all full-time matriculated undergraduates who enrolled in 2018, 50 Federal Work-Study jobs (averaging $3500).
Applying *Options:* electronic application, deferred entrance. *Application fee:* $30. *Required:* high school transcript, minimum 2.0 GPA.
Freshman Application Contact Charlene Graham, Assistant Director of Admissions, Georgia Highlands College, 3175 Cedartown Highway, Rome, GA 30161. *Phone:* 706-295-6339. *Toll-free phone:* 800-332-2406. *Fax:* 706-295-6341. *E-mail:* cgraham@highlands.edu. *Website:* http://www.highlands.edu/.

Georgia Military College

Milledgeville, Georgia

Freshman Application Contact Georgia Military College, 201 East Greene Street, Old Capitol Building, Milledgeville, GA 31061-3398. *Phone:* 478-387-4890. *Toll-free phone:* 800-342-0413. *Website:* http://www.gmc.edu/.

Georgia Northwestern Technical College

Rome, Georgia

Freshman Application Contact Georgia Northwestern Technical College, One Maurice Culberson Drive, Rome, GA 30161. *Phone:* 706-295-6933. *Toll-free phone:* 866-983-GNTC. *Website:* http://www.gntc.edu/.

Georgia Piedmont Technical College

Clarkston, Georgia

Freshman Application Contact Georgia Piedmont Technical College, 495 North Indian Creek Drive, Clarkston, GA 30021-2397. *Phone:* 404-297-9522 Ext. 1229. *Website:* http://www.gptc.edu/.

Gordon State College

Barnesville, Georgia

Freshman Application Contact Gordon State College, 419 College Drive, Barnesville, GA 30204-1762. *Phone:* 678-359-5021. *Toll-free phone:* 800-282-6504. *Website:* http://www.gordonstate.edu/.

Gupton-Jones College of Funeral Service

Decatur, Georgia

Freshman Application Contact Gupton-Jones College of Funeral Service, 5141 Snapfinger Woods Drive, Decatur, GA 30035-4022. *Phone:* 770-593-2257. *Toll-free phone:* 800-848-5352. *Website:* http://www.gupton-jones.edu/.

Gwinnett College
Lilburn, Georgia

Admissions Office Contact Gwinnett College, 4230 Lawrenceville Highway, Suite 11, Lilburn, GA 30047. *Website:* http://www.gwinnettcollege.edu/.

Gwinnett College
Marietta, Georgia

Admissions Office Contact Gwinnett College, 1130 Northchase Parkway, Suite 100, Marietta, GA 30067. *Website:* http://www.gwinnettcollege.edu/locations/marietta/.

Gwinnett College
Sandy Springs, Georgia

Admissions Office Contact Gwinnett College, 6690 Roswell Road NE, Suite 2200, Sandy Springs, GA 30328. *Website:* http://www.gwinnettcollege.edu/locations/sandy-springs/.

Gwinnett Technical College
Lawrenceville, Georgia

Freshman Application Contact Gwinnett Technical College, 5150 Sugarloaf Parkway, Lawrenceville, GA 30043-5702. *Phone:* 678-762-7580 Ext. 434. *Website:* http://www.gwinnetttech.edu/.

Interactive College of Technology
Chamblee, Georgia

Freshman Application Contact Director of Admissions, Interactive College of Technology, 5303 New Peachtree Road, Chamblee, GA 30341. *Phone:* 770-216-2960. *Toll-free phone:* 800-447-2011. *Fax:* 770-216-2988. *Website:* http://ict.edu/.

Interactive College of Technology
Gainesville, Georgia

Freshman Application Contact Interactive College of Technology, 2323 Browns Bridge Road, Gainesville, GA 30504. *Website:* http://ict.edu/.

Interactive College of Technology
Morrow, Georgia

Admissions Office Contact Interactive College of Technology, 1580 Southlake Parkway, Suite C, Morrow, GA 30260. *Website:* http://ict.edu/.

Lanier Technical College
Oakwood, Georgia

Freshman Application Contact Lanier Technical College, 2990 Landrum Education Drive, PO Box 58, Oakwood, GA 30566. *Phone:* 770-531-6332. *Website:* http://www.laniertech.edu/.

Lincoln College of Technology - Marietta
Marietta, Georgia

Admissions Office Contact Lincoln College of Technology - Marietta, 2359 Windy Hill Road, Marietta, GA 30067. *Toll-free phone:* 844-215-1513. *Website:* http://www.lincolntech.edu/.

Miller-Motte College - Augusta
Augusta, Georgia

Admissions Office Contact Miller-Motte College - Augusta, 621 Frontage Road NW, Augusta, GA 30907. *Toll-free phone:* 800-705-9182. *Website:* http://www.miller-motte.edu/.

Miller-Motte College - Columbus
Columbus, Georgia

Admissions Office Contact Miller-Motte College - Columbus, 1800 Box Road, Columbus, GA 31907. *Toll-free phone:* 800-705-9182. *Website:* http://www.miller-motte.edu/.

Miller-Motte Technical College - Macon
Macon, Georgia

Admissions Office Contact Miller-Motte Technical College - Macon, 175 Tom Hill Sr. Boulevard, Macon, GA 31210. *Toll-free phone:* 800-705-9182. *Website:* http://www.miller-motte.edu/.

North Georgia Technical College
Clarkesville, Georgia

Freshman Application Contact North Georgia Technical College, 1500 Georgia Highway 197, North, PO Box 65, Clarkesville, GA 30523. *Phone:* 706-754-7724. *Website:* http://www.northgatech.edu/.

Oconee Fall Line Technical College
Sandersville, Georgia

Freshman Application Contact Oconee Fall Line Technical College, 1189 Deepstep Road, Sandersville, GA 31082. *Phone:* 478-553-2050. *Toll-free phone:* 877-399-8324. *Website:* http://www.oftc.edu/.

Ogeechee Technical College
Statesboro, Georgia

Freshman Application Contact Ogeechee Technical College, One Joe Kennedy Boulevard, Statesboro, GA 30458. *Phone:* 912-871-1600. *Toll-free phone:* 800-646-1316. *Website:* http://www.ogeecheetech.edu/.

SAE Institute Atlanta
Atlanta, Georgia

Admissions Office Contact SAE Institute Atlanta, 215 Peachtree Street NE, Atlanta, GA 30303. *Website:* http://www.sae.edu/.

Savannah Technical College
Savannah, Georgia

Freshman Application Contact Savannah Technical College, 5717 White Bluff Road, Savannah, GA 31405. *Phone:* 912-443-5711. *Toll-free phone:* 800-769-6362. *Website:* http://www.savannahtech.edu/.

Southeastern Technical College
Vidalia, Georgia

Freshman Application Contact Southeastern Technical College, 3001 East First Street, Vidalia, GA 30474. *Phone:* 912-538-3121. *Website:* http://www.southeasterntech.edu/.

Southern Crescent Technical College
Griffin, Georgia

Freshman Application Contact Southern Crescent Technical College, 501 Varsity Road, Griffin, GA 30223. *Phone:* 770-646-6160. *Website:* http://www.sctech.edu/.

Southern Regional Technical College
Thomasville, Georgia

Freshman Application Contact Southern Regional Technical College, 15689 US 19 North, Thomasville, GA 31792. *Phone:* 229-225-5089. *Website:* http://www.southwestgatech.edu/.

South Georgia State College
Douglas, Georgia

Freshman Application Contact South Georgia State College, 100 West College Park Drive, Douglas, GA 31533-5098. *Phone:* 912-260-4409. *Toll-free phone:* 800-342-6364. *Website:* http://sgsc.edu.

South Georgia Technical College
Americus, Georgia

Freshman Application Contact South Georgia Technical College, 900 South Georgia Tech Parkway, Americus, GA 31709. *Phone:* 229-931-2299. *Website:* http://www.southgatech.edu/.

West Georgia Technical College

Waco, Georgia

Freshman Application Contact West Georgia Technical College, 176 Murphy Campus Boulevard, Waco, GA 30182. *Phone:* 770-537-5719. *Website:* http://www.westgatech.edu/.

Wiregrass Georgia Technical College

Valdosta, Georgia

Freshman Application Contact Wiregrass Georgia Technical College, 4089 Val Tech Road, Valdosta, GA 31602. *Phone:* 229-468-2278. *Website:* http://www.wiregrass.edu/.

GUAM

Guam Community College

Mangilao, Guam

Freshman Application Contact Dr. Julie Ulloa-Heath, Registrar, Guam Community College, PO Box 23069 GMF, Barrigada, GU 96921. *Phone:* 671-735-5561. *Fax:* 671-735-5531. *E-mail:* julie.ulloaheath@guamcc.edu. *Website:* http://www.guamcc.edu/.

HAWAII

Hawaii Community College

Hilo, Hawaii

Director of Admissions Mrs. Tammy M. Tanaka, Admissions Specialist, Hawaii Community College, 1175 Manono Street, Hilo, HI 96720-5096. *Phone:* 808-974-7661. *Website:* http://www.hawcc.hawaii.edu/.

Hawaii Tokai International College

Kapolei, Hawaii

- **Independent** 2-year, founded 1992, part of Tokai University Educational System
- **Suburban** 7-acre campus with easy access to Honolulu
- **Coed,** 64 undergraduate students, 100% full-time, 50% women, 50% men

Undergraduates 64 full-time. Students come from 2 states and territories; 3 other countries; 7% are from out of state; 11% Asian, non-Hispanic/Latino; 2% Native Hawaiian or other Pacific Islander, non-Hispanic/Latino; 8% Two or more races, non-Hispanic/Latino; 78% international; 30% live on campus. *Retention:* 75% of full-time freshmen returned.
Freshmen *Admission:* 41 applied, 35 admitted. *Average high school GPA:* 3.1.
Faculty *Total:* 13, 46% full-time, 38% with terminal degrees. *Student/faculty ratio:* 6:1.
Majors Liberal arts and sciences/liberal studies.
Academics *Calendar:* quarters. *Degree:* certificates, diplomas, and associate. *Special study options:* academic remediation for entering students, advanced placement credit, English as a second language, internships, part-time degree program, services for LD students, study abroad, summer session for credit.
Library Library and Learning Center plus 1 other. *Books:* 7,807 (physical); *Serial titles:* 30 (physical); *Databases:* 48. Weekly public service hours: 68; students can reserve study rooms.
Student Life *Housing Options:* men-only, women-only, special housing for students with disabilities. Campus housing is university owned. Freshman applicants given priority for college housing. *Activities and Organizations:* Basketball Club, International Friendship Association, Music Club, Hula Club, Phi Theta Kappa International Honor Society. *Campus security:* 24-hour emergency response devices and patrols, controlled dormitory access. *Student services:* health clinic, personal/psychological counseling.
Costs (2020–21) *One-time required fee:* $20. *Comprehensive fee:* $22,545 includes full-time tuition ($12,750), mandatory fees ($795), and room and board ($9000). Part-time tuition: $475 per credit hour. Part-time tuition and fees vary according to course load. *Required fees:* $265 per term part-time. *Room and board:* Room and board charges vary according to board plan. *Payment plan:* tuition prepayment. *Waivers:* employees or children of employees.
Applying *Options:* electronic application, deferred entrance. *Application fee:* $50. *Required:* essay or personal statement, high school transcript, minimum 2.5 GPA. *Required for some:* interview. *Recommended:* letters of recommendation. *Application deadlines:* rolling (freshmen), rolling (transfers). *Notification:* continuous (freshmen), continuous (transfers).
Freshman Application Contact Mr. Darrell Kicker, Director of Admissions, Hawaii Tokai International College, 91-971 Farrington Highway, Kapolei, HI 96707. *Phone:* 808-983-4202. *Fax:* 808-983-4107. *E-mail:* admissions@tokai.edu.
Website: http://www.htic.edu/.

Honolulu Community College

Honolulu, Hawaii

- **State-supported** 2-year, founded 1920, part of University of Hawaii System
- **Urban** 20-acre campus
- **Coed**

Undergraduates 1,632 full-time, 2,736 part-time. Students come from 26 states and territories; 12 other countries; 4% are from out of state; 2% Black or African American, non-Hispanic/Latino; 9% Hispanic/Latino; 42% Asian, non-Hispanic/Latino; 9% Native Hawaiian or other Pacific Islander, non-Hispanic/Latino; 0.2% American Indian or Alaska Native, non-Hispanic/Latino; 28% Two or more races, non-Hispanic/Latino; 0.7% Race/ethnicity unknown; 1% international; 9% transferred in. *Retention:* 59% of full-time freshmen returned.
Faculty *Student/faculty ratio:* 15:1.
Academics *Calendar:* semesters. *Degree:* certificates and associate. *Special study options:* academic remediation for entering students, accelerated degree program, advanced placement credit, cooperative education, distance learning, English as a second language, internships, part-time degree program, services for LD students, student-designed majors, summer session for credit. *ROTC:* Army (c), Air Force (c).
Library Honolulu Community College Library plus 1 other.
Student Life *Campus security:* 24-hour emergency response devices.
Standardized Tests *Required for some:* TOEFL for international applicants.
Financial Aid Of all full-time matriculated undergraduates who enrolled in 2018, 30 Federal Work-Study jobs (averaging $1600).
Applying *Options:* early admission. *Application fee:* $25.
Freshman Application Contact Admissions Office, Honolulu Community College, 874 Dillingham Boulevard, Honolulu, HI 96817. *Phone:* 808-845-9129. *E-mail:* honcc@hawaii.edu. *Website:* http://www.honolulu.hawaii.edu/.

Kapiolani Community College

Honolulu, Hawaii

- **State-supported** 2-year, founded 1957, part of University of Hawaii System
- **Urban** 52-acre campus
- **Coed**

Undergraduates 4% are from out of state. *Retention:* 63% of full-time freshmen returned.
Faculty *Student/faculty ratio:* 17:1.
Academics *Calendar:* semesters. *Degree:* certificates and associate. *Special study options:* academic remediation for entering students, adult/continuing education programs, advanced placement credit, cooperative education, distance learning, English as a second language, honors programs, internships, off-campus study, part-time degree program, services for LD students, student-designed majors, summer session for credit. *ROTC:* Army (c), Air Force (c).
Library Lama Library.
Student Life *Campus security:* 24-hour patrols.
Financial Aid Of all full-time matriculated undergraduates who enrolled in 2011, 6 Federal Work-Study jobs (averaging $1686).
Applying *Options:* early admission. *Application fee:* $25.
Freshman Application Contact Kapiolani Community College, 4303 Diamond Head Road, Honolulu, HI 96816-4421. *Phone:* 808-734-9555. *Website:* http://www.kapiolani.hawaii.edu/.

Kauai Community College

Lihue, Hawaii

- **State-supported** 2-year, founded 1965, part of University of Hawaii System
- **Small-town** 100-acre campus
- **Coed**

Undergraduates 1% are from out of state. *Retention:* 68% of full-time freshmen returned.
Faculty *Student/faculty ratio:* 11:1.
Academics *Calendar:* semesters. *Degree:* certificates and associate. *Special study options:* accelerated degree program, advanced placement credit,

cooperative education, distance learning, English as a second language, internships, part-time degree program, services for LD students, summer session for credit.
Library S. W. Wilcox II Learning Resource Center plus 1 other.
Student Life *Campus security:* student patrols, 6-hour evening patrols by trained security personnel.
Financial Aid Of all full-time matriculated undergraduates who enrolled in 2018, 10 Federal Work-Study jobs (averaging $3000). 30 state and other part-time jobs (averaging $3000).
Applying *Options:* early admission. *Application fee:* $25. *Required for some:* high school transcript. *Recommended:* high school transcript.
Freshman Application Contact Mr. Leighton Oride, Admissions Officer and Registrar, Kauai Community College, 3-1901 Kaumualii Highway, Lihue, HI 96766. *Phone:* 808-245-8225. *Fax:* 808-245-8297. *E-mail:* arkauai@hawaii.edu. *Website:* http://kauai.hawaii.edu/.

Leeward Community College
Pearl City, Hawaii

- **State-supported** 2-year, founded 1968, part of University of Hawaii System
- **Suburban** 49-acre campus with easy access to Honolulu
- **Coed**

Undergraduates 3,296 full-time, 4,646 part-time. Students come from 13 other countries; 0.8% are from out of state; 2% Black or African American, non-Hispanic/Latino; 11% Hispanic/Latino; 37% Asian, non-Hispanic/Latino; 12% Native Hawaiian or other Pacific Islander, non-Hispanic/Latino; 0.3% American Indian or Alaska Native, non-Hispanic/Latino; 26% Two or more races, non-Hispanic/Latino; 1% Race/ethnicity unknown; 0.5% international; 7% transferred in. *Retention:* 65% of full-time freshmen returned.
Faculty *Student/faculty ratio:* 23:1.
Academics *Calendar:* semesters. *Degree:* certificates and associate. *Special study options:* academic remediation for entering students, advanced placement credit, cooperative education, distance learning, English as a second language, honors programs, independent study, internships, off-campus study, part-time degree program, services for LD students, study abroad, summer session for credit. *ROTC:* Air Force (c).
Student Life *Campus security:* 24-hour emergency response devices and patrols, late-night transport/escort service.
Applying *Options:* electronic application, early admission. *Application fee:* $25. *Required for some:* high school transcript.
Freshman Application Contact Ms. Sheryl Higa, Assistant Registrar, Leeward Community College, 96-045 Ala Ike, Pearl City, HI 96782-3393. *Phone:* 808-455-0643. *Website:* http://www.leeward.hawaii.edu/.

Remington College–Honolulu Campus
Honolulu, Hawaii

Director of Admissions Louis LaMair, Director of Recruitment, Remington College–Honolulu Campus, 1111 Bishop Street, Suite 400, Honolulu, HI 96813. *Phone:* 808-942-1000. *Toll-free phone:* 800-323-8122. *Fax:* 808-533-3064. *E-mail:* louis.lamair@remingtoncollege.edu. *Website:* http://www.remingtoncollege.edu/.

University of Hawaii Maui College
Kahului, Hawaii

Freshman Application Contact Mr. Stephen Kameda, Director of Admissions and Records, University of Hawaii Maui College, 310 Kaahumanu Avenue, Kahului, HI 96732. *Phone:* 808-984-3267. *Toll-free phone:* 800-479-6692. *Fax:* 808-984-3872. *E-mail:* skameda@hawaii.edu. *Website:* http://maui.hawaii.edu/.

Windward Community College
Kaneohe, Hawaii

Director of Admissions Geri Imai, Registrar, Windward Community College, 45-720 Keaahala Road, Kaneohe, HI 96744-3528. *Phone:* 808-235-7430. *E-mail:* gerii@hawaii.edu. *Website:* http://www.windward.hawaii.edu/.

IDAHO

Carrington College–Boise
Boise, Idaho

- **Proprietary** 2-year, founded 1980, part of Carrington Colleges Group, Inc.
- **Coed**

Undergraduates 395 full-time, 51 part-time. 16% are from out of state; 4% Black or African American, non-Hispanic/Latino; 17% Hispanic/Latino; 7% Asian, non-Hispanic/Latino; 0.2% Native Hawaiian or other Pacific Islander, non-Hispanic/Latino; 0.9% American Indian or Alaska Native, non-Hispanic/Latino; 2% Two or more races, non-Hispanic/Latino; 0.5% Race/ethnicity unknown; 18% transferred in. *Retention:* 67% of full-time freshmen returned.
Faculty *Student/faculty ratio:* 15:1.
Academics *Degree:* certificates and associate.
Standardized Tests *Required:* institutional entrance exam (for admission).
Applying *Required:* essay or personal statement, high school transcript, interview.
Freshman Application Contact Carrington College–Boise, 1122 North Liberty Street, Boise, ID 83704. *Website:* http://www.carrington.edu/.

College of Eastern Idaho
Idaho Falls, Idaho

- **State-supported** 2-year, founded 1969
- **Small-town** 60-acre campus
- **Coed,** 1,595 undergraduate students, 34% full-time, 64% women, 36% men

Undergraduates 548 full-time, 1,047 part-time. Students come from 4 states and territories; 0.3% are from out of state; 0.8% Black or African American, non-Hispanic/Latino; 14% Hispanic/Latino; 0.8% Asian, non-Hispanic/Latino; 0.4% Native Hawaiian or other Pacific Islander, non-Hispanic/Latino; 0.8% American Indian or Alaska Native, non-Hispanic/Latino; 0.8% Two or more races, non-Hispanic/Latino; 2% Race/ethnicity unknown; 101% transferred in.
Freshmen *Admission:* 210 enrolled.
Faculty *Total:* 144, 40% full-time. *Student/faculty ratio:* 10:1.
Majors Accounting; administrative assistant and secretarial science; automobile/automotive mechanics technology; computer and information systems security; computer systems networking and telecommunications; diesel mechanics technology; electrician; fire science/firefighting; legal assistant/paralegal; liberal arts and sciences/liberal studies; marketing/marketing management; medical/clinical assistant; registered nursing/registered nurse; surgical technology; web page, digital/multimedia and information resources design; welding technology.
Academics *Calendar:* semesters. *Degree:* certificates and associate. *Special study options:* academic remediation for entering students, adult/continuing education programs, advanced placement credit, distance learning, English as a second language, part-time degree program, services for LD students, summer session for credit.
Library Richard and Lila Jordan Library plus 1 other.
Student Life *Housing:* college housing not available. *Activities and Organizations:* drama/theater group. *Campus security:* 24-hour emergency response devices and patrols, late-night transport/escort service. *Student services:* personal/psychological counseling, veterans affairs office.
Standardized Tests *Required for some:* ACT Compass, ACT ASSET, or CPT.
Costs (2020–21) *Tuition:* $129 per credit hour part-time; state resident $179 per credit hour part-time; nonresident $258 per credit hour part-time. *Required fees:* $15 per term part-time. *Payment plan:* installment. *Waivers:* employees or children of employees.
Financial Aid Of all full-time matriculated undergraduates who enrolled in 2018, 37 Federal Work-Study jobs (averaging $1176). 11 state and other part-time jobs (averaging $1619).
Applying *Options:* electronic application, deferred entrance. *Required:* high school transcript. *Required for some:* essay or personal statement, interview. *Application deadline:* rolling (freshmen).
Freshman Application Contact Hailey Mack, Career Placement and Recruiting Coordinator, College of Eastern Idaho, 1600 South 25th East, Idaho Falls, ID 83404. *Phone:* 208-524-5337 Ext. 35337. *Toll-free phone:* 800-662-0261. *Fax:* 208-524-0429. *E-mail:* hailey.mack@cei.edu. *Website:* http://www.citc.edu/.

College of Southern Idaho
Twin Falls, Idaho

- **State and locally supported** 2-year, founded 1964
- **Small-town** 287-acre campus
- **Coed**

Undergraduates 1,937 full-time, 4,969 part-time. 7% are from out of state; 1% Black or African American, non-Hispanic/Latino; 28% Hispanic/Latino; 2% Asian, non-Hispanic/Latino; 0.3% Native Hawaiian or other Pacific Islander, non-Hispanic/Latino; 1% American Indian or Alaska Native, non-Hispanic/Latino; 2% Two or more races, non-Hispanic/Latino; 1% Race/ethnicity unknown; 2% international; 6% transferred in; 5% live on campus.
Faculty *Student/faculty ratio:* 19:1.
Academics *Calendar:* semesters. *Degree:* certificates and associate. *Special study options:* academic remediation for entering students, adult/continuing education programs, advanced placement credit, cooperative education, distance learning, English as a second language, honors programs, independent study, internships, part-time degree program, services for LD students, summer session for credit.
Library College of Southern Idaho Library.
Student Life *Campus security:* 24-hour emergency response devices and patrols, controlled dormitory access.
Athletics Member NJCAA.
Costs (2019–20) *Tuition:* area resident $2850 full-time, $140 per credit hour part-time; state resident $3360 full-time, $190 per credit hour part-time; nonresident $6840 full-time, $285 per credit hour part-time. Full-time tuition and fees vary according to course load. Part-time tuition and fees vary according to course load. *Required fees:* $1350 full-time. *Room and board:* $5500; room only: $2500. Room and board charges vary according to board plan.
Applying *Application fee:* $10. *Required:* high school transcript. *Required for some:* interview.
Freshman Application Contact Director of Admissions, Registration, and Records, College of Southern Idaho, PO Box 1238, Twin Falls, ID 83303-1238. *Phone:* 208-732-6232. *Toll-free phone:* 800-680-0274. *Fax:* 208-736-3014. *Website:* http://www.csi.edu/.

College of Western Idaho
Nampa, Idaho

- **State-supported** 2-year, founded 2007
- **Rural** campus with easy access to Boise
- **Coed**

Undergraduates 2% Black or African American, non-Hispanic/Latino; 14% Hispanic/Latino; 1% Asian, non-Hispanic/Latino; 0.7% Native Hawaiian or other Pacific Islander, non-Hispanic/Latino; 1% American Indian or Alaska Native, non-Hispanic/Latino; 2% Two or more races, non-Hispanic/Latino; 13% Race/ethnicity unknown.
Faculty *Student/faculty ratio:* 22:1.
Academics *Calendar:* semesters. *Degree:* certificates and associate. *Special study options:* academic remediation for entering students, advanced placement credit, cooperative education, English as a second language, honors programs, internships, part-time degree program, services for LD students, summer session for credit.
Standardized Tests *Recommended:* SAT or ACT (for admission), ACT Compass.
Applying *Options:* electronic application. *Application fee:* $25. *Required:* high school transcript.
Freshman Application Contact College of Western Idaho, 6056 Birch Lane, Nampa, ID 83687. *Website:* http://cwidaho.cc/.

North Idaho College
Coeur d'Alene, Idaho

- **State and locally supported** 2-year, founded 1933
- **Small-town** 42-acre campus
- **Coed,** 5,723 undergraduate students, 60% full-time, 59% women, 41% men

Undergraduates 3,437 full-time, 2,286 part-time. 0.9% Black or African American, non-Hispanic/Latino; 3% Hispanic/Latino; 1% Asian, non-Hispanic/Latino; 0.3% Native Hawaiian or other Pacific Islander, non-Hispanic/Latino; 2% American Indian or Alaska Native, non-Hispanic/Latino; 8% Two or more races, non-Hispanic/Latino.
Freshmen *Admission:* 2,684 applied, 1,565 admitted, 1,224 enrolled.
Faculty *Total:* 447, 36% full-time, 8% with terminal degrees. *Student/faculty ratio:* 17:1.
Majors Administrative assistant and secretarial science; American Indian/Native American studies; anthropology; art; astronomy; athletic training; automobile/automotive mechanics technology; biological and physical sciences; biology/biological sciences; botany/plant biology; business administration and management; business teacher education; carpentry; chemistry; clinical laboratory science/medical technology; commercial and advertising art; computer and information sciences and support services related; computer and information sciences related; computer programming; computer science; criminal justice/law enforcement administration; criminal justice/police science; culinary arts; developmental and child psychology; drafting and design technology; dramatic/theater arts; education; electrical, electronic and communications engineering technology; elementary education; engineering; English; environmental health; fishing and fisheries sciences and management; forestry; French; geology/earth science; German; health/health-care administration; heating, air conditioning, ventilation and refrigeration maintenance technology; heavy equipment maintenance technology; history; hospitality administration; human services; journalism; legal administrative assistant/secretary; legal assistant/paralegal; liberal arts and sciences/liberal studies; licensed practical/vocational nurse training; machine tool technology; marine maintenance and ship repair technology; mass communication/media; mathematics; medical administrative assistant and medical secretary; music; music teacher education; physical sciences; physics; political science and government; psychology; registered nursing/registered nurse; social sciences; sociology; Spanish; welding technology; wildlife biology; wildlife, fish and wildlands science and management; zoology/animal biology.
Academics *Calendar:* semesters. *Degree:* certificates and associate. *Special study options:* academic remediation for entering students, adult/continuing education programs, advanced placement credit, cooperative education, distance learning, English as a second language, independent study, internships, off-campus study, part-time degree program, services for LD students, summer session for credit. *ROTC:* Army (c).
Library Molstead Library Computer Center.
Student Life *Housing Options:* coed. Campus housing is university owned. *Activities and Organizations:* drama/theater group, student-run newspaper, choral group, Ski Club, Fusion, Baptist student ministries, Journalism Club, Phi Theta Kappa. *Campus security:* 24-hour emergency response devices and patrols, late-night transport/escort service. *Student services:* health clinic, personal/psychological counseling, women's center, legal services.
Athletics Member NJCAA. *Intercollegiate sports:* basketball M(s)/W(s), cheerleading M(s)/W(s), soccer M(s)/W(s), softball W(s), volleyball W(s), wrestling M(s). *Intramural sports:* basketball M/W, bowling M/W, cheerleading M/W, crew M(c)/W(c), cross-country running M(c)/W(c), football M/W, golf M/W, racquetball M/W, sailing M(c)/W(c), skiing (cross-country) M(c)/W(c), skiing (downhill) M(c)/W(c), soccer M(c)/W(c), softball M/W, table tennis M/W, tennis M/W, track and field M(c)/W(c), volleyball M/W.
Costs (2019–20) *Tuition:* area resident $2436 full-time, $203 per credit part-time; state resident $4000 full-time, $350 per credit part-time; nonresident $7776 full-time, $648 per credit part-time. Full-time tuition and fees vary according to course load and reciprocity agreements. Part-time tuition and fees vary according to course load and reciprocity agreements. *Required fees:* $960 full-time, $40 per credit part-time, $240 per credit part-time. *Room and board:* $7200. Room and board charges vary according to board plan. *Payment plan:* installment. *Waivers:* senior citizens and employees or children of employees.
Financial Aid Of all full-time matriculated undergraduates who enrolled in 2019, 1,290 applied for aid, 1,057 were judged to have need, 191 had their need fully met. In 2019, 204 non-need-based awards were made. *Average percent of need met:* 67%. *Average financial aid package:* $8235. *Average need-based loan:* $3969. *Average need-based gift aid:* $5336. *Average non-need-based aid:* $1580.
Applying *Options:* electronic application, early admission, deferred entrance. *Application fee:* $25. *Required for some:* essay or personal statement, high school transcript, county residency certificate. *Application deadlines:* 8/20 (freshmen), 8/20 (transfers).
Freshman Application Contact Cardinal Central, North Idaho College, 1000 West Garden Avenue, Coeur d Alene, ID 83814-2199. *Phone:* 208-769-3311. *Toll-free phone:* 877-404-4536 Ext. 3311. *Fax:* 208-769-3399. *E-mail:* cardinalcentral@nic.edu.
Website: http://www.nic.edu/.

ILLINOIS

Ambria College of Nursing
Hoffman Estates, Illinois

Admissions Office Contact Ambria College of Nursing, 5210 Trillium Boulevard, Hoffman Estates, IL 60192. *Website:* http://www.ambria.edu/.

Black Hawk College

Moline, Illinois

- **State and locally supported** 2-year, founded 1946
- **Urban** 232-acre campus
- **Coed,** 4,472 undergraduate students, 35% full-time, 61% women, 39% men

Undergraduates 1,562 full-time, 2,910 part-time. Students come from 14 states and territories; 10 other countries; 7% are from out of state; 11% Black or African American, non-Hispanic/Latino; 16% Hispanic/Latino; 3% Asian, non-Hispanic/Latino; 0.1% American Indian or Alaska Native, non-Hispanic/Latino; 4% Two or more races, non-Hispanic/Latino; 1% Race/ethnicity unknown; 0.4% international; 4% transferred in.
Freshmen *Admission:* 902 applied, 902 admitted, 803 enrolled.
Faculty *Total:* 197, 49% full-time, 14% with terminal degrees. *Student/faculty ratio:* 19:1.
Majors Accounting; administrative assistant and secretarial science; agricultural business and management; agricultural mechanics and equipment technology; agricultural production; agriculture; applied horticulture/horticulture operations; automobile/automotive mechanics technology; biological and physical sciences; child-care provision; criminal justice/police science; crop production; design and visual communications; emergency medical technology (EMT paramedic); equestrian studies; general studies; health information/medical records technology; horse husbandry/equine science and management; information technology; liberal arts and sciences/liberal studies; manufacturing engineering technology; physical therapy technology; radiologic technology/science; registered nursing/registered nurse; retailing; small business administration; surgical technology; veterinary/animal health technology.
Academics *Calendar:* semesters. *Degree:* certificates and associate. *Special study options:* academic remediation for entering students, advanced placement credit, distance learning, English as a second language, independent study, internships, part-time degree program, services for LD students, summer session for credit.
Library Quad City Campus Library plus 1 other. *Books:* 29,086 (physical), 202,920 (digital/electronic); *Serial titles:* 127 (physical), 57,357 (digital/electronic); *Databases:* 39. Weekly public service hours: 56; students can reserve study rooms.
Student Life *Housing:* college housing not available. *Activities and Organizations:* choral group, National Student Nurses Association, Wellness Club, Student Ambassadors, Association of Lation American Students, Clean Sphere. *Campus security:* 24-hour patrols. *Student services:* personal/psychological counseling, veterans affairs office.
Athletics Member NJCAA. *Intercollegiate sports:* baseball M(s), basketball M(s)/W(s), golf M(s), softball W(s), volleyball W(s). *Intramural sports:* soccer M.
Costs (2019–20) *Tuition:* area resident $4470 full-time, $149 per credit hour part-time; state resident $7500 full-time, $250 per credit hour part-time; nonresident $7650 full-time, $255 per credit hour part-time. *Payment plan:* installment. *Waivers:* senior citizens and employees or children of employees.
Financial Aid Of all full-time matriculated undergraduates who enrolled in 2018, 157 Federal Work-Study jobs (averaging $1437). 176 state and other part-time jobs (averaging $1023).
Applying *Options:* electronic application, early admission, deferred entrance. *Application fee:* $20. *Recommended:* high school transcript. *Application deadlines:* rolling (freshmen), rolling (out-of-state freshmen), rolling (transfers), rolling (early action). *Early decision deadline:* rolling (for plan 1), rolling (for plan 2). *Notification:* continuous (freshmen), continuous (out-of-state freshmen), continuous (transfers), rolling (early decision plan 1), rolling (early decision plan 2), rolling (early action).
Freshman Application Contact Ms. Gabriella Hurtado, Recruitment Coordinator/Admissions Advisor, Black Hawk College, 6600-34th Avenue, Moline, IL 61265. *Phone:* 309-796-5341. *Toll-free phone:* 800-334-1311. *E-mail:* ghurtado@bhc.edu.
Website: http://www.bhc.edu/.

Carl Sandburg College

Galesburg, Illinois

- **State and locally supported** 2-year, founded 1967, part of Illinois Community College Board
- **Small-town** 105-acre campus
- **Coed**

Undergraduates *Retention:* 65% of full-time freshmen returned.
Faculty *Student/faculty ratio:* 15:1.
Academics *Calendar:* semesters. *Degree:* certificates and associate. *Special study options:* academic remediation for entering students, adult/continuing education programs, advanced placement credit, cooperative education, English as a second language, internships, part-time degree program, services for LD students, student-designed majors, summer session for credit. *ROTC:* Army (c).
Library Learning Resource Center plus 1 other.
Student Life *Campus security:* 24-hour emergency response devices and patrols.
Athletics Member NJCAA.
Financial Aid Of all full-time matriculated undergraduates who enrolled in 2018, 80 Federal Work-Study jobs (averaging $3000).
Applying *Options:* early admission, deferred entrance. *Required:* high school transcript.
Director of Admissions Ms. Carol Kreider, Dean of Student Support Services, Carl Sandburg College, 2400 Tom L. Wilson Boulevard, Galesburg, IL 61401-9576. *Phone:* 309-341-5234. *Website:* http://www.sandburg.edu/.

City Colleges of Chicago, Harold Washington College

Chicago, Illinois

- **State and locally supported** 2-year, founded 1962, part of City Colleges of Chicago
- **Urban** 1-acre campus
- **Coed**

Faculty *Student/faculty ratio:* 33:1.
Academics *Calendar:* semesters. *Degree:* certificates and associate. *Special study options:* academic remediation for entering students, accelerated degree program, adult/continuing education programs, advanced placement credit, cooperative education, distance learning, double majors, English as a second language, independent study, internships, off-campus study, part-time degree program, services for LD students, summer session for credit.
Library Harold Washington College Library plus 1 other.
Student Life *Campus security:* 24-hour emergency response devices and patrols.
Financial Aid Of all full-time matriculated undergraduates who enrolled in 2018, 100 Federal Work-Study jobs (averaging $3500).
Applying *Options:* early admission, deferred entrance.
Freshman Application Contact Admissions Office, City Colleges of Chicago, Harold Washington College, 30 East Lake Street, Chicago, IL 60601-2449. *Phone:* 312-553-6010. *Website:* http://hwashington.ccc.edu/.

City Colleges of Chicago, Harry S. Truman College

Chicago, Illinois

- **State and locally supported** 2-year, founded 1956, part of City Colleges of Chicago
- **Urban** 5-acre campus
- **Coed**

Faculty *Student/faculty ratio:* 34:1.
Academics *Calendar:* semesters. *Degree:* certificates, diplomas, and associate. *Special study options:* academic remediation for entering students, adult/continuing education programs, advanced placement credit, cooperative education, distance learning, English as a second language, honors programs, internships, part-time degree program, services for LD students, summer session for credit.
Student Life *Campus security:* 24-hour patrols, late-night transport/escort service.
Athletics Member NJCAA.
Financial Aid Of all full-time matriculated undergraduates who enrolled in 2018, 150 Federal Work-Study jobs (averaging $3000).
Applying *Options:* early admission, deferred entrance.
Freshman Application Contact City Colleges of Chicago, Harry S. Truman College, 1145 West Wilson Avenue, Chicago, IL 60640-5616. *Phone:* 773-907-4000 Ext. 1112. *Website:* http://www.trumancollege.edu/.

City Colleges of Chicago, Kennedy-King College

Chicago, Illinois

- **State and locally supported** 2-year, founded 1935, part of City Colleges of Chicago
- **Urban** 40-acre campus with easy access to Chicago
- **Coed**

Undergraduates 1,584 full-time, 1,234 part-time. Students come from 20 states and territories; 8 other countries; 1% are from out of state; 78% Black or African American, non-Hispanic/Latino; 14% Hispanic/Latino; 1% Asian, non-Hispanic/Latino; 0.1% American Indian or Alaska Native, non-

Hispanic/Latino; 3% Two or more races, non-Hispanic/Latino; 0.6% Race/ethnicity unknown; 1% transferred in. *Retention:* 34% of full-time freshmen returned.
Faculty *Student/faculty ratio:* 30:1.
Academics *Calendar:* semesters. *Degree:* certificates and associate. *Special study options:* academic remediation for entering students, adult/continuing education programs, advanced placement credit, cooperative education, distance learning, English as a second language, honors programs, internships, part-time degree program, summer session for credit.
Library Harold Washington College Library.
Student Life *Campus security:* late-night transport/escort service.
Athletics Member NJCAA.
Financial Aid Of all full-time matriculated undergraduates who enrolled in 2018, 148 Federal Work-Study jobs (averaging $1539).
Applying *Options:* electronic application. *Required:* high school transcript.
Freshman Application Contact Nicholas Ambrose, Assistant Registrar, City Colleges of Chicago, Kennedy-King College, 6301 South Halsted Street, W-110, Chicago, IL 60621. *Phone:* 773-602-5090. *Fax:* 773-602-5055. *E-mail:* nambrose1@ccc.edu. *Website:* http://www.ccc.edu/colleges/kennedy/.

City Colleges of Chicago, Malcolm X College

Chicago, Illinois

- **State and locally supported** 2-year, founded 1911, part of City Colleges of Chicago
- **Urban** 20-acre campus
- **Coed**

Undergraduates 2,522 full-time, 3,509 part-time.
Faculty *Student/faculty ratio:* 25:1.
Academics *Calendar:* semesters. *Degree:* certificates and associate. *Special study options:* academic remediation for entering students, adult/continuing education programs, advanced placement credit, cooperative education, distance learning, English as a second language, part-time degree program, services for LD students, summer session for credit.
Library The Carter G. Woodson Library.
Student Life *Campus security:* 24-hour emergency response devices and patrols.
Athletics Member NJCAA.
Applying *Options:* electronic application. *Required:* high school transcript, minimum 2.0 GPA. *Required for some:* essay or personal statement, interview.
Freshman Application Contact Ms. Kimberly Hollingsworth, Dean of Student Services, City Colleges of Chicago, Malcolm X College, 1900 West Van Buren Street, Chicago, IL 60612-3145. *Phone:* 312-850-7120. *Fax:* 312-850-7119. *E-mail:* khollingsworth@ccc.edu. *Website:* http://malcolmx.ccc.edu/.

City Colleges of Chicago, Olive-Harvey College

Chicago, Illinois

Freshman Application Contact Nailah Alexandar, Assistant Registrar, City Colleges of Chicago, Olive-Harvey College, 10001 South Woodlawn Avenue, Room 1405, Chicago, IL 60628. *Phone:* 773-291-6384. *E-mail:* nalexander17@ccc.edu. *Website:* http://oliveharvey.ccc.edu/.

City Colleges of Chicago, Richard J. Daley College

Chicago, Illinois

Freshman Application Contact City Colleges of Chicago, Richard J. Daley College, 7500 South Pulaski Road, Chicago, IL 60652-1242. *Phone:* 773-838-7606. *Website:* http://daley.ccc.edu/.

City Colleges of Chicago, Wilbur Wright College

Chicago, Illinois

- **State and locally supported** 2-year, founded 1934, part of City Colleges of Chicago
- **Urban** 20-acre campus
- **Coed**

Undergraduates 2,214 full-time, 4,612 part-time.
Faculty *Student/faculty ratio:* 23:1.
Academics *Calendar:* semesters. *Degree:* certificates and associate. *Special study options:* academic remediation for entering students, accelerated degree program, adult/continuing education programs, distance learning, English as a second language, part-time degree program, summer session for credit.
Library Learning Resource Center plus 1 other.
Student Life *Campus security:* 24-hour emergency response devices and patrols, student patrols, late-night transport/escort service.
Athletics Member NJCAA.
Financial Aid Of all full-time matriculated undergraduates who enrolled in 2018, 67 Federal Work-Study jobs (averaging $1000).
Applying *Options:* electronic application, early admission, deferred entrance.
Freshman Application Contact Ms. Amy Aiello, Assistant Dean of Student Services, City Colleges of Chicago, Wilbur Wright College, Chicago, IL 60634. *Phone:* 773-481-8207. *Fax:* 773-481-8185. *E-mail:* aaiello@ccc.edu. *Website:* http://wright.ccc.edu/.

College of DuPage

Glen Ellyn, Illinois

- **State and locally supported** 2-year, founded 1967
- **Suburban** 297-acre campus with easy access to Chicago
- **Coed,** 23,903 undergraduate students, 33% full-time, 54% women, 46% men

Undergraduates 7,793 full-time, 16,110 part-time. Students come from 17 states and territories; 7% Black or African American, non-Hispanic/Latino; 27% Hispanic/Latino; 12% Asian, non-Hispanic/Latino; 0.2% American Indian or Alaska Native, non-Hispanic/Latino; 3% Two or more races, non-Hispanic/Latino; 2% Race/ethnicity unknown; 1% international; 8% transferred in. *Retention:* 68% of full-time freshmen returned.
Freshmen *Admission:* 3,360 applied, 2,918 admitted, 3,229 enrolled.
Faculty *Total:* 1,322, 21% full-time, 19% with terminal degrees. *Student/faculty ratio:* 21:1.
Majors Accounting; administrative assistant and secretarial science; automobile/automotive mechanics technology; baking and pastry arts; biological and physical sciences; building/property maintenance; business administration and management; child-care and support services management; child-care provision; child development; cinematography and film/video production; commercial and advertising art; communications systems installation and repair technology; communications technology; computer installation and repair technology; computer programming (specific applications); computer typography and composition equipment operation; corrections; criminal justice/law enforcement administration; criminal justice/police science; culinary arts; data entry/microcomputer applications related; dental hygiene; design and visual communications; desktop publishing and digital imaging design; drafting and design technology; drafting/design engineering technologies related; electrical, electronic and communications engineering technology; electrical/electronics equipment installation and repair; electromechanical technology; emergency medical technology (EMT paramedic); engineering; fashion and fabric consulting; fashion/apparel design; fashion merchandising; fire science/firefighting; graphic and printing equipment operation/production; health/health-care administration; health information/medical records administration; health information/medical records technology; heating, air conditioning, ventilation and refrigeration maintenance technology; hospital and health-care facilities administration; hospitality administration; hotel/motel administration; human services; industrial electronics technology; industrial technology; interior design; landscaping and groundskeeping; legal administrative assistant/secretary; liberal arts and sciences/liberal studies; library and archives assisting; library and information science; machine tool technology; manufacturing engineering technology; marketing/marketing management; massage therapy; medical radiologic technology; merchandising; nuclear medical technology; occupational therapist assistant; occupational therapy; office management; ornamental horticulture; photography; physical therapy technology; plastics and polymer engineering technology; precision production trades; registered nursing/registered nurse; respiratory care therapy; restaurant, culinary, and catering management; retailing; robotics technology; sales, distribution, and marketing operations; selling skills and sales; speech-language pathology; substance abuse/addiction counseling; surgical technology; tourism and travel services management; tourism and travel services marketing; tourism promotion; transportation and materials moving related; welding technology.
Academics *Calendar:* semesters. *Degree:* certificates and associate. *Special study options:* academic remediation for entering students, adult/continuing education programs, advanced placement credit, cooperative education, distance learning, English as a second language, external degree program, honors programs, independent study, internships, off-campus study, part-time degree program, services for LD students, student-designed majors, study abroad, summer session for credit.
Library College of DuPage Library. *Books:* 324,124 (physical); *Serial titles:* 182,304 (physical); *Databases:* 142. Students can reserve study rooms.

Student Life *Housing:* college housing not available. *Activities and Organizations:* drama/theater group, student-run newspaper, choral group, Latino Ethnic Awareness Association, The Christian Group, Phi Theta Kappa, International Students Organization, Muslim Student Association. *Campus security:* 24-hour emergency response devices and patrols, student patrols, late-night transport/escort service. *Student services:* health clinic, personal/psychological counseling.
Athletics Member USCAA, NJCAA. *Intercollegiate sports:* baseball M, basketball M/W, football M, golf M, soccer M/W, softball M/W, volleyball W. *Intramural sports:* basketball M/W, cross-country running M/W, ice hockey M, racquetball M/W, soccer M/W, softball W, tennis M/W, track and field M/W, volleyball W.
Costs (2020–21) *Tuition:* area resident $3155 full-time; state resident $9750 full-time. *Required fees:* $986 full-time.
Financial Aid Of all full-time matriculated undergraduates who enrolled in 2018, 424 Federal Work-Study jobs (averaging $4135).
Applying *Options:* early admission, deferred entrance. *Application fee:* $20. *Application deadlines:* rolling (freshmen), rolling (transfers). *Notification:* continuous (freshmen), continuous (transfers).
Freshman Application Contact College of DuPage, IL. *E-mail:* admissions@cod.edu.
Website: http://www.cod.edu/.

College of Lake County
Grayslake, Illinois

- **District-supported** 2-year, founded 1967, part of Illinois Community College Board
- **Suburban** 226-acre campus with easy access to Chicago, Milwaukee
- **Coed**

Undergraduates 4,945 full-time, 12,632 part-time. Students come from 42 other countries; 1% are from out of state; 5% Black or African American, non-Hispanic/Latino; 34% Hispanic/Latino; 4% Asian, non-Hispanic/Latino; 0.2% Native Hawaiian or other Pacific Islander, non-Hispanic/Latino; 0.1% American Indian or Alaska Native, non-Hispanic/Latino; 2% Two or more races, non-Hispanic/Latino; 3% Race/ethnicity unknown; 1% international. *Retention:* 70% of full-time freshmen returned.
Faculty *Student/faculty ratio:* 17:1.
Academics *Calendar:* semesters. *Degree:* certificates and associate. *Special study options:* academic remediation for entering students, adult/continuing education programs, advanced placement credit, cooperative education, distance learning, double majors, English as a second language, honors programs, independent study, internships, off-campus study, part-time degree program, services for LD students, student-designed majors, study abroad, summer session for credit.
Library College of Lake County Library plus 1 other.
Student Life *Campus security:* 24-hour emergency response devices and patrols, late-night transport/escort service.
Athletics Member NJCAA.
Financial Aid Of all full-time matriculated undergraduates who enrolled in 2018, 98 Federal Work-Study jobs (averaging $1311).
Applying *Options:* electronic application, early admission, deferred entrance. *Required for some:* high school transcript, interview.
Freshman Application Contact Director, Student Recruitment, College of Lake County, Grayslake, IL 60030-1198. *Phone:* 847-543-2383. *Fax:* 847-543-3061. *Website:* http://www.clcillinois.edu/.

Coyne College
Chicago, Illinois

Freshman Application Contact Coyne College, 1 North State Street, Suite 400, Chicago, IL 60602. *Phone:* 773-577-8100 Ext. 8102. *Toll-free phone:* 800-707-1922. *Website:* http://www.coynecollege.edu/.

Danville Area Community College
Danville, Illinois

- **State and locally supported** 2-year, founded 1946, part of Illinois Community College Board
- **Small-town** 72-acre campus
- **Endowment** $15.0 million
- **Coed,** 2,279 undergraduate students, 39% full-time, 58% women, 42% men

Undergraduates 883 full-time, 1,396 part-time. Students come from 5 states and territories; 3 other countries; 5% are from out of state; 15% Black or African American, non-Hispanic/Latino; 4% Hispanic/Latino; 1% Asian, non-Hispanic/Latino; 0.1% Native Hawaiian or other Pacific Islander, non-Hispanic/Latino; 0.2% American Indian or Alaska Native, non-Hispanic/Latino; 2% Two or more races, non-Hispanic/Latino; 6% Race/ethnicity unknown; 22% transferred in. *Retention:* 58% of full-time freshmen returned.
Freshmen *Admission:* 335 enrolled.
Faculty *Total:* 129, 49% full-time, 16% with terminal degrees. *Student/faculty ratio:* 16:1.
Majors Accounting technology and bookkeeping; agricultural business and management; art; art teacher education; automobile/automotive mechanics technology; biological and physical sciences; business automation/technology/data entry; CAD/CADD drafting/design technology; child-care provision; computer programming (specific applications); computer systems networking and telecommunications; corrections; criminal justice/police science; energy management and systems technology; engineering; executive assistant/executive secretary; fire science/firefighting; floriculture/floristry management; general studies; health information/medical records technology; industrial electronics technology; industrial mechanics and maintenance technology; juvenile corrections; liberal arts and sciences/liberal studies; manufacturing engineering technology; medical administrative assistant and medical secretary; radiologic technology/science; registered nursing/registered nurse; selling skills and sales; teacher assistant/aide; turf and turfgrass management.
Academics *Calendar:* semesters. *Degree:* certificates and associate. *Special study options:* academic remediation for entering students, adult/continuing education programs, advanced placement credit, cooperative education, distance learning, double majors, English as a second language, independent study, internships, off-campus study, part-time degree program, services for LD students, summer session for credit.
Library Danville Area Community College Library. *Books:* 22,716 (physical), 245,636 (digital/electronic); *Serial titles:* 363 (physical), 48,844 (digital/electronic); *Databases:* 119. Weekly public service hours: 45; students can reserve study rooms.
Student Life *Housing:* college housing not available. *Activities and Organizations:* drama/theater group, student-run newspaper, choral group, Phi Theta Kappa International Honor Society, The Guild, Powerhouse Campus Ministry, Rad Tech Club, Ag Club. *Campus security:* 24-hour emergency response devices and patrols. *Student services:* personal/psychological counseling, veterans affairs office.
Athletics Member NJCAA. *Intercollegiate sports:* baseball M(s), basketball M(s)/W(s), cheerleading W, cross-country running M(s)/W(s), softball W(s).
Costs (2020–21) *Tuition:* area resident $4200 full-time, $140 per credit hour part-time; state resident $7500 full-time, $250 per credit hour part-time; nonresident $7500 full-time, $250 per credit hour part-time. Full-time tuition and fees vary according to program. Part-time tuition and fees vary according to program. *Required fees:* $825 full-time, $60 per credit hour part-time. *Payment plan:* installment. *Waivers:* senior citizens and employees or children of employees.
Financial Aid Of all full-time matriculated undergraduates who enrolled in 2019, 60 Federal Work-Study jobs (averaging $3500). 60 state and other part-time jobs (averaging $3500).
Applying *Options:* early admission, deferred entrance. *Required:* high school transcript. *Application deadlines:* rolling (freshmen), rolling (transfers).
Freshman Application Contact Cristin Prince, Coordinator of Recruitment, Danville Area Community College, 2000 East Main Street, Danville, IL 61832-5199. *Phone:* 217-443-8864. *Fax:* 217-443-8337. *E-mail:* cprince@dacc.edu.
Website: http://www.dacc.edu/.

Elgin Community College
Elgin, Illinois

Freshman Application Contact Admissions, Recruitment, and Student Life, Elgin Community College, 1700 Spartan Drive, Elgin, IL 60123. *Phone:* 847-214-7414. *E-mail:* admissions@elgin.edu. *Website:* http://www.elgin.edu/.

Fox College
Bedford Park, Illinois

- **Private** 2-year, founded 1932
- **Suburban** campus
- **Coed,** 443 undergraduate students

Majors Administrative assistant and secretarial science; dental hygiene; medical/clinical assistant; occupational therapist assistant; physical therapy technology; veterinary/animal health technology.
Academics *Calendar:* semesters. *Degree:* diplomas and associate. *Special study options:* accelerated degree program, internships.
Student Life *Housing:* college housing not available.
Freshman Application Contact Admissions Office, Fox College, 6640 South Cicero, Bedford Park, IL 60638. *Phone:* 708-444-4500.
Website: http://www.foxcollege.edu/.

Harper College

Palatine, Illinois

- **State and locally supported** 2-year, founded 1965, part of Illinois Community College Board
- **Suburban** 200-acre campus with easy access to Chicago
- **Coed,** 13,477 undergraduate students, 34% full-time, 55% women, 45% men

Undergraduates 4,519 full-time, 8,958 part-time. 0.5% are from out of state; 5% Black or African American, non-Hispanic/Latino; 29% Hispanic/Latino; 12% Asian, non-Hispanic/Latino; 0.2% American Indian or Alaska Native, non-Hispanic/Latino; 2% Two or more races, non-Hispanic/Latino; 2% Race/ethnicity unknown; 0.9% international; 4% transferred in. *Retention:* 75% of full-time freshmen returned.

Freshmen *Admission:* 2,586 enrolled. *Average high school GPA:* 2.9.

Faculty *Total:* 638, 32% full-time, 18% with terminal degrees. *Student/faculty ratio:* 22:1.

Majors Accounting; administrative assistant and secretarial science; architectural drafting and CAD/CADD; architectural engineering technology; art; banking and financial support services; biology/biological sciences; business administration and management; cardiovascular technology; chemistry; child-care provision; computer and information sciences; computer programming; computer programming (specific applications); computer science; criminal justice/law enforcement administration; cyber/computer forensics and counterterrorism; dental hygiene; diagnostic medical sonography and ultrasound technology; dietetics; dietetic technology; early childhood education; electrical, electronic and communications engineering technology; elementary education; engineering; English; environmental studies; fashion and fabric consulting; fashion/apparel design; fashion merchandising; finance; fine/studio arts; fire science/firefighting; food service systems administration; health teacher education; heating, air conditioning, ventilation and refrigeration maintenance technology; history; homeland security; hospitality administration; humanities; human services; interior design; international business/trade/commerce; legal administrative assistant/secretary; legal assistant/paralegal; liberal arts and sciences/liberal studies; marketing/marketing management; mathematics; medical administrative assistant and medical secretary; medical/clinical assistant; music; nanotechnology; philosophy; physical education teaching and coaching; physical sciences; psychology; public relations, advertising, and applied communication related; radiologic technology/science; registered nursing/registered nurse; sales, distribution, and marketing operations; small business administration; sociology and anthropology; speech communication and rhetoric; theater/theater arts management; web page, digital/multimedia and information resources design.

Academics *Calendar:* semesters. *Degree:* certificates and associate. *Special study options:* academic remediation for entering students, accelerated degree program, adult/continuing education programs, advanced placement credit, cooperative education, distance learning, English as a second language, freshman honors college, honors programs, independent study, internships, part-time degree program, services for LD students, study abroad, summer session for credit.

Library Harper College Library.

Student Life *Housing:* college housing not available. *Activities and Organizations:* drama/theater group, student-run newspaper, radio station, choral group, Student Radio Station, Program Board, Student Senate, Nursing Club, Phi Theta Kappa. *Campus security:* 24-hour emergency response devices and patrols, late-night transport/escort service. *Student services:* health clinic, personal/psychological counseling, women's center, legal services.

Athletics Member NJCAA. *Intercollegiate sports:* baseball M, basketball M/W, cross-country running M/W, soccer M/W, softball W, track and field M/W, volleyball W, wrestling M. *Intramural sports:* baseball M, basketball M, football M, racquetball M/W, softball M/W, table tennis M/W, tennis M/W, volleyball M/W.

Costs (2019–20) *Tuition:* area resident $4005 full-time, $134 per credit hour part-time; state resident $11,715 full-time, $391 per credit hour part-time; nonresident $13,980 full-time, $466 per credit hour part-time. Full-time tuition and fees vary according to course load and program. Part-time tuition and fees vary according to course load and program. *Required fees:* $684 full-time, $19 per credit hour part-time. *Payment plans:* installment, deferred payment. *Waivers:* senior citizens and employees or children of employees.

Financial Aid Of all full-time matriculated undergraduates who enrolled in 2018, 2,768 applied for aid, 2,224 were judged to have need, 50 had their need fully met. In 2018, 28 non-need-based awards were made. *Average percent of need met:* 42%. *Average financial aid package:* $5913. *Average need-based loan:* $3056. *Average need-based gift aid:* $5712. *Average non-need-based aid:* $3141.

Applying *Options:* electronic application. *Application fee:* $25. *Required:* high school transcript. *Application deadlines:* rolling (freshmen), rolling (transfers). *Notification:* continuous (freshmen), continuous (transfers).

Freshman Application Contact Harper College, 1200 West Algonquin Road, Palatine, IL 60067-7398. *Phone:* 847-925-6649.
Website: http://www.harpercollege.edu/.

Heartland Community College

Normal, Illinois

- **State and locally supported** 2-year, founded 1990, part of Illinois Community College Board
- **Urban** 145-acre campus
- **Coed**

Undergraduates 1,816 full-time, 2,906 part-time. Students come from 27 states and territories; 13 other countries; 1% are from out of state; 9% Black or African American, non-Hispanic/Latino; 7% Hispanic/Latino; 2% Asian, non-Hispanic/Latino; 0.1% American Indian or Alaska Native, non-Hispanic/Latino; 5% Two or more races, non-Hispanic/Latino; 1% Race/ethnicity unknown; 1% international; 10% transferred in. *Retention:* 55% of full-time freshmen returned.

Faculty *Student/faculty ratio:* 19:1.

Academics *Calendar:* semesters. *Degree:* certificates and associate. *Special study options:* academic remediation for entering students, adult/continuing education programs, advanced placement credit, cooperative education, distance learning, double majors, English as a second language, honors programs, independent study, internships, part-time degree program, services for LD students, study abroad, summer session for credit.

Library Heartland Community College Library. *Books:* 19,860 (physical); *Serial titles:* 22,933 (physical), 99,327 (digital/electronic); *Databases:* 20. Weekly public service hours: 61.

Student Life *Campus security:* 24-hour emergency response devices and patrols.

Athletics Member NJCAA.

Costs (2019–20) *Tuition:* area resident $4500 full-time, $150 per credit hour part-time; state resident $9000 full-time, $300 per credit hour part-time; nonresident $13,500 full-time, $450 per credit hour part-time. *Required fees:* $240 full-time, $8 per credit hour part-time.

Financial Aid Of all full-time matriculated undergraduates who enrolled in 2018, 75 Federal Work-Study jobs (averaging $1500).

Applying *Options:* electronic application. *Recommended:* high school transcript.

Freshman Application Contact Ms. Amanda Garard, Coordinator of Admissions, Heartland Community College, 1500 West Raab Road, Normal, IL 61761. *Phone:* 309-268-8010. *Fax:* 309-268-7992. *E-mail:* Amanda.Rambo@heartland.edu. *Website:* http://www.heartland.edu/.

Highland Community College

Freeport, Illinois

Freshman Application Contact Mr. Jeremy Bradt, Director, Enrollment and Records, Highland Community College, 2998 West Pearl City Road, Freeport, IL 61032. *Phone:* 815-235-6121 Ext. 3500. *Fax:* 815-235-6130. *E-mail:* jeremy.bradt@highland.edu. *Website:* http://www.highland.edu/.

Illinois Central College

East Peoria, Illinois

Freshman Application Contact Emily Points, Dean of Students, Illinois Central College, 1 College Drive, East Peoria, IL 61635. *Phone:* 309-694-8501. *E-mail:* emily.points@icc.edu. *Website:* http://www.icc.edu/.

Illinois Eastern Community Colleges, Frontier Community College

Fairfield, Illinois

Freshman Application Contact Ms. Amy Loss, Coordinator of Registration and Records, Illinois Eastern Community Colleges, Frontier Community College, 2 Frontier Drive, Fairfield, IL 62837. *Phone:* 618-842-3711 Ext. 4114. *Toll-free phone:* 877-464-3687. *Fax:* 618-842-6340. *E-mail:* lossa@iecc.edu. *Website:* http://www.iecc.edu/fcc/.

Illinois Eastern Community Colleges, Lincoln Trail College
Robinson, Illinois

Freshman Application Contact Ms. Megan Scott, Director of Admissions, Illinois Eastern Community Colleges, Lincoln Trail College, 11220 State Highway 1, Robinson, IL 62454. *Phone:* 618-544-8657 Ext. 1137. *Toll-free phone:* 866-582-4322. *Fax:* 618-544-7423. *E-mail:* scottm@iecc.edu. *Website:* http://www.iecc.edu/ltc/.

Illinois Eastern Community Colleges, Olney Central College
Olney, Illinois

Freshman Application Contact Ms. Andrea Pampe, Assistant Dean for Student Services, Illinois Eastern Community Colleges, Olney Central College, 305 North West Street, Olney, IL 62450. *Phone:* 618-395-7777 Ext. 2005. *Toll-free phone:* 866-622-4322. *Fax:* 618-392-5212. *E-mail:* pampea@iecc.edu. *Website:* http://www.iecc.edu/occ/.

Illinois Eastern Community Colleges, Wabash Valley College
Mount Carmel, Illinois

Freshman Application Contact Mrs. Tiffany Cowger, Assistant Dean for Student Services, Illinois Eastern Community Colleges, Wabash Valley College, 2200 College Drive, Mt. Carmel, IL 62863. *Phone:* 618-262-8641 Ext. 3101. *Toll-free phone:* 866-982-4322. *Fax:* 618-262-8647. *E-mail:* cowgert@iecc.edu. *Website:* http://www.iecc.edu/wvc/.

Illinois Valley Community College
Oglesby, Illinois

Freshman Application Contact Mr. Quintin Overocker, Director of Admissions and Records, Illinois Valley Community College, Oglesby, IL 61348. *Phone:* 815-224-0437. *Fax:* 815-224-3033. *E-mail:* quintin_overocker@ivcc.edu. *Website:* http://www.ivcc.edu/.

John A. Logan College
Carterville, Illinois

Director of Admissions Mr. Terry Crain, Dean of Student Services, John A. Logan College, 700 Logan College Road, Carterville, IL 62918-9900. *Phone:* 618-985-3741 Ext. 8382. *Fax:* 618-985-4433. *E-mail:* terrycrain@jalc.edu. *Website:* http://www.jalc.edu/.

John Wood Community College
Quincy, Illinois

Freshman Application Contact Mr. Lee Wibbell, Director of Admissions, John Wood Community College, Quincy, IL 62305-8736. *Phone:* 217-641-4339. *Fax:* 217-224-4208. *E-mail:* admissions@jwcc.edu. *Website:* http://www.jwcc.edu/.

Joliet Junior College
Joliet, Illinois

Freshman Application Contact Ms. Jennifer Kloberdanz, Director of Admissions and Recruitment, Joliet Junior College, 1215 Houbolt Road, Joliet, IL 60431. *Phone:* 815-729-9020 Ext. 2414. *E-mail:* admission@jjc.edu. *Website:* http://www.jjc.edu/.

Kankakee Community College
Kankakee, Illinois

- **State and locally supported** 2-year, founded 1966, part of Illinois Community College Board
- **Small-town** 185-acre campus with easy access to Chicago
- **Endowment** $6.5 million
- **Coed**

Undergraduates 1,222 full-time, 2,084 part-time. Students come from 17 states and territories; 7 other countries; 1% are from out of state; 12% Black or African American, non-Hispanic/Latino; 13% Hispanic/Latino; 1% Asian, non-Hispanic/Latino; 0.1% Native Hawaiian or other Pacific Islander, non-Hispanic/Latino; 0.8% American Indian or Alaska Native, non-Hispanic/Latino; 1% Two or more races, non-Hispanic/Latino; 2% Race/ethnicity unknown; 0.2% international; 2% transferred in. *Retention:* 68% of full-time freshmen returned.
Faculty *Student/faculty ratio:* 14:1.
Academics *Calendar:* semesters. *Degrees:* certificates, diplomas, and associate (also offers continuing education program with significant enrollment not reflected in profile). *Special study options:* academic remediation for entering students, advanced placement credit, distance learning, English as a second language, honors programs, independent study, internships, off-campus study, part-time degree program, services for LD students, student-designed majors, study abroad, summer session for credit. *ROTC:* Army (c).
Library Kankakee Community College Learning Resource Center.
Student Life *Campus security:* 24-hour patrols, late-night transport/escort service.
Athletics Member NJCAA.
Financial Aid Of all full-time matriculated undergraduates who enrolled in 2018, 70 Federal Work-Study jobs (averaging $1100). *Financial aid deadline:* 10/1.
Applying *Options:* electronic application, early admission. *Required:* high school transcript.
Freshman Application Contact Ms. Kim Harpin, Director of Support Services, Kankakee Community College, 100 College Drive, Kankakee, IL 60901. *Phone:* 815-802-8472. *Fax:* 815-802-8472. *E-mail:* kharpin@kcc.edu. *Website:* http://www.kcc.edu/.

Kaskaskia College
Centralia, Illinois

- **State and locally supported** 2-year, founded 1966, part of Illinois Community College Board
- **Rural** 195-acre campus with easy access to St. Louis
- **Endowment** $7.7 million
- **Coed,** 3,248 undergraduate students, 40% full-time, 61% women, 39% men

Undergraduates 1,295 full-time, 1,953 part-time. Students come from 9 states and territories; 0.4% are from out of state; 5% Black or African American, non-Hispanic/Latino; 2% Hispanic/Latino; 0.5% Asian, non-Hispanic/Latino; 0.1% Native Hawaiian or other Pacific Islander, non-Hispanic/Latino; 0.2% American Indian or Alaska Native, non-Hispanic/Latino; 2% Two or more races, non-Hispanic/Latino; 0.2% Race/ethnicity unknown; 11% transferred in.
Freshmen *Admission:* 269 applied, 269 admitted, 305 enrolled. *Average high school GPA:* 3.6.
Faculty *Total:* 141, 51% full-time, 9% with terminal degrees. *Student/faculty ratio:* 17:1.
Majors Accounting; agriculture; animal sciences; applied horticulture/horticulture operations; architectural drafting and CAD/CADD; automobile/automotive mechanics technology; biological and physical sciences; business automation/technology/data entry; business/commerce; carpentry; child-care provision; clinical/medical laboratory technology; construction management; cosmetology; criminal justice/law enforcement administration; culinary arts; dental assisting; electrical, electronic and communications engineering technology; emergency medical technology (EMT paramedic); engineering; executive assistant/executive secretary; food service and dining room management; general studies; health information/medical records technology; heating, air conditioning, ventilation and refrigeration maintenance technology; industrial mechanics and maintenance technology; juvenile corrections; liberal arts and sciences/liberal studies; library and archives assisting; music; network and system administration; occupational therapist assistant; physical therapy technology; radiologic technology/science; registered nursing/registered nurse; respiratory care therapy; robotics technology; teacher assistant/aide; veterinary/animal health technology; web/multimedia management and webmaster; welding technology.
Academics *Calendar:* semesters. *Degree:* certificates and associate. *Special study options:* academic remediation for entering students, accelerated degree program, adult/continuing education programs, cooperative education, distance learning, double majors, English as a second language, honors programs, independent study, internships, off-campus study, part-time degree program, services for LD students, summer session for credit. *ROTC:* Army (c).
Library Kaskaskia College Library. *Books:* 17,285 (physical), 24,433 (digital/electronic); *Serial titles:* 24 (physical); *Databases:* 86. Weekly public service hours: 47.
Student Life *Housing:* college housing not available. *Activities and Organizations:* drama/theater group, choral group, SNO, SPNO, Veterans, Radiology, CJ. *Campus security:* 24-hour emergency response devices and patrols, late-night transport/escort service. *Student services:* personal/psychological counseling, veterans affairs office.

Athletics Member NJCAA. *Intercollegiate sports:* baseball M(s), basketball M(s)/W(s), cheerleading M(s)/W(s), cross-country running M(s)/W(s), soccer W(s), softball W(s), tennis M(s)/W(s), volleyball W(s).
Standardized Tests *Recommended:* SAT or ACT (for admission).
Costs (2020–21) *Tuition:* area resident $4560 full-time, $152 per credit hour part-time; state resident $7530 full-time, $251 per credit hour part-time; nonresident $12,330 full-time, $411 per credit hour part-time. *Required fees:* $480 full-time, $16 per credit hour part-time. *Waivers:* employees or children of employees.
Financial Aid Of all full-time matriculated undergraduates who enrolled in 2018, 758 applied for aid, 625 were judged to have need, 51 had their need fully met. 46 Federal Work-Study jobs (averaging $2754). 31 state and other part-time jobs (averaging $2914). In 2018, 127 non-need-based awards were made. *Average percent of need met:* 60%. *Average financial aid package:* $4637. *Average need-based gift aid:* $3815. *Average non-need-based aid:* $4126.
Applying *Options:* electronic application, early admission, deferred entrance. *Required:* high school transcript. *Required for some:* interview. *Application deadlines:* rolling (freshmen), rolling (transfers). *Notification:* continuous (freshmen), continuous (transfers).
Freshman Application Contact Jenna Lammers, Registrar, Kaskaskia College, 27210 College Road, Centralia, IL 62801. *Phone:* 618-545-3044. *Toll-free phone:* 800-642-0859. *Fax:* 618-532-1990. *E-mail:* jlammers@kaskaskia.edu.
Website: http://www.kaskaskia.edu/.

Kishwaukee College
Malta, Illinois

- **State and locally supported** 2-year, founded 1967, part of Illinois Community College Board
- **Rural** 120-acre campus with easy access to Chicago
- **Coed,** 3,775 undergraduate students, 43% full-time, 53% women, 47% men

Undergraduates 1,634 full-time, 2,141 part-time. 15% Black or African American, non-Hispanic/Latino; 15% Hispanic/Latino; 2% Asian, non-Hispanic/Latino; 0.1% Native Hawaiian or other Pacific Islander, non-Hispanic/Latino; 0.5% American Indian or Alaska Native, non-Hispanic/Latino; 3% Two or more races, non-Hispanic/Latino; 2% Race/ethnicity unknown. *Retention:* 59% of full-time freshmen returned.
Freshmen *Admission:* 614 enrolled.
Faculty *Total:* 236, 32% full-time, 6% with terminal degrees. *Student/faculty ratio:* 16:1.
Majors Administrative assistant and secretarial science; agricultural mechanization; airline pilot and flight crew; applied horticulture/horticulture operations; art; autobody/collision and repair technology; automobile/automotive mechanics technology; biological and physical sciences; business administration and management; CAD/CADD drafting/design technology; child-care and support services management; child-care provision; criminal justice/police science; criminal justice/safety; diesel mechanics technology; education (multiple levels); electrical, electronic and communications engineering technology; emergency medical technology (EMT paramedic); engineering; fine/studio arts; forensic science and technology; information technology; landscaping and groundskeeping; liberal arts and sciences/liberal studies; network and system administration; ornamental horticulture; radiologic technology/science; registered nursing/registered nurse; teacher assistant/aide.
Academics *Calendar:* semesters. *Degree:* certificates, diplomas, and associate. *Special study options:* academic remediation for entering students, adult/continuing education programs, advanced placement credit, cooperative education, distance learning, double majors, English as a second language, external degree program, freshman honors college, honors programs, independent study, internships, off-campus study, part-time degree program, services for LD students, study abroad, summer session for credit.
Library Kishwaukee College Library. Students can reserve study rooms.
Student Life *Activities and Organizations:* drama/theater group, student-run newspaper, choral group. *Campus security:* 24-hour emergency response devices and patrols. *Student services:* health clinic, personal/psychological counseling, veterans affairs office.
Athletics Member NJCAA. *Intercollegiate sports:* baseball M(s), basketball M(s)/W(s), bowling M, cross-country running M(s)/W(s), golf M(s)/W(s), soccer M(s), softball W(s), volleyball W(s).
Costs (2020–21) *Tuition:* area resident $4440 full-time, $149 per credit hour part-time; state resident $8880 full-time, $298 per credit hour part-time; nonresident $13,320 full-time, $447 per credit hour part-time. Full-time tuition and fees vary according to program and reciprocity agreements. Part-time tuition and fees vary according to program and reciprocity agreements. *Required fees:* $570 full-time, $17 per credit hour part-time. *Room and board:* $6040; room only: $3100. *Payment plans:* installment, deferred payment. *Waivers:* senior citizens and employees or children of employees.
Financial Aid *Average indebtedness upon graduation:* $4375.
Applying *Options:* electronic application, early admission, deferred entrance. *Required for some:* high school transcript. *Recommended:* high school transcript, transcripts from all other colleges or universities previously attended. *Application deadlines:* rolling (freshmen), rolling (transfers). *Notification:* continuous (freshmen), continuous (transfers).
Freshman Application Contact Ms. Graciela Horta, Coordinator, Student Outreach, Kishwaukee College, 21193 Malta Road, Malta, IL 60150. *Phone:* 815-825-1711. *E-mail:* ghorta@kish.edu.
Website: http://www.kish.edu/.

Lake Land College
Mattoon, Illinois

Freshman Application Contact Mr. Jon VanDyke, Dean of Admissions Services, Lake Land College, Mattoon, IL 61938-9366. *Phone:* 217-234-5378. *E-mail:* admissions@lakeland.cc.il.us. *Website:* http://www.lakelandcollege.edu/.

Lewis and Clark Community College
Godfrey, Illinois

Freshman Application Contact Lewis and Clark Community College, 5800 Godfrey Road, Godfrey, IL 62035-2466. *Phone:* 618-468-5100. *Toll-free phone:* 800-YES-LCCC. *Website:* http://www.lc.edu/.

Lincoln College of Technology - Melrose Park
Melrose Park, Illinois

Admissions Office Contact Lincoln College of Technology - Melrose Park, 8317 West North Avenue, Melrose Park, IL 60160. *Toll-free phone:* 844-215-1513. *Website:* http://www.lincolntech.edu/.

Lincoln Land Community College
Springfield, Illinois

Freshman Application Contact Mr. Ron Gregoire, Executive Director of Admissions and Records, Lincoln Land Community College, 5250 Shepherd Road, PO Box 19256, Springfield, IL 62794-9256. *Phone:* 217-786-2243. *Toll-free phone:* 800-727-4161. *Fax:* 217-786-2492. *E-mail:* ron.gregoire@llcc.edu. *Website:* http://www.llcc.edu/.

MacCormac College
Chicago, Illinois

Director of Admissions Mr. David Grassi, Director of Admissions, MacCormac College, 506 South Wabash Avenue, Chicago, IL 60605-1667. *Phone:* 312-922-1884 Ext. 102. *Website:* http://www.maccormac.edu/.

McHenry County College
Crystal Lake, Illinois

- **State and locally supported** 2-year, founded 1967, part of Illinois Community College Board
- **Suburban** 168-acre campus with easy access to Chicago
- **Coed,** 7,031 undergraduate students, 31% full-time, 52% women, 48% men

Undergraduates 2,169 full-time, 4,862 part-time. 1% are from out of state; 2% Black or African American, non-Hispanic/Latino; 19% Hispanic/Latino; 2% Asian, non-Hispanic/Latino; 0.1% Native Hawaiian or other Pacific Islander, non-Hispanic/Latino; 0.2% American Indian or Alaska Native, non-Hispanic/Latino; 3% Two or more races, non-Hispanic/Latino; 5% Race/ethnicity unknown; 0.2% international; 10% transferred in.
Freshmen *Admission:* 1,694 applied, 1,694 admitted, 956 enrolled. *Average high school GPA:* 2.3.
Faculty *Total:* 329, 28% full-time, 65% with terminal degrees. *Student/faculty ratio:* 23:1.
Majors Accounting; administrative assistant and secretarial science; animation, interactive technology, video graphics and special effects; applied horticulture/horticulture operations; biological and physical sciences; business administration and management; child-care provision; commercial photography; computer systems networking and telecommunications; construction management; criminal justice/police science; emergency medical technology (EMT paramedic); engineering; fine/studio arts; fire science/firefighting; general studies; health and physical education/fitness; information technology; liberal arts and sciences/liberal studies; music;

occupational therapist assistant; operations management; registered nursing/registered nurse; restaurant, culinary, and catering management; selling skills and sales; special education.

Academics *Calendar:* semesters. *Degree:* certificates and associate. *Special study options:* academic remediation for entering students, accelerated degree program, adult/continuing education programs, advanced placement credit, cooperative education, distance learning, English as a second language, independent study, internships, part-time degree program, services for LD students, study abroad, summer session for credit.

Library McHenry County College Library. *Books:* 36,034 (physical), 10,808 (digital/electronic); *Serial titles:* 59 (physical), 33,250 (digital/electronic); *Databases:* 120.

Student Life *Housing:* college housing not available. *Activities and Organizations:* drama/theater group, student-run newspaper, radio station, choral group, Phi Theta Kappa, Student Senate, Equality Club, Writer's Block, Latinos Unidos. *Campus security:* 24-hour emergency response devices and patrols, late-night transport/escort service.

Athletics Member NJCAA. *Intercollegiate sports:* baseball M(s), basketball M(s)/W(s), soccer M(s), softball W(s), tennis M(s)/W(s), volleyball W(s).

Costs (2020–21) *Tuition:* area resident $3345 full-time, $112 per credit hour part-time; state resident $11,345 full-time, $378 per credit hour part-time; nonresident $14,104 full-time, $470 per credit hour part-time. Full-time tuition and fees vary according to course load. Part-time tuition and fees vary according to course load. *Required fees:* $284 full-time, $9 per credit hour part-time, $7 per term part-time. *Payment plan:* installment. *Waivers:* senior citizens and employees or children of employees.

Financial Aid Of all full-time matriculated undergraduates who enrolled in 2018, 200 Federal Work-Study jobs (averaging $3700). 130 state and other part-time jobs (averaging $2000).

Applying *Options:* electronic application, early admission, deferred entrance. *Application fee:* $15. *Recommended:* high school transcript. *Application deadlines:* rolling (freshmen), rolling (out-of-state freshmen), rolling (transfers). *Notification:* continuous (freshmen), continuous (out-of-state freshmen), continuous (transfers).

Freshman Application Contact Amy Carzoli, Director of Admissions and Recruitment, McHenry County College, 8900 US Highway 14, Crystal Lake, IL 60012-2761. *Phone:* 815-455-8670. *E-mail:* admissions@mchenry.edu. *Website:* http://www.mchenry.edu/.

Midwestern Career College

Chicago, Illinois

Admissions Office Contact Midwestern Career College, 20 North Wacker Drive #3800, Chicago, IL 60606. *Website:* http://www.mccollege.edu/.

Moraine Valley Community College

Palos Hills, Illinois

Freshman Application Contact Mr. Andrew Sarata, Director, Admissions and Recruitment, Moraine Valley Community College, 9000 West College Parkway, Palos Hills, IL 60465-0937. *Phone:* 708-974-5357. *Fax:* 708-974-0681. *E-mail:* sarataa@morainevalley.edu. *Website:* http://www.morainevalley.edu/.

Morrison Institute of Technology

Morrison, Illinois

Admissions Office Contact Morrison Institute of Technology, 701 Portland Avenue, Morrison, IL 61270-0410. *Website:* http://www.morrisontech.edu/.

Morton College

Cicero, Illinois

- **State and locally supported** 2-year, founded 1924, part of Illinois Community College Board
- **Suburban** 25-acre campus with easy access to Chicago
- **Coed,** 4,439 undergraduate students, 26% full-time, 58% women, 42% men

Undergraduates 1,162 full-time, 3,277 part-time. Students come from 8 states and territories; 7 other countries; 1% are from out of state; ####% Black or African American, non-Hispanic/Latino; 85% Hispanic/Latino; 1% Asian, non-Hispanic/Latino; 0.3% American Indian or Alaska Native, non-Hispanic/Latino; 0.5% Two or more races, non-Hispanic/Latino; 5% Race/ethnicity unknown.

Freshmen *Admission:* 630 enrolled.

Faculty *Total:* 208, 33% full-time, 18% with terminal degrees. *Student/faculty ratio:* 19:1.

Majors Accounting; administrative assistant and secretarial science; art; automobile/automotive mechanics technology; biological and physical sciences; business administration and management; CAD/CADD drafting/design technology; child-care provision; computer support specialist; criminal justice/police science; data processing and data processing technology; drafting and design technology; early childhood education; finance; fine/studio arts; fire science/firefighting; health information/medical records technology; heating, air conditioning, ventilation and refrigeration maintenance technology; information technology; legal administrative assistant/secretary; liberal arts and sciences/liberal studies; marketing/marketing management; medical administrative assistant and medical secretary; music; physical therapy; physical therapy technology; registered nursing/registered nurse; web/multimedia management and webmaster.

Academics *Calendar:* semesters. *Degree:* certificates and associate. *Special study options:* academic remediation for entering students, adult/continuing education programs, advanced placement credit, distance learning, English as a second language, independent study, internships, part-time degree program, services for LD students, student-designed majors, study abroad, summer session for credit.

Library Learning Resource Center. Students can reserve study rooms.

Student Life *Housing:* college housing not available. *Activities and Organizations:* drama/theater group, student-run radio station, Student Government Association, Phi Theta Kappa Honor Society, Nursing Student Association, Physical Therapy Assistants Club, National Society of Leadership and Success. *Campus security:* 24-hour emergency response devices and patrols, security cameras. *Student services:* personal/psychological counseling.

Athletics Member NJCAA. *Intercollegiate sports:* baseball M(s), basketball M(s)/W(s), cross-country running M(s)/W(s), soccer M(s)/W(s), softball W(s), volleyball W(s).

Costs (2019–20) *Tuition:* area resident $2496 full-time, $104 per credit hour part-time; state resident $5568 full-time, $232 per credit hour part-time; nonresident $7104 full-time, $296 per credit hour part-time. *Required fees:* $980 full-time, $40 per credit hour part-time, $10 per term part-time. *Payment plan:* installment. *Waivers:* senior citizens and employees or children of employees.

Financial Aid Of all full-time matriculated undergraduates who enrolled in 2018, 963 applied for aid, 917 were judged to have need.

Applying *Options:* electronic application. *Application fee:* $10. *Required:* high school transcript. *Application deadlines:* rolling (freshmen), rolling (out-of-state freshmen), rolling (transfers).

Freshman Application Contact Morton College, 3801 South Central Avenue, Cicero, IL 60804-4398. *Website:* http://www.morton.edu/.

Northwestern College–Bridgeview Campus

Bridgeview, Illinois

Admissions Office Contact Northwestern College–Bridgeview Campus, 7725 South Harlem Avenue, Bridgeview, IL 60645. *Toll-free phone:* 888-205-2283. *Website:* http://www.nc.edu/locations/bridgeview-campus/.

Northwestern College–Chicago Campus

Chicago, Illinois

- **Proprietary** 2-year, founded 1902
- **Urban** 3-acre campus with easy access to Chicago, IL
- **Coed,** 1,082 undergraduate students, 44% full-time, 83% women, 17% men

Undergraduates 472 full-time, 610 part-time. 2% are from out of state; 40% Black or African American, non-Hispanic/Latino; 21% Hispanic/Latino; 1% Asian, non-Hispanic/Latino; 0.2% Native Hawaiian or other Pacific Islander, non-Hispanic/Latino; 2% American Indian or Alaska Native, non-Hispanic/Latino; 8% Two or more races, non-Hispanic/Latino; 6% Race/ethnicity unknown.

Freshmen *Admission:* 555 applied, 530 admitted, 256 enrolled.

Majors Accounting technology and bookkeeping; business administration and management; criminal justice/law enforcement administration; diagnostic medical sonography and ultrasound technology; health information/medical records technology; legal assistant/paralegal; massage therapy; medical/clinical assistant; radiologic technology/science; registered nursing/registered nurse.

Academics *Calendar:* quarters. *Degree:* profile includes branch campuses in Bridgeview and Naperville, IL. *Special study options:* academic remediation for entering students, cooperative education, honors programs, independent study, internships, part-time degree program, summer session for credit.

Library Edward G. Schumacher Memorial Library.

Student Life *Housing:* college housing not available. *Student services:* personal/psychological counseling.
Standardized Tests *Recommended:* SAT or ACT (for admission).
Costs (2019–20) *Tuition:* $18,475 full-time. Full-time tuition and fees vary according to program. *Required fees:* $1548 full-time. *Payment plan:* installment. *Waivers:* employees or children of employees.
Applying *Options:* electronic application. *Application fee:* $25.
Freshman Application Contact Northwestern College–Chicago Campus, 4829 North Lipps Avenue, Chicago, IL 60630. *Phone:* 708-233-5000. *Toll-free phone:* 888-205-2283.
Website: http://www.nc.edu/locations/chicago-campus/.

Oakton Community College
Des Plaines, Illinois

- **District-supported** 2-year, founded 1969, part of Illinois Community College Board
- **Suburban** 193-acre campus with easy access to Chicago
- **Coed,** 7,652 undergraduate students

Undergraduates 8% Black or African American, non-Hispanic/Latino; 18% Hispanic/Latino; 24% Asian, non-Hispanic/Latino; 0.3% American Indian or Alaska Native, non-Hispanic/Latino; 5% Race/ethnicity unknown.
Majors Accounting technology and bookkeeping; administrative assistant and secretarial science; architectural drafting and CAD/CADD; automobile/automotive mechanics technology; banking and financial support services; biological and physical sciences; building/construction finishing, management, and inspection related; child-care provision; clinical/medical laboratory technology; computer programming; criminal justice/police science; electrical, electronic and communications engineering technology; engineering; fire science/firefighting; graphic design; health information/medical records administration; heating, ventilation, air conditioning and refrigeration engineering technology; information technology; liberal arts and sciences/liberal studies; manufacturing engineering technology; marketing/marketing management; mechanical engineering/mechanical technology; music; operations management; real estate; registered nursing/registered nurse; sales, distribution, and marketing operations; social work; substance abuse/addiction counseling.
Academics *Calendar:* semesters. *Degree:* certificates and associate. *Special study options:* academic remediation for entering students, adult/continuing education programs, advanced placement credit, distance learning, English as a second language, honors programs, independent study, internships, off-campus study, part-time degree program, services for LD students, study abroad, summer session for credit.
Library Oakton Community College Library plus 1 other.
Student Life *Housing:* college housing not available. *Activities and Organizations:* drama/theater group, student-run newspaper, choral group. *Campus security:* 24-hour emergency response devices and patrols, student patrols, late-night transport/escort service. *Student services:* health clinic, personal/psychological counseling, veterans affairs office.
Athletics Member NJCAA. *Intercollegiate sports:* baseball M, basketball M/W, cross-country running M/W, soccer M/W, softball W, tennis M/W, track and field M/W, volleyball W. *Intramural sports:* basketball M/W, cheerleading W, soccer M, table tennis M/W, volleyball M/W.
Costs (2020–21) *Tuition:* area resident $3270 full-time; state resident $8808 full-time; nonresident $10,536 full-time. *Waivers:* senior citizens and employees or children of employees.
Applying *Options:* electronic application. *Application fee:* $25. *Required for some:* interview. *Recommended:* high school transcript. *Application deadlines:* rolling (freshmen), rolling (transfers). *Notification:* continuous (freshmen), continuous (transfers).
Freshman Application Contact Ms. Rebel Barber, Admissions Specialist, Oakton Community College, 1600 East Golf Road, Des Plaines, IL 60016-1268. *Phone:* 847-635-1703. *Fax:* 847-635-1890. *E-mail:* rcampbel@oakton.edu.
Website: http://www.oakton.edu/.

Parkland College
Champaign, Illinois

Freshman Application Contact Mr. Tim Wendt, Director of Enrollment Services, Parkland College, Champaign, IL 61821-1899. *Phone:* 217-351-2482. *Toll-free phone:* 800-346-8089. *Fax:* 217-353-2640. *E-mail:* admissions@parkland.edu. *Website:* http://www.parkland.edu/.

Prairie State College
Chicago Heights, Illinois

Freshman Application Contact Jaime Miller, Director of Admissions, Prairie State College, 202 South Halsted Street, Chicago Heights, IL 60411. *Phone:* 708-709-3513. *E-mail:* jmmiller@prairiestate.edu. *Website:* http://www.prairiestate.edu/.

Rend Lake College
Ina, Illinois

- **State-supported** 2-year, founded 1967, part of Illinois Community College Board
- **Rural** 350-acre campus
- **Coed,** 2,317 undergraduate students, 48% full-time, 57% women, 43% men

Undergraduates 1,123 full-time, 1,194 part-time. Students come from 3 states and territories; 5 other countries; 5% Black or African American, non-Hispanic/Latino; 1% Hispanic/Latino; 0.7% Asian, non-Hispanic/Latino; 0.1% Native Hawaiian or other Pacific Islander, non-Hispanic/Latino; 0.3% American Indian or Alaska Native, non-Hispanic/Latino; 0.6% Race/ethnicity unknown; 3% transferred in.
Freshmen *Admission:* 511 admitted, 511 enrolled.
Faculty *Total:* 120, 45% full-time, 12% with terminal degrees. *Student/faculty ratio:* 20:1.
Majors Agricultural business and management; agricultural mechanics and equipment technology; agricultural mechanization; agricultural production; architectural drafting and CAD/CADD; automobile/automotive mechanics technology; barbering; biological and physical sciences; biomedical technology; business/commerce; child-care provision; computer and information systems security; computer programming; computer technology/computer systems technology; cosmetology; criminal justice/police science; culinary arts; emergency medical technology (EMT paramedic); engineering; fine/studio arts; graphic design; health information/medical records technology; heavy equipment maintenance technology; industrial mechanics and maintenance technology; liberal arts and sciences/liberal studies; manufacturing engineering technology; medical/clinical assistant; medical radiologic technology; music; operations management; registered nursing/registered nurse; welding technology.
Academics *Calendar:* semesters. *Degree:* certificates and associate. *Special study options:* academic remediation for entering students, adult/continuing education programs, advanced placement credit, cooperative education, distance learning, double majors, English as a second language, honors programs, independent study, internships, off-campus study, part-time degree program, services for LD students, study abroad, summer session for credit.
Library Learning Resource Center. *Books:* 10,953 (physical), 45,587 (digital/electronic); *Serial titles:* 35 (physical), 23,148 (digital/electronic); *Databases:* 62. Weekly public service hours: 54; students can reserve study rooms.
Student Life *Housing:* college housing not available. *Activities and Organizations:* drama/theater group, choral group, Fellowship of Christian Athletes, Agriculture, Culinary Arts, Thespians Club, Radiology Club. *Campus security:* 24-hour emergency response devices and patrols, late-night transport/escort service. *Student services:* personal/psychological counseling, veterans affairs office.
Athletics Member NJCAA. *Intercollegiate sports:* baseball M(s), basketball M(s)/W(s), golf M(s)/W(s), softball W(s), volleyball W(s).
Costs (2020–21) *Tuition:* area resident $3300 full-time, $110 per credit hour part-time; state resident $5250 full-time, $175 per credit hour part-time; nonresident $6000 full-time, $200 per credit hour part-time. Full-time tuition and fees vary according to course level, course load, program, and reciprocity agreements. Part-time tuition and fees vary according to course level, course load, program, and reciprocity agreements. *Required fees:* $750 full-time, $25 per credit hour part-time. *Payment plan:* installment. *Waivers:* senior citizens and employees or children of employees.
Financial Aid Of all full-time matriculated undergraduates who enrolled in 2018, 25 Federal Work-Study jobs (averaging $1860). 42 state and other part-time jobs (averaging $2041).
Applying *Options:* electronic application, deferred entrance. *Required:* high school transcript. *Application deadlines:* 8/24 (freshmen), 8/24 (out-of-state freshmen), 8/24 (transfers).
Freshman Application Contact Mrs. Jena Jensik, Director of Academic Advisement, Rend Lake College, 468 North Ken Gray Parkway, Ina, IL 62846-9801. *Phone:* 618-437-5321 Ext. 1293. *Toll-free phone:* 800-369-5321. *Fax:* 618-437-5677. *E-mail:* jensikj@rlc.edu.
Website: http://www.rlc.edu/.

Richland Community College
Decatur, Illinois

Freshman Application Contact Ms. Catherine Sebok, Director of Admissions and Records, Richland Community College, Decatur, IL 62521. *Phone:* 217-875-7200 Ext. 558. *Fax:* 217-875-7783. *E-mail:* csebok@richland.edu. *Website:* http://www.richland.edu/.

Rockford Career College
Rockford, Illinois

Director of Admissions Ms. Barbara Holliman, Director of Admissions, Rockford Career College, 1130 South Alpine Road, Suite 100, Rockford, IL 61108. *Phone:* 815-965-8616 Ext. 16. *Website:* http://www.rockfordcareercollege.edu/.

Rock Valley College
Rockford, Illinois

- **District-supported** 2-year, founded 1964, part of Illinois Community College Board
- **Suburban** 217-acre campus with easy access to Chicago
- **Coed,** 6,092 undergraduate students, 45% full-time, 55% women, 45% men

Undergraduates 2,728 full-time, 3,364 part-time. 9% Black or African American, non-Hispanic/Latino; 22% Hispanic/Latino; 7% Asian, non-Hispanic/Latino; 0.1% Native Hawaiian or other Pacific Islander, non-Hispanic/Latino; 0.3% American Indian or Alaska Native, non-Hispanic/Latino; 2% Two or more races, non-Hispanic/Latino; 4% Race/ethnicity unknown; 0.4% international.
Freshmen *Admission:* 941 enrolled.
Faculty *Total:* 398, 32% full-time. *Student/faculty ratio:* 16:1.
Majors Accounting; administrative assistant and secretarial science; automobile/automotive mechanics technology; avionics maintenance technology; business administration and management; child development; computer engineering technology; computer science; computer systems networking and telecommunications; construction engineering technology; criminal justice/law enforcement administration; dental hygiene; drafting/design engineering technologies related; electrical, electronic and communications engineering technology; electrician; energy management and systems technology; fire science/firefighting; graphic and printing equipment operation/production; human services; industrial and product design; industrial technology; liberal arts and sciences/liberal studies; marketing/marketing management; pre-engineering; registered nursing/registered nurse; respiratory care therapy; sheet metal technology; sport and fitness administration/management; surgical technology; tool and die technology; welding technology.
Academics *Calendar:* semesters. *Degree:* certificates, diplomas, and associate. *Special study options:* academic remediation for entering students, adult/continuing education programs, advanced placement credit, cooperative education, distance learning, English as a second language, honors programs, independent study, internships, part-time degree program, services for LD students, student-designed majors, study abroad, summer session for credit.
Library Educational Resource Center plus 1 other.
Student Life *Housing:* college housing not available. *Activities and Organizations:* drama/theater group, student-run newspaper, choral group, Black Student Alliance, Phi Theta Kappa, Adults on Campus, Inter-Varsity Club, Christian Fellowship. *Campus security:* 24-hour emergency response devices and patrols, late-night transport/escort service. *Student services:* personal/psychological counseling.
Athletics Member NJCAA. *Intercollegiate sports:* baseball M, basketball M/W, bowling M/W, soccer M/W, softball W, volleyball W.
Costs (2020–21) *Tuition:* area resident $3600 full-time, $115 per credit hour part-time; state resident $8970 full-time, $294 per credit hour part-time; nonresident $16,530 full-time, $546 per credit hour part-time. *Required fees:* $314 full-time, $314 per credit hour part-time, $314 per credit hour part-time. *Payment plan:* deferred payment. *Waivers:* employees or children of employees.
Financial Aid Of all full-time matriculated undergraduates who enrolled in 2018, 120 Federal Work-Study jobs (averaging $1800).
Applying *Required:* high school transcript.
Freshman Application Contact Sam Morgan, Dean of Enrollment and Retention, Rock Valley College, 3301 North Mulford Road, Rockford, IL 61008. *Phone:* -815-921-4262. *Toll-free phone:* 800-973-7821. *E-mail:* s.morgan@rockvalleycollege.edu.
Website: http://www.rockvalleycollege.edu/.

SAE Institute Chicago
Chicago, Illinois

Admissions Office Contact SAE Institute Chicago, 820 North Orleans Street #125, Chicago, IL 60610. *Website:* http://www.sae.edu/.

Sauk Valley Community College
Dixon, Illinois

Freshman Application Contact Sauk Valley Community College, 173 Illinois Route 2, Dixon, IL 61021. *Phone:* 815-288-5511 Ext. 378. *Website:* http://www.svcc.edu/.

Shawnee Community College
Ullin, Illinois

- **State and locally supported** 2-year, founded 1967, part of Illinois Community College Board
- **Rural** 163-acre campus
- **Coed,** 1,083 undergraduate students, 59% full-time, 66% women, 34% men

Undergraduates 644 full-time, 439 part-time. Students come from 4 states and territories; 3% are from out of state; 13% Black or African American, non-Hispanic/Latino; 5% Hispanic/Latino; 0.5% Asian, non-Hispanic/Latino; 0.1% Native Hawaiian or other Pacific Islander, non-Hispanic/Latino; 1% American Indian or Alaska Native, non-Hispanic/Latino; 7% Race/ethnicity unknown; 3% transferred in. *Retention:* 55% of full-time freshmen returned.
Freshmen *Admission:* 646 applied, 646 admitted, 269 enrolled.
Faculty *Total:* 77, 43% full-time, 5% with terminal degrees. *Student/faculty ratio:* 16:1.
Majors Accounting; agricultural business and management; automobile/automotive mechanics technology; biological and physical sciences; business administration and management; business automation/technology/data entry; child-care provision; clinical/medical laboratory technology; executive assistant/executive secretary; forensic science and technology; general studies; information technology; logistics, materials, and supply chain management; occupational therapist assistant; registered nursing/registered nurse; sheet metal technology; social work; veterinary/animal health technology; wildlife, fish and wildlands science and management.
Academics *Calendar:* semesters. *Degree:* certificates, diplomas, and associate. *Special study options:* academic remediation for entering students, accelerated degree program, adult/continuing education programs, advanced placement credit, cooperative education, distance learning, double majors, English as a second language, external degree program, independent study, internships, off-campus study, part-time degree program, services for LD students, summer session for credit.
Library Shawnee Community College Library. *Books:* 34,273 (physical), 11,763 (digital/electronic); *Serial titles:* 34 (physical), 10 (digital/electronic); *Databases:* 42. Students can reserve study rooms.
Student Life *Housing:* college housing not available. *Activities and Organizations:* drama/theater group, choral group, Phi Theta Kappa, Phi Beta Lambda, Music Club, Student Senate, Future Teachers Organization. *Campus security:* 24-hour patrols. *Student services:* personal/psychological counseling, veterans affairs office.
Athletics Member NJCAA. *Intercollegiate sports:* baseball M(s), basketball M(s)/W(s), softball W(s).
Standardized Tests *Required for some:* SAT (for admission). *Recommended:* SAT (for admission).
Costs (2020–21) *Tuition:* $115 per credit hour part-time; state resident $176 per credit hour part-time; nonresident $192 per credit hour part-time. Full-time tuition and fees vary according to location. Part-time tuition and fees vary according to location. *Required fees:* $10 per credit hour part-time. *Payment plans:* installment, deferred payment. *Waivers:* senior citizens and employees or children of employees.
Financial Aid Of all full-time matriculated undergraduates who enrolled in 2018, 60 Federal Work-Study jobs (averaging $2000). 50 state and other part-time jobs (averaging $2000).
Applying *Options:* electronic application, early admission, deferred entrance. *Required:* high school transcript. *Application deadlines:* rolling (freshmen), rolling (transfers). *Notification:* continuous (freshmen), continuous (transfers), rolling (early decision).
Freshman Application Contact Mrs. Erin King, Recruiter/Advisor, Shawnee Community College, 8364 Shawnee College Road, Ullin, IL 62992. *Phone:* 618-634-3200. *Toll-free phone:* 800-481-2242. *Fax:* 618-634-3300. *E-mail:* erink@shawneecc.edu.
Website: http://www.shawneecc.edu/.

Southeastern Illinois College
Harrisburg, Illinois

Freshman Application Contact Dr. David Nudo, Director of Counseling, Southeastern Illinois College, 3575 College Road, Harrisburg, IL 62946-4925. *Phone:* 618-252-5400 Ext. 2430. *Toll-free phone:* 866-338-2742. *Website:* http://www.sic.edu/.

South Suburban College

South Holland, Illinois

- **State and locally supported** 2-year, founded 1927, part of Illinois Community College Board
- **Suburban** 5-acre campus with easy access to Chicago
- **Coed,** 4,073 undergraduate students, 26% full-time, 63% women, 37% men

Undergraduates 1,041 full-time, 3,032 part-time. 3% are from out of state; 53% Black or African American, non-Hispanic/Latino; 21% Hispanic/Latino; 1% Asian, non-Hispanic/Latino; 0.1% Native Hawaiian or other Pacific Islander, non-Hispanic/Latino; 0.5% American Indian or Alaska Native, non-Hispanic/Latino; 3% Two or more races, non-Hispanic/Latino; 2% Race/ethnicity unknown; 0.3% international. *Retention:* 20% of full-time freshmen returned.
Freshmen *Average high school GPA:* 2.3.
Faculty *Total:* 237, 33% full-time. *Student/faculty ratio:* 14:1.
Majors Accounting; accounting technology and bookkeeping; architectural drafting and CAD/CADD; biological and physical sciences; building/home/construction inspection; CAD/CADD drafting/design technology; child-care provision; construction engineering technology; court reporting; criminal justice/safety; electrical, electronic and communications engineering technology; executive assistant/executive secretary; fine/studio arts; information technology; kinesiology and exercise science; legal assistant/paralegal; liberal arts and sciences/liberal studies; nursing administration; occupational therapist assistant; office management; radiologic technology/science; small business administration; social work.
Academics *Calendar:* semesters. *Degree:* certificates and associate. *Special study options:* academic remediation for entering students, adult/continuing education programs, advanced placement credit, cooperative education, distance learning, English as a second language, honors programs, internships, off-campus study, part-time degree program, services for LD students, study abroad, summer session for credit.
Library South Suburban College Library plus 1 other. *Books:* 25,563 (physical); *Serial titles:* 56 (physical); *Databases:* 25. Weekly public service hours: 60; students can reserve study rooms.
Student Life *Housing:* college housing not available. *Activities and Organizations:* drama/theater group, choral group. *Campus security:* 24-hour emergency response devices and patrols.
Athletics Member NJCAA. *Intercollegiate sports:* baseball M, basketball M/W, soccer M/W, softball W, volleyball W.
Costs (2020–21) *Tuition:* area resident $4560 full-time; state resident $10,500 full-time; nonresident $12,150 full-time. *Required fees:* $558 full-time. *Waivers:* employees or children of employees.
Applying *Options:* early admission, deferred entrance. *Required:* high school transcript. *Required for some:* essay or personal statement. *Recommended:* essay or personal statement, minimum 2.0 GPA. *Application deadlines:* rolling (freshmen), rolling (transfers). *Notification:* continuous (freshmen), continuous (transfers).
Freshman Application Contact Ms. Tiffane Jones, Director of Enrollment Services, South Suburban College, 15800 South State Street, South Holland, IL 60473. *Phone:* 708-596-2000 Ext. 2158. *E-mail:* admissionsquestions@ssc.edu.
Website: http://www.ssc.edu/.

Southwestern Illinois College

Belleville, Illinois

Freshman Application Contact Southwestern Illinois College, 2500 Carlyle Avenue, Belleville, IL 62221-5899. *Toll-free phone:* 866-942-SWIC. *Website:* http://www.swic.edu/.

Spoon River College

Canton, Illinois

Freshman Application Contact Ms. Missy Wilkinson, Dean of Student Services, Spoon River College, 23235 North County 22, Canton, IL 61520-9801. *Phone:* 309-649-6305. *Toll-free phone:* 800-334-7337. *Fax:* 309-649-6235. *E-mail:* info@src.edu. *Website:* http://www.src.edu/.

Taylor Business Institute

Chicago, Illinois

Director of Admissions Mr. Rashed Jahangir, Taylor Business Institute, 318 West Adams, Chicago, IL 60606. *Website:* http://www.tbiil.edu/.

Tribeca Flashpoint College

Chicago, Illinois

Admissions Office Contact Tribeca Flashpoint College, 28 North Clark Street, Chicago, IL 60602. *Website:* http://www.tribecaflashpoint.edu/.

Triton College

River Grove, Illinois

Freshman Application Contact Ms. Mary-Rita Moore, Dean of Admissions, Triton College, 2000 Fifth Avenue, River Grove, IL 60171. *Phone:* 708-456-0300 Ext. 3679. *Fax:* 708-583-3162. *E-mail:* mpatrice@triton.edu. *Website:* http://www.triton.edu/.

Vet Tech Institute at Fox College

Tinley Park, Illinois

Freshman Application Contact Admissions Office, Vet Tech Institute at Fox College, 18020 South Oak Park Avenue, Tinley Park, IL 60477. *Phone:* 888-884-3694. *Toll-free phone:* 888-884-3694. *Website:* http://chicago.vettechinstitute.edu/.

Waubonsee Community College

Sugar Grove, Illinois

- **District-supported** 2-year, founded 1966, part of Illinois Community College Board
- **Small-town** 243-acre campus with easy access to Chicago
- **Coed**

Undergraduates 3,469 full-time, 7,252 part-time. 7% Black or African American, non-Hispanic/Latino; 33% Hispanic/Latino; 3% Asian, non-Hispanic/Latino; 0.1% Native Hawaiian or other Pacific Islander, non-Hispanic/Latino; 0.1% American Indian or Alaska Native, non-Hispanic/Latino; 2% Two or more races, non-Hispanic/Latino; 3% Race/ethnicity unknown; 2% transferred in. *Retention:* 67% of full-time freshmen returned.
Faculty *Student/faculty ratio:* 22:1.
Academics *Calendar:* semesters. *Degree:* certificates and associate. *Special study options:* academic remediation for entering students, accelerated degree program, advanced placement credit, distance learning, English as a second language, honors programs, independent study, internships, off-campus study, part-time degree program, services for LD students, study abroad, summer session for credit. *ROTC:* Army (c).
Library Todd Library plus 3 others.
Student Life *Campus security:* 24-hour emergency response devices and patrols, late-night transport/escort service.
Athletics Member NJCAA.
Financial Aid Of all full-time matriculated undergraduates who enrolled in 2018, 23 Federal Work-Study jobs (averaging $2000).
Applying *Options:* electronic application.
Freshman Application Contact Joy Sanders, Admissions Manager, Waubonsee Community College, Route 47 at Waubonsee Drive, Sugar Grove, IL 60554. *Phone:* 630-466-7900 Ext. 5756. *Fax:* 630-466-6663. *E-mail:* admissions@waubonsee.edu. *Website:* http://www.waubonsee.edu/.

Worsham College of Mortuary Science

Wheeling, Illinois

Director of Admissions President, Worsham College of Mortuary Science, 495 Northgate Parkway, Wheeling, IL 60090-2646. *Phone:* 847-808-8444. *Website:* http://www.worsham.edu/.

INDIANA

Ancilla College

Donaldson, Indiana

Freshman Application Contact Ms. Ericka Taylor-Joseph, Executive Director of Admissions, Ancilla College, PO Box 1, 9601 Union Road, Donaldson, IN 46513. *Phone:* 574-936-8898 Ext. 326. *Toll-free phone:* 866-ANCILLA. *Fax:* 574-935-1773. *E-mail:* admissions@ancilla.edu. *Website:* http://www.ancilla.edu/.

College of Court Reporting

Valparaiso, Indiana

Freshman Application Contact Ms. Nicky Rodriquez, Director of Admissions, College of Court Reporting, 455 West Lincolnway, Valparaiso, IN 46385. *Phone:* 219-942-1459 Ext. 222. *Toll-free phone:* 866-294-3974. *Fax:* 219-942-1631. *E-mail:* nrodriquez@ccr.edu. *Website:* http://www.ccr.edu/.

Fortis College

Indianapolis, Indiana

Freshman Application Contact Mr. Alex Teitelbaum, Vice President Systems and Administration, Fortis College, 9001 North Wesleyan Road, Suite 101, Indianapolis, IN 46268. *Phone:* 410-633-2929. *Toll-free phone:* 855-4-FORTIS. *E-mail:* kbennett@edaff.com. *Website:* http://www.fortis.edu/.

International Business College

Indianapolis, Indiana

Freshman Application Contact Admissions Office, International Business College, 7205 Shadeland Station, Indianapolis, IN 46256. *Phone:* 317-813-2300. *Toll-free phone:* 800-589-6500. *Website:* http://www.ibcindianapolis.edu/.

Ivy Tech Community College–Bloomington

Bloomington, Indiana

Freshman Application Contact Mr. Neil Frederick, Assistant Director of Admissions, Ivy Tech Community College–Bloomington, 200 Daniels Way, Bloomington, IN 47404. *Phone:* 812-330-6026. *Toll-free phone:* 888-IVY-LINE. *Fax:* 812-332-8147. *E-mail:* nfrederi@ivytech.edu. *Website:* http://www.ivytech.edu/.

Ivy Tech Community College–Central Indiana

Indianapolis, Indiana

Freshman Application Contact Ms. Tracy Funk, Director of Admissions, Ivy Tech Community College–Central Indiana, 50 West Fall Creek Parkway North Drive, Indianapolis, IN 46208-4777. *Phone:* 317-921-4371. *Toll-free phone:* 888-IVYLINE. *Fax:* 317-917-5919. *E-mail:* tfunk@ivytech.edu. *Website:* http://www.ivytech.edu/.

Ivy Tech Community College–Columbus

Columbus, Indiana

Freshman Application Contact Alisa Deck, Director of Admissions, Ivy Tech Community College–Columbus, 4475 Central Avenue, Columbus, IN 47203-1868. *Phone:* 812-374-5129. *Toll-free phone:* 888-IVY-LINE. *Fax:* 812-372-0331. *E-mail:* adeck@ivytech.edu. *Website:* http://www.ivytech.edu/.

Ivy Tech Community College–East Central

Muncie, Indiana

Freshman Application Contact Ms. Mary Lewellen, Ivy Tech Community College–East Central, 4301 South Cowan Road, Muncie, IN 47302-9448. *Phone:* 765-289-2291 Ext. 1391. *Toll-free phone:* 888-IVY-LINE. *Fax:* 765-289-2292. *E-mail:* mlewelle@ivytech.edu. *Website:* http://www.ivytech.edu/.

Ivy Tech Community College–Kokomo

Kokomo, Indiana

Freshman Application Contact Mr. Mike Federspill, Director of Admissions, Ivy Tech Community College–Kokomo, 1815 East Morgan Street, Kokomo, IN 46903-1373. *Phone:* 765-459-0561 Ext. 233. *Toll-free phone:* 888-IVY-LINE. *Fax:* 765-454-5111. *E-mail:* mfedersp@ivytech.edu. *Website:* http://www.ivytech.edu/.

Ivy Tech Community College–Lafayette

Lafayette, Indiana

Freshman Application Contact Mr. Ivan Hernanadez, Director of Admissions, Ivy Tech Community College–Lafayette, 3101 South Creasy Lane, PO Box 6299, Lafayette, IN 47903. *Phone:* 765-269-5116. *Toll-free phone:* 888-IVY-LINE. *Fax:* 765-772-9293. *E-mail:* ihernand@ivytech.edu. *Website:* http://www.ivytech.edu/.

Ivy Tech Community College–North Central

South Bend, Indiana

Freshman Application Contact Darryl Williams, Bi-Regional Director of Admissions, Ivy Tech Community College–North Central, 220 Dean Johnson Boulevard, South Bend, IN 46601-3415. *Toll-free phone:* 888-IVY-LINE. *E-mail:* dwilliams770@ivytech.edu. *Website:* http://www.ivytech.edu/.

Ivy Tech Community College–Northeast

Fort Wayne, Indiana

Freshman Application Contact Robyn Boss, Director of Admissions, Ivy Tech Community College–Northeast, 3800 North Anthony Boulevard, Ft. Wayne, IN 46805-1489. *Phone:* 260-480-4211. *Toll-free phone:* 888-IVY-LINE. *Fax:* 260-480-2053. *E-mail:* rboss1@ivytech.edu. *Website:* http://www.ivytech.edu/.

Ivy Tech Community College–Northwest

Gary, Indiana

Freshman Application Contact Darryl Williams, Bi-Regional Director of Admissions, Ivy Tech Community College–Northwest, 1440 East 35th Avenue, Gary, IN 46409-499. *Phone:* 219-981-1111. *Toll-free phone:* 888-IVY-LINE. *E-mail:* dwilliams770@ivytech.edu. *Website:* http://www.ivytech.edu/.

Ivy Tech Community College–Richmond

Richmond, Indiana

Freshman Application Contact Linda Przybysz, Director of Admissions, Ivy Tech Community College–Richmond, 2325 Chester Boulevard, Richmond, IN 47374-1298. *Phone:* 765-966-2656 Ext. 1246. *Toll-free phone:* 888-IVY-LINE. *E-mail:* lprzybys@ivytech.edu. *Website:* http://www.ivytech.edu/.

Ivy Tech Community College–Sellersburg

Sellersburg, Indiana

Freshman Application Contact Ben Harris, Director of Admissions, Ivy Tech Community College–Sellersburg, 8204 Highway 311, Sellersburg, IN 47172-1897. *Phone:* 812-246-3301 Ext. 4137. *Toll-free phone:* 888-IVY-LINE. *Fax:* 812-246-9905. *E-mail:* bharris88@ivytech.edu. *Website:* http://www.ivytech.edu/.

Ivy Tech Community College–Southeast

Madison, Indiana

Freshman Application Contact Shakira Grubbs, Director Express Enrollment Center, Ivy Tech Community College–Southeast, 590 Ivy Tech Drive, Madison, IN 47250-1881. *Phone:* 812-537-4010. *Toll-free phone:* 888-IVY-LINE. *E-mail:* sgrubbs5@ivytech.edu. *Website:* http://www.ivytech.edu/.

Ivy Tech Community College–Southwest

Evansville, Indiana

Freshman Application Contact Ms. Denise Johnson-Kincade, Director of Admissions, Ivy Tech Community College–Southwest, 3501 First Avenue, Evansville, IN 47710-3398. *Phone:* 812-429-1430. *Toll-free phone:* 888-IVY-LINE. *Fax:* 812-429-9878. *E-mail:* ajohnson@ivytech.edu. *Website:* http://www.ivytech.edu/.

Ivy Tech Community College–Wabash Valley

Terre Haute, Indiana

Freshman Application Contact Nina Storey, Director of Admissions, Ivy Tech Community College–Wabash Valley, 7999 U.S. Highway 41 South, Terre Haute, IN 47802-4898. *Phone:* 812-298-2288. *Toll-free phone:* 888-IVY-LINE. *E-mail:* nstorey@ivytech.edu. *Website:* http://www.ivytech.edu/.

Lincoln College of Technology - Indianapolis

Indianapolis, Indiana

Director of Admissions Ms. Cindy Ryan, Director of Admissions, Lincoln College of Technology - Indianapolis, 7225 Winton Drive, Building 128, Indianapolis, IN 46268. *Phone:* 317-632-5553. *Toll-free phone:* 844-215-1513. *Website:* http://www.lincolntech.edu/.

Mid-America College of Funeral Service

Jeffersonville, Indiana

Freshman Application Contact Mr. Richard Nelson, Dean of Students, Mid-America College of Funeral Service, 3111 Hamburg Pike, Jeffersonville, IN 47130-9630. *Phone:* 812-288-8878. *Toll-free phone:* 800-221-6158. *Fax:* 812-288-5942. *E-mail:* macfs@mindspring.com. *Website:* http://www.mid-america.edu/.

Vet Tech Institute at International Business College

Fort Wayne, Indiana

Freshman Application Contact Admissions Office, Vet Tech Institute at International Business College, 5699 Coventry Lane, Fort Wayne, IN 46804. *Phone:* 800-589-6363. *Toll-free phone:* 800-589-6363. *Website:* http://ftwayne.vettechinstitute.edu/.

Vet Tech Institute at International Business College

Indianapolis, Indiana

Freshman Application Contact Admissions Office, Vet Tech Institute at International Business College, 7205 Shadeland Station, Indianapolis, IN 46256. *Phone:* 800-589-6500. *Toll-free phone:* 800-589-6500. *Website:* http://indianapolis.vettechinstitute.edu/.

Vincennes University

Vincennes, Indiana

- **State-supported** primarily 2-year, founded 1801
- **Small-town** 160-acre campus
- **Coed,** 17,239 undergraduate students, 55% full-time, 76% women, 24% men

Undergraduates 9,543 full-time, 7,696 part-time. 14% are from out of state; 8% Black or African American, non-Hispanic/Latino; 13% Hispanic/Latino; 0.8% Asian, non-Hispanic/Latino; 0.2% Native Hawaiian or other Pacific Islander, non-Hispanic/Latino; 0.4% American Indian or Alaska Native, non-Hispanic/Latino; 2% Two or more races, non-Hispanic/Latino; 3% Race/ethnicity unknown; 0.7% international; 0.8% transferred in; 37% live on campus. *Retention:* 32% of full-time freshmen returned.

Freshmen *Admission:* 4,631 applied, 3,566 admitted, 1,602 enrolled.

Faculty *Total:* 817, 22% full-time. *Student/faculty ratio:* 22:1.

Majors Accounting technology and bookkeeping; agricultural business and management; aircraft powerplant technology; airline pilot and flight crew; American Sign Language (ASL); applied horticulture/horticulture operations; architectural drafting and CAD/CADD; art; art teacher education; autobody/collision and repair technology; automation engineer technology; automobile/automotive mechanics technology; behavioral sciences; biological and biomedical sciences related; building/construction finishing, management, and inspection related; business administration and management; business/commerce; business teacher education; chemistry related; chemistry teacher education; child-care and support services management; commercial and advertising art; communications technologies and support services related; computer/information technology services administration related; computer programming; computer science; computer systems networking and telecommunications; cosmetology; criminal justice/police science; culinary arts; design and applied arts related; diesel mechanics technology; dietetics; dramatic/theater arts; early childhood education; electrical, electronic and communications engineering technology; elementary education; engineering science; English; English/language arts teacher education; environmental studies; family and consumer sciences/home economics teacher education; family and consumer sciences/human sciences; fashion merchandising; fire science/firefighting; foreign languages and literatures; funeral service and mortuary science; health and physical education/fitness; health information/medical records technology; health teacher education; history; hotel/motel administration; industrial technology; information technology; journalism; legal assistant/paralegal; liberal arts and sciences and humanities related; liberal arts and sciences/liberal studies; logistics, materials, and supply chain management; manufacturing engineering technology; mathematics teacher education; mechanical drafting and CAD/CADD; mining technology; music; natural resources/conservation; occupational therapy; pharmacy technician; philosophy; photojournalism; physical education teaching and coaching; physical therapy technology; pre-law studies; public relations/image management; radio and television broadcasting technology; recording arts technology; registered nursing, nursing administration, nursing research and clinical nursing related; registered nursing/registered nurse; restaurant, culinary, and catering management; science teacher education; secondary education; securities services administration; social work; special education; surgical technology; surveying technology; technology/industrial arts teacher education; tool and die technology; welding technology.

Academics *Calendar:* semesters. *Degrees:* certificates, associate, and bachelor's. *Special study options:* academic remediation for entering students, accelerated degree program, adult/continuing education programs, advanced placement credit, distance learning, double majors, English as a second language, external degree program, freshman honors college, honors programs, independent study, internships, off-campus study, part-time degree program, services for LD students, student-designed majors, summer session for credit. *ROTC:* Army (c).

Library Shake Learning Resource Center. *Books:* 85,614 (physical), 104,859 (digital/electronic); *Serial titles:* 1,377 (physical); *Databases:* 99.

Student Life *Housing:* on-campus residence required for freshman year. *Options:* coed, men-only, women-only, special housing for students with disabilities. Campus housing is university owned. Freshman campus housing is guaranteed. *Activities and Organizations:* drama/theater group, student-run newspaper, radio and television station, choral group, national fraternities, national sororities. *Campus security:* 24-hour emergency response devices and patrols, student patrols, late-night transport/escort service, controlled dormitory access. *Student services:* health clinic, personal/psychological counseling.

Athletics Member NJCAA. *Intercollegiate sports:* baseball M, basketball M/W, bowling M, cross-country running M/W, golf M, track and field M/W, volleyball W.

Costs (2019–20) *Tuition:* area resident $5581 full-time, $186 per credit hour part-time; state resident $5581 full-time, $186 per credit hour part-time; nonresident $13,871 full-time, $462 per credit hour part-time. Full-time tuition and fees vary according to course level, course load, location, program, reciprocity agreements, and student level. Part-time tuition and fees vary according to course level, course load, location, program, reciprocity agreements, and student level. *Required fees:* $493 full-time, $7 per credit hour part-time, $270 per year part-time. *Room and board:* $10,590. Room and board charges vary according to board plan and housing facility. *Payment plan:* installment. *Waivers:* senior citizens and employees or children of employees.

Applying *Options:* electronic application, deferred entrance. *Application fee:* $20. *Required:* high school transcript. *Required for some:* interview. *Application deadlines:* rolling (freshmen), rolling (transfers). *Notification:* continuous until 8/1 (freshmen), continuous (transfers).

Freshman Application Contact Vincennes University, 1002 North First Street, Vincennes, IN 47591. *Phone:* 812-888-4313. *Toll-free phone:* 800-742-9198.
Website: http://www.vinu.edu/.

IOWA

Clinton Community College

Clinton, Iowa

Freshman Application Contact Mr. Gary Mohr, Executive Director of Enrollment Management and Marketing, Clinton Community College, 1000 Lincoln Boulevard, Clinton, IA 52732-6299. *Phone:* 563-336-3322. *Toll-free phone:* 800-462-3255. *Fax:* 563-336-3350. *E-mail:* gmohr@eicc.edu. *Website:* http://www.eicc.edu/about-eicc/colleges-and-centers/clinton-community-college.aspx.

Des Moines Area Community College
Ankeny, Iowa

- **State and locally supported** 2-year, founded 1966, part of Iowa Area Community Colleges System
- **Small-town** 362-acre campus
- **Endowment** $4.8 million
- **Coed,** 23,258 undergraduate students, 26% full-time, 56% women, 44% men

Undergraduates 6,146 full-time, 17,112 part-time. Students come from 52 states and territories; 14 other countries; 2% are from out of state; 6% Black or African American, non-Hispanic/Latino; 8% Hispanic/Latino; 4% Asian, non-Hispanic/Latino; 0.1% Native Hawaiian or other Pacific Islander, non-Hispanic/Latino; 0.2% American Indian or Alaska Native, non-Hispanic/Latino; 2% Two or more races, non-Hispanic/Latino; 9% Race/ethnicity unknown; 0.5% international; 15% transferred in. *Retention:* 59% of full-time freshmen returned.

Freshmen *Admission:* 2,871 enrolled.

Faculty *Total:* 1,177, 30% full-time. *Student/faculty ratio:* 19:1.

Majors Accounting; accounting and business/management; accounting technology and bookkeeping; agricultural/farm supplies retailing and wholesaling; apparel and accessories marketing; applied horticulture/horticultural business services related; architectural drafting and CAD/CADD; autobody/collision and repair technology; automobile/automotive mechanics technology; biomedical technology; business administration and management; child-care provision; civil engineering technology; clinical/medical laboratory technology; commercial and advertising art; communications systems installation and repair technology; computer and information sciences and support services related; computer engineering technology; computer programming (specific applications); criminal justice/law enforcement administration; culinary arts; dental hygiene; desktop publishing and digital imaging design; diesel mechanics technology; electrical, electronic and communications engineering technology; fire prevention and safety technology; funeral service and mortuary science; health/health-care administration; heating, air conditioning, ventilation and refrigeration maintenance technology; hospitality administration; industrial electronics technology; industrial mechanics and maintenance technology; information technology; language interpretation and translation; legal assistant/paralegal; liberal arts and sciences/liberal studies; licensed practical/vocational nurse training; machine tool technology; marketing/marketing management; mechanical drafting and CAD/CADD; medical administrative assistant and medical secretary; medical/clinical assistant; office management; registered nursing/registered nurse; respiratory care therapy; sales, distribution, and marketing operations; sport and fitness administration/management; surveying engineering; tool and die technology; veterinary/animal health technology.

Academics *Calendar:* semesters. *Degrees:* certificates, diplomas, and associate (profile also includes information from the Boone, Carroll, Des Moines, and Newton campuses). *Special study options:* academic remediation for entering students, adult/continuing education programs, advanced placement credit, cooperative education, distance learning, English as a second language, honors programs, off-campus study, part-time degree program, services for LD students, student-designed majors, summer session for credit.

Library DMACC District Library plus 4 others.

Student Life *Housing Options:* coed. Campus housing is university owned. *Activities and Organizations:* drama/theater group, student-run newspaper, choral group, Agri-Business Club, Horticulture Club, Hospitality Arts Club, Iowa Delta Epsilon Chi, Dental Hygienist Club. *Campus security:* 24-hour emergency response devices and patrols, late-night transport/escort service. *Student services:* health clinic, personal/psychological counseling.

Athletics Member NJCAA. *Intercollegiate sports:* baseball M(s), basketball M(s)/W(s), cross-country running W(s), golf M(s)/W(s), volleyball W(s). *Intramural sports:* badminton M/W, basketball M/W, football M/W, golf M/W, soccer M/W, volleyball M/W.

Standardized Tests *Required for some:* SAT or ACT (for admission), ACT Compass.

Costs (2020–21) *Tuition:* state resident $5100 full-time; nonresident $10,200 full-time. Full-time tuition and fees vary according to course load and reciprocity agreements. *Room and board:* $7276; room only: $4800. Room and board charges vary according to location. *Payment plan:* installment. *Waivers:* senior citizens and employees or children of employees.

Financial Aid Of all full-time matriculated undergraduates who enrolled in 2018, 377 Federal Work-Study jobs (averaging $1055).

Applying *Options:* electronic application, early admission, deferred entrance. *Required for some:* high school transcript, interview. *Application deadlines:* rolling (freshmen), rolling (transfers).

Freshman Application Contact Mr. Michael Lentsch, Director of Program Development, Des Moines Area Community College, 2006 South Ankeny Boulevard, Ankeny, IA 50021-8995. *Phone:* 515-965-7086. *Toll-free phone:* 800-362-2127. *E-mail:* mjleutsch@dmacc.edu.
Website: http://www.dmacc.edu/.

Ellsworth Community College
Iowa Falls, Iowa

Director of Admissions Mrs. Nancy Walters, Registrar, Ellsworth Community College, 1100 College Avenue, Iowa Falls, IA 50126-1199. *Phone:* 641-648-4611. *Toll-free phone:* 800-ECC-9235. *Website:* http://ecc.iavalley.edu/.

Hawkeye Community College
Waterloo, Iowa

- **State and locally supported** 2-year, founded 1966
- **Rural** 320-acre campus
- **Endowment** $2.3 million
- **Coed,** 5,391 undergraduate students, 39% full-time, 58% women, 42% men

Undergraduates 2,097 full-time, 3,294 part-time. Students come from 9 states and territories; 17 other countries; 1% are from out of state; 9% Black or African American, non-Hispanic/Latino; 5% Hispanic/Latino; 1% Asian, non-Hispanic/Latino; 0.2% Native Hawaiian or other Pacific Islander, non-Hispanic/Latino; 0.2% American Indian or Alaska Native, non-Hispanic/Latino; 3% Two or more races, non-Hispanic/Latino; 1% international; 13% transferred in.

Freshmen *Admission:* 1,514 applied, 1,420 admitted, 928 enrolled. *Test scores:* ACT scores over 18: 50%; ACT scores over 24: 14%; ACT scores over 30: 3%.

Faculty *Total:* 283, 39% full-time, 9% with terminal degrees. *Student/faculty ratio:* 19:1.

Majors Accounting; agricultural/farm supplies retailing and wholesaling; agricultural power machinery operation; animal/livestock husbandry and production; autobody/collision and repair technology; automation engineer technology; automobile/automotive mechanics technology; carpentry; child-care provision; civil engineering technology; clinical/medical laboratory technology; commercial photography; computer/information technology services administration related; computer systems networking and telecommunications; criminal justice/police science; dental hygiene; desktop publishing and digital imaging design; diesel mechanics technology; digital communication and media/multimedia; electrical, electronic and communications engineering technology; emergency medical technology (EMT paramedic); golf course operation and grounds management; hospitality administration; human resources management; landscaping and groundskeeping; liberal arts and sciences/liberal studies; machine tool technology; medical administrative assistant and medical secretary; medical insurance coding; multi/interdisciplinary studies related; natural resources management and policy; occupational therapist assistant; physical therapy technology; registered nursing/registered nurse; respiratory care therapy; sales, distribution, and marketing operations; web page, digital/multimedia and information resources design; welding technology.

Academics *Calendar:* semesters. *Degree:* certificates, diplomas, and associate. *Special study options:* academic remediation for entering students, accelerated degree program, adult/continuing education programs, advanced placement credit, cooperative education, distance learning, English as a second language, external degree program, part-time degree program, services for LD students, study abroad, summer session for credit. *ROTC:* Army (c).

Library Hawkeye Community College Library. *Books:* 23,087 (physical), 188,106 (digital/electronic); *Serial titles:* 89 (physical), 17 (digital/electronic); *Databases:* 62. Weekly public service hours: 70; students can reserve study rooms.

Student Life *Housing:* college housing not available. *Activities and Organizations:* drama/theater group, choral group, Student Ambassadors, Phi Theta Kappa, Student American Dental Assistant Association, Photography. *Campus security:* 24-hour patrols. *Student services:* health clinic, personal/psychological counseling, women's center, veterans affairs office.

Athletics Member NJCAA. *Intercollegiate sports:* cross-country running M(s)/W(s), golf M(s), soccer M(s)/W(s), track and field M(s)/W(s), volleyball W(s). *Intramural sports:* badminton M/W, basketball M/W, bowling M/W, football M/W, softball M/W, table tennis M/W.

Standardized Tests *Required:* ACT ACCUPLACER or the equivalent from ACT or accredited college course(s) (for admission). *Required for some:* ACT (for admission).

Costs (2019–20) *Tuition:* state resident $5236 full-time, $187 per credit hour part-time; nonresident $5936 full-time, $212 per credit hour part-time. *Required fees:* $238 full-time, $9 per credit hour part-time. *Payment plan:* installment.

Applying *Options:* electronic application, deferred entrance. *Required:* high school transcript. *Application deadlines:* rolling (freshmen), rolling (transfers). *Notification:* continuous (freshmen), continuous (transfers).
Freshman Application Contact Ms. Holly Grimm, Associate Director, Admissions and Recruitment, Hawkeye Community College, PO Box 8015, Waterloo, IA 50704-8015. *Phone:* 319-296-4277. *Toll-free phone:* 800-670-4769. *Fax:* 319-296-2505. *E-mail:* holly.grimm@hawkeyecollege.edu. *Website:* http://www.hawkeyecollege.edu/.

Indian Hills Community College

Ottumwa, Iowa

Freshman Application Contact Mrs. Jane Sapp, Admissions Officer, Indian Hills Community College, 525 Grandview Avenue, Building #1, Ottumwa, IA 52501-1398. *Phone:* 641-683-5155. *Toll-free phone:* 800-726-2585. *Website:* http://www.ihcc.cc.ia.us/.

Iowa Central Community College

Fort Dodge, Iowa

- **State and locally supported** 2-year, founded 1966
- **Small-town** 110-acre campus
- **Coed,** 5,237 undergraduate students, 49% full-time, 50% women, 50% men

Undergraduates 2,544 full-time, 2,693 part-time. Students come from 41 states and territories; 39 other countries; 9% are from out of state; 10% Black or African American, non-Hispanic/Latino; 10% Hispanic/Latino; 2% Asian, non-Hispanic/Latino; 0.3% Native Hawaiian or other Pacific Islander, non-Hispanic/Latino; 0.8% American Indian or Alaska Native, non-Hispanic/Latino; 2% Two or more races, non-Hispanic/Latino; 5% Race/ethnicity unknown; 2% international; 6% transferred in; 48% live on campus.
Freshmen *Admission:* 1,256 applied, 1,210 enrolled.
Faculty *Total:* 391, 23% full-time. *Student/faculty ratio:* 17:1.
Majors Accounting; administrative assistant and secretarial science; agribusiness; agricultural business and management; agricultural teacher education; agronomy and crop science; animal sciences; autobody/collision and repair technology; automobile/automotive mechanics technology; biology/biological sciences; business administration and management; chemistry; clinical/medical laboratory technology; commercial photography; computer systems networking and telecommunications; cooking and related culinary arts; cosmetology; criminal justice/police science; criminal justice/safety; dental hygiene; desktop publishing and digital imaging design; diesel mechanics technology; digital communication and media/multimedia; early childhood education; emergency medical technology (EMT paramedic); engineering technology; fire science/firefighting; health/health-care administration; industrial electronics technology; liberal arts and sciences/liberal studies; licensed practical/vocational nurse training; logistics, materials, and supply chain management; machine tool technology; mathematics; medical/clinical assistant; multi/interdisciplinary studies related; occupational therapy; parks, recreation and leisure facilities management; physics; psychology; radio and television broadcasting technology; radiologic technology/science; robotics technology; secondary education; social work; sociology; turf and turfgrass management; vehicle maintenance and repair technologies related; web page, digital/multimedia and information resources design.
Academics *Calendar:* semesters. *Degree:* certificates, diplomas, and associate. *Special study options:* academic remediation for entering students, adult/continuing education programs, advanced placement credit, cooperative education, distance learning, English as a second language, honors programs, independent study, internships, part-time degree program, services for LD students, study abroad, summer session for credit.
Library Iowa Central Community College Library plus 1 other. Students can reserve study rooms.
Student Life *Housing Options:* men-only, women-only. Campus housing is university owned. *Activities and Organizations:* drama/theater group, student-run newspaper, radio station, choral group, marching band, Student Senate, BPA, Phi Theta Kappa, Art & Photography Club, Collegian. *Campus security:* 24-hour emergency response devices and patrols, student patrols, late-night transport/escort service, controlled dormitory access. *Student services:* health clinic, personal/psychological counseling, veterans affairs office.
Athletics Member NJCAA. *Intercollegiate sports:* baseball M(s), basketball M(s)/W(s), bowling M(s)/W(s), cheerleading M(s)/W(s), cross-country running M(s)/W(s), equestrian sports M(s)/W(s), football M(s), golf M(s)/W(s), rugby M(s), soccer M(s)/W(s), softball W(s), swimming and diving M(s)/W(s), tennis M(s)/W(s), track and field M(s)/W(s), volleyball W(s), wrestling M(s). *Intramural sports:* basketball M/W, football M, golf M/W, softball W, table tennis M/W, tennis M/W, volleyball M/W, weight lifting M, wrestling M.
Costs (2020–21) *Tuition:* state resident $4980 full-time, $198 per credit hour part-time; nonresident $7480 full-time, $281 per semester hour part-time. Full-time tuition and fees vary according to course load and program. Part-time tuition and fees vary according to course load and program. *Required fees:* $720 full-time, $30 per credit hour part-time. *Room and board:* $6900. *Payment plan:* deferred payment. *Waivers:* employees or children of employees.
Applying *Options:* electronic application, early admission, deferred entrance. *Required for some:* high school transcript, letters of recommendation, interview. *Recommended:* high school transcript. *Application deadlines:* rolling (freshmen), rolling (transfers). *Notification:* continuous (freshmen), continuous (transfers).
Freshman Application Contact Carmin Miller, Enrollment Management and Student Development Secretary, Iowa Central Community College, One Triton Circle, Fort Dodge, IA 50501. *Phone:* 515-574-1023. *Toll-free phone:* 800-362-2793. *Fax:* 515-576-7207. *E-mail:* miller_c@iowacentral.edu. *Website:* http://www.iowacentral.edu/.

Iowa Lakes Community College

Estherville, Iowa

Freshman Application Contact Iowa Lakes Community College, IA. *Phone:* 712-362-7923 Ext. 7923. *Toll-free phone:* 800-521-5054. *E-mail:* info@iowalakes.edu. *Website:* http://www.iowalakes.edu/.

Iowa Western Community College

Council Bluffs, Iowa

Freshman Application Contact Ms. Tori Christie, Director of Admissions, Iowa Western Community College, 2700 College Road, Box 4-C, Council Bluffs, IA 51502. *Phone:* 712-325-3288. *Toll-free phone:* 800-432-5852. *E-mail:* admissions@iwcc.edu. *Website:* http://www.iwcc.edu/.

Kirkwood Community College

Cedar Rapids, Iowa

Freshman Application Contact Kirkwood Community College, PO Box 2068, Cedar Rapids, IA 52406-2068. *Phone:* 319-398-5517. *Toll-free phone:* 800-332-2055. *Website:* http://www.kirkwood.edu/.

Marshalltown Community College

Marshalltown, Iowa

Freshman Application Contact Ms. Deana Inman, Director of Admissions, Marshalltown Community College, 3700 South Center Street, Marshalltown, IA 50158-4760. *Phone:* 641-752-7106. *Toll-free phone:* 866-622-4748. *Fax:* 641-752-8149. *Website:* http://mcc.iavalley.edu/.

Muscatine Community College

Muscatine, Iowa

Freshman Application Contact Gary Mohr, Executive Director of Enrollment Management and Marketing, Muscatine Community College, 152 Colorado Street, Muscatine, IA 52761-5396. *Phone:* 563-336-3322. *Toll-free phone:* 800-351-4669. *Fax:* 563-336-3350. *E-mail:* gmohr@eicc.edu. *Website:* http://www.eicc.edu/about-eicc/colleges-and-centers/muscatine-community-college.aspx.

Northeast Iowa Community College

Calmar, Iowa

- **State and locally supported** 2-year, founded 1966, part of Iowa Area Community Colleges System
- **Rural** 210-acre campus
- **Coed,** 4,408 undergraduate students, 26% full-time, 59% women, 41% men

Undergraduates 1,128 full-time, 3,280 part-time. 12% are from out of state; 5% Black or African American, non-Hispanic/Latino; 3% Hispanic/Latino; 1% Asian, non-Hispanic/Latino; 0.7% Native Hawaiian or other Pacific Islander, non-Hispanic/Latino; 0.2% American Indian or Alaska Native, non-Hispanic/Latino; 1% Two or more races, non-Hispanic/Latino; 4% Race/ethnicity unknown; 0.1% international; 4% transferred in. *Retention:* 63% of full-time freshmen returned.
Freshmen *Admission:* 1,156 applied, 1,156 admitted, 501 enrolled.
Faculty *Total:* 262, 37% full-time. *Student/faculty ratio:* 13:1.
Majors Accounting; administrative assistant and secretarial science; agribusiness; agricultural and food products processing; agricultural power

machinery operation; agricultural production; automobile/automotive mechanics technology; business administration and management; business automation/technology/data entry; clinical/medical laboratory technology; computer programming (specific applications); construction trades; cosmetology; crop production; dairy husbandry and production; desktop publishing and digital imaging design; electrical, electronic and communications engineering technology; electrician; emergency medical technology (EMT paramedic); energy management and systems technology; fire science/firefighting; health information/medical records technology; liberal arts and sciences/liberal studies; plumbing technology; radiologic technology/science; registered nursing/registered nurse; respiratory care therapy; sales, distribution, and marketing operations; social work.
Academics *Calendar:* semesters. *Degree:* certificates, diplomas, and associate. *Special study options:* academic remediation for entering students, adult/continuing education programs, advanced placement credit, cooperative education, distance learning, double majors, English as a second language, external degree program, honors programs, internships, off-campus study, part-time degree program, services for LD students, summer session for credit.
Library Wilder Resource Center and Burton Payne Library plus 2 others.
Student Life *Housing:* college housing not available. *Activities and Organizations:* national fraternities, national sororities. *Campus security:* security personnel on weeknights. *Student services:* personal/psychological counseling.
Athletics *Intramural sports:* basketball M/W, bowling M/W, football M, golf M/W, riflery M/W, skiing (downhill) M/W, softball M/W, volleyball M/W.
Costs (2019–20) *Tuition:* state resident $5220 full-time, $174 per credit hour part-time; nonresident $5940 full-time, $198 per credit hour part-time. Full-time tuition and fees vary according to course load. Part-time tuition and fees vary according to course load. *Required fees:* $720 full-time, $24 per credit hour part-time, $24 per credit hour part-time. *Payment plan:* installment. *Waivers:* employees or children of employees.
Applying *Options:* electronic application, deferred entrance. *Recommended:* high school transcript.
Freshman Application Contact Blake Moen, Admissions Representative, Northeast Iowa Community College, Calmar, IA 52132. *Phone:* 844-642-2338 Ext. 1153. *Toll-free phone:* 800-728-CALMAR. *Fax:* 563-562-4369. *E-mail:* moenb@nicc.edu.
Website: http://www.nicc.edu/.

North Iowa Area Community College
Mason City, Iowa

Freshman Application Contact Ms. Rachel McGuire, Director of Enrollment Services, North Iowa Area Community College, 500 College Drive, Mason City, IA 50401. *Phone:* 641-422-4104. *Toll-free phone:* 888-GO NIACC Ext. 4245. *Fax:* 641-422-4385. *E-mail:* request@niacc.edu. *Website:* http://www.niacc.edu/.

Northwest Iowa Community College
Sheldon, Iowa

- **State-supported** 2-year, founded 1966, part of Iowa Department of Education Division of Community Colleges
- **Small-town** 263-acre campus with easy access to Sioux City, IA and Sioux Falls, SD
- **Coed**

Undergraduates 10% are from out of state. *Retention:* 69% of full-time freshmen returned.
Faculty *Student/faculty ratio:* 12:1.
Academics *Calendar:* semesters. *Degree:* certificates, diplomas, and associate. *Special study options:* academic remediation for entering students, adult/continuing education programs, cooperative education, distance learning, double majors, English as a second language, off-campus study, part-time degree program, services for LD students, study abroad.
Library Northwest Iowa Community College Library plus 1 other.
Student Life *Campus security:* 24-hour emergency response devices.
Standardized Tests *Required:* ACT Compass (for admission).
Financial Aid Of all full-time matriculated undergraduates who enrolled in 2018, 60 Federal Work-Study jobs (averaging $900).
Applying *Options:* electronic application. *Application fee:* $10. *Required:* high school transcript. *Required for some:* minimum 2.0 GPA.
Director of Admissions Ms. Lisa Story, Director of Enrollment Management, Northwest Iowa Community College, 603 West Park Street, Sheldon, IA 51201-1046. *Phone:* 712-324-5061 Ext. 115. *Toll-free phone:* 800-352-4907. *E-mail:* lstory@nwicc.edu. *Website:* http://www.nwicc.edu/.

Ross College
Bettendorf, Iowa

Freshman Application Contact Ross College, 2119 East Kimberly Road, Bettendorf, IA 52722. *Phone:* 563-344-1500. *Toll-free phone:* 866-815-5578. *Website:* http://www.rosseducation.edu/.

St. Luke's College
Sioux City, Iowa

- **Independent** primarily 2-year, founded 1967
- **Rural** 3-acre campus with easy access to Omaha
- **Endowment** $1.2 million
- **Coed**, 235 undergraduate students, 52% full-time, 93% women, 7% men

Undergraduates 123 full-time, 112 part-time. Students come from 21 states and territories; 39% are from out of state; 2% Black or African American, non-Hispanic/Latino; 8% Hispanic/Latino; 3% Asian, non-Hispanic/Latino; 0.9% Native Hawaiian or other Pacific Islander, non-Hispanic/Latino; 2% American Indian or Alaska Native, non-Hispanic/Latino; 2% Two or more races, non-Hispanic/Latino; 0.4% Race/ethnicity unknown; 23% transferred in. *Retention:* 100% of full-time freshmen returned.
Freshmen *Admission:* 53 applied, 8 admitted, 6 enrolled. *Average high school GPA:* 3.3.
Faculty *Total:* 41, 61% full-time, 12% with terminal degrees. *Student/faculty ratio:* 5:1.
Majors Health services/allied health/health sciences; radiologic technology/science; registered nursing/registered nurse; respiratory care therapy.
Academics *Calendar:* semesters. *Degrees:* certificates, associate, and bachelor's. *Special study options:* advanced placement credit, distance learning, internships, services for LD students, summer session for credit.
Library St. Luke's College Library. *Books:* 1,435 (physical), 4,700 (digital/electronic); *Databases:* 5. Weekly public service hours: 56.
Student Life *Housing:* college housing not available. *Campus security:* 24-hour emergency response devices and patrols, late-night transport/escort service. *Student services:* health clinic, personal/psychological counseling.
Standardized Tests *Required:* SAT or ACT (for admission).
Costs (2020–21) *Tuition:* $19,440 full-time, $540 per credit hour part-time. Full-time tuition and fees vary according to degree level and program. Part-time tuition and fees vary according to degree level and program. *Required fees:* $1650 full-time, $1650 per year part-time. *Payment plan:* installment.
Financial Aid Of all full-time matriculated undergraduates who enrolled in 2018, 98 applied for aid, 98 were judged to have need. 3 Federal Work-Study jobs (averaging $1367). *Average percent of need met:* 80%. *Average financial aid package:* $12,750. *Average need-based loan:* $6500. *Average need-based gift aid:* $5250. *Average indebtedness upon graduation:* $21,027.
Applying *Options:* electronic application. *Required:* essay or personal statement, high school transcript, minimum 2.5 GPA, interview. *Notification:* continuous (freshmen), continuous (out-of-state freshmen), continuous (transfers), rolling (early decision plan 1), rolling (early decision plan 2), rolling (early action).
Freshman Application Contact Ms. Sherry McCarthy, Admissions Coordinator, St. Luke's College, 2720 Stone Park Boulevard, Sioux City, IA 51104. *Phone:* 712-279-3149. *Toll-free phone:* 800-352-4660 Ext. 3149. *Fax:* 712-233-8017. *E-mail:* sherry.mccarthy@stlukescollege.edu. *Website:* http://stlukescollege.edu/.

Scott Community College
Bettendorf, Iowa

Freshman Application Contact Mr. Gary Mohr, Executive Director of Enrollment Management and Marketing, Scott Community College, 500 Belmont Road, Bettendorf, IA 52722-6804. *Phone:* 563-336-3322. *Toll-free phone:* 800-895-0811. *Fax:* 563-336-3350. *E-mail:* gmohr@eicc.edu. *Website:* http://www.eicc.edu/about-eicc/colleges-and-centers/scott-community-college.aspx.

Southeastern Community College
West Burlington, Iowa

- **State and locally supported** 2-year, founded 1968, part of Iowa Department of Education Division of Community Colleges
- **Small-town** 160-acre campus
- **Coed**

Undergraduates 1,312 full-time, 1,532 part-time. 16% are from out of state; 5% Black or African American, non-Hispanic/Latino; 5% Hispanic/Latino; 1% Asian, non-Hispanic/Latino; 0.1% Native Hawaiian or other Pacific Islander, non-Hispanic/Latino; 0.7% American Indian or Alaska Native, non-

Hispanic/Latino; 4% Two or more races, non-Hispanic/Latino; 6% Race/ethnicity unknown; 0.9% international; 2% transferred in; 2% live on campus. *Retention:* 60% of full-time freshmen returned.
Faculty *Student/faculty ratio:* 16:1.
Academics *Calendar:* semesters. *Degree:* certificates, diplomas, and associate. *Special study options:* adult/continuing education programs, part-time degree program.
Library Yohe Memorial Library.
Student Life *Campus security:* controlled dormitory access, night patrols by trained security personnel.
Athletics Member NJCAA.
Financial Aid Of all full-time matriculated undergraduates who enrolled in 2018, 979 applied for aid, 800 were judged to have need. In 2018, 16. *Average financial aid package:* $6892. *Average need-based loan:* $3155. *Average need-based gift aid:* $5409. *Average non-need-based aid:* $6686.
Applying *Options:* early admission, deferred entrance.
Freshman Application Contact Ms. Stacy White, Admissions, Southeastern Community College, 1500 West Agency Road, West Burlington, IA 52655-0180. *Phone:* 319-752-2731 Ext. 8137. *Toll-free phone:* 866-722-4692. *E-mail:* admoff@scciowa.edu. *Website:* http://www.scciowa.edu/.

Southwestern Community College

Creston, Iowa

- **State-supported** 2-year, founded 1966, part of Iowa Department of Education Division of Community Colleges
- **Rural** 406-acre campus
- **Coed,** 1,856 undergraduate students, 51% full-time, 66% women, 34% men

Undergraduates 952 full-time, 904 part-time. Students come from 13 states and territories; 5 other countries; 14% are from out of state; 8% Black or African American, non-Hispanic/Latino; 6% Hispanic/Latino; 0.9% Asian, non-Hispanic/Latino; 0.1% Native Hawaiian or other Pacific Islander, non-Hispanic/Latino; 0.1% American Indian or Alaska Native, non-Hispanic/Latino; 2% Two or more races, non-Hispanic/Latino; 1% Race/ethnicity unknown; 3% international; 5% transferred in; 6% live on campus. *Retention:* 62% of full-time freshmen returned.
Freshmen *Admission:* 415 enrolled.
Faculty *Total:* 123, 35% full-time, 2% with terminal degrees. *Student/faculty ratio:* 15:1.
Majors Accounting technology and bookkeeping; agribusiness; autobody/collision and repair technology; automobile/automotive mechanics technology; business administration and management; carpentry; computer systems networking and telecommunications; criminal justice/safety; electrician; industrial mechanics and maintenance technology; liberal arts and sciences/liberal studies; library and information science; music; registered nursing/registered nurse; web page, digital/multimedia and information resources design; welding technology.
Academics *Calendar:* semesters. *Degree:* certificates, diplomas, and associate. *Special study options:* academic remediation for entering students, adult/continuing education programs, advanced placement credit, distance learning, double majors, independent study, part-time degree program, summer session for credit.
Library Learning Resource Center. *Books:* 15,796 (physical), 28,886 (digital/electronic); *Databases:* 60. Weekly public service hours: 58.
Student Life *Housing Options:* coed, men-only, women-only. Campus housing is university owned. *Activities and Organizations:* drama/theater group, choral group. *Campus security:* 24-hour emergency response devices, controlled dormitory access. *Student services:* personal/psychological counseling.
Athletics Member NCAA, NJCAA. All NCAA Division II. *Intercollegiate sports:* baseball M(s), basketball M(s)/W(s), cross-country running M/W, golf M, softball W, track and field M/W, volleyball W. *Intramural sports:* basketball M/W, football M, volleyball M/W.
Standardized Tests *Required for some:* SAT or ACT (for admission), ACCUPLACER.
Financial Aid Of all full-time matriculated undergraduates who enrolled in 2018, 84 Federal Work-Study jobs (averaging $1075). 42 state and other part-time jobs (averaging $1080).
Applying *Options:* electronic application, early admission. *Required:* high school transcript. *Application deadline:* 9/5 (transfers). *Notification:* continuous (freshmen), continuous (transfers).
Freshman Application Contact Ms. Cait Maitlen, Director of Admissions, Southwestern Community College, 1501 West Townline Street, Creston, IA 50801. *Phone:* 641-782-7081 Ext. 453. *Toll-free phone:* 800-247-4023. *Fax:* 641-782-3312. *E-mail:* maitlen@swcciowa.edu. *Website:* http://www.swcciowa.edu/.

Western Iowa Tech Community College

Sioux City, Iowa

- **State-supported** 2-year, founded 1966, part of Iowa Department of Education Division of Community Colleges
- **Suburban** 143-acre campus
- **Endowment** $3.0 million
- **Coed,** 5,976 undergraduate students, 30% full-time, 60% women, 40% men

Undergraduates 1,792 full-time, 4,184 part-time. Students come from 28 states and territories; 13 other countries; 18% are from out of state; 5% Black or African American, non-Hispanic/Latino; 18% Hispanic/Latino; 2% Asian, non-Hispanic/Latino; 0.1% Native Hawaiian or other Pacific Islander, non-Hispanic/Latino; 1% American Indian or Alaska Native, non-Hispanic/Latino; 10% Two or more races, non-Hispanic/Latino; 3% Race/ethnicity unknown; 10% international; 5% transferred in; 5% live on campus. *Retention:* 50% of full-time freshmen returned.
Freshmen *Admission:* 929 enrolled. *Test scores:* ACT scores over 18: 74%; ACT scores over 24: 12%; ACT scores over 30: 1%.
Faculty *Total:* 535, 14% full-time, 8% with terminal degrees. *Student/faculty ratio:* 16:1.
Majors Accounting; accounting technology and bookkeeping; administrative assistant and secretarial science; agricultural business and management; agricultural/farm supplies retailing and wholesaling; agronomy and crop science; animation, interactive technology, video graphics and special effects; architectural engineering technology; autobody/collision and repair technology; automobile/automotive mechanics technology; biomedical technology; business administration and management; business automation/technology/data entry; chemistry; child-care provision; cinematography and film/video production; commercial photography; communication; computer/information technology services administration related; computer programming (specific applications); criminal justice/police science; crisis/emergency/disaster management; dental assisting; desktop publishing and digital imaging design; early childhood education; elementary education; emergency medical technology (EMT paramedic); energy management and systems technology; English; finance; fine arts related; fire science/firefighting; game and interactive media design; human resources management; industrial mechanics and maintenance technology; legal assistant/paralegal; liberal arts and sciences/liberal studies; mathematics; mechanical drafting and CAD/CADD; medical office management; multi/interdisciplinary studies related; musical instrument fabrication and repair; physical therapy technology; psychology; recording arts technology; registered nursing/registered nurse; secondary education; sociology; surgical technology; web page, digital/multimedia and information resources design; welding technology.
Academics *Calendar:* semesters. *Degree:* certificates, diplomas, and associate. *Special study options:* academic remediation for entering students, accelerated degree program, advanced placement credit, cooperative education, distance learning, double majors, English as a second language, honors programs, independent study, internships, off-campus study, part-time degree program, services for LD students, student-designed majors, study abroad, summer session for credit.
Library Western Iowa Tech Community College Library Services plus 1 other. *Books:* 22,896 (physical), 13,260 (digital/electronic); *Serial titles:* 145 (physical), 66 (digital/electronic); *Databases:* 81. Weekly public service hours: 60.
Student Life *Housing Options:* coed. Campus housing is university owned. *Activities and Organizations:* choral group, Shakespeare Overseas Traveling Club, Habitat for Humanity, Anime Club, Leadership Academy, Police Science Club. *Campus security:* 24-hour emergency response devices and patrols, controlled dormitory access. *Student services:* health clinic, personal/psychological counseling.
Athletics *Intramural sports:* basketball M/W, bowling M/W, football M/W, rugby M/W, soccer M/W, softball M/W, volleyball M/W, wrestling M/W.
Standardized Tests *Recommended:* ACT (for admission), SAT or ACT (for admission).
Costs (2020–21) *Tuition:* area resident $4740 full-time; state resident $4740 full-time; nonresident $4770 full-time. *Required fees:* $870 full-time. *Room and board:* $5950; room only: $3950. Room and board charges vary according to housing facility. *Payment plan:* installment. *Waivers:* employees or children of employees.
Financial Aid Of all full-time matriculated undergraduates who enrolled in 2018, 148 Federal Work-Study jobs (averaging $1000). 2 state and other part-time jobs (averaging $2500).
Applying *Options:* electronic application, early admission, deferred entrance. *Recommended:* high school transcript. *Application deadlines:* rolling

(freshmen), rolling (transfers). *Notification:* continuous (freshmen), continuous (transfers).
Freshman Application Contact Western Iowa Tech Community College, 4647 Stone Avenue, PO Box 5199, Sioux City, IA 51102-5199. *Phone:* 712-274-8733 Ext. 1491. *Toll-free phone:* 800-352-4649 Ext. 6403.
Website: http://www.witcc.edu/.

KANSAS

Allen Community College
Iola, Kansas

Freshman Application Contact Rebecca Bilderback, Director of Admissions, Allen Community College, 1801 North Cottonwood, Iola, KS 66749. *Phone:* 620-365-5116 Ext. 267. *Fax:* 620-365-7406. *E-mail:* bilderback@allencc.edu. *Website:* http://www.allencc.edu/.

Barton County Community College
Great Bend, Kansas

Freshman Application Contact Ms. Tana Cooper, Director of Admissions and Promotions, Barton County Community College, 245 Northeast 30th Road, Great Bend, KS 67530. *Phone:* 620-792-9241. *Toll-free phone:* 800-722-6842. *Fax:* 620-786-1160. *E-mail:* admissions@bartonccc.edu. *Website:* http://www.bartonccc.edu/.

Butler Community College
El Dorado, Kansas

Freshman Application Contact Mr. Glenn Lygrisse, Interim Director of Enrollment Management, Butler Community College, 901 South Haverhill Road, El Dorado, KS 67042. *Phone:* 316-321-2222. *Fax:* 316-322-3109. *E-mail:* admissions@butlercc.edu. *Website:* http://www.butlercc.edu/.

Cloud County Community College
Concordia, Kansas

- **State and locally supported** 2-year, founded 1965, part of Kansas Community College System
- **Rural** 35-acre campus
- **Coed**

Undergraduates 814 full-time, 1,059 part-time. Students come from 26 states and territories; 33 other countries; 7% are from out of state; 4% Black or African American, non-Hispanic/Latino; 4% Hispanic/Latino; 0.7% Asian, non-Hispanic/Latino; 0.1% Native Hawaiian or other Pacific Islander, non-Hispanic/Latino; 0.5% American Indian or Alaska Native, non-Hispanic/Latino; 3% Two or more races, non-Hispanic/Latino; 3% Race/ethnicity unknown; 4% international; 7% transferred in. *Retention:* 64% of full-time freshmen returned.
Faculty *Student/faculty ratio:* 11:1.
Academics *Calendar:* semesters. *Degree:* certificates, diplomas, and associate. *Special study options:* academic remediation for entering students, adult/continuing education programs, advanced placement credit, cooperative education, distance learning, English as a second language, freshman honors college, honors programs, internships, part-time degree program, services for LD students, summer session for credit.
Library Cloud County Community College Library. *Books:* 16,807 (physical), 9,784 (digital/electronic); *Databases:* 45. Weekly public service hours: 40.
Student Life *Campus security:* 24-hour emergency response devices.
Athletics Member NJCAA.
Costs (2019–20) *Tuition:* area resident $2130 full-time, $71 per credit hour part-time; state resident $2340 full-time, $78 per credit hour part-time; nonresident $2520 full-time, $84 per credit hour part-time. Full-time tuition and fees vary according to course level, course load, location, program, reciprocity agreements, and student level. Part-time tuition and fees vary according to course level, course load, location, program, reciprocity agreements, and student level. *Required fees:* $1050 full-time, $25 per credit hour part-time. *Room and board:* $5900. Room and board charges vary according to board plan and housing facility.
Financial Aid Of all full-time matriculated undergraduates who enrolled in 2018, 122 Federal Work-Study jobs (averaging $800).
Applying *Options:* early admission, deferred entrance. *Required:* high school transcript.
Freshman Application Contact Shane Olson, Director of Admissions, Cloud County Community College, 2221 Campus Drive, PO Box 1002, Concordia, KS 66901-1002. *Phone:* 785-243-1435 Ext. 213. *Toll-free phone:* 800-729-5101. *E-mail:* solson@cloud.edu. *Website:* http://www.cloud.edu/.

Coffeyville Community College
Coffeyville, Kansas

Freshman Application Contact Stacia Meek, Admissions Counselor/Marketing Event Coordinator, Coffeyville Community College, 400 West 11th Street, Coffeyville, KS 67337-5063. *Phone:* 620-252-7100. *Toll-free phone:* 877-51-RAVEN. *E-mail:* staciam@coffeyville.edu. *Website:* http://www.coffeyville.edu/.

Colby Community College
Colby, Kansas

Freshman Application Contact Ms. Nikol Nolan, Admissions Director, Colby Community College, Colby, KS 67701-4099. *Phone:* 785-462-3984 Ext. 5496. *Toll-free phone:* 888-634-9350. *Fax:* 785-460-4691. *E-mail:* admissions@colbycc.edu. *Website:* http://www.colbycc.edu/.

Cowley County Community College and Area Vocational–Technical School
Arkansas City, Kansas

Freshman Application Contact Ms. Lory West, Director of Admissions, Cowley County Community College and Area Vocational–Technical School, PO Box 1147, Arkansas City, KS 67005. *Phone:* 620-441-5594. *Toll-free phone:* 800-593-CCCC. *Fax:* 620-441-5350. *E-mail:* admissions@cowley.edu. *Website:* http://www.cowley.edu/.

Dodge City Community College
Dodge City, Kansas

Freshman Application Contact Dodge City Community College, 2501 North 14th Avenue, Dodge City, KS 67801-2399. *Phone:* 620-225-1321. *Website:* http://www.dc3.edu/.

Donnelly College
Kansas City, Kansas

- **Independent Roman Catholic** primarily 2-year, founded 1949
- **Urban** 4-acre campus
- **Coed,** 303 undergraduate students, 54% full-time, 71% women, 29% men

Undergraduates 164 full-time, 139 part-time. Students come from 2 states and territories; 32% are from out of state; 35% Black or African American, non-Hispanic/Latino; 38% Hispanic/Latino; 8% Asian, non-Hispanic/Latino; 0.3% Native Hawaiian or other Pacific Islander, non-Hispanic/Latino; 2% American Indian or Alaska Native, non-Hispanic/Latino; 3% Two or more races, non-Hispanic/Latino; 1% Race/ethnicity unknown; 1% international; 16% transferred in. *Retention:* 73% of full-time freshmen returned.
Freshmen *Admission:* 59 enrolled.
Faculty *Total:* 34, 41% full-time. *Student/faculty ratio:* 11:1.
Majors Business administration and management; computer and information sciences; computer and information systems security; elementary education; information technology; liberal arts and sciences/liberal studies; nonprofit management; registered nursing/registered nurse.
Academics *Calendar:* semesters. *Degrees:* certificates, associate, and bachelor's. *Special study options:* academic remediation for entering students, advanced placement credit, cooperative education, distance learning, English as a second language, external degree program, honors programs, independent study, internships, part-time degree program, services for LD students, summer session for credit.
Library Dean-Loyoza Family Academic Resource Center plus 1 other.
Student Life *Housing:* college housing not available. *Activities and Organizations:* Organization of Student Leadership, Student Ambassadors, Healthy Student Task Force, Men's Soccer Club, Women's Soccer Club. *Campus security:* 24-hour emergency response devices. *Student services:* personal/psychological counseling.
Athletics *Intramural sports:* soccer M/W.
Applying *Options:* electronic application. *Recommended:* high school transcript. *Application deadlines:* rolling (freshmen), rolling (transfers).
Freshman Application Contact Donnelly College, 608 North 18th Street, Kansas City, KS 66102. *Phone:* 913-621-8762. *Fax:* 913-621-8719. *E-mail:* admissions@donnelly.edu.
Website: http://www.donnelly.edu/.

Flint Hills Technical College

Emporia, Kansas

Freshman Application Contact Admissions Office, Flint Hills Technical College, 3301 West 18th Avenue, Emporia, KS 66801. *Phone:* 620-341-1325. *Toll-free phone:* 800-711-6947. *Website:* http://www.fhtc.edu/.

Fort Scott Community College

Fort Scott, Kansas

Director of Admissions Mrs. Mert Barrows, Director of Admissions, Fort Scott Community College, 2108 South Horton, Fort Scott, KS 66701. *Phone:* 620-223-2700 Ext. 353. *Toll-free phone:* 800-874-3722. *Website:* http://www.fortscott.edu/.

Garden City Community College

Garden City, Kansas

- **County-supported** 2-year, founded 1919, part of Kansas Board of Regents
- **Rural** 63-acre campus
- **Endowment** $5.9 million
- **Coed**

Undergraduates 1,069 full-time, 928 part-time. Students come from 5 other countries; 24% are from out of state; 7% Black or African American, non-Hispanic/Latino; 39% Hispanic/Latino; 3% Asian, non-Hispanic/Latino; 0.1% Native Hawaiian or other Pacific Islander, non-Hispanic/Latino; 0.8% American Indian or Alaska Native, non-Hispanic/Latino; 3% Race/ethnicity unknown; 0.4% international; 4% transferred in. *Retention:* 58% of full-time freshmen returned.
Faculty *Student/faculty ratio:* 16:1.
Academics *Calendar:* semesters. *Degree:* certificates and associate. *Special study options:* academic remediation for entering students, adult/continuing education programs, advanced placement credit, distance learning, English as a second language, external degree program, part-time degree program, services for LD students, student-designed majors, summer session for credit.
Library Saffell Library.
Student Life *Campus security:* 24-hour emergency response devices and patrols, student patrols, late-night transport/escort service, controlled dormitory access.
Athletics Member NJCAA.
Standardized Tests *Required:* ACT Compass (for admission). *Recommended:* ACT (for admission).
Financial Aid Of all full-time matriculated undergraduates who enrolled in 2018, 90 Federal Work-Study jobs (averaging $1000). 100 state and other part-time jobs (averaging $900).
Applying *Required:* high school transcript.
Freshman Application Contact Office of Admissions, Garden City Community College, 801 Campus Drive, Garden City, KS 67846. *Phone:* 620-276-9531. *Toll-free phone:* 800-658-1696. *Fax:* 620-276-9650. *E-mail:* admissions@gcccks.edu. *Website:* http://www.gcccks.edu/.

Hesston College

Hesston, Kansas

- **Independent Mennonite** primarily 2-year, founded 1909
- **Small-town** 50-acre campus with easy access to Wichita
- **Endowment** $13.9 million
- **Coed,** 378 undergraduate students, 91% full-time, 58% women, 42% men

Undergraduates 343 full-time, 35 part-time. Students come from 25 states and territories; 23 other countries; 39% are from out of state; 6% Black or African American, non-Hispanic/Latino; 13% Hispanic/Latino; 2% Asian, non-Hispanic/Latino; 0.8% American Indian or Alaska Native, non-Hispanic/Latino; 2% Two or more races, non-Hispanic/Latino; 0.3% Race/ethnicity unknown; 15% international; 13% transferred in; 69% live on campus. *Retention:* 86% of full-time freshmen returned.
Freshmen *Admission:* 595 applied, 308 admitted, 130 enrolled. *Average high school GPA:* 3.4. *Test scores:* SAT evidence-based reading and writing scores over 500: 54%; SAT math scores over 500: 63%; ACT scores over 18: 86%; SAT evidence-based reading and writing scores over 600: 30%; SAT math scores over 600: 30%; ACT scores over 24: 23%; SAT evidence-based reading and writing scores over 700: 3%; SAT math scores over 700: 3%; ACT scores over 30: 1%.
Faculty *Total:* 52, 69% full-time, 21% with terminal degrees. *Student/faculty ratio:* 7:1.
Majors Aeronautics/aviation/aerospace science and technology; airline pilot and flight crew; air traffic control; biblical studies; business administration and management; computer/information technology services administration related; general studies; kindergarten/preschool education; liberal arts and sciences/liberal studies; pastoral studies/counseling; registered nursing/registered nurse; youth ministry.
Academics *Calendar:* semesters. *Degrees:* associate and bachelor's. *Special study options:* academic remediation for entering students, adult/continuing education programs, advanced placement credit, cooperative education, double majors, English as a second language, independent study, internships, part-time degree program, services for LD students, summer session for credit.
Library Mary Miller Library. *Books:* 28,000 (physical); *Serial titles:* 101 (physical); *Databases:* 88. Weekly public service hours: 87; students can reserve study rooms.
Student Life *Housing:* on-campus residence required through sophomore year. *Options:* men-only, women-only. Campus housing is university owned. Freshman campus housing is guaranteed. *Activities and Organizations:* drama/theater group, student-run newspaper, choral group, Peace and Service Club, Intramural Sports, Ministry Assistants. *Campus security:* 24-hour emergency response devices, controlled dormitory access. *Student services:* personal/psychological counseling.
Athletics Member NJCAA. *Intercollegiate sports:* baseball M(s), basketball M(s)/W(s), cross-country running M(s)/W(s), golf M(s), soccer M(s)/W(s), softball W(s), track and field M(s)/W(s), volleyball W(s). *Intramural sports:* basketball M/W, golf M(c)/W(c), sand volleyball M/W, soccer M/W, ultimate Frisbee M/W, volleyball M/W.
Standardized Tests *Required:* SAT or ACT (for admission).
Costs (2020–21) *Comprehensive fee:* $37,920 includes full-time tuition ($27,984), mandatory fees ($456), and room and board ($9480). Full-time tuition and fees vary according to course load and program. Part-time tuition: $1166 per credit hour. Part-time tuition and fees vary according to course load and program. *Required fees:* $114 per term part-time. *Room and board:* Room and board charges vary according to board plan and housing facility. *Payment plans:* installment, deferred payment. *Waivers:* employees or children of employees.
Financial Aid Of all full-time matriculated undergraduates who enrolled in 2018, 120 Federal Work-Study jobs (averaging $800).
Applying *Options:* electronic application, early admission, deferred entrance. *Required:* high school transcript. *Required for some:* 2 letters of recommendation, interview. *Application deadlines:* rolling (freshmen), rolling (transfers).
Freshman Application Contact Del Hershberger, Vice President of Admissions, Hesston College, Hesston, KS 67062. *Phone:* 620-327-8206. *Toll-free phone:* 800-995-2757. *Fax:* 620-327-8300. *E-mail:* admissions@hesston.edu.
Website: http://www.hesston.edu/.

Highland Community College

Highland, Kansas

Director of Admissions Ms. Cheryl Rasmussen, Vice President of Student Services, Highland Community College, 606 West Main Street, Highland, KS 66035. *Phone:* 785-442-6020. *Fax:* 785-442-6106. *Website:* http://www.highlandcc.edu/.

Hutchinson Community College

Hutchinson, Kansas

- **State and locally supported** 2-year, founded 1928
- **Small-town** 47-acre campus with easy access to Wichita
- **Coed,** 5,574 undergraduate students, 37% full-time, 55% women, 45% men

Undergraduates 2,055 full-time, 3,519 part-time. Students come from 43 states and territories; 10 other countries; 8% are from out of state; 6% Black or African American, non-Hispanic/Latino; 12% Hispanic/Latino; 0.7% Asian, non-Hispanic/Latino; 0.1% Native Hawaiian or other Pacific Islander, non-Hispanic/Latino; 1% American Indian or Alaska Native, non-Hispanic/Latino; 3% Two or more races, non-Hispanic/Latino; 7% Race/ethnicity unknown; 0.6% international; 8% transferred in; 10% live on campus.
Freshmen *Admission:* 2,405 applied, 2,405 admitted, 943 enrolled. *Average high school GPA:* 3.1.
Faculty *Total:* 268, 40% full-time, 11% with terminal degrees. *Student/faculty ratio:* 16:1.
Majors Accounting technology and bookkeeping; administrative assistant and secretarial science; agricultural mechanics and equipment technology; agriculture; architectural drafting and CAD/CADD; autobody/collision and repair technology; automation engineer technology; automobile/automotive mechanics technology; biology/biological sciences; business and personal/financial services marketing; business/commerce; carpentry; clinical/medical laboratory technology; communications technology; computer and information sciences; computer support specialist; computer systems

analysis; computer systems networking and telecommunications; cosmetology; criminal justice/police science; design and visual communications; education; electrical/electronics equipment installation and repair; electrician; emergency medical technology (EMT paramedic); engineering; English; family and consumer sciences/human sciences; farm and ranch management; fire science/firefighting; foreign languages and literatures; graphic communications; health information/medical records technology; legal assistant/paralegal; liberal arts and sciences/liberal studies; machine tool technology; manufacturing engineering technology; mathematics; mechanical drafting and CAD/CADD; natural resources management and policy; physical sciences; physical therapy technology; psychology; radio and television broadcasting technology; radiologic technology/science; registered nursing/registered nurse; respiratory care therapy; retailing; small business administration; social sciences; speech communication and rhetoric; sport and fitness administration/management; surgical technology; visual and performing arts; web page, digital/multimedia and information resources design; welding technology.

Academics *Calendar:* semesters. *Degree:* certificates and associate. *Special study options:* academic remediation for entering students, advanced placement credit, cooperative education, distance learning, double majors, English as a second language, honors programs, independent study, internships, part-time degree program, services for LD students, summer session for credit.

Library John F. Kennedy Library plus 1 other. *Books:* 33,604 (physical), 14,281 (digital/electronic); *Serial titles:* 101 (physical); *Databases:* 98. Weekly public service hours: 65.

Student Life *Housing Options:* men-only, women-only. Campus housing is university owned. *Activities and Organizations:* drama/theater group, student-run newspaper, choral group, CKI (Circle K), Honors Club, DragonLAN (Computer/technology club), HutchCC Bigs (Big Brothres/Big Sisters), Collegiate 4-H. *Campus security:* 24-hour emergency response devices and patrols, late-night transport/escort service, controlled dormitory access. *Student services:* health clinic, personal/psychological counseling, veterans affairs office.

Athletics Member NJCAA. *Intercollegiate sports:* baseball M(s), basketball M(s)/W(s), cheerleading M(s)/W(s), cross-country running M(s)/W(s), football M(s), golf M(s), soccer W(s), softball W(s), track and field M(s)/W(s), volleyball W(s). *Intramural sports:* basketball M/W, football M/W, soccer M/W, table tennis M/W, tennis M/W, volleyball M/W.

Costs (2020–21) *Tuition:* area resident $2490 full-time, $83 per credit hour part-time; state resident $2790 full-time, $93 per credit hour part-time; nonresident $3720 full-time, $124 per credit hour part-time. *Required fees:* $690 full-time, $23 per credit hour part-time. *Room and board:* $6200. Room and board charges vary according to board plan and housing facility. *Payment plan:* installment. *Waivers:* employees or children of employees.

Financial Aid Of all full-time matriculated undergraduates who enrolled in 2018, 1,502 applied for aid, 1,216 were judged to have need, 197 had their need fully met. 80 Federal Work-Study jobs (averaging $3600). In 2018, 358 non-need-based awards were made. *Average percent of need met:* 80%. *Average financial aid package:* $7047. *Average need-based loan:* $2896. *Average need-based gift aid:* $4996. *Average non-need-based aid:* $2141.

Applying *Options:* electronic application, early admission, deferred entrance. *Required:* high school transcript. *Required for some:* interview. *Application deadlines:* rolling (freshmen), rolling (transfers). *Notification:* continuous (freshmen), continuous (transfers).

Freshman Application Contact Mr. Corbin Strobel, Director of Admissions, Hutchinson Community College, 1300 North Plum, Hutchinson, KS 67501. *Phone:* 620-665-3536. *Toll-free phone:* 888-GO-HUTCH. *Fax:* 620-665-3301. *E-mail:* strobelc@hutchcc.edu. *Website:* http://www.hutchcc.edu/.

Independence Community College

Independence, Kansas

Freshman Application Contact Ms. Brittany Thornton, Admissions Coordinator, Independence Community College, PO Box 708, 1057 W. College Avenue, Independence, KS 673001. *Phone:* 620-332-5495. *Toll-free phone:* 800-842-6063. *Fax:* 620-331-0946. *E-mail:* bthornton@indycc.edu. *Website:* http://www.indycc.edu/.

Johnson County Community College

Overland Park, Kansas

Freshman Application Contact Johnson County Community College, 12345 College Boulevard, Overland Park, KS 66210-1299. *Phone:* 913-469-8500 Ext. 3865. *Website:* http://www.jccc.edu/.

Kansas City Kansas Community College

Kansas City, Kansas

Freshman Application Contact Dr. Denise McDowell, Dean of Enrollment Management/Registrar, Kansas City Kansas Community College, Admissions Office, 7250 State Avenue, Kansas City, KS 66112. *Phone:* 913-288-7694. *Fax:* 913-288-7648. *E-mail:* dmcdowell@kckcc.edu. *Website:* http://www.kckcc.edu/.

Labette Community College

Parsons, Kansas

Freshman Application Contact Ms. Tammy Fuentez, Director of Admission, Labette Community College, 200 South 14th Street, Parsons, KS 67357-4299. *Phone:* 620-421-6700. *Toll-free phone:* 888-522-3883. *Fax:* 620-421-0180. *Website:* http://www.labette.edu/.

Manhattan Area Technical College

Manhattan, Kansas

Freshman Application Contact Mr. Neil Ross, Director of Admissions, Manhattan Area Technical College, 3136 Dickens Avenue, Manhattan, KS 66503. *Phone:* 785-320-4554. *Toll-free phone:* 800-352-7575. *Fax:* 785-587-2804. *E-mail:* neilross@manhattantech.edu. *Website:* http://www.manhattantech.edu/.

Neosho County Community College

Chanute, Kansas

Freshman Application Contact Ms. Lisa Last, Dean of Student Development, Neosho County Community College, 800 West 14th Street, Chanute, KS 66720. *Phone:* 620-431-2820 Ext. 213. *Toll-free phone:* 800-729-6222. *Fax:* 620-431-0082. *E-mail:* llast@neosho.edu. *Website:* http://www.neosho.edu/.

North Central Kansas Technical College

Beloit, Kansas

Freshman Application Contact Ms. Judy Heidrick, Director of Admissions, North Central Kansas Technical College, PO Box 507, 3033 US Highway 24, Beloit, KS 67420. *Toll-free phone:* 800-658-4655. *E-mail:* jheidrick@ ncktc.tec.ks.us. *Website:* http://www.ncktc.edu/.

Northwest Kansas Technical College

Goodland, Kansas

Admissions Office Contact Northwest Kansas Technical College, PO Box 668, 1209 Harrison Street, Goodland, KS 67735. *Toll-free phone:* 800-316-4127. *Website:* http://www.nwktc.edu/.

Pratt Community College

Pratt, Kansas

Freshman Application Contact Ms. Theresa Ziehr, Office Assistant, Student Services, Pratt Community College, 348 Northeast State Road 61, Pratt, KS 67124. *Phone:* 620-450-2217. *Toll-free phone:* 800-794-3091. *Fax:* 620-672-5288. *E-mail:* theresaz@prattcc.edu. *Website:* http://www.prattcc.edu/.

Salina Area Technical College

Salina, Kansas

Freshman Application Contact Mrs. Rebekah Ohlde, Director of Academic Advising, Salina Area Technical College, 2562 Centennial Road, Salina, KS 67401. *Phone:* 785-309-3119. *Fax:* 785-309-3101. *E-mail:* rebekah.ohlde@ salinatech.edu. *Website:* http://www.salinatech.edu/.

Seward County Community College and Area Technical School

Liberal, Kansas

Director of Admissions Dr. Gerald Harris, Dean of Student Services, Seward County Community College and Area Technical School, PO Box 1137, Liberal, KS 67905-1137. *Phone:* 620-624-1951 Ext. 617. *Toll-free phone:* 800-373-9951. *Website:* http://www.sccc.edu/.

Wichita Technical Institute
Wichita, Kansas
Admissions Office Contact Wichita Technical Institute, 2051 S. Meridian Avenue, Wichita, KS 67213. *Website:* http://www.wti.edu/.

WSU Tech
Wichita, Kansas
Freshman Application Contact Mr. Andy McFayden, Director, Admissions, WSU Tech, 4004 N. Webb Road, Suite 100, Wichita, KS 67226 . *Phone:* 316-677-9400. *Fax:* 316-677-9555. *E-mail:* info@watc.edu. *Website:* http://wsutech.edu/.

KENTUCKY

American National University - Louisville
Louisville, Kentucky
- **Proprietary** primarily 2-year, founded 1990, part of National College of Business and Technology
- **Coed**

Faculty *Student/faculty ratio:* 7:1.
Academics *Calendar:* quarters. *Degrees:* diplomas, associate, and bachelor's. *Special study options:* advanced placement credit, double majors, honors programs, internships, part-time degree program, services for LD students, summer session for credit.
Financial Aid Of all full-time matriculated undergraduates who enrolled in 2018, 2 Federal Work-Study jobs.
Applying *Options:* electronic application. *Required for some:* high school transcript. *Recommended:* interview.
Director of Admissions Vincent C. Tinebra, Campus Director, American National University - Louisville, 4205 Dixie Highway, Louisville, KY 40216. *Phone:* 502-447-7634. *Toll-free phone:* 888-9-JOBREADY. *Website:* http://www.an.edu/.

American National University - Pikeville
Pikeville, Kentucky
- **Proprietary** 2-year, founded 1976, part of National College of Business and Technology
- **Rural** campus
- **Coed**

Academics *Calendar:* quarters. *Degree:* diplomas and associate. *Special study options:* advanced placement credit, double majors, honors programs, internships, part-time degree program, services for LD students, summer session for credit.
Financial Aid Of all full-time matriculated undergraduates who enrolled in 2018, 4 Federal Work-Study jobs.
Applying *Required for some:* high school transcript. *Recommended:* interview.
Director of Admissions Tammy Riley, Campus Director, American National University - Pikeville, 50 National College Boulevard, Pikeville, KY 41501. *Phone:* 606-478-7200. *Toll-free phone:* 888-9-JOBREADY. *Website:* http://www.an.edu/.

Ashland Community and Technical College
Ashland, Kentucky
Freshman Application Contact Ashland Community and Technical College, 1400 College Drive, Ashland, KY 41101-3683. *Phone:* 606-326-2008. *Toll-free phone:* 800-928-4256. *Website:* http://www.ashland.kctcs.edu/.

ATA College
Louisville, Kentucky
Freshman Application Contact Admissions Office, ATA College, 10180 Linn Station Road, Suite A200, Louisville, KY 40223. *Phone:* 502-371-8330. *Fax:* 502-371-8598. *Website:* http://www.ata.edu/.

Beckfield College
Florence, Kentucky
Freshman Application Contact Mrs. Leah Boerger, Director of Admissions, Beckfield College, 16 Spiral Drive, Florence, KY 41042. *Phone:* 859-371-9393. *E-mail:* lboerger@beckfield.edu. *Website:* http://www.beckfield.edu/.

Big Sandy Community and Technical College
Prestonsburg, Kentucky
Director of Admissions Jimmy Wright, Director of Admissions, Big Sandy Community and Technical College, One Bert T. Combs Drive, Prestonsburg, KY 41653-1815. *Phone:* 606-886-3863. *Toll-free phone:* 888-641-4132. *E-mail:* jimmy.wright@kctcs.edu. *Website:* http://www.bigsandy.kctcs.edu/.

Bluegrass Community and Technical College
Lexington, Kentucky
Freshman Application Contact Mrs. Shelbie Hugle, Director of Admission Services, Bluegrass Community and Technical College, 470 Cooper Drive, Lexington, KY 40506. *Phone:* 859-246-6216. *Toll-free phone:* 800-744-4872 (in-state); 866-744-4872 (out-of-state). *E-mail:* shelbie.hugle@kctcs.edu. *Website:* http://www.bluegrass.kctcs.edu/.

Daymar College
Bowling Green, Kentucky
- **Proprietary** 2-year, founded 1989
- **Suburban** campus with easy access to Nashville
- **Coed, primarily women**

Undergraduates 6% are from out of state.
Faculty *Student/faculty ratio:* 18:1.
Academics *Calendar:* semesters. *Degree:* diplomas and associate. *Special study options:* adult/continuing education programs, part-time degree program.
Student Life *Campus security:* 24-hour emergency response devices.
Financial Aid Of all full-time matriculated undergraduates who enrolled in 2018, 2 Federal Work-Study jobs (averaging $4950).
Applying *Required:* high school transcript.
Freshman Application Contact Mrs. Traci Henderson, Admissions Director, Daymar College, 2421 Fitzgerald Industrial Drive, Bowling Green, KY 42101. *Phone:* 270-843-6750. *Toll-free phone:* 877-258-7796. *E-mail:* thenderson@daymarcollege.edu. *Website:* http://www.daymarcollege.edu/.

Elizabethtown Community and Technical College
Elizabethtown, Kentucky
Freshman Application Contact Elizabethtown Community and Technical College, 620 College Street Road, Elizabethtown, KY 42701. *Phone:* 270-706-8800. *Toll-free phone:* 877-246-2322. *Website:* http://www.elizabethtown.kctcs.edu/.

Galen College of Nursing
Hazard, Kentucky
Admissions Office Contact Galen College of Nursing, 100 Airport Gardens Drive, Hazard, KY 41701. *Website:* http://www.galencollege.edu/.

Galen College of Nursing
Louisville, Kentucky
Admissions Office Contact Galen College of Nursing, 1031 Zorn Avenue, Suite 400, Louisville, KY 40207. *Toll-free phone:* 877-223-7040. *Website:* http://www.galencollege.edu/.

Gateway Community and Technical College

Florence, Kentucky

- **State-supported** 2-year, founded 1961, part of Kentucky Community and Technical College System
- **Suburban** campus with easy access to Cincinnati
- **Coed,** 4,766 undergraduate students, 27% full-time, 49% women, 50% men

Undergraduates 1,266 full-time, 3,453 part-time. 3% are from out of state; 5% Black or African American, non-Hispanic/Latino; 5% Hispanic/Latino; 1% Asian, non-Hispanic/Latino; 0.1% Native Hawaiian or other Pacific Islander, non-Hispanic/Latino; 0.1% American Indian or Alaska Native, non-Hispanic/Latino; 4% Two or more races, non-Hispanic/Latino; 3% Race/ethnicity unknown; 17% transferred in.

Freshmen *Admission:* 1,789 applied, 1,773 admitted, 433 enrolled. *Average high school GPA:* 2.4. *Test scores:* ACT scores over 18: 56%; ACT scores over 24: 8%; ACT scores over 30: 1%.

Faculty *Total:* 269, 28% full-time. *Student/faculty ratio:* 18:1.

Majors Automobile/automotive mechanics technology; business administration and management; child-care provision; computer and information sciences; criminal justice/law enforcement administration; diesel mechanics technology; electrician; emergency medical technology (EMT paramedic); energy management and systems technology; fire science/firefighting; health information/medical records technology; health services/allied health/health sciences; heating, air conditioning, ventilation and refrigeration maintenance technology; human services; industrial mechanics and maintenance technology; industrial technology; interdisciplinary studies; liberal arts and sciences/liberal studies; logistics, materials, and supply chain management; machine shop technology; manufacturing engineering technology; massage therapy; medical/clinical assistant; registered nursing/registered nurse; teacher assistant/aide; welding technology.

Academics *Calendar:* semesters. *Degree:* certificates, diplomas, and associate. *Special study options:* academic remediation for entering students, cooperative education, distance learning, internships, part-time degree program, services for LD students, summer session for credit.

Library Main Library plus 3 others.

Student Life *Housing:* college housing not available. *Activities and Organizations:* National Technical Honor Society, Student Government Association, Speech Team, Phi Theta Kappa. *Campus security:* 24-hour emergency response devices, campus security during hours of operation. *Student services:* personal/psychological counseling, veterans affairs office.

Standardized Tests *Required:* ACT or SAT; KYOTE (Math); TABE-Advanced (Reading and Writing); Ed-Ready (for admission).

Costs (2019–20) *Tuition:* state resident $4176 full-time, $174 per credit hour part-time; nonresident $14,616 full-time, $609 per course part-time. Full-time tuition and fees vary according to course load. Part-time tuition and fees vary according to course load. *Required fees:* $8 per credit hour part-time, $40 per term part-time. *Payment plan:* installment. *Waivers:* senior citizens and employees or children of employees.

Applying *Options:* electronic application, early admission, deferred entrance. *Required:* high school transcript. *Application deadlines:* rolling (freshmen), rolling (out-of-state freshmen), rolling (transfers). *Notification:* continuous (freshmen), continuous (transfers).

Freshman Application Contact Gateway Community and Technical College, 500 Technology Way, Florence, KY 41042. *Phone:* 859-442-4176. *E-mail:* andre.washington@kctcs.edu.
Website: http://www.gateway.kctcs.edu/.

Hazard Community and Technical College

Hazard, Kentucky

Freshman Application Contact Director of Admissions, Hazard Community and Technical College, 1 Community College Drive, Hazard, KY 41701-2403. *Phone:* 606-487-3102. *Toll-free phone:* 800-246-7521. *Website:* http://www.hazard.kctcs.edu/.

Henderson Community College

Henderson, Kentucky

- **State-supported** 2-year, founded 1963, part of Kentucky Community and Technical College System
- **Small town** 120-acre campus
- **Coed**

Undergraduates 506 full-time, 1,080 part-time. Students come from 9 states and territories; 9% are from out of state; 10% Black or African American, non-Hispanic/Latino; 4% Hispanic/Latino; 0.4% Asian, non-Hispanic/Latino; 0.1% Native Hawaiian or other Pacific Islander, non-Hispanic/Latino; 0.1% American Indian or Alaska Native, non-Hispanic/Latino; 5% Two or more races, non-Hispanic/Latino; 0.5% Race/ethnicity unknown; 3% transferred in. *Retention:* 52% of full-time freshmen returned.

Academics *Calendar:* semesters. *Degree:* certificates, diplomas, and associate. *Special study options:* academic remediation for entering students, accelerated degree program, adult/continuing education programs, advanced placement credit, cooperative education, distance learning, double majors, English as a second language, external degree program, independent study, internships, off-campus study, part-time degree program, summer session for credit.

Library Hartfield Learning Resource Center plus 1 other.

Student Life *Campus security:* 24-hour emergency response devices.

Costs (2019–20) *Tuition:* area resident $169 full-time; state resident $169 full-time; nonresident $592 full-time.

Applying *Required:* high school transcript. *Required for some:* essay or personal statement, interview.

Freshman Application Contact Mr. Chad Phillips, Registrar/Director of Admissions, Henderson Community College, 2660 Green Street, Henderson, KY 42420. *Phone:* 270-827-1867. *Toll-free phone:* 800-696-9958. *E-mail:* chad.phillips@kctcs.edu. *Website:* http://www.henderson.kctcs.edu/.

Hopkinsville Community College

Hopkinsville, Kentucky

- **State-supported** 2-year, founded 1965, part of Kentucky Community and Technical College System
- **Small-town** 69-acre campus with easy access to Nashville
- **Coed,** 3,120 undergraduate students, 40% full-time, 63% women, 37% men

Undergraduates 1,245 full-time, 1,875 part-time. 22% Black or African American, non-Hispanic/Latino; 9% Hispanic/Latino; 1% Asian, non-Hispanic/Latino; 0.8% Native Hawaiian or other Pacific Islander, non-Hispanic/Latino; 0.5% American Indian or Alaska Native, non-Hispanic/Latino; 4% Two or more races, non-Hispanic/Latino; 2% Race/ethnicity unknown; 0.2% international; 7% transferred in. *Retention:* 43% of full-time freshmen returned.

Freshmen *Admission:* 273 enrolled.

Faculty *Total:* 158, 36% full-time. *Student/faculty ratio:* 12:1.

Majors Administrative assistant and secretarial science; agricultural production; business administration and management; child-care provision; computer and information sciences; criminal justice/law enforcement administration; electrical, electronic and communications engineering technology; executive assistant/executive secretary; human services; industrial technology; liberal arts and sciences/liberal studies; multi/interdisciplinary studies related; registered nursing/registered nurse; social work.

Academics *Calendar:* semesters. *Degree:* certificates, diplomas, and associate. *Special study options:* academic remediation for entering students, advanced placement credit, cooperative education, distance learning, honors programs, independent study, part-time degree program, services for LD students, summer session for credit.

Library Learning Resource Center.

Student Life *Housing:* college housing not available. *Activities and Organizations:* student-run newspaper, Ag Tech, Amateur Radio, Ballroom Dance, Baptist Campus Ministries, Black Men United. *Campus security:* 24-hour emergency response devices, late-night transport/escort service, security provided by trained security personnel during hours of normal operation. *Student services:* veterans affairs office.

Athletics *Intramural sports:* basketball M, football M, golf M, table tennis M/W, volleyball M/W.

Costs (2019–20) *Tuition:* state resident $4056 full-time, $174 per credit hour part-time; nonresident $14,208 full-time, $609 per credit hour part-time. Full-time tuition and fees vary according to reciprocity agreements. Part-time tuition and fees vary according to reciprocity agreements. *Required fees:* $340 full-time. *Payment plan:* installment. *Waivers:* senior citizens and employees or children of employees.

Applying *Options:* electronic application, deferred entrance. *Recommended:* high school transcript. *Application deadlines:* rolling (freshmen), rolling (transfers). *Notification:* continuous (freshmen), continuous (transfers).

Freshman Application Contact Hopkinsville Community College, KY. *Phone:* 270-707-3811. *Toll-free phone:* 866-534-2224.
Website: http://hopkinsville.kctcs.edu/.

Interactive College of Technology

Newport, Kentucky

Freshman Application Contact Diana Mamas, Interactive College of Technology, 76 Carothers Road, Newport, KY 41071. *Phone:* 859-282-8989. *Fax:* 859-282-8475. *E-mail:* dmamas@ict.edu. *Website:* http://ict.edu/.

Jefferson Community and Technical College

Louisville, Kentucky

Freshman Application Contact Ms. Melanie Vaughan-Cooke, Admissions Coordinator, Jefferson Community and Technical College, Louisville, KY 40202. *Phone:* 502-213-4000. *Fax:* 502-213-2540. *Website:* http://www.jefferson.kctcs.edu/.

Madisonville Community College

Madisonville, Kentucky

Director of Admissions Mr. Jay Parent, Registrar, Madisonville Community College, 2000 College Drive, Madisonville, KY 42431-9185. *Phone:* 270-821-2250. *Website:* http://www.madisonville.kctcs.edu/.

Maysville Community and Technical College

Maysville, Kentucky

- **State-supported** 2-year, founded 1967, part of Kentucky Community and Technical College System
- **Rural** 12-acre campus
- **Coed,** 3,889 undergraduate students, 35% full-time, 61% women, 39% men

Undergraduates 1,349 full-time, 2,540 part-time. 2% Black or African American, non-Hispanic/Latino; 3% Hispanic/Latino; 0.2% Asian, non-Hispanic/Latino; 0.1% Native Hawaiian or other Pacific Islander, non-Hispanic/Latino; 0.2% American Indian or Alaska Native, non-Hispanic/Latino; 3% Two or more races, non-Hispanic/Latino; 4% Race/ethnicity unknown.
Freshmen *Admission:* 614 enrolled.
Faculty *Student/faculty ratio:* 20:1.
Majors Business administration and management; child-care provision; clinical/medical laboratory technology; computer and information sciences; criminal justice/law enforcement administration; culinary arts; electromechanical technology; engineering technology; executive assistant/executive secretary; family systems; industrial mechanics and maintenance technology; interdisciplinary studies; liberal arts and sciences/liberal studies; machine shop technology; medical administrative assistant and medical secretary; registered nursing/registered nurse; respiratory care therapy.
Academics *Calendar:* semesters. *Degree:* certificates, diplomas, and associate. *Special study options:* academic remediation for entering students, adult/continuing education programs, advanced placement credit, cooperative education, distance learning, English as a second language, external degree program, honors programs, independent study, internships, off-campus study, part-time degree program, services for LD students, summer session for credit.
Library Finch Library.
Student Life *Housing:* college housing not available. *Campus security:* 24-hour emergency response devices, Full-time or Part-time security personnel on each campus. *Student services:* personal/psychological counseling, veterans affairs office.
Financial Aid Of all full-time matriculated undergraduates who enrolled in 2018, 30 Federal Work-Study jobs (averaging $1960).
Applying *Options:* electronic application, early admission. *Required:* high school transcript. *Application deadlines:* rolling (freshmen), rolling (transfers). *Notification:* continuous (freshmen), continuous (transfers).
Freshman Application Contact Maysville Community and Technical College, 1755 US 68, Maysville, KY 41056. *Phone:* 606-759-7141 Ext. 66271.
Website: http://www.maysville.kctcs.edu/.

Maysville Community and Technical College

Morehead, Kentucky

Director of Admissions Patee Massie, Registrar, Maysville Community and Technical College, 609 Viking Drive, Morehead, KY 40351. *Phone:* 606-759-7141 Ext. 66184. *Website:* http://www.maysville.kctcs.edu/.

Owensboro Community and Technical College

Owensboro, Kentucky

- **State-supported** 2-year, founded 1986, part of Kentucky Community and Technical College System
- **Suburban** 102-acre campus
- **Coed,** 4,004 undergraduate students, 41% full-time, 55% women, 45% men

Undergraduates 1,622 full-time, 2,382 part-time. Students come from 25 states and territories; 7% are from out of state; 4% Black or African American, non-Hispanic/Latino; 2% Hispanic/Latino; 1% Asian, non-Hispanic/Latino; 0.1% Native Hawaiian or other Pacific Islander, non-Hispanic/Latino; 0.2% American Indian or Alaska Native, non-Hispanic/Latino; 3% Two or more races, non-Hispanic/Latino; 0.5% Race/ethnicity unknown; 4% transferred in. *Retention:* 62% of full-time freshmen returned.
Freshmen *Admission:* 638 enrolled.
Faculty *Total:* 143, 54% full-time, 13% with terminal degrees. *Student/faculty ratio:* 24:1.
Majors Agricultural production; automobile/automotive mechanics technology; building/property maintenance; business administration and management; child-care provision; computer and information sciences; criminal justice/law enforcement administration; diesel mechanics technology; dramatic/theater arts; electrical and electronic engineering technologies related; electrician; emergency medical technology (EMT paramedic); executive assistant/executive secretary; fine/studio arts; fire science/firefighting; heating, air conditioning, ventilation and refrigeration maintenance technology; industrial mechanics and maintenance technology; liberal arts and sciences/liberal studies; machine shop technology; medical administrative assistant and medical secretary; medical/clinical assistant; radiologic technology/science; registered nursing/registered nurse; surgical technology; veterinary/animal health technology; welding technology.
Academics *Calendar:* semesters. *Degree:* certificates, diplomas, and associate. *Special study options:* academic remediation for entering students, adult/continuing education programs, advanced placement credit, cooperative education, distance learning, double majors, English as a second language, external degree program, honors programs, independent study, internships, off-campus study, part-time degree program, services for LD students, student-designed majors, study abroad, summer session for credit. *ROTC:* Army (b).
Library Main Campus Library plus 1 other. *Books:* 25,113 (physical), 18,771 (digital/electronic); *Serial titles:* 19 (physical), 56,406 (digital/electronic); *Databases:* 56. Weekly public service hours: 48.
Student Life *Housing:* college housing not available. *Activities and Organizations:* drama/theater group, choral group, Student Government Association, OCTC Speech & Debate Society. *Campus security:* 24-hour emergency response devices, late-night transport/escort service. *Student services:* personal/psychological counseling, veterans affairs office.
Costs (2019–20) *Tuition:* state resident $5220 full-time, $174 per credit hour part-time; nonresident $18,270 full-time, $609 per credit hour part-time. Full-time tuition and fees vary according to course load and reciprocity agreements. Part-time tuition and fees vary according to course load and reciprocity agreements. *Required fees:* $240 full-time, $8 per credit hour part-time. *Payment plan:* installment. *Waivers:* senior citizens and employees or children of employees.
Financial Aid Of all full-time matriculated undergraduates who enrolled in 2019, 1,238 applied for aid, 831 were judged to have need. 27 Federal Work-Study jobs (averaging $4849). *Average need-based gift aid:* $3700. *Financial aid deadline:* 7/1.
Applying *Options:* electronic application. *Required:* high school transcript. *Required for some:* college transcripts for transfer students. *Application deadlines:* rolling (freshmen), rolling (out-of-state freshmen), rolling (transfers). *Notification:* continuous (freshmen), continuous (out-of-state freshmen), continuous (transfers).
Freshman Application Contact Ms. Barbara Tipmore, Director of Counseling Services, Owensboro Community and Technical College, 4800 New Hartford Road, Owensboro, KY 42303. *Phone:* 270-686-4530. *Toll-free phone:* 866-755-6282. *E-mail:* barb.tipmore@kctcs.edu.
Website: http://www.owensboro.kctcs.edu/.

Ross College

Hopkinsville, Kentucky

Freshman Application Contact Ross College, 4001 Fort Cambell Boulevard, Hopkinsville, KY 42240. *Phone:* 270-886-1302. *Toll-free phone:* 866-815-5578. *Website:* http://www.rosseducation.edu/.

Somerset Community College
Somerset, Kentucky

- **State-supported** 2-year, founded 1965, part of Kentucky Community and Technical College System
- **Small-town** 70-acre campus
- **Coed,** 5,657 undergraduate students, 39% full-time, 61% women, 39% men

Undergraduates 2,205 full-time, 3,452 part-time. 1% are from out of state; 1% Black or African American, non-Hispanic/Latino; 2% Hispanic/Latino; 0.5% Asian, non-Hispanic/Latino; 0.1% Native Hawaiian or other Pacific Islander, non-Hispanic/Latino; 0.2% American Indian or Alaska Native, non-Hispanic/Latino; 2% Two or more races, non-Hispanic/Latino; 0.5% Race/ethnicity unknown; 0.1% international. *Retention:* 56% of full-time freshmen returned.

Faculty *Total:* 267, 52% full-time. *Student/faculty ratio:* 24:1.

Majors Aircraft powerplant technology; business administration and management; child-care provision; clinical/medical laboratory assistant; computer and information sciences; criminal justice/law enforcement administration; culinary arts; electrical and electronic engineering technologies related; emergency medical technology (EMT paramedic); engineering technology; executive assistant/executive secretary; industrial mechanics and maintenance technology; liberal arts and sciences/liberal studies; medical administrative assistant and medical secretary; medical radiologic technology; multi/interdisciplinary studies related; physical therapy technology; radiologic technology/science; registered nursing/registered nurse; respiratory care therapy; surgical technology; teacher assistant/aide.

Academics *Calendar:* semesters. *Degree:* certificates, diplomas, and associate. *Special study options:* academic remediation for entering students, adult/continuing education programs, advanced placement credit, distance learning, English as a second language, honors programs, independent study, part-time degree program, services for LD students, summer session for credit.

Library Somerset Community College Learning Commons plus 1 other. Weekly public service hours: 45; students can reserve study rooms.

Student Life *Housing:* college housing not available. *Activities and Organizations:* drama/theater group, student-run newspaper. *Student services:* veterans affairs office.

Costs (2020–21) *Tuition:* area resident $5220 full-time, $174 per credit hour part-time; state resident $5220 full-time, $174 per credit hour part-time; nonresident $18,270 full-time, $609 per credit hour part-time. Full-time tuition and fees vary according to course load. Part-time tuition and fees vary according to course load. *Required fees:* $240 full-time, $8 per credit hour part-time. *Payment plan:* installment. *Waivers:* senior citizens and employees or children of employees.

Applying *Options:* electronic application, early admission. *Required:* high school transcript. *Application deadlines:* rolling (freshmen), rolling (transfers). *Notification:* continuous (freshmen), continuous (transfers).

Freshman Application Contact Director of Admission, Somerset Community College, 808 Monticello Street, Somerset, KY 42501-2973. *Phone:* 606-451-6630. *Toll-free phone:* 877-629-9722. *E-mail:* somerset-admissions@kctcs.edu.
Website: http://www.somerset.kctcs.edu/.

Southcentral Kentucky Community and Technical College
Bowling Green, Kentucky

Freshman Application Contact Southcentral Kentucky Community and Technical College, 1845 Loop Drive, Bowling Green, KY 42101. *Phone:* 270-901-1114. *Toll-free phone:* 800-790-0990. *Website:* http://southcentral.kctcs.edu/.

Southeast Kentucky Community and Technical College
Cumberland, Kentucky

Freshman Application Contact Southeast Kentucky Community and Technical College, 700 College Road, Cumberland, KY 40823-1099. *Phone:* 606-589-2145 Ext. 13018. *Toll-free phone:* 888-274-SECC. *Website:* http://www.southeast.kctcs.edu/.

West Kentucky Community and Technical College
Paducah, Kentucky

- **State-supported** 2-year, founded 1932, part of Kentucky Community and Technical College System
- **Small-town** 117-acre campus
- **Coed,** 4,985 undergraduate students, 41% full-time, 55% women, 45% men

Undergraduates 2,068 full-time, 2,917 part-time. Students come from 25 states and territories; 2 other countries; 8% Black or African American, non-Hispanic/Latino; 5% Hispanic/Latino; 0.6% Asian, non-Hispanic/Latino; 0.1% Native Hawaiian or other Pacific Islander, non-Hispanic/Latino; 0.4% American Indian or Alaska Native, non-Hispanic/Latino; 5% Two or more races, non-Hispanic/Latino; 0.6% Race/ethnicity unknown; 0.1% international. *Retention:* 54% of full-time freshmen returned.

Freshmen *Admission:* 900 enrolled.

Faculty *Total:* 121. *Student/faculty ratio:* 18:1.

Majors Animation, interactive technology, video graphics and special effects; automobile/automotive mechanics technology; business administration and management; child-care provision; clinical/medical laboratory technology; computer and information sciences; criminal justice/law enforcement administration; culinary arts; diagnostic medical sonography and ultrasound technology; electrician; emergency medical technology (EMT paramedic); fine/studio arts; fire science/firefighting; health services/allied health/health sciences; homeland security, law enforcement, firefighting and protective services related; industrial mechanics and maintenance technology; liberal arts and sciences/liberal studies; logistics, materials, and supply chain management; machine shop technology; marine transportation related; mechanic and repair technologies related; medical administrative assistant and medical secretary; multi/interdisciplinary studies related; physical therapy technology; registered nursing/registered nurse; surgical technology.

Academics *Calendar:* semesters. *Degree:* certificates, diplomas, and associate. *Special study options:* academic remediation for entering students, accelerated degree program, adult/continuing education programs, cooperative education, distance learning, English as a second language, external degree program, honors programs, independent study, part-time degree program, services for LD students, study abroad, summer session for credit.

Library WKCTC Matheson Library.

Student Life *Housing:* college housing not available. *Campus security:* 24-hour patrols. *Student services:* personal/psychological counseling, veterans affairs office.

Athletics *Intramural sports:* basketball M.

Costs (2020–21) *Tuition:* area resident $4176 full-time, $174 per credit hour part-time; state resident $4176 full-time, $174 per credit hour part-time; nonresident $14,616 full-time, $609 per credit hour part-time. *Required fees:* $192 full-time, $8 per credit hour part-time. *Waivers:* senior citizens and employees or children of employees.

Financial Aid Of all full-time matriculated undergraduates who enrolled in 2018, 50 Federal Work-Study jobs (averaging $1650).

Applying *Options:* electronic application, early admission. *Required:* high school transcript. *Application deadlines:* rolling (freshmen), rolling (transfers). *Notification:* continuous (freshmen), continuous (transfers).

Freshman Application Contact Mr. Trent Johnson, Director of Admission, West Kentucky Community and Technical College, 4810 Alben Barkley Drive, Paducah, KY 42001. *E-mail:* trent.johnson@kctcs.edu.
Website: http://www.westkentucky.kctcs.edu/.

LOUISIANA

Baton Rouge Community College
Baton Rouge, Louisiana

- **State-supported** 2-year, founded 1995
- **Coed**

Undergraduates 1% are from out of state. *Retention:* 52% of full-time freshmen returned.

Faculty *Student/faculty ratio:* 29:1.

Academics *Calendar:* semesters. *Degree:* associate.

Athletics Member NJCAA.

Applying *Application fee:* $7.

Director of Admissions Nancy Clay, Interim Executive Director for Enrollment Services, Baton Rouge Community College, 201 Community College Drive, Baton Rouge, LA 70806. *Phone:* 225-216-8700. *Toll-free phone:* 800-601-4558. *Website:* http://www.mybrcc.edu/.

Baton Rouge School of Computers
Baton Rouge, Louisiana

Freshman Application Contact Admissions Office, Baton Rouge School of Computers, 9352 Interline Avenue, Baton Rouge, LA 70809. *Phone:* 225-923-2524. *Toll-free phone:* 888-920-2772. *Fax:* 225-923-2979. *E-mail:* admissions@brsc.net. *Website:* http://www.brsc.edu/.

Bossier Parish Community College
Bossier City, Louisiana

- **State-supported** 2-year, founded 1967, part of Louisiana Community and Technical College System
- **Urban** 64-acre campus with easy access to Shreveport
- **Coed,** 7,865 undergraduate students, 42% full-time, 74% women, 26% men

Undergraduates 3,313 full-time, 4,552 part-time. 7% are from out of state; 41% Black or African American, non-Hispanic/Latino; 2% Hispanic/Latino; 0.3% Asian, non-Hispanic/Latino; 0.1% Native Hawaiian or other Pacific Islander, non-Hispanic/Latino; 0.4% American Indian or Alaska Native, non-Hispanic/Latino; 4% Two or more races, non-Hispanic/Latino; 2% Race/ethnicity unknown; 0.2% international; 11% transferred in. *Retention:* 15% of full-time freshmen returned.
Freshmen *Admission:* 4,611 applied, 4,496 admitted, 1,306 enrolled. *Average high school GPA:* 2.4.
Faculty *Total:* 168, 60% full-time, 10% with terminal degrees. *Student/faculty ratio:* 21:1.
Majors Administrative assistant and secretarial science; audiovisual communications technologies related; business/commerce; child-care provision; computer/information technology services administration related; construction engineering; construction engineering technology; criminal justice/safety; culinary arts; drafting and design technology; dramatic/theater arts; education; educational/instructional technology; emergency medical technology (EMT paramedic); engineering; foods, nutrition, and wellness; general studies; hospital and health-care facilities administration; industrial mechanics and maintenance technology; industrial technology; information science/studies; liberal arts and sciences and humanities related; liberal arts and sciences/liberal studies; medical/clinical assistant; music; natural sciences; occupational therapist assistant; petroleum technology; pharmacy technician; physical therapy; physical therapy technology; recording arts technology; registered nursing/registered nurse; respiratory care therapy; visual and performing arts related.
Academics *Calendar:* semesters. *Degree:* certificates, diplomas, and associate. *Special study options:* academic remediation for entering students, adult/continuing education programs, advanced placement credit, distance learning, double majors, part-time degree program, services for LD students, summer session for credit.
Library Bossier Parish Community College Library.
Student Life *Housing:* college housing not available. *Activities and Organizations:* drama/theater group, student-run newspaper, choral group. *Campus security:* student patrols. *Student services:* personal/psychological counseling.
Athletics Member NJCAA. *Intercollegiate sports:* baseball M(s), basketball M(s), soccer W, softball W(s). *Intramural sports:* badminton M/W, bowling M/W, football M, racquetball M, softball M, table tennis M/W, volleyball M/W.
Financial Aid Of all full-time matriculated undergraduates who enrolled in 2019, 2,831 applied for aid, 2,591 were judged to have need, 68 had their need fully met. In 2019, 15 non-need-based awards were made. *Average percent of need met:* 42%. *Average financial aid package:* $9876. *Average need-based loan:* $2145. *Average need-based gift aid:* $2199. *Average non-need-based aid:* $750.
Freshman Application Contact Mr. Richard Cockerham, Registrar, Bossier Parish Community College, 6220 East Texas Street, Bossier City, LA 71111. *Phone:* 318-678-6093. *Fax:* 318-678-6390.
Website: http://www.bpcc.edu/.

Cameron College
New Orleans, Louisiana

Admissions Office Contact Cameron College, 2740 Canal Street, New Orleans, LA 70119. *Website:* http://www.cameroncollege.com/.

Central Louisiana Technical Community College
Alexandria, Louisiana

Freshman Application Contact Heather Renier, Director of Student Affairs and Services, Central Louisiana Technical Community College, 4311 South MacArthur Drive, Alexandria, LA 71302. *Phone:* 318-487-5443 Ext. 1129. *Fax:* 318-487-5970. *E-mail:* meredithclark@cltcc.edu. *Website:* http://www.cltcc.edu/.

Delgado Community College
New Orleans, Louisiana

- **State-supported** 2-year, founded 1921, part of Louisiana Community and Technical College System
- **Urban** 57-acre campus
- **Endowment** $2.0 million
- **Coed**

Undergraduates 7,906 full-time, 10,792 part-time. Students come from 20 states and territories; 45% Black or African American, non-Hispanic/Latino; 8% Hispanic/Latino; 3% Asian, non-Hispanic/Latino; 0.1% Native Hawaiian or other Pacific Islander, non-Hispanic/Latino; 0.4% American Indian or Alaska Native, non-Hispanic/Latino; 2% Two or more races, non-Hispanic/Latino; 7% Race/ethnicity unknown; 0.8% international. *Retention:* 57% of full-time freshmen returned.
Faculty *Student/faculty ratio:* 42:1.
Academics *Calendar:* semesters. *Degree:* certificates and associate. *Special study options:* academic remediation for entering students, advanced placement credit, cooperative education, distance learning, double majors, English as a second language, honors programs, off-campus study, part-time degree program, services for LD students, summer session for credit. *ROTC:* Army (c), Air Force (c).
Library Moss Memorial Library.
Student Life *Campus security:* 24-hour patrols, late-night transport/escort service.
Athletics Member NJCAA.
Financial Aid Of all full-time matriculated undergraduates who enrolled in 2018, 308 Federal Work-Study jobs (averaging $1375).
Applying *Options:* electronic application. *Application fee:* $25. *Required for some:* high school transcript. *Recommended:* high school transcript, proof of immunization.
Freshman Application Contact Ms. Gwen Boute, Director of Admissions, Delgado Community College, 615 City Park Avenue, New Orleans, LA 70119. *Phone:* 504-671-5010. *Fax:* 504-483-1895. *E-mail:* enroll@dcc.edu. *Website:* http://www.dcc.edu/.

Fletcher Technical Community College
Schriever, Louisiana

Director of Admissions Admissions Office, Fletcher Technical Community College, 1407 Highway 311, Schriever, LA 70395. *Phone:* 985-857-3659. *Website:* http://www.fletcher.edu/.

Fortis College
Baton Rouge, Louisiana

Director of Admissions Ms. Sheri Kirley, Associate Director of Admissions, Fortis College, 9255 Interline Avenue, Baton Rouge, LA 70809. *Phone:* 225-248-1015. *Toll-free phone:* 855-4-FORTIS. *Website:* http://www.fortis.edu/.

ITI Technical College
Baton Rouge, Louisiana

Freshman Application Contact Mr. Shawn Norris, Admissions Director, ITI Technical College, 13944 Airline Highway, Baton Rouge, LA 70817. *Phone:* 225-752-4230 Ext. 261. *Toll-free phone:* 888-211-7165. *Fax:* 225-756-0903. *E-mail:* snorris@iticollege.edu. *Website:* http://www.iticollege.edu/.

Louisiana Culinary Institute
Baton Rouge, Louisiana

Admissions Office Contact Louisiana Culinary Institute, 10550 Airline Highway, Baton Rouge, LA 70816. *Toll-free phone:* 877-533-3198. *Website:* http://www.lci.edu/.

Louisiana Delta Community College

Monroe, Louisiana

Freshman Application Contact Ms. Kathy Gardner, Interim Dean of Enrollment Services, Louisiana Delta Community College, 7500 Millhaven Drive, Monroe, LA 71203. *Phone:* 318-345-9261. *Toll-free phone:* 866-500-LDCC. *Website:* http://www.ladelta.edu/.

Louisiana State University at Eunice

Eunice, Louisiana

Freshman Application Contact Ms. Tasha Naquin, Admissions Counselor, Louisiana State University at Eunice, PO Box 1129, Eunice, LA 70535. *Phone:* 337-550-1329. *Toll-free phone:* 888-367-5783. *E-mail:* admissions@lsue.edu. *Website:* http://www.lsue.edu/.

McCann School of Business & Technology

Monroe, Louisiana

Freshman Application Contact Mrs. Susan Boudreaux, Admissions Office, McCann School of Business & Technology, 2319 Louisville Avenue, Monroe, LA 71201. *Phone:* 318-323-2889. *Toll-free phone:* 866-865-8065. *Fax:* 318-324-9883. *E-mail:* susan.boudreaux@careertc.edu. *Website:* http://www.mccann.edu/.

Northshore Technical Community College

Bogalusa, Louisiana

Director of Admissions Admissions Office, Northshore Technical Community College, 1710 Sullivan Drive, Bogalusa, LA 70427. *Phone:* 985-732-6640. *Website:* http://www.northshorecollege.edu/.

Northwest Louisiana Technical College

Minden, Louisiana

Director of Admissions Ms. Helen Deville, Admissions Office, Northwest Louisiana Technical College, 9500 Industrial Drive, Minden, LA 71055. *Phone:* 318-371-3035. *Toll-free phone:* 800-529-1387. *Fax:* 318-371-3155. *Website:* http://www.nwltc.edu/.

Nunez Community College

Chalmette, Louisiana

- **State-supported** 2-year, founded 1992, part of Louisiana Community and Technical College System
- **Suburban** 20-acre campus with easy access to New Orleans
- **Endowment** $1.2 million
- **Coed**

Undergraduates 986 full-time, 1,613 part-time. Students come from 15 states and territories; 9 other countries; 1% are from out of state; 40% Black or African American, non-Hispanic/Latino; 7% Hispanic/Latino; 2% Asian, non-Hispanic/Latino; 0.2% Native Hawaiian or other Pacific Islander, non-Hispanic/Latino; 0.7% American Indian or Alaska Native, non-Hispanic/Latino; 3% Two or more races, non-Hispanic/Latino; 4% Race/ethnicity unknown; 0.6% international; 16% transferred in. *Retention:* 20% of full-time freshmen returned.
Faculty *Student/faculty ratio:* 20:1.
Academics *Calendar:* semesters. *Degree:* certificates, diplomas, and associate. *Special study options:* academic remediation for entering students, accelerated degree program, adult/continuing education programs, advanced placement credit, cooperative education, distance learning, double majors, independent study, internships, off-campus study, part-time degree program, services for LD students, student-designed majors, summer session for credit.
Library Nunez Community College Library.
Student Life *Campus security:* late-night transport/escort service, security cameras.
Athletics Member NJCAA.
Financial Aid Of all full-time matriculated undergraduates who enrolled in 2016, 2,599 applied for aid, 2,175 were judged to have need. 37 Federal Work-Study jobs (averaging $2567). *Average financial aid package:* $6229. *Average need-based loan:* $2703. *Average need-based gift aid:* $3526.
Applying *Options:* electronic application, early admission, deferred entrance. *Application fee:* $20. *Required for some:* high school transcript.
Freshman Application Contact Mrs. Becky Maillet, Nunez Community College, 3710 Paris Road, Chalmette, LA 70043. *Phone:* 504-278-6477. *E-mail:* bmaillet@nunez.edu. *Website:* http://www.nunez.edu/.

Remington College–Baton Rouge Campus

Baton Rouge, Louisiana

Director of Admissions Monica Butler-Johnson, Director of Recruitment, Remington College–Baton Rouge Campus, 4520 South Sherwood Forrest Boulevard, Baton Rouge, LA 70816. *Phone:* 225-236-3200. *Toll-free phone:* 800-323-8122. *Fax:* 225-922-3250. *E-mail:* monica.johnson@remingtoncollege.edu. *Website:* http://www.remingtoncollege.edu/.

Remington College–Lafayette Campus

Lafayette, Louisiana

Freshman Application Contact Remington College–Lafayette Campus, 303 Rue Louis XIV, Lafayette, LA 70508. *Phone:* 337-981-4010. *Toll-free phone:* 800-323-8122. *Website:* http://www.remingtoncollege.edu/.

Remington College–Shreveport

Shreveport, Louisiana

Freshman Application Contact Mr. Marc Wright, Remington College–Shreveport, 2106 West Bert Kouns Industrial Loop, Shreveport, LA 71118. *Phone:* 318-671-4000. *Toll-free phone:* 800-323-8122. *Website:* http://www.remingtoncollege.edu/.

River Parishes Community College

Gonzales, Louisiana

Director of Admissions Ms. Allison Dauzat, Dean of Students and Enrollment Management, River Parishes Community College, 925 West Edenborne Parkway, Gonzales, LA 70737. *Phone:* 225-675-8270. *Fax:* 225-675-5478. *E-mail:* adauzat@rpcc.cc.la.us. *Website:* http://www.rpcc.edu/.

South Central Louisiana Technical College

Morgan City, Louisiana

Director of Admissions Ms. Melanie Henry, Admissions Office, South Central Louisiana Technical College, 900 Youngs Road, Morgan City, LA 70380. *Phone:* 504-380-2436. *Fax:* 504-380-2440. *Website:* http://www.scl.edu/.

Southern University at Shreveport

Shreveport, Louisiana

- **State-supported** 2-year, founded 1964, part of Southern University System
- **Urban** 103-acre campus
- **Endowment** $619,644
- **Coed**
- 74% of applicants were admitted

Undergraduates 1,511 full-time, 1,140 part-time. Students come from 25 states and territories; 3 other countries; 3% are from out of state; 91% Black or African American, non-Hispanic/Latino; 0.2% Hispanic/Latino; 0.4% Asian, non-Hispanic/Latino; 0.3% American Indian or Alaska Native, non-Hispanic/Latino; 0.3% Two or more races, non-Hispanic/Latino; 3% international; 7% transferred in; 7% live on campus. *Retention:* 41% of full-time freshmen returned.
Faculty *Student/faculty ratio:* 21:1.
Academics *Calendar:* semesters. *Degree:* certificates and associate. *Special study options:* academic remediation for entering students, adult/continuing education programs, advanced placement credit, cooperative education, distance learning, double majors, English as a second language, honors programs, internships, part-time degree program, services for LD students, student-designed majors, summer session for credit. *ROTC:* Army (c).
Library Library/Learning Resources Center plus 1 other. *Books:* 56,043 (physical), 11,097 (digital/electronic); *Serial titles:* 164 (physical); *Databases:* 86. Students can reserve study rooms.
Student Life *Campus security:* 24-hour emergency response devices and patrols, controlled dormitory access.

Athletics Member NJCAA.
Standardized Tests *Required for some:* SAT or ACT (for admission). *Recommended:* ACT (for admission).
Costs (2019–20) *One-time required fee:* $175. *Tuition:* area resident $2618 full-time; state resident $2618 full-time; nonresident $5918 full-time. Full-time tuition and fees vary according to program. Part-time tuition and fees vary according to program. *Required fees:* $1732 full-time. *Room and board:* $11,728; room only: $8500. Room and board charges vary according to board plan and housing facility.
Applying *Application fee:* $25. *Recommended:* high school transcript.
Freshman Application Contact Ms. Danielle Anderson, Admissions Advisor, Southern University at Shreveport, 3050 Martin Luther King Jr. Drive, Shreveport, LA 71107. *Phone:* 318-670-9211. *Toll-free phone:* 800-458-1472. *Fax:* 318-670-6483. *E-mail:* danderson@susla.edu. *Website:* http://www.susla.edu/.

South Louisiana Community College
Lafayette, Louisiana

Freshman Application Contact Director of Admissions, South Louisiana Community College, 1101 Bertrand Drive, Lafayette, LA 70506. *Phone:* 337-521-8953. *E-mail:* admissions@solacc.edu. *Website:* http://www.solacc.edu/.

Sowela Technical Community College
Lake Charles, Louisiana

- **State-supported** 2-year, founded 1938, part of Louisiana Community and Technical College System
- **Urban** 84-acre campus
- **Endowment** $1.0 million
- **Coed**
- 100% of applicants were admitted

Undergraduates 1,796 full-time, 1,663 part-time. Students come from 21 states and territories; 15 other countries; 2% are from out of state; 24% Black or African American, non-Hispanic/Latino; 4% Hispanic/Latino; 0.7% Asian, non-Hispanic/Latino; 0.8% Native Hawaiian or other Pacific Islander, non-Hispanic/Latino; 1% American Indian or Alaska Native, non-Hispanic/Latino; 4% Two or more races, non-Hispanic/Latino; 3% Race/ethnicity unknown; 0.5% international; 12% transferred in. *Retention:* 54% of full-time freshmen returned.
Faculty *Student/faculty ratio:* 24:1.
Academics *Calendar:* semesters. *Degree:* certificates, diplomas, and associate. *Special study options:* academic remediation for entering students, accelerated degree program, adult/continuing education programs, advanced placement credit, distance learning, double majors, external degree program, internships, off-campus study, part-time degree program, services for LD students, summer session for credit.
Library Library and Learning Resource Center plus 3 others. *Books:* 7,767 (physical), 11,150 (digital/electronic); *Serial titles:* 21 (physical), 32,295 (digital/electronic); *Databases:* 64. Weekly public service hours: 50; students can reserve study rooms.
Student Life *Campus security:* security guard on duty.
Costs (2019–20) *Tuition:* area resident $3335 full-time, $139 per credit hour part-time; state resident $3335 full-time, $139 per credit hour part-time; nonresident $6762 full-time, $282 per credit hour part-time. Full-time tuition and fees vary according to course load and reciprocity agreements. Part-time tuition and fees vary according to course load and reciprocity agreements. *Required fees:* $930 full-time, $35 per credit hour part-time, $45 per term part-time. *Payment plans:* installment, deferred payment.
Applying *Options:* electronic application, early admission. *Required:* proof of immunization, proof of Selective Service status. *Required for some:* high school transcript.
Director of Admissions Allison Dering, Executive Director of Enrollment Services and Student Affairs, Sowela Technical Community College, 3820 Senator J. Bennett Johnston Avenue, Lake Charles, LA 70615. *Phone:* 337-421-6955. *Toll-free phone:* 800-256-0483. *Fax:* 337-491-2443. *E-mail:* allison.dering@sowela.edu. *Website:* http://www.sowela.edu/.

MAINE

Beal College
Bangor, Maine

Freshman Application Contact Tasha Sullivan, Admissions Representative, Beal College, 99 Farm Road, Bangor, ME 04401. *Phone:* 207-947-4591. *Toll-free phone:* 800-660-7351. *Fax:* 207-947-0208. *E-mail:* admissions@bealcollege.edu. *Website:* http://www.bealcollege.edu/.

Central Maine Community College
Auburn, Maine

- **State-supported** 2-year, founded 1964, part of Maine Community College System
- **Small-town** 135-acre campus
- **Endowment** $1.0 million
- **Coed,** 3,219 undergraduate students, 37% full-time, 54% women, 46% men

Undergraduates 1,199 full-time, 2,020 part-time. Students come from 21 states and territories; 10 other countries; 3% are from out of state; 10% Black or African American, non-Hispanic/Latino; 2% Hispanic/Latino; 0.5% Asian, non-Hispanic/Latino; 0.1% Native Hawaiian or other Pacific Islander, non-Hispanic/Latino; 0.5% American Indian or Alaska Native, non-Hispanic/Latino; 2% Two or more races, non-Hispanic/Latino; 5% Race/ethnicity unknown; 2% international; 6% transferred in; 8% live on campus. *Retention:* 57% of full-time freshmen returned.
Freshmen *Admission:* 741 enrolled.
Faculty *Total:* 252, 21% full-time, 6% with terminal degrees. *Student/faculty ratio:* 16:1.
Majors Accounting; administrative assistant and secretarial science; arts, entertainment, and media management; biology/biological sciences; building construction technology; building/property maintenance; business administration and management; civil engineering technology; computer and information systems security; criminal justice/safety; criminology; culinary arts; early childhood education; electromechanical technology; forensic science and technology; general studies; graphic and printing equipment operation/production; graphic communications; heating, air conditioning, ventilation and refrigeration maintenance technology; human services; liberal arts and sciences/liberal studies; machine tool technology; medical/clinical assistant; medical insurance coding; multi/interdisciplinary studies related; network and system administration; parts, warehousing, and inventory management; physical fitness technician; plumbing technology; registered nursing/registered nurse; restaurant, culinary, and catering management; teacher assistant/aide.
Academics *Calendar:* semesters. *Degree:* certificates and associate. *Special study options:* academic remediation for entering students, accelerated degree program, adult/continuing education programs, advanced placement credit, cooperative education, distance learning, honors programs, independent study, internships, part-time degree program, services for LD students, study abroad, summer session for credit.
Library The Learning Commons. *Books:* 7,810 (physical); *Serial titles:* 10 (physical); *Databases:* 130. Weekly public service hours: 57; students can reserve study rooms.
Student Life *Housing Options:* coed, men-only, women-only. Campus housing is university owned. Freshman applicants given priority for college housing. *Campus security:* 24-hour emergency response devices, student patrols, controlled dormitory access, night patrols by police. *Student services:* personal/psychological counseling, veterans affairs office.
Athletics Member USCAA. *Intercollegiate sports:* baseball M, basketball M/W, cross-country running M/W, ice hockey M, soccer M/W, softball W, volleyball W.
Standardized Tests *Recommended:* SAT and SAT Subject Tests or ACT (for admission).
Costs (2020–21) *Tuition:* area resident $2820 full-time, $94 per credit hour part-time; state resident $2820 full-time, $94 per credit hour part-time; nonresident $5640 full-time, $188 per credit hour part-time. *Required fees:* $964 full-time. *Room and board:* $9340. *Payment plan:* installment. *Waivers:* employees or children of employees.
Financial Aid Of all full-time matriculated undergraduates who enrolled in 2018, 89 Federal Work-Study jobs (averaging $1200). *Financial aid deadline:* 8/1.
Applying *Options:* electronic application, deferred entrance. *Application fee:* $20. *Required:* high school transcript. *Recommended:* essay or personal statement. *Application deadlines:* rolling (freshmen), rolling (transfers). *Notification:* continuous (freshmen), continuous (transfers).
Freshman Application Contact Ms. Joan Nichols, Admissions Assistant, Central Maine Community College, 1250 Turner Street, Auburn, ME 04210. *Phone:* 207-755-5273. *Toll-free phone:* 800-891-2002. *Fax:* 207-755-5493. *E-mail:* enroll@cmcc.edu.
Website: http://www.cmcc.edu/.

Eastern Maine Community College
Bangor, Maine

Freshman Application Contact Mr. W. Gregory Swett, Director of Admissions, Eastern Maine Community College, 354 Hogan Road, Bangor, ME 04401. *Phone:* 207-974-4680. *Toll-free phone:* 800-286-9357. *Fax:* 207-974-4683. *E-mail:* admissions@emcc.edu. *Website:* http://www.emcc.edu/.

Kennebec Valley Community College
Fairfield, Maine

Freshman Application Contact Mr. Crichton McKenna, Assistant Director of Admissions, Kennebec Valley Community College, 92 Western Avenue, Fairfield, ME 04937-1367. *Phone:* 207-453-5155. *Toll-free phone:* 800-528-5882. *Fax:* 207-453-5011. *E-mail:* admissions@kvcc.me.edu. *Website:* http://www.kvcc.me.edu/.

The Landing School
Arundel, Maine

Freshman Application Contact Kristin Potter, Admissions Representative, The Landing School, 286 River Road, Arundel, ME 04046. *Phone:* 207-985-7976. *E-mail:* info@landingschool.edu. *Website:* http://www.landingschool.edu/.

Maine College of Health Professions
Lewiston, Maine

Freshman Application Contact Ms. Erica Watson, Admissions Director, Maine College of Health Professions, 70 Middle Street, Lewiston, ME 04240. *Phone:* 207-795-2843. *Fax:* 207-795-2849. *E-mail:* watsoner@mchp.edu. *Website:* http://www.mchp.edu/.

Northern Maine Community College
Presque Isle, Maine

Freshman Application Contact Ms. Nicole Poulin, Admissions Specialist, Northern Maine Community College, 33 Edgemont Drive, Presque Isle, ME 04769-2016. *Phone:* 207-768-2785. *Toll-free phone:* 800-535-6682. *Fax:* 207-768-2848. *E-mail:* nnpoulin@nmcc.edu. *Website:* http://www.nmcc.edu/.

Southern Maine Community College
South Portland, Maine

- **State-supported** 2-year, founded 1946, part of Maine Community College System
- **Suburban** 80-acre campus
- **Coed,** 8,491 undergraduate students, 40% full-time, 69% women, 31% men

Undergraduates 3,424 full-time, 5,067 part-time. Students come from 15 states and territories; 10 other countries; 5% live on campus. *Retention:* 55% of full-time freshmen returned.
Freshmen *Admission:* 1,664 enrolled.
Majors Agroecology and sustainable agriculture; allied health and medical assisting services related; automobile/automotive mechanics technology; biotechnology; building construction technology; business administration and management; cardiovascular technology; computer and information systems security; computer engineering technology; computer science; criminal justice/safety; culinary arts; dietetic technology; digital communication and media/multimedia; drafting and design technology; early childhood education; education; electrical, electronic and communications engineering technology; emergency medical technology (EMT paramedic); engineering; fire science/firefighting; health services/allied health/health sciences; heating, air conditioning, ventilation and refrigeration maintenance technology; human services; liberal arts and sciences and humanities related; liberal arts and sciences/liberal studies; machine tool technology; marine biology and biological oceanography; materials engineering; medical/clinical assistant; network and system administration; plumbing technology; radiologic technology/science; registered nursing/registered nurse; respiratory care therapy; surgical technology.
Academics *Calendar:* semesters. *Degree:* certificates and associate. *Special study options:* academic remediation for entering students, advanced placement credit, distance learning, double majors, English as a second language, honors programs, independent study, internships, off-campus study, part-time degree program, services for LD students, study abroad, summer session for credit.
Library Southern Maine Community College Library. Weekly public service hours: 68; students can reserve study rooms.
Student Life *Housing Options:* coed, men-only. Campus housing is university owned. *Activities and Organizations:* drama/theater group, student-run newspaper, choral group, Student Senate. *Campus security:* 24-hour patrols, student patrols, late-night transport/escort service, controlled dormitory access. *Student services:* personal/psychological counseling.
Athletics *Intercollegiate sports:* baseball M, basketball M/W, golf M, soccer M/W, softball W.
Costs (2020–21) *Tuition:* $94 per credit hour part-time; state resident $2820 full-time, $94 per credit hour part-time; nonresident $5640 full-time, $188 per credit hour part-time. *Required fees:* $1000 full-time, $33 per credit hour part-time, $25 per term part-time. *Room and board:* $9488. Room and board charges vary according to location. *Payment plan:* installment. *Waivers:* senior citizens and employees or children of employees.
Applying *Options:* electronic application. *Application fee:* $20. *Required:* high school transcript. *Application deadlines:* rolling (freshmen), rolling (out-of-state freshmen), rolling (transfers). *Notification:* continuous (freshmen), continuous (out-of-state freshmen), continuous (transfers).
Freshman Application Contact Amy Lee, Assistant Dean of Enrollment Management, Southern Maine Community College, 2 Fort Road, South Portland, ME 04106. *Phone:* 207-741-5800. *Toll-free phone:* 877-282-2182. *Fax:* 207-741-5760. *E-mail:* alee@smccme.edu. *Website:* http://www.smccme.edu/.

Washington County Community College
Calais, Maine

Freshman Application Contact Washington County Community College, One College Drive, Calais, ME 04619. *Phone:* 207-454-1000. *Toll-free phone:* 800-210-6932. *Website:* http://www.wccc.me.edu/.

York County Community College
Wells, Maine

Freshman Application Contact Fred Quistgard, Director of Admissions, York County Community College, 112 College Drive, Wells, ME 04090. *Phone:* 207-216-4406. *Toll-free phone:* 800-580-3820. *Fax:* 207-641-0837. *Website:* http://www.yccc.edu/.

MARYLAND

Allegany College of Maryland
Cumberland, Maryland

Freshman Application Contact Ms. Cathy Nolan, Director of Admissions and Registration, Allegany College of Maryland, Cumberland, MD 21502. *Phone:* 301-784-5000 Ext. 5202. *Fax:* 301-784-5220. *E-mail:* cnolan@allegany.edu. *Website:* http://www.allegany.edu/.

Anne Arundel Community College
Arnold, Maryland

Freshman Application Contact Mr. Thomas McGinn, Director of Enrollment Development and Admissions, Anne Arundel Community College, 101 College Parkway, Arnold, MD 21012-1895. *Phone:* 410-777-2240. *Fax:* 410-777-2246. *E-mail:* 4info@aacc.edu. *Website:* http://www.aacc.edu/.

Baltimore City Community College
Baltimore, Maryland

- **State-supported** 2-year, founded 1947
- **Urban** 19-acre campus
- **Coed**

Undergraduates 1% are from out of state. *Retention:* 39% of full-time freshmen returned.
Faculty *Student/faculty ratio:* 18:1.
Academics *Calendar:* semesters. *Degree:* certificates and associate. *Special study options:* academic remediation for entering students, adult/continuing education programs, advanced placement credit, cooperative education, distance learning, double majors, English as a second language, honors programs, internships, part-time degree program, services for LD students, study abroad, summer session for credit.
Library Bard Library.
Athletics Member NJCAA.
Standardized Tests *Required:* ACCUPLACER (for admission).

Financial Aid Of all full-time matriculated undergraduates who enrolled in 2018, 331 Federal Work-Study jobs (averaging $1879).
Applying *Options:* early admission, deferred entrance. *Application fee:* $10. *Required:* high school transcript. *Recommended:* interview.
Freshman Application Contact Baltimore City Community College, 2901 Liberty Heights Avenue, Baltimore, MD 21215-7893. *Phone:* 410-462-8311. *Toll-free phone:* 888-203-1261. *Website:* http://www.bccc.edu/.

Carroll Community College

Westminster, Maryland

Freshman Application Contact Ms. Candace Edwards, Director of Admissions, Carroll Community College, 1601 Washington Road, Westminster, MD 21157. *Phone:* 410-386-8405. *Toll-free phone:* 888-221-9748. *Fax:* 410-386-8446. *E-mail:* cedwards@carrollcc.edu. *Website:* http://www.carrollcc.edu/.

Cecil College

North East, Maryland

Freshman Application Contact Dr. Christy Dryer, Cecil College, One Seahawk Drive, North East, MD 21901-1999. *Phone:* 410-287-6060. *Fax:* 410-287-1001. *E-mail:* cdryer@cecil.edu. *Website:* http://www.cecil.edu/.

Chesapeake College

Wye Mills, Maryland

- **State and locally supported** 2-year, founded 1965
- **Rural** 170-acre campus with easy access to Baltimore and Washington, DC
- **Coed,** 2,184 undergraduate students, 26% full-time, 66% women, 34% men

Undergraduates 563 full-time, 1,621 part-time. Students come from 8 states and territories; 44% Black or African American, non-Hispanic/Latino; 20% Hispanic/Latino; 5% Asian, non-Hispanic/Latino; 0.6% Native Hawaiian or other Pacific Islander, non-Hispanic/Latino; 3% American Indian or Alaska Native, non-Hispanic/Latino; 8% Two or more races, non-Hispanic/Latino; 14% Race/ethnicity unknown; 5% international; 3% transferred in. *Retention:* 52% of full-time freshmen returned.
Freshmen *Admission:* 493 enrolled.
Faculty *Total:* 105, 51% full-time, 25% with terminal degrees.
Majors Accounting technology and bookkeeping; agricultural production; biology/biological sciences; business administration and management; business/commerce; child-care and support services management; computer and information sciences and support services related; computer and information systems security; computer science; corrections and criminal justice related; early childhood education; education; elementary education; emergency medical technology (EMT paramedic); engineering-related technologies; engineering technologies and engineering related; environmental science; hospitality administration; hospitality administration related; landscape architecture; legal assistant/paralegal; liberal arts and sciences and humanities related; mental and social health services and allied professions related; physical therapy technology; registered nursing/registered nurse.
Academics *Calendar:* semesters. *Degree:* certificates and associate. *Special study options:* academic remediation for entering students, adult/continuing education programs, advanced placement credit, distance learning, English as a second language, honors programs, independent study, internships, part-time degree program, services for LD students, summer session for credit.
Library Learning Resource Center. *Books:* 44,000 (physical), 300,000 (digital/electronic); *Serial titles:* 38 (physical), 25,500 (digital/electronic); *Databases:* 56. Weekly public service hours: 51.
Student Life *Housing:* college housing not available. *Activities and Organizations:* drama/theater group, Student Senate, Geek club, Green Team, Phi Theta Kappa, UHURU. *Campus security:* 24-hour emergency response devices. *Student services:* veterans affairs office.
Athletics Member NJCAA. *Intercollegiate sports:* baseball M, basketball M/W, soccer M, softball W, volleyball W.
Costs (2019–20) *Tuition:* area resident $3750 full-time, $125 per credit hour part-time; state resident $5790 full-time, $193 per credit hour part-time; nonresident $8100 full-time, $270 per credit hour part-time. *Required fees:* $1100 full-time, $35 per credit hour part-time, $25 per term part-time. *Payment plan:* installment. *Waivers:* senior citizens and employees or children of employees.
Financial Aid Of all full-time matriculated undergraduates who enrolled in 2018, 32 Federal Work-Study jobs (averaging $1482).
Applying *Options:* electronic application. *Required:* high school transcript. *Application deadlines:* rolling (freshmen), rolling (transfers). *Notification:* continuous (freshmen), continuous (transfers).
Freshman Application Contact Ms. Angela Denherder, Director of Student Recruitment and Outreach, Chesapeake College, 1000 College Circle, Wye Mills, MD 21679. *Phone:* 410-827-5856. *E-mail:* adenherder@chesapeake.edu.
Website: http://www.chesapeake.edu/.

College of Southern Maryland

La Plata, Maryland

- **State and locally supported** 2-year, founded 1958
- **Rural** 175-acre campus with easy access to Washington, DC
- **Coed**

Undergraduates 3,087 full-time, 5,324 part-time. 26% Black or African American, non-Hispanic/Latino; 6% Hispanic/Latino; 3% Asian, non-Hispanic/Latino; 0.3% Native Hawaiian or other Pacific Islander, non-Hispanic/Latino; 0.5% American Indian or Alaska Native, non-Hispanic/Latino; 5% Two or more races, non-Hispanic/Latino; 2% Race/ethnicity unknown; 0.4% international; 7% transferred in.
Faculty *Student/faculty ratio:* 19:1.
Academics *Calendar:* semesters. *Degree:* certificates and associate. *Special study options:* academic remediation for entering students, accelerated degree program, adult/continuing education programs, advanced placement credit, cooperative education, distance learning, honors programs, independent study, part-time degree program, services for LD students, study abroad, summer session for credit.
Library College of Southern Maryland Library.
Student Life *Campus security:* 24-hour emergency response devices and patrols.
Athletics Member NJCAA.
Financial Aid Of all full-time matriculated undergraduates who enrolled in 2013, 2,067 applied for aid, 1,496 were judged to have need, 10 had their need fully met. In 2013, 12. *Average percent of need met:* 35. *Average financial aid package:* $5727. *Average need-based loan:* $3115. *Average need-based gift aid:* $5347. *Average non-need-based aid:* $1090.
Applying *Options:* electronic application, early admission, deferred entrance. *Recommended:* high school transcript.
Freshman Application Contact Admissions Department, College of Southern Maryland, PO Box 910, La Plata, MD 20646-0910. *Phone:* 301-934-2251. *Toll-free phone:* 800-933-9177. *Fax:* 301-934-7698. *E-mail:* askme@csmd.edu. *Website:* http://www.csmd.edu/.

Community College of Baltimore County

Baltimore, Maryland

- **County-supported** 2-year, founded 1957
- **Suburban** 350-acre campus with easy access to Baltimore
- **Coed,** 18,833 undergraduate students, 27% full-time, 62% women, 38% men

Undergraduates 5,081 full-time, 13,752 part-time. 39% Black or African American, non-Hispanic/Latino; 5% Hispanic/Latino; 6% Asian, non-Hispanic/Latino; 0.2% Native Hawaiian or other Pacific Islander, non-Hispanic/Latino; 0.3% American Indian or Alaska Native, non-Hispanic/Latino; 3% Two or more races, non-Hispanic/Latino; 0.9% Race/ethnicity unknown; 6% international.
Freshmen *Admission:* 3,424 enrolled.
Faculty *Total:* 1,132, 37% full-time, 11% with terminal degrees.
Majors Accounting technology and bookkeeping; aeronautics/aviation/aerospace science and technology; airline pilot and flight crew; air traffic control; anesthesiologist assistant; applied horticulture/horticulture operations; architectural drafting and CAD/CADD; automobile/automotive mechanics technology; aviation/airway management; biological and physical sciences; building/construction finishing, management, and inspection related; building/construction site management; business administration and management; business/commerce; chemistry teacher education; child-care and support services management; clinical/medical laboratory technology; commercial and advertising art; communications technologies and support services related; computer and information sciences; computer and information systems security; computer engineering; computer systems networking and telecommunications; criminal justice/police science; deaf studies; dental hygiene; early childhood education; education; electrical and electronics engineering; elementary education; emergency medical technology (EMT paramedic); engineering; engineering technologies and engineering related; English/language arts teacher education; funeral service and mortuary science; health services/allied health/health sciences; heating, ventilation, air conditioning and refrigeration engineering technology; histologic technology/histotechnologist; hydraulics and fluid power

technology; legal assistant/paralegal; liberal arts and sciences and humanities related; liberal arts and sciences/liberal studies; management information systems; massage therapy; mathematics teacher education; medical administrative assistant and medical secretary; medical informatics; medical radiologic technology; occupational therapy; parks, recreation, leisure, and fitness studies related; physics teacher education; registered nursing/registered nurse; respiratory care therapy; sign language interpretation and translation; Spanish language teacher education; substance abuse/addiction counseling; transportation/mobility management; veterinary/animal health technology; visual and performing arts.
Academics *Calendar:* semesters. *Degree:* certificates and associate. *Special study options:* academic remediation for entering students, advanced placement credit, cooperative education, distance learning, English as a second language, honors programs, independent study, internships, off-campus study, part-time degree program, services for LD students, study abroad, summer session for credit.
Student Life *Housing:* college housing not available. *Activities and Organizations:* drama/theater group, student-run newspaper, choral group. *Campus security:* 24-hour emergency response devices and patrols, late-night transport/escort service. *Student services:* veterans affairs office.
Athletics Member NJCAA. *Intercollegiate sports:* baseball M(s), basketball M(s)/W(s), cross-country running M(s)/W(s), lacrosse M(s)/W(s), soccer M(s)/W(s), softball W(s), volleyball W(s). *Intramural sports:* bowling M/W.
Costs (2020–21) *Tuition:* area resident $3660 full-time, $122 per credit hour part-time; state resident $7230 full-time, $241 per credit hour part-time; nonresident $11,160 full-time, $372 per credit hour part-time. Full-time tuition and fees vary according to course load. Part-time tuition and fees vary according to course load. *Required fees:* $1326 full-time. *Payment plan:* installment. *Waivers:* minority students, senior citizens, and employees or children of employees.
Applying *Options:* electronic application. *Required:* high school transcript. *Application deadlines:* rolling (freshmen), rolling (transfers).
Freshman Application Contact Ms. Diane Drake, Director of Admissions, Community College of Baltimore County, 7201 Rossville Boulevard, Baltimore, MD 21237-3899. *Phone:* 443-840-4392. *E-mail:* ddrake@ccbcmd.edu.
Website: http://www.ccbcmd.edu/.

Fortis College
Landover, Maryland

Admissions Office Contact Fortis College, 4351 Garden City Drive, Landover, MD 20785. *Toll-free phone:* 855-4-FORTIS. *Website:* http://www.fortis.edu/.

Frederick Community College
Frederick, Maryland

Freshman Application Contact Ms. Lisa A. Freel, Director of Admissions, Frederick Community College, 7932 Opossumtown Pike, Frederick, MD 21702. *Phone:* 301-846-2468. *Fax:* 301-624-2799. *E-mail:* admissions@frederick.edu. *Website:* http://www.frederick.edu/.

Garrett College
McHenry, Maryland

Freshman Application Contact Mrs. Shauna McQuade, Director of Enrollment Management, Garrett College, 687 Mosser Road, McHenry, MD 21541. *Phone:* 301-387-3739. *Toll-free phone:* 866-55-GARRETT. *E-mail:* admissions@garrettcollege.edu. *Website:* http://www.garrettcollege.edu/.

Hagerstown Community College
Hagerstown, Maryland

- **State and locally supported** 2-year, founded 1946
- **Suburban** 319-acre campus with easy access to Baltimore and Washington, DC
- **Coed,** 3,848 undergraduate students, 28% full-time, 65% women, 35% men

Undergraduates 1,061 full-time, 2,787 part-time. 21% are from out of state; 12% Black or African American, non-Hispanic/Latino; 8% Hispanic/Latino; 2% Asian, non-Hispanic/Latino; 0.1% Native Hawaiian or other Pacific Islander, non-Hispanic/Latino; 0.2% American Indian or Alaska Native, non-Hispanic/Latino; 5% Two or more races, non-Hispanic/Latino; 2% Race/ethnicity unknown; 1% international; 8% transferred in. *Retention:* 59% of full-time freshmen returned.
Freshmen *Admission:* 742 enrolled.
Faculty *Total:* 220, 35% full-time. *Student/faculty ratio:* 17:1.
Majors Accounting technology and bookkeeping; animation, interactive technology, video graphics and special effects; biology/biotechnology laboratory technician; business administration and management; business/commerce; child-care and support services management; commercial and advertising art; computer and information sciences; computer and information systems security; criminal justice/police science; dental hygiene; early childhood education; education; electrical, electronic and communications engineering technology; elementary education; emergency medical technology (EMT paramedic); engineering; engineering technologies and engineering related; English/language arts teacher education; environmental studies; industrial electronics technology; instrumentation technology; liberal arts and sciences and humanities related; liberal arts and sciences/liberal studies; management information systems; mechanical engineering/mechanical technology; medical radiologic technology; psychiatric/mental health services technology; registered nursing/registered nurse; transportation/mobility management; web page, digital/multimedia and information resources design.
Academics *Calendar:* semesters. *Degree:* certificates and associate. *Special study options:* academic remediation for entering students, accelerated degree program, adult/continuing education programs, advanced placement credit, cooperative education, distance learning, double majors, English as a second language, honors programs, independent study, internships, off-campus study, part-time degree program, services for LD students, summer session for credit.
Library William M. Brish Library plus 2 others. *Books:* 4,289 (physical), 210,763 (digital/electronic); *Serial titles:* 7 (physical), 127,152 (digital/electronic); *Databases:* 98. Students can reserve study rooms.
Student Life *Housing:* college housing not available. *Activities and Organizations:* drama/theater group, student-run newspaper, choral group, Phi Theta Kappa, Robinwood Players Theater Club, Association of Nursing Students, Radiography Club, Art and Design Club. *Campus security:* 24-hour patrols, student patrols. *Student services:* personal/psychological counseling, veterans affairs office.
Athletics Member NJCAA. *Intercollegiate sports:* baseball M(s), basketball M(s)/W(s), cross-country running M(s)/W(s), golf M(s), soccer M(s)/W(s), softball W(s), track and field M(s)/W(s), volleyball W(s).
Costs (2020–21) *Tuition:* area resident $3690 full-time, $121 per credit hour part-time; state resident $5760 full-time, $190 per credit hour part-time; nonresident $7560 full-time, $250 per credit hour part-time. Full-time tuition and fees vary according to course load, program, and reciprocity agreements. Part-time tuition and fees vary according to course load, program, and reciprocity agreements. *Required fees:* $480 full-time, $14 per credit hour part-time, $30 per term part-time. *Payment plan:* installment. *Waivers:* senior citizens and employees or children of employees.
Financial Aid Of all full-time matriculated undergraduates who enrolled in 2016, 721 applied for aid, 587 were judged to have need, 31 had their need fully met. 43 Federal Work-Study jobs (averaging $2054). 170 state and other part-time jobs (averaging $2797). In 2016, 23 non-need-based awards were made. *Average percent of need met:* 44%. *Average financial aid package:* $5889. *Average need-based loan:* $2995. *Average need-based gift aid:* $4473. *Average non-need-based aid:* $964.
Applying *Options:* electronic application, deferred entrance. *Required for some:* high school transcript. *Application deadlines:* rolling (freshmen), rolling (transfers). *Notification:* continuous (freshmen), continuous (transfers).
Freshman Application Contact Hagerstown Community College, 11400 Robinwood Drive, Hagerstown, MD 21742-6590. *Phone:* 240-500-2238. *Fax:* 301-791-9165. *E-mail:* admissions@hagerstowncc.edu.
Website: http://www.hagerstowncc.edu/.

Harford Community College
Bel Air, Maryland

- **State and locally supported** 2-year, founded 1957
- **Small-town** 352-acre campus with easy access to Baltimore
- **Coed**

Undergraduates 2,183 full-time, 3,917 part-time. Students come from 23 states and territories; 51 other countries; 4% are from out of state; 16% Black or African American, non-Hispanic/Latino; 5% Hispanic/Latino; 2% Asian, non-Hispanic/Latino; 0.2% Native Hawaiian or other Pacific Islander, non-Hispanic/Latino; 0.3% American Indian or Alaska Native, non-Hispanic/Latino; 4% Two or more races, non-Hispanic/Latino; 0.8% Race/ethnicity unknown; 1% international.
Faculty *Student/faculty ratio:* 21:1.
Academics *Calendar:* semesters. *Degree:* certificates, diplomas, and associate. *Special study options:* academic remediation for entering students, adult/continuing education programs, advanced placement credit, cooperative education, distance learning, double majors, English as a second language, honors programs, independent study, internships, part-time degree program, services for LD students, student-designed majors, study abroad, summer session for credit.

Library Harford Community College Library. *Books:* 43,126 (physical), 324,718 (digital/electronic); *Serial titles:* 828 (physical), 75 (digital/electronic); *Databases:* 79.
Student Life *Campus security:* 24-hour patrols, late-night transport/escort service.
Athletics Member NJCAA.
Financial Aid Of all full-time matriculated undergraduates who enrolled in 2016, 1,286 applied for aid, 889 were judged to have need. 57 Federal Work-Study jobs (averaging $1984).
Applying *Options:* electronic application.
Admissions Office Contact Harford Community College, 401 Thomas Run Road, Bel Air, MD 21015-1698. *Website:* http://www.harford.edu/.

Howard Community College

Columbia, Maryland

Freshman Application Contact Aaron Alder, Assistant Director of Admissions, Howard Community College, 10901 Little Patuxent Parkway, Columbia, MD 21044-3197. *Phone:* 443-518-4599. *Fax:* 443-518-4589. *E-mail:* admissions@howardcc.edu. *Website:* http://www.howardcc.edu/.

Lincoln College of Technology - Columbia

Columbia, Maryland

Admissions Office Contact Lincoln College of Technology - Columbia, 9325 Snowden River Parkway, Columbia, MD 21046. *Toll-free phone:* 844-215-1513. *Website:* http://www.lincolntech.edu/.

Montgomery College

Rockville, Maryland

- **State and locally supported** 2-year, founded 1946
- **Suburban** 333-acre campus with easy access to Washington, DC
- **Endowment** $26.1 million
- **Coed,** 21,132 undergraduate students, 34% full-time, 54% women, 46% men

Undergraduates 7,260 full-time, 13,872 part-time. 3% are from out of state; 25% Black or African American, non-Hispanic/Latino; 26% Hispanic/Latino; 12% Asian, non-Hispanic/Latino; 0.2% Native Hawaiian or other Pacific Islander, non-Hispanic/Latino; 0.3% American Indian or Alaska Native, non-Hispanic/Latino; 3% Two or more races, non-Hispanic/Latino; 0.4% Race/ethnicity unknown; 10% international; 3% transferred in. *Retention:* 74% of full-time freshmen returned.
Freshmen *Admission:* 4,836 applied, 3,870 admitted, 2,979 enrolled.
Faculty *Total:* 1,296, 36% full-time, 32% with terminal degrees. *Student/faculty ratio:* 16:1.
Majors Accounting technology and bookkeeping; American Sign Language (ASL); animation, interactive technology, video graphics and special effects; applied horticulture/horticulture operations; architectural drafting and CAD/CADD; art; automobile/automotive mechanics technology; biology/biotechnology laboratory technician; building/construction finishing, management, and inspection related; business/commerce; chemistry teacher education; child-care provision; commercial and advertising art; commercial photography; communications technologies and support services related; computer and information sciences; computer and information systems security; computer technology/computer systems technology; criminal justice/police science; crisis/emergency/disaster management; data entry/microcomputer applications; diagnostic medical sonography and ultrasound technology; early childhood education; elementary education; engineering; English/language arts teacher education; fire prevention and safety technology; geography; health information/medical records technology; hotel/motel administration; interior design; legal assistant/paralegal; liberal arts and sciences and humanities related; liberal arts and sciences/liberal studies; mathematics teacher education; medical radiologic technology; physical therapy technology; physics teacher education; psychiatric/mental health services technology; registered nursing/registered nurse; Spanish language teacher education; speech communication and rhetoric; surgical technology; web page, digital/multimedia and information resources design.
Academics *Calendar:* semesters. *Degree:* certificates, diplomas, and associate. *Special study options:* academic remediation for entering students, accelerated degree program, adult/continuing education programs, advanced placement credit, distance learning, double majors, English as a second language, honors programs, internships, off-campus study, part-time degree program, services for LD students, study abroad, summer session for credit. *ROTC:* Air Force (c).
Library Montgomery College Library plus 3 others. *Books:* 211,641 (physical), 57,782 (digital/electronic); *Serial titles:* 9,356 (physical), 104,416 (digital/electronic); *Databases:* 176. Weekly public service hours: 73; students can reserve study rooms.
Student Life *Housing:* college housing not available. *Activities and Organizations:* drama/theater group, student-run newspaper, radio and television station, choral group, marching band, Math Club, Engineers without Borders (EWB), STEM Education Community Club, Cyber Security Club, Animation and Drone Club. *Campus security:* 24-hour emergency response devices and patrols.
Athletics Member NJCAA. *Intercollegiate sports:* baseball M, basketball M/W, cross-country running M/W, soccer M/W, softball W, swimming and diving M/W, tennis M/W, track and field M/W, volleyball W. *Intramural sports:* baseball M, basketball M/W, cheerleading W, cross-country running M/W, golf M, soccer M/W, softball W, swimming and diving M/W, tennis M/W, track and field M/W, volleyball W, wrestling M.
Costs (2020–21) *Comprehensive fee:* $13,430 includes mandatory fees ($2724).
Applying *Options:* electronic application, early admission. *Application fee:* $25. *Recommended:* high school transcript, interview. *Application deadlines:* rolling (freshmen), rolling (transfers). *Notification:* continuous (freshmen), continuous (transfers).
Freshman Application Contact Montgomery College, 51 Mannakee Street, Rockville, MD 20850. *Phone:* 240-567-5036.
Website: http://www.montgomerycollege.edu/.

Prince George's Community College

Largo, Maryland

- **County-supported** 2-year, founded 1958
- **Suburban** 150-acre campus with easy access to Washington, DC
- **Coed**

Undergraduates 3,007 full-time, 8,854 part-time. Students come from 20 states and territories; 98 other countries; 4% are from out of state; 8% transferred in. *Retention:* 60% of full-time freshmen returned.
Faculty *Student/faculty ratio:* 16:1.
Academics *Calendar:* semesters plus 2 summer sessions. *Degree:* certificates and associate. *Special study options:* academic remediation for entering students, adult/continuing education programs, advanced placement credit, cooperative education, distance learning, English as a second language, external degree program, honors programs, part-time degree program, services for LD students, summer session for credit. *ROTC:* Army (c).
Library Accokeek Hall.
Student Life *Campus security:* 24-hour emergency response devices and patrols, late-night transport/escort service.
Athletics Member NJCAA.
Financial Aid Of all full-time matriculated undergraduates who enrolled in 2018, 99 Federal Work-Study jobs (averaging $2000).
Applying *Options:* early admission. *Application fee:* $25. *Required for some:* high school transcript. *Recommended:* minimum 2.0 GPA.
Freshman Application Contact Ms. Vera Bagley, Director of Admissions and Records, Prince George's Community College, 301 Largo Road, Largo, MD 20774-2199. *Phone:* 301-322-0801. *Fax:* 301-322-0119. *E-mail:* enrollmentservices@pgcc.edu. *Website:* http://www.pgcc.edu/.

Wor-Wic Community College

Salisbury, Maryland

- **State and locally supported** 2-year, founded 1976
- **Small-town** 202-acre campus
- **Endowment** $19.3 million
- **Coed,** 2,894 undergraduate students, 25% full-time, 64% women, 36% men

Undergraduates 712 full-time, 2,182 part-time. Students come from 9 states and territories; 9 other countries; 3% are from out of state; 27% Black or African American, non-Hispanic/Latino; 6% Hispanic/Latino; 2% Asian, non-Hispanic/Latino; 0.1% Native Hawaiian or other Pacific Islander, non-Hispanic/Latino; 0.1% American Indian or Alaska Native, non-Hispanic/Latino; 4% Two or more races, non-Hispanic/Latino; 2% Race/ethnicity unknown; 0.5% international; 7% transferred in.
Freshmen *Admission:* 865 applied, 865 admitted, 544 enrolled.
Faculty *Total:* 151, 47% full-time, 19% with terminal degrees. *Student/faculty ratio:* 15:1.
Majors Administrative assistant and secretarial science; biology/biological sciences; business administration and management; business/commerce; child-care and support services management; computer and information sciences; computer systems analysis; criminal justice/police science; early childhood education; education; elementary education; emergency medical technology (EMT paramedic); hospitality administration; liberal arts and sciences and humanities related; medical radiologic technology; occupational therapist

assistant; physical therapy technology; registered nursing/registered nurse; science technologies related; substance abuse/addiction counseling.
Academics *Calendar:* semesters. *Degree:* certificates and associate. *Special study options:* academic remediation for entering students, adult/continuing education programs, advanced placement credit, distance learning, double majors, English as a second language, honors programs, independent study, part-time degree program, services for LD students, summer session for credit.
Library Patricia M. Hazel Resource Center plus 4 others. *Databases:* 56. Weekly public service hours: 70.
Student Life *Housing:* college housing not available. *Activities and Organizations:* The Gaming Association, Phi Theta Kappa (PTK): Alpha Nu Omicron, Criminal Justice Club, Veterans - Military Association, Gay Straight Alliance. *Campus security:* 24-hour emergency response devices, late-night transport/escort service, patrols by trained security personnel 7:00 am to 11:00 pm. *Student services:* personal/psychological counseling, veterans affairs office.
Costs (2019–20) *Tuition:* area resident $3600 full-time, $120 per credit part-time; state resident $7230 full-time, $241 per credit part-time; nonresident $9060 full-time, $302 per credit part-time. *Required fees:* $570 full-time, $19 per credit part-time. *Payment plan:* installment. *Waivers:* senior citizens and employees or children of employees.
Applying *Options:* electronic application, early admission. *Recommended:* high school transcript. *Application deadlines:* rolling (freshmen), rolling (transfers).
Freshman Application Contact Ms. Angie N. Hayden, Director of Admissions and Records, Wor-Wic Community College, 32000 Campus Drive, Salisbury, MD 21804. *Phone:* 410-572-8712. *Fax:* 410-334-2954. *E-mail:* admissions@worwic.edu.
Website: http://www.worwic.edu/.

MASSACHUSETTS

Bay State College
Boston, Massachusetts

Freshman Application Contact Kimberly Odusami, Director of Admissions, Bay State College, 122 Commonwealth Avenue, Boston, MA 02116. *Phone:* 617-217-9186. *Toll-free phone:* 800-81-LEARN. *E-mail:* admissions@baystate.edu. *Website:* http://www.baystate.edu/.

Benjamin Franklin Institute of Technology
Boston, Massachusetts

- **Independent** primarily 2-year, founded 1908
- **Urban** 3-acre campus
- **Coed,** 597 undergraduate students, 78% full-time, 15% women, 85% men

Undergraduates 466 full-time, 131 part-time. 3% are from out of state; 36% Black or African American, non-Hispanic/Latino; 28% Hispanic/Latino; 6% Asian, non-Hispanic/Latino; 0.4% Native Hawaiian or other Pacific Islander, non-Hispanic/Latino; 1% American Indian or Alaska Native, non-Hispanic/Latino; 2% Two or more races, non-Hispanic/Latino; 8% Race/ethnicity unknown; 2% international; 11% transferred in.
Freshmen *Admission:* 725 applied, 514 admitted, 208 enrolled. *Average high school GPA:* 2.3.
Majors Architectural drafting and CAD/CADD; architectural engineering technology; automobile/automotive mechanics technology; automotive engineering technology; bioengineering and biomedical engineering; biomedical technology; computer engineering technology; computer science; computer technology/computer systems technology; drafting and design technology; electrical and electronic engineering technologies related; electrical and power transmission installation; electrical, electronic and communications engineering technology; engineering technology; mechanical engineering/mechanical technology; opticianry.
Academics *Calendar:* semesters. *Degrees:* certificates, associate, and bachelor's. *Special study options:* academic remediation for entering students, accelerated degree program, adult/continuing education programs, advanced placement credit, independent study, internships, off-campus study, part-time degree program, services for LD students, summer session for credit.
Library Lufkin Memorial Library.
Student Life *Housing:* college housing not available. *Activities and Organizations:* Phi Theta Kappa, Student Government and Leadership, yearbook and video club, Green Technology Club, Women's Forum. *Campus security:* 24-hour emergency response devices. *Student services:* personal/psychological counseling.
Athletics Member NJCAA. *Intercollegiate sports:* soccer M. *Intramural sports:* basketball M/W, table tennis M/W.
Financial Aid ***Average percent of need met:*** 45%. *Average financial aid package:* $11,677. *Average need-based gift aid:* $8581.
Applying *Options:* electronic application, early action, deferred entrance. *Application fee:* $25. *Required:* high school transcript. *Recommended:* essay or personal statement, minimum 2.0 GPA, interview. *Application deadline:* 12/14 (early action). *Notification:* 12/21 (early action).
Freshman Application Contact Ms. Brittainy Johnson, Associate Director of Admissions, Benjamin Franklin Institute of Technology, Boston, MA 02116. *Phone:* 617-423-4630 Ext. 122. *Toll-free phone:* 877-400-BFIT. *Fax:* 617-482-3706. *E-mail:* bjohnson@bfit.edu.
Website: http://www.bfit.edu/.

Berkshire Community College
Pittsfield, Massachusetts

Freshman Application Contact Ms. Tina Schettini, Senior Admissions Counselor, Berkshire Community College, 1350 West Street, Pittsfield, MA 01201-5786. *Phone:* 413-236-1635. *Toll-free phone:* 800-816-1233. *Fax:* 413-496-9511. *E-mail:* tschetti@berkshirecc.edu. *Website:* http://www.berkshirecc.edu/.

Bristol Community College
Fall River, Massachusetts

- **State-supported** 2-year, founded 1965, part of Massachusetts Community College System
- **Urban** 102-acre campus with easy access to Boston
- **Endowment** $9.5 million
- **Coed,** 7,637 undergraduate students

Undergraduates Students come from 7 other countries; 13% are from out of state; 8% Black or African American, non-Hispanic/Latino; 9% Hispanic/Latino; 2% Asian, non-Hispanic/Latino; 0.1% Native Hawaiian or other Pacific Islander, non-Hispanic/Latino; 0.2% American Indian or Alaska Native, non-Hispanic/Latino; 6% Two or more races, non-Hispanic/Latino; 5% Race/ethnicity unknown.
Faculty *Student/faculty ratio:* 16:1.
Majors Accounting; American Sign Language (ASL); banking and financial support services; biology/biological sciences; business administration and management; business, management, and marketing related; business operations support and secretarial services related; civil engineering technology; clinical/medical laboratory technology; computer and information sciences; computer and information sciences related; computer programming; computer science; computer systems analysis; computer systems networking and telecommunications; criminal justice/safety; culinary arts related; data processing and data processing technology; dental hygiene; design and visual communications; dramatic/theater arts; electrical, electronic and communications engineering technology; electromechanical technology; elementary education; engineering; engineering science; engineering technologies and engineering related; entrepreneurship; environmental engineering technology; environmental studies; finance and financial management services related; fine/studio arts; fire science/firefighting; general studies; graphic design; health information/medical records technology; hospitality administration; humanities; information science/studies; intermedia/multimedia; kindergarten/preschool education; legal assistant/paralegal; legal professions and studies related; liberal arts and sciences and humanities related; liberal arts and sciences/liberal studies; manufacturing engineering; marketing/marketing management; mathematics and statistics related; mechanical engineering; mechanical engineering/mechanical technology; medical administrative assistant and medical secretary; occupational therapist assistant; real estate; receptionist; registered nursing/registered nurse; small business administration; social sciences; social work; speech communication and rhetoric; structural engineering; veterinary/animal health technology.
Academics *Calendar:* semesters. *Degree:* certificates and associate. *Special study options:* academic remediation for entering students, accelerated degree program, advanced placement credit, cooperative education, distance learning, English as a second language, freshman honors college, honors programs, independent study, internships, off-campus study, part-time degree program, services for LD students, student-designed majors, summer session for credit.
Library Learning Resources Center plus 3 others. *Books:* 50,394 (physical), 49,459 (digital/electronic); *Databases:* 85. Students can reserve study rooms.
Student Life *Housing:* college housing not available. *Activities and Organizations:* drama/theater group, student-run newspaper, International Club, STEM, Dental Hygiene, Medical Assisting, Seeds of Sustainability (SOS). *Campus security:* 24-hour emergency response devices and patrols, late-night transport/escort service. *Student services:* health clinic, personal/psychological counseling, women's center, veterans affairs office.

Athletics Member NJCAA. *Intramural sports:* basketball M/W, cross-country running M/W, golf M/W, soccer M/W, tennis M/W.
Applying *Options:* electronic application, deferred entrance. *Application fee:* $10. *Required:* high school transcript. *Notification:* continuous (freshmen), continuous (transfers).
Freshman Application Contact Bristol Community College, 777 Elsbree Street, Fall River, MA 02720-7395. *Phone:* 774-3572947 Ext. 2947. *Website:* http://www.bristolcc.edu/.

Bunker Hill Community College
Boston, Massachusetts

- **State-supported** 2-year, founded 1973
- **Urban** 21-acre campus
- **Endowment** $4.6 million
- **Coed**
- 89% of applicants were admitted

Undergraduates 4,185 full-time, 8,472 part-time. 26% Black or African American, non-Hispanic/Latino; 27% Hispanic/Latino; 11% Asian, non-Hispanic/Latino; 0.1% Native Hawaiian or other Pacific Islander, non-Hispanic/Latino; 0.3% American Indian or Alaska Native, non-Hispanic/Latino; 2% Two or more races, non-Hispanic/Latino; 8% Race/ethnicity unknown; 5% international.
Faculty *Student/faculty ratio:* 22:1.
Academics *Calendar:* semesters. *Degree:* certificates and associate. *Special study options:* academic remediation for entering students, accelerated degree program, advanced placement credit, cooperative education, distance learning, English as a second language, external degree program, honors programs, independent study, internships, part-time degree program, services for LD students, study abroad, summer session for credit.
Library Bunker Hill Community College Library. *Books:* 40,964 (physical), 80,596 (digital/electronic); *Serial titles:* 92 (physical), 39 (digital/electronic); *Databases:* 105.
Student Life *Campus security:* 24-hour emergency response devices and patrols, late-night transport/escort service.
Athletics Member NJCAA.
Costs (2019–20) *Tuition:* state resident $576 full-time, $24 per credit hour part-time; nonresident $5520 full-time, $230 per credit hour part-time. *Required fees:* $4128 full-time, $172 per credit hour part-time.
Financial Aid Of all full-time matriculated undergraduates who enrolled in 2017, 159 Federal Work-Study jobs (averaging $2712).
Applying *Options:* electronic application. *Required:* high school transcript.
Director of Admissions Francine S. Kupferman, Director of Admissions and Recruitment, Bunker Hill Community College, 250 New Rutherford Avenue, Boston, MA 02129. *Phone:* 617-228-3398. *Fax:* 617-228-3481. *E-mail:* Admissions@bhcc.mass.edu. *Website:* http://www.bhcc.mass.edu/.

Cape Cod Community College
West Barnstable, Massachusetts

- **State-supported** 2-year, founded 1961, part of Massachusetts Public Higher Education System
- **Rural** 120-acre campus with easy access to Boston
- **Coed**

Undergraduates 1% are from out of state.
Faculty *Student/faculty ratio:* 18:1.
Academics *Calendar:* semesters. *Degree:* certificates and associate. *Special study options:* academic remediation for entering students, adult/continuing education programs, advanced placement credit, cooperative education, distance learning, English as a second language, freshman honors college, honors programs, independent study, internships, off-campus study, part-time degree program, services for LD students, study abroad, summer session for credit.
Library Cape Cod Community College Learning Resource Center.
Student Life *Campus security:* 24-hour patrols.
Applying *Options:* deferred entrance. *Required:* high school transcript. *Required for some:* essay or personal statement.
Freshman Application Contact Director of Admissions, Cape Cod Community College, 2240 Iyannough Road, West Barnstable, MA 02668-1599. *Phone:* 508-362-2131 Ext. 4311. *Toll-free phone:* 877-846-3672. *Fax:* 508-375-4089. *E-mail:* admiss@capecod.edu. *Website:* http://www.capecod.edu/.

FINE Mortuary College, LLC
Norwood, Massachusetts

Freshman Application Contact FINE Mortuary College, LLC, 150 Kerry Place, Norwood, MA 02062. *Phone:* 781-762-1211. *Website:* http://www.fmc.edu/.

Greenfield Community College
Greenfield, Massachusetts

Freshman Application Contact Ms. Colleen Kucinski, Assistant Director of Admission, Greenfield Community College, 1 College Drive, Greenfield, MA 01301-9739. *Phone:* 413-775-1000. *Fax:* 413-773-5129. *E-mail:* admission@gcc.mass.edu. *Website:* http://www.gcc.mass.edu/.

Holyoke Community College
Holyoke, Massachusetts

Freshman Application Contact Ms. Renee Tastad, Director of Admissions and Transfer Affairs, Holyoke Community College, Admission Office, Holyoke, MA 01040. *Phone:* 413-552-2321. *Fax:* 413-552-2045. *E-mail:* admissions@hcc.edu. *Website:* http://www.hcc.edu/.

Labouré College
Milton, Massachusetts

Director of Admissions Ms. Gina M. Morrissette, Director of Admissions, Labouré College, 303 Adams Street, Milton, MA 02186. *Phone:* 617-296-8300. *Website:* http://www.laboure.edu/.

Lawrence Memorial/Regis College
Medford, Massachusetts

Admissions Office Contact Lawrence Memorial/Regis College, 170 Governors Avenue, Medford, MA 02155. *Website:* http://www.lmregis.org/.

Massachusetts Bay Community College
Wellesley Hills, Massachusetts

- **State-supported** 2-year, founded 1961
- **Suburban** 84-acre campus with easy access to Boston
- **Coed**

Undergraduates 1,471 full-time, 2,897 part-time. Students come from 10 states and territories; 73 other countries; 1% are from out of state; 16% Black or African American, non-Hispanic/Latino; 21% Hispanic/Latino; 4% Asian, non-Hispanic/Latino; 0.1% Native Hawaiian or other Pacific Islander, non-Hispanic/Latino; 0.4% American Indian or Alaska Native, non-Hispanic/Latino; 2% Two or more races, non-Hispanic/Latino; 5% Race/ethnicity unknown; 2% international; 6% transferred in. *Retention:* 57% of full-time freshmen returned.
Faculty *Student/faculty ratio:* 17:1.
Academics *Calendar:* semesters. *Degree:* certificates and associate. *Special study options:* academic remediation for entering students, adult/continuing education programs, advanced placement credit, cooperative education, distance learning, double majors, English as a second language, honors programs, independent study, internships, part-time degree program, services for LD students, study abroad, summer session for credit.
Library Perkins Library plus 1 other. *Books:* 20,790 (physical), 6,806 (digital/electronic); *Serial titles:* 27 (physical), 322,824 (digital/electronic); *Databases:* 117. Weekly public service hours: 66.
Student Life *Campus security:* 24-hour emergency response devices and patrols.
Athletics Member NJCAA.
Applying *Options:* electronic application, deferred entrance. *Required for some:* high school transcript.
Freshman Application Contact Ms. Alison McCarty, Director of Admissions, Massachusetts Bay Community College, 50 Oakland Street, Wellesley Hills, MA 02481. *Phone:* 781-239-2506. *E-mail:* amccarty1@massbay.edu. *Website:* http://www.massbay.edu/.

Massasoit Community College
Brockton, Massachusetts

Freshman Application Contact Michelle Hughes, Director of Admissions, Massasoit Community College, 1 Massasoit Boulevard, Brockton, MA 02302-3996. *Phone:* 508-588-9100. *Toll-free phone:* 800-CAREERS. *Website:* http://www.massasoit.mass.edu/.

Middlesex Community College
Bedford, Massachusetts

Freshman Application Contact Middlesex Community College, 591 Springs Road, Bedford, MA 01730-1655. *Phone:* 978-656-3211. *Toll-free phone:* 800-818-3434. *Website:* http://www.middlesex.mass.edu/.

Mount Wachusett Community College
Gardner, Massachusetts

- **State-supported** 2-year, founded 1963, part of Massachusetts Public Higher Education System
- **Small-town** 270-acre campus with easy access to Boston
- **Endowment** $7.4 million
- **Coed,** 3,674 undergraduate students, 33% full-time, 65% women, 35% men

Undergraduates 1,217 full-time, 2,457 part-time. Students come from 8 states and territories; 7 other countries; 5% are from out of state; 9% Black or African American, non-Hispanic/Latino; 17% Hispanic/Latino; 3% Asian, non-Hispanic/Latino; 0.2% American Indian or Alaska Native, non-Hispanic/Latino; 1% Two or more races, non-Hispanic/Latino; 3% Race/ethnicity unknown; 0.8% international; 23% transferred in.

Freshmen *Admission:* 1,882 applied, 1,858 admitted, 663 enrolled. *Average high school GPA:* 2.5.

Faculty *Total:* 289, 22% full-time, 14% with terminal degrees. *Student/faculty ratio:* 15:1.

Majors Allied health and medical assisting services related; alternative and complementary medical support services related; art; automobile/automotive mechanics technology; biology/biological sciences; biotechnology; business administration and management; business/commerce; chemistry; child-care and support services management; child development; clinical/medical laboratory technology; computer and information sciences; corrections; criminal justice/law enforcement administration; criminal justice/safety; dental hygiene; dramatic/theater arts; elementary education; energy management and systems technology; environmental studies; fire prevention and safety technology; history; human services; interdisciplinary studies; kinesiology and exercise science; legal assistant/paralegal; liberal arts and sciences/liberal studies; mass communication/media; mathematics; medical/clinical assistant; pharmacy; pharmacy, pharmaceutical sciences, and administration related; physical sciences; physical therapy technology; physics; plastics and polymer engineering technology; radio and television broadcasting technology; registered nursing/registered nurse; veterinary/animal health technology; web page, digital/multimedia and information resources design.

Academics *Calendar:* semesters. *Degree:* certificates, diplomas, and associate. *Special study options:* academic remediation for entering students, accelerated degree program, adult/continuing education programs, advanced placement credit, cooperative education, distance learning, double majors, English as a second language, honors programs, independent study, internships, part-time degree program, services for LD students, study abroad, summer session for credit. *ROTC:* Army (c).

Library LaChance Library. *Books:* 33,368 (physical), 144,567 (digital/electronic); *Serial titles:* 27 (physical); *Databases:* 68. Weekly public service hours: 57; students can reserve study rooms.

Student Life *Housing:* college housing not available. *Activities and Organizations:* drama/theater group, student-run newspaper, Student Nurse Association, Dental Hygienist Club, Early Childhood and Elementary Education Club, Art Club, ALANA. *Campus security:* 24-hour emergency response devices and patrols, late-night transport/escort service, security cameras, access cards for laboratory access. *Student services:* health clinic, personal/psychological counseling, veterans affairs office.

Athletics *Intramural sports:* badminton M/W, basketball M/W, football M/W, soccer M/W, softball M/W, table tennis M/W, volleyball M/W, water polo M/W.

Costs (2019–20) *Tuition:* state resident $600 full-time, $25 per credit hour part-time; nonresident $5520 full-time, $230 per credit hour part-time. Full-time tuition and fees vary according to program and reciprocity agreements. Part-time tuition and fees vary according to program and reciprocity agreements. *Required fees:* $5068 full-time, $197 per credit hour part-time, $125 per term part-time. *Payment plan:* installment. *Waivers:* senior citizens and employees or children of employees.

Financial Aid Of all full-time matriculated undergraduates who enrolled in 2018, 1,067 applied for aid, 826 were judged to have need, 35 had their need fully met. In 2018, 31 non-need-based awards were made. *Average percent of need met:* 96%. *Average financial aid package:* $6225. *Average need-based loan:* $1895. *Average need-based gift aid:* $5572. *Average non-need-based aid:* $983.

Applying *Options:* electronic application, deferred entrance. *Required:* high school transcript. *Required for some:* GED is accepted. *Application deadlines:* 9/11 (freshmen), rolling (transfers). *Notification:* continuous (freshmen), continuous (transfers).

Freshman Application Contact Ms. Marcia Rosbury-Henne, Dean of Admissions and Enrollment, Mount Wachusett Community College, 444 Green Street, Gardner, MA 01440-1378. *Phone:* 978-632-6600 Ext. 337. *Fax:* 978-630-9558. *E-mail:* admissions@mwcc.mass.edu.
Website: http://www.mwcc.edu/.

Northern Essex Community College
Haverhill, Massachusetts

- **State-supported** 2-year, founded 1960
- **Suburban** 106-acre campus with easy access to Boston
- **Endowment** $3.8 million
- **Coed,** 4,932 undergraduate students, 32% full-time, 61% women, 39% men

Undergraduates 1,595 full-time, 3,337 part-time. Students come from 9 states and territories; 1 other country; 12% are from out of state; 5% Black or African American, non-Hispanic/Latino; 46% Hispanic/Latino; 2% Asian, non-Hispanic/Latino; 0.4% Native Hawaiian or other Pacific Islander, non-Hispanic/Latino; 0.2% American Indian or Alaska Native, non-Hispanic/Latino; 2% Two or more races, non-Hispanic/Latino; 2% Race/ethnicity unknown; 1% international; 5% transferred in. *Retention:* 58% of full-time freshmen returned.

Freshmen *Admission:* 3,181 applied, 3,099 admitted, 956 enrolled.

Faculty *Total:* 381, 24% full-time. *Student/faculty ratio:* 19:1.

Majors Accounting; biology/biological sciences; business administration and management; business administration, management and operations related; business/commerce; business teacher education; civil engineering technology; commercial and advertising art; community health services counseling; computer and information sciences; computer programming; computer programming related; computer programming (specific applications); computer science; computer systems networking and telecommunications; computer technology/computer systems technology; criminal justice/police science; data processing and data processing technology; dental assisting; education; electrical, electronic and communications engineering technology; elementary education; emergency medical technology (EMT paramedic); engineering science; general studies; health and physical education/fitness; health information/medical records administration; hotel/motel administration; human services; industrial radiologic technology; journalism; kindergarten/preschool education; liberal arts and sciences/liberal studies; logistics, materials, and supply chain management; machine tool technology; marketing/marketing management; materials science; medical administrative assistant and medical secretary; medical radiologic technology; medical transcription; music; parks, recreation and leisure; physical education teaching and coaching; physical science technologies related; political science and government; psychiatric/mental health services technology; psychology; public health; radiologic technology/science; registered nursing/registered nurse; respiratory care therapy; respiratory therapy technician; science technologies; sign language interpretation and translation; telecommunications technology; web/multimedia management and webmaster; web page, digital/multimedia and information resources design.

Academics *Calendar:* semesters. *Degree:* certificates and associate. *Special study options:* academic remediation for entering students, adult/continuing education programs, advanced placement credit, cooperative education, distance learning, double majors, English as a second language, freshman honors college, honors programs, independent study, internships, off-campus study, part-time degree program, services for LD students, study abroad, summer session for credit. *ROTC:* Air Force (c).

Library Bentley Library. *Books:* 40,687 (physical), 107,724 (digital/electronic); *Serial titles:* 2,097 (physical), 27,741 (digital/electronic); *Databases:* 61.

Student Life *Housing:* college housing not available. *Activities and Organizations:* drama/theater group, student-run newspaper, choral group. *Campus security:* 24-hour emergency response devices and patrols. *Student services:* veterans affairs office.

Athletics Member NJCAA. *Intercollegiate sports:* baseball M, basketball M/W, cross-country running M/W, golf M/W, soccer M, softball W, track and field M/W, volleyball W. *Intramural sports:* basketball M/W, cheerleading W(c), cross-country running M/W, football M/W, soccer M/W, volleyball M/W, weight lifting M/W.

Financial Aid Of all full-time matriculated undergraduates who enrolled in 2018, 74 Federal Work-Study jobs (averaging $1759).

Applying *Options:* early admission. *Required:* high school transcript. *Application deadlines:* rolling (freshmen), rolling (transfers). *Notification:* continuous (freshmen), continuous (transfers).

Freshman Application Contact Northern Essex Community College, 100 Elliott Street, Haverhill, MA 01830. *Phone:* 978-556-3616.
Website: http://www.necc.mass.edu/.

North Shore Community College

Danvers, Massachusetts

Freshman Application Contact Mrs. Gissel Lopez, Academic Counselor, North Shore Community College, Danvers, MA 01923. *Phone:* 978-762-4000 Ext. 2108. *Fax:* 978-762-4015. *E-mail:* gilopez@northshore.edu. *Website:* http://www.northshore.edu/.

Quincy College

Quincy, Massachusetts

Freshman Application Contact Quincy College, 1250 Hancock Street, Quincy, MA 02169. *Phone:* 617-984-1710. *Toll-free phone:* 800-698-1700. *Website:* http://www.quincycollege.edu/.

Quinsigamond Community College

Worcester, Massachusetts

- **State-supported** 2-year, founded 1963, part of Massachusetts System of Higher Education
- **Urban** 57-acre campus with easy access to Boston
- **Endowment** $585,572
- **Coed,** 7,293 undergraduate students, 34% full-time, 59% women, 41% men

Undergraduates 2,456 full-time, 4,837 part-time. Students come from 14 states and territories; 35 other countries; 1% are from out of state; 14% Black or African American, non-Hispanic/Latino; 21% Hispanic/Latino; 5% Asian, non-Hispanic/Latino; 0.1% Native Hawaiian or other Pacific Islander, non-Hispanic/Latino; 0.4% American Indian or Alaska Native, non-Hispanic/Latino; 3% Two or more races, non-Hispanic/Latino; 5% Race/ethnicity unknown; 0.4% international; 6% transferred in.

Freshmen *Admission:* 3,123 applied, 2,082 admitted, 1,333 enrolled.

Faculty *Total:* 558, 24% full-time, 12% with terminal degrees. *Student/faculty ratio:* 15:1.

Majors Automation engineer technology; automobile/automotive mechanics technology; biology/biological sciences; biotechnology; business administration and management; business/commerce; chemistry; community health and preventive medicine; computer and information sciences; computer and information systems security; computer engineering technology; computer graphics; computer programming; computer science; computer support specialist; computer systems analysis; criminal justice/police science; data modeling/warehousing and database administration; deaf studies; dental hygiene; dental services and allied professions related; directing and theatrical production; early childhood education; electrical, electronic and communications engineering technology; elementary education; emergency medical technology (EMT paramedic); energy management and systems technology; English; environmental science; executive assistant/executive secretary; fire services administration; game and interactive media design; general studies; health/health-care administration; health information/medical records technology; health services/allied health/health sciences; history; hospitality administration; human services; laser and optical technology; liberal arts and sciences/liberal studies; manufacturing engineering technology; mass communication/media; medical administrative assistant and medical secretary; medical office management; music; nursing assistant/aide and patient care assistant/aide; occupational therapist assistant; pre-engineering; pre-pharmacy studies; psychology; radiologic technology/science; registered nursing/registered nurse; respiratory care therapy; restaurant/food services management; sociology; surgical technology; web page, digital/multimedia and information resources design.

Academics *Calendar:* semesters. *Degree:* certificates and associate. *Special study options:* academic remediation for entering students, accelerated degree program, advanced placement credit, cooperative education, distance learning, double majors, English as a second language, honors programs, independent study, internships, off-campus study, part-time degree program, services for LD students, summer session for credit. *ROTC:* Army (c).

Library Alden Library plus 1 other. *Books:* 44,051 (physical), 129,831 (digital/electronic); *Serial titles:* 20 (physical), 65,000 (digital/electronic); *Databases:* 57. Weekly public service hours: 67; students can reserve study rooms.

Student Life *Housing:* college housing not available. *Activities and Organizations:* drama/theater group, student-run newspaper, Academic-Related Clubs, Phi Theta Kappa, Student Senate, Anime Club, Psi Beta Club. *Campus security:* 24-hour emergency response devices and patrols, late-night transport/escort service. *Student services:* personal/psychological counseling, veterans affairs office.

Athletics Member NJCAA. *Intercollegiate sports:* baseball M, basketball M/W. *Intramural sports:* basketball M/W, cheerleading W(c), soccer M/W, table tennis M/W, ultimate Frisbee M/W, volleyball M/W.

Costs (2020–21) *Tuition:* state resident $720 full-time, $24 per credit part-time; nonresident $6900 full-time, $230 per credit part-time. Full-time tuition and fees vary according to course load and program. Part-time tuition and fees vary according to course load and program. *Required fees:* $6150 full-time, $178 per credit part-time, $390 per term part-time. *Payment plan:* installment. *Waivers:* senior citizens and employees or children of employees.

Applying *Options:* electronic application. *Application fee:* $20. *Required:* high school transcript. *Required for some:* interview. *Application deadlines:* rolling (freshmen), rolling (transfers). *Notification:* continuous (freshmen), continuous (transfers).

Freshman Application Contact Quinsigamond Community College, 670 West Boylston Street, Worcester, MA 01606-2092. *Phone:* 508-854-4354. *Website:* http://www.qcc.edu/.

Roxbury Community College

Roxbury Crossing, Massachusetts

Director of Admissions Nancy Santos, Director, Admissions, Roxbury Community College, 1234 Columbus Avenue, Roxbury Crossing, MA 02120-3400. *Phone:* 617-541-5310. *Website:* http://www.rcc.mass.edu/.

Springfield Technical Community College

Springfield, Massachusetts

- **State-supported** 2-year, founded 1967
- **Urban** 34-acre campus
- **Coed,** 5,066 undergraduate students, 43% full-time, 59% women, 41% men

Undergraduates 2,177 full-time, 2,889 part-time. Students come from 12 states and territories; 71 other countries; 3% are from out of state; 14% Black or African American, non-Hispanic/Latino; 31% Hispanic/Latino; 4% Asian, non-Hispanic/Latino; 0.1% Native Hawaiian or other Pacific Islander, non-Hispanic/Latino; 0.2% American Indian or Alaska Native, non-Hispanic/Latino; 3% Two or more races, non-Hispanic/Latino; 6% Race/ethnicity unknown; 1% international; 8% transferred in.

Freshmen *Admission:* 3,224 applied, 2,600 admitted, 1,102 enrolled.

Faculty *Total:* 366, 40% full-time. *Student/faculty ratio:* 14:1.

Majors Administrative assistant and secretarial science; animation, interactive technology, video graphics and special effects; architectural and building sciences; automobile/automotive mechanics technology; biology/biological sciences; biotechnology; building/construction finishing, management, and inspection related; business administration and management; business/commerce; chemistry; civil engineering technology; clinical/medical laboratory technology; commercial and advertising art; commercial photography; computer and information systems security; computer engineering technology; computer programming (specific applications); computer science; criminal justice/police science; dental hygiene; diagnostic medical sonography and ultrasound technology; early childhood education; electrical, electronic and communications engineering technology; electromechanical technology; elementary education; engineering; fine/studio arts; fire prevention and safety technology; health information/medical records technology; heating, air conditioning, ventilation and refrigeration maintenance technology; landscaping and groundskeeping; laser and optical technology; liberal arts and sciences/liberal studies; mathematics; mechanical engineering/mechanical technology; medical administrative assistant and medical secretary; medical/clinical assistant; medical insurance coding; occupational therapist assistant; physical therapy technology; physics; premedical studies; radio and television broadcasting technology; radiologic technology/science; registered nursing/registered nurse; respiratory care therapy; secondary education; small business administration; surgical technology; telecommunications technology.

Academics *Calendar:* semesters. *Degree:* certificates and associate. *Special study options:* academic remediation for entering students, adult/continuing education programs, advanced placement credit, cooperative education, distance learning, English as a second language, honors programs, independent study, internships, off-campus study, part-time degree program, services for LD students, summer session for credit.

Library Springfield Technical Community College Library. *Books:* 45,975 (physical), 9,270 (digital/electronic); *Serial titles:* 159 (physical), 12 (digital/electronic); *Databases:* 93. Weekly public service hours: 60.

Student Life *Housing:* college housing not available. *Activities and Organizations:* drama/theater group, student-run newspaper, Gay Lesbian Bisexual Transgender Alliance (GLBTA), Respiratory Care Club, Cosmetology Club, Anime Club, Dental Hygiene Club. *Campus security:* 24-hour emergency response devices and patrols, late-night transport/escort service. *Student services:* health clinic, personal/psychological counseling, legal services, veterans affairs office.

Athletics Member NJCAA. *Intercollegiate sports:* basketball M/W, soccer M/W, wrestling M/W.
Standardized Tests *Required for some:* SAT (for admission).
Costs (2020–21) *Tuition:* area resident $750 full-time, $25 per credit part-time; state resident $750 full-time, $25 per credit part-time; nonresident $7260 full-time, $242 per credit part-time. Full-time tuition and fees vary according to course load and reciprocity agreements. Part-time tuition and fees vary according to course load and reciprocity agreements. No tuition increase for student's term of enrollment. *Required fees:* $5856 full-time, $188 per credit part-time, $108 per term part-time. *Payment plan:* installment. *Waivers:* senior citizens and employees or children of employees.
Applying *Options:* electronic application. *Required:* high school transcript. *Required for some:* interview. *Application deadlines:* rolling (freshmen), rolling (transfers). *Notification:* continuous (freshmen), continuous (transfers).
Freshman Application Contact Springfield Technical Community College, 1 Armory Square, Suite 1, PO Box 9000, Springfield, MA 01102. *Phone:* 413-781-7822 Ext. 4380.
Website: http://www.stcc.edu/.

Urban College of Boston
Boston, Massachusetts

Admissions Office Contact Urban College of Boston, 2 Boylston Street, 2nd Floor, Boston, MA 02116. *Website:* http://www.urbancollege.edu/.

MICHIGAN

Alpena Community College
Alpena, Michigan

Freshman Application Contact Mr. Mike Kollien, Director of Admissions, Alpena Community College, 665 Johnson, Alpena, MI 49707. *Phone:* 989-358-7339. *Toll-free phone:* 888-468-6222. *Fax:* 989-358-7540. *E-mail:* kollienm@alpenacc.edu. *Website:* http://www.alpenacc.edu/.

Bay de Noc Community College
Escanaba, Michigan

- **County-supported** 2-year, founded 1963, part of Michigan Department of Education
- **Rural** 150-acre campus
- **Endowment** $10.4 million
- **Coed,** 1,820 undergraduate students, 39% full-time, 62% women, 38% men

Undergraduates 716 full-time, 1,104 part-time. Students come from 6 states and territories; 4 other countries; 4% are from out of state; 1% Black or African American, non-Hispanic/Latino; 3% Hispanic/Latino; 0.7% Asian, non-Hispanic/Latino; 0.2% Native Hawaiian or other Pacific Islander, non-Hispanic/Latino; 3% American Indian or Alaska Native, non-Hispanic/Latino; 4% Two or more races, non-Hispanic/Latino; 0.4% Race/ethnicity unknown; 3% transferred in; 4% live on campus. *Retention:* 59% of full-time freshmen returned.
Freshmen *Admission:* 342 enrolled.
Faculty *Total:* 128, 32% full-time. *Student/faculty ratio:* 16:1.
Majors Accounting; administrative assistant and secretarial science; automobile/automotive mechanics technology; biochemistry, biophysics and molecular biology related; business administration and management; business/commerce; child-care and support services management; computer software and media applications related; computer systems networking and telecommunications; computer technology/computer systems technology; criminal justice/law enforcement administration; criminal justice/safety; electromechanical technology; emergency medical technology (EMT paramedic); environmental engineering technology; fine/studio arts; general studies; human services; liberal arts and sciences/liberal studies; medical administrative assistant and medical secretary; natural resources/conservation; pre-engineering; premedical studies; registered nursing/registered nurse; small business administration; surveying technology; water quality and wastewater treatment management and recycling technology.
Academics *Calendar:* semesters. *Degree:* certificates and associate. *Special study options:* academic remediation for entering students, adult/continuing education programs, advanced placement credit, cooperative education, distance learning, double majors, independent study, internships, part-time degree program, services for LD students, summer session for credit.
Library Library/Learning Resources Center. *Books:* 31,671 (physical), 46 (digital/electronic); *Serial titles:* 9 (physical), 2,576 (digital/electronic). Weekly public service hours: 52; students can reserve study rooms.
Student Life *Housing Options:* coed. Campus housing is university owned. *Activities and Organizations:* drama/theater group, Phi Theta Kappa, Art Club, Bay Area Water Tech Association (BAWA), Gaming Galaxy, Bay Business Professionals in America (BPA). *Campus security:* resident assistants in housing. *Student services:* personal/psychological counseling, veterans affairs office.
Athletics Member NJCAA. *Intercollegiate sports:* baseball M, basketball M/W, cross-country running M/W, softball W.
Applying *Options:* electronic application, early admission, deferred entrance. *Recommended:* high school transcript. *Application deadlines:* rolling (freshmen), rolling (transfers). *Notification:* continuous (freshmen), continuous (transfers).
Freshman Application Contact Ms. Jessica LeMarch, Director of Admissions, Bay de Noc Community College, 2001 North Lincoln Road, Escanaba, MI 49829. *Phone:* 906-217-4010. *Toll-free phone:* 800-221-2001. *Fax:* 906-217-1714. *E-mail:* jessica.lamarch@baycollege.edu.
Website: http://www.baycollege.edu/.

Bay Mills Community College
Brimley, Michigan

- **District-supported** 2-year, founded 1984
- **Rural** campus
- **Coed**

Undergraduates *Retention:* 49% of full-time freshmen returned.
Academics *Calendar:* semesters. *Degree:* certificates, diplomas, and associate. *Special study options:* academic remediation for entering students, internships, part-time degree program.
Student Life *Campus security:* 24-hour emergency response devices.
Applying *Options:* early admission. *Required:* high school transcript.
Freshman Application Contact Ms. Elaine Lehre, Admissions Officer, Bay Mills Community College, 12214 West Lakeshore Drive, Brimley, MI 49715. *Phone:* 906-248-3354. *Toll-free phone:* 800-844-BMCC. *Fax:* 906-248-3351. *Website:* http://www.bmcc.edu/.

Career Quest Learning Center–Jackson
Jackson, Michigan

Admissions Office Contact Career Quest Learning Center–Jackson, 209 East Washington Avenue, Suite 241, Jackson, MI 49201. *Website:* http://www.careerquest.edu/.

Career Quest Learning Center–Lansing
Lansing, Michigan

Admissions Office Contact Career Quest Learning Center–Lansing, 3215 South Pennsylvania Avenue, Lansing, MI 48910. *Website:* http://www.careerquest.edu/.

Career Quest Learning Center–Mt. Pleasant
Mount Pleasant, Michigan

Admissions Office Contact Career Quest Learning Center–Mt. Pleasant, 2116 South Mission Street, Mount Pleasant, MI 48858. *Website:* http://www.careerquest.edu/.

Delta College
University Center, Michigan

- **District-supported** 2-year, founded 1961
- **Rural** 640-acre campus
- **Endowment** $20.1 million
- **Coed,** 7,819 undergraduate students, 35% full-time, 58% women, 42% men

Undergraduates 2,737 full-time, 5,082 part-time. Students come from 9 states and territories; 1 other country; 0.1% are from out of state; 8% Black or African American, non-Hispanic/Latino; 8% Hispanic/Latino; 0.8% Asian, non-Hispanic/Latino; 0.1% Native Hawaiian or other Pacific Islander, non-Hispanic/Latino; 0.5% American Indian or Alaska Native, non-Hispanic/Latino; 3% Two or more races, non-Hispanic/Latino; 4% Race/ethnicity unknown; 0.2% international; 4% transferred in.
Freshmen *Admission:* 1,547 applied, 1,547 admitted, 1,547 enrolled.
Faculty *Total:* 488, 36% full-time. *Student/faculty ratio:* 16:1.
Majors Accounting technology and bookkeeping; administrative assistant and secretarial science; agriculture and agriculture operations related; architectural engineering technology; automobile/automotive mechanics technology;

building/construction finishing, management, and inspection related; building/property maintenance; business administration and management; carpentry; chemical technology; child-care provision; computer and information sciences related; computer and information systems security; computer installation and repair technology; computer programming; computer systems networking and telecommunications; construction engineering technology; corrections; criminal justice/police science; dental assisting; dental hygiene; diagnostic medical sonography and ultrasound technology; diesel mechanics technology; electrician; energy management and systems technology; environmental engineering technology; fine/studio arts; fire prevention and safety technology; general studies; heating, air conditioning, ventilation and refrigeration maintenance technology; industrial mechanics and maintenance technology; journalism; legal assistant/paralegal; liberal arts and sciences/liberal studies; machine shop technology; manufacturing engineering technology; marketing/marketing management; mechanical engineering/mechanical technology; mechatronics, robotics, and automation engineering; medical administrative assistant and medical secretary; medical radiologic technology; peace studies and conflict resolution; physical therapy technology; pipefitting and sprinkler fitting; plumbing technology; precision metal working related; precision production related; radio and television; registered nursing/registered nurse; respiratory care therapy; salon/beauty salon management; security and loss prevention; sheet metal technology; small business administration; sport and fitness administration/management; surgical technology; technology/industrial arts teacher education; tool and die technology; water quality and wastewater treatment management and recycling technology; web/multimedia management and webmaster; welding technology.

Academics *Calendar:* semesters. *Degree:* certificates and associate. *Special study options:* academic remediation for entering students, adult/continuing education programs, advanced placement credit, cooperative education, distance learning, double majors, freshman honors college, honors programs, independent study, internships, off-campus study, part-time degree program, services for LD students, study abroad, summer session for credit.

Library Library Learning Information Center. *Books:* 52,885 (physical), 2 (digital/electronic); *Serial titles:* 215 (physical); *Databases:* 89. Weekly public service hours: 65.

Student Life *Housing:* college housing not available. *Activities and Organizations:* drama/theater group, student-run newspaper, choral group, DECA, Phi Theta Kappa, DCSNA (student nursing association), Physical Therapy Assistant (PTA) Club, Honors. *Campus security:* 24-hour emergency response devices, student patrols, late-night transport/escort service. *Student services:* personal/psychological counseling, veterans affairs office.

Athletics Member NJCAA. *Intercollegiate sports:* baseball M, basketball M(s)/W(s), golf M, soccer W, softball W(s). *Intramural sports:* basketball M/W, cross-country running M/W, soccer M/W.

Costs (2020–21) *Tuition:* area resident $3510 full-time, $117 per contact hour part-time; state resident $5970 full-time, $199 per contact hour part-time; nonresident $11,190 full-time, $373 per contact hour part-time. Full-time tuition and fees vary according to course load. Part-time tuition and fees vary according to course load. *Required fees:* $710 full-time, $21 per contact hour part-time, $40 per term part-time. *Payment plan:* installment. *Waivers:* senior citizens and employees or children of employees.

Financial Aid Of all full-time matriculated undergraduates who enrolled in 2018, 115 Federal Work-Study jobs (averaging $2307). 67 state and other part-time jobs (averaging $2214).

Applying *Options:* electronic application, early admission, deferred entrance. *Required for some:* essay or personal statement. *Recommended:* high school transcript. *Application deadlines:* rolling (freshmen), rolling (transfers). *Notification:* continuous (freshmen), continuous (transfers).

Freshman Application Contact Mr. Jason Premo, Director of Admissions and Career Development, Delta College, 1961 Delta Road, University Center, MI 48710. *Phone:* 989-686-9584. *Fax:* 989-667-2202. *E-mail:* admit@delta.edu.
Website: http://www.delta.edu/.

Glen Oaks Community College

Centreville, Michigan

- **State and locally supported** 2-year, founded 1965
- **Rural** 300-acre campus
- **Coed**

Undergraduates 531 full-time, 690 part-time. 6% are from out of state; 6% Black or African American, non-Hispanic/Latino; 6% Hispanic/Latino; 1% Asian, non-Hispanic/Latino; 0.4% American Indian or Alaska Native, non-Hispanic/Latino; 3% Race/ethnicity unknown; 0.1% international; 4% transferred in. *Retention:* 56% of full-time freshmen returned.

Faculty *Student/faculty ratio:* 22:1.

Academics *Calendar:* semesters. *Degree:* certificates and associate. *Special study options:* academic remediation for entering students, advanced placement credit, distance learning, internships, part-time degree program, services for LD students, summer session for credit.

Library E. J. Shaheen Library.

Student Life *Campus security:* 24-hour emergency response devices.

Athletics Member NJCAA.

Financial Aid Of all full-time matriculated undergraduates who enrolled in 2018, 70 Federal Work-Study jobs (averaging $1100). 38 state and other part-time jobs (averaging $1200).

Applying *Options:* electronic application. *Required:* high school transcript.

Freshman Application Contact Ms. Beverly M. Andrews, Director of Admissions/Registrar, Glen Oaks Community College, 62249 Shimmel Road, Centreville, MI 49032-9719. *Phone:* 269-294-4249. *Toll-free phone:* 888-994-7818. *Fax:* 269-467-4114. *E-mail:* thowden@glenoaks.edu. *Website:* http://www.glenoaks.edu/.

Gogebic Community College

Ironwood, Michigan

Freshman Application Contact Ms. Kim Zeckovich, Director of Admissions, Marketing, and Public Relations, Gogebic Community College, E. 4946 Jackson Road, Ironwood, MI 49938. *Phone:* 906-932-4231 Ext. 347. *Toll-free phone:* 800-682-5910. *Fax:* 906-932-2339. *E-mail:* jeanneg@gogebic.edu. *Website:* http://www.gogebic.edu/.

Grand Rapids Community College

Grand Rapids, Michigan

- **District-supported** 2-year, founded 1914, part of Michigan Department of Education
- **Urban** 35-acre campus
- **Endowment** $39.2 million
- **Coed,** 13,252 undergraduate students, 30% full-time, 53% women, 47% men

Undergraduates 4,017 full-time, 9,235 part-time. Students come from 6 states and territories; 6 other countries; 1% are from out of state; 9% Black or African American, non-Hispanic/Latino; 15% Hispanic/Latino; 4% Asian, non-Hispanic/Latino; 0.1% Native Hawaiian or other Pacific Islander, non-Hispanic/Latino; 0.5% American Indian or Alaska Native, non-Hispanic/Latino; 3% Two or more races, non-Hispanic/Latino; 6% Race/ethnicity unknown; 0.4% international; 7% transferred in.

Freshmen *Admission:* 8,687 applied, 2,777 enrolled. *Average high school GPA:* 2.8.

Faculty *Total:* 667, 32% full-time. *Student/faculty ratio:* 19:1.

Majors Accounting technology and bookkeeping; architectural technology; architecture; art; automation engineer technology; automobile/automotive mechanics technology; business administration and management; chemical technology; child-care and support services management; commercial and advertising art; computer programming; computer support specialist; computer systems networking and telecommunications; corrections; criminal justice/police science; culinary arts; dental assisting; dental hygiene; electrical, electronic and communications engineering technology; fashion merchandising; fine/studio arts; heating, air conditioning, ventilation and refrigeration maintenance technology; industrial mechanics and maintenance technology; interior design; landscaping and groundskeeping; liberal arts and sciences/liberal studies; manufacturing engineering technology; music; music teacher education; plastics and polymer engineering technology; quality control technology; registered nursing/registered nurse; restaurant, culinary, and catering management; web page, digital/multimedia and information resources design; welding technology.

Academics *Calendar:* semesters. *Degree:* certificates and associate. *Special study options:* academic remediation for entering students, adult/continuing education programs, advanced placement credit, cooperative education, distance learning, English as a second language, honors programs, independent study, internships, off-campus study, part-time degree program, services for LD students, study abroad, summer session for credit.

Library Arthur Andrews Memorial Library. *Books:* 67,050 (physical), 168,882 (digital/electronic); *Serial titles:* 357 (physical), 25,196 (digital/electronic); *Databases:* 100. Students can reserve study rooms.

Student Life *Housing:* college housing not available. *Activities and Organizations:* drama/theater group, student-run newspaper, choral group, Student Alliance, Phi Theta Kappa, Hispanic Student Organization, Student Gamers Association, Foreign Affairs Club. *Campus security:* 24-hour emergency response devices, late-night transport/escort service. *Student services:* personal/psychological counseling, veterans affairs office.

Athletics Member NJCAA. *Intercollegiate sports:* baseball M(s), basketball M(s)/W(s), cross-country running M/W, golf M(s), softball W(s), volleyball W(s).

Costs (2019–20) *Tuition:* area resident $3450 full-time, $115 per contact hour part-time; state resident $7350 full-time, $245 per contact hour part-time;

nonresident $10,950 full-time, $365 per contact hour part-time. Full-time tuition and fees vary according to course load and program. Part-time tuition and fees vary according to course load and program. *Required fees:* $459 full-time, $15 per contact hour part-time, $90 per contact part-time. *Payment plan:* installment. *Waivers:* employees or children of employees.
Financial Aid Of all full-time matriculated undergraduates who enrolled in 2008, 6,142 applied for aid, 4,896 were judged to have need, 1,012 had their need fully met. In 2008, 96 non-need-based awards were made. *Average financial aid package:* $4850. *Average need-based loan:* $2764. *Average need-based gift aid:* $3984. *Average non-need-based aid:* $1051.
Applying *Options:* electronic application, deferred entrance. *Required:* high school transcript. *Application deadline:* rolling (transfers). *Notification:* continuous (freshmen), continuous (transfers).
Freshman Application Contact Ms. Lori Cook, Director of Admissions, Grand Rapids Community College, Grand Rapids, MI 49503-3201. *Phone:* 616-234-4100. *Fax:* 616-234-4005. *E-mail:* lcook@grcc.edu.
Website: http://www.grcc.edu/.

Henry Ford College
Dearborn, Michigan

Freshman Application Contact Admissions Office, Henry Ford College, 5101 Evergreen Road, Dearborn, MI 48128-1495. *Phone:* 313-845-6403. *Toll-free phone:* 800-585-HFCC. *Fax:* 313-845-6464. *E-mail:* enroll@hfcc.edu. *Website:* http://www.hfcc.edu/.

Jackson College
Jackson, Michigan

Freshman Application Contact Mr. Daniel Vainner, Registrar, Jackson College, 2111 Emmons Road, Jackson, MI 49201. *Phone:* 517-796-8425. *Toll-free phone:* 888-522-7344. *Fax:* 517-796-8446. *E-mail:* admissions@jccmi.edu. *Website:* http://www.jccmi.edu/.

Kalamazoo Valley Community College
Kalamazoo, Michigan

Freshman Application Contact Kalamazoo Valley Community College, PO Box 4070, Kalamazoo, MI 49003-4070. *Phone:* 269-488-4207. *Website:* http://www.kvcc.edu/.

Kellogg Community College
Battle Creek, Michigan

Freshman Application Contact Ms. Nicole Jewell, Director of Admissions, Kellogg Community College, 450 North Avenue, Battle Creek, MI 49017. *Phone:* 269-965-3931. *Fax:* 269-965-4133. *E-mail:* jewelln@kellogg.edu. *Website:* http://www.kellogg.edu/.

Keweenaw Bay Ojibwa Community College
Baraga, Michigan

Freshman Application Contact Ms. Megan Shanahan, Admissions Officer, Keweenaw Bay Ojibwa Community College, 111 Beartown Road, Baraga, MI 49908. *Phone:* 909-353-4600. *E-mail:* megan@kbocc.org. *Website:* http://www.kbocc.edu/.

Kirtland Community College
Roscommon, Michigan

- **District-supported** 2-year, founded 1966
- **Rural** 180-acre campus
- **Coed,** 1,460 undergraduate students, 31% full-time, 58% women, 42% men

Undergraduates 447 full-time, 1,013 part-time. Students come from 4 states and territories; 1% Black or African American, non-Hispanic/Latino; 2% Hispanic/Latino; 0.9% Asian, non-Hispanic/Latino; 0.1% Native Hawaiian or other Pacific Islander, non-Hispanic/Latino; 1% American Indian or Alaska Native, non-Hispanic/Latino; 1% Two or more races, non-Hispanic/Latino; 3% Race/ethnicity unknown; 0.1% international.
Freshmen *Admission:* 468 applied, 468 admitted, 191 enrolled.
Faculty *Total:* 92, 30% full-time. *Student/faculty ratio:* 16:1.
Majors Accounting technology and bookkeeping; automobile/automotive mechanics technology; business administration and management; cardiovascular technology; cosmetology; criminal justice/law enforcement administration; criminal justice/police science; electrical, electronic and communications engineering technology; electromechanical technology; general studies; graphic design; health information/medical records technology; heating, air conditioning, ventilation and refrigeration maintenance technology; liberal arts and sciences/liberal studies; management information systems; medical/clinical assistant; registered nursing/registered nurse; robotics technology; surgical technology; welding technology; wood science and wood products/pulp and paper technology.
Academics *Calendar:* semesters. *Degree:* certificates and associate. *Special study options:* academic remediation for entering students, adult/continuing education programs, advanced placement credit, cooperative education, distance learning, honors programs, independent study, internships, part-time degree program, services for LD students, summer session for credit.
Library Kirtland Community College Library plus 1 other. *Books:* 20,064 (physical), 1,307 (digital/electronic); *Serial titles:* 70 (physical); *Databases:* 51. Weekly public service hours: 40; students can reserve study rooms.
Student Life *Housing:* college housing not available. *Campus security:* 24-hour emergency response devices, student patrols, late-night transport/escort service, campus warning siren, uniformed armed police officers, RAVE alert system (text, email, voice).
Athletics Member NJCAA. *Intercollegiate sports:* bowling M(s)/W(s), cross-country running M(s)/W(s), golf M(s)/W(s).
Standardized Tests *Recommended:* SAT or ACT (for admission).
Costs (2019–20) *Tuition:* area resident $3630 full-time, $121 per contact hour part-time; state resident $5460 full-time, $182 per contact hour part-time; nonresident $7800 full-time, $260 per contact hour part-time. *Required fees:* $630 full-time, $21 per contact hour part-time. *Payment plan:* installment. *Waivers:* senior citizens and employees or children of employees.
Financial Aid Of all full-time matriculated undergraduates who enrolled in 2018, 50 Federal Work-Study jobs (averaging $1253). 28 state and other part-time jobs (averaging $1647).
Applying *Options:* electronic application. *Required:* high school transcript. *Application deadlines:* rolling (freshmen), rolling (transfers). *Notification:* continuous until 8/15 (freshmen), continuous until 8/15 (transfers).
Freshman Application Contact Ms. Michelle Vyskocil, Dean of Student Services, Kirtland Community College, 4800 W 4 Mile Road, Grayling, MI 49738. *Phone:* 989-275-5000 Ext. 248. *Fax:* 989-275-6789. *E-mail:* registrar@kirtland.edu.
Website: http://www.kirtland.edu/.

Lake Michigan College
Benton Harbor, Michigan

Freshman Application Contact Mr. Louis Thomas, Lead Admissions Specialist, Lake Michigan College, 2755 East Napier Avenue, Benton Harbor, MI 49022-1899. *Phone:* 269-927-6584. *Toll-free phone:* 800-252-1LMC. *Fax:* 269-927-6718. *E-mail:* thomas@lakemichigancollege.edu. *Website:* http://www.lakemichigancollege.edu/.

Lansing Community College
Lansing, Michigan

Freshman Application Contact Ms. Tammy Grossbauer, Director of Admissions/Registrar, Lansing Community College, 1121 Enrollment Services, PO BOX 40010, Lansing, MI 48901. *Phone:* 517-483-1200. *Toll-free phone:* 800-644-4LCC. *Fax:* 517-483-1170. *E-mail:* grossbt@lcc.edu. *Website:* http://www.lcc.edu/.

Macomb Community College
Warren, Michigan

Freshman Application Contact Mr. Brian Bouwman, Coordinator of Admissions and Transfer Credit, Macomb Community College, 14500 East 12 Mile Road, Warren, MI 48088-3896. *Phone:* 586-445-7246. *Toll-free phone:* 866-MACOMB1. *Fax:* 586-445-7140. *E-mail:* stevensr@macomb.edu. *Website:* http://www.macomb.edu/.

MIAT College of Technology
Canton, Michigan

Admissions Office Contact MIAT College of Technology, 2955 South Haggerty Road, Canton, MI 48188. *Website:* http://www.miat.edu/.

Mid Michigan Community College
Harrison, Michigan

Freshman Application Contact Jennifer Casebeer, Admissions Specialist, Mid Michigan Community College, 1375 South Clare Avenue, Harrison, MI

48625-9447. *Phone:* 989-386-6661. *E-mail:* apply@midmich.edu. *Website:* http://www.midmich.edu/.

Monroe County Community College

Monroe, Michigan

- **County-supported** 2-year, founded 1964, part of Michigan Department of Education
- **Small-town** 150-acre campus with easy access to Detroit, Toledo
- **Coed**

Undergraduates 954 full-time, 2,190 part-time. Students come from 2 other countries; 4% are from out of state; 18% Black or African American, non-Hispanic/Latino; 10% Hispanic/Latino; 4% Asian, non-Hispanic/Latino; 0.4% American Indian or Alaska Native, non-Hispanic/Latino; 4% Two or more races, non-Hispanic/Latino; 8% Race/ethnicity unknown; 1% international. *Retention:* 61% of full-time freshmen returned.
Academics *Calendar:* semesters. *Degree:* certificates and associate. *Special study options:* academic remediation for entering students, advanced placement credit, distance learning, honors programs, independent study, part-time degree program, services for LD students, study abroad, summer session for credit.
Library Campbell Learning Resource Center.
Student Life *Campus security:* police patrols during open hours.
Standardized Tests *Required:* ACT, ACT Compass, SAT, ACCUPLACER (for admission). *Recommended:* SAT (for admission), ACT (for admission).
Costs (2019–20) *Tuition:* area resident $3174 full-time, $132 per credit hour part-time; state resident $5268 full-time, $220 per credit hour part-time; nonresident $5808 full-time, $242 per credit hour part-time. Full-time tuition and fees vary according to reciprocity agreements. Part-time tuition and fees vary according to reciprocity agreements. *Required fees:* $80 full-time, $40 per term part-time.
Applying *Options:* early admission, deferred entrance. *Required:* high school transcript.
Freshman Application Contact Mr. Ryan Rafko, Director of Admissions and Guidance Services, Monroe County Community College, 1555 South Raisinville Road, Monroe, MI 48161. *Phone:* 734-384-4261. *Toll-free phone:* 877-YES-MCCC. *Fax:* 734-242-9711. *E-mail:* rrafko@monroeccc.edu. *Website:* http://www.monroeccc.edu/.

Montcalm Community College

Sidney, Michigan

Freshman Application Contact Ms. Debra Alexander, Associate Dean of Student Services, Montcalm Community College, 2800 College Drive, SW, Sidney, MI 48885. *Phone:* 989-328-1276. *Toll-free phone:* 877-328-2111. *E-mail:* admissions@montcalm.edu. *Website:* http://www.montcalm.edu/.

Mott Community College

Flint, Michigan

Freshman Application Contact Ms. Regina Broomfield, Director, Admissions, Mott Community College, 1401 East Court Street, Flint, MI 48503. *Phone:* 810-762-0358. *Toll-free phone:* 800-852-8614. *Fax:* 810-232-9442. *E-mail:* regina.broomfield@mcc.edu. *Website:* http://www.mcc.edu/.

Muskegon Community College

Muskegon, Michigan

- **State and locally supported** 2-year, founded 1926, part of Michigan Department of Education
- **Small-town** 112-acre campus with easy access to Grand Rapids
- **Coed**

Undergraduates 1,488 full-time, 3,018 part-time. Students come from 4 states and territories; 9% Black or African American, non-Hispanic/Latino; 3% Hispanic/Latino; 0.8% Asian, non-Hispanic/Latino; 0.1% Native Hawaiian or other Pacific Islander, non-Hispanic/Latino; 0.9% American Indian or Alaska Native, non-Hispanic/Latino; 4% Two or more races, non-Hispanic/Latino; 5% Race/ethnicity unknown; 0.4% international; 5% transferred in. *Retention:* 62% of full-time freshmen returned.
Faculty *Student/faculty ratio:* 19:1.
Academics *Calendar:* semesters. *Degree:* associate. *Special study options:* academic remediation for entering students, adult/continuing education programs, cooperative education, honors programs, part-time degree program, student-designed majors, summer session for credit.
Library Hendrik Meijer and Technology Center.
Student Life *Campus security:* 24-hour emergency response devices, on-campus security officer.
Athletics Member NJCAA.
Financial Aid Of all full-time matriculated undergraduates who enrolled in 2018, 250 Federal Work-Study jobs (averaging $2500). 50 state and other part-time jobs (averaging $2500).
Applying *Options:* electronic application, early admission, deferred entrance. *Required:* high school transcript.
Freshman Application Contact Mr. Johnathon Skidmore, Senior Clerk 1 Admissions, Muskegon Community College, 221 South Quarterline Road, Muskegon, MI 49442-1493. *Phone:* 231-777-0366. *Toll-free phone:* 866-711-4622. *E-mail:* johnathon.skidmore@muskegoncc.edu. *Website:* http://www.muskegoncc.edu/.

North Central Michigan College

Petoskey, Michigan

Director of Admissions Ms. Julieanne Tobin, Director of Enrollment Management, North Central Michigan College, 1515 Howard Street, Petoskey, MI 49770-8717. *Phone:* 231-439-6511. *Toll-free phone:* 888-298-6605. *E-mail:* jtobin@ncmich.edu. *Website:* http://www.ncmich.edu/.

Northwestern Michigan College

Traverse City, Michigan

Freshman Application Contact Catheryn Claerhout, Director of Admissions, Northwestern Michigan College, 1701 E. Front Street, Traverse City, MI 49686. *Phone:* 231-995-1034. *Toll-free phone:* 800-748-0566. *E-mail:* c.claerhout@nmc.edu. *Website:* http://www.nmc.edu/.

Oakland Community College

Bloomfield Hills, Michigan

Freshman Application Contact Stephan M. Linden, Registrar, Oakland Community College, 2480 Opdyke Road, Bloomfield Hills, MI 48304-2266. *Phone:* 248-341-2192. *Fax:* 248-341-2099. *E-mail:* smlinden@oaklandcc.edu. *Website:* http://www.oaklandcc.edu/.

Saginaw Chippewa Tribal College

Mount Pleasant, Michigan

Freshman Application Contact Ms. Amanda Flaugher, Admissions Officer/Registrar/Financial Aid, Saginaw Chippewa Tribal College, 2274 Enterprise Drive, Mount Pleasant, MI 48858. *Phone:* 989-317-4760. *Fax:* 989-317-4781. *E-mail:* aflaugher@sagchip.edu. *Website:* http://www.sagchip.edu/.

St. Clair County Community College

Port Huron, Michigan

Freshman Application Contact St. Clair County Community College, 323 Erie Street, PO Box 5015, Port Huron, MI 48061-5015. *Phone:* 810-989-5501. *Toll-free phone:* 800-553-2427. *Website:* http://www.sc4.edu/.

Schoolcraft College

Livonia, Michigan

- **District-supported** primarily 2-year, founded 1961, part of Michigan Department of Education
- **Suburban** campus with easy access to Detroit
- **Coed,** 9,230 undergraduate students, 24% full-time, 54% women, 46% men

Undergraduates 2,240 full-time, 6,990 part-time. 14% Black or African American, non-Hispanic/Latino; 5% Hispanic/Latino; 5% Asian, non-Hispanic/Latino; 0.1% Native Hawaiian or other Pacific Islander, non-Hispanic/Latino; 0.4% American Indian or Alaska Native, non-Hispanic/Latino; 3% Two or more races, non-Hispanic/Latino; 6% Race/ethnicity unknown; 2% international; 9% transferred in. *Retention:* 66% of full-time freshmen returned.
Freshmen *Admission:* 1,744 enrolled. *Average high school GPA:* 2.8.
Faculty *Total:* 482, 18% full-time. *Student/faculty ratio:* 20:1.
Majors Accounting technology and bookkeeping; arts, entertainment, and media management; biomedical technology; business administration and management; business automation/technology/data entry; business/commerce; child development; computer graphics; computer programming; computer programming (specific applications); computer support specialist; computer systems networking and telecommunications; criminal justice/police science; culinary arts; drafting and design technology; education; electrical, electronic and communications engineering technology; emergency medical technology (EMT paramedic); engineering; environmental engineering technology; fine

arts related; fire science/firefighting; fire services administration; foods and nutrition related; general studies; health/health-care administration; health information/medical records technology; health services/allied health/health sciences; homeland security, law enforcement, firefighting and protective services related; manufacturing engineering technology; marketing/marketing management; massage therapy; mechatronics, robotics, and automation engineering; metallurgical technology; physical fitness technician; plastics and polymer engineering technology; pre-pharmacy studies; radio and television broadcasting technology; recording arts technology; registered nursing/registered nurse; salon/beauty salon management; small business administration; web page, digital/multimedia and information resources design; welding technology.

Academics *Calendar:* semesters. *Degrees:* certificates, associate, and bachelor's. *Special study options:* academic remediation for entering students, advanced placement credit, distance learning, English as a second language, honors programs, independent study, internships, part-time degree program, services for LD students, study abroad, summer session for credit.

Library Bradner Library plus 1 other. *Books:* 64,514 (physical), 319,132 (digital/electronic); *Serial titles:* 351 (physical); *Databases:* 142. Students can reserve study rooms.

Student Life *Housing:* college housing not available. *Activities and Organizations:* drama/theater group, student-run newspaper, Phi Theta Kappa, Early Childhood/Special Education Student Educators, Health Information Technology Club, Otaku Anime Japanese Animation Club, Student Nurse Association. *Campus security:* 24-hour emergency response devices and patrols, late-night transport/escort service. *Student services:* health clinic, personal/psychological counseling, women's center, veterans affairs office.

Athletics Member NJCAA. *Intercollegiate sports:* baseball M, basketball M(s)/W(s), bowling M/W, soccer M/W, softball W, volleyball W.

Costs (2020–21) *Tuition:* area resident $3198 full-time, $123 per credit hour part-time; state resident $4602 full-time, $177 per credit hour part-time; nonresident $6760 full-time, $260 per credit hour part-time. *Required fees:* $26 per credit hour part-time, $43 per term part-time. *Payment plan:* installment. *Waivers:* senior citizens and employees or children of employees.

Financial Aid Of all full-time matriculated undergraduates who enrolled in 2017, 124 Federal Work-Study jobs (averaging $4000).

Applying *Options:* electronic application, early admission, deferred entrance. *Required for some:* high school transcript. *Recommended:* high school transcript. *Application deadlines:* rolling (freshmen), rolling (transfers).

Freshman Application Contact Ms. Lisa Bushaw, Director of Admissions, Schoolcraft College, 18600 Haggerty Road, Livonia, MI 48152-2696. *Phone:* 734-462-4683. *E-mail:* admissions@schoolcraft.edu.
Website: http://www.schoolcraft.edu/.

Southwestern Michigan College

Dowagiac, Michigan

- **State and locally supported** 2-year, founded 1964
- **Rural** 240-acre campus
- **Coed,** 2,141 undergraduate students, 43% full-time, 60% women, 40% men

Undergraduates 910 full-time, 1,231 part-time. Students come from 12 states and territories; 1 other country; 17% are from out of state; 14% Black or African American, non-Hispanic/Latino; 5% Hispanic/Latino; 2% Asian, non-Hispanic/Latino; 0.1% Native Hawaiian or other Pacific Islander, non-Hispanic/Latino; 1% American Indian or Alaska Native, non-Hispanic/Latino; 4% Two or more races, non-Hispanic/Latino; 6% Race/ethnicity unknown; 0.1% international; 5% transferred in; 24% live on campus. *Retention:* 51% of full-time freshmen returned.

Freshmen *Admission:* 2,081 applied, 2,081 admitted, 573 enrolled.

Faculty *Total:* 111, 51% full-time, 26% with terminal degrees. *Student/faculty ratio:* 18:1.

Majors Accounting technology and bookkeeping; agricultural production; automation engineer technology; automobile/automotive mechanics technology; business administration and management; carpentry; computer programming; computer systems networking and telecommunications; criminal justice/safety; early childhood education; engineering technology; fire science/firefighting; general studies; graphic design; health information/medical records technology; industrial mechanics and maintenance technology; legal assistant/paralegal; liberal arts and sciences/liberal studies; medical/clinical assistant; registered nursing/registered nurse; social work; sport and fitness administration/management.

Academics *Calendar:* semesters. *Degree:* certificates and associate. *Special study options:* academic remediation for entering students, accelerated degree program, adult/continuing education programs, advanced placement credit, double majors, honors programs, independent study, internships, part-time degree program, services for LD students, summer session for credit.

Library Fred L. Mathews Library. *Books:* 20,028 (physical), 808 (digital/electronic); *Serial titles:* 4 (physical), 33,873 (digital/electronic); *Databases:* 49. Weekly public service hours: 61; students can reserve study rooms.

Student Life *Housing Options:* coed. Campus housing is university owned. *Activities and Organizations:* drama/theater group, choral group, Phi Theta Kappa Club, Black Student Union Club, SMC Cheer Club, Business Club, SMC Honors Club. *Campus security:* 24-hour emergency response devices and patrols, controlled dormitory access, Day and Evening police patrols. *Student services:* personal/psychological counseling.

Athletics *Intramural sports:* basketball M/W, football M/W, rock climbing M(c)/W(c), soccer M/W, softball M/W, ultimate Frisbee M/W, volleyball M/W.

Costs (2020–21) *Tuition:* area resident $3765 full-time, $126 per contact hour part-time; state resident $4943 full-time, $165 per contact hour part-time; nonresident $5385 full-time, $180 per contact hour part-time. *Required fees:* $1613 full-time, $54 per contact hour part-time. *Room and board:* $9450; room only: $6550. *Payment plan:* installment. *Waivers:* employees or children of employees.

Financial Aid Of all full-time matriculated undergraduates who enrolled in 2018, 125 Federal Work-Study jobs (averaging $1000). 75 state and other part-time jobs (averaging $1000).

Applying *Options:* electronic application, deferred entrance. *Required:* high school transcript. *Required for some:* interview. *Application deadlines:* rolling (freshmen), rolling (out-of-state freshmen), rolling (transfers). *Notification:* continuous (freshmen), continuous (out-of-state freshmen), continuous (transfers).

Freshman Application Contact Dr. Lucian Leone, Director of Admissions, Southwestern Michigan College, Dowagiac, MI 49047. *Phone:* 269-782-1000 Ext. 1238. *Toll-free phone:* 800-456-8675. *Fax:* 269-782-1371. *E-mail:* lleone@swmich.edu.
Website: http://www.swmich.edu/.

Washtenaw Community College

Ann Arbor, Michigan

Freshman Application Contact Washtenaw Community College, 4800 East Huron River Drive, PO Box D-1, Ann Arbor, MI 48106. *Phone:* 734-973-3315. *Website:* http://www.wccnet.edu/.

Wayne County Community College District

Detroit, Michigan

- **State and locally supported** 2-year, founded 1967
- **Urban** campus
- **Coed**

Undergraduates 2,005 full-time, 12,952 part-time. 69% Black or African American, non-Hispanic/Latino; 2% Hispanic/Latino; 0.6% Asian, non-Hispanic/Latino; 0.1% Native Hawaiian or other Pacific Islander, non-Hispanic/Latino; 0.2% American Indian or Alaska Native, non-Hispanic/Latino; 5% Two or more races, non-Hispanic/Latino; 6% Race/ethnicity unknown; 0.6% international; 10% transferred in.

Faculty *Student/faculty ratio:* 17:1.

Academics *Calendar:* semesters. *Degree:* certificates and associate. *Special study options:* academic remediation for entering students, adult/continuing education programs, advanced placement credit, cooperative education, distance learning, English as a second language, honors programs, internships, part-time degree program, services for LD students, study abroad, summer session for credit.

Library Learning Resource Center.

Student Life *Campus security:* 24-hour emergency response devices.

Athletics Member NJCAA.

Financial Aid Of all full-time matriculated undergraduates who enrolled in 2018, 239 Federal Work-Study jobs (averaging $2360). 147 state and other part-time jobs (averaging $1200).

Applying *Options:* electronic application, early admission, deferred entrance. *Required:* high school transcript.

Freshman Application Contact Mr. Adrian Phillips, District Associate Vice Chancellor of Student Services, Wayne County Community College District, 801 West Fort Street, Detroit, MI 48226-9975. *Phone:* 313-496-2820. *Fax:* 313-962-1643. *E-mail:* aphilli1@wcccd.edu. *Website:* http://www.wcccd.edu/.

West Shore Community College

Scottville, Michigan

Freshman Application Contact Wendy Fought, Director of Admissions, West Shore Community College, PO Box 277, 3000 North Stiles Road, Scottville, MI 49454-0277. *Phone:* 231-843-5503. *Fax:* 231-845-3944. *E-mail:* admissions@westshore.edu. *Website:* http://www.westshore.edu/.

MINNESOTA

Alexandria Technical and Community College

Alexandria, Minnesota

- **State-supported** 2-year, founded 1961, part of Minnesota State Colleges and Universities System
- **Small-town** 98-acre campus
- **Coed,** 2,481 undergraduate students, 44% full-time, 54% women, 46% men

Undergraduates 1,101 full-time, 1,380 part-time. Students come from 18 states and territories; 5% are from out of state; 1% Black or African American, non-Hispanic/Latino; 3% Hispanic/Latino; 1% Asian, non-Hispanic/Latino; 0.1% Native Hawaiian or other Pacific Islander, non-Hispanic/Latino; 1% American Indian or Alaska Native, non-Hispanic/Latino; 0.5% Race/ethnicity unknown.

Faculty *Total:* 93, 69% full-time, 5% with terminal degrees. *Student/faculty ratio:* 22:1.

Majors Accounting; automation engineer technology; business administration and management; business/commerce; clinical/medical laboratory technology; commercial and advertising art; computer systems networking and telecommunications; criminal justice/police science; diesel mechanics technology; early childhood education; fashion merchandising; human services; information science/studies; interior design; legal administrative assistant/secretary; legal assistant/paralegal; liberal arts and sciences/liberal studies; mechanical drafting and CAD/CADD; medical administrative assistant and medical secretary; multi/interdisciplinary studies related; office management; physical fitness technician; registered nursing/registered nurse; sales, distribution, and marketing operations; speech-language pathology assistant.

Academics *Calendar:* semesters. *Degree:* certificates, diplomas, and associate. *Special study options:* academic remediation for entering students, advanced placement credit, distance learning, double majors, independent study, internships, part-time degree program, services for LD students, student-designed majors, summer session for credit.

Library Learning Resource Center. *Books:* 7,532 (physical), 13,392 (digital/electronic); *Serial titles:* 26 (physical); *Databases:* 47. Weekly public service hours: 55; students can reserve study rooms.

Student Life *Housing:* college housing not available. *Activities and Organizations:* SkillsUSA, Collegiate DECA, Business Professionals of America (BPA), Phi Theta Kappa (PTK), HOSA-Future Health Professionals. *Campus security:* student patrols, late-night transport/escort service. *Student services:* personal/psychological counseling, veterans affairs office.

Athletics *Intramural sports:* basketball M/W, football M/W, softball M/W, volleyball M/W.

Costs (2019–20) *Tuition:* state resident $4963 full-time, $165 per credit part-time; nonresident $4963 full-time, $165 per credit part-time. *Required fees:* $603 full-time, $20 per credit part-time. *Payment plan:* installment. *Waivers:* senior citizens and employees or children of employees.

Applying *Options:* electronic application, early admission, deferred entrance. *Application fee:* $20. *Required for some:* high school transcript, interview. *Recommended:* interview. *Application deadlines:* rolling (freshmen), rolling (out-of-state freshmen), rolling (transfers). *Notification:* continuous (freshmen), continuous (out-of-state freshmen), continuous (transfers).

Freshman Application Contact Vicki Sward, Information Center Manager, Alexandria Technical and Community College, 1601 Jefferson Street, Alexandria, MN 56308. *Phone:* 320-762-4600. *Toll-free phone:* 888-234-1222. *Fax:* 320-762-4501. *E-mail:* info@alextech.edu.
Website: http://www.alextech.edu/.

Anoka-Ramsey Community College

Coon Rapids, Minnesota

- **State-supported** 2-year, founded 1965, part of Minnesota State Colleges and Universities System
- **Suburban** 230-acre campus with easy access to Minneapolis-St. Paul
- **Coed,** 8,834 undergraduate students, 38% full-time, 61% women, 39% men

Undergraduates 3,334 full-time, 5,474 part-time. 12% Black or African American, non-Hispanic/Latino; 7% Hispanic/Latino; 7% Asian, non-Hispanic/Latino; 0.2% Native Hawaiian or other Pacific Islander, non-Hispanic/Latino; 0.6% American Indian or Alaska Native, non-Hispanic/Latino; 5% Two or more races, non-Hispanic/Latino; 0.6% Race/ethnicity unknown; 0.6% international; 31% transferred in. *Retention:* 61% of full-time freshmen returned.

Freshmen *Admission:* 1,026 enrolled.

Faculty *Total:* 248, 51% full-time. *Student/faculty ratio:* 32:1.

Majors Accounting; accounting technology and bookkeeping; art; bioengineering and biomedical engineering; biology/biological sciences; biomedical technology; business administration and management; business/commerce; chemistry; community health and preventive medicine; computer and information systems security; computer science; computer systems networking and telecommunications; creative writing; dramatic/theater arts; elementary education; environmental science; fine/studio arts; health services/allied health/health sciences; holistic health; human resources management; interdisciplinary studies; kinesiology and exercise science; liberal arts and sciences/liberal studies; music; pharmacy technician; physical fitness technician; physical therapy technology; pre-engineering; registered nursing/registered nurse; sales, distribution, and marketing operations; special education; substance abuse/addiction counseling; visual and performing arts.

Academics *Calendar:* semesters. *Degree:* certificates and associate. *Special study options:* academic remediation for entering students, accelerated degree program, advanced placement credit, cooperative education, distance learning, double majors, English as a second language, honors programs, independent study, internships, off-campus study, part-time degree program, services for LD students, study abroad, summer session for credit. *ROTC:* Air Force (c).

Library Coon Rapids Campus Library plus 1 other. *Books:* 37,400 (physical), 17,311 (digital/electronic); *Serial titles:* 129 (physical); *Databases:* 31. Weekly public service hours: 63.

Student Life *Housing:* college housing not available. *Activities and Organizations:* drama/theater group, student-run newspaper, choral group, Student Nursing Association, Art Club, Psychology Club, Photography Club, Basketball. *Campus security:* 24-hour emergency response devices, late-night transport/escort service. *Student services:* health clinic, personal/psychological counseling, veterans affairs office.

Athletics Member NJCAA. *Intercollegiate sports:* baseball M, basketball M/W, soccer M/W, softball W, volleyball W. *Intramural sports:* badminton M/W, basketball M/W, bowling M/W, football M/W, golf M/W, ice hockey M/W, soccer M/W, softball M/W, tennis M/W, volleyball M/W.

Costs (2020–21) *Tuition:* state resident $4479 full-time, $149 per credit hour part-time; nonresident $4479 full-time, $149 per credit hour part-time. Full-time tuition and fees vary according to course load and program. Part-time tuition and fees vary according to course load and program. *Required fees:* $740 full-time, $25 per credit hour part-time. *Payment plans:* installment, deferred payment. *Waivers:* senior citizens and employees or children of employees.

Applying *Options:* electronic application, early admission, deferred entrance. *Required for some:* high school transcript. *Application deadlines:* rolling (freshmen), rolling (transfers). *Notification:* continuous (freshmen), continuous (transfers).

Freshman Application Contact Admissions Department, Anoka-Ramsey Community College, 11200 Mississippi Boulevard NW, Coon Rapids, MN 55433-3470. *Phone:* 763-433-1300. *Fax:* 763-433-1521. *E-mail:* admissions@anokaramsey.edu.
Website: http://www.anokaramsey.edu/.

Anoka Technical College

Anoka, Minnesota

- **State-supported** 2-year, founded 1967, part of Minnesota State Colleges and Universities System
- **Small-town** 23-acre campus with easy access to Minneapolis-St. Paul
- **Coed,** 1,838 undergraduate students, 39% full-time, 44% women, 39% men

Undergraduates 714 full-time, 813 part-time. 12% Black or African American, non-Hispanic/Latino; 5% Hispanic/Latino; 5% Asian, non-Hispanic/Latino; 0.4% American Indian or Alaska Native, non-Hispanic/Latino; 5% Two or more races, non-Hispanic/Latino; 0.8% Race/ethnicity unknown; 27% transferred in. *Retention:* 61% of full-time freshmen returned.

Freshmen *Admission:* 286 enrolled.

Faculty *Total:* 88, 60% full-time. *Student/faculty ratio:* 18:1.

Majors Accounting; administrative assistant and secretarial science; architectural drafting and CAD/CADD; automobile/automotive mechanics technology; biomedical technology; computer numerically controlled (CNC) machinist technology; computer technology/computer systems technology; court reporting; data processing and data processing technology; developmental services worker; electrical, electronic and communications engineering technology; golf course operation and grounds management; health information/medical records technology; landscaping and groundskeeping; legal administrative assistant/secretary; mechanical drafting and CAD/CADD; medical administrative assistant and medical secretary; medical/clinical assistant; occupational therapist assistant; office management; surgical technology; welding technology.

Academics *Calendar:* semesters. *Degree:* certificates, diplomas, and associate. *Special study options:* academic remediation for entering students, advanced placement credit, cooperative education, distance learning, double majors, English as a second language, internships, part-time degree program, services for LD students.
Library Anoka Technical College Library. *Books:* 7,402 (physical), 8,635 (digital/electronic); *Serial titles:* 17 (physical), 2 (digital/electronic); *Databases:* 41. Weekly public service hours: 59; students can reserve study rooms.
Student Life *Housing:* college housing not available. *Campus security:* 24-hour emergency response devices, late-night transport/escort service. *Student services:* personal/psychological counseling, veterans affairs office.
Costs (2020–21) *Tuition:* state resident $172 per credit hour part-time; nonresident $172 per credit hour part-time. Full-time tuition and fees vary according to course load, program, and reciprocity agreements. Part-time tuition and fees vary according to course load, program, and reciprocity agreements. *Payment plans:* installment, deferred payment. *Waivers:* senior citizens and employees or children of employees.
Applying *Options:* electronic application, deferred entrance. *Required:* high school transcript. *Required for some:* interview.
Freshman Application Contact Enrollment Services, Anoka Technical College, 1355 West Highway 10, Anoka, MN 55303. *Phone:* 763-576-7710. *E-mail:* enrollmentservices@anokatech.edu.
Website: http://www.anokatech.edu/.

Central Lakes College
Brainerd, Minnesota

- **State-supported** 2-year, founded 1938, part of Minnesota State Colleges and Universities System
- **Small-town** campus
- **Endowment** $7.3 million
- **Coed,** 4,357 undergraduate students, 37% full-time, 59% women, 41% men

Undergraduates 1,622 full-time, 2,735 part-time. Students come from 26 states and territories; 2% are from out of state. *Retention:* 58% of full-time freshmen returned.
Faculty *Total:* 135, 69% full-time. *Student/faculty ratio:* 20:1.
Majors Accounting; administrative assistant and secretarial science; applied horticulture/horticulture operations; business administration and management; child-care and support services management; commercial and advertising art; computer systems networking and telecommunications; computer technology/computer systems technology; conservation biology; criminalistics and criminal science; criminal justice/police science; criminal justice/safety; developmental and child psychology; diesel mechanics technology; engineering; horticultural science; industrial electronics technology; industrial engineering; kindergarten/preschool education; legal administrative assistant/secretary; liberal arts and sciences/liberal studies; machine tool technology; marketing/marketing management; mechanical drafting and CAD/CADD; medical administrative assistant and medical secretary; natural resources/conservation; photographic and film/video technology; registered nursing/registered nurse; robotics technology; welding technology.
Academics *Calendar:* semesters. *Degree:* certificates, diplomas, and associate. *Special study options:* academic remediation for entering students, advanced placement credit, distance learning, English as a second language, external degree program, independent study, internships, off-campus study, part-time degree program, services for LD students, summer session for credit.
Library Learning Resource Center.
Student Life *Housing:* college housing not available. *Activities and Organizations:* drama/theater group, student-run newspaper, television station, choral group. *Campus security:* 24-hour emergency response devices and patrols, student patrols, late-night transport/escort service. *Student services:* health clinic, personal/psychological counseling, veterans affairs office.
Athletics Member NJCAA. *Intercollegiate sports:* baseball M, basketball M/W, football M, softball W, volleyball W. *Intramural sports:* basketball M/W, bowling M/W, football M, softball M/W, tennis M/W, volleyball M/W.
Costs (2019–20) *Tuition:* state resident $4916 full-time, $164 per credit hour part-time; nonresident $4916 full-time, $164 per credit hour part-time. Full-time tuition and fees vary according to course load and program. Part-time tuition and fees vary according to course load and program. *Required fees:* $760 full-time, $25 per credit hour part-time. *Payment plan:* installment. *Waivers:* senior citizens and employees or children of employees.
Applying *Options:* electronic application, deferred entrance. *Application fee:* $20. *Required:* high school transcript. *Application deadlines:* rolling (freshmen), rolling (transfers).
Freshman Application Contact Ms. Tambera Topp, Central Lakes College, 501 West College Drive, Brainerd, MN 56401-3904. *Phone:* 218-855-8036. *Toll-free phone:* 800-933-0346. *Fax:* 218-855-8220. *E-mail:* tambera.topp@clcmn.edu.
Website: http://www.clcmn.edu/.

Century College
White Bear Lake, Minnesota

- **State-supported** 2-year, founded 1970, part of Minnesota State Colleges and Universities System
- **Suburban** 170-acre campus with easy access to Minneapolis-St. Paul
- **Coed,** 8,653 undergraduate students, 40% full-time, 57% women, 43% men

Undergraduates 3,477 full-time, 5,176 part-time. Students come from 37 states and territories; 50 other countries; 6% are from out of state; 11% Black or African American, non-Hispanic/Latino; 10% Hispanic/Latino; 19% Asian, non-Hispanic/Latino; 0.1% Native Hawaiian or other Pacific Islander, non-Hispanic/Latino; 0.3% American Indian or Alaska Native, non-Hispanic/Latino; 5% Two or more races, non-Hispanic/Latino; 0.9% Race/ethnicity unknown; 2% international; 12% transferred in.
Freshmen *Admission:* 3,017 applied, 3,017 admitted, 1,146 enrolled. *Average high school GPA:* 2.7.
Faculty *Total:* 362, 46% full-time, 17% with terminal degrees. *Student/faculty ratio:* 22:1.
Majors Accounting; administrative assistant and secretarial science; animation, interactive technology, video graphics and special effects; applied horticulture/horticulture operations; art; autobody/collision and repair technology; biology/biological sciences; building/property maintenance; business administration and management; business/commerce; CAD/CADD drafting/design technology; chemistry; cinematography and film/video production; commercial photography; computer and information systems security; computer science; computer systems networking and telecommunications; cosmetology; criminal justice/police science; criminal justice/safety; crisis/emergency/disaster management; cyber/computer forensics and counterterrorism; data processing and data processing technology; dental assisting; dental hygiene; dramatic/theater arts; e-commerce; education; elementary education; emergency medical technology (EMT paramedic); energy management and systems technology; engineering technology; fire science/firefighting; geology/earth science; graphic design; health services/allied health/health sciences; heating, air conditioning, ventilation and refrigeration maintenance technology; horticultural science; human services; interior design; kinesiology and exercise science; liberal arts and sciences/liberal studies; marketing/marketing management; medical administrative assistant and medical secretary; multi/interdisciplinary studies related; music; orthotics/prosthetics; pre-engineering; radiologic technology/science; registered nursing/registered nurse; special education; substance abuse/addiction counseling; web page, digital/multimedia and information resources design.
Academics *Calendar:* semesters. *Degree:* certificates, diplomas, and associate. *Special study options:* academic remediation for entering students, advanced placement credit, distance learning, double majors, English as a second language, honors programs, independent study, internships, part-time degree program, services for LD students, student-designed majors, study abroad, summer session for credit. *ROTC:* Air Force (c).
Library Century College Library. *Books:* 58,144 (physical), 224,404 (digital/electronic); *Serial titles:* 204 (physical), 58,900 (digital/electronic); *Databases:* 72. Weekly public service hours: 65; students can reserve study rooms.
Student Life *Housing:* college housing not available. *Activities and Organizations:* drama/theater group, student-run newspaper, choral group, Anime Club, Phi Theta Kappa, Planning Activities Committee, Spanish Club, Nursing. *Campus security:* late-night transport/escort service, day patrols. *Student services:* health clinic, personal/psychological counseling, veterans affairs office.
Athletics Member NJCAA. *Intercollegiate sports:* baseball M, softball W. *Intramural sports:* badminton M/W, basketball M/W, bowling M/W, football M/W, ice hockey M/W, skiing (downhill) M/W, soccer M/W, softball M/W, table tennis M/W, ultimate Frisbee M/W, volleyball M/W.
Costs (2020–21) *Tuition:* area resident $4962 full-time, $165 per credit part-time; state resident $4962 full-time, $165 per credit part-time; nonresident $165 per credit part-time. Full-time tuition and fees vary according to class time, program, and reciprocity agreements. Part-time tuition and fees vary according to class time, program, and reciprocity agreements. *Required fees:* $616 full-time, $20 per credit part-time. *Payment plan:* installment. *Waivers:* senior citizens and employees or children of employees.
Financial Aid Of all full-time matriculated undergraduates who enrolled in 2018, 81 Federal Work-Study jobs (averaging $2763). 85 state and other part-time jobs (averaging $2646).
Applying *Options:* electronic application, deferred entrance. *Application fee:* $20. *Required:* high school transcript. *Application deadlines:* rolling (freshmen), rolling (out-of-state freshmen), rolling (transfers). *Notification:* continuous (freshmen), continuous (out-of-state freshmen), continuous (transfers).
Freshman Application Contact Robert Beaver, Assistant Admissions Director, Century College, 3300 Century Avenue North, White Bear Lake, MN

55110. *Phone:* 651-779-5744. *Toll-free phone:* 800-228-1978. *Fax:* 651-773-1796. *E-mail:* admissions@century.edu.
Website: http://www.century.edu/.

Dakota County Technical College
Rosemount, Minnesota

- **State-supported** 2-year, founded 1970, part of Minnesota State Colleges and Universities System
- **Suburban** 100-acre campus with easy access to Minneapolis-St. Paul
- **Endowment** $3.2 million
- **Coed**

Undergraduates 1,690 full-time, 1,982 part-time. Students come from 8 states and territories; 28 other countries; 3% are from out of state; 7% Black or African American, non-Hispanic/Latino; 3% Hispanic/Latino; 3% Asian, non-Hispanic/Latino; 0.8% American Indian or Alaska Native, non-Hispanic/Latino; 6% Race/ethnicity unknown; 0.8% international; 17% transferred in.
Faculty *Student/faculty ratio:* 30:1.
Academics *Calendar:* semesters. *Degree:* certificates, diplomas, and associate. *Special study options:* academic remediation for entering students, cooperative education, distance learning, double majors, English as a second language, independent study, internships, part-time degree program, services for LD students, student-designed majors, summer session for credit.
Library DCTC Library.
Student Life *Campus security:* 24-hour emergency response devices, late-night transport/escort service.
Athletics Member NJCAA.
Applying *Options:* electronic application. *Application fee:* $20. *Required for some:* high school transcript.
Freshman Application Contact Mr. Patrick Lair, Admissions Director, Dakota County Technical College, 1300 East 145th Street, Rosemount, MN 55068. *Phone:* 651-423-8399. *Toll-free phone:* 877-YES-DCTC. *Fax:* 651-423-8775. *E-mail:* admissions@dctc.mnscu.edu. *Website:* http://www.dctc.edu/.

Dunwoody College of Technology
Minneapolis, Minnesota

- **Independent** primarily 2-year, founded 1914
- **Urban** 11-acre campus with easy access to Minneapolis-St. Paul
- **Endowment** $23.3 million
- **Coed, primarily men,** 1,358 undergraduate students, 82% full-time, 18% women, 82% men

Undergraduates 1,109 full-time, 249 part-time. Students come from 3 other countries; 3% are from out of state; 4% Black or African American, non-Hispanic/Latino; 3% Hispanic/Latino; 5% Asian, non-Hispanic/Latino; 0.1% Native Hawaiian or other Pacific Islander, non-Hispanic/Latino; 0.7% American Indian or Alaska Native, non-Hispanic/Latino; 5% Two or more races, non-Hispanic/Latino; 15% Race/ethnicity unknown; 0.2% international; 16% transferred in; 1% live on campus. *Retention:* 86% of full-time freshmen returned.
Freshmen *Admission:* 672 applied, 434 admitted, 237 enrolled. *Average high school GPA:* 2.8.
Faculty *Total:* 161, 55% full-time, 24% with terminal degrees. *Student/faculty ratio:* 11:1.
Majors Architectural technology; architecture; autobody/collision and repair technology; automobile/automotive mechanics technology; building/construction site management; business administration and management; CAD/CADD drafting/design technology; civil engineering technology; computer numerically controlled (CNC) machinist technology; computer software engineering; computer systems analysis; computer systems networking and telecommunications; construction management; desktop publishing and digital imaging design; electrical and electronics engineering; electrical, electronic and communications engineering technology; electrical/electronics drafting and CAD/CADD; electrician; facilities planning and management; graphic design; heating, air conditioning, ventilation and refrigeration maintenance technology; heating, ventilation, air conditioning and refrigeration engineering technology; interior design; manufacturing engineering; mechanical engineering; medical radiologic technology; web page, digital/multimedia and information resources design; welding technology.
Academics *Calendar:* semesters. *Degrees:* certificates, associate, and bachelor's. *Special study options:* academic remediation for entering students, adult/continuing education programs, cooperative education, distance learning, double majors, independent study, internships, study abroad, summer session for credit.
Library Learning Resource Center plus 1 other. *Books:* 8,000 (physical), 188,153 (digital/electronic); *Serial titles:* 136 (physical); *Databases:* 26. Weekly public service hours: 55.
Student Life *Housing Options:* coed. Campus housing is university owned. *Activities and Organizations:* Phi Theta Kappa, Historic Green, Dunwoody Motorsports Club, Architectural Institute of America Student Chapter, Professional Association for Design. *Campus security:* 24-hour emergency response devices, late-night transport/escort service. *Student services:* women's center.
Standardized Tests *Required for some:* SAT or ACT (for admission).
Costs (2020–21) *Tuition:* $21,941 full-time, $815 per credit hour part-time. Full-time tuition and fees vary according to course load and program. Part-time tuition and fees vary according to course load and program. *Required fees:* $1729 full-time. *Room only:* $1100. *Payment plan:* installment.
Financial Aid Of all full-time matriculated undergraduates who enrolled in 2018, 1,186 applied for aid, 985 were judged to have need, 32 had their need fully met. 17 Federal Work-Study jobs (averaging $6029). 26 state and other part-time jobs (averaging $6611). In 2018, 24 non-need-based awards were made. *Average percent of need met:* 34%. *Average financial aid package:* $12,031. *Average need-based loan:* $3562. *Average need-based gift aid:* $10,271. *Average non-need-based aid:* $4541. *Average indebtedness upon graduation:* $16,342.
Applying *Options:* electronic application, deferred entrance. *Application fee:* $50. *Required:* essay or personal statement, high school transcript, interview. *Required for some:* 1 letter of recommendation, ACT scores and Resumes. *Recommended:* minimum 2.5 GPA, interview. *Application deadlines:* rolling (freshmen), rolling (transfers). *Notification:* continuous (freshmen), continuous (transfers).
Freshman Application Contact Kelly O'Brien, Director of Admissions, Dunwoody College of Technology, 818 Dunwoody Boulevard, Minneapolis, MN 55403. *Phone:* 612-381-3302. *Toll-free phone:* 800-292-4625. *Fax:* 612-677-3131. *E-mail:* kobrien@dunwoody.edu.
Website: http://www.dunwoody.edu/.

Fond du Lac Tribal and Community College
Cloquet, Minnesota

Freshman Application Contact Kathie Jubie, Admissions Representative, Fond du Lac Tribal and Community College, 2101 14th Street, Cloquet, MN 55720. *Phone:* 218-879-0808. *Toll-free phone:* 800-657-3712. *E-mail:* admissions@fdltcc.edu. *Website:* http://www.fdltcc.edu/.

Hennepin Technical College
Brooklyn Park, Minnesota

Freshman Application Contact Admissions, Hennepin Technical College, 9000 Brooklyn Boulevard, Brooklyn Park, MN 55445. *Phone:* 763-488-2580. *Toll-free phone:* 800-345-4655 (in-state); 800-645-4655 (out-of-state). *Fax:* 763-550-2113. *E-mail:* info@hennepintech.edu. *Website:* http://www.hennepintech.edu/.

Herzing University
Minneapolis, Minnesota

Freshman Application Contact Ms. Shelly Larson, Director of Admissions, Herzing University, 5700 West Broadway, Minneapolis, MN 55428. *Phone:* 763-231-3155. *Toll-free phone:* 800-596-0724. *Fax:* 763-535-9205. *E-mail:* info@mpls.herzing.edu. *Website:* http://www.herzing.edu/minneapolis.

Hibbing Community College
Hibbing, Minnesota

Freshman Application Contact Admissions, Hibbing Community College, 1515 East 25th Street, Hibbing, MN 55746. *Phone:* 218-262-7200. *Toll-free phone:* 800-224-4HCC. *Fax:* 218-262-6717. *E-mail:* admissions@hibbing.edu. *Website:* http://www.hcc.mnscu.edu/.

The Institute of Production and Recording
Minneapolis, Minnesota

Freshman Application Contact The Institute of Production and Recording, 300 North 1st Avenue, Suite 500, Minneapolis, MN 55401. *Website:* http://www.ipr.edu/.

Inver Hills Community College

Inver Grove Heights, Minnesota

- **State-supported** 2-year, founded 1969, part of Minnesota State Colleges and Universities System
- **Suburban** 100-acre campus with easy access to Minneapolis-St. Paul
- **Coed**

Undergraduates 2,502 full-time, 3,840 part-time. Students come from 19 states and territories; 2% are from out of state; 11% Black or African American, non-Hispanic/Latino; 5% Hispanic/Latino; 6% Asian, non-Hispanic/Latino; 0.3% Native Hawaiian or other Pacific Islander, non-Hispanic/Latino; 1% American Indian or Alaska Native, non-Hispanic/Latino; 2% Race/ethnicity unknown; 0.6% international; 5% transferred in.

Academics *Calendar:* semesters. *Degree:* certificates and associate. *Special study options:* academic remediation for entering students, accelerated degree program, advanced placement credit, cooperative education, distance learning, English as a second language, external degree program, honors programs, independent study, internships, off-campus study, part-time degree program, services for LD students, summer session for credit. *ROTC:* Army (c), Air Force (c).

Student Life *Campus security:* late-night transport/escort service, evening police patrol.

Financial Aid Of all full-time matriculated undergraduates who enrolled in 2009, 3,600 applied for aid, 3,250 were judged to have need. 175 Federal Work-Study jobs (averaging $2300). 153 state and other part-time jobs (averaging $2300). *Average percent of need met:* 48. *Average financial aid package:* $4300. *Average need-based loan:* $4200. *Average need-based gift aid:* $3800.

Applying *Options:* electronic application. *Application fee:* $20. *Required for some:* high school transcript. *Recommended:* high school transcript.

Freshman Application Contact Mr. Casey Carmody, Admissions Representative, Inver Hills Community College, 2500 East 80th Street, Inver Grove Heights, MN 55076-3224. *Phone:* 651-450-3589. *Fax:* 651-450-3677. *E-mail:* admissions@inverhills.edu. *Website:* http://www.inverhills.edu/.

Itasca Community College

Grand Rapids, Minnesota

Freshman Application Contact Ms. Candace Perry, Director of Enrollment Services, Itasca Community College, Grand Rapids, MN 55744. *Phone:* 218-322-2340. *Toll-free phone:* 800-996-6422. *Fax:* 218-327-4350. *E-mail:* iccinfo@itascacc.edu. *Website:* http://www.itascacc.edu/.

Lake Superior College

Duluth, Minnesota

- **State-supported** 2-year, founded 1995, part of Minnesota State
- **Urban** 105-acre campus
- **Coed**

Undergraduates 1,849 full-time, 2,841 part-time. Students come from 34 states and territories; 13 other countries; 13% are from out of state; 3% Black or African American, non-Hispanic/Latino; 3% Hispanic/Latino; 2% Asian, non-Hispanic/Latino; 0.1% Native Hawaiian or other Pacific Islander, non-Hispanic/Latino; 2% American Indian or Alaska Native, non-Hispanic/Latino; 5% Two or more races, non-Hispanic/Latino; 0.7% Race/ethnicity unknown; 2% international; 34% transferred in.

Faculty *Student/faculty ratio:* 18:1.

Academics *Calendar:* semesters. *Degree:* certificates, diplomas, and associate. *Special study options:* academic remediation for entering students, advanced placement credit, distance learning, double majors, independent study, internships, part-time degree program, services for LD students, study abroad, summer session for credit.

Library Harold P. Erickson Library. Students can reserve study rooms.

Student Life *Campus security:* 24-hour emergency response devices, late-night transport/escort service.

Athletics Member NJCAA.

Applying *Options:* electronic application. *Application fee:* $20. *Required:* high school transcript.

Freshman Application Contact Ms. Sherry Sanchez Tibbetz, Interim Director of Admissions, Lake Superior College, 2101 Trinity Road, Duluth, MN 55811. *Phone:* 218-733-7601. *Toll-free phone:* 800-432-2884. *E-mail:* enroll@lsc.edu. *Website:* http://www.lsc.edu/.

Leech Lake Tribal College

Cass Lake, Minnesota

Freshman Application Contact Ms. Shelly Braford, Recruiter, Leech Lake Tribal College, PO Box 180, 6945 Littlewolf Road NW, Cass Lake, MN 56633. *Phone:* 218-335-4200 Ext. 4270. *Fax:* 218-335-4217. *E-mail:* shelly.braford@lltc.edu. *Website:* http://www.lltc.edu/.

Mesabi Range College

Virginia, Minnesota

- **State-supported** 2-year, founded 1918, part of Minnesota State
- **Small-town** 30-acre campus
- **Coed,** 1,169 undergraduate students, 52% full-time, 49% women, 51% men

Undergraduates 604 full-time, 561 part-time. Students come from 6 states and territories; 2 other countries; 10% Black or African American, non-Hispanic/Latino; 1% Hispanic/Latino; 0.7% Asian, non-Hispanic/Latino; 0.1% Native Hawaiian or other Pacific Islander, non-Hispanic/Latino; 5% American Indian or Alaska Native, non-Hispanic/Latino; 6% Race/ethnicity unknown; 10% live on campus.

Faculty *Total:* 135, 25% full-time. *Student/faculty ratio:* 22:1.

Majors Administrative assistant and secretarial science; business/commerce; computer graphics; computer/information technology services administration related; computer programming related; computer programming (specific applications); computer software and media applications related; computer systems networking and telecommunications; electrical/electronics equipment installation and repair; human services; information technology; instrumentation technology; liberal arts and sciences/liberal studies; pre-engineering; substance abuse/addiction counseling; web page, digital/multimedia and information resources design.

Academics *Calendar:* semesters. *Degree:* certificates, diplomas, and associate. *Special study options:* academic remediation for entering students, adult/continuing education programs, advanced placement credit, cooperative education, distance learning, independent study, internships, off-campus study, part-time degree program, services for LD students, student-designed majors, study abroad, summer session for credit.

Library Mesabi Library.

Student Life *Housing Options:* coed. Campus housing is university owned. *Activities and Organizations:* drama/theater group, Student Senate, Human Services Club, Career Program Clubs, Student Life Club, Gaming Club. *Student services:* personal/psychological counseling, veterans affairs office.

Athletics Member NJCAA. *Intercollegiate sports:* baseball M, basketball M/W, football M, softball W, volleyball W. *Intramural sports:* basketball M/W, ice hockey M/W, volleyball M/W.

Costs (2019–20) *Tuition:* area resident $4870 full-time, $162 per credit hour part-time; state resident $4870 full-time, $162 per credit hour part-time; nonresident $6087 full-time, $203 per credit hour part-time. Full-time tuition and fees vary according to program. *Required fees:* $600 full-time, $20 per credit hour part-time. *Room and board:* $6526; room only: $4726. *Waivers:* senior citizens and employees or children of employees.

Financial Aid Of all full-time matriculated undergraduates who enrolled in 2011, 168 Federal Work-Study jobs (averaging $1227). 82 state and other part-time jobs (averaging $1380).

Applying *Options:* electronic application, early admission, deferred entrance. *Application fee:* $20. *Required:* high school transcript. *Application deadlines:* rolling (freshmen), rolling (transfers). *Notification:* continuous (freshmen), continuous (transfers).

Freshman Application Contact Ms. Brenda Kochevar, Enrollment Services Director, Mesabi Range College, Virginia, MN 55792. *Phone:* 218-749-0314. *Toll-free phone:* 800-657-3860. *Fax:* 218-749-0318. *E-mail:* b.kochevar@mesabirange.edu.
Website: http://www.mesabirange.edu/.

Minneapolis Business College

Roseville, Minnesota

Freshman Application Contact Admissions Office, Minneapolis Business College, 1711 West County Road B, Roseville, MN 55113. *Phone:* 651-636-7406. *Toll-free phone:* 800-279-5200. *Website:* http://www.minneapolisbusinesscollege.edu/.

Minneapolis Community and Technical College

Minneapolis, Minnesota

Freshman Application Contact Minneapolis Community and Technical College, 1501 Hennepin Avenue, Minneapolis, MN 55403. *Phone:* 612-659-6200. *Toll-free phone:* 800-247-0911. *E-mail:* admissions.office@minneapolis.edu. *Website:* http://www.minneapolis.edu/.

Minnesota State College–Southeast Technical

Winona, Minnesota

- **State-supported** 2-year, founded 1992, part of Minnesota State Colleges and Universities System
- **Small-town** 132-acre campus with easy access to Minneapolis-St. Paul
- **Coed**

Undergraduates 710 full-time, 1,104 part-time. 26% are from out of state; 4% Black or African American, non-Hispanic/Latino; 4% Hispanic/Latino; 3% Asian, non-Hispanic/Latino; 0.1% Native Hawaiian or other Pacific Islander, non-Hispanic/Latino; 0.5% American Indian or Alaska Native, non-Hispanic/Latino; 4% Two or more races, non-Hispanic/Latino; 0.8% Race/ethnicity unknown; 0.4% international; 10% transferred in.
Faculty *Student/faculty ratio:* 15:1.
Academics *Calendar:* semesters. *Degree:* certificates, diplomas, and associate. *Special study options:* distance learning, double majors, internships.
Library Learning Resource Center.
Student Life *Campus security:* 24-hour emergency response devices, late-night transport/escort service.
Costs (2019–20) *Tuition:* state resident $5020 full-time, $172 per credit hour part-time; nonresident $5020 full-time, $172 per credit hour part-time. Full-time tuition and fees vary according to program. Part-time tuition and fees vary according to program. *Required fees:* $666 full-time, $17 per credit hour part-time. *Room and board:* $7448.
Financial Aid Of all full-time matriculated undergraduates who enrolled in 2017, 618 applied for aid, 542 were judged to have need, 19 had their need fully met. In 2017, 27. *Average percent of need met:* 38. *Average financial aid package:* $6659. *Average need-based loan:* $3227. *Average need-based gift aid:* $5021. *Average non-need-based aid:* $2012.
Applying *Options:* electronic application. *Application fee:* $20. *Required:* high school transcript. *Recommended:* interview.
Director of Admissions Tammy Vondrasek, Director of Enrollment Services, Minnesota State College–Southeast Technical, 1250 Homer Road, PO Box 409, Winona, MN 55987. *Phone:* 507-453-2639. *Toll-free phone:* 800-372-8164. *E-mail:* tvondrasek@southeastmn.edu. *Website:* http://www.southeastmn.edu/.

Minnesota State Community and Technical College

Fergus Falls, Minnesota

- **State-supported** 2-year, founded 1960, part of Minnesota State Colleges and Universities System
- **Rural** campus
- **Coed,** 2,429 undergraduate students, 16% full-time, 62% women, 38% men

Undergraduates 385 full-time, 2,044 part-time. 2% live on campus.
Freshmen *Admission:* 142 enrolled.
Majors Accounting; administrative assistant and secretarial science; agricultural and food products processing; architectural drafting and CAD/CADD; art; autobody/collision and repair technology; automobile/automotive mechanics technology; banking and financial support services; biochemistry and molecular biology; biology/biological sciences; building/construction site management; business administration and management; business automation/technology/data entry; business/commerce; cardiovascular technology; carpentry; chemistry; civil engineering technology; clinical/medical laboratory technology; computer and information systems security; computer engineering technology; computer programming; computer systems networking and telecommunications; computer technology/computer systems technology; construction management; cooking and related culinary arts; cosmetology; criminal justice/safety; dental assisting; dental hygiene; diesel mechanics technology; electrical and electronic engineering technologies related; electrical, electronic and communications engineering technology; environmental studies; equestrian studies; fashion merchandising; financial planning and services; fire services administration; graphic design; health information/medical records technology; heating, ventilation, air conditioning and refrigeration engineering technology; horse husbandry/equine science and management; human resources management; industrial mechanics and maintenance technology; information technology; legal administrative assistant/secretary; legal assistant/paralegal; liberal arts and sciences/liberal studies; licensed practical/vocational nurse training; lineworker; manufacturing engineering technology; marine maintenance and ship repair technology; marketing/marketing management; mechanical drafting and CAD/CADD; medical administrative assistant and medical secretary; merchandising, sales, and marketing operations related (general); multi/interdisciplinary studies related; music; office management; pharmacy technician; plumbing technology; pre-engineering; radiologic technology/science; registered nursing/registered nurse; sales, distribution, and marketing operations; sign language interpretation and translation; surgical technology; teacher assistant/aide; telecommunications technology; web page, digital/multimedia and information resources design.
Academics *Calendar:* semesters. *Degree:* certificates, diplomas, and associate. *Special study options:* academic remediation for entering students, accelerated degree program, advanced placement credit, cooperative education, distance learning, double majors, English as a second language, freshman honors college, honors programs, independent study, internships, off-campus study, part-time degree program, services for LD students, study abroad, summer session for credit.
Library Minnesota State Community and Technical College - Fergus Falls Library plus 4 others.
Student Life *Housing Options:* coed. Campus housing is university owned. *Activities and Organizations:* drama/theater group, choral group, Student Senate, Students In Free Enterprise (SIFE), Phi Theta Kappa, Business Professionals of America, SkillsUSA–VICA. *Campus security:* 24-hour emergency response devices, late-night transport/escort service, security for special events. *Student services:* personal/psychological counseling, women's center.
Financial Aid Of all full-time matriculated undergraduates who enrolled in 2017, 6,298 applied for aid. 95 Federal Work-Study jobs, 103 state and other part-time jobs. *Average financial aid package:* $7816. *Average need-based loan:* $3500. *Average need-based gift aid:* $750. *Financial aid deadline:* 7/1.
Applying *Options:* electronic application, early admission, deferred entrance. *Application fee:* $20.
Freshman Application Contact Minnesota State Community and Technical College, 1414 College Way, Fergus Falls, MN 56537-1009. *Toll-free phone:* 877-450-3322.
Website: http://www.minnesota.edu/.

Minnesota State Community and Technical College–Detroit Lakes

Detroit Lakes, Minnesota

- **State-supported** 2-year, founded 1966, part of Minnesota State Colleges and Universities System
- **Small-town** campus
- **Coed,** 755 undergraduate students, 41% full-time, 71% women, 29% men

Undergraduates 309 full-time, 446 part-time. Students come from 36 states and territories; 12% Black or African American, non-Hispanic/Latino; 5% Hispanic/Latino; 3% Asian, non-Hispanic/Latino; 0.1% Native Hawaiian or other Pacific Islander, non-Hispanic/Latino; 2% American Indian or Alaska Native, non-Hispanic/Latino; 5% Two or more races, non-Hispanic/Latino; 0.4% Race/ethnicity unknown.
Freshmen *Admission:* 119 enrolled.
Majors Accounting; administrative assistant and secretarial science; architectural drafting and CAD/CADD; architectural technology; civil engineering technology; computer and information systems security; early childhood education; engineering technology; entrepreneurship; legal assistant/paralegal; liberal arts and sciences/liberal studies; licensed practical/vocational nurse training; marine maintenance and ship repair technology; marketing/marketing management; multi/interdisciplinary studies related; nursing practice; office management; radiologic technology/science; registered nursing/registered nurse; sales, distribution, and marketing operations; teacher assistant/aide.
Academics *Calendar:* semesters. *Degree:* certificates, diplomas, and associate.
Student Life *Housing:* college housing not available.
Costs (2019–20) *One-time required fee:* $20. *Tuition:* state resident $4965 full-time, $166 per credit hour part-time; nonresident $4965 full-time, $166 per credit hour part-time. Full-time tuition and fees vary according to location and program. Part-time tuition and fees vary according to location and program. *Required fees:* $514 full-time. *Waivers:* senior citizens and employees or children of employees.
Applying *Application fee:* $20. *Required:* high school transcript, immunization record.
Freshman Application Contact Minnesota State Community and Technical College–Detroit Lakes, 900 Highway 34, E, Detroit Lakes, MN 56501. *Phone:* 218-846-3777. *Toll-free phone:* 800-492-4836.
Website: http://www.minnesota.edu/.

Minnesota State Community and Technical College–Moorhead

Moorhead, Minnesota

- **State-supported** 2-year, part of Minnesota State Colleges and Universities System
- **Rural** campus
- **Coed,** 2,276 undergraduate students, 50% full-time, 55% women, 45% men
- 64% of applicants were admitted

Undergraduates 1,139 full-time, 1,137 part-time. Students come from 36 states and territories; 12% Black or African American, non-Hispanic/Latino; 5% Hispanic/Latino; 3% Asian, non-Hispanic/Latino; 0.1% Native Hawaiian or other Pacific Islander, non-Hispanic/Latino; 2% American Indian or Alaska Native, non-Hispanic/Latino; 5% Two or more races, non-Hispanic/Latino; 0.4% Race/ethnicity unknown.
Freshmen *Admission:* 3,849 applied, 2,467 admitted, 484 enrolled.
Faculty *Total:* 276, 56% full-time.
Majors Accounting; administrative assistant and secretarial science; automobile/automotive mechanics technology; automotive engineering technology; biology/biological sciences; business administration and management; business/commerce; cardiovascular technology; chemistry; computer programming; computer systems networking and telecommunications; construction management; criminal justice/law enforcement administration; criminal justice/safety; dental assisting; dental hygiene; diesel mechanics technology; dramatic/theater arts; engineering; environmental studies; graphic design; human resources development; human resources management; information technology; liberal arts and sciences/liberal studies; licensed practical/vocational nurse training; mechanical drafting and CAD/CADD; medical administrative assistant and medical secretary; multi/interdisciplinary studies related; nursing practice; office management; plumbing technology; pre-engineering; registered nursing/registered nurse; sales, distribution, and marketing operations; sign language interpretation and translation; surgical technology.
Academics *Calendar:* semesters. *Degree:* certificates, diplomas, and associate.
Athletics Member NJCAA. *Intercollegiate sports:* baseball M, basketball M/W, football M, golf M/W, softball W, volleyball W.
Costs (2020–21) *One-time required fee:* $20. *Tuition:* $166 per credit hour part-time; state resident $4965 full-time, $166 per credit hour part-time; nonresident $4965 full-time, $166 per credit hour part-time. Full-time tuition and fees vary according to location and program. Part time tuition and fees vary according to location and program. *Required fees:* $620 full-time. *Room and board:* $6724. Room and board charges vary according to board plan, housing facility, and location. *Waivers:* senior citizens and employees or children of employees.
Applying *Application fee:* $20. *Required:* high school transcript, immunization record.
Freshman Application Contact Minnesota State Community and Technical College–Moorhead, 1900 28th Avenue, South, Moorhead, MN 56560. *Phone:* 218-299-6824. *Toll-free phone:* 800-426-5603.
Website: http://www.minnesota.edu/.

Minnesota State Community and Technical College–Wadena

Wadena, Minnesota

- **State-supported** 2-year, part of Minnesota State Colleges and Universities
- **Small-town** campus
- **Coed,** 548 undergraduate students, 61% full-time, 56% women, 44% men

Undergraduates 332 full-time, 216 part-time. Students come from 36 states and territories.
Freshmen *Admission:* 165 enrolled.
Majors Electrical and power transmission installation related; industrial mechanics and maintenance technology; liberal arts and sciences/liberal studies; licensed practical/vocational nurse training; lineworker; medical administrative assistant and medical secretary; multi/interdisciplinary studies related; network and system administration; nursing practice; office management; registered nursing/registered nurse.
Academics *Calendar:* semesters. *Degree:* certificates, diplomas, and associate.
Costs (2019–20) *One-time required fee:* $20. *Tuition:* state resident $4965 full-time, $166 per credit hour part-time; nonresident $4965 full-time, $166 per credit hour part-time. Full-time tuition and fees vary according to location and program. Part-time tuition and fees vary according to location and program. *Required fees:* $514 full-time. *Room and board:* $6724. Room and board charges vary according to housing facility and location. *Waivers:* senior citizens and employees or children of employees.
Applying *Application fee:* $20. *Required:* high school transcript, immunization record.
Freshman Application Contact Minnesota State Community and Technical College–Wadena, 405 Colfax Avenue, SW, PO Box 566, Wadena, MN 56482. *Phone:* 218-631-7818. *Toll-free phone:* 800-247-2007.
Website: http://www.minnesota.edu/.

Minnesota West Community and Technical College

Pipestone, Minnesota

Freshman Application Contact Ms. Crystal Strouth, College Registrar, Minnesota West Community and Technical College, 1450 Collegeway, Worthington, MN 56187. *Phone:* 507-372-3451. *Toll-free phone:* 800-658-2330. *Fax:* 507-372-5803. *E-mail:* crystal.strouth@mnwest.edu. *Website:* http://www.mnwest.edu/.

Normandale Community College

Bloomington, Minnesota

- **State-supported** 2-year, founded 1968, part of Minnesota State Colleges and Universities System
- **Suburban** 90-acre campus with easy access to Minneapolis-St. Paul
- **Coed**

Faculty *Student/faculty ratio:* 27:1.
Academics *Calendar:* semesters. *Degree:* certificates and associate. *Special study options:* academic remediation for entering students, adult/continuing education programs, advanced placement credit, cooperative education, distance learning, English as a second language, external degree program, independent study, internships, off-campus study, part-time degree program, services for LD students, student-designed majors, study abroad, summer session for credit.
Library Library plus 1 other.
Student Life *Campus security:* 24-hour emergency response devices, student patrols, late-night transport/escort service.
Applying *Options:* electronic application, deferred entrance. *Application fee:* $20. *Required for some:* high school transcript.
Freshman Application Contact Admissions Office, Normandale Community College, 9700 France Avenue South, Bloomington, MN 55431. *Phone:* 952-358-8201. *Toll-free phone:* 800-481-5412. *Fax:* 952-358-8230. *E-mail:* information@normandale.edu. *Website:* http://www.normandale.edu/.

North Hennepin Community College

Brooklyn Park, Minnesota

Freshman Application Contact Mr. Sean Olson, Associate Director of Admissions and Outreach, North Hennepin Community College, 7411 85th Avenue North, Brooklyn Park, MN 55445. *Phone:* 763-424-0724. *Toll-free phone:* 800-818-0395. *Fax:* 763-493-0563. *E-mail:* solson2@nhcc.edu. *Website:* http://www.nhcc.edu/.

Northland Community and Technical College

Thief River Falls, Minnesota

- **State-supported** 2-year, founded 1949, part of Minnesota State Colleges and Universities System
- **Small-town** 239-acre campus
- **Coed,** 3,190 undergraduate students, 40% full-time, 58% women, 41% men

Undergraduates 1,273 full-time, 1,883 part-time. Students come from 37 states and territories; 6 other countries; 33% are from out of state; 6% Black or African American, non-Hispanic/Latino; 3% Hispanic/Latino; 0.9% Asian, non-Hispanic/Latino; 1% American Indian or Alaska Native, non-Hispanic/Latino; 3% Two or more races, non-Hispanic/Latino; 2% Race/ethnicity unknown; 0.3% international; 36% transferred in.
Freshmen *Admission:* 1,246 applied, 789 admitted, 424 enrolled.
Faculty *Total:* 134, 66% full-time. *Student/faculty ratio:* 18:1.
Majors Accounting technology and bookkeeping; administrative assistant and secretarial science; agricultural mechanics and equipment technology; agriculture; airframe mechanics and aircraft maintenance technology; architectural drafting and CAD/CADD; autobody/collision and repair technology; automation engineer technology; automobile/automotive mechanics technology; business administration and management; computer support specialist; computer systems networking and telecommunications;

criminal justice/police science; dietetic technology; emergency medical technology (EMT paramedic); fire prevention and safety technology; health services/allied health/health sciences; heating, air conditioning, ventilation and refrigeration maintenance technology; liberal arts and sciences/liberal studies; manufacturing engineering technology; medical administrative assistant and medical secretary; medical insurance coding; occupational therapist assistant; pharmacy technician; physical therapy technology; radiologic technology/science; registered nursing/registered nurse; respiratory care therapy; sales, distribution, and marketing operations; signal/geospatial intelligence; special products marketing; surgical technology; teacher assistant/aide.

Academics *Calendar:* semesters. *Degree:* certificates, diplomas, and associate. *Special study options:* academic remediation for entering students, adult/continuing education programs, advanced placement credit, cooperative education, distance learning, double majors, external degree program, internships, off-campus study, part-time degree program, services for LD students, summer session for credit.

Library Northland Community and Technical College Library plus 1 other. *Books:* 24,000 (physical), 19,000 (digital/electronic); *Serial titles:* 55 (physical); *Databases:* 47. Weekly public service hours: 82; students can reserve study rooms.

Student Life *Housing:* college housing not available. *Activities and Organizations:* student-run radio station, choral group, Student Senate, PAMA, AD Nursing, PN Nursing, Fire Tech. *Campus security:* student patrols, late-night transport/escort service. *Student services:* personal/psychological counseling, women's center, veterans affairs office.

Athletics Member NJCAA. *Intercollegiate sports:* baseball M, basketball M/W, softball W, volleyball W, wrestling M. *Intramural sports:* basketball M/W, table tennis M/W, volleyball M/W, weight lifting M/W.

Financial Aid Of all full-time matriculated undergraduates who enrolled in 2011, 98 Federal Work-Study jobs (averaging $2701). 68 state and other part-time jobs (averaging $2839).

Applying *Options:* electronic application, early admission, deferred entrance. *Required:* high school transcript. *Application deadlines:* 8/28 (freshmen), 8/28 (transfers). *Notification:* continuous (freshmen), continuous (transfers).

Freshman Application Contact Mrs. Nicki Carlson, Director of Admissions & Enrollment Management, Northland Community and Technical College, 1101 Highway One East, Thief River Falls, MN 56701. *Phone:* 218-683-8546. *Toll-free phone:* 800-959-6282. *Fax:* 218-683-8980. *E-mail:* nicki.carlson@northlandcollege.edu.
Website: http://www.northlandcollege.edu/.

Northwest Technical College

Bemidji, Minnesota

Freshman Application Contact Ms. Kari Kantack-Miller, Diversity and Enrollment Representative, Northwest Technical College, 905 Grant Avenue, Southeast, Bemidji, MN 56601. *Phone:* 218-333-6645. *Toll-free phone:* 800-942-8324. *Fax:* 218-333-6694. *E-mail:* kari.kantack@ntcmn.edu. *Website:* http://www.ntcmn.edu/.

Pine Technical and Community College

Pine City, Minnesota

Freshman Application Contact Pine Technical and Community College, 900 4th Street SE, Pine City, MN 55063. *Phone:* 320-629-5100. *Toll-free phone:* 800-521-7463. *Website:* http://www.pine.edu/.

Rainy River Community College

International Falls, Minnesota

Freshman Application Contact Ms. Berta Wilcox, Registrar, Rainy River Community College, 1501 Highway 71, International Falls, MN 56649. *Phone:* 218-285-2207. *Toll-free phone:* 800-456-3996. *Fax:* 218-285-2314. *E-mail:* berta.wilcox@rainyriver.edu. *Website:* http://www.rainyriver.edu/.

Ridgewater College

Willmar, Minnesota

- **State-supported** 2-year, founded 1961, part of Minnesota State Colleges and Universities System
- **Small-town** 83-acre campus
- **Coed,** 2,586 students

Faculty *Total:* 159, 62% full-time. *Student/faculty ratio:* 20:1.

Majors Accounting; administrative assistant and secretarial science; agribusiness; agricultural production; agriculture; agronomy and crop science; animal/livestock husbandry and production; autobody/collision and repair technology; automobile/automotive mechanics technology; biology/biological sciences; business administration and management; carpentry; chemistry; commercial photography; computer programming; computer science; computer systems networking and telecommunications; computer technology/computer systems technology; cosmetology; criminal justice/police science; crop production; dairy husbandry and production; desktop publishing and digital imaging design; digital communication and media/multimedia; electrical, electronic and communications engineering technology; electrician; electromechanical technology; health information/medical records technology; instrumentation technology; legal administrative assistant/secretary; liberal arts and sciences and humanities related; liberal arts and sciences/liberal studies; machine tool technology; marketing/marketing management; mechanical drafting and CAD/CADD; medical administrative assistant and medical secretary; medical/clinical assistant; network and system administration; radiologic technology/science; recording arts technology; registered nursing/registered nurse; sales, distribution, and marketing operations; selling skills and sales; teacher assistant/aide; telecommunications technology; therapeutic recreation; tool and die technology; veterinary/animal health technology; web page, digital/multimedia and information resources design; welding technology.

Academics *Calendar:* semesters. *Degree:* certificates, diplomas, and associate. *Special study options:* academic remediation for entering students, advanced placement credit, cooperative education, distance learning, double majors, external degree program, independent study, internships, off-campus study, part-time degree program, services for LD students, summer session for credit.

Student Life *Housing:* college housing not available. *Campus security:* 24-hour emergency response devices. *Student services:* personal/psychological counseling, veterans affairs office.

Athletics Member NJCAA. *Intercollegiate sports:* baseball M, basketball M/W, softball W, volleyball W, wrestling M.

Financial Aid Of all full-time matriculated undergraduates who enrolled in 2018, 350 Federal Work-Study jobs (averaging $3000). 133 state and other part-time jobs (averaging $2400).

Applying *Options:* electronic application. *Required:* high school transcript.

Freshman Application Contact Ms. Linda Duering, Admissions Assistant, Ridgewater College, 2101 15th Avenue NW, Willmar, MN 56201. *Phone:* 320-222-5976. *Toll-free phone:* 800-722-1151. *E-mail:* linda.duering@ridgewater.edu.
Website: http://www.ridgewater.edu/.

Riverland Community College

Austin, Minnesota

Freshman Application Contact Riverland Community College, 1900 8th Avenue, NW, Austin, MN 55912. *Phone:* 507-433-0600. *Toll-free phone:* 800-247-5039. *Website:* http://www.riverland.edu/.

Rochester Community and Technical College

Rochester, Minnesota

Director of Admissions Mr. Troy Tynsky, Director of Admissions, Rochester Community and Technical College, 851 30th Avenue, SE, Rochester, MN 55904-4999. *Phone:* 507-280-3509. *Website:* http://www.rctc.edu/.

St. Cloud Technical & Community College

St. Cloud, Minnesota

Freshman Application Contact Ms. Jodi Elness, Admissions Office, St. Cloud Technical & Community College, 1540 Northway Drive, St. Cloud, MN 56303. *Phone:* 320-308-5089. *Toll-free phone:* 800-222-1009. *Fax:* 320-308-5981. *E-mail:* jelness@sctcc.edu. *Website:* http://www.sctcc.edu/.

Saint Paul College–A Community & Technical College

St. Paul, Minnesota

- **State-related** 2-year, founded 1919, part of Minnesota State Colleges and Universities System
- **Urban** campus
- **Coed**

Undergraduates 2,454 full-time, 3,474 part-time. 8% are from out of state; 13% transferred in.

Faculty *Student/faculty ratio:* 18:1.

Academics *Calendar:* semesters. *Degree:* certificates, diplomas, and associate. *Special study options:* academic remediation for entering students, adult/continuing education programs, distance learning, English as a second language, honors programs, internships, off-campus study, part-time degree program, summer session for credit.
Library Saint Paul College Library.
Student Life *Campus security:* late-night transport/escort service.
Standardized Tests *Required:* ACCUPLACER (for admission).
Financial Aid Of all full-time matriculated undergraduates who enrolled in 2018, 48 Federal Work-Study jobs (averaging $2500). 94 state and other part-time jobs (averaging $2500).
Applying *Options:* electronic application, early admission. *Application fee:* $20. *Required for some:* high school transcript, interview.
Freshman Application Contact Ms. Sarah Carrico, Saint Paul College–A Community & Technical College, 235 Marshall Avenue, Saint Paul, MN 55102. *Phone:* 651-846-1424. *Toll-free phone:* 800-227-6029. *Fax:* 651-846-1703. *E-mail:* admissions@saintpaul.edu. *Website:* http://www.saintpaul.edu/.

South Central College
North Mankato, Minnesota

Freshman Application Contact Ms. Beverly Herda, Director of Admissions, South Central College, 1920 Lee Boulevard, North Mankato, MN 56003. *Phone:* 507-389-7334. *Fax:* 507-388-9951. *Website:* http://southcentral.edu/.

Vermilion Community College
Ely, Minnesota

Freshman Application Contact Mr. Todd Heiman, Director of Enrollment Services, Vermilion Community College, 1900 East Camp Street, Ely, MN 55731-1996. *Phone:* 218-365-7224. *Toll-free phone:* 800-657-3608. *Website:* http://www.vcc.edu/.

White Earth Tribal and Community College
Mahnomen, Minnesota

Admissions Office Contact White Earth Tribal and Community College, 102 3rd Street NE, Mahnomen, MN 56557. *Website:* http://www.wetcc.edu/.

MISSISSIPPI

Coahoma Community College
Clarksdale, Mississippi

- **State and locally supported** 2-year, founded 1949, part of Mississippi State Board for Community and Junior Colleges
- **Rural** 29-acre campus with easy access to Memphis
- **Coed**

Undergraduates 1,962 full-time, 254 part-time. 22% live on campus. *Retention:* 58% of full-time freshmen returned.
Faculty *Student/faculty ratio:* 19:1.
Academics *Calendar:* semesters. *Degree:* certificates and associate. *Special study options:* academic remediation for entering students, accelerated degree program, adult/continuing education programs, advanced placement credit, cooperative education, distance learning, off-campus study, part-time degree program, student-designed majors.
Library Dickerson-Johnson Library.
Student Life *Campus security:* 24-hour patrols, controlled dormitory access.
Athletics Member NJCAA.
Financial Aid Of all full-time matriculated undergraduates who enrolled in 2018, 350 Federal Work-Study jobs (averaging $600). 45 state and other part-time jobs (averaging $1000).
Applying *Required:* high school transcript. *Required for some:* interview.
Freshman Application Contact Mrs. Wanda Holmes, Director of Admissions and Records, Coahoma Community College, Clarksdale, MS 38614-9799. *Phone:* 662-621-4205. *Toll-free phone:* 866-470-1CCC. *Website:* http://www.coahomacc.edu/.

Concorde Career College
Southaven, Mississippi

Admissions Office Contact Concorde Career College, 7900 Airways Boulevard, Suite 103, Southaven, MS 38671. *Website:* http://www.concorde.edu/.

Copiah-Lincoln Community College
Wesson, Mississippi

Freshman Application Contact Ms. Gay Langham, Student Records Manager, Copiah-Lincoln Community College, PO Box 649, Wesson, MS 39191-0457. *Phone:* 601-643-8307. *E-mail:* gay.langham@colin.edu. *Website:* http://www.colin.edu/.

East Central Community College
Decatur, Mississippi

- **State and locally supported** 2-year, founded 1928, part of Mississippi State Board for Community and Junior Colleges
- **Rural** 200-acre campus
- **Coed**

Academics *Calendar:* semesters. *Degree:* certificates and associate. *Special study options:* academic remediation for entering students, adult/continuing education programs, advanced placement credit, honors programs, part-time degree program, services for LD students, summer session for credit.
Library Burton Library.
Student Life *Campus security:* 24-hour patrols.
Athletics Member NJCAA.
Financial Aid Of all full-time matriculated undergraduates who enrolled in 2018, 90 Federal Work-Study jobs (averaging $850). 38 state and other part-time jobs (averaging $1020).
Applying *Options:* early admission. *Required:* high school transcript.
Director of Admissions Ms. Donna Luke, Director of Admissions, Records, and Research, East Central Community College, PO Box 129, Decatur, MS 39327-0129. *Phone:* 601-635-2111 Ext. 206. *Toll-free phone:* 877-462-3222. *Website:* http://www.eccc.edu/.

East Mississippi Community College
Scooba, Mississippi

Director of Admissions Ms. Melinda Sciple, Admissions Officer, East Mississippi Community College, PO Box 158, Scooba, MS 39358-0158. *Phone:* 662-476-5041. *Website:* http://www.eastms.edu/.

Hinds Community College
Raymond, Mississippi

Freshman Application Contact Hinds Community College, PO Box 1100, Raymond, MS 39154-1100. *Phone:* 601-857-3280. *Toll-free phone:* 800-HINDSCC. *Website:* http://www.hindscc.edu/.

Holmes Community College
Goodman, Mississippi

Director of Admissions Dr. Lynn Wright, Dean of Admissions and Records, Holmes Community College, PO Box 369, Goodman, MS 39079-0369. *Phone:* 601-472-2312 Ext. 1023. *Toll-free phone:* 800-HOLMES-4. *Website:* http://www.holmescc.edu/.

Itawamba Community College
Fulton, Mississippi

Freshman Application Contact Mr. Larry Boggs, Director of Student Recruitment and Scholarships, Itawamba Community College, 602 West Hill Street, Fulton, MS 38843. *Phone:* 601-862-8252. *E-mail:* laboggs@iccms.edu. *Website:* http://www.iccms.edu/.

Jones County Junior College
Ellisville, Mississippi

Director of Admissions Mrs. Dianne Speed, Director of Admissions and Records, Jones County Junior College, 900 South Court Street, Ellisville, MS 39437-3901. *Phone:* 601-477-4025. *Website:* http://www.jcjc.edu/.

Meridian Community College

Meridian, Mississippi

- **State and locally supported** 2-year, founded 1937, part of Mississippi Community College Board
- **Small-town** 91-acre campus
- **Endowment** $15.7 million
- **Coed,** 3,402 undergraduate students, 67% full-time, 68% women, 32% men

Undergraduates 2,291 full-time, 1,111 part-time. Students come from 6 states and territories; 6 other countries; 44% Black or African American, non-Hispanic/Latino; 1% Hispanic/Latino; 0.7% Asian, non-Hispanic/Latino; 1% American Indian or Alaska Native, non-Hispanic/Latino; 1% Two or more races, non-Hispanic/Latino; 5% Race/ethnicity unknown; 34% transferred in; 12% live on campus. *Retention:* 56% of full-time freshmen returned.

Freshmen *Admission:* 683 enrolled.

Faculty *Total:* 217, 62% full-time, 4% with terminal degrees. *Student/faculty ratio:* 17:1.

Majors Administrative assistant and secretarial science; broadcast journalism; business, management, and marketing related; clinical/medical laboratory technology; communication and media related; computer programming; computer systems networking and telecommunications; culinary arts; dental hygiene; early childhood education; electrical, electronic and communications engineering technology; electrical/electronics drafting and CAD/CADD; emergency medical technology (EMT paramedic); fire science/firefighting; graphic design; health information/medical records administration; hotel, motel, and restaurant management; machine tool technology; marketing/marketing management; medical office assistant; medical office management; physical therapy technology; precision production trades; registered nursing/registered nurse; respiratory care therapy; telecommunications technology; welding technology.

Academics *Calendar:* semesters. *Degree:* certificates and associate. *Special study options:* academic remediation for entering students, accelerated degree program, adult/continuing education programs, advanced placement credit, cooperative education, distance learning, double majors, English as a second language, freshman honors college, honors programs, independent study, internships, part-time degree program, services for LD students, summer session for credit.

Library L.O. Todd-Billy C. Beal Learning Resources Center. *Books:* 49,287 (physical), 189,470 (digital/electronic); *Serial titles:* 173 (physical), 9 (digital/electronic); *Databases:* 3.

Student Life *Housing Options:* coed, men-only, women-only. Campus housing is university owned. *Activities and Organizations:* drama/theater group, student-run radio station, choral group, Phi Theta Kappa, VICA (Vocational Industrial Clubs of America), Health Occupations Students of America, Organization of Student Nurses, Distributive Education Clubs of America. *Campus security:* 24-hour patrols by law enforcement officers. *Student services:* personal/psychological counseling, veterans affairs office.

Athletics Member NJCAA. *Intercollegiate sports:* baseball M(s), basketball M(s)/W(s), cross-country running M(s)/W(s), golf M(s), soccer M(s)/W(s), softball W(s), tennis M(s)/W(s), track and field M(s)/W(s). *Intramural sports:* basketball M/W, cross-country running M/W, swimming and diving M/W, tennis M/W, volleyball M/W.

Standardized Tests *Required:* ACT or ACCUPLACER (for admission).

Costs (2020–21) *Tuition:* state resident $3024 full-time, $160 per credit hour part-time; nonresident $4004 full-time, $187 per credit hour part-time. Full-time tuition and fees vary according to program. Part-time tuition and fees vary according to program. *Required fees:* $300 full-time, $6 per credit hour part-time, $15 per term part-time. *Room and board:* $5280. Room and board charges vary according to housing facility. *Waivers:* employees or children of employees.

Applying *Options:* early admission. *Required:* high school transcript, minimum 2.0 GPA. *Application deadlines:* rolling (freshmen), rolling (out-of-state freshmen), rolling (transfers). *Notification:* continuous (freshmen), continuous (out-of-state freshmen), continuous (transfers).

Freshman Application Contact Ms. Angela Payne, Director of Admissions, Meridian Community College, 910 Highway 19 North, Meridian, MS 39307. *Phone:* 601-484-8357. *Toll-free phone:* 800-MCC-THE-1. *E-mail:* apayne@meridiancc.edu.

Website: http://www.meridiancc.edu/.

Mississippi Delta Community College

Moorhead, Mississippi

- **District-supported** 2-year, founded 1926, part of Mississippi State Board for Community and Junior Colleges
- **Small-town** 425-acre campus
- **Coed,** 1,944 undergraduate students, 86% full-time, 64% women, 36% men

Undergraduates 1,670 full-time, 274 part-time. Students come from 6 states and territories; 67% Black or African American, non-Hispanic/Latino; 2% Hispanic/Latino; 0.4% Asian, non-Hispanic/Latino; 0.1% American Indian or Alaska Native, non-Hispanic/Latino; 2% Race/ethnicity unknown; 12% transferred in; 25% live on campus. *Retention:* 45% of full-time freshmen returned.

Freshmen *Admission:* 909 applied, 909 admitted, 565 enrolled. *Test scores:* ACT scores over 18: 31%; ACT scores over 24: 3%.

Faculty *Total:* 208, 54% full-time, 8% with terminal degrees. *Student/faculty ratio:* 18:1.

Majors Accounting; administrative assistant and secretarial science; advertising; agricultural business and management; agricultural economics; American studies; architectural engineering technology; art teacher education; behavioral sciences; biology/biological sciences; business machine repair; civil engineering technology; clinical/medical laboratory technology; computer engineering technology; criminal justice/law enforcement administration; dental hygiene; design and applied arts related; developmental and child psychology; dramatic/theater arts; economics; education; electrical, electronic and communications engineering technology; elementary education; English; family and consumer sciences/human sciences; geography; graphic and printing equipment operation/production; health information/medical records administration; health teacher education; history; horticultural science; liberal arts and sciences/liberal studies; management information systems; masonry; mathematics; medical office computer specialist; medical radiologic technology; music; music teacher education; physical education teaching and coaching; political science and government; registered nursing/registered nurse; science teacher education; social work.

Academics *Calendar:* semesters. *Degree:* certificates, diplomas, and associate. *Special study options:* academic remediation for entering students, adult/continuing education programs, advanced placement credit, part-time degree program, summer session for credit.

Library Stanny Sanders Library.

Student Life *Housing Options:* men-only, women-only. Campus housing is university owned. *Activities and Organizations:* choral group, marching band, Phi Theta Kappa, SkillsUSA, Phi Beta Lambda, Student Government Association, Nursing Club. *Campus security:* 24-hour emergency response devices and patrols, late-night transport/escort service, controlled dormitory access. *Student services:* personal/psychological counseling.

Athletics Member NJCAA. *Intercollegiate sports:* baseball M(s), basketball M(s)/W(s), football M(s), softball W(s).

Standardized Tests *Required for some:* ACT (for admission).

Financial Aid Of all full-time matriculated undergraduates who enrolled in 2019, 1,670 applied for aid, 1,670 were judged to have need, 1,475 had their need fully met. In 2019, 390 non-need-based awards were made. *Average percent of need met:* 50%. *Average financial aid package:* $3033. *Average need-based gift aid:* $8355. *Average non-need-based aid:* $9534. *Financial aid deadline:* 9/15.

Applying *Options:* deferred entrance. *Required:* high school transcript. *Application deadlines:* 7/27 (freshmen), rolling (out-of-state freshmen), 7/27 (transfers). *Notification:* continuous (freshmen), continuous (out-of-state freshmen), continuous (transfers).

Freshman Application Contact Mississippi Delta Community College, PO Box 668, Highway 3 and Cherry Street, Moorhead, MS 38761-0668. *Phone:* 662-246-6302.

Website: http://www.msdelta.edu/.

Mississippi Gulf Coast Community College

Perkinston, Mississippi

Freshman Application Contact Mrs. Nichol Green, Director of Admissions, Mississippi Gulf Coast Community College, PO Box 548, Perkinston, MS 39573. *Phone:* 601-928-6264. *Fax:* 601-928-6345. *Website:* http://www.mgccc.edu/.

Northeast Mississippi Community College

Booneville, Mississippi

- **State-supported** 2-year, founded 1948, part of Mississippi State Board for Community and Junior Colleges
- **Small-town** 100-acre campus
- **Coed**

Undergraduates 3% are from out of state. *Retention:* 68% of full-time freshmen returned.
Faculty *Student/faculty ratio:* 22:1.
Academics *Calendar:* semesters. *Degree:* certificates and associate. *Special study options:* academic remediation for entering students, adult/continuing education programs, advanced placement credit, cooperative education, part-time degree program, services for LD students, student-designed majors, summer session for credit.
Library Eula Dees Library.
Student Life *Campus security:* 24-hour patrols, student patrols, controlled dormitory access.
Athletics Member NJCAA.
Standardized Tests *Required for some:* SAT or ACT (for admission).
Applying *Options:* early admission.
Freshman Application Contact Office of Enrollment Services, Northeast Mississippi Community College, 101 Cunningham Boulevard, Booneville, MS 38829. *Phone:* 662-720-7239. *Toll-free phone:* 800-555-2154. *E-mail:* admitme@nemcc.edu. *Website:* http://www.nemcc.edu/.

Northwest Mississippi Community College

Senatobia, Mississippi

Freshman Application Contact Northwest Mississippi Community College, 4975 Highway 51 North, Senatobia, MS 38668-1701. *Phone:* 662-562-8217. *Website:* http://www.northwestms.edu/.

Pearl River Community College

Poplarville, Mississippi

Freshman Application Contact Mr. J. Dow Ford, Director of Admissions, Pearl River Community College, 101 Highway 11 North, Poplarville, MS 39470. *Phone:* 601-403-1000. *E-mail:* dford@prcc.edu. *Website:* http://www.prcc.edu/.

Southwest Mississippi Community College

Summit, Mississippi

Freshman Application Contact Mr. Matthew Calhoun, Vice President of Admissions and Records, Southwest Mississippi Community College, 1156 College Drive, Summit, MS 39666. *Phone:* 601-276-2001. *Fax:* 601-276-3888. *E-mail:* mattc@smcc.edu. *Website:* http://www.smcc.cc.ms.us/.

MISSOURI

American Trade School

Saint Ann, Missouri

Admissions Office Contact American Trade School, 3925 Industrial Drive, Saint Ann, MO 63074. *Website:* http://www.americantradeschool.edu/.

Bolivar Technical College

Bolivar, Missouri

Admissions Office Contact Bolivar Technical College, 1135 North Oakland Avenue, Bolivar, MO 65613. *Website:* http://www.bolivarcollege.org/.

Concorde Career College

Kansas City, Missouri

Freshman Application Contact Deborah Crow, Director, Concorde Career College, 3239 Broadway Street, Kansas City, MO 64111. *Phone:* 816-531-5223. *Fax:* 816-756-3231. *E-mail:* dcrow@concorde.edu. *Website:* http://www.concorde.edu/.

Cottey College

Nevada, Missouri

- **Independent** primarily 2-year, founded 1884
- **Small-town** 51-acre campus
- **Endowment** $108.8 million
- **Women only**

Undergraduates 260 full-time, 5 part-time. Students come from 32 states and territories; 18 other countries; 85% are from out of state; 5% Black or African American, non-Hispanic/Latino; 8% Hispanic/Latino; 0.4% Asian, non-Hispanic/Latino; 0.4% Native Hawaiian or other Pacific Islander, non-Hispanic/Latino; 2% American Indian or Alaska Native, non-Hispanic/Latino; 5% Two or more races, non-Hispanic/Latino; 15% international; 4% transferred in; 90% live on campus. *Retention:* 70% of full-time freshmen returned.
Faculty *Student/faculty ratio:* 7:1.
Academics *Calendar:* semesters. *Degrees:* associate and bachelor's. *Special study options:* advanced placement credit, distance learning, independent study, internships, part-time degree program, services for LD students, study abroad.
Library Blanche Skiff Ross Memorial Library plus 1 other. Weekly public service hours: 88.
Student Life *Campus security:* 24-hour emergency response devices and patrols, late-night transport/escort service, controlled dormitory access.
Athletics Member NJCAA.
Standardized Tests *Required:* SAT or ACT (for admission). *Required for some:* TOEFL, IELTS.
Costs (2019–20) *Comprehensive fee:* $29,910 includes full-time tuition ($20,500), mandatory fees ($1360), and room and board ($8050). Part-time tuition: $550 per credit hour. Part-time tuition and fees vary according to course load. *Room and board:* college room only: $4300. Room and board charges vary according to housing facility.
Financial Aid Of all full-time matriculated undergraduates who enrolled in 2019, 223 applied for aid, 191 were judged to have need, 64 had their need fully met. In 2019, 59. *Average percent of need met:* 87. *Average financial aid package:* $23,100. *Average need-based loan:* $2594. *Average need-based gift aid:* $19,804. *Average non-need-based aid:* $13,741. *Average indebtedness upon graduation:* $20,406.
Applying *Options:* electronic application, early admission, deferred entrance. *Application fee:* $20. *Required:* essay or personal statement, high school transcript, 1 letter of recommendation. *Recommended:* minimum 2.6 GPA, interview.
Freshman Application Contact Mrs. Angela Moore, Enrollment Office, Cottey College, 1000 West Austin Boulevard, Nevada, MO 64772. *Phone:* 417-667-8181. *Toll-free phone:* 888-526-8839. *Fax:* 417-667-8103. *E-mail:* amoore@cottey.edu. *Website:* http://www.cottey.edu/.

Crowder College

Neosho, Missouri

- **State and locally supported** 2-year, founded 1963, part of Missouri Coordinating Board for Higher Education
- **Rural** 608-acre campus
- **Coed,** 4,401 undergraduate students, 43% full-time, 62% women, 38% men

Undergraduates 1,875 full-time, 2,526 part-time. Students come from 23 states and territories; 4 other countries; 8% are from out of state; 1% Black or African American, non-Hispanic/Latino; 11% Hispanic/Latino; 1% Asian, non-Hispanic/Latino; 0.9% Native Hawaiian or other Pacific Islander, non-Hispanic/Latino; 2% American Indian or Alaska Native, non-Hispanic/Latino; 5% Two or more races, non-Hispanic/Latino; 2% Race/ethnicity unknown; 15% international; 6% transferred in; 10% live on campus. *Retention:* 58% of full-time freshmen returned.
Freshmen *Admission:* 944 enrolled.
Faculty *Total:* 343, 35% full-time, 8% with terminal degrees. *Student/faculty ratio:* 13:1.
Majors Administrative assistant and secretarial science; agribusiness; agricultural mechanization; agriculture; art; autobody/collision and repair technology; automobile/automotive mechanics technology; biology/biological sciences; business administration and management; business automation/technology/data entry; computer systems analysis; computer systems networking and telecommunications; construction engineering technology; construction trades; drafting and design technology; dramatic/theater arts; education; electrical, electronic and communications engineering technology; elementary education; emergency medical technology (EMT paramedic); energy management and systems technology; environmental engineering technology; executive assistant/executive secretary; farm and ranch management; fire science/firefighting; general studies; health information/medical records technology; industrial technology;

legal administrative assistant/secretary; liberal arts and sciences/liberal studies; manufacturing engineering technology; mass communication/media; mathematics; mathematics and computer science; medical administrative assistant and medical secretary; music; occupational therapist assistant; physical education teaching and coaching; physical sciences; pre-engineering; psychology; public relations/image management; registered nursing/registered nurse; solar energy technology; veterinary/animal health technology; welding technology.
Academics *Calendar:* semesters. *Degree:* certificates and associate. *Special study options:* academic remediation for entering students, adult/continuing education programs, advanced placement credit, cooperative education, English as a second language, freshman honors college, honors programs, independent study, part-time degree program, student-designed majors, study abroad, summer session for credit.
Library Bill & Margot Lee Library. *Books:* 39,022 (physical), 237,481 (digital/electronic); *Serial titles:* 82 (physical); *Databases:* 53. Weekly public service hours: 62.
Student Life *Housing Options:* men-only, women-only, special housing for students with disabilities. Campus housing is university owned. *Activities and Organizations:* drama/theater group, student-run newspaper, Phi Theta Kappa, Students in Free Enterprise (SIFE), Baptist Student Union, Aggies, Student Ambassadors. *Campus security:* 24-hour patrols. *Student services:* personal/psychological counseling, veterans affairs office.
Athletics Member NJCAA. *Intercollegiate sports:* baseball M(s), basketball W(s), soccer M(s).
Costs (2019–20) *Tuition:* area resident $2760 full-time, $90 per credit hour part-time; state resident $4440 full-time, $143 per credit hour part-time; nonresident $4440 full-time, $143 per credit hour part-time. Full-time tuition and fees vary according to program. Part-time tuition and fees vary according to program. *Required fees:* $990 full-time, $33 per credit hour part-time. *Room and board:* $6579; room only: $4290. Room and board charges vary according to board plan and housing facility. *Payment plan:* installment. *Waivers:* senior citizens and employees or children of employees.
Applying *Application fee:* $25. *Required:* high school transcript. *Application deadlines:* rolling (freshmen), rolling (transfers). *Notification:* continuous (freshmen).
Freshman Application Contact Mr. James P. Dickey, Admissions Coordinator, Crowder College, Neosho, MO 64850. *Phone:* 417-451-3223 Ext. 5466. *Toll-free phone:* 866-238-7788. *Fax:* 417-455-5731. *E-mail:* jamesdickey@crowder.edu.
Website: http://www.crowder.edu/.

East Central College
Union, Missouri

- **District-supported** 2-year, founded 1959
- **Rural** 207-acre campus with easy access to St. Louis
- **Coed**

Undergraduates 1,219 full-time, 1,410 part-time. 1% Black or African American, non-Hispanic/Latino; 2% Hispanic/Latino; 0.9% Asian, non-Hispanic/Latino; 0.5% American Indian or Alaska Native, non-Hispanic/Latino; 2% Two or more races, non-Hispanic/Latino; 1% Race/ethnicity unknown; 0.5% international.
Academics *Calendar:* semesters. *Degree:* certificates and associate. *Special study options:* academic remediation for entering students, adult/continuing education programs, advanced placement credit, distance learning, English as a second language, honors programs, independent study, internships, off-campus study, part-time degree program, services for LD students, study abroad, summer session for credit.
Library East Central College Library. Students can reserve study rooms.
Student Life *Campus security:* 24-hour emergency response devices, late-night transport/escort service.
Athletics Member NJCAA.
Costs (2019–20) *Tuition:* area resident $2448 full-time, $102 per credit hour part-time; state resident $3528 full-time, $147 per credit hour part-time; nonresident $5232 full-time, $218 per credit hour part-time. Full-time tuition and fees vary according to program. Part-time tuition and fees vary according to program. *Required fees:* $648 full-time, $27 per credit hour part-time.
Applying *Options:* electronic application, early admission, deferred entrance. *Required:* high school transcript.
Freshman Application Contact Mr. JC Crane, Director, Admissions, East Central College, 1964 Prairie Dell Road, Union, MO 63084. *Phone:* 636-584-6552. *E-mail:* jc.crane@eastcentral.edu. *Website:* http://www.eastcentral.edu/.

Jefferson College
Hillsboro, Missouri

Freshman Application Contact Dr. Kimberly Harvey, Director of Student Records and Admissions Services, Jefferson College, 1000 Viking Drive, Hillsboro, MO 63050-2441. *Phone:* 636-481-3205 Ext. 3205. *Fax:* 636-789-5103. *E-mail:* admissions@jeffco.edu. *Website:* http://www.jeffco.edu/.

Metropolitan Community College–Kansas City
Kansas City, Missouri

- **State and locally supported** 2-year, founded 1969, part of Metropolitan Community Colleges System
- **Suburban** 420-acre campus with easy access to Kansas City
- **Endowment** $4.5 million
- **Coed**

Undergraduates 7,734 full-time, 11,500 part-time. Students come from 19 states and territories; 74 other countries; 1% are from out of state; 17% Black or African American, non-Hispanic/Latino; 9% Hispanic/Latino; 3% Asian, non-Hispanic/Latino; 0.3% Native Hawaiian or other Pacific Islander, non-Hispanic/Latino; 0.3% American Indian or Alaska Native, non-Hispanic/Latino; 6% Two or more races, non-Hispanic/Latino; 0.7% Race/ethnicity unknown; 4% transferred in. *Retention:* 52% of full-time freshmen returned.
Faculty *Student/faculty ratio:* 26:1.
Academics *Calendar:* semesters. *Degree:* certificates and associate. *Special study options:* academic remediation for entering students, accelerated degree program, adult/continuing education programs, advanced placement credit, cooperative education, distance learning, English as a second language, honors programs, independent study, internships, off-campus study, part-time degree program, services for LD students, summer session for credit.
Library College Library.
Student Life *Campus security:* 24-hour emergency response devices and patrols, late-night transport/escort service.
Athletics Member NJCAA.
Standardized Tests *Recommended:* ACT (for admission).
Applying *Options:* electronic application, early admission, deferred entrance.
Freshman Application Contact Dr. Tuesday Stanley, Vice Chancellor of Student Development and Enrollment Services, Metropolitan Community College–Kansas City, 3200 Broadway, Kansas City, MO 64111-2429. *Phone:* 816-604-1253. *E-mail:* tuesday.stanley@mcckc.edu. *Website:* http://www.mcckc.edu/.

Midwest Institute
Fenton, Missouri

Freshman Application Contact Admissions Office, Midwest Institute, 964 South Highway Drive, Fenton, MO 63026. *Toll-free phone:* 800-695-5550. *Website:* http://www.midwestinstitute.com/.

Midwest Institute
St. Louis, Missouri

Freshman Application Contact Admissions Office, Midwest Institute, 4260 Shoreline Drive, St. Louis, MO 63045. *Phone:* 314-344-4440. *Toll-free phone:* 800-695-5550. *Fax:* 314-344-0495. *Website:* http://www.midwestinstitute.com/.

Mineral Area College
Park Hills, Missouri

Freshman Application Contact Pam Reeder, Registrar, Mineral Area College, PO Box 1000, Park Hills, MO 63601-1000. *Phone:* 573-518-2204. *Fax:* 573-518-2166. *E-mail:* preeder@mineralarea.edu. *Website:* http://www.mineralarea.edu/.

Missouri State University-West Plains
West Plains, Missouri

- **State-supported** 2-year, founded 1963, part of Missouri State University
- **Small-town** 20-acre campus
- **Endowment** $8.3 million
- **Coed**

Undergraduates 806 full-time, 1,103 part-time. Students come from 18 states and territories; 15 other countries; 3% are from out of state; 1% Black or African American, non-Hispanic/Latino; 3% Hispanic/Latino; 0.1% Asian,

non-Hispanic/Latino; 84% Native Hawaiian or other Pacific Islander, non-Hispanic/Latino; 5% American Indian or Alaska Native, non-Hispanic/Latino; 3% Two or more races, non-Hispanic/Latino; 3% Race/ethnicity unknown; 0.7% international; 4% transferred in; 10% live on campus.
Faculty *Student/faculty ratio:* 20:1.
Academics *Calendar:* semesters. *Degree:* certificates and associate. *Special study options:* academic remediation for entering students, adult/continuing education programs, advanced placement credit, cooperative education, distance learning, honors programs, internships, off-campus study, part-time degree program, services for LD students, study abroad, summer session for credit.
Library Garnett Library. *Books:* 42,808 (physical), 234,677 (digital/electronic); *Serial titles:* 118 (physical), 5,877 (digital/electronic); *Databases:* 239. Weekly public service hours: 67.
Student Life *Campus security:* 24-hour emergency response devices, student patrols, late-night transport/escort service, controlled dormitory access, access only with key, agreement with city police for patrols.
Athletics Member NJCAA.
Financial Aid Of all full-time matriculated undergraduates who enrolled in 2018, 63 Federal Work-Study jobs (averaging $2000).
Applying *Options:* electronic application. *Required for some:* high school transcript.
Freshman Application Contact Ms. Melissa Jett, Coordinator of Admissions, Missouri State University-West Plains, 128 Garfield, West Plains, MO 65775. *Phone:* 417-255-7955. *Toll-free phone:* 888-466-7897. *Fax:* 417-255-7959. *E-mail:* melissajett@missouristate.edu. *Website:* http://wp.missouristate.edu/.

Moberly Area Community College
Moberly, Missouri

Freshman Application Contact Dr. James Grant, Dean of Student Services, Moberly Area Community College, Moberly, MO 65270-1304. *Phone:* 660-263-4110 Ext. 235. *Toll-free phone:* 800-622-2070. *Fax:* 660-263-2406. *E-mail:* info@macc.edu. *Website:* http://www.macc.edu/.

North Central Missouri College
Trenton, Missouri

Freshman Application Contact Jamie Cunningham, Admissions Recruiter, North Central Missouri College, Trenton, MO 64683. *Phone:* 660-359-3948 Ext. 1414. *E-mail:* jcunningham@mail.ncmissouri.edu. *Website:* http://www.ncmissouri.edu/.

Ozarks Technical Community College
Springfield, Missouri

- **District-supported** 2-year, founded 1990, part of Missouri Coordinating Board for Higher Education
- **Urban** campus
- **Endowment** $2.8 million
- **Coed**

Undergraduates 5,826 full-time, 7,434 part-time. Students come from 31 states and territories; 2% are from out of state; 3% Black or African American, non-Hispanic/Latino; 5% Hispanic/Latino; 1% Asian, non-Hispanic/Latino; 0.2% Native Hawaiian or other Pacific Islander, non-Hispanic/Latino; 0.5% American Indian or Alaska Native, non-Hispanic/Latino; 5% Two or more races, non-Hispanic/Latino; 2% Race/ethnicity unknown.
Faculty *Student/faculty ratio:* 21:1.
Academics *Calendar:* semesters. *Degree:* certificates, diplomas, and associate. *Special study options:* academic remediation for entering students, adult/continuing education programs, cooperative education, distance learning, double majors, English as a second language, honors programs, internships, off-campus study, part-time degree program, services for LD students, summer session for credit.
Library Main Library plus 1 other.
Student Life *Campus security:* 24-hour emergency response devices.
Costs (2019–20) *Tuition:* area resident $2712 full-time, $113 per credit hour part-time; state resident $3936 full-time, $164 per credit hour part-time; nonresident $5040 full-time, $210 per credit hour part-time. Full-time tuition and fees vary according to program. Part-time tuition and fees vary according to program. *Required fees:* $862 full-time, $26 per credit hour part-time, $100 per term part-time. *Payment plans:* installment, deferred payment.
Financial Aid Of all full-time matriculated undergraduates who enrolled in 2016, 180 Federal Work-Study jobs (averaging $1533).
Applying *Options:* electronic application. *Required:* high school transcript.
Freshman Application Contact Ozarks Technical Community College, 1001 E. Chestnut Expressway, Springfield, MO 65802. *Website:* http://www.otc.edu/.

Pinnacle Career Institute
Kansas City, Missouri

- **Proprietary** 2-year, founded 1953
- **Coed**

Undergraduates *Retention:* 72% of full-time freshmen returned.
Faculty *Student/faculty ratio:* 10:1.
Academics *Degree:* certificates and associate.
Applying *Application fee:* $50.
Director of Admissions Ms. Ruth Matous, Director of Admissions, Pinnacle Career Institute, 10301 Hickman Mills Drive, Kansas City, MO 64137. *Phone:* 816-331-5700 Ext. 212. *Toll-free phone:* 877-241-3097. *Website:* http://www.pcitraining.edu/.

Pinnacle Career Institute - North Kansas City
Kansas City, Missouri

- **Proprietary** 2-year, part of Pinnacle Career Institute
- **Suburban** campus with easy access to Kansas City
- **Coed**

Undergraduates 14% Black or African American, non-Hispanic/Latino; 9% Hispanic/Latino; 0.7% American Indian or Alaska Native, non-Hispanic/Latino; 4% Two or more races, non-Hispanic/Latino; 0.7% Race/ethnicity unknown. *Retention:* 72% of full-time freshmen returned.
Academics *Calendar:* monthly modules. *Degree:* certificates, diplomas, and associate.
Applying *Options:* electronic application. *Required:* high school transcript, interview.
Freshman Application Contact Pinnacle Career Institute - North Kansas City, 11500 NW Ambassador Drive, Suite 221, Kansas City, MO 64153. *Phone:* 816-331-5700. *Toll-free phone:* 877-241-3097. *Website:* http://www.pcitraining.edu/.

Ranken Technical College
St. Louis, Missouri

Freshman Application Contact Ranken Technical College, 4431 Finney Avenue, St. Louis, MO 63113. *Phone:* 314-371-0233 Ext. 4811. *Toll-free phone:* 866-4-RANKEN. *Website:* http://www.ranken.edu/.

St. Charles Community College
Cottleville, Missouri

- **State-supported** 2-year, founded 1986
- **Suburban** 228-acre campus with easy access to St. Louis
- **Endowment** $86,607
- **Coed,** 6,363 undergraduate students, 51% full-time, 58% women, 42% men

Undergraduates 3,222 full-time, 3,141 part-time. Students come from 23 states and territories; 47 other countries; 8% Black or African American, non-Hispanic/Latino; 6% Hispanic/Latino; 3% Asian, non-Hispanic/Latino; 0.1% Native Hawaiian or other Pacific Islander, non-Hispanic/Latino; 0.2% American Indian or Alaska Native, non-Hispanic/Latino; 4% Two or more races, non-Hispanic/Latino; 4% Race/ethnicity unknown; 0.6% international; 11% transferred in.
Freshmen *Admission:* 1,699 applied, 1,619 admitted, 1,290 enrolled.
Faculty *Total:* 455, 22% full-time, 21% with terminal degrees. *Student/faculty ratio:* 20:1.
Majors Accounting technology and bookkeeping; agriculture; biology/biological sciences; chemistry; child-care and support services management; commercial and advertising art; computer programming; creative writing; criminal justice/police science; drafting and design technology; education (specific subject areas) related; emergency medical technology (EMT paramedic); environmental health; general studies; health information/medical records technology; human services; industrial technology; liberal arts and sciences/liberal studies; manufacturing engineering technology; marketing/marketing management; music; music teacher education; occupational therapist assistant; office management; precision production related; pre-engineering; pre-pharmacy studies; registered nursing/registered nurse; teacher assistant/aide; welding technology.
Academics *Calendar:* semesters. *Degree:* certificates and associate. *Special study options:* academic remediation for entering students, adult/continuing education programs, advanced placement credit, cooperative education, distance learning, double majors, English as a second language, external degree program, honors programs, independent study, internships, part-time degree program, services for LD students, study abroad, summer session for credit.

Library Paul and Helen Schnare Library. *Books:* 56,633 (physical), 262,413 (digital/electronic); *Serial titles:* 349 (physical), 389,199 (digital/electronic); *Databases:* 50. Weekly public service hours: 68.
Student Life *Housing Options:* coed. Campus housing is university owned. *Activities and Organizations:* drama/theater group, student-run newspaper, choral group, Phi Theta Kappa, Missouri State Teachers Association-SCC Chapter, Student Nursing Association, Occupational Therapy Assistant Club, GAMES Club. *Campus security:* 24-hour emergency response devices and patrols, late-night transport/escort service, campus police officers on duty 24 hours a day, 365 days a year. *Student services:* personal/psychological counseling, veterans affairs office.
Athletics Member NJCAA. *Intercollegiate sports:* baseball M(s), cross-country running M/W, soccer M(s)/W(s), softball W(s), track and field M/W. *Intramural sports:* table tennis M(c)/W(c), tennis M(c)/W(c), ultimate Frisbee M(c)/W(c).
Financial Aid Of all full-time matriculated undergraduates who enrolled in 2017, 20 Federal Work-Study jobs (averaging $2567).
Applying *Options:* electronic application, deferred entrance. *Application fee:* $10. *Required for some:* high school transcript, minimum 2.5 GPA. *Application deadlines:* rolling (freshmen), rolling (transfers). *Notification:* continuous (freshmen), continuous (transfers).
Freshman Application Contact Kelli Lile, Admissions and Recruitment Manager, St. Charles Community College, 4601 Mid Rivers Mall Drive, Cottleville, MO 63376-0975. *Phone:* 636-922-8226. *Fax:* 636-922-8236. *E-mail:* klile@stchas.edu.
Website: http://www.stchas.edu/.

St. Louis College of Health Careers - Fenton

Fenton, Missouri

Admissions Office Contact St. Louis College of Health Careers - Fenton, 1297 North Highway Drive, Fenton, MO 63026. *Toll-free phone:* 866-529-2070. *Website:* http://www.slchc.com/.

St. Louis College of Health Careers - St. Louis

St. Louis, Missouri

Freshman Application Contact Admissions Office, St. Louis College of Health Careers - St. Louis, 909 South Taylor Avenue, St. Louis, MO 63110. *Phone:* 314-652-0300. *Toll-free phone:* 866-529-2070. *Fax:* 314-652-4825. *Website:* http://www.slchc.com/.

St. Louis Community College

St. Louis, Missouri

- **Public** 2-year, founded 1962, part of St. Louis Community College
- **Suburban** campus with easy access to St. Louis
- **Coed**

Undergraduates 6,580 full-time, 11,577 part-time. Students come from 31 states and territories; 110 other countries; 2% are from out of state; 33% Black or African American, non-Hispanic/Latino; 3% Hispanic/Latino; 3% Asian, non-Hispanic/Latino; 0.1% Native Hawaiian or other Pacific Islander, non-Hispanic/Latino; 0.2% American Indian or Alaska Native, non-Hispanic/Latino; 5% Two or more races, non-Hispanic/Latino; 2% Race/ethnicity unknown; 2% international; 7% transferred in. *Retention:* 58% of full-time freshmen returned.
Faculty *Student/faculty ratio:* 17:1.
Academics *Calendar:* semesters. *Degree:* certificates and associate. *Special study options:* academic remediation for entering students, accelerated degree program, adult/continuing education programs, advanced placement credit, distance learning, English as a second language, honors programs, independent study, internships, part-time degree program, services for LD students, study abroad, summer session for credit.
Student Life *Campus security:* 24-hour emergency response devices, late-night transport/escort service.
Athletics Member NJCAA.
Applying *Options:* electronic application. *Required for some:* high school transcript, interview.
Admissions Office Contact St. Louis Community College, 300 South Broadway, St. Louis, MO 63102. *Website:* http://www.stlcc.edu/.

Southeast Missouri Hospital College of Nursing and Health Sciences

Cape Girardeau, Missouri

Freshman Application Contact Southeast Missouri Hospital College of Nursing and Health Sciences, 2001 William Street, Cape Girardeau, MO 63701. *Phone:* 573-334-6825 Ext. 12. *Website:* http://www.sehcollege.edu/.

State Fair Community College

Sedalia, Missouri

Freshman Application Contact State Fair Community College, 3201 West 16th Street, Sedalia, MO 65301-2199. *Phone:* 660-596-7379. *Toll-free phone:* 877-311-7322. *Website:* http://www.sfccmo.edu/.

State Technical College of Missouri

Linn, Missouri

- **State-supported** 2-year, founded 1961
- **Rural** 350-acre campus
- **Coed, primarily men,** 1,724 undergraduate students, 83% full-time, 20% women, 80% men

Undergraduates 1,425 full-time, 299 part-time. Students come from 5 states and territories; 1 other country; 3% are from out of state; 1% Black or African American, non-Hispanic/Latino; 2% Hispanic/Latino; 0.5% Asian, non-Hispanic/Latino; 0.2% American Indian or Alaska Native, non-Hispanic/Latino; 2% Two or more races, non-Hispanic/Latino; 2% Race/ethnicity unknown; 8% transferred in; 8% live on campus.
Freshmen *Admission:* 718 enrolled.
Faculty *Total:* 134, 70% full-time, 1% with terminal degrees. *Student/faculty ratio:* 14:1.
Majors Agricultural mechanization; aircraft powerplant technology; autobody/collision and repair technology; automobile/automotive mechanics technology; civil engineering technology; computer programming; computer systems networking and telecommunications; construction trades; drafting and design technology; electrical/electronics equipment installation and repair; electrician; heating, air conditioning, ventilation and refrigeration maintenance technology; heavy equipment maintenance technology; lineworker; machine tool technology; manufacturing engineering technology; medium/heavy vehicle and truck technology; multi/interdisciplinary studies related; nuclear/nuclear power technology; office management; physical therapy technology; radiologic technology/science; registered nursing/registered nurse; turf and turfgrass management; welding technology.
Academics *Calendar:* semesters. *Degree:* certificates and associate. *Special study options:* academic remediation for entering students, adult/continuing education programs, advanced placement credit, cooperative education, distance learning, double majors, external degree program, independent study, internships, off-campus study, part-time degree program, services for LD students, summer session for credit.
Library State Technical College of Missouri Library plus 1 other. *Books:* 12,511 (physical), 172,100 (digital/electronic); *Serial titles:* 87 (physical); *Databases:* 42. Weekly public service hours: 64; students can reserve study rooms.
Student Life *Housing Options:* coed, men-only, women-only, special housing for students with disabilities. Campus housing is university owned. *Activities and Organizations:* SkillsUSA, Phi Theta Kappa, Student Government Association, Aviation Club, Electricity Club. *Campus security:* 24-hour emergency response devices, student patrols, controlled dormitory access, indoor and outdoor surveillance cameras. *Student services:* health clinic, personal/psychological counseling.
Athletics *Intramural sports:* archery M/W, basketball M/W, football M/W, riflery M/W, sand volleyball M/W, softball M/W, table tennis M/W, volleyball M/W.
Standardized Tests *Required:* SAT and SAT Subject Tests or ACT (for admission), ACCUPLACER (for admission). *Required for some:* ACT (for admission).
Costs (2019–20) *Tuition:* area resident $175 full-time, $175 per credit hour part-time; state resident $175 full-time, $175 per credit hour part-time; nonresident $351 full-time, $351 per credit hour part-time. *Required fees:* $36 full-time, $36 per credit hour part-time. *Room and board:* $5900; room only: $3600. *Payment plan:* installment. *Waivers:* employees or children of employees.
Financial Aid Of all full-time matriculated undergraduates who enrolled in 2018, 70 Federal Work-Study jobs (averaging $769).
Applying *Options:* electronic application, early admission, early decision, early action. *Required:* high school transcript. *Required for some:* essay or personal statement, 2 letters of recommendation, interview, Clinical

Observation Hours. *Application deadlines:* rolling (freshmen), rolling (transfers). *Notification:* continuous (freshmen), continuous (transfers).
Freshman Application Contact State Technical College of Missouri, One Technology Drive, Linn, MO 65051-9606. *Phone:* 573-897-5196. *Toll-free phone:* 800-743-TECH.
Website: http://www.statetechmo.edu/.

Texas County Technical College
Houston, Missouri

Admissions Office Contact Texas County Technical College, 6915 S. Hwy 63, Houston, MO 65483. *Website:* http://www.texascountytech.edu/.

Three Rivers College
Poplar Bluff, Missouri

Freshman Application Contact Three Rivers College, 2080 Three Rivers Boulevard, Poplar Bluff, MO 63901-2393. *Toll-free phone:* 877-TRY-TRCC. *Website:* http://www.trcc.edu/.

WellSpring School of Allied Health
Kansas City, Missouri

Admissions Office Contact WellSpring School of Allied Health, 9140 Ward Parkway, Suite 100, Kansas City, MO 64114. *Website:* http://www.wellspring.edu/.

MONTANA

Aaniiih Nakoda College
Harlem, Montana

Freshman Application Contact Aaniiih Nakoda College, PO Box 159, Harlem, MT 59526-0159. *Phone:* 406-353-2607 Ext. 233. *Website:* http://www.ancollege.edu/.

Blackfeet Community College
Browning, Montana

Freshman Application Contact Ms. Deana M. McNabb, Registrar and Admissions Officer, Blackfeet Community College, PO Box 819, Browning, MT 59417-0819. *Phone:* 406-338-5421. *Toll-free phone:* 800-549-7457. *Fax:* 406-338-3272. *Website:* http://www.bfcc.edu/.

Chief Dull Knife College
Lame Deer, Montana

Freshman Application Contact Director of Admissions, Chief Dull Knife College, PO Box 98, 1 College Drive, Lame Deer, MT 59043-0098. *Phone:* 406-477-6215. *Website:* http://www.cdkc.edu/.

Dawson Community College
Glendive, Montana

- **State and locally supported** 2-year, founded 1940, part of Montana University System
- **Rural** 300-acre campus
- **Endowment** $3.5 million
- **Coed,** 380 undergraduate students, 73% full-time, 55% women, 45% men

Undergraduates 278 full-time, 197 part-time. Students come from 19 states and territories; 5 other countries; 80% are from out of state; 9% Black or African American, non-Hispanic/Latino; 7% Hispanic/Latino; 2% Asian, non-Hispanic/Latino; 8% American Indian or Alaska Native, non-Hispanic/Latino; 3% Two or more races, non-Hispanic/Latino; 3% Race/ethnicity unknown; 7% international; 9% transferred in.
Freshmen *Admission:* 326 applied, 326 admitted, 105 enrolled. *Average high school GPA:* 3.0. *Test scores:* ACT scores over 18: 84%; ACT scores over 24: 18%.
Faculty *Total:* 32, 41% full-time, 16% with terminal degrees. *Student/faculty ratio:* 17:1.
Majors Agricultural business and management; business/commerce; child-care provision; clinical/medical social work; community psychology; computer and information sciences; computer and information sciences related; criminal justice/police science; industrial production technologies related; liberal arts and sciences/liberal studies; music; substance abuse/addiction counseling; welding technology.
Academics *Calendar:* semesters. *Degree:* certificates and associate. *Special study options:* academic remediation for entering students, adult/continuing education programs, distance learning, independent study, internships, part-time degree program, services for LD students, summer session for credit.
Library Jane Carey Memorial Library plus 1 other. *Books:* 33,477 (physical), 13,359 (digital/electronic); *Serial titles:* 81 (physical); *Databases:* 118. Weekly public service hours: 40; students can reserve study rooms.
Student Life *Housing Options:* coed. Campus housing is university owned. *Activities and Organizations:* drama/theater group, choral group, Phi Theta Kappa, Associated Student Body, Rodeo Club, Intervarsity, FFA. *Campus security:* 24-hour emergency response devices.
Athletics Member NJCAA. *Intercollegiate sports:* baseball M(s), basketball M(s)/W(s), cross-country running M(s)/W(s), equestrian sports M(s)/W(s), softball W(s), track and field M(s)/W(s), volleyball W(s). *Intramural sports:* basketball M/W, bowling M/W, softball M/W.
Costs (2020–21) *Tuition:* area resident $2160 full-time, $72 per credit hour part-time; state resident $3720 full-time, $124 per credit hour part-time; nonresident $6300 full-time, $210 per credit hour part-time. *Required fees:* $1710 full-time, $57 per credit hour part-time. *Room and board:* $7676. Room and board charges vary according to board plan. *Payment plan:* deferred payment. *Waivers:* senior citizens and employees or children of employees.
Financial Aid Of all full-time matriculated undergraduates who enrolled in 2016, 158 applied for aid, 158 were judged to have need. 35 Federal Work-Study jobs (averaging $2200). 8 state and other part-time jobs (averaging $2200).
Applying *Options:* electronic application, deferred entrance. *Application fee:* $30. *Required:* high school transcript. *Application deadlines:* rolling (freshmen), rolling (transfers). *Notification:* continuous (freshmen), continuous (transfers).
Freshman Application Contact Ms. Julie Brandt, Admissions Specialist, Dawson Community College, 300 College Drive, Glendive, MT 59330. *Phone:* 406-377-9411. *Toll-free phone:* 800-821-8320. *Fax:* 406-377-8132. *E-mail:* jbrandt@dawson.edu.
Website: http://www.dawson.edu/.

Flathead Valley Community College
Kalispell, Montana

Freshman Application Contact Ms. Marlene C. Stoltz, Admissions/Graduation Coordinator, Flathead Valley Community College, 777 Grandview Drive, Kalispell, MT 59901-2622. *Phone:* 406-756-3846. *Toll-free phone:* 800-313-3822. *E-mail:* mstoltz@fvcc.cc.mt.us. *Website:* http://www.fvcc.edu/.

Fort Peck Community College
Poplar, Montana

Director of Admissions Mr. Robert McAnally, Vice President for Student Services, Fort Peck Community College, PO Box 398, Poplar, MT 59255-0398. *Phone:* 406-768-6329. *Website:* http://www.fpcc.edu/.

Great Falls College Montana State University
Great Falls, Montana

- **State-supported** 2-year, founded 1969, part of Montana University System
- **Small-town** 40-acre campus
- **Endowment** $11,300
- **Coed,** 1,315 undergraduate students, 40% full-time, 69% women, 31% men

Undergraduates 524 full-time, 791 part-time. Students come from 25 states and territories; 2 other countries; 4% are from out of state; 1% Black or African American, non-Hispanic/Latino; 5% Hispanic/Latino; 1% Asian, non-Hispanic/Latino; 0.1% Native Hawaiian or other Pacific Islander, non-Hispanic/Latino; 4% American Indian or Alaska Native, non-Hispanic/Latino; 9% Two or more races, non-Hispanic/Latino; 1% Race/ethnicity unknown; 0.1% international; 6% transferred in.
Freshmen *Admission:* 379 applied, 378 admitted, 155 enrolled.
Faculty *Total:* 106, 35% full-time, 8% with terminal degrees. *Student/faculty ratio:* 13:1.
Majors Accounting; computer programming; computer systems analysis; computer systems networking and telecommunications; dental hygiene; emergency medical technology (EMT paramedic); energy management and systems technology; health information/medical records administration; health

information/medical records technology; information technology; liberal arts and sciences and humanities related; physical therapy technology; registered nursing/registered nurse; surgical technology; welding technology.
Academics *Calendar:* semesters. *Degree:* certificates and associate. *Special study options:* academic remediation for entering students, advanced placement credit, distance learning, double majors, independent study, internships, part-time degree program, services for LD students, summer session for credit.
Library Weaver Library plus 1 other. *Books:* 9,239 (physical), 266,102 (digital/electronic); *Serial titles:* 60 (physical), 121,995 (digital/electronic); *Databases:* 55. Students can reserve study rooms.
Student Life *Housing:* college housing not available. *Activities and Organizations:* choral group, The Associated Students of Great Falls College Montana State University, Phi Theta Kappa, Medical Assistant Club, Dental Hygiene Club, Nursing Club. *Campus security:* 24-hour emergency response devices, patrol by security personnel. *Student services:* veterans affairs office.
Costs (2020–21) *Tuition:* area resident $2752 full-time, $115 per credit hour part-time; state resident $2752 full-time, $115 per credit hour part-time; nonresident $9644 full-time, $402 per credit hour part-time. Full-time tuition and fees vary according to course load, location, and program. Part-time tuition and fees vary according to course load, location, and program. *Required fees:* $728 full-time, $60 per credit hour part-time, $30 per term part-time. *Payment plan:* deferred payment. *Waivers:* minority students, senior citizens, and employees or children of employees.
Financial Aid Of all full-time matriculated undergraduates who enrolled in 2018, 534 applied for aid, 467 were judged to have need, 99 had their need fully met. 28 Federal Work-Study jobs (averaging $2517). 16 state and other part-time jobs (averaging $2368). In 2018, 11 non-need-based awards were made. *Average percent of need met:* 73%. *Average financial aid package:* $8576. *Average need-based loan:* $5667. *Average need-based gift aid:* $4849. *Average non-need-based aid:* $727.
Applying *Options:* electronic application, deferred entrance. *Application fee:* $30. *Required:* high school transcript, proof of immunization. *Application deadlines:* rolling (freshmen), rolling (transfers). *Notification:* continuous (freshmen), continuous (transfers).
Freshman Application Contact Ms. Shannon Marr, Director of Recruitment & Enrollment, Great Falls College Montana State University, 2100 16th Avenue South, Great Falls, MT 59405. *Phone:* 406-771-4408. *Toll-free phone:* 800-446-2698. *Fax:* 406-268-3700. *E-mail:* shannon.marr1@gfcmsu.edu.
Website: http://www.gfcmsu.edu/.

Helena College University of Montana
Helena, Montana
Freshman Application Contact Mr. Ryan Loomis, Admissions Representative/Recruiter, Helena College University of Montana, 1115 North Roberts Street, Helena, MT 59601. *Phone:* 406-447-6904. *Toll-free phone:* 800-241-4882. *Website:* http://www.umhelena.edu/.

Highlands College of Montana Tech
Butte, Montana
Admissions Office Contact Highlands College of Montana Tech, 25 Basin Creek Road, Butte, MT 59701. *Website:* http://www.mtech.edu/academics/highlands/.

Little Big Horn College
Crow Agency, Montana
Freshman Application Contact Ms. Ann Bullis, Dean of Student Services, Little Big Horn College, Box 370, 1 Forest Lane, Crow Agency, MT 59022-0370. *Phone:* 406-638-2228 Ext. 50. *Website:* http://www.lbhc.edu/.

Miles Community College
Miles City, Montana
Freshman Application Contact Mr. Haley Anderson, Admissions Representative, Miles Community College, 2715 Dickinson Street, Miles City, MT 59301. *Phone:* 406-874-6178. *Toll-free phone:* 800-541-9281. *E-mail:* andersonh@milescc.edu. *Website:* http://www.milescc.edu/.

Pima Medical Institute - Dillon
Dillon, Montana
Admissions Office Contact Pima Medical Institute - Dillon, 434 East Poindexter Street, Dillon, MT 59725. *Website:* http://www.pmi.edu/.

Salish Kootenai College
Pablo, Montana
Freshman Application Contact Ms. Jackie Moran, Admissions Officer, Salish Kootenai College, PO Box 70, Pablo, MT 59855-0117. *Phone:* 406-275-4866. *Fax:* 406-275-4810. *E-mail:* jackie_moran@skc.edu. *Website:* http://www.skc.edu/.

Stone Child College
Box Elder, Montana
Director of Admissions Mr. Ted Whitford, Director of Admissions/Registrar, Stone Child College, 8294 Upper Box Elder Road, Box Elder, MT 59521. *Phone:* 406-395-4313 Ext. 110. *E-mail:* uanet337@quest.ocsc.montana.edu. *Website:* http://www.stonechild.edu/.

NEBRASKA

CHI Health School of Radiologic Technology
Omaha, Nebraska
Freshman Application Contact CHI Health School of Radiologic Technology, 6911 North 68th Plaza, Omaha, NE 68122. *Phone:* 402-572-3650. *Website:* http://www.chihealth.com/school-of-radiologic-technology.

Little Priest Tribal College
Winnebago, Nebraska
Freshman Application Contact Little Priest Tribal College, PO Box 270, Winnebago, NE 68071. *Phone:* 402-878-2380 Ext. 112. *Website:* http://www.littlepriest.edu/.

Metropolitan Community College
Omaha, Nebraska
- **State and locally supported** 2-year, founded 1974, part of Nebraska Coordinating Commission for Postsecondary Education
- **Urban** 172-acre campus
- **Endowment** $1.4 million
- **Coed**

Undergraduates 7,095 full-time, 9,908 part-time. 3% are from out of state; 17% transferred in. *Retention:* 50% of full-time freshmen returned.
Faculty *Student/faculty ratio:* 16:1.
Academics *Calendar:* quarters. *Degree:* certificates, diplomas, and associate. *Special study options:* academic remediation for entering students, adult/continuing education programs, advanced placement credit, cooperative education, distance learning, English as a second language, independent study, internships, part-time degree program, services for LD students, summer session for credit. *ROTC:* Army (c).
Library Metropolitan Community College plus 2 others.
Student Life *Campus security:* 24-hour emergency response devices and patrols, late-night transport/escort service, controlled dormitory access, security on duty 9 pm to 6 am.
Applying *Options:* early admission. *Recommended:* high school transcript.
Freshman Application Contact Ms. Maria Vazquez, Associate Vice President for Student Affairs, Metropolitan Community College, PO Box 3777, Omaha, NE 69103-0777. *Phone:* 402-457-2430. *Toll-free phone:* 800-228-9553. *Fax:* 402-457-2238. *E-mail:* mvazquez@mccneb.edu. *Website:* http://www.mccneb.edu/.

Mid-Plains Community College
North Platte, Nebraska
Freshman Application Contact Ms. Sandy Ablard, Admissions Specialist, Mid-Plains Community College, 1101 Halligan Drive, North Platte, NE 69101. *Phone:* 308-535-3609. *Toll-free phone:* 800-658-4308 (in-state); 800-658-4348 (out-of-state). *Fax:* 308-534-5767. *E-mail:* ablards@mpcc.edu. *Website:* http://www.mpcc.edu/.

Myotherapy Institute
Lincoln, Nebraska

Freshman Application Contact Admissions Office, Myotherapy Institute, 4001 Pioneers Woods Drive, Lincoln, NE 68506. *Phone:* 402-421-7410. *Website:* http://www.myotherapy.edu/.

Nebraska College of Technical Agriculture
Curtis, Nebraska

Freshman Application Contact Kevin Martin, Assistant Admissions Coordinator, Nebraska College of Technical Agriculture, 404 East 7th Street, Curtis, NE 69025. *Phone:* 308-367-4124. *Toll-free phone:* 800-3CURTIS. *Website:* http://www.ncta.unl.edu/.

Nebraska Indian Community College
Macy, Nebraska

- **Federally supported** 2-year, founded 1979
- **Rural** 22-acre campus with easy access to Omaha
- **Coed**
- 100% of applicants were admitted

Undergraduates 47 full-time, 133 part-time. Students come from 3 states and territories; 13% are from out of state; 2% transferred in. *Retention:* 59% of full-time freshmen returned.
Faculty *Student/faculty ratio:* 5:1.
Academics *Calendar:* semesters. *Degree:* certificates and associate. *Special study options:* academic remediation for entering students, adult/continuing education programs, distance learning, double majors, independent study, internships, part-time degree program, services for LD students, study abroad, summer session for credit.
Library Macy Library plus 1 other. *Books:* 17,555 (physical), 370 (digital/electronic). Weekly public service hours: 40.
Applying *Options:* electronic application, early admission. *Required:* high school transcript. *Required for some:* certificate of tribal enrollment.
Freshman Application Contact Troy Munhofen, Registrar, Nebraska Indian Community College, PO Box 428, Macy, NE 68039. *Phone:* 402-241-5922. *Toll-free phone:* 844-440-NICC. *Fax:* 402-837-4183. *E-mail:* tmunhofen@thenicc.edu. *Website:* http://www.thenicc.edu/.

Northeast Community College
Norfolk, Nebraska

Freshman Application Contact Tiffany Hopper, Admissions Specialist, Northeast Community College, 801 East Benjamin Avenue, PO Box 469, Norfolk, NE 68702-0469. *Phone:* 402-844-7260. *Toll-free phone:* 800-348-9033 Ext. 7260. *E-mail:* admission@northeast.edu. *Website:* http://www.northeast.edu/.

Omaha School of Massage and Healthcare of Herzing University
Omaha, Nebraska

Admissions Office Contact Omaha School of Massage and Healthcare of Herzing University, 9748 Park Drive, Omaha, NE 68127. *Website:* http://www.osmhc.com/.

Southeast Community College, Beatrice Campus
Beatrice, Nebraska

Freshman Application Contact Admissions Office, Southeast Community College, Beatrice Campus, 4771 West Scott Road, Beatrice, NE 68310. *Phone:* 402-228-3468. *Toll-free phone:* 800-233-5027. *Fax:* 402-228-2218. *Website:* http://www.southeast.edu/.

Southeast Community College, Lincoln Campus
Lincoln, Nebraska

Freshman Application Contact Admissions Office, Southeast Community College, Lincoln Campus, 8800 O Street, Lincoln, NE 68520. *Phone:* 402-471-3333. *Toll-free phone:* 800-642-4075. *Fax:* 402-437-2404. *E-mail:* admissions@southeast.edu. *Website:* http://www.southeast.edu/.

Southeast Community College, Milford Campus
Milford, Nebraska

Freshman Application Contact Admissions Office, Southeast Community College, Milford Campus, 600 State Street, Milford, NE 68405. *Phone:* 402-761-2131. *Toll-free phone:* 800-933-7223. *Fax:* 402-761-2324. *E-mail:* admissions@southeast.edu. *Website:* http://www.southeast.edu/.

Universal College of Healing Arts
Omaha, Nebraska

Admissions Office Contact Universal College of Healing Arts, 8702 North 30th Street, Omaha, NE 68112-1810. *Website:* http://www.ucha.edu/.

Western Nebraska Community College
Sidney, Nebraska

Director of Admissions Mr. Troy Archuleta, Admissions and Recruitment Director, Western Nebraska Community College, 371 College Drive, Sidney, NE 69162. *Phone:* 308-635-6015. *Toll-free phone:* 800-222-9682. *E-mail:* rhovey@wncc.net. *Website:* http://www.wncc.net/.

NEVADA

Career College of Northern Nevada
Sparks, Nevada

Freshman Application Contact Ms. Maria Clark, Director of Admissions, Career College of Northern Nevada, 1421 Pullman Dr, Sparks, NV 89434. *Phone:* 775-856-2266. *Fax:* 775-856-0935. *E-mail:* mclark@ccnn4u.com. *Website:* http://www.ccnn.edu/.

Carrington College–Las Vegas
Las Vegas, Nevada

Freshman Application Contact Carrington College–Las Vegas, 5740 South Eastern Avenue, Suite 140, Las Vegas, NV 89119. *Website:* http://www.carrington.edu/.

Carrington College–Reno
Reno, Nevada

Freshman Application Contact Carrington College–Reno, 5580 Kietzke Lane, Reno, NV 89511. *Phone:* 775-335-2900. *Website:* http://www.carrington.edu/.

College of Southern Nevada
Las Vegas, Nevada

- **State-supported** primarily 2-year, founded 1971, part of University and Community College System of Nevada
- **Suburban** 89-acre campus with easy access to Las Vegas
- **Coed**

Academics *Calendar:* semesters. *Degrees:* certificates, associate, and bachelor's. *Special study options:* academic remediation for entering students, accelerated degree program, adult/continuing education programs, advanced placement credit, cooperative education, distance learning, double majors, English as a second language, honors programs, independent study, internships, part-time degree program, services for LD students, summer session for credit. *ROTC:* Army (b).
Library Learning Assistance Center.
Student Life *Campus security:* 24-hour emergency response devices and patrols.
Athletics Member NJCAA.
Financial Aid Of all full-time matriculated undergraduates who enrolled in 2018, 199 Federal Work-Study jobs (averaging $1753). 170 state and other part-time jobs (averaging $2154).
Applying *Options:* early admission. *Required:* student data form.
Freshman Application Contact Admissions and Records, College of Southern Nevada, 6375 West Charleston Boulevard, Las Vegas, NV 89146. *Phone:* 702-651-4060. *Website:* http://www.csn.edu/.

Great Basin College

Elko, Nevada

Freshman Application Contact Ms. Jan King, Director of Admissions and Registrar, Great Basin College, 1500 College Parkway, Elko, NV 89801. *Phone:* 775-753-2102. *E-mail:* jan.king@gbcnv.edu. *Website:* http://www.gbcnv.edu/.

Northwest Career College

Las Vegas, Nevada

Admissions Office Contact Northwest Career College, 7398 Smoke Ranch Road, Suite 100, Las Vegas, NV 89128. *Website:* http://www.northwestcareercollege.edu/.

Pima Medical Institute - Las Vegas

Las Vegas, Nevada

Freshman Application Contact Admissions Office, Pima Medical Institute - Las Vegas, 3333 East Flamingo Road, Las Vegas, NV 89121. *Phone:* 702-458-9650 Ext. 202. *Toll-free phone:* 800-477-PIMA. *Website:* http://www.pmi.edu/.

Truckee Meadows Community College

Reno, Nevada

- **State-supported** primarily 2-year, founded 1971, part of Nevada System of Higher Education
- **Suburban** 63-acre campus
- **Endowment** $11.2 million
- **Coed,** 11,316 undergraduate students, 27% full-time, 46% women, 54% men

Undergraduates 3,065 full-time, 8,251 part-time. Students come from 27 states and territories; 18 other countries; 6% are from out of state; 3% Black or African American, non-Hispanic/Latino; 33% Hispanic/Latino; 6% Asian, non-Hispanic/Latino; 0.1% Native Hawaiian or other Pacific Islander, non-Hispanic/Latino; 1% American Indian or Alaska Native, non-Hispanic/Latino; 4% Two or more races, non-Hispanic/Latino; 2% Race/ethnicity unknown; 0.3% international; 5% transferred in. *Retention:* 66% of full-time freshmen returned.
Freshmen *Admission:* 3,265 applied, 3,265 admitted, 1,638 enrolled.
Faculty *Total:* 640, 26% full-time. *Student/faculty ratio:* 19:1.
Majors Anthropology; architectural drafting and CAD/CADD; architecture; automobile/automotive mechanics technology; biology/biological sciences; business/commerce; chemistry; civil engineering; commercial and advertising art; computer programming (specific applications); computer systems networking and telecommunications; cooking and related culinary arts; criminal justice/police science; criminal justice/safety; crisis/emergency/disaster management; dental assisting; dental hygiene; diesel mechanics technology; dietetics; drafting and design technology; elementary education; energy management and systems technology; engineering; engineering technologies and engineering related; English; entrepreneurial and small business related; environmental science; fine arts related; fire prevention and safety technology; foods, nutrition, and wellness; general studies; geology/earth science; heating, air conditioning, ventilation and refrigeration maintenance technology; history; kindergarten/preschool education; landscape architecture; legal assistant/paralegal; liberal arts and sciences/liberal studies; logistics, materials, and supply chain management; management information systems and services related; manufacturing engineering technology; mathematics; medical radiologic technology; mental health counseling; music; music performance; natural resources/conservation; philosophy; physics; psychology; registered nursing/registered nurse; science, technology and society; veterinary/animal health technology; welding technology.
Academics *Calendar:* semesters. *Degrees:* certificates, associate, and bachelor's. *Special study options:* academic remediation for entering students, accelerated degree program, adult/continuing education programs, advanced placement credit, cooperative education, distance learning, double majors, English as a second language, independent study, internships, part-time degree program, services for LD students, summer session for credit. *ROTC:* Army (c).
Library Elizabeth Sturm Library plus 3 others. *Books:* 49,012 (physical); *Serial titles:* 32 (digital/electronic); *Databases:* 93. Weekly public service hours: 143; students can reserve study rooms.
Student Life *Housing:* college housing not available. *Activities and Organizations:* drama/theater group, student-run newspaper, Entrepreneurship Club, International Club, Phi Theta Kappa, Student Government Association, Student Media and Broadcasting Club. *Campus security:* 24-hour emergency response devices and patrols, late-night transport/escort service. *Student services:* personal/psychological counseling, veterans affairs office.
Athletics Member NJCAA. *Intercollegiate sports:* soccer M/W.
Costs (2019–20) *Tuition:* state resident $2466 full-time, $103 per credit part-time; nonresident $9656 full-time, $113 per credit part-time. Full-time tuition and fees vary according to course level, course load, degree level, and program. Part-time tuition and fees vary according to course level, course load, degree level, and program. *Required fees:* $300 full-time, $13 per credit part-time. *Payment plan:* installment. *Waivers:* employees or children of employees.
Applying *Options:* electronic application, early admission. *Application fee:* $20. *Application deadlines:* rolling (freshmen), rolling (transfers). *Notification:* continuous (freshmen), continuous (transfers).
Freshman Application Contact Truckee Meadows Community College, 7000 Dandini Boulevard, Reno, NV 89512-3901. *Phone:* 775-673-7240. *Website:* http://www.tmcc.edu/.

Western Nevada College

Carson City, Nevada

- **State-supported** primarily 2-year, founded 1971, part of Nevada System of Higher Education
- **Small-town** 200-acre campus
- **Endowment** $250,000
- **Coed,** 3,702 undergraduate students, 33% full-time, 58% women, 42% men

Undergraduates 1,227 full-time, 2,475 part-time. Students come from 10 states and territories; 20 other countries; 4% are from out of state; 2% Black or African American, non-Hispanic/Latino; 25% Hispanic/Latino; 2% Asian, non-Hispanic/Latino; 0.3% Native Hawaiian or other Pacific Islander, non-Hispanic/Latino; 2% American Indian or Alaska Native, non-Hispanic/Latino; 4% Two or more races, non-Hispanic/Latino; 6% Race/ethnicity unknown; 5% transferred in.
Freshmen *Admission:* 612 applied, 612 admitted, 613 enrolled.
Faculty *Total:* 246, 22% full-time. *Student/faculty ratio:* 18:1.
Majors Accounting; automobile/automotive mechanics technology; building construction technology; business administration and management; business/commerce; commercial and advertising art; computer and information sciences; construction management; criminal justice/law enforcement administration; deaf studies; general studies; industrial technology; liberal arts and sciences/liberal studies; machine tool technology; management information systems; manufacturing engineering technology; physical sciences; registered nursing/registered nurse; welding technology.
Academics *Calendar:* semesters. *Degrees:* certificates, associate, and bachelor's. *Special study options:* academic remediation for entering students, adult/continuing education programs, advanced placement credit, cooperative education, distance learning, double majors, English as a second language, independent study, internships, part-time degree program, services for LD students, summer session for credit.
Library Western Nevada College Library and Media Services plus 1 other. *Books:* 35,923 (physical), 4,544 (digital/electronic); *Serial titles:* 2,725 (physical); *Databases:* 33. Weekly public service hours: 61; students can reserve study rooms.
Student Life *Housing:* college housing not available. *Activities and Organizations:* drama/theater group, choral group, Associated Students of Western Nevada, Soccer Club, Veterans Club, National Student Nurses Association, American Sign Language Club. *Campus security:* late-night transport/escort service. *Student services:* personal/psychological counseling, veterans affairs office.
Athletics *Intramural sports:* soccer M(c)/W(c).
Costs (2019–20) *Tuition:* state resident $3428 full-time; nonresident $10,618 full-time. Full-time tuition and fees vary according to course level. Part-time tuition and fees vary according to course level. *Payment plans:* tuition prepayment, installment. *Waivers:* employees or children of employees.
Financial Aid Of all full-time matriculated undergraduates who enrolled in 2019, 658 applied for aid, 597 were judged to have need. *Average financial aid package:* $13,467. *Average need-based loan:* $7016. *Average need-based gift aid:* $9740.
Applying *Options:* electronic application, early admission. *Application fee:* $15. *Required for some:* high school transcript. *Recommended:* high school transcript. *Application deadlines:* rolling (freshmen), rolling (out-of-state freshmen), rolling (transfers). *Notification:* continuous (freshmen), continuous (out-of-state freshmen), continuous (transfers).
Freshman Application Contact Admissions and Records, Western Nevada College, 2201 West College Parkway, Carson City, NV 89703. *Phone:* 775-445-2377. *Fax:* 775-445-3147. *E-mail:* wncc_aro@wncc.edu. *Website:* http://www.wnc.edu/.

NEW HAMPSHIRE

Great Bay Community College

Portsmouth, New Hampshire

Freshman Application Contact Mr. Matt Thornton, Admissions Coordinator, Great Bay Community College, 320 Corporate Drive, Portsmouth, NH 03801. *Phone:* 603-427-7605. *Toll-free phone:* 800-522-1194. *E-mail:* askgreatbay@ccsnh.edu. *Website:* http://www.greatbay.edu/.

Lakes Region Community College

Laconia, New Hampshire

Admissions Office Contact Lakes Region Community College, 379 Belmont Road, Laconia, NH 03246. *Toll-free phone:* 800-357-2992. *Website:* http://www.lrcc.edu/.

Manchester Community College

Manchester, New Hampshire

Freshman Application Contact Ms. Jacquie Poirier, Coordinator of Admissions, Manchester Community College, 1066 Front Street, Manchester, NH 03102-8518. *Phone:* 603-668-6706 Ext. 283. *Toll-free phone:* 800-924-3445. *E-mail:* jpoirier@nhctc.edu. *Website:* http://www.mccnh.edu/.

Nashua Community College

Nashua, New Hampshire

Freshman Application Contact Ms. Patricia Goodman, Vice President of Student Services, Nashua Community College, Nashua, NH 03063. *Phone:* 603-882-6923 Ext. 1529. *Fax:* 603-882-8690. *E-mail:* pgoodman@ccsnh.edu. *Website:* http://www.nashuacc.edu/.

NHTI, Concord's Community College

Concord, New Hampshire

Freshman Application Contact NHTI, Concord's Community College, 31 College Drive, Concord, NH 03301-7412. *Toll-free phone:* 800-247-0179. *Website:* http://www.nhti.edu/.

River Valley Community College

Claremont, New Hampshire

Freshman Application Contact River Valley Community College, 1 College Place, Claremont, NH 03743. *Phone:* 603-542-7744 Ext. 5323. *Toll-free phone:* 800-837-0658. *Website:* http://www.rivervalley.edu/.

St. Joseph School of Nursing

Nashua, New Hampshire

Freshman Application Contact Mrs. L. Nadeau, Admissions, St. Joseph School of Nursing, 5 Woodward Avenue, Nashua, NH 03060. *Toll-free phone:* 800-370-3169. *Website:* http://www.sjson.edu/.

White Mountains Community College

Berlin, New Hampshire

Freshman Application Contact Ms. Amanda Gaeb, Admissions Counselor, White Mountains Community College, 2020 Riverside Drive, Berlin, NH 03570. *Phone:* 603-342-3006. *Toll-free phone:* 800-445-4525. *Fax:* 603-752-6335. *E-mail:* agaeb@ccsnh.edu. *Website:* http://www.wmcc.edu/.

NEW JERSEY

Assumption College for Sisters

Denville, New Jersey

- **Independent Roman Catholic** 2-year, founded 1953
- **Rural** 112-acre campus with easy access to New York City
- **Women only**

Undergraduates 20% are from out of state. *Retention:* 100% of full-time freshmen returned.
Faculty *Student/faculty ratio:* 8:1.
Academics *Calendar:* semesters. *Degree:* certificates and associate. *Special study options:* academic remediation for entering students, advanced placement credit, English as a second language, part-time degree program, services for LD students, summer session for credit.
Library Assumption College for Sisters Library.
Student Life *Campus security:* 24-hour emergency response devices.
Applying *Application fee:* $50. *Required:* high school transcript, 1 letter of recommendation, women religious or women in religious formation.
Freshman Application Contact Sr. Gerardine Tantsits, Academic Dean/Registrar, Assumption College for Sisters, 350 Bernardsville Road, Mendham, NJ 07945-2923. *Phone:* 973-543-6528 Ext. 228. *Fax:* 973-543-1738. *E-mail:* deanregistrar@acs350.org. *Website:* http://www.acs350.org/.

Atlantic Cape Community College

Mays Landing, New Jersey

Freshman Application Contact Mrs. Linda McLeod, Assistant Director, Admissions and College Recruitment, Atlantic Cape Community College, 5100 Black Horse Pike, Mays Landing, NJ 08330-2699. *Phone:* 609-343-5009. *Fax:* 609-343-4921. *E-mail:* accadmit@atlantic.edu. *Website:* http://www.atlantic.edu/.

Bergen Community College

Paramus, New Jersey

- **County-supported** 2-year, founded 1965
- **Suburban** 167-acre campus with easy access to New York City
- **Coed**

Undergraduates 1% are from out of state.
Faculty *Student/faculty ratio:* 22:1.
Academics *Calendar:* semesters. *Degree:* certificates and associate. *Special study options:* academic remediation for entering students, adult/continuing education programs, cooperative education, distance learning, English as a second language, honors programs, internships, part-time degree program, services for LD students, study abroad, summer session for credit.
Library Sidney Silverman Library and Learning Resources Center plus 1 other.
Student Life *Campus security:* 24-hour patrols.
Athletics Member NJCAA.
Financial Aid Of all full-time matriculated undergraduates who enrolled in 2018, 236 Federal Work-Study jobs (averaging $1410).
Freshman Application Contact Admissions Office, Bergen Community College, 400 Paramus Road, Paramus, NJ 07652-1595. *Phone:* 201-447-7195. *E-mail:* admsoffice@bergen.edu. *Website:* http://www.bergen.edu/.

Brookdale Community College

Lincroft, New Jersey

- **County-supported** 2-year, founded 1967, part of New Jersey Commission on Higher Education
- **Small-town** 221-acre campus with easy access to New York City
- **Coed**

Undergraduates *Retention:* 72% of full-time freshmen returned.
Faculty *Student/faculty ratio:* 20:1.
Academics *Calendar:* semesters plus 1 ten-week and 2 six-week summer terms. *Degree:* certificates and associate. *Special study options:* academic remediation for entering students, adult/continuing education programs, advanced placement credit, cooperative education, distance learning, English as a second language, honors programs, independent study, internships, part-time degree program, services for LD students, study abroad, summer session for credit. *ROTC:* Army (c), Air Force (c).
Library Brookdale Community College Library.
Student Life *Campus security:* 24-hour emergency response devices and patrols.
Athletics Member NJCAA.
Applying *Options:* early admission, deferred entrance. *Application fee:* $25. *Required:* high school transcript.
Director of Admissions Ms. Kim Toomey, Registrar, Brookdale Community College, 765 Newman Springs Road, Lincroft, NJ 07738-1597. *Phone:* 732-224-2268. *Website:* http://www.brookdalecc.edu/.

Camden County College

Blackwood, New Jersey

- **State and locally supported** 2-year, founded 1967, part of New Jersey Office of the Secretary of Higher Education
- **Suburban** 320-acre campus with easy access to Philadelphia
- **Coed**, 9,735 undergraduate students, 43% full-time, 61% women, 39% men

Undergraduates 4,200 full-time, 5,535 part-time. Students come from 8 states and territories; 1% are from out of state; 21% Black or African American, non-Hispanic/Latino; 19% Hispanic/Latino; 6% Asian, non-Hispanic/Latino; 0.1% Native Hawaiian or other Pacific Islander, non-Hispanic/Latino; 1% American Indian or Alaska Native, non-Hispanic/Latino; 0.5% Two or more races, non-Hispanic/Latino; 4% Race/ethnicity unknown; 2% international; 8% transferred in.

Freshmen *Admission:* 6,383 applied, 1,580 enrolled.

Majors Accounting technology and bookkeeping; administrative assistant and secretarial science; automotive engineering technology; biology/biotechnology laboratory technician; business administration and management; cinematography and film/video production; clinical/medical laboratory technology; computer and information sciences; criminal justice/police science; dental assisting; dental hygiene; desktop publishing and digital imaging design; dietetic technology; drafting and design technology; early childhood education; education (multiple levels); electrical, electronic and communications engineering technology; electromechanical technology; emergency medical technology (EMT paramedic); engineering science; engineering technologies and engineering related; fine/studio arts; fire prevention and safety technology; fire services administration; health information/medical records administration; health services/allied health/health sciences; hospitality administration; industrial production technologies related; legal assistant/paralegal; liberal arts and sciences/liberal studies; management information systems; marketing/marketing management; massage therapy; mechanical engineering/mechanical technology; mechanical engineering technologies related; occupational therapist assistant; opticianry; radio and television broadcasting technology; registered nursing/registered nurse; rehabilitation and therapeutic professions related; sign language interpretation and translation; social work; sport and fitness administration/management; substance abuse/addiction counseling; veterinary/animal health technology; web page, digital/multimedia and information resources design.

Academics *Calendar:* semesters. *Degree:* certificates and associate. *Special study options:* academic remediation for entering students, adult/continuing education programs, advanced placement credit, cooperative education, distance learning, double majors, English as a second language, external degree program, freshman honors college, honors programs, independent study, internships, off-campus study, part-time degree program, services for LD students, study abroad, summer session for credit.

Library Wolverton Center Library. Students can reserve study rooms.

Student Life *Housing:* college housing not available. *Activities and Organizations:* drama/theater group, student-run newspaper, radio station, choral group. *Campus security:* 24-hour emergency response devices and patrols, late-night transport/escort service. *Student services:* health clinic, veterans affairs office.

Athletics Member NJCAA. *Intercollegiate sports:* baseball M, basketball M/W, cross-country running M/W, golf M/W, soccer M/W, softball W, tennis W, wrestling M.

Costs (2020–21) *Tuition:* area resident $3210 full-time, $107 per credit hour part-time; state resident $3330 full-time, $111 per credit hour part-time; nonresident $3330 full-time, $111 per credit hour part-time. Full-time tuition and fees vary according to course load and program. Part-time tuition and fees vary according to course load and program. *Required fees:* $1110 full-time, $37 per credit hour part-time. *Payment plans:* installment, deferred payment. *Waivers:* senior citizens and employees or children of employees.

Financial Aid Of all full-time matriculated undergraduates who enrolled in 2018, 117 Federal Work-Study jobs (averaging $1126).

Applying *Options:* electronic application, early admission. *Required for some:* high school transcript. *Application deadlines:* rolling (freshmen), rolling (transfers).

Freshman Application Contact Mr. Donald Delaney, Director of Program Outreach, Camden County College, PO Box 200, Blackwood, NJ 08012-0200. *Phone:* 856-227-7200 Ext. 4660. *Fax:* 856-374-4916. *E-mail:* ddelaney@camdencc.edu.
Website: http://www.camdencc.edu/.

County College of Morris

Randolph, New Jersey

- **County-supported** 2-year, founded 1966
- **Suburban** 218-acre campus with easy access to New York City
- **Endowment** $5.4 million
- **Coed**

Undergraduates 3,819 full-time, 4,130 part-time. Students come from 6 states and territories; 0.4% are from out of state; 5% Black or African American, non-Hispanic/Latino; 21% Hispanic/Latino; 6% Asian, non-Hispanic/Latino; 0.2% Native Hawaiian or other Pacific Islander, non-Hispanic/Latino; 0.4% American Indian or Alaska Native, non-Hispanic/Latino; 2% Two or more races, non-Hispanic/Latino; 6% Race/ethnicity unknown; 2% international; 5% transferred in. *Retention:* 72% of full-time freshmen returned.

Academics *Calendar:* semesters. *Degree:* certificates and associate. *Special study options:* academic remediation for entering students, accelerated degree program, advanced placement credit, cooperative education, distance learning, double majors, English as a second language, independent study, internships, services for LD students, study abroad, summer session for credit.

Library Learning Resource Center plus 1 other. *Books:* 38,594 (physical), 3,508 (digital/electronic); *Serial titles:* 26 (physical), 5 (digital/electronic); *Databases:* 123. Weekly public service hours: 68.

Student Life *Campus security:* 24-hour emergency response devices and patrols, late-night transport/escort service.

Athletics Member NJCAA.

Costs (2019–20) *Tuition:* area resident $4110 full-time, $137 per credit hour part-time; state resident $8220 full-time, $274 per credit hour part-time; nonresident $11,790 full-time, $393 per credit hour part-time. Full-time tuition and fees vary according to class time, course load, and program. Part-time tuition and fees vary according to class time, course load, and program. *Required fees:* $1080 full-time, $29 per credit hour part-time, $21 per course part-time.

Financial Aid Of all full-time matriculated undergraduates who enrolled in 2018, 588 Federal Work-Study jobs (averaging $1947).

Applying *Options:* electronic application. *Application fee:* $30. *Required:* high school transcript.

Freshman Application Contact County College of Morris, 214 Center Grove Road, Randolph, NJ 07869-2086. *Phone:* 973-328-5096. *Website:* http://www.ccm.edu/.

Cumberland County College

Vineland, New Jersey

Freshman Application Contact Ms. Anne Daly-Eimer, Director of Admissions and Registration, Cumberland County College, 3322 College Drive, Vineland, NJ 08360. *Phone:* 856-691-8600. *Website:* http://www.cccnj.edu/.

Eastern International College

Belleville, New Jersey

- **Proprietary** primarily 2-year
- **Urban** campus with easy access to Manhattan, New York
- **Coed**

Academics *Degrees:* associate and bachelor's.

Freshman Application Contact Eastern International College, 251 Washington Avenue, Belleville, NJ 07109. *Website:* http://www.eicollege.edu/.

Eastern International College

Jersey City, New Jersey

Admissions Office Contact Eastern International College, 684 Newark Avenue, Jersey City, NJ 07306. *Website:* http://www.eicollege.edu/.

Eastwick College - Hackensack

Hackensack, New Jersey

Admissions Office Contact Eastwick College - Hackensack, 250 Moore Street, Hackensack, NJ 07601. *Website:* http://eastwick.edu.

Eastwick College - Nutley

Nutley, New Jersey

Admissions Office Contact Eastwick College - Nutley, 103 Park Avenue, Nutley, NJ 07110. *Website:* http://eastwick.edu.

Eastwick College - Ramsey

Ramsey, New Jersey

Admissions Office Contact Eastwick College - Ramsey, 10 South Franklin Turnpike, Ramsey, NJ 07446. *Website:* http://eastwick.edu.

Essex County College

Newark, New Jersey

- **County-supported** 2-year, founded 1966, part of New Jersey Commission on Higher Education
- **Urban** 22-acre campus with easy access to New York City
- **Coed**

Undergraduates 6,569 full-time, 5,410 part-time. Students come from 9 states and territories; 49 other countries; 1% are from out of state; 48% Black or African American, non-Hispanic/Latino; 24% Hispanic/Latino; 4% Asian, non-Hispanic/Latino; 0.1% Native Hawaiian or other Pacific Islander, non-Hispanic/Latino; 0.2% American Indian or Alaska Native, non-Hispanic/Latino; 0.5% Two or more races, non-Hispanic/Latino; 6% Race/ethnicity unknown; 8% international; 2% transferred in. *Retention:* 52% of full-time freshmen returned.
Faculty *Student/faculty ratio:* 29:1.
Academics *Calendar:* semesters. *Degree:* certificates and associate. *Special study options:* academic remediation for entering students, accelerated degree program, adult/continuing education programs, advanced placement credit, cooperative education, distance learning, double majors, English as a second language, independent study, internships, off-campus study, part-time degree program, services for LD students, summer session for credit. *ROTC:* Army (c).
Library Martin Luther King, Jr. Library.
Student Life *Campus security:* 24-hour emergency response devices and patrols.
Athletics Member NJCAA.
Financial Aid Of all full-time matriculated undergraduates who enrolled in 2009, 256 Federal Work-Study jobs (averaging $2488).
Applying *Options:* electronic application, deferred entrance. *Application fee:* $25. *Required:* high school transcript.
Freshman Application Contact Ms. Marva Mack, Director of Admissions, Essex County College, 303 University Avenue, Newark, NJ 07102. *Phone:* 973-877-3119. *Fax:* 973-623-6449. *Website:* http://www.essex.edu/.

Hudson County Community College

Jersey City, New Jersey

Freshman Application Contact Hudson County Community College, 70 Sip Avenue, Jersey City, NJ 07306. *Phone:* 201-360-4111. *Website:* http://www.hccc.edu/.

Jersey College

Teterboro, New Jersey

Freshman Application Contact Jersey College, 546 US Highway 46, Teterboro, NJ 07608. *Website:* http://www.jerseycollege.edu/.

Mercer County Community College

Trenton, New Jersey

- **State and locally supported** 2-year, founded 1966
- **Suburban** 292-acre campus with easy access to New York City, Philadelphia
- **Coed**

Undergraduates 3,077 full-time, 4,902 part-time. Students come from 7 states and territories; 89 other countries; 1% are from out of state; 22% Black or African American, non-Hispanic/Latino; 18% Hispanic/Latino; 6% Asian, non-Hispanic/Latino; 0.2% Native Hawaiian or other Pacific Islander, non-Hispanic/Latino; 0.2% American Indian or Alaska Native, non-Hispanic/Latino; 2% Two or more races, non-Hispanic/Latino; 9% Race/ethnicity unknown; 4% international; 3% transferred in. *Retention:* 71% of full-time freshmen returned.
Faculty *Student/faculty ratio:* 18:1.
Academics *Calendar:* semesters. *Degree:* certificates and associate. *Special study options:* academic remediation for entering students, accelerated degree program, adult/continuing education programs, advanced placement credit, cooperative education, distance learning, double majors, English as a second language, external degree program, independent study, internships, part-time degree program, services for LD students, student-designed majors, summer session for credit. *ROTC:* Army (c), Air Force (c).
Library Mercer County Community College Library plus 1 other.
Student Life *Campus security:* 24-hour emergency response devices and patrols.
Athletics Member NJCAA.
Financial Aid Of all full-time matriculated undergraduates who enrolled in 2016, 76 Federal Work-Study jobs (averaging $2348). 10 state and other part-time jobs (averaging $1952).
Applying *Options:* electronic application, deferred entrance. *Required:* high school transcript. *Recommended:* interview.
Freshman Application Contact Dr. L. Campbell, Dean for Student and Academic Services, Mercer County Community College, 1200 Old Trenton Road, PO Box B, Trenton, NJ 08690-1004. *Phone:* 609-586-4800 Ext. 3222. *Toll-free phone:* 800-392-MCCC. *Fax:* 609-586-6944. *E-mail:* admiss@mccc.edu. *Website:* http://www.mccc.edu/.

Middlesex County College

Edison, New Jersey

- **County-supported** 2-year, founded 1964
- **Suburban** 200-acre campus with easy access to New York City
- **Coed,** 11,673 undergraduate students

Undergraduates 11% Black or African American, non-Hispanic/Latino; 30% Hispanic/Latino; 14% Asian, non-Hispanic/Latino; 0.5% Native Hawaiian or other Pacific Islander, non-Hispanic/Latino; 0.4% American Indian or Alaska Native, non-Hispanic/Latino; 3% Two or more races, non-Hispanic/Latino; 7% Race/ethnicity unknown; 2% international. *Retention:* 62% of full-time freshmen returned.
Faculty *Student/faculty ratio:* 24:1.
Majors Accounting; administrative assistant and secretarial science; automotive engineering technology; biology/biotechnology laboratory technician; biotechnology; business administration and management; civil engineering technology; clinical/medical laboratory technology; communications technologies and support services related; computer and information sciences; criminal justice/police science; dental hygiene; dietitian assistant; electrical, electronic and communications engineering technology; energy management and systems technology; engineering science; engineering technologies and engineering related; environmental control technologies related; fire prevention and safety technology; geology/earth science; graphic communications related; health professions related; health services/allied health/health sciences; hotel/motel administration; industrial production technologies related; legal assistant/paralegal; liberal arts and sciences/liberal studies; marketing/marketing management; mechanical engineering/mechanical technology; mechanical engineering technologies related; medical radiologic technology; merchandising, sales, and marketing operations related (specialized); physical sciences; registered nursing/registered nurse; rehabilitation and therapeutic professions related; respiratory care therapy; small business administration; surveying technology; teacher assistant/aide; visual and performing arts.
Academics *Calendar:* semesters. *Degree:* certificates and associate. *Special study options:* academic remediation for entering students, adult/continuing education programs, advanced placement credit, cooperative education, distance learning, English as a second language, independent study, internships, off-campus study, part-time degree program, services for LD students, study abroad, summer session for credit. *ROTC:* Army (c).
Library Middlesex County College Library plus 1 other.
Student Life *Housing:* college housing not available. *Activities and Organizations:* drama/theater group, student-run newspaper, radio station, choral group. *Campus security:* 24-hour emergency response devices and patrols. *Student services:* health clinic, personal/psychological counseling, veterans affairs office.
Athletics Member NJCAA. *Intercollegiate sports:* baseball M, basketball M/W, cross-country running M/W, soccer M/W, softball W, track and field M/W, wrestling M.
Financial Aid Of all full-time matriculated undergraduates who enrolled in 2018, 4,804 applied for aid. 90 Federal Work-Study jobs (averaging $300,095). In 2018, 97 non-need-based awards were made. *Average financial aid package:* $1578. *Average need-based gift aid:* $2490. *Average non-need-based aid:* $2647.
Applying *Options:* early admission, deferred entrance. *Application fee:* $25. *Required:* high school transcript. *Application deadlines:* rolling (freshmen), rolling (transfers). *Notification:* continuous (freshmen), continuous (transfers).
Freshman Application Contact Middlesex County College, 2600 Woodbridge Avenue, PO Box 3050, Edison, NJ 08818-3050. *Website:* http://www.middlesexcc.edu/.

Ocean County College

Toms River, New Jersey

Freshman Application Contact Ms. Sheenah Hartigan, CRM Communications Administrator, Ocean County College, College Drive, PO

Box 2001, Toms River, NJ 08754-2001. *Phone:* 732-255-0400 Ext. 2189. *E-mail:* shartigan@ocean.edu. *Website:* http://www.ocean.edu/.

Passaic County Community College

Paterson, New Jersey

- **County-supported** 2-year, founded 1968
- **Urban** 6-acre campus with easy access to New York City
- **Endowment** $78,695
- **Coed**

Undergraduates 1% are from out of state.
Academics *Calendar:* semesters. *Degree:* certificates and associate. *Special study options:* academic remediation for entering students, advanced placement credit, cooperative education, distance learning, double majors, English as a second language, honors programs, independent study, internships, part-time degree program, study abroad, summer session for credit. *ROTC:* Army (c).
Library Passaic County Community College Learning Resource Center plus 1 other.
Student Life *Campus security:* late-night transport/escort service.
Athletics Member NJCAA.
Financial Aid Of all full-time matriculated undergraduates who enrolled in 2018, 100 Federal Work-Study jobs (averaging $3000).
Applying *Options:* early admission, deferred entrance.
Freshman Application Contact Mr. Patrick Noonan, Director of Admissions, Passaic County Community College, One College Boulevard, Paterson, NJ 07505-1179. *Phone:* 973-684-6304. *Website:* http://www.pccc.cc.nj.us/.

Raritan Valley Community College

Branchburg, New Jersey

- **State and locally supported** 2-year, founded 1965
- **Suburban** 240-acre campus with easy access to New York City, Philadelphia
- **Endowment** $1.1 million
- **Coed,** 7,793 undergraduate students, 38% full-time, 50% women, 50% men
- 100% of applicants were admitted

Undergraduates 2,992 full-time, 4,801 part-time. Students come from 6 states and territories; 1% are from out of state; 13% Black or African American, non-Hispanic/Latino; 24% Hispanic/Latino; 6% Asian, non-Hispanic/Latino; 0.4% Native Hawaiian or other Pacific Islander, non-Hispanic/Latino; 0.2% American Indian or Alaska Native, non-Hispanic/Latino; 2% Two or more races, non-Hispanic/Latino; 6% Race/ethnicity unknown; 2% international; 5% transferred in. *Retention:* 68% of full-time freshmen returned.
Freshmen *Admission:* 2,369 applied, 2,369 admitted, 1,548 enrolled.
Faculty *Total:* 459, 27% full-time. *Student/faculty ratio:* 20:1.
Majors Accounting related; allied health and medical assisting services related; animation, interactive technology, video graphics and special effects; automotive engineering technology; business administration and management; business/commerce; child-care provision; communication and media related; computer and information sciences; computer programming; computer systems networking and telecommunications; construction engineering technology; criminal justice/law enforcement administration; crisis/emergency/disaster management; dance; dental hygiene; design and applied arts related; energy management and systems technology; engineering science; engineering technologies and engineering related; English; fine/studio arts; game and interactive media design; health information/medical records technology; health services/allied health/health sciences; heating, ventilation, air conditioning and refrigeration engineering technology; human computer interaction; human services; information technology; interior design; intermedia/multimedia; kindergarten/preschool education; kinesiology and exercise science; legal assistant/paralegal; liberal arts and sciences/liberal studies; lineworker; management information systems; manufacturing engineering technology; medical/clinical assistant; meeting and event planning; modeling, virtual environments and simulation; multi/interdisciplinary studies related; music; occupational therapist assistant; opticianry; optometric technician; registered nursing/registered nurse; rehabilitation and therapeutic professions related; respiratory care therapy; restaurant, culinary, and catering management; small business administration; web/multimedia management and webmaster.
Academics *Calendar:* semesters. *Degree:* certificates and associate. *Special study options:* academic remediation for entering students, adult/continuing education programs, advanced placement credit, cooperative education, distance learning, double majors, English as a second language, freshman honors college, honors programs, independent study, internships, off-campus study, part-time degree program, services for LD students, summer session for credit. *ROTC:* Army (c), Air Force (c).
Library Evelyn S. Field Library. *Books:* 62,257 (physical), 121,737 (digital/electronic); *Serial titles:* 98 (physical), 45,229 (digital/electronic); *Databases:* 70.
Student Life *Housing:* college housing not available. *Activities and Organizations:* drama/theater group, student-run newspaper, radio station, choral group, National Society for Leadership and Success, Phi Theta Kappa, Rotary, Student Nurses Association, Orgullo Latino (OLC). *Campus security:* 24-hour emergency response devices and patrols, late-night transport/escort service. *Student services:* personal/psychological counseling, veterans affairs office.
Athletics Member NJCAA. *Intercollegiate sports:* baseball M(s), basketball M(s)/W(s), cross-country running M/W, golf M, soccer M/W, volleyball W. *Intramural sports:* basketball M/W, soccer M/W, softball W, volleyball W.
Costs (2019–20) *Tuition:* area resident $4860 full-time, $162 per credit hour part-time; state resident $6360 full-time, $212 per credit hour part-time; nonresident $6360 full-time, $212 per credit hour part-time. *Required fees:* $1126 full-time, $27 per credit hour part-time, $113 per term part-time.
Financial Aid Of all full-time matriculated undergraduates who enrolled in 2018, 12 Federal Work-Study jobs (averaging $2500).
Applying *Options:* electronic application. *Application fee:* $25. *Required:* high school transcript. *Application deadlines:* rolling (freshmen), rolling (transfers). *Notification:* continuous (freshmen), continuous (out-of-state freshmen), continuous (transfers).
Freshman Application Contact Mr. John Wheeler, Registrar, Enrollment Services, Raritan Valley Community College, 118 Lamington Road, Branchburg, NJ 08876. *Phone:* 908-526-1200 Ext. 8339. *Fax:* 908-704-3442. *E-mail:* jwheeler@raritanval.edu. *Website:* http://www.raritanval.edu/.

Rowan College at Burlington County

Pemberton, New Jersey

Freshman Application Contact Rowan College at Burlington County, 601 Pemberton Browns Mills Road, Pemberton, NJ 08068. *Phone:* 609-894-9311 Ext. 1200. *Website:* http://www.rcbc.edu/.

Rowan College at Gloucester County

Sewell, New Jersey

Freshman Application Contact Ms. Judy Atkinson, Registrar/Admissions, Rowan College at Gloucester County, 1400 Tanyard Road, Sewell, NJ 08080. *Phone:* 856-415-2209. *E-mail:* jatkinso@gccnj.edu. *Website:* http://www.rcgc.edu/.

Salem Community College

Carneys Point, New Jersey

Freshman Application Contact Kelly McShay, Director of Retention and Admissions, Salem Community College, 460 Hollywood Avenue, Carneys Point, NJ 08069. *Phone:* 856-351-2919. *E-mail:* kmcshay@salemcc.edu. *Website:* http://www.salemcc.edu/.

Sussex County Community College

Newton, New Jersey

Freshman Application Contact Mr. Todd Poltersdorf, Director of Admissions, Sussex County Community College, 1 College Hill Road, Newton, NJ 07860. *Phone:* 973-300-2253. *E-mail:* tpoltersdorf@sussex.edu. *Website:* http://www.sussex.edu/.

Union County College

Cranford, New Jersey

- **State and locally supported** 2-year, founded 1933
- **Suburban** 48-acre campus with easy access to New York City
- **Coed,** 9,181 undergraduate students, 46% full-time, 62% women, 38% men
- 100% of applicants were admitted

Undergraduates 4,226 full-time, 4,955 part-time. 29% Black or African American, non-Hispanic/Latino; 40% Hispanic/Latino; 4% Asian, non-Hispanic/Latino; 0.4% Native Hawaiian or other Pacific Islander, non-Hispanic/Latino; 0.3% American Indian or Alaska Native, non-Hispanic/Latino; 2% Two or more races, non-Hispanic/Latino; 6% Race/ethnicity unknown; 1% international; 7% transferred in.
Freshmen *Admission:* 4,822 applied, 4,822 admitted, 1,835 enrolled.
Faculty *Student/faculty ratio:* 22:1.
Majors Accounting technology and bookkeeping; American Sign Language (ASL); automobile/automotive mechanics technology; biology/biological

sciences; business administration and management; business/commerce; chemistry; computer and information sciences and support services related; computer science; criminal justice/law enforcement administration; cyber/computer forensics and counterterrorism; diagnostic medical sonography and ultrasound technology; electromechanical technology; emergency medical technology (EMT paramedic); engineering; engineering technologies and engineering related; English; fire prevention and safety technology; health services/allied health/health sciences; history; hospitality administration; human services; information technology; legal assistant/paralegal; liberal arts and sciences/liberal studies; logistics, materials, and supply chain management; marketing/marketing management; mass communication/media; mathematics; physical therapy technology; radiologic technology/science; registered nursing/registered nurse; rehabilitation and therapeutic professions related; respiratory care therapy; sport and fitness administration/management.

Academics *Calendar:* semesters. *Degree:* certificates and associate. *Special study options:* academic remediation for entering students, adult/continuing education programs, advanced placement credit, distance learning, English as a second language, honors programs, independent study, internships, off-campus study, part-time degree program, services for LD students, summer session for credit. *ROTC:* Air Force (c).

Library MacKay Library plus 2 others. *Books:* 77,364 (physical), 260,603 (digital/electronic); *Serial titles:* 222 (physical), 396,957 (digital/electronic); *Databases:* 105.

Student Life *Housing:* college housing not available. *Activities and Organizations:* drama/theater group, student-run newspaper, radio station. *Campus security:* 24-hour emergency response devices and patrols. *Student services:* veterans affairs office.

Athletics Member NJCAA. *Intercollegiate sports:* baseball M, basketball M/W(s), bowling W, cross-country running M/W, golf M/W, lacrosse M(s), soccer M/W, track and field M/W, volleyball W, wrestling M.

Costs (2020–21) *Tuition:* area resident $5281 full-time, $214 per credit hour part-time; state resident $10,562 full-time, $428 per credit hour part-time; nonresident $10,562 full-time, $428 per credit hour part-time. Full-time tuition and fees vary according to course load. Part-time tuition and fees vary according to course load. *Payment plan:* installment. *Waivers:* senior citizens and employees or children of employees.

Applying *Options:* electronic application. *Application fee:* $10. *Required:* high school transcript, immunization records. *Required for some:* essay or personal statement, interview. *Application deadlines:* rolling (freshmen), rolling (transfers). *Notification:* continuous (freshmen), continuous (transfers).

Freshman Application Contact Ms. Beatriz Rodriguez, Director of Enrollment Services, Union County College, Cranford, NJ 07016. *Phone:* 908-709-7000. *E-mail:* rodriguez@ucc.edu. *Website:* http://www.ucc.edu/.

Warren County Community College

Washington, New Jersey

Freshman Application Contact Shannon Horwath, Associate Director of Admissions, Warren County Community College, 475 Route 57 West, Washington, NJ 07882-9605. *Phone:* 908-835-2300. *E-mail:* shorwath@warren.edu. *Website:* http://www.warren.edu/.

NEW MEXICO

Carrington College–Albuquerque

Albuquerque, New Mexico

- **Proprietary** 2-year, part of Carrington Colleges Group, Inc.
- **Coed**

Undergraduates 400 full-time, 34 part-time. 2% are from out of state; 2% Black or African American, non-Hispanic/Latino; 48% Hispanic/Latino; 1% Asian, non-Hispanic/Latino; 31% American Indian or Alaska Native, non-Hispanic/Latino; 1% Two or more races, non-Hispanic/Latino; 0.7% Race/ethnicity unknown; 25% transferred in. *Retention:* 78% of full-time freshmen returned.

Faculty *Student/faculty ratio:* 21:1.

Academics *Degree:* certificates and associate.

Standardized Tests *Required:* institutional entrance exam (for admission).

Applying *Required:* essay or personal statement, high school transcript, interview.

Freshman Application Contact Carrington College–Albuquerque, 1001 Menaul Boulevard NE, Albuquerque, NM 87107. *Website:* http://www.carrington.edu/.

Central New Mexico Community College

Albuquerque, New Mexico

- **State-supported** 2-year, founded 1965
- **Urban** 304-acre campus
- **Endowment** $1.9 million
- **Coed**

Undergraduates 6,538 full-time, 17,179 part-time. Students come from 18 other countries; 1% are from out of state; 3% Black or African American, non-Hispanic/Latino; 52% Hispanic/Latino; 2% Asian, non-Hispanic/Latino; 0.2% Native Hawaiian or other Pacific Islander, non-Hispanic/Latino; 6% American Indian or Alaska Native, non-Hispanic/Latino; 2% Two or more races, non-Hispanic/Latino; 7% Race/ethnicity unknown; 0.2% international; 4% transferred in.

Faculty *Student/faculty ratio:* 23:1.

Academics *Calendar:* trimesters. *Degree:* certificates and associate. *Special study options:* academic remediation for entering students, accelerated degree program, adult/continuing education programs, advanced placement credit, cooperative education, distance learning, English as a second language, honors programs, independent study, internships, off-campus study, part-time degree program, services for LD students, summer session for credit. *ROTC:* Army (c), Navy (c), Air Force (c).

Library Main Campus Library plus 5 others. *Books:* 37,327 (physical), 246,604 (digital/electronic); *Serial titles:* 173 (physical), 1,511 (digital/electronic); *Databases:* 83.

Student Life *Campus security:* 24-hour emergency response devices and patrols, late-night transport/escort service.

Costs (2019–20) *Tuition:* state resident $1344 full-time, $56 per credit hour part-time; nonresident $7104 full-time, $296 per credit hour part-time. *Required fees:* $306 full-time, $9 per credit hour part-time, $45 per term part-time.

Financial Aid Of all full-time matriculated undergraduates who enrolled in 2017, 4,897 applied for aid, 4,384 were judged to have need. *Average need-based loan:* $2862. *Average need-based gift aid:* $2232.

Applying *Options:* electronic application.

Freshman Application Contact Glenn Damiani, Senior Director, Enrollment Services, Central New Mexico Community College, Albuquerque, NM 87106. *Phone:* 505-224-4000 Ext. 1104. *E-mail:* gdamiani@cnm.edu. *Website:* http://www.cnm.edu/.

Clovis Community College

Clovis, New Mexico

- **State-supported** 2-year, founded 1990
- **Small-town** 25-acre campus
- **Endowment** $740,423
- **Coed**

Undergraduates 995 full-time, 3,180 part-time. 14% are from out of state; 8% transferred in. *Retention:* 43% of full-time freshmen returned.

Faculty *Student/faculty ratio:* 21:1.

Academics *Calendar:* semesters. *Degree:* certificates and associate. *Special study options:* academic remediation for entering students, adult/continuing education programs, advanced placement credit, cooperative education, distance learning, double majors, English as a second language, independent study, internships, part-time degree program, services for LD students, summer session for credit.

Library Clovis Community College Library and Learning Resources Center.

Student Life *Campus security:* student patrols, late-night transport/escort service.

Applying *Required:* high school transcript. *Required for some:* interview.

Freshman Application Contact Ms. Rosie Corrie, Director of Admissions and Records/Registrar, Clovis Community College, Clovis, NM 88101-8381. *Phone:* 575-769-4962. *Toll-free phone:* 800-769-1409. *Fax:* 575-769-4190. *E-mail:* admissions@clovis.edu. *Website:* http://www.clovis.edu/.

Doña Ana Community College

Las Cruces, New Mexico

- **State and locally supported** 2-year, founded 1973, part of New Mexico State University System
- **Urban** 15-acre campus with easy access to El Paso
- **Endowment** $18,682
- **Coed**

Undergraduates 4,037 full-time, 4,854 part-time. Students come from 14 states and territories; 1 other country; 12% are from out of state; 3% Black or African American, non-Hispanic/Latino; 65% Hispanic/Latino; 1% Asian, non-Hispanic/Latino; 2% American Indian or Alaska Native, non-Hispanic/Latino; 5% Race/ethnicity unknown; 2% international; 2% transferred in. *Retention:* 85% of full-time freshmen returned.

Faculty *Student/faculty ratio:* 21:1.
Academics *Calendar:* semesters. *Degree:* certificates and associate. *Special study options:* academic remediation for entering students, adult/continuing education programs, advanced placement credit, cooperative education, distance learning, English as a second language, freshman honors college, honors programs, internships, part-time degree program, services for LD students, summer session for credit. *ROTC:* Army (c), Air Force (c).
Library Library/Media Center.
Student Life *Campus security:* 24-hour emergency response devices and patrols, late-night transport/escort service, controlled dormitory access.
Standardized Tests *Recommended:* ACT, ACT ASSET, or ACT Compass.
Financial Aid Of all full-time matriculated undergraduates who enrolled in 2018, 15 Federal Work-Study jobs (averaging $2800). 106 state and other part-time jobs (averaging $2800). *Financial aid deadline:* 6/30.
Applying *Options:* electronic application, deferred entrance. *Application fee:* $20. *Required:* high school transcript.
Freshman Application Contact Mrs. Ricci Montes, Admissions Advisor, Doña Ana Community College, MSC-3DA, Box 30001, 3400 South Espina Street, Las Cruces, NM 88003-8001. *Phone:* 575-527-7683. *Toll-free phone:* 800-903-7503. *Fax:* 575-527-7515. *Website:* http://dacc.nmsu.edu/.

Eastern New Mexico University–Roswell

Roswell, New Mexico

- **State-supported** 2-year, founded 1958, part of Eastern New Mexico University System
- **Small-town** 241-acre campus
- **Coed**

Undergraduates 10% are from out of state.
Faculty *Student/faculty ratio:* 20:1.
Academics *Calendar:* semesters. *Degree:* certificates and associate. *Special study options:* academic remediation for entering students, adult/continuing education programs, advanced placement credit, cooperative education, distance learning, English as a second language, independent study, internships, off-campus study, part-time degree program, services for LD students, summer session for credit. *ROTC:* Army (c), Navy (c), Air Force (c).
Library Learning Resource Center.
Student Life *Campus security:* 24-hour emergency response devices, student patrols, late-night transport/escort service.
Standardized Tests *Recommended:* ACT (for admission).
Financial Aid Of all full-time matriculated undergraduates who enrolled in 2018, 100 Federal Work-Study jobs (averaging $5400). 60 state and other part-time jobs (averaging $5400).
Applying *Options:* early admission. *Required:* high school transcript.
Freshman Application Contact Eastern New Mexico University–Roswell, PO Box 6000, Roswell, NM 88202-6000. *Phone:* 505-624-7142. *Toll-free phone:* 800-243-6687 (in-state); 800-624-7000 (out-of-state). *Website:* http://www.roswell.enmu.edu/.

IntelliTec College - Albuquerque

Albuquerque, New Mexico

Admissions Office Contact IntelliTec College - Albuquerque, 5001 Montgomery Boulevard NE, Suite A24, Albuquerque, NM 87109. *Website:* http://www.intelliteccollege.edu/.

Luna Community College

Las Vegas, New Mexico

Freshman Application Contact Ms. Henrietta Griego, Director of Admissions, Recruitment, and Retention, Luna Community College, PO Box 1510, Las Vegas, NM 87701. *Phone:* 505-454-2020. *Toll-free phone:* 800-588-7232. *Fax:* 505-454-2588. *E-mail:* hgriego@luna.cc.nm.us. *Website:* http://www.luna.edu/.

Mesalands Community College

Tucumcari, New Mexico

Freshman Application Contact Mesalands Community College, 911 South Tenth Street, Tucumcari, NM 88401. *Phone:* 575-461-4413. *Website:* http://www.mesalands.edu/.

New Mexico Junior College

Hobbs, New Mexico

Freshman Application Contact New Mexico Junior College, 5317 Lovington Highway, Hobbs, NM 88240-9123. *Phone:* 575-492-2587. *Toll-free phone:* 800-657-6260. *Website:* http://www.nmjc.edu/.

New Mexico Military Institute

Roswell, New Mexico

Freshman Application Contact New Mexico Military Institute, Roswell, NM 88201-5173. *Phone:* 505-624-8050. *Toll-free phone:* 800-421-5376. *Fax:* 505-624-8058. *E-mail:* admissions@nmmi.edu. *Website:* http://www.nmmi.edu/.

New Mexico State University–Alamogordo

Alamogordo, New Mexico

Freshman Application Contact Ms. Elma Hernandez, Coordinator of Admissions and Records, New Mexico State University–Alamogordo, 2400 North Scenic Drive, Alamogordo, NM 88311-0477. *Phone:* 575-439-3700. *E-mail:* advisor@nmsu.edu. *Website:* http://nmsua.edu/.

New Mexico State University–Carlsbad

Carlsbad, New Mexico

Freshman Application Contact Ms. Everal Shannon, Records Specialist, New Mexico State University–Carlsbad, 1500 University Drive, Carlsbad, NM 88220. *Phone:* 575-234-9222. *Fax:* 575-885-4951. *E-mail:* eshannon@nmsu.edu. *Website:* http://www.cavern.nmsu.edu/.

New Mexico State University–Grants

Grants, New Mexico

- **State-supported** 2-year, founded 1968, part of New Mexico State University System
- **Small-town** campus
- **Coed**

Undergraduates 9,712 full-time, 1,975 part-time. 26% are from out of state; 2% Black or African American, non-Hispanic/Latino; 61% Hispanic/Latino; 1% Asian, non-Hispanic/Latino; 0.1% Native Hawaiian or other Pacific Islander, non-Hispanic/Latino; 2% American Indian or Alaska Native, non-Hispanic/Latino; 2% Two or more races, non-Hispanic/Latino; 1% Race/ethnicity unknown; 4% international; 5% transferred in; 22% live on campus. *Retention:* 74% of full-time freshmen returned.
Faculty *Student/faculty ratio:* 17:1.
Academics *Calendar:* semesters. *Degree:* certificates and associate. *Special study options:* part-time degree program, summer session for credit. *ROTC:* Army (b), Air Force (b).
Standardized Tests *Required:* CPT (for admission).
Financial Aid Of all full-time matriculated undergraduates who enrolled in 2018, 3 Federal Work-Study jobs (averaging $1800). 6 state and other part-time jobs (averaging $1500).
Applying *Options:* early admission. *Application fee:* $20. *Required:* high school transcript.
Director of Admissions Ms. Irene Lutz, Campus Student Services Officer, New Mexico State University–Grants, 1500 3rd Street, Grants, NM 87020-2025. *Phone:* 505-287-7981. *Website:* http://grants.nmsu.edu/.

Pima Medical Institute - Albuquerque

Albuquerque, New Mexico

Freshman Application Contact Admissions Office, Pima Medical Institute - Albuquerque, 4400 Cutler Avenue NE, Albuquerque, NM 87110. *Phone:* 505-881-1234. *Toll-free phone:* 800-477-PIMA. *Fax:* 505-881-5329. *Website:* http://www.pmi.edu/.

San Juan College

Farmington, New Mexico

- **State-supported** 2-year, founded 1958, part of New Mexico Higher Education Department
- **Small-town** 698-acre campus
- **Endowment** $15.2 million
- **Coed,** 6,741 undergraduate students, 35% full-time, 67% women, 33% men

Undergraduates 2,376 full-time, 4,365 part-time. Students come from 52 states and territories; 23 other countries; 30% are from out of state; 1% Black or African American, non-Hispanic/Latino; 17% Hispanic/Latino; 1% Asian, non-Hispanic/Latino; 0.1% Native Hawaiian or other Pacific Islander, non-Hispanic/Latino; 36% American Indian or Alaska Native, non-Hispanic/Latino; 2% Two or more races, non-Hispanic/Latino; 4% Race/ethnicity unknown; 1% international; 7% transferred in.

Freshmen *Admission:* 817 admitted, 817 enrolled.
Faculty *Total:* 469, 32% full-time. *Student/faculty ratio:* 16:1.
Majors Accounting technology and bookkeeping; American Indian/Native American studies; autobody/collision and repair technology; automobile/automotive mechanics technology; biology/biological sciences; business administration and management; carpentry; chemistry; child-care provision; clinical/medical laboratory technology; commercial and advertising art; cosmetology; criminal justice/police science; data processing and data processing technology; dental hygiene; diesel mechanics technology; drafting and design technology; electrical, electronic and communications engineering technology; elementary education; emergency medical technology (EMT paramedic); engineering; engineering technology; fire science/firefighting; general studies; health and physical education/fitness; health information/medical records technology; industrial mechanics and maintenance technology; industrial technology; instrumentation technology; legal assistant/paralegal; liberal arts and sciences/liberal studies; mathematics; occupational safety and health technology; occupational therapist assistant; parks, recreation and leisure; physical sciences; physical therapy technology; physics; premedical studies; psychology; registered nursing/registered nurse; respiratory care therapy; secondary education; social work; special education; surgical technology; theater design and technology; veterinary/animal health technology; welding technology.
Academics *Calendar:* semesters. *Degrees:* certificates, diplomas, associate, and postbachelor's certificates. *Special study options:* academic remediation for entering students, accelerated degree program, adult/continuing education programs, advanced placement credit, cooperative education, distance learning, double majors, English as a second language, freshman honors college, honors programs, independent study, internships, off-campus study, part-time degree program, services for LD students, summer session for credit.
Library San Juan College Library. *Books:* 79,433 (physical), 218,153 (digital/electronic); *Serial titles:* 208 (physical), 34,990 (digital/electronic); *Databases:* 96. Weekly public service hours: 69.
Student Life *Housing:* college housing not available. *Activities and Organizations:* drama/theater group, student-run newspaper, choral group, National Society of Leadership and Success (NSLS), Geeks and Gamers, Social & Behavioral Sciences Club (PSI BETA), All Nations Leadership Association, CLEAR CREW, national fraternities, national sororities. *Campus security:* 24-hour emergency response devices and patrols, late-night transport/escort service. *Student services:* personal/psychological counseling, veterans affairs office.
Athletics *Intramural sports:* basketball M/W, volleyball M/W.
Costs (2020–21) *Tuition:* area resident $1470 full-time, $49 per credit hour part-time; state resident $1470 full-time, $49 per credit hour part-time; nonresident $4650 full-time, $155 per credit hour part-time. Full-time tuition and fees vary according to reciprocity agreements. Part-time tuition and fees vary according to course load and reciprocity agreements. *Required fees:* $415 full-time, $78 per term part-time. *Payment plan:* installment. *Waivers:* minority students, senior citizens, and employees or children of employees.
Financial Aid Of all full-time matriculated undergraduates who enrolled in 2018, 138 Federal Work-Study jobs (averaging $1460). 140 state and other part-time jobs (averaging $1363). *Average percent of need met:* 7%.
Applying *Options:* electronic application, early admission, deferred entrance. *Application fee:* $10. *Required:* high school transcript. *Application deadlines:* rolling (freshmen), rolling (out-of-state freshmen), rolling (transfers). *Notification:* continuous (freshmen), continuous (out-of-state freshmen), continuous (transfers).
Freshman Application Contact Mrs. Roxanna Hughes, Admission Technician, San Juan College, 4601 College Boulevard, Farmington, NM 87402. *Phone:* 505-566-3479. *Fax:* 505-566-3500. *E-mail:* hughesr@sanjuancollege.edu.
Website: http://www.sanjuancollege.edu/.

Santa Fe Community College
Santa Fe, New Mexico

Freshman Application Contact Marcos Maez, Student Recruitment and Outreach Administrator, Santa Fe Community College, 6401 Richards Avenue, Santa Fe, NM 87508. *Phone:* 505-428-1779. *E-mail:* marcos.maez@sfcc.edu. *Website:* http://www.sfcc.edu/.

Southwestern Indian Polytechnic Institute
Albuquerque, New Mexico

Freshman Application Contact Tawna Harrison, First Year Counselor, Southwestern Indian Polytechnic Institute, PO Box 10146, 9169 Coors Road NW, Albuquerque, NM 87184. *Phone:* 505-922-6516. *Toll-free phone:* 800-586-7474. *E-mail:* tawna.harrison@bie.edu. *Website:* http://www.sipi.edu/.

University of New Mexico–Gallup
Gallup, New Mexico

Freshman Application Contact University of New Mexico–Gallup, 705 Gurley Avenue, Gallup, NM 87301. *Phone:* 505-863-7576. *Website:* http://www.gallup.unm.edu/.

University of New Mexico–Los Alamos Branch
Los Alamos, New Mexico

Freshman Application Contact Mrs. Irene K. Martinez, Enrollment Representative, University of New Mexico–Los Alamos Branch, 4000 University Drive, Los Alamos, NM 87544-2233. *Phone:* 505-662-0332. *E-mail:* l65130@unm.edu. *Website:* http://losalamos.unm.edu/.

University of New Mexico–Taos
Taos, New Mexico

Director of Admissions Vickie Alvarez, Student Enrollment Associate, University of New Mexico–Taos, 115 Civic Plaza Drive, Taos, NM 87571. *Phone:* 575-737-6425. *E-mail:* valvarez@unm.edu. *Website:* http://taos.unm.edu/.

University of New Mexico–Valencia Campus
Los Lunas, New Mexico

Director of Admissions Richard M. Hulett, Director of Admissions and Recruitment, University of New Mexico–Valencia Campus, 280 La Entrada, Los Lunas, NM 87031-7633. *Phone:* 505-277-2446. *E-mail:* mhulett@unm.edu. *Website:* http://valencia.unm.edu/.

NEW YORK

Adirondack Community College
Queensbury, New York

- **State and locally supported** 2-year, founded 1960, part of State University of New York System
- **Small-town** 141-acre campus
- **Endowment** $3.9 million
- **Coed,** 3,468 undergraduate students, 55% full-time, 57% women, 43% men

Undergraduates 1,906 full-time, 1,562 part-time. Students come from 10 states and territories; 5 other countries; 1% are from out of state; 5% Black or African American, non-Hispanic/Latino; 5% Hispanic/Latino; 1% Asian, non-Hispanic/Latino; 0.1% Native Hawaiian or other Pacific Islander, non-Hispanic/Latino; 0.6% American Indian or Alaska Native, non-Hispanic/Latino; 3% Two or more races, non-Hispanic/Latino; 0.1% Race/ethnicity unknown; 0.1% international; 7% transferred in. *Retention:* 56% of full-time freshmen returned.
Freshmen *Admission:* 2,006 applied, 1,947 admitted, 826 enrolled.
Faculty *Total:* 256, 35% full-time. *Student/faculty ratio:* 17:1.
Majors Accounting; business administration and management; computer science; computer systems networking and telecommunications; cooking and related culinary arts; creative writing; criminal justice/police science; design and visual communications; electrical, electronic and communications engineering technology; engineering; hospitality administration; information technology; liberal arts and sciences/liberal studies; marketing/marketing management; music; music performance; parks, recreation and leisure facilities management; radio and television broadcasting technology; registered nursing/registered nurse; sport and fitness administration/management; substance abuse/addiction counseling; tourism and travel services management.
Academics *Calendar:* semesters. *Degree:* certificates and associate. *Special study options:* academic remediation for entering students, accelerated degree program, adult/continuing education programs, advanced placement credit, cooperative education, distance learning, double majors, English as a second language, independent study, internships, part-time degree program, services for LD students, study abroad, summer session for credit.
Library SUNY Adirondack Library. *Books:* 33,139 (physical); *Serial titles:* 136 (physical). Students can reserve study rooms.

Student Life *Housing Options:* coed. *Activities and Organizations:* drama/theater group, student-run radio and television station, choral group, E-Sports, Adventure Sports, ABA, College Activity Board, Media. *Campus security:* 24-hour emergency response devices and patrols, controlled dormitory access, last night escort service, patrols by trained security personnel 8 am to 10 pm. *Student services:* personal/psychological counseling, veterans affairs office.
Athletics Member NJCAA. *Intercollegiate sports:* baseball M, basketball M/W, bowling M/W, golf M/W, soccer M/W, softball W, volleyball W. *Intramural sports:* badminton M/W, basketball M/W, volleyball M/W.
Costs (2019–20) *One-time required fee:* $35. *Tuition:* area resident $4800 full-time; state resident $4800 full-time, $200 per credit hour part-time; nonresident $9600 full-time, $400 per credit hour part-time. Full-time tuition and fees vary according to course load and program. Part-time tuition and fees vary according to course load and program. *Required fees:* $938 full-time, $34 per credit hour part-time. *Room and board:* $11,900; room only: $8160. Room and board charges vary according to board plan. *Payment plan:* installment. *Waivers:* senior citizens and employees or children of employees.
Financial Aid Of all full-time matriculated undergraduates who enrolled in 2018, 98 Federal Work-Study jobs (averaging $462).
Applying *Options:* electronic application. *Application fee:* $35.
Freshman Application Contact Office of Admissions, Adirondack Community College, 640 Bay Road, Queensbury, NY 12804. *Phone:* 518-743-2264. *Toll-free phone:* 888-SUNY-ADK. *Fax:* 518-743-2200. *Website:* http://www.sunyacc.edu/.

American Academy McAllister Institute of Funeral Service

New York, New York

- **Independent** 2-year, founded 1926, part of ABSFE
- **Urban** campus
- **Coed,** 460 undergraduate students, 14% full-time, 68% women, 32% men

Undergraduates 64 full-time, 396 part-time. Students come from 14 states and territories; 1 other country; 45% are from out of state; 25% Black or African American, non-Hispanic/Latino; 14% Hispanic/Latino; 0.7% Asian, non-Hispanic/Latino; 0.4% Native Hawaiian or other Pacific Islander, non-Hispanic/Latino; 1% American Indian or Alaska Native, non-Hispanic/Latino; 7% Race/ethnicity unknown; 21% transferred in. *Retention:* 19% of full-time freshmen returned.
Freshmen *Admission:* 162 applied, 97 admitted, 49 enrolled.
Faculty *Total:* 30. *Student/faculty ratio:* 22:1.
Majors Funeral service and mortuary science.
Academics *Calendar:* semesters. *Degree:* associate. *Special study options:* distance learning, part-time degree program, summer session for credit.
Library American Academy MacAllister Institute Library. *Books:* 5,000 (physical). Weekly public service hours: 35.
Student Life *Housing:* college housing not available. *Campus security:* 24-hour emergency response devices. *Student services:* veterans affairs office.
Costs (2020–21) *Tuition:* $17,850 full-time, $525 per credit hour part-time. *Required fees:* $200 full-time, $25 per term part-time. *Payment plan:* installment.
Applying *Options:* electronic application, deferred entrance. *Application fee:* $50. *Required:* high school transcript. *Application deadlines:* rolling (freshmen), rolling (out-of-state freshmen), rolling (transfers). *Notification:* continuous (freshmen), continuous (out-of-state freshmen), continuous (transfers).
Freshman Application Contact Ms. Rene Hernandez, Assistant Director of Admissions, American Academy McAllister Institute of Funeral Service, 619 W. 54th Street, 2nd Floor, New York, NY 10019. *Phone:* 212-757-1190. *Toll-free phone:* 866-932-2264. *Fax:* 212-765-5923. *E-mail:* rhernandez@aami.edu.
Website: http://www.funeraleducation.org/.

The American Academy of Dramatic Arts–New York

New York, New York

Freshman Application Contact Kerin Reilly, Director of Admissions, The American Academy of Dramatic Arts–New York, 120 Madison Avenue, New York, NY 10016. *Phone:* 212-686-9244 Ext. 333. *Toll-free phone:* 800-463-8990. *E-mail:* kreilly@aada.edu. *Website:* http://www.aada.edu/.

ASA College

Brooklyn, New York

Freshman Application Contact Admissions Office, ASA College, 81 Willoughby Street, Brooklyn, NY 11201. *Phone:* 718-522-9073. *Toll-free phone:* 877-679-8772. *Website:* http://www.asa.edu/.

The Belanger School of Nursing

Schenectady, New York

Freshman Application Contact Carolyn Lansing, Student Services Manager, The Belanger School of Nursing, 650 McClellan Street, Schenectady, NY 12304. *Phone:* 518-831-8810. *Fax:* 518-243-4470. *E-mail:* lansingc@ellismedicine.org. *Website:* http://www.ellismedicine.org/school-of-nursing/.

Bill and Sandra Pomeroy College of Nursing at Crouse Hospital

Syracuse, New York

Freshman Application Contact Ms. Amy Graham, Enrollment Management Supervisor, Bill and Sandra Pomeroy College of Nursing at Crouse Hospital, 765 Irving Avenue, Syracuse, NY 13210. *Phone:* 315-470-7481. *Fax:* 315-470-7925. *E-mail:* amygraham@crouse.org. *Website:* http://www.crouse.org/nursing/.

Borough of Manhattan Community College of the City University of New York

New York, New York

- **State and locally supported** 2-year, founded 1963, part of City University of New York System
- **Urban** 5-acre campus
- **Coed,** 25,500 undergraduate students, 70% full-time, 57% women, 43% men

Undergraduates 17,772 full-time, 7,728 part-time. 3% are from out of state; 26% Black or African American, non-Hispanic/Latino; 44% Hispanic/Latino; 11% Asian, non-Hispanic/Latino; 0.2% Native Hawaiian or other Pacific Islander, non-Hispanic/Latino; 0.3% American Indian or Alaska Native, non-Hispanic/Latino; 2% Two or more races, non-Hispanic/Latino; 7% international; 7% transferred in.
Freshmen *Admission:* 33,325 applied, 30,974 admitted, 6,567 enrolled.
Faculty *Total:* 1,768, 29% full-time. *Student/faculty ratio:* 22:1.
Majors Accounting; accounting technology and bookkeeping; administrative assistant and secretarial science; animation, interactive technology, video graphics and special effects; art history, criticism and conservation; biotechnology; business administration and management; community organization and advocacy; computer and information sciences; computer science; criminal justice/police science; economics; emergency medical technology (EMT paramedic); engineering; English; ethnic, cultural minority, gender, and group studies related; finance; fine/studio arts; foreign languages and literatures; forensic science and technology; general studies; geographic information science and cartography; gerontology; health information/medical records technology; health services/allied health/health sciences; history; liberal arts and sciences/liberal studies; linguistics; mass communication/media; mathematics; music; physical sciences; psychology; public health; public health education and promotion; radio and television broadcasting technology; registered nursing/registered nurse; respiratory therapy technician; small business administration; sociology; teacher assistant/aide; visual and performing arts; web page, digital/multimedia and information resources design; women's studies.
Academics *Calendar:* semesters. *Degree:* certificates and associate. *Special study options:* academic remediation for entering students, accelerated degree program, adult/continuing education programs, advanced placement credit, cooperative education, distance learning, English as a second language, honors programs, independent study, internships, off-campus study, part-time degree program, services for LD students, study abroad, summer session for credit.
Library A. Philip Randolph Library plus 1 other. *Books:* 113,472 (physical), 580,303 (digital/electronic); *Serial titles:* 1,061 (physical), 114,687 (digital/electronic); *Databases:* 169. Weekly public service hours: 80; students can reserve study rooms.
Student Life *Activities and Organizations:* drama/theater group, choral group, Bangladeshi Student Association, Health Information Technology, Muslim Students Association, Resurgence in Christ, Urban Mentors and Leaders Association. *Campus security:* 24-hour patrols. *Student services:* health clinic, personal/psychological counseling, women's center, veterans affairs office.

Athletics Member NJCAA. *Intercollegiate sports:* baseball M, basketball M/W, soccer M/W, volleyball W.
Costs (2019–20) *Tuition:* area resident $4800 full-time, $210 per credit part-time; state resident $4800 full-time, $210 per credit part-time; nonresident $7680 full-time, $320 per credit part-time. *Required fees:* $369 full-time, $100 part-time.
Applying *Options:* electronic application, deferred entrance. *Application fee:* $65. *Required:* high school transcript. *Application deadlines:* rolling (freshmen), rolling (transfers). *Notification:* continuous (freshmen), continuous (transfers).
Freshman Application Contact Ms. Lisa Kasper, Director of Enrollment Management, Borough of Manhattan Community College of the City University of New York, 199 Chambers Street, Room S-310, New York, NY 10007. *Phone:* 212-220-1272. *Toll-free phone:* 866-583-5729. *Fax:* 212-220-2366. *E-mail:* admissions@bmcc.cuny.edu. *Website:* http://www.bmcc.cuny.edu/.

Bronx Community College of the City University of New York

Bronx, New York

- **State and locally supported** 2-year, founded 1959, part of City University of New York System
- **Urban** 50-acre campus with easy access to New York City
- **Endowment** $469,572
- **Coed**

Undergraduates 6,598 full-time, 4,770 part-time. Students come from 119 other countries; 4% are from out of state; 8% transferred in. *Retention:* 65% of full-time freshmen returned.
Faculty *Student/faculty ratio:* 26:1.
Academics *Calendar:* semesters. *Degree:* certificates and associate. *Special study options:* academic remediation for entering students, accelerated degree program, adult/continuing education programs, advanced placement credit, cooperative education, distance learning, double majors, English as a second language, honors programs, independent study, internships, off-campus study, part-time degree program, services for LD students, study abroad, summer session for credit.
Library Library & Gerald S. Lieblich Learning Resources Center.
Student Life *Campus security:* 24-hour emergency response devices and patrols, late-night transport/escort service, free shuttle bus service provides transportation from campus to subway and bus lines between 5 pm-11 pm.
Athletics Member NJCAA.
Standardized Tests *Recommended:* SAT or ACT (for admission).
Applying *Options:* early admission. *Application fee:* $65. *Required:* high school transcript.
Freshman Application Contact Ms. Patricia A. Ramos, Admissions Officer, Bronx Community College of the City University of New York, 2155 University Avenue, Bronx, NY 10453. *Phone:* 718-289-5888. *E-mail:* admission@bcc.cuny.edu. *Website:* http://www.bcc.cuny.edu/.

Bryant & Stratton College–Albany Campus

Albany, New York

Freshman Application Contact Mr. Robert Ferrell, Director of Admissions, Bryant & Stratton College–Albany Campus, 1259 Central Avenue, Albany, NY 12205. *Phone:* 518-437-1802 Ext. 205. *Fax:* 518-437-1048. *Website:* http://www.bryantstratton.edu/.

Bryant & Stratton College–Amherst Campus

Clarence, New York

Freshman Application Contact Mr. Brian K. Dioguardi, Director of Admissions, Bryant & Stratton College–Amherst Campus, Audubon Business Center, 40 Hazelwood Drive, Amherst, NY 14228. *Phone:* 716-691-0012. *Fax:* 716-691-0012. *E-mail:* bkdioguardi@bryantstratton.edu. *Website:* http://www.bryantstratton.edu/.

Bryant & Stratton College–Buffalo Campus

Buffalo, New York

Freshman Application Contact Mr. Philip J. Struebel, Director of Admissions, Bryant & Stratton College–Buffalo Campus, 465 Main Street, Suite 400, Buffalo, NY 14203. *Phone:* 716-884-9120. *Fax:* 716-884-0091. *E-mail:* pjstruebel@bryantstratton.edu. *Website:* http://www.bryantstratton.edu/.

Bryant & Stratton College–Greece Campus

Rochester, New York

Freshman Application Contact Bryant & Stratton College–Greece Campus, 854 Long Pond Road, Rochester, NY 14612. *Phone:* 585-720-0660. *Website:* http://www.bryantstratton.edu/.

Bryant & Stratton College–Henrietta Campus

Rochester, New York

Freshman Application Contact Bryant & Stratton College–Henrietta Campus, 1225 Jefferson Road, Rochester, NY 14623. *Phone:* 585-292-5627 Ext. 101. *Website:* http://www.bryantstratton.edu/.

Bryant & Stratton College–Orchard Park Campus

Orchard Park, New York

Freshman Application Contact Bryant & Stratton College–Orchard Park Campus, 200 Redtail Road, Orchard Park, NY 14127. *Phone:* 716-677-9500. *Website:* http://www.bryantstratton.edu/.

Bryant & Stratton College–Syracuse Campus

Syracuse, New York

Freshman Application Contact Ms. Dawn Rajkowski, Director of High School Enrollments, Bryant & Stratton College–Syracuse Campus, 953 James Street, Syracuse, NY 13203-2502. *Phone:* 315-472-6603 Ext. 248. *Fax:* 315-474-4383. *Website:* http://www.bryantstratton.edu/.

Bryant & Stratton College–Syracuse North Campus

Liverpool, New York

Freshman Application Contact Ms. Heather Macnik, Director of Admissions, Bryant & Stratton College–Syracuse North Campus, 8687 Carling Road, Liverpool, NY 13090. *Phone:* 315-652-6500. *Website:* http://www.bryantstratton.edu/.

Cayuga County Community College

Auburn, New York

- **State and locally supported** 2-year, founded 1953, part of State University of New York System
- **Small-town** 50-acre campus with easy access to Rochester, Syracuse
- **Endowment** $14.4 million
- **Coed,** 3,669 undergraduate students, 37% full-time, 60% women, 40% men

Undergraduates 1,368 full-time, 2,301 part-time. Students come from 17 states and territories; 11 other countries; 0.9% are from out of state; 8% Black or African American, non-Hispanic/Latino; 3% Hispanic/Latino; 0.8% Asian, non-Hispanic/Latino; 0.1% Native Hawaiian or other Pacific Islander, non-Hispanic/Latino; 0.7% American Indian or Alaska Native, non-Hispanic/Latino; 0.5% Two or more races, non-Hispanic/Latino; 9% Race/ethnicity unknown; 1% international; 7% transferred in.
Freshmen *Admission:* 670 applied, 605 enrolled. *Average high school GPA:* 2.5.
Faculty *Total:* 189, 33% full-time. *Student/faculty ratio:* 23:1.
Majors Accounting technology and bookkeeping; art; business administration and management; child-care and support services management; communications systems installation and repair technology; computer and information sciences; computer and information sciences and support services related; corrections; criminal justice/police science; culinary arts; data processing and data processing technology; drafting and design technology; education (multiple levels); electrical, electronic and communications engineering technology; environmental science; fine/studio arts; game and interactive media design; geographic information science and cartography; health services/allied health/health sciences; humanities; information

science/studies; information technology; liberal arts and sciences and humanities related; liberal arts and sciences/liberal studies; mass communication/media; mechanical engineering/mechanical technology; music related; occupational therapist assistant; radio and television broadcasting technology; radio, television, and digital communication related; registered nursing/registered nurse; sport and fitness administration/management; telecommunications technology; wine steward/sommelier; writing.

Academics *Calendar:* semesters. *Degree:* certificates and associate. *Special study options:* academic remediation for entering students, advanced placement credit, cooperative education, distance learning, honors programs, internships, off-campus study, part-time degree program, services for LD students, study abroad, summer session for credit.

Library Norman F. Bourke Memorial Library plus 1 other. *Books:* 69,726 (physical), 216,738 (digital/electronic); *Serial titles:* 429 (physical), 67,522 (digital/electronic); *Databases:* 116. Weekly public service hours: 58; students can reserve study rooms.

Student Life *Housing:* college housing not available. *Activities and Organizations:* drama/theater group, student-run newspaper, radio and television station, choral group, Student Activity Board, Student Government, Criminal Justice Club, Tutor Club, Early Childhood Club. *Student services:* health clinic, personal/psychological counseling, veterans affairs office.

Athletics Member NJCAA. *Intercollegiate sports:* baseball M, basketball M/W, cross-country running M/W, golf M/W, lacrosse M/W, soccer M/W, softball W, volleyball W. *Intramural sports:* basketball M/W.

Costs (2020–21) *Tuition:* state resident $4844 full-time, $202 per credit hour part-time; nonresident $9688 full-time, $404 per credit hour part-time. Full-time tuition and fees vary according to course load, location, and program. Part-time tuition and fees vary according to course load, location, and program. *Required fees:* $608 full-time. *Payment plan:* installment. *Waivers:* employees or children of employees.

Financial Aid Of all full-time matriculated undergraduates who enrolled in 2018, 150 Federal Work-Study jobs (averaging $2000). 200 state and other part-time jobs (averaging $1000).

Applying *Options:* electronic application. *Required:* high school transcript. *Required for some:* specific additional requirements for nursing and occupational therapy programs. *Application deadlines:* rolling (freshmen), rolling (transfers). *Notification:* continuous (freshmen), continuous (transfers).

Freshman Application Contact Cayuga County Community College, 197 Franklin Street, Auburn, NY 13021-3099. *Phone:* 315-255-1743 Ext. 2244. *Toll-free phone:* 866-598-8883.
Website: http://www.cayuga-cc.edu/.

Clinton Community College
Plattsburgh, New York

Freshman Application Contact Clinton Community College, 136 Clinton Point Drive, Plattsburgh, NY 12901-9573. *Phone:* 518-562-4171. *Toll-free phone:* 800-552-1160. *Website:* http://www.clinton.edu/.

Cochran School of Nursing
Yonkers, New York

Freshman Application Contact Brandy Haughton, Admissions Counselor, Cochran School of Nursing, 967 North Broadway, Yonkers, NY 10701. *Phone:* 914-964-4606. *Fax:* 914-964-4796. *E-mail:* bhaughton@riversidehealth.org. *Website:* http://www.cochranschoolofnursing.us/.

The College of Westchester
White Plains, New York

- **Proprietary** primarily 2-year, founded 1915
- **Suburban** campus with easy access to New York City
- **Coed,** 906 undergraduate students, 80% full-time, 67% women, 33% men

Undergraduates 728 full-time, 178 part-time. Students come from 9 states and territories; 5% are from out of state; 40% Black or African American, non-Hispanic/Latino; 47% Hispanic/Latino; 2% Asian, non-Hispanic/Latino; 0.1% Native Hawaiian or other Pacific Islander, non-Hispanic/Latino; 0.1% American Indian or Alaska Native, non-Hispanic/Latino; 1% Two or more races, non-Hispanic/Latino; 2% Race/ethnicity unknown; 12% transferred in. *Retention:* 63% of full-time freshmen returned.

Freshmen *Admission:* 824 applied, 796 admitted, 155 enrolled.

Majors Accounting; business administration and management; commercial and advertising art; computer software and media applications related; health/health-care administration; health information/medical records administration; information technology; medical/clinical assistant; network and system administration; web page, digital/multimedia and information resources design.

Academics *Calendar:* semesters. *Degrees:* certificates, associate, and bachelor's. *Special study options:* academic remediation for entering students, accelerated degree program, adult/continuing education programs, cooperative education, distance learning, double majors, honors programs, internships, part-time degree program, summer session for credit.

Library Dr. William R. Papallo Library.

Student Life *Housing:* college housing not available. *Activities and Organizations:* student-run newspaper. *Student services:* personal/psychological counseling, veterans affairs office.

Standardized Tests *Recommended:* SAT (for admission).

Costs (2019–20) *Tuition:* $21,060 full-time, $780 per credit part-time. *Required fees:* $1350 full-time, $150 per course part-time. *Payment plan:* installment. *Waivers:* employees or children of employees.

Applying *Options:* electronic application, deferred entrance. *Application fee:* $40. *Required:* high school transcript, interview. *Required for some:* essay or personal statement. *Application deadlines:* rolling (freshmen), rolling (transfers).

Freshman Application Contact Mr. Matt Curtis, Vice President, Enrollment Management, The College of Westchester, 325 Central Avenue, PO Box 710, White Plains, NY 10602. *Phone:* 914-948-4442 Ext. 313. *Toll-free phone:* 855-403-7722. *Fax:* 914-948-5441. *E-mail:* admissions@cw.edu.
Website: http://www.cw.edu/.

Columbia-Greene Community College
Hudson, New York

- **State and locally supported** 2-year, founded 1966, part of State University of New York System
- **Rural** 143-acre campus
- **Coed,** 1,461 undergraduate students, 36% full-time, 62% women, 38% men

Undergraduates 528 full-time, 933 part-time. Students come from 3 states and territories; 10% Black or African American, non-Hispanic/Latino; 9% Hispanic/Latino; 2% Asian, non-Hispanic/Latino; 0.2% American Indian or Alaska Native, non-Hispanic/Latino; 4% Two or more races, non-Hispanic/Latino; 2% Race/ethnicity unknown; 5% transferred in. *Retention:* 61% of full-time freshmen returned.

Freshmen *Admission:* 363 applied, 361 admitted, 252 enrolled.

Faculty *Total:* 79, 52% full-time. *Student/faculty ratio:* 15:1.

Majors Accounting technology and bookkeeping; automobile/automotive mechanics technology; business administration and management; business/commerce; computer and information sciences; criminal justice/law enforcement administration; cyber/computer forensics and counterterrorism; environmental studies; fine/studio arts; general studies; humanities; human services; information technology; liberal arts and sciences/liberal studies; medical/clinical assistant; registered nursing/registered nurse.

Academics *Calendar:* semesters. *Degree:* certificates and associate. *Special study options:* academic remediation for entering students, advanced placement credit, cooperative education, distance learning, English as a second language, honors programs, independent study, internships, part-time degree program, services for LD students, summer session for credit.

Library Columbia-Greene Library plus 1 other.

Student Life *Housing:* college housing not available. *Activities and Organizations:* student-run radio station, Criminal Justice Club, Human Services Club, Psychology Club, Student Senate, Animal Advocates. *Campus security:* 24-hour emergency response devices and patrols, student patrols, late-night transport/escort service. *Student services:* personal/psychological counseling, veterans affairs office.

Athletics Member NCAA, NJCAA. All NCAA Division III. *Intercollegiate sports:* baseball M, basketball M, softball W. *Intramural sports:* basketball M/W.

Costs (2019–20) *Tuition:* state resident $4824 full-time, $201 per credit hour part-time; nonresident $9648 full-time, $402 per credit hour part-time. Full-time tuition and fees vary according to course load and program. Part-time tuition and fees vary according to course load and program. *Required fees:* $504 full-time, $22 per semester hour part-time. *Payment plan:* installment. *Waivers:* senior citizens and employees or children of employees.

Applying *Options:* electronic application, early admission, deferred entrance. *Required:* high school transcript. *Required for some:* interview. *Application deadlines:* rolling (freshmen), rolling (out-of-state freshmen), rolling (transfers).

Freshman Application Contact Ms. Ann Bruno, Acting Assistant Dean of Enrollment management, Columbia-Greene Community College, 4400 Route 23, Hudson, NY 12534. *Phone:* 518-828-4181 Ext. 3361. *Fax:* 518-822-2015. *E-mail:* ann.bruno@sunycgcc.edu.
Website: http://www.sunycgcc.edu/.

Corning Community College
Corning, New York

Freshman Application Contact Corning Community College, One Academic Drive, Corning, NY 14830-3297. *Phone:* 607-962-9540. *Toll-free phone:* 800-358-7171. *Website:* http://www.corning-cc.edu/.

Dutchess Community College
Poughkeepsie, New York

- **State and locally supported** 2-year, founded 1957, part of State University of New York System
- **Suburban** 130-acre campus with easy access to New York City
- **Coed,** 8,691 undergraduate students, 40% full-time, 56% women, 44% men

Undergraduates 3,514 full-time, 5,177 part-time. Students come from 29 states and territories; 49 other countries; 1% are from out of state; 11% Black or African American, non-Hispanic/Latino; 21% Hispanic/Latino; 4% Asian, non-Hispanic/Latino; 0.1% Native Hawaiian or other Pacific Islander, non-Hispanic/Latino; 0.2% American Indian or Alaska Native, non-Hispanic/Latino; 4% Two or more races, non-Hispanic/Latino; 3% Race/ethnicity unknown; 0.6% international; 3% transferred in; 5% live on campus.
Freshmen *Admission:* 5,732 applied, 4,040 admitted, 1,675 enrolled. *Average high school GPA:* 2.8.
Faculty *Total:* 463, 27% full-time, 9% with terminal degrees. *Student/faculty ratio:* 21:1.
Majors Accounting; accounting technology and bookkeeping; airline pilot and flight crew; architectural engineering technology; art; aviation/airway management; business administration and management; child-care and support services management; clinical/medical laboratory technology; commercial and advertising art; communications systems installation and repair technology; community health services counseling; computer/information technology services administration related; computer science; construction trades related; criminal justice/police science; electrical, electronic and communications engineering technology; emergency medical technology (EMT paramedic); engineering; fire services administration; general studies; humanities; human services; information science/studies; legal assistant/paralegal; liberal arts and sciences and humanities related; liberal arts and sciences/liberal studies; physical education teaching and coaching; registered nursing/registered nurse; speech communication and rhetoric; visual and performing arts.
Academics *Calendar:* semesters. *Degree:* certificates and associate. *Special study options:* academic remediation for entering students, adult/continuing education programs, advanced placement credit, distance learning, English as a second language, freshman honors college, honors programs, internships, off-campus study, part-time degree program, services for LD students, summer session for credit.
Library Dutchess Library plus 1 other. *Books:* 92,029 (physical), 189,102 (digital/electronic); *Serial titles:* 128 (physical), 86,535 (digital/electronic); *Databases:* 116. Weekly public service hours: 70.
Student Life *Housing Options:* coed, men-only, women-only, special housing for students with disabilities. Campus housing is university owned. *Activities and Organizations:* drama/theater group, student-run newspaper, radio station, choral group, Rap, Poetry and Music, Outdoor Adventure, Student Government Association, Gamers Club, Masquer's Guild Theatre Club. *Campus security:* 24-hour emergency response devices and patrols, late-night transport/escort service, controlled dormitory access, Mass Notification System. *Student services:* health clinic, personal/psychological counseling, veterans affairs office.
Athletics Member NJCAA. *Intercollegiate sports:* baseball M, basketball M/W, cross-country running M/W, soccer M, softball W, volleyball W.
Costs (2020–21) *Tuition:* area resident $4150 full-time; nonresident $8300 full-time. *Required fees:* $540 full-time, $173 per credit hour part-time. *Room and board:* $12,106.
Applying *Options:* electronic application, early admission, deferred entrance. *Required:* high school transcript. *Application deadlines:* rolling (freshmen), rolling (transfers). *Notification:* continuous (freshmen), continuous (transfers).
Freshman Application Contact Dutchess Community College, 53 Pendell Road, Poughkeepsie, NY 12601-1595. *Phone:* 845-431-8010. *Website:* http://www.sunydutchess.edu/.

Elim Bible Institute and College
Lima, New York

- **Independent Christian** 2-year
- **Rural** 17-acre campus
- **Coed,** 109 undergraduate students, 82% full-time, 46% women, 54% men

Undergraduates 89 full-time, 20 part-time. Students come from 11 states and territories; 7 other countries; 27% are from out of state; 11% Black or African American, non-Hispanic/Latino; 13% Hispanic/Latino; 1% Asian, non-Hispanic/Latino; 2% Two or more races, non-Hispanic/Latino; 6% Race/ethnicity unknown; 5% international; 55% transferred in. *Retention:* 67% of full-time freshmen returned.
Freshmen *Admission:* 28 enrolled.
Faculty *Student/faculty ratio:* 10:1.
Majors Biblical studies.
Academics *Degree:* certificates and associate.
Library S. Joy Niswander Library.
Student Life *Housing Options:* Campus housing is university owned. Freshman campus housing is guaranteed. *Campus security:* 24-hour emergency response devices.
Standardized Tests *Recommended:* SAT (for admission).
Costs (2020–21) *One-time required fee:* $1476. *Comprehensive fee:* $16,880 includes full-time tuition ($9480), mandatory fees ($500), and room and board ($6900). Part-time tuition: $316 per credit. No tuition increase for student's term of enrollment. *Required fees:* $500 per year part-time. *Room and board:* college room only: $3000. Room and board charges vary according to housing facility. *Payment plans:* installment, deferred payment. *Waivers:* employees or children of employees.
Applying *Options:* electronic application. *Required:* high school transcript. *Application deadlines:* 8/1 (freshmen), 8/1 (out-of-state freshmen). *Notification:* continuous (freshmen), continuous (out-of-state freshmen).
Freshman Application Contact Ms. Krista Vann, Associate Admissions Director, Elim Bible Institute and College, 7245 College St, Lima, NY 14485. *Phone:* 585-5828265. *E-mail:* info@elim.edu. *Website:* http://www.elim.edu/.

Elmira Business Institute
Elmira, New York

Freshman Application Contact Ms. Lindsay Dull, Director of Student services, Elmira Business Institute, Elmira, NY 14901. *Phone:* 607-733-7177. *Toll-free phone:* 800-843-1812. *E-mail:* info@ebi-college.com. *Website:* http://www.ebi.edu/.

Elyon College
Brooklyn, New York

Admissions Office Contact Elyon College, 1400 West 6th Street, Brooklyn, NY 11204. *Website:* http://www.elyon.edu/.

Erie Community College
Buffalo, New York

Freshman Application Contact Erie Community College, 45 Oak Street, Buffalo, NY 14203-2620. *Phone:* 716-851-1155. *Fax:* 716-270-2821. *E-mail:* admissions@ecc.edu. *Website:* http://www.ecc.edu/.

Erie Community College, North Campus
Williamsville, New York

Freshman Application Contact Erie Community College, North Campus, 6205 Main Street, Williamsville, NY 14221-7095. *Phone:* 716-851-1455. *Fax:* 716-270-2961. *E-mail:* admissions@ecc.edu. *Website:* http://www.ecc.edu/.

Erie Community College, South Campus
Orchard Park, New York

Freshman Application Contact Erie Community College, South Campus, 4041 Southwestern Boulevard, Orchard Park, NY 14127-2199. *Phone:* 716-851-1655. *Fax:* 716-851-1687. *E-mail:* admissions@ecc.edu. *Website:* http://www.ecc.edu/.

Eugenio María de Hostos Community College of the City University of New York

Bronx, New York

Freshman Application Contact Mr. Roland Velez, Director of Admissions, Eugenio María de Hostos Community College of the City University of New York, 120 149th Street, Bronx, NY 10451. *Phone:* 718-319-7968. *Fax:* 718-319-7919. *E-mail:* admissions@hostos.cuny.edu. *Website:* http://www.hostos.cuny.edu/.

Finger Lakes Community College

Canandaigua, New York

- **State and locally supported** 2-year, founded 1965, part of State University of New York System
- **Small-town** 300-acre campus with easy access to Rochester
- **Coed**

Undergraduates 2,587 full-time, 3,934 part-time. Students come from 15 states and territories; 2 other countries; 0.3% are from out of state; 5% Black or African American, non-Hispanic/Latino; 5% Hispanic/Latino; 1% Asian, non-Hispanic/Latino; 0.3% American Indian or Alaska Native, non-Hispanic/Latino; 3% Two or more races, non-Hispanic/Latino; 13% Race/ethnicity unknown; 3% transferred in.
Faculty *Student/faculty ratio:* 22:1.
Academics *Calendar:* semesters. *Degree:* certificates and associate. *Special study options:* academic remediation for entering students, accelerated degree program, advanced placement credit, distance learning, double majors, honors programs, independent study, internships, off-campus study, part-time degree program, services for LD students, study abroad, summer session for credit. *ROTC:* Air Force (c).
Library Charles Meder Library. Students can reserve study rooms.
Student Life *Campus security:* 24-hour emergency response devices and patrols, late-night transport/escort service.
Athletics Member NJCAA.
Financial Aid Of all full-time matriculated undergraduates who enrolled in 2016, 2,180 applied for aid, 2,109 were judged to have need. In 2016, 7. *Average non-need-based aid:* $1837.
Applying *Options:* electronic application, early admission, deferred entrance. *Application fee:* $20. *Required:* high school transcript.
Freshman Application Contact Ms. Bonnie B. Ritts, Director of Admissions, Finger Lakes Community College, 3325 Marvin Sands Drive, Canandaigua, NY 14424-8395. *Phone:* 585-785-1279. *Fax:* 585-785-1734. *E-mail:* admissions@flcc.edu. *Website:* http://www.flcc.edu/.

Finger Lakes Health College of Nursing

Geneva, New York

Admissions Office Contact Finger Lakes Health College of Nursing, 196 North Street, Geneva, NY 14456. *Website:* http://www.flhcon.edu/.

Fiorello H. LaGuardia Community College of the City University of New York

Long Island City, New York

- **State and locally supported** 2-year, founded 1970, part of City University of New York System
- **Urban** 25-acre campus with easy access to New York City
- **Endowment** $6.8 million
- **Coed,** 18,285 undergraduate students, 56% full-time, 42% women, 58% men

Undergraduates 10,225 full-time, 8,060 part-time. Students come from 17 states and territories; 148 other countries; 0.4% are from out of state; 19% Black or African American, non-Hispanic/Latino; 40% Hispanic/Latino; 21% Asian, non-Hispanic/Latino; 0.4% American Indian or Alaska Native, non-Hispanic/Latino; 7% international; 9% transferred in. *Retention:* 62% of full-time freshmen returned.
Freshmen *Admission:* 21,388 applied, 19,585 admitted, 3,006 enrolled.
Faculty *Total:* 1,052, 38% full-time, 31% with terminal degrees. *Student/faculty ratio:* 21:1.
Majors Accounting technology and bookkeeping; administrative assistant and secretarial science; adult development and aging; biology/biological sciences; business administration and management; civil engineering; commercial photography; computer and information sciences and support services related; computer installation and repair technology; computer programming; computer science; computer systems networking and telecommunications; criminal justice/safety; dietetic technology; digital arts; dramatic/theater arts; electrical and electronics engineering; emergency medical technology (EMT paramedic); energy management and systems technology; English; environmental science; fine/studio arts; industrial and product design; Japanese; legal assistant/paralegal; liberal arts and sciences/liberal studies; licensed practical/vocational nurse training; mechanical engineering; medical radiologic technology; occupational therapist assistant; philosophy; physical therapy technology; psychiatric/mental health services technology; psychology; recording arts technology; registered nursing/registered nurse; restaurant/food services management; Spanish; speech communication and rhetoric; teacher assistant/aide; tourism and travel services management; veterinary/animal health technology; visual and performing arts.
Academics *Calendar:* enhanced semester. *Degree:* certificates and associate. *Special study options:* academic remediation for entering students, accelerated degree program, adult/continuing education programs, advanced placement credit, cooperative education, distance learning, double majors, English as a second language, honors programs, independent study, internships, off-campus study, part-time degree program, services for LD students, student-designed majors, study abroad, summer session for credit.
Library Fiorello H. LaGuardia Community College Library Media Resources Center plus 1 other. *Books:* 88,566 (physical), 775,784 (digital/electronic); *Serial titles:* 1,168 (physical), 148,208 (digital/electronic); *Databases:* 79,440. Weekly public service hours: 82; students can reserve study rooms.
Student Life *Housing:* college housing not available. *Activities and Organizations:* drama/theater group, student-run newspaper, radio station, Bangladesh Student Association, Christian Club, Chinese Club, Web Radio, Black Student Union. *Campus security:* 24-hour emergency response devices and patrols, late-night transport/escort service. *Student services:* health clinic, personal/psychological counseling, women's center, legal services.
Athletics *Intramural sports:* basketball M/W, soccer M/W, swimming and diving M/W, table tennis M/W, volleyball M/W.
Costs (2020–21) *One-time required fee:* $417. *Tuition:* area resident $4800 full-time; nonresident $9600 full-time. *Payment plan:* installment.
Applying *Options:* electronic application, early admission, deferred entrance. *Application fee:* $70. *Required:* high school transcript. *Application deadlines:* rolling (freshmen), rolling (transfers). *Notification:* continuous (freshmen), continuous (transfers).
Freshman Application Contact Ms. LaVora Desvigne, Director of Admissions, Fiorello H. LaGuardia Community College of the City University of New York, RM-147, 31-10 Thomson Avenue, Long Island City, NY 11101. *Phone:* 718-482-5114. *Fax:* 718-482-5112. *E-mail:* admissions@lagcc.cuny.edu.
Website: http://www.lagcc.cuny.edu/.

Fulton-Montgomery Community College

Johnstown, New York

- **State and locally supported** 2-year, founded 1964, part of State University of New York System
- **Rural** 195-acre campus
- **Endowment** $1.7 million
- **Coed**

Undergraduates 1,863 full-time, 970 part-time. Students come from 6 states and territories; 18 other countries; 1% are from out of state; 2% transferred in. *Retention:* 57% of full-time freshmen returned.
Faculty *Student/faculty ratio:* 18:1.
Academics *Calendar:* semesters plus winter session. *Degree:* certificates and associate. *Special study options:* academic remediation for entering students, accelerated degree program, adult/continuing education programs, advanced placement credit, cooperative education, distance learning, double majors, English as a second language, external degree program, honors programs, independent study, internships, off-campus study, part-time degree program, services for LD students, student-designed majors, study abroad, summer session for credit.
Library Evans Library.
Student Life *Campus security:* weekend and night security.
Athletics Member NJCAA.
Applying *Options:* electronic application, early admission, deferred entrance. *Required:* high school transcript.
Freshman Application Contact Fulton-Montgomery Community College, 2805 State Highway 67, Johnstown, NY 12095-3790. *Phone:* 518-762-4651 Ext. 8301. *Website:* http://www.fmcc.suny.edu/.

Genesee Community College

Batavia, New York

Freshman Application Contact Mrs. Tanya Lane-Martin, Director of Admissions, Genesee Community College, Batavia, NY 14020. *Phone:* 585-

343-0055 Ext. 6413. *Toll-free phone:* 866-CALL GCC. *Fax:* 585-345-6892. *E-mail:* tmlanemartin@genesee.edu. *Website:* http://www.genesee.edu/.

Helene Fuld College of Nursing

New York, New York

Freshman Application Contact Helene Fuld College of Nursing, 24 East 120th Street, New York, NY 10035. *Phone:* 212-616-7271. *Website:* http://www.helenefuld.edu/.

Herkimer County Community College

Herkimer, New York

Freshman Application Contact Herkimer County Community College, 100 Reservoir Road, Herkimer, NY 13350. *Phone:* 315-866-0300 Ext. 8278. *Toll-free phone:* 888-464-4222 Ext. 8278. *Website:* http://www.herkimer.edu/.

Hudson Valley Community College

Troy, New York

Freshman Application Contact Ms. Marie Claire Bauer, Director of Admissions, Hudson Valley Community College, 80 Vandenburgh Avenue, Troy, NY 12180-6096. *Phone:* 518-629-7309. *Toll-free phone:* 877-325-HVCC. *Website:* http://www.hvcc.edu/.

Island Drafting and Technical Institute

Amityville, New York

Freshman Application Contact Larry Basile, Island Drafting and Technical Institute, 128 Broadway, Amityville, NY 11701. *Phone:* 631-691-8733 Ext. 114. *Fax:* 631-691-8738. *E-mail:* info@idti.edu. *Website:* http://www.idti.edu/.

Jamestown Business College

Jamestown, New York

Freshman Application Contact Mrs. Brenda Salemme, Director of Admissions, Jamestown Business College, 7 Fairmount Avenue, Box 429, Jamestown, NY 14702-0429. *Phone:* 716-664-5100. *Fax:* 716-664-3144. *E-mail:* brendasalemme@jbc.edu. *Website:* http://www.jbc.edu/.

Jamestown Community College

Jamestown, New York

- **State and locally supported** 2-year, founded 1950, part of State University of New York
- **Small-town** 107-acre campus
- **Coed,** 4,467 undergraduate students, 44% full-time, 59% women, 41% men

Undergraduates 1,973 full-time, 2,494 part-time. Students come from 17 states and territories; 26 other countries; 13% are from out of state; 4% Black or African American, non-Hispanic/Latino; 7% Hispanic/Latino; 0.8% Asian, non-Hispanic/Latino; 0.1% Native Hawaiian or other Pacific Islander, non-Hispanic/Latino; 2% American Indian or Alaska Native, non-Hispanic/Latino; 3% Two or more races, non-Hispanic/Latino; 1% Race/ethnicity unknown; 2% international; 4% transferred in; 13% live on campus.

Freshmen *Admission:* 1,713 applied, 1,707 admitted, 811 enrolled. *Average high school GPA:* 3.3.

Faculty *Total:* 260, 27% full-time. *Student/faculty ratio:* 15:1.

Majors Accounting technology and bookkeeping; administrative assistant and secretarial science; biology/biotechnology laboratory technician; business administration and management; computer and information sciences; criminal justice/law enforcement administration; criminal justice/police science; engineering; environmental science; fine/studio arts; general studies; health and physical education/fitness; health information/medical records technology; homeland security; humanities; human services; information science/studies; information technology; international/global studies; liberal arts and sciences and humanities related; liberal arts and sciences/liberal studies; mechanical engineering/mechanical technology; music; music management; occupational therapist assistant; registered nursing/registered nurse; speech communication and rhetoric; sport and fitness administration/management; substance abuse/addiction counseling; teacher assistant/aide; welding technology.

Academics *Calendar:* semesters. *Degree:* certificates and associate. *Special study options:* academic remediation for entering students, adult/continuing education programs, advanced placement credit, cooperative education, distance learning, English as a second language, honors programs, independent study, internships, off-campus study, part-time degree program, services for LD students, study abroad, summer session for credit.

Library Hultquist Library plus 1 other. *Books:* 68,789 (physical), 2,129 (digital/electronic); *Serial titles:* 486 (physical); *Databases:* 106. Weekly public service hours: 50.

Student Life *Housing Options:* coed. Campus housing is university owned. *Activities and Organizations:* drama/theater group, choral group. *Campus security:* 24-hour emergency response devices, controlled dormitory access. *Student services:* health clinic.

Athletics Member NJCAA. *Intercollegiate sports:* baseball M, basketball M/W, golf M/W, soccer M/W, softball W, swimming and diving M/W, volleyball W, wrestling M. *Intramural sports:* basketball M/W, bowling M/W, cross-country running M/W, softball M/W, volleyball M/W.

Costs (2020–21) *Tuition:* state resident $5220 full-time, $218 per credit hour part-time; nonresident $10,440 full-time, $435 per credit hour part-time. *Required fees:* $1060 full-time, $250 per term part-time. *Room and board:* $10,980. Room and board charges vary according to board plan. *Payment plan:* installment. *Waivers:* employees or children of employees.

Financial Aid Of all full-time matriculated undergraduates who enrolled in 2018, 1,666 applied for aid, 1,453 were judged to have need, 23 had their need fully met. In 2018, 71 non-need-based awards were made. *Average non-need-based aid:* $3075.

Applying *Options:* electronic application, deferred entrance. *Required:* high school transcript. *Application deadlines:* rolling (freshmen), rolling (out-of-state freshmen), rolling (transfers). *Notification:* continuous (freshmen), continuous (out-of-state freshmen), continuous (transfers).

Freshman Application Contact Ms. Corrine Case, Director of Admissions, Jamestown Community College, 525 Falconer Street, PO Box 20, Jamestown, NY 14702-0020. *Phone:* 716-338-1072. *Toll-free phone:* 800-388-8557. *E-mail:* admissions@mail.sunyjcc.edu.
Website: http://www.sunyjcc.edu/.

Jefferson Community College

Watertown, New York

Freshman Application Contact Sandra L. Spadoni, Dean for Enrollment, Jefferson Community College, 1220 Coffeen Street, Watertown, NY 13601. *Phone:* 315-786-2437. *Toll-free phone:* 888-435-6522. *Fax:* 315-786-2349. *E-mail:* admissions@sunyjefferson.edu. *Website:* http://www.sunyjefferson.edu/.

Kingsborough Community College of the City University of New York

Brooklyn, New York

Freshman Application Contact Mr. Javier Morgades, Director of Admissions Information Center, Kingsborough Community College of the City University of New York, 2001 Oriental Boulevard, Brooklyn, NY 11235. *Phone:* 718-368-4600. *E-mail:* info@kbcc.cuny.edu. *Website:* http://www.kbcc.cuny.edu/.

Long Island Business Institute

Flushing, New York

Freshman Application Contact Mr. Keith Robertson, Director of Admissions, Long Island Business Institute, 408 Broadway, 2nd Floor, New York, NY 10013. *Phone:* 212-226-7300. *E-mail:* krobertson@libi.edu. *Website:* http://www.libi.edu/.

Mandl School

New York, New York

Admissions Office Contact Mandl School, 254 West 54th Street, 9th Floor, New York, NY 10019. *Website:* http://www.mandl.edu/.

Memorial College of Nursing

Albany, New York

Freshman Application Contact Admissions Office, Memorial College of Nursing, 600 Northern Boulevard, Albany, NY 12204. *Website:* http://www.nehealth.com/son/.

Mildred Elley–New York City

New York, New York

Admissions Office Contact Mildred Elley–New York City, 25 Broadway, 16th Floor, New York, NY 10004-1010. *Website:* http://www.mildred-elley.edu/.

Mildred Elley School
Albany, New York

Director of Admissions Mr. Michael Cahalan, Enrollment Manager, Mildred Elley School, 855 Central Avenue, Albany, NY 12206. *Phone:* 518-786-3171 Ext. 227. *Toll-free phone:* 800-622-6327. *Website:* http://www.mildred-elley.edu/.

Mohawk Valley Community College
Utica, New York

Freshman Application Contact Kirsten Edwards, Technical Assistant, Admissions, Mohawk Valley Community College, 1101 Sherman Drive, Utica, NY 13501. *Phone:* 315-792-5640. *Toll-free phone:* 800-SEE-MVCC. *Fax:* 315-792-5527. *E-mail:* kedwards@mvcc.edu. *Website:* http://www.mvcc.edu/.

Monroe Community College
Rochester, New York

Freshman Application Contact Ms. Sarah Hagreen, Interim Director of Admissions, Monroe Community College, 1000 East Henrietta Road, Rochester, NY 14623. *Phone:* 585-292-2222. *Fax:* 585-292-3860. *E-mail:* admissions@monroecc.edu. *Website:* http://www.monroecc.edu/.

Montefiore School of Nursing
Mount Vernon, New York

Director of Admissions Sandra Farrior, Coordinator of Student Services, Montefiore School of Nursing, 53 Valentine Street, Mount Vernon, NY 10550. *Phone:* 914-361-6472. *E-mail:* hopferadmissions@sshsw.org. *Website:* http://www.montefiorehealthsystem.org/landing.cfm?id=19.

Nassau Community College
Garden City, New York

- **State and locally supported** 2-year, founded 1959, part of State University of New York System
- **Suburban** 225-acre campus with easy access to New York City
- **Coed,** 17,278 undergraduate students, 57% full-time, 51% women, 49% men

Undergraduates 9,844 full-time, 7,434 part-time. Students come from 19 states and territories; 21% Black or African American, non-Hispanic/Latino; 29% Hispanic/Latino; 7% Asian, non-Hispanic/Latino; 0.3% Native Hawaiian or other Pacific Islander, non-Hispanic/Latino; 0.2% American Indian or Alaska Native, non-Hispanic/Latino; 2% Two or more races, non-Hispanic/Latino; 4% Race/ethnicity unknown; 0.8% international.

Freshmen *Admission:* 3,542 enrolled. *Average high school GPA:* 2.5.

Faculty *Total:* 1,129, 34% full-time. *Student/faculty ratio:* 21:1.

Majors Accounting; accounting technology and bookkeeping; administrative assistant and secretarial science; African American/Black studies; art; business administration and management; civil engineering technology; clinical/medical laboratory technology; commercial and advertising art; computer and information sciences; computer and information sciences related; computer graphics; computer science; computer systems networking and telecommunications; criminal justice/law enforcement administration; criminal justice/safety; dance; data processing and data processing technology; design and visual communications; dramatic/theater arts; engineering; entrepreneurship; fashion/apparel design; fashion merchandising; funeral service and mortuary science; general studies; hotel/motel administration; instrumentation technology; insurance; interior design; kindergarten/preschool education; legal administrative assistant/secretary; legal assistant/paralegal; liberal arts and sciences/liberal studies; management information systems; marketing/marketing management; mass communication/media; mathematics; medical administrative assistant and medical secretary; medical radiologic technology; music performance; photography; physical therapy technology; real estate; registered nursing/registered nurse; rehabilitation and therapeutic professions related; respiratory care therapy; retailing; speech communication and rhetoric; surgical technology; theater design and technology; transportation and materials moving related; visual and performing arts.

Academics *Calendar:* semesters. *Degree:* certificates and associate. *Special study options:* academic remediation for entering students, adult/continuing education programs, advanced placement credit, cooperative education, distance learning, English as a second language, honors programs, internships, off-campus study, part-time degree program, services for LD students, summer session for credit.

Library A. Holly Patterson Library.

Student Life *Housing:* college housing not available. *Activities and Organizations:* drama/theater group, student-run newspaper, radio station, choral group, Muslim Student Association, Make a Difference Club, Interact Club, Political Science Club, Investment Club. *Campus security:* 24-hour emergency response devices and patrols, late-night transport/escort service. *Student services:* personal/psychological counseling, women's center.

Athletics Member NJCAA. *Intercollegiate sports:* baseball M, basketball M/W, cross-country running M/W, football M, golf. M/W, lacrosse M/W, soccer M/W, softball W, tennis M/W, track and field M/W, volleyball W, wrestling M. *Intramural sports:* badminton M/W, baseball M, basketball M/W, cheerleading M/W, racquetball M/W, soccer M/W, softball M/W, swimming and diving M/W, table tennis M/W, tennis M/W, volleyball M/W.

Costs (2019–20) *Tuition:* area resident $5600 full-time, $234 per credit part-time; state resident $11,200 full-time, $468 per credit part-time; nonresident $11,200 full-time, $468 per credit part-time. Full-time tuition and fees vary according to program. Part-time tuition and fees vary according to program. *Required fees:* $220 full-time, $12 per credit part-time.

Financial Aid Of all full-time matriculated undergraduates who enrolled in 2018, 400 Federal Work-Study jobs (averaging $3000).

Applying *Options:* electronic application, deferred entrance. *Application fee:* $40. *Required:* high school transcript. *Required for some:* minimum 3.0 GPA, interview. *Recommended:* minimum 2.0 GPA. *Application deadline:* 8/7 (transfers). *Notification:* continuous (freshmen), continuous (transfers).

Freshman Application Contact Nassau Community College, 1 Education Drive, Garden City, NY 11530-6793. *Phone:* 516-572-7345. *Website:* http://www.ncc.edu/.

Niagara County Community College
Sanborn, New York

- **State and locally supported** 2-year, founded 1962, part of State University of New York
- **Rural** 287-acre campus
- **Endowment** $11.3 million
- **Coed,** 4,997 undergraduate students, 55% full-time, 58% women, 42% men

Undergraduates 2,756 full-time, 2,241 part-time. 13% Black or African American, non-Hispanic/Latino; 5% Hispanic/Latino; 2% Asian, non-Hispanic/Latino; 2% American Indian or Alaska Native, non-Hispanic/Latino; 4% Two or more races, non-Hispanic/Latino; 3% Race/ethnicity unknown; 0.6% international.

Freshmen *Admission:* 1,031 enrolled.

Majors Accounting; administrative assistant and secretarial science; animal sciences; baking and pastry arts; biological and physical sciences; business administration and management; business, management, and marketing related; chemical technology; computer science; consumer merchandising/retailing management; criminal justice/law enforcement administration; culinary arts; design and applied arts related; drafting and design technology; drafting/design engineering technologies related; dramatic/theater arts; elementary education; fine/studio arts; general studies; hospitality administration; humanities; human services; information science/studies; liberal arts and sciences/liberal studies; massage therapy; mass communication/media; mathematics; medical/clinical assistant; medical radiologic technology; music; natural resources/conservation; occupational health and industrial hygiene; parks, recreation and leisure; physical education teaching and coaching; physical therapy technology; registered nursing/registered nurse; social sciences; sport and fitness administration/management; surgical technology; tourism and travel services management; web page, digital/multimedia and information resources design; wine steward/sommelier.

Academics *Calendar:* semesters. *Degree:* certificates, diplomas, and associate. *Special study options:* academic remediation for entering students, adult/continuing education programs, advanced placement credit, cooperative education, distance learning, double majors, honors programs, independent study, internships, off-campus study, part-time degree program, services for LD students, student-designed majors, study abroad, summer session for credit.

Library Students can reserve study rooms.

Student Life *Campus security:* 24-hour emergency response devices and patrols.

Athletics Member NJCAA.

Financial Aid Of all full-time matriculated undergraduates who enrolled in 2018, 2,979 applied for aid, 2,979 were judged to have need. 74 Federal Work-Study jobs (averaging $1390). *Average percent of need met:* 85%. *Average financial aid package:* $5877. *Average need-based loan:* $3183. *Average need-based gift aid:* $5180.

Applying *Options:* early admission. *Required:* high school transcript. *Required for some:* minimum 2.0 GPA.

Freshman Application Contact Robert McKeown, Assistant Vice President of Enrollment Management, Niagara County Community College, 3111

Saunders Settlement Road, Sanborn, NY 14132. *Phone:* 716-614-6200. *Fax:* 716-614-6820. *E-mail:* admissions@niagaracc.suny.edu. *Website:* http://www.niagaracc.suny.edu/.

North Country Community College

Saranac Lake, New York

Freshman Application Contact Enrollment Management Assistant, North Country Community College, 23 Santanoni Avenue, PO Box 89, Saranac Lake, NY 12983-0089. *Phone:* 518-891-2915 Ext. 686. *Toll-free phone:* 800-TRY-NCCC (in-state); 888-TRY-NCCC (out-of-state). *Fax:* 518-891-0898. *E-mail:* info@nccc.edu. *Website:* http://www.nccc.edu/.

Onondaga Community College

Syracuse, New York

- **State and locally supported** 2-year, founded 1962, part of State University of New York System
- **Suburban** 280-acre campus
- **Endowment** $10.5 million
- **Coed**

Undergraduates 5,895 full-time, 5,991 part-time. Students come from 25 states and territories; 19 other countries; 1% are from out of state; 13% Black or African American, non-Hispanic/Latino; 6% Hispanic/Latino; 4% Asian, non-Hispanic/Latino; 0.1% Native Hawaiian or other Pacific Islander, non-Hispanic/Latino; 1% American Indian or Alaska Native, non-Hispanic/Latino; 3% Two or more races, non-Hispanic/Latino; 13% Race/ethnicity unknown; 0.4% international; 3% transferred in; 6% live on campus.

Faculty *Student/faculty ratio:* 24:1.

Academics *Calendar:* semesters. *Degree:* certificates, diplomas, and associate. *Special study options:* academic remediation for entering students, accelerated degree program, adult/continuing education programs, advanced placement credit, cooperative education, distance learning, double majors, English as a second language, external degree program, honors programs, internships, part-time degree program, services for LD students, study abroad, summer session for credit. *ROTC:* Air Force (c).

Library Sidney B. Coulter Library plus 1 other. *Books:* 84,742 (physical), 542 (digital/electronic); *Serial titles:* 194 (physical), 10 (digital/electronic); *Databases:* 92. Weekly public service hours: 67; students can reserve study rooms.

Student Life *Campus security:* 24-hour emergency response devices and patrols, controlled dormitory access.

Athletics Member NJCAA.

Financial Aid Of all full-time matriculated undergraduates who enrolled in 2014, 5,594 applied for aid, 5,025 were judged to have need, 227 had their need fully met. 99 Federal Work-Study jobs (averaging $3161). *Average percent of need met:* 1. *Average financial aid package:* $6747. *Average need-based loan:* $3000. *Average need-based gift aid:* $5539.

Applying *Options:* electronic application. *Required:* high school transcript. *Required for some:* minimum 2.0 GPA, interview.

Freshman Application Contact Mr. Denny Nicholson, Onondaga Community College, 4585 West Seneca Turnpike, Syracuse, NY 13215. *Phone:* 315-488-2912. *Fax:* 315-488-2107. *E-mail:* admissions@sunyocc.edu. *Website:* http://www.sunyocc.edu/.

Orange County Community College

Middletown, New York

Freshman Application Contact Michael Roe, Director of Admissions and Recruitment, Orange County Community College, 115 South Street, Middletown, NY 10940. *Phone:* 845-341-4205. *Fax:* 845-343-1228. *E-mail:* apply@sunyorange.edu. *Website:* http://www.sunyorange.edu/.

Phillips Beth Israel School of Nursing

New York, New York

Freshman Application Contact Mrs. Bernice Pass-Stern, Assistant Dean, Phillips Beth Israel School of Nursing, 776 Sixth Avenue, 4th Floor, New York, NY 10010-6354. *Phone:* 212-614-6176. *Fax:* 212-614-6109. *E-mail:* bstern@chpnet.org. *Website:* http://www.mountsinai.org/locations/beth-israel/pson.

Plaza College

Forest Hills, New York

Freshman Application Contact Dean Vanessa Lopez, Dean of Admissions, Plaza College, 118-33 Queens Boulevard, Forest Hills, NY 11375. *Phone:* 718-779-1430. *E-mail:* info@plazacollege.edu. *Website:* http://www.plazacollege.edu/.

Queensborough Community College of the City University of New York

Bayside, New York

- **State and locally supported** 2-year, founded 1958, part of City University of New York
- **Urban** 37-acre campus with easy access to New York City
- **Coed,** 14,035 undergraduate students, 60% full-time, 53% women, 47% men

Undergraduates 8,411 full-time, 5,624 part-time. Students come from 123 other countries; 2% are from out of state; 23% Black or African American, non-Hispanic/Latino; 33% Hispanic/Latino; 23% Asian, non-Hispanic/Latino; 0.7% Native Hawaiian or other Pacific Islander, non-Hispanic/Latino; 1% American Indian or Alaska Native, non-Hispanic/Latino; 2% Two or more races, non-Hispanic/Latino; 6% international; 8% transferred in. *Retention:* 62% of full-time freshmen returned.

Freshmen *Admission:* 16,089 applied, 14,797 admitted, 3,203 enrolled.

Faculty *Total:* 946, 43% full-time, 51% with terminal degrees. *Student/faculty ratio:* 18:1.

Majors Accounting; accounting technology and bookkeeping; administrative assistant and secretarial science; architectural drafting and CAD/CADD; art; biotechnology; business administration and management; chemistry; cinematography and film/video production; computer and information sciences; computer engineering technology; criminal justice/law enforcement administration; dance; data processing and data processing technology; digital arts; dramatic/theater arts; electrical, electronic and communications engineering technology; engineering; engineering science; environmental science; forensic science and technology; health services/allied health/health sciences; information technology; liberal arts and sciences/liberal studies; massage therapy; mechanical engineering/mechanical technology; medical/clinical assistant; museum studies; music history, literature, and theory; physical sciences; psychology; public health; recording arts technology; registered nursing/registered nurse; telecommunications technology.

Academics *Calendar:* semesters. *Degree:* certificates and associate. *Special study options:* academic remediation for entering students, accelerated degree program, advanced placement credit, cooperative education, distance learning, double majors, English as a second language, independent study, internships, off-campus study, part-time degree program, services for LD students, student-designed majors, study abroad, summer session for credit. *ROTC:* Army (c).

Library The Kurt R. Schmeller Library. *Books:* 109,962 (physical), 581,791 (digital/electronic); *Serial titles:* 1,195 (physical), 103,782 (digital/electronic); *Databases:* 145. Weekly public service hours: 77.

Student Life *Housing:* college housing not available. *Activities and Organizations:* drama/theater group, student-run newspaper, choral group, Phi Theta kappa, Student Organization for Disability Awareness (SODA), ASAP Club, CSTEP Club, Chemistry Club. *Campus security:* 24-hour emergency response devices and patrols, Security cameras. *Student services:* health clinic, personal/psychological counseling, legal services, veterans affairs office.

Athletics Member NJCAA. *Intercollegiate sports:* baseball M, basketball M/W, cross-country running M/W, soccer M, swimming and diving M/W, track and field M/W, volleyball W. *Intramural sports:* badminton M/W, basketball M/W, swimming and diving M(c)/W(c), table tennis M/W, tennis M/W, volleyball M/W, weight lifting M/W.

Costs (2020–21) *Tuition:* area resident $4800 full-time, $210 per credit part-time; state resident $4800 full-time, $210 per credit part-time; nonresident $9600 full-time, $320 per credit part-time. *Required fees:* $409 full-time, $106 per term part-time. *Payment plan:* installment. *Waivers:* senior citizens and employees or children of employees.

Applying *Options:* electronic application, deferred entrance. *Application fee:* $65. *Required:* high school transcript. *Required for some:* a New York State High School Equivalency Diploma (GED/TASC) is required in lieu of high school diploma. *Application deadlines:* 2/1 (freshmen), 2/1 (transfers). *Notification:* continuous (freshmen), continuous (transfers).

Freshman Application Contact Ms. Linda Evangleou, Director of Admissions & Recruitment, Queensborough Community College of the City University of New York, 222-05 56th Avenue, Bayside, NY 11364. *Phone:* 718-281-5000 Ext. 1. *Fax:* 718-281-5189. *E-mail:* admissions@qcc.cuny.edu. *Website:* http://www.qcc.cuny.edu/.

Rockland Community College
Suffern, New York

- **State and locally supported** 2-year, founded 1959, part of State University of New York System
- **Suburban** 150-acre campus with easy access to New York City
- **Coed**

Undergraduates 4,189 full-time, 3,245 part-time. Students come from 5 states and territories; 78 other countries; 1% are from out of state; 18% Black or African American, non-Hispanic/Latino; 22% Hispanic/Latino; 5% Asian, non-Hispanic/Latino; 0.3% Native Hawaiian or other Pacific Islander, non-Hispanic/Latino; 0.2% American Indian or Alaska Native, non-Hispanic/Latino; 2% Two or more races, non-Hispanic/Latino; 12% Race/ethnicity unknown; 1% international; 6% transferred in. *Retention:* 70% of full-time freshmen returned.
Faculty *Student/faculty ratio:* 22:1.
Academics *Calendar:* semesters. *Degree:* certificates and associate. *Special study options:* academic remediation for entering students, accelerated degree program, adult/continuing education programs, advanced placement credit, cooperative education, distance learning, double majors, English as a second language, external degree program, freshman honors college, honors programs, independent study, internships, off-campus study, part-time degree program, services for LD students, study abroad, summer session for credit.
Library Rockland Community College Library.
Student Life *Campus security:* 24-hour emergency response devices and patrols, student patrols, late-night transport/escort service.
Athletics Member NJCAA.
Financial Aid Of all full-time matriculated undergraduates who enrolled in 2015, 64 Federal Work-Study jobs (averaging $2953). *Average need-based loan:* $4492. *Average need-based gift aid:* $4361.
Applying *Options:* early admission, deferred entrance. *Application fee:* $30. *Required:* high school transcript.
Freshman Application Contact Rockland Community College, 145 College Road, Suffern, NY 10901-3699. *Phone:* 845-574-4484. *Toll-free phone:* 800-722-7666. *Website:* http://www.sunyrockland.edu/.

St. Elizabeth College of Nursing
Utica, New York

Freshman Application Contact Donna Ernst, Director of Recruitment, St. Elizabeth College of Nursing, 2215 Genesee Street, Utica, NY 13501. *Phone:* 315-798-8189. *E-mail:* dernst@secon.edu. *Website:* http://www.secon.edu/.

St. Joseph's College of Nursing
Syracuse, New York

Freshman Application Contact Ms. Felicia Corp, Recruiter, St. Joseph's College of Nursing, 206 Prospect Avenue, Syracuse, NY 13203. *Phone:* 315-448-5040. *Fax:* 315-448-5745. *E-mail:* collegeofnursing@sjhsyr.org. *Website:* http://www.sjhcon.edu/.

St. Paul's School of Nursing
Queens, New York

Director of Admissions Nancy Wolinski, Chairperson of Admissions, St. Paul's School of Nursing, 97-77 Queens Boulevard, Queens, NY 11374. *Phone:* 718-357-0500 Ext. 131. *E-mail:* nwolinski@svcmcny.org. *Website:* http://www.stpaulsschoolofnursing.edu/.

St. Paul's School of Nursing
Staten Island, New York

Admissions Office Contact St. Paul's School of Nursing, Corporate Commons Two, 2 Teleport Drive, Suite 203, Staten Island, NY 10311. *Website:* http://www.stpaulsschoolofnursing.edu/.

Samaritan Hospital School of Nursing
Troy, New York

Director of Admissions Ms. Diane Dyer, Student Services Coordinator, Samaritan Hospital School of Nursing, 1300 Massachusetts Avenue, Troy, NY 12180. *Phone:* 518-271-3734. *Fax:* 518-271-3303. *E-mail:* marronej@nehealth.com. *Website:* http://www.nehealth.com/.

Schenectady County Community College
Schenectady, New York

- **State and locally supported** 2-year, founded 1969, part of State University of New York System
- **Urban** 50-acre campus
- **Coed**

Undergraduates 2,184 full-time, 4,450 part-time. 14% Black or African American, non-Hispanic/Latino; 7% Hispanic/Latino; 7% Asian, non-Hispanic/Latino; 0.4% Native Hawaiian or other Pacific Islander, non-Hispanic/Latino; 0.8% American Indian or Alaska Native, non-Hispanic/Latino; 1% Two or more races, non-Hispanic/Latino; 3% Race/ethnicity unknown; 5% transferred in.
Faculty *Student/faculty ratio:* 21:1.
Academics *Calendar:* semesters. *Degree:* certificates and associate. *Special study options:* academic remediation for entering students, adult/continuing education programs, advanced placement credit, distance learning, double majors, English as a second language, honors programs, internships, off-campus study, part-time degree program, services for LD students, summer session for credit.
Library Begley Library.
Student Life *Campus security:* 24-hour emergency response devices and patrols, late-night transport/escort service.
Athletics Member NJCAA.
Financial Aid Of all full-time matriculated undergraduates who enrolled in 2018, 50 Federal Work-Study jobs (averaging $2400).
Applying *Options:* electronic application, early admission, deferred entrance. *Required:* high school transcript.
Freshman Application Contact Mr. David Sampson, Director of Admissions, Schenectady County Community College, 78 Washington Avenue, Schenectady, NY 12305-2294. *Phone:* 518-381-1370 Ext. 1370. *E-mail:* sampsodg@gw.sunysccc.edu. *Website:* http://www.sunysccc.edu/.

State University of New York Broome Community College
Binghamton, New York

Freshman Application Contact Ms. Jenae Norris, Director of Admissions, State University of New York Broome Community College, PO Box 1017, Upper Front Street, Binghamton, NY 13902. *Phone:* 607-778-5001. *Fax:* 607-778-5394. *E-mail:* admissions@sunybroome.edu. *Website:* http://www.sunybroome.edu/.

State University of New York College of Technology at Alfred
Alfred, New York

- **State-supported** primarily 2-year, founded 1908, part of State University of New York System
- **Rural** 1084-acre campus with easy access to Rochester
- **Endowment** $5.9 million
- **Coed,** 3,780 undergraduate students, 92% full-time, 37% women, 63% men

Undergraduates 3,482 full-time, 298 part-time. Students come from 29 states and territories; 7 other countries; 4% are from out of state; 13% Black or African American, non-Hispanic/Latino; 9% Hispanic/Latino; 1% Asian, non-Hispanic/Latino; 0.1% Native Hawaiian or other Pacific Islander, non-Hispanic/Latino; 0.3% American Indian or Alaska Native, non-Hispanic/Latino; 3% Two or more races, non-Hispanic/Latino; 2% Race/ethnicity unknown; 0.3% international; 7% transferred in; 61% live on campus. *Retention:* 78% of full-time freshmen returned.
Freshmen *Admission:* 6,683 applied, 4,460 admitted, 1,180 enrolled. *Average high school GPA:* ####. *Test scores:* SAT evidence-based reading and writing scores over 500: 63%; SAT math scores over 500: 67%; ACT scores over 18: 78%; SAT evidence-based reading and writing scores over 600: 19%; SAT math scores over 600: 22%; ACT scores over 24: 36%; SAT evidence-based reading and writing scores over 700: 2%; SAT math scores over 700: 3%; ACT scores over 30: 5%.
Faculty *Total:* 258, 65% full-time, 32% with terminal degrees. *Student/faculty ratio:* 18:1.
Majors Accounting technology and bookkeeping; agribusiness; agricultural business and management; agricultural mechanics and equipment technology; agriculture; animation, interactive technology, video graphics and special effects; architectural engineering technology; architecture; autobody/collision and repair technology; automobile/automotive mechanics technology; biology/biological sciences; business administration and management;

business, management, and marketing related; computer and information sciences; computer and information systems security; computer engineering technology; computer programming (specific applications); construction engineering technology; construction management; construction trades related; court reporting; criminal justice/law enforcement administration; criminal justice/safety; culinary arts; diagnostic medical sonography and ultrasound technology; diesel mechanics technology; drafting and design technology; electrical and power transmission installation; electrical, electronic and communications engineering technology; electromechanical technology; engineering; engineering technologies and engineering related; environmental engineering technology; financial planning and services; forensic science and technology; game and interactive media design; general studies; graphic design; health/health-care administration; health information/medical records technology; health services/allied health/health sciences; heating, air conditioning, ventilation and refrigeration maintenance technology; heavy/industrial equipment maintenance technologies related; humanities; human resources management; human services; information science/studies; interior design; intermedia/multimedia; liberal arts and sciences and humanities related; liberal arts and sciences/liberal studies; machine shop technology; masonry; mechanical engineering/mechanical technology; motorcycle maintenance and repair technology; multi/interdisciplinary studies related; nursing practice; radiologic technology/science; registered nursing/registered nurse; sales, distribution, and marketing operations; sport and fitness administration/management; surveying technology; system, networking, and LAN/WAN management; vehicle maintenance and repair technologies related; veterinary/animal health technology; web/multimedia management and webmaster; welding technology.

Academics *Calendar:* semesters. *Degrees:* certificates, associate, and bachelor's. *Special study options:* academic remediation for entering students, accelerated degree program, adult/continuing education programs, advanced placement credit, cooperative education, distance learning, double majors, English as a second language, honors programs, independent study, internships, off-campus study, part-time degree program, services for LD students, student-designed majors, study abroad, summer session for credit. *ROTC:* Army (c).

Library Walter C. Hinkle Memorial Library plus 1 other. *Books:* 34,991 (physical), 1,901 (digital/electronic); *Serial titles:* 162 (physical); *Databases:* 228. Weekly public service hours: 88.

Student Life *Housing Options:* coed, men-only, women-only, special housing for students with disabilities. Campus housing is university owned. Freshman campus housing is guaranteed. *Activities and Organizations:* drama/theater group, student-run newspaper, radio station, choral group, Outdoor Recreation Club, Caribbean Student Association, Alfred Programming Board, Pioneer Woodsmen, Disaster Relief Team. *Campus security:* 24-hour emergency response devices and patrols, late-night transport/escort service, controlled dormitory access, residence hall entrance guards. *Student services:* health clinic, personal/psychological counseling, veterans affairs office.

Athletics Member NCAA, USCAA. All Division III. *Intercollegiate sports:* baseball M, basketball M/W, cross-country running M/W, equestrian sports M/W, football M, lacrosse M, soccer M/W, softball W, swimming and diving M/W, track and field M/W, volleyball W, wrestling M. *Intramural sports:* archery M(c)/W(c), basketball M/W, cheerleading M(c)/W(c), equestrian sports M(c)/W(c), football M, golf M/W, ice hockey M(c), rock climbing M/W, soccer M/W, softball M/W, swimming and diving M/W, tennis M/W, ultimate Frisbee M/W, volleyball M/W.

Standardized Tests *Required for some:* SAT or ACT (for admission). *Recommended:* SAT or ACT (for admission).

Costs (2019–20) *One-time required fee:* $150. *Tuition:* area resident $7070 full-time, $295 per credit hour part-time; state resident $7070 full-time, $295 per credit hour part-time; nonresident $16,980 full-time, $460 per credit hour part-time. *Required fees:* $1782 full-time, $66 per credit hour part-time, $10 per credit hour part-time. *Room and board:* $13,060; room only: $7990. Room and board charges vary according to board plan, housing facility, and location. *Payment plans:* installment, deferred payment. *Waivers:* employees or children of employees.

Financial Aid Of all full-time matriculated undergraduates who enrolled in 2018, 3,232 applied for aid, 2,864 were judged to have need, 308 had their need fully met. In 2018, 176 non-need-based awards were made. *Average percent of need met:* 57%. *Average financial aid package:* $11,164. *Average need-based loan:* $3677. *Average need-based gift aid:* $7392. *Average non-need-based aid:* $5663. *Average indebtedness upon graduation:* $34,177.

Applying *Options:* electronic application. *Application fee:* $50. *Required:* high school transcript, minimum 2.0 GPA, Common Application with essay on supplemental application. *Recommended:* essay or personal statement, interview. *Application deadlines:* rolling (freshmen), rolling (transfers). *Notification:* continuous (freshmen), continuous (transfers).

Freshman Application Contact Ms. Betsy Penrose, Vice President for Enrollment Management, State University of New York College of Technology at Alfred, Huntington Administration Building, 10 Upper College Drive, Alfred, NY 14802. *Phone:* 607-587-3945. *Toll-free phone:* 800-4-ALFRED. *Fax:* 607-587-4299. *E-mail:* admissions@alfredstate.edu. *Website:* http://www.alfredstate.edu/.

Stella and Charles Guttman Community College

New York, New York

Admissions Office Contact Stella and Charles Guttman Community College, 50 West 40th Street, New York, NY 10018. *Website:* http://guttman.cuny.edu/.

Suffolk County Community College

Selden, New York

Freshman Application Contact Suffolk County Community College, 533 College Road, Selden, NY 11784-2899. *Phone:* 631-451-4000. *Website:* http://www.sunysuffolk.edu/.

Sullivan County Community College

Loch Sheldrake, New York

- **State and locally supported** 2-year, founded 1962, part of State University of New York System
- **Rural** 405-acre campus
- **Endowment** $921,102
- **Coed**

Undergraduates 782 full-time, 756 part-time. Students come from 2 states and territories; 9 other countries; 1% are from out of state; 16% Black or African American, non-Hispanic/Latino; 24% Hispanic/Latino; 2% Asian, non-Hispanic/Latino; 0.1% Native Hawaiian or other Pacific Islander, non-Hispanic/Latino; 0.4% American Indian or Alaska Native, non-Hispanic/Latino; 4% Two or more races, non-Hispanic/Latino; 6% Race/ethnicity unknown; 1% international; 6% transferred in; 16% live on campus.

Faculty *Student/faculty ratio:* 21:1.

Academics *Calendar:* semesters. *Degree:* certificates and associate. *Special study options:* academic remediation for entering students, adult/continuing education programs, advanced placement credit, cooperative education, distance learning, double majors, honors programs, independent study, internships, off-campus study, part-time degree program, services for LD students, summer session for credit.

Library Hermann Memorial Library plus 1 other. *Books:* 59,923 (physical), 169,353 (digital/electronic); *Serial titles:* 128 (physical), 3 (digital/electronic); *Databases:* 94. Weekly public service hours: 62.

Student Life *Campus security:* 24-hour emergency response devices and patrols, student patrols, controlled dormitory access.

Athletics Member NJCAA.

Costs (2019–20) *Tuition:* state resident $5016 full-time, $209 per credit hour part-time; nonresident $10,032 full-time, $418 per credit hour part-time. *Required fees:* $909 full-time, $37 per credit hour part-time. *Room and board:* $9948; room only: $6228.

Financial Aid Of all full-time matriculated undergraduates who enrolled in 2017, 643 applied for aid, 628 were judged to have need, 628 had their need fully met. 52 Federal Work-Study jobs (averaging $737). 11 state and other part-time jobs (averaging $949). *Average percent of need met:* 100. *Average financial aid package:* $4327. *Average need-based loan:* $1756. *Average need-based gift aid:* $3706.

Applying *Options:* electronic application, early admission, deferred entrance. *Required:* high school transcript.

Freshman Application Contact Mr. Steven Alhona, Director of Admissions, Sullivan County Community College, 112 College Road, Loch Sheldrake, NY 12759. *Phone:* 845-434-5750 Ext. 4356. *Toll-free phone:* 800-577-5243. *Fax:* 845-434-4806. *E-mail:* salhona@sunysullivan.edu. *Website:* http://www.sunysullivan.edu/.

Tompkins Cortland Community College

Dryden, New York

Admissions Office Contact Tompkins Cortland Community College, 170 North Street, PO Box 139, Dryden, NY 13053-0139. *Toll-free phone:* 888-567-8211. *Website:* http://www.tompkinscortland.edu/.

Trocaire College
Buffalo, New York
Freshman Application Contact Trocaire College, 360 Choate Avenue, Buffalo, NY 14220-2094. *Phone:* 716-826-2558. *Website:* http://www.trocaire.edu/.

Ulster County Community College
Stone Ridge, New York
Freshman Application Contact Admissions Office, Ulster County Community College, 491 Cottekill Road, Stone Ridge, NY 12484. *Phone:* 845-687-5022. *Toll-free phone:* 800-724-0833. *E-mail:* admissionsoffice@sunyulster.edu. *Website:* http://www.sunyulster.edu/.

Westchester Community College
Valhalla, New York
- **State and locally supported** 2-year, founded 1946, part of State University of New York System
- **Suburban** 218-acre campus with easy access to New York City
- **Coed**

Majors Accounting; accounting technology and bookkeeping; administrative assistant and secretarial science; animal sciences; art; business administration and management; child-care and support services management; civil engineering technology; commercial and advertising art; community organization and advocacy; computer and information sciences; computer and information sciences and support services related; computer and information systems security; corrections; design and applied arts related; dietitian assistant; digital arts; digital communication and media/multimedia; drafting and design technology; electrical, electronic and communications engineering technology; emergency medical technology (EMT paramedic); environmental control technologies related; environmental science; environmental studies; food service systems administration; health and physical education/fitness; health information/medical records technology; health professions related; humanities; information science/studies; international business/trade/commerce; journalism; legal assistant/paralegal; liberal arts and sciences and humanities related; liberal arts and sciences/liberal studies; marketing related; mechanical engineering/mechanical technology; medical administrative assistant and medical secretary; medical radiologic technology; merchandising, sales, and marketing operations related (general); practical nursing, vocational nursing and nursing assistants related; registered nursing/registered nurse; respiratory care therapy; restaurant, culinary, and catering management; retailing; small business administration; speech communication and rhetoric; substance abuse/addiction counseling; teacher assistant/aide; visual and performing arts.

Academics *Calendar:* semesters. *Degree:* certificates and associate. *Special study options:* academic remediation for entering students, adult/continuing education programs, advanced placement credit, cooperative education, distance learning, double majors, English as a second language, honors programs, independent study, internships, off-campus study, part-time degree program, services for LD students, study abroad, summer session for credit.

Library Harold L. Drimmer Library.

Student Life *Housing:* college housing not available. *Activities and Organizations:* student-run newspaper, radio station, choral group, Accounting Club, Future Nurses Club, Law Society, Chemistry Club, Respiratory Therapy. *Campus security:* 24-hour emergency response devices and patrols, late-night transport/escort service. *Student services:* health clinic, personal/psychological counseling, women's center, veterans affairs office.

Athletics Member NJCAA. *Intercollegiate sports:* baseball M, basketball M/W, bowling M/W, golf M, soccer M, softball W, volleyball W. *Intramural sports:* badminton M/W, basketball M/W, softball M/W, swimming and diving M/W, tennis M/W, volleyball M/W, weight lifting M/W.

Costs (2019–20) *Tuition:* area resident $4580 full-time, $191 per credit hour part-time; state resident $4580 full-time, $191 per credit hour part-time; nonresident $11,770 full-time, $493 per credit hour part-time. Full-time tuition and fees vary according to program. Part-time tuition and fees vary according to program. *Required fees:* $456 full-time, $12 per credit hour part-time, $50 per term part-time. *Waivers:* employees or children of employees.

Applying *Options:* electronic application, early action. *Application fee:* $35. *Required:* high school transcript. *Required for some:* interview. *Application deadline:* rolling (freshmen).

Freshman Application Contact Ms. Gloria De La Paz, Director of Admissions, Westchester Community College, 75 Grasslands Road, Administration Building, Valhalla, NY 10595-1698. *Phone:* 914-606-6735. *Fax:* 914-606-6540. *E-mail:* admissions@sunywcc.edu.
Website: http://www.sunywcc.edu/.

Yeshiva Sholom Shachna
Brooklyn, New York
Admissions Office Contact Yeshiva Sholom Shachna, 401 Elmwood Avenue, Brooklyn, NY 11230.

NORTH CAROLINA

Alamance Community College
Graham, North Carolina
- **State-supported** 2-year, founded 1958, part of North Carolina Community College System
- **Small-town** 48-acre campus
- **Endowment** $2.9 million
- **Coed,** 4,233 undergraduate students, 61% full-time, 60% women, 40% men

Undergraduates 2,565 full-time, 1,668 part-time. Students come from 7 states and territories; 6 other countries; 1% are from out of state; 21% Black or African American, non-Hispanic/Latino; 9% Hispanic/Latino; 2% Asian, non-Hispanic/Latino; 0.2% Native Hawaiian or other Pacific Islander, non-Hispanic/Latino; 0.4% American Indian or Alaska Native, non-Hispanic/Latino; 2% Two or more races, non-Hispanic/Latino; 0.6% international; 28% transferred in.

Freshmen *Admission:* 448 enrolled.

Faculty *Total:* 435, 26% full-time, 3% with terminal degrees. *Student/faculty ratio:* 20:1.

Majors Accounting technology and bookkeeping; animal sciences; applied horticulture/horticulture operations; automobile/automotive mechanics technology; banking and financial support services; biotechnology; business administration and management; carpentry; clinical/medical laboratory technology; commercial and advertising art; criminal justice/safety; culinary arts; electrical, electronic and communications engineering technology; executive assistant/executive secretary; heating, ventilation, air conditioning and refrigeration engineering technology; information science/studies; kindergarten/preschool education; legal administrative assistant/secretary; liberal arts and sciences/liberal studies; machine tool technology; mechanical engineering/mechanical technology; medical administrative assistant and medical secretary; medical/clinical assistant; office occupations and clerical services; registered nursing/registered nurse; retailing; teacher assistant/aide; welding technology.

Academics *Calendar:* semesters. *Degree:* certificates, diplomas, and associate. *Special study options:* academic remediation for entering students, adult/continuing education programs, cooperative education, distance learning, double majors, English as a second language, independent study, off-campus study, part-time degree program, services for LD students, summer session for credit.

Library Learning Resources Center. Weekly public service hours: 64; students can reserve study rooms.

Student Life *Housing:* college housing not available. *Campus security:* 24-hour emergency response devices and patrols, student patrols, late-night transport/escort service. *Student services:* personal/psychological counseling, veterans affairs office.

Costs (2020–21) *Tuition:* state resident $2432 full-time, $76 per credit hour part-time; nonresident $8576 full-time, $268 per credit hour part-time. Full-time tuition and fees vary according to course load. Part-time tuition and fees vary according to course load. *Required fees:* $30 full-time, $5 per credit hour part-time. *Payment plan:* installment.

Financial Aid Of all full-time matriculated undergraduates who enrolled in 2010, 4,000 applied for aid, 3,000 were judged to have need. 200 Federal Work-Study jobs (averaging $1250). *Average percent of need met:* 30%. *Average financial aid package:* $4500. *Average need-based gift aid:* $4500. *Average indebtedness upon graduation:* $2500.

Applying *Options:* electronic application. *Required:* high school transcript. *Application deadlines:* rolling (freshmen), rolling (transfers). *Notification:* continuous (freshmen), continuous (transfers).

Freshman Application Contact Ms. Elizabeth Brehler, Director for Enrollment Management, Alamance Community College, Graham, NC 27253-8000. *Phone:* 336-506-4120. *Fax:* 336-506-4264. *E-mail:* brehlere@alamancecc.edu.
Website: http://www.alamancecc.edu/.

Asheville-Buncombe Technical Community College
Asheville, North Carolina

- **State-supported** 2-year, founded 1959, part of North Carolina Community College System
- **Urban** 126-acre campus
- **Coed**

Majors Accounting; automobile/automotive mechanics technology; baking and pastry arts; biology/biotechnology laboratory technician; building/property maintenance; business administration and management; CAD/CADD drafting/design technology; civil engineering technology; clinical/medical laboratory technology; clinical/medical social work; computer and information systems security; computer engineering technology; computer software and media applications related; computer systems networking and telecommunications; criminal justice/safety; culinary arts; dental hygiene; diagnostic medical sonography and ultrasound technology; diesel mechanics technology; drafting/design engineering technologies related; early childhood education; electrical, electronic and communications engineering technology; electrician; electromechanical and instrumentation and maintenance technologies related; elementary education; emergency medical technology (EMT paramedic); general studies; heating, air conditioning, ventilation and refrigeration maintenance technology; human resources management; information science/studies; information technology; liberal arts and sciences/liberal studies; machine shop technology; marketing/marketing management; mechanical engineering technologies related; office management; radiologic technology/science; registered nursing/registered nurse; surgical technology; surveying technology; veterinary/animal health technology; welding technology.
Academics *Calendar:* semesters. *Degree:* certificates, diplomas, and associate. *Special study options:* academic remediation for entering students, adult/continuing education programs, advanced placement credit, cooperative education, distance learning, double majors, English as a second language, external degree program, honors programs, independent study, internships, part-time degree program, services for LD students, study abroad, summer session for credit.
Library Locke Learning Resources Center. Students can reserve study rooms.
Student Life *Housing:* college housing not available. *Activities and Organizations:* drama/theater group, choral group. *Campus security:* 24-hour emergency response devices and patrols. *Student services:* health clinic, personal/psychological counseling, veterans affairs office.
Financial Aid Of all full-time matriculated undergraduates who enrolled in 2018, 55 Federal Work-Study jobs (averaging $2000).
Applying *Required for some:* high school transcript. *Application deadlines:* rolling (freshmen), rolling (out-of-state freshmen), rolling (transfers).
Freshman Application Contact Asheville-Buncombe Technical Community College, 340 Victoria Road, Asheville, NC 28801-4897. *Phone:* 828-398-7900 Ext. 7887.
Website: http://www.abtech.edu/.

Beaufort County Community College
Washington, North Carolina

Freshman Application Contact Mr. Gary Burbage, Director of Admissions, Beaufort County Community College, PO Box 1069, 5337 US Highway 264 East, Washington, NC 27889-1069. *Phone:* 252-940-6233. *Fax:* 252-940-6393. *E-mail:* garyb@beaufortccc.edu. *Website:* http://www.beaufortccc.edu/.

Bladen Community College
Dublin, North Carolina

Freshman Application Contact Ms. Andrea Fisher, Enrollment Specialist, Bladen Community College, PO Box 266, Dublin, NC 28332. *Phone:* 910-879-5593. *Fax:* 910-879-5564. *E-mail:* acarterfisher@bladencc.edu. *Website:* http://www.bladencc.edu/.

Blue Ridge Community College
Flat Rock, North Carolina

Freshman Application Contact Blue Ridge Community College, 180 West Campus Drive, Flat Rock, NC 28731. *Phone:* 828-694-1810. *Website:* http://www.blueridge.edu/.

Brunswick Community College
Supply, North Carolina

- **State-supported** 2-year, founded 1979, part of North Carolina Community College System
- **Rural** 266-acre campus
- **Coed**

Undergraduates 4% are from out of state.
Faculty *Student/faculty ratio:* 12:1.
Academics *Calendar:* semesters. *Degree:* certificates, diplomas, and associate. *Special study options:* academic remediation for entering students, advanced placement credit, cooperative education, distance learning, English as a second language, independent study, internships, part-time degree program, services for LD students, summer session for credit.
Library Brunswick Community College Library plus 1 other.
Student Life *Campus security:* late-night transport/escort service, campus police.
Athletics Member NJCAA.
Applying *Options:* electronic application. *Required:* high school transcript. *Required for some:* interview.
Freshman Application Contact Admissions Counselor, Brunswick Community College, 50 College Road, PO Box 30, Supply, NC 28462-0030. *Phone:* 910-755-7300. *Toll-free phone:* 800-754-1050. *Fax:* 910-754-9609. *E-mail:* admissions@brunswickcc.edu. *Website:* http://www.brunswickcc.edu/.

Caldwell Community College and Technical Institute
Hudson, North Carolina

Freshman Application Contact Patricia Brinkley, Admissions Representative, Caldwell Community College and Technical Institute, 2855 Hickory Boulevard, Hudson, NC 28638. *Phone:* 828-726-2700. *Fax:* 828-726-2709. *E-mail:* pbrinkley@cccti.edu. *Website:* http://www.cccti.edu/.

Cape Fear Community College
Wilmington, North Carolina

Freshman Application Contact Ms. Linda Kasyan, Director of Admissions, Cape Fear Community College, 411 North Front Street, Wilmington, NC 28401-3993. *Phone:* 910-362-7054. *Toll-free phone:* 877-799-2322. *Fax:* 910-362-7080. *E-mail:* admissions@cfcc.edu. *Website:* http://www.cfcc.edu/.

Carolinas College of Health Sciences
Charlotte, North Carolina

- **Public** 2-year, founded 1990
- **Urban** 3-acre campus with easy access to Charlotte
- **Endowment** $2.4 million
- **Coed**

Undergraduates 49 full-time, 384 part-time. Students come from 12 states and territories; 10% are from out of state; 10% Black or African American, non-Hispanic/Latino; 6% Hispanic/Latino; 3% Asian, non-Hispanic/Latino; 0.5% Native Hawaiian or other Pacific Islander, non-Hispanic/Latino; 0.2% American Indian or Alaska Native, non-Hispanic/Latino; 3% Two or more races, non-Hispanic/Latino; 4% Race/ethnicity unknown.
Faculty *Student/faculty ratio:* 9:1.
Academics *Calendar:* semesters. *Degree:* certificates, diplomas, and associate. *Special study options:* advanced placement credit, distance learning, independent study, off-campus study, part-time degree program, services for LD students, study abroad, summer session for credit.
Library AHEC Library. Study areas open 24 hours, 5–7 days a week; students can reserve study rooms.
Student Life *Campus security:* 24-hour emergency response devices and patrols, late-night transport/escort service.
Standardized Tests *Required for some:* SAT or ACT (for admission).
Financial Aid Of all full-time matriculated undergraduates who enrolled in 2014, 7 Federal Work-Study jobs (averaging $3569).
Applying *Options:* electronic application. *Application fee:* $50. *Required:* minimum 2.5 GPA. *Required for some:* high school transcript, 3 letters of recommendation, interview.
Freshman Application Contact Ms. Merritt Newman, Admissions Representative, Carolinas College of Health Sciences, 1200 Blythe Boulevard, Charlotte, NC 28203. *Phone:* 704-355-5583. *Fax:* 704-355-9336. *E-mail:* merritt.newman@carolinascollege.edu. *Website:* http://www.carolinascollege.edu/.

Carteret Community College
Morehead City, North Carolina

- **State-supported** 2-year, founded 1963, part of North Carolina Community College System
- **Small-town** 41-acre campus
- **Endowment** $4.8 million
- **Coed**

Undergraduates 571 full-time, 792 part-time. Students come from 8 states and territories; 1% are from out of state; 9% Black or African American, non-Hispanic/Latino; 4% Hispanic/Latino; 1% Asian, non-Hispanic/Latino; 0.4% Native Hawaiian or other Pacific Islander, non-Hispanic/Latino; 1% American Indian or Alaska Native, non-Hispanic/Latino; 4% Two or more races, non-Hispanic/Latino; 2% Race/ethnicity unknown; 11% transferred in.
Faculty *Student/faculty ratio:* 11:1.
Academics *Calendar:* semesters. *Degrees:* certificates, diplomas, associate, and postbachelor's certificates. *Special study options:* academic remediation for entering students, adult/continuing education programs, cooperative education, distance learning, double majors, internships, part-time degree program, services for LD students, summer session for credit.
Library Michael J. Smith Learning Resource Center. *Books:* 18,182 (physical), 173,614 (digital/electronic); *Databases:* 74. Weekly public service hours: 63.
Student Life *Campus security:* late-night transport/escort service, security service from 7 am until 11:30 pm.
Athletics Member NCAA. All Division I.
Costs (2019–20) *Tuition:* state resident $1900 full-time, $76 per credit hour part-time; nonresident $6432 full-time, $268 per credit hour part-time. Full-time tuition and fees vary according to course load and program. Part-time tuition and fees vary according to course load and program. *Required fees:* $115 full-time, $31 per term part-time.
Applying *Options:* electronic application. *Required for some:* high school transcript.
Admissions Office Contact Carteret Community College, 3505 Arendell Street, Morehead City, NC 28557-2989. *Website:* http://www.carteret.edu/.

Catawba Valley Community College
Hickory, North Carolina

Freshman Application Contact Catawba Valley Community College, 2550 Highway 70 SE, Hickory, NC 28602-9699. *Phone:* 828-327-7000 Ext. 4618. *Website:* http://www.cvcc.edu/.

Central Carolina Community College
Sanford, North Carolina

Freshman Application Contact Mrs. Jamie Tyson Childress, Dean of Enrollment/Registrar, Central Carolina Community College, 1105 Kelly Drive, Sanford, NC 27330-9000. *Phone:* 919-718-7239. *Toll-free phone:* 800-682-8353. *Fax:* 919-718-7380. *Website:* http://www.cccc.edu/.

Central Piedmont Community College
Charlotte, North Carolina

- **State and locally supported** 2-year, founded 1963, part of North Carolina Community College System
- **Urban** 37-acre campus
- **Endowment** $16.7 million
- **Coed**

Undergraduates 7,630 full-time, 11,734 part-time. Students come from 13 states and territories; 117 other countries; 3% are from out of state; 11% transferred in. *Retention:* 55% of full-time freshmen returned.
Faculty *Student/faculty ratio:* 19:1.
Academics *Calendar:* semesters. *Degree:* certificates, diplomas, and associate. *Special study options:* academic remediation for entering students, accelerated degree program, advanced placement credit, cooperative education, distance learning, English as a second language, honors programs, off-campus study, part-time degree program, services for LD students, student-designed majors, summer session for credit.
Library Hagemeyer Learning Center plus 5 others.
Student Life *Campus security:* 24-hour emergency response devices and patrols.
Athletics Member NJCAA.
Financial Aid Of all full-time matriculated undergraduates who enrolled in 2018, 99 Federal Work-Study jobs (averaging $2988).
Applying *Required:* high school transcript.
Freshman Application Contact Ms. Linda McComb, Associate Dean, Central Piedmont Community College, PO Box 35009, Charlotte, NC 28235-5009. *Phone:* 704-330-6784. *Fax:* 704-330-6136. *Website:* http://www.cpcc.edu/.

Cleveland Community College
Shelby, North Carolina

- **State-supported** 2-year, founded 1965, part of North Carolina Community College System
- **Small-town** 43-acre campus with easy access to Charlotte
- **Coed,** 2,536 undergraduate students, 27% full-time, 64% women, 36% men

Undergraduates 696 full-time, 1,840 part-time. 18% Black or African American, non-Hispanic/Latino; 5% Hispanic/Latino; 1% Asian, non-Hispanic/Latino; 0.1% Native Hawaiian or other Pacific Islander, non-Hispanic/Latino; 0.4% American Indian or Alaska Native, non-Hispanic/Latino; 2% Two or more races, non-Hispanic/Latino; 3% Race/ethnicity unknown; 0.6% international.
Freshmen *Admission:* 306 enrolled.
Faculty *Student/faculty ratio:* 14:1.
Majors Automation engineer technology; biotechnology; business administration and management; criminal justice/safety; early childhood education; electrical, electronic and communications engineering technology; electrician; elementary education; emergency medical technology (EMT paramedic); fire prevention and safety technology; general studies; information technology; liberal arts and sciences and humanities related; liberal arts and sciences/liberal studies; mechanical drafting and CAD/CADD; medical/clinical assistant; medical office management; office management; radio and television broadcasting technology; radiologic technology/science; registered nursing/registered nurse.
Academics *Calendar:* semesters. *Degree:* certificates, diplomas, and associate. *Special study options:* academic remediation for entering students, adult/continuing education programs, advanced placement credit, cooperative education, distance learning, double majors, English as a second language, independent study, off-campus study, part-time degree program, summer session for credit.
Library Jim & Patsy Rose Library.
Student Life *Housing:* college housing not available. *Activities and Organizations:* drama/theater group, student-run television station. *Campus security:* security personnel during hours of operation. *Student services:* personal/psychological counseling, veterans affairs office.
Athletics Member NJCAA. *Intercollegiate sports:* cross-country running M/W, softball W.
Financial Aid Of all full-time matriculated undergraduates who enrolled in 2018, 20 Federal Work-Study jobs.
Applying *Options:* electronic application, deferred entrance. *Required:* high school transcript. *Application deadlines:* rolling (freshmen), rolling (transfers). *Notification:* continuous (freshmen), continuous (transfers).
Freshman Application Contact Cleveland Community College, 137 South Post Road, Shelby, NC 28152. *Phone:* 704-669-4321. *Website:* http://www.clevelandcc.edu/.

Coastal Carolina Community College
Jacksonville, North Carolina

Freshman Application Contact Ms. Heather Calihan, Counseling Coordinator, Coastal Carolina Community College, Jacksonville, NC 28546. *Phone:* 910-938-6241. *Fax:* 910-455-2767. *E-mail:* calihanh@coastal.cc.nc.us. *Website:* http://www.coastalcarolina.edu/.

College of The Albemarle
Elizabeth City, North Carolina

- **State-supported** 2-year, founded 1960, part of North Carolina Community College System
- **Small-town** 40-acre campus with easy access to Norfolk, VA
- **Coed,** 3,191 undergraduate students, 34% full-time, 65% women, 35% men

Undergraduates 1,074 full-time, 2,117 part-time. Students come from 4 states and territories; 16% Black or African American, non-Hispanic/Latino; 6% Hispanic/Latino; 0.7% Asian, non-Hispanic/Latino; 0.1% Native Hawaiian or other Pacific Islander, non-Hispanic/Latino; 0.7% American Indian or Alaska Native, non-Hispanic/Latino; 4% Two or more races, non-Hispanic/Latino; 2% Race/ethnicity unknown; 5% international; 3% transferred in. *Retention:* 74% of full-time freshmen returned.
Freshmen *Admission:* 2,370 applied, 1,260 admitted, 251 enrolled.
Faculty *Student/faculty ratio:* 13:1.
Majors Architectural engineering technology; art; aviation/airway management; biotechnology; business administration and management;

computer engineering technology; computer programming; computer programming (specific applications); construction trades; crafts, folk art and artisanry; criminal justice/law enforcement administration; culinary arts; data entry/microcomputer applications; drafting/design engineering technologies related; dramatic/theater arts; education; health and physical education/fitness; information science/studies; information technology; liberal arts and sciences/liberal studies; licensed practical/vocational nurse training; medical administrative assistant and medical secretary; metal and jewelry arts; music; phlebotomy technology; registered nursing/registered nurse; teacher assistant/aide.
Academics *Calendar:* semesters. *Degree:* certificates, diplomas, and associate. *Special study options:* academic remediation for entering students, accelerated degree program, adult/continuing education programs, advanced placement credit, cooperative education, distance learning, double majors, English as a second language, part-time degree program, services for LD students, study abroad, summer session for credit.
Library Learning Resources Center. Students can reserve study rooms.
Student Life *Housing:* college housing not available. *Activities and Organizations:* drama/theater group, Phi Beta Lambda, Phi Theta Kappa. *Campus security:* 24-hour emergency response devices and patrols. *Student services:* personal/psychological counseling, veterans affairs office.
Athletics *Intramural sports:* archery M/W, baseball M/W, basketball M/W, football M/W, golf M/W, gymnastics M/W, sailing M/W, soccer M(c), softball M/W, swimming and diving M/W, table tennis M/W, tennis M/W, volleyball M/W.
Costs (2019–20) *Tuition:* state resident $2098 full-time, $76 per credit hour part-time; nonresident $7601 full-time, $268 per credit hour part-time. Full-time tuition and fees vary according to program. Part-time tuition and fees vary according to program. *Required fees:* $147 full-time, $45 per term part-time. *Payment plan:* installment.
Applying *Options:* electronic application, early admission, deferred entrance. *Required:* high school transcript. *Application deadlines:* rolling (freshmen), rolling (transfers). *Notification:* continuous (freshmen), continuous (transfers).
Freshman Application Contact Megan Dross, Director of Admissions and Recruitment, College of The Albemarle, PO Box 2327, Elizabeth City, NC 27906-2327. *Phone:* 252-335-0821 Ext. 2220.
Website: http://www.albemarle.edu/.

Craven Community College
New Bern, North Carolina

- **State-supported** 2-year, founded 1965, part of North Carolina Community College System
- **Suburban** 100-acre campus
- **Coed,** 2,961 undergraduate students, 31% full-time, 58% women, 42% men

Undergraduates 932 full-time, 2,029 part-time. 17% Black or African American, non-Hispanic/Latino; 10% Hispanic/Latino; 4% Asian, non-Hispanic/Latino; 0.3% Native Hawaiian or other Pacific Islander, non-Hispanic/Latino; 0.4% American Indian or Alaska Native, non-Hispanic/Latino; 4% Two or more races, non-Hispanic/Latino; 4% Race/ethnicity unknown; 1% international; 10% transferred in.
Freshmen *Admission:* 358 enrolled.
Faculty *Total:* 205, 33% full-time. *Student/faculty ratio:* 14:1.
Majors Accounting; airframe mechanics and aircraft maintenance technology; automobile/automotive mechanics technology; banking and financial support services; business administration and management; computer and information systems security; computer programming (specific applications); computer systems networking and telecommunications; criminal justice/law enforcement administration; criminal justice/safety; early childhood education; electrical, electronic and communications engineering technology; electromechanical technology; elementary education; entrepreneurship; general studies; health information/medical records technology; heating, air conditioning, ventilation and refrigeration maintenance technology; hotel, motel, and restaurant management; information technology; legal administrative assistant/secretary; liberal arts and sciences and humanities related; liberal arts and sciences/liberal studies; machine shop technology; mechanical engineering/mechanical technology; medical administrative assistant and medical secretary; medical/clinical assistant; medical office management; office management; physical therapy technology; pre-engineering; registered nursing/registered nurse; special education; system, networking, and LAN/WAN management; tool and die technology; welding technology.
Academics *Calendar:* semesters. *Degree:* certificates, diplomas, and associate. *Special study options:* academic remediation for entering students, adult/continuing education programs, advanced placement credit, cooperative education, distance learning, double majors, English as a second language, honors programs, independent study, internships, part-time degree program, services for LD students, study abroad, summer session for credit.
Library R. C. Godwin Memorial Library. *Books:* 17,065 (physical), 240,000 (digital/electronic); *Serial titles:* 27 (physical), 18,759 (digital/electronic); *Databases:* 86. Students can reserve study rooms.
Student Life *Housing:* college housing not available. *Activities and Organizations:* choral group. *Campus security:* 24-hour emergency response devices and patrols. *Student services:* personal/psychological counseling, legal services, veterans affairs office.
Costs (2020–21) *Tuition:* state resident $1824 full-time, $76 per credit hour part-time; nonresident $6432 full-time, $268 per credit hour part-time. Full-time tuition and fees vary according to course load. Part-time tuition and fees vary according to course load. *Required fees:* $199 full-time, $100 per term part-time. *Payment plan:* installment. *Waivers:* senior citizens.
Applying *Options:* electronic application. *Required:* high school transcript. *Application deadlines:* rolling (freshmen), rolling (transfers).
Freshman Application Contact Craven Community College, 800 College Court, New Bern, NC 28562. *Phone:* 252-638-4597.
Website: http://www.cravencc.edu/.

Davidson County Community College
Lexington, North Carolina

- **State and locally supported** 2-year, founded 1958, part of North Carolina Community College System
- **Rural** 83-acre campus
- **Coed**

Faculty *Student/faculty ratio:* 20:1.
Academics *Calendar:* semesters. *Degree:* certificates, diplomas, and associate. *Special study options:* academic remediation for entering students, adult/continuing education programs, advanced placement credit, cooperative education, double majors, internships, off-campus study, part-time degree program, services for LD students, summer session for credit.
Library Grady E. Love Learning Resource Center.
Student Life *Campus security:* 24-hour patrols, late-night transport/escort service, security guards.
Athletics Member NJCAA.
Costs (2019–20) *Tuition:* state resident $1824 full-time, $76 per credit hour part-time; nonresident $6432 full-time, $268 per credit hour part-time. Full-time tuition and fees vary according to course load and program. Part-time tuition and fees vary according to course load and program. *Required fees:* $155 full-time, $6 per credit hour part-time.
Financial Aid Of all full-time matriculated undergraduates who enrolled in 2018, 15 Federal Work-Study jobs (averaging $1600).
Applying *Options:* early admission, deferred entrance. *Required:* high school transcript. *Required for some:* interview.
Freshman Application Contact Davidson County Community College, PO Box 1287, Lexington, NC 27293-1287. *Phone:* 336-249-8186 Ext. 6715. *Fax:* 336-224-0240. *E-mail:* admissions@davidsonccc.edu. *Website:* http://www.davidsonccc.edu/.

Durham Technical Community College
Durham, North Carolina

Director of Admissions Ms. Penny Augustine, Director of Admissions and Testing, Durham Technical Community College, 1637 Lawson Street, Durham, NC 27703-5023. *Phone:* 919-686-3619. *Website:* http://www.durhamtech.edu/.

Edgecombe Community College
Tarboro, North Carolina

Freshman Application Contact Ms. Jackie Heath, Admissions Officer, Edgecombe Community College, 2009 West Wilson Street, Tarboro, NC 27886-9399. *Phone:* 252-823-5166 Ext. 254. *Website:* http://www.edgecombe.edu/.

Fayetteville Technical Community College
Fayetteville, North Carolina

- **State-supported** 2-year, founded 1961, part of North Carolina Community College System
- **Suburban** 207-acre campus with easy access to Raleigh
- **Endowment** $39,050
- **Coed,** 12,021 undergraduate students, 39% full-time, 61% women, 39% men

Undergraduates 4,646 full-time, 7,375 part-time. Students come from 29 states and territories; 13 other countries; 24% are from out of state; 37% Black or African American, non-Hispanic/Latino; 13% Hispanic/Latino; 2% Asian, non-Hispanic/Latino; 0.4% Native Hawaiian or other Pacific Islander, non-Hispanic/Latino; 2% American Indian or Alaska Native, non-Hispanic/Latino; 5% Two or more races, non-Hispanic/Latino; 4% Race/ethnicity unknown; 0.8% international; 10% transferred in.

Freshmen *Admission:* 3,091 applied, 3,091 admitted, 1,458 enrolled. *Average high school GPA:* 2.6.

Faculty *Total:* 492, 58% full-time, 8% with terminal degrees. *Student/faculty ratio:* 20:1.

Majors Accounting and finance; applied horticulture/horticulture operations; architectural engineering technology; autobody/collision and repair technology; automobile/automotive mechanics technology; building/construction finishing, management, and inspection related; business administration and management; civil engineering technology; commercial and advertising art; cosmetology; criminal justice/safety; crisis/emergency/disaster management; culinary arts; dental hygiene; early childhood education; electrical, electronic and communications engineering technology; electrician; electromechanical and instrumentation and maintenance technologies related; elementary education; emergency medical technology (EMT paramedic); entrepreneurship; fire prevention and safety technology; forensic science and technology; funeral service and mortuary science; game and interactive media design; gunsmithing; health and physical education related; heating, air conditioning, ventilation and refrigeration maintenance technology; hotel, motel, and restaurant management; information technology; intelligence; legal assistant/paralegal; liberal arts and sciences and humanities related; liberal arts and sciences/liberal studies; logistics, materials, and supply chain management; machine shop technology; medical office management; office management; pharmacy technician; physical therapy technology; pre-engineering; radiologic technology/science; registered nursing/registered nurse; respiratory care therapy; speech-language pathology assistant; surgical technology; surveying technology.

Academics *Calendar:* semesters. *Degree:* certificates, diplomas, and associate. *Special study options:* academic remediation for entering students, accelerated degree program, adult/continuing education programs, advanced placement credit, cooperative education, distance learning, double majors, English as a second language, freshman honors college, honors programs, independent study, internships, off-campus study, part-time degree program, services for LD students, summer session for credit. *ROTC:* Air Force (c).

Library Paul H. Thompson Library plus 1 other. *Books:* 39,806 (physical), 300,000 (digital/electronic); *Serial titles:* 53 (physical), 5 (digital/electronic); *Databases:* 147.

Student Life *Housing:* college housing not available. *Activities and Organizations:* choral group, Parents for Higher Education, Phi Theta Kappa, Phi Beta Lambda, National Society for Leadership and Success, Student Veterans of America. *Campus security:* 24-hour emergency response devices and patrols, late-night transport/escort service, campus-wide emergency notification system. *Student services:* personal/psychological counseling, veterans affairs office.

Athletics Member NJCAA. *Intercollegiate sports:* baseball M, basketball M/W, golf M/W, softball W, volleyball W. *Intramural sports:* basketball M/W, tennis M/W.

Costs (2019–20) *One-time required fee:* $21. *Tuition:* state resident $2432 full-time, $76 per credit hour part-time; nonresident $8576 full-time, $268 per credit hour part-time. Full-time tuition and fees vary according to course load. Part-time tuition and fees vary according to course load. *Required fees:* $112 full-time, $66 per term part-time. *Payment plan:* installment. *Waivers:* employees or children of employees.

Financial Aid Of all full-time matriculated undergraduates who enrolled in 2018, 3,895 applied for aid, 3,338 were judged to have need, 2,768 had their need fully met. 60 Federal Work-Study jobs (averaging $2363). *Average percent of need met:* 94%. *Average financial aid package:* $7468. *Average need-based loan:* $3504. *Average need-based gift aid:* $6341.

Applying *Options:* electronic application, deferred entrance. *Required:* high school transcript. *Required for some:* essay or personal statement, interview. *Application deadlines:* rolling (freshmen), rolling (transfers). *Notification:* continuous (freshmen), continuous (transfers).

Freshman Application Contact Dr. Louanna Castleman, Director of Admissions & Counseling, Fayetteville Technical Community College, 2201 Hull Road, PO Box 35236, Fayetteville, NC 28303-0236. *Phone:* 910-678-0141. *Fax:* 910-678-0085. *E-mail:* castleml@faytechcc.edu. *Website:* http://www.faytechcc.edu/.

Forsyth Technical Community College
Winston-Salem, North Carolina

Freshman Application Contact Admissions Office, Forsyth Technical Community College, 2100 Silas Creek Parkway, Winston-Salem, NC 27103-5197. *Phone:* 336-734-7556. *E-mail:* admissions@forsythtech.edu. *Website:* http://www.forsythtech.edu/.

Gaston College
Dallas, North Carolina

- **State and locally supported** 2-year, founded 1963, part of North Carolina Community College System
- **Small-town** 166-acre campus with easy access to Charlotte
- **Coed**

Undergraduates 1% are from out of state. *Retention:* 74% of full-time freshmen returned.

Faculty *Student/faculty ratio:* 19:1.

Academics *Calendar:* semesters. *Degree:* certificates, diplomas, and associate. *Special study options:* academic remediation for entering students, advanced placement credit, cooperative education, English as a second language, off-campus study, part-time degree program, services for LD students, summer session for credit.

Library Gaston College Library.

Student Life *Campus security:* 24-hour patrols, late-night transport/escort service.

Standardized Tests *Required:* ACT Compass (for admission). *Required for some:* SAT and SAT Subject Tests or ACT (for admission).

Financial Aid Of all full-time matriculated undergraduates who enrolled in 2018, 50 Federal Work-Study jobs (averaging $1800). 30 state and other part-time jobs (averaging $1533).

Applying *Required:* high school transcript.

Freshman Application Contact Terry Basier, Director of Enrollment Management and Admissions, Gaston College, 201 Highway 321 South, Dallas, NC 28034. *Phone:* 704-922-6214. *Fax:* 704-922-6443. *Website:* http://www.gaston.edu/.

Guilford Technical Community College
Jamestown, North Carolina

Freshman Application Contact Guilford Technical Community College, PO Box 309, Jamestown, NC 27282-0309. *Phone:* 336-334-4822 Ext. 50125. *Website:* http://www.gtcc.edu/.

Halifax Community College
Weldon, North Carolina

- **State and locally supported** 2-year, founded 1967, part of North Carolina Community College System
- **Rural** 109-acre campus
- **Coed,** 1,087 undergraduate students, 41% full-time, 64% women, 36% men
- 67% of applicants were admitted

Undergraduates 442 full-time, 645 part-time. Students come from 2 states and territories.

Freshmen *Admission:* 509 applied, 341 admitted, 161 enrolled.

Faculty *Total:* 81, 51% full-time, 11% with terminal degrees. *Student/faculty ratio:* 13:1.

Majors Automobile/automotive mechanics technology; business administration and management; commercial and advertising art; cosmetology; criminal justice/safety; dental hygiene; early childhood education; electromechanical and instrumentation and maintenance technologies related; engineering; human services; industrial mechanics and maintenance technology; information technology; legal assistant/paralegal; liberal arts and sciences and humanities related; liberal arts and sciences/liberal studies; medical administrative assistant and medical secretary; medical office management; mental and social health services and allied professions related; office management; registered nursing/registered nurse; welding technology.

Academics *Calendar:* semesters. *Degree:* certificates, diplomas, and associate. *Special study options:* academic remediation for entering students, cooperative education, distance learning, double majors, English as a second language, independent study, internships, part-time degree program, services for LD students, summer session for credit.

Library Learning Resources Center. *Books:* 23,686 (physical), 202,576 (digital/electronic); *Serial titles:* 86 (physical), 1,382 (digital/electronic); *Databases:* 89. Weekly public service hours: 52.

Student Life *Housing:* college housing not available. *Activities and Organizations:* Phi Theta Kappa, PRIDE, Women of Excellence. *Campus security:* 24-hour emergency response devices, 12-hour patrols by trained security personnel. *Student services:* health clinic, veterans affairs office.

Costs (2019–20) *Tuition:* state resident $2296 full-time, $76 per credit hour part-time; nonresident $7672 full-time, $268 per credit hour part-time. *Required fees:* $176 full-time, $2 per credit hour part-time, $56 per term part-time. *Payment plan:* installment.

Applying *Options:* electronic application. *Required:* high school transcript. *Application deadlines:* rolling (freshmen), rolling (out-of-state freshmen),

rolling (transfers). *Notification:* continuous (freshmen), continuous (out-of-state freshmen), continuous (transfers).
Freshman Application Contact Mr. Antonio Squire, Coordinator of Admissions, Halifax Community College, P.O. Drawer 809, 100 College Drive, Weldon, NC 27890. *Phone:* 252-536-7225. *E-mail:* asquire374@halifaxcc.edu.
Website: http://www.halifaxcc.edu/.

Haywood Community College
Clyde, North Carolina

- **State and locally supported** 2-year, founded 1965, part of North Carolina Community College System
- **Rural** 85-acre campus
- **Endowment** $9.1 million
- **Coed,** 1,632 undergraduate students, 37% full-time, 63% women, 37% men

Undergraduates 601 full-time, 1,031 part-time. Students come from 3 states and territories; 0.4% are from out of state; 5% Black or African American, non-Hispanic/Latino; 5% Hispanic/Latino; 0.7% Asian, non-Hispanic/Latino; 0.2% Native Hawaiian or other Pacific Islander, non-Hispanic/Latino; 2% American Indian or Alaska Native, non-Hispanic/Latino; 1% Two or more races, non-Hispanic/Latino; 3% Race/ethnicity unknown; 0.2% international; 9% transferred in. *Retention:* 70% of full-time freshmen returned.
Freshmen *Admission:* 1,632 admitted, 279 enrolled.
Faculty *Total:* 254, 22% full-time. *Student/faculty ratio:* 13:1.
Majors Accounting; accounting technology and bookkeeping; applied horticulture/horticulture operations; autobody/collision and repair technology; automobile/automotive mechanics technology; building/construction finishing, management, and inspection related; business administration and management; child-care and support services management; computer systems networking and telecommunications; cosmetology; crafts, folk art and artisanry; criminal justice/law enforcement administration; criminal justice/safety; early childhood education; electrical, electronic and communications engineering technology; electrician; electromechanical and instrumentation and maintenance technologies related; elementary education; entrepreneurship; fiber, textile and weaving arts; forest technology; information technology; liberal arts and sciences and humanities related; liberal arts and sciences/liberal studies; medical/clinical assistant; medical office management; metal and jewelry arts; pre-engineering; registered nursing/registered nurse; welding technology; wildlife, fish and wildlands science and management.
Academics *Calendar:* semesters. *Degree:* certificates, diplomas, and associate. *Special study options:* academic remediation for entering students, adult/continuing education programs, advanced placement credit, cooperative education, distance learning, double majors, English as a second language, honors programs, independent study, internships, part-time degree program, services for LD students, study abroad, summer session for credit.
Library Freedlander Learning Resource Center. *Books:* 36,213 (physical), 382,812 (digital/electronic); *Serial titles:* 123 (physical), 23,465 (digital/electronic); *Databases:* 91. Weekly public service hours: 47; students can reserve study rooms.
Student Life *Activities and Organizations:* student-run newspaper, Wildlife Society, Timbersport Forestry Club, Student Association of Medical Assistants (SAMA), HCC Student Nurses Association, HCC Skills USA Club. *Campus security:* Emergency Phone and Patrols while campus is open. *Student services:* veterans affairs office.
Costs (2020–21) *Tuition:* area resident $2580 full-time; state resident $2580 full-time, $76 per credit hour part-time; nonresident $8724 full-time, $268 per credit hour part-time. Full-time tuition and fees vary according to course load. Part-time tuition and fees vary according to course load. *Required fees:* $148 full-time, $148 per year part-time. *Room and board:* $9861; room only: $7602. *Payment plan:* installment.
Financial Aid Of all full-time matriculated undergraduates who enrolled in 2019, 543 applied for aid, 498 were judged to have need, 27 had their need fully met. In 2019, 7 non-need-based awards were made. *Average percent of need met:* 58%. *Average financial aid package:* $8093. *Average need-based loan:* $7348. *Average need-based gift aid:* $8107. *Average non-need-based aid:* $586.
Applying *Options:* electronic application. *Required:* high school transcript. *Required for some:* interview. *Application deadlines:* rolling (freshmen), rolling (transfers).
Freshman Application Contact Haywood Community College, 185 Freedlander Drive, Clyde, NC 28721-9453. *Phone:* 828-627-4507. *Toll-free phone:* 866-GOTOHCC.
Website: http://www.haywood.edu/.

Isothermal Community College
Spindale, North Carolina

Freshman Application Contact Ms. Vickie Searcy, Enrollment Management Office, Isothermal Community College, PO Box 804, Spindale, NC 28160-0804. *Phone:* 828-286-3636 Ext. 251. *Fax:* 828-286-8109. *E-mail:* vsearcy@isothermal.edu. *Website:* http://www.isothermal.edu/.

James Sprunt Community College
Kenansville, North Carolina

- **State-supported** 2-year, founded 1964, part of North Carolina Community College System
- **Rural** 51-acre campus with easy access to Raleigh, Wilmington
- **Endowment** $1.5 million
- **Coed,** 1,266 undergraduate students, 32% full-time, 67% women, 33% men

Undergraduates 402 full-time, 864 part-time. Students come from 4 states and territories; 1% are from out of state; 27% Black or African American, non-Hispanic/Latino; 25% Hispanic/Latino; 0.3% Asian, non-Hispanic/Latino; 0.1% Native Hawaiian or other Pacific Islander, non-Hispanic/Latino; 0.5% American Indian or Alaska Native, non-Hispanic/Latino; 1% Two or more races, non-Hispanic/Latino; 2% Race/ethnicity unknown; 2% international; 4% transferred in.
Freshmen *Admission:* 53 applied, 53 admitted, 128 enrolled.
Faculty *Total:* 72, 47% full-time. *Student/faculty ratio:* 10:1.
Majors Accounting and finance; agribusiness; animal/livestock husbandry and production; animal sciences; business administration and management; child development; commercial and advertising art; cosmetology; criminal justice/safety; early childhood education; elementary education; general studies; information technology; institutional food workers; liberal arts and sciences and humanities related; liberal arts and sciences/liberal studies; livestock management; medium/heavy vehicle and truck technology; office management; prenursing studies; registered nursing/registered nurse.
Academics *Calendar:* semesters. *Degree:* certificates, diplomas, and associate. *Special study options:* academic remediation for entering students, accelerated degree program, advanced placement credit, cooperative education, distance learning, double majors, English as a second language, independent study, internships, part-time degree program, services for LD students, summer session for credit.
Library James Sprunt Community College Library. *Books:* 24,785 (physical), 214,329 (digital/electronic); *Serial titles:* 34 (physical), 24,504 (digital/electronic); *Databases:* 91. Weekly public service hours: 48; students can reserve study rooms.
Student Life *Housing:* college housing not available. *Activities and Organizations:* student-run newspaper, Student Government Association, Phi Theta Kappa, Scholarly Men of Success, Scholarly Women of Tomorrow, national sororities. *Campus security:* day, evening, and Saturday trained security personnel. *Student services:* personal/psychological counseling, veterans affairs office.
Athletics *Intramural sports:* basketball M/W, soccer M/W.
Costs (2020–21) *Tuition:* state resident $2570 full-time, $76 per semester hour part-time; nonresident $8714 full-time, $268 per semester hour part-time. Full-time tuition and fees vary according to course load. Part-time tuition and fees vary according to course load. *Required fees:* $76 full-time, $68 per term part-time. *Waivers:* senior citizens.
Applying *Options:* electronic application. *Required:* high school transcript. *Application deadlines:* rolling (freshmen), rolling (transfers). *Notification:* continuous (freshmen), continuous (transfers).
Freshman Application Contact Ms. Wanda Edwards, Admissions Specialist, James Sprunt Community College, PO Box 398, 133 James Sprunt Drive, Kenansville, NC 28349. *Phone:* 910-275-6364. *Fax:* 910-296-1222. *E-mail:* wedwards@jamessprunt.edu.
Website: http://www.jamessprunt.edu/.

Johnston Community College
Smithfield, North Carolina

- **State-supported** 2-year, founded 1969, part of North Carolina Community College System
- **Rural** 100-acre campus
- **Endowment** $6.4 million
- **Coed**

Undergraduates 1,546 full-time, 2,606 part-time. 13% Black or African American, non-Hispanic/Latino; 14% Hispanic/Latino; 0.7% Asian, non-Hispanic/Latino; 0.1% Native Hawaiian or other Pacific Islander, non-Hispanic/Latino; 0.6% American Indian or Alaska Native, non-Hispanic/Latino; 2% Two or more races, non-Hispanic/Latino; 7% Race/ethnicity unknown; 1% international.

Academics *Calendar:* semesters. *Degree:* certificates, diplomas, and associate. *Special study options:* academic remediation for entering students, adult/continuing education programs, advanced placement credit, cooperative education, distance learning, double majors, honors programs, independent study, part-time degree program, services for LD students, summer session for credit.
Library Johnston Community College Library plus 1 other. *Books:* 27,174 (physical), 202,576 (digital/electronic); *Serial titles:* 64 (physical), 23,465 (digital/electronic); *Databases:* 131. Weekly public service hours: 57; students can reserve study rooms.
Student Life *Campus security:* 24-hour patrols.
Athletics Member NJCAA.
Standardized Tests *Required:* NC DAP (for admission). *Recommended:* SAT or ACT (for admission).
Costs (2019–20) *Tuition:* area resident $2432 full-time, $76 per credit hour part-time; state resident $2432 full-time, $76 per credit hour part-time; nonresident $8576 full-time, $268 per credit hour part-time. Full-time tuition and fees vary according to course load. Part-time tuition and fees vary according to course load. *Required fees:* $225 full-time.
Financial Aid Of all full-time matriculated undergraduates who enrolled in 2018, 33 Federal Work-Study jobs (averaging $1754).
Applying *Options:* electronic application. *Required:* high school transcript, interview.
Freshman Application Contact Megan L. Shaner, Director of Enrollment Management & Retention, Johnston Community College, 245 College Road, PO Box 2350, Smithfield, NC 27577. *Phone:* 919-209-2201. *Fax:* 919-989-7862. *E-mail:* mlshaner@johnstoncc.edu. *Website:* http://www.johnstoncc.edu/.

Lenoir Community College

Kinston, North Carolina

- **State-supported** 2-year, founded 1960, part of North Carolina Community College System
- **Small-town** 86-acre campus
- **Coed,** 2,526 undergraduate students, 34% full-time, 64% women, 36% men

Undergraduates 850 full-time, 1,676 part-time. Students come from 14 states and territories; 1 other country; 1% are from out of state; 31% Black or African American, non-Hispanic/Latino; 9% Hispanic/Latino; 0.5% Asian, non-Hispanic/Latino; 0.1% Native Hawaiian or other Pacific Islander, non-Hispanic/Latino; 0.5% American Indian or Alaska Native, non-Hispanic/Latino; 2% Two or more races, non-Hispanic/Latino; 2% international; 6% transferred in.
Freshmen *Admission:* 1,631 applied, 1,472 admitted, 279 enrolled.
Faculty *Total:* 115, 72% full-time, 9% with terminal degrees. *Student/faculty ratio:* 15:1.
Majors Accounting and finance; agricultural teacher education; agroecology and sustainable agriculture; airline pilot and flight crew; applied horticulture/horticulture operations; autobody/collision and repair technology; automobile/automotive mechanics technology; business administration and management; commercial and advertising art; computer engineering technology; cosmetology; criminal justice/safety; crisis/emergency/disaster management; culinary arts; dental assisting; dental hygiene; early childhood education; electromechanical and instrumentation and maintenance technologies related; electroneurodiagnostic/electroencephalographic technology; emergency medical technology (EMT paramedic); general studies; graphic design; gunsmithing; information technology; liberal arts and sciences and humanities related; liberal arts and sciences/liberal studies; machine shop technology; mechanical engineering/mechanical technology; medical/clinical assistant; medical office management; mental and social health services and allied professions related; office management; polysomnography; pre-engineering; prenursing studies; radiologic technology/science; registered nursing/registered nurse; trade and industrial teacher education; welding technology.
Academics *Calendar:* semesters. *Degree:* certificates, diplomas, and associate. *Special study options:* academic remediation for entering students, adult/continuing education programs, advanced placement credit, cooperative education, distance learning, double majors, English as a second language, independent study, part-time degree program, services for LD students, summer session for credit.
Library Learning Resources Center plus 1 other. *Books:* 22,929 (physical), 415,829 (digital/electronic); *Serial titles:* 24 (physical), 88,716 (digital/electronic); *Databases:* 150. Weekly public service hours: 38; students can reserve study rooms.
Student Life *Activities and Organizations:* drama/theater group, choral group, Student Government Association, Surgical Technology, Computer Engineering, Nightingals, Transitional and Career Studies. *Campus security:* 24-hour emergency response devices and patrols, student patrols. *Student services:* personal/psychological counseling, veterans affairs office.
Athletics Member NJCAA. *Intercollegiate sports:* baseball M, basketball M/W, volleyball W.
Standardized Tests *Recommended:* SAT or ACT (for admission).
Costs (2020–21) *Tuition:* area resident $2432 full-time; state resident $2432 full-time; nonresident $8576 full-time. *Required fees:* $136 full-time. *Room and board:* $6364.
Applying *Options:* electronic application, early admission. *Required:* high school transcript. *Application deadlines:* rolling (freshmen), rolling (transfers). *Notification:* continuous (freshmen), continuous (transfers).
Freshman Application Contact Mr. Dusk Stroud, Director of Admissions & Enrollment Management, Lenoir Community College, 231 Highway 58 South, Kinston, NC 28502-0188. *Phone:* 252-527-6223 Ext. 394. *Fax:* 252-233-6895. *E-mail:* dostroud89@lenoircc.edu.
Website: http://www.lenoircc.edu/.

Louisburg College

Louisburg, North Carolina

Freshman Application Contact Ms. Stephanie Tolbert, Vice President for Enrollment Management, Louisburg College, 501 North Main Street, Louisburg, NC 27549-2399. *Phone:* 919-497-3233. *Toll-free phone:* 800-775-0208. *Fax:* 919-496-1788. *E-mail:* admissions@louisburg.edu. *Website:* http://www.louisburg.edu/.

Martin Community College

Williamston, North Carolina

Freshman Application Contact Martin Community College, 1161 Kehukee Park Road, Williamston, NC 27892. *Phone:* 252-792-1521 Ext. 244. *Website:* http://www.martincc.edu/.

Mayland Community College

Spruce Pine, North Carolina

- **State and locally supported** 2-year, founded 1971, part of North Carolina Community College System
- **Rural** 38-acre campus
- **Coed,** 1,472 undergraduate students

Faculty *Student/faculty ratio:* 13:1.
Majors Applied horticulture/horticulture operations; business administration and management; computer engineering technology; cosmetology; criminal justice/safety; electrical, electronic and communications engineering technology; general studies; industrial electronics technology; liberal arts and sciences/liberal studies; management information systems; medical administrative assistant and medical secretary; medical/clinical assistant; registered nursing/registered nurse.
Academics *Calendar:* semesters. *Degree:* certificates, diplomas, and associate. *Special study options:* academic remediation for entering students, adult/continuing education programs, advanced placement credit, cooperative education, distance learning, double majors, independent study, internships, part-time degree program, services for LD students, summer session for credit.
Library Carolyn Munro Wilson Learning Resources Center plus 1 other.
Student Life *Housing:* college housing not available. *Student services:* personal/psychological counseling.
Standardized Tests *Required for some:* CPT for nursing program.
Financial Aid Of all full-time matriculated undergraduates who enrolled in 2009, 16 Federal Work-Study jobs (averaging $1800).
Applying *Options:* electronic application, deferred entrance. *Required:* high school transcript. *Application deadlines:* rolling (freshmen), rolling (transfers). *Notification:* continuous (freshmen), continuous (transfers).
Freshman Application Contact Mayland Community College, PO Box 547, Spruce Pine, NC 28777-0547. *Phone:* 828-766-1251. *Toll-free phone:* 800-462-9526.
Website: http://www.mayland.edu/.

McDowell Technical Community College

Marion, North Carolina

Freshman Application Contact Mr. Rick L. Wilson, Director of Admissions, McDowell Technical Community College, 54 College Drive, Marion, NC 28752. *Phone:* 828-652-0632. *Fax:* 828-652-1014. *E-mail:* rickw@mcdowelltech.edu. *Website:* http://www.mcdowelltech.edu/.

Miller-Motte College - Cary
Cary, North Carolina

Admissions Office Contact Miller-Motte College - Cary, 2205 Walnut Street, Cary, NC 27518. *Toll-free phone:* 800-705-9182. *Website:* http://www.miller-motte.edu/.

Miller-Motte College - Fayetteville
Fayetteville, North Carolina

Admissions Office Contact Miller-Motte College - Fayetteville, 3725 Ramsey Street, Fayetteville, NC 28311. *Toll-free phone:* 800-705-9182. *Website:* http://www.miller-motte.edu/.

Miller-Motte College - Jacksonville
Jacksonville, North Carolina

Admissions Office Contact Miller-Motte College - Jacksonville, 1291 Hargett Street, Jacksonville, NC 28540. *Toll-free phone:* 800-705-9182. *Website:* http://www.miller-motte.edu/.

Miller-Motte College - Raleigh
Raleigh, North Carolina

Admissions Office Contact Miller-Motte College - Raleigh, 3901 Capital Boulevard, Suite 151, Raleigh, NC 27604. *Toll-free phone:* 800-705-9182. *Website:* http://www.miller-motte.edu/.

Miller-Motte College - Wilmington
Wilmington, North Carolina

Freshman Application Contact Admissions Office, Miller-Motte College - Wilmington, 5000 Market Street, Wilmington, NC 28405. *Toll-free phone:* 800-705-9182. *Website:* http://www.miller-motte.edu/.

Mitchell Community College
Statesville, North Carolina

- **State-supported** 2-year, founded 1852, part of North Carolina Community College System
- **Small-town** 14-acre campus with easy access to Charlotte
- **Endowment** $18.4 million
- **Coed**

Undergraduates 974 full-time, 2,190 part-time. 11% Black or African American, non-Hispanic/Latino; 11% Hispanic/Latino; 2% Asian, non-Hispanic/Latino; 0.1% Native Hawaiian or other Pacific Islander, non-Hispanic/Latino; 0.4% American Indian or Alaska Native, non-Hispanic/Latino; 2% Two or more races, non-Hispanic/Latino; 1% Race/ethnicity unknown; 0.9% international; 6% transferred in. *Retention:* 51% of full-time freshmen returned.
Faculty *Student/faculty ratio:* 18:1.
Academics *Calendar:* semesters. *Degree:* certificates, diplomas, and associate. *Special study options:* academic remediation for entering students, adult/continuing education programs, advanced placement credit, cooperative education, distance learning, English as a second language, part-time degree program, services for LD students, summer session for credit.
Library Huskins Library. *Books:* 14,669 (physical), 203,337 (digital/electronic); *Serial titles:* 2 (physical), 23,468 (digital/electronic); *Databases:* 93. Students can reserve study rooms.
Student Life *Campus security:* late-night transport/escort service, day and evening security guards.
Costs (2019–20) *Tuition:* state resident $2432 full-time, $76 per credit hour part-time; nonresident $8576 full-time, $268 per credit hour part-time. *Required fees:* $219 full-time, $6 per credit hour part-time, $36 per term part-time.
Financial Aid Of all full-time matriculated undergraduates who enrolled in 2018, 30 Federal Work-Study jobs.
Applying *Options:* electronic application. *Required:* high school transcript.
Director of Admissions Porter Brannon, Dean of Student Services, Mitchell Community College, 500 West Broad Street, Statesville, NC 28677. *Phone:* 704-878-3281. *Website:* http://www.mitchellcc.edu/.

Montgomery Community College
Troy, North Carolina

Admissions Office Contact Montgomery Community College, 1011 Page Street, Troy, NC 27371. *Toll-free phone:* 877-572-6222. *Website:* http://www.montgomery.edu/.

Nash Community College
Rocky Mount, North Carolina

Freshman Application Contact Ms. Dorothy Gardner, Admissions Officer, Nash Community College, PO Box 7488, Rocky Mount, NC 27804. *Phone:* 252-451-8300. *E-mail:* dgardner@nashcc.edu. *Website:* http://www.nashcc.edu/.

Pamlico Community College
Grantsboro, North Carolina

Director of Admissions Mr. Floyd H. Hardison, Admissions Counselor, Pamlico Community College, PO Box 185, Grantsboro, NC 28529-0185. *Phone:* 252-249-1851 Ext. 28. *Website:* http://www.pamlicocc.edu/.

Piedmont Community College
Roxboro, North Carolina

- **State-supported** 2-year, founded 1970, part of North Carolina Community College System
- **Small-town** 178-acre campus
- **Coed,** 1,414 undergraduate students, 28% full-time, 63% women, 37% men

Undergraduates 396 full-time, 1,018 part-time.
Faculty *Student/faculty ratio:* 12:1.
Majors Accounting; business administration and management; child-care and support services management; criminal justice/safety; early childhood education; electrical and power transmission installation; electrician; electromechanical and instrumentation and maintenance technologies related; general studies; graphic communications; health professions related; historic preservation and conservation; industrial technology; information technology; liberal arts and sciences and humanities related; liberal arts and sciences/liberal studies; medical administrative assistant and medical secretary; medical/clinical assistant; medical office management; mental and social health services and allied professions related; office management; registered nursing/registered nurse.
Academics *Calendar:* semesters. *Degree:* certificates, diplomas, and associate. *Special study options:* academic remediation for entering students, adult/continuing education programs, advanced placement credit, cooperative education, distance learning, double majors, English as a second language, off-campus study, part-time degree program, summer session for credit.
Library Learning Commons.
Student Life *Housing:* college housing not available. *Activities and Organizations:* drama/theater group. *Campus security:* routine patrols by the local sheriff department. *Student services:* veterans affairs office.
Applying *Options:* electronic application, early admission, deferred entrance. *Required for some:* high school transcript. *Application deadlines:* rolling (freshmen), rolling (out-of-state freshmen), rolling (transfers). *Notification:* continuous (freshmen), continuous (out-of-state freshmen), continuous (transfers).
Freshman Application Contact Piedmont Community College, PO Box 1197, Roxboro, NC 27573-1197. *Phone:* 336-599-1181. *Website:* http://www.piedmontcc.edu/.

Pitt Community College
Winterville, North Carolina

- **State and locally supported** 2-year, founded 1961, part of North Carolina Community College System
- **Small-town** 294-acre campus
- **Coed**

Undergraduates 4,670 full-time, 4,232 part-time. 28% Black or African American, non-Hispanic/Latino; 2% Hispanic/Latino; 0.5% Asian, non-Hispanic/Latino; 0.1% Native Hawaiian or other Pacific Islander, non-Hispanic/Latino; 0.3% American Indian or Alaska Native, non-Hispanic/Latino; 0.2% Two or more races, non-Hispanic/Latino; 39% Race/ethnicity unknown; 0.7% international. *Retention:* 59% of full-time freshmen returned.
Faculty *Student/faculty ratio:* 19:1.
Academics *Calendar:* semesters. *Degree:* certificates, diplomas, and associate. *Special study options:* academic remediation for entering students,

adult/continuing education programs, advanced placement credit, cooperative education, distance learning, double majors, English as a second language, external degree program, independent study, internships, part-time degree program, services for LD students, summer session for credit. *ROTC:* Army (b).
Library Pitt Community College Library.
Student Life *Campus security:* 24-hour patrols, student patrols, late-night transport/escort service.
Athletics Member NJCAA.
Costs (2019–20) *Tuition:* state resident $2432 full-time, $76 per credit hour part-time; nonresident $8576 full-time, $268 per credit hour part-time. Full-time tuition and fees vary according to course load. Part-time tuition and fees vary according to course load. *Required fees:* $148 full-time, $148 per year part-time.
Financial Aid Of all full-time matriculated undergraduates who enrolled in 2014, 103 Federal Work-Study jobs (averaging $2949). *Average percent of need met:* 100. *Average financial aid package:* $5772.
Applying *Options:* electronic application, deferred entrance. *Required:* high school transcript.
Freshman Application Contact Dr. Kimberly Williamson, Interim Coordinator of Counseling, Pitt Community College, PO Drawer 7007, Greenville, NC 27835-7007. *Phone:* 252-493-7217. *Fax:* 252-321-4612. *E-mail:* pittadm@pcc.pitt.cc.nc.us. *Website:* http://www.pittcc.edu/.

Randolph Community College
Asheboro, North Carolina

Freshman Application Contact Ms. Hillary D Pritchard, Director of Admissions, Records and Registration, Randolph Community College, 629 Industrial Park Avenue, Asheboro, NC 27205-7333. *Phone:* 336-633-0122. *Fax:* 336-629-9547. *E-mail:* hdpritchard@randolph.edu. *Website:* http://www.randolph.edu/.

Richmond Community College
Hamlet, North Carolina

- **State-supported** 2-year, founded 1964, part of North Carolina Community College System
- **Rural** 163-acre campus
- **Coed,** 2,586 undergraduate students, 38% full-time, 65% women, 35% men

Undergraduates 989 full-time, 1,597 part-time. 0.5% are from out of state; 24% Black or African American, non-Hispanic/Latino; 6% Hispanic/Latino; 1% Asian, non-Hispanic/Latino; 0.1% Native Hawaiian or other Pacific Islander, non-Hispanic/Latino; 10% American Indian or Alaska Native, non-Hispanic/Latino; 3% Two or more races, non-Hispanic/Latino; 17% Race/ethnicity unknown; 0.3% international; 21% transferred in.
Freshmen *Admission:* 290 enrolled.
Faculty *Total:* 215, 49% full-time, 9% with terminal degrees. *Student/faculty ratio:* 15:1.
Majors Accounting and finance; business administration and management; computer engineering technology; criminal justice/safety; early childhood education; electrical and power transmission installation; electrical, electronic and communications engineering technology; electromechanical and instrumentation and maintenance technologies related; electromechanical technology; health information/medical records technology; heating, air conditioning, ventilation and refrigeration maintenance technology; information technology; liberal arts and sciences/liberal studies; mechanical engineering/mechanical technology; medical/clinical assistant; medical office management; mental and social health services and allied professions related; office management; pre-engineering; registered nursing/registered nurse; substance abuse/addiction counseling.
Academics *Calendar:* semesters. *Degree:* certificates, diplomas, and associate. *Special study options:* academic remediation for entering students, adult/continuing education programs, advanced placement credit, cooperative education, distance learning, double majors, English as a second language, independent study, internships, part-time degree program, student-designed majors, summer session for credit.
Library Richmond Community College Library. Students can reserve study rooms.
Student Life *Housing:* college housing not available. *Activities and Organizations:* choral group, SGA, HOSA, HVAC, Leadership and Mentoring, Campus Crusade. *Campus security:* 24-hour emergency response devices. *Student services:* personal/psychological counseling.
Costs (2019–20) *Tuition:* state resident $2462 full-time, $76 per credit hour part-time; nonresident $8576 full-time, $268 per credit hour part-time. Full-time tuition and fees vary according to course load. Part-time tuition and fees vary according to course load. *Required fees:* $84 full-time, $35 per term part-time. *Payment plan:* installment. *Waivers:* employees or children of employees.
Financial Aid Of all full-time matriculated undergraduates who enrolled in 2018, 23 Federal Work-Study jobs (averaging $2322).
Applying *Options:* electronic application, deferred entrance. *Required:* high school transcript. *Application deadlines:* rolling (freshmen), rolling (transfers). *Notification:* continuous (freshmen), continuous (transfers).
Freshman Application Contact Cayce Holmes, Registrar, Richmond Community College, PO Box 1189, 1042 W. Hamlet Avenue, Hamlet, NC 28345. *Phone:* 910-410-1737. *Fax:* 910-582-7102. *E-mail:* ccholmes@richmondcc.edu.
Website: http://www.richmondcc.edu/.

Roanoke-Chowan Community College
Ahoskie, North Carolina

Director of Admissions Miss Sandra Copeland, Director, Counseling Services, Roanoke-Chowan Community College, 109 Community College Road, Ahoskie, NC 27910. *Phone:* 252-862-1225. *Website:* http://www.roanokechowan.edu/.

Robeson Community College
Lumberton, North Carolina

Freshman Application Contact Ms. Patricia Locklear, College Recruiter, Robeson Community College, PO Box 1420, Lumberton, NC 28359. *Phone:* 910-272-3356 Ext. 251. *Fax:* 910-618-5686. *E-mail:* plocklear@robeson.edu. *Website:* http://www.robeson.edu/.

Rockingham Community College
Wentworth, North Carolina

Freshman Application Contact Mr. Derrick Satterfield, Director of Enrollment Services, Rockingham Community College, PO Box 38, Wentworth, NC 27375-0038. *Phone:* 336-342-4261 Ext. 2114. *Fax:* 336-342-1809. *E-mail:* admissions@rockinghamcc.edu. *Website:* http://www.rockinghamcc.edu/.

Rowan-Cabarrus Community College
Salisbury, North Carolina

Freshman Application Contact Rowan-Cabarrus Community College, 1333 Jake Alexander Boulevard South, Salisbury, NC 28146. *Website:* http://www.rccc.edu/.

Sampson Community College
Clinton, North Carolina

Director of Admissions Mr. William R. Jordan, Director of Admissions, Sampson Community College, PO Box 318, 1801 Sunset Avenue, Highway 24 West, Clinton, NC 28329-0318. *Phone:* 910-592-8084 Ext. 2022. *Website:* http://www.sampsoncc.edu/.

Sandhills Community College
Pinehurst, North Carolina

Freshman Application Contact Mr. Isai Robledo, Recruiter, Sandhills Community College, 3395 Airport Road, Pinehurst, NC 28374-8299. *Phone:* 910-246-5365. *Toll-free phone:* 800-338-3944. *Fax:* 910-695-3981. *E-mail:* robledoi@sandhills.edu. *Website:* http://www.sandhills.edu/.

Southeastern Community College
Whiteville, North Carolina

Freshman Application Contact Ms. Sylvia McQueen, Registrar, Southeastern Community College, PO Box 151, Whiteville, NC 28472. *Phone:* 910-642-7141 Ext. 249. *Fax:* 910-642-5658. *Website:* http://www.sccnc.edu/.

South Piedmont Community College
Polkton, North Carolina

Freshman Application Contact Ms. Amanda Secrest, Assistant Director Admissions and Testing, South Piedmont Community College, PO Box 126, Polkton, NC 28135. *Phone:* 704-290-5847. *Toll-free phone:* 800-766-0319. *E-mail:* asecrest@spcc.edu. *Website:* http://www.spcc.edu/.

Southwestern Community College

Sylva, North Carolina

- **State-supported** 2-year, founded 1964, part of North Carolina Community College System
- **Small-town** 77-acre campus
- **Coed,** 2,324 undergraduate students, 31% full-time, 61% women, 39% men

Undergraduates 721 full-time, 1,603 part-time. 3% Black or African American, non-Hispanic/Latino; 7% Hispanic/Latino; 0.7% Asian, non-Hispanic/Latino; 0.2% Native Hawaiian or other Pacific Islander, non-Hispanic/Latino; 11% American Indian or Alaska Native, non-Hispanic/Latino; 4% Two or more races, non-Hispanic/Latino; 1% Race/ethnicity unknown; 1% international.
Freshmen *Admission:* 184 enrolled.
Faculty *Student/faculty ratio:* 16:1.
Majors Accounting; automobile/automotive mechanics technology; business administration and management; child development; clinical/medical laboratory technology; commercial and advertising art; computer engineering technology; cosmetology; criminal justice/police science; culinary arts; electrical, electronic and communications engineering technology; emergency medical technology (EMT paramedic); health information/medical records administration; health information/medical records technology; information science/studies; legal assistant/paralegal; liberal arts and sciences/liberal studies; massage therapy; mechatronics, robotics, and automation engineering; medical office management; medical radiologic technology; mental health counseling; occupational therapist assistant; office management; parks, recreation, leisure, and fitness studies related; physical therapy technology; registered nursing/registered nurse; respiratory care therapy; substance abuse/addiction counseling; system, networking, and LAN/WAN management.
Academics *Calendar:* semesters. *Degree:* certificates, diplomas, and associate. *Special study options:* academic remediation for entering students, adult/continuing education programs, advanced placement credit, cooperative education, distance learning, double majors, English as a second language, honors programs, independent study, off-campus study, part-time degree program, services for LD students, summer session for credit.
Library Holt Library.
Student Life *Housing:* college housing not available. *Campus security:* security during hours of operation. *Student services:* personal/psychological counseling, veterans affairs office.
Costs (2019–20) *Tuition:* state resident $2212 full-time, $76 per credit hour part-time; nonresident $7588 full-time, $268 per credit hour part-time. Full-time tuition and fees vary according to course load and program. Part-time tuition and fees vary according to course load and program. *Required fees:* $85 full-time, $3 per credit hour part-time, $1 per year part-time. *Payment plan:* installment.
Applying *Options:* electronic application. *Required:* high school transcript. *Required for some:* minimum 2.5 GPA, interview.
Freshman Application Contact Mark Ellison, Director of Enrollment Management, Southwestern Community College, 447 College Drive, Sylva, NC 28779. *Phone:* 828-339-4229. *Toll-free phone:* 800-447-4091 (in-state); 800-447-7091 (out-of-state). *E-mail:* m_ellison@southwesterncc.edu. *Website:* http://www.southwesterncc.edu/.

Stanly Community College

Albemarle, North Carolina

Freshman Application Contact Mrs. Denise B. Ross, Associate Dean, Admissions, Stanly Community College, 141 College Drive, Albemarle, NC 28001. *Phone:* 704-982-0121 Ext. 264. *Fax:* 704-982-0255. *E-mail:* dross7926@stanly.edu. *Website:* http://www.stanly.edu/.

Surry Community College

Dobson, North Carolina

Freshman Application Contact Renita Hazelwood, Director of Admissions, Surry Community College, 630 South Main Street, Dobson, NC 27017. *Phone:* 336-386-3392. *Fax:* 336-386-3690. *E-mail:* hazelwoodr@surry.edu. *Website:* http://www.surry.edu/.

Tri-County Community College

Murphy, North Carolina

Freshman Application Contact Mrs. Samantha Jones, First Year Success Coach and Retention Specialist, Tri-County Community College, 21 Campus Circle, Murphy, NC 28906-7919. *Phone:* 828-837-6810. *Fax:* 828-837-3266. *E-mail:* sjones@tricountycc.edu. *Website:* http://www.tricountycc.edu/.

Vance-Granville Community College

Henderson, North Carolina

- **State-supported** 2-year, founded 1969, part of North Carolina Community College System
- **Rural** 83-acre campus with easy access to Raleigh
- **Endowment** $3.0 million
- **Coed**

Undergraduates 1,718 full-time, 2,339 part-time. Students come from 10 states and territories; 15 other countries; 2% are from out of state; 2% transferred in.
Faculty *Student/faculty ratio:* 9:1.
Academics *Calendar:* semesters. *Degree:* certificates, diplomas, and associate. *Special study options:* academic remediation for entering students, accelerated degree program, adult/continuing education programs, advanced placement credit, cooperative education, distance learning, double majors, English as a second language, internships, part-time degree program, services for LD students, summer session for credit.
Library Vance-Granville Community College Learning Resource Center plus 1 other.
Student Life *Campus security:* 24-hour emergency response devices and patrols.
Financial Aid Of all full-time matriculated undergraduates who enrolled in 2018, 38 Federal Work-Study jobs (averaging $1750).
Applying *Options:* early admission, deferred entrance. *Required:* high school transcript.
Freshman Application Contact Ms. Kathy Kutl, Admissions Officer, Vance-Granville Community College, PO Box 917, State Road 1126, Henderson, NC 27536. *Phone:* 252-492-2061 Ext. 3265. *Fax:* 252-430-0460. *Website:* http://www.vgcc.edu/.

Wake Technical Community College

Raleigh, North Carolina

Director of Admissions Ms. Susan Bloomfield, Director of Admissions, Wake Technical Community College, 9101 Fayetteville Road, Raleigh, NC 27603-5696. *Phone:* 919-866-5452. *E-mail:* srbloomfield@waketech.edu. *Website:* http://www.waketech.edu/.

Wayne Community College

Goldsboro, North Carolina

Freshman Application Contact Mrs. Lea Matthews, Associate Director of Admissions and Records, Wayne Community College, PO Box 8002, Goldsboro, NC 27533. *Phone:* 919-735-5151 Ext. 6717. *Fax:* 919-736-9425. *E-mail:* rlmatthews@waynecc.edu. *Website:* http://www.waynecc.edu/.

Western Piedmont Community College

Morganton, North Carolina

Freshman Application Contact Susan Williams, Director of Admissions, Western Piedmont Community College, 1001 Burkemont Avenue, Morganton, NC 28655-4511. *Phone:* 828-438-6051. *Fax:* 828-438-6065. *E-mail:* swilliams@wpcc.edu. *Website:* http://www.wpcc.edu/.

Wilkes Community College

Wilkesboro, North Carolina

Freshman Application Contact Mr. Mac Warren, Director of Admissions, Wilkes Community College, PO Box 120, Wilkesboro, NC 28697. *Phone:* 336-838-6141. *Fax:* 336-838-6547. *E-mail:* mac.warren@wilkescc.edu. *Website:* http://www.wilkescc.edu/.

Wilson Community College

Wilson, North Carolina

Freshman Application Contact Mrs. Maegan Williams, Admissions Technician, Wilson Community College, Wilson, NC 27893-0305. *Phone:* 252-246-1275. *Fax:* 252-243-7148. *E-mail:* mwilliams@wilsoncc.edu. *Website:* http://www.wilsoncc.edu/.

NORTH DAKOTA

Bismarck State College
Bismarck, North Dakota

Freshman Application Contact Karen Erickson, Director of Admissions and Enrollment Services, Bismarck State College, PO Box 5587, Bismarck, ND 58506. *Phone:* 701-224-5424. *Toll-free phone:* 800-445-5073. *Fax:* 701-224-5643. *E-mail:* karen.erickson@bismarckstate.edu. *Website:* http://www.bismarckstate.edu/.

Cankdeska Cikana Community College
Fort Totten, North Dakota

- **Federally supported** 2-year, founded 1974
- **Small-town** 1-acre campus
- **Coed**

Undergraduates 157 full-time, 94 part-time. *Retention:* 53% of full-time freshmen returned.
Faculty *Student/faculty ratio:* 9:1.
Academics *Calendar:* semesters. *Degree:* certificates and associate. *Special study options:* academic remediation for entering students, adult/continuing education programs, cooperative education, off-campus study, part-time degree program, services for LD students, student-designed majors, summer session for credit.
Student Life *Campus security:* late-night transport/escort service.
Applying *Options:* early admission, deferred entrance.
Director of Admissions DeShawn Lawrence, Registrar, Cankdeska Cikana Community College, PO Box 269, Fort Totten, ND 58335-0269. *Phone:* 701-766-1342. *Toll-free phone:* 888-783-1463. *Website:* http://www.littlehoop.edu/.

Dakota College at Bottineau
Bottineau, North Dakota

- **State-supported** 2-year, founded 1906, part of North Dakota University System
- **Rural** 35-acre campus
- **Coed**

Undergraduates 9% Black or African American, non-Hispanic/Latino; 5% Hispanic/Latino; 0.3% Asian, non-Hispanic/Latino; 0.1% Native Hawaiian or other Pacific Islander, non-Hispanic/Latino; 4% American Indian or Alaska Native, non-Hispanic/Latino; 5% Two or more races, non-Hispanic/Latino; 5% Race/ethnicity unknown.
Faculty *Student/faculty ratio:* 8:1.
Academics *Calendar:* semesters. *Degree:* certificates, diplomas, and associate. *Special study options:* academic remediation for entering students, advanced placement credit, cooperative education, distance learning, double majors, off-campus study, part-time degree program, services for LD students, summer session for credit.
Library Dakota College at Bottineau Library plus 1 other.
Student Life *Campus security:* controlled dormitory access, security cameras, night security personnel.
Athletics Member NJCAA.
Financial Aid Of all full-time matriculated undergraduates who enrolled in 2015, 296 applied for aid, 246 were judged to have need, 62 had their need fully met. 65 Federal Work-Study jobs (averaging $668). In 2015, 26. *Average percent of need met:* 70. *Average financial aid package:* $10,004. *Average need-based loan:* $5400. *Average need-based gift aid:* $5196. *Average non-need-based aid:* $2012. *Average indebtedness upon graduation:* $12,305.
Applying *Options:* electronic application, early admission, deferred entrance. *Application fee:* $35. *Required:* high school transcript, immunization records, previous college official transcripts.
Freshman Application Contact Mrs. Heidi Hauf, Admissions Clerk, Dakota College at Bottineau, 105 Simrall Boulevard, Bottineau, ND 58318. *Phone:* 701-228-5487. *Toll-free phone:* 800-542-6866. *Fax:* 701-228-5499. *E-mail:* heidi.hauf@dakotacollege.edu. *Website:* http://www.dakotacollege.edu/.

Lake Region State College
Devils Lake, North Dakota

- **State-supported** 2-year, founded 1941, part of North Dakota University System
- **Small-town** 120-acre campus
- **Coed,** 1,982 undergraduate students, 26% full-time, 58% women, 42% men

Undergraduates 515 full-time, 1,467 part-time. Students come from 36 states and territories; 16 other countries; 19% are from out of state; 4% Black or African American, non-Hispanic/Latino; 6% Hispanic/Latino; 0.9% Asian, non-Hispanic/Latino; 0.3% Native Hawaiian or other Pacific Islander, non-Hispanic/Latino; 4% American Indian or Alaska Native, non-Hispanic/Latino; 7% Two or more races, non-Hispanic/Latino; 2% Race/ethnicity unknown; 5% international; 5% transferred in; 12% live on campus. *Retention:* 64% of full-time freshmen returned.
Freshmen *Admission:* 206 enrolled.
Faculty *Total:* 108, 41% full-time, 12% with terminal degrees. *Student/faculty ratio:* 14:1.
Majors Agricultural business and management; automobile/automotive mechanics technology; business administration and management; child-care provision; computer installation and repair technology; criminal justice/police science; electrical and electronic engineering technologies related; language interpretation and translation; liberal arts and sciences/liberal studies; management information systems; merchandising, sales, and marketing operations related (general); physical fitness technician; registered nursing/registered nurse; speech-language pathology.
Academics *Calendar:* semesters. *Degree:* certificates, diplomas, and associate. *Special study options:* academic remediation for entering students, cooperative education, distance learning, double majors, honors programs, off-campus study, part-time degree program, services for LD students, summer session for credit.
Library Paul Hoghaug Library. *Books:* 11,909 (physical), 282,761 (digital/electronic); *Databases:* 63. Students can reserve study rooms.
Student Life *Housing Options:* coed, men-only, women-only. Campus housing is university owned. *Activities and Organizations:* drama/theater group, choral group, Royal Ambassadors, Student Senate, DECA, Phi Theta Kappa, Student Nurse Organization. *Campus security:* 24-hour emergency response devices, controlled dormitory access. *Student services:* personal/psychological counseling.
Athletics Member NJCAA. *Intercollegiate sports:* baseball M(s), basketball M(s)/W(s), softball W(s), volleyball W(s). *Intramural sports:* riflery M(c)/W(c).
Costs (2020–21) *Tuition:* state resident $3929 full-time, $164 per credit part-time; nonresident $3929 full-time, $164 per credit part-time. *Required fees:* $914 full-time, $30 per credit part-time. *Room and board:* $7050. Room and board charges vary according to board plan and housing facility. *Payment plan:* installment. *Waivers:* minority students, senior citizens, and employees or children of employees.
Financial Aid Of all full-time matriculated undergraduates who enrolled in 2019, 391 applied for aid, 311 were judged to have need, 101 had their need fully met. In 2019, 106 non-need-based awards were made. *Average percent of need met:* 76%. *Average financial aid package:* $10,912. *Average need-based loan:* $5770. *Average need-based gift aid:* $6444. *Average non-need-based aid:* $1327. *Average indebtedness upon graduation:* $12,477.
Applying *Options:* electronic application. *Application fee:* $35. *Required for some:* high school transcript, immunization records, college transcripts. *Application deadlines:* rolling (freshmen), rolling (transfers). *Notification:* continuous (freshmen), continuous (transfers).
Freshman Application Contact Merissa Halvorson, Admissions Associate, Lake Region State College, 1801 College Drive North, Devils Lake, ND 58301. *Phone:* 701-662-1519. *Toll-free phone:* 800-443-1313. *Fax:* 701-662-1581. *E-mail:* merissa.halvorson@lrsc.edu.
Website: http://www.lrsc.edu/.

North Dakota State College of Science
Wahpeton, North Dakota

- **State-supported** 2-year, founded 1903, part of North Dakota University System
- **Rural** 128-acre campus
- **Endowment** $18.4 million
- **Coed,** 2,977 undergraduate students, 51% full-time, 47% women, 53% men

Undergraduates 1,522 full-time, 1,455 part-time. 46% are from out of state; 9% Black or African American, non-Hispanic/Latino; 3% Hispanic/Latino; 1% Asian, non-Hispanic/Latino; 0.1% Native Hawaiian or other Pacific Islander, non-Hispanic/Latino; 1% American Indian or Alaska Native, non-Hispanic/Latino; 4% Two or more races, non-Hispanic/Latino; 0.7%

Race/ethnicity unknown; 1% international; 5% transferred in; 72% live on campus. *Retention:* 71% of full-time freshmen returned.
Freshmen *Admission:* 1,156 applied, 772 admitted, 690 enrolled.
Faculty *Total:* 287, 37% full-time, 7% with terminal degrees. *Student/faculty ratio:* 12:1.
Majors Agricultural business and management; agricultural business technology; agricultural mechanics and equipment technology; animal sciences; architectural engineering technology; autobody/collision and repair technology; automobile/automotive mechanics technology; building construction technology; business administration and management; civil engineering technology; computer and information sciences; computer systems networking and telecommunications; construction engineering technology; culinary arts; dental assisting; dental hygiene; diesel mechanics technology; electrical and electronic engineering technologies related; emergency medical technology (EMT paramedic); entrepreneurship; health information/medical records technology; heating, air conditioning, ventilation and refrigeration maintenance technology; heating, ventilation, air conditioning and refrigeration engineering technology; industrial production technologies related; liberal arts and sciences/liberal studies; licensed practical/vocational nurse training; livestock management; machine tool technology; manufacturing engineering technology; marketing/marketing management; occupational therapist assistant; pharmacy technician; registered nursing/registered nurse; restaurant/food services management; small engine mechanics and repair technology; vehicle maintenance and repair technologies related; web page, digital/multimedia and information resources design; welding technology.
Academics *Calendar:* semesters. *Degree:* certificates, diplomas, and associate. *Special study options:* academic remediation for entering students, cooperative education, distance learning, English as a second language, external degree program, independent study, internships, part-time degree program, services for LD students, student-designed majors, summer session for credit.
Library Mildred Johnson Library. *Books:* 57,489 (physical), 15,859 (digital/electronic); *Serial titles:* 204 (physical), 23,940 (digital/electronic); *Databases:* 80.
Student Life *Housing:* on-campus residence required for freshman year. *Options:* coed, men-only, women-only, special housing for students with disabilities. Campus housing is university owned. Freshman campus housing is guaranteed. *Activities and Organizations:* drama/theater group, choral group, SkillsUSA, Welding Club, Dental Club, Diesel Club, HVAC. *Campus security:* 24-hour patrols, late-night transport/escort service, controlled dormitory access. *Student services:* health clinic, personal/psychological counseling, veterans affairs office.
Athletics Member NJCAA. *Intercollegiate sports:* basketball M(s)/W(s), football M(s), softball W, volleyball W(s). *Intramural sports:* basketball M/W, football M, racquetball M/W, softball M/W, ultimate Frisbee M/W, volleyball M/W.
Costs (2020–21) *Tuition:* $140 per credit hour part-time; state resident $140 per credit hour part-time; nonresident $168 per credit hour part-time. *Room and board:* Room and board charges vary according to board plan and housing facility. *Waivers:* employees or children of employees.
Financial Aid Of all full-time matriculated undergraduates who enrolled in 2018, 1,345 applied for aid, 1,002 were judged to have need, 345 had their need fully met. In 2018, 90 non-need-based awards were made. *Average percent of need met:* 58%. *Average financial aid package:* $10,800. *Average need-based loan:* $5753. *Average need-based gift aid:* $5259. *Average non-need-based aid:* $1207. *Average indebtedness upon graduation:* $17,202.
Applying *Options:* electronic application. *Application fee:* $35. *Required:* high school transcript. *Application deadlines:* rolling (freshmen), rolling (transfers). *Notification:* continuous (freshmen), continuous (transfers).
Freshman Application Contact Mr. Justin Grams, Director of Admissions, North Dakota State College of Science, 800 North 6th Street, Wahpeton, ND 58076. *Phone:* 701-671-2189. *Toll-free phone:* 800-342-4325. *E-mail:* justin.grams@ndscs.edu.
Website: http://www.ndscs.edu/.

Nueta Hidatsa Sahnish College

New Town, North Dakota

Freshman Application Contact Office of Admissions, Nueta Hidatsa Sahnish College, PO Box 490, 220 8th Avenue North, New Town, ND 58763-0490. *Phone:* 701-627-4738 Ext. 295. *Website:* http://www.nhsc.edu/.

Turtle Mountain Community College

Belcourt, North Dakota

Director of Admissions Ms. Joni LaFontaine, Admissions/Records Officer, Turtle Mountain Community College, Box 340, Belcourt, ND 58316-0340. *Phone:* 701-477-5605 Ext. 217. *E-mail:* jlafontaine@tm.edu. *Website:* http://www.tm.edu/.

United Tribes Technical College

Bismarck, North Dakota

Freshman Application Contact Ms. Vivian Gillette, Director of Admissions, United Tribes Technical College, Bismarck, ND 58504. *Phone:* 701-255-3285 Ext. 1334. *Fax:* 701-530-0640. *E-mail:* vgillette@uttc.edu. *Website:* http://www.uttc.edu/.

Williston State College

Williston, North Dakota

Freshman Application Contact Ms. Jamee Robbins, Enrollment Services Associate, Williston State College, 1410 University Avenue, Williston, ND 58801. *Phone:* 701-774-4278. *Toll-free phone:* 888-863-9455. *E-mail:* wsc.admission@willistonstate.edu. *Website:* http://www.willistonstate.edu/.

NORTHERN MARIANA ISLANDS

Northern Marianas College

Saipan, Northern Mariana Islands

Freshman Application Contact Ms. Leilani M. Basa-Alam, Admission Specialist, Northern Marianas College, PO Box 501250, Saipan, MP 96950-1250. *Phone:* 670-234-3690 Ext. 1539. *Fax:* 670-235-4967. *E-mail:* leilanib@nmcnet.edu. *Website:* http://www.marianas.edu/.

OHIO

American Institute of Alternative Medicine

Columbus, Ohio

Admissions Office Contact American Institute of Alternative Medicine, 6685 Doubletree Avenue, Columbus, OH 43229. *Website:* http://www.aiam.edu/.

Beckfield College

Cincinnati, Ohio

Freshman Application Contact Beckfield College, 225 Pictoria Drive, Suite 200, Cincinnati, OH 45246. *Website:* http://www.beckfield.edu/.

Belmont College

St. Clairsville, Ohio

Director of Admissions Michael Sterling, Director of Recruitment, Belmont College, 120 Fox Shannon Place, St. Clairsville, OH 43950-9735. *Phone:* 740-695-9500 Ext. 1563. *Toll-free phone:* 800-423-1188. *E-mail:* msterling@btc.edu. *Website:* http://www.belmontcollege.edu/.

Bowling Green State University–Firelands College

Huron, Ohio

- **State-supported** primarily 2-year, founded 1968, part of Bowling Green State University System
- **Rural** 216-acre campus with easy access to Cleveland, Toledo
- **Coed**

Undergraduates 936 full-time, 1,034 part-time. Students come from 6 states and territories; 1 other country; 1% are from out of state; 6% Black or African American, non-Hispanic/Latino; 5% Hispanic/Latino; 0.8% Asian, non-Hispanic/Latino; 0.2% American Indian or Alaska Native, non-Hispanic/Latino; 4% Two or more races, non-Hispanic/Latino; 5% Race/ethnicity unknown; 0.1% international. *Retention:* 53% of full-time freshmen returned.
Faculty *Student/faculty ratio:* 20:1.
Academics *Calendar:* semesters. *Degrees:* certificates, associate, and bachelor's (also offers some upper-level and graduate courses). *Special study*

options: academic remediation for entering students, adult/continuing education programs, advanced placement credit, cooperative education, distance learning, double majors, honors programs, independent study, internships, part-time degree program, services for LD students, student-designed majors, study abroad, summer session for credit. *ROTC:* Army (c), Air Force (c).
Library BGSU Firelands College Library.
Student Life *Campus security:* 24-hour emergency response devices, late-night transport/escort service, patrols by trained security personnel.
Applying *Options:* electronic application, early admission, deferred entrance. *Application fee:* $45. *Required:* high school transcript.
Freshman Application Contact Dr. Megan Zahler, Assistant Dean for Strategic Enrollment Planning, Bowling Green State University–Firelands College, One University Drive, Huron, OH 44839-9791. *Phone:* 419-433-5560. *Toll-free phone:* 800-322-4787. *Fax:* 419-372-0604. *E-mail:* mzahler@bgsu.edu. *Website:* http://www.firelands.bgsu.edu/.

Bradford School
Columbus, Ohio

Freshman Application Contact Admissions Office, Bradford School, 2469 Stelzer Road, Columbus, OH 43219. *Phone:* 614-416-6200. *Toll-free phone:* 800-678-7981. *Website:* http://www.bradfordschoolcolumbus.edu/.

Bryant & Stratton College–Eastlake Campus
Eastlake, Ohio

Freshman Application Contact Ms. Melanie Pettit, Director of Admissions, Bryant & Stratton College–Eastlake Campus, 35350 Curtis Boulevard, Eastlake, OH 44095. *Phone:* 440-510-1112. *Website:* http://www.bryantstratton.edu/.

Bryant & Stratton College–Parma Campus
Parma, Ohio

Freshman Application Contact Bryant & Stratton College–Parma Campus, 12955 Snow Road, Parma, OH 44130-1005. *Phone:* 216-265-3151. *Toll-free phone:* 866-948-0571. *Website:* http://www.bryantstratton.edu/.

Central Ohio Technical College
Newark, Ohio

- **State-supported** 2-year, founded 1971, part of Ohio Department of Higher Education
- **Small-town** 177-acre campus with easy access to Columbus
- **Endowment** $3.4 million
- **Coed,** 3,468 undergraduate students, 19% full-time, 67% women, 33% men

Undergraduates 672 full-time, 2,796 part-time. Students come from 31 states and territories; 6 other countries; 0.6% are from out of state; 13% Black or African American, non-Hispanic/Latino; 2% Hispanic/Latino; 3% Asian, non-Hispanic/Latino; 0.3% American Indian or Alaska Native, non-Hispanic/Latino; 4% Two or more races, non-Hispanic/Latino; 6% Race/ethnicity unknown; 0.2% international; 8% transferred in.
Freshmen *Admission:* 625 applied, 625 admitted, 316 enrolled.
Faculty *Total:* 188, 30% full-time, 80% with terminal degrees. *Student/faculty ratio:* 16:1.
Majors Accounting; advertising; architectural drafting and CAD/CADD; business administration and management; CAD/CADD drafting/design technology; civil drafting and CAD/CADD; civil engineering technology; computer graphics; computer programming; computer support specialist; criminal justice/law enforcement administration; criminal justice/police science; culinary arts; diagnostic medical sonography and ultrasound technology; early childhood education; emergency medical technology (EMT paramedic); fire science/firefighting; human services; liberal arts and sciences/liberal studies; manufacturing engineering technology; mechanical engineering/mechanical technology; radiologic technology/science; registered nursing/registered nurse; surgical technology; web page, digital/multimedia and information resources design.
Academics *Calendar:* semesters. *Degree:* certificates and associate. *Special study options:* academic remediation for entering students, accelerated degree program, adult/continuing education programs, advanced placement credit, cooperative education, distance learning, double majors, external degree program, internships, off-campus study, part-time degree program, services for LD students, student-designed majors, summer session for credit.
Library Newark Campus Library. Weekly public service hours: 69; students can reserve study rooms.
Student Life *Housing Options:* Campus housing is university owned. *Activities and Organizations:* drama/theater group, choral group, Society of Engineering Technology, Radiologic Technology Student Organization, Phi Theta Kappa, Community Outreach Committee, Journey Campus Ministry. *Campus security:* 24-hour emergency response devices and patrols, late-night transport/escort service. *Student services:* personal/psychological counseling, veterans affairs office.
Athletics *Intramural sports:* badminton M/W, basketball M/W, football M/W, golf M/W, sand volleyball M/W, soccer M/W, softball M/W, table tennis M/W, ultimate Frisbee M/W, volleyball M/W, weight lifting M/W.
Costs (2020–21) *One-time required fee:* $80. *Tuition:* state resident $4776 full-time, $199 per credit hour part-time; nonresident $7536 full-time, $314 per credit hour part-time. Full-time tuition and fees vary according to course load. Part-time tuition and fees vary according to course load. *Payment plan:* installment. *Waivers:* senior citizens and employees or children of employees.
Financial Aid Of all full-time matriculated undergraduates who enrolled in 2018, 43 Federal Work-Study jobs (averaging $4000).
Applying *Options:* electronic application, deferred entrance. *Required for some:* high school transcript. *Application deadlines:* rolling (freshmen), rolling (out-of-state freshmen), rolling (transfers).
Freshman Application Contact Melanie Garrabrant, Central Ohio Technical College, 1179 University Drive, Newark, OH 43055. *Phone:* 740-755-7109. *Toll-free phone:* 800-9NEWARK. *E-mail:* garrabrant.34@mail.cotc.edu. *Website:* http://www.cotc.edu/.

Chatfield College
St. Martin, Ohio

Freshman Application Contact Chatfield College, 20918 State Route 251, St. Martin, OH 45118-9705. *Phone:* 513-875-3344 Ext. 138. *Website:* http://www.chatfield.edu/.

The Christ College of Nursing and Health Sciences
Cincinnati, Ohio

Freshman Application Contact Mr. Bradley Jackson, Admissions, The Christ College of Nursing and Health Sciences, 2139 Auburn Avenue, Cincinnati, OH 45219. *Phone:* 513-585-0016. *E-mail:* bradley.jackson@thechristcollege.edu. *Website:* http://www.thechristcollege.edu/.

Cincinnati State Technical and Community College
Cincinnati, Ohio

- **State-supported** 2-year, founded 1966, part of Ohio Board of Regents
- **Urban** 46-acre campus
- **Coed**

Undergraduates 2,873 full-time, 6,757 part-time. 9% are from out of state; 26% Black or African American, non-Hispanic/Latino; 2% Hispanic/Latino; 2% Asian, non-Hispanic/Latino; 0.1% Native Hawaiian or other Pacific Islander, non-Hispanic/Latino; 0.4% American Indian or Alaska Native, non-Hispanic/Latino; 3% Two or more races, non-Hispanic/Latino; 5% Race/ethnicity unknown; 2% international; 7% transferred in. *Retention:* 50% of full-time freshmen returned.
Faculty *Student/faculty ratio:* 13:1.
Academics *Calendar:* 5 10-week terms. *Degree:* certificates and associate. *Special study options:* academic remediation for entering students, advanced placement credit, cooperative education, distance learning, double majors, English as a second language, honors programs, independent study, internships, off-campus study, part-time degree program, services for LD students, student-designed majors, summer session for credit. *ROTC:* Army (c).
Library Johnnie Mae Berry Library.
Student Life *Campus security:* 24-hour emergency response devices and patrols, late-night transport/escort service.
Athletics Member NJCAA.
Financial Aid Of all full-time matriculated undergraduates who enrolled in 2018, 100 Federal Work-Study jobs (averaging $3500).
Applying *Options:* electronic application, deferred entrance. *Required:* high school transcript.
Freshman Application Contact Ms. Gabriele Boeckermann, Director of Admission, Cincinnati State Technical and Community College, Office of Admissions, 3520 Central Parkway, Cincinnati, OH 45223-2690. *Phone:* 513-569-1550. *Toll-free phone:* 877-569-0115. *Fax:* 513-569-1562. *E-mail:* adm@cincinnatistate.edu. *Website:* http://www.cincinnatistate.edu/.

Clark State Community College

Springfield, Ohio

Freshman Application Contact Admissions Office, Clark State Community College, PO Box 570, Springfield, OH 45501-0570. *Phone:* 937-328-3858. *Fax:* 937-328-6133. *E-mail:* admissions@clarkstate.edu. *Website:* http://www.clarkstate.edu/.

Columbus Culinary Institute at Bradford School

Columbus, Ohio

Freshman Application Contact Admissions Office, Columbus Culinary Institute at Bradford School, 2435 Stelzer Road, Columbus, OH 43219. *Phone:* 614-944-4200. *Toll-free phone:* 877-506-5006. *Website:* http://www.columbusculinary.com/.

Columbus State Community College

Columbus, Ohio

Freshman Application Contact Director of Admissions, Columbus State Community College, 550 E. Spring Street, Columbus, OH 43215. *Phone:* 614-287-2669. *Toll-free phone:* 800-621-6407 Ext. 2669. *Fax:* 614-287-6019. *Website:* http://www.cscc.edu/.

Cuyahoga Community College

Cleveland, Ohio

Freshman Application Contact Mr. Kevin McDaniel, Director of Admissions and Records, Cuyahoga Community College, Cleveland, OH 44115. *Phone:* 216-987-4030. *Toll-free phone:* 800-954-8742. *Fax:* 216-696-2567. *Website:* http://www.tri-c.edu/.

Davis College

Toledo, Ohio

Freshman Application Contact Mr. Timothy Brunner, Davis College, 4747 Monroe Street, Toledo, OH 43623-4307. *Phone:* 419-473-2700. *Toll-free phone:* 800-477-7021. *Fax:* 419-473-2472. *E-mail:* tbrunner@daviscollege.edu. *Website:* http://www.daviscollege.edu/.

Daymar College

Columbus, Ohio

- **Proprietary** 2-year, founded 1984
- **Coed**

Faculty *Student/faculty ratio:* 11:1.
Academics *Calendar:* quarters. *Degree:* associate.
Applying *Application fee:* $125.
Freshman Application Contact Holly Hankinson, Admissions Office, Daymar College, 2745 Winchester Pike, Columbus, OH 43232. *Phone:* 740-687-6126. *Toll-free phone:* 877-258-7796. *E-mail:* hhankinson@daymarcollege.edu. *Website:* http://www.daymarcollege.edu/.

Eastern Gateway Community College

Steubenville, Ohio

- **State and locally supported** 2-year, founded 1966, part of Ohio Board of Regents
- **Small-town** 83-acre campus with easy access to Pittsburgh
- **Endowment** $448,293
- **Coed,** 25,648 undergraduate students, 22% full-time, 68% women, 32% men

Undergraduates 5,672 full-time, 19,976 part-time. Students come from 50 states and territories; 1 other country; 82% are from out of state; 20% Black or African American, non-Hispanic/Latino; 16% Hispanic/Latino; 2% Asian, non-Hispanic/Latino; 0.5% Native Hawaiian or other Pacific Islander, non-Hispanic/Latino; 0.5% American Indian or Alaska Native, non-Hispanic/Latino; 4% Two or more races, non-Hispanic/Latino; 1% Race/ethnicity unknown; 0.3% transferred in. *Retention:* 52% of full-time freshmen returned.
Freshmen *Admission:* 5,545 enrolled.
Faculty *Total:* 977, 6% full-time. *Student/faculty ratio:* 33:1.
Majors Accounting; administrative assistant and secretarial science; business administration and management; child-care and support services management; computer engineering related; corrections; criminal justice/police science; data processing and data processing technology; dental assisting; drafting and design technology; electrical, electronic and communications engineering technology; emergency medical technology (EMT paramedic); industrial radiologic technology; industrial technology; legal administrative assistant/secretary; licensed practical/vocational nurse training; mechanical engineering/mechanical technology; medical administrative assistant and medical secretary; medical/clinical assistant; real estate; respiratory care therapy.
Academics *Calendar:* semesters. *Degree:* certificates and associate. *Special study options:* academic remediation for entering students, adult/continuing education programs, advanced placement credit, cooperative education, distance learning, double majors, external degree program, honors programs, independent study, internships, off-campus study, part-time degree program, services for LD students, student-designed majors, summer session for credit.
Library Eastern Gateway Community College Library plus 1 other.
Student Life *Housing:* college housing not available. *Activities and Organizations:* Phi Theta Kappa, IT Club. *Campus security:* 24-hour emergency response devices, controlled dormitory access, day and evening security. *Student services:* personal/psychological counseling, veterans affairs office.
Athletics Member NJCAA. *Intercollegiate sports:* baseball M, volleyball W.
Financial Aid Of all full-time matriculated undergraduates who enrolled in 2018, 30 Federal Work-Study jobs (averaging $1500).
Applying *Options:* electronic application. *Required for some:* high school transcript. *Application deadlines:* 10/12 (freshmen), 10/12 (out-of-state freshmen), 10/12 (transfers). *Notification:* continuous (freshmen), continuous (out-of-state freshmen), continuous (transfers).
Freshman Application Contact Ms. Cristen Tarquinio, Coordinator of Enrollment Services, Eastern Gateway Community College, 110 John Scott Highway, Steubenville, OH 43952. *Phone:* 740-2645591 Ext. 1926. *Toll-free phone:* 800-68-COLLEGE. *E-mail:* Cjtarquinio@egcc.edu. *Website:* http://www.egcc.edu/.

Edison State Community College

Piqua, Ohio

- **State-supported** 2-year, founded 1973, part of Ohio Board of Regents
- **Small-town** 131-acre campus with easy access to Dayton, Columbus, Cincinnati
- **Coed,** 3,248 undergraduate students, 23% full-time, 60% women, 40% men

Undergraduates 753 full-time, 2,495 part-time. Students come from 8 states and territories; 12% are from out of state; 5% Black or African American, non-Hispanic/Latino; 2% Hispanic/Latino; 0.9% Asian, non-Hispanic/Latino; 0.3% Native Hawaiian or other Pacific Islander, non-Hispanic/Latino; 0.2% American Indian or Alaska Native, non-Hispanic/Latino; 2% Two or more races, non-Hispanic/Latino; 2% Race/ethnicity unknown; 0.4% transferred in. *Retention:* 83% of full-time freshmen returned.
Freshmen *Admission:* 462 enrolled. *Average high school GPA:* 2.9.
Faculty *Total:* 178, 28% full-time, 9% with terminal degrees. *Student/faculty ratio:* 17:1.
Majors Accounting; agribusiness; art; banking and financial support services; biology/biological sciences; business administration and management; business/commerce; child development; clinical/medical laboratory technology; computer and information sciences; computer and information systems security; computer programming; computer systems networking and telecommunications; criminal justice/police science; dramatic/theater arts; economics; education; electrical, electronic and communications engineering technology; electromechanical technology; English; executive assistant/executive secretary; geology/earth science; health/medical preparatory programs related; heating, ventilation, air conditioning and refrigeration engineering technology; history; human resources management; human services; industrial technology; legal assistant/paralegal; liberal arts and sciences/liberal studies; logistics, materials, and supply chain management; manufacturing engineering technology; marketing/marketing management; mathematics; mechanical drafting and CAD/CADD; medical administrative assistant and medical secretary; medical/clinical assistant; medium/heavy vehicle and truck technology; philosophy and religious studies related; physical therapy technology; prenursing studies; psychology; registered nursing/registered nurse; social work; speech communication and rhetoric; veterinary/animal health technology; web page, digital/multimedia and information resources design.
Academics *Calendar:* semesters. *Degrees:* certificates, associate, and postbachelor's certificates. *Special study options:* academic remediation for entering students, accelerated degree program, adult/continuing education programs, advanced placement credit, distance learning, double majors, English as a second language, honors programs, independent study, internships, off-campus study, part-time degree program, services for LD students, student-designed majors, summer session for credit.

Library Edison Community College Library. *Books:* 18,825 (physical), 112,623 (digital/electronic); *Serial titles:* 61 (physical), 11,044 (digital/electronic); *Databases:* 149. Weekly public service hours: 50; students can reserve study rooms.
Student Life *Housing:* college housing not available. *Activities and Organizations:* drama/theater group, student-run newspaper. *Campus security:* late-night transport/escort service, 18-hour patrols by trained security personnel. *Student services:* health clinic, veterans affairs office.
Athletics *Intercollegiate sports:* baseball M(s), basketball M(s)/W(s), softball W, volleyball W(s).
Financial Aid Of all full-time matriculated undergraduates who enrolled in 2018, 42 Federal Work-Study jobs (averaging $3000).
Applying *Options:* electronic application.
Freshman Application Contact Dr. Loleta Collins, Director of Student Services, Edison State Community College, 1973 Edison Drive, Piqua, OH 45356. *Phone:* 937-778-7983. *E-mail:* lcollins@edisonohio.edu. *Website:* http://www.edisonohio.edu/.

ETI Technical College of Niles
Niles, Ohio

Freshman Application Contact Ms. Diane Marsteller, Director of Admissions, ETI Technical College of Niles, 2076 Youngstown-Warren Road, Niles, OH 44446-4398. *Phone:* 330-652-9919 Ext. 16. *Fax:* 330-652-4399. *E-mail:* dianemarsteller@eticollege.edu. *Website:* http://eticollege.edu/.

Fortis College
Centerville, Ohio

Freshman Application Contact Fortis College, 555 East Alex Bell Road, Centerville, OH 45459. *Phone:* 937-433-3410. *Toll-free phone:* 855-4-FORTIS. *Website:* http://www.fortis.edu/.

Fortis College
Cincinnati, Ohio

Admissions Office Contact Fortis College, 11499 Chester Road, Suite 200, Cincinnati, OH 45246. *Toll-free phone:* 855-4-FORTIS. *Website:* http://www.fortis.edu/.

Fortis College
Cuyahoga Falls, Ohio

Freshman Application Contact Admissions Office, Fortis College, 2545 Bailey Road, Cuyahoga Falls, OH 44221. *Phone:* 330-923-9959. *Toll-free phone:* 855-4-FORTIS. *Fax:* 330-923-0886. *Website:* http://www.fortis.edu/.

Fortis College
Ravenna, Ohio

Freshman Application Contact Admissions Office, Fortis College, 653 Enterprise Parkway, Ravenna, OH 44266. *Toll-free phone:* 855-4-FORTIS. *Website:* http://www.fortis.edu/.

Fortis College
Westerville, Ohio

Admissions Office Contact Fortis College, 4151 Executive Parkway, Suite 120, Westerville, OH 43081. *Toll-free phone:* 855-4-FORTIS. *Website:* http://www.fortis.edu/.

Good Samaritan College of Nursing and Health Science
Cincinnati, Ohio

Freshman Application Contact Admissions Office, Good Samaritan College of Nursing and Health Science, 375 Dixmyth Avenue, Cincinnati, OH 45220. *Phone:* 513-862-2743. *Fax:* 513-862-3572. *Website:* http://www.gscollege.edu/.

Herzing University
Akron, Ohio

Admissions Office Contact Herzing University, 1600 South Arlington Street, Suite 100, Akron, OH 44306. *Toll-free phone:* 800-596-0724. *Website:* http://www.herzing.edu/akron.

Herzing University
Toledo, Ohio

Admissions Office Contact Herzing University, 5212 Hill Avenue, Toledo, OH 43615. *Toll-free phone:* 800-596-0724. *Website:* http://www.herzing.edu/toledo.

Hocking College
Nelsonville, Ohio

Freshman Application Contact Hocking College, 3301 Hocking Parkway, Nelsonville, OH 45764-9588. *Phone:* 740-753-3591 Ext. 7080. *Website:* http://www.hocking.edu/.

Hondros College
Westerville, Ohio

Director of Admissions Ms. Carol Thomas, Operations Manager, Hondros College, 4140 Executive Parkway, Westerville, OH 43081-3855. *Phone:* 614-508-7244. *Toll-free phone:* 888-HONDROS. *Website:* http://www.hondros.edu/.

International College of Broadcasting
Dayton, Ohio

Freshman Application Contact International College of Broadcasting, 6 South Smithville Road, Dayton, OH 45431-1833. *Phone:* 937-258-8251. *Toll-free phone:* 800-517-7284. *Website:* http://www.icb.edu/.

James A. Rhodes State College
Lima, Ohio

- **State-supported** 2-year, founded 1971
- **Small-town** 565-acre campus
- **Endowment** $1.7 million
- **Coed**

Undergraduates 1,548 full-time, 2,335 part-time. Students come from 4 states and territories; 1% are from out of state; 7% Black or African American, non-Hispanic/Latino; 1% Hispanic/Latino; 0.5% Asian, non-Hispanic/Latino; 0.7% American Indian or Alaska Native, non-Hispanic/Latino; 0.7% Two or more races, non-Hispanic/Latino; 4% Race/ethnicity unknown; 7% transferred in. *Retention:* 55% of full-time freshmen returned.
Faculty *Student/faculty ratio:* 15:1.
Academics *Calendar:* quarters. *Degree:* certificates and associate. *Special study options:* academic remediation for entering students, adult/continuing education programs, advanced placement credit, cooperative education, distance learning, independent study, internships, off-campus study, part-time degree program, services for LD students, student-designed majors, summer session for credit.
Library Rhodes State/Ohio State Library.
Student Life *Campus security:* 24-hour emergency response devices and patrols, student patrols, late-night transport/escort service.
Financial Aid Of all full-time matriculated undergraduates who enrolled in 2018, 110 Federal Work-Study jobs (averaging $1000).
Applying *Options:* electronic application, early admission, deferred entrance. *Application fee:* $25. *Required:* high school transcript.
Freshman Application Contact Traci Cox, Director, Office of Admissions, James A. Rhodes State College, Lima, OH 45804-3597. *Phone:* 419-995-8040. *E-mail:* cox.t@rhodesstate.edu. *Website:* http://www.rhodesstate.edu/.

Kent State University at Ashtabula
Ashtabula, Ohio

- **State-supported** primarily 2-year, founded 1958, part of Kent State University System
- **Small-town** 83-acre campus with easy access to Cleveland
- **Coed**

Undergraduates 1,029 full-time, 997 part-time. Students come from 25 states and territories; 3 other countries; 4% are from out of state; 5% Black or African American, non-Hispanic/Latino; 5% Hispanic/Latino; 0.8% Asian, non-Hispanic/Latino; 0.1% Native Hawaiian or other Pacific Islander, non-Hispanic/Latino; 0.2% American Indian or Alaska Native, non-Hispanic/Latino; 3% Two or more races, non-Hispanic/Latino; 3% Race/ethnicity unknown; 0.5% international; 4% transferred in. *Retention:* 51% of full-time freshmen returned.
Faculty *Student/faculty ratio:* 22:1.
Academics *Calendar:* semesters. *Degrees:* certificates, associate, and bachelor's (also offers some upper-level and graduate courses). *Special study*

options: academic remediation for entering students, advanced placement credit, distance learning, double majors, independent study, internships, part-time degree program, services for LD students, student-designed majors, study abroad, summer session for credit. *ROTC:* Army (c), Air Force (c).
Library Kent State at Ashtabula Library. Weekly public service hours: 56.
Student Life *Campus security:* 24-hour emergency response devices.
Standardized Tests *Required for some:* SAT or ACT (for admission). *Recommended:* SAT or ACT (for admission).
Financial Aid Of all full-time matriculated undergraduates who enrolled in 2019, 448 applied for aid, 385 were judged to have need, 9 had their need fully met. 16 Federal Work-Study jobs (averaging $2576). In 2019, 31. *Average percent of need met:* 55. *Average financial aid package:* $8076. *Average need-based loan:* $3698. *Average need-based gift aid:* $5386. *Average non-need-based aid:* $1606.
Applying *Options:* electronic application, deferred entrance. *Application fee:* $40. *Required:* high school transcript.
Freshman Application Contact Megan Krippel, Admissions Coordinator, Kent State University at Ashtabula, 3300 Lake Road West, Ashtabula, OH 44004. *Phone:* 440-964-4277. *Fax:* 440-964-4269. *E-mail:* ashtabula_admissions@kent.edu. *Website:* http://www.ashtabula.kent.edu/.

Kent State University at East Liverpool
East Liverpool, Ohio

- **State-supported** primarily 2-year, founded 1967, part of Kent State University System
- **Small-town** 3-acre campus with easy access to Pittsburgh, Youngstown
- **Coed**

Undergraduates 567 full-time, 553 part-time. Students come from 13 states and territories; 10 other countries; 6% are from out of state; 5% Black or African American, non-Hispanic/Latino; 2% Hispanic/Latino; 1% Asian, non-Hispanic/Latino; 0.3% American Indian or Alaska Native, non-Hispanic/Latino; 3% Two or more races, non-Hispanic/Latino; 3% Race/ethnicity unknown; 0.8% international; 3% transferred in. *Retention:* 42% of full-time freshmen returned.
Faculty *Student/faculty ratio:* 26:1.
Academics *Calendar:* semesters. *Degrees:* certificates, associate, and bachelor's. *Special study options:* academic remediation for entering students, accelerated degree program, adult/continuing education programs, advanced placement credit, distance learning, double majors, freshman honors college, honors programs, independent study, internships, part-time degree program, services for LD students, student-designed majors, study abroad, summer session for credit. *ROTC:* Army (c), Air Force (c).
Library Paul Blair Memorial Library. Weekly public service hours: 46.
Student Life *Campus security:* 24-hour emergency response devices, student patrols, late-night transport/escort service.
Standardized Tests *Required for some:* SAT or ACT (for admission). *Recommended:* SAT or ACT (for admission).
Financial Aid Of all full-time matriculated undergraduates who enrolled in 2019, 129 applied for aid, 113 were judged to have need, 8 had their need fully met. In 2019, 9. *Average percent of need met:* 59. *Average financial aid package:* $7965. *Average need-based loan:* $3794. *Average need-based gift aid:* $5430. *Average non-need-based aid:* $878.
Applying *Options:* electronic application, deferred entrance. *Application fee:* $40. *Required:* high school transcript.
Freshman Application Contact Office of Admissions, Kent State University at East Liverpool, 400 East 4th Street, East Liverpool, OH 43920-3497. *Phone:* 330-385-3805. *Website:* http://www.eliv.kent.edu/.

Kent State University at Salem
Salem, Ohio

- **State-supported** primarily 2-year, founded 1966, part of Kent State University System
- **Rural** 100-acre campus with easy access to Youngstown
- **Coed**

Undergraduates 1,017 full-time, 680 part-time. Students come from 7 states and territories; 2% are from out of state; 4% Black or African American, non-Hispanic/Latino; 2% Hispanic/Latino; 1% Asian, non-Hispanic/Latino; 0.3% American Indian or Alaska Native, non-Hispanic/Latino; 3% Two or more races, non-Hispanic/Latino; 2% Race/ethnicity unknown; 0.9% international; 4% transferred in. *Retention:* 58% of full-time freshmen returned.
Faculty *Student/faculty ratio:* 21:1.
Academics *Calendar:* semesters. *Degrees:* certificates, associate, and bachelor's (also offers some upper-level and graduate courses). *Special study options:* academic remediation for entering students, accelerated degree program, adult/continuing education programs, advanced placement credit, cooperative education, distance learning, double majors, freshman honors college, honors programs, independent study, part-time degree program, services for LD students, student-designed majors, study abroad, summer session for credit. *ROTC:* Army (c), Air Force (c).
Library Kent State Salem Library. *Books:* 23,500 (physical); *Serial titles:* 4,500 (physical).
Student Life *Campus security:* 24-hour emergency response devices, late-night transport/escort service.
Standardized Tests *Required for some:* SAT or ACT (for admission). *Recommended:* SAT or ACT (for admission).
Financial Aid Of all full-time matriculated undergraduates who enrolled in 2019, 543 applied for aid, 420 were judged to have need, 34 had their need fully met. 18 Federal Work-Study jobs (averaging $2425). In 2019, 73. *Average percent of need met:* 60. *Average financial aid package:* $7523. *Average need-based loan:* $3684. *Average need-based gift aid:* $4803. *Average non-need-based aid:* $887.
Applying *Options:* electronic application, deferred entrance. *Application fee:* $40. *Required:* high school transcript. *Required for some:* essay or personal statement.
Freshman Application Contact Office of Admissions, Kent State University at Salem, 2491 State Route 45 South, Salem, OH 44460-9412. *Phone:* 330-332-0361. *Website:* http://www.salem.kent.edu/.

Kent State University at Trumbull
Warren, Ohio

- **State-supported** primarily 2-year, founded 1954, part of Kent State University System
- **Suburban** 438-acre campus with easy access to Akron, Youngstown
- **Coed**

Undergraduates 1,476 full-time, 801 part-time. Students come from 6 states and territories; 3% are from out of state; 8% Black or African American, non-Hispanic/Latino; 3% Hispanic/Latino; 0.9% Asian, non-Hispanic/Latino; 0.1% Native Hawaiian or other Pacific Islander, non-Hispanic/Latino; 0.2% American Indian or Alaska Native, non-Hispanic/Latino; 3% Two or more races, non-Hispanic/Latino; 3% Race/ethnicity unknown; 0.4% international; 5% transferred in. *Retention:* 60% of full-time freshmen returned.
Faculty *Student/faculty ratio:* 25:1.
Academics *Calendar:* semesters. *Degrees:* associate and bachelor's (also offers some upper-level and graduate courses). *Special study options:* academic remediation for entering students, adult/continuing education programs, advanced placement credit, distance learning, double majors, freshman honors college, honors programs, independent study, internships, part-time degree program, services for LD students, student-designed majors, summer session for credit. *ROTC:* Army (c), Air Force (c).
Library Gelbke Library at Kent State Trumbull. *Books:* 40,000 (physical), 100,000 (digital/electronic); *Serial titles:* 40 (physical); *Databases:* 459. Weekly public service hours: 56.
Student Life *Campus security:* 24-hour emergency response devices, late-night transport/escort service, patrols by trained security personnel during hours of operation.
Standardized Tests *Recommended:* SAT or ACT (for admission).
Financial Aid Of all full-time matriculated undergraduates who enrolled in 2019, 606 applied for aid, 516 were judged to have need, 40 had their need fully met. 20 Federal Work-Study jobs (averaging $2989). In 2019, 54. *Average percent of need met:* 60. *Average financial aid package:* $8081. *Average need-based loan:* $3706. *Average need-based gift aid:* $5469. *Average non-need-based aid:* $2215.
Applying *Options:* electronic application, deferred entrance. *Application fee:* $40. *Required:* high school transcript.
Freshman Application Contact Office of Enrollment Management, Kent State University at Trumbull, 4314 Mahoning Avenue, NW, Warren, OH 44483-1998. *Phone:* 330-675-8860. *E-mail:* trumbullinfo@kent.edu. *Website:* http://www.trumbull.kent.edu/.

Kent State University at Tuscarawas
New Philadelphia, Ohio

- **State-supported** primarily 2-year, founded 1962, part of Kent State University System
- **Small-town** 180-acre campus with easy access to Akron, Canton
- **Coed,** 2,168 undergraduate students, 63% full-time, 58% women, 42% men

Undergraduates 1,360 full-time, 808 part-time. Students come from 8 states and territories; 3 other countries; 2% are from out of state; 4% Black or African American, non-Hispanic/Latino; 2% Hispanic/Latino; 0.7% Asian, non-Hispanic/Latino; 0.2% American Indian or Alaska Native, non-Hispanic/Latino; 3% Two or more races, non-Hispanic/Latino; 3% Race/ethnicity unknown; 0.9% international; 4% transferred in. *Retention:* 64% of full-time freshmen returned.

Freshmen *Admission:* 459 applied, 459 admitted, 305 enrolled. *Average high school GPA:* 3.1.
Faculty *Total:* 126, 40% full-time. *Student/faculty ratio:* 22:1.
Majors Accounting technology and bookkeeping; administrative assistant and secretarial science; agribusiness; business administration and management; business/commerce; CAD/CADD drafting/design technology; computer programming (specific applications); criminal justice/safety; early childhood education; education related; electrical and electronic engineering technologies related; engineering technology; English; general studies; industrial technology; liberal arts and sciences and humanities related; mechanical engineering/mechanical technology; psychology; registered nursing/registered nurse; speech communication and rhetoric; veterinary/animal health technology.
Academics *Calendar:* semesters. *Degrees:* certificates, diplomas, associate, and bachelor's (also offers some upper-level and graduate courses). *Special study options:* academic remediation for entering students, accelerated degree program, adult/continuing education programs, advanced placement credit, distance learning, double majors, freshman honors college, honors programs, independent study, internships, part-time degree program, services for LD students, student-designed majors, study abroad, summer session for credit. *ROTC:* Army (c), Air Force (c).
Library Kent State Tuscarawas Library. *Books:* 52,500 (physical), 12 (digital/electronic); *Serial titles:* 540 (physical).
Student Life *Housing:* college housing not available. *Activities and Organizations:* choral group, Student Nurses Association, Technology Club, Vet Tech Student Chapter, Realms of Roleplay, Vision. *Campus security:* 24-hour emergency response devices.
Athletics Member USCAA. *Intercollegiate sports:* baseball M, basketball M/W, cross-country running M/W, golf M/W, softball W, track and field M/W, volleyball W, wrestling M.
Standardized Tests *Recommended:* SAT or ACT (for admission).
Financial Aid Of all full-time matriculated undergraduates who enrolled in 2019, 661 applied for aid, 529 were judged to have need, 66 had their need fully met. 21 Federal Work-Study jobs (averaging $2804). In 2019, 96 non-need-based awards were made. *Average percent of need met:* 64%. *Average financial aid package:* $7265. *Average need-based loan:* $3539. *Average need-based gift aid:* $4692. *Average non-need-based aid:* $1267.
Applying *Options:* electronic application, deferred entrance. *Application fee:* $40. *Required:* high school transcript. *Application deadlines:* 8/15 (freshmen), 8/15 (transfers). *Notification:* continuous (freshmen), continuous (transfers).
Freshman Application Contact Office of Admissions, Kent State University at Tuscarawas, 330 University Drive NE, New Philadelphia, OH 44663-9403. *Phone:* 330-339-3391. *E-mail:* infotusc@kent.edu.
Website: http://www.tusc.kent.edu/.

Lakeland Community College
Kirtland, Ohio

- **State and locally supported** 2-year, founded 1967, part of Ohio Department of Higher Education
- **Suburban** 380-acre campus with easy access to Cleveland
- **Endowment** $35,367
- **Coed,** 6,524 undergraduate students, 28% full-time, 60% women, 40% men

Undergraduates 1,847 full-time, 4,677 part-time. Students come from 7 states and territories; 1 other country; 15% Black or African American, non-Hispanic/Latino; 5% Hispanic/Latino; 1% Asian, non-Hispanic/Latino; 0.1% Native Hawaiian or other Pacific Islander, non-Hispanic/Latino; 0.3% American Indian or Alaska Native, non-Hispanic/Latino; 3% Two or more races, non-Hispanic/Latino; 3% Race/ethnicity unknown; 0.2% international; 4% transferred in.
Freshmen *Admission:* 861 enrolled.
Faculty *Total:* 405, 25% full-time. *Student/faculty ratio:* 17:1.
Majors Accounting; administrative assistant and secretarial science; biotechnology; business administration and management; child-care provision; civil engineering technology; clinical/medical laboratory technology; commercial and advertising art; computer engineering technology; computer programming (specific applications); computer systems analysis; computer systems networking and telecommunications; computer technology/computer systems technology; corrections; criminal justice/police science; dental hygiene; electrical, electronic and communications engineering technology; energy management and systems technology; fire prevention and safety technology; health professions related; homeland security, law enforcement, firefighting and protective services related; hospitality administration; instrumentation technology; legal assistant/paralegal; liberal arts and sciences/liberal studies; management information systems; marketing/marketing management; mechanical engineering/mechanical technology; medical radiologic technology; nuclear medical technology; ophthalmic technology; quality control technology; registered nursing/registered nurse; respiratory care therapy; restaurant, culinary, and catering management; sign language interpretation and translation; social work; surgical technology; tourism and travel services management.
Academics *Calendar:* semesters. *Degree:* certificates and associate. *Special study options:* academic remediation for entering students, adult/continuing education programs, advanced placement credit, cooperative education, distance learning, English as a second language, external degree program, independent study, internships, off-campus study, part-time degree program, services for LD students, study abroad, summer session for credit.
Library Lakeland Community College Library. Students can reserve study rooms.
Student Life *Housing:* college housing not available. *Activities and Organizations:* drama/theater group, student-run newspaper, radio station, choral group, Campus Activities Board, Lakeland Student Government, Lakeland Signers, Gamer's Guild. *Campus security:* 24-hour emergency response devices and patrols, student patrols, late-night transport/escort service. *Student services:* health clinic, personal/psychological counseling, women's center, veterans affairs office.
Athletics Member NJCAA. *Intercollegiate sports:* baseball M(s), basketball M(s)/W(s), soccer M(s), softball W(s), volleyball W(s).
Standardized Tests *Required:* ACT Compass (for admission).
Costs (2020–21) *Tuition:* area resident $2932 full-time, $113 per credit hour part-time; state resident $3667 full-time, $141 per credit hour part-time; nonresident $8295 full-time, $319 per credit hour part-time. Full-time tuition and fees vary according to course load. Part-time tuition and fees vary according to course load. *Required fees:* $550 full-time, $34 per term part-time, $34 per term part-time. *Payment plans:* installment, deferred payment. *Waivers:* senior citizens and employees or children of employees.
Financial Aid Of all full-time matriculated undergraduates who enrolled in 2015, 3,430 applied for aid, 2,959 were judged to have need, 469 had their need fully met. 63 Federal Work-Study jobs (averaging $3489). *Average percent of need met:* 56%. *Average financial aid package:* $7024. *Average need-based loan:* $3232. *Average need-based gift aid:* $5250.
Applying *Options:* electronic application, early admission, deferred entrance. *Application fee:* $15. *Required:* high school transcript. *Application deadlines:* 9/1 (freshmen), 9/1 (transfers). *Notification:* continuous until 9/1 (freshmen), continuous until 9/1 (transfers).
Freshman Application Contact Lakeland Community College, 7700 Clocktower Drive, Kirtland, OH 44094-5198. *Phone:* 440-525-7230. *Toll-free phone:* 800-589-8520.
Website: http://www.lakelandcc.edu/.

Lorain County Community College
Elyria, Ohio

Freshman Application Contact Lorain County Community College, 1005 Abbe Road, North, Elyria, OH 44035. *Phone:* 440-366-7622. *Toll-free phone:* 800-995-5222 Ext. 4032. *Website:* http://www.lorainccc.edu/.

Marion Technical College
Marion, Ohio

Freshman Application Contact Mr. Joel Liles, Dean of Enrollment Services, Marion Technical College, 1467 Mount Vernon Avenue, Marion, OH 43302. *Phone:* 740-389-4636 Ext. 249. *Fax:* 740-389-6136. *E-mail:* enroll@mtc.edu. *Website:* http://www.mtc.edu/.

The Modern College of Design
Kettering, Ohio

Freshman Application Contact Mrs. Mariesa Brewster, Director of Admissions, The Modern College of Design, 1725 E. David Road, Kettering, OH 45440. *Phone:* 937-294-0592. *Toll-free phone:* 877-300-9866. *Fax:* 937-294-5869. *E-mail:* mariesa.brewster@themodern.edu. *Website:* http://www.themoderncollegeofdesign.com/.

North Central State College
Mansfield, Ohio

Freshman Application Contact Ms. Nikia L. Fletcher, Director of Admissions, North Central State College, 2441 Kenwood Circle, PO Box 698, Mansfield, OH 44901-0698. *Phone:* 419-755-4813. *Toll-free phone:* 888-755-4899. *E-mail:* nfletcher@ncstatecollege.edu. *Website:* http://www.ncstatecollege.edu/.

Northwest State Community College

Archbold, Ohio

- **State-supported** 2-year, founded 1968, part of Ohio Board of Regents
- **Rural** 80-acre campus with easy access to Toledo
- **Coed,** 2,857 undergraduate students, 19% full-time, 44% women, 56% men

Undergraduates 541 full-time, 2,316 part-time. Students come from 5 states and territories; 10 other countries; 3% are from out of state; 2% Black or African American, non-Hispanic/Latino; 12% Hispanic/Latino; 0.3% Asian, non-Hispanic/Latino; 0.6% American Indian or Alaska Native, non-Hispanic/Latino; 1% Two or more races, non-Hispanic/Latino; 6% Race/ethnicity unknown; 2% transferred in.
Freshmen *Admission:* 1,367 applied, 1,367 admitted, 248 enrolled. *Average high school GPA:* 3.1.
Faculty *Total:* 86, 43% full-time, 59% with terminal degrees. *Student/faculty ratio:* 24:1.
Majors Accounting; accounting related; administrative assistant and secretarial science; agribusiness; business administration and management; business/commerce; CAD/CADD drafting/design technology; child-care and support services management; computer and information systems security; computer engineering; computer engineering technology; computer programming; construction engineering technology; corrections and criminal justice related; criminal justice/police science; criminal justice/safety; data entry/microcomputer applications; design and visual communications; electrical, electronic and communications engineering technology; energy management and systems technology; engineering related; engineering technologies and engineering related; entrepreneurship; history; human development and family studies related; human resources management; industrial electronics technology; industrial mechanics and maintenance technology; industrial production technologies related; international business/trade/commerce; kindergarten/preschool education; legal administrative assistant/secretary; legal assistant/paralegal; liberal arts and sciences/liberal studies; logistics, materials, and supply chain management; machine tool technology; marketing/marketing management; mechanical engineering; mechanical engineering/mechanical technology; medical administrative assistant and medical secretary; medical/clinical assistant; network and system administration; nonprofit management; office management; plastics and polymer engineering technology; precision metal working related; registered nursing/registered nurse; social work; soil science and agronomy; teacher assistant/aide; web page, digital/multimedia and information resources design.
Academics *Calendar:* semesters. *Degree:* certificates and associate. *Special study options:* academic remediation for entering students, adult/continuing education programs, advanced placement credit, cooperative education, distance learning, double majors, external degree program, independent study, internships, off-campus study, part-time degree program, services for LD students, student-designed majors, summer session for credit.
Library Northwest State Community College Library plus 1 other. *Books:* 11,150 (physical), 74,200 (digital/electronic); *Serial titles:* 8 (physical); *Databases:* 805. Weekly public service hours: 50; students can reserve study rooms.
Student Life *Housing:* college housing not available. *Activities and Organizations:* drama/theater group, Student Body Organziation (SBO), Students for Community Outreach and Awareness (SCOA), Phi Theta Kappa (PTK), Kappa Beta Delta (KBD), ev/Motorsports. *Campus security:* 24-hour emergency response devices, security patrols. *Student services:* personal/psychological counseling, veterans affairs office.
Athletics *Intramural sports:* basketball M/W, bowling M/W, soccer M/W, table tennis M/W, volleyball M/W.
Costs (2020–21) *Tuition:* state resident $4256 full-time, $177 per semester hour part-time; nonresident $8368 full-time, $349 per semester hour part-time. Full-time tuition and fees vary according to reciprocity agreements. Part-time tuition and fees vary according to reciprocity agreements. *Required fees:* $82 full-time, $41 per term part-time. *Payment plan:* installment. *Waivers:* employees or children of employees.
Financial Aid Of all full-time matriculated undergraduates who enrolled in 2018, 43 Federal Work-Study jobs (averaging $1077).
Applying *Options:* electronic application, early admission, deferred entrance. *Required:* high school transcript. *Required for some:* minimum 2.5 GPA, interview, NLN PAX with a relative score greater than or equal to 50 in each of the 3 sections for nursing. *Application deadlines:* rolling (freshmen), rolling (out-of-state freshmen), rolling (transfers). *Notification:* continuous (freshmen), continuous (transfers).
Freshman Application Contact Mrs. Cassie Rickenberg, Director of Advising Center, Northwest State Community College, 22600 State Route 34, Archbold, OH 43502. *Phone:* 419-267-1334. *Toll-free phone:* 855-267-5511. *Fax:* 419-267-3688. *E-mail:* crickenberg@northweststate.edu. *Website:* http://www.northweststate.edu/.

Ohio Business College

Sandusky, Ohio

- **Proprietary** 2-year, founded 1982
- **Small-town** 1-acre campus with easy access to Cleveland, Toledo
- **Coed**

Undergraduates 170 full-time, 95 part-time. Students come from 1 other state; 22% Black or African American, non-Hispanic/Latino; 5% Hispanic/Latino; 0.4% Asian, non-Hispanic/Latino; 0.4% American Indian or Alaska Native, non-Hispanic/Latino; 0.4% Two or more races, non-Hispanic/Latino; 2% Race/ethnicity unknown. *Retention:* 73% of full-time freshmen returned.
Faculty *Student/faculty ratio:* 8:1.
Academics *Calendar:* quarters. *Degree:* diplomas and associate. *Special study options:* academic remediation for entering students, independent study, internships, part-time degree program, summer session for credit.
Library Main Library plus 1 other.
Applying *Required:* high school transcript.
Freshman Application Contact Ohio Business College, 5202 Timber Commons Drive, Sandusky, OH 44870. *Phone:* 419-627-8345. *Toll-free phone:* 888-627-8345. *Website:* http://www.ohiobusinesscollege.edu/.

Ohio Business College

Sheffield Village, Ohio

- **Proprietary** 2-year, founded 1903, part of Tri State Educational Systems
- **Suburban** campus with easy access to Cleveland
- **Coed**

Undergraduates *Retention:* 54% of full-time freshmen returned.
Faculty *Student/faculty ratio:* 8:1.
Academics *Calendar:* quarters. *Degree:* diplomas and associate. *Special study options:* academic remediation for entering students, accelerated degree program, adult/continuing education programs, advanced placement credit, double majors, external degree program, independent study, internships, part-time degree program, summer session for credit.
Library Ohio Business College Library.
Applying *Options:* electronic application. *Application fee:* $25. *Required:* high school transcript, interview.
Freshman Application Contact Ohio Business College, 5095 Waterford Drive, Sheffield Village, OH 44035. *Toll-free phone:* 888-514-3126. *Website:* http://www.ohiobusinesscollege.edu/.

The Ohio State University Agricultural Technical Institute

Wooster, Ohio

Freshman Application Contact Ms. Julia Morris, Admissions Counselor, The Ohio State University Agricultural Technical Institute, 1328 Dover Road, Wooster, OH 44691. *Phone:* 330-287-1327. *Toll-free phone:* 800-647-8283 Ext. 1327. *Fax:* 330-287-1333. *E-mail:* morris.878@osu.edu. *Website:* http://www.ati.osu.edu/.

Ohio Technical College

Cleveland, Ohio

- **Proprietary** 2-year, founded 1969
- **Urban** 18-acre campus
- **Coed,** 944 undergraduate students, 100% full-time, 10% women, 90% men
- 100% of applicants were admitted

Undergraduates 944 full-time. Students come from 25 states and territories; 57% are from out of state; 21% Black or African American, non-Hispanic/Latino; 7% Hispanic/Latino; 0.3% Asian, non-Hispanic/Latino; 0.2% Native Hawaiian or other Pacific Islander, non-Hispanic/Latino; 0.7% American Indian or Alaska Native, non-Hispanic/Latino; 4% Two or more races, non-Hispanic/Latino; 0.3% Race/ethnicity unknown; 6% transferred in. *Retention:* 81% of full-time freshmen returned.
Freshmen *Admission:* 509 applied, 509 admitted, 509 enrolled.
Faculty *Total:* 54, 81% full-time. *Student/faculty ratio:* 16:1.
Majors Autobody/collision and repair technology; automobile/automotive mechanics technology; diesel mechanics technology; high performance and custom engine technology; mechanic and repair technologies related; motorcycle maintenance and repair technology; vehicle maintenance and repair technologies; welding technology.
Academics *Degree:* certificates, diplomas, and associate.
Library Ohio Technical College Library Resource Center. *Books:* 3,859 (physical), 21 (digital/electronic); *Databases:* 6. Weekly public service hours: 40.

Student Life *Housing Options:* Campus housing is university owned. *Campus security:* late-night transport/escort service. *Student services:* personal/psychological counseling.
Costs (2020–21) *One-time required fee:* $50. *Tuition:* $28,500 full-time. Full-time tuition and fees vary according to degree level and program. No tuition increase for student's term of enrollment. *Payment plans:* tuition prepayment, installment. *Waivers:* employees or children of employees.
Financial Aid Of all full-time matriculated undergraduates who enrolled in 2018, 769 applied for aid, 726 were judged to have need. *Average percent of need met:* 40%. *Average financial aid package:* $6070. *Average need-based loan:* $2715. *Average need-based gift aid:* $3354.
Applying *Options:* electronic application. *Required:* high school transcript, interview. *Application deadlines:* rolling (freshmen), rolling (out-of-state freshmen).
Freshman Application Contact Ohio Technical College, 1374 East 51st Street, Cleveland, OH 44103. *Phone:* 216-881-1700. *Toll-free phone:* 800-322-7000.
Website: http://www.ohiotech.edu/.

Ohio Valley College of Technology
East Liverpool, Ohio

Freshman Application Contact Mr. Scott S. Rogers, Director, Ohio Valley College of Technology, 15258 State Route 170, East Liverpool, OH 43920. *Phone:* 330-385-1070. *Website:* http://www.ovct.edu/.

Owens Community College
Toledo, Ohio

- **State-supported** 2-year, founded 1966
- **Suburban** 420-acre campus with easy access to Detroit
- **Endowment** $1.7 million
- **Coed**

Undergraduates 4,257 full-time, 8,315 part-time. Students come from 25 states and territories; 6 other countries; 3% are from out of state; 15% Black or African American, non-Hispanic/Latino; 7% Hispanic/Latino; 1% Asian, non-Hispanic/Latino; 0.4% American Indian or Alaska Native, non-Hispanic/Latino; 3% Two or more races, non-Hispanic/Latino; 2% Race/ethnicity unknown; 1% international; 0.7% transferred in.
Faculty *Student/faculty ratio:* 16:1.
Academics *Calendar:* semesters. *Degree:* certificates and associate. *Special study options:* academic remediation for entering students, accelerated degree program, adult/continuing education programs, advanced placement credit, cooperative education, distance learning, double majors, English as a second language, honors programs, independent study, internships, part-time degree program, services for LD students, study abroad, summer session for credit.
Library Owens Community College Library plus 1 other.
Student Life *Campus security:* 24-hour emergency response devices and patrols, student patrols, classroom doors lock from inside, campus alert system.
Athletics Member NJCAA.
Applying *Options:* electronic application, early admission, deferred entrance. *Application fee:* $20. *Required for some:* minimum 2.0 GPA, interview.
Freshman Application Contact Ms. Meghan L. Schmidbauer, Director, Admissions, Owens Community College, PO Box 10000, Toledo, OH 43699. *Phone:* 567-661-2155. *Toll-free phone:* 800-GO-OWENS. *Fax:* 567-661-7734. *E-mail:* meghan_schmidbauer@owens.edu. *Website:* http://www.owens.edu/.

Professional Skills Institute
Maumee, Ohio

Director of Admissions Ms. Hope Finch, Director of Marketing, Professional Skills Institute, 1505 Holland Road, Maumee, OH 43537. *Phone:* 419-531-9610. *Website:* http://www.proskills.edu/.

Remington College–Cleveland Campus
Cleveland, Ohio

Director of Admissions Director of Recruitment, Remington College–Cleveland Campus, 14445 Broadway Avenue, Cleveland, OH 44125. *Phone:* 216-475-7520. *Toll-free phone:* 800-323-8122. *Fax:* 216-475-6055. *Website:* http://www.remingtoncollege.edu/.

Rosedale Bible College
Irwin, Ohio

Freshman Application Contact Rosedale Bible College, 2270 Rosedale Road, Irwin, OH 43029-9501. *Phone:* 740-857-1311. *Website:* http://www.rosedale.edu/.

Ross College
Canton, Ohio

Freshman Application Contact Ross College, 4300 Munson Street NW, Canton, OH 44718. *Phone:* 330-494-1214. *Toll-free phone:* 866-815-5578. *Website:* http://www.rosseducation.edu/.

Ross College
Sylvania, Ohio

Admissions Office Contact Ross College, 5834 Monroe Street, Suite F-J, Sylvania, OH 43560. *Toll-free phone:* 866-815-5578. *Website:* http://www.rosseducation.edu/.

Sinclair Community College
Dayton, Ohio

Freshman Application Contact Ms. Sara Smith, Director and Systems Manager, Outreach Services, Sinclair Community College, 444 West Third Street, Dayton, OH 45402-1460. *Phone:* 937-512-3060. *Toll-free phone:* 800-315-3000. *Fax:* 937-512-2393. *E-mail:* ssmith@sinclair.edu. *Website:* http://www.sinclair.edu/.

Southern State Community College
Hillsboro, Ohio

Freshman Application Contact Ms. Wendy Johnson, Director of Admissions, Southern State Community College, Hillsboro, OH 45133. *Phone:* 937-393-3431 Ext. 2720. *Toll-free phone:* 800-628-7722. *Fax:* 937-393-6682. *E-mail:* wjohnson@sscc.edu. *Website:* http://www.sscc.edu/.

Stark State College
North Canton, Ohio

- **State-related** 2-year, founded 1960, part of University System of Ohio
- **Suburban** 100-acre campus with easy access to Cleveland
- **Endowment** $6.9 million
- **Coed,** 11,833 undergraduate students, 26% full-time, 59% women, 41% men

Undergraduates 3,053 full-time, 8,780 part-time. Students come from 27 states and territories; 1 other country; 1% are from out of state; 17% Black or African American, non-Hispanic/Latino; 2% Hispanic/Latino; 3% Asian, non-Hispanic/Latino; 0.2% Native Hawaiian or other Pacific Islander, non-Hispanic/Latino; 0.4% American Indian or Alaska Native, non-Hispanic/Latino; 3% Two or more races, non-Hispanic/Latino; 2% Race/ethnicity unknown; 0.1% international; 8% transferred in.
Freshmen *Admission:* 8,328 applied, 8,321 admitted, 1,649 enrolled. *Average high school GPA:* 2.8.
Faculty *Total:* 518, 34% full-time. *Student/faculty ratio:* 20:1.
Majors Accounting; accounting and finance; administrative assistant and secretarial science; biomedical technology; business administration and management; civil engineering technology; clinical/medical laboratory technology; computer and information sciences; computer programming (specific applications); computer systems networking and telecommunications; court reporting; dental hygiene; finance; health information/medical records administration; human services; industrial technology; legal administrative assistant/secretary; marketing/marketing management; mechanical engineering/mechanical technology; medical/clinical assistant; occupational therapy; operations management; physical therapy; registered nursing/registered nurse; respiratory care therapy; substance abuse/addiction counseling; surgical technology; web page, digital/multimedia and information resources design.
Academics *Calendar:* semesters. *Degree:* certificates and associate. *Special study options:* academic remediation for entering students, adult/continuing education programs, cooperative education, distance learning, double majors, external degree program, independent study, internships, off-campus study, part-time degree program, services for LD students, student-designed majors, summer session for credit.
Library Learning Resource Center plus 1 other.
Student Life *Housing:* college housing not available. *Activities and Organizations:* drama/theater group, student-run newspaper, Phi Theta Kappa,

Business Student Club, Institute of Management Accountants, Stark State College Association of Medical Assistants, Student Health Information Management Association. *Campus security:* 24-hour emergency response devices and patrols, student patrols, late-night transport/escort service, patrols by trained security personnel during hours of operation. *Student services:* personal/psychological counseling, veterans affairs office.
Financial Aid Of all full-time matriculated undergraduates who enrolled in 2014, 1,939 applied for aid, 1,697 were judged to have need, 6 had their need fully met. 74 Federal Work-Study jobs (averaging $2306). *Average need-based loan:* $2537. *Average need-based gift aid:* $4317.
Applying *Options:* electronic application. *Required:* high school transcript. *Application deadlines:* rolling (freshmen), rolling (out-of-state freshmen), rolling (transfers). *Notification:* continuous (freshmen), continuous (out-of-state freshmen), continuous (transfers).
Freshman Application Contact J. P. Cooney, Executive Director to Recruitment, Admissions and Marketing, Stark State College, 6200 Frank Road NE, Canton, OH 44720. *Phone:* 330-494-6170 Ext. 4401. *Toll-free phone:* 800-797-8275. *E-mail:* info@starkstate.edu.
Website: http://www.starkstate.edu/.

Stautzenberger College - Brecksville
Brecksville, Ohio

Admissions Office Contact Stautzenberger College - Brecksville, 8001 Katherine Boulevard, Brecksville, OH 44141. *Toll-free phone:* 800-437-2997. *Website:* http://www.sctoday.edu/.

Stautzenberger College - Maumee
Maumee, Ohio

Director of Admissions Ms. Karen Fitzgerald, Director of Admissions and Marketing, Stautzenberger College - Maumee, 1796 Indian Wood Circle, Maumee, OH 43537. *Phone:* 419-866-0261. *Toll-free phone:* 800-552-5099. *Fax:* 419-867-9821. *E-mail:* klfitzgerald@stautzenberger.com. *Website:* http://www.sctoday.edu/maumee/.

Terra State Community College
Fremont, Ohio

Freshman Application Contact Mr. Heath Martin, Director of Admissions and Enrollment Services, Terra State Community College, 2830 Napoleon Road, Fremont, OH 43420. *Phone:* 419-559-2154. *Toll-free phone:* 866-AT-TERRA. *Fax:* 419-559-2352. *Website:* http://www.terra.edu/.

The University of Akron Wayne College
Orrville, Ohio

- **State-supported** primarily 2-year, founded 1972, part of The University of Akron
- **Rural** 157-acre campus
- **Coed**

Undergraduates 1,109 full-time, 1,244 part-time. Students come from 2 states and territories; 2 other countries; 3% Black or African American, non-Hispanic/Latino; 1% Hispanic/Latino; 0.6% Asian, non-Hispanic/Latino; 0.1% Native Hawaiian or other Pacific Islander, non-Hispanic/Latino; 0.3% American Indian or Alaska Native, non-Hispanic/Latino; 2% Two or more races, non-Hispanic/Latino; 4% Race/ethnicity unknown; 2% transferred in. *Retention:* 60% of full-time freshmen returned.
Faculty *Student/faculty ratio:* 20:1.
Academics *Calendar:* semesters. *Degrees:* certificates, associate, and bachelor's. *Special study options:* academic remediation for entering students, adult/continuing education programs, advanced placement credit, cooperative education, distance learning, double majors, honors programs, independent study, internships, off-campus study, part-time degree program, services for LD students, summer session for credit. *ROTC:* Army (c), Air Force (c).
Library Wayne College Library.
Student Life *Campus security:* 24-hour emergency response devices, late-night transport/escort service.
Standardized Tests *Required for some:* SAT or ACT (for admission), ACT Compass. *Recommended:* SAT or ACT (for admission), ACT Compass.
Financial Aid Of all full-time matriculated undergraduates who enrolled in 2018, 8 Federal Work-Study jobs (averaging $2200).
Applying *Options:* electronic application, early admission, deferred entrance. *Application fee:* $50. *Required for some:* high school transcript.
Freshman Application Contact Ms. Alicia Broadus, Student Services Counselor, The University of Akron Wayne College, Orrville, OH 44667. *Phone:* 800-221-8308 Ext. 8901. *Toll-free phone:* 800-221-8308. *Fax:* 330-684-8989. *E-mail:* wayneadmissions@uakron.edu. *Website:* http://www.wayne.uakron.edu/.

University of Cincinnati Blue Ash College
Cincinnati, Ohio

Freshman Application Contact University of Cincinnati Blue Ash College, 9555 Plainfield Road, Cincinnati, OH 45236-1007. *Phone:* 513-745-5700. *Website:* http://www.ucblueash.edu/.

University of Cincinnati Clermont College
Batavia, Ohio

- **State-supported** primarily 2-year, founded 1972, part of University of Cincinnati System
- **Rural** 91-acre campus with easy access to Cincinnati
- **Coed**

Undergraduates 23,121 full-time, 3,821 part-time. 17% are from out of state; 7% Black or African American, non-Hispanic/Latino; 3% Hispanic/Latino; 4% Asian, non-Hispanic/Latino; 0.1% American Indian or Alaska Native, non-Hispanic/Latino; 4% Two or more races, non-Hispanic/Latino; 3% Race/ethnicity unknown; 4% international; 5% transferred in; 24% live on campus. *Retention:* 86% of full-time freshmen returned.
Faculty *Student/faculty ratio:* 16:1.
Academics *Calendar:* semesters. *Degrees:* certificates, associate, bachelor's, and postbachelor's certificates. *Special study options:* academic remediation for entering students, adult/continuing education programs, advanced placement credit, cooperative education, distance learning, double majors, external degree program, independent study, internships, off-campus study, part-time degree program, services for LD students, student-designed majors, study abroad, summer session for credit. *ROTC:* Army (b), Air Force (b).
Library UC Clermont College Library. Students can reserve study rooms.
Student Life *Campus security:* 24-hour emergency response devices and patrols.
Athletics Member USCAA.
Costs (2019–20) *Tuition:* state resident $4898 full-time, $235 per credit hour part-time; nonresident $12,130 full-time, $536 per credit hour part-time. Full-time tuition and fees vary according to course level, degree level, program, and reciprocity agreements. Part-time tuition and fees vary according to course level, degree level, program, and reciprocity agreements. No tuition increase for student's term of enrollment. *Required fees:* $368 full-time.
Financial Aid Of all full-time matriculated undergraduates who enrolled in 2018, 1,129 applied for aid, 941 were judged to have need, 18 had their need fully met. 64 Federal Work-Study jobs (averaging $3002). In 2018, 93. *Average percent of need met:* 35. *Average financial aid package:* $6273. *Average need-based loan:* $3498. *Average need-based gift aid:* $4834. *Average non-need-based aid:* $1611.
Applying *Options:* electronic application, deferred entrance. *Application fee:* $50. *Required:* high school transcript.
Freshman Application Contact Mrs. Jamie Adkins, University Services Associate, University of Cincinnati Clermont College, 4200 Clermont College Drive, Batavia, OH 45103. *Phone:* 513-732-5294. *Toll-free phone:* 866-446-2822. *Fax:* 513-732-5303. *E-mail:* jamie.adkins@uc.edu. *Website:* http://www.ucclermont.edu/.

Valor Christian College
Canal Winchester, Ohio

Admissions Office Contact Valor Christian College, 4595 Gender Road, PO Box 800, Canal Winchester, OH 43110. *Website:* http://www.valorcollege.edu/.

Vet Tech Institute at Bradford School
Columbus, Ohio

Freshman Application Contact Admissions Office, Vet Tech Institute at Bradford School, 2469 Stelzer Road, Columbus, OH 43219. *Phone:* 800-678-7981. *Toll-free phone:* 800-678-7981. *Website:* http://columbus.vettechinstitute.edu/.

Washington State Community College
Marietta, Ohio

Freshman Application Contact Ms. Rebecca Peroni, Director of Admissions, Washington State Community College, 110 Colegate Drive, Marietta, OH

45750. *Phone:* 740-374-8716. *Fax:* 740-376-0257. *E-mail:* rperoni@wscc.edu. *Website:* http://www.wscc.edu/.

Zane State College
Zanesville, Ohio

- **State and locally supported** 2-year, founded 1969
- **Small-town** 170-acre campus with easy access to Columbus
- **Coed**

Undergraduates *Retention:* 65% of full-time freshmen returned.
Faculty *Student/faculty ratio:* 18:1.
Academics *Calendar:* quarters. *Degree:* certificates and associate. *Special study options:* academic remediation for entering students, adult/continuing education programs, cooperative education, honors programs, internships, off-campus study, part-time degree program, services for LD students, student-designed majors, summer session for credit.
Standardized Tests *Recommended:* SAT or ACT (for admission).
Financial Aid Of all full-time matriculated undergraduates who enrolled in 2018, 65 Federal Work-Study jobs (averaging $2010).
Applying *Options:* early admission. *Application fee:* $25. *Required:* high school transcript. *Required for some:* interview.
Director of Admissions Mr. Paul Young, Director of Admissions, Zane State College, 1555 Newark Road, Zanesville, OH 43701-2626. *Phone:* 740-454-2501 Ext. 1225. *Toll-free phone:* 800-686-8324. *E-mail:* pyoung@zanestate.edu. *Website:* http://www.zanestate.edu/.

OKLAHOMA

Carl Albert State College
Poteau, Oklahoma

- **State-supported** 2-year, founded 1934, part of Oklahoma State Regents for Higher Education
- **Small-town** 78-acre campus
- **Coed**

Undergraduates 1,320 full-time, 874 part-time. Students come from 9 states and territories; 3% Black or African American, non-Hispanic/Latino; 7% Hispanic/Latino; 0.3% Asian, non-Hispanic/Latino; 25% American Indian or Alaska Native, non-Hispanic/Latino; 6% Two or more races, non-Hispanic/Latino; 1% Race/ethnicity unknown; 1% international; 12% live on campus. *Retention:* 46% of full-time freshmen returned.
Faculty *Student/faculty ratio:* 21:1.
Academics *Calendar:* semesters. *Degree:* certificates and associate. *Special study options:* academic remediation for entering students, adult/continuing education programs, cooperative education, part-time degree program.
Library Joe E. White Library.
Student Life *Campus security:* security guards.
Athletics Member NJCAA.
Standardized Tests *Recommended:* SAT or ACT (for admission).
Financial Aid Of all full-time matriculated undergraduates who enrolled in 2018, 112 Federal Work-Study jobs (averaging $2100).
Applying *Required:* high school transcript.
Admissions Office Contact Carl Albert State College, 1507 South McKenna, Poteau, OK 74953-5208. *Website:* http://www.carlalbert.edu/.

Clary Sage College
Tulsa, Oklahoma

Freshman Application Contact Dr. Raye Mahlberg, Campus Director, Clary Sage College, 3131 South Sheridan, Tulsa, OK 74145. *Phone:* 918-298-8200 Ext. 1025. *E-mail:* rmahlberg@clarysagecollege.com. *Website:* http://www.clarysagecollege.com/.

College of the Muscogee Nation
Okmulgee, Oklahoma

Admissions Office Contact College of the Muscogee Nation, 2170 Raven Circle, Okmulgee, OK 74447-0917. *Website:* http://www.cmn.edu/.

Community Care College
Tulsa, Oklahoma

Freshman Application Contact Dr. Kevin Kirk, President, Community Care College, 4242 South Sheridan, Tulsa, OK 74145. *Phone:* 918-610-0027 Ext. 2003. *Fax:* 918-610-0029. *E-mail:* kkirk@communitycarecollege.edu. *Website:* http://www.communitycarecollege.edu/.

Connors State College
Warner, Oklahoma

Freshman Application Contact Ms. Sonya Baker, Registrar, Connors State College, Route 1 Box 1000, Warner, OK 74469-9700. *Phone:* 918-463-6233. *Website:* http://www.connorsstate.edu/.

Eastern Oklahoma State College
Wilburton, Oklahoma

- **State-supported** 2-year, founded 1908, part of Oklahoma State Regents for Higher Education
- **Rural** 4000-acre campus
- **Coed**

Academics *Calendar:* semesters. *Degree:* certificates and associate. *Special study options:* academic remediation for entering students, adult/continuing education programs, advanced placement credit, cooperative education, double majors, honors programs, internships, off-campus study, part-time degree program, summer session for credit.
Library Bill H. Hill Library.
Athletics Member NJCAA.
Financial Aid Of all full-time matriculated undergraduates who enrolled in 2018, 111 Federal Work-Study jobs (averaging $825). 125 state and other part-time jobs (averaging $721).
Applying *Options:* early admission, deferred entrance. *Application fee:* $10. *Required:* high school transcript.
Freshman Application Contact Ms. Leah McLaughlin, Director of Admissions, Eastern Oklahoma State College, 1301 West Main, Wilburton, OK 74578-4999. *Phone:* 918-465-1811. *Toll-free phone:* 855-534-3672. *Fax:* 918-465-2431. *E-mail:* lmiller@eosc.edu. *Website:* http://www.eosc.edu/.

Murray State College
Tishomingo, Oklahoma

Freshman Application Contact Murray State College, One Murray Campus, Tishomingo, OK 73460. *Phone:* 580-371-2371 Ext. 171. *Website:* http://www.mscok.edu/.

Northeastern Oklahoma Agricultural and Mechanical College
Miami, Oklahoma

Freshman Application Contact Amy Ishmael, Vice President for Enrollment Management, Northeastern Oklahoma Agricultural and Mechanical College, 200 I Street, NE, Miami, OK 74354-6434. *Phone:* 918-540-6212. *Toll-free phone:* 800-464-6636. *Fax:* 918-540-6946. *E-mail:* neoadmission@neo.edu. *Website:* http://www.neo.edu/.

Northern Oklahoma College
Tonkawa, Oklahoma

Freshman Application Contact Ms. Sheri Snyder, Director of College Relations, Northern Oklahoma College, 1220 East Grand Avenue, PO Box 310, Tonkawa, OK 74653-0310. *Phone:* 580-628-6290. *Website:* http://www.noc.edu/.

Oklahoma City Community College
Oklahoma City, Oklahoma

Freshman Application Contact Ms. Jillian C. Hibblen, Acting Director of Recruitment and Admissions, Oklahoma City Community College, 7777 South May Avenue, Oklahoma City, OK 73159. *Phone:* 405-682-7743. *Fax:* 405-682-7817. *E-mail:* jhibblen@occc.edu. *Website:* http://www.occc.edu/.

Oklahoma State University Institute of Technology

Okmulgee, Oklahoma

- **State-supported** primarily 2-year, founded 1946, part of Oklahoma State University
- **Small-town** 160-acre campus with easy access to Tulsa
- **Endowment** $7.8 million
- **Coed,** 2,309 undergraduate students, 63% full-time, 35% women, 65% men

Undergraduates 1,464 full-time, 845 part-time. Students come from 26 states and territories; 11 other countries; 9% are from out of state; 3% Black or African American, non-Hispanic/Latino; 7% Hispanic/Latino; 0.6% Asian, non-Hispanic/Latino; 12% American Indian or Alaska Native, non-Hispanic/Latino; 15% Two or more races, non-Hispanic/Latino; 5% Race/ethnicity unknown; 1% international; 9% transferred in; 26% live on campus. *Retention:* 59% of full-time freshmen returned.

Freshmen *Admission:* 2,518 applied, 734 admitted, 587 enrolled. *Average high school GPA:* 3.1. *Test scores:* ACT scores over 18: 52%; ACT scores over 24: 8%; ACT scores over 30: 1%.

Faculty *Total:* 135, 69% full-time, 7% with terminal degrees. *Student/faculty ratio:* 16:1.

Majors Automobile/automotive mechanics technology; business/commerce; computer and information systems security; construction trades; culinary arts related; diesel mechanics technology; education (multiple levels); electrical and power transmission installation; engineering technology; graphic design; health services/allied health/health sciences; heating, air conditioning, ventilation and refrigeration maintenance technology; industrial mechanics and maintenance technology; information technology; instrumentation technology; interdisciplinary studies; intermedia/multimedia; lineworker; mechanical engineering/mechanical technology; multi/interdisciplinary studies related; operations management; orthotics/prosthetics; petroleum technology; registered nursing/registered nurse.

Academics *Calendar:* trimesters. *Degrees:* associate and bachelor's. *Special study options:* academic remediation for entering students, adult/continuing education programs, advanced placement credit, distance learning, double majors, independent study, internships, part-time degree program, services for LD students, summer session for credit.

Library Oklahoma State University Institute of Technology Library. *Books:* 11,292 (physical), 152,731 (digital/electronic); *Serial titles:* 107 (physical), 98,630 (digital/electronic); *Databases:* 111. Weekly public service hours: 73; students can reserve study rooms.

Student Life *Housing:* on-campus residence required for freshman year. *Options:* coed, men-only, special housing for students with disabilities. Campus housing is university owned. Freshman applicants given priority for college housing. *Activities and Organizations:* Phi Theta Kappa, Visual Communications Collective, Air Conditioning and Refrigeration Club, Future Chefs Association, Association of Information Technology Professionals. *Campus security:* 24-hour emergency response devices and patrols, late-night transport/escort service, controlled dormitory access. *Student services:* health clinic, personal/psychological counseling, veterans affairs office.

Athletics *Intramural sports:* basketball M/W, football M/W, racquetball M/W, soccer M/W, softball M/W, table tennis M/W, volleyball M/W.

Standardized Tests *Required for some:* SAT or ACT (for admission). *Recommended:* ACT (for admission).

Costs (2019–20) *Tuition:* state resident $4350 full-time, $145 per credit hour part-time; nonresident $9960 full-time, $332 per credit hour part-time. Full-time tuition and fees vary according to class time, course level, course load, degree level, location, program, and student level. Part-time tuition and fees vary according to class time, course level, course load, degree level, location, program, and student level. *Required fees:* $1200 full-time, $40 per credit hour part-time. *Room and board:* $7016. Room and board charges vary according to board plan and housing facility. *Payment plan:* installment. *Waivers:* senior citizens and employees or children of employees.

Financial Aid Of all full-time matriculated undergraduates who enrolled in 2019, 1,201 applied for aid, 1,044 were judged to have need, 14 had their need fully met. In 2019, 19 non-need-based awards were made. *Average percent of need met:* 57%. *Average financial aid package:* $11,363. *Average need-based loan:* $3585. *Average need-based gift aid:* $7385. *Average non-need-based aid:* $2091.

Applying *Options:* deferred entrance. *Required:* high school transcript. *Application deadlines:* rolling (freshmen), rolling (out-of-state freshmen), rolling (transfers).

Freshman Application Contact Kyle Gregorio, Assistant Registrar, Oklahoma State University Institute of Technology, 1801 E. 4th Street, Okmulgee, OK 74447. *Phone:* 918-293-5274. *Toll-free phone:* 800-722-4471. *Fax:* 918-293-4643. *E-mail:* kyleg@okstate.edu. *Website:* http://www.osuit.edu/.

Oklahoma State University–Oklahoma City

Oklahoma City, Oklahoma

Freshman Application Contact Mr. Kyle Williams, Senior Director of Enrollment Management, Oklahoma State University–Oklahoma City, 900 North Portland Avenue, AD202, Oklahoma City, OK 73107. *Phone:* 405-945-9152. *Toll-free phone:* 800-560-4099. *E-mail:* wilkylw@osuokc.edu. *Website:* http://www.osuokc.edu/.

Oklahoma Technical College

Tulsa, Oklahoma

Freshman Application Contact Mr. Jeremy Cooper, Campus Director, Oklahoma Technical College, 4444 South Sheridan Road, Tulsa, OK 74145. *Phone:* 918-895-7500 Ext. 3007. *Fax:* 918-895-7885. *E-mail:* jcooper@oklahomatechnicalcollege.com. *Website:* http://www.oklahomatechnicalcollege.com/.

Platt College

Moore, Oklahoma

Admissions Office Contact Platt College, 201 North Eastern Avenue, Moore, OK 73160. *Toll-free phone:* 877-392-6616. *Website:* http://www.plattcolleges.edu/.

Platt College

Oklahoma City, Oklahoma

Admissions Office Contact Platt College, 2727 West Memorial Road, Oklahoma City, OK 73134. *Toll-free phone:* 877-392-6616. *Website:* http://www.plattcolleges.edu/.

Platt College

Tulsa, Oklahoma

Director of Admissions Mrs. Susan Rone, Director, Platt College, 3801 South Sheridan Road, Tulsa, OK 74145. *Phone:* 918-663-9000. *Toll-free phone:* 877-392-6616. *Fax:* 918-622-1240. *E-mail:* susanr@plattcollege.org. *Website:* http://www.plattcolleges.edu/.

Redlands Community College

El Reno, Oklahoma

Freshman Application Contact Redlands Community College, 1300 South Country Club Road, El Reno, OK 73036-5304. *Phone:* 405-262-2552 Ext. 1263. *Toll-free phone:* 866-415-6367. *Website:* http://www.redlandscc.edu/.

Rose State College

Midwest City, Oklahoma

Freshman Application Contact Ms. Mechelle Aitson-Roessler, Registrar and Director of Admissions, Rose State College, 6420 Southeast 15th Street, Midwest City, OK 73110-2799. *Phone:* 405-733-7308. *Toll-free phone:* 866-621-0987. *Fax:* 405-736-0203. *E-mail:* maitson@ms.rose.cc.ok.us. *Website:* http://www.rose.edu/.

Seminole State College

Seminole, Oklahoma

- **State-supported** 2-year, founded 1931, part of Oklahoma State Regents for Higher Education
- **Small-town** 40-acre campus with easy access to Oklahoma City
- **Endowment** $3.1 million
- **Coed,** 1,531 undergraduate students, 54% full-time, 69% women, 31% men

Undergraduates 831 full-time, 700 part-time. Students come from 8 states and territories; 8 other countries; 1% are from out of state; 7% Black or African American, non-Hispanic/Latino; 6% Hispanic/Latino; 0.7% Asian, non-Hispanic/Latino; 0.3% Native Hawaiian or other Pacific Islander, non-Hispanic/Latino; 25% American Indian or Alaska Native, non-Hispanic/Latino; 0.3% Two or more races, non-Hispanic/Latino; 1% Race/ethnicity unknown; 0.5% international; 0.4% transferred in; 10% live on campus.

Freshmen *Admission:* 319 applied, 319 admitted, 330 enrolled.

Faculty *Total:* 84, 52% full-time, 4% with terminal degrees. *Student/faculty ratio:* 19:1.
Majors Accounting; art; behavioral sciences; biological and biomedical sciences related; biology/biological sciences; business administration and management; business/commerce; child development; clinical/medical laboratory technology; computer science; criminal justice/law enforcement administration; criminal justice/police science; elementary education; engineering; English; fine arts related; general studies; humanities; liberal arts and sciences/liberal studies; management information systems and services related; mathematics; physical education teaching and coaching; physical sciences; pre-engineering; psychology related; registered nursing/registered nurse; social sciences.
Academics *Calendar:* semesters. *Degree:* certificates, diplomas, and associate. *Special study options:* academic remediation for entering students, adult/continuing education programs, advanced placement credit, cooperative education, distance learning, double majors, English as a second language, independent study, off-campus study, part-time degree program, services for LD students, study abroad, summer session for credit.
Library Boren Library plus 1 other. *Books:* 29,131 (physical); *Serial titles:* 35 (physical), 11 (digital/electronic); *Databases:* 8. Weekly public service hours: 48.
Student Life *Housing:* on-campus residence required through sophomore year. *Options:* coed, special housing for students with disabilities. Campus housing is university owned. *Activities and Organizations:* Student Government Association, Native American Student Association, Psi Beta Honor Society, Student Nurses Association, Phi Theta Kappa. *Campus security:* 24-hour emergency response devices and patrols, student patrols, late-night transport/escort service, controlled dormitory access, police department staffed with state certified officers. *Student services:* veterans affairs office.
Athletics Member NJCAA. *Intercollegiate sports:* baseball M(s), basketball M(s)/W(s), golf M(s)/W(s), soccer W, softball W(s), tennis M(s)/W(s), volleyball W(s).
Costs (2019–20) *One-time required fee:* $25. *Tuition:* state resident $3120 full-time, $104 per credit hour part-time; nonresident $9450 full-time, $315 per credit hour part-time. Full-time tuition and fees vary according to course load, location, and program. Part-time tuition and fees vary according to course load, location, and program. *Required fees:* $1620 full-time, $54 per credit hour part-time. *Room and board:* $7070. *Payment plan:* installment. *Waivers:* senior citizens and employees or children of employees.
Applying *Options:* early admission, deferred entrance. *Application fee:* $15. *Recommended:* high school transcript. *Application deadlines:* rolling (freshmen), rolling (transfers). *Notification:* continuous (freshmen), continuous (transfers).
Freshman Application Contact Seminole State College, 2701 Boren Boulevard, PO Box 351, Seminole, OK 74818-0351. *Phone:* 405-3829501. *Website:* http://www.sscok.edu/.

Spartan College of Aeronautics and Technology
Tulsa, Oklahoma

Freshman Application Contact Mr. Mark Fowler, Vice President of Student Records and Finance, Spartan College of Aeronautics and Technology, 8820 East Pine Street, Tulsa, OK 74115. *Phone:* 918-836-6886. *Toll-free phone:* 800-331-1204. *Website:* http://www.spartan.edu/.

Tulsa Community College
Tulsa, Oklahoma

- **State-supported** 2-year, founded 1968, part of Oklahoma State Regents for Higher Education
- **Urban** 160-acre campus
- **Coed**

Undergraduates 4,833 full-time, 1,755 part-time. 6% are from out of state; 18% Black or African American, non-Hispanic/Latino; 13% Hispanic/Latino; 9% Asian, non-Hispanic/Latino; 0.1% Native Hawaiian or other Pacific Islander, non-Hispanic/Latino; 0.2% American Indian or Alaska Native, non-Hispanic/Latino; 5% Two or more races, non-Hispanic/Latino; 1% Race/ethnicity unknown; 4% international; 9% transferred in; 9% live on campus. *Retention:* 71% of full-time freshmen returned.
Faculty *Student/faculty ratio:* 19:1.
Academics *Calendar:* semesters. *Degree:* certificates and associate. *Special study options:* academic remediation for entering students, accelerated degree program, adult/continuing education programs, advanced placement credit, cooperative education, distance learning, English as a second language, freshman honors college, honors programs, independent study, internships, off-campus study, part-time degree program, services for LD students, student-designed majors, study abroad, summer session for credit. *ROTC:* Army (c), Navy (c), Air Force (c).
Student Life *Campus security:* 24-hour emergency response devices and patrols, student patrols, late-night transport/escort service.
Costs (2019–20) *Tuition:* state resident $4307 full-time, $113 per credit hour part-time; nonresident $11,057 full-time, $338 per credit hour part-time. *Required fees:* $930 full-time, $29 per credit hour part-time, $5 per term part-time.
Financial Aid Of all full-time matriculated undergraduates who enrolled in 2019, 4,455 applied for aid, 3,272 were judged to have need, 162 had their need fully met. In 2019, 659. *Average percent of need met:* 62. *Average financial aid package:* $5595. *Average need-based loan:* $2871. *Average need-based gift aid:* $5146. *Average non-need-based aid:* $3277.
Applying *Options:* electronic application, early admission. *Application fee:* $25. *Required:* high school transcript.
Freshman Application Contact Ms. Traci Heck, Dean of Enrollment Management, Tulsa Community College, 6111 East Skelly Drive, Tulsa, OK 74135. *Phone:* 918-595-3411. *E-mail:* traci.heck@tulsacc.edu. *Website:* http://www.tulsacc.edu/.

Tulsa Welding School
Tulsa, Oklahoma

Freshman Application Contact Mrs. Debbie Renee Burke, Vice President/Executive Director, Tulsa Welding School, 2545 East 11th Street, Tulsa, OK 74104. *Phone:* 918-587-6789 Ext. 2258. *Toll-free phone:* 888-765-5555. *Fax:* 918-295-6812. *E-mail:* dburke@twsweld.com. *Website:* http://www.tulsaweldingschool.com/.

Western Oklahoma State College
Altus, Oklahoma

Freshman Application Contact Dean Chad E. Wiginton, Dean of Student Support Services, Western Oklahoma State College, 2801 North Main, Altus, OK 73521. *Phone:* 580-477-7918. *Fax:* 580-477-7716. *E-mail:* chad.wiginton@wosc.edu. *Website:* http://www.wosc.edu/.

OREGON

Blue Mountain Community College
Pendleton, Oregon

Director of Admissions Ms. Theresa Bosworth, Director of Admissions, Blue Mountain Community College, 2411 Northwest Carden Avenue, PO Box 100, Pendleton, OR 97801-1000. *Phone:* 541-278-5774. *E-mail:* tbosworth@bluecc.edu. *Website:* http://www.bluecc.edu/.

Central Oregon Community College
Bend, Oregon

- **District-supported** 2-year, founded 1949, part of Oregon Community College Association
- **Small-town** 193-acre campus
- **Endowment** $21.3 million
- **Coed,** 4,871 undergraduate students, 47% full-time, 53% women, 47% men

Undergraduates 2,303 full-time, 2,568 part-time. 0.6% Black or African American, non-Hispanic/Latino; 12% Hispanic/Latino; 1% Asian, non-Hispanic/Latino; 0.3% Native Hawaiian or other Pacific Islander, non-Hispanic/Latino; 2% American Indian or Alaska Native, non-Hispanic/Latino; 4% Two or more races, non-Hispanic/Latino; 7% Race/ethnicity unknown; 9% transferred in. *Retention:* 61% of full-time freshmen returned.
Freshmen *Admission:* 979 applied, 979 admitted, 1,139 enrolled.
Faculty *Total:* 290, 44% full-time, 2% with terminal degrees. *Student/faculty ratio:* 17:1.
Majors Accounting; agriculture; airline pilot and flight crew; alternative fuel vehicle technology; anthropology; art; automobile/automotive mechanics technology; baking and pastry arts; biological and physical sciences; biology/biological sciences; business administration and management; CAD/CADD drafting/design technology; chemistry; child-care and support services management; computer and information sciences; computer and information sciences related; computer science; computer systems networking and telecommunications; cooking and related culinary arts; criminal justice/safety; criminology; culinary arts; customer service management; dental assisting; dental hygiene; dietetics; drafting and design technology; early childhood education; education; electrical, electronic and communications engineering technology; emergency medical technology

(EMT paramedic); engineering; English; entrepreneurship; fine/studio arts; fire science/firefighting; fire services administration; foreign languages and literatures; forest/forest resources management; forestry; forest technology; general studies; geographic information science and cartography; geography; geology/earth science; health and physical education/fitness; health information/medical records technology; health/medical preparatory programs related; history; hospitality administration; hotel/motel administration; humanities; industrial technology; kinesiology and exercise science; liberal arts and sciences/liberal studies; licensed practical/vocational nurse training; management information systems; manufacturing engineering technology; marketing/marketing management; massage therapy; mathematics; medical/clinical assistant; music; natural resources/conservation; outdoor education; physical sciences; physical therapy; physics; political science and government; polymer/plastics engineering; pre-law studies; premedical studies; pre-pharmacy studies; public health; radiologic technology/science; registered nursing/registered nurse; retailing; social sciences; speech communication and rhetoric; sport and fitness administration/management; substance abuse/addiction counseling; veterinary/animal health technology; web page, digital/multimedia and information resources design; welding engineering technology.

Academics *Calendar:* quarters. *Degree:* certificates, diplomas, and associate. *Special study options:* academic remediation for entering students, cooperative education, distance learning, double majors, English as a second language, independent study, internships, part-time degree program, services for LD students, student-designed majors, study abroad, summer session for credit. *ROTC:* Army (c).

Library COCC Barber Library plus 1 other. *Books:* 58,892 (physical), 236,191 (digital/electronic); *Serial titles:* 5,544 (physical), 126,380 (digital/electronic); *Databases:* 135. Weekly public service hours: 79.

Student Life *Housing Options:* coed, special housing for students with disabilities. Campus housing is university owned. *Activities and Organizations:* drama/theater group, student-run newspaper, choral group, Club Sports, Latinx Club, Criminal Justice Club, Aviation Club, Native American Club. *Campus security:* 24-hour emergency response devices and patrols, late-night transport/escort service, controlled dormitory access. *Student services:* personal/psychological counseling, veterans affairs office.

Athletics *Intercollegiate sports:* golf M. *Intramural sports:* baseball M, basketball M/W, cross-country running M/W, football M, rugby M, skiing (cross-country) M/W, skiing (downhill) M/W, soccer M/W, track and field M/W, volleyball M/W, weight lifting M/W.

Costs (2020–21) *Tuition:* area resident $5388 full-time, $106 per credit hour part-time; state resident $7301 full-time, $149 per credit hour part-time; nonresident $14,528 full-time, $309 per credit hour part-time. *Required fees:* $754 full-time. *Room and board:* $11,511. Room and board charges vary according to board plan. *Payment plan:* installment. *Waivers:* employees or children of employees.

Applying *Options:* electronic application. *Application fee:* $25. *Application deadlines:* rolling (freshmen), rolling (transfers). *Notification:* continuous (freshmen), continuous (transfers).

Freshman Application Contact Central Oregon Community College, 2600 Northwest College Way, Bend, OR 97703. *Phone:* 541-383-7500. *Website:* http://www.cocc.edu/.

Chemeketa Community College

Salem, Oregon

- **State and locally supported** 2-year, founded 1955
- **Urban** 72-acre campus with easy access to Portland
- **Endowment** $3.7 million
- **Coed**

Undergraduates 6,225 full-time, 6,146 part-time. Students come from 21 states and territories; 20 other countries; 5% are from out of state; 1% Black or African American, non-Hispanic/Latino; 18% Hispanic/Latino; 2% Asian, non-Hispanic/Latino; 0.8% Native Hawaiian or other Pacific Islander, non-Hispanic/Latino; 2% American Indian or Alaska Native, non-Hispanic/Latino; 4% Two or more races, non-Hispanic/Latino; 4% Race/ethnicity unknown; 0.6% international; 1% transferred in. *Retention:* 61% of full-time freshmen returned.

Faculty *Student/faculty ratio:* 26:1.

Academics *Calendar:* quarters. *Degree:* certificates, diplomas, and associate. *Special study options:* academic remediation for entering students, adult/continuing education programs, advanced placement credit, cooperative education, distance learning, double majors, English as a second language, independent study, internships, part-time degree program, services for LD students, study abroad, summer session for credit.

Library Chemeketa Community College Library (CCRLS).

Student Life *Campus security:* 24-hour emergency response devices and patrols, late-night transport/escort service.

Applying *Required for some:* high school transcript, interview.

Freshman Application Contact Admissions Office, Chemeketa Community College, PO Box 14009, Salem, OR 97309. *Phone:* 503-399-5001. *E-mail:* admissions@chemeketa.edu. *Website:* http://www.chemeketa.edu/.

Clackamas Community College

Oregon City, Oregon

- **District-supported** 2-year, founded 1966
- **Suburban** 175-acre campus with easy access to Portland
- **Endowment** $16.9 million
- **Coed,** 6,270 undergraduate students, 38% full-time, 47% women, 53% men

Undergraduates 2,358 full-time, 3,912 part-time. Students come from 9 states and territories; 10 other countries; 1% are from out of state; 2% Black or African American, non-Hispanic/Latino; 13% Hispanic/Latino; 2% Asian, non-Hispanic/Latino; 0.3% Native Hawaiian or other Pacific Islander, non-Hispanic/Latino; 1% American Indian or Alaska Native, non-Hispanic/Latino; 5% Two or more races, non-Hispanic/Latino; 16% Race/ethnicity unknown; 0.4% international; 14% transferred in. *Retention:* 62% of full-time freshmen returned.

Freshmen *Admission:* 1,588 enrolled.

Faculty *Total:* 374, 34% full-time. *Student/faculty ratio:* 17:1.

Majors Accounting; administrative assistant and secretarial science; applied horticulture/horticulture operations; architectural drafting and CAD/CADD; autobody/collision and repair technology; automobile/automotive mechanics technology; CAD/CADD drafting/design technology; child-care and support services management; community organization and advocacy; computer programming (specific applications); computer systems networking and telecommunications; computer technology/computer systems technology; construction trades; corrections; criminal justice/police science; digital communication and media/multimedia; drafting and design technology; electrical and power transmission installation; electrical, electronic and communications engineering technology; emergency medical technology (EMT paramedic); fire science/firefighting; general studies; industrial engineering; industrial technology; landscaping and groundskeeping; liberal arts and sciences/liberal studies; machine tool technology; manufacturing engineering technology; marketing/marketing management; office management; operations management; ornamental horticulture; registered nursing/registered nurse; retailing; social work; surveying technology; water quality and wastewater treatment management and recycling technology; web/multimedia management and webmaster; welding technology.

Academics *Calendar:* quarters. *Degree:* certificates, diplomas, and associate. *Special study options:* academic remediation for entering students, accelerated degree program, adult/continuing education programs, advanced placement credit, cooperative education, distance learning, double majors, English as a second language, honors programs, independent study, internships, part-time degree program, services for LD students, study abroad, summer session for credit.

Library Dye Learning Resource Center plus 1 other. Students can reserve study rooms.

Student Life *Activities and Organizations:* drama/theater group, student-run newspaper, choral group, Phi Theta Kappa, STEM, Student Nurses, Horticulture Club, American Sign Language, national fraternities. *Campus security:* 24-hour emergency response devices, late-night transport/escort service. *Student services:* personal/psychological counseling, veterans affairs office.

Athletics Member NJCAA. *Intercollegiate sports:* baseball M(s), basketball M(s)/W(s), cross-country running M(s)/W(s), soccer W, softball W(s), track and field M(s)/W(s), volleyball W(s), wrestling M(s). *Intramural sports:* basketball M/W, soccer W.

Costs (2020–21) *Tuition:* area resident $4860 full-time, $108 per credit part-time; state resident $4860 full-time, $108 per credit part-time; nonresident $12,330 full-time, $274 per credit part-time. *Required fees:* $474 full-time, $9 per credit part-time, $30 per term part-time. *Room and board:* $5130. *Payment plan:* deferred payment. *Waivers:* employees or children of employees.

Applying *Options:* electronic application, early admission. *Application deadlines:* rolling (freshmen), rolling (transfers).

Freshman Application Contact Admissions Center, Clackamas Community College, 19600 South Molalla Avenue, Oregon City, OR 97045. *Phone:* 503-594-3284. *E-mail:* campustour@clackamas.edu. *Website:* http://www.clackamas.edu/.

Clatsop Community College
Astoria, Oregon

- **County-supported** 2-year, founded 1958
- **Small-town** 20-acre campus
- **Coed**

Undergraduates 455 full-time, 616 part-time. Students come from 5 states and territories; 20% are from out of state; 0.6% Black or African American, non-Hispanic/Latino; 12% Hispanic/Latino; 1% Asian, non-Hispanic/Latino; 0.2% Native Hawaiian or other Pacific Islander, non-Hispanic/Latino; 2% American Indian or Alaska Native, non-Hispanic/Latino; 2% Two or more races, non-Hispanic/Latino; 8% Race/ethnicity unknown; 5% transferred in. *Retention:* 51% of full-time freshmen returned.
Faculty *Student/faculty ratio:* 13:1.
Academics *Calendar:* quarters. *Degree:* certificates and associate. *Special study options:* academic remediation for entering students, adult/continuing education programs, advanced placement credit, cooperative education, distance learning, English as a second language, freshman honors college, honors programs, independent study, internships, part-time degree program, services for LD students, summer session for credit.
Library Dora Badollet Library.
Student Life *Campus security:* 24-hour emergency response devices, late-night transport/escort service.
Financial Aid Of all full-time matriculated undergraduates who enrolled in 2018, 220 Federal Work-Study jobs (averaging $2175).
Applying *Options:* electronic application. *Application fee:* $15. *Recommended:* high school transcript.
Freshman Application Contact Ms. Monica Van Steenberg, Recruiting Coordinator, Clatsop Community College, 1651 Lexington Avenue, Astoria, OR 97103. *Phone:* 503-338-2417. *Toll-free phone:* 855-252-8767. *Fax:* 503-325-5738. *E-mail:* admissions@clatsopcc.edu. *Website:* http://www.clatsopcc.edu/.

Columbia Gorge Community College
The Dalles, Oregon

- **State-supported** 2-year, founded 1977
- **Small-town** 78-acre campus
- **Coed**

Undergraduates 542 full-time, 703 part-time. Students come from 24 states and territories; 195% are from out of state; 0.6% Black or African American, non-Hispanic/Latino; 7% Hispanic/Latino; 0.8% Asian, non-Hispanic/Latino; 0.1% Native Hawaiian or other Pacific Islander, non-Hispanic/Latino; 5% American Indian or Alaska Native, non-Hispanic/Latino; 0.3% Two or more races, non-Hispanic/Latino; 17% Race/ethnicity unknown; 3% transferred in. *Retention:* 49% of full-time freshmen returned.
Faculty *Student/faculty ratio:* 12:1.
Academics *Calendar:* quarters. *Degree:* certificates, diplomas, and associate. *Special study options:* academic remediation for entering students, cooperative education, distance learning, English as a second language, honors programs, independent study, part-time degree program, services for LD students, summer session for credit.
Library Columbia Gorge Community College Library.
Student Life *Campus security:* 24-hour emergency response devices.
Applying *Options:* electronic application.
Freshman Application Contact Columbia Gorge Community College, 400 East Scenic Drive, The Dalles, OR 97058. *Phone:* 541-506-6025. *Website:* http://www.cgcc.edu/.

Concorde Career College
Portland, Oregon

Admissions Office Contact Concorde Career College, 1425 NE Irving Street, Portland, OR 97232. *Website:* http://www.concorde.edu/.

Klamath Community College
Klamath Falls, Oregon

Freshman Application Contact Tammi Garlock, Retention Coordinator, Klamath Community College, 7390 South 6th Street, Klamath Falls, OR 97603. *Phone:* 541-882-3521. *Fax:* 541-885-7758. *E-mail:* garlock@klamathcc.edu. *Website:* http://www.klamathcc.edu/.

Lane Community College
Eugene, Oregon

Freshman Application Contact Lane Community College, 4000 East 30th Avenue, Eugene, OR 97405-0640. *Phone:* 541-747-4501 Ext. 2686. *Website:* http://www.lanecc.edu/.

Linn-Benton Community College
Albany, Oregon

- **State and locally supported** 2-year, founded 1966
- **Small-town** 104-acre campus
- **Coed**

Undergraduates 2,604 full-time, 3,013 part-time. 3% are from out of state; 1% Black or African American, non-Hispanic/Latino; 8% Hispanic/Latino; 2% Asian, non-Hispanic/Latino; 0.5% Native Hawaiian or other Pacific Islander, non-Hispanic/Latino; 2% American Indian or Alaska Native, non-Hispanic/Latino; 3% Two or more races, non-Hispanic/Latino; 4% Race/ethnicity unknown; 2% international; 10% transferred in. *Retention:* 55% of full-time freshmen returned.
Academics *Calendar:* quarters. *Degree:* certificates and associate. *Special study options:* academic remediation for entering students, advanced placement credit, cooperative education, distance learning, English as a second language, independent study, internships, part-time degree program, services for LD students, student-designed majors, study abroad, summer session for credit. *ROTC:* Army (c), Navy (c), Air Force (c).
Library Linn-Benton Community College Library.
Student Life *Campus security:* 24-hour emergency response devices and patrols, student patrols, late-night transport/escort service.
Financial Aid Of all full-time matriculated undergraduates who enrolled in 2018, 290 Federal Work-Study jobs (averaging $1800).
Applying *Options:* electronic application, deferred entrance. *Application fee:* $30.
Freshman Application Contact Ms. Kim Sullivan, Outreach Coordinator, Linn-Benton Community College, 6500 Pacific Boulevard, SW, Albany, OR 97321. *Phone:* 541-917-4847. *Fax:* 541-917-4838. *E-mail:* admissions@linnbenton.edu. *Website:* http://www.linnbenton.edu/.

Mt. Hood Community College
Gresham, Oregon

Director of Admissions Dr. Craig Kolins, Associate Vice President of Enrollment Services, Mt. Hood Community College, 26000 Southeast Stark Street, Gresham, OR 97030-3300. *Phone:* 503-491-7265. *Website:* http://www.mhcc.edu/.

Oregon Coast Community College
Newport, Oregon

Freshman Application Contact Student Services, Oregon Coast Community College, 400 SE College Way, Newport, OR 97366. *Phone:* 541-265-2283. *Fax:* 541-265-3820. *E-mail:* webinfo@occc.cc.or.us. *Website:* http://www.oregoncoastcc.org/.

Pacific Bible College
Medford, Oregon

Admissions Office Contact Pacific Bible College, 28 South Fir Street, Medford, OR 97501. *Website:* http://www.pacificbible.com/.

Portland Community College
Portland, Oregon

- **State and locally supported** 2-year, founded 1961
- **Urban** 400-acre campus
- **Endowment** $17.8 million
- **Coed,** 20,000 undergraduate students

Majors Accounting; administrative assistant and secretarial science; agricultural power machinery operation; airframe mechanics and aircraft maintenance technology; airline pilot and flight crew; architectural drafting and CAD/CADD; autobody/collision and repair technology; automobile/automotive mechanics technology; biology/biotechnology laboratory technician; building/home/construction inspection; business administration and management; child-care and support services management; civil engineering technology; clinical/medical laboratory technology; commercial and advertising art; computer programming; computer technology/computer systems technology; construction engineering technology; construction trades related; criminal justice/safety; dental hygiene;

dental laboratory technology; diesel mechanics technology; electrical, electronic and communications engineering technology; emergency medical technology (EMT paramedic); fire prevention and safety technology; general studies; gerontology; health and physical education related; health information/medical records administration; heating, air conditioning, ventilation and refrigeration maintenance technology; homeland security, law enforcement, firefighting and protective services related; interior design; landscaping and groundskeeping; legal assistant/paralegal; liberal arts and sciences/liberal studies; machine tool technology; management information systems; mechanical engineering/mechanical technology; medical radiologic technology; multi/interdisciplinary studies related; office management; optometric technician; registered nursing/registered nurse; special education; substance abuse/addiction counseling; teacher assistant/aide; veterinary/animal health technology; welding technology.

Academics *Calendar:* quarters. *Degree:* certificates, diplomas, and associate. *Special study options:* academic remediation for entering students, adult/continuing education programs, advanced placement credit, cooperative education, distance learning, double majors, English as a second language, external degree program, independent study, internships, off-campus study, part-time degree program, services for LD students, study abroad, summer session for credit.

Library PCC Library plus 4 others.

Student Life *Housing:* college housing not available. *Activities and Organizations:* drama/theater group, student-run newspaper, television station, choral group. *Campus security:* 24-hour emergency response devices and patrols, late-night transport/escort service. *Student services:* personal/psychological counseling, women's center, veterans affairs office.

Athletics Member NJCAA. *Intercollegiate sports:* basketball M(s)/W(s). *Intramural sports:* archery M/W, badminton M/W, baseball M, basketball M/W, bowling M/W, cross-country running M/W, racquetball M/W, skiing (cross-country) M/W, skiing (downhill) M/W, soccer M/W, softball W, swimming and diving M/W, table tennis M/W, track and field M/W, ultimate Frisbee M/W, volleyball M/W, weight lifting M/W, wrestling M.

Applying *Options:* electronic application. *Application fee:* $25. *Application deadline:* rolling (freshmen).

Freshman Application Contact Admissions and Registration Office, Portland Community College, PO Box 19000, Portland, OR 97280. *Phone:* 503-977-8888. *Toll-free phone:* 866-922-1010. *Website:* http://www.pcc.edu/.

Rogue Community College

Grants Pass, Oregon

Freshman Application Contact Mr. John Duarte, Director of Enrollment Services, Rogue Community College, 3345 Redwood Highway, Grants Pass, OR 97527-9291. *Phone:* 541-956-7176. *Fax:* 541-471-3585. *E-mail:* jduarte@roguecc.edu. *Website:* http://www.roguecc.edu/.

Southwestern Oregon Community College

Coos Bay, Oregon

Freshman Application Contact Ms. Brenda Rogers, Admissions, Southwestern Oregon Community College, 1988 Newmark Avenue, Coos Bay, OR 97420. *Phone:* 541-888-7636. *Toll-free phone:* 800-962-2838. *E-mail:* lwells@socc.edu. *Website:* http://www.socc.edu/.

Sumner College

Portland, Oregon

- **Proprietary** 2-year, founded 1974
- **Urban** campus with easy access to Portland
- **Coed, primarily women**

Undergraduates 261 full-time. 10% are from out of state; 15% Black or African American, non-Hispanic/Latino; 6% Hispanic/Latino; 7% Asian, non-Hispanic/Latino; 0.8% Race/ethnicity unknown.

Faculty *Student/faculty ratio:* 15:1.

Academics *Calendar:* quarters. *Degree:* diplomas and associate. *Special study options:* academic remediation for entering students, distance learning.

Library Main Library plus 1 other. *Books:* 800 (physical); *Serial titles:* 100 (digital/electronic); *Databases:* 2. Weekly public service hours: 50; students can reserve study rooms.

Costs (2019–20) *Comprehensive fee:* $38,430 includes full-time tuition ($27,180), mandatory fees ($2340), and room and board ($8910).

Applying *Required:* high school transcript, interview. *Required for some:* essay or personal statement, Entrance exam.

Admissions Office Contact Sumner College, 15115 SW Sequoia Parkway, Suite 200, Portland, OR 97224. *Website:* http://www.sumnercollege.edu/.

Tillamook Bay Community College

Tillamook, Oregon

Freshman Application Contact Rhoda Hanson, Director of Student Services, Tillamook Bay Community College, 4301 Third Street, Tillamook, OR 97224. *Phone:* 503-842-8222 Ext. 1110. *Fax:* 503-842-8334. *E-mail:* rhodahanson@tillamookbaycc.edu. *Website:* http://www.tillamookbaycc.edu/.

Treasure Valley Community College

Ontario, Oregon

- **State and locally supported** 2-year, founded 1962
- **Rural** 90-acre campus with easy access to Boise
- **Endowment** $5.9 million
- **Coed**

Undergraduates 807 full-time, 1,059 part-time. Students come from 15 states and territories; 2 other countries; 67% are from out of state; 2% Black or African American, non-Hispanic/Latino; 25% Hispanic/Latino; 0.7% Asian, non-Hispanic/Latino; 0.3% Native Hawaiian or other Pacific Islander, non-Hispanic/Latino; 1% American Indian or Alaska Native, non-Hispanic/Latino; 3% Two or more races, non-Hispanic/Latino; 4% Race/ethnicity unknown; 0.4% international; 6% transferred in; 4% live on campus. *Retention:* 40% of full-time freshmen returned.

Faculty *Student/faculty ratio:* 21:1.

Academics *Calendar:* quarters. *Degree:* certificates and associate. *Special study options:* academic remediation for entering students, accelerated degree program, adult/continuing education programs, advanced placement credit, cooperative education, distance learning, English as a second language, honors programs, independent study, internships, off-campus study, part-time degree program, services for LD students, summer session for credit.

Library Treasure Valley Community College Library. *Books:* 26,100 (physical), 1.5 million (digital/electronic); *Serial titles:* 47 (physical), 3 (digital/electronic); *Databases:* 10. Weekly public service hours: 72; students can reserve study rooms.

Student Life *Campus security:* 24-hour emergency response devices, late-night transport/escort service, controlled dormitory access.

Costs (2019–20) *Tuition:* state resident $4590 full-time, $102 per credit part-time; nonresident $5040 full-time, $112 per credit part-time. *Required fees:* $990 full-time, $22 per credit part-time. *Room and board:* $7373; room only: $3926.

Financial Aid Of all full-time matriculated undergraduates who enrolled in 2018, 90 Federal Work-Study jobs (averaging $1500).

Applying *Options:* electronic application, early admission, deferred entrance.

Freshman Application Contact Mr. Travis McFetridge, Director of Admissions and Student Success, Treasure Valley Community College, 650 College Boulevard, Ontario, OR 97914. *Phone:* 541-881-5825. *E-mail:* tmcfetri@tvcc.cc. *Website:* http://www.tvcc.cc/.

Umpqua Community College

Roseburg, Oregon

Freshman Application Contact Admissions Office, Umpqua Community College, PO Box 967, Roseburg, OR 97470-0226. *Phone:* 541-440-7743. *Fax:* 541-440-4612. *Website:* http://www.umpqua.edu/.

PENNSYLVANIA

All-State Career School–Essington Campus

Essington, Pennsylvania

Admissions Office Contact All-State Career School–Essington Campus, 50 West Powhattan Ave, Essington, PA 19029. *Website:* http://www.allstatecareer.edu/.

ASPIRA City College

Philadelphia, Pennsylvania

Freshman Application Contact Admissions Office, ASPIRA City College, 4322 North 5th Street, Philadelphia, PA 19140. *Phone:* 215-568-7861. *Website:* http://www.aspiracitycollege.org/.

Berks Technical Institute
Wyomissing, Pennsylvania

Freshman Application Contact Mr. Allan Brussolo, Academic Dean, Berks Technical Institute, 2205 Ridgewood Road, Wyomissing, PA 19610-1168. *Phone:* 610-372-1722. *Toll-free phone:* 866-591-8384. *Fax:* 610-376-4684. *E-mail:* abrussolo@berks.edu. *Website:* http://www.berks.edu/.

Bidwell Training Center
Pittsburgh, Pennsylvania

Freshman Application Contact Admissions Office, Bidwell Training Center, 1815 Metropolitan Street, Pittsburgh, PA 15233. *Phone:* 412-322-1773. *Toll-free phone:* 800-516-1800. *E-mail:* admissions@mcg-btc.org. *Website:* http://www.bidwelltraining.edu/.

Bucks County Community College
Newtown, Pennsylvania

- **County-supported** 2-year, founded 1964
- **Suburban** 200-acre campus with easy access to Philadelphia
- **Endowment** $8.0 million
- **Coed,** 7,480 undergraduate students, 36% full-time, 57% women, 43% men

Undergraduates 2,702 full-time, 4,778 part-time. Students come from 17 states and territories; 1% are from out of state; 6% Black or African American, non-Hispanic/Latino; 10% Hispanic/Latino; 5% Asian, non-Hispanic/Latino; 0.2% Native Hawaiian or other Pacific Islander, non-Hispanic/Latino; 0.3% American Indian or Alaska Native, non-Hispanic/Latino; 3% Two or more races, non-Hispanic/Latino; 6% Race/ethnicity unknown; 0.5% international; 6% transferred in. *Retention:* 70% of full-time freshmen returned.

Freshmen *Admission:* 3,491 applied, 3,333 admitted, 1,478 enrolled.

Faculty *Total:* 602, 23% full-time, 24% with terminal degrees. *Student/faculty ratio:* 15:1.

Majors Accounting technology and bookkeeping; art history, criticism and conservation; baking and pastry arts; biology/biotechnology laboratory technician; business administration and management; business/commerce; cabinetmaking and millwork; chemical technology; child-care provision; cinematography and film/video production; clinical/medical laboratory technology; commercial and advertising art; commercial photography; computer and information sciences; computer and information systems security; computer systems networking and telecommunications; criminal justice/safety; critical infrastructure protection; culinary arts; early childhood education; engineering; engineering technology; English; environmental science; fire services administration; general studies; health professions related; health services/allied health/health sciences; history; history teacher education; hospitality administration; information science/studies; journalism; kinesiology and exercise science; legal professions and studies related; liberal arts and sciences and humanities related; liberal arts and sciences/liberal studies; mathematics; mathematics teacher education; medical/clinical assistant; medical insurance coding; meeting and event planning; multi/interdisciplinary studies related; music; network and system administration; neuroscience; physical education teaching and coaching; psychology; radiologic technology/science; registered nursing/registered nurse; small business administration; social sciences; social work; speech communication and rhetoric; sport and fitness administration/management; visual and performing arts; web page, digital/multimedia and information resources design.

Academics *Calendar:* semesters. *Degree:* certificates and associate. *Special study options:* academic remediation for entering students, adult/continuing education programs, advanced placement credit, cooperative education, distance learning, English as a second language, external degree program, independent study, internships, part-time degree program, services for LD students, student-designed majors, summer session for credit.

Library Bucks County Community College Library. *Books:* 109,895 (physical), 9,498 (digital/electronic); *Serial titles:* 166 (physical), 63 (digital/electronic); *Databases:* 58. Weekly public service hours: 73; students can reserve study rooms.

Student Life *Housing:* college housing not available. *Activities and Organizations:* drama/theater group, student-run newspaper, radio and television station, choral group, BC3 Anime Club, Bucks Gaming Club, Glass Arts Club, Future Teachers Organization (FTO), National Society of Leadership & Success (NSLS). *Campus security:* 24-hour emergency response devices and patrols, late-night transport/escort service. *Student services:* personal/psychological counseling, women's center, veterans affairs office.

Athletics Member NJCAA. *Intercollegiate sports:* baseball M, basketball M/W, equestrian sports W, golf M, soccer M/W, softball W, volleyball W. *Intramural sports:* baseball M, basketball M/W, cheerleading M(c)/W(c), cross-country running M(c)/W(c), equestrian sports W(c), football M, soccer M/W, tennis M/W, volleyball M(c).

Financial Aid Of all full-time matriculated undergraduates who enrolled in 2016, 147 Federal Work-Study jobs (averaging $1708).

Applying *Options:* electronic application, early admission. *Required:* high school transcript. *Required for some:* essay or personal statement, interview.

Freshman Application Contact Ms. Marlene Barlow, Director of Admissions, Bucks County Community College, 275 Swamp Rd., Newtown, PA 18940. *Phone:* 215-968-8137. *E-mail:* marlene.barlow@bucks.edu. *Website:* http://www.bucks.edu/.

Butler County Community College
Butler, Pennsylvania

Freshman Application Contact Mr. Robert Morris, Director of Admissions, Butler County Community College, College Drive, PO Box 1205, Butler, PA 16003-1203. *Phone:* 724-287-8711 Ext. 344. *Toll-free phone:* 888-826-2829. *Fax:* 724-287-4961. *E-mail:* robert.morris@bc3.edu. *Website:* http://www.bc3.edu/.

Central Pennsylvania Institute of Science and Technology
Pleasant Gap, Pennsylvania

Admissions Office Contact Central Pennsylvania Institute of Science and Technology, 540 North Harrison Road, Pleasant Gap, PA 16823. *Website:* http://www.cpi.edu/.

Commonwealth Technical Institute
Johnstown, Pennsylvania

Freshman Application Contact Mr. Jason Gies, Admissions Supervisor, Commonwealth Technical Institute, Hiram G. Andrews Center, 727 Goucher Street, Johnstown, PA 15905. *Phone:* 814-255-8200 Ext. 0564. *Toll-free phone:* 800-762-4211. *Fax:* 814-255-8283. *E-mail:* jgies@pa.gov. *Website:* http://www.dli.pa.gov/Individuals/Disability-Services/hgac/Pages/default.aspx.

Community College of Allegheny County
Pittsburgh, Pennsylvania

- **County-supported** 2-year, founded 1966
- **Urban** 242-acre campus
- **Coed,** 16,076 undergraduate students, 32% full-time, 53% women, 47% men

Undergraduates 5,145 full-time, 10,931 part-time. 16% Black or African American, non-Hispanic/Latino; 3% Hispanic/Latino; 3% Asian, non-Hispanic/Latino; 0.1% Native Hawaiian or other Pacific Islander, non-Hispanic/Latino; 0.4% American Indian or Alaska Native, non-Hispanic/Latino; 3% Two or more races, non-Hispanic/Latino; 13% Race/ethnicity unknown.

Freshmen *Admission:* 3,720 enrolled.

Faculty *Student/faculty ratio:* 18:1.

Majors Accounting technology and bookkeeping; administrative assistant and secretarial science; airline pilot and flight crew; anesthesiologist assistant; architectural drafting and CAD/CADD; art; automobile/automotive mechanics technology; automotive engineering technology; aviation/airway management; banking and financial support services; biology/biological sciences; biotechnology; building construction technology; building/property maintenance; business administration and management; business machine repair; business, management, and marketing related; CAD/CADD drafting/design technology; chemical technology; chemistry; child-care provision; civil drafting and CAD/CADD; civil engineering technology; clinical/medical laboratory technology; computer and information sciences; computer and information systems security; computer engineering technology; computer programming; computer technology/computer systems technology; court reporting; critical infrastructure protection; culinary arts; diagnostic medical sonography and ultrasound technology; dramatic/theater arts; electrical and power transmission installation; electrical, electronic and communications engineering technology; electrician; emergency medical technology (EMT paramedic); engineering science; fire prevention and safety technology; game and interactive media design; general studies; graphic design; health and physical education/fitness; health information/medical records technology; heating, air conditioning, ventilation and refrigeration maintenance technology; homeland security, law enforcement, firefighting and protective services related; human resources management; industrial and product design; legal assistant/paralegal; liberal arts and sciences/liberal studies; management information systems; management science;

manufacturing engineering technology; marketing/marketing management; massage therapy; mathematics; mechanical drafting and CAD/CADD; mechanical engineering/mechanical technology; mechatronics, robotics, and automation engineering; medical/clinical assistant; medical radiologic technology; middle school education; music; nanotechnology; nuclear medical technology; occupational therapist assistant; pharmacy technician; physical therapy technology; physics; psychiatric/mental health services technology; psychology; registered nursing/registered nurse; respiratory care therapy; sheet metal technology; sign language interpretation and translation; sociology; substance abuse/addiction counseling; surgical technology; teacher assistant/aide; therapeutic recreation; tourism and travel services management.
Academics *Calendar:* semesters. *Degree:* certificates, diplomas, and associate. *Special study options:* academic remediation for entering students, accelerated degree program, distance learning, English as a second language, honors programs, off-campus study, part-time degree program, services for LD students, study abroad, summer session for credit. *ROTC:* Army (c), Navy (c), Air Force (c).
Library Community College of Allegheny County Libraries. *Books:* 119,791 (physical), 60,213 (digital/electronic); *Serial titles:* 595 (physical), 32 (digital/electronic); *Databases:* 120. Weekly public service hours: 12.
Student Life *Housing:* college housing not available. *Activities and Organizations:* drama/theater group, student-run newspaper, radio and television station, choral group, Art Club, Veterans Club, Computer Science Club, Phi Theta Kappa, Women on a Mission. *Campus security:* 24-hour emergency response devices and patrols, late-night transport/escort service. *Student services:* health clinic, personal/psychological counseling, veterans affairs office.
Athletics Member NJCAA. *Intercollegiate sports:* baseball M, basketball M/W, bowling M/W, cross-country running M/W, golf M/W. *Intramural sports:* ice hockey M/W, soccer M/W.
Costs (2019–20) *Tuition:* area resident $3480 full-time, $116 per credit hour part-time; state resident $6960 full-time, $232 per credit hour part-time; nonresident $10,440 full-time, $348 per credit hour part-time. Full-time tuition and fees vary according to course load and program. Part-time tuition and fees vary according to course load and program. *Payment plan:* installment. *Waivers:* senior citizens and employees or children of employees.
Applying *Recommended:* high school transcript.
Freshman Application Contact Community College of Allegheny County, 800 Allegheny Avenue, Pittsburgh, PA 15233-1894.
Website: http://www.ccac.edu/.

Community College of Beaver County

Monaca, Pennsylvania

- **State-supported** 2-year, founded 1966
- **Small-town** 75-acre campus with easy access to Pittsburgh
- **Coed**

Undergraduates 2% are from out of state. *Retention:* 43% of full-time freshmen returned.
Faculty *Student/faculty ratio:* 16:1.
Academics *Calendar:* semesters. *Degree:* certificates, diplomas, and associate. *Special study options:* academic remediation for entering students, adult/continuing education programs, advanced placement credit, cooperative education, distance learning, double majors, independent study, internships, off-campus study, part-time degree program, services for LD students, summer session for credit.
Library Community College of Beaver County Library.
Student Life *Campus security:* 24-hour emergency response devices and patrols, late-night transport/escort service.
Athletics Member NJCAA.
Applying *Options:* early admission. *Required:* interview. *Recommended:* high school transcript.
Freshman Application Contact Enrollment Management, Community College of Beaver County, One Campus Drive, Monaca, PA 15061-2588. *Phone:* 724-480-3500. *Toll-free phone:* 800-335-0222. *E-mail:* admissions@ccbc.edu. *Website:* http://www.ccbc.edu/.

Community College of Philadelphia

Philadelphia, Pennsylvania

- **State and locally supported** 2-year, founded 1964
- **Urban** 14-acre campus with easy access to Philadelphia
- **Coed**

Undergraduates Students come from 50 other countries.
Academics *Calendar:* semesters. *Degree:* certificates, diplomas, and associate. *Special study options:* academic remediation for entering students, accelerated degree program, adult/continuing education programs, advanced placement credit, cooperative education, distance learning, English as a second language, external degree program, honors programs, independent study, internships, off-campus study, part-time degree program, services for LD students, student-designed majors, study abroad, summer session for credit. *ROTC:* Army (c).
Library Main Campus Library plus 2 others. *Books:* 84,000 (physical); *Databases:* 40. Weekly public service hours: 30; students can reserve study rooms.
Student Life *Campus security:* 24-hour emergency response devices and patrols, late-night transport/escort service, phone/alert systems in classrooms/buildings, electronic messages/alerts, ID required to enter buildings.
Athletics Member NJCAA.
Costs (2019–20) *Tuition:* $159 per credit hour part-time; state resident $318 per credit hour part-time; nonresident $477 per credit hour part-time. Full-time tuition and fees vary according to course load and program. Part-time tuition and fees vary according to course load and program.
Applying *Options:* electronic application, early admission, deferred entrance. *Required for some:* high school transcript, specific entry requirements for allied health and nursing programs.
Freshman Application Contact Community College of Philadelphia, 1700 Spring Garden Street, Philadelphia, PA 19130-3991. *Phone:* 215-751-8010. *Website:* http://www.ccp.edu/.

Delaware County Community College

Media, Pennsylvania

- **State and locally supported** 2-year, founded 1967
- **Suburban** 123-acre campus with easy access to Philadelphia
- **Endowment** $3.8 million
- **Coed**

Undergraduates 5,360 full-time, 7,888 part-time. Students come from 9 states and territories; 53 other countries; 1% are from out of state; 25% Black or African American, non-Hispanic/Latino; 3% Hispanic/Latino; 4% Asian, non-Hispanic/Latino; 0.1% Native Hawaiian or other Pacific Islander, non-Hispanic/Latino; 0.3% American Indian or Alaska Native, non-Hispanic/Latino; 3% Two or more races, non-Hispanic/Latino; 4% Race/ethnicity unknown. *Retention:* 61% of full-time freshmen returned.
Faculty *Student/faculty ratio:* 24:1.
Academics *Calendar:* semesters. *Degree:* certificates and associate. *Special study options:* academic remediation for entering students, adult/continuing education programs, advanced placement credit, cooperative education, distance learning, double majors, English as a second language, independent study, internships, part-time degree program, services for LD students, student-designed majors, summer session for credit.
Library Delaware County Community College Library.
Student Life *Campus security:* 24-hour emergency response devices and patrols, late-night transport/escort service.
Athletics Member NJCAA.
Financial Aid Of all full-time matriculated undergraduates who enrolled in 2018, 95 Federal Work-Study jobs (averaging $900).
Applying *Options:* early admission. *Application fee:* $25. *Required:* high school transcript.
Freshman Application Contact Ms. Hope Diehl, Director of Admissions and Enrollment Services, Delaware County Community College, 901 South Media Line Road, Media, PA 19063-1094. *Phone:* 610-359-5050. *Fax:* 610-723-1530. *E-mail:* admiss@dccc.edu. *Website:* http://www.dccc.edu/.

Douglas Education Center

Monessen, Pennsylvania

- **Proprietary** 2-year, founded 1904
- **Small-town** campus with easy access to Pittsburgh
- **Coed**

Undergraduates 334 full-time. Students come from 4 other countries; 32% are from out of state; 4% Black or African American, non-Hispanic/Latino; 4% Hispanic/Latino; 0.6% Asian, non-Hispanic/Latino; 0.6% Native Hawaiian or other Pacific Islander, non-Hispanic/Latino; 0.6% American Indian or Alaska Native, non-Hispanic/Latino; 1% Two or more races, non-Hispanic/Latino; 1% Race/ethnicity unknown; 1% international. *Retention:* 87% of full-time freshmen returned.
Faculty *Student/faculty ratio:* 16:1.
Academics *Degree:* diplomas and associate. *Special study options:* advanced placement credit.
Library Douglas Education Center Library / Learning Resource Center plus 2 others.
Student Life *Campus security:* 24-hour emergency response devices.
Standardized Tests *Required:* Wonderlic aptitude test (for admission).
Financial Aid Of all full-time matriculated undergraduates who enrolled in 2018, 5 Federal Work-Study jobs (averaging $2500).

Applying *Application fee:* $50. *Required:* high school transcript, interview.
Freshman Application Contact Ms. Sherry Lee Walters, Director of Enrollment Services, Douglas Education Center, 130 Seventh Street, Monessen, PA 15062. *Phone:* 724-684-3684 Ext. 2181. *Toll-free phone:* 800-413-6013. *Website:* http://www.dec.edu/.

Erie Institute of Technology
Erie, Pennsylvania

Freshman Application Contact Erie Institute of Technology, 940 Millcreek Mall, Erie, PA 16565. *Phone:* 814-868-9900. *Toll-free phone:* 866-868-3743. *Website:* http://www.erieit.edu/.

Fortis Institute
Erie, Pennsylvania

Director of Admissions Guy M. Euliano, President, Fortis Institute, 5757 West 26th Street, Erie, PA 16506. *Phone:* 814-838-7673. *Toll-free phone:* 855-4-FORTIS. *Fax:* 814-838-8642. *E-mail:* geuliano@tsbi.org. *Website:* http://www.fortis.edu/.

Fortis Institute
Forty Fort, Pennsylvania

Freshman Application Contact Admissions Office, Fortis Institute, 166 Slocum Street, Forty Fort, PA 18704. *Phone:* 570-288-8400. *Toll-free phone:* 855-4-FORTIS. *Website:* http://www.fortis.edu/.

Fortis Institute
Scranton, Pennsylvania

Director of Admissions Ms. Heather Contardi, Director of Admissions, Fortis Institute, 517 Ash Street, Scranton, PA 18509. *Phone:* 570-558-1818. *Toll-free phone:* 855-4-FORTIS. *Fax:* 570-342-4537. *E-mail:* heatherp@markogroup.com. *Website:* http://www.fortis.edu/.

Great Lakes Institute of Technology
Erie, Pennsylvania

Admissions Office Contact Great Lakes Institute of Technology, 5100 Peach Street, Erie, PA 16509. *Website:* http://www.glit.edu/.

Harcum College
Bryn Mawr, Pennsylvania

Freshman Application Contact Office of Enrollment Management, Harcum College, 750 Montgomery Avenue, Bryn Mawr, PA 19010-3476. *Phone:* 610-526-6050. *E-mail:* enroll@harcum.edu. *Website:* http://www.harcum.edu/.

Harrisburg Area Community College
Harrisburg, Pennsylvania

- **State and locally supported** 2-year, founded 1964
- **Urban** 212-acre campus
- **Coed,** 17,422 undergraduate students, 28% full-time, 65% women, 35% men

Undergraduates 4,886 full-time, 12,536 part-time. 5% are from out of state; 11% Black or African American, non-Hispanic/Latino; 14% Hispanic/Latino; 4% Asian, non-Hispanic/Latino; 0.1% Native Hawaiian or other Pacific Islander, non-Hispanic/Latino; 0.3% American Indian or Alaska Native, non-Hispanic/Latino; 4% Two or more races, non-Hispanic/Latino; 2% Race/ethnicity unknown; 2% international; 7% transferred in.
Freshmen *Admission:* 12,306 applied, 12,306 admitted, 2,832 enrolled.
Faculty *Total:* 981, 32% full-time, 57% with terminal degrees. *Student/faculty ratio:* 17:1.
Majors Administrative assistant and secretarial science; adult development and aging; architectural engineering technology; automobile/automotive mechanics technology; biology/biological sciences; business administration and management; business/commerce; cardiovascular technology; chemistry; civil engineering technology; clinical/medical laboratory technology; communication and journalism related; computer and information sciences; computer and information systems security; computer science; computer systems networking and telecommunications; construction engineering technology; criminal justice/law enforcement administration; criminal justice/police science; culinary arts; dental hygiene; design and visual communications; dramatic/theater arts; early childhood education; electrical, electronic and communications engineering technology; electrician; engineering; engineering technologies and engineering related; environmental science; fire science/firefighting; general studies; geographic information science and cartography; graphic design; health and physical education/fitness; health/health-care administration; health professions related; health services administration; heating, air conditioning, ventilation and refrigeration maintenance technology; hospitality administration related; human services; international relations and affairs; legal assistant/paralegal; mathematics; mechanical engineering/mechanical technology; mechatronics, robotics, and automation engineering; medical informatics; music management; philosophy; photography; physical sciences; psychology; radiologic technology/science; registered nursing/registered nurse; respiratory care therapy; secondary education; social sciences; social work; structural engineering; surgical technology; visual and performing arts; web page, digital/multimedia and information resources design.
Academics *Calendar:* semesters. *Degree:* certificates, diplomas, and associate. *Special study options:* academic remediation for entering students, adult/continuing education programs, advanced placement credit, distance learning, double majors, English as a second language, honors programs, independent study, internships, part-time degree program, services for LD students, summer session for credit. *ROTC:* Army (b).
Library McCormick Library.
Student Life *Housing:* college housing not available. *Activities and Organizations:* drama/theater group, student-run newspaper, Student Government Association, Phi Theta Kappa, African-American Student Association, Mosiaco Club, Fourth Estate. *Campus security:* 24-hour emergency response devices and patrols, late-night transport/escort service. *Student services:* veterans affairs office.
Athletics *Intercollegiate sports:* basketball M/W, golf M, soccer M, volleyball M/W.
Costs (2019–20) *Tuition:* area resident $5408 full-time, $180 per credit hour part-time; state resident $6660 full-time, $222 per credit hour part-time; nonresident $8010 full-time, $267 per credit hour part-time. Full-time tuition and fees vary according to location and program. Part-time tuition and fees vary according to location and program. *Required fees:* $1275 full-time, $43 per credit hour part-time. *Payment plan:* installment. *Waivers:* employees or children of employees.
Financial Aid Of all full-time matriculated undergraduates who enrolled in 2018, 3,996 applied for aid, 3,120 were judged to have need. *Average need-based loan:* $3358.
Applying *Options:* electronic application. *Required for some:* high school transcript, 1 letter of recommendation, interview.
Freshman Application Contact Harrisburg Area Community College, 1 HACC Drive, Harrisburg, PA 17110-2999. *Toll-free phone:* 800-ABC-HACC. *Website:* http://www.hacc.edu/.

JNA Institute of Culinary Arts
Philadelphia, Pennsylvania

Freshman Application Contact Admissions Office, JNA Institute of Culinary Arts, 1212 South Broad Street, Philadelphia, PA 19146. *Website:* http://www.culinaryarts.com/.

Johnson College
Scranton, Pennsylvania

Freshman Application Contact Johnson College, 3427 North Main Avenue, Scranton, PA 18508-1495. *Phone:* 570-702-8911. *Toll-free phone:* 800-2WE-WORK. *Website:* http://www.johnson.edu/.

Lackawanna College
Scranton, Pennsylvania

- **Independent** primarily 2-year, founded 1894
- **Urban** 4-acre campus
- **Endowment** $5.7 million
- **Coed,** 1,991 undergraduate students, 67% full-time, 56% women, 44% men

Undergraduates 1,335 full-time, 656 part-time. Students come from 16 states and territories; 8% are from out of state; 12% Black or African American, non-Hispanic/Latino; 12% Hispanic/Latino; 1% Asian, non-Hispanic/Latino; 0.2% Native Hawaiian or other Pacific Islander, non-Hispanic/Latino; 0.4% American Indian or Alaska Native, non-Hispanic/Latino; 2% Two or more races, non-Hispanic/Latino; 11% Race/ethnicity unknown; 1% international; 11% transferred in; 17% live on campus. *Retention:* 100% of full-time freshmen returned.
Freshmen *Admission:* 1,627 applied, 570 admitted, 466 enrolled.
Faculty *Total:* 193, 17% full-time, 5% with terminal degrees. *Student/faculty ratio:* 19:1.

Majors Accounting; administrative assistant and secretarial science; banking and financial support services; biology/biological sciences; biology/biotechnology laboratory technician; business administration and management; business administration, management and operations related; business/commerce; cardiovascular science; child-care provision; communication and media related; criminal justice/law enforcement administration; criminal justice/police science; criminal justice/safety; culinary arts; diagnostic medical sonography and ultrasound technology; dramatic/theater arts and stagecraft related; e-commerce; education; emergency medical technology (EMT paramedic); environmental science; financial planning and services; health information/medical records technology; health professions related; hospitality administration; hotel/motel administration; human services; industrial mechanics and maintenance technology; industrial technology; legal assistant/paralegal; liberal arts and sciences and humanities related; liberal arts and sciences/liberal studies; management information systems; medical administrative assistant and medical secretary; mental and social health services and allied professions related; multi/interdisciplinary studies related; organizational behavior; petroleum technology; physical therapy technology; psychology; psychology related; surgical technology.

Academics *Calendar:* semesters. *Degrees:* certificates, diplomas, associate, and bachelor's. *Special study options:* academic remediation for entering students, adult/continuing education programs, cooperative education, double majors, English as a second language, internships, part-time degree program, services for LD students, summer session for credit.

Library Albright Memorial Library plus 1 other. Students can reserve study rooms.

Student Life *Housing:* on-campus residence required through sophomore year. *Options:* coed, men-only. Campus housing is university owned. *Activities and Organizations:* Student Government Association, V.O.L.C. (Volunteers of Lackawanna College), Falcon Ambassador Board (FAB), COMMunity Club, Pineapple Club (Hospitality & Culinary Club). *Campus security:* 24-hour emergency response devices and patrols, late-night transport/escort service, controlled dormitory access, patrols by college liaison staff. *Student services:* personal/psychological counseling, veterans affairs office.

Athletics Member NJCAA. *Intercollegiate sports:* baseball M(s), basketball M(s)/W(s), cross-country running M(s)/W(s), football M(s), golf M(s), soccer M(s)/W(s), softball W(s), tennis W(s), volleyball W(s), wrestling M(s). *Intramural sports:* cheerleading W.

Standardized Tests *Recommended:* SAT or ACT (for admission).

Costs (2019–20) *Comprehensive fee:* $26,430 includes full-time tuition ($15,300), mandatory fees ($830), and room and board ($10,300). Full-time tuition and fees vary according to course load, location, and program. Part-time tuition: $535 per credit. Part-time tuition and fees vary according to course load, location, and program. *Required fees:* $415 per term part-time. *Room and board:* college room only: $6700. Room and board charges vary according to board plan. *Payment plans:* installment, deferred payment. *Waivers:* employees or children of employees.

Financial Aid Of all full-time matriculated undergraduates who enrolled in 2018, 2,718 applied for aid, 2,448 were judged to have need, 33 had their need fully met. In 2018, 27 non-need-based awards were made. *Average percent of need met:* 27%. *Average financial aid package:* $8291. *Average need-based loan:* $3331. *Average need-based gift aid:* $6733. *Average non-need-based aid:* $4987. *Average indebtedness upon graduation:* $9496.

Applying *Options:* electronic application, deferred entrance. *Application fee:* $35. *Required:* high school transcript, interview. *Application deadlines:* rolling (freshmen), rolling (transfers).

Freshman Application Contact Mr. Eddie Perry, Admissions Advisor, Lackawanna College, 501 Vine Street, Scranton, PA 18509. *Phone:* 570-961-7889. *Toll-free phone:* 877-346-3552. *E-mail:* perrye@lackawanna.edu. *Website:* http://www.lackawanna.edu/.

Lancaster County Career and Technology Center

Willow Street, Pennsylvania

Admissions Office Contact Lancaster County Career and Technology Center, 1730 Hans Herr Drive, Willow Street, PA 17584. *Website:* http://www.lancasterctc.edu/.

Lansdale School of Business

North Wales, Pennsylvania

Freshman Application Contact Lansdale School of Business, 290 Wissahickon Avenue, North Wales, PA 19454. *Phone:* 215-699-5700 Ext. 112. *Toll-free phone:* 800-219-0486. *Website:* http://www.lsb.edu/.

Laurel Business Institute

Uniontown, Pennsylvania

Freshman Application Contact Mrs. Lisa Dolan, Laurel Business Institute, 11 East Penn Street, PO Box 877, Uniontown, PA 15401. *Phone:* 724-439-4900 Ext. 158. *Fax:* 724-439-3607. *E-mail:* ldolan@laurel.edu. *Website:* http://www.laurel.edu/locations/uniontown.

Laurel Technical Institute

Sharon, Pennsylvania

Freshman Application Contact Irene Lewis, Laurel Technical Institute, 200 Sterling Avenue, Sharon, PA 16146. *Phone:* 724-983-0700. *Fax:* 724-983-8355. *E-mail:* info@biop.edu. *Website:* http://www.laurel.edu/locations/sharon.

Lehigh Carbon Community College

Schnecksville, Pennsylvania

- **State and locally supported** 2-year, founded 1966
- **Suburban** 254-acre campus with easy access to Philadelphia
- **Endowment** $5.7 million
- **Coed**

Undergraduates 2,476 full-time, 4,477 part-time. Students come from 11 states and territories; 18 other countries; 0.4% are from out of state; 7% Black or African American, non-Hispanic/Latino; 22% Hispanic/Latino; 2% Asian, non-Hispanic/Latino; 0.1% American Indian or Alaska Native, non-Hispanic/Latino; 4% Two or more races, non-Hispanic/Latino; 3% Race/ethnicity unknown; 0.4% international; 53% transferred in. *Retention:* 45% of full-time freshmen returned.

Faculty *Student/faculty ratio:* 18:1.

Academics *Calendar:* semesters. *Degree:* certificates, diplomas, and associate. *Special study options:* academic remediation for entering students, advanced placement credit, cooperative education, distance learning, English as a second language, external degree program, honors programs, independent study, internships, off-campus study, part-time degree program, services for LD students, summer session for credit. *ROTC:* Army (c).

Library Rothrock Library. *Books:* 48,142 (physical), 68,508 (digital/electronic); *Serial titles:* 220 (physical), 182 (digital/electronic); *Databases:* 46. Weekly public service hours: 71.

Student Life *Campus security:* 24-hour emergency response devices.

Athletics Member NJCAA.

Applying *Options:* electronic application. *Required for some:* essay or personal statement, high school transcript, interview.

Freshman Application Contact Ms. Nancy Kelley, Admission Representative, Lehigh Carbon Community College, 4525 Education Park Drive, Schnecksville, PA 18078. *Phone:* 610-799-1558. *Fax:* 610-799-1527. *E-mail:* admissions@lccc.edu. *Website:* http://www.lccc.edu/.

Lincoln Technical Institute

Allentown, Pennsylvania

Freshman Application Contact Admissions Office, Lincoln Technical Institute, 5151 Tilghman Street, Allentown, PA 18104. *Phone:* 610-398-5301. *Toll-free phone:* 844-215-1513. *Website:* http://www.lincolntech.edu/.

Lincoln Technical Institute

Philadelphia, Pennsylvania

Director of Admissions Mr. James Kuntz, Executive Director, Lincoln Technical Institute, 9191 Torresdale Avenue, Philadelphia, PA 19136. *Phone:* 215-335-0800. *Toll-free phone:* 844-215-1513. *Fax:* 215-335-1443. *E-mail:* jkuntz@lincolntech.com. *Website:* http://www.lincolntech.edu/.

Luzerne County Community College

Nanticoke, Pennsylvania

- **County-supported** 2-year, founded 1966
- **Suburban** 122-acre campus
- **Coed,** 4,920 undergraduate students, 40% full-time, 61% women, 39% men

Undergraduates 1,955 full-time, 2,965 part-time. 6% Black or African American, non-Hispanic/Latino; 16% Hispanic/Latino; 2% Asian, non-Hispanic/Latino; 0.1% Native Hawaiian or other Pacific Islander, non-Hispanic/Latino; 0.3% American Indian or Alaska Native, non-Hispanic/Latino; 1% Two or more races, non-Hispanic/Latino; 10% Race/ethnicity unknown.

Freshmen *Admission:* 2,177 applied, 2,177 admitted, 1,074 enrolled.

Majors Accounting; administrative assistant and secretarial science; architectural engineering; architectural engineering technology; automobile/automotive mechanics technology; baking and pastry arts; banking and financial support services; biological and physical sciences; building/property maintenance; business administration and management; child-care provision; commercial and advertising art; commercial photography; computer and information sciences; computer and information sciences related; computer graphics; computer programming related; computer science; computer systems networking and telecommunications; computer technology/computer systems technology; court reporting; criminal justice/law enforcement administration; culinary arts; data entry/microcomputer applications; data processing and data processing technology; dental hygiene; drafting and design technology; drafting/design engineering technologies related; drawing; early childhood education; education; electrical, electronic and communications engineering technology; electrician; emergency medical technology (EMT paramedic); engineering technology; executive assistant/executive secretary; fire science/firefighting; food technology and processing; funeral service and mortuary science; general studies; graphic and printing equipment operation/production; graphic design; health and physical education/fitness; health/health-care administration; heating, air conditioning, ventilation and refrigeration maintenance technology; hospitality and recreation marketing; hotel/motel administration; humanities; human services; industrial and product design; international business/trade/commerce; journalism; legal assistant/paralegal; liberal arts and sciences and humanities related; liberal arts and sciences/liberal studies; mathematics; medical administrative assistant and medical secretary; painting; photography; physical education teaching and coaching; plumbing technology; pre-pharmacy studies; radio and television broadcasting technology; registered nursing/registered nurse; respiratory care therapy; social sciences; surgical technology.
Academics *Calendar:* semesters. *Degree:* certificates, diplomas, and associate. *Special study options:* academic remediation for entering students, accelerated degree program, advanced placement credit, cooperative education, distance learning, English as a second language, external degree program, honors programs, internships, part-time degree program, services for LD students, summer session for credit. *ROTC:* Army (c).
Library Learning Resources Center plus 1 other. Students can reserve study rooms.
Student Life *Housing:* college housing not available. *Activities and Organizations:* drama/theater group, student-run radio and television station, choral group, Student Government, Circle K, Nursing Forum, Science Club, SADAH. *Campus security:* 24-hour patrols.
Athletics Member NJCAA. *Intercollegiate sports:* baseball M, basketball M/W, cross-country running M/W, softball M/W, volleyball W. *Intramural sports:* basketball M/W, bowling M/W, softball M/W, volleyball M/W.
Applying *Options:* electronic application. *Recommended:* high school transcript. *Application deadlines:* rolling (freshmen), rolling (out-of-state freshmen), rolling (transfers). *Notification:* continuous (freshmen), continuous (out-of-state freshmen), continuous (transfers).
Freshman Application Contact Mr. James Domzalski, Director of Enrollment Management, Luzerne County Community College, 1333 South Prospect Street, Nanticoke, PA 18634. *Phone:* 570-740-0342. *Toll-free phone:* 800-377-5222 Ext. 7337. *Fax:* 570-740-0238. *E-mail:* admissions@luzerne.edu.
Website: http://www.luzerne.edu/.

Manor College
Jenkintown, Pennsylvania

- **Independent Byzantine Catholic** primarily 2-year, founded 1947
- **Suburban** 35-acre campus with easy access to Philadelphia
- **Endowment** $2.8 million
- **Coed**

Undergraduates 480 full-time, 260 part-time. Students come from 6 states and territories; 2 other countries; 3% are from out of state; 34% Black or African American, non-Hispanic/Latino; 14% Hispanic/Latino; 3% Asian, non-Hispanic/Latino; 0.3% Native Hawaiian or other Pacific Islander, non-Hispanic/Latino; 1% American Indian or Alaska Native, non-Hispanic/Latino; 2% Two or more races, non-Hispanic/Latino; 5% Race/ethnicity unknown; 0.3% international; 10% transferred in; 11% live on campus. *Retention:* 58% of full-time freshmen returned.
Faculty *Student/faculty ratio:* 10:1.
Academics *Calendar:* semesters. *Degrees:* certificates, associate, bachelor's, and postbachelor's certificates. *Special study options:* academic remediation for entering students, accelerated degree program, advanced placement credit, distance learning, double majors, honors programs, independent study, internships, part-time degree program, services for LD students, summer session for credit.
Library Basileiad Library. *Books:* 27,188 (physical), 5,037 (digital/electronic); *Serial titles:* 3 (physical); *Databases:* 14. Weekly public service hours: 65.
Student Life *Campus security:* 24-hour emergency response devices and patrols, late-night transport/escort service.
Athletics Member NJCAA.
Standardized Tests *Recommended:* SAT or ACT (for admission).
Costs (2019–20) *Comprehensive fee:* $25,984 includes full-time tuition ($16,922), mandatory fees ($1100), and room and board ($7962). Full-time tuition and fees vary according to course load and program. Part-time tuition: $689 per credit. Part-time tuition and fees vary according to course load and program. *Required fees:* $275 per term part-time.
Financial Aid Of all full-time matriculated undergraduates who enrolled in 2009, 35 Federal Work-Study jobs (averaging $3000). 10 state and other part-time jobs (averaging $3600).
Applying *Options:* electronic application, deferred entrance. *Required:* high school transcript, minimum 2.0 GPA. *Required for some:* essay or personal statement, letters of recommendation, interview.
Freshman Application Contact Angelica Crespo, Admissions Office Manager, Manor College, 700 Fox Chase Road, Jenkintown, PA 19046. *Phone:* 215-885-2216 Ext. 212. *Fax:* 215-576-6564. *E-mail:* swalker@manor.edu. *Website:* http://www.manor.edu/.

McCann School of Business & Technology
Allentown, Pennsylvania

Admissions Office Contact McCann School of Business & Technology, 2200 North Irving Street, Allentown, PA 18109. *Website:* http://www.mccann.edu/.

McCann School of Business & Technology
Lewisburg, Pennsylvania

Admissions Office Contact McCann School of Business & Technology, 7495 Westbranch Highway, Lewisburg, PA 17837. *Toll-free phone:* 866-865-8065. *Website:* http://www.mccann.edu/.

Mercyhurst North East
North East, Pennsylvania

Director of Admissions Travis Lindahl, Director of Admissions, Mercyhurst North East, 16 West Division Street, North East, PA 16428. *Phone:* 814-725-6217. *Toll-free phone:* 866-846-6042. *Fax:* 814-725-6251. *E-mail:* neadmiss@mercyhurst.edu. *Website:* http://northeast.mercyhurst.edu/.

Montgomery County Community College
Blue Bell, Pennsylvania

- **County-supported** 2-year, founded 1964
- **Suburban** 186-acre campus with easy access to Philadelphia
- **Coed,** 10,309 undergraduate students, 31% full-time, 57% women, 43% men

Undergraduates 3,147 full-time, 7,162 part-time. Students come from 14 states and territories; 4 other countries; 1% are from out of state; 16% Black or African American, non-Hispanic/Latino; 9% Hispanic/Latino; 6% Asian, non-Hispanic/Latino; 0.2% Native Hawaiian or other Pacific Islander, non-Hispanic/Latino; 0.2% American Indian or Alaska Native, non-Hispanic/Latino; 4% Two or more races, non-Hispanic/Latino; 5% Race/ethnicity unknown; 1% international. *Retention:* 65% of full-time freshmen returned.
Freshmen *Admission:* 8,455 applied, 8,455 admitted, 1,688 enrolled.
Faculty *Total:* 603, 30% full-time. *Student/faculty ratio:* 16:1.
Majors Accounting technology and bookkeeping; administrative assistant and secretarial science; applied behavior analysis; art; automobile/automotive mechanics technology; baking and pastry arts; biology/biotechnology laboratory technician; biotechnology; business administration and management; business/commerce; child-care and support services management; clinical/medical laboratory technology; computer programming; computer science; computer technology/computer systems technology; criminal justice/police science; culinary arts; dance; dental hygiene; drafting and design technology; electrical and electronics engineering; electrical, electronic and communications engineering technology; elementary education; engineering science; engineering technologies and engineering related; environmental studies; fire prevention and safety technology; food service and dining room management; game and interactive media design; health and physical education/fitness; hospitality and recreation marketing; information technology; liberal arts and sciences/liberal studies; mathematics; mechanical engineering; mechanical engineering/mechanical technology; medical office management; middle school education; music teacher education;

nanotechnology; network and system administration; physical education teaching and coaching; physical sciences; psychiatric/mental health services technology; public health; radiologic technology/science; radio, television, and digital communication related; real estate; recording arts technology; registered nursing/registered nurse; sales, distribution, and marketing operations; science technologies related; secondary education; securities services administration; social sciences; speech communication and rhetoric; substance abuse/addiction counseling; surgical technology; teacher assistant/aide; tourism and travel services marketing; web/multimedia management and webmaster; web page, digital/multimedia and information resources design.

Academics *Calendar:* semesters plus winter term. *Degree:* certificates and associate. *Special study options:* academic remediation for entering students, accelerated degree program, adult/continuing education programs, advanced placement credit, cooperative education, distance learning, English as a second language, honors programs, independent study, internships, part-time degree program, services for LD students, student-designed majors, study abroad, summer session for credit.

Library The Brendlinger Library. *Books:* 73,691 (physical), 98,911 (digital/electronic); *Serial titles:* 237 (physical), 19,750 (digital/electronic); *Databases:* 37. Weekly public service hours: 76; students can reserve study rooms.

Student Life *Housing Options:* Campus housing is university owned. *Activities and Organizations:* drama/theater group, student-run newspaper, radio and television station, choral group, CRU, Phi Theta Kappa, West End Student Theater, Drama Club, Montco Radio. *Campus security:* 24-hour emergency response devices and patrols, late-night transport/escort service, bicycle patrol. *Student services:* health clinic, personal/psychological counseling, veterans affairs office.

Athletics Member NJCAA. *Intercollegiate sports:* baseball M, basketball M/W, soccer M/W, softball W, volleyball W. *Intramural sports:* basketball M/W, soccer M/W.

Costs (2020–21) *Tuition:* area resident $4320 full-time, $144 per credit hour part-time; state resident $8640 full-time, $288 per credit hour part-time; nonresident $12,960 full-time, $432 per credit hour part-time. Full-time tuition and fees vary according to program. Part-time tuition and fees vary according to program. *Required fees:* $1410 full-time, $47 per credit hour part-time. *Room and board:* $6050. Room and board charges vary according to board plan. *Payment plans:* installment, deferred payment. *Waivers:* senior citizens and employees or children of employees.

Financial Aid Of all full-time matriculated undergraduates who enrolled in 2018, 60 Federal Work-Study jobs (averaging $2500).

Applying *Options:* electronic application, early admission, deferred entrance. *Required:* high school transcript. *Required for some:* interview. *Application deadline:* rolling (transfers). *Notification:* continuous (freshmen), continuous (transfers).

Freshman Application Contact Montgomery County Community College, Blue Bell, PA 19422. *Phone:* 215-641-6551. *Fax:* 215-619-7188. *E-mail:* admrec@admin.mc3.edu.
Website: http://www.mc3.edu/.

New Castle School of Trades

New Castle, Pennsylvania

Freshman Application Contact Mr. Joe Blazak, Admissions Director, New Castle School of Trades, 4117 Pulaski Road, New Castle, PA 16101. *Phone:* 724-964-8811. *Toll-free phone:* 800-837-8299. *Fax:* 724-964-8177. *Website:* http://www.ncstrades.edu/.

Northampton Community College

Bethlehem, Pennsylvania

- **State and locally supported** 2-year, founded 1967
- **Suburban** 165-acre campus with easy access to Philadelphia
- **Coed**, 9,769 undergraduate students, 44% full-time, 61% women, 39% men

Undergraduates 4,255 full-time, 5,514 part-time. 2% are from out of state; 9% transferred in; 6% live on campus.

Freshmen *Admission:* 5,630 applied, 5,630 admitted, 1,839 enrolled.

Majors Accounting technology and bookkeeping; acting; administrative assistant and secretarial science; applied psychology; architectural engineering technology; athletic training; automobile/automotive mechanics technology; biology/biological sciences; biotechnology; business administration and management; business/commerce; CAD/CADD drafting/design technology; chemistry; computer and information systems security; computer programming; computer science; computer support specialist; computer systems networking and telecommunications; construction management; criminal justice/safety; culinary arts; dental hygiene; diagnostic medical sonography and ultrasound technology; early childhood education; electrical, electronic and communications engineering technology; electrician; electromechanical technology; engineering; environmental science; fine/studio arts; fire science/firefighting; fire services administration; funeral service and mortuary science; general studies; graphic design; heating, air conditioning, ventilation and refrigeration maintenance technology; hotel/motel administration; industrial electronics technology; interior design; international/global studies; journalism; legal assistant/paralegal; liberal arts and sciences and humanities related; liberal arts and sciences/liberal studies; marketing/marketing management; mathematics; medical administrative assistant and medical secretary; meeting and event planning; middle school education; physics; psychology; public health education and promotion; quality control technology; radio and television broadcasting technology; radiologic technology/science; registered nursing/registered nurse; restaurant/food services management; secondary education; social work; speech communication and rhetoric; sport and fitness administration/management; teacher assistant/aide; veterinary/animal health technology; web page, digital/multimedia and information resources design; welding technology.

Academics *Calendar:* semesters. *Degree:* certificates, diplomas, and associate. *Special study options:* academic remediation for entering students, adult/continuing education programs, advanced placement credit, distance learning, English as a second language, honors programs, independent study, internships, off-campus study, part-time degree program, services for LD students, student-designed majors, study abroad, summer session for credit.

Library Paul & Harriett Mack Library plus 1 other. Weekly public service hours: 83; students can reserve study rooms.

Student Life *Housing Options:* coed. Campus housing is university owned. *Activities and Organizations:* student-run newspaper, radio station, choral group, Phi Theta Kappa, Student Senate, Nursing Student Organization, American Dental Hygiene Association (ADHA), International Student Organization. *Campus security:* 24-hour emergency response devices and patrols, controlled dormitory access. *Student services:* health clinic, personal/psychological counseling, veterans affairs office.

Athletics Member NJCAA. *Intercollegiate sports:* baseball M, basketball M/W, cross-country running M/W, golf M, lacrosse M, soccer M/W, softball W, tennis W, volleyball W. *Intramural sports:* basketball M/W, cheerleading M(c)/W(c), soccer M/W, volleyball M/W.

Costs (2020–21) *Tuition:* area resident $3210 full-time, $107 per credit hour part-time; state resident $6420 full-time, $214 per credit hour part-time; nonresident $9630 full-time, $321 per credit hour part-time. Full-time tuition and fees vary according to course load. Part-time tuition and fees vary according to course load. *Required fees:* $1320 full-time, $44 per credit hour part-time. *Room and board:* $9348; room only: $5628. Room and board charges vary according to board plan and housing facility. *Payment plan:* installment. *Waivers:* senior citizens and employees or children of employees.

Financial Aid Of all full-time matriculated undergraduates who enrolled in 2018, 201 Federal Work-Study jobs (averaging $2400). 148 state and other part-time jobs (averaging $2000).

Applying *Options:* electronic application, deferred entrance. *Application fee:* $25. *Required for some:* high school transcript, minimum 2.5 GPA, interview, interview for radiography and veterinary programs. *Application deadlines:* rolling (freshmen), rolling (transfers). *Notification:* continuous (freshmen), continuous (transfers).

Freshman Application Contact Mr. Brandon Kwatiek, Associate Director of Admissions, Northampton Community College, 3835 Green Pond Road, Bethlehem, PA 18020-7599. *Phone:* 610-861-4174. *Fax:* 610-861-5551. *E-mail:* bkwatiek@northampton.edu.
Website: http://www.northampton.edu/.

Penn Commercial Business and Technical School

Washington, Pennsylvania

Director of Admissions Mr. Michael John Joyce, Director of Admissions, Penn Commercial Business and Technical School, 242 Oak Spring Road, Washington, PA 15301. *Phone:* 724-222-5330 Ext. 1. *Toll-free phone:* 888-309-7484. *E-mail:* mjoyce@penn-commercial.com. *Website:* http://www.penncommercial.edu/.

Pennco Tech

Bristol, Pennsylvania

Freshman Application Contact Pennco Tech, 3815 Otter Street, Bristol, PA 19007-3696. *Phone:* 215-785-0111. *Toll-free phone:* 800-575-9399. *Website:* http://www.penncotech.edu/.

Penn State DuBois
DuBois, Pennsylvania

- **State-related** primarily 2-year, founded 1935, part of Pennsylvania State University
- **Small-town** campus
- **Coed,** 563 undergraduate students, 78% full-time, 41% women, 59% men

Undergraduates 441 full-time, 122 part-time. 5% are from out of state; 3% Black or African American, non-Hispanic/Latino; 2% Hispanic/Latino; 1% Asian, non-Hispanic/Latino; 0.2% Native Hawaiian or other Pacific Islander, non-Hispanic/Latino; 0.2% American Indian or Alaska Native, non-Hispanic/Latino; 1% Two or more races, non-Hispanic/Latino; 0.4% Race/ethnicity unknown; 6% transferred in. *Retention:* 86% of full-time freshmen returned.

Freshmen *Admission:* 561 applied, 403 admitted, 123 enrolled. *Test scores:* SAT evidence-based reading and writing scores over 500: 75%; SAT math scores over 500: 73%; ACT scores over 18: 80%; SAT evidence-based reading and writing scores over 600: 28%; SAT math scores over 600: 30%; SAT evidence-based reading and writing scores over 700: 1%; SAT math scores over 700: 4%.

Faculty *Total:* 63, 63% full-time, 37% with terminal degrees. *Student/faculty ratio:* 10:1.

Majors Accounting; acting; actuarial science; adult and continuing education administration; advertising; aerospace, aeronautical and astronautical/space engineering; African American/Black studies; agribusiness; agricultural and extension education; agricultural business and management related; agricultural engineering; agricultural mechanization; agriculture; agronomy and crop science; animal sciences; animal sciences related; anthropology; applied economics; archeology; architectural engineering; art; art history, criticism and conservation; art teacher education; Asian studies (East); astronomy; atmospheric sciences and meteorology; biochemistry; bioengineering and biomedical engineering; biological and biomedical sciences related; biological and physical sciences; biology/biological sciences; biology/biotechnology laboratory technician; biomedical technology; business administration and management; business/commerce; business/managerial economics; chemical engineering; chemistry; civil engineering; classics and classical languages; clinical/medical laboratory technology; communication and journalism related; communication sciences and disorders; comparative literature; computer and information sciences; computer engineering; criminal justice/law enforcement administration; economics; electrical and electronics engineering; electrical, electronic and communications engineering technology; elementary education; engineering science; English; environmental/environmental health engineering; film/cinema/video studies; finance; food science; foreign language teacher education; forest sciences and biology; forest technology; French; geography; geological and earth sciences/geosciences related; geology/earth science; German; graphic design; health/health-care administration; history; horticultural science; hospitality administration related; human development and family studies; human nutrition; industrial engineering; information science/studies; international business/trade/commerce; international relations and affairs; Italian; Japanese; Jewish/Judaic studies; journalism; kinesiology and exercise science; labor and industrial relations; landscaping and groundskeeping; Latin American studies; liberal arts and sciences/liberal studies; management information systems; marketing/marketing management; materials science; mathematics; mechanical engineering; mechanical engineering/mechanical technology; medical microbiology and bacteriology; medieval and Renaissance studies; metallurgical technology; mining and mineral engineering; music; natural resources and conservation related; natural resources/conservation; nuclear engineering; occupational therapist assistant; organizational behavior; parks, recreation and leisure facilities management; petroleum engineering; philosophy; physical therapy technology; physics; political science and government; premedical studies; psychology; registered nursing/registered nurse; rehabilitation and therapeutic professions related; religious studies; Russian; secondary education; sociology; soil science and agronomy; Spanish; special education; speech communication and rhetoric; statistics; telecommunications technology; theater design and technology; toxicology; turf and turfgrass management; visual and performing arts; wildlife, fish and wildlands science and management; women's studies.

Academics *Calendar:* semesters. *Degrees:* certificates, associate, and bachelor's. *Special study options:* adult/continuing education programs, distance learning, double majors, external degree program, honors programs, independent study, internships, student-designed majors, study abroad.

Student Life *Housing:* college housing not available.

Athletics Member NJCAA. *Intercollegiate sports:* basketball M, cross-country running M/W, golf M/W, volleyball W. *Intramural sports:* basketball M/W, football M, soccer M/W, table tennis M/W, volleyball M/W.

Standardized Tests *Required:* SAT or ACT (for admission).

Costs (2020–21) *Tuition:* area resident $12,718 full-time, $524 per credit hour part-time; state resident $12,718 full-time, $524 per credit hour part-time; nonresident $21,310 full-time, $888 per credit hour part-time. Full-time tuition and fees vary according to course level, degree level, location, program, and student level. Part-time tuition and fees vary according to course level, course load, degree level, location, program, and student level. *Required fees:* $992 full-time. *Payment plans:* installment, deferred payment. *Waivers:* senior citizens and employees or children of employees.

Financial Aid Of all full-time matriculated undergraduates who enrolled in 2018, 411 applied for aid, 359 were judged to have need, 67 had their need fully met. In 2018, 32 non-need-based awards were made. *Average percent of need met:* 57%. *Average financial aid package:* $10,140. *Average need-based loan:* $3846. *Average need-based gift aid:* $5423. *Average non-need-based aid:* $2724. *Average indebtedness upon graduation:* $33,943.

Applying *Options:* electronic application, early admission, early action, deferred entrance. *Application fee:* $65. *Required:* high school transcript. *Required for some:* interview. *Recommended:* essay or personal statement. *Application deadlines:* rolling (freshmen), rolling (transfers), 11/1 (early action). *Notification:* continuous (freshmen), continuous (transfers), 12/24 (early action).

Freshman Application Contact Admissions Office, Penn State DuBois, 1 College Place, DuBois, PA 15801. *Phone:* 814-375-4720. *Toll-free phone:* 800-346-7627. *Fax:* 814-375-4784. *E-mail:* duboisinfo@psi.edu.
Website: http://www.ds.psu.edu/.

Penn State Fayette, The Eberly Campus
Lemont Furnace, Pennsylvania

- **State-related** primarily 2-year, founded 1934, part of Pennsylvania State University
- **Small-town** campus
- **Coed,** 589 undergraduate students, 89% full-time, 55% women, 45% men

Undergraduates 525 full-time, 64 part-time. 5% are from out of state; 3% Black or African American, non-Hispanic/Latino; 3% Hispanic/Latino; 0.9% Asian, non-Hispanic/Latino; 1% Native Hawaiian or other Pacific Islander, non-Hispanic/Latino; 0.5% American Indian or Alaska Native, non-Hispanic/Latino; 3% Two or more races, non-Hispanic/Latino; 0.9% Race/ethnicity unknown; 0.3% international; 6% transferred in. *Retention:* 76% of full-time freshmen returned.

Freshmen *Admission:* 638 applied, 401 admitted, 165 enrolled. *Test scores:* SAT evidence-based reading and writing scores over 500: 73%; SAT math scores over 500: 70%; ACT scores over 18: 80%; SAT evidence-based reading and writing scores over 600: 19%; SAT math scores over 600: 21%; ACT scores over 24: 20%; SAT evidence-based reading and writing scores over 700: 3%; SAT math scores over 700: 1%; ACT scores over 30: 10%.

Faculty *Total:* 75, 53% full-time, 29% with terminal degrees. *Student/faculty ratio:* 11:1.

Majors Accounting; acting; actuarial science; adult and continuing education administration; advertising; aerospace, aeronautical and astronautical/space engineering; African American/Black studies; agribusiness; agricultural and extension education; agricultural business and management related; agricultural engineering; agricultural mechanization; agriculture; agronomy and crop science; animal sciences; animal sciences related; anthropology; applied economics; archeology; architectural engineering; architectural engineering technology; art; art history, criticism and conservation; art teacher education; Asian studies (East); astronomy; atmospheric sciences and meteorology; biochemistry; bioengineering and biomedical engineering; biological and biomedical sciences related; biological and physical sciences; biology/biological sciences; biology/biotechnology laboratory technician; biomedical technology; business administration and management; business/commerce; business/managerial economics; chemical engineering; chemistry; civil engineering; classics and classical languages; communication and journalism related; communication sciences and disorders; comparative literature; computer and information sciences; computer engineering; criminal justice/law enforcement administration; criminal justice/safety; economics; electrical and electronics engineering; electrical, electronic and communications engineering technology; elementary education; engineering science; English; environmental/environmental health engineering; film/cinema/video studies; finance; food science; foreign language teacher education; forest sciences and biology; forest technology; French; geography; geological and earth sciences/geosciences related; geology/earth science; German; graphic design; health/health-care administration; history; horticultural science; hospitality administration related; human development and family studies; human nutrition; industrial engineering; information science/studies; international relations and affairs; Italian; Japanese; Jewish/Judaic studies; journalism; kinesiology and exercise science; labor and industrial relations; landscaping and groundskeeping; Latin American studies; liberal arts and sciences/liberal studies; logistics, materials, and supply chain management; management information systems; manufacturing engineering; marketing/marketing management; materials science; mathematics; mechanical engineering; medical microbiology and bacteriology; medieval and Renaissance studies; metallurgical technology; mining and mineral engineering; natural resources and conservation related; natural resources/conservation; nuclear engineering; organizational behavior; parks, recreation and leisure facilities management; petroleum engineering; philosophy; physics; political science and government; premedical studies; psychology; registered nursing/registered nurse; rehabilitation and therapeutic professions related; religious studies; Russian; secondary education; sociology; soil science and agronomy; Spanish; special education; speech communication and rhetoric; statistics; telecommunications technology; theater design and technology; toxicology; turf and turfgrass management; visual and performing arts; women's studies.

Academics *Calendar:* semesters. *Degrees:* certificates, associate, and bachelor's. *Special study options:* accelerated degree program, adult/continuing education programs, distance learning, double majors, external degree program, honors programs, independent study, internships, study abroad.

Student Life *Housing:* college housing not available. *Activities and Organizations:* drama/theater group. *Campus security:* student patrols, 8-hour patrols by trained security personnel.

Athletics Member NJCAA. *Intercollegiate sports:* baseball M, basketball M, softball W, volleyball W. *Intramural sports:* badminton M/W, basketball M/W, cheerleading M(c)/W(c), equestrian sports M(c)/W(c), football M/W, golf M(c)/W(c), softball M/W, tennis M/W, volleyball M/W, weight lifting M/W.

Standardized Tests *Required:* SAT or ACT (for admission).

Costs (2020–21) *Tuition:* area resident $12,718 full-time, $524 per credit hour part-time; state resident $12,718 full-time, $524 per credit hour part-time; nonresident $21,310 full-time, $888 per credit hour part-time. Full-time tuition and fees vary according to course level, degree level, location, program, and student level. Part-time tuition and fees vary according to course level, course load, degree level, location, program, and student level. *Required fees:* $992 full-time. *Payment plans:* installment, deferred payment. *Waivers:* senior citizens and employees or children of employees.

Financial Aid Of all full-time matriculated undergraduates who enrolled in 2018, 527 applied for aid, 456 were judged to have need, 76 had their need fully met. In 2018, 55 non-need-based awards were made. *Average percent of need met:* 61%. *Average financial aid package:* $11,145. *Average need-based loan:* $3975. *Average need-based gift aid:* $6060. *Average non-need-based aid:* $2567. *Average indebtedness upon graduation:* $36,499.

Applying *Options:* electronic application, early admission, early action, deferred entrance. *Application fee:* $65. *Required:* high school transcript. *Required for some:* interview. *Recommended:* essay or personal statement. *Application deadlines:* rolling (freshmen), rolling (transfers), 11/1 (early action). *Notification:* continuous (freshmen), continuous (transfers), 12/24 (early action).

Freshman Application Contact Admissions Office, Penn State Fayette, The Eberly Campus, 2201 University Drive, Lemont Furnace, PA 15456. *Phone:* 724-430-4130. *Toll-free phone:* 877-568-4130. *Fax:* 724-430-4175. *E-mail:* feadm@psu.edu.
Website: http://www.fe.psu.edu/.

Penn State Mont Alto

Mont Alto, Pennsylvania

- **State-related** primarily 2-year, founded 1929, part of Pennsylvania State University
- **Small-town** campus
- **Coed,** 730 undergraduate students, 80% full-time, 58% women, 42% men

Undergraduates 587 full-time, 143 part-time. 15% are from out of state; 5% Black or African American, non-Hispanic/Latino; 7% Hispanic/Latino; 2% Asian, non-Hispanic/Latino; 5% Two or more races, non-Hispanic/Latino; 0.9% Race/ethnicity unknown; 0.4% international; 5% transferred in; 22% live on campus. *Retention:* 84% of full-time freshmen returned.

Freshmen *Admission:* 712 applied, 550 admitted, 188 enrolled. *Test scores:* SAT evidence-based reading and writing scores over 500: 74%; SAT math scores over 500: 76%; ACT scores over 18: 57%; SAT evidence-based reading and writing scores over 600: 20%; SAT math scores over 600: 20%; ACT scores over 24: 29%; SAT math scores over 700: 4%.

Faculty *Total:* 114, 50% full-time, 25% with terminal degrees. *Student/faculty ratio:* 8:1.

Majors Accounting; acting; actuarial science; adult and continuing education administration; advertising; aerospace, aeronautical and astronautical/space engineering; African American/Black studies; agribusiness; agricultural and extension education; agricultural business and management related; agricultural engineering; agricultural mechanization; agriculture; agronomy and crop science; animal sciences; animal sciences related; anthropology; applied economics; archeology; architectural engineering; art; art history, criticism and conservation; art teacher education; Asian studies (East); astronomy; atmospheric sciences and meteorology; biochemistry; bioengineering and biomedical engineering; biological and biomedical sciences related; biological and physical sciences; biology/biological sciences; biology/biotechnology laboratory technician; business administration and management; business/commerce; business/managerial economics; chemical engineering; chemistry; civil engineering; classics and classical languages; communication and journalism related; communication sciences and disorders; comparative literature; computer and information sciences; computer engineering; criminal justice/law enforcement administration; economics; electrical and electronics engineering; elementary education; engineering science; English; environmental/environmental health engineering; film/cinema/video studies; finance; food science; foreign language teacher education; forest sciences and biology; forest technology; French; geography; geological and earth sciences/geosciences related; geology/earth science; German; graphic design; health/health-care administration; history; horticultural science; hospitality administration related; human development and family studies; human nutrition; industrial engineering; information science/studies; international relations and affairs; Italian; Japanese; Jewish/Judaic studies; journalism; kinesiology and exercise science; labor and industrial relations; landscaping and groundskeeping; Latin American studies; liberal arts and sciences/liberal studies; management information systems; marketing/marketing management; materials science; mathematics; mechanical engineering; medical microbiology and bacteriology; medieval and Renaissance studies; mining and mineral engineering; music; natural resources and conservation related; natural resources/conservation; nuclear engineering; occupational therapist assistant; occupational therapy; organizational behavior; parks, recreation and leisure facilities management; petroleum engineering; philosophy; physical therapy technology; physics; political science and government; premedical studies; psychology; registered nursing/registered nurse; rehabilitation and therapeutic professions related; religious studies; Russian; secondary education; sociology; soil science and agronomy; Spanish; special education; speech communication and rhetoric; statistics; theater design and technology; toxicology; turf and turfgrass management; visual and performing arts; women's studies.

Academics *Calendar:* semesters. *Degrees:* certificates, associate, and bachelor's. *Special study options:* adult/continuing education programs, distance learning, double majors, external degree program, honors programs, independent study, internships, study abroad. *ROTC:* Army (c).

Student Life *Housing Options:* coed, special housing for students with disabilities. Campus housing is university owned. Freshman campus housing is guaranteed. *Activities and Organizations:* drama/theater group, student-run newspaper, choral group. *Campus security:* 24-hour patrols, controlled dormitory access.

Athletics Member NJCAA. *Intercollegiate sports:* basketball M/W, cheerleading M/W, cross-country running M/W, golf M/W, soccer M/W, softball W, tennis M/W, volleyball W. *Intramural sports:* badminton M/W, basketball M/W, cheerleading M(c)/W(c), racquetball M/W, soccer M/W, softball W, volleyball M/W.

Standardized Tests *Required:* SAT or ACT (for admission).

Costs (2020–21) *Tuition:* area resident $12,718 full-time, $524 per credit hour part-time; state resident $12,718 full-time, $524 per credit hour part-time; nonresident $21,310 full-time, $888 per credit hour part-time. Full-time tuition and fees vary according to course level, degree level, location, program, and student level. Part-time tuition and fees vary according to course level, course load, degree level, location, program, and student level. *Required fees:* $992 full-time. *Room and board:* $11,510; room only: $6180. Room and board charges vary according to board plan, housing facility, and location. *Payment plans:* installment, deferred payment. *Waivers:* senior citizens and employees or children of employees.

Financial Aid Of all full-time matriculated undergraduates who enrolled in 2018, 529 applied for aid, 456 were judged to have need, 116 had their need fully met. In 2018, 43 non-need-based awards were made. *Average percent of need met:* 62%. *Average financial aid package:* $10,768. *Average need-based loan:* $3798. *Average need-based gift aid:* $5354. *Average non-need-based aid:* $3860. *Average indebtedness upon graduation:* $42,611.

Applying *Options:* electronic application, early admission, early action, deferred entrance. *Application fee:* $65. *Required:* high school transcript. *Required for some:* interview. *Recommended:* essay or personal statement. *Application deadlines:* rolling (freshmen), rolling (transfers), 11/1 (early action). *Notification:* continuous (freshmen), continuous (transfers), 12/24 (early action).

Freshman Application Contact Admissions Office, Penn State Mont Alto, 1 Campus Drive, Mont Alto, PA 17237. *Phone:* 717-749-6130. *Toll-free phone:* 800-392-6173. *Fax:* 717-749-6132. *E-mail:* psuma@psu.edu.
Website: http://www.ma.psu.edu/.

Pennsylvania Highlands Community College

Johnstown, Pennsylvania

Freshman Application Contact Mr. Jeff Maul, Admissions Officer, Pennsylvania Highlands Community College, 101 Community College Way, Johnstown, PA 15904. *Phone:* 814-262-6431. *Toll-free phone:* 888-385-7325. *Fax:* 814-269-9743. *E-mail:* jmaul@pennhighlands.edu. *Website:* http://www.pennhighlands.edu/.

Pennsylvania Institute of Health and Technology

Mount Braddock, Pennsylvania

Admissions Office Contact Pennsylvania Institute of Health and Technology, 1015 Mount Braddock Road, Mount Braddock, PA 15465. *Website:* http://www.piht.edu/.

Pennsylvania Institute of Technology

Media, Pennsylvania

Freshman Application Contact Mr. Matthew Meyers, Director of Admissions, Pennsylvania Institute of Technology, 800 Manchester Avenue, Media, PA 19063-4036. *Phone:* 610-892-1543. *Toll-free phone:* 800-422-0025. *Fax:* 610-892-1510. *E-mail:* info@pit.edu. *Website:* http://www.pit.edu/.

Pittsburgh Career Institute

Pittsburgh, Pennsylvania

- **Proprietary** 2-year, founded 1980
- **Urban** campus
- **Coed**

Undergraduates *Retention:* 55% of full-time freshmen returned.
Faculty *Student/faculty ratio:* 136:1.
Academics *Calendar:* continuous. *Degree:* associate. *Special study options:* academic remediation for entering students, accelerated degree program, adult/continuing education programs, advanced placement credit, cooperative education, English as a second language, internships, services for LD students.
Library Campus Library.
Student Life *Campus security:* 24-hour emergency response devices, 14-hour security patrols Monday through Friday.
Standardized Tests *Recommended:* SAT or ACT (for admission), SAT Subject Tests (for admission).
Financial Aid Of all full-time matriculated undergraduates who enrolled in 2018, 25 Federal Work-Study jobs (averaging $1200).
Applying *Options:* electronic application, early admission, deferred entrance. *Application fee:* $25. *Required:* high school transcript, interview.
Freshman Application Contact Pittsburgh Career Institute, 421 Seventh Avenue, Pittsburgh, PA 15219-1907. *Phone:* 412-281-2600. *Toll-free phone:* 800-333-6607. *Website:* http://www.pci.edu/.

Pittsburgh Institute of Aeronautics

Pittsburgh, Pennsylvania

Freshman Application Contact Steven D. Sabold, Director of Admissions, Pittsburgh Institute of Aeronautics, PO Box 10897, Pittsburgh, PA 15236-0897. *Phone:* 412-346-2100. *Toll-free phone:* 800-444-1440. *Fax:* 412-466-5013. *E-mail:* admissions@pia.edu. *Website:* http://www.pia.edu/.

Pittsburgh Institute of Mortuary Science, Incorporated

Pittsburgh, Pennsylvania

Freshman Application Contact Ms. Karen Rocco, Registrar, Pittsburgh Institute of Mortuary Science, Incorporated, 5808 Baum Boulevard, Pittsburgh, PA 15206-3706. *Phone:* 412-362-8500 Ext. 105. *Fax:* 412-362-1684. *E-mail:* pims5808@aol.com. *Website:* http://www.pims.edu/.

Pittsburgh Technical College

Oakdale, Pennsylvania

Freshman Application Contact Ms. Nancy Goodlin, Admissions Office Assistant, Pittsburgh Technical College, 1111 McKee Road, Oakdale, PA 15071. *Phone:* 412-809-5100. *Toll-free phone:* 800-784-9675. *Fax:* 412-809-5351. *E-mail:* goodlin.nancy@ptcollege.edu. *Website:* http://www.ptcollege.edu/.

Reading Area Community College

Reading, Pennsylvania

Freshman Application Contact Ms. Debbie Hettinger, Enrollment Services Coordinator/Communications Specialist, Reading Area Community College, PO Box 1706, Reading, PA 19603-1706. *Phone:* 610-372-4721 Ext. 5130. *E-mail:* dhettinger@racc.edu. *Website:* http://www.racc.edu/.

The Restaurant School at Walnut Hill College

Philadelphia, Pennsylvania

Freshman Application Contact Mr. John English, Director of Admissions, The Restaurant School at Walnut Hill College, 4207 Walnut Street, Philadelphia, PA 19104-3518. *Phone:* 267-295-2353. *Fax:* 215-222-4219. *E-mail:* jenglish@walnuthillcollege.edu. *Website:* http://www.walnuthillcollege.edu/.

Rosedale Technical Institute

Pittsburgh, Pennsylvania

Freshman Application Contact Ms. Debbie Bier, Director of Admissions, Rosedale Technical Institute, 215 Beecham Drive, Suite 2, Pittsburgh, PA 15205-9791. *Phone:* 412-521-6200. *Toll-free phone:* 800-521-6262. *Fax:* 412-521-2520. *E-mail:* admissions@rosedaletech.org. *Website:* http://www.rosedaletech.org/.

South Hills School of Business & Technology

State College, Pennsylvania

Freshman Application Contact Mr. Troy R. Otradovec, Regional Director of Admissions, South Hills School of Business & Technology, 480 Waupelani Drive, State College, PA 16801-4516. *Phone:* 814-234-7755 Ext. 2020. *Toll-free phone:* 888-282-7427. *Fax:* 814-234-0926. *E-mail:* admissions@southhills.edu. *Website:* http://www.southhills.edu/.

Thaddeus Stevens College of Technology

Lancaster, Pennsylvania

Freshman Application Contact Ms. Amy Kwiatkowski, Thaddeus Stevens College of Technology, 750 East King Street, Lancaster, PA 17055. *Phone:* 717-391-3540. *Toll-free phone:* 800-842-3832. *E-mail:* kwiatkowski@stevenscollege.edu. *Website:* http://www.stevenscollege.edu/.

Triangle Tech, Bethlehem

Bethlehem, Pennsylvania

Freshman Application Contact Triangle Tech, Bethlehem, 3184 Airport Road, Bethlehem, PA 18017. *Website:* http://www.triangle-tech.edu/.

Triangle Tech, DuBois

Falls Creek, Pennsylvania

Freshman Application Contact Terry Kucic, Director of Admissions, Triangle Tech, DuBois, PO Box 551, DuBois, PA 15801. *Phone:* 814-371-2090. *Toll-free phone:* 800-874-8324. *Fax:* 814-371-9227. *E-mail:* tkucic@triangle-tech.com. *Website:* http://www.triangle-tech.edu/.

Triangle Tech, Erie

Erie, Pennsylvania

Freshman Application Contact Admissions Representative, Triangle Tech, Erie, 2000 Liberty Street, Erie, PA 16502-2594. *Phone:* 814-453-6016. *Toll-free phone:* 800-874-8324 (in-state); 800-TRI-TECH (out-of-state). *Website:* http://www.triangle-tech.edu/.

Triangle Tech, Greensburg

Greensburg, Pennsylvania

Freshman Application Contact Mr. John Mazzarese, Vice President of Admissions, Triangle Tech, Greensburg, 222 East Pittsburgh Street, Greensburg, PA 15601. *Phone:* 412-359-1000. *Toll-free phone:* 800-874-8324. *Website:* http://www.triangle-tech.edu/.

Triangle Tech, Pittsburgh

Pittsburgh, Pennsylvania

Freshman Application Contact Director of Admissions, Triangle Tech, Pittsburgh, 1940 Perrysville Avenue, Pittsburgh, PA 15214-3897. *Phone:* 412-359-1000. *Toll-free phone:* 800-874-8324. *Fax:* 412-359-1012. *E-mail:* info@triangle-tech.edu. *Website:* http://www.triangle-tech.edu/.

Triangle Tech, Sunbury

Sunbury, Pennsylvania

Freshman Application Contact Triangle Tech, Sunbury, 191 Performance Road, Sunbury, PA 17801. *Phone:* 412-359-1000. *Website:* http://www.triangle-tech.edu/.

University of Pittsburgh at Titusville

Titusville, Pennsylvania

- **State-related** 2-year, founded 1963, part of University of Pittsburgh System
- **Small-town** 10-acre campus
- **Endowment** $850,000
- **Coed**

Undergraduates 187 full-time, 38 part-time. Students come from 15 states and territories; 4% are from out of state; 13% Black or African American, non-Hispanic/Latino; 2% Hispanic/Latino; 0.9% Asian, non-Hispanic/Latino; 4% Two or more races, non-Hispanic/Latino; 10% transferred in; 52% live on campus.

Faculty *Student/faculty ratio:* 7:1.

Academics *Calendar:* semesters. *Degree:* associate. *Special study options:* academic remediation for entering students, advanced placement credit, distance learning, external degree program, internships, part-time degree program, summer session for credit.

Library Haskell Memorial Library.

Student Life *Campus security:* 24-hour emergency response devices and patrols, late-night transport/escort service, controlled dormitory access.

Athletics Member NJCAA.

Standardized Tests *Required:* SAT or ACT (for admission).

Costs (2019–20) *Tuition:* area resident $11,176 full-time, $465 per credit hour part-time; state resident $11,176 full-time, $465 per credit hour part-time; nonresident $21,116 full-time, $879 per credit hour part-time. Full-time tuition and fees vary according to program. Part-time tuition and fees vary according to program. *Required fees:* $830 full-time. *Room and board:* $11,142; room only: $5800. Room and board charges vary according to board plan.

Financial Aid Of all full-time matriculated undergraduates who enrolled in 2018, 181 applied for aid, 168 were judged to have need, 7 had their need fully met. In 2018, 13. *Average percent of need met:* 55. *Average financial aid package:* $11,629. *Average need-based loan:* $3453. *Average need-based gift aid:* $8493. *Average non-need-based aid:* $3116.

Applying *Required:* high school transcript, minimum 2.0 GPA. *Required for some:* essay or personal statement. *Recommended:* interview.

Freshman Application Contact Ms. Colleen R. Motter, Admissions Counselor, University of Pittsburgh at Titusville, 504 East Main Street, Titusville, PA 16354. *Phone:* 814-827-4408. *Toll-free phone:* 888-878-0462. *Fax:* 814-827-4519. *E-mail:* motter@pitt.edu. *Website:* http://www.upt.pitt.edu/.

Valley Forge Military College

Wayne, Pennsylvania

Freshman Application Contact Maj. Greg Potts, Dean of Enrollment Management, Valley Forge Military College, 1001 Eagle Road, Wayne, PA 19087-3695. *Phone:* 610-989-1300. *Toll-free phone:* 800-234-8362. *Fax:* 610-688-1545. *E-mail:* admissions@vfmac.edu. *Website:* http://www.vfmac.edu/.

Vet Tech Institute

Pittsburgh, Pennsylvania

Freshman Application Contact Admissions Office, Vet Tech Institute, 125 7th Street, Pittsburgh, PA 15222-3400. *Phone:* 412-391-7021. *Toll-free phone:* 800-570-0693. *Website:* http://pittsburgh.vettechinstitute.edu/.

Westmoreland County Community College

Youngwood, Pennsylvania

- **County-supported** 2-year, founded 1970
- **Rural** 85-acre campus with easy access to Pittsburgh
- **Endowment** $2.4 million
- **Coed,** 4,645 undergraduate students, 37% full-time, 63% women, 37% men

Undergraduates 1,701 full-time, 2,944 part-time. Students come from 7 states and territories; 0.3% are from out of state; 4% Black or African American, non-Hispanic/Latino; 3% Hispanic/Latino; 0.4% Asian, non-Hispanic/Latino; 0.2% American Indian or Alaska Native, non-Hispanic/Latino; 4% Two or more races, non-Hispanic/Latino; 0.7% international; 4% transferred in.

Freshmen *Admission:* 3,344 applied, 3,344 admitted, 706 enrolled.

Faculty *Total:* 369, 22% full-time, 4% with terminal degrees. *Student/faculty ratio:* 14:1.

Majors Accounting technology and bookkeeping; administrative assistant and secretarial science; architectural drafting and CAD/CADD; baking and pastry arts; banking and financial support services; biology/biological sciences; business/commerce; computer and information systems security; computer programming; computer support specialist; computer systems networking and telecommunications; criminal justice/police science; criminal justice/safety; criminology; culinary arts; dental assisting; dental hygiene; desktop publishing and digital imaging design; diagnostic medical sonography and ultrasound technology; dietetic technology; early childhood education; electrical, electronic and communications engineering technology; fine arts related; fine/studio arts; graphic design; health services/allied health/health sciences; heating, air conditioning, ventilation and refrigeration maintenance technology; hotel/motel administration; human resources management; human services; industrial mechanics and maintenance technology; instrumentation technology; legal assistant/paralegal; liberal arts and sciences/liberal studies; machine tool technology; manufacturing engineering technology; mathematics; mechanical drafting and CAD/CADD; mechanical engineering/mechanical technology; medical administrative assistant and medical secretary; photographic and film/video technology; physics; plumbing technology; psychology; radiologic technology/science; real estate; registered nursing/registered nurse; restaurant, culinary, and catering management; sales, distribution, and marketing operations; small business administration; web page, digital/multimedia and information resources design; welding technology.

Academics *Calendar:* semesters. *Degree:* certificates, diplomas, and associate. *Special study options:* academic remediation for entering students, advanced placement credit, cooperative education, distance learning, double majors, English as a second language, honors programs, independent study, internships, part-time degree program, services for LD students, summer session for credit.

Library Westmoreland County Community College Learning Resources Center. *Books:* 25,150 (physical), 202,718 (digital/electronic); *Serial titles:* 24 (physical), 53,023 (digital/electronic); *Databases:* 31. Weekly public service hours: 59; students can reserve study rooms.

Student Life *Housing:* college housing not available. *Activities and Organizations:* Phi Theta Kappa, Sigma Alpha Pi Leadership Society, Criminal Justice Fraternity, SNAP, SADAA/SADHA. *Campus security:* 24-hour emergency response devices and patrols, county police office on campus. *Student services:* personal/psychological counseling, veterans affairs office.

Athletics Member NJCAA. *Intercollegiate sports:* baseball M, basketball M/W, bowling M/W, cross-country running M/W, golf M/W, soccer M/W, softball W, volleyball W. *Intramural sports:* basketball M/W, soccer M/W, volleyball M/W.

Costs (2020–21) *Tuition:* area resident $5598 full-time, $133 per credit hour part-time; state resident $9732 full-time, $266 per credit hour part-time; nonresident $13,722 full-time, $399 per credit hour part-time. *Required fees:* $67 per credit hour part-time. *Payment plan:* installment. *Waivers:* senior citizens and employees or children of employees.

Applying *Options:* electronic application, early admission. *Required:* high school transcript. *Application deadlines:* rolling (freshmen), rolling (transfers). *Notification:* continuous (freshmen), continuous (transfers).

Freshman Application Contact Ms. Ashlee Lee, Admissions Coordinator, Westmoreland County Community College, 145 Pavillon Lane, Youngwood,

PA 15697. *Phone:* 724-925-4077. *Toll-free phone:* 800-262-2103. *Fax:* 724-925-4292. *E-mail:* leeas@westmoreland.edu. *Website:* http://www.westmoreland.edu/.

Williamson College of the Trades

Media, Pennsylvania

Freshman Application Contact Mr. Jay Merillat, Dean of Admissions, Williamson College of the Trades, 106 South New Middletown Road, Media, PA 19063. *Phone:* 610-566-1776 Ext. 235. *E-mail:* jmerillat@williamson.edu. *Website:* http://www.williamson.edu/.

YTI Career Institute–Altoona

Altoona, Pennsylvania

Admissions Office Contact YTI Career Institute–Altoona, 2900 Fairway Drive, Altoona, PA 16602. *Website:* http://www.yti.edu/.

YTI Career Institute–Lancaster

Lancaster, Pennsylvania

Admissions Office Contact YTI Career Institute–Lancaster, 3050 Hempland Road, Lancaster, PA 17601. *Website:* http://www.yti.edu/.

YTI Career Institute - York

York, Pennsylvania

Freshman Application Contact YTI Career Institute - York, 1405 Williams Road, York, PA 17402-9017. *Phone:* 717-757-1100 Ext. 318. *Toll-free phone:* 800-557-6335. *Website:* http://www.yti.edu/.

PUERTO RICO

The Center of Cinematography, Arts and Television

Bayamon, Puerto Rico

Admissions Office Contact The Center of Cinematography, Arts and Television, 51 Dr. Veve Street, Degetau Street Corner, Bayamon, PR 00960. *Website:* http://ccatmiami.com/.

Centro de Estudios Multidisciplinarios - Mayaguez

Mayaguez, Puerto Rico

Admissions Office Contact Centro de Estudios Multidisciplinarios - Mayaguez, Calle Cristy #56, Mayaguez, PR 00680. *Website:* http://www.cemcollege.edu/.

Centro de Estudios Multidisciplinarios - San Juan

Rio Piedras, Puerto Rico

Director of Admissions Admissions Department, Centro de Estudios Multidisciplinarios - San Juan, Calle 13 #1206, Ext. San Agustin, Rio Piedras, PR 00926. *Phone:* 787-765-4210 Ext. 115. *Toll-free phone:* 877-779-CDEM. *Website:* http://www.cemcollege.edu/.

Dewey University–Bayamón

Bayamón, Puerto Rico

Admissions Office Contact Dewey University–Bayamón, Carr. #2, Km. 15.9, Parque Industrial Corujo, Hato Tejas, Bayamón, PR 00959. *Website:* http://www.dewey.edu/.

Dewey University–Carolina

Carolina, Puerto Rico

Admissions Office Contact Dewey University–Carolina, Carr. #3, Km. 11, Parque Industrial de Carolina, Lote 7, Carolina, PR 00986. *Website:* http://www.dewey.edu/.

Dewey University–Fajardo

Fajardo, Puerto Rico

Admissions Office Contact Dewey University–Fajardo, 267 Calle General Valero, Fajardo, PR 00910. *Website:* http://www.dewey.edu/.

Dewey University–Hato Rey

Hato Rey, Puerto Rico

Admissions Office Contact Dewey University–Hato Rey, 427 Avenida Barbosa, Hato Rey, PR 00923. *Website:* http://www.dewey.edu/.

Dewey University–Juana Diaz

Juana Diaz, Puerto Rico

Admissions Office Contact Dewey University–Juana Diaz, Carr. 149, Km. 55.9, Parque Industrial Lomas, Juana Diaz, PR 00910. *Website:* http://www.dewey.edu/.

Dewey University–Manati

Manati, Puerto Rico

Admissions Office Contact Dewey University–Manati, Carr. 604, Km. 49.1 Barrio Tierras Nuevas, Salientes, Manati, PR 00674. *Toll-free phone:* 866-773-3939. *Website:* http://www.dewey.edu/.

Dewey University–Mayaguez

Mayaguez, Puerto Rico

Admissions Office Contact Dewey University–Mayaguez, Carr. #64 Km 6.6 Barrio Algarrobo, Mayaguez, PR 00682. *Website:* http://www.dewey.edu/.

EDIC College

Caguas, Puerto Rico

Admissions Office Contact EDIC College, Ave. Rafael Cordero Calle Génova Urb. Caguas Norte, Caguas, PR 00726. *Website:* http://www.ediccollege.edu/.

Huertas College

Caguas, Puerto Rico

Director of Admissions Mrs. Barbara Hassim López, Director of Admissions, Huertas College, PO Box 8429, Caguas, PR 00726. *Phone:* 787-743-1242. *Fax:* 787-743-0203. *E-mail:* huertas@huertas.org. *Website:* http://www.huertas.edu/.

Humacao Community College

Humacao, Puerto Rico

Freshman Application Contact Mrs. Arlene Osorio, Recruitment and Promotion Official, Humacao Community College, PO Box 9139, Humacao, PR 00792, Puerto Rico. *Phone:* 787-852-1430 Ext. 225. *Fax:* 787-850-1577. *E-mail:* arlene.osorio@hccpr.edu. *Website:* http://www.hccpr.edu/.

ICPR Junior College–Hato Rey Campus

Hato Rey, Puerto Rico

Freshman Application Contact Admissions Office, ICPR Junior College–Hato Rey Campus, 558 Munoz Rivera Avenue, PO Box 190304, Hato Rey, PR 00919-0304. *Phone:* 787-753-6335. *Website:* http://www.icprjc.edu/.

Ponce Paramedical College

Ponce, Puerto Rico

Admissions Office Contact Ponce Paramedical College, L-15 Acacia Street Villa Flores Urbanizacion, Ponce, PR 00731. *Website:* http://www.popac.edu/.

RHODE ISLAND

Community College of Rhode Island

Warwick, Rhode Island

Freshman Application Contact Community College of Rhode Island, Flanagan Campus, 1762 Louisquisset Pike, Lincoln, RI 02865-4585. *Phone:* 401-333-7490. *Fax:* 401-333-7122. *E-mail:* webadmission@ccri.edu. *Website:* http://www.ccri.edu/.

SOUTH CAROLINA

Aiken Technical College

Graniteville, South Carolina

Freshman Application Contact Jessica Moon, Director of Enrollment Services, Aiken Technical College, 2276 J. Davis Highway, Graniteville, SC 29829. *Phone:* 803-508-7262 Ext. 156. *E-mail:* moonj@atc.edu. *Website:* http://www.atc.edu/.

Central Carolina Technical College

Sumter, South Carolina

- **State-supported** 2-year, founded 1963, part of South Carolina State Board for Technical and Comprehensive Education
- **Small-town** 70-acre campus with easy access to Columbia
- **Endowment** $1.4 million
- **Coed**

Undergraduates 1,607 full-time, 2,915 part-time. 1% are from out of state; 48% Black or African American, non-Hispanic/Latino; 2% Hispanic/Latino; 0.8% Asian, non-Hispanic/Latino; 0.1% American Indian or Alaska Native, non-Hispanic/Latino; 0.6% Two or more races, non Hispanic/Latino; 5% Race/ethnicity unknown; 7% transferred in.
Faculty *Student/faculty ratio:* 17:1.
Academics *Calendar:* semesters. *Degree:* certificates, diplomas, and associate. *Special study options:* academic remediation for entering students, accelerated degree program, adult/continuing education programs, advanced placement credit, cooperative education, distance learning, external degree program, independent study, internships, part-time degree program, services for LD students, summer session for credit.
Library Central Carolina Technical College Library.
Student Life *Campus security:* 24-hour emergency response devices, student patrols, security patrols parking lots and halls during working hours and off-duty police officers are deployed on main campus during peak hours.
Standardized Tests *Required:* ACT Compass/ACT ASSET (for admission). *Required for some:* SAT or ACT (for admission).
Applying *Options:* electronic application. *Required for some:* high school transcript.
Freshman Application Contact Ms. Barbara Wright, Director of Admissions and Counseling, Central Carolina Technical College, 506 North Guignard Drive, Sumter, SC 29150. *Phone:* 803-778-6695. *Toll-free phone:* 800-221-8711. *Fax:* 803-778-6696. *E-mail:* wrightb@cctech.edu. *Website:* http://www.cctech.edu/.

Centura College

Columbia, South Carolina

Admissions Office Contact Centura College, 7500 Two Notch Road, Columbia, SC 29223. *Website:* http://www.centuracollege.edu/.

Clinton College

Rock Hill, South Carolina

- **Independent** 2-year, founded 1894, affiliated with African Methodist Episcopal Zion Church
- **Coed**

Undergraduates 45% are from out of state.
Faculty *Student/faculty ratio:* 15:1.
Academics *Calendar:* semesters. *Degree:* associate.
Athletics Member NJCAA.
Applying *Application fee:* $25.
Director of Admissions Robert M. Copeland, Vice President for Student Affairs, Clinton College, 1029 Crawford Road, Rock Hill, SC 29730. *Phone:* 803-327-7402. *Toll-free phone:* 877-837-9645. *Fax:* 803-327-3261. *E-mail:* rcopeland@clintonjrcollege.org. *Website:* http://www.clintoncollege.edu/.

Denmark Technical College

Denmark, South Carolina

- **State-supported** 2-year, founded 1948, part of South Carolina State Board for Technical and Comprehensive Education
- **Rural** 53-acre campus
- **Coed**

Undergraduates 655 full-time, 388 part-time. 4% are from out of state; 92% Black or African American, non-Hispanic/Latino; 0.8% Hispanic/Latino; 0.2% Asian, non-Hispanic/Latino; 0.2% American Indian or Alaska Native, non-Hispanic/Latino; 0.4% Race/ethnicity unknown; 0.8% transferred in. *Retention:* 28% of full-time freshmen returned.
Faculty *Student/faculty ratio:* 20:1.
Academics *Calendar:* semesters. *Degree:* certificates, diplomas, and associate. *Special study options:* academic remediation for entering students, adult/continuing education programs, advanced placement credit, cooperative education, distance learning, independent study, internships, off-campus study, part-time degree program, services for LD students, summer session for credit.
Library Denmark Technical College Learning Resources Center. *Books:* 9,810 (physical); *Databases:* 2. Weekly public service hours: 40; study areas open 24 hours, 5–7 days a week; students can reserve study rooms.
Student Life *Campus security:* 24-hour emergency response devices and patrols, late-night transport/escort service.
Athletics Member NJCAA.
Standardized Tests *Required:* ACT ASSET, ACCUPLACER, and TEAS (for nursing) (for admission). *Recommended:* SAT or ACT (for admission).
Financial Aid Of all full-time matriculated undergraduates who enrolled in 2018, 250 Federal Work-Study jobs (averaging $2000).
Applying *Options:* electronic application, early admission, deferred entrance. *Application fee:* $10. *Required:* high school transcript. *Required for some:* essay or personal statement, criminal background check, drug test, PPD test for LPN.
Freshman Application Contact Ms. Kara Troy, Administrative Specialist II, Denmark Technical College, PO Box 327, 1126 Solomon Blatt Boulevard, Denmark, SC 29042. *Phone:* 803-793-5180. *Fax:* 803-793-5942. *E-mail:* troyk@denmarktech.edu. *Website:* http://www.denmarktech.edu/.

Florence-Darlington Technical College

Florence, South Carolina

Director of Admissions Shelley Fortin, Vice President for Enrollment Management and Student Services, Florence-Darlington Technical College, 2715 West Lucas Street, PO Box 100548, Florence, SC 29501-0548. *Phone:* 843-661-8111 Ext. 117. *Toll-free phone:* 800-228-5745. *E-mail:* shelley.fortin@fdtc.edu. *Website:* http://www.fdtc.edu/.

Forrest College

Anderson, South Carolina

Freshman Application Contact Ms. Janie Turmon, Admissions and Placement Coordinator/Representative, Forrest College, 601 East River Street, Anderson, SC 29624. *Phone:* 864-225-7653. *Fax:* 864-261-7471. *E-mail:* janieturmon@forrestcollege.edu. *Website:* http://www.forrestcollege.edu/.

Fortis College

Columbia, South Carolina

Admissions Office Contact Fortis College, 246 Stoneridge Drive, Suite 101, Columbia, SC 29210. *Toll-free phone:* 855-4-FORTIS. *Website:* http://www.fortis.edu/.

Greenville Technical College

Greenville, South Carolina

- **State-supported** 2-year, founded 1962, part of South Carolina State Board for Technical and Comprehensive Education
- **Urban** 604-acre campus
- **Coed,** 11,745 undergraduate students, 41% full-time, 60% women, 40% men

Undergraduates 4,809 full-time, 6,936 part-time. 1% are from out of state.
Freshmen *Admission:* 4,922 applied, 4,911 admitted, 2,240 enrolled.
Majors Accounting; administrative assistant and secretarial science; architectural engineering technology; autobody/collision and repair technology; automobile/automotive mechanics technology; business administration and management; child-care and support services management;

clinical/medical laboratory technology; computer numerically controlled (CNC) machinist technology; construction engineering technology; criminal justice/safety; culinary arts; data processing and data processing technology; dental hygiene; diagnostic medical sonography and ultrasound technology; drafting and design technology; electrical, electronic and communications engineering technology; electromechanical and instrumentation and maintenance technologies related; emergency medical technology (EMT paramedic); health information/medical records technology; human services; legal assistant/paralegal; liberal arts and sciences/liberal studies; machine tool technology; mechanical engineering/mechanical technology; mechanic and repair technologies related; medical radiologic technology; multi/interdisciplinary studies related; occupational therapist assistant; physical therapy technology; purchasing, procurement/acquisitions and contracts management; registered nursing/registered nurse; respiratory care therapy; sales, distribution, and marketing operations.
Academics *Calendar:* semesters. *Degree:* certificates, diplomas, and associate. *Special study options:* academic remediation for entering students, advanced placement credit, cooperative education, distance learning, double majors, English as a second language, honors programs, independent study, internships, part-time degree program, services for LD students, summer session for credit.
Library J. Verne Smith Library plus 3 others. Weekly public service hours: 59.
Student Life *Housing Options:* coed. Campus housing is university owned. *Activities and Organizations:* Phi Theta Kappa, Kappa Omega Sigma - Cosmetology Club, Student Government Association (SGA). *Campus security:* 24-hour emergency response devices and patrols, late-night transport/escort service. *Student services:* veterans affairs office.
Athletics *Intramural sports:* basketball M(c)/W(c), bowling M(c)/W(c), football M(c)/W(c), softball M(c)/W(c), table tennis M(c)/W(c), tennis M(c)/W(c), volleyball M(c)/W(c).
Costs (2019–20) *Tuition:* area resident $5520 full-time, $184 per credit hour part-time; state resident $6030 full-time, $201 per credit hour part-time; nonresident $11,310 full-time, $377 per credit hour part-time. Full-time tuition and fees vary according to course load and program. Part-time tuition and fees vary according to course load and program. *Required fees:* $410 full-time, $8 per credit hour part-time, $85 per term part-time. *Payment plans:* installment, deferred payment. *Waivers:* senior citizens.
Applying *Options:* electronic application, early admission, deferred entrance. *Application deadlines:* rolling (freshmen), rolling (transfers). *Notification:* continuous until 8/18 (freshmen), continuous until 8/18 (transfers).
Freshman Application Contact Greenville Technical College, PO Box 5616, Greenville, SC 29606-5616. *Phone:* 864-250-8107. *Toll-free phone:* 800-992-1183 (in-state); 800-723-0673 (out-of-state).
Website: http://www.gvltec.edu/.

Horry-Georgetown Technical College

Conway, South Carolina

Freshman Application Contact Cynthia Johnston, Assistant Vice President for Enrollment Services, Horry-Georgetown Technical College, 2050 Highway 501 East, PO Box 261966, Conway, SC 29528-6066. *Phone:* 843-349-7835. *Fax:* 843-349-7588. *E-mail:* cynthia.johnston@hgtc.edu. *Website:* http://www.hgtc.edu/.

Midlands Technical College

Columbia, South Carolina

- **State and locally supported** 2-year, founded 1974, part of South Carolina State Board for Technical and Comprehensive Education
- **Suburban** 156-acre campus
- **Endowment** $6.9 million
- **Coed**

Undergraduates 4,981 full-time, 5,965 part-time. Students come from 30 states and territories; 65 other countries; 2% are from out of state; 36% Black or African American, non-Hispanic/Latino; 5% Hispanic/Latino; 2% Asian, non-Hispanic/Latino; 0.2% Native Hawaiian or other Pacific Islander, non-Hispanic/Latino; 0.3% American Indian or Alaska Native, non-Hispanic/Latino; 5% Two or more races, non-Hispanic/Latino; 5% Race/ethnicity unknown; 10% transferred in.
Faculty *Student/faculty ratio:* 20:1.
Academics *Calendar:* semesters. *Degree:* certificates, diplomas, and associate. *Special study options:* academic remediation for entering students, adult/continuing education programs, advanced placement credit, cooperative education, distance learning, double majors, English as a second language, internships, part-time degree program, services for LD students, student-designed majors, summer session for credit. *ROTC:* Army (c), Navy (c), Air Force (c).
Library Midlands Technical College Library plus 5 others. *Books:* 50,329 (physical), 354,481 (digital/electronic); *Serial titles:* 295 (physical); *Databases:* 111. Weekly public service hours: 58; students can reserve study rooms.
Student Life *Campus security:* 24-hour emergency response devices and patrols, late-night transport/escort service.
Standardized Tests *Required for some:* ACT ASSET. *Recommended:* SAT or ACT (for admission).
Financial Aid Of all full-time matriculated undergraduates who enrolled in 2011, 4,794 applied for aid, 4,160 were judged to have need, 118 had their need fully met. 154 Federal Work-Study jobs (averaging $2775). *Average percent of need met:* 13. *Average financial aid package:* $6098. *Average need-based loan:* $3089. *Average need-based gift aid:* $4370.
Applying *Options:* electronic application, early admission, deferred entrance. *Application fee:* $35. *Recommended:* high school transcript.
Freshman Application Contact Ms. Sylvia Littlejohn, Director of Admissions, Midlands Technical College, PO Box 2408, Columbia, SC 29202. *Phone:* 803-738-8324. *Toll-free phone:* 800-922-8038. *Fax:* 803-790-7524. *E-mail:* admissions@midlandstech.edu. *Website:* http://www.midlandstech.edu/.

Miller-Motte College - Charleston

North Charleston, South Carolina

Freshman Application Contact Ms. Elaine Cue, Campus President, Miller-Motte College - Charleston, 8085 Rivers Avenue, North Charleston, SC 29406. *Phone:* 843-574-0101. *Toll-free phone:* 800-705-9182. *Fax:* 843-266-3424. *E-mail:* juliasc@miller-mott.net. *Website:* http://www.miller-motte.edu/.

Miller-Motte Technical College - Conway

Conway, South Carolina

Admissions Office Contact Miller-Motte Technical College - Conway, 2451 Highway 501 East, Conway, SC 29526. *Toll-free phone:* 800-705-9182. *Website:* http://www.miller-motte.edu/.

Northeastern Technical College

Cheraw, South Carolina

Freshman Application Contact Mrs. Joy L. Hicks, Admissions Administrative Specialist, Northeastern Technical College, 1201 Chesterfield Highway, Cheraw, SC 29520-1007. *Phone:* 843-921-1461. *Toll-free phone:* 800-921-7399. *Fax:* 843-921-1476. *E-mail:* jhicks@netc.edu. *Website:* http://www.netc.edu/.

Orangeburg-Calhoun Technical College

Orangeburg, South Carolina

Freshman Application Contact Mr. Dana Rickards, Director of Recruitment, Orangeburg-Calhoun Technical College, 3250 St Matthews Road, NE, Orangeburg, SC 29118-8299. *Phone:* 803-535-1219. *Toll-free phone:* 800-813-6519. *Website:* http://www.octech.edu/.

Piedmont Technical College

Greenwood, South Carolina

Director of Admissions Mr. Steve Coleman, Director of Admissions, Piedmont Technical College, 620 North Emerald Road, PO Box 1467, Greenwood, SC 29648-1467. *Phone:* 864-941-8603. *Toll-free phone:* 800-868-5528. *Website:* http://www.ptc.edu/.

Spartanburg Community College

Spartanburg, South Carolina

Freshman Application Contact Ms. Sabrina Sims, Admissions Counselor, Spartanburg Community College, PO Box 4386, Spartanburg, SC 29305. *Phone:* 864-592-4816. *Toll-free phone:* 866-591-3700. *Fax:* 864-592-4564. *E-mail:* admissions@sccsc.edu. *Website:* http://www.sccsc.edu/.

Spartanburg Methodist College

Spartanburg, South Carolina

- **Independent Methodist** 2-year, founded 1911
- **Suburban** 110-acre campus with easy access to Charlotte
- **Endowment** $22.0 million
- **Coed**

Undergraduates 784 full-time, 6 part-time. Students come from 16 states and territories; 3 other countries; 9% are from out of state; 38% Black or African American, non-Hispanic/Latino; 8% Hispanic/Latino; 0.9% Asian, non-

Hispanic/Latino; 0.3% American Indian or Alaska Native, non-Hispanic/Latino; 3% Two or more races, non-Hispanic/Latino; 0.4% international; 5% transferred in; 61% live on campus.
Faculty *Student/faculty ratio:* 20:1.
Academics *Calendar:* semesters. *Degree:* associate. *Special study options:* academic remediation for entering students, advanced placement credit, English as a second language, honors programs, independent study, part-time degree program, services for LD students, summer session for credit.
Library Marie Blair Burgess Library. *Books:* 46,541 (physical), 155,060 (digital/electronic); *Databases:* 80. Weekly public service hours: 72; students can reserve study rooms.
Student Life *Campus security:* 24-hour emergency response devices and patrols, student patrols, late-night transport/escort service, controlled dormitory access.
Athletics Member NJCAA.
Standardized Tests *Required:* SAT or ACT (for admission).
Costs (2019–20) *One-time required fee:* $200. *Comprehensive fee:* $26,810 includes full-time tuition ($15,750), mandatory fees ($1560), and room and board ($9500). Full-time tuition and fees vary according to course load. Part-time tuition: $425 per credit hour. Part-time tuition and fees vary according to course load.
Financial Aid Of all full-time matriculated undergraduates who enrolled in 2018, 80 Federal Work-Study jobs (averaging $1600). 90 state and other part-time jobs (averaging $1600). *Financial aid deadline:* 8/30.
Applying *Options:* electronic application, deferred entrance. *Application fee:* $25. *Required:* essay or personal statement, high school transcript, minimum 2.0 GPA. *Required for some:* interview. *Recommended:* interview.
Freshman Application Contact Mr. Wells Shepard, Vice President for Enrollment, Spartanburg Methodist College, 1000 Powell Mill Road, Spartanburg, SC 29301-5899. *Phone:* 864-587-4254. *Toll-free phone:* 800-772-7286. *Fax:* 864-587-4355. *E-mail:* admiss@smcsc.edu. *Website:* http://www.smcsc.edu/.

Technical College of the Lowcountry
Beaufort, South Carolina

Freshman Application Contact Rhonda Cole, Admissions Services Manager, Technical College of the Lowcountry, 921 Ribaut Road, PO Box 1288, Beaufort, SC 29901-1288. *Phone:* 843-525-8229. *Fax:* 843-525-8285. *E-mail:* rcole@tcl.edu. *Website:* http://www.tcl.edu/.

Tri-County Technical College
Pendleton, South Carolina

Freshman Application Contact Tri-County Technical College, PO Box 587, 7900 Highway 76, Pendleton, SC 29670-0587. *Phone:* 864-646-1550. *Website:* http://www.tctc.edu/.

Trident Technical College
Charleston, South Carolina

- **State and locally supported** 2-year, founded 1964, part of South Carolina State Board for Technical and Comprehensive Education
- **Urban** campus
- **Coed,** 201,388 undergraduate students, 96% full-time, 4% women, 96% men

Undergraduates 193,654 full-time, 7,734 part-time. Students come from 28 states and territories; 62 other countries; 1% are from out of state; 26% Black or African American, non-Hispanic/Latino; 7% Hispanic/Latino; 2% Asian, non-Hispanic/Latino; 0.5% Native Hawaiian or other Pacific Islander, non-Hispanic/Latino; 0.5% American Indian or Alaska Native, non-Hispanic/Latino; 4% Two or more races, non-Hispanic/Latino; 2% Race/ethnicity unknown; 0.5% transferred in.
Freshmen *Admission:* 1,918 enrolled.
Faculty *Total:* 560, 47% full-time, 8% with terminal degrees. *Student/faculty ratio:* 19:1.
Majors Accounting; administrative assistant and secretarial science; airframe mechanics and aircraft maintenance technology; automobile/automotive mechanics technology; biological and physical sciences; business administration and management; child-care provision; civil engineering technology; clinical/medical laboratory technology; commercial and advertising art; computer engineering technology; computer graphics; computer/information technology services administration related; computer programming (specific applications); computer systems networking and telecommunications; criminal justice/law enforcement administration; culinary arts; dental hygiene; electrical, electronic and communications engineering technology; engineering technology; horticultural science; hotel/motel administration; human services; industrial technology; legal assistant/paralegal; legal studies; liberal arts and sciences/liberal studies; machine tool technology; marketing/marketing management; mechanical engineering/mechanical technology; medical administrative assistant and medical secretary; occupational therapy; physical therapy; registered nursing/registered nurse; respiratory care therapy; telecommunications technology; veterinary/animal health technology; web/multimedia management and webmaster; web page, digital/multimedia and information resources design.
Academics *Calendar:* semesters. *Degree:* certificates, diplomas, and associate. *Special study options:* academic remediation for entering students, advanced placement credit, cooperative education, distance learning, double majors, English as a second language, internships, off-campus study, part-time degree program, services for LD students, study abroad, summer session for credit.
Library Learning Resource Center plus 2 others. Students can reserve study rooms.
Student Life *Housing:* college housing not available. *Activities and Organizations:* drama/theater group, student-run newspaper, radio station, Phi Theta Kappa, Lex Artis Paralegal Society, Hospitality and Culinary Student Association, Partnership for Change in Communities and Families. *Campus security:* 24-hour emergency response devices and patrols, late-night transport/escort service. *Student services:* personal/psychological counseling.
Costs (2020–21) *Tuition:* area resident $4648 full-time, $189 per credit hour part-time; state resident $5143 full-time, $209 per credit hour part-time; nonresident $8690 full-time, $357 per credit hour part-time.
Applying *Options:* electronic application, early admission. *Application fee:* $30. *Required for some:* high school transcript. *Application deadlines:* 8/6 (freshmen), 8/6 (transfers). *Notification:* continuous (freshmen), continuous (transfers).
Freshman Application Contact Mr. Richard Waring, Interim Admissions Director, Trident Technical College, Charleston, SC 29423-8067. *Phone:* 843-574-6386. *Fax:* 843-574-6109. *E-mail:* robert.waring@tridenttech.edu. *Website:* http://www.tridenttech.edu/.

University of South Carolina Lancaster
Lancaster, South Carolina

- **State-supported** primarily 2-year, founded 1959, part of University of South Carolina System
- **Small-town** 17-acre campus with easy access to Charlotte
- **Coed,** 1,593 undergraduate students, 50% full-time, 60% women, 40% men

Undergraduates 794 full-time, 799 part-time. Students come from 10 states and territories; 2 other countries; 1% are from out of state.
Freshmen *Admission:* 557 applied, 555 admitted.
Faculty *Total:* 105, 60% full-time, 44% with terminal degrees. *Student/faculty ratio:* 14:1.
Majors Business administration and management; criminal justice/law enforcement administration; liberal arts and sciences/liberal studies; registered nursing/registered nurse.
Academics *Calendar:* semesters. *Degrees:* associate and bachelor's. *Special study options:* academic remediation for entering students, advanced placement credit, distance learning, honors programs, independent study, internships, part-time degree program, services for LD students.
Library Medford Library. Students can reserve study rooms.
Student Life *Housing:* college housing not available. *Activities and Organizations:* drama/theater group, student-run newspaper. *Student services:* personal/psychological counseling.
Athletics Member NJCAA. *Intercollegiate sports:* baseball M(s), soccer M(s)/W(s), volleyball W(s).
Standardized Tests *Required:* SAT or ACT (for admission).
Applying *Options:* electronic application, early admission. *Application fee:* $40. *Required:* high school transcript, Standardized test scores. *Application deadlines:* rolling (freshmen), rolling (out-of-state freshmen), rolling (transfers). *Notification:* continuous (freshmen), continuous (out-of-state freshmen), continuous (transfers).
Freshman Application Contact Jennifer Blackmon, Admissions Processor, University of South Carolina Lancaster, PO Box 889, Lancaster, SC 29721. *Phone:* 803-313-7073. *Fax:* 803-313-7116. *E-mail:* jblackmo@mailbox.sc.edu.
Website: http://usclancaster.sc.edu/.

University of South Carolina Salkehatchie
Allendale, South Carolina

Freshman Application Contact Ms. Carmen Brown, Admissions Coordinator, University of South Carolina Salkehatchie, PO Box 617, Allendale, SC 29810. *Phone:* 803-584-3446. *Toll-free phone:* 800-922-5500.

Fax: 803-584-3884. *E-mail:* cdbrown@mailbox.sc.edu. *Website:* http://uscsalkehatchie.sc.edu/.

University of South Carolina Sumter
Sumter, South Carolina

Freshman Application Contact Mr. Keith Britton, Director of Admissions, University of South Carolina Sumter, 200 Miller Road, Sumter, SC 29150-2498. *Phone:* 803-938-3882. *Fax:* 803-938-3901. *E-mail:* kbritton@usc.sumter.edu. *Website:* http://www.uscsumter.edu/.

University of South Carolina Union
Union, South Carolina

- **State-supported** primarily 2-year, founded 1965, part of University of South Carolina System
- **Small-town** 7-acre campus with easy access to Charlotte, North Carolina
- **Endowment** $1.2 million
- **Coed**

Undergraduates 487 full-time, 418 part-time. Students come from 3 states and territories; 1 other country; 2% are from out of state; 43% Black or African American, non-Hispanic/Latino; 3% Hispanic/Latino.
Faculty *Student/faculty ratio:* 18:1.
Academics *Calendar:* semesters. *Degrees:* associate and bachelor's. *Special study options:* advanced placement credit, cooperative education, distance learning, double majors, independent study, internships, part-time degree program, study abroad, summer session for credit.
Library Union Carnegie Library plus 1 other. Study areas open 24 hours, 5–7 days a week.
Student Life *Campus security:* 24-hour emergency response devices.
Athletics Member NJCAA.
Standardized Tests *Required:* SAT or ACT (for admission).
Financial Aid Of all full-time matriculated undergraduates who enrolled in 2018, 16 Federal Work-Study jobs (averaging $3400).
Applying *Options:* electronic application. *Application fee:* $40. *Required:* high school transcript.
Freshman Application Contact Mr. Michael B. Greer, Director of Enrollment Services, University of South Carolina Union, PO Drawer 729, Union, SC 29379-0729. *Phone:* 864-424-8039. *E-mail:* greerm@mailbox.sc.edu. *Website:* http://uscunion.sc.edu/.

Williamsburg Technical College
Kingstree, South Carolina

- **State-supported** 2-year, founded 1969, part of South Carolina State Board for Technical and Comprehensive Education
- **Rural** 41-acre campus
- **Coed,** 732 undergraduate students, 27% full-time, 61% women, 39% men

Undergraduates 194 full-time, 538 part-time. Students come from 1 other state; 76% Black or African American, non-Hispanic/Latino; 0.3% Asian, non-Hispanic/Latino; 0.1% American Indian or Alaska Native, non-Hispanic/Latino; 0.4% Race/ethnicity unknown; 4% transferred in. *Retention:* 45% of full-time freshmen returned.
Freshmen *Admission:* 103 enrolled.
Faculty *Total:* 49, 37% full-time. *Student/faculty ratio:* 12:1.
Majors Administrative assistant and secretarial science; business/commerce; child-care and support services management; interdisciplinary studies; liberal arts and sciences/liberal studies.
Academics *Calendar:* semesters. *Degree:* certificates, diplomas, and associate. *Special study options:* academic remediation for entering students, advanced placement credit, distance learning, double majors, independent study, part-time degree program, services for LD students, summer session for credit.
Library Learning Resource Center. *Books:* 18,002 (physical), 391,203 (digital/electronic); *Serial titles:* 91 (physical); *Databases:* 44. Students can reserve study rooms.
Student Life *Housing:* college housing not available. *Activities and Organizations:* Phi Theta Kappa, Student Government Association. *Student services:* personal/psychological counseling, veterans affairs office.
Costs (2019–20) *Tuition:* area resident $4296 full-time, $179 per credit hour part-time; state resident $4416 full-time, $184 per credit hour part-time; nonresident $8208 full-time, $342 per credit hour part-time. *Required fees:* $192 full-time, $8 per credit hour part-time. *Payment plans:* installment, deferred payment. *Waivers:* senior citizens and employees or children of employees.
Applying *Options:* electronic application, early admission, deferred entrance. *Required:* high school transcript. *Application deadlines:* rolling (freshmen), rolling (transfers). *Notification:* continuous (freshmen), continuous (transfers).
Freshman Application Contact Ms. Cheryl DuBose, Director of Admissions, Williamsburg Technical College, 601 MLK Jr. Avenue, Kingstree, SC 29556-4197. *Phone:* 843-355-4165. *Toll-free phone:* 800-768-2021. *Fax:* 843-355-4289. *E-mail:* dubosec@wiltech.edu. *Website:* http://www.wiltech.edu/.

York Technical College
Rock Hill, South Carolina

Freshman Application Contact Mr. Kenny Aldridge, Admissions Department Manager, York Technical College, Rock Hill, SC 29730. *Phone:* 803-327-8008. *Toll-free phone:* 800-922-8324. *Fax:* 803-981-7237. *E-mail:* kaldridge@yorktech.com. *Website:* http://www.yorktech.edu/.

SOUTH DAKOTA

Lake Area Technical Institute
Watertown, South Dakota

- **State-supported** 2-year, founded 1965, part of South Dakota Department of Education
- **Small-town** 40-acre campus
- **Endowment** $3.4 million
- **Coed,** 2,228 undergraduate students, 68% full-time, 48% women, 52% men

Undergraduates 1,507 full-time, 721 part-time. Students come from 19 states and territories; 4 other countries; 19% are from out of state; 1% Black or African American, non-Hispanic/Latino; 2% Hispanic/Latino; 0.9% Asian, non-Hispanic/Latino; 0.1% Native Hawaiian or other Pacific Islander, non-Hispanic/Latino; 2% American Indian or Alaska Native, non-Hispanic/Latino; 0.1% Two or more races, non-Hispanic/Latino; 3% Race/ethnicity unknown; 0.2% international; 12% transferred in.
Freshmen *Admission:* 630 enrolled. *Test scores:* ACT scores over 18: 66%; ACT scores over 24: 13%; ACT scores over 30: 1%.
Faculty *Total:* 146, 74% full-time. *Student/faculty ratio:* 17:1.
Majors Agricultural business and management; aircraft powerplant technology; airline pilot and flight crew; autobody/collision and repair technology; automobile/automotive mechanics technology; banking and financial support services; building construction technology; clinical/medical laboratory technology; community health services counseling; computer science; construction engineering technology; construction/heavy equipment/earthmoving equipment operation; criminal justice/police science; dental assisting; diesel mechanics technology; electrical, electronic and communications engineering technology; emergency medical technology (EMT paramedic); engine machinist; environmental science; human services; machine tool technology; manufacturing engineering technology; marketing/marketing management; medical/clinical assistant; occupational therapist assistant; physical therapy technology; registered nursing/registered nurse; robotics technology; welding technology.
Academics *Calendar:* semesters. *Degree:* certificates, diplomas, and associate. *Special study options:* academic remediation for entering students, advanced placement credit, cooperative education, distance learning, double majors, English as a second language, independent study, internships, off-campus study, part-time degree program, services for LD students, summer session for credit.
Library Leonard H. Timmerman Library. *Books:* 2,500 (physical), 250,000 (digital/electronic); *Serial titles:* 25 (physical); *Databases:* 40. Weekly public service hours: 58.
Student Life *Housing:* college housing not available. *Activities and Organizations:* Campus Crusades, Student Voice, Student Ambassador, SkillsUSA, Campus Activities Board. *Campus security:* 24-hour emergency response devices, partnership with local police department. *Student services:* personal/psychological counseling, veterans affairs office.
Athletics *Intramural sports:* basketball M/W, bowling M/W, equestrian sports M/W, football M, softball M/W, volleyball M/W.
Standardized Tests *Recommended:* ACT (for admission), SAT or ACT (for admission), only 1 of ACCUPLACER or ACT or SAT is required.
Costs (2019–20) *Tuition:* state resident $3630 full-time, $121 per credit part-time; nonresident $3630 full-time, $121 per credit part-time. Full-time tuition and fees vary according to course load and program. Part-time tuition and fees vary according to course load and program. *Required fees:* $2952 full-time, $107 per credit part-time. *Payment plan:* installment. *Waivers:* employees or children of employees.

Financial Aid Of all full-time matriculated undergraduates who enrolled in 2018, 1,358 applied for aid, 1,123 were judged to have need, 92 had their need fully met. 184 Federal Work-Study jobs (averaging $1987). In 2018, 57 non-need-based awards were made. *Average percent of need met:* 48%. *Average financial aid package:* $8214. *Average need-based loan:* $3680. *Average need-based gift aid:* $5709. *Average non-need-based aid:* $1075.
Applying *Options:* electronic application. *Application fee:* $25. *Required:* high school transcript. *Required for some:* essay or personal statement, interview. *Application deadlines:* rolling (freshmen), rolling (transfers). *Notification:* continuous (freshmen), continuous (transfers).
Freshman Application Contact Ms. LuAnn Strait, Director of Student Services, Lake Area Technical Institute, 1201 Arrow Avenue, PO Box 730, Watertown, SD 57201. *Phone:* 605-882-5284 Ext. 241. *Toll-free phone:* 800-657-4344. *Fax:* 605-882-6299. *E-mail:* straitl@lakeareatech.edu.
Website: http://www.lakeareatech.edu/.

Mitchell Technical Institute
Mitchell, South Dakota

- **State-supported** 2-year, founded 1968, part of South Dakota Board of Technical Education
- **Small-town** 90-acre campus
- **Coed**

Undergraduates 840 full-time, 358 part-time. Students come from 19 states and territories; 10% are from out of state; 0.8% Black or African American, non-Hispanic/Latino; 2% Hispanic/Latino; 1% Asian, non-Hispanic/Latino; 0.1% Native Hawaiian or other Pacific Islander, non-Hispanic/Latino; 3% American Indian or Alaska Native, non-Hispanic/Latino; 2% Two or more races, non-Hispanic/Latino; 2% Race/ethnicity unknown; 10% transferred in. *Retention:* 81% of full-time freshmen returned.
Faculty *Student/faculty ratio:* 13:1.
Academics *Calendar:* semesters. *Degree:* certificates, diplomas, and associate. *Special study options:* academic remediation for entering students, advanced placement credit, cooperative education, distance learning, double majors, internships, part-time degree program, services for LD students, summer session for credit.
Library Center for Student Success. *Books:* 187 (physical), 929 (digital/electronic); *Databases:* 17. Weekly public service hours: 45.
Student Life *Campus security:* 24-hour emergency response devices.
Standardized Tests *Required:* ACCUPLACER (for admission). *Recommended:* ACT (for admission).
Costs (2019–20) *Tuition:* state resident $3872 full-time, $121 per credit hour part-time; nonresident $3872 full-time, $121 per credit hour part-time. Full-time tuition and fees vary according to course load and program. Part-time tuition and fees vary according to course load and program. *Required fees:* $3072 full-time, $96 per credit hour part-time.
Financial Aid Of all full-time matriculated undergraduates who enrolled in 2018, 778 applied for aid, 778 were judged to have need, 155 had their need fully met. In 2018, 51. *Average percent of need met:* 20. *Average financial aid package:* $5151. *Average need-based loan:* $3389. *Average need-based gift aid:* $5026. *Average non-need-based aid:* $1081.
Applying *Options:* electronic application. *Required:* high school transcript. *Required for some:* essay or personal statement, interview. *Recommended:* minimum 2.0 GPA.
Freshman Application Contact Mr. Clayton Deuter, Dean of Enrollment Services, Mitchell Technical Institute, 1800 East Spruce Street, Mitchell, SD 57301. *Phone:* 605-995-3025. *Toll-free phone:* 800-684-1969. *Fax:* 605-995-3067. *E-mail:* clayton.deuter@mitchelltech.edu. *Website:* http://www.mitchelltech.edu/.

Sisseton-Wahpeton College
Sisseton, South Dakota

Freshman Application Contact Sisseton-Wahpeton College, Old Agency Box 689, Sisseton, SD 57262. *Phone:* 605-698-3966 Ext. 1180. *Website:* http://www.swc.tc/.

Southeast Technical Institute
Sioux Falls, South Dakota

Freshman Application Contact Mr. Scott Dorman, Recruiter, Southeast Technical Institute, Sioux Falls, SD 57107. *Phone:* 605-367-4458. *Toll-free phone:* 800-247-0789. *Fax:* 605-367-8305. *E-mail:* scott.dorman@southeasttech.edu. *Website:* http://www.southeasttech.edu/.

Western Dakota Technical Institute
Rapid City, South Dakota

- **State-supported** 2-year, founded 1968
- **Small-town** 5-acre campus
- **Endowment** $187,302
- **Coed,** 1,214 undergraduate students, 50% full-time, 58% women, 42% men

Undergraduates 603 full-time, 611 part-time. 4% are from out of state; 2% Black or African American, non-Hispanic/Latino; 6% Hispanic/Latino; 1% Asian, non-Hispanic/Latino; 0.5% Native Hawaiian or other Pacific Islander, non-Hispanic/Latino; 12% American Indian or Alaska Native, non-Hispanic/Latino; 3% Two or more races, non-Hispanic/Latino; 0.1% Race/ethnicity unknown; 30% transferred in. *Retention:* 63% of full-time freshmen returned.
Freshmen *Admission:* 997 applied, 613 admitted, 190 enrolled. *Average high school GPA:* 2.7.
Faculty *Total:* 96, 48% full-time, 10% with terminal degrees. *Student/faculty ratio:* 12:1.
Majors Accounting; business administration and management; clinical/medical laboratory technology; computer systems networking and telecommunications; criminal justice/police science; criminal justice/safety; drafting and design technology; electrician; emergency medical technology (EMT paramedic); environmental control technologies related; fire science/firefighting; health services/allied health/health sciences; heating, air conditioning, ventilation and refrigeration maintenance technology; interdisciplinary studies; library and archives assisting; licensed practical/vocational nurse training; machine tool technology; medical/clinical assistant; medical transcription; pharmacy technician; surgical technology; vehicle maintenance and repair technologies related; welding technology.
Academics *Calendar:* semesters. *Degree:* certificates, diplomas, and associate. *Special study options:* academic remediation for entering students, advanced placement credit, distance learning, double majors, internships, part-time degree program, services for LD students, summer session for credit.
Library Western Dakota Technical Institute Library plus 1 other. *Books:* 3,500 (physical), 158,080 (digital/electronic); *Databases:* 12. Weekly public service hours: 48.
Student Life *Housing:* college housing not available. *Campus security:* 24-hour video surveillance.
Costs (2020–21) *Tuition:* area resident $3780 full-time, $126 per credit hour part-time; state resident $3780 full-time, $126 per credit hour part-time; nonresident $3780 full-time, $126 per credit hour part-time. Full-time tuition and fees vary according to course load and program. Part-time tuition and fees vary according to course load and program. *Required fees:* $4830 full-time. *Payment plans:* installment, deferred payment. *Waivers:* employees or children of employees.
Financial Aid Of all full-time matriculated undergraduates who enrolled in 2019, 531 applied for aid, 483 were judged to have need, 24 had their need fully met. 35 Federal Work-Study jobs (averaging $1269). In 2019, 15 non-need-based awards were made. *Average percent of need met:* 72%. *Average financial aid package:* $13,394. *Average need-based loan:* $3668. *Average need-based gift aid:* $7945. *Average non-need-based aid:* $2166.
Applying *Options:* electronic application. *Required:* high school transcript. *Required for some:* essay or personal statement, 3 letters of recommendation, interview. *Recommended:* minimum 2.0 GPA. *Application deadlines:* 8/1 (freshmen), 8/1 (transfers). *Notification:* continuous until 8/15 (freshmen), continuous until 8/15 (transfers).
Freshman Application Contact Ms. Jill Elder, Admissions Coordinator, Western Dakota Technical Institute, 800 Mickelson Drive, Rapid City, SD 57703. *Phone:* 605-718-2411. *Toll-free phone:* 800-544-8765. *Fax:* 605-394-2204. *E-mail:* jill.elder@wdt.edu.
Website: http://www.wdt.edu/.

TENNESSEE

Chattanooga College–Medical, Dental and Technical Careers
Chattanooga, Tennessee

Freshman Application Contact Chattanooga College–Medical, Dental and Technical Careers, 248 Northgate Mall Drive, Suite 130, Chattanooga, TN 37415. *Phone:* 423-305-7781. *Toll-free phone:* 877-313-2373. *Website:* http://www.chattanoogacollege.edu/.

Chattanooga State Community College
Chattanooga, Tennessee

- **State-supported** 2-year, founded 1965, part of Tennessee Board of Regents
- **Urban** 100-acre campus
- **Endowment** $6.8 million
- **Coed**

Undergraduates 4,775 full-time, 5,663 part-time. Students come from 23 states and territories; 9 other countries; 11% are from out of state; 12% Black or African American, non-Hispanic/Latino; 6% Hispanic/Latino; 2% Asian, non-Hispanic/Latino; 0.1% Native Hawaiian or other Pacific Islander, non-Hispanic/Latino; 0.2% American Indian or Alaska Native, non-Hispanic/Latino; 4% Two or more races, non-Hispanic/Latino; 0.4% Race/ethnicity unknown; 40% transferred in. *Retention:* 55% of full-time freshmen returned.
Faculty *Student/faculty ratio:* 19:1.
Academics *Calendar:* semesters. *Degree:* certificates, diplomas, and associate. *Special study options:* academic remediation for entering students, accelerated degree program, adult/continuing education programs, advanced placement credit, cooperative education, distance learning, double majors, external degree program, honors programs, independent study, internships, part-time degree program, services for LD students, summer session for credit.
Library Augusta R. Kolwyck Library.
Student Life *Campus security:* 24-hour emergency response devices and patrols, late-night transport/escort service.
Athletics Member NJCAA.
Applying *Options:* electronic application, early admission, deferred entrance. *Application fee:* $15. *Required for some:* high school transcript, interview. *Recommended:* high school transcript.
Freshman Application Contact Brad McCormick, Director of Admissions and Records, Chattanooga State Community College, 4501 Amnicola Highway, Chattanooga, TN 37406. *Phone:* 423-697-4401 Ext. 3264. *Toll-free phone:* 866-547-3733. *Fax:* 423-697-4709. *E-mail:* brad.mccormick@chattanoogastate.edu. *Website:* http://www.chattanoogastate.edu/.

Cleveland State Community College
Cleveland, Tennessee

- **State-supported** 2-year, founded 1967, part of Tennessee Board of Regents
- **Suburban** 83-acre campus
- **Endowment** $8.2 million
- **Coed,** 3,370 undergraduate students, 53% full-time, 57% women, 43% men

Undergraduates 1,793 full-time, 1,577 part-time. Students come from 10 states and territories; 1% are from out of state; 6% Black or African American, non-Hispanic/Latino; 6% Hispanic/Latino; 1% Asian, non-Hispanic/Latino; 0.1% Native Hawaiian or other Pacific Islander, non-Hispanic/Latino; 0.3% American Indian or Alaska Native, non-Hispanic/Latino; 0.7% Two or more races, non-Hispanic/Latino; 1% Race/ethnicity unknown; 5% transferred in.
Freshmen *Admission:* 1,897 applied, 1,897 admitted, 844 enrolled. *Average high school GPA:* 3.2.
Faculty *Total:* 204, 38% full-time, 17% with terminal degrees. *Student/faculty ratio:* 19:1.
Majors Administrative assistant and secretarial science; business administration and management; child development; computer and information sciences; criminal justice/police science; education; electrical, electronic and communications engineering technology; electromechanical technology; emergency medical technology (EMT paramedic); engineering technology; general studies; health professions related; industrial technology; information technology; liberal arts and sciences/liberal studies; medical/clinical assistant; medical informatics; multi/interdisciplinary studies related; music performance; public administration and social service professions related; registered nursing/registered nurse; science technologies related.
Academics *Calendar:* semesters. *Degree:* certificates and associate. *Special study options:* academic remediation for entering students, adult/continuing education programs, advanced placement credit, cooperative education, distance learning, double majors, external degree program, honors programs, independent study, internships, off-campus study, part-time degree program, services for LD students, study abroad, summer session for credit.
Library Cleveland State Community College Library plus 1 other. *Books:* 50,326 (physical), 250,777 (digital/electronic); *Serial titles:* 426 (physical); *Databases:* 76.
Student Life *Housing:* college housing not available. *Activities and Organizations:* drama/theater group, choral group, Human Services/Social Work, Computer-Aided Design, Phi Theta Kappa, Student Nursing Association, Early Childhood Education. *Campus security:* 24-hour emergency response devices and patrols. *Student services:* personal/psychological counseling, veterans affairs office.
Athletics Member NJCAA. *Intercollegiate sports:* baseball M(s), basketball M(s)/W(s), cross-country running M(s)/W(s), golf M(s), softball W(s), volleyball W(s). *Intramural sports:* archery M/W, basketball M/W, bowling M/W, cheerleading M(c)/W(c), softball W, table tennis M/W, volleyball M/W.
Financial Aid Of all full-time matriculated undergraduates who enrolled in 2019, 1,651 applied for aid, 1,299 were judged to have need, 56 had their need fully met. 35 Federal Work-Study jobs (averaging $1904). In 2019, 417 non-need-based awards were made. *Average percent of need met:* 55%. *Average financial aid package:* $3562. *Average need-based loan:* $1519. *Average need-based gift aid:* $2719. *Average non-need-based aid:* $1577.
Applying *Options:* electronic application, early admission, deferred entrance. *Required:* high school transcript. *Application deadline:* 8/12 (out-of-state freshmen). *Notification:* continuous (freshmen).
Freshman Application Contact Mrs. Cate Green, Director of Admissions, Recruiting, and High School Relations, Cleveland State Community College, PO Box 3570, Cleveland, TN 37320-3570. *Phone:* 423-472-7141 Ext. 743. *Toll-free phone:* 800-604-2722. *E-mail:* cgreen16@clevelandstatecc.edu. *Website:* http://www.clevelandstatecc.edu/.

Columbia State Community College
Columbia, Tennessee

Freshman Application Contact Mr. Joey Scruggs, Coordinator of Recruitment, Columbia State Community College, 1665 Hampshire Pike, Columbia, TN 38401. *Phone:* 931-540-2540. *E-mail:* scruggs@coscc.cc.tn.us. *Website:* http://www.columbiastate.edu/.

Concorde Career College
Memphis, Tennessee

Freshman Application Contact Dee Vickers, Director, Concorde Career College, 5100 Poplar Avenue, Suite 132, Memphis, TN 38137. *Phone:* 901-761-9494. *Fax:* 901-761-3293. *E-mail:* dvickers@concorde.edu. *Website:* http://www.concorde.edu/.

Daymar College
Clarksville, Tennessee

- **Proprietary** primarily 2-year, founded 1987
- **Small-town** campus
- **Coed**

Undergraduates 381 full-time, 151 part-time. Students come from 12 states and territories; 2 other countries; 16% are from out of state.
Faculty *Student/faculty ratio:* 7:1.
Academics *Calendar:* quarters. *Degrees:* certificates, diplomas, associate, and bachelor's. *Special study options:* cooperative education, distance learning, double majors, honors programs, independent study, internships, part-time degree program, services for LD students.
Financial Aid Of all full-time matriculated undergraduates who enrolled in 2018, 20 Federal Work-Study jobs (averaging $1000).
Applying *Required:* high school transcript, interview.
Freshman Application Contact Daymar College, 2691 Trenton Road, Clarksville, TN 37040. *Phone:* 931-552-7600 Ext. 204. *Website:* http://www.daymarcollege.edu/.

Daymar College
Murfreesboro, Tennessee

- **Proprietary** primarily 2-year
- **Coed**

Academics *Degrees:* certificates, associate, and bachelor's.
Admissions Office Contact Daymar College, 415 Golden Bear Court, Murfreesboro, TN 37128. *Website:* http://www.daymarcollege.edu/.

Daymar College
Nashville, Tennessee

- **Proprietary** 2-year, founded 1884
- **Suburban** 5-acre campus
- **Coed**

Academics *Calendar:* semesters. *Degree:* associate. *Special study options:* academic remediation for entering students, internships, part-time degree program, summer session for credit.
Student Life *Campus security:* 24-hour emergency response devices.
Financial Aid Of all full-time matriculated undergraduates who enrolled in 2018, 26 Federal Work-Study jobs (averaging $2975).

Applying *Options:* deferred entrance. *Required:* high school transcript.
Director of Admissions Admissions Office, Daymar College, 560 Royal Parkway, Nashville, TN 37214. *Phone:* 615-361-7555. *Fax:* 615-367-2736. *Website:* http://www.daymarcollege.edu/.

Dyersburg State Community College

Dyersburg, Tennessee

- **State-supported** 2-year, founded 1969, part of Tennessee Board of Regents
- **Small-town** 115-acre campus with easy access to Memphis
- **Endowment** $4.0 million
- **Coed,** 2,816 undergraduate students, 44% full-time, 65% women, 35% men
- 100% of applicants were admitted

Undergraduates 1,253 full-time, 1,563 part-time. Students come from 4 states and territories; 1 other country; 19% Black or African American, non-Hispanic/Latino; 3% Hispanic/Latino; 1% Asian, non-Hispanic/Latino; 0.4% American Indian or Alaska Native, non-Hispanic/Latino; 2% Two or more races, non-Hispanic/Latino; 1% Race/ethnicity unknown; 0.2% international; 5% transferred in. *Retention:* 50% of full-time freshmen returned.
Freshmen *Admission:* 1,421 applied, 1,421 admitted, 609 enrolled. *Average high school GPA:* 3.0. *Test scores:* ACT scores over 18: 68%; ACT scores over 24: 15%; ACT scores over 30: 1%.
Faculty *Total:* 130, 41% full-time, 9% with terminal degrees. *Student/faculty ratio:* 21:1.
Majors Agriculture; automation engineer technology; business administration and management; child development; computer and information sciences; computer and information systems security; criminal justice/police science; criminal justice/safety; education; emergency medical technology (EMT paramedic); general studies; health information/medical records technology; health services/allied health/health sciences; industrial electronics technology; industrial mechanics and maintenance technology; information science/studies; information technology; liberal arts and sciences/liberal studies; registered nursing/registered nurse.
Academics *Calendar:* semesters. *Degree:* certificates and associate. *Special study options:* academic remediation for entering students, accelerated degree program, adult/continuing education programs, advanced placement credit, cooperative education, distance learning, double majors, honors programs, independent study, internships, off-campus study, part-time degree program, services for LD students, study abroad, summer session for credit.
Library Learning Resource Center plus 2 others. *Books:* 17,817 (physical), 225,400 (digital/electronic); *Serial titles:* 29 (digital/electronic); *Databases:* 121. Weekly public service hours: 66; students can reserve study rooms.
Student Life *Housing:* college housing not available. *Activities and Organizations:* drama/theater group, choral group, Psychology Club, Phi Theta Kappa, Student Government, Student Nurses Association, Criminal Justice Association. *Campus security:* 24-hour emergency response devices and patrols. *Student services:* personal/psychological counseling, veterans affairs office.
Athletics Member NJCAA. *Intercollegiate sports:* baseball M(s), basketball M(s)/W(s), cheerleading M(s)/W(s), softball W(s). *Intramural sports:* soccer M/W, table tennis M/W, ultimate Frisbee M/W, volleyball M/W.
Standardized Tests *Required:* SAT or ACT (for admission). *Required for some:* ACT Compass for students who are over 21.
Costs (2019–20) *Tuition:* state resident $4032 full-time, $168 per credit hour part-time; nonresident $16,608 full-time, $692 per credit hour part-time. Full-time tuition and fees vary according to course load. Part-time tuition and fees vary according to course load. *Required fees:* $306 full-time, $153 per term part-time. *Payment plan:* deferred payment. *Waivers:* senior citizens and employees or children of employees.
Financial Aid Of all full-time matriculated undergraduates who enrolled in 2019, 30 Federal Work-Study jobs (averaging $2114). 84 state and other part-time jobs (averaging $1277).
Applying *Options:* electronic application. *Required:* high school transcript. *Application deadlines:* rolling (freshmen), rolling (out-of-state freshmen), rolling (transfers).
Freshman Application Contact Mrs. Heather Page, Director of Admissions and Records, Dyersburg State Community College, Dyersburg, TN 38024. *Phone:* 731-286-3331. *Fax:* 731-286-3325. *E-mail:* page@dscc.edu. *Website:* http://www.dscc.edu/.

Fortis Institute

Cookeville, Tennessee

Director of Admissions Ms. Sharon Mellott, Director of Admissions, Fortis Institute, 1025 Highway 111, Cookeville, TN 38501. *Phone:* 931-526-3660. *Toll-free phone:* 855-4-FORTIS. *Website:* http://www.fortis.edu/.

Fortis Institute

Nashville, Tennessee

Admissions Office Contact Fortis Institute, 3354 Perimeter Hill Drive, Suite 105, Nashville, TN 37211. *Toll-free phone:* 855-4-FORTIS. *Website:* http://www.fortis.edu/.

Hiwassee College

Madisonville, Tennessee

Director of Admissions Jamie Williamson, Director of Admission, Hiwassee College, 225 Hiwassee College Drive, Madisonville, TN 37354. *Phone:* 423-420-1891. *Toll-free phone:* 800-356-2187. *Website:* http://www.hiwassee.edu/.

Jackson State Community College

Jackson, Tennessee

Freshman Application Contact Ms. Andrea Winchester, Director of High School Initiatives, Jackson State Community College, 2046 North Parkway, Jackson, TN 38301-3797. *Phone:* 731-424-3520 Ext. 50484. *Toll-free phone:* 800-355-5722. *Fax:* 731-425-9559. *E-mail:* awinchester@jscc.edu. *Website:* http://www.jscc.edu/.

John A. Gupton College

Nashville, Tennessee

Freshman Application Contact John A. Gupton College, 1616 Church Street, Nashville, TN 37203-2920. *Phone:* 615-327-3927. *Website:* http://www.guptoncollege.edu/.

Lincoln College of Technology - Nashville

Nashville, Tennessee

Freshman Application Contact Ms. Tanya Smith, Director of Admissions, Lincoln College of Technology - Nashville, 1524 Gallatin Road, Nashville, TN 37206. *Phone:* 615-226-3990 Ext. 71703. *Toll-free phone:* 844-215-1513. *Fax:* 615-262-8466. *E-mail:* tlegg-smith@lincolntech.com. *Website:* http://www.lincolntech.edu/.

Miller-Motte College - Chattanooga

Chattanooga, Tennessee

Admissions Office Contact Miller-Motte College - Chattanooga, 6397 Lee Highway, Suite 100, Chattanooga, TN 37421. *Toll-free phone:* 800-705-9182. *Website:* http://www.miller-motte.edu/.

Motlow State Community College

Tullahoma, Tennessee

- **State-supported** 2-year, founded 1969, part of Tennessee Board of Regents
- **Rural** 187-acre campus with easy access to Nashville
- **Endowment** $7.1 million
- **Coed,** 6,991 undergraduate students, 49% full-time, 62% women, 38% men

Undergraduates 3,438 full-time, 3,553 part-time. 12% Black or African American, non-Hispanic/Latino; 10% Hispanic/Latino; 3% Asian, non-Hispanic/Latino; 0.2% Native Hawaiian or other Pacific Islander, non-Hispanic/Latino; 0.3% American Indian or Alaska Native, non-Hispanic/Latino; 3% Two or more races, non-Hispanic/Latino; 0.8% Race/ethnicity unknown; 0.2% international; 4% transferred in. *Retention:* 53% of full-time freshmen returned.
Freshmen *Admission:* 3,996 applied, 3,996 admitted, 1,817 enrolled. *Average high school GPA:* 3.1. *Test scores:* ACT scores over 18: 64%; ACT scores over 24: 13%.
Majors Business administration and management; child development; clinical/medical laboratory technology; education; electromechanical technology; emergency medical technology (EMT paramedic); interdisciplinary studies; liberal arts and sciences/liberal studies; music performance; registered nursing/registered nurse; web page, digital/multimedia and information resources design.
Academics *Calendar:* semesters. *Degree:* certificates and associate. *Special study options:* academic remediation for entering students, accelerated degree program, adult/continuing education programs, advanced placement credit, cooperative education, distance learning, double majors, honors programs,

independent study, part-time degree program, services for LD students, study abroad, summer session for credit.
Library Clayton-Glass Library. *Books:* 63,642 (physical), 419,239 (digital/electronic); *Serial titles:* 94 (physical), 37,886 (digital/electronic); *Databases:* 58. Students can reserve study rooms.
Student Life *Housing:* college housing not available. *Activities and Organizations:* drama/theater group, student-run newspaper, choral group, Phi Theta Kappa, Student Government Association, Baptist Collegiate Ministries, Art Club, Psi Beta. *Campus security:* 24-hour patrols, late-night transport/escort service. *Student services:* personal/psychological counseling, veterans affairs office.
Athletics Member NJCAA. *Intercollegiate sports:* baseball M(s), basketball M(s)/W(s), soccer W(s), softball W(s). *Intramural sports:* basketball M/W.
Standardized Tests *Required:* SAT or ACT (for admission).
Costs (2019–20) *Tuition:* area resident $4344 full-time; state resident $4344 full-time; nonresident $16,920 full-time. Full-time tuition and fees vary according to course load and program. Part-time tuition and fees vary according to program. *Required fees:* $312 full-time. *Payment plans:* installment, deferred payment. *Waivers:* senior citizens and employees or children of employees.
Financial Aid Of all full-time matriculated undergraduates who enrolled in 2017, 2,991 applied for aid, 2,294 were judged to have need, 238 had their need fully met. In 2017, 642 non-need-based awards were made. *Average percent of need met:* 55%. *Average financial aid package:* $6067. *Average need-based gift aid:* $5058. *Average non-need-based aid:* $3957.
Applying *Options:* electronic application, deferred entrance. *Required:* high school transcript. *Notification:* continuous (freshmen), continuous (transfers).
Freshman Application Contact Motlow State Community College, PO Box 8500, Lynchburg, TN 37352-8500. *Phone:* 931-393-1530. *Toll-free phone:* 800-654-4877.
Website: http://www.mscc.edu/.

Nashville State Community College

Nashville, Tennessee

Freshman Application Contact Mr. Tyler White, Coordinator of Recruitment, Nashville State Community College, 120 White Bridge Road, Nashville, TN 37209-4515. *Phone:* 615-353-3265. *Toll-free phone:* 800-272-7363. *E-mail:* recruiting@nscc.edu. *Website:* http://www.nscc.edu/.

National College

Bristol, Tennessee

Freshman Application Contact National College, 1328 Highway 11 West, Bristol, TN 37620. *Phone:* 423-878-4440. *Toll-free phone:* 888-9-JOBREADY. *Website:* http://www.national-college.edu/.

National College

Nashville, Tennessee

Director of Admissions Jerry Lafferty, Campus Director, National College, 1638 Bell Road, Nashville, TN 37211. *Phone:* 615-333-3344. *Toll-free phone:* 888-9-JOBREADY. *Website:* http://www.national-college.edu/.

North Central Institute

Clarksville, Tennessee

Freshman Application Contact Dale Wood, Director of Admissions, North Central Institute, 168 Jack Miller Boulevard, Clarksville, TN 37042. *Phone:* 931-431-9700. *Toll-free phone:* 800-603-4116. *Fax:* 931-431-9771. *E-mail:* admissions@nci.edu. *Website:* http://www.nci.edu/.

Northeast State Community College

Blountville, Tennessee

- **State-supported** 2-year, founded 1966, part of Tennessee Board of Regents
- **Small-town** 95-acre campus
- **Endowment** $9.9 million
- **Coed,** 6,085 undergraduate students, 53% full-time, 54% women, 46% men

Undergraduates 3,251 full-time, 2,834 part-time. Students come from 3 states and territories; 3 other countries; 2% are from out of state; 2% Black or African American, non-Hispanic/Latino; 3% Hispanic/Latino; 0.8% Asian, non-Hispanic/Latino; 0.1% Native Hawaiian or other Pacific Islander, non-Hispanic/Latino; 0.4% American Indian or Alaska Native, non-Hispanic/Latino; 3% Two or more races, non-Hispanic/Latino; 2% Race/ethnicity unknown; 0.1% international; 5% transferred in. *Retention:* 57% of full-time freshmen returned.
Freshmen *Admission:* 1,346 enrolled. *Average high school GPA:* 3.1.
Majors Administrative assistant and secretarial science; aircraft powerplant technology; business administration and management; cardiovascular technology; child development; criminal justice/safety; education; electrical, electronic and communications engineering technology; emergency medical technology (EMT paramedic); general studies; health professions related; industrial technology; information technology; interdisciplinary studies; liberal arts and sciences/liberal studies; recording arts technology; registered nursing/registered nurse; surgical technology.
Academics *Calendar:* semesters. *Degree:* certificates and associate.
Financial Aid Of all full-time matriculated undergraduates who enrolled in 2018, 109 Federal Work-Study jobs (averaging $1318). 35 state and other part-time jobs.
Applying *Required:* high school transcript.
Freshman Application Contact Northeast State Community College, PO Box 246, Blountville, TN 37617-0246. *Toll-free phone:* 800-836-7822.
Website: http://www.northeaststate.edu/.

Pellissippi State Community College

Knoxville, Tennessee

- **State-supported** 2-year, founded 1974, part of Tennessee Board of Regents
- **Suburban** 144-acre campus
- **Coed**

Undergraduates 1% are from out of state. *Retention:* 60% of full-time freshmen returned.
Faculty *Student/faculty ratio:* 24:1.
Academics *Calendar:* semesters. *Degree:* associate. *Special study options:* academic remediation for entering students, adult/continuing education programs, advanced placement credit, cooperative education, distance learning, double majors, English as a second language, freshman honors college, honors programs, internships, part-time degree program, services for LD students, student-designed majors, summer session for credit.
Library Educational Resources Center plus 1 other.
Student Life *Campus security:* 24-hour patrols.
Standardized Tests *Required for some:* SAT or ACT (for admission).
Financial Aid Of all full-time matriculated undergraduates who enrolled in 2018, 175 Federal Work-Study jobs.
Applying *Options:* electronic application, early admission, deferred entrance. *Application fee:* $20. *Required:* high school transcript.
Freshman Application Contact Director of Admissions and Records, Pellissippi State Community College, PO Box 22990, Knoxville, TN 37933-0990. *Phone:* 865-694-6400. *Fax:* 865-539-7217. *Website:* http://www.pstcc.edu/.

Remington College–Memphis Campus

Memphis, Tennessee

Director of Admissions Randal Hayes, Director of Recruitment, Remington College–Memphis Campus, 2710 Nonconnah Boulevard, Memphis, TN 38132. *Phone:* 901-345-1000. *Toll-free phone:* 800-323-8122. *Fax:* 901-396-8310. *E-mail:* randal.hayes@remingtoncollege.edu. *Website:* http://www.remingtoncollege.edu/.

Remington College–Nashville Campus

Nashville, Tennessee

Director of Admissions Mr. Frank Vivelo, Campus President, Remington College–Nashville Campus, 441 Donelson Pike, Suite 150, Nashville, TN 37214. *Phone:* 615-889-5520. *Toll-free phone:* 800-323-8122. *Fax:* 615-889-5528. *E-mail:* frank.vivelo@remingtoncollege.edu. *Website:* http://www.remingtoncollege.edu/.

Roane State Community College

Harriman, Tennessee

Freshman Application Contact Admissions Office, Roane State Community College, 276 Patton Lane, Harriman, TN 37748. *Phone:* 865-882-4523. *Toll-free phone:* 866-462-7722 Ext. 4554. *E-mail:* admissionsrecords@roanestate.edu. *Website:* http://www.roanestate.edu/.

SAE Institute Nashville

Nashville, Tennessee

Admissions Office Contact SAE Institute Nashville, 7 Music Circle N, Nashville, TN 37203. *Website:* http://www.sae.edu/.

Southwest Tennessee Community College

Memphis, Tennessee

- **State-supported** 2-year, founded 2000, part of Tennessee Board of Regents
- **Urban** 100-acre campus
- **Coed**

Undergraduates 4,183 full-time, 5,984 part-time. Students come from 13 states and territories; 8 other countries; 2% are from out of state; 6% transferred in. *Retention:* 50% of full-time freshmen returned.

Academics *Calendar:* semesters. *Degree:* certificates and associate. *Special study options:* academic remediation for entering students, accelerated degree program, adult/continuing education programs, advanced placement credit, cooperative education, distance learning, double majors, English as a second language, internships, part-time degree program, services for LD students, student-designed majors, summer session for credit. *ROTC:* Army (c), Air Force (c).

Library Infonet Library plus 4 others.

Student Life *Campus security:* 24-hour emergency response devices and patrols, late-night transport/escort service.

Athletics Member NJCAA.

Financial Aid Of all full-time matriculated undergraduates who enrolled in 2018, 201 Federal Work-Study jobs (averaging $2600).

Applying *Options:* early admission, deferred entrance. *Application fee:* $10. *Required:* high school transcript.

Freshman Application Contact Mrs. Vanessa Dowdy, Southwest Tennessee Community College, 5983 Macon Cove, Memphis, TN 38134. *Phone:* 901-333-4275. *Toll-free phone:* 877-717-STCC. *E-mail:* vdowdy@southwest.tn.edu. *Website:* http://www.southwest.tn.edu/.

Volunteer State Community College

Gallatin, Tennessee

- **State-supported** 2-year, founded 1970, part of Tennessee Board of Regents
- **Suburban** 110-acre campus with easy access to Nashville
- **Endowment** $5.6 million
- **Coed,** 9,144 undergraduate students, 52% full-time, 62% women, 38% men

Undergraduates 4,779 full-time, 4,365 part-time. Students come from 8 states and territories; 10 other countries; 1% are from out of state; 10% Black or African American, non-Hispanic/Latino; 8% Hispanic/Latino; 1% Asian, non-Hispanic/Latino; 0.2% Native Hawaiian or other Pacific Islander, non-Hispanic/Latino; 0.3% American Indian or Alaska Native, non-Hispanic/Latino; 3% Two or more races, non-Hispanic/Latino; 3% Race/ethnicity unknown; 0.2% international; 6% transferred in.

Freshmen *Admission:* 3,090 applied, 3,090 admitted, 2,258 enrolled. *Average high school GPA:* 3.0. *Test scores:* ACT scores over 18: 64%; ACT scores over 24: 13%; ACT scores over 30: 1%.

Faculty *Total:* 475, 40% full-time, 14% with terminal degrees. *Student/faculty ratio:* 22:1.

Majors Business administration and management; clinical/medical laboratory technology; criminal justice/safety; digital arts; education; electromechanical technology; fire science/firefighting; health information/medical records technology; health professions related; information technology; liberal arts and sciences/liberal studies; medical/clinical assistant; medical radiologic technology; music performance; ophthalmic technology; physical therapy technology; registered nursing/registered nurse; respiratory care therapy; veterinary/animal health technology.

Academics *Calendar:* semesters. *Degree:* certificates and associate. *Special study options:* academic remediation for entering students, accelerated degree program, adult/continuing education programs, advanced placement credit, cooperative education, distance learning, double majors, English as a second language, honors programs, independent study, internships, part-time degree program, services for LD students, study abroad, summer session for credit.

Library Thigpen Library. *Books:* 44,419 (physical), 265,497 (digital/electronic); *Serial titles:* 67 (physical), 37,241 (digital/electronic); *Databases:* 93. Weekly public service hours: 71; students can reserve study rooms.

Student Life *Housing:* college housing not available. *Activities and Organizations:* drama/theater group, student-run newspaper, radio station, choral group. *Campus security:* 24-hour emergency response devices and patrols, late-night transport/escort service. *Student services:* personal/psychological counseling, veterans affairs office.

Athletics Member NJCAA. *Intercollegiate sports:* baseball M, basketball M/W, softball W.

Standardized Tests *Required for some:* SAT or ACT (for admission).

Financial Aid Of all full-time matriculated undergraduates who enrolled in 2018, 4,589 applied for aid, 3,186 were judged to have need, 173 had their need fully met. 29 Federal Work-Study jobs (averaging $2077). In 2018, 54 non-need-based awards were made. *Average percent of need met:* 51%. *Average financial aid package:* $5713. *Average need-based loan:* $2837. *Average need-based gift aid:* $4849. *Average non-need-based aid:* $1827.

Applying *Options:* electronic application, early admission, deferred entrance. *Required:* high school transcript. *Required for some:* minimum 2.0 GPA, interview. *Application deadlines:* 8/25 (freshmen), 8/25 (transfers). *Notification:* continuous (freshmen), continuous (transfers).

Freshman Application Contact Mr. Tim Amyx, Director of Admissions/College Registrar, Volunteer State Community College, 1480 Nashville Pike, Gallatin, TN 37066-3188. *Phone:* 615-452-8600 Ext. 3614. *Toll-free phone:* 888-335-8722. *Fax:* 615-230-4875. *E-mail:* admissions@volstate.edu.
Website: http://www.volstate.edu/.

Walters State Community College

Morristown, Tennessee

- **State-supported** 2-year, founded 1970, part of Tennessee Board of Regents
- **Small-town** 100-acre campus
- **Coed,** 6,280 undergraduate students, 52% full-time, 64% women, 36% men

Undergraduates 3,242 full-time, 3,038 part-time. 1% are from out of state; 3% Black or African American, non-Hispanic/Latino; 6% Hispanic/Latino; 1% Asian, non-Hispanic/Latino; 0.1% Native Hawaiian or other Pacific Islander, non-Hispanic/Latino; 0.3% American Indian or Alaska Native, non-Hispanic/Latino; 3% Two or more races, non-Hispanic/Latino; 0.4% Race/ethnicity unknown; 0.4% international.

Freshmen *Admission:* 3,847 applied, 3,847 admitted, 1,601 enrolled. *Average high school GPA:* 3.2.

Faculty *Total:* 387, 43% full-time, 24% with terminal degrees. *Student/faculty ratio:* 17:1.

Majors Business administration and management; child development; computer and information sciences; criminal justice/police science; criminal justice/safety; data processing and data processing technology; education; energy management and systems technology; general studies; health information/medical records technology; industrial technology; liberal arts and sciences/liberal studies; music performance; occupational therapist assistant; ornamental horticulture; physical therapy technology; registered nursing/registered nurse; respiratory care therapy; surgical technology; web page, digital/multimedia and information resources design.

Academics *Calendar:* semesters. *Degree:* certificates and associate. *Special study options:* academic remediation for entering students, accelerated degree program, advanced placement credit, cooperative education, distance learning, English as a second language, external degree program, freshman honors college, honors programs, independent study, internships, off-campus study, part-time degree program, services for LD students, student-designed majors, study abroad, summer session for credit. *ROTC:* Army (c).

Library Walters State Library.

Student Life *Housing:* college housing not available. *Activities and Organizations:* drama/theater group, choral group, Baptist Collegiate Ministry, Phi Theta Kappa, Debate Club, Student Government Association, Service Learners Club. *Campus security:* 24-hour emergency response devices and patrols, late-night transport/escort service, security cameras. *Student services:* health clinic, personal/psychological counseling.

Athletics Member NJCAA. *Intercollegiate sports:* baseball M(s), basketball M(s)/W(s), golf M(s), softball W(s), volleyball W(s). *Intramural sports:* baseball M, basketball M/W.

Financial Aid Of all full-time matriculated undergraduates who enrolled in 2018, 2,796 applied for aid, 2,401 were judged to have need, 149 had their need fully met. In 2018, 333 non-need-based awards were made. *Average percent of need met:* 41%. *Average financial aid package:* $6172. *Average need-based gift aid:* $5025. *Average non-need-based aid:* $4769.

Applying *Options:* electronic application, early admission. *Required:* high school transcript. *Application deadlines:* rolling (freshmen), rolling (transfers). *Notification:* continuous (freshmen), continuous (transfers).

Freshman Application Contact Mr. Michael Campbell, Assistant Vice President for Student Affairs, Walters State Community College, 500 South Davy Crockett Parkway, Morristown, TN 37813-6899. *Phone:* 423-585-2682.

Toll-free phone: 800-225-4770. *Fax:* 423-585-6876. *E-mail:* mike.campbell@ws.edu.
Website: http://www.ws.edu/.

West Tennessee Business College
Jackson, Tennessee

Admissions Office Contact West Tennessee Business College, 1186 Highway 45 Bypass, Jackson, TN 38343. *Website:* http://www.wtbc.edu/.

TEXAS

Alvin Community College
Alvin, Texas

- **State and locally supported** 2-year, founded 1949
- **Suburban** 114-acre campus with easy access to Houston
- **Coed,** 5,573 undergraduate students, 23% full-time, 57% women, 43% men

Undergraduates 1,302 full-time, 4,271 part-time. Students come from 10 states and territories; 38 other countries; 1% are from out of state; 11% Black or African American, non-Hispanic/Latino; 36% Hispanic/Latino; 4% Asian, non-Hispanic/Latino; 0.2% Native Hawaiian or other Pacific Islander, non-Hispanic/Latino; 0.8% American Indian or Alaska Native, non-Hispanic/Latino; 1% Race/ethnicity unknown; 2% international. *Retention:* 52% of full-time freshmen returned.

Freshmen *Admission:* 965 enrolled.

Faculty *Total:* 322, 34% full-time, 15% with terminal degrees. *Student/faculty ratio:* 17:1.

Majors Accounting; administrative assistant and secretarial science; aeronautics/aviation/aerospace science and technology; art; automobile/automotive mechanics technology; biology/biological sciences; business administration and management; business/commerce; chemical technology; child development; computer engineering technology; computer programming; corrections; criminalistics and criminal science; criminal justice/police science; criminal justice/safety; culinary arts; desktop publishing and digital imaging design; diagnostic medical sonography and ultrasound technology; drafting and design technology; dramatic/theater arts; early childhood education; electrical, electronic and communications engineering technology; electroneurodiagnostic/electroencephalographic technology; emergency medical technology (EMT paramedic); executive assistant/executive secretary; general studies; health and physical education/fitness; health/health-care administration; health services/allied health/health sciences; history; legal administrative assistant/secretary; legal assistant/paralegal; legal studies; liberal arts and sciences/liberal studies; licensed practical/vocational nurse training; marketing/marketing management; mathematics; medical administrative assistant and medical secretary; mental health counseling; middle school education; music; office occupations and clerical services; pharmacy technician; physical education teaching and coaching; physical sciences; psychiatric/mental health services technology; psychology; radio and television; registered nursing/registered nurse; respiratory care therapy; secondary education; sociology; substance abuse/addiction counseling; voice and opera.

Academics *Calendar:* semesters. *Degree:* certificates, diplomas, and associate. *Special study options:* academic remediation for entering students, accelerated degree program, adult/continuing education programs, advanced placement credit, cooperative education, distance learning, double majors, English as a second language, external degree program, honors programs, independent study, internships, part-time degree program, services for LD students, student-designed majors, study abroad, summer session for credit.

Library Alvin Community College Library. *Books:* 11,000 (physical), 30,000 (digital/electronic); *Databases:* 80. Weekly public service hours: 67; students can reserve study rooms.

Student Life *Housing:* college housing not available. *Activities and Organizations:* drama/theater group, student-run radio and television station, choral group. *Campus security:* 24-hour patrols, late-night transport/escort service, Vehicle Assist, emergency messages. *Student services:* personal/psychological counseling, veterans affairs office.

Athletics Member NJCAA. *Intercollegiate sports:* baseball M(s), softball W(s).

Costs (2020–21) *One-time required fee:* $30. *Tuition:* area resident $1410 full-time, $47 per credit hour part-time; state resident $2820 full-time, $94 per credit hour part-time; nonresident $4290 full-time, $143 per credit hour part-time. Full-time tuition and fees vary according to program. Part-time tuition and fees vary according to program. *Required fees:* $620 full-time, $259 per credit hour part-time. *Payment plans:* installment, deferred payment. *Waivers:* senior citizens.

Financial Aid Of all full-time matriculated undergraduates who enrolled in 2018, 21 Federal Work-Study jobs (averaging $2629). 1 state and other part-time job (averaging $2051). *Average financial aid package:* $3940. *Average need-based loan:* $2231.

Applying *Options:* electronic application. *Application fee:* $30. *Required for some:* high school transcript. *Application deadlines:* rolling (freshmen), rolling (out-of-state freshmen), rolling (transfers), rolling (early action). *Early decision deadline:* rolling (for plan 1), rolling (for plan 2). *Notification:* continuous (freshmen), continuous (out-of-state freshmen), continuous (transfers), rolling (early decision plan 1), rolling (early decision plan 2), rolling (early action).

Freshman Application Contact Alvin Community College, 3110 Mustang Road, Alvin, TX 77511-4898. *Phone:* 281-756-3501.
Website: http://www.alvincollege.edu/.

Amarillo College
Amarillo, Texas

- **State and locally supported** 2-year, founded 1929
- **Urban** 1542-acre campus
- **Endowment** $40.0 million
- **Coed**

Undergraduates 5% Black or African American, non-Hispanic/Latino; 39% Hispanic/Latino; 3% Asian, non-Hispanic/Latino; 0.1% Native Hawaiian or other Pacific Islander, non-Hispanic/Latino; 0.5% American Indian or Alaska Native, non-Hispanic/Latino; 2% Two or more races, non-Hispanic/Latino; 1% Race/ethnicity unknown. *Retention:* 52% of full-time freshmen returned.

Faculty *Total:* 775, 25% full-time, 4% with terminal degrees.

Majors Accounting; administrative assistant and secretarial science; airframe mechanics and aircraft maintenance technology; architectural engineering technology; art; automobile/automotive mechanics technology; behavioral sciences; biblical studies; biology/biological sciences; broadcast journalism; business administration and management; business teacher education; chemical technology; chemistry; child development; clinical laboratory science/medical technology; commercial and advertising art; computer engineering technology; computer programming; computer science; computer systems analysis; corrections; criminal justice/law enforcement administration; criminal justice/police science; dental hygiene; drafting and design technology; dramatic/theater arts; electrical, electronic and communications engineering technology; elementary education; emergency medical technology (EMT paramedic); engineering; English; environmental health; fine/studio arts; fire science/firefighting; funeral service and mortuary science; general studies; geology/earth science; health information/medical records administration; heating, air conditioning, ventilation and refrigeration maintenance technology; heavy equipment maintenance technology; history; industrial radiologic technology; information science/studies; instrumentation technology; interior design; journalism; laser and optical technology; legal administrative assistant/secretary; liberal arts and sciences/liberal studies; licensed practical/vocational nurse training; machine tool technology; mass communication/media; mathematics; medical administrative assistant and medical secretary; modern languages; music; music teacher education; natural sciences; nuclear medical technology; occupational therapy; photography; physical education teaching and coaching; physical sciences; physical therapy; physics; pre-engineering; pre-pharmacy studies; psychology; public relations/image management; radio and television; radiologic technology/science; real estate; registered nursing/registered nurse; religious studies; respiratory care therapy; rhetoric and composition; social sciences; social work; substance abuse/addiction counseling; telecommunications technology; tourism and travel services management; visual and performing arts.

Academics *Calendar:* semesters. *Degree:* certificates and associate. *Special study options:* academic remediation for entering students, adult/continuing education programs, advanced placement credit, cooperative education, distance learning, English as a second language, freshman honors college, honors programs, part-time degree program, services for LD students, summer session for credit.

Library Lynn Library Learning Center plus 2 others. Students can reserve study rooms.

Student Life *Housing:* college housing not available. *Activities and Organizations:* drama/theater group, student-run newspaper, radio station, choral group. *Campus security:* 24-hour emergency response devices, late-night transport/escort service, campus police patrol Monday through Saturday 7 am-11 pm. *Student services:* personal/psychological counseling, legal services, veterans affairs office.

Athletics *Intramural sports:* basketball M/W, soccer M/W, softball M/W, tennis M/W, volleyball M/W.

Costs (2020–21) *Tuition:* area resident $2670 full-time, $89 per credit hour part-time; state resident $3960 full-time, $132 per credit hour part-time; nonresident $5880 full-time, $196 per credit hour part-time. Full-time tuition and fees vary according to course load. Part-time tuition and fees vary

according to course load. *Required fees:* $1260 full-time, $42 per semester hour part-time. *Payment plan:* installment. *Waivers:* senior citizens and employees or children of employees.
Financial Aid Of all full-time matriculated undergraduates who enrolled in 2018, 4,715 applied for aid, 4,293 were judged to have need. 128 Federal Work-Study jobs (averaging $4922). 12 state and other part-time jobs (averaging $4538). *Average indebtedness upon graduation:* $6611.
Applying *Options:* early admission, deferred entrance. *Required:* high school transcript. *Notification:* continuous (freshmen), continuous (transfers).
Freshman Application Contact Amarillo College, PO Box 447, Amarillo, TX 79178-0001. *Phone:* 806-371-5000. *Toll-free phone:* 800-227-8784. *Fax:* 806-371-5497. *E-mail:* askac@actx.edu.
Website: http://www.actx.edu/.

Angelina College
Lufkin, Texas

Freshman Application Contact Angelina College, PO Box 1768, Lufkin, TX 75902-1768. *Phone:* 936-633-5213. *Website:* http://www.angelina.edu/.

Auguste Escoffier School of Culinary Arts
Austin, Texas

Admissions Office Contact Auguste Escoffier School of Culinary Arts, 6020-B Dillard, Austin, TX 78752. *Website:* http://www.escoffier.edu/.

Austin Community College District
Austin, Texas

- **State and locally supported** primarily 2-year, founded 1972
- **Urban** campus with easy access to Austin
- **Endowment** $8.7 million
- **Coed,** 41,056 undergraduate students, 22% full-time, 57% women, 43% men

Undergraduates 8,939 full-time, 32,117 part-time. Students come from 54 states and territories; 101 other countries; 2% are from out of state; 8% Black or African American, non-Hispanic/Latino; 40% Hispanic/Latino; 5% Asian, non-Hispanic/Latino; 0.2% Native Hawaiian or other Pacific Islander, non-Hispanic/Latino; 0.6% American Indian or Alaska Native, non-Hispanic/Latino; 3% Two or more races, non-Hispanic/Latino; 0.9% Race/ethnicity unknown; 2% international; 10% transferred in.
Freshmen *Admission:* 5,505 enrolled.
Faculty *Total:* 1,893, 32% full-time, 24% with terminal degrees. *Student/faculty ratio:* 19:1.
Majors Accounting; accounting technology and bookkeeping; administrative assistant and secretarial science; agriculture; agroecology and sustainable agriculture; animation, interactive technology, video graphics and special effects; anthropology; Arabic; archeology; art; art history, criticism and conservation; autobody/collision and repair technology; automobile/automotive mechanics technology; biology/biological sciences; biology/biotechnology laboratory technician; biomedical technology; business administration and management; business/commerce; carpentry; chemistry; child development; Chinese; civil engineering; clinical/medical laboratory technology; commercial photography; computer and information sciences; computer programming; computer systems networking and telecommunications; corrections; creative writing; criminal justice/police science; crisis/emergency/disaster management; culinary arts; dance; dental hygiene; design and visual communications; diagnostic medical sonography and ultrasound technology; digital arts; drafting and design technology; dramatic/theater arts; early childhood education; economics; electrical, electronic and communications engineering technology; emergency medical technology (EMT paramedic); engineering; English; entrepreneurship; environmental engineering technology; environmental science; fashion/apparel design; fire prevention and safety technology; French; general studies; geographic information science and cartography; geography; geology/earth science; German; health and physical education/fitness; health information/medical records technology; heating, ventilation, air conditioning and refrigeration engineering technology; history; hospitality administration; hotel/motel administration; international business/trade/commerce; Italian; Japanese; journalism; kinesiology and exercise science; Latin; legal assistant/paralegal; logistics, materials, and supply chain management; marketing/marketing management; mathematics; mental health counseling; middle school education; multi/interdisciplinary studies related; music; music management; occupational therapist assistant; pharmacy technician; philosophy; photographic and film/video technology; physical fitness technician; physical therapy technology; physics; political science and government; premedical studies; professional, technical, business, and scientific writing; psychology; radio and television; radiologic technology/science; real estate; registered nursing/registered nurse; rhetoric and composition; Russian; secondary education; sign language interpretation and translation; social work; sociology; Spanish; substance abuse/addiction counseling; surgical technology; surveying technology; theater design and technology; therapeutic recreation; tourism and travel services management; veterinary/animal health technology; watchmaking and jewelrymaking; welding technology.
Academics *Calendar:* semesters. *Degrees:* certificates, associate, bachelor's, and postbachelor's certificates. *Special study options:* academic remediation for entering students, accelerated degree program, adult/continuing education programs, advanced placement credit, cooperative education, distance learning, English as a second language, honors programs, independent study, internships, part-time degree program, services for LD students, summer session for credit. *ROTC:* Army (c), Air Force (c).
Library Main Library plus 11 others. *Books:* 148,059 (physical), 36,660 (digital/electronic); *Serial titles:* 402 (physical), 94,538 (digital/electronic); *Databases:* 104. Weekly public service hours: 83; students can reserve study rooms.
Student Life *Housing:* college housing not available. *Activities and Organizations:* Intramurals, Students for Environmental Outreach, Phi Theta Kappa (PTK), National Society of Collegiate Scholars, Students for Community Involvement. *Campus security:* 24-hour emergency response devices and patrols, late-night transport/escort service. *Student services:* personal/psychological counseling, veterans affairs office.
Athletics *Intramural sports:* basketball M/W, soccer M/W, softball M/W, volleyball W.
Costs (2019–20) *Tuition:* area resident $2010 full-time, $67 per credit hour part-time; state resident $10,290 full-time, $343 per credit hour part-time; nonresident $12,480 full-time, $416 per credit hour part-time. Full-time tuition and fees vary according to course load. Part-time tuition and fees vary according to course load. *Required fees:* $540 full-time, $18 per credit hour part-time. *Payment plan:* installment. *Waivers:* senior citizens and employees or children of employees.
Financial Aid Of all full-time matriculated undergraduates who enrolled in 2019, 4,771 applied for aid, 3,941 were judged to have need. 167 Federal Work-Study jobs (averaging $2987). 15 state and other part-time jobs (averaging $2185). *Average need-based loan:* $3286. *Average need-based gift aid:* $4779.
Applying *Options:* electronic application. *Required:* high school transcript. *Application deadlines:* rolling (freshmen), rolling (transfers).
Freshman Application Contact Mrs. Linda Terry, Executive Director, Admissions and Records, Austin Community College District, 5930 Middle Fiskville Road, Austin, TX 78752. *Phone:* 512-223-7503. *Fax:* 512-223-7963. *E-mail:* admission@austincc.edu.
Website: http://www.austincc.edu/.

Blinn College
Brenham, Texas

- **State and locally supported** 2-year, founded 1883
- **Rural** 100-acre campus with easy access to Houston
- **Endowment** $10.3 million
- **Coed,** 21,372 undergraduate students, 47% full-time, 51% women, 49% men

Undergraduates 10,070 full-time, 11,302 part-time. Students come from 42 other countries; 3% are from out of state; 10% Black or African American, non-Hispanic/Latino; 22% Hispanic/Latino; 2% Asian, non-Hispanic/Latino; 0.1% Native Hawaiian or other Pacific Islander, non-Hispanic/Latino; 0.4% American Indian or Alaska Native, non-Hispanic/Latino; 3% Two or more races, non-Hispanic/Latino; 1% Race/ethnicity unknown; 0.6% international; 26% transferred in; 95% live on campus. *Retention:* 47% of full-time freshmen returned.
Freshmen *Admission:* 52,910 applied, 52,830 admitted, 7,192 enrolled.
Faculty *Total:* 742, 62% full-time, 18% with terminal degrees. *Student/faculty ratio:* 40:1.
Majors Accounting; administrative assistant and secretarial science; agriculture; anthropology; architectural and building sciences; biology/biological sciences; biology/biotechnology laboratory technician; business administration and management; chemistry; child development; comparative literature; computer science; computer systems networking and telecommunications; criminal justice/law enforcement administration; criminal justice/safety; dental hygiene; dramatic/theater arts; economics; education; engineering; English; fire science/firefighting; French; general studies; geography; geology/earth science; German; health and physical education/fitness; health information/medical records technology; history; industrial radiologic technology; legal administrative assistant/secretary; mass communication/media; mathematics; mental health counseling; music; natural sciences; philosophy; physical education teaching and coaching; physical therapy technology; physics; psychology; real estate; registered

nursing/registered nurse; rhetoric and composition; secondary education; social sciences; Spanish; welding technology.
Academics *Calendar:* semesters. *Degree:* certificates, diplomas, and associate. *Special study options:* academic remediation for entering students, adult/continuing education programs, advanced placement credit, distance learning, double majors, English as a second language, freshman honors college, part-time degree program, services for LD students, summer session for credit.
Library W. L. Moody, Jr. Library plus 1 other. *Books:* 116,309 (physical), 267,677 (digital/electronic); *Serial titles:* 1,706 (physical), 6,529 (digital/electronic).
Student Life *Housing Options:* coed, men-only, women-only, special housing for students with disabilities. Campus housing is university owned. *Activities and Organizations:* drama/theater group, student-run newspaper, choral group, marching band, Student Government Association, Phi Theta Kappa, Baptist student ministries, Blinn Ethnic Student Organization, Circle K. *Campus security:* 24-hour emergency response devices and patrols, controlled dormitory access. *Student services:* personal/psychological counseling.
Athletics Member NJCAA. *Intercollegiate sports:* baseball M(s), basketball M(s)/W(s), cheerleading M(s)/W(s), football M(s), soccer M/W, softball W(s), volleyball W(s). *Intramural sports:* basketball M/W, bowling M/W, football M, golf M, softball W, table tennis M/W, volleyball M/W, weight lifting M/W.
Costs (2019–20) *Tuition:* area resident $1650 full-time, $55 per credit hour part-time; state resident $3360 full-time, $112 per credit hour part-time; nonresident $8160 full-time, $272 per credit hour part-time. Full-time tuition and fees vary according to course load. Part-time tuition and fees vary according to course load. *Required fees:* $2114 full-time, $67 per credit hour part-time. *Room and board:* $8199; room only: $5399. Room and board charges vary according to board plan and housing facility. *Payment plan:* installment.
Financial Aid Of all full-time matriculated undergraduates who enrolled in 2018, 162 Federal Work-Study jobs (averaging $1803).
Applying *Options:* electronic application, early admission, deferred entrance. *Required:* high school transcript. *Application deadlines:* rolling (freshmen), rolling (transfers).
Freshman Application Contact Ms. Elaine Abshire, Director Prospective Student Relations/Community Outreach, Blinn College, 902 College Avenue, Brenham, TX 77833-4049. *Phone:* 979-209-7547. *E-mail:* eabshire@blinn.edu.
Website: http://www.blinn.edu/.

Brazosport College
Lake Jackson, Texas

- **State and locally supported** primarily 2-year, founded 1968
- **Small-town** 160-acre campus with easy access to Houston
- **Coed**

Undergraduates Students come from 1 other state. *Retention:* 52% of full-time freshmen returned.
Faculty *Student/faculty ratio:* 17:1.
Academics *Calendar:* semesters. *Degrees:* certificates, associate, and bachelor's. *Special study options:* academic remediation for entering students, adult/continuing education programs, advanced placement credit, cooperative education, distance learning, honors programs, internships, part-time degree program, summer session for credit.
Library Brazosport College Library.
Student Life *Campus security:* 24-hour patrols.
Applying *Options:* early admission, deferred entrance. *Required for some:* high school transcript.
Freshman Application Contact Brazosport College, 500 College Drive, Lake Jackson, TX 77566-3199. *Phone:* 979-230-3020. *Website:* http://www.brazosport.edu/.

Brookhaven College
Farmers Branch, Texas

Freshman Application Contact Admissions Office, Brookhaven College, 3939 Valley View Lane, Farmers Branch, TX 75244-4997. *Phone:* 972-860-4883. *Fax:* 972-860-4886. *E-mail:* bhcadmissions@dcccd.edu. *Website:* http://www.brookhavencollege.edu/.

Carrington College–Mesquite
Mesquite, Texas

Admissions Office Contact Carrington College–Mesquite, 3733 West Emporium Circle, Mesquite, TX 75150-6509. *Website:* http://www.carrington.edu/.

Cedar Valley College
Lancaster, Texas

Freshman Application Contact Admissions Office, Cedar Valley College, Lancaster, TX 75134-3799. *Phone:* 972-860-8206. *Fax:* 972-860-8207. *Website:* http://www.cedarvalleycollege.edu/.

Center for Advanced Legal Studies
Houston, Texas

Freshman Application Contact Mr. James Scheffer, Center for Advanced Legal Studies, 3910 Kirby, Suite 200, Houston, TX 77098. *Phone:* 713-529-2778. *Toll-free phone:* 800-446-6931. *Fax:* 713-523-2715. *E-mail:* james.scheffer@paralegal.edu. *Website:* http://www.paralegal.edu/.

Central Texas College
Killeen, Texas

- **State and locally supported** 2-year, founded 1967
- **Suburban** 500-acre campus with easy access to Austin
- **Endowment** $8.2 million
- **Coed**

Undergraduates 4,355 full-time, 11,718 part-time. Students come from 54 states and territories; 31% are from out of state; 27% Black or African American, non-Hispanic/Latino; 25% Hispanic/Latino; 3% Asian, non-Hispanic/Latino; 1% Native Hawaiian or other Pacific Islander, non-Hispanic/Latino; 0.6% American Indian or Alaska Native, non-Hispanic/Latino; 5% Two or more races, non-Hispanic/Latino; 3% Race/ethnicity unknown; 0.4% international; 7% transferred in; 1% live on campus. *Retention:* 52% of full-time freshmen returned.
Faculty *Student/faculty ratio:* 17:1.
Academics *Calendar:* semesters. *Degree:* certificates and associate. *Special study options:* academic remediation for entering students, accelerated degree program, adult/continuing education programs, advanced placement credit, cooperative education, distance learning, English as a second language, external degree program, internships, part-time degree program, services for LD students, student-designed majors, summer session for credit. *ROTC:* Army (b).
Library Oveta Culp Hobby Memorial Library. *Books:* 37,738 (physical), 279,575 (digital/electronic); *Serial titles:* 126 (physical); *Databases:* 82. Weekly public service hours: 85; students can reserve study rooms.
Student Life *Campus security:* 24-hour emergency response devices and patrols.
Standardized Tests *Required for some:* TSI Assessment required for those that are not TSI exempt or waived.
Costs (2019–20) *Tuition:* area resident $2700 full-time, $90 per credit hour part-time; state resident $3390 full-time, $113 per credit hour part-time; nonresident $7050 full-time, $235 per credit hour part-time. Full-time tuition and fees vary according to location and program. Part-time tuition and fees vary according to location and program. *Room and board:* $5794. Room and board charges vary according to board plan.
Financial Aid Of all full-time matriculated undergraduates who enrolled in 2018, 68 Federal Work-Study jobs (averaging $3658).
Applying *Options:* electronic application, early admission, deferred entrance. *Required:* high school transcript.
Director of Admissions Shannon Bralley, Director, Admissions and Recruitment, Central Texas College, PO Box 1800, Killeen, TX 76540-1800. *Phone:* 254-526-1934. *Toll-free phone:* 800-223-4760 (in-state); 800-792-3348 (out-of-state). *E-mail:* shannon.bralley@ctcd.edu. *Website:* http://www.ctcd.edu/.

Cisco College
Cisco, Texas

- **State and locally supported** 2-year, founded 1940
- **Rural** 40-acre campus
- **Coed**

Undergraduates 1,601 full-time, 2,421 part-time. 12% live on campus. *Retention:* 56% of full-time freshmen returned.
Faculty *Student/faculty ratio:* 18:1.
Academics *Calendar:* semesters. *Degree:* certificates and associate. *Special study options:* academic remediation for entering students, advanced placement credit, part-time degree program, summer session for credit. *ROTC:* Army (c).
Library Maner Library.
Student Life *Campus security:* late-night transport/escort service.
Athletics Member NJCAA.
Standardized Tests *Recommended:* SAT (for admission), ACT (for admission).

Applying *Options:* early admission. *Required:* high school transcript.
Freshman Application Contact Mr. Olin O. Odom III, Dean of Admission/Registrar, Cisco College, 101 College Heights, Cisco, TX 76437-9321. *Phone:* 254-442-2567 Ext. 5130. *E-mail:* oodom@cjc.edu. *Website:* http://www.cisco.edu/.

Clarendon College
Clarendon, Texas

Freshman Application Contact Ms. Martha Smith, Admissions Director, Clarendon College, PO Box 968, Clarendon, TX 79226. *Phone:* 806-874-3571 Ext. 106. *Toll-free phone:* 800-687-9737. *Fax:* 806-874-3201. *E-mail:* martha.smith@clarendoncollege.edu. *Website:* http://www.clarendoncollege.edu/.

Coastal Bend College
Beeville, Texas

- **County-supported** 2-year, founded 1965
- **Rural** 100-acre campus
- **Endowment** $514,263
- **Coed**

Undergraduates 1,353 full-time, 2,423 part-time. Students come from 2 states and territories; 1 other country; 1% are from out of state; 5% transferred in; 5% live on campus.
Faculty *Student/faculty ratio:* 13:1.
Academics *Calendar:* semesters. *Degree:* certificates and associate. *Special study options:* academic remediation for entering students, adult/continuing education programs, advanced placement credit, cooperative education, distance learning, internships, part-time degree program, services for LD students, summer session for credit.
Library Grady C. Hogue Learning Resource Center.
Student Life *Campus security:* 24-hour emergency response devices, night security.
Athletics Member NJCAA.
Financial Aid Of all full-time matriculated undergraduates who enrolled in 2018, 80 Federal Work-Study jobs (averaging $1484). 11 state and other part-time jobs (averaging $1159).
Applying *Options:* electronic application, deferred entrance. *Required:* high school transcript.
Freshman Application Contact Mrs. Tammy Adams, Director of Admissions/Registrar, Coastal Bend College, Beeville, TX 78102-2197. *Phone:* 361-354-2245. *Toll-free phone:* 866-722-2838 (in-state); 866-262-2838 (out-of-state). *Fax:* 361-354-2254. *E-mail:* tadams@coastalbend.edu. *Website:* http://www.coastalbend.edu/.

The College of Health Care Professions
Austin, Texas

Admissions Office Contact The College of Health Care Professions, 6505 Airport Boulevard, Austin, TX 78752. *Website:* http://www.chcp.edu/.

The College of Health Care Professions
Fort Worth, Texas

Admissions Office Contact The College of Health Care Professions, 4248 North Freeway, Fort Worth, TX 76137-5021. *Website:* http://www.chcp.edu/.

The College of Health Care Professions
Houston, Texas

Freshman Application Contact Admissions Office, The College of Health Care Professions, 240 Northwest Mall Boulevard, Houston, TX 77092. *Phone:* 713-425-3100. *Toll-free phone:* 800-487-6728. *Fax:* 713-425-3193. *Website:* http://www.chcp.edu/.

The College of Health Care Professions
McAllen, Texas

Admissions Office Contact The College of Health Care Professions, 1917 Nolana Avenue, Suite 100, McAllen, TX 78504. *Website:* http://www.chcp.edu/.

The College of Health Care Professions
San Antonio, Texas

Admissions Office Contact The College of Health Care Professions, 4738 NW Loop 410, San Antonio, TX 78229. *Website:* http://www.chcp.edu/.

College of the Mainland
Texas City, Texas

- **State and locally supported** 2-year, founded 1967
- **Suburban** 128-acre campus with easy access to Houston
- **Coed**

Undergraduates 1,121 full-time, 3,067 part-time. Students come from 3 states and territories; 18% Black or African American, non-Hispanic/Latino; 35% Hispanic/Latino; 3% Asian, non-Hispanic/Latino; 0.2% Native Hawaiian or other Pacific Islander, non-Hispanic/Latino; 0.4% American Indian or Alaska Native, non-Hispanic/Latino; 0.5% Two or more races, non-Hispanic/Latino; 3% Race/ethnicity unknown; 5% transferred in. *Retention:* 54% of full-time freshmen returned.
Faculty *Student/faculty ratio:* 15:1.
Academics *Calendar:* semesters. *Degree:* certificates, diplomas, and associate. *Special study options:* academic remediation for entering students, adult/continuing education programs, cooperative education, distance learning, English as a second language, honors programs, internships, part-time degree program, services for LD students, summer session for credit. *ROTC:* Air Force (c).
Library COM Library plus 1 other.
Student Life *Campus security:* 24-hour emergency response devices and patrols, student patrols, late-night transport/escort service, vehicular assistance for lock outs, jump starts.
Standardized Tests *Recommended:* SAT or ACT (for admission).
Financial Aid Of all full-time matriculated undergraduates who enrolled in 2018, 343 applied for aid, 303 were judged to have need, 5 had their need fully met. *Average percent of need met:* 57. *Average financial aid package:* $6102. *Average need-based loan:* $630. *Average need-based gift aid:* $5272.
Applying *Options:* electronic application, early admission, deferred entrance. *Required for some:* high school transcript.
Freshman Application Contact Mr. Martin Perez, Director of Admissions/International Affairs, College of the Mainland, 1200 Amburn Road, Texas City, TX 77591. *Phone:* 409-933-8653. *Toll-free phone:* 888-258-8859 Ext. 8264. *E-mail:* mperez@com.edu. *Website:* http://www.com.edu/.

Collin County Community College District
McKinney, Texas

- **State and locally supported** primarily 2-year, founded 1985
- **Suburban** 406-acre campus with easy access to Dallas-Fort Worth
- **Endowment** $11.7 million
- **Coed,** 35,144 undergraduate students, 31% full-time, 56% women, 44% men
- 100% of applicants were admitted

Undergraduates 10,760 full-time, 24,384 part-time. 72% are from out of state; 13% Black or African American, non-Hispanic/Latino; 23% Hispanic/Latino; 11% Asian, non-Hispanic/Latino; 0.2% Native Hawaiian or other Pacific Islander, non-Hispanic/Latino; 0.3% American Indian or Alaska Native, non-Hispanic/Latino; 4% Two or more races, non-Hispanic/Latino; 2% Race/ethnicity unknown; 3% international; 5% transferred in. *Retention:* 66% of full-time freshmen returned.
Freshmen *Admission:* 9,625 applied, 9,625 admitted, 5,566 enrolled.
Faculty *Total:* 1,442, 32% full-time, 28% with terminal degrees. *Student/faculty ratio:* 25:1.
Majors Administrative assistant and secretarial science; baking and pastry arts; business administration and management; business/commerce; child-care provision; child development; commercial and advertising art; commercial photography; computer and information sciences; computer and information systems security; computer science; computer systems networking and telecommunications; criminal justice/law enforcement administration; criminal justice/safety; culinary arts; dental hygiene; drafting and design technology; early childhood education; electrical, electronic and communications engineering technology; electroneurodiagnostic/electroencephalographic technology; emergency medical technology (EMT paramedic); engineering; fire prevention and safety technology; fire science/firefighting; game and interactive media design; geographic information science and cartography; graphic design; health information/medical records technology; health services/allied health/health sciences; heating, ventilation, air conditioning and refrigeration engineering

technology; hospitality administration; illustration; interior design; legal assistant/paralegal; liberal arts and sciences/liberal studies; logistics, materials, and supply chain management; medical insurance coding; middle school education; music; music management; network and system administration; real estate; registered nursing/registered nurse; respiratory care therapy; retail management; secondary education; sign language interpretation and translation; speech communication and rhetoric; surgical technology; system, networking, and LAN/WAN management; telecommunications technology; web page, digital/multimedia and information resources design; welding technology.

Academics *Calendar:* semesters. *Degrees:* certificates, associate, and bachelor's. *Special study options:* academic remediation for entering students, adult/continuing education programs, advanced placement credit, cooperative education, distance learning, English as a second language, honors programs, internships, part-time degree program, services for LD students, summer session for credit. *ROTC:* Army (c), Air Force (c).

Library Collin College Library plus 2 others. *Books:* 248,662 (physical), 53,569 (digital/electronic); *Serial titles:* 741 (physical), 176 (digital/electronic); *Databases:* 185. Weekly public service hours: 75; students can reserve study rooms.

Student Life *Activities and Organizations:* drama/theater group, choral group, Student Government Association, Phi Theta Kappa, Fellowship of Christian University Students, Collin Organized Geek Society, Society of Women Engineers. *Campus security:* 24-hour emergency response devices and patrols, late-night transport/escort service. *Student services:* personal/psychological counseling, veterans affairs office.

Athletics Member NJCAA. *Intercollegiate sports:* basketball M(s)/W(s), tennis M(s)/W(s). *Intramural sports:* basketball M/W, soccer M/W, volleyball M/W.

Costs (2020–21) *Tuition:* area resident $1560 full-time, $52 per credit hour part-time; state resident $2940 full-time, $98 per credit hour part-time; nonresident $4950 full-time, $165 per credit hour part-time. *Required fees:* $64 full-time. *Room and board:* $11,655. *Payment plan:* installment. *Waivers:* senior citizens and employees or children of employees.

Financial Aid Of all full-time matriculated undergraduates who enrolled in 2018, 4,909 applied for aid, 3,782 were judged to have need, 12 had their need fully met. In 2018, 144 non-need-based awards were made. *Average percent of need met:* 37%. *Average financial aid package:* $5797. *Average need-based loan:* $2941. *Average need-based gift aid:* $4949. *Average non-need-based aid:* $1180.

Applying *Options:* electronic application. *Application deadlines:* rolling (freshmen), rolling (transfers). *Notification:* continuous (freshmen), continuous (out-of-state freshmen), continuous (transfers).

Freshman Application Contact Mr. Todd E. Fields, Dean Admission/District Registrar, Collin County Community College District, 2800 E. Spring Creek Parkway, Plano, TX 75074. *Phone:* 972-881-5174. *Fax:* 972-881-5175. *E-mail:* tfields@collin.edu.
Website: http://www.collin.edu/.

Commonwealth Institute of Funeral Service

Houston, Texas

Freshman Application Contact Ms. Patricia Moreno, Registrar, Commonwealth Institute of Funeral Service, 415 Barren Springs Drive, Houston, TX 77090. *Phone:* 281-873-0262. *Toll-free phone:* 800-628-1580. *Fax:* 281-873-5232. *E-mail:* p.moreno@commonwealth.edu. *Website:* http://www.commonwealth.edu/.

Concorde Career College

Dallas, Texas

Admissions Office Contact Concorde Career College, 12606 Greenville Avenue, Suite 130, Dallas, TX 75243. *Website:* http://www.concorde.edu/.

Concorde Career College

Grand Prairie, Texas

Admissions Office Contact Concorde Career College, 3015 West Interstate 20, Grand Prairie, TX 75052. *Toll-free phone:* 800-693-7010. *Website:* http://www.concorde.edu/.

Concorde Career College

San Antonio, Texas

Admissions Office Contact Concorde Career College, 4803 NW Loop 410, Suite 200, San Antonio, TX 78229. *Website:* http://www.concorde.edu/.

Culinary Institute LeNotre

Houston, Texas

Freshman Application Contact Ellen Hogaboom, Admissions Manager, Culinary Institute LeNotre, 7070 Allensby Street, Houston, TX 77022. *Phone:* 713-692-0077. *Toll-free phone:* 888-LENOTRE. *Fax:* 713-692-7399. *E-mail:* ehogaboom@ciaml.com. *Website:* http://www.culinaryinstitute.edu/.

Dallas Institute of Funeral Service

Dallas, Texas

Freshman Application Contact Olga Retana, Admissions Representative, Dallas Institute of Funeral Service, 3909 South Buckner Boulevard, Dallas, TX 75227. *Phone:* 214-388-5466 Ext. 817. *Toll-free phone:* 800-235-5444. *Fax:* 214-388-0316. *E-mail:* oretana@dallasinstitute.edu. *Website:* http://www.dallasinstitute.edu/.

Dallas Nursing Institute

Dallas, Texas

Admissions Office Contact Dallas Nursing Institute, 12170 N. Abrams Road, Suite 200, Dallas, TX 75243. *Website:* http://www.dni.edu/.

Del Mar College

Corpus Christi, Texas

- **State and locally supported** 2-year, founded 1935
- **Urban** 159-acre campus
- **Coed**

Undergraduates 2,671 full-time, 9,162 part-time. Students come from 41 states and territories; 30 other countries; 2% are from out of state; 3% Black or African American, non-Hispanic/Latino; 67% Hispanic/Latino; 2% Asian, non-Hispanic/Latino; 0.2% Native Hawaiian or other Pacific Islander, non-Hispanic/Latino; 0.2% American Indian or Alaska Native, non-Hispanic/Latino; 3% Two or more races, non-Hispanic/Latino; 0.4% Race/ethnicity unknown; 0.2% international; 6% transferred in. *Retention:* 56% of full-time freshmen returned.

Faculty *Student/faculty ratio:* 18:1.

Academics *Calendar:* semesters. *Degree:* certificates and associate. *Special study options:* academic remediation for entering students, accelerated degree program, adult/continuing education programs, advanced placement credit, cooperative education, distance learning, double majors, English as a second language, freshman honors college, honors programs, internships, off-campus study, part-time degree program, services for LD students, summer session for credit. *ROTC:* Army (b).

Library White Library plus 1 other. *Books:* 145,107 (physical), 192,073 (digital/electronic); *Serial titles:* 1,635 (physical), 74,730 (digital/electronic); *Databases:* 172.

Student Life *Campus security:* 24-hour emergency response devices and patrols.

Costs (2019–20) *Tuition:* $65 per semester hour part-time; state resident $105 per semester hour part-time; nonresident $152 per semester hour part-time. *Required fees:* $36 per semester hour part-time, $77 per term part-time.

Financial Aid Of all full-time matriculated undergraduates who enrolled in 2018, 259 Federal Work-Study jobs (averaging $960). 449 state and other part-time jobs (averaging $1082).

Applying *Options:* electronic application, early admission, deferred entrance. *Required:* high school transcript.

Freshman Application Contact Del Mar College, 101 Baldwin Boulevard, Corpus Christi, TX 78404-3897. *Phone:* 361-698-1248. *Toll-free phone:* 800-652-3357. *Website:* http://www.delmar.edu/.

Eastfield College

Mesquite, Texas

- **State and locally supported** 2-year, founded 1970, part of Dallas County Community College District System
- **Suburban** 244-acre campus with easy access to Dallas-Fort Worth
- **Coed**

Undergraduates 3,026 full-time, 9,377 part-time. Students come from 7 states and territories; 26 other countries; 0.6% are from out of state; 2% transferred in.

Faculty *Student/faculty ratio:* 24:1.

Academics *Calendar:* semesters. *Degree:* certificates and associate. *Special study options:* academic remediation for entering students, adult/continuing education programs, advanced placement credit, cooperative education, distance learning, English as a second language, honors programs, part-time degree program, services for LD students, summer session for credit.

Library Eastfield College Learning Resource Center.
Student Life *Campus security:* 24-hour emergency response devices and patrols.
Athletics Member NJCAA.
Applying *Options:* early admission, deferred entrance. *Recommended:* high school transcript.
Freshman Application Contact Ms. Glynis Miller, Director of Admissions/Registrar, Eastfield College, 3737 Motley Drive, Mesquite, TX 75150-2099. *Phone:* 972-860-7010. *Fax:* 972-860-8306. *E-mail:* efc@dcccd.edu. *Website:* http://www.eastfieldcollege.edu/.

El Centro College
Dallas, Texas

Freshman Application Contact Ms. Rebecca Garza, Director of Admissions and Registrar, El Centro College, Dallas, TX 75202. *Phone:* 214-860-2618. *Fax:* 214-860-2233. *E-mail:* rgarza@dcccd.edu. *Website:* http://www.elcentrocollege.edu/.

El Paso Community College
El Paso, Texas

Freshman Application Contact Cassandra Lachica-Chavez, Executive Director Admission and Registrar, El Paso Community College, PO Box 20500, El Paso, TX 79998. *Phone:* 915-831-2580. *E-mail:* clachica@epcc.edu. *Website:* http://www.epcc.edu/.

Florida Career College
Houston, Texas

Admissions Office Contact Florida Career College, 70-A Farm to Market Road 1960 West, Houston, TX 77090. *Website:* http://www.floridacareercollege.edu/.

Fortis College
Grand Prairie, Texas

Admissions Office Contact Fortis College, 401 East Palace Parkway, Suite 100, Grand Prairie, TX 75050. *Toll-free phone:* 855-4-FORTIS. *Website:* http://www.fortis.edu/.

Fortis College
Houston, Texas

Admissions Office Contact Fortis College, 1201 West Oaks Mall, Houston, TX 77082. *Toll-free phone:* 855-4-FORTIS. *Website:* http://www.fortis.edu/.

Frank Phillips College
Borger, Texas

Freshman Application Contact Ms. Michele Stevens, Director of Enrollment Management, Frank Phillips College, PO Box 5118, Borger, TX 79008-5118. *Phone:* 806-457-4200 Ext. 707. *Fax:* 806-457-4225. *E-mail:* mstevens@fpctx.edu. *Website:* http://www.fpctx.edu/.

Galen College of Nursing
San Antonio, Texas

Admissions Office Contact Galen College of Nursing, 7411 John Smith Drive, Suite 1400, San Antonio, TX 78229. *Toll-free phone:* 877-223-7040. *Website:* http://www.galencollege.edu/.

Galveston College
Galveston, Texas

- **State and locally supported** primarily 2-year, founded 1967
- **Small-town** 11-acre campus with easy access to Houston, Texas
- **Coed,** 2,306 undergraduate students, 32% full-time, 61% women, 39% men

Undergraduates 731 full-time, 1,575 part-time. Students come from 28 states and territories; 17 other countries; 3% are from out of state; 16% Black or African American, non-Hispanic/Latino; 41% Hispanic/Latino; 3% Asian, non-Hispanic/Latino; 0.3% Native Hawaiian or other Pacific Islander, non-Hispanic/Latino; 0.3% American Indian or Alaska Native, non-Hispanic/Latino; 1% Two or more races, non-Hispanic/Latino; 2% Race/ethnicity unknown; 0.9% international; 9% transferred in. *Retention:* 55% of full-time freshmen returned.
Freshmen *Admission:* 353 enrolled.
Faculty *Total:* 105, 56% full-time, 21% with terminal degrees. *Student/faculty ratio:* 17:1.
Majors Art; behavioral sciences; biological and physical sciences; biology/biological sciences; business administration and management; chemistry; civil engineering; clinical laboratory science/medical technology; computer and information sciences; computer science; cosmetology; criminal justice/police science; criminal justice/safety; culinary arts; diagnostic medical sonography and ultrasound technology; dramatic/theater arts; education; electrical and electronics engineering; electrical and power transmission installation; electromechanical technology; emergency medical technology (EMT paramedic); English; general studies; health and physical education/fitness; health/health-care administration; heating, air conditioning, ventilation and refrigeration maintenance technology; history; humanities; liberal arts and sciences/liberal studies; mathematics; mechanical engineering; medical administrative assistant and medical secretary; medical radiologic technology; music; natural sciences; nuclear medical technology; occupational therapy; physical education teaching and coaching; physics; political science and government; psychology; radiologic technology/science; registered nursing/registered nurse; rhetoric and composition; social sciences; social work; sociology; surgical technology; welding technology.
Academics *Calendar:* semesters. *Degrees:* certificates, associate, and bachelor's. *Special study options:* academic remediation for entering students, adult/continuing education programs, advanced placement credit, cooperative education, distance learning, double majors, honors programs, internships, part-time degree program, services for LD students, study abroad, summer session for credit.
Library David Glenn Hunt Memorial Library. *Books:* 35,214 (physical), 227,610 (digital/electronic); *Serial titles:* 67 (physical), 34,344 (digital/electronic); *Databases:* 117. Students can reserve study rooms.
Student Life *Housing Options:* Campus housing is university owned. *Activities and Organizations:* drama/theater group, choral group, Fishing Club, Associate Degree in Nursing (ADN) Club, Radiography Club. *Campus security:* 24-hour emergency response devices and patrols, late-night transport/escort service. *Student services:* personal/psychological counseling, veterans affairs office.
Athletics Member NJCAA. *Intercollegiate sports:* baseball M(s), softball W(s). *Intramural sports:* badminton M/W, basketball M/W, soccer M/W, tennis M/W, volleyball M/W.
Costs (2020–21) *Tuition:* area resident $1350 full-time, $45 per credit hour part-time; state resident $2010 full-time, $67 per credit hour part-time; nonresident $4260 full-time, $142 per credit hour part-time. Full-time tuition and fees vary according to course load. Part-time tuition and fees vary according to course load. *Required fees:* $940 full-time, $25 per credit hour part-time, $95 per term part-time. *Room and board:* $3194; room only: $1894. *Payment plan:* installment. *Waivers:* senior citizens.
Financial Aid Of all full-time matriculated undergraduates who enrolled in 2016, 27 Federal Work-Study jobs (averaging $3000). 3 state and other part-time jobs (averaging $3000).
Applying *Options:* electronic application. *Required for some:* high school transcript. *Application deadlines:* rolling (freshmen), rolling (transfers). *Notification:* continuous (freshmen), continuous (transfers).
Freshman Application Contact Galveston College, 4015 Avenue Q, Galveston, TX 77550. *Phone:* 409-944-1216.
Website: http://www.gc.edu/.

Grayson College
Denison, Texas

Freshman Application Contact Charles Leslie, Enrollment Advisor, Grayson College, 6101Grayson Drive, Denison, TX 75020. *Phone:* 903-415-2532. *Fax:* 903-463-5284. *E-mail:* lesliec@grayson.edu. *Website:* http://www.grayson.edu/.

Hill College
Hillsboro, Texas

Freshman Application Contact Enrollment Management, Hill College, 112 Lamar Drive, Hillsboro, TX 76645. *Phone:* 254-659-7600. *Fax:* 254-582-7591. *E-mail:* enrollmentinfo@hillcollege.edu. *Website:* http://www.hillcollege.edu/.

Houston Community College
Houston, Texas

- **State and locally supported** 2-year, founded 1971
- **Urban** campus with easy access to Houston
- **Coed,** 56,151 undergraduate students, 29% full-time, 60% women, 40% men

Undergraduates 16,397 full-time, 39,754 part-time. 7% are from out of state; 27% Black or African American, non-Hispanic/Latino; 37% Hispanic/Latino; 10% Asian, non-Hispanic/Latino; 0.1% Native Hawaiian or other Pacific Islander, non-Hispanic/Latino; 0.1% American Indian or Alaska Native, non-Hispanic/Latino; 2% Two or more races, non-Hispanic/Latino; 2% Race/ethnicity unknown; 10% international; 8% transferred in. *Retention:* 64% of full-time freshmen returned.
Freshmen *Admission:* 8,342 applied, 8,342 admitted, 8,342 enrolled.
Faculty *Total:* 2,826, 31% full-time.
Majors Accounting; animation, interactive technology, video graphics and special effects; anthropology; applied horticulture/horticulture operations; automobile/automotive mechanics technology; banking and financial support services; biology/biological sciences; biology/biotechnology laboratory technician; business administration and management; business automation/technology/data entry; business/corporate communications; cardiovascular technology; chemical technology; chemistry; child development; cinematography and film/video production; clinical/medical laboratory science and allied professions related; clinical/medical laboratory technology; commercial photography; computer engineering technology; computer programming; computer programming (specific applications); computer science; computer systems networking and telecommunications; construction engineering technology; cosmetology; court reporting; criminal justice/police science; culinary arts; desktop publishing and digital imaging design; drafting and design technology; early childhood education; education (multiple levels); emergency medical technology (EMT paramedic); energy management and systems technology; engineering science; English; fashion/apparel design; fashion merchandising; fine/studio arts; fire prevention and safety technology; general studies; health and physical education/fitness; health information/medical records technology; health services/allied health/health sciences; histologic technician; hotel/motel administration; instrumentation technology; interior design; international business/trade/commerce; legal assistant/paralegal; logistics, materials, and supply chain management; manufacturing engineering technology; marketing/marketing management; mathematics; music management; music performance; music theory and composition; network and system administration; nuclear medical technology; occupational safety and health technology; occupational therapist assistant; petroleum technology; physical therapy technology; physics; psychiatric/mental health services technology; public administration; radio and television broadcasting technology; radiologic technology/science; real estate; registered nursing/registered nurse; respiratory care therapy; secondary education; sign language interpretation and translation; speech communication and rhetoric; tourism and travel services management; turf and turfgrass management.
Academics *Calendar:* semesters. *Degree:* certificates and associate. *Special study options:* academic remediation for entering students, advanced placement credit, cooperative education, distance learning, English as a second language, honors programs, internships, part-time degree program, services for LD students, study abroad, summer session for credit. *ROTC:* Army (c), Air Force (c).
Library Houston Community College Libraries plus 15 others. *Books:* 195,417 (physical), 287,522 (digital/electronic); *Serial titles:* 465 (physical), 37,745 (digital/electronic); *Databases:* 171. Students can reserve study rooms.
Student Life *Housing:* college housing not available. *Activities and Organizations:* student-run newspaper. *Campus security:* 24-hour emergency response devices and patrols, late-night transport/escort service, crime prevention services. *Student services:* veterans affairs office.
Costs (2019–20) *Tuition:* area resident $1848 full-time, $465 per term part-time; state resident $4152 full-time, $1041 per term part-time; nonresident $5268 full-time, $1320 per term part-time. Full-time tuition and fees vary according to course load and location. Part-time tuition and fees vary according to course load and location. *Payment plan:* installment. *Waivers:* senior citizens and employees or children of employees.
Financial Aid Of all full-time matriculated undergraduates who enrolled in 2018, 302 Federal Work-Study jobs (averaging $3602). 284 state and other part-time jobs (averaging $4251).
Applying *Options:* electronic application. *Required for some:* high school transcript, interview. *Application deadlines:* rolling (freshmen), rolling (transfers).
Freshman Application Contact Ms. Mary Lemburg, Registrar, Houston Community College, 3100 Main Street, PO Box 667517, Houston, TX 77266-7517. *Phone:* 713-718-2000. *Toll-free phone:* 877-422-6111. *Fax:* 713-718-2111. *E-mail:* student.info@hccs.edu.
Website: http://www.hccs.edu/.

Howard College
Big Spring, Texas

Freshman Application Contact Ms. TaNeal Richardson, Assistant Registrar, Howard College, 1001 Birdwell Lane, Big Spring, TX 79720-3702. *Phone:* 432-264-5105. *Toll-free phone:* 866-HC-HAWKS. *Fax:* 432-264-5604. *E-mail:* trichardson@howardcollege.edu. *Website:* http://www.howardcollege.edu/.

Interactive College of Technology
Houston, Texas

Freshman Application Contact Interactive College of Technology, 4473 I-45 N. Freeway, Airline Plaza, Houston, TX 77022. *Website:* http://ict.edu/.

Interactive College of Technology
Houston, Texas

Freshman Application Contact Interactive College of Technology, 6200 Hillcroft Avenue, Suite 200, Houston, TX 77081. *Website:* http://ict.edu/.

Interactive College of Technology
Pasadena, Texas

Freshman Application Contact Interactive College of Technology, 213 West Southmore Street, Suite 101, Pasadena, TX 77502. *Website:* http://ict.edu/.

International Business College
El Paso, Texas

Admissions Office Contact International Business College, 1155 North Zaragosa Road, El Paso, TX 79907. *Website:* http://www.ibcelpaso.edu/.

International Business College
El Paso, Texas

Admissions Office Contact International Business College, 1156 Barranca Drive, El Paso, TX 79935. *Website:* http://www.ibcelpaso.edu/.

Jacksonville College
Jacksonville, Texas

Freshman Application Contact Danny Morris, Director of Admissions, Jacksonville College, 105 B.J. Albritton Drive, Jacksonville, TX 75766. *Phone:* 903-589-7110. *Toll-free phone:* 800-256-8522. *E-mail:* admissions@jacksonville-college.org. *Website:* http://www.jacksonville-college.edu/.

KD Conservatory College of Film and Dramatic Arts
Dallas, Texas

Freshman Application Contact Mr. Michael Schraeder, Director of Education and Acting Program Chair, KD Conservatory College of Film and Dramatic Arts, 2600 Stemmons Freeway, Suite 117, Dallas, TX 75207. *Phone:* 214-638-0484. *Toll-free phone:* 877-278-2283. *Fax:* 214-630-5140. *E-mail:* mschraeder@kdstudio.com. *Website:* http://www.kdstudio.com/.

Kilgore College
Kilgore, Texas

Freshman Application Contact Kilgore College, 1100 Broadway Boulevard, Kilgore, TX 75662-3299. *Phone:* 903-983-8200. *E-mail:* register@kilgore.cc.tx.us. *Website:* http://www.kilgore.edu/.

Lamar Institute of Technology
Beaumont, Texas

- **State-supported** 2-year, founded 1995
- **Urban** 11-acre campus
- **Coed**

Undergraduates 1,365 full-time, 2,200 part-time. Students come from 3 states and territories; 27% Black or African American, non-Hispanic/Latino; 19% Hispanic/Latino; 3% Asian, non-Hispanic/Latino; 0.1% Native Hawaiian or other Pacific Islander, non-Hispanic/Latino; 0.7% American Indian or Alaska Native, non-Hispanic/Latino; 2% Two or more races, non-Hispanic/Latino.

Academics *Calendar:* semesters. *Degree:* certificates and associate.
Library The Mary and John Gray Library. *Books:* 621,094 (physical), 71,446 (digital/electronic); *Serial titles:* 19,735 (physical), 46,546 (digital/electronic); *Databases:* 127. Weekly public service hours: 93.
Student Life *Campus security:* 24-hour emergency response devices and patrols, late-night transport/escort service, controlled dormitory access.
Financial Aid ***Financial aid deadline:*** 4/1.
Freshman Application Contact Julie Pitts, Student Services Assistant, Lamar Institute of Technology, 855 East Lavaca, Beaumont, TX 77705. *Phone:* 409-880-8858. *Toll-free phone:* 800-950-6989. *Fax:* 409-880-1711. *E-mail:* jrpitts@lit.edu. *Website:* http://www.lit.edu/.

Lamar State College–Orange

Orange, Texas

Freshman Application Contact Kerry Olson, Director of Admissions and Financial Aid, Lamar State College–Orange, 410 Front Street, Orange, TX 77632. *Phone:* 409-882-3362. *Fax:* 409-882-3374. *Website:* http://www.lsco.edu/.

Lamar State College–Port Arthur

Port Arthur, Texas

Freshman Application Contact Ms. Connie Nicholas, Registrar, Lamar State College–Port Arthur, PO Box 310, Port Arthur, TX 77641-0310. *Phone:* 409-984-6165. *Toll-free phone:* 800-477-5872. *Fax:* 409-984-6025. *E-mail:* nichoca@lamarpa.edu. *Website:* http://www.lamarpa.edu/.

Laredo College

Laredo, Texas

Freshman Application Contact Ms. Josie Soliz, Admissions Records Supervisor, Laredo College, Laredo, TX 78040-4395. *Phone:* 956-721-5177. *Fax:* 956-721-5493. *Website:* http://www.laredo.edu/.

Lee College

Baytown, Texas

Director of Admissions Ms. Becki Griffith, Registrar, Lee College, PO Box 818, Baytown, TX 77522-0818. *Phone:* 281-425-6399. *E-mail:* bgriffit@lee.edu. *Website:* http://www.lee.edu/.

Lincoln College of Technology - Grand Prairie

Grand Prairie, Texas

Admissions Office Contact Lincoln College of Technology - Grand Prairie, 2915 Alouette Drive, Grand Prairie, TX 75052. *Toll-free phone:* 844-215-1513. *Website:* http://www.lincolntech.edu/.

Lone Star College–CyFair

Cypress, Texas

- **State and locally supported** 2-year, founded 2002, part of Lone Star College
- **Suburban** campus with easy access to Houston
- **Coed**

Undergraduates 152,012 full-time, 49,080 part-time. Students come from 67 other countries; 13% Black or African American, non-Hispanic/Latino; 43% Hispanic/Latino; 11% Asian, non-Hispanic/Latino; 0.2% American Indian or Alaska Native, non-Hispanic/Latino; 3% Two or more races, non-Hispanic/Latino; 3% Race/ethnicity unknown; 3% transferred in.
Faculty *Student/faculty ratio:* 21:1.
Academics *Calendar:* semesters. *Degree:* certificates, diplomas, and associate. *Special study options:* academic remediation for entering students, accelerated degree program, adult/continuing education programs, advanced placement credit, cooperative education, distance learning, double majors, English as a second language, honors programs, independent study, internships, part-time degree program, services for LD students, study abroad, summer session for credit.
Library LSC–CyFair Library.
Student Life *Campus security:* 24-hour emergency response devices and patrols, late-night transport/escort service.
Costs (2019–20) *Tuition:* area resident $1352 full-time, $44 per credit hour part-time; state resident $4202 full-time, $139 per credit hour part-time; nonresident $5252 full-time, $174 per credit hour part-time. *Required fees:* $664 full-time.
Applying *Options:* electronic application, early admission. *Recommended:* high school transcript.
Freshman Application Contact Admissions Office, Lone Star College–CyFair, 9191 Barker Cypress Road, Cypress, TX 77433-1383. *Phone:* 281-290-3200. *E-mail:* cfc.info@lonestar.edu. *Website:* http://www.lonestar.edu/cyfair.

Lone Star College–Kingwood

Kingwood, Texas

- **State and locally supported** 2-year, founded 1984, part of Lone Star College
- **Suburban** 264-acre campus with easy access to Houston
- **Coed**

Undergraduates 152,012 full-time, 46,253 part-time. Students come from 48 other countries; 14% Black or African American, non-Hispanic/Latino; 35% Hispanic/Latino; 4% Asian, non-Hispanic/Latino; 0.3% American Indian or Alaska Native, non-Hispanic/Latino; 3% Two or more races, non-Hispanic/Latino; 4% Race/ethnicity unknown; 2% transferred in.
Faculty *Student/faculty ratio:* 21:1.
Academics *Calendar:* semesters. *Degree:* certificates and associate. *Special study options:* academic remediation for entering students, accelerated degree program, adult/continuing education programs, advanced placement credit, cooperative education, distance learning, double majors, English as a second language, honors programs, independent study, internships, part-time degree program, services for LD students, study abroad, summer session for credit.
Library LSC–Kingwood Library.
Student Life *Campus security:* 24-hour emergency response devices and patrols, late-night transport/escort service.
Costs (2019–20) *Tuition:* area resident $1352 full-time, $44 per credit hour part-time; state resident $4202 full-time, $139 per credit hour part-time; nonresident $5252 full-time, $174 per credit hour part-time. *Required fees:* $664 full-time.
Financial Aid Of all full-time matriculated undergraduates who enrolled in 2009, 28 Federal Work-Study jobs (averaging $3394). 6 state and other part-time jobs (averaging $2606). *Financial aid deadline:* 4/1.
Applying *Options:* electronic application, early admission. *Recommended:* high school transcript.
Freshman Application Contact Admissions Office, Lone Star College–Kingwood, 20000 Kingwood Drive, Kingwood, TX 77339. *Phone:* 281-312-1525. *Fax:* 281-312-1477. *E-mail:* kingwoodadvising@lonestar.edu. *Website:* http://www.lonestar.edu/kingwood.htm.

Lone Star College–Montgomery

Conroe, Texas

- **State and locally supported** 2-year, founded 1995, part of Lone Star College
- **Suburban** campus with easy access to Houston
- **Coed**

Undergraduates 152,012 full-time, 47,023 part-time. Students come from 63 other countries; 10% Black or African American, non-Hispanic/Latino; 30% Hispanic/Latino; 4% Asian, non-Hispanic/Latino; 0.3% American Indian or Alaska Native, non-Hispanic/Latino; 3% Two or more races, non-Hispanic/Latino; 4% Race/ethnicity unknown; 2% transferred in.
Faculty *Student/faculty ratio:* 21:1.
Academics *Calendar:* semesters. *Degree:* certificates and associate. *Special study options:* academic remediation for entering students, adult/continuing education programs, advanced placement credit, cooperative education, distance learning, double majors, English as a second language, honors programs, independent study, internships, part-time degree program, services for LD students, study abroad, summer session for credit.
Library LSC–Montgomery Library.
Student Life *Campus security:* 24-hour emergency response devices and patrols, late-night transport/escort service.
Costs (2019–20) *Tuition:* area resident $1352 full-time, $44 per credit hour part-time; state resident $4202 full-time, $139 per credit hour part-time; nonresident $5252 full-time, $174 per credit hour part-time. *Required fees:* $664 full-time.
Financial Aid Of all full-time matriculated undergraduates who enrolled in 2018, 25 Federal Work-Study jobs (averaging $2500). 4 state and other part-time jobs.
Applying *Options:* electronic application, early admission. *Recommended:* high school transcript.
Freshman Application Contact Lone Star College–Montgomery, 3200 College Park Drive, Conroe, TX 77384. *Phone:* 281-290-2721. *Website:* http://www.lonestar.edu/montgomery.

Lone Star College–North Harris
Houston, Texas

- **State and locally supported** 2-year, founded 1972, part of Lone Star College
- **Suburban** campus with easy access to Houston
- **Coed**

Undergraduates 152,012 full-time, 47,404 part-time. Students come from 49 other countries; 26% Black or African American, non-Hispanic/Latino; 46% Hispanic/Latino; 5% Asian, non-Hispanic/Latino; 0.2% American Indian or Alaska Native, non-Hispanic/Latino; 3% Two or more races, non-Hispanic/Latino; 5% Race/ethnicity unknown; 2% transferred in.
Faculty *Student/faculty ratio:* 21:1.
Academics *Calendar:* semesters. *Degree:* certificates and associate. *Special study options:* academic remediation for entering students, adult/continuing education programs, advanced placement credit, cooperative education, distance learning, double majors, English as a second language, honors programs, independent study, internships, part-time degree program, services for LD students, study abroad, summer session for credit.
Library LSC–North Harris Library.
Student Life *Campus security:* 24-hour emergency response devices and patrols, late-night transport/escort service.
Costs (2019–20) *Tuition:* area resident $1352 full-time, $44 per credit hour part-time; state resident $4202 full-time, $139 per credit hour part-time; nonresident $5252 full-time, $174 per credit hour part-time. *Required fees:* $664 full-time.
Applying *Options:* electronic application, early admission.
Freshman Application Contact Admissions Office, Lone Star College–North Harris, 2700 W. W. Thorne Drive, Houston, TX 77073-3499. *Phone:* 281-618-5410. *E-mail:* nhcounselor@lonestar.edu. *Website:* http://www.lonestar.edu/northharris.

Lone Star College–Tomball
Tomball, Texas

- **State and locally supported** 2-year, founded 1988, part of Lone Star College
- **Suburban** campus with easy access to Houston
- **Coed**

Undergraduates 152,012 full-time, 45,660 part-time. Students come from 44 other countries; 13% Black or African American, non-Hispanic/Latino; 29% Hispanic/Latino; 5% Asian, non-Hispanic/Latino; 0.3% American Indian or Alaska Native, non-Hispanic/Latino; 3% Two or more races, non-Hispanic/Latino; 5% Race/ethnicity unknown; 1% transferred in.
Faculty *Student/faculty ratio:* 21:1.
Academics *Calendar:* semesters. *Degree:* certificates and associate. *Special study options:* academic remediation for entering students, adult/continuing education programs, advanced placement credit, cooperative education, distance learning, double majors, English as a second language, honors programs, independent study, internships, part-time degree program, services for LD students, study abroad, summer session for credit.
Library LSC–Tomball Community Library.
Student Life *Campus security:* 24-hour emergency response devices and patrols, late-night transport/escort service, trained security personnel during hours of operation.
Costs (2019–20) *Tuition:* area resident $1352 full-time, $44 per credit hour part-time; state resident $4202 full-time, $139 per credit hour part-time; nonresident $5252 full-time, $174 per credit hour part-time. *Required fees:* $664 full-time.
Financial Aid Of all full-time matriculated undergraduates who enrolled in 2018, 34 Federal Work-Study jobs (averaging $3000).
Applying *Options:* electronic application, early admission. *Recommended:* high school transcript.
Freshman Application Contact Admissions Office, Lone Star College–Tomball, 30555 Tomball Parkway, Tomball, TX 77375-4036. *Phone:* 281-351-3310. *E-mail:* tcinfo@lonestar.edu. *Website:* http://www.lonestar.edu/tomball.

Lone Star College–University Park
Houston, Texas

Freshman Application Contact Lone Star College–University Park, 20515 SH 249, Houston, TX 77070. *Phone:* 281-290-2721. *Website:* http://www.lonestar.edu/universitypark.

McLennan Community College
Waco, Texas

- **County-supported** 2-year, founded 1965
- **Urban** 200-acre campus
- **Endowment** $15.3 million
- **Coed,** 8,705 undergraduate students, 32% full-time, 66% women, 34% men

Undergraduates 2,746 full-time, 5,959 part-time. Students come from 17 states and territories; 2% are from out of state; 12% Black or African American, non-Hispanic/Latino; 30% Hispanic/Latino; 1% Asian, non-Hispanic/Latino; 0.4% American Indian or Alaska Native, non-Hispanic/Latino; 3% Two or more races, non-Hispanic/Latino; 1% Race/ethnicity unknown; 6% transferred in. *Retention:* 52% of full-time freshmen returned.
Freshmen *Admission:* 2,362 applied, 2,362 admitted, 1,437 enrolled.
Majors Accounting; administrative assistant and secretarial science; art teacher education; business administration and management; clinical/medical laboratory technology; computer engineering technology; criminal justice/law enforcement administration; criminal justice/police science; developmental and child psychology; finance; health information/medical records administration; industrial radiologic technology; information science/studies; kindergarten/preschool education; legal administrative assistant/secretary; legal assistant/paralegal; liberal arts and sciences/liberal studies; medical administrative assistant and medical secretary; mental health counseling; music; physical education teaching and coaching; physical therapy; real estate; registered nursing/registered nurse; respiratory care therapy; sign language interpretation and translation.
Academics *Calendar:* semesters. *Degree:* certificates and associate. *Special study options:* academic remediation for entering students, adult/continuing education programs, advanced placement credit, cooperative education, distance learning, honors programs, internships, off-campus study, part-time degree program, services for LD students, study abroad, summer session for credit. *ROTC:* Air Force (c).
Library McLennan Community College Library. Students can reserve study rooms.
Student Life *Housing:* college housing not available. *Activities and Organizations:* drama/theater group, student-run newspaper, choral group. *Campus security:* 24-hour emergency response devices and patrols. *Student services:* personal/psychological counseling.
Athletics Member NCAA, NJCAA. All NCAA Division I. *Intercollegiate sports:* baseball M(s), basketball M(s)/W(s), golf M(s)/W(s), softball W(s). *Intramural sports:* basketball M/W, volleyball M/W.
Costs (2019–20) *Tuition:* area resident $3180 full-time, $106 per semester hour part-time; state resident $3720 full-time, $124 per semester hour part-time; nonresident $5430 full-time, $181 per semester hour part-time. *Required fees:* $270 full-time, $9 per semester hour part-time. *Payment plan:* installment. *Waivers:* employees or children of employees.
Financial Aid Of all full-time matriculated undergraduates who enrolled in 2018, 265 Federal Work-Study jobs (averaging $850). 35 state and other part-time jobs (averaging $1000).
Applying *Options:* electronic application, early admission. *Required:* high school transcript. *Application deadlines:* rolling (freshmen), rolling (transfers). *Notification:* continuous until 9/2 (freshmen), continuous until 9/2 (transfers).
Freshman Application Contact Amanda Straten, Coordinator of Student Admissions, McLennan Community College, 1400 College Drive, Waco, TX 76708. *Phone:* 254-299-8657. *Fax:* 254-299-8694. *E-mail:* astraten@mclennan.edu.
Website: http://www.mclennan.edu/.

MediaTech Institute
Dallas, Texas

Admissions Office Contact MediaTech Institute, 13300 Branch View Lane, Dallas, TX 75234. *Toll-free phone:* 866-498-1122. *Website:* http://www.mediatech.edu/.

Mountain View College
Dallas, Texas

Freshman Application Contact Ms. Glenda Hall, Director of Admissions, Mountain View College, 4849 West Illinois Avenue, Dallas, TX 75211-6599. *Phone:* 214-860-8666. *Fax:* 214-860-8570. *E-mail:* ghall@dcccd.edu. *Website:* http://www.mountainviewcollege.edu/.

Navarro College

Corsicana, Texas

- **State and locally supported** 2-year, founded 1946
- **Small-town** 275-acre campus with easy access to Dallas-Fort Worth
- **Coed,** 8,268 undergraduate students, 36% full-time, 60% women, 40% men

Undergraduates 3,014 full-time, 5,254 part-time. Students come from 31 states and territories; 31 other countries; 1% are from out of state; 16% Black or African American, non-Hispanic/Latino; 19% Hispanic/Latino; 1% Asian, non-Hispanic/Latino; 0.3% Native Hawaiian or other Pacific Islander, non-Hispanic/Latino; 0.5% American Indian or Alaska Native, non-Hispanic/Latino; 4% Two or more races, non-Hispanic/Latino; 1% Race/ethnicity unknown; 0.7% international; 10% live on campus.
Freshmen *Admission:* 1,196 enrolled.
Faculty *Total:* 366, 30% full-time, 10% with terminal degrees. *Student/faculty ratio:* 24:1.
Majors Accounting; administrative assistant and secretarial science; agricultural mechanization; art; biological and physical sciences; biology/biological sciences; business administration and management; chemistry; clinical/medical laboratory technology; commercial and advertising art; computer graphics; computer programming; computer science; consumer merchandising/retailing management; corrections; criminal justice/law enforcement administration; criminal justice/police science; data processing and data processing technology; developmental and child psychology; drafting and design technology; dramatic/theater arts; education; elementary education; engineering; English; fire science/firefighting; industrial technology; legal administrative assistant/secretary; legal assistant/paralegal; legal studies; licensed practical/vocational nurse training; marketing/marketing management; mathematics; music; occupational therapy; pharmacy; physical education teaching and coaching; physical sciences; physics; pre-engineering; psychology; registered nursing/registered nurse; rhetoric and composition; social sciences; sociology; voice and opera.
Academics *Calendar:* semesters. *Degree:* certificates, diplomas, and associate. *Special study options:* academic remediation for entering students, adult/continuing education programs, advanced placement credit, cooperative education, distance learning, freshman honors college, honors programs, part-time degree program, services for LD students, student-designed majors, summer session for credit.
Library Richard M. Sanchez Library.
Student Life *Housing Options:* men-only, women-only. Campus housing is university owned. *Activities and Organizations:* drama/theater group, choral group, marching band, Student Government Association, Phi Theta Kappa, Ebony Club, Que Pasa. *Campus security:* 24-hour emergency response devices and patrols, Campus police. *Student services:* health clinic, personal/psychological counseling, veterans affairs office.
Athletics Member NJCAA. *Intercollegiate sports:* baseball M(s), basketball M(s), cheerleading M(s)/W(s), football M(s), soccer W, softball W, volleyball W(s). *Intramural sports:* basketball M/W, bowling M/W, football M, soccer M, softball M/W, volleyball M/W.
Costs (2020–21) *Tuition:* area resident $675 full-time, $135 per credit hour part-time; state resident $1620 full-time, $162 per credit hour part-time; nonresident $3390 full-time, $339 per credit hour part-time. *Required fees:* $1392 full-time, $128 per credit hour part-time. *Room and board:* $6300.
Applying *Options:* electronic application, early admission. *Required:* high school transcript.
Freshman Application Contact Tammy Adams, Registrar, Navarro College, 3200 West 7th Avenue, Corsicana, TX 75110-4899. *Phone:* 903-875-7348. *Toll-free phone:* 800-NAVARRO (in-state); 800-628-2776 (out-of-state). *Fax:* 903-875-7353. *E-mail:* tammy.adams@navarrocollege.edu. *Website:* http://www.navarrocollege.edu/.

North Central Texas College

Gainesville, Texas

Freshman Application Contact Melinda Carroll, Director of Admissions/Registrar, North Central Texas College, 1525 West California, Gainesville, TX 76240-4699. *Phone:* 940-668-7731. *Fax:* 940-668-7075. *E-mail:* mcarroll@nctc.edu. *Website:* http://www.nctc.edu/.

Northeast Lakeview College

Universal City, Texas

Admissions Office Contact Northeast Lakeview College, 1201 Kitty Hawk Road, Universal City, TX 78145. *Website:* http://www.alamo.edu/.

Northeast Texas Community College

Mount Pleasant, Texas

Freshman Application Contact Linda Bond, Admissions Specialist, Northeast Texas Community College, PO Box 1307, Mount Pleasant, TX 75456-1307. *Phone:* 903-434-8140. *Toll-free phone:* 800-870-0142. *E-mail:* lbond@ntcc.edu. *Website:* http://www.ntcc.edu/.

North Lake College

Irving, Texas

Freshman Application Contact Admissions/Registration Office, North Lake College, 5001 North MacArthur Boulevard, Irving, TX 75038. *Phone:* 972-273-3183. *Website:* http://www.northlakecollege.edu/.

Northwest Vista College

San Antonio, Texas

Freshman Application Contact Ms. Robin Sandberg, Director of Enrollment Management, Northwest Vista College, 3535 North Ellison Drive, San Antonio, TX 78251. *Phone:* 210-486-4134. *Fax:* 210-486-9091. *E-mail:* rsandberg@alamo.edu. *Website:* http://www.alamo.edu/nvc/.

Odessa College

Odessa, Texas

Freshman Application Contact Ms. Tracy Avery, Director of Recruitment, Odessa College, 201 West University Avenue, Odessa, TX 79764. *Phone:* 432-335-6765. *Fax:* 432-335-6303. *E-mail:* tavery@odessa.edu. *Website:* http://www.odessa.edu/.

Palo Alto College

San Antonio, Texas

- **District-supported** 2-year, founded 1987, part of Alamo Community College District System
- **Urban** campus
- **Coed**

Undergraduates 1,533 full-time, 6,843 part-time. Students come from 15 states and territories; 0.3% are from out of state; 3% Black or African American, non-Hispanic/Latino; 69% Hispanic/Latino; 1% Asian, non-Hispanic/Latino; 0.2% Native Hawaiian or other Pacific Islander, non-Hispanic/Latino; 0.3% American Indian or Alaska Native, non-Hispanic/Latino; 2% Two or more races, non-Hispanic/Latino; 3% Race/ethnicity unknown; 0.1% international; 34% transferred in. *Retention:* 62% of full-time freshmen returned.
Faculty *Student/faculty ratio:* 24:1.
Academics *Calendar:* semesters. *Degree:* certificates and associate. *Special study options:* academic remediation for entering students, adult/continuing education programs, cooperative education, English as a second language, part-time degree program, summer session for credit.
Library Ozuna Learning and Resource Center.
Student Life *Campus security:* 24-hour emergency response devices and patrols.
Financial Aid Of all full-time matriculated undergraduates who enrolled in 2018, 272 Federal Work-Study jobs (averaging $2000).
Applying *Options:* early admission. *Required:* high school transcript.
Freshman Application Contact Ms. Elizabeth Aguilar-Villarreal, Director of Enrollment Management, Palo Alto College, 1400 West Villaret Boulevard, San Antonio, TX 78224. *Phone:* 210-486-3713. *E-mail:* eaguilar-villarr@alamo.edu. *Website:* http://www.alamo.edu/pac/.

Panola College

Carthage, Texas

Freshman Application Contact Mr. Jeremy Dorman, Registrar/Director of Admissions, Panola College, 1109 West Panola Street, Carthage, TX 75633-2397. *Phone:* 903-693-2009. *Fax:* 903-693-2031. *E-mail:* bsimpson@panola.edu. *Website:* http://www.panola.edu/.

Paris Junior College
Paris, Texas

- **State and locally supported** 2-year, founded 1924
- **Rural** 54-acre campus with easy access to Dallas-Fort Worth
- **Endowment** $20.4 million
- **Coed,** 4,858 undergraduate students, 34% full-time, 61% women, 39% men

Undergraduates 1,667 full-time, 3,191 part-time. Students come from 31 states and territories; 5 other countries; 3% are from out of state; 12% Black or African American, non-Hispanic/Latino; 19% Hispanic/Latino; 1% Asian, non-Hispanic/Latino; 0.4% Native Hawaiian or other Pacific Islander, non-Hispanic/Latino; 1% American Indian or Alaska Native, non-Hispanic/Latino; 2% Two or more races, non-Hispanic/Latino; 1% Race/ethnicity unknown; 1% international; 5% transferred in; 4% live on campus. *Retention:* 59% of full-time freshmen returned.
Freshmen *Admission:* 815 enrolled.
Faculty *Total:* 189, 44% full-time. *Student/faculty ratio:* 21:1.
Majors Accounting; administrative assistant and secretarial science; agriculture; art; biological and physical sciences; biology/biological sciences; business administration and management; business automation/technology/data entry; business/commerce; chemistry; computer and information sciences; computer engineering technology; computer typography and composition equipment operation; cosmetology; criminal justice/safety; criminology; cyber/computer forensics and counterterrorism; drafting and design technology; dramatic/theater arts; early childhood education; education; education (multiple levels); electrical, electronic and communications engineering technology; electromechanical technology; elementary education; emergency medical technology (EMT paramedic); engineering; English; foreign languages and literatures; general studies; health information/medical records technology; health services/allied health/health sciences; heating, air conditioning, ventilation and refrigeration maintenance technology; history; information science/studies; journalism; kinesiology and exercise science; liberal arts and sciences/liberal studies; mathematics; medical office management; music; nursing administration; office occupations and clerical services; physical sciences; physics; political science and government; practical nursing, vocational nursing and nursing assistants related; pre-law studies; premedical studies; prenursing studies; pre-pharmacy studies; psychology; radiologic technology/science; registered nursing/registered nurse; rhetoric and composition; secondary education; social sciences; social work; sociology; speech communication and rhetoric; sport and fitness administration/management; surgical technology; system, networking, and LAN/WAN management; watchmaking and jewelrymaking; welding technology.
Academics *Calendar:* semesters. *Degree:* certificates, diplomas, and associate. *Special study options:* academic remediation for entering students, adult/continuing education programs, advanced placement credit, cooperative education, distance learning, double majors, part-time degree program, services for LD students, summer session for credit.
Library Mike Rheudasil Learning Center. *Books:* 85,521 (physical), 331 (digital/electronic); *Serial titles:* 278 (physical), 278 (digital/electronic); *Databases:* 6,227. Weekly public service hours: 72.
Student Life *Housing Options:* men-only, women-only. Campus housing is university owned. *Activities and Organizations:* drama/theater group, student-run newspaper, choral group, Student Government Organization, PTK, African American Student Union, HARTS, Delta Psi Omega. *Campus security:* 24-hour emergency response devices and patrols, late-night transport/escort service, controlled dormitory access. *Student services:* personal/psychological counseling, veterans affairs office.
Athletics Member NJCAA. *Intercollegiate sports:* baseball M(s), basketball M(s)/W(s), cheerleading M(s)/W(s), golf M(s), soccer M(s)/W(s), softball W(s), volleyball W(s). *Intramural sports:* basketball M/W, table tennis M/W, tennis M/W.
Costs (2020–21) *Tuition:* area resident $1710 full-time, $57 per credit hour part-time; state resident $1710 full-time, $107 per credit hour part-time; nonresident $4710 full-time, $157 per credit hour part-time. Full-time tuition and fees vary according to course load and program. Part-time tuition and fees vary according to course load and program. *Required fees:* $750 full-time, $25 per credit hour part-time. *Room and board:* $5340. Room and board charges vary according to housing facility. *Payment plan:* installment. *Waivers:* senior citizens and employees or children of employees.
Financial Aid Of all full-time matriculated undergraduates who enrolled in 2018, 64 Federal Work-Study jobs (averaging $2015). 16 state and other part-time jobs (averaging $1421).
Applying *Options:* electronic application, early admission. *Required:* high school transcript. *Application deadlines:* rolling (freshmen), rolling (out-of-state freshmen), rolling (transfers). *Notification:* continuous (freshmen), continuous (out-of-state freshmen), continuous (transfers).
Freshman Application Contact Paris Junior College, 2400 Clarksville Street, Paris, TX 75460-6298. *Phone:* 903-782-0211. *Toll-free phone:* 800-232-5804.
Website: http://www.parisjc.edu/.

Pima Medical Institute - El Paso
El Paso, Texas

Admissions Office Contact Pima Medical Institute - El Paso, 6926 Gateway Boulevard East, El Paso, TX 79915. *Website:* http://www.pmi.edu/.

Pima Medical Institute - Houston
Houston, Texas

Freshman Application Contact Mr. Christopher Luebke, Corporate Director of Admissions, Pima Medical Institute - Houston, 2160 South Power Road, Mesa, AZ 85209. *Phone:* 480-610-6063. *Toll-free phone:* 800-477-PIMA. *E-mail:* cluebke@pmi.edu. *Website:* http://www.pmi.edu/.

Quest College
San Antonio, Texas

Admissions Office Contact Quest College, 5430 Fredericksburg Road, Suite 310, San Antonio, TX 78229. *Website:* http://www.questcollege.edu/.

Ranger College
Ranger, Texas

Freshman Application Contact Dr. Jim Davis, Dean of Students, Ranger College, 1100 College Circle, Ranger, TX 76470. *Phone:* 254-647-3234 Ext. 110. *Website:* http://www.rangercollege.edu/.

Remington College–Dallas Campus
Garland, Texas

Director of Admissions Ms. Shonda Wisenhunt, Remington College–Dallas Campus, 1800 Eastgate Drive, Garland, TX 75041. *Phone:* 972-686-7878. *Toll-free phone:* 800-323-8122. *Fax:* 972-686-5116. *E-mail:* shonda.wisenhunt@remingtoncollege.edu. *Website:* http://www.remingtoncollege.edu/.

Remington College–Fort Worth Campus
Fort Worth, Texas

Director of Admissions Marcia Kline, Director of Recruitment, Remington College–Fort Worth Campus, 300 East Loop 820, Fort Worth, TX 76112. *Phone:* 817-451-0017. *Toll-free phone:* 800-323-8122. *Fax:* 817-496-1257. *E-mail:* marcia.kline@remingtoncollege.edu. *Website:* http://www.remingtoncollege.edu/.

Remington College–Houston Southeast Campus
Webster, Texas

Director of Admissions Lori Minor, Director of Recruitment, Remington College–Houston Southeast Campus, 20985 Gulf Freeway, Webster, TX 77598. *Phone:* 281-554-1700. *Toll-free phone:* 800-323-8122. *Fax:* 281-554-1765. *E-mail:* lori.minor@remingtoncollege.edu. *Website:* http://www.remingtoncollege.edu/.

Remington College–North Houston Campus
Houston, Texas

Director of Admissions Edmund Flores, Director of Recruitment, Remington College–North Houston Campus, 11310 Greens Crossing Boulevard, Suite 300, Houston, TX 77067. *Phone:* 281-885-4450. *Toll-free phone:* 800-323-8122. *Fax:* 281-875-9964. *E-mail:* edmund.flores@remingtoncollege.edu. *Website:* http://www.remingtoncollege.edu/.

Richland College

Dallas, Texas

Freshman Application Contact Richland College, 12800 Abrams Road, Dallas, TX 75243. *Phone:* 972-328-6948. *E-mail:* rlcadmissions@dcccd.edu. *Website:* http://www.richlandcollege.edu/.

St. Philip's College

San Antonio, Texas

Freshman Application Contact Ms. Angela Molina, Coordinator, Student Success, St. Philip's College, 1801 Martin Luther King Drive, San Antonio, TX 78203-2098. *Phone:* 210-486-2403. *Fax:* 210-486-2103. *E-mail:* amolina@alamo.edu. *Website:* http://www.alamo.edu/spc/.

San Antonio College

San Antonio, Texas

Director of Admissions Mr. J. Martin Ortega, Director of Admissions and Records, San Antonio College, 1819 North Main Avenue, San Antonio, TX 78212-3941. *Phone:* 210-733-2582. *Toll-free phone:* 844-202-5266. *Website:* http://www.alamo.edu/sac/.

San Jacinto College

Pasadena, Texas

- **State and locally supported** 2-year, founded 1961
- **Suburban** 483-acre campus with easy access to Houston
- **Endowment** $7.3 million
- **Coed,** 32,452 undergraduate students, 28% full-time, 59% women, 41% men

Undergraduates 9,244 full-time, 23,208 part-time. Students come from 38 states and territories; 67 other countries; 1% are from out of state; 9% Black or African American, non-Hispanic/Latino; 60% Hispanic/Latino; 5% Asian, non-Hispanic/Latino; 0.1% Native Hawaiian or other Pacific Islander, non-Hispanic/Latino; 0.2% American Indian or Alaska Native, non-Hispanic/Latino; 2% Two or more races, non-Hispanic/Latino; 0.5% Race/ethnicity unknown; 1% international; 4% transferred in. *Retention:* 63% of full-time freshmen returned.

Freshmen *Admission:* 12,946 applied, 4,389 admitted, 5,827 enrolled.

Faculty *Total:* 1,136, 41% full-time, 8% with terminal degrees. *Student/faculty ratio:* 21:1.

Majors Accounting; administrative assistant and secretarial science; agribusiness; agriculture; art; autobody/collision and repair technology; automobile/automotive mechanics technology; baking and pastry arts; behavioral sciences; biology/biological sciences; business administration and management; business/commerce; cardiovascular technology; chemical process technology; chemistry; child development; clinical/medical laboratory technology; commercial and advertising art; computer and information sciences; construction engineering technology; cosmetology; cosmetology, barber/styling, and nail instruction; criminal justice/police science; culinary arts; dance; diagnostic medical sonography and ultrasound technology; diesel mechanics technology; digital communication and media/multimedia; drafting and design technology; dramatic/theater arts; electrical and power transmission installation; electrical, electronic and communications engineering technology; emergency medical technology (EMT paramedic); engineering; English; environmental science; fire science/firefighting; foreign languages and literatures; general studies; geology/earth science; health and physical education/fitness; health information/medical records technology; heating, air conditioning, ventilation and refrigeration maintenance technology; Hispanic-American, Puerto Rican, and Mexican-American/Chicano studies; history; instrumentation technology; interior design; international business/trade/commerce; journalism; legal assistant/paralegal; management information systems; marine science/merchant marine officer; mathematics; medical/clinical assistant; music; occupational safety and health technology; occupational therapy; optometric technician; pharmacy technician; philosophy; physical sciences; physical therapy technology; physics; political science and government; psychiatric/mental health services technology; psychology; radio and television broadcasting technology; radiologic technology/science; real estate; registered nursing/registered nurse; respiratory care therapy; restaurant, culinary, and catering management; rhetoric and composition; science teacher education; secondary education; social sciences; sociology; surgical technology; welding technology.

Academics *Calendar:* semesters. *Degree:* certificates, diplomas, and associate. *Special study options:* academic remediation for entering students, accelerated degree program, adult/continuing education programs, advanced placement credit, cooperative education, distance learning, double majors, English as a second language, honors programs, part-time degree program, services for LD students, student-designed majors, study abroad, summer session for credit. *ROTC:* Army (c), Air Force (c).

Library Lee Davis Library(Central),Edwin E. Lehr(North),Parker Williams(South). *Books:* 369,191 (physical), 1,925 (digital/electronic); *Serial titles:* 1,825 (physical), 16 (digital/electronic); *Databases:* 154. Weekly public service hours: 68; students can reserve study rooms.

Student Life *Housing:* college housing not available. *Activities and Organizations:* drama/theater group, student-run newspaper, choral group, Phi Theta Kappa honor society, Phi Beta Lambda, Student Government Association, Nurses Association, Divers Student Populations. *Campus security:* 24-hour emergency response devices and patrols, late-night transport/escort service. *Student services:* personal/psychological counseling, veterans affairs office.

Athletics Member NJCAA. *Intercollegiate sports:* baseball M(s), basketball M/W. *Intramural sports:* soccer M/W, softball W, volleyball M/W, weight lifting M/W.

Applying *Options:* electronic application, early admission. *Required:* high school transcript. *Required for some:* interview. *Recommended:* interview for nursing program and EMT program. *Application deadlines:* rolling (freshmen), rolling (out-of-state freshmen), rolling (transfers). *Notification:* continuous (freshmen), continuous (out-of-state freshmen), continuous (transfers).

Freshman Application Contact San Jacinto College, 4624 Fairmont Parkway, Pasadena, TX 77504-3323. *Phone:* 281-998-6150. *Website:* http://www.sanjac.edu/.

School of Automotive Machinists & Technology

Houston, Texas

Admissions Office Contact School of Automotive Machinists & Technology, 1911 Antoine Drive, Houston, TX 77055. *Website:* http://www.samtech.edu/.

South Plains College

Levelland, Texas

- **State and locally supported** 2-year, founded 1958
- **Small-town** 177-acre campus
- **Endowment** $3.0 million
- **Coed**

Undergraduates 4,605 full-time, 4,448 part-time. Students come from 31 states and territories; 28 other countries; 2% are from out of state; 6% Black or African American, non-Hispanic/Latino; 45% Hispanic/Latino; 1% Asian, non-Hispanic/Latino; 0.1% Native Hawaiian or other Pacific Islander, non-Hispanic/Latino; 0.4% American Indian or Alaska Native, non-Hispanic/Latino; 0.9% international; 29% transferred in; 10% live on campus. *Retention:* 8% of full-time freshmen returned.

Faculty *Student/faculty ratio:* 20:1.

Academics *Calendar:* semesters. *Degree:* certificates and associate. *Special study options:* academic remediation for entering students, accelerated degree program, adult/continuing education programs, advanced placement credit, distance learning, double majors, internships, off-campus study, part-time degree program, services for LD students, study abroad, summer session for credit. *ROTC:* Army (c), Air Force (c).

Library South Plains College Library plus 1 other. Weekly public service hours: 57; students can reserve study rooms.

Student Life *Campus security:* 24-hour emergency response devices and patrols, controlled dormitory access.

Athletics Member NJCAA.

Standardized Tests *Recommended:* SAT or ACT (for admission).

Costs (2019–20) *Tuition:* area resident $1652 full-time; state resident $2700 full-time; nonresident $3180 full-time. Full-time tuition and fees vary according to course load and location. Part-time tuition and fees vary according to course load and location. *Required fees:* $2197 full-time. *Room and board:* $4418. Room and board charges vary according to housing facility.

Financial Aid Of all full-time matriculated undergraduates who enrolled in 2018, 80 Federal Work-Study jobs (averaging $2000). 22 state and other part-time jobs (averaging $2000).

Applying *Options:* electronic application, early admission. *Required:* high school transcript, proof of meningitis vaccination.

Freshman Application Contact Mrs. Andrea Rangel, Dean of Admissions and Records, South Plains College, 1401 College Avenue, Levelland, TX 78336. *Phone:* 806-894-9611 Ext. 2370. *Fax:* 806-897-3167. *E-mail:* arangel@southplainscollege.edu. *Website:* http://www.southplainscollege.edu/.

South Texas College

McAllen, Texas

Freshman Application Contact Mr. Matthew Hebbard, Director of Enrollment Services and Registrar, South Texas College, 3201 West Pecan, McAllen, TX 78501. *Phone:* 956-872-2147. *Toll-free phone:* 800-742-7822. *E-mail:* mshebbar@southtexascollege.edu. *Website:* http://www.southtexascollege.edu/.

Southwest Texas Junior College

Uvalde, Texas

- **State and locally supported** 2-year, founded 1946
- **Small-town** 97-acre campus with easy access to San Antonio
- **Coed,** 7,049 undergraduate students, 100% full-time, 68% women, 32% men

Undergraduates 7,049 full-time. Students come from 129 other countries; 1% Black or African American, non-Hispanic/Latino; 86% Hispanic/Latino; 3% Two or more races, non-Hispanic/Latino; 4% transferred in; 9% live on campus.

Freshmen *Admission:* 1,065 applied, 1,065 admitted.

Faculty *Total:* 195, 66% full-time.

Majors Agricultural mechanization; autobody/collision and repair technology; automobile/automotive mechanics technology; business administration and management; business automation/technology/data entry; child development; computer and information sciences; computer engineering technology; construction trades; cosmetology; criminal justice/law enforcement administration; criminal justice/police science; criminal justice/safety; data processing and data processing technology; diesel mechanics technology; education; emergency medical technology (EMT paramedic); engineering; farm and ranch management; general studies; heating, air conditioning, ventilation and refrigeration maintenance technology; liberal arts and sciences/liberal studies; radiologic technology/science; registered nursing/registered nurse; wildlife, fish and wildlands science and management.

Academics *Calendar:* semesters. *Degree:* certificates and associate. *Special study options:* academic remediation for entering students, adult/continuing education programs, advanced placement credit, distance learning, English as a second language, external degree program, part-time degree program, summer session for credit.

Library Will C. Miller Memorial Library.

Student Life *Housing Options:* coed, women-only. Campus housing is university owned. *Activities and Organizations:* drama/theater group, student-run newspaper, Catholic Students Club, Business Administration Club. *Campus security:* 24-hour patrols, controlled dormitory access. *Student services:* health clinic, personal/psychological counseling, veterans affairs office.

Athletics *Intercollegiate sports:* basketball M/W, cross-country running M/W, equestrian sports M/W. *Intramural sports:* basketball M/W, equestrian sports M/W, football M, golf M/W, racquetball M/W, swimming and diving M/W, tennis M/W, volleyball M/W.

Financial Aid Of all full-time matriculated undergraduates who enrolled in 2018, 150 Federal Work-Study jobs (averaging $1250). 75 state and other part-time jobs (averaging $1250).

Applying *Options:* electronic application, early admission, deferred entrance. *Required:* high school transcript. *Application deadlines:* rolling (freshmen), rolling (transfers). *Notification:* continuous (freshmen), continuous (transfers).

Freshman Application Contact Southwest Texas Junior College, 2401 Garner Field Road, Uvalde, TX 78801-6297. *Phone:* 830-278-4401 Ext. 7280. *Website:* http://www.swtjc.edu/.

Tarrant County College District

Fort Worth, Texas

- **County-supported** 2-year, founded 1967
- **Urban** 667-acre campus with easy access to Dallas-Fort Worth
- **Endowment** $5.8 million
- **Coed,** 51,100 undergraduate students, 27% full-time, 59% women, 41% men

Undergraduates 13,979 full-time, 37,121 part-time. Students come from 42 states and territories; 17% Black or African American, non-Hispanic/Latino; 35% Hispanic/Latino; 6% Asian, non-Hispanic/Latino; 0.1% Native Hawaiian or other Pacific Islander, non-Hispanic/Latino; 0.4% American Indian or Alaska Native, non-Hispanic/Latino; 3% Two or more races, non-Hispanic/Latino; 2% Race/ethnicity unknown; 1% international; 4% transferred in.

Freshmen *Admission:* 7,927 applied, 7,927 admitted, 7,927 enrolled.

Faculty *Total:* 2,194, 34% full-time. *Student/faculty ratio:* 22:1.

Majors Accounting; administrative assistant and secretarial science; architectural engineering technology; automobile/automotive mechanics technology; avionics maintenance technology; business administration and management; clinical laboratory science/medical technology; clinical/medical laboratory technology; computer programming; computer science; construction engineering technology; consumer merchandising/retailing management; criminal justice/law enforcement administration; dental hygiene; developmental and child psychology; dietetics; drafting and design technology; educational/instructional technology; electrical, electronic and communications engineering technology; electromechanical technology; emergency medical technology (EMT paramedic); fashion merchandising; fire science/firefighting; food technology and processing; graphic and printing equipment operation/production; health information/medical records administration; heating, air conditioning, ventilation and refrigeration maintenance technology; horticultural science; industrial radiologic technology; legal assistant/paralegal; liberal arts and sciences/liberal studies; machine tool technology; marketing/marketing management; mechanical engineering/mechanical technology; mental health counseling; physical therapy; quality control technology; registered nursing/registered nurse; respiratory care therapy; sign language interpretation and translation; surgical technology; welding technology.

Academics *Calendar:* semesters. *Degree:* certificates and associate. *Special study options:* academic remediation for entering students, adult/continuing education programs, advanced placement credit, distance learning, English as a second language, honors programs, part-time degree program, services for LD students, summer session for credit. *ROTC:* Army (c), Air Force (c).

Library Main Library plus 5 others. *Books:* 135,046 (physical), 368,488 (digital/electronic); *Serial titles:* 1,157 (physical), 92,344 (digital/electronic); *Databases:* 243.

Student Life *Housing:* college housing not available. *Activities and Organizations:* drama/theater group, student-run newspaper, choral group. *Campus security:* 24-hour emergency response devices and patrols, late-night transport/escort service. *Student services:* health clinic, personal/psychological counseling, veterans affairs office.

Athletics *Intramural sports:* basketball M/W, football M/W, golf M, table tennis M, tennis M/W, volleyball M/W.

Costs (2019–20) *Tuition:* area resident $1661 full-time, $64 per credit hour part-time; state resident $3132 full-time, $126 per credit hour part-time; nonresident $7560 full-time, $305 per credit hour part-time. Full-time tuition and fees vary according to course load and program. Part-time tuition and fees vary according to course load and program. *Payment plans:* installment, deferred payment. *Waivers:* senior citizens and employees or children of employees.

Financial Aid Of all full-time matriculated undergraduates who enrolled in 2016, 7,182 applied for aid, 6,589 were judged to have need. 296 Federal Work-Study jobs (averaging $1624). 75 state and other part-time jobs (averaging $2677). In 2016, 56 non-need-based awards were made. *Average need-based loan:* $985. *Average need-based gift aid:* $5032. *Average non-need-based aid:* $1413.

Applying *Options:* electronic application. *Application deadlines:* rolling (freshmen), rolling (transfers).

Freshman Application Contact Ms. Rebecca Griffith, District Director of Admissions and Records, Tarrant County College District, 300 Trinity Campus Circle, Fort Worth, TX 76102. *Phone:* 817-515-1581. *E-mail:* rebecca.griffith@tccd.edu. *Website:* http://www.tccd.edu/.

Temple College

Temple, Texas

Freshman Application Contact Ms. Toni Cuellar, Director of Admissions and Records, Temple College, 2600 South First Street, Temple, TX 76504. *Phone:* 254-298-8303. *Toll-free phone:* 800-460-4636. *E-mail:* carey.rose@templejc.edu. *Website:* http://www.templejc.edu/.

Texarkana College

Texarkana, Texas

- **State and locally supported** 2-year, founded 1927
- **Urban** 105-acre campus
- **Coed**

Undergraduates 1,516 full-time, 2,723 part-time. 22% Black or African American, non-Hispanic/Latino; 8% Hispanic/Latino; 1% Asian, non-Hispanic/Latino; 0.1% Native Hawaiian or other Pacific Islander, non-Hispanic/Latino; 0.9% American Indian or Alaska Native, non-Hispanic/Latino; 5% Two or more races, non-Hispanic/Latino; 2% Race/ethnicity unknown; 0.9% international; 20% transferred in; 1% live on campus.

Faculty *Student/faculty ratio:* 22:1.

Academics *Calendar:* semesters. *Degree:* certificates and associate. *Special study options:* academic remediation for entering students, adult/continuing

education programs, advanced placement credit, cooperative education, distance learning, freshman honors college, honors programs, independent study, internships, part-time degree program, services for LD students, study abroad, summer session for credit.
Library Palmer Memorial Library. *Books:* 46,602 (physical), 28,549 (digital/electronic); *Serial titles:* 143 (physical), 2 (digital/electronic); *Databases:* 101.
Student Life *Campus security:* 24-hour patrols.
Costs (2019–20) *Tuition:* area resident $1344 full-time, $56 per credit hour part-time; state resident $2688 full-time, $112 per credit hour part-time; nonresident $4008 full-time, $167 per credit hour part-time. Full-time tuition and fees vary according to program. Part-time tuition and fees vary according to program. *Required fees:* $964 full-time, $36 per credit hour part-time, $50 per term part-time. *Room and board:* $6717.
Financial Aid Of all full-time matriculated undergraduates who enrolled in 2018, 30 Federal Work-Study jobs (averaging $3090).
Applying *Options:* electronic application, early admission, deferred entrance. *Required:* high school transcript. *Recommended:* interview for nursing program, meningitis vaccine.
Freshman Application Contact Mr. Lee Williams, Director of Admissions, Texarkana College, 2500 North Robison Road, Texarkana, TX 75599-0001. *Phone:* 903-823-3016. *Fax:* 903-823-3451. *E-mail:* lee.williams@texarkanacollege.edu. *Website:* http://www.texarkanacollege.edu/.

Texas Southmost College
Brownsville, Texas

Freshman Application Contact New Student Relations, Texas Southmost College, 80 Fort Brown, Brownsville, TX 78520-4991. *Phone:* 956-882-8860. *Toll-free phone:* 877-882-8721. *Fax:* 956-882-8959. *Website:* http://www.utb.edu/.

Texas State Technical College
Waco, Texas

Freshman Application Contact Mrs. Paula Arredondo, Registrar/Director of Admission and Records, Texas State Technical College, 3801 Campus Drive, Waco, TX 76705. *Phone:* 254-867-3363. *Toll-free phone:* 800-792-8784 Ext. 2362. *E-mail:* mary.daniel@tstc.edu. *Website:* http://www.tstc.edu/.

Trinity Valley Community College
Athens, Texas

- **State and locally supported** 2-year, founded 1946
- **Rural** 65-acre campus with easy access to Dallas-Fort Worth
- **Coed**

Undergraduates 1,950 full-time, 2,499 part-time. Students come from 28 states and territories; 15 other countries; 1% are from out of state; 17% Black or African American, non-Hispanic/Latino; 2% Hispanic/Latino; 0.5% Asian, non-Hispanic/Latino; 0.1% Native Hawaiian or other Pacific Islander, non-Hispanic/Latino; 0.2% American Indian or Alaska Native, non-Hispanic/Latino; 21% Two or more races, non-Hispanic/Latino; 1% Race/ethnicity unknown; 0.0% international; 6% live on campus.
Faculty *Student/faculty ratio:* 19:1.
Academics *Calendar:* semesters. *Degree:* certificates, diplomas, and associate. *Special study options:* academic remediation for entering students, adult/continuing education programs, advanced placement credit, cooperative education, distance learning, double majors, English as a second language, honors programs, independent study, internships, part-time degree program, services for LD students, summer session for credit.
Library Ginger Murchison Learning Resource Center plus 3 others. *Books:* 47,948 (physical), 49,908 (digital/electronic); *Serial titles:* 124 (physical), 3 (digital/electronic); *Databases:* 68.
Student Life *Campus security:* 24-hour emergency response devices and patrols, controlled dormitory access.
Athletics Member NJCAA.
Costs (2019–20) *Tuition:* area resident $1170 full-time, $39 per credit hour part-time; state resident $3450 full-time, $115 per credit hour part-time; nonresident $4500 full-time, $150 per credit hour part-time. *Required fees:* $1470 full-time, $49 per credit hour part-time. *Room and board:* $6584.
Financial Aid Of all full-time matriculated undergraduates who enrolled in 2014, 90 Federal Work-Study jobs (averaging $1176). 56 state and other part-time jobs (averaging $660).
Applying *Options:* electronic application, early admission. *Required:* high school transcript.
Freshman Application Contact Ms. Tammy Denney, Registrar, Trinity Valley Community College, 100 Cardinal Drive, Athens, TX 75751. *Phone:* 903-675-6209 Ext. 209. *Website:* http://www.tvcc.edu/.

Tyler Junior College
Tyler, Texas

- **State and locally supported** primarily 2-year, founded 1926
- **Suburban** 137-acre campus
- **Endowment** $42.2 million
- **Coed**

Undergraduates 6,026 full-time, 4,080 part-time. Students come from 27 states and territories; 31 other countries; 3% are from out of state; 21% Black or African American, non-Hispanic/Latino; 26% Hispanic/Latino; 2% Asian, non-Hispanic/Latino; 0.1% Native Hawaiian or other Pacific Islander, non-Hispanic/Latino; 0.9% American Indian or Alaska Native, non-Hispanic/Latino; 0.5% Two or more races, non-Hispanic/Latino; 0.7% Race/ethnicity unknown; 0.4% international; 6% transferred in; 11% live on campus. *Retention:* 54% of full-time freshmen returned.
Faculty *Student/faculty ratio:* 20:1.
Academics *Calendar:* semesters. *Degrees:* certificates, diplomas, associate, and bachelor's. *Special study options:* academic remediation for entering students, accelerated degree program, adult/continuing education programs, advanced placement credit, distance learning, freshman honors college, honors programs, part-time degree program, services for LD students, study abroad, summer session for credit.
Library Vaughn Library and Learning Resource Center. *Books:* 85,418 (physical), 135,816 (digital/electronic); *Databases:* 100. Weekly public service hours: 74.
Student Life *Campus security:* 24-hour emergency response devices and patrols, controlled dormitory access.
Athletics Member NJCAA.
Costs (2019–20) *Tuition:* $32 per credit hour part-time; state resident $32 per credit hour part-time; nonresident $56 per credit hour part-time. *Required fees:* $59 per credit hour part-time, $120 per term part-time. *Room and board:* Room and board charges vary according to housing facility.
Financial Aid Of all full-time matriculated undergraduates who enrolled in 2018, 4,359 applied for aid, 3,789 were judged to have need, 50 had their need fully met. In 2018, 647. *Average percent of need met:* 57. *Average financial aid package:* $3822. *Average need-based loan:* $1017. *Average need-based gift aid:* $2700. *Average non-need-based aid:* $1227. *Average indebtedness upon graduation:* $14,743. *Financial aid deadline:* 6/1.
Applying *Options:* electronic application, early admission. *Required:* high school transcript.
Admissions Office Contact Tyler Junior College, PO Box 9020, Tyler, TX 75711-9020. *Toll-free phone:* 800-687-5680. *Website:* http://www.tjc.edu/.

Vernon College
Vernon, Texas

Director of Admissions Mr. Joe Hite, Dean of Admissions/Registrar, Vernon College, 4400 College Drive, Vernon, TX 76384-4092. *Phone:* 940-552-6291 Ext. 2204. *Website:* http://www.vernoncollege.edu/.

Vet Tech Institute of Houston
Houston, Texas

Freshman Application Contact Admissions Office, Vet Tech Institute of Houston, 4669 Southwest Freeway, Suite 100, Houston, TX 77027. *Phone:* 800-275-2736. *Toll-free phone:* 800-275-2736. *Website:* http://houston.vettechinstitute.edu/.

Victoria College
Victoria, Texas

Freshman Application Contact Madelyne Tolliver, Registrar, Victoria College, 2200 E. Red River, Victoria, TX 77901. *Phone:* 361-572-6400. *Toll-free phone:* 877-843-4369. *Fax:* 361-582-2525. *E-mail:* registrar@victoriacollege.edu. *Website:* http://www.victoriacollege.edu/.

Vista College
El Paso, Texas

Director of Admissions Ms. Sarah Hernandez, Registrar, Vista College, 6101 Montana Avenue, El Paso, TX 79925. *Phone:* 915-779-8031. *Toll-free phone:* 866-442-4197. *Website:* http://www.vistacollege.edu/.

Vista College–Online Campus

Richardson, Texas

Admissions Office Contact Vista College–Online Campus, 300 North Coit Road, Suite 300, Richardson, TX 75080. *Website:* http://www.vistacollege.edu/.

Wade College

Dallas, Texas

Freshman Application Contact Wade College, Infomart, 1950 North Stemmons Freeway, Suite 4080, LB 562, Dallas, TX 75207. *Phone:* 214-637-3530. *Toll-free phone:* 800-624-4850. *Website:* http://www.wadecollege.edu/.

Weatherford College

Weatherford, Texas

- **State and locally supported** primarily 2-year, founded 1869
- **Small-town** 94-acre campus with easy access to Dallas-Fort Worth
- **Coed,** 5,637 undergraduate students

Undergraduates Students come from 28 other countries; 7% live on campus.
Faculty *Total:* 220, 43% full-time. *Student/faculty ratio:* 22:1.
Majors Biological and physical sciences; business administration and management; computer graphics; computer programming; cosmetology; criminal justice/law enforcement administration; diagnostic medical sonography and ultrasound technology; education; emergency medical technology (EMT paramedic); fire science/firefighting; information science/studies; liberal arts and sciences/liberal studies; occupational therapist assistant; physical therapy technology; radiologic technology/science; registered nursing/registered nurse; respiratory care therapy; substance abuse/addiction counseling; veterinary/animal health technology.
Academics *Calendar:* semesters. *Degrees:* certificates, diplomas, associate, and bachelor's. *Special study options:* academic remediation for entering students, adult/continuing education programs, cooperative education, distance learning, freshman honors college, honors programs, internships, part-time degree program, services for LD students, student-designed majors, summer session for credit. *ROTC:* Army (c), Air Force (c).
Library Speaker Jim Wright Library. *Books:* 50,220 (physical). Students can reserve study rooms.
Student Life *Housing Options:* coed. Campus housing is university owned. *Activities and Organizations:* drama/theater group, choral group, Black Awareness Student Organization, Criminal Justice Club, Phi Theta Kappa. *Campus security:* 24-hour emergency response devices and patrols, late-night transport/escort service. *Student services:* personal/psychological counseling, veterans affairs office.
Athletics Member NJCAA. *Intercollegiate sports:* baseball M(s), basketball M(s)/W(s), cheerleading M(s)/W(s), equestrian sports M(s)/W(s), softball W(s).
Costs (2019–20) *Tuition:* area resident $2136 full-time, $89 per semester hour part-time; state resident $3432 full-time, $143 per semester hour part-time; nonresident $4848 full-time, $202 per semester hour part-time. Full-time tuition and fees vary according to course load and program. Part-time tuition and fees vary according to course load and program. *Required fees:* $240 full-time, $10 per semester hour part-time. *Room and board:* $7673. Room and board charges vary according to board plan. *Payment plan:* installment. *Waivers:* senior citizens and employees or children of employees.
Applying *Options:* electronic application, early admission. *Recommended:* high school transcript. *Application deadline:* rolling (transfers). *Notification:* continuous (freshmen), continuous (transfers).
Freshman Application Contact Mr. Ralph Willingham, Director of Admissions, Weatherford College, 225 College Park Drive, Weatherford, TX 76086-5699. *Phone:* 817-598-6248. *Toll-free phone:* 800-287-5471. *Fax:* 817-598-6205. *E-mail:* rwillingham@wc.edu.
Website: http://www.wc.edu/.

Western Technical College

El Paso, Texas

Freshman Application Contact Ms. Laura Pena, Director of Admissions, Western Technical College, 9451 Diana Drive, El Paso, TX 79930-2610. *Phone:* 915-566-9621. *Toll-free phone:* 800-201-9232. *E-mail:* lpena@westerntech.edu. *Website:* http://www.westerntech.edu/.

Western Technical College

El Paso, Texas

Freshman Application Contact Mr. Bill Terrell, Chief Admissions Officer, Western Technical College, 9624 Plaza Circle, El Paso, TX 79927. *Phone:* 915-532-3737 Ext. 117. *Fax:* 915-532-6946. *E-mail:* bterrell@wtc-ep.edu. *Website:* http://www.westerntech.edu/.

Western Texas College

Snyder, Texas

Freshman Application Contact Donna Morris, Registrar, Western Texas College, 6200 S. College Avenue, Snyder, TX 79549. *Phone:* 325-573-8511. *Toll-free phone:* 888-GO-TO-WTC. *Fax:* 325-573-9321. *E-mail:* dmorris@wtc.edu. *Website:* http://www.wtc.edu/.

Wharton County Junior College

Wharton, Texas

Freshman Application Contact Mr. Albert Barnes, Dean of Admissions and Registration, Wharton County Junior College, 911 Boling Highway, Wharton, TX 77488-3298. *Phone:* 979-532-6381. *E-mail:* albertb@wcjc.edu. *Website:* http://www.wcjc.edu/.

UTAH

Ameritech College of Healthcare

Draper, Utah

Admissions Office Contact Ameritech College of Healthcare, 12257 South Business Park Drive, Suite 108, Draper, UT 84020-6545. *Website:* http://www.ameritech.edu/.

Fortis College

Salt Lake City, Utah

Admissions Office Contact Fortis College, 3949 South 700 East, Suite 150, Salt Lake City, UT 84107. *Toll-free phone:* 855-4-FORTIS. *Website:* http://www.fortis.edu/.

LDS Business College

Salt Lake City, Utah

Freshman Application Contact Kristen Whittaker, Director of Enrollment Management, LDS Business College, 95 North 300 West, Salt Lake City, UT 84101-3500. *Phone:* 801-524-8145. *Toll-free phone:* 800-999-5767. *E-mail:* admissions@ldsbc.edu. *Website:* http://www.ldsbc.edu/.

Nightingale College

Ogden, Utah

- **Proprietary** primarily 2-year
- **Suburban** campus with easy access to Salt Lake City
- **Coed**
- 75% of applicants were admitted

Undergraduates *Retention:* 43% of full-time freshmen returned.
Faculty *Student/faculty ratio:* 7:1.
Academics *Calendar:* semesters. *Degrees:* diplomas, associate, and bachelor's. *Special study options:* part-time degree program.
Standardized Tests *Required:* Nightingale Entrance Exam (for admission).
Applying *Options:* electronic application, early admission. *Application fee:* $100. *Required:* essay or personal statement, high school transcript, interview.
Freshman Application Contact Nightingale College, 4155 Harrison Boulevard #100, Ogden, UT 84403. *Website:* http://www.nightingale.edu/.

Provo College

Provo, Utah

Director of Admissions Mr. Gordon Peters, College Director, Provo College, 1450 West 820 North, Provo, UT 84601. *Phone:* 801-375-1861. *Toll-free phone:* 877-777-5886. *Fax:* 801-375-9728. *E-mail:* gordonp@provocollege.org. *Website:* http://www.provocollege.edu/.

Salt Lake Community College

Salt Lake City, Utah

- **State-supported** 2-year, founded 1948, part of Utah System of Higher Education
- **Urban** 114-acre campus with easy access to Salt Lake City
- **Endowment** $837,612
- **Coed**

Undergraduates 7,811 full-time, 21,809 part-time. 2% Black or African American, non-Hispanic/Latino; 18% Hispanic/Latino; 4% Asian, non-Hispanic/Latino; 1% Native Hawaiian or other Pacific Islander, non-Hispanic/Latino; 0.8% American Indian or Alaska Native, non-Hispanic/Latino; 3% Two or more races, non-Hispanic/Latino; 2% Race/ethnicity unknown; 1% international; 7% transferred in.
Faculty *Student/faculty ratio:* 18:1.
Academics *Calendar:* semesters. *Degree:* certificates, diplomas, and associate. *Special study options:* academic remediation for entering students, advanced placement credit, cooperative education, distance learning, double majors, English as a second language, internships, part-time degree program, services for LD students, student-designed majors, study abroad, summer session for credit. *ROTC:* Army (c), Air Force (c).
Library Markosian Library plus 2 others.
Student Life *Campus security:* 24-hour emergency response devices and patrols, late-night transport/escort service.
Athletics Member NJCAA.
Applying *Options:* electronic application, early admission. *Application fee:* $40.
Admissions Office Contact Salt Lake Community College, PO Box 30808, Salt Lake City, UT 84130-0808. *Website:* http://www.slcc.edu/.

Snow College

Ephraim, Utah

- **State-supported** 2-year, founded 1888, part of Utah System of Higher Education
- **Rural** 50-acre campus
- **Endowment** $8.9 million
- **Coed**
- 100% of applicants were admitted

Undergraduates 3,227 full-time, 2,347 part-time. Students come from 35 states and territories; 42 other countries; 5% are from out of state; 0.6% Black or African American, non-Hispanic/Latino; 7% Hispanic/Latino; 0.4% Asian, non-Hispanic/Latino; 2% Native Hawaiian or other Pacific Islander, non-Hispanic/Latino; 1% American Indian or Alaska Native, non-Hispanic/Latino; 0.4% Two or more races, non-Hispanic/Latino; 0.2% Race/ethnicity unknown; 3% international; 0.6% transferred in; 20% live on campus. *Retention:* 46% of full-time freshmen returned.
Faculty *Student/faculty ratio:* 21:1.
Academics *Calendar:* semesters. *Degree:* certificates, diplomas, and associate. *Special study options:* academic remediation for entering students, adult/continuing education programs, advanced placement credit, cooperative education, distance learning, English as a second language, external degree program, honors programs, independent study, part-time degree program, services for LD students, summer session for credit.
Library Karen Huntsman Library plus 1 other. *Books:* 57,726 (physical); *Serial titles:* 775 (physical); *Databases:* 85. Weekly public service hours: 66.
Student Life *Campus security:* 24-hour emergency response devices and patrols, student patrols, late-night transport/escort service, controlled dormitory access.
Athletics Member NJCAA.
Standardized Tests *Recommended:* SAT or ACT (for admission).
Costs (2019–20) *Room and board:* $2400; room only: $1900.
Financial Aid ***Average financial aid package:*** $2351. *Average need-based loan:* $2903. *Average need-based gift aid:* $2395.
Applying *Options:* electronic application, early admission. *Application fee:* $30. *Required:* high school transcript.
Freshman Application Contact Rachel Wade, Admissions Advisor, Snow College, 150 East College Avenue, Ephraim, UT 84627. *Phone:* 435-283-7159. *Fax:* 435-283-7157. *E-mail:* rachel.wade@snow.edu. *Website:* http://www.snow.edu/.

VERMONT

Community College of Vermont

Montpelier, Vermont

Freshman Application Contact Community College of Vermont, 660 Elm Street, Montpelier, VT 05602. *Phone:* 802-654-0505. *Toll-free phone:* 800-CCV-6686. *Website:* http://www.ccv.edu/.

Landmark College

Putney, Vermont

Freshman Application Contact Admissions Main Desk, Landmark College, Admissions Office, River Road South, Putney, VT 05346. *Phone:* 802-387-6718. *Fax:* 802-387-6868. *E-mail:* admissions@landmark.edu. *Website:* http://www.landmark.edu/.

New England Culinary Institute

Montpelier, Vermont

- **Proprietary** primarily 2-year, founded 1980
- **Small-town** campus
- **Coed**

Undergraduates 257 full-time, 43 part-time. Students come from 39 states and territories; 6 other countries; 80% are from out of state; 8% Black or African American, non-Hispanic/Latino; 5% Hispanic/Latino; 4% Asian, non-Hispanic/Latino; 1% American Indian or Alaska Native, non-Hispanic/Latino; 1% Two or more races, non-Hispanic/Latino; 13% Race/ethnicity unknown; 6% transferred in. *Retention:* 100% of full-time freshmen returned.
Faculty *Student/faculty ratio:* 6:1.
Academics *Calendar:* quarters. *Degrees:* certificates, associate, and bachelor's. *Special study options:* academic remediation for entering students, accelerated degree program, advanced placement credit, cooperative education, distance learning, honors programs, internships, services for LD students.
Library New England Culinary Institute Library.
Student Life *Campus security:* 24-hour emergency response devices, student patrols.
Standardized Tests *Recommended:* SAT or ACT (for admission).
Financial Aid Of all full-time matriculated undergraduates who enrolled in 2018, 320 Federal Work-Study jobs (averaging $1000).
Applying *Options:* electronic application, early admission, deferred entrance. *Application fee:* $35. *Required:* essay or personal statement, high school transcript, 1 letter of recommendation, interview. *Recommended:* culinary experience.
Freshman Application Contact Adonica Williams, New England Culinary Institute, 7 School Street, Montpelier, VT 05602-3115. *Phone:* 802-225-3210. *Toll-free phone:* 877-223-6324. *Fax:* 802-225-3280. *E-mail:* admissions@neci.edu. *Website:* http://www.neci.edu/.

VIRGINIA

Advanced Technology Institute

Virginia Beach, Virginia

Freshman Application Contact Admissions Office, Advanced Technology Institute, 5700 Southern Boulevard, Suite 100, Virginia Beach, VA 23462. *Phone:* 757-490-1241. *Toll-free phone:* 888-468-1093. *Website:* http://www.auto.edu/.

American National University - Danville

Danville, Virginia

- **Proprietary** primarily 2-year, founded 1975, part of National College of Business and Technology
- **Small-town** campus
- **Coed**

Academics *Calendar:* quarters. *Degrees:* diplomas, associate, and bachelor's. *Special study options:* part-time degree program, summer session for credit.
Financial Aid Of all full-time matriculated undergraduates who enrolled in 2018, 3 Federal Work-Study jobs.

Applying *Options:* electronic application. *Required for some:* high school transcript. *Recommended:* interview.
Freshman Application Contact Admissions Office, American National University - Danville, 336 Old Riverside Drive, Danville, VA 24541. *Phone:* 434-793-6822. *Toll-free phone:* 888-9-JOBREADY. *Website:* http://www.an.edu/.

Blue Ridge Community College
Weyers Cave, Virginia

- **State-supported** 2-year, founded 1967, part of Virginia Community College System
- **Rural** 65-acre campus
- **Coed**

Undergraduates 1% are from out of state. *Retention:* 59% of full-time freshmen returned.
Faculty *Student/faculty ratio:* 20:1.
Academics *Calendar:* semesters. *Degree:* certificates, diplomas, and associate. *Special study options:* academic remediation for entering students, adult/continuing education programs, advanced placement credit, cooperative education, distance learning, double majors, English as a second language, honors programs, internships, off-campus study, part-time degree program, services for LD students, study abroad, summer session for credit.
Library Houff Library.
Student Life *Campus security:* 24-hour emergency response devices and patrols, late-night transport/escort service.
Standardized Tests *Required:* College Preparedness Test (for admission).
Financial Aid Of all full-time matriculated undergraduates who enrolled in 2018, 40 Federal Work-Study jobs (averaging $1500).
Applying *Options:* electronic application, early admission. *Required for some:* high school transcript, interview.
Freshman Application Contact Blue Ridge Community College, PO Box 80, Weyers Cave, VA 24486-0080. *Phone:* 540-453-2217. *Toll-free phone:* 888-750-2722. *Website:* http://www.brcc.edu/.

Bryant & Stratton College–Richmond Campus
Richmond, Virginia

Freshman Application Contact Mr. David K. Mayle, Director of Admissions, Bryant & Stratton College–Richmond Campus, 8141 Hull Street Road, Richmond, VA 23235-6411. *Phone:* 804-745-2444. *Fax:* 804-745-6884. *E-mail:* tlawson@bryanstratton.edu. *Website:* http://www.bryantstratton.edu/.

Bryant & Stratton College–Virginia Beach Campus
Virginia Beach, Virginia

Freshman Application Contact Bryant & Stratton College–Virginia Beach Campus, 301 Centre Pointe Drive, Virginia Beach, VA 23462. *Phone:* 757-499-7900 Ext. 173. *Website:* http://www.bryantstratton.edu/.

Centra College of Nursing
Lynchburg, Virginia

Admissions Office Contact Centra College of Nursing, 905 Lakeside Drive, Suite A, Lynchburg, VA 24501. *Website:* http://www.centrahealth.com/facilities/centra-college-nursing/.

Central Virginia Community College
Lynchburg, Virginia

Freshman Application Contact Admissions Office, Central Virginia Community College, 3506 Wards Road, Lynchburg, VA 24502. *Phone:* 434-832-7633. *Toll-free phone:* 800-562-3060. *Fax:* 434-832-7793. *Website:* http://www.centralvirginia.edu/.

Centura College
Chesapeake, Virginia

Director of Admissions Director of Admissions, Centura College, 932 Ventures Way, Chesapeake, VA 23320. *Phone:* 757-549-2121. *Toll-free phone:* 877-575-5627. *Fax:* 575-549-1196. *Website:* http://www.centuracollege.edu/.

Centura College
Newport News, Virginia

Director of Admissions Victoria Whitehead, Director of Admissions, Centura College, 616 Denbigh Boulevard, Newport News, VA 23608. *Phone:* 757-874-2121. *Toll-free phone:* 877-575-5627. *Fax:* 757-874-3857. *E-mail:* admdircpen@centura.edu. *Website:* http://www.centuracollege.edu/.

Centura College
Norfolk, Virginia

Director of Admissions Director of Admissions, Centura College, 7020 North Military Highway, Norfolk, VA 23518. *Phone:* 757-853-2121. *Toll-free phone:* 877-575-5627. *Fax:* 757-852-9017. *Website:* http://www.centuracollege.edu/.

Centura College
North Chesterfield, Virginia

Freshman Application Contact Admissions Office, Centura College, 7914 Midlothian Turnpike, North Chesterfield, VA 23235. *Phone:* 804-330-0111. *Toll-free phone:* 877-575-5627. *Fax:* 804-330-3809. *Website:* http://www.centuracollege.edu/.

Centura College
Virginia Beach, Virginia

Freshman Application Contact Admissions Office, Centura College, 2697 Dean Drive, Suite 100, Virginia Beach, VA 23452. *Phone:* 757-340-2121. *Toll-free phone:* 877-575-5627. *Fax:* 757-340-9704. *Website:* http://www.centuracollege.edu/.

Chester Career College
Chester, Virginia

Admissions Office Contact Chester Career College, 751 West Hundred Road, Chester, VA 23836. *Website:* http://www.chestercareercollege.edu/.

Columbia College
Vienna, Virginia

Admissions Office Contact Columbia College, 8620 Westwood Center Drive, Vienna, VA 22182. *Website:* http://www.ccdc.edu/.

Dabney S. Lancaster Community College
Clifton Forge, Virginia

- **State-supported** 2-year, founded 1964, part of Virginia Community College System
- **Rural** 117-acre campus
- **Endowment** $6.6 million
- **Coed**

Undergraduates 428 full-time, 758 part-time. Students come from 3 states and territories; 4% are from out of state; 4% Black or African American, non-Hispanic/Latino; 2% Hispanic/Latino; 0.6% Asian, non-Hispanic/Latino; 0.7% American Indian or Alaska Native, non-Hispanic/Latino; 4% Two or more races, non-Hispanic/Latino; 0.6% Race/ethnicity unknown; 0.1% international; 29% transferred in. *Retention:* 77% of full-time freshmen returned.
Faculty *Student/faculty ratio:* 10:1.
Academics *Calendar:* semesters. *Degree:* certificates and associate. *Special study options:* academic remediation for entering students, adult/continuing education programs, advanced placement credit, cooperative education, distance learning, double majors, independent study, internships, off-campus study, part-time degree program, services for LD students, summer session for credit.
Library DSLCC Library. *Books:* 35,154 (physical), 74,281 (digital/electronic); *Serial titles:* 5 (physical), 95,157 (digital/electronic); *Databases:* 117. Weekly public service hours: 60; students can reserve study rooms.
Student Life *Campus security:* 24-hour emergency response devices, Security Cameras at Rockbridge Regional Center.
Standardized Tests *Required for some:* SAT and SAT Subject Tests or ACT (for admission).
Costs (2019–20) *Tuition:* $154 per credit hour part-time; state resident $3696 full-time; nonresident $9918 full-time. *Required fees:* $84 full-time, $4 per credit hour part-time.

Applying *Options:* electronic application. *Recommended:* high school transcript.
Freshman Application Contact Ms. Suzanne Ostling, Admissions Officer, Dabney S. Lancaster Community College, 1000 Dabney Drive, Clifton Forge, VA 24422. *Phone:* 540-863-2826. *Toll-free phone:* 877-73-DSLCC. *Fax:* 540-863-2915. *E-mail:* sostling@dslcc.edu. *Website:* http://www.dslcc.edu/.

Danville Community College
Danville, Virginia

- **State-supported** 2-year, founded 1967, part of Virginia Community College System
- **Urban** 76-acre campus
- **Coed**

Undergraduates 1% are from out of state.
Faculty *Student/faculty ratio:* 18:1.
Academics *Calendar:* semesters. *Degree:* certificates, diplomas, and associate. *Special study options:* academic remediation for entering students, adult/continuing education programs, advanced placement credit, cooperative education, distance learning, honors programs, part-time degree program, summer session for credit.
Library Learning Resource Center.
Student Life *Campus security:* 24-hour patrols.
Financial Aid Of all full-time matriculated undergraduates who enrolled in 2018, 40 Federal Work-Study jobs (averaging $1700).
Applying *Options:* early admission, deferred entrance. *Required:* high school transcript.
Freshman Application Contact Cathy Pulliam, Coordinator of Student Recruitment and Enrollment, Danville Community College, 1008 South Main Street, Danville, VA 24541-4088. *Phone:* 434-797-8538. *Toll-free phone:* 800-560-4291. *E-mail:* cpulliam@dcc.vccs.edu. *Website:* http://www.dcc.vccs.edu/.

Eastern Shore Community College
Melfa, Virginia

Freshman Application Contact Ms. Cheryll Mills, Coordinator of Student Services, Eastern Shore Community College, 29300 Lankford Highway, Melfa, VA 23410. *Phone:* 757-789-1730. *Toll-free phone:* 877-871-8455. *Fax:* 757-789-1737. *E-mail:* cmills@es.vccs.edu. *Website:* http://www.es.vccs.edu/.

Eastern Virginia Career College
Fredericksburg, Virginia

Admissions Office Contact Eastern Virginia Career College, 10304 Spotsylvania Avenue, Suite 400, Fredericksburg, VA 22408. *Website:* http://www.evcc.edu/.

Fortis College
Norfolk, Virginia

Admissions Office Contact Fortis College, 6300 Center Drive, Suite 100, Norfolk, VA 23502. *Toll-free phone:* 855-4-FORTIS. *Website:* http://www.fortis.edu/.

Fortis College
Richmond, Virginia

Admissions Office Contact Fortis College, 2000 Westmoreland Street, Suite A, Richmond, VA 23230. *Toll-free phone:* 855-4-FORTIS. *Website:* http://www.fortis.edu/.

Germanna Community College
Locust Grove, Virginia

Freshman Application Contact Ms. Rita Dunston, Registrar, Germanna Community College, 10000 Germanna Point Drive, Fredericksburg, VA 22408. *Phone:* 540-891-3020. *Fax:* 540-891-3092. *Website:* http://www.germanna.edu/.

John Tyler Community College
Chester, Virginia

- **State-supported** 2 year, founded 1967, part of Virginia Community College System
- **Suburban** 160-acre campus with easy access to Richmond
- **Coed**

Undergraduates 2,431 full-time, 7,713 part-time. 3% are from out of state; 22% Black or African American, non-Hispanic/Latino; 10% Hispanic/Latino; 3% Asian, non-Hispanic/Latino; 0.2% Native Hawaiian or other Pacific Islander, non-Hispanic/Latino; 0.4% American Indian or Alaska Native, non-Hispanic/Latino; 5% Two or more races, non-Hispanic/Latino; 1% Race/ethnicity unknown.
Faculty *Student/faculty ratio:* 20:1.
Academics *Calendar:* semesters. *Degree:* certificates and associate. *Special study options:* academic remediation for entering students, adult/continuing education programs, advanced placement credit, distance learning, external degree program, honors programs, off-campus study, part-time degree program, services for LD students, study abroad, summer session for credit. *ROTC:* Army (c).
Library John Tyler Community College Learning Resource and Technology Center.
Student Life *Campus security:* 24-hour emergency response devices and patrols.
Costs (2019–20) *Tuition:* state resident $4650 full-time, $155 per credit hour part-time; nonresident $9948 full-time, $332 per credit hour part-time. Full-time tuition and fees vary according to course load. Part-time tuition and fees vary according to course load. *Required fees:* $150 full-time, $5 per credit hour part-time.
Financial Aid Of all full-time matriculated undergraduates who enrolled in 2018, 45 Federal Work-Study jobs (averaging $2590).
Applying *Options:* electronic application, early admission, deferred entrance. *Recommended:* high school transcript.
Freshman Application Contact Mr. Leigh Baxter, Director Admissions and Records and Registrar, John Tyler Community College, Office of Admissions and Records, 800 Charter Colony Parkway, Midlothian, VA 23831. *Phone:* 804-594-1549. *Toll-free phone:* 800-552-3490. *Fax:* 804-594-1543. *E-mail:* lbaxter@jtcc.edu. *Website:* http://www.jtcc.edu/.

J. Sargeant Reynolds Community College
Richmond, Virginia

Admissions Office Contact J. Sargeant Reynolds Community College, PO Box 85622, Richmond, VA 23285-5622. *Website:* http://www.reynolds.edu/.

Lord Fairfax Community College
Middletown, Virginia

Freshman Application Contact Karen Bucher, Director of Enrollment Management, Lord Fairfax Community College, 173 Skirmisher Lane, Middletown, VA 22645. *Phone:* 540-868-7132. *Toll-free phone:* 800-906-LFCC. *Fax:* 540-868-7005. *E-mail:* kbucher@lfcc.edu. *Website:* http://www.lfcc.edu/.

Mountain Empire Community College
Big Stone Gap, Virginia

Freshman Application Contact Mountain Empire Community College, 3441 Mountain Empire Road, Big Stone Gap, VA 24219. *Phone:* 276-523-2400 Ext. 219. *Website:* http://www.mecc.edu/.

New River Community College
Dublin, Virginia

Freshman Application Contact Mrs. Tammy L. Smith, Coordinator, Admissions and Records, New River Community College, 5251 College Drive, Dublin, VA 24084. *Phone:* 540-674-3600 Ext. 4203. *Toll-free phone:* 866-462-6722. *Fax:* 540-674-3644. *E-mail:* tsmith@nr.edu. *Website:* http://www.nr.edu/.

Northern Virginia Community College
Annandale, Virginia

Freshman Application Contact Northern Virginia Community College, 8333 Little River Turnpike, Annandale, VA 22003. *Phone:* 703-323-3195. *Website:* http://www.nvcc.edu/.

Patrick Henry Community College

Martinsville, Virginia

Freshman Application Contact Mr. Travis Tisdale, Coordinator, Admissions and Records, Patrick Henry Community College, 645 Patriot Avenue, Martinsville, VA 24112. *Phone:* 276-656-0311. *Toll-free phone:* 800-232-7997. *Fax:* 276-656-0352. *Website:* http://www.patrickhenry.edu/.

Paul D. Camp Community College

Franklin, Virginia

Freshman Application Contact Mrs. Trina Jones, Dean Student Services, Paul D. Camp Community College, PO Box 737, 100 N. College Drive, Franklin, VA 23851. *Phone:* 757-569-6720. *E-mail:* tjones@pdc.edu. *Website:* http://www.pdc.edu/.

Piedmont Virginia Community College

Charlottesville, Virginia

- **State-supported** 2-year, founded 1972, part of Virginia Community College System
- **Suburban** 114-acre campus with easy access to Richmond
- **Endowment** $6.8 million
- **Coed,** 5,358 undergraduate students, 21% full-time, 58% women, 42% men

Undergraduates 1,119 full-time, 4,239 part-time.

Majors Accounting; art; biotechnology; business administration and management; computer and information sciences; computer and information systems security; computer technology/computer systems technology; criminal justice/police science; culinary arts; diagnostic medical sonography and ultrasound technology; education; emergency medical technology (EMT paramedic); engineering; general studies; information technology; liberal arts and sciences and humanities related; management science; music; nursing science; radiologic technology/science; theater literature, history and criticism.

Academics *Calendar:* semesters. *Degree:* certificates and associate. *Special study options:* academic remediation for entering students, adult/continuing education programs, advanced placement credit, distance learning, double majors, English as a second language, external degree program, honors programs, independent study, internships, part-time degree program, services for LD students, study abroad, summer session for credit. *ROTC:* Army (c), Air Force (c).

Library Jessup Library.

Student Life *Housing:* college housing not available. *Activities and Organizations:* drama/theater group, student-run newspaper, choral group. *Campus security:* 24-hour emergency response devices and patrols, late-night transport/escort service, establishment of Campus Police. *Student services:* veterans affairs office.

Athletics *Intramural sports:* basketball M/W, golf M/W, soccer M/W, table tennis M/W, tennis M/W, ultimate Frisbee M/W, volleyball M/W, weight lifting M/W.

Costs (2020–21) *Tuition:* area resident $4650 full-time, $155 per credit hour part-time; state resident $4650 full-time, $155 per credit hour part-time; nonresident $9948 full-time, $331 per credit hour part-time. Full-time tuition and fees vary according to course load. Part-time tuition and fees vary according to course load. *Required fees:* $140 full-time. *Payment plan:* installment. *Waivers:* senior citizens and employees or children of employees.

Applying *Options:* electronic application, deferred entrance. *Required for some:* high school transcript, prerequisite courses for nursing, practical nursing, radiography, sonography, surgical technology, emergency medical services, health information management, and patient admissions coordination. *Application deadlines:* rolling (freshmen), rolling (transfers). *Notification:* continuous (freshmen), continuous (transfers).

Freshman Application Contact Ms. Mary Lee Walsh, Dean of Student Services, Piedmont Virginia Community College, 501 College Drive, Charlottesville, VA 22902-7589. *Phone:* 434-961-6540. *Fax:* 434-961-5425. *E-mail:* mwalsh@pvcc.edu.
Website: http://www.pvcc.edu/.

Rappahannock Community College

Glenns, Virginia

Freshman Application Contact Ms. Felicia Packett, Admissions and Records Officer, Rappahannock Community College, 12745 College Drive, Glenns, VA 23149-0287. *Phone:* 804-758-6740. *Toll-free phone:* 800-836-9381. *Website:* http://www.rappahannock.edu/.

Richard Bland College of The College of William and Mary

Petersburg, Virginia

Freshman Application Contact Office of Admissions, Richard Bland College of The College of William and Mary, 8311 Halifax Road, Petersburg, VA 23805. *Phone:* 804-862-6100 Ext. 6249. *E-mail:* apply@rbc.edu. *Website:* http://www.rbc.edu/.

Riverside College of Health Careers

Newport News, Virginia

Admissions Office Contact Riverside College of Health Careers, 316 Main Street, Newport News, VA 23601. *Website:* http://www.riverside.edu/.

Saint Michael College of Allied Health

Alexandria, Virginia

Admissions Office Contact Saint Michael College of Allied Health, 8305 Richmond Highway, Alexandria, VA 22309. *Website:* http://www.stmichaelcollegeva.edu/.

Southside Regional Medical Center Professional Schools

Colonial Heights, Virginia

Admissions Office Contact Southside Regional Medical Center Professional Schools, 430 Clairmont Court, Suite 200, Colonial Heights, VA 23834. *Website:* http://www.srmconline.com/Southside-Regional-Medical-Center/nursingeducation.aspx.

Southside Virginia Community College

Alberta, Virginia

Freshman Application Contact Mr. Brent Richey, Dean of Enrollment Management, Southside Virginia Community College, 109 Campus Drive, Alberta, VA 23821. *Phone:* 434-949-1012. *Fax:* 434-949-7863. *E-mail:* rhina.jones@sv.vccs.edu. *Website:* http://www.southside.edu/.

Southwest Virginia Community College

Richlands, Virginia

Freshman Application Contact Ms. Dionne Cook, Admissions Counselor, Southwest Virginia Community College, Box SVCC, Richlands, VA 24641. *Phone:* 276-964-7301. *Toll-free phone:* 800-822-7822. *Fax:* 276-964-7716. *E-mail:* dionne.cook@sw.edu. *Website:* http://www.sw.edu/.

Sovah Health School of Health Professions

Danville, Virginia

Admissions Office Contact Sovah Health School of Health Professions, 142 South Main Street, Danville, VA 24541. *Website:* http://www.danvilleregional.com/for-healthcare-professionals/radiologic-technology-program.

Standard Healthcare Services, College of Nursing

Falls Church, Virginia

Admissions Office Contact Standard Healthcare Services, College of Nursing, 7704 Leesburg Pike, Suite 1000, Falls Church, VA 22043. *Website:* http://www.standardcollege.edu/.

Thomas Nelson Community College

Hampton, Virginia

Freshman Application Contact Ms. Geraldine Newson, Senior Admission Specialist, Thomas Nelson Community College, PO Box 9407, Hampton, VA 23670-0407. *Phone:* 757-825-2800. *Fax:* 757-825-2763. *E-mail:* admissions@tncc.edu. *Website:* http://www.tncc.edu/.

Tidewater Community College
Norfolk, Virginia

- **State-supported** 2-year, founded 1968, part of Virginia Community College System
- **Suburban** 520-acre campus
- **Endowment** $7.1 million
- **Coed**

Undergraduates 7,375 full-time, 13,566 part-time. 17% are from out of state; 30% Black or African American, non-Hispanic/Latino; 9% Hispanic/Latino; 4% Asian, non-Hispanic/Latino; 0.5% Native Hawaiian or other Pacific Islander, non-Hispanic/Latino; 0.4% American Indian or Alaska Native, non-Hispanic/Latino; 6% Two or more races, non-Hispanic/Latino; 1% Race/ethnicity unknown; 0.7% international. *Retention:* 54% of full-time freshmen returned.
Faculty *Student/faculty ratio:* 20:1.
Academics *Calendar:* semesters. *Degree:* certificates and associate. *Special study options:* academic remediation for entering students, accelerated degree program, adult/continuing education programs, advanced placement credit, cooperative education, distance learning, English as a second language, honors programs, independent study, internships, off-campus study, part-time degree program, services for LD students, summer session for credit.
Library Main Library plus 5 others.
Student Life *Campus security:* 24-hour patrols.
Costs (2019–20) *Tuition:* state resident $4056 full-time, $156 per credit hour part-time; nonresident $8648 full-time, $333 per credit hour part-time. *Required fees:* $763 full-time, $29 per credit hour part-time.
Financial Aid Of all full-time matriculated undergraduates who enrolled in 2018, 64 Federal Work-Study jobs (averaging $2000).
Applying *Options:* electronic application, early admission, deferred entrance.
Admissions Office Contact Tidewater Community College, 121 College Place, Norfolk, VA 23510. *Website:* http://www.tcc.edu/.

Virginia Highlands Community College
Abingdon, Virginia

Freshman Application Contact Karen Cheers, Acting Director of Admissions, Records, and Financial Aid, Virginia Highlands Community College, PO Box 828, 100 VHCC Drive Abingdon, Abingdon, VA 24212. *Phone:* 276-739-2490. *Toll-free phone:* 877-207-6115. *E-mail:* kcheers@vhcc.edu. *Website:* http://www.vhcc.edu/.

Virginia Western Community College
Roanoke, Virginia

- **State-supported** 2-year, founded 1966, part of Virginia Community College System
- **Suburban** 70-acre campus
- **Coed**

Undergraduates 2,139 full-time, 5,398 part-time. Students come from 34 states and territories; 62 other countries; 6% are from out of state; 12% Black or African American, non-Hispanic/Latino; 4% Hispanic/Latino; 4% Asian, non-Hispanic/Latino; 0.1% Native Hawaiian or other Pacific Islander, non-Hispanic/Latino; 0.1% American Indian or Alaska Native, non-Hispanic/Latino; 4% Two or more races, non-Hispanic/Latino; 0.5% Race/ethnicity unknown; 0.6% international; 4% transferred in. *Retention:* 53% of full-time freshmen returned.
Faculty *Student/faculty ratio:* 25:1.
Academics *Calendar:* semesters. *Degree:* certificates and associate. *Special study options:* academic remediation for entering students, advanced placement credit, cooperative education, distance learning, double majors, English as a second language, honors programs, independent study, internships, part-time degree program, services for LD students, summer session for credit.
Library Brown Library.
Student Life *Campus security:* 24-hour emergency response devices and patrols, late-night transport/escort service.
Costs (2019–20) *Tuition:* area resident $4680 full-time, $156 per credit hour part-time; state resident $4680 full-time, $156 per credit hour part-time; nonresident $9978 full-time, $333 per credit hour part-time. *Required fees:* $675 full-time, $22 per credit hour part-time.
Applying *Options:* electronic application, early admission, deferred entrance. *Required for some:* high school transcript. *Recommended:* high school transcript.
Freshman Application Contact Admissions Office, Virginia Western Community College, PO Box 14007, Roanoke, VA 24038. *Phone:* 540-857-7231. *Website:* http://www.virginiawestern.edu/.

Wave Leadership College
Virginia Beach, Virginia

Admissions Office Contact Wave Leadership College, 1000 North Great Neck Road, Virginia Beach, VA 23454. *Website:* http://www.wavecollege.com/.

Wytheville Community College
Wytheville, Virginia

Freshman Application Contact Wytheville Community College, 1000 East Main Street, Wytheville, VA 24382-3308. *Phone:* 276-223-4701. *Toll-free phone:* 800-468-1195. *Website:* http://www.wcc.vccs.edu/.

WASHINGTON

Bates Technical College
Tacoma, Washington

Director of Admissions Director of Admissions, Bates Technical College, 1101 South Yakima Avenue, Tacoma, WA 98405-4895. *Phone:* 253-680-7000. *E-mail:* registration@bates.ctc.edu. *Website:* http://www.bates.ctc.edu/.

Bellevue College
Bellevue, Washington

- **State-supported** primarily 2-year, founded 1966, part of Washington State Board for Community and Technical Colleges
- **Suburban** 96-acre campus with easy access to Seattle
- **Coed**

Undergraduates 1,839 full-time, 2,316 part-time.
Academics *Calendar:* quarters. *Degrees:* certificates, associate, and bachelor's. *Special study options:* academic remediation for entering students, advanced placement credit, cooperative education, distance learning, English as a second language, honors programs, independent study, internships, part-time degree program, services for LD students, summer session for credit.
Library Bellevue Community College Library.
Financial Aid Of all full-time matriculated undergraduates who enrolled in 2018, 65 Federal Work-Study jobs (averaging $3400). 43 state and other part-time jobs (averaging $3000).
Applying *Options:* electronic application. *Application fee:* $28.
Freshman Application Contact Morenika Jacobs, Associate Dean of Enrollment Services, Bellevue College, 3000 Landerholm Circle, SE, Bellevue, WA 98007-6484. *Phone:* 425-564-2205. *Fax:* 425-564-4065. *Website:* http://www.bellevuecollege.edu/.

Bellingham Technical College
Bellingham, Washington

- **State-supported** 2-year, founded 1957, part of Washington State Board for Community and Technical Colleges
- **Suburban** 21-acre campus with easy access to Vancouver, BC; Seattle, WA
- **Coed,** 2,864 undergraduate students

Freshmen *Admission:* 2,562 applied, 2,562 admitted.
Faculty *Total:* 189, 67% full-time. *Student/faculty ratio:* 24:1.
Majors Accounting technology and bookkeeping; autobody/collision and repair technology; automobile/automotive mechanics technology; building/property maintenance; civil engineering technology; communications systems installation and repair technology; computer systems networking and telecommunications; culinary arts; data entry/microcomputer applications; diesel mechanics technology; electrician; executive assistant/executive secretary; fishing and fisheries sciences and management; heating, air conditioning, ventilation and refrigeration maintenance technology; heavy/industrial equipment maintenance technologies related; industrial mechanics and maintenance technology; instrumentation technology; legal assistant/paralegal; machine tool technology; marketing/marketing management; medical radiologic technology; registered nursing/registered nurse; surgical technology; surveying technology; welding technology.
Academics *Calendar:* quarters. *Degree:* certificates and associate. *Special study options:* academic remediation for entering students, distance learning, English as a second language, internships, part-time degree program, services for LD students, summer session for credit.

Library Bellingham Technical College Library. *Books:* 15,500 (physical), 120,000 (digital/electronic); *Serial titles:* 90 (physical); *Databases:* 13. Weekly public service hours: 70; students can reserve study rooms.
Student Life *Housing:* college housing not available. *Student services:* personal/psychological counseling.
Financial Aid Of all full-time matriculated undergraduates who enrolled in 2016, 17 Federal Work-Study jobs (averaging $2866). 35 state and other part-time jobs (averaging $2096).
Applying *Options:* electronic application, early admission, deferred entrance. *Required for some:* high school transcript, prerequisite courses. *Application deadlines:* rolling (freshmen), rolling (transfers).
Freshman Application Contact Bellingham Technical College, 3028 Lindbergh Avenue, Bellingham, WA 98225. *Phone:* 360-752-8324.
Website: http://www.btc.edu/.

Big Bend Community College
Moses Lake, Washington

Freshman Application Contact Candis Lacher, Associate Vice President of Student Services, Big Bend Community College, 7662 Chanute Street NE, Moses Lake, WA 98837. *Phone:* 509-793-2061. *Toll-free phone:* 877-745-1212. *Fax:* 509-793-6243. *E-mail:* admissions@bigbend.edu. *Website:* http://www.bigbend.edu/.

Carrington College–Spokane
Spokane, Washington

- **Proprietary** 2-year, founded 1976, part of Carrington Colleges Group, Inc.
- **Coed**

Undergraduates 407 full-time. 18% are from out of state; 2% Black or African American, non-Hispanic/Latino; 12% Hispanic/Latino; 2% Asian, non-Hispanic/Latino; 0.5% Native Hawaiian or other Pacific Islander, non-Hispanic/Latino; 3% American Indian or Alaska Native, non-Hispanic/Latino; 4% Two or more races, non-Hispanic/Latino; 0.7% Race/ethnicity unknown; 19% transferred in. *Retention:* 69% of full-time freshmen returned.
Faculty *Student/faculty ratio:* 18:1.
Academics *Degree:* certificates and associate.
Standardized Tests *Required:* institutional entrance exam (for admission).
Applying *Required:* essay or personal statement, high school transcript, interview.
Freshman Application Contact Carrington College–Spokane, 10102 East Knox Avenue, Suite 200, Spokane, WA 99206. *Website:* http://www.carrington.edu/.

Cascadia College
Bothell, Washington

- **State-supported** primarily 2-year, founded 1999, part of Washington State Board for Community and Technical Colleges
- **Suburban** 128-acre campus with easy access to Seattle, WA
- **Coed,** 3,757 undergraduate students, 41% full-time, 36% women, 37% men

Undergraduates 1,529 full-time, 1,230 part-time. Students come from 12 states and territories; 3% Black or African American, non-Hispanic/Latino; 18% Hispanic/Latino; 15% Asian, non-Hispanic/Latino; 0.4% Native Hawaiian or other Pacific Islander, non-Hispanic/Latino; 0.8% American Indian or Alaska Native, non-Hispanic/Latino; 16% Two or more races, non-Hispanic/Latino; 17% Race/ethnicity unknown; 12% international.
Freshmen *Admission:* 2,939 applied.
Faculty *Total:* 129, 24% full-time.
Majors Liberal arts and sciences and humanities related; liberal arts and sciences/liberal studies; science technologies related; sustainability studies.
Academics *Calendar:* quarters. *Degrees:* certificates, diplomas, associate, and bachelor's. *Special study options:* academic remediation for entering students, accelerated degree program, adult/continuing education programs, advanced placement credit, cooperative education, distance learning, double majors, English as a second language, independent study, internships, off-campus study, part-time degree program, services for LD students, study abroad, summer session for credit.
Library Campus Library. *Books:* 90,000 (physical), 600,000 (digital/electronic); *Serial titles:* 600 (physical), 100,000 (digital/electronic); *Databases:* 600. Weekly public service hours: 86; students can reserve study rooms.
Student Life *Housing:* college housing not available. *Activities and Organizations:* drama/theater group, student-run newspaper. *Campus security:* 24-hour emergency response devices, late-night transport/escort service. *Student services:* personal/psychological counseling, veterans affairs office.
Athletics *Intramural sports:* basketball M/W, football M/W, soccer M/W.
Applying *Options:* electronic application. *Application fee:* $30. *Application deadlines:* rolling (freshmen), rolling (transfers). *Notification:* continuous (freshmen), continuous (transfers).
Freshman Application Contact Ms. Erin Blakeney, Dean for Student Success, Cascadia College, 18345 Campus Way, NE, Bothell, WA 98011. *Phone:* 425-352-8000. *Fax:* 425-352-8137. *E-mail:* admissions@cascadia.edu.
Website: http://www.cascadia.edu/.

Centralia College
Centralia, Washington

Freshman Application Contact Admissions Office, Centralia College, Centralia, WA 98531. *Phone:* 360-736-9391 Ext. 221. *Fax:* 360-330-7503. *E-mail:* admissions@centralia.edu. *Website:* http://www.centralia.edu/.

Clark College
Vancouver, Washington

Freshman Application Contact Ms. Vanessa Watkins, Associate Director of Entry Services, Clark College, Vancouver, WA 98663. *Phone:* 360-992-2308. *Fax:* 360-992-2867. *E-mail:* admissions@clark.edu. *Website:* http://www.clark.edu/.

Clover Park Technical College
Lakewood, Washington

- **State-supported** 2-year, founded 1942, part of Washington State Board for Community and Technical Colleges
- **Coed**

Academics *Degree:* certificates and associate. *Special study options:* academic remediation for entering students, accelerated degree program, cooperative education, distance learning, English as a second language, internships, part-time degree program, services for LD students.
Library CPTC Library.
Student Life *Campus security:* 24-hour patrols, late-night transport/escort service.
Financial Aid ***Financial aid deadline:*** 4/11.
Applying *Options:* electronic application. *Application fee:* $41. *Required for some:* high school transcript, interview.
Director of Admissions Ms. Judy Richardson, Registrar, Clover Park Technical College, 4500 Steilacoom Boulevard, SW, Lakewood, WA 98499. *Phone:* 253-589-5570. *Website:* http://www.cptc.edu/.

Columbia Basin College
Pasco, Washington

Freshman Application Contact Admissions Department, Columbia Basin College, 2600 North 20th Avenue, Pasco, WA 99301-3397. *Phone:* 509-542-4524. *Fax:* 509-544-2023. *E-mail:* admissions@columbiabasin.edu. *Website:* http://www.columbiabasin.edu/.

Edmonds Community College
Lynnwood, Washington

- **State and locally supported** 2-year, founded 1967, part of Washington State Board for Community and Technical Colleges
- **Suburban** 115-acre campus with easy access to Seattle
- **Endowment** $2.7 million
- **Coed**

Undergraduates 3,656 full-time, 4,779 part-time. Students come from 55 other countries; 6% are from out of state; 0.5% transferred in. *Retention:* 64% of full-time freshmen returned.
Faculty *Student/faculty ratio:* 21:1.
Academics *Calendar:* quarters. *Degree:* certificates and associate. *Special study options:* academic remediation for entering students, adult/continuing education programs, advanced placement credit, cooperative education, distance learning, English as a second language, honors programs, internships, off-campus study, part-time degree program, services for LD students, student-designed majors, study abroad, summer session for credit.
Library Edmonds Community College Library.
Student Life *Campus security:* 24-hour emergency response devices and patrols, student patrols, late-night transport/escort service.
Applying *Options:* electronic application, early admission, deferred entrance. *Application fee:* $18.
Freshman Application Contact Ms. Nancy Froemming, Enrollment Services Office Manager, Edmonds Community College, 20000 68th Avenue West,

Lynwood, WA 98036-5999. *Phone:* 425-640-1853. *Fax:* 425-640-1159. *E-mail:* nanci.froemming@edcc.edu. *Website:* http://www.edcc.edu/.

Everett Community College
Everett, Washington

Freshman Application Contact Ms. Linda Baca, Entry Services Manager, Everett Community College, 2000 Tower Street, Everett, WA 98201-1327. *Phone:* 425-388-9219. *Fax:* 425-388-9173. *E-mail:* admissions@everettcc.edu. *Website:* http://www.everettcc.edu/.

Grays Harbor College
Aberdeen, Washington

Freshman Application Contact Ms. Brenda Dell, Admissions Officer, Grays Harbor College, 1620 Edward P. Smith Drive, Aberdeen, WA 98520. *Phone:* 360-532-4216. *Toll-free phone:* 800-562-4830. *Website:* http://www.ghc.edu/.

Green River College
Auburn, Washington

Freshman Application Contact Ms. Peggy Morgan, Program Support Supervisor, Green River College, 12401 Southeast 320th Street, Auburn, WA 98092-3699. *Phone:* 253-833-9111. *Fax:* 253-288-3454. *Website:* http://www.greenriver.edu/.

Highline College
Des Moines, Washington

Freshman Application Contact Ms. Michelle Kuwasaki, Director of Admissions, Highline College, 2400 South 240th Street, Des Moines, WA 98198-9800. *Phone:* 206-878-3710 Ext. 9800. *Website:* http://www.highline.edu/.

Lake Washington Institute of Technology
Kirkland, Washington

Freshman Application Contact Shawn Miller, Registrar, Enrollment Services, Lake Washington Institute of Technology, 11605 132nd Avenue NE, Kirkland, WA 98034-8506. *Phone:* 425-739-8104. *E-mail:* info@lwtc.edu. *Website:* http://www.lwtech.edu/.

Lower Columbia College
Longview, Washington

Freshman Application Contact Ms. Nichole Seroshek, Director of Registration, Lower Columbia College, 1600 Maple Street, Longview, WA 98632. *Phone:* 360-442-2372. *Toll-free phone:* 866-900-2311. *Fax:* 360-442-2379. *E-mail:* registration@lowercolumbia.edu. *Website:* http://www.lowercolumbia.edu/.

North Seattle College
Seattle, Washington

- **State-supported** 2-year, founded 1970, part of Seattle Community College District System
- **Urban** 65-acre campus
- **Endowment** $4.4 million
- **Coed**

Undergraduates 1,953 full-time, 4,350 part-time. Students come from 39 other countries; 5% are from out of state; 20% Black or African American, non-Hispanic/Latino; 22% Hispanic/Latino; 29% Asian, non-Hispanic/Latino; 1% Native Hawaiian or other Pacific Islander, non-Hispanic/Latino; 1% American Indian or Alaska Native, non-Hispanic/Latino; 17% Two or more races, non-Hispanic/Latino; 63% Race/ethnicity unknown; 23% transferred in.
Faculty *Student/faculty ratio:* 20:1.
Academics *Calendar:* quarters. *Degree:* certificates, diplomas, and associate. *Special study options:* academic remediation for entering students, adult/continuing education programs, advanced placement credit, cooperative education, distance learning, English as a second language, external degree program, independent study, internships, part-time degree program, services for LD students, study abroad, summer session for credit. *ROTC:* Army (c).
Library North Seattle Community College Library.
Student Life *Campus security:* 24-hour emergency response devices, late-night transport/escort service, patrols by security.
Applying *Options:* electronic application, early admission, deferred entrance. *Required:* high school transcript. *Required for some:* essay or personal statement.
Freshman Application Contact Ms. Betsy Abts, Registrar, North Seattle College, Seattle, WA 98103-3599. *Phone:* 206-934-3663. *Fax:* 206-934-3671. *E-mail:* arrc@seattlecolleges.edu. *Website:* http://www.northseattle.edu/.

Northwest Indian College
Bellingham, Washington

Freshman Application Contact Office of Admissions, Northwest Indian College, 2522 Kwina Road, Bellingham, WA 98226. *Phone:* 360-676-2772. *Toll-free phone:* 866-676-2772. *Fax:* 360-392-4333. *E-mail:* admissions@nwic.edu. *Website:* http://www.nwic.edu/.

Northwest School of Wooden Boatbuilding
Port Hadlock, Washington

- **Independent** 2-year, founded 1980
- **Small-town** 7-acre campus
- **Coed**

Undergraduates Students come from 15 states and territories; 2 other countries; 45% are from out of state.
Faculty *Total:* 8, 75% full-time. *Student/faculty ratio:* 12:1.
Majors Marine maintenance and ship repair technology.
Academics *Calendar:* quarters. *Degree:* diplomas and associate.
Library School Library.
Student Life *Housing:* college housing not available.
Applying *Options:* electronic application. *Required:* essay or personal statement, high school transcript.
Freshman Application Contact Northwest School of Wooden Boatbuilding, 42 North Water Street, Port Hadlock, WA 98339. *Phone:* 360-385-4948 Ext. 305.
Website: http://www.nwswb.edu/.

Olympic College
Bremerton, Washington

- **State-supported** primarily 2-year, founded 1946, part of Washington State Board for Community and Technical Colleges
- **Suburban** 33-acre campus with easy access to Seattle, Tacoma
- **Coed**

Undergraduates 5% Black or African American, non-Hispanic/Latino; 8% Hispanic/Latino; 10% Asian, non-Hispanic/Latino; 2% American Indian or Alaska Native, non-Hispanic/Latino; 2% international; 1% live on campus.
Academics *Calendar:* quarters. *Degrees:* certificates, diplomas, associate, and bachelor's. *Special study options:* academic remediation for entering students, adult/continuing education programs, advanced placement credit, cooperative education, distance learning, English as a second language, independent study, internships, off-campus study, part-time degree program, services for LD students, study abroad, summer session for credit.
Library Haselwood Library plus 1 other. Students can reserve study rooms.
Student Life *Campus security:* 24-hour emergency response devices and patrols, student patrols, late-night transport/escort service.
Financial Aid Of all full-time matriculated undergraduates who enrolled in 2018, 105 Federal Work-Study jobs (averaging $2380). 31 state and other part-time jobs (averaging $2880).
Applying *Options:* electronic application. *Required for some:* essay or personal statement, high school transcript, 2 letters of recommendation.
Freshman Application Contact Ms. Nora Downard, Program Manager, Olympic College, 1600 Chester Avenue, Bremerton, WA 98337-1699. *Phone:* 360-475-7445. *Toll-free phone:* 800-259-6718. *Fax:* 360-475-7202. *E-mail:* ndownard@olympic.edu. *Website:* http://www.olympic.edu/.

Peninsula College
Port Angeles, Washington

Freshman Application Contact Ms. Pauline Marvin, Peninsula College, 1502 East Lauridsen Boulevard, Port Angeles, WA 98362. *Phone:* 360-417-6596. *Toll-free phone:* 877-452-9277. *Fax:* 360-457-8100. *E-mail:* admissions@pencol.edu. *Website:* http://www.pencol.edu/.

Perry Technical Institute
Yakima, Washington

Admissions Office Contact Perry Technical Institute, 2011 West Washington Avenue, Yakima, WA 98903-1296. *Website:* http://www.perrytech.edu/.

Pierce College Fort Steilacoom
Lakewood, Washington

Freshman Application Contact Admissions Office, Pierce College Fort Steilacoom, 9401 Farwest Drive SW, Lakewood, WA 98498. *Phone:* 253-964-6501. *E-mail:* admiss1@pierce.ctc.edu. *Website:* http://www.pierce.ctc.edu/.

Pierce College Puyallup
Puyallup, Washington

Freshman Application Contact Pierce College Puyallup, 1601 39th Avenue Southeast, Puyallup, WA 98374. *Phone:* 253-840-8400. *Website:* http://www.pierce.ctc.edu/.

Pima Medical Institute - Renton
Renton, Washington

Freshman Application Contact Pima Medical Institute - Renton, 555 South Renton Village Place, Renton, WA 98057. *Phone:* 425-228-9600. *Toll-free phone:* 800-477-PIMA. *Website:* http://www.pmi.edu/.

Pima Medical Institute - Seattle
Seattle, Washington

Freshman Application Contact Admissions Office, Pima Medical Institute - Seattle, 9709 Third Avenue NE, Suite 400, Seattle, WA 98115. *Phone:* 206-322-6100. *Toll-free phone:* 800-477-PIMA. *Website:* http://www.pmi.edu/.

Renton Technical College
Renton, Washington

- **State-supported** primarily 2-year, founded 1942, part of Washington State Board for Community and Technical Colleges
- **Suburban** 30-acre campus with easy access to Seattle
- **Endowment** $837,103
- **Coed**

Undergraduates 1,245 full-time, 2,301 part-time. 16% Black or African American, non-Hispanic/Latino; 13% Hispanic/Latino; 19% Asian, non-Hispanic/Latino; 1% Native Hawaiian or other Pacific Islander, non-Hispanic/Latino; 0.5% American Indian or Alaska Native, non-Hispanic/Latino; 6% Two or more races, non-Hispanic/Latino; 6% Race/ethnicity unknown; 0.9% international.
Faculty *Student/faculty ratio:* 16:1.
Academics *Calendar:* quarters. *Degrees:* certificates, diplomas, associate, and bachelor's. *Special study options:* academic remediation for entering students, adult/continuing education programs, advanced placement credit, cooperative education, distance learning, English as a second language, internships, off-campus study, part-time degree program, services for LD students, summer session for credit.
Library Renton Technical College Library. *Books:* 24,464 (physical), 64,437 (digital/electronic); *Serial titles:* 354 (physical), 19,981 (digital/electronic); *Databases:* 22. Weekly public service hours: 62.
Student Life *Campus security:* patrols by security, security system.
Standardized Tests *Required for some:* ACT ASSET, CLEP, ACCUPLACER, DSP.
Applying *Options:* electronic application, early admission. *Application fee:* $30. *Required for some:* essay or personal statement, high school transcript, interview.
Director of Admissions Patrick Brown, Director of Enrollment Services/Registrar, Renton Technical College, 3000 NE Fourth Street, Renton, WA 98056. *Phone:* 425-2352352 Ext. 5537. *E-mail:* pbrown@rtc.edu. *Website:* http://www.rtc.edu/.

Seattle Central College
Seattle, Washington

Freshman Application Contact Admissions Office, Seattle Central College, 1701 Broadway, Seattle, WA 98122-2400. *Phone:* 206-587-5450. *Website:* http://www.seattlecentral.edu/.

Shoreline Community College
Shoreline, Washington

Freshman Application Contact Shoreline Community College, 16101 Greenwood Avenue North, Shoreline, WA 98133-5696. *Phone:* 206-546-4613. *Website:* http://www.shoreline.edu/.

Skagit Valley College
Mount Vernon, Washington

Freshman Application Contact Ms. Karen Marie Bade, Admissions and Recruitment Coordinator, Skagit Valley College, 2405 College Way, Mount Vernon, WA 98273-5899. *Phone:* 360-416-7620. *E-mail:* karenmarie.bade@skagit.edu. *Website:* http://www.skagit.edu/.

South Puget Sound Community College
Olympia, Washington

Freshman Application Contact Ms. Heidi Dearborn, South Puget Sound Community College, 2011 Mottman Road, SW, Olympia, WA 98512-6292. *Phone:* 360-754-7711 Ext. 5358. *E-mail:* hdearborn@spcc.edu. *Website:* http://www.spscc.edu/.

South Seattle College
Seattle, Washington

Director of Admissions Ms. Kim Manderbach, Dean of Student Services/Registration, South Seattle College, 6000 16th Avenue, SW, Seattle, WA 98106-1499. *Phone:* 206-764-5378. *Fax:* 206-764-7947. *E-mail:* kimmanderb@sccd.ctc.edu. *Website:* http://southseattle.edu/.

Spokane Community College
Spokane, Washington

Freshman Application Contact Ann Hightower-Chavez, Researcher, District Institutional Research, Spokane Community College, Spokane, WA 99217-5399. *Phone:* 509-434-5242. *Toll-free phone:* 800-248-5644. *Fax:* 509-434-5249. *E-mail:* mlee@ccs.spokane.edu. *Website:* http://www.scc.spokane.edu/.

Spokane Falls Community College
Spokane, Washington

Freshman Application Contact Admissions Office, Spokane Falls Community College, Admissions MS 3011, 3410 West Fort George Wright Drive, Spokane, WA 99224. *Phone:* 509-533-3401. *Toll-free phone:* 888-509-7944. *Fax:* 509-533-3852. *Website:* http://www.spokanefalls.edu/.

Tacoma Community College
Tacoma, Washington

Freshman Application Contact Enrollment Services, Tacoma Community College, 6501 South 19th Street, Tacoma, WA 98466. *Phone:* 253-566-5325. *Fax:* 253-566-6034. *Website:* http://www.tacomacc.edu/.

Walla Walla Community College
Walla Walla, Washington

Freshman Application Contact Walla Walla Community College, 500 Tausick Way, Walla Walla, WA 99362-9267. *Phone:* 509-522-2500. *Toll-free phone:* 877-992-9922. *Website:* http://www.wwcc.edu/.

Wenatchee Valley College
Wenatchee, Washington

Freshman Application Contact Wenatchee Valley College, 1300 Fifth Street, Wenatchee, WA 98801-1799. *Phone:* 509-682-6835. *Toll-free phone:* 877-982-4968. *Website:* http://www.wvc.edu/.

Whatcom Community College
Bellingham, Washington

Freshman Application Contact Entry and Advising Center, Whatcom Community College, 237 West Kellogg Road, Bellingham, WA 98226-8003. *Phone:* 360-676-2170. *Fax:* 360-676-2171. *E-mail:* admit@whatcom.ctc.edu. *Website:* http://www.whatcom.ctc.edu/.

Yakima Valley Community College
Yakima, Washington

Freshman Application Contact Ms. Denise Anderson, Registrar and Director for Enrollment Services, Yakima Valley Community College, PO Box 1647, Yakima, WA 98907-1647. *Phone:* 509-574-4702. *Fax:* 509-574-6879. *E-mail:* admis@yvcc.edu. *Website:* http://www.yvcc.edu/.

WEST VIRGINIA

Blue Ridge Community and Technical College
Martinsburg, West Virginia

- **State-supported** 2-year, founded 1974, part of Community and Technical College System of West Virginia
- **Small-town** 46-acre campus
- **Coed,** 6,532 undergraduate students, 16% full-time, 62% women, 38% men

Undergraduates 1,041 full-time, 5,491 part-time. 10% are from out of state; 5% Black or African American, non-Hispanic/Latino; 2% Hispanic/Latino; 2% Asian, non-Hispanic/Latino; 0.3% Native Hawaiian or other Pacific Islander, non-Hispanic/Latino; 0.3% American Indian or Alaska Native, non-Hispanic/Latino; 2% Two or more races, non-Hispanic/Latino; 5% Race/ethnicity unknown.
Freshmen *Admission:* 409 enrolled.
Faculty *Total:* 208, 43% full-time, 14% with terminal degrees. *Student/faculty ratio:* 22:1.
Majors Accounting; allied health and medical assisting services related, automation engineer technology; baking and pastry arts; business administration and management; business administration, management and operations related; clinical/medical laboratory technology; computer and information systems security; criminal justice/safety; culinary arts; data entry/microcomputer applications related; electrical and electronic engineering technologies related; emergency medical technology (EMT paramedic); general studies; information technology; legal assistant/paralegal; liberal arts and sciences/liberal studies; medical/clinical assistant; multi/interdisciplinary studies related; operations management; physical therapy technology; registered nursing/registered nurse; restaurant, culinary, and catering management; science technologies related.
Academics *Calendar:* semesters. *Degree:* certificates and associate. *Special study options:* academic remediation for entering students, accelerated degree program, adult/continuing education programs, advanced placement credit, double majors, English as a second language, independent study, internships, part-time degree program, services for LD students.
Student Life *Housing:* college housing not available. *Activities and Organizations:* drama/theater group, Student Government Association, Drama Club, Phi Theta Kappa, Phi Beta Lambda, Student Nurses Association. *Campus security:* 24-hour emergency response devices, late-night transport/escort service. *Student services:* personal/psychological counseling.
Standardized Tests *Recommended:* SAT and SAT Subject Tests or ACT (for admission).
Costs (2019–20) *Tuition:* state resident $4128 full-time, $172 per credit hour part-time; nonresident $7464 full-time, $311 per credit hour part-time. Full-time tuition and fees vary according to class time and course load. Part-time tuition and fees vary according to class time and course load. *Payment plan:* installment. *Waivers:* senior citizens and employees or children of employees.
Applying *Options:* electronic application, deferred entrance. *Application fee:* $25. *Required:* high school transcript. *Required for some:* interview.
Freshman Application Contact Brenda K. Neal, Dean of Students, Blue Ridge Community and Technical College, 13650 Apple Harvest Drive, Martinsburg, WV 25403. *Phone:* 304-260-4380 Ext. 2109. *Fax:* 304-260-4376. *E-mail:* bneal@blueridgectc.edu.
Website: http://www.blueridgectc.edu/.

BridgeValley Community and Technical College
Montgomery, West Virginia

Director of Admissions Ms. Lisa Graham, Director of Admissions, BridgeValley Community and Technical College, 619 2nd Avenue, Montgomery, WV 25136. *Phone:* 304-442-3167. *Website:* http://www.bridgevalley.edu/.

BridgeValley Community and Technical College
South Charleston, West Virginia

Freshman Application Contact Mr. Bryce Casto, Vice President, Student Affairs, BridgeValley Community and Technical College, 2001 Union Carbide Drive, South Charleston, WV 25303. *Phone:* 304-766-3140. *Fax:* 304-766-4158. *E-mail:* castosb@wvstateu.edu. *Website:* http://www.bridgevalley.edu/.

Eastern West Virginia Community and Technical College
Moorefield, West Virginia

- **State-supported** 2-year, founded 1999
- **Rural** campus
- **Coed**

Faculty *Student/faculty ratio:* 20:1.
Academics *Calendar:* semesters. *Degree:* certificates and associate. *Special study options:* academic remediation for entering students, advanced placement credit, distance learning, double majors, external degree program, independent study, internships, part-time degree program, services for LD students, student-designed majors.
Financial Aid Of all full-time matriculated undergraduates who enrolled in 2019, 168 applied for aid, 140 were judged to have need, 138 had their need fully met. *Average percent of need met:* 36. *Average financial aid package:* $7544. *Average need-based loan:* $2110. *Average need-based gift aid:* $5792.
Freshman Application Contact Learner Support Services, Eastern West Virginia Community and Technical College, HC 65 Box 402, Moorefield, WV 26836. *Phone:* 304-434-8000. *Toll-free phone:* 877-982-2322. *Fax:* 304-434-7000. *E-mail:* askeast@eastern.wvnet.edu. *Website:* http://www.eastern.wvnet.edu/.

Huntington Junior College
Huntington, West Virginia

Director of Admissions Mr. James Garrett, Educational Services Director, Huntington Junior College, 900 Fifth Avenue, Huntington, WV 25701-2004. *Phone:* 304-697-7550. *Toll-free phone:* 800-344-4522. *Website:* http://www.huntingtonjuniorcollege.com/.

Martinsburg College
Martinsburg, West Virginia

Admissions Office Contact Martinsburg College, 341 Aikens Center, Martinsburg, WV 25404. *Website:* http://www.martinsburgcollege.edu/.

Mountain State College
Parkersburg, West Virginia

Freshman Application Contact Ms. Judith Sutton, President, Mountain State College, 1508 Spring Street, Parkersburg, WV 26101-3993. *Phone:* 304-485-5487. *Toll-free phone:* 800-841-0201. *Fax:* 304-485-3524. *E-mail:* jsutton@msc.edu. *Website:* http://www.msc.edu/.

Mountwest Community & Technical College
Huntington, West Virginia

Freshman Application Contact Dr. Tammy Johnson, Admissions Director, Mountwest Community & Technical College, 1 John Marshall Drive, Huntington, WV 25755. *Phone:* 304-696-3160. *Toll-free phone:* 866-676-5533. *Fax:* 304-696-3135. *E-mail:* admissions@marshall.edu. *Website:* http://www.mctc.edu/.

New River Community and Technical College
Beaver, West Virginia

Director of Admissions Dr. Allen B. Withers, Vice President, Student Services, New River Community and Technical College, 280 University Drive, Beaver, WV 25813. *Phone:* 304-929-5011. *Toll-free phone:* 866-349-3739. *E-mail:* awithers@newriver.edu. *Website:* http://www.newriver.edu/.

Pierpont Community & Technical College

Fairmont, West Virginia

- **State-supported** 2-year, founded 1974
- **Small-town** 90-acre campus
- **Endowment** $9.9 million
- **Coed**

Undergraduates 1,156 full-time, 782 part-time. Students come from 14 states and territories; 6 other countries; 4% are from out of state; 6% Black or African American, non-Hispanic/Latino; 2% Hispanic/Latino; 0.6% Asian, non-Hispanic/Latino; 0.5% American Indian or Alaska Native, non-Hispanic/Latino; 3% Two or more races, non-Hispanic/Latino; 0.1% Race/ethnicity unknown; 0.1% international; 10% transferred in; 14% live on campus. *Retention:* 44% of full-time freshmen returned.
Faculty *Student/faculty ratio:* 14:1.
Academics *Calendar:* semesters. *Degree:* certificates and associate. *Special study options:* adult/continuing education programs, part-time degree program, summer session for credit. *ROTC:* Army (c), Air Force (c).
Athletics Member NCAA.
Standardized Tests *Required:* SAT or ACT (for admission).
Applying *Options:* electronic application, deferred entrance. *Recommended:* high school transcript.
Freshman Application Contact Mr. Steve Leadman, Director of Admissions and Recruiting, Pierpont Community & Technical College, 1201 Locust Avenue, Fairmont, WV 26554. *Phone:* 304-367-4892. *Toll-free phone:* 800-641-5678. *Fax:* 304-367-4789. *Website:* http://www.pierpont.edu/.

Potomac State College of West Virginia University

Keyser, West Virginia

- **State-supported** primarily 2-year, founded 1901, part of West Virginia Higher Education Policy Commission
- **Small-town** 18-acre campus
- **Coed**

Undergraduates 1,018 full-time, 322 part-time. 20% are from out of state; 8% Black or African American, non-Hispanic/Latino; 3% Hispanic/Latino; 1% Asian, non-Hispanic/Latino; 0.1% Native Hawaiian or other Pacific Islander, non-Hispanic/Latino; 0.2% American Indian or Alaska Native, non-Hispanic/Latino; 4% Two or more races, non-Hispanic/Latino; 1% Race/ethnicity unknown; 0.4% international; 4% transferred in; 52% live on campus. *Retention:* 39% of full-time freshmen returned.
Faculty *Student/faculty ratio:* 22:1.
Academics *Calendar:* semesters. *Degrees:* associate and bachelor's. *Special study options:* academic remediation for entering students, adult/continuing education programs, advanced placement credit, cooperative education, distance learning, double majors, honors programs, independent study, internships, part-time degree program, services for LD students, study abroad, summer session for credit.
Library Mary F. Shipper Library. *Books:* 7,011 (physical), 617,383 (digital/electronic); *Serial titles:* 19 (physical), 93,783 (digital/electronic); *Databases:* 687.
Student Life *Campus security:* 24-hour patrols, late-night transport/escort service, controlled dormitory access.
Athletics Member NJCAA.
Costs (2019–20) *Tuition:* state resident $4536 full-time, $189 per credit hour part-time; nonresident $11,544 full-time, $481 per credit hour part-time. Full-time tuition and fees vary according to degree level and program. Part-time tuition and fees vary according to degree level. *Room and board:* $8780. Room and board charges vary according to board plan and housing facility.
Financial Aid Of all full-time matriculated undergraduates who enrolled in 2017, 1,059 applied for aid, 843 were judged to have need, 73 had their need fully met. In 2017, 57. *Average percent of need met:* 65. *Average financial aid package:* $4355. *Average need-based loan:* $3039. *Average need-based gift aid:* $3418. *Average non-need-based aid:* $1907. *Average indebtedness upon graduation:* $18,208.
Applying *Options:* electronic application. *Required:* high school transcript.
Freshman Application Contact Ms. Beth Little, Director of Enrollment Services, Potomac State College of West Virginia University, 75 Arnold Street, Keyser, WV 26726. *Phone:* 304-788-6820. *Toll-free phone:* 800-262-7332 Ext. 6820. *Fax:* 304-788-6939. *E-mail:* go2psc@mail.wvu.edu. *Website:* http://www.potomacstatecollege.edu/.

Southern West Virginia Community and Technical College

Mount Gay, West Virginia

Freshman Application Contact Mr. Roy Simmons, Registrar, Southern West Virginia Community and Technical College, PO Box 2900, Mt. Gay, WV 25637. *Phone:* 304-792-7160 Ext. 120. *Fax:* 304-792-7096. *E-mail:* admissions@southern.wvnet.edu. *Website:* http://southernwv.edu/.

Valley College - Martinsburg

Martinsburg, West Virginia

Freshman Application Contact Ms. Gail Kennedy, Admissions Director, Valley College - Martinsburg, 287 Aikens Center, Martinsburg, WV 25404. *Phone:* 304-263-0878. *Fax:* 304-263-2413. *E-mail:* gkennedy@vct.edu. *Website:* http://www.valley.edu/.

West Virginia Junior College - Bridgeport

Bridgeport, West Virginia

Freshman Application Contact Ms. Kristen Kirk, High School Admissions Representative, West Virginia Junior College - Bridgeport, 176 Thompson Drive, Bridgeport, WV 26330. *Phone:* 304-842-4007. *Toll-free phone:* 800-470-5627. *Fax:* 304-842-8191. *E-mail:* kkirk@wvjc.edu. *Website:* http://www.wvjc.edu/.

West Virginia Junior College - Charleston

Charleston, West Virginia

Freshman Application Contact West Virginia Junior College - Charleston, 1000 Virginia Street East, Charleston, WV 25301-2817. *Phone:* 304-345-2820. *Toll-free phone:* 800-924-5208. *Website:* http://www.wvjc.edu/.

West Virginia Junior College–Morgantown

Morgantown, West Virginia

Freshman Application Contact Admissions Office, West Virginia Junior College–Morgantown, 148 Willey Street, Morgantown, WV 26505-5521. *Phone:* 304-296-8282. *Website:* http://www.wvjcmorgantown.edu/.

West Virginia Northern Community College

Wheeling, West Virginia

Freshman Application Contact Mrs. Janet Fike, Vice President of Student Services, West Virginia Northern Community College, 1704 Market Street, Wheeling, WV 26003. *Phone:* 304-214-8837. *E-mail:* jfike@northern.wvnet.edu. *Website:* http://www.wvncc.edu/.

West Virginia University at Parkersburg

Parkersburg, West Virginia

Freshman Application Contact Christine Post, Associate Dean of Enrollment Management, West Virginia University at Parkersburg, 300 Campus Drive, Parkersburg, WV 26104. *Phone:* 304-424-8223 Ext. 223. *Toll-free phone:* 800-WVA-WVUP. *Fax:* 304-424-8332. *E-mail:* christine.post@mail.wvu.edu. *Website:* http://www.wvup.edu/.

WISCONSIN

Blackhawk Technical College

Janesville, Wisconsin

Freshman Application Contact Blackhawk Technical College, 6004 South County Road G, Janesville, WI 53546-9458. *Phone:* 608-757-7713. *Website:* http://www.blackhawk.edu/.

Bryant & Stratton College–Bayshore Campus
Glendale, Wisconsin

Admissions Office Contact Bryant & Stratton College–Bayshore Campus, 500 West Silver Spring Drive, Bayshore Town Center, Suite K340, Glendale, WI 53217. *Website:* http://www.bryantstratton.edu/.

Bryant & Stratton College–Milwaukee Campus
Milwaukee, Wisconsin

Freshman Application Contact Mr. Dan Basile, Director of Admissions, Bryant & Stratton College–Milwaukee Campus, 310 West Wisconsin Avenue, Suite 500 East, Milwaukee, WI 53203-2214. *Phone:* 414-276-5200. *Website:* http://www.bryantstratton.edu/.

Chippewa Valley Technical College
Eau Claire, Wisconsin

Freshman Application Contact Admissions Office, Chippewa Valley Technical College, 620 W. Clairemont Avenue, Eau Claire, WI 54701. *Phone:* 715-833-6200. *Toll-free phone:* 800-547-2882. *Fax:* 715-833-6470. *E-mail:* infocenter@cvtc.edu. *Website:* http://www.cvtc.edu/.

College of Menominee Nation
Keshena, Wisconsin

Director of Admissions Tessa James, Admissions Coordinator, College of Menominee Nation, PO Box 1179, Keshena, WI 54135. *Phone:* 715-799-5600 Ext. 3053. *Toll-free phone:* 800-567-2344. *E-mail:* tjames@menominee.edu. *Website:* http://www.menominee.edu/.

Fox Valley Technical College
Appleton, Wisconsin

- **State and locally supported** 2-year, founded 1967, part of Wisconsin Technical College System
- **Suburban** 100-acre campus
- **Endowment** $4.7 million
- **Coed,** 12,239 undergraduate students, 17% full-time, 45% women, 55% men
- 72% of applicants were admitted

Undergraduates 2,092 full-time, 10,147 part-time. Students come from 14 states and territories; 2 other countries; 1% are from out of state; 2% Black or African American, non-Hispanic/Latino; 5% Hispanic/Latino; 4% Asian, non-Hispanic/Latino; 0.1% Native Hawaiian or other Pacific Islander, non-Hispanic/Latino; 0.9% American Indian or Alaska Native, non-Hispanic/Latino; 0.7% Two or more races, non-Hispanic/Latino; 8% Race/ethnicity unknown; 0.8% international.
Freshmen *Admission:* 1,584 applied, 1,146 admitted, 672 enrolled.
Faculty *Total:* 1,040, 30% full-time. *Student/faculty ratio:* 11:1.
Majors Accounting; administrative assistant and secretarial science; agricultural/farm supplies retailing and wholesaling; agricultural mechanization; agronomy and crop science; airline pilot and flight crew; animal/livestock husbandry and production; autobody/collision and repair technology; automation engineer technology; automobile/automotive mechanics technology; avionics maintenance technology; banking and financial support services; biology/biotechnology laboratory technician; building/construction site management; business administration and management; clinical/medical laboratory technology; computer and information systems security; computer programming; computer support specialist; computer systems networking and telecommunications; court reporting; criminal justice/police science; critical infrastructure protection; culinary arts; dental hygiene; diesel mechanics technology; early childhood education; electrical and electronic engineering technologies related; electrical, electronic and communications engineering technology; electromechanical technology; electroneurodiagnostic/electroencephalographic technology; entrepreneurship; fire science/firefighting; forensic science and technology; health information/medical records technology; hospitality administration; human resources management; industrial safety technology; interior design; knowledge management; legal assistant/paralegal; logistics, materials, and supply chain management; manufacturing engineering technology; marketing/marketing management; mechanical drafting and CAD/CADD; medical office management; meeting and event planning; multi/interdisciplinary studies related; natural resources/conservation; occupational therapist assistant; office management; professional, technical, business, and scientific writing; psychiatric/mental health services technology; radio, television, and digital communication related; registered nursing/registered nurse; substance abuse/addiction counseling; veterinary/animal health technology; web/multimedia management and webmaster; welding technology; wildland/forest firefighting and investigation.
Academics *Calendar:* semesters. *Degree:* certificates, diplomas, and associate. *Special study options:* academic remediation for entering students, accelerated degree program, advanced placement credit, cooperative education, distance learning, double majors, English as a second language, independent study, internships, off-campus study, part-time degree program, services for LD students, student-designed majors, study abroad, summer session for credit.
Library Student Success Center Library. *Books:* 9,454 (physical), 415,953 (digital/electronic); *Serial titles:* 30 (physical), 45,301 (digital/electronic); *Databases:* 135. Weekly public service hours: 63; students can reserve study rooms.
Student Life *Housing:* college housing not available. *Activities and Organizations:* student-run newspaper, Student Government Association, Phi Theta Kappa, Culinary Arts Club, Machine Tool Club, Post Secondary Agribusiness Club. *Campus security:* 24-hour emergency response devices, late-night transport/escort service, trained security personnel patrol during hours of operation. *Student services:* health clinic, personal/psychological counseling, veterans affairs office.
Standardized Tests *Required for some:* ACT or ACCUPLACER, TEAS, Bennett Mechanical Comprehension Test.
Costs (2019–20) *Tuition:* state resident $4095 full-time, $137 per credit part-time; nonresident $6143 full-time, $205 per credit part-time. *Required fees:* $545 full-time, $18 per credit part-time. *Payment plan:* installment.
Applying *Options:* electronic application. *Application fee:* $30. *Required for some:* high school transcript, interview. *Application deadlines:* rolling (freshmen), rolling (transfers).
Freshman Application Contact Admissions Center, Fox Valley Technical College, 1825 North Bluemound Drive, PO Box 2277, Appleton, WI 54912-2277. *Phone:* 920-735-5643. *Toll-free phone:* 800-735-3882. *Fax:* 920-735-2582.
Website: http://www.fvtc.edu/.

Gateway Technical College
Kenosha, Wisconsin

Freshman Application Contact Admissions, Gateway Technical College, 3520 30th Avenue, Kenosha, WI 53144-1690. *Phone:* 262-564-2300. *Fax:* 262-564-2301. *E-mail:* admissions@gtc.edu. *Website:* http://www.gtc.edu/.

Lac Courte Oreilles Ojibwa Community College
Hayward, Wisconsin

Freshman Application Contact Ms. Annette Wiggins, Registrar, Lac Courte Oreilles Ojibwa Community College, 13466 West Trepania Road, Hayward, WI 54843-2181. *Phone:* 715-634-4790 Ext. 104. *Toll-free phone:* 888-526-6221. *Website:* http://www.lco.edu/.

Lakeshore Technical College
Cleveland, Wisconsin

Freshman Application Contact Lakeshore Technical College, 1290 North Avenue, Cleveland, WI 53015. *Phone:* 920-693-1339. *Toll-free phone:* 888-GO TO LTC. *Fax:* 920-693-3561. *Website:* http://www.gotoltc.edu/.

Madison Area Technical College
Madison, Wisconsin

Freshman Application Contact Ms. Lori Sebranek, Dean, Enrollment Services, Madison Area Technical College, 1701 Wright Street, Madison, WI 53704. *Phone:* 608-243-4185. *Toll-free phone:* 800-322-6282. *Fax:* 608-243-4353. *E-mail:* enrollmentservices@madisoncollege.edu. *Website:* http://madisoncollege.edu/.

Madison Media Institute
Madison, Wisconsin

Freshman Application Contact Mr. Chris K. Hutchings, President/Director, Madison Media Institute, 2702 Agriculture Drive, Madison, WI 53718. *Phone:* 608-237-8301. *Toll-free phone:* 800-236-4997. *Website:* http://www.mediainstitute.edu/.

Mid-State Technical College

Wisconsin Rapids, Wisconsin

Freshman Application Contact Ms. Carole Prochnow, Admissions Assistant, Mid-State Technical College, 500 32nd Street North, Wisconsin Rapids, WI 54494-5599. *Phone:* 715-422-5444. *Website:* http://www.mstc.edu/.

Milwaukee Area Technical College

Milwaukee, Wisconsin

- **District-supported** 2-year, founded 1912, part of Wisconsin Technical College System
- **Urban** campus
- **Coed**

Undergraduates 7,048 full-time, 13,167 part-time. Students come from 16 states and territories; 50 other countries; 1% are from out of state; 16% transferred in. *Retention:* 54% of full-time freshmen returned.
Faculty *Student/faculty ratio:* 14:1.
Academics *Calendar:* semesters. *Degree:* certificates, diplomas, and associate. *Special study options:* academic remediation for entering students, accelerated degree program, adult/continuing education programs, advanced placement credit, cooperative education, distance learning, double majors, English as a second language, external degree program, freshman honors college, honors programs, independent study, internships, off-campus study, part-time degree program, services for LD students, student-designed majors, study abroad, summer session for credit.
Library William F. Rasche Library plus 4 others.
Student Life *Campus security:* 24-hour emergency response devices and patrols, student patrols, late-night transport/escort service.
Athletics Member NJCAA.
Standardized Tests *Required:* ACCUPLACER (for admission).
Financial Aid Of all full-time matriculated undergraduates who enrolled in 2018, 300 Federal Work-Study jobs (averaging $3900).
Applying *Options:* electronic application. *Application fee:* $30. *Required:* high school transcript.
Freshman Application Contact Sarah Adams, Director, Enrollment Services, Milwaukee Area Technical College, 700 West State Street, Milwaukee, WI 53233-1443. *Phone:* 414-297-6595. *Fax:* 414-297-7800. *E-mail:* adamss4@matc.edu. *Website:* http://www.matc.edu/.

Milwaukee Career College

Milwaukee, Wisconsin

Admissions Office Contact Milwaukee Career College, 3077 N. Mayfair Road, Suite 300, Milwaukee, WI 53222. *Website:* http://www.mkecc.edu/.

Moraine Park Technical College

Fond du Lac, Wisconsin

Freshman Application Contact Karen Jarvis, Student Services, Moraine Park Technical College, 235 North National Avenue, Fond du Lac, WI 54935. *Phone:* 920-924-3200. *Toll-free phone:* 800-472-4554. *Fax:* 920-924-3421. *E-mail:* kjarvis@morainepark.edu. *Website:* http://www.morainepark.edu/.

Nicolet Area Technical College

Rhinelander, Wisconsin

Freshman Application Contact Ms. Susan Kordula, Director of Admissions, Nicolet Area Technical College, PO Box 518, Rhinelander, WI 54501. *Phone:* 715-365-4451. *Toll-free phone:* 800-544-3039. *E-mail:* inquire@nicoletcollege.edu. *Website:* http://www.nicoletcollege.edu/.

Northcentral Technical College

Wausau, Wisconsin

Freshman Application Contact Northcentral Technical College, 1000 West Campus Drive, Wausau, WI 54401-1899. *Phone:* 715-675-3331. *Website:* http://www.ntc.edu/.

Northeast Wisconsin Technical College

Green Bay, Wisconsin

- **State and locally supported** 2-year, founded 1913, part of Wisconsin Technical College System
- **Suburban** 192-acre campus
- **Coed,** 8,105 undergraduate students

Majors Accounting; administrative assistant and secretarial science; agroecology and sustainable agriculture; architectural engineering technology; autobody/collision and repair technology; automobile/automotive mechanics technology; biology/biotechnology laboratory technician; biomedical technology; building/construction site management; business administration and management; civil engineering technology; clinical/medical laboratory technology; community health services counseling; computer and information sciences and support services related; computer and information systems security; computer programming; computer systems networking and telecommunications; construction trades; corrections; court reporting; criminal justice/police science; dental hygiene; desktop publishing and digital imaging design; diagnostic medical sonography and ultrasound technology; early childhood education; electrical and electronic engineering technologies related; electrical, electronic and communications engineering technology; electromechanical and instrumentation and maintenance technologies related; electromechanical technology; emergency medical technology (EMT paramedic); energy management and systems technology; entrepreneurship; environmental control technologies related; farm and ranch management; fire systems technology; gerontology; health and wellness; health/health-care administration; health information/medical records technology; heating, ventilation, air conditioning and refrigeration engineering technology; heavy equipment maintenance technology; hospitality administration; human resources management; interdisciplinary studies; knowledge management; landscaping and groundskeeping; legal assistant/paralegal; logistics, materials, and supply chain management; machine shop technology; manufacturing engineering technology; marketing/marketing management; marketing related; mechanical drafting and CAD/CADD; medical insurance/medical billing; medical radiologic technology; meeting and event planning; multi/interdisciplinary studies related; naval architecture and marine engineering; nuclear/nuclear power technology; office management; operations management; physical therapy technology; psychiatric/mental health services technology; quality control and safety technologies related; quality control technology; radiation protection/health physics technology; radio, television, and digital communication related; registered nursing/registered nurse; respiratory care therapy; teacher assistant/aide; viticulture and enology; web/multimedia management and webmaster; web page, digital/multimedia and information resources design.
Academics *Calendar:* semesters. *Degree:* certificates, diplomas, and associate. *Special study options:* academic remediation for entering students, accelerated degree program, adult/continuing education programs, advanced placement credit, distance learning, English as a second language, part-time degree program, services for LD students, student-designed majors, summer session for credit.
Student Life *Campus security:* 24-hour emergency response devices, late-night transport/escort service. *Student services:* health clinic, personal/psychological counseling.
Athletics *Intramural sports:* basketball M/W, football M/W, volleyball M/W.
Costs (2019–20) *Tuition:* area resident $4095 full-time, $137 per credit hour part-time; state resident $4095 full-time, $137 per credit hour part-time; nonresident $6143 full-time, $205 per credit hour part-time. *Required fees:* $482 full-time, $16 per credit hour part-time. *Room and board:* $7410. *Payment plan:* installment. *Waivers:* senior citizens.
Applying *Options:* early admission. *Application fee:* $30. *Application deadline:* rolling (freshmen). *Notification:* continuous (transfers).
Freshman Application Contact Christine Lemerande, Program Enrollment Supervisor, Northeast Wisconsin Technical College, 2740 W Mason Street, PO Box 19042, Green Bay, WI 54307-9042. *Phone:* 920-498-5444. *Toll-free phone:* 888-385-6982. *Fax:* 920-498-6882.
Website: http://www.nwtc.edu/.

Southwest Wisconsin Technical College

Fennimore, Wisconsin

- **State and locally supported** 2-year, founded 1967, part of Wisconsin Technical College System
- **Rural** 53-acre campus
- **Endowment** $2.7 million
- **Coed,** 2,640 undergraduate students, 27% full-time, 56% women, 44% men

Undergraduates 722 full-time, 1,918 part-time. Students come from 42 states and territories; 14% are from out of state; 2% Black or African American, non-Hispanic/Latino; 2% Hispanic/Latino; 0.5% Asian, non-Hispanic/Latino; 0.8%

American Indian or Alaska Native, non-Hispanic/Latino; 3% Two or more races, non-Hispanic/Latino; 2% Race/ethnicity unknown; 20% transferred in; 7% live on campus.
Freshmen *Admission:* 870 applied, 856 admitted, 410 enrolled.
Faculty *Total:* 123, 63% full-time. *Student/faculty ratio:* 15:1.
Majors Accounting; agribusiness; agricultural/farm supplies retailing and wholesaling; agronomy and crop science; animal/livestock husbandry and production; computer systems networking and telecommunications; criminal justice/police science; criminal justice/safety; culinary arts; direct entry midwifery; early childhood education; electromechanical technology; golf course operation and grounds management; health information/medical records technology; instrumentation technology; interdisciplinary studies; registered nursing/registered nurse; restaurant, culinary, and catering management; web page, digital/multimedia and information resources design.
Academics *Calendar:* semesters. *Degree:* certificates, diplomas, and associate. *Special study options:* academic remediation for entering students, advanced placement credit, distance learning, double majors, English as a second language, independent study, internships, off-campus study, part-time degree program, services for LD students, student-designed majors, summer session for credit.
Library Knox Learning Center. *Books:* 11,470 (physical), 180,598 (digital/electronic); *Serial titles:* 31 (physical); *Databases:* 42. Weekly public service hours: 58; students can reserve study rooms.
Student Life *Housing Options:* coed, special housing for students with disabilities. Campus housing is university owned. *Activities and Organizations:* Student Senate, Student Ambassadors, Phi Theta Kappa. *Campus security:* 24-hour emergency response devices. *Student services:* personal/psychological counseling.
Athletics Member NJCAA. *Intercollegiate sports:* golf M. *Intramural sports:* basketball M/W, volleyball M/W.
Costs (2019–20) *Tuition:* area resident $4095 full-time; state resident $4095 full-time; nonresident $6143 full-time. Full-time tuition and fees vary according to course load, degree level, program, and reciprocity agreements. Part-time tuition and fees vary according to course load, degree level, program, and reciprocity agreements. *Required fees:* $338 full-time. *Room and board:* $7511. Room and board charges vary according to housing facility. *Payment plans:* installment, deferred payment.
Applying *Options:* electronic application, early admission. *Application fee:* $30. *Required:* high school transcript, interview. *Application deadlines:* rolling (freshmen), rolling (out-of-state freshmen), rolling (transfers). *Notification:* continuous (freshmen), continuous (out-of-state freshmen), continuous (transfers).
Freshman Application Contact Danielle Seippel, Registrar, Southwest Wisconsin Technical College, 1800 Bronson Boulevard, Fennimore, WI 53809. *Phone:* 608-822-2317 Ext. 2317. *Toll-free phone:* 800-362-3322. *E-mail:* dseippel@swtc.edu.
Website: http://www.swtc.edu/.

University of Wisconsin–Baraboo/Sauk County
Baraboo, Wisconsin

Freshman Application Contact University of Wisconsin–Baraboo/Sauk County, 1006 Connie Road, Baraboo, WI 53913. *Website:* http://www.baraboo.uwc.edu/.

University of Wisconsin–Barron County
Rice Lake, Wisconsin

Freshman Application Contact University of Wisconsin–Barron County, 1800 College Drive, Rice Lake, WI 54868. *Website:* http://www.barron.uwc.edu/.

University of Wisconsin Colleges Online
Madison, Wisconsin

Admissions Office Contact University of Wisconsin Colleges Online, 34 Schroeder Court, Suite 200, Madison, WI 53711. *Toll-free phone:* 877-449-1877. *Website:* http://www.online.uwc.edu/.

University of Wisconsin–Fond du Lac
Fond du Lac, Wisconsin

Freshman Application Contact University of Wisconsin–Fond du Lac, 400 University Drive, Fond du Lac, WI 54935. *Website:* http://www.fdl.uwc.edu/.

University of Wisconsin–Fox Valley
Menasha, Wisconsin

Freshman Application Contact University of Wisconsin–Fox Valley, 1478 Midway Road, Menasha, WI 54952. *Website:* http://www.uwfox.uwc.edu/.

University of Wisconsin–Manitowoc
Manitowoc, Wisconsin

Freshman Application Contact University of Wisconsin–Manitowoc, 705 Viebahn Street, Manitowoc, WI 54220. *Website:* http://www.manitowoc.uwc.edu/.

University of Wisconsin–Marathon County
Wausau, Wisconsin

Freshman Application Contact University of Wisconsin–Marathon County, 518 South 7th Avenue, Wausau, WI 54401. *Toll-free phone:* 888-367-8962. *Website:* http://www.uwmc.uwc.edu/.

University of Wisconsin–Marinette
Marinette, Wisconsin

Freshman Application Contact University of Wisconsin–Marinette, 750 West Bay Shore, Marinette, WI 54143. *Website:* http://www.marinette.uwc.edu/.

University of Wisconsin–Marshfield/Wood County
Marshfield, Wisconsin

Freshman Application Contact University of Wisconsin–Marshfield/Wood County, 2000 West 5th Street, Marshfield, WI 54449. *Website:* http://marshfield.uwc.edu/.

University of Wisconsin–Richland
Richland Center, Wisconsin

Freshman Application Contact University of Wisconsin–Richland, 1200 Highway 14 West, Richland Center, WI 53581. *Website:* http://richland.uwc.edu/.

University of Wisconsin–Rock County
Janesville, Wisconsin

Freshman Application Contact University of Wisconsin–Rock County, 2909 Kellogg Avenue, Janesville, WI 53546. *Toll-free phone:* 888-INFO-UWC. *Website:* http://rock.uwc.edu/.

University of Wisconsin–Sheboygan
Sheboygan, Wisconsin

Freshman Application Contact University of Wisconsin–Sheboygan, One University Drive, Sheboygan, WI 53081. *Website:* http://www.sheboygan.uwc.edu/.

University of Wisconsin–Washington County
West Bend, Wisconsin

Freshman Application Contact University of Wisconsin–Washington County, 400 University Drive, West Bend, WI 53095. *Website:* http://www.washington.uwc.edu/.

University of Wisconsin–Waukesha
Waukesha, Wisconsin

Freshman Application Contact University of Wisconsin–Waukesha, 1500 North University Drive, Waukesha, WI 53188. *Website:* http://www.waukesha.uwc.edu/.

Waukesha County Technical College

Pewaukee, Wisconsin

Freshman Application Contact Waukesha County Technical College, 800 Main Street, Pewaukee, WI 53072-4601. *Phone:* 262-691-5464. *Website:* http://www.wctc.edu/.

Western Technical College

La Crosse, Wisconsin

Freshman Application Contact Ms. Jane Wells, Manager of Admissions, Registration, and Records, Western Technical College, PO Box 908, La Crosse, WI 54602-0908. *Phone:* 608-785-9158. *Toll-free phone:* 800-322-9982. *Fax:* 608-785-9094. *E-mail:* mildes@wwtc.edu. *Website:* http://www.westerntc.edu/.

Wisconsin Indianhead Technical College

Shell Lake, Wisconsin

Freshman Application Contact Mr. Steve Bitzer, Vice President, Student Affairs and Campus Administrator, Wisconsin Indianhead Technical College, 2100 Beaser Avenue, Ashland, WI 54806. *Phone:* 715-468-2815 Ext. 3149. *Toll-free phone:* 800-243-9482. *Fax:* 715-468-2819. *E-mail:* steve.bitzer@witc.edu. *Website:* http://www.witc.edu/.

WYOMING

Casper College

Casper, Wyoming

- **State and locally supported** 2-year, founded 1945
- **Small-town** 200-acre campus
- **Coed**

Undergraduates 1,733 full-time, 1,893 part-time. Students come from 37 states and territories; 17 other countries; 10% are from out of state; 1% Black or African American, non-Hispanic/Latino; 7% Hispanic/Latino; 0.9% Asian, non-Hispanic/Latino; 0.2% Native Hawaiian or other Pacific Islander, non-Hispanic/Latino; 0.9% American Indian or Alaska Native, non-Hispanic/Latino; 2% Two or more races, non-Hispanic/Latino; 3% Race/ethnicity unknown; 0.5% international; 2% transferred in; 16% live on campus.
Faculty *Student/faculty ratio:* 14:1.
Academics *Calendar:* semesters. *Degree:* certificates and associate. *Special study options:* academic remediation for entering students, accelerated degree program, advanced placement credit, cooperative education, distance learning, English as a second language, honors programs, independent study, internships, off-campus study, part-time degree program, services for LD students, summer session for credit.
Library Goodstein Foundation Library. *Books:* 66,488 (physical), 184,000 (digital/electronic); *Serial titles:* 4,300 (physical); *Databases:* 415. Weekly public service hours: 82; students can reserve study rooms.
Student Life *Campus security:* 24-hour emergency response devices and patrols, late-night transport/escort service.
Athletics Member NJCAA.
Financial Aid Of all full-time matriculated undergraduates who enrolled in 2018, 80 Federal Work-Study jobs (averaging $2000).
Applying *Options:* electronic application, early admission. *Required:* high school transcript.
Freshman Application Contact Ms. Kyla Foltz, Director of Admissions Services, Casper College, 125 College Drive, Casper, WY 82601. *Phone:* 307-268-2111. *Toll-free phone:* 800-442-2963. *Fax:* 307-268-2611. *E-mail:* kfoltz@caspercollege.edu. *Website:* http://www.caspercollege.edu/.

Central Wyoming College

Riverton, Wyoming

Freshman Application Contact Mr. Patrick Edwards, Director of Admissions, Central Wyoming College, 2660 Peck Avenue, Riverton, WY 82501-2273. *Phone:* 307-855-2022. *Toll-free phone:* 800-735-8418. *Fax:* 307-855-2065. *E-mail:* pedwards@cwc.edu. *Website:* http://www.cwc.edu/.

Eastern Wyoming College

Torrington, Wyoming

Freshman Application Contact Dr. Rex Cogdill, Vice President for Students Services, Eastern Wyoming College, 3200 West C Street, Torrington, WY 82240. *Phone:* 307-532-8257. *Toll-free phone:* 866-327-8996. *Fax:* 307-532-8222. *E-mail:* rex.cogdill@ewc.wy.edu. *Website:* http://www.ewc.wy.edu/.

Laramie County Community College

Cheyenne, Wyoming

- **District-supported** 2-year, founded 1968, part of Wyoming Community College Commission
- **Small-town** 271-acre campus
- **Coed,** 4,284 undergraduate students, 37% full-time, 59% women, 41% men
- 100% of applicants were admitted

Undergraduates 1,604 full-time, 2,680 part-time. 16% are from out of state; 2% Black or African American, non-Hispanic/Latino; 14% Hispanic/Latino; 0.8% Asian, non-Hispanic/Latino; 0.1% Native Hawaiian or other Pacific Islander, non-Hispanic/Latino; 0.8% American Indian or Alaska Native, non-Hispanic/Latino; 3% Two or more races, non-Hispanic/Latino; 17% Race/ethnicity unknown; 0.6% international; 3% transferred in.
Freshmen *Admission:* 1,759 applied, 1,759 admitted, 678 enrolled. *Average high school GPA:* 3.0.
Faculty *Total:* 250, 48% full-time, 11% with terminal degrees. *Student/faculty ratio:* 15:1.
Academics *Calendar:* semesters. *Degree:* certificates, diplomas, and associate. *ROTC:* Army (c), Air Force (c).
Student Life *Housing Options:* coed. *Activities and Organizations:* drama/theater group, student-run newspaper, choral group.
Costs (2020–21) *Tuition:* area resident $2970 full-time, $99 per credit hour part-time; state resident $2970 full-time, $99 per credit hour part-time; nonresident $8910 full-time, $297 per credit hour part-time. *Required fees:* $1463 full-time. *Room and board:* $8276.
Financial Aid Of all full-time matriculated undergraduates who enrolled in 2018, 1,215 applied for aid, 893 were judged to have need, 138 had their need fully met. In 2018, 609 non-need-based awards were made. *Average percent of need met:* 65%. *Average financial aid package:* $7179. *Average need-based loan:* $3004. *Average need-based gift aid:* $4638. *Average non-need-based aid:* $1355.
Applying *Options:* deferred entrance. *Required for some:* high school transcript, interview.
Freshman Application Contact Laramie County Community College, 1400 East College Drive, Cheyenne, WY 82007-3299. *Toll-free phone:* 800-522-2993 Ext. 1357.
Website: http://www.lccc.wy.edu/.

Northwest College

Powell, Wyoming

Freshman Application Contact Mr. West Hernandez, Admissions Manager, Northwest College, 231 W. 6th Street, Orendorff Building 1, Powell, WY 82435-1898. *Phone:* 307-754-6103. *Toll-free phone:* 800-560-4692. *Fax:* 307-754-6249. *E-mail:* west.hernandez@nwc.edu. *Website:* http://www.nwc.edu/.

Sheridan College

Sheridan, Wyoming

Freshman Application Contact Mr. Matt Adams, Admissions Coordinator, Sheridan College, PO Box 1500, Sheridan, WY 82801-1500. *Phone:* 307-674-6446 Ext. 2005. *Toll-free phone:* 800-913-9139 Ext. 2002. *Fax:* 307-674-3373. *E-mail:* madams@sheridan.edu. *Website:* http://www.sheridan.edu/.

Western Wyoming Community College

Rock Springs, Wyoming

- **State and locally supported** 2-year, founded 1959
- **Small-town** 342-acre campus
- **Endowment** $23.7 million
- **Coed**

Undergraduates 1,096 full-time, 2,087 part-time. Students come from 15 states and territories; 16 other countries; 16% are from out of state; 2% Black or African American, non-Hispanic/Latino; 12% Hispanic/Latino; 0.9% Asian, non-Hispanic/Latino; 0.1% Native Hawaiian or other Pacific Islander, non-Hispanic/Latino; 0.6% American Indian or Alaska Native, non-

Hispanic/Latino; 3% Two or more races, non-Hispanic/Latino; 0.8% Race/ethnicity unknown; 2% international; 10% live on campus.
Faculty *Student/faculty ratio:* 11:1.
Academics *Calendar:* semesters. *Degree:* certificates, diplomas, and associate. *Special study options:* academic remediation for entering students, advanced placement credit, cooperative education, distance learning, English as a second language, honors programs, independent study, internships, part-time degree program, services for LD students, summer session for credit.
Library Hay Library. *Books:* 93,144 (physical), 747,995 (digital/electronic); *Serial titles:* 136 (physical), 63,272 (digital/electronic); *Databases:* 412. Weekly public service hours: 81; students can reserve study rooms.
Student Life *Campus security:* 24-hour emergency response devices and patrols, late-night transport/escort service, controlled dormitory access.
Athletics Member NJCAA.
Costs (2019–20) *Tuition:* area resident $2970 full-time, $99 per credit hour part-time; state resident $2970 full-time, $99 per credit hour part-time; nonresident $8910 full-time, $297 per credit hour part-time. *Required fees:* $951 full-time, $40 per credit hour part-time. *Room and board:* $5720; room only: $2680. Room and board charges vary according to board plan and housing facility.
Financial Aid Of all full-time matriculated undergraduates who enrolled in 2018, 20 Federal Work-Study jobs (averaging $1500).
Applying *Options:* electronic application, early admission, deferred entrance. *Recommended:* high school transcript.
Freshman Application Contact Mr. Kurtis Wilkinson, Director of Admissions, Western Wyoming Community College, 2500 College Drive, Rock Springs, WY 82901. *Phone:* 307-382-1647. *Toll-free phone:* 800-226-1181. *Fax:* 307-382-1636. *E-mail:* admissions@westernwyoming.edu. *Website:* http://www.westernwyoming.edu/.

CANADA

CANADA

Southern Alberta Institute of Technology
Calgary, Alberta, Canada

Freshman Application Contact Southern Alberta Institute of Technology, 1301 16th Avenue NW, Calgary, AB T2M 0L4, Canada. *Phone:* 403-284-8857. *Toll-free phone:* 877-284-SAIT. *Website:* http://www.sait.ca/.

BERMUDA

Bermuda College
Paget, Bermuda

Admissions Office Contact Bermuda College, 21 Stonington Avenue, South Road, Paget PG 04, Bermuda. *Website:* http://www.college.bm/.

MARSHALL ISLANDS

College of the Marshall Islands
Majuro, Marshall Islands

- **State-supported** 2-year
- **Rural** campus
- **Endowment** $1.2 million
- **Coed**

Undergraduates 693 full-time, 302 part-time. 1% are from out of state; 100% Native Hawaiian or other Pacific Islander, non-Hispanic/Latino; 0.3% American Indian or Alaska Native, non-Hispanic/Latino; 0.4% international; 0.5% transferred in.
Faculty *Student/faculty ratio:* 12:1.
Academics *Degree:* associate.
Financial Aid Of all full-time matriculated undergraduates who enrolled in 2015, 984 applied for aid, 984 were judged to have need. *Average financial aid package:* $4372. *Average need-based gift aid:* $4372. *Financial aid deadline:* 7/15.
Applying *Application fee:* $5. *Required:* high school transcript, minimum 2.0 GPA, health examination form.
Freshman Application Contact Ms. Jomi Monica Capelle, Director of Admissions and Records, College of the Marshall Islands, PO Box 1258, Majuro 96960, Marshall Islands. *Phone:* 692-625-6823. *Fax:* 692-625-7203. *E-mail:* cmiadmissions@cmi.edu. *Website:* http://www.cmi.edu/.

MICRONESIA

College of Micronesia–FSM
Kolonia Pohnpei, Micronesia

- **Territory-supported** 2-year, founded 1963
- **Rural** 70-acre campus
- **Coed**

Undergraduates *Retention:* 58% of full-time freshmen returned.
Faculty *Student/faculty ratio:* 15:1.
Academics *Calendar:* semesters. *Degree:* certificates and associate. *Special study options:* academic remediation for entering students, adult/continuing education programs, double majors, English as a second language, independent study, internships, summer session for credit.
Library Learning Resources Center plus 1 other.
Applying *Options:* deferred entrance. *Application fee:* $10. *Required:* high school transcript, minimum 2.0 GPA.
Freshman Application Contact Rita Hinga, Student Services Specialist, College of Micronesia–FSM, PO Box 159, Kolonia Pohnpei, FM 96941, Micronesia. *Phone:* 691-320-3795 Ext. 15. *E-mail:* rhinga@comfsm.fm. *Website:* http://www.comfsm.fm/.

PALAU

Palau Community College
Koror, Palau

Freshman Application Contact Ms. Dahlia Katosang, Director of Admissions and Financial Aid, Palau Community College, PO Box 9, Koror 96940-0009, Palau. *Phone:* 680-488-2471 Ext. 233. *Fax:* 680-488-4468. *E-mail:* dahliapcc@palaunet.com. *Website:* http://www.palau.edu/.

Indexes

Associate Degree Programs at Two-Year Colleges

ACCOUNTING
Adirondack Comm Coll (NY)
Alexandria Tech and Comm Coll (MN)
Alvin Comm Coll (TX)
Amarillo Coll (TX)
Anoka-Ramsey Comm Coll (MN)
Anoka Tech Coll (MN)
Asheville-Buncombe Tech Comm Coll (NC)
Austin Comm Coll District (TX)
Bay de Noc Comm Coll (MI)
Black Hawk Coll, Moline (IL)
Blinn Coll (TX)
Blue Ridge Comm and Tech Coll (WV)
Borough of Manhattan Comm Coll of the City U of New York (NY)
Bristol Comm Coll (MA)
Central Lakes Coll (MN)
Central Maine Comm Coll (ME)
Central Ohio Tech Coll (OH)
Central Oregon Comm Coll (OR)
Century Coll (MN)
Chandler-Gilbert Comm Coll (AZ)
Clackamas Comm Coll (OR)
Coll of DuPage (IL)
Coll of Eastern Idaho (ID)
The Coll of Westchester (NY)
Craven Comm Coll (NC)
De Anza Coll (CA)
Des Moines Area Comm Coll (IA)
Dutchess Comm Coll (NY)
Eastern Gateway Comm Coll (OH)
Edison State Comm Coll (OH)
Fox Valley Tech Coll (WI)
Great Falls Coll Montana State U (MT)
Greenville Tech Coll (SC)
Harper Coll (IL)
Hawkeye Comm Coll (IA)
Haywood Comm Coll (NC)
Housatonic Comm Coll (CT)
Houston Comm Coll (TX)
Iowa Central Comm Coll (IA)
Kaskaskia Coll (IL)
Lackawanna Coll (PA)
Lakeland Comm Coll (OH)
Los Angeles City Coll (CA)
Los Angeles Mission Coll (CA)
Luzerne County Comm Coll (PA)
Manchester Comm Coll (CT)
McHenry County Coll (IL)
McLennan Comm Coll (TX)
Middlesex Comm Coll (CT)
Middlesex County Coll (NJ)
Minnesota State Comm and Tech Coll (MN)
Minnesota State Comm and Tech Coll–Detroit Lakes (MN)
Minnesota State Comm and Tech Coll–Moorhead (MN)
Mississippi Delta Comm Coll (MS)
Morton Coll (IL)
Mt. San Antonio Coll (CA)
Nassau Comm Coll (NY)
Navarro Coll (TX)
Niagara County Comm Coll (NY)
Northeastern Jr Coll (CO)
Northeast Iowa Comm Coll (IA)
Northeast Wisconsin Tech Coll (WI)
Northern Essex Comm Coll (MA)
Northwest State Comm Coll (OH)
Paris Jr Coll (TX)
Pensacola State Coll (FL)
Piedmont Comm Coll (NC)
Piedmont Virginia Comm Coll (VA)
Portland Comm Coll (OR)
Queensborough Comm Coll of the City U of New York (NY)
Ridgewater Coll (MN)
Rock Valley Coll (IL)
San Jacinto Coll (TX)
San Joaquin Delta Coll (CA)
Seminole State Coll (OK)
Shawnee Comm Coll (IL)
Sierra Coll (CA)
South Suburban Coll (IL)
Southwestern Comm Coll (NC)
Southwest Wisconsin Tech Coll (WI)
Stark State Coll (OH)
Tarrant County Coll District (TX)
Trident Tech Coll (SC)
Westchester Comm Coll (NY)
Western Dakota Tech Inst (SD)
Western Iowa Tech Comm Coll (IA)
Western Nevada Coll (NV)

ACCOUNTING AND BUSINESS/MANAGEMENT
Des Moines Area Comm Coll (IA)

ACCOUNTING AND FINANCE
Fayetteville Tech Comm Coll (NC)
James Sprunt Comm Coll (NC)
Lenoir Comm Coll (NC)
Richmond Comm Coll (NC)
Stark State Coll (OH)

ACCOUNTING RELATED
Northwest State Comm Coll (OH)
Raritan Valley Comm Coll (NJ)

ACCOUNTING TECHNOLOGY AND BOOKKEEPING
Alamance Comm Coll (NC)
Anoka-Ramsey Comm Coll (MN)
Arapahoe Comm Coll (CO)
Austin Comm Coll District (TX)
Bellingham Tech Coll (WA)
Borough of Manhattan Comm Coll of the City U of New York (NY)
Bucks County Comm Coll (PA)
Camden County Coll (NJ)
Cayuga County Comm Coll (NY)
Chandler-Gilbert Comm Coll (AZ)
Chesapeake Coll (MD)
Columbia-Greene Comm Coll (NY)
Comm Coll of Allegheny County (PA)
Comm Coll of Baltimore County (MD)
Comm Coll of Denver (CO)
Danville Area Comm Coll (IL)
Daytona State Coll (FL)
Delta Coll (MI)
Des Moines Area Comm Coll (IA)
Dutchess Comm Coll (NY)
Fiorello H. LaGuardia Comm Coll of the City U of New York (NY)
Florida SouthWestern State Coll (FL)
Front Range Comm Coll (CO)
Fullerton Coll (CA)
Grand Rapids Comm Coll (MI)
Gulf Coast State Coll (FL)
Hagerstown Comm Coll (MD)
Haywood Comm Coll (NC)
Hillsborough Comm Coll (FL)
Hutchinson Comm Coll (KS)
IBMC Coll, Fort Collins (CO)
Jamestown Comm Coll (NY)
Kent State U at Tuscarawas (OH)
Kirtland Comm Coll (MI)
Los Angeles City Coll (CA)
Miami Dade Coll (FL)
MiraCosta Coll (CA)
Montgomery Coll (MD)
Montgomery County Comm Coll (PA)
Nassau Comm Coll (NY)
Northampton Comm Coll (PA)
Northland Comm and Tech Coll (MN)
Northwestern Coll–Chicago Campus (IL)
Northwest-Shoals Comm Coll (AL)
Oakton Comm Coll (IL)
Pensacola State Coll (FL)
Queensborough Comm Coll of the City U of New York (NY)
St. Charles Comm Coll (MO)
San Juan Coll (NM)
Schoolcraft Coll (MI)
South Suburban Coll (IL)
Southwestern Comm Coll (IA)
Southwestern Michigan Coll (MI)
State U of New York Coll of Technology at Alfred (NY)
Union County Coll (NJ)
Vincennes U (IN)
Westchester Comm Coll (NY)
Western Iowa Tech Comm Coll (IA)
Westmoreland County Comm Coll (PA)

ACTING
Northampton Comm Coll (PA)

ADMINISTRATIVE ASSISTANT AND SECRETARIAL SCIENCE
Alvin Comm Coll (TX)
Amarillo Coll (TX)
Anoka Tech Coll (MN)
Austin Comm Coll District (TX)
Bay de Noc Comm Coll (MI)
Bevill State Comm Coll (AL)
Black Hawk Coll, Moline (IL)
Black River Tech Coll (AR)
Blinn Coll (TX)
Borough of Manhattan Comm Coll of the City U of New York (NY)
Bossier Parish Comm Coll (LA)
Camden County Coll (NJ)
Central Lakes Coll (MN)
Central Maine Comm Coll (ME)
Century Coll (MN)
Chandler-Gilbert Comm Coll (AZ)
Citrus Coll (CA)
Clackamas Comm Coll (OR)
Cleveland State Comm Coll (TN)
Coll of DuPage (IL)
Coll of Eastern Idaho (ID)
Collin County Comm Coll District (TX)
Comm Coll of Allegheny County (PA)
Comm Coll of Denver (CO)
Crowder Coll (MO)
De Anza Coll (CA)
Delta Coll (MI)
Eastern Arizona Coll (AZ)
Eastern Gateway Comm Coll (OH)
Fiorello H. LaGuardia Comm Coll of the City U of New York (NY)
Fox Coll (IL)
Fox Valley Tech Coll (WI)
Fullerton Coll (CA)
Greenville Tech Coll (SC)
Harper Coll (IL)
Harrisburg Area Comm Coll (PA)
Hopkinsville Comm Coll (KY)
Housatonic Comm Coll (CT)
Hutchinson Comm Coll (KS)
Iowa Central Comm Coll (IA)
Jamestown Comm Coll (NY)
Kent State U at Tuscarawas (OH)
Kishwaukee Coll (IL)
Lackawanna Coll (PA)
Lakeland Comm Coll (OH)
Los Angeles City Coll (CA)
Los Angeles Mission Coll (CA)
Lurleen B. Wallace Comm Coll (AL)
Luzerne County Comm Coll (PA)
Manchester Comm Coll (CT)
McHenry County Coll (IL)
McLennan Comm Coll (TX)
Meridian Comm Coll (MS)
Mesabi Range Coll (MN)
Middlesex Comm Coll (CT)
Middlesex County Coll (NJ)
Minnesota State Comm and Tech Coll (MN)
Minnesota State Comm and Tech Coll–Detroit Lakes (MN)
Minnesota State Comm and Tech Coll–Moorhead (MN)
MiraCosta Coll (CA)
Mississippi Delta Comm Coll (MS)
Montgomery County Comm Coll (PA)
Morton Coll (IL)
Mt. San Antonio Coll (CA)
Nassau Comm Coll (NY)
Navarro Coll (TX)
Niagara County Comm Coll (NY)
Northampton Comm Coll (PA)
Northeast Iowa Comm Coll (IA)
Northeast State Comm Coll (TN)
Northeast Wisconsin Tech Coll (WI)
North Idaho Coll (ID)
Northland Comm and Tech Coll (MN)
Northwest-Shoals Comm Coll (AL)
Northwest State Comm Coll (OH)
Oakton Comm Coll (IL)
Paris Jr Coll (TX)
Pensacola State Coll (FL)
Portland Comm Coll (OR)
Queensborough Comm Coll of the City U of New York (NY)
Ridgewater Coll (MN)
Rock Valley Coll (IL)
San Jacinto Coll (TX)
Sierra Coll (CA)
South Arkansas Comm Coll (AR)
Springfield Tech Comm Coll (MA)
Stark State Coll (OH)
Tarrant County Coll District (TX)
Trident Tech Coll (SC)
Westchester Comm Coll (NY)
Western Iowa Tech Comm Coll (IA)
Westmoreland County Comm Coll (PA)
Williamsburg Tech Coll (SC)
Wor-Wic Comm Coll (MD)

ADULT DEVELOPMENT AND AGING
Fiorello H. LaGuardia Comm Coll of the City U of New York (NY)
Harrisburg Area Comm Coll (PA)
MiraCosta Coll (CA)

ADVERTISING
Central Ohio Tech Coll (OH)
Mississippi Delta Comm Coll (MS)
Mt. San Antonio Coll (CA)

AERONAUTICAL/AEROSPACE ENGINEERING TECHNOLOGY
Daytona State Coll (FL)

AERONAUTICS/AVIATION/AEROSPACE SCIENCE AND TECHNOLOGY
Alvin Comm Coll (TX)
Comm Coll of Baltimore County (MD)
Hesston Coll (KS)
Miami Dade Coll (FL)

AFRICAN AMERICAN/BLACK STUDIES
Nassau Comm Coll (NY)

AGRIBUSINESS
Crowder Coll (MO)
Edison State Comm Coll (OH)
Iowa Central Comm Coll (IA)
James Sprunt Comm Coll (NC)
Northeast Iowa Comm Coll (IA)
Northwest State Comm Coll (OH)
Ridgewater Coll (MN)
San Jacinto Coll (TX)
Southwestern Comm Coll (IA)
Southwest Wisconsin Tech Coll (WI)
State U of New York Coll of Technology at Alfred (NY)

AGRICULTURAL AND FOOD PRODUCTS PROCESSING
Minnesota State Comm and Tech Coll (MN)
Northeast Iowa Comm Coll (IA)

AGRICULTURAL BUSINESS AND MANAGEMENT
Black Hawk Coll, Moline (IL)
Danville Area Comm Coll (IL)
Dawson Comm Coll (MT)
Iowa Central Comm Coll (IA)
Lake Area Tech Inst (SD)
Lake Region State Coll (ND)
Mississippi Delta Comm Coll (MS)
Mt. San Antonio Coll (CA)
North Dakota State Coll of Science (ND)
Northeastern Jr Coll (CO)
Pensacola State Coll (FL)
Rend Lake Coll (IL)
San Joaquin Delta Coll (CA)
Shawnee Comm Coll (IL)
Vincennes U (IN)
Western Iowa Tech Comm Coll (IA)

AGRICULTURAL BUSINESS AND MANAGEMENT RELATED
Penn State DuBois (PA)
Penn State Fayette, The Eberly Campus (PA)
Penn State Mont Alto (PA)

AGRICULTURAL BUSINESS TECHNOLOGY
North Dakota State Coll of Science (ND)

AGRICULTURAL ECONOMICS
Mississippi Delta Comm Coll (MS)

AGRICULTURAL/FARM SUPPLIES RETAILING AND WHOLESALING
Des Moines Area Comm Coll (IA)
Fox Valley Tech Coll (WI)
Hawkeye Comm Coll (IA)
Southwest Wisconsin Tech Coll (WI)
Western Iowa Tech Comm Coll (IA)

AGRICULTURAL MECHANICS AND EQUIPMENT TECHNOLOGY
Black Hawk Coll, Moline (IL)
Hutchinson Comm Coll (KS)
North Dakota State Coll of Science (ND)
Northland Comm and Tech Coll (MN)
Rend Lake Coll (IL)
State U of New York Coll of Technology at Alfred (NY)

AGRICULTURAL MECHANIZATION
Crowder Coll (MO)
Fox Valley Tech Coll (WI)
Kishwaukee Coll (IL)
Navarro Coll (TX)
Rend Lake Coll (IL)
San Joaquin Delta Coll (CA)
Southwest Texas Jr Coll (TX)
State Tech Coll of Missouri (MO)

AGRICULTURAL POWER MACHINERY OPERATION
Hawkeye Comm Coll (IA)
Northeast Iowa Comm Coll (IA)
Portland Comm Coll (OR)

AGRICULTURAL PRODUCTION
Black Hawk Coll, Moline (IL)
Chesapeake Coll (MD)
Hopkinsville Comm Coll (KY)
Northeast Iowa Comm Coll (IA)
Owensboro Comm and Tech Coll (KY)
Rend Lake Coll (IL)
Ridgewater Coll (MN)
Southwestern Michigan Coll (MI)

AGRICULTURAL TEACHER EDUCATION
Iowa Central Comm Coll (IA)
Lenoir Comm Coll (NC)
Northeastern Jr Coll (CO)

AGRICULTURE
Austin Comm Coll District (TX)
Black Hawk Coll, Moline (IL)
Blinn Coll (TX)
Central Oregon Comm Coll (OR)
Crowder Coll (MO)
Dyersburg State Comm Coll (TN)
Feather River Coll (CA)
Hutchinson Comm Coll (KS)
Kaskaskia Coll (IL)
Miami Dade Coll (FL)
Mt. San Antonio Coll (CA)
Northeastern Jr Coll (CO)
Northland Comm and Tech Coll (MN)
Paris Jr Coll (TX)
Pensacola State Coll (FL)
Ridgewater Coll (MN)
St. Charles Comm Coll (MO)
San Jacinto Coll (TX)
San Joaquin Delta Coll (CA)
Sierra Coll (CA)
State U of New York Coll of Technology at Alfred (NY)

AGRICULTURE AND AGRICULTURE OPERATIONS RELATED
Delta Coll (MI)

AGROECOLOGY AND SUSTAINABLE AGRICULTURE
Austin Comm Coll District (TX)
Lenoir Comm Coll (NC)
Northeast Wisconsin Tech Coll (WI)
Southern Maine Comm Coll (ME)

AGRONOMY AND CROP SCIENCE
Fox Valley Tech Coll (WI)
Iowa Central Comm Coll (IA)
Northeastern Jr Coll (CO)
Ridgewater Coll (MN)
Southwest Wisconsin Tech Coll (WI)
Western Iowa Tech Comm Coll (IA)

AIRCRAFT POWERPLANT TECHNOLOGY
Black River Tech Coll (AR)
Chandler-Gilbert Comm Coll (AZ)
Lake Area Tech Inst (SD)
Northeast State Comm Coll (TN)
Somerset Comm Coll (KY)
State Tech Coll of Missouri (MO)
Vincennes U (IN)

AIRFRAME MECHANICS AND AIRCRAFT MAINTENANCE TECHNOLOGY
Amarillo Coll (TX)
Chandler-Gilbert Comm Coll (AZ)
Craven Comm Coll (NC)
Mt. San Antonio Coll (CA)
Northland Comm and Tech Coll (MN)
Portland Comm Coll (OR)
Trident Tech Coll (SC)

AIRLINE PILOT AND FLIGHT CREW
Central Oregon Comm Coll (OR)
Chandler-Gilbert Comm Coll (AZ)
Comm Coll of Allegheny County (PA)
Comm Coll of Baltimore County (MD)
Dutchess Comm Coll (NY)
Fox Valley Tech Coll (WI)
Hesston Coll (KS)
Kishwaukee Coll (IL)
Lake Area Tech Inst (SD)
Lenoir Comm Coll (NC)
Miami Dade Coll (FL)
Mt. San Antonio Coll (CA)
Portland Comm Coll (OR)
Vincennes U (IN)

AIR TRAFFIC CONTROL
Comm Coll of Baltimore County (MD)
Hesston Coll (KS)
Miami Dade Coll (FL)
Mt. San Antonio Coll (CA)

ALLIED HEALTH AND MEDICAL ASSISTING SERVICES RELATED
Blue Ridge Comm and Tech Coll (WV)
Mount Wachusett Comm Coll (MA)
Raritan Valley Comm Coll (NJ)
Southern Maine Comm Coll (ME)

ALTERNATIVE AND COMPLEMENTARY MEDICAL SUPPORT SERVICES RELATED
Mount Wachusett Comm Coll (MA)

ALTERNATIVE FUEL VEHICLE TECHNOLOGY
Central Oregon Comm Coll (OR)

AMERICAN INDIAN/NATIVE AMERICAN STUDIES
Chandler-Gilbert Comm Coll (AZ)
North Idaho Coll (ID)
San Juan Coll (NM)

AMERICAN SIGN LANGUAGE (ASL)
Bristol Comm Coll (MA)
Montgomery Coll (MD)
Sierra Coll (CA)
Union County Coll (NJ)
Vincennes U (IN)

AMERICAN STUDIES
Miami Dade Coll (FL)
Mississippi Delta Comm Coll (MS)

ANESTHESIOLOGIST ASSISTANT
Comm Coll of Allegheny County (PA)
Comm Coll of Baltimore County (MD)

ANIMAL/LIVESTOCK HUSBANDRY AND PRODUCTION
Fox Valley Tech Coll (WI)
Hawkeye Comm Coll (IA)
James Sprunt Comm Coll (NC)
Mt. San Antonio Coll (CA)
Ridgewater Coll (MN)
Sierra Coll (CA)
Southwest Wisconsin Tech Coll (WI)

ANIMAL SCIENCES
Alamance Comm Coll (NC)
Iowa Central Comm Coll (IA)
James Sprunt Comm Coll (NC)
Kaskaskia Coll (IL)
Mt. San Antonio Coll (CA)
Niagara County Comm Coll (NY)
North Dakota State Coll of Science (ND)
Northeastern Jr Coll (CO)
San Joaquin Delta Coll (CA)
Westchester Comm Coll (NY)

ANIMATION, INTERACTIVE TECHNOLOGY, VIDEO GRAPHICS AND SPECIAL EFFECTS
Austin Comm Coll District (TX)
Borough of Manhattan Comm Coll of the City U of New York (NY)
Century Coll (MN)
Front Range Comm Coll (CO)
Hagerstown Comm Coll (MD)
Houston Comm Coll (TX)
McHenry County Coll (IL)
Miami Dade Coll (FL)
Montgomery Coll (MD)
Raritan Valley Comm Coll (NJ)
Springfield Tech Comm Coll (MA)
State U of New York Coll of Technology at Alfred (NY)
Western Iowa Tech Comm Coll (IA)
West Kentucky Comm and Tech Coll (KY)

ANTHROPOLOGY
Austin Comm Coll District (TX)
Blinn Coll (TX)
Central Oregon Comm Coll (OR)
Chandler-Gilbert Comm Coll (AZ)
Eastern Arizona Coll (AZ)
Feather River Coll (CA)
Fullerton Coll (CA)
Houston Comm Coll (TX)
Miami Dade Coll (FL)
Northeastern Jr Coll (CO)
North Idaho Coll (ID)
San Joaquin Delta Coll (CA)
Truckee Meadows Comm Coll (NV)

APPAREL AND ACCESSORIES MARKETING
Des Moines Area Comm Coll (IA)

APPAREL AND TEXTILE MANUFACTURING
Sierra Coll (CA)

APPAREL AND TEXTILE MARKETING MANAGEMENT
Fullerton Coll (CA)
Sierra Coll (CA)

APPAREL AND TEXTILES
Fullerton Coll (CA)
Mt. San Antonio Coll (CA)

APPLIED BEHAVIOR ANALYSIS
Montgomery County Comm Coll (PA)

APPLIED HORTICULTURE/ HORTICULTURAL BUSINESS SERVICES RELATED
Des Moines Area Comm Coll (IA)

APPLIED HORTICULTURE/ HORTICULTURE OPERATIONS
Alamance Comm Coll (NC)
Black Hawk Coll, Moline (IL)
Central Lakes Coll (MN)
Century Coll (MN)
Clackamas Comm Coll (OR)
Comm Coll of Baltimore County (MD)
Fayetteville Tech Comm Coll (NC)
Front Range Comm Coll (CO)
Fullerton Coll (CA)
Haywood Comm Coll (NC)
Houston Comm Coll (TX)
Kaskaskia Coll (IL)
Kishwaukee Coll (IL)
Lenoir Comm Coll (NC)
Mayland Comm Coll (NC)
McHenry County Coll (IL)
Montgomery Coll (MD)
Mt. San Antonio Coll (CA)
Sierra Coll (CA)
Vincennes U (IN)

APPLIED PSYCHOLOGY
Northampton Comm Coll (PA)

AQUACULTURE
Hillsborough Comm Coll (FL)

ARABIC
Austin Comm Coll District (TX)

ARCHEOLOGY
Austin Comm Coll District (TX)

ARCHITECTURAL AND BUILDING SCIENCES
Blinn Coll (TX)
Springfield Tech Comm Coll (MA)

ARCHITECTURAL DRAFTING AND CAD/CADD
Anoka Tech Coll (MN)
Benjamin Franklin Inst of Technology (MA)
Central Ohio Tech Coll (OH)
Clackamas Comm Coll (OR)
Comm Coll of Allegheny County (PA)
Comm Coll of Baltimore County (MD)
Des Moines Area Comm Coll (IA)
Harper Coll (IL)
Hutchinson Comm Coll (KS)
Kaskaskia Coll (IL)
Miami Dade Coll (FL)
Minnesota State Comm and Tech Coll (MN)
Minnesota State Comm and Tech Coll–Detroit Lakes (MN)
Montgomery Coll (MD)
Northland Comm and Tech Coll (MN)
Oakton Comm Coll (IL)
Portland Comm Coll (OR)
Queensborough Comm Coll of the City U of New York (NY)
Rend Lake Coll (IL)
Sierra Coll (CA)
South Suburban Coll (IL)
Truckee Meadows Comm Coll (NV)
Vincennes U (IN)
Westmoreland County Comm Coll (PA)

ARCHITECTURAL ENGINEERING
Luzerne County Comm Coll (PA)

ARCHITECTURAL ENGINEERING TECHNOLOGY
Amarillo Coll (TX)
Arapahoe Comm Coll (CO)
Benjamin Franklin Inst of Technology (MA)
Coll of The Albemarle (NC)
Delta Coll (MI)
Dutchess Comm Coll (NY)
Fayetteville Tech Comm Coll (NC)
Front Range Comm Coll (CO)
Greenville Tech Coll (SC)
Harper Coll (IL)
Harrisburg Area Comm Coll (PA)
Hillsborough Comm Coll (FL)
Luzerne County Comm Coll (PA)
Miami Dade Coll (FL)
Mississippi Delta Comm Coll (MS)
Mt. San Antonio Coll (CA)
Northampton Comm Coll (PA)
North Dakota State Coll of Science (ND)
Northeast Wisconsin Tech Coll (WI)
Penn State Fayette, The Eberly Campus (PA)
State U of New York Coll of Technology at Alfred (NY)
Tarrant County Coll District (TX)
Western Iowa Tech Comm Coll (IA)

ARCHITECTURAL TECHNOLOGY
Dunwoody Coll of Technology (MN)
Florida SouthWestern State Coll (FL)
Fullerton Coll (CA)
Grand Rapids Comm Coll (MI)
Hillsborough Comm Coll (FL)
Miami Dade Coll (FL)
Minnesota State Comm and Tech Coll–Detroit Lakes (MN)
MiraCosta Coll (CA)
Pensacola State Coll (FL)

ARCHITECTURE
Grand Rapids Comm Coll (MI)
Truckee Meadows Comm Coll (NV)

AREA STUDIES RELATED
Fullerton Coll (CA)

ART
Alvin Comm Coll (TX)
Amarillo Coll (TX)
Anoka-Ramsey Comm Coll (MN)
Austin Comm Coll District (TX)
Cayuga County Comm Coll (NY)
Central Oregon Comm Coll (OR)
Century Coll (MN)
Citrus Coll (CA)
Coll of The Albemarle (NC)
Comm Coll of Allegheny County (PA)
Crowder Coll (MO)
Danville Area Comm Coll (IL)
De Anza Coll (CA)
Dutchess Comm Coll (NY)
Eastern Arizona Coll (AZ)
Edison State Comm Coll (OH)
Fullerton Coll (CA)
Galveston Coll (TX)
Grand Rapids Comm Coll (MI)
Harper Coll (IL)
Housatonic Comm Coll (CT)
Kishwaukee Coll (IL)
Los Angeles City Coll (CA)
Miami Dade Coll (FL)
Minnesota State Comm and Tech Coll (MN)
MiraCosta Coll (CA)
Montgomery Coll (MD)
Montgomery County Comm Coll (PA)
Morton Coll (IL)
Mount Wachusett Comm Coll (MA)
Nassau Comm Coll (NY)
Navarro Coll (TX)
Northeastern Jr Coll (CO)
North Idaho Coll (ID)
Paris Jr Coll (TX)
Pensacola State Coll (FL)
Piedmont Virginia Comm Coll (VA)
Queensborough Comm Coll of the City U of New York (NY)
San Jacinto Coll (TX)
San Joaquin Delta Coll (CA)
Seminole State Coll (OK)
Sierra Coll (CA)
Vincennes U (IN)
Westchester Comm Coll (NY)

ART HISTORY, CRITICISM AND CONSERVATION
Austin Comm Coll District (TX)
Borough of Manhattan Comm Coll of the City U of New York (NY)
Bucks County Comm Coll (PA)
De Anza Coll (CA)
Northeastern Jr Coll (CO)

ARTS, ENTERTAINMENT, AND MEDIA MANAGEMENT
Central Maine Comm Coll (ME)
Schoolcraft Coll (MI)

ART TEACHER EDUCATION
Danville Area Comm Coll (IL)
McLennan Comm Coll (TX)
Mississippi Delta Comm Coll (MS)
Pensacola State Coll (FL)
Vincennes U (IN)

ASIAN STUDIES
Miami Dade Coll (FL)

ASTRONOMY
Chandler-Gilbert Comm Coll (AZ)
Fullerton Coll (CA)
North Idaho Coll (ID)

ATHLETIC TRAINING
Northampton Comm Coll (PA)
North Idaho Coll (ID)

AUDIOLOGY AND SPEECH-LANGUAGE PATHOLOGY
Miami Dade Coll (FL)

AUDIOVISUAL COMMUNICATIONS TECHNOLOGIES RELATED
Bossier Parish Comm Coll (LA)

AUTOBODY/COLLISION AND REPAIR TECHNOLOGY
Austin Comm Coll District (TX)
Bellingham Tech Coll (WA)
Century Coll (MN)
Clackamas Comm Coll (OR)
Crowder Coll (MO)
Des Moines Area Comm Coll (IA)
Dunwoody Coll of Technology (MN)
Fayetteville Tech Comm Coll (NC)
Fox Valley Tech Coll (WI)
Greenville Tech Coll (SC)
Hawkeye Comm Coll (IA)
Haywood Comm Coll (NC)
Hutchinson Comm Coll (KS)
Iowa Central Comm Coll (IA)
Kishwaukee Coll (IL)
Lake Area Tech Inst (SD)
Lenoir Comm Coll (NC)
Minnesota State Comm and Tech Coll (MN)
North Dakota State Coll of Science (ND)
Northeast Wisconsin Tech Coll (WI)
Northland Comm and Tech Coll (MN)
Ohio Tech Coll (OH)
Portland Comm Coll (OR)
Ridgewater Coll (MN)
San Jacinto Coll (TX)

San Juan Coll (NM)
Southwestern Comm Coll (IA)
Southwest Texas Jr Coll (TX)
State Tech Coll of Missouri (MO)
State U of New York Coll of Technology at Alfred (NY)
Vincennes U (IN)
Western Iowa Tech Comm Coll (IA)

AUTOMATION ENGINEER TECHNOLOGY
Alexandria Tech and Comm Coll (MN)
Arapahoe Comm Coll (CO)
Blue Ridge Comm and Tech Coll (WV)
Cleveland Comm Coll (NC)
Dyersburg State Comm Coll (TN)
Fox Valley Tech Coll (WI)
Front Range Comm Coll (CO)
Grand Rapids Comm Coll (MI)
Gulf Coast State Coll (FL)
Hawkeye Comm Coll (IA)
Hutchinson Comm Coll (KS)
Miami Dade Coll (FL)
Northland Comm and Tech Coll (MN)
Quinsigamond Comm Coll (MA)
Southwestern Michigan Coll (MI)
Vincennes U (IN)

AUTOMOBILE/AUTOMOTIVE MECHANICS TECHNOLOGY
Alamance Comm Coll (NC)
Alvin Comm Coll (TX)
Amarillo Coll (TX)
Anoka Tech Coll (MN)
Arapahoe Comm Coll (CO)
Asheville-Buncombe Tech Comm Coll (NC)
Austin Comm Coll District (TX)
Bay de Noc Comm Coll (MI)
Bellingham Tech Coll (WA)
Benjamin Franklin Inst of Technology (MA)
Black Hawk Coll, Moline (IL)
Central Oregon Comm Coll (OR)
Citrus Coll (CA)
Clackamas Comm Coll (OR)
Coll of DuPage (IL)
Coll of Eastern Idaho (ID)
Columbia-Greene Comm Coll (NY)
Comm Coll of Allegheny County (PA)
Comm Coll of Baltimore County (MD)
Craven Comm Coll (NC)
Crowder Coll (MO)
Danville Area Comm Coll (IL)
De Anza Coll (CA)
Delta Coll (MI)
Des Moines Area Comm Coll (IA)
Dunwoody Coll of Technology (MN)
Eastern Arizona Coll (AZ)
Fayetteville Tech Comm Coll (NC)
Fox Valley Tech Coll (WI)
Front Range Comm Coll (CO)
Fullerton Coll (CA)
Gateway Comm and Tech Coll (KY)
Grand Rapids Comm Coll (MI)
Greenville Tech Coll (SC)
Halifax Comm Coll (NC)
Harrisburg Area Comm Coll (PA)
Hawkeye Comm Coll (IA)
Haywood Comm Coll (NC)
Houston Comm Coll (TX)
Hutchinson Comm Coll (KS)
Iowa Central Comm Coll (IA)
Kaskaskia Coll (IL)
Kirtland Comm Coll (MI)
Kishwaukee Coll (IL)
Lake Area Tech Inst (SD)
Lake Region State Coll (ND)
Lenoir Comm Coll (NC)
Luzerne County Comm Coll (PA)
Minnesota State Comm and Tech Coll (MN)
Minnesota State Comm and Tech Coll–Moorhead (MN)
Montgomery Coll (MD)
Montgomery County Comm Coll (PA)
Morton Coll (IL)
Mount Wachusett Comm Coll (MA)
Northampton Comm Coll (PA)
North Dakota State Coll of Science (ND)
Northeastern Jr Coll (CO)
Northeast Iowa Comm Coll (IA)
Northeast Wisconsin Tech Coll (WI)
North Idaho Coll (ID)
Northland Comm and Tech Coll (MN)
Oakton Comm Coll (IL)
Ohio Tech Coll (OH)
Oklahoma State U Inst of Technology (OK)
Owensboro Comm and Tech Coll (KY)
Portland Comm Coll (OR)
Quinsigamond Comm Coll (MA)
Rend Lake Coll (IL)
Ridgewater Coll (MN)
Rock Valley Coll (IL)
San Jacinto Coll (TX)
San Joaquin Delta Coll (CA)
San Juan Coll (NM)
Shawnee Comm Coll (IL)
Sierra Coll (CA)
Southern Maine Comm Coll (ME)
Southwestern Comm Coll (IA)
Southwestern Comm Coll (NC)
Southwestern Michigan Coll (MI)
Southwest Texas Jr Coll (TX)
Springfield Tech Comm Coll (MA)
State Tech Coll of Missouri (MO)
State U of New York Coll of Technology at Alfred (NY)
Tarrant County Coll District (TX)
Trident Tech Coll (SC)
Truckee Meadows Comm Coll (NV)
Union County Coll (NJ)
Vincennes U (IN)
Western Iowa Tech Comm Coll (IA)
Western Nevada Coll (NV)
West Kentucky Comm and Tech Coll (KY)

AUTOMOTIVE ENGINEERING TECHNOLOGY
Benjamin Franklin Inst of Technology (MA)
Camden County Coll (NJ)
Comm Coll of Allegheny County (PA)
Middlesex County Coll (NJ)
Minnesota State Comm and Tech Coll–Moorhead (MN)
Raritan Valley Comm Coll (NJ)

AVIATION/AIRWAY MANAGEMENT
Coll of The Albemarle (NC)
Comm Coll of Allegheny County (PA)
Comm Coll of Baltimore County (MD)
Dutchess Comm Coll (NY)
Miami Dade Coll (FL)

AVIONICS MAINTENANCE TECHNOLOGY
Fox Valley Tech Coll (WI)
Housatonic Comm Coll (CT)
Mt. San Antonio Coll (CA)
Rock Valley Coll (IL)
Tarrant County Coll District (TX)

BAKING AND PASTRY ARTS
Asheville-Buncombe Tech Comm Coll (NC)
Blue Ridge Comm and Tech Coll (WV)
Bucks County Comm Coll (PA)
Central Oregon Comm Coll (OR)
Coll of DuPage (IL)
Collin County Comm Coll District (TX)
Luzerne County Comm Coll (PA)
Montgomery County Comm Coll (PA)
Niagara County Comm Coll (NY)
San Jacinto Coll (TX)
Westmoreland County Comm Coll (PA)

BANKING AND FINANCIAL SUPPORT SERVICES
Alamance Comm Coll (NC)
Bristol Comm Coll (MA)
Comm Coll of Allegheny County (PA)
Craven Comm Coll (NC)
Edison State Comm Coll (OH)
Fox Valley Tech Coll (WI)
Harper Coll (IL)
Houston Comm Coll (TX)
Lackawanna Coll (PA)
Lake Area Tech Inst (SD)
Los Angeles City Coll (CA)
Luzerne County Comm Coll (PA)
Miami Dade Coll (FL)
Minnesota State Comm and Tech Coll (MN)
Oakton Comm Coll (IL)
Westmoreland County Comm Coll (PA)

BARBERING
Rend Lake Coll (IL)

BEHAVIORAL SCIENCES
Amarillo Coll (TX)
Citrus Coll (CA)
De Anza Coll (CA)
Galveston Coll (TX)
Miami Dade Coll (FL)
Mississippi Delta Comm Coll (MS)
San Jacinto Coll (TX)
Seminole State Coll (OK)
Vincennes U (IN)

BIBLICAL STUDIES
Amarillo Coll (TX)
Elim Bible Inst and Coll (NY)
Hesston Coll (KS)

BIOCHEMISTRY
Chandler-Gilbert Comm Coll (AZ)
Pensacola State Coll (FL)

BIOCHEMISTRY AND MOLECULAR BIOLOGY
Minnesota State Comm and Tech Coll (MN)

BIOCHEMISTRY, BIOPHYSICS AND MOLECULAR BIOLOGY RELATED
Bay de Noc Comm Coll (MI)

BIOENGINEERING AND BIOMEDICAL ENGINEERING
Anoka-Ramsey Comm Coll (MN)
Benjamin Franklin Inst of Technology (MA)

BIOLOGICAL AND BIOMEDICAL SCIENCES RELATED
Seminole State Coll (OK)
Vincennes U (IN)

BIOLOGICAL AND PHYSICAL SCIENCES
Black Hawk Coll, Moline (IL)
Central Oregon Comm Coll (OR)
Citrus Coll (CA)
Coll of DuPage (IL)
Comm Coll of Baltimore County (MD)
Danville Area Comm Coll (IL)
Fullerton Coll (CA)
Galveston Coll (TX)
Kaskaskia Coll (IL)
Kishwaukee Coll (IL)
Los Angeles City Coll (CA)
Luzerne County Comm Coll (PA)
McHenry County Coll (IL)
Middlesex Comm Coll (CT)
MiraCosta Coll (CA)
Morton Coll (IL)
Mt. San Antonio Coll (CA)
Navarro Coll (TX)
Niagara County Comm Coll (NY)
North Idaho Coll (ID)
Oakton Comm Coll (IL)
Paris Jr Coll (TX)
Penn State DuBois (PA)
Penn State Fayette, The Eberly Campus (PA)
Rend Lake Coll (IL)
Shawnee Comm Coll (IL)
Sierra Coll (CA)
South Suburban Coll (IL)
Trident Tech Coll (SC)
Weatherford Coll (TX)

BIOLOGY/BIOLOGICAL SCIENCES
Alvin Comm Coll (TX)
Amarillo Coll (TX)
Anoka-Ramsey Comm Coll (MN)
Austin Comm Coll District (TX)
Blinn Coll (TX)
Bristol Comm Coll (MA)
Central Maine Comm Coll (ME)
Central Oregon Comm Coll (OR)
Century Coll (MN)
Chandler-Gilbert Comm Coll (AZ)
Chesapeake Coll (MD)
Citrus Coll (CA)
Comm Coll of Allegheny County (PA)
Crowder Coll (MO)
De Anza Coll (CA)
Eastern Arizona Coll (AZ)
Edison State Comm Coll (OH)
Feather River Coll (CA)
Fiorello H. LaGuardia Comm Coll of the City U of New York (NY)
Fullerton Coll (CA)
Galveston Coll (TX)
Harper Coll (IL)
Harrisburg Area Comm Coll (PA)
Houston Comm Coll (TX)
Hutchinson Comm Coll (KS)
Iowa Central Comm Coll (IA)
Lackawanna Coll (PA)
Los Angeles Mission Coll (CA)
Miami Dade Coll (FL)
Minnesota State Comm and Tech Coll (MN)
Minnesota State Comm and Tech Coll–Moorhead (MN)
Mississippi Delta Comm Coll (MS)
Mount Wachusett Comm Coll (MA)
Navarro Coll (TX)
Northampton Comm Coll (PA)
Northeastern Jr Coll (CO)
Northern Essex Comm Coll (MA)
North Idaho Coll (ID)
Paris Jr Coll (TX)
Pensacola State Coll (FL)
Quinsigamond Comm Coll (MA)
Ridgewater Coll (MN)
St. Charles Comm Coll (MO)
San Jacinto Coll (TX)
San Joaquin Delta Coll (CA)
San Juan Coll (NM)
Seminole State Coll (OK)
Sierra Coll (CA)
Springfield Tech Comm Coll (MA)
State U of New York Coll of Technology at Alfred (NY)
Tohono O'odham Comm Coll (AZ)
Truckee Meadows Comm Coll (NV)
Union County Coll (NJ)
Westmoreland County Comm Coll (PA)
Wor-Wic Comm Coll (MD)

BIOLOGY/BIOTECHNOLOGY LABORATORY TECHNICIAN
Asheville-Buncombe Tech Comm Coll (NC)
Austin Comm Coll District (TX)
Blinn Coll (TX)
Bucks County Comm Coll (PA)
Camden County Coll (NJ)
Florida SouthWestern State Coll (FL)
Fox Valley Tech Coll (WI)
Hagerstown Comm Coll (MD)
Houston Comm Coll (TX)
Jamestown Comm Coll (NY)
Lackawanna Coll (PA)
Middlesex Comm Coll (CT)
Middlesex County Coll (NJ)
Montgomery Coll (MD)
Montgomery County Comm Coll (PA)
Northeast Wisconsin Tech Coll (WI)
Portland Comm Coll (OR)

BIOMEDICAL TECHNOLOGY
Anoka-Ramsey Comm Coll (MN)
Anoka Tech Coll (MN)
Austin Comm Coll District (TX)
Benjamin Franklin Inst of Technology (MA)
Des Moines Area Comm Coll (IA)
Fullerton Coll (CA)
Miami Dade Coll (FL)
MiraCosta Coll (CA)
Northeast Wisconsin Tech Coll (WI)
Penn State DuBois (PA)
Penn State Fayette, The Eberly Campus (PA)
Rend Lake Coll (IL)
Schoolcraft Coll (MI)
Stark State Coll (OH)
Western Iowa Tech Comm Coll (IA)

BIOTECHNOLOGY
Alamance Comm Coll (NC)
Borough of Manhattan Comm Coll of the City U of New York (NY)
Cleveland Comm Coll (NC)
Coll of The Albemarle (NC)
Comm Coll of Allegheny County (PA)
Hillsborough Comm Coll (FL)
Lakeland Comm Coll (OH)
Miami Dade Coll (FL)
Middlesex County Coll (NJ)
Montgomery County Comm Coll (PA)
Mount Wachusett Comm Coll (MA)
Northampton Comm Coll (PA)
Piedmont Virginia Comm Coll (VA)
Queensborough Comm Coll of the City U of New York (NY)
Quinsigamond Comm Coll (MA)
Southern Maine Comm Coll (ME)
Springfield Tech Comm Coll (MA)

BOTANY/PLANT BIOLOGY
North Idaho Coll (ID)
Pensacola State Coll (FL)

BROADCAST JOURNALISM
Amarillo Coll (TX)
Meridian Comm Coll (MS)
Middlesex Comm Coll (CT)
San Joaquin Delta Coll (CA)

BUILDING/CONSTRUCTION FINISHING, MANAGEMENT, AND INSPECTION RELATED
Comm Coll of Baltimore County (MD)
Delta Coll (MI)
Fayetteville Tech Comm Coll (NC)
Haywood Comm Coll (NC)
Montgomery Coll (MD)
Mt. San Antonio Coll (CA)
Oakton Comm Coll (IL)
Springfield Tech Comm Coll (MA)
Vincennes U (IN)

BUILDING/CONSTRUCTION SITE MANAGEMENT
Arapahoe Comm Coll (CO)
Comm Coll of Baltimore County (MD)
Dunwoody Coll of Technology (MN)
Fox Valley Tech Coll (WI)
Fullerton Coll (CA)
Minnesota State Comm and Tech Coll (MN)
Northeast Wisconsin Tech Coll (WI)

BUILDING CONSTRUCTION TECHNOLOGY
Central Maine Comm Coll (ME)
Comm Coll of Allegheny County (PA)
Lake Area Tech Inst (SD)
North Dakota State Coll of Science (ND)
Southern Maine Comm Coll (ME)
Western Nevada Coll (NV)

BUILDING/HOME/ CONSTRUCTION INSPECTION
Fullerton Coll (CA)
Portland Comm Coll (OR)
South Suburban Coll (IL)

BUILDING/PROPERTY MAINTENANCE
Asheville-Buncombe Tech Comm Coll (NC)
Bellingham Tech Coll (WA)
Central Maine Comm Coll (ME)
Century Coll (MN)
Coll of DuPage (IL)
Comm Coll of Allegheny County (PA)
Delta Coll (MI)
Luzerne County Comm Coll (PA)
Owensboro Comm and Tech Coll (KY)
Pensacola State Coll (FL)

BUSINESS ADMINISTRATION AND MANAGEMENT
Adirondack Comm Coll (NY)
Alamance Comm Coll (NC)
Alexandria Tech and Comm Coll (MN)
Alvin Comm Coll (TX)
Amarillo Coll (TX)
Anoka-Ramsey Comm Coll (MN)
Arapahoe Comm Coll (CO)
Asheville-Buncombe Tech Comm Coll (NC)
Austin Comm Coll District (TX)
Bay de Noc Comm Coll (MI)
Blinn Coll (TX)
Blue Ridge Comm and Tech Coll (WV)
Borough of Manhattan Comm Coll of the City U of New York (NY)
Bristol Comm Coll (MA)
Bucks County Comm Coll (PA)
Camden County Coll (NJ)
Cayuga County Comm Coll (NY)
Central Lakes Coll (MN)
Central Maine Comm Coll (ME)
Central Ohio Tech Coll (OH)
Central Oregon Comm Coll (OR)
Century Coll (MN)
Chandler-Gilbert Comm Coll (AZ)
Chesapeake Coll (MD)
Citrus Coll (CA)
Cleveland Comm Coll (NC)
Cleveland State Comm Coll (TN)
Coll of DuPage (IL)
Coll of The Albemarle (NC)
The Coll of Westchester (NY)
Collin County Comm Coll District (TX)
Columbia-Greene Comm Coll (NY)
Comm Coll of Allegheny County (PA)
Comm Coll of Baltimore County (MD)
Comm Coll of Denver (CO)
Craven Comm Coll (NC)
Crowder Coll (MO)
Daytona State Coll (FL)

De Anza Coll (CA)
Delta Coll (MI)
Des Moines Area Comm Coll (IA)
Donnelly Coll (KS)
Dutchess Comm Coll (NY)
Dyersburg State Comm Coll (TN)
Eastern Arizona Coll (AZ)
Eastern Gateway Comm Coll (OH)
Edison State Comm Coll (OH)
Fayetteville Tech Comm Coll (NC)
Fiorello H. LaGuardia Comm Coll of the City U of New York (NY)
Florida SouthWestern State Coll (FL)
Fox Valley Tech Coll (WI)
Front Range Comm Coll (CO)
Fullerton Coll (CA)
Galveston Coll (TX)
Gateway Comm and Tech Coll (KY)
Grand Rapids Comm Coll (MI)
Greenville Tech Coll (SC)
Gulf Coast State Coll (FL)
Hagerstown Comm Coll (MD)
Halifax Comm Coll (NC)
Harper Coll (IL)
Harrisburg Area Comm Coll (PA)
Haywood Comm Coll (NC)
Hesston Coll (KS)
Hillsborough Comm Coll (FL)
Hopkinsville Comm Coll (KY)
Housatonic Comm Coll (CT)
Houston Comm Coll (TX)
IBMC Coll, Fort Collins (CO)
Iowa Central Comm Coll (IA)
James Sprunt Comm Coll (NC)
Jamestown Comm Coll (NY)
Kirtland Comm Coll (MI)
Kishwaukee Coll (IL)
Lackawanna Coll (PA)
Lakeland Comm Coll (OH)
Lake Region State Coll (ND)
Lenoir Comm Coll (NC)
Los Angeles City Coll (CA)
Los Angeles Mission Coll (CA)
Luzerne County Comm Coll (PA)
Manchester Comm Coll (CT)
Mayland Comm Coll (NC)
Maysville Comm and Tech Coll, Maysville (KY)
McHenry County Coll (IL)
McLennan Comm Coll (TX)
Miami Dade Coll (FL)
Middlesex Comm Coll (CT)
Middlesex County Coll (NJ)
Minnesota State Comm and Tech Coll (MN)
Minnesota State Comm and Tech Coll–Moorhead (MN)
MiraCosta Coll (CA)
Montgomery County Comm Coll (PA)
Morton Coll (IL)
Motlow State Comm Coll (TN)
Mt. San Antonio Coll (CA)
Mount Wachusett Comm Coll (MA)
Nassau Comm Coll (NY)
Navarro Coll (TX)
Niagara County Comm Coll (NY)
Northampton Comm Coll (PA)
North Dakota State Coll of Science (ND)
Northeastern Jr Coll (CO)
Northeast Iowa Comm Coll (IA)
Northeast State Comm Coll (TN)
Northeast Wisconsin Tech Coll (WI)
Northern Essex Comm Coll (MA)
North Idaho Coll (ID)
Northland Comm and Tech Coll (MN)
Northwestern Coll–Chicago Campus (IL)
Northwest State Comm Coll (OH)
Owensboro Comm and Tech Coll (KY)
Paris Jr Coll (TX)
Pensacola State Coll (FL)
Piedmont Comm Coll (NC)
Piedmont Virginia Comm Coll (VA)
Portland Comm Coll (OR)
Queensborough Comm Coll of the City U of New York (NY)
Quinsigamond Comm Coll (MA)
Raritan Valley Comm Coll (NJ)
Richmond Comm Coll (NC)
Ridgewater Coll (MN)
Rock Valley Coll (IL)
San Jacinto Coll (TX)
San Joaquin Delta Coll (CA)
San Juan Coll (NM)
Schoolcraft Coll (MI)
Seminole State Coll (OK)
Shawnee Comm Coll (IL)
Sierra Coll (CA)
Somerset Comm Coll (KY)
Southern Maine Comm Coll (ME)
Southwestern Comm Coll (IA)
Southwestern Comm Coll (NC)
Southwestern Michigan Coll (MI)
Southwest Texas Jr Coll (TX)
Springfield Tech Comm Coll (MA)
Stark State Coll (OH)
State U of New York Coll of Technology at Alfred (NY)
Tarrant County Coll District (TX)
Tohono O'odham Comm Coll (AZ)
Trident Tech Coll (SC)
Union County Coll (NJ)
U of Alaska Anchorage, Kenai Peninsula Coll (AK)
U of South Carolina Lancaster (SC)
Vincennes U (IN)
Volunteer State Comm Coll (TN)
Walters State Comm Coll (TN)
Weatherford Coll (TX)
Westchester Comm Coll (NY)
Western Dakota Tech Inst (SD)
Western Iowa Tech Comm Coll (IA)
Western Nevada Coll (NV)
West Kentucky Comm and Tech Coll (KY)
Wor-Wic Comm Coll (MD)

BUSINESS ADMINISTRATION, MANAGEMENT AND OPERATIONS RELATED
Blue Ridge Comm and Tech Coll (WV)
Chandler-Gilbert Comm Coll (AZ)
Lackawanna Coll (PA)
Northern Essex Comm Coll (MA)
Pensacola State Coll (FL)

BUSINESS AND PERSONAL/ FINANCIAL SERVICES MARKETING
Hutchinson Comm Coll (KS)

BUSINESS AUTOMATION/ TECHNOLOGY/DATA ENTRY
Crowder Coll (MO)
Danville Area Comm Coll (IL)
De Anza Coll (CA)
Houston Comm Coll (TX)
Kaskaskia Coll (IL)
Miami Dade Coll (FL)
Minnesota State Comm and Tech Coll (MN)
Northeast Iowa Comm Coll (IA)
Paris Jr Coll (TX)
Schoolcraft Coll (MI)
Shawnee Comm Coll (IL)
Southwest Texas Jr Coll (TX)
Western Iowa Tech Comm Coll (IA)

BUSINESS/COMMERCE
Alexandria Tech and Comm Coll (MN)
Alvin Comm Coll (TX)
Anoka-Ramsey Comm Coll (MN)
Austin Comm Coll District (TX)
Bay de Noc Comm Coll (MI)
Bossier Parish Comm Coll (LA)
Bucks County Comm Coll (PA)
Century Coll (MN)
Chandler-Gilbert Comm Coll (AZ)
Chesapeake Coll (MD)
Citrus Coll (CA)
Collin County Comm Coll District (TX)
Columbia-Greene Comm Coll (NY)
Comm Coll of Baltimore County (MD)
Dawson Comm Coll (MT)
Eastern Arizona Coll (AZ)
Edison State Comm Coll (OH)
Feather River Coll (CA)
Hagerstown Comm Coll (MD)
Harrisburg Area Comm Coll (PA)
Hutchinson Comm Coll (KS)
Kaskaskia Coll (IL)
Kent State U at Tuscarawas (OH)
Lackawanna Coll (PA)
Mesabi Range Coll (MN)
Minnesota State Comm and Tech Coll (MN)
Minnesota State Comm and Tech Coll–Moorhead (MN)
Montgomery Coll (MD)
Montgomery County Comm Coll (PA)
Mount Wachusett Comm Coll (MA)
Northampton Comm Coll (PA)
Northern Essex Comm Coll (MA)
Northwest State Comm Coll (OH)
Oklahoma State U Inst of Technology (OK)
Paris Jr Coll (TX)
Penn State DuBois (PA)
Penn State Fayette, The Eberly Campus (PA)
Penn State Mont Alto (PA)
Pensacola State Coll (FL)
Quinsigamond Comm Coll (MA)
Raritan Valley Comm Coll (NJ)
Rend Lake Coll (IL)
San Jacinto Coll (TX)
Schoolcraft Coll (MI)
Seminole State Coll (OK)
Sierra Coll (CA)
South Arkansas Comm Coll (AR)
Springfield Tech Comm Coll (MA)
Truckee Meadows Comm Coll (NV)
Union County Coll (NJ)
Vincennes U (IN)
Western Nevada Coll (NV)
Westmoreland County Comm Coll (PA)
Williamsburg Tech Coll (SC)
Wor-Wic Comm Coll (MD)

BUSINESS/CORPORATE COMMUNICATIONS
Houston Comm Coll (TX)

BUSINESS MACHINE REPAIR
Comm Coll of Allegheny County (PA)
De Anza Coll (CA)
Mississippi Delta Comm Coll (MS)

BUSINESS, MANAGEMENT, AND MARKETING RELATED
Bristol Comm Coll (MA)
Chandler-Gilbert Comm Coll (AZ)
Comm Coll of Allegheny County (PA)
Eastern Arizona Coll (AZ)
Meridian Comm Coll (MS)
Niagara County Comm Coll (NY)
South Arkansas Comm Coll (AR)

BUSINESS OPERATIONS SUPPORT AND SECRETARIAL SERVICES RELATED
Bristol Comm Coll (MA)
Eastern Arizona Coll (AZ)

BUSINESS TEACHER EDUCATION
Amarillo Coll (TX)
Eastern Arizona Coll (AZ)
Mt. San Antonio Coll (CA)
Northern Essex Comm Coll (MA)
North Idaho Coll (ID)
Vincennes U (IN)

CABINETMAKING AND MILLWORK
Bucks County Comm Coll (PA)
Sierra Coll (CA)

CAD/CADD DRAFTING/DESIGN TECHNOLOGY
Asheville-Buncombe Tech Comm Coll (NC)
Central Ohio Tech Coll (OH)
Central Oregon Comm Coll (OR)
Century Coll (MN)
Clackamas Comm Coll (OR)
Comm Coll of Allegheny County (PA)
Danville Area Comm Coll (IL)
Dunwoody Coll of Technology (MN)
Front Range Comm Coll (CO)
Gulf Coast State Coll (FL)
Kent State U at Tuscarawas (OH)
Kishwaukee Coll (IL)
Miami Dade Coll (FL)
Morton Coll (IL)
Northampton Comm Coll (PA)
Northwest State Comm Coll (OH)
South Suburban Coll (IL)

CARDIOVASCULAR SCIENCE
Lackawanna Coll (PA)

CARDIOVASCULAR TECHNOLOGY
Florida SouthWestern State Coll (FL)
Harper Coll (IL)
Harrisburg Area Comm Coll (PA)
Hillsborough Comm Coll (FL)
Houston Comm Coll (TX)
Kirtland Comm Coll (MI)
Minnesota State Comm and Tech Coll (MN)
Minnesota State Comm and Tech Coll–Moorhead (MN)
Northeast State Comm Coll (TN)
San Jacinto Coll (TX)
Southern Maine Comm Coll (ME)

CARPENTRY
Alamance Comm Coll (NC)
Austin Comm Coll District (TX)
Delta Coll (MI)
Fullerton Coll (CA)
Hawkeye Comm Coll (IA)
Hutchinson Comm Coll (KS)
Kaskaskia Coll (IL)
Minnesota State Comm and Tech Coll (MN)
North Idaho Coll (ID)
Ridgewater Coll (MN)
San Juan Coll (NM)
Southwestern Comm Coll (IA)
Southwestern Michigan Coll (MI)
Tohono O'odham Comm Coll (AZ)

CERAMIC ARTS AND CERAMICS
De Anza Coll (CA)

CHEMICAL PROCESS TECHNOLOGY
San Jacinto Coll (TX)

CHEMICAL TECHNOLOGY
Alvin Comm Coll (TX)
Amarillo Coll (TX)
Bucks County Comm Coll (PA)
Comm Coll of Allegheny County (PA)
Delta Coll (MI)
Florida SouthWestern State Coll (FL)
Fullerton Coll (CA)
Grand Rapids Comm Coll (MI)
Houston Comm Coll (TX)
Niagara County Comm Coll (NY)
Pensacola State Coll (FL)
South Arkansas Comm Coll (AR)

CHEMISTRY
Amarillo Coll (TX)
Anoka-Ramsey Comm Coll (MN)
Austin Comm Coll District (TX)
Blinn Coll (TX)
Central Oregon Comm Coll (OR)
Century Coll (MN)
Chandler-Gilbert Comm Coll (AZ)
Comm Coll of Allegheny County (PA)
Eastern Arizona Coll (AZ)
Fullerton Coll (CA)
Galveston Coll (TX)
Harper Coll (IL)
Harrisburg Area Comm Coll (PA)
Houston Comm Coll (TX)
Iowa Central Comm Coll (IA)
Los Angeles City Coll (CA)
Miami Dade Coll (FL)
Minnesota State Comm and Tech Coll (MN)
Minnesota State Comm and Tech Coll–Moorhead (MN)
Mount Wachusett Comm Coll (MA)
Navarro Coll (TX)
Northampton Comm Coll (PA)
Northeastern Jr Coll (CO)
North Idaho Coll (ID)
Paris Jr Coll (TX)
Pensacola State Coll (FL)
Queensborough Comm Coll of the City U of New York (NY)
Quinsigamond Comm Coll (MA)
Ridgewater Coll (MN)
St. Charles Comm Coll (MO)
San Jacinto Coll (TX)
San Joaquin Delta Coll (CA)
San Juan Coll (NM)
Sierra Coll (CA)
Springfield Tech Comm Coll (MA)
Truckee Meadows Comm Coll (NV)
Union County Coll (NJ)
Western Iowa Tech Comm Coll (IA)

CHEMISTRY RELATED
Vincennes U (IN)

CHEMISTRY TEACHER EDUCATION
Comm Coll of Baltimore County (MD)
Daytona State Coll (FL)
Montgomery Coll (MD)
Vincennes U (IN)

CHILD-CARE AND SUPPORT SERVICES MANAGEMENT
Bay de Noc Comm Coll (MI)
Bevill State Comm Coll (AL)
Cayuga County Comm Coll (NY)
Central Lakes Coll (MN)
Central Oregon Comm Coll (OR)
Chesapeake Coll (MD)
Clackamas Comm Coll (OR)
Coll of DuPage (IL)
Comm Coll of Baltimore County (MD)
Dutchess Comm Coll (NY)
Eastern Gateway Comm Coll (OH)
Grand Rapids Comm Coll (MI)
Greenville Tech Coll (SC)
Hagerstown Comm Coll (MD)
Haywood Comm Coll (NC)
Hillsborough Comm Coll (FL)
Kishwaukee Coll (IL)
Lurleen B. Wallace Comm Coll (AL)
MiraCosta Coll (CA)
Montgomery County Comm Coll (PA)
Mount Wachusett Comm Coll (MA)
Northwest-Shoals Comm Coll (AL)
Northwest State Comm Coll (OH)
Pensacola State Coll (FL)
Piedmont Comm Coll (NC)
Portland Comm Coll (OR)
St. Charles Comm Coll (MO)
Vincennes U (IN)
Westchester Comm Coll (NY)
Williamsburg Tech Coll (SC)
Wor-Wic Comm Coll (MD)

CHILD-CARE PROVISION
Black Hawk Coll, Moline (IL)
Bossier Parish Comm Coll (LA)
Bucks County Comm Coll (PA)
Coll of DuPage (IL)
Collin County Comm Coll District (TX)
Comm Coll of Allegheny County (PA)
Danville Area Comm Coll (IL)
Dawson Comm Coll (MT)
Delta Coll (MI)
Des Moines Area Comm Coll (IA)
Feather River Coll (CA)
Florida SouthWestern State Coll (FL)
Fullerton Coll (CA)
Gateway Comm and Tech Coll (KY)
Gulf Coast State Coll (FL)
Harper Coll (IL)
Hawkeye Comm Coll (IA)
Hopkinsville Comm Coll (KY)
Kaskaskia Coll (IL)
Kishwaukee Coll (IL)
Lackawanna Coll (PA)
Lakeland Comm Coll (OH)
Lake Region State Coll (ND)
Luzerne County Comm Coll (PA)
Maysville Comm and Tech Coll, Maysville (KY)
McHenry County Coll (IL)
Miami Dade Coll (FL)
MiraCosta Coll (CA)
Montgomery Coll (MD)
Morton Coll (IL)
Oakton Comm Coll (IL)
Owensboro Comm and Tech Coll (KY)
Pensacola State Coll (FL)
Raritan Valley Comm Coll (NJ)
Rend Lake Coll (IL)
San Juan Coll (NM)
Shawnee Comm Coll (IL)
Somerset Comm Coll (KY)
South Suburban Coll (IL)
Trident Tech Coll (SC)
Western Iowa Tech Comm Coll (IA)
West Kentucky Comm and Tech Coll (KY)

CHILD DEVELOPMENT
Alvin Comm Coll (TX)
Amarillo Coll (TX)
Austin Comm Coll District (TX)
Blinn Coll (TX)
Citrus Coll (CA)
Cleveland State Comm Coll (TN)
Coll of DuPage (IL)
Collin County Comm Coll District (TX)
De Anza Coll (CA)
Dyersburg State Comm Coll (TN)
Edison State Comm Coll (OH)
Houston Comm Coll (TX)
James Sprunt Comm Coll (NC)
Los Angeles City Coll (CA)

Miami Dade Coll (FL)
Motlow State Comm Coll (TN)
Mt. San Antonio Coll (CA)
Mount Wachusett Comm Coll (MA)
Northeastern Jr Coll (CO)
Northeast State Comm Coll (TN)
Northwest-Shoals Comm Coll (AL)
Rock Valley Coll (IL)
San Jacinto Coll (TX)
Schoolcraft Coll (MI)
Seminole State Coll (OK)
Sierra Coll (CA)
Southwestern Comm Coll (NC)
Southwest Texas Jr Coll (TX)
Walters State Comm Coll (TN)

CHINESE
Austin Comm Coll District (TX)
Los Angeles City Coll (CA)

CINEMATOGRAPHY AND FILM/ VIDEO PRODUCTION
Bucks County Comm Coll (PA)
Camden County Coll (NJ)
Century Coll (MN)
Coll of DuPage (IL)
Houston Comm Coll (TX)
Los Angeles City Coll (CA)
Miami Dade Coll (FL)
Queensborough Comm Coll of the City U of New York (NY)
South Arkansas Comm Coll (AR)
Western Iowa Tech Comm Coll (IA)

CIVIL DRAFTING AND CAD/ CADD
Central Ohio Tech Coll (OH)
Comm Coll of Allegheny County (PA)

CIVIL ENGINEERING
Austin Comm Coll District (TX)
Fiorello H. LaGuardia Comm Coll of the City U of New York (NY)
Galveston Coll (TX)
Truckee Meadows Comm Coll (NV)

CIVIL ENGINEERING TECHNOLOGY
Asheville-Buncombe Tech Comm Coll (NC)
Bellingham Tech Coll (WA)
Bristol Comm Coll (MA)
Central Maine Comm Coll (ME)
Central Ohio Tech Coll (OH)
Comm Coll of Allegheny County (PA)
Des Moines Area Comm Coll (IA)
Dunwoody Coll of Technology (MN)
Eastern Arizona Coll (AZ)
Fayetteville Tech Comm Coll (NC)
Florida SouthWestern State Coll (FL)
Gulf Coast State Coll (FL)
Harrisburg Area Comm Coll (PA)
Hawkeye Comm Coll (IA)
Lakeland Comm Coll (OH)
Miami Dade Coll (FL)
Middlesex County Coll (NJ)
Minnesota State Comm and Tech Coll (MN)
Minnesota State Comm and Tech Coll–Detroit Lakes (MN)
Mississippi Delta Comm Coll (MS)
Mt. San Antonio Coll (CA)
Nassau Comm Coll (NY)
North Dakota State Coll of Science (ND)
Northeast Wisconsin Tech Coll (WI)
Northern Essex Comm Coll (MA)
Pensacola State Coll (FL)
Portland Comm Coll (OR)
San Joaquin Delta Coll (CA)
Springfield Tech Comm Coll (MA)
Stark State Coll (OH)
State Tech Coll of Missouri (MO)
Trident Tech Coll (SC)
Westchester Comm Coll (NY)

CLINICAL LABORATORY SCIENCE/MEDICAL TECHNOLOGY
Amarillo Coll (TX)
De Anza Coll (CA)
Galveston Coll (TX)
North Idaho Coll (ID)
Tarrant County Coll District (TX)

CLINICAL/MEDICAL LABORATORY ASSISTANT
Somerset Comm Coll (KY)

CLINICAL/MEDICAL LABORATORY SCIENCE AND ALLIED PROFESSIONS RELATED
Houston Comm Coll (TX)

CLINICAL/MEDICAL LABORATORY TECHNOLOGY
Alamance Comm Coll (NC)
Alexandria Tech and Comm Coll (MN)
Arapahoe Comm Coll (CO)
Asheville-Buncombe Tech Comm Coll (NC)
Austin Comm Coll District (TX)
Blue Ridge Comm and Tech Coll (WV)
Bristol Comm Coll (MA)
Bucks County Comm Coll (PA)
Camden County Coll (NJ)
Comm Coll of Allegheny County (PA)
Comm Coll of Baltimore County (MD)
Des Moines Area Comm Coll (IA)
Dutchess Comm Coll (NY)
Edison State Comm Coll (OH)
Fox Valley Tech Coll (WI)
Greenville Tech Coll (SC)
Harrisburg Area Comm Coll (PA)
Hawkeye Comm Coll (IA)
Houston Comm Coll (TX)
Hutchinson Comm Coll (KS)
Iowa Central Comm Coll (IA)
Kaskaskia Coll (IL)
Lake Area Tech Inst (SD)
Lakeland Comm Coll (OH)
Manchester Comm Coll (CT)
Maysville Comm and Tech Coll, Maysville (KY)
McLennan Comm Coll (TX)
Meridian Comm Coll (MS)
Miami Dade Coll (FL)
Middlesex County Coll (NJ)
Minnesota State Comm and Tech Coll (MN)
Mississippi Delta Comm Coll (MS)
Montgomery County Comm Coll (PA)
Motlow State Comm Coll (TN)
Mount Wachusett Comm Coll (MA)
Nassau Comm Coll (NY)
Navarro Coll (TX)
Northeast Iowa Comm Coll (IA)
Northeast Wisconsin Tech Coll (WI)
Oakton Comm Coll (IL)
Portland Comm Coll (OR)
San Jacinto Coll (TX)
San Juan Coll (NM)
Seminole State Coll (OK)
Shawnee Comm Coll (IL)
South Arkansas Comm Coll (AR)
Southwestern Comm Coll (NC)
Springfield Tech Comm Coll (MA)
Stark State Coll (OH)
Tarrant County Coll District (TX)
Trident Tech Coll (SC)
Volunteer State Comm Coll (TN)
Western Dakota Tech Inst (SD)
West Kentucky Comm and Tech Coll (KY)

CLINICAL/MEDICAL SOCIAL WORK
Asheville-Buncombe Tech Comm Coll (NC)
Dawson Comm Coll (MT)

CLINICAL RESEARCH COORDINATOR
Hillsborough Comm Coll (FL)

COMMERCIAL AND ADVERTISING ART
Alamance Comm Coll (NC)
Alexandria Tech and Comm Coll (MN)
Amarillo Coll (TX)
Bucks County Comm Coll (PA)
Central Lakes Coll (MN)
Chandler-Gilbert Comm Coll (AZ)
Coll of DuPage (IL)
Collin County Comm Coll District (TX)
Comm Coll of Baltimore County (MD)
De Anza Coll (CA)
Des Moines Area Comm Coll (IA)
Dutchess Comm Coll (NY)
Eastern Arizona Coll (AZ)
Fayetteville Tech Comm Coll (NC)
Grand Rapids Comm Coll (MI)
Hagerstown Comm Coll (MD)
Halifax Comm Coll (NC)
Housatonic Comm Coll (CT)
James Sprunt Comm Coll (NC)
Lakeland Comm Coll (OH)
Lenoir Comm Coll (NC)
Luzerne County Comm Coll (PA)
Manchester Comm Coll (CT)
Miami Dade Coll (FL)
Middlesex Comm Coll (CT)
Montgomery Coll (MD)
Mt. San Antonio Coll (CA)
Nassau Comm Coll (NY)
Navarro Coll (TX)
Northern Essex Comm Coll (MA)
North Idaho Coll (ID)
Pensacola State Coll (FL)
Portland Comm Coll (OR)
St. Charles Comm Coll (MO)
San Jacinto Coll (TX)
San Joaquin Delta Coll (CA)
San Juan Coll (NM)
Southwestern Comm Coll (NC)
Springfield Tech Comm Coll (MA)
Trident Tech Coll (SC)
Truckee Meadows Comm Coll (NV)
Vincennes U (IN)
Westchester Comm Coll (NY)
Western Nevada Coll (NV)

COMMERCIAL PHOTOGRAPHY
Arapahoe Comm Coll (CO)
Austin Comm Coll District (TX)
Bucks County Comm Coll (PA)
Century Coll (MN)
Chandler-Gilbert Comm Coll (AZ)
Collin County Comm Coll District (TX)
Fiorello H. LaGuardia Comm Coll of the City U of New York (NY)
Hawkeye Comm Coll (IA)
Houston Comm Coll (TX)
Iowa Central Comm Coll (IA)
Luzerne County Comm Coll (PA)
McHenry County Coll (IL)
Montgomery Coll (MD)
Ridgewater Coll (MN)
Sierra Coll (CA)
Springfield Tech Comm Coll (MA)
Western Iowa Tech Comm Coll (IA)

COMMUNICATION
De Anza Coll (CA)
Northeastern Jr Coll (CO)
Western Iowa Tech Comm Coll (IA)

COMMUNICATION AND JOURNALISM RELATED
Harrisburg Area Comm Coll (PA)

COMMUNICATION AND MEDIA RELATED
Chandler-Gilbert Comm Coll (AZ)
Lackawanna Coll (PA)
Meridian Comm Coll (MS)
Raritan Valley Comm Coll (NJ)

COMMUNICATIONS SYSTEMS INSTALLATION AND REPAIR TECHNOLOGY
Bellingham Tech Coll (WA)
Cayuga County Comm Coll (NY)
Coll of DuPage (IL)
Des Moines Area Comm Coll (IA)
Dutchess Comm Coll (NY)

COMMUNICATIONS TECHNOLOGIES AND SUPPORT SERVICES RELATED
Comm Coll of Baltimore County (MD)
Middlesex County Coll (NJ)
Montgomery Coll (MD)
Vincennes U (IN)

COMMUNICATIONS TECHNOLOGY
Coll of DuPage (IL)
Gulf Coast State Coll (FL)
Hutchinson Comm Coll (KS)
Pensacola State Coll (FL)

COMMUNITY HEALTH AND PREVENTIVE MEDICINE
Anoka-Ramsey Comm Coll (MN)
Quinsigamond Comm Coll (MA)

COMMUNITY HEALTH SERVICES COUNSELING
Daytona State Coll (FL)
Dutchess Comm Coll (NY)
Florida SouthWestern State Coll (FL)
Hillsborough Comm Coll (FL)
Lake Area Tech Inst (SD)
Miami Dade Coll (FL)
Northeast Wisconsin Tech Coll (WI)
Northern Essex Comm Coll (MA)

COMMUNITY ORGANIZATION AND ADVOCACY
Borough of Manhattan Comm Coll of the City U of New York (NY)
Clackamas Comm Coll (OR)
Westchester Comm Coll (NY)

COMMUNITY PSYCHOLOGY
Dawson Comm Coll (MT)

COMPARATIVE LITERATURE
Blinn Coll (TX)
Miami Dade Coll (FL)
San Joaquin Delta Coll (CA)

COMPUTER AND INFORMATION SCIENCES
Arapahoe Comm Coll (CO)
Austin Comm Coll District (TX)
Bevill State Comm Coll (AL)
Borough of Manhattan Comm Coll of the City U of New York (NY)
Bristol Comm Coll (MA)
Bucks County Comm Coll (PA)
Camden County Coll (NJ)
Cayuga County Comm Coll (NY)
Central Oregon Comm Coll (OR)
Chandler-Gilbert Comm Coll (AZ)
Cleveland State Comm Coll (TN)
Collin County Comm Coll District (TX)
Columbia-Greene Comm Coll (NY)
Comm Coll of Allegheny County (PA)
Comm Coll of Baltimore County (MD)
Comm Coll of Denver (CO)
Dawson Comm Coll (MT)
Donnelly Coll (KS)
Dyersburg State Comm Coll (TN)
Edison State Comm Coll (OH)
Front Range Comm Coll (CO)
Galveston Coll (TX)
Gateway Comm and Tech Coll (KY)
Hagerstown Comm Coll (MD)
Harper Coll (IL)
Harrisburg Area Comm Coll (PA)
Hopkinsville Comm Coll (KY)
Hutchinson Comm Coll (KS)
Jamestown Comm Coll (NY)
Lurleen B. Wallace Comm Coll (AL)
Luzerne County Comm Coll (PA)
Maysville Comm and Tech Coll, Maysville (KY)
Middlesex County Coll (NJ)
Montgomery Coll (MD)
Mt. San Antonio Coll (CA)
Mount Wachusett Comm Coll (MA)
Nassau Comm Coll (NY)
North Dakota State Coll of Science (ND)
Northern Essex Comm Coll (MA)
Northwest-Shoals Comm Coll (AL)
Owensboro Comm and Tech Coll (KY)
Paris Jr Coll (TX)
Pensacola State Coll (FL)
Piedmont Virginia Comm Coll (VA)
Queensborough Comm Coll of the City U of New York (NY)
Quinsigamond Comm Coll (MA)
Raritan Valley Comm Coll (NJ)
San Jacinto Coll (TX)
Somerset Comm Coll (KY)
Southwest Texas Jr Coll (TX)
Stark State Coll (OH)
State U of New York Coll of Technology at Alfred (NY)
Walters State Comm Coll (TN)
Westchester Comm Coll (NY)
Western Nevada Coll (NV)
West Kentucky Comm and Tech Coll (KY)
Wor-Wic Comm Coll (MD)

COMPUTER AND INFORMATION SCIENCES AND SUPPORT SERVICES RELATED
Cayuga County Comm Coll (NY)
Chandler-Gilbert Comm Coll (AZ)
Chesapeake Coll (MD)
Des Moines Area Comm Coll (IA)
Fiorello H. LaGuardia Comm Coll of the City U of New York (NY)
Los Angeles City Coll (CA)
Northeast Wisconsin Tech Coll (WI)
North Idaho Coll (ID)
Sierra Coll (CA)
Union County Coll (NJ)
Westchester Comm Coll (NY)

COMPUTER AND INFORMATION SCIENCES RELATED
Bristol Comm Coll (MA)
Central Oregon Comm Coll (OR)
Citrus Coll (CA)
Dawson Comm Coll (MT)
Delta Coll (MI)
Los Angeles City Coll (CA)
Luzerne County Comm Coll (PA)
Nassau Comm Coll (NY)
North Idaho Coll (ID)
Pensacola State Coll (FL)

COMPUTER AND INFORMATION SYSTEMS SECURITY
Anoka-Ramsey Comm Coll (MN)
Arapahoe Comm Coll (CO)
Asheville-Buncombe Tech Comm Coll (NC)
Blue Ridge Comm and Tech Coll (WV)
Bucks County Comm Coll (PA)
Central Maine Comm Coll (ME)
Century Coll (MN)
Chandler-Gilbert Comm Coll (AZ)
Chesapeake Coll (MD)
Coll of Eastern Idaho (ID)
Collin County Comm Coll District (TX)
Comm Coll of Allegheny County (PA)
Comm Coll of Baltimore County (MD)
Craven Comm Coll (NC)
Delta Coll (MI)
Donnelly Coll (KS)
Dyersburg State Comm Coll (TN)
Edison State Comm Coll (OH)
Fox Valley Tech Coll (WI)
Hagerstown Comm Coll (MD)
Harrisburg Area Comm Coll (PA)
Hillsborough Comm Coll (FL)
Minnesota State Comm and Tech Coll (MN)
Minnesota State Comm and Tech Coll–Detroit Lakes (MN)
Montgomery Coll (MD)
Northampton Comm Coll (PA)
Northeast Wisconsin Tech Coll (WI)
Northwest State Comm Coll (OH)
Pensacola State Coll (FL)
Piedmont Virginia Comm Coll (VA)
Quinsigamond Comm Coll (MA)
Rend Lake Coll (IL)
Southern Maine Comm Coll (ME)
Springfield Tech Comm Coll (MA)
Westchester Comm Coll (NY)
Westmoreland County Comm Coll (PA)

COMPUTER ENGINEERING
Comm Coll of Baltimore County (MD)
Northwest State Comm Coll (OH)
Pensacola State Coll (FL)

COMPUTER ENGINEERING RELATED
Eastern Gateway Comm Coll (OH)

COMPUTER ENGINEERING TECHNOLOGY
Alvin Comm Coll (TX)
Amarillo Coll (TX)
Asheville-Buncombe Tech Comm Coll (NC)
Benjamin Franklin Inst of Technology (MA)
Coll of The Albemarle (NC)
Comm Coll of Allegheny County (PA)
Daytona State Coll (FL)
Des Moines Area Comm Coll (IA)
Hillsborough Comm Coll (FL)
Houston Comm Coll (TX)
Lakeland Comm Coll (OH)
Lenoir Comm Coll (NC)
Los Angeles City Coll (CA)
Mayland Comm Coll (NC)
McLennan Comm Coll (TX)
Miami Dade Coll (FL)
Minnesota State Comm and Tech Coll (MN)
Mississippi Delta Comm Coll (MS)
Mt. San Antonio Coll (CA)
Northwest State Comm Coll (OH)
Paris Jr Coll (TX)
Queensborough Comm Coll of the City U of New York (NY)
Quinsigamond Comm Coll (MA)
Richmond Comm Coll (NC)
Rock Valley Coll (IL)
Southern Maine Comm Coll (ME)
Southwestern Comm Coll (NC)

Southwest Texas Jr Coll (TX)
Springfield Tech Comm Coll (MA)
State U of New York Coll of Technology at Alfred (NY)
Trident Tech Coll (SC)

COMPUTER GRAPHICS
Central Ohio Tech Coll (OH)
Citrus Coll (CA)
De Anza Coll (CA)
Luzerne County Comm Coll (PA)
Mesabi Range Coll (MN)
Miami Dade Coll (FL)
Mt. San Antonio Coll (CA)
Nassau Comm Coll (NY)
Navarro Coll (TX)
Pensacola State Coll (FL)
Quinsigamond Comm Coll (MA)
Schoolcraft Coll (MI)
Trident Tech Coll (SC)
Weatherford Coll (TX)

COMPUTER/INFORMATION TECHNOLOGY SERVICES ADMINISTRATION RELATED
Bossier Parish Comm Coll (LA)
Dutchess Comm Coll (NY)
Hawkeye Comm Coll (IA)
Hesston Coll (KS)
Mesabi Range Coll (MN)
Trident Tech Coll (SC)
Vincennes U (IN)
Western Iowa Tech Comm Coll (IA)

COMPUTER INSTALLATION AND REPAIR TECHNOLOGY
Chandler-Gilbert Comm Coll (AZ)
Coll of DuPage (IL)
Delta Coll (MI)
Fiorello H. LaGuardia Comm Coll of the City U of New York (NY)
Lake Region State Coll (ND)
Miami Dade Coll (FL)
Sierra Coll (CA)

COMPUTER NUMERICALLY CONTROLLED (CNC) MACHINIST TECHNOLOGY
Anoka Tech Coll (MN)
De Anza Coll (CA)
Dunwoody Coll of Technology (MN)
Greenville Tech Coll (SC)

COMPUTER PROGRAMMING
Alvin Comm Coll (TX)
Amarillo Coll (TX)
Austin Comm Coll District (TX)
Bristol Comm Coll (MA)
Central Ohio Tech Coll (OH)
Chandler-Gilbert Comm Coll (AZ)
Coll of The Albemarle (NC)
Comm Coll of Allegheny County (PA)
Daytona State Coll (FL)
De Anza Coll (CA)
Delta Coll (MI)
Edison State Comm Coll (OH)
Feather River Coll (CA)
Fiorello H. LaGuardia Comm Coll of the City U of New York (NY)
Florida SouthWestern State Coll (FL)
Fox Valley Tech Coll (WI)
Grand Rapids Comm Coll (MI)
Great Falls Coll Montana State U (MT)
Gulf Coast State Coll (FL)
Harper Coll (IL)
Hillsborough Comm Coll (FL)
Houston Comm Coll (TX)
Los Angeles Mission Coll (CA)
Meridian Comm Coll (MS)
Miami Dade Coll (FL)
Middlesex Comm Coll (CT)
Minnesota State Comm and Tech Coll (MN)
Minnesota State Comm and Tech Coll–Moorhead (MN)
MiraCosta Coll (CA)
Montgomery County Comm Coll (PA)
Navarro Coll (TX)
Northampton Comm Coll (PA)
Northeast Wisconsin Tech Coll (WI)
Northern Essex Comm Coll (MA)
North Idaho Coll (ID)
Northwest State Comm Coll (OH)
Oakton Comm Coll (IL)
Pensacola State Coll (FL)
Portland Comm Coll (OR)
Quinsigamond Comm Coll (MA)
Raritan Valley Comm Coll (NJ)
Rend Lake Coll (IL)
Ridgewater Coll (MN)
St. Charles Comm Coll (MO)
Schoolcraft Coll (MI)
Sierra Coll (CA)
Southwestern Michigan Coll (MI)
State Tech Coll of Missouri (MO)
Tarrant County Coll District (TX)
Vincennes U (IN)
Weatherford Coll (TX)
Westmoreland County Comm Coll (PA)

COMPUTER PROGRAMMING RELATED
Luzerne County Comm Coll (PA)
Mesabi Range Coll (MN)
Northern Essex Comm Coll (MA)

COMPUTER PROGRAMMING (SPECIFIC APPLICATIONS)
Arapahoe Comm Coll (CO)
Clackamas Comm Coll (OR)
Coll of DuPage (IL)
Coll of The Albemarle (NC)
Craven Comm Coll (NC)
Danville Area Comm Coll (IL)
Daytona State Coll (FL)
Des Moines Area Comm Coll (IA)
Harper Coll (IL)
Hillsborough Comm Coll (FL)
Houston Comm Coll (TX)
Kent State U at Tuscarawas (OH)
Lakeland Comm Coll (OH)
Mesabi Range Coll (MN)
Miami Dade Coll (FL)
Northeast Iowa Comm Coll (IA)
Northern Essex Comm Coll (MA)
Pensacola State Coll (FL)
Schoolcraft Coll (MI)
Springfield Tech Comm Coll (MA)
Stark State Coll (OH)
Trident Tech Coll (SC)
Truckee Meadows Comm Coll (NV)
Western Iowa Tech Comm Coll (IA)

COMPUTER PROGRAMMING (VENDOR/PRODUCT CERTIFICATION)
Chandler-Gilbert Comm Coll (AZ)
Gulf Coast State Coll (FL)
Miami Dade Coll (FL)
Pensacola State Coll (FL)

COMPUTER SCIENCE
Adirondack Comm Coll (NY)
Amarillo Coll (TX)
Anoka-Ramsey Comm Coll (MN)
Benjamin Franklin Inst of Technology (MA)
Blinn Coll (TX)
Borough of Manhattan Comm Coll of the City U of New York (NY)
Bristol Comm Coll (MA)
Central Oregon Comm Coll (OR)
Century Coll (MN)
Chandler-Gilbert Comm Coll (AZ)
Chesapeake Coll (MD)
Citrus Coll (CA)
Collin County Comm Coll District (TX)
De Anza Coll (CA)
Dutchess Comm Coll (NY)
Fiorello H. LaGuardia Comm Coll of the City U of New York (NY)
Fullerton Coll (CA)
Galveston Coll (TX)
Harper Coll (IL)
Harrisburg Area Comm Coll (PA)
Houston Comm Coll (TX)
Lake Area Tech Inst (SD)
Los Angeles City Coll (CA)
Luzerne County Comm Coll (PA)
Miami Dade Coll (FL)
MiraCosta Coll (CA)
Montgomery County Comm Coll (PA)
Mt. San Antonio Coll (CA)
Nassau Comm Coll (NY)
Navarro Coll (TX)
Niagara County Comm Coll (NY)
Northampton Comm Coll (PA)
Northern Essex Comm Coll (MA)
North Idaho Coll (ID)
Pensacola State Coll (FL)
Quinsigamond Comm Coll (MA)
Ridgewater Coll (MN)
Rock Valley Coll (IL)
San Joaquin Delta Coll (CA)
Seminole State Coll (OK)
Southern Maine Comm Coll (ME)
Springfield Tech Comm Coll (MA)
Tarrant County Coll District (TX)
Union County Coll (NJ)
Vincennes U (IN)

COMPUTER SOFTWARE AND MEDIA APPLICATIONS RELATED
Asheville-Buncombe Tech Comm Coll (NC)
Bay de Noc Comm Coll (MI)
The Coll of Westchester (NY)
Mesabi Range Coll (MN)

COMPUTER SOFTWARE TECHNOLOGY
Miami Dade Coll (FL)

COMPUTER SUPPORT SPECIALIST
Central Ohio Tech Coll (OH)
Fox Valley Tech Coll (WI)
Grand Rapids Comm Coll (MI)
Hutchinson Comm Coll (KS)
Miami Dade Coll (FL)
Morton Coll (IL)
Northampton Comm Coll (PA)
Northland Comm and Tech Coll (MN)
Quinsigamond Comm Coll (MA)
Schoolcraft Coll (MI)
Westmoreland County Comm Coll (PA)

COMPUTER SYSTEMS ANALYSIS
Amarillo Coll (TX)
Bristol Comm Coll (MA)
Chandler-Gilbert Comm Coll (AZ)
Crowder Coll (MO)
Great Falls Coll Montana State U (MT)
Hutchinson Comm Coll (KS)
Lakeland Comm Coll (OH)
Pensacola State Coll (FL)
Quinsigamond Comm Coll (MA)
Wor-Wic Comm Coll (MD)

COMPUTER SYSTEMS NETWORKING AND TELECOMMUNICATIONS
Adirondack Comm Coll (NY)
Alexandria Tech and Comm Coll (MN)
Anoka-Ramsey Comm Coll (MN)
Arapahoe Comm Coll (CO)
Asheville-Buncombe Tech Comm Coll (NC)
Austin Comm Coll District (TX)
Bay de Noc Comm Coll (MI)
Bellingham Tech Coll (WA)
Blinn Coll (TX)
Bristol Comm Coll (MA)
Bucks County Comm Coll (PA)
Central Lakes Coll (MN)
Central Oregon Comm Coll (OR)
Century Coll (MN)
Chandler-Gilbert Comm Coll (AZ)
Clackamas Comm Coll (OR)
Coll of Eastern Idaho (ID)
Collin County Comm Coll District (TX)
Comm Coll of Baltimore County (MD)
Craven Comm Coll (NC)
Crowder Coll (MO)
Danville Area Comm Coll (IL)
Delta Coll (MI)
Dunwoody Coll of Technology (MN)
Edison State Comm Coll (OH)
Fiorello H. LaGuardia Comm Coll of the City U of New York (NY)
Florida SouthWestern State Coll (FL)
Fox Valley Tech Coll (WI)
Front Range Comm Coll (CO)
Grand Rapids Comm Coll (MI)
Great Falls Coll Montana State U (MT)
Gulf Coast State Coll (FL)
Harrisburg Area Comm Coll (PA)
Hawkeye Comm Coll (IA)
Haywood Comm Coll (NC)
Houston Comm Coll (TX)
Hutchinson Comm Coll (KS)
Iowa Central Comm Coll (IA)
Lakeland Comm Coll (OH)
Luzerne County Comm Coll (PA)
McHenry County Coll (IL)
Meridian Comm Coll (MS)
Mesabi Range Coll (MN)
Miami Dade Coll (FL)
Minnesota State Comm and Tech Coll (MN)
Minnesota State Comm and Tech Coll–Moorhead (MN)
MiraCosta Coll (CA)
Nassau Comm Coll (NY)
Northampton Comm Coll (PA)
North Dakota State Coll of Science (ND)
Northeast Wisconsin Tech Coll (WI)
Northern Essex Comm Coll (MA)
Northland Comm and Tech Coll (MN)
Raritan Valley Comm Coll (NJ)
Ridgewater Coll (MN)
Rock Valley Coll (IL)
Schoolcraft Coll (MI)
Sierra Coll (CA)
Southeastern Coll–West Palm Beach (FL)
Southwestern Comm Coll (IA)
Southwestern Michigan Coll (MI)
Southwest Wisconsin Tech Coll (WI)
Stark State Coll (OH)
State Tech Coll of Missouri (MO)
Trident Tech Coll (SC)
Truckee Meadows Comm Coll (NV)
Vincennes U (IN)
Western Dakota Tech Inst (SD)
Westmoreland County Comm Coll (PA)

COMPUTER TECHNOLOGY/ COMPUTER SYSTEMS TECHNOLOGY
Anoka Tech Coll (MN)
Bay de Noc Comm Coll (MI)
Benjamin Franklin Inst of Technology (MA)
Central Lakes Coll (MN)
Clackamas Comm Coll (OR)
Comm Coll of Allegheny County (PA)
De Anza Coll (CA)
Lakeland Comm Coll (OH)
Luzerne County Comm Coll (PA)
Miami Dade Coll (FL)
Minnesota State Comm and Tech Coll (MN)
Montgomery Coll (MD)
Montgomery County Comm Coll (PA)
Northern Essex Comm Coll (MA)
Piedmont Virginia Comm Coll (VA)
Portland Comm Coll (OR)
Rend Lake Coll (IL)
Ridgewater Coll (MN)

COMPUTER TYPOGRAPHY AND COMPOSITION EQUIPMENT OPERATION
Coll of DuPage (IL)
Paris Jr Coll (TX)

CONSERVATION BIOLOGY
Central Lakes Coll (MN)

CONSTRUCTION ENGINEERING
Bossier Parish Comm Coll (LA)

CONSTRUCTION ENGINEERING TECHNOLOGY
Bossier Parish Comm Coll (LA)
Crowder Coll (MO)
Daytona State Coll (FL)
De Anza Coll (CA)
Delta Coll (MI)
Greenville Tech Coll (SC)
Gulf Coast State Coll (FL)
Harrisburg Area Comm Coll (PA)
Houston Comm Coll (TX)
Lake Area Tech Inst (SD)
Miami Dade Coll (FL)
North Dakota State Coll of Science (ND)
Northwest State Comm Coll (OH)
Pensacola State Coll (FL)
Portland Comm Coll (OR)
Raritan Valley Comm Coll (NJ)
Rock Valley Coll (IL)
San Jacinto Coll (TX)
San Joaquin Delta Coll (CA)
South Suburban Coll (IL)
State U of New York Coll of Technology at Alfred (NY)
Tarrant County Coll District (TX)

CONSTRUCTION/HEAVY EQUIPMENT/EARTHMOVING EQUIPMENT OPERATION
Lake Area Tech Inst (SD)

CONSTRUCTION MANAGEMENT
Kaskaskia Coll (IL)
McHenry County Coll (IL)
Minnesota State Comm and Tech Coll (MN)
Minnesota State Comm and Tech Coll–Moorhead (MN)
Northampton Comm Coll (PA)

CONSTRUCTION TRADES
Clackamas Comm Coll (OR)
Coll of The Albemarle (NC)
Crowder Coll (MO)
Northeast Iowa Comm Coll (IA)
Northeast Wisconsin Tech Coll (WI)
Oklahoma State U Inst of Technology (OK)
Sierra Coll (CA)
Southwest Texas Jr Coll (TX)
State Tech Coll of Missouri (MO)

CONSTRUCTION TRADES RELATED
Citrus Coll (CA)
Dutchess Comm Coll (NY)
Fullerton Coll (CA)
Portland Comm Coll (OR)
State U of New York Coll of Technology at Alfred (NY)

CONSUMER MERCHANDISING/ RETAILING MANAGEMENT
Navarro Coll (TX)
Niagara County Comm Coll (NY)
Tarrant County Coll District (TX)

CONSUMER SERVICES AND ADVOCACY
Pensacola State Coll (FL)

COOKING AND RELATED CULINARY ARTS
Adirondack Comm Coll (NY)
Central Oregon Comm Coll (OR)
Feather River Coll (CA)
Iowa Central Comm Coll (IA)
Miami Dade Coll (FL)
Minnesota State Comm and Tech Coll (MN)
Pensacola State Coll (FL)
Truckee Meadows Comm Coll (NV)

CORRECTIONS
Alvin Comm Coll (TX)
Amarillo Coll (TX)
Austin Comm Coll District (TX)
Cayuga County Comm Coll (NY)
Clackamas Comm Coll (OR)
Coll of DuPage (IL)
Danville Area Comm Coll (IL)
De Anza Coll (CA)
Delta Coll (MI)
Eastern Gateway Comm Coll (OH)
Grand Rapids Comm Coll (MI)
Lakeland Comm Coll (OH)
Miami Dade Coll (FL)
Mt. San Antonio Coll (CA)
Mount Wachusett Comm Coll (MA)
Navarro Coll (TX)
Northeast Wisconsin Tech Coll (WI)
San Joaquin Delta Coll (CA)
Westchester Comm Coll (NY)

CORRECTIONS AND CRIMINAL JUSTICE RELATED
Chesapeake Coll (MD)
Feather River Coll (CA)
Miami Dade Coll (FL)
Northwest State Comm Coll (OH)

COSMETOLOGY
Arapahoe Comm Coll (CO)
Century Coll (MN)
Citrus Coll (CA)
Eastern Arizona Coll (AZ)
Fayetteville Tech Comm Coll (NC)
Fullerton Coll (CA)
Galveston Coll (TX)
Halifax Comm Coll (NC)
Haywood Comm Coll (NC)
Houston Comm Coll (TX)
Hutchinson Comm Coll (KS)
Iowa Central Comm Coll (IA)
James Sprunt Comm Coll (NC)
Kaskaskia Coll (IL)

Kirtland Comm Coll (MI)
Lenoir Comm Coll (NC)
Mayland Comm Coll (NC)
Minnesota State Comm and Tech Coll (MN)
Northeastern Jr Coll (CO)
Northeast Iowa Comm Coll (IA)
Paris Jr Coll (TX)
Rend Lake Coll (IL)
Ridgewater Coll (MN)
San Jacinto Coll (TX)
San Juan Coll (NM)
Southwestern Comm Coll (NC)
Southwest Texas Jr Coll (TX)
Vincennes U (IN)
Weatherford Coll (TX)

COSMETOLOGY, BARBER/ STYLING, AND NAIL INSTRUCTION
San Jacinto Coll (TX)

COURT REPORTING
Anoka Tech Coll (MN)
Comm Coll of Allegheny County (PA)
Fox Valley Tech Coll (WI)
Houston Comm Coll (TX)
Luzerne County Comm Coll (PA)
Miami Dade Coll (FL)
Northeast Wisconsin Tech Coll (WI)
South Suburban Coll (IL)
Stark State Coll (OH)
State U of New York Coll of Technology at Alfred (NY)

CRAFTS, FOLK ART AND ARTISANRY
Coll of The Albemarle (NC)
Haywood Comm Coll (NC)

CREATIVE WRITING
Adirondack Comm Coll (NY)
Anoka-Ramsey Comm Coll (MN)
Austin Comm Coll District (TX)
Chandler-Gilbert Comm Coll (AZ)
St. Charles Comm Coll (MO)

CRIMINALISTICS AND CRIMINAL SCIENCE
Alvin Comm Coll (TX)
Central Lakes Coll (MN)

CRIMINAL JUSTICE/LAW ENFORCEMENT ADMINISTRATION
Amarillo Coll (TX)
Arapahoe Comm Coll (CO)
Bay de Noc Comm Coll (MI)
Black River Tech Coll (AR)
Blinn Coll (TX)
Central Ohio Tech Coll (OH)
Citrus Coll (CA)
Coll of DuPage (IL)
Coll of The Albemarle (NC)
Collin County Comm Coll District (TX)
Columbia-Greene Comm Coll (NY)
Craven Comm Coll (NC)
Daytona State Coll (FL)
De Anza Coll (CA)
Des Moines Area Comm Coll (IA)
Eastern Arizona Coll (AZ)
Florida SouthWestern State Coll (FL)
Gateway Comm and Tech Coll (KY)
Gulf Coast State Coll (FL)
Harper Coll (IL)
Harrisburg Area Comm Coll (PA)
Haywood Comm Coll (NC)
Hillsborough Comm Coll (FL)
Hopkinsville Comm Coll (KY)
Housatonic Comm Coll (CT)
Jamestown Comm Coll (NY)
Kaskaskia Coll (IL)
Kirtland Comm Coll (MI)
Lackawanna Coll (PA)
Los Angeles City Coll (CA)
Luzerne County Comm Coll (PA)
Manchester Comm Coll (CT)
Maysville Comm and Tech Coll, Maysville (KY)
McLennan Comm Coll (TX)
Miami Dade Coll (FL)
Minnesota State Comm and Tech Coll–Moorhead (MN)
Mississippi Delta Comm Coll (MS)
Mount Wachusett Comm Coll (MA)
Nassau Comm Coll (NY)
Navarro Coll (TX)
Niagara County Comm Coll (NY)
North Idaho Coll (ID)
Northwestern Coll–Chicago Campus (IL)
Owensboro Comm and Tech Coll (KY)
Pensacola State Coll (FL)
Queensborough Comm Coll of the City U of New York (NY)
Raritan Valley Comm Coll (NJ)
Rock Valley Coll (IL)
Seminole State Coll (OK)
Somerset Comm Coll (KY)
Southwest Texas Jr Coll (TX)
Tarrant County Coll District (TX)
Trident Tech Coll (SC)
Union County Coll (NJ)
U of South Carolina Lancaster (SC)
Weatherford Coll (TX)
Western Nevada Coll (NV)
West Kentucky Comm and Tech Coll (KY)

CRIMINAL JUSTICE/POLICE SCIENCE
Adirondack Comm Coll (NY)
Alexandria Tech and Comm Coll (MN)
Alvin Comm Coll (TX)
Amarillo Coll (TX)
Austin Comm Coll District (TX)
Black Hawk Coll, Moline (IL)
Black River Tech Coll (AR)
Borough of Manhattan Comm Coll of the City U of New York (NY)
Camden County Coll (NJ)
Cayuga County Comm Coll (NY)
Central Lakes Coll (MN)
Central Ohio Tech Coll (OH)
Century Coll (MN)
Chandler-Gilbert Comm Coll (AZ)
Citrus Coll (CA)
Clackamas Comm Coll (OR)
Cleveland State Comm Coll (TN)
Coll of DuPage (IL)
Comm Coll of Baltimore County (MD)
Danville Area Comm Coll (IL)
Dawson Comm Coll (MT)
De Anza Coll (CA)
Delta Coll (MI)
Dutchess Comm Coll (NY)
Dyersburg State Comm Coll (TN)
Eastern Arizona Coll (AZ)
Eastern Gateway Comm Coll (OH)
Edison State Comm Coll (OH)
Fox Valley Tech Coll (WI)
Front Range Comm Coll (CO)
Fullerton Coll (CA)
Galveston Coll (TX)
Grand Rapids Comm Coll (MI)
Hagerstown Comm Coll (MD)
Harrisburg Area Comm Coll (PA)
Hawkeye Comm Coll (IA)
Houston Comm Coll (TX)
Hutchinson Comm Coll (KS)
Iowa Central Comm Coll (IA)
Jamestown Comm Coll (NY)
Kirtland Comm Coll (MI)
Kishwaukee Coll (IL)
Lackawanna Coll (PA)
Lake Area Tech Inst (SD)
Lakeland Comm Coll (OH)
Lake Region State Coll (ND)
Los Angeles City Coll (CA)
Los Angeles Mission Coll (CA)
McHenry County Coll (IL)
McLennan Comm Coll (TX)
Miami Dade Coll (FL)
Middlesex Comm Coll (CT)
Middlesex County Coll (NJ)
MiraCosta Coll (CA)
Montgomery Coll (MD)
Montgomery County Comm Coll (PA)
Morton Coll (IL)
Mt. San Antonio Coll (CA)
Navarro Coll (TX)
Northeastern Jr Coll (CO)
Northeast Wisconsin Tech Coll (WI)
Northern Essex Comm Coll (MA)
North Idaho Coll (ID)
Northland Comm and Tech Coll (MN)
Northwest-Shoals Comm Coll (AL)
Northwest State Comm Coll (OH)
Oakton Comm Coll (IL)
Piedmont Virginia Comm Coll (VA)
Quinsigamond Comm Coll (MA)
Rend Lake Coll (IL)
Ridgewater Coll (MN)
St. Charles Comm Coll (MO)
San Jacinto Coll (TX)
San Joaquin Delta Coll (CA)
San Juan Coll (NM)
Schoolcraft Coll (MI)
Seminole State Coll (OK)
Sierra Coll (CA)
South Arkansas Comm Coll (AR)
Southwestern Comm Coll (NC)
Southwest Texas Jr Coll (TX)
Southwest Wisconsin Tech Coll (WI)
Springfield Tech Comm Coll (MA)
Truckee Meadows Comm Coll (NV)
Vincennes U (IN)
Walters State Comm Coll (TN)
Western Dakota Tech Inst (SD)
Western Iowa Tech Comm Coll (IA)
Westmoreland County Comm Coll (PA)
Wor-Wic Comm Coll (MD)

CRIMINAL JUSTICE/SAFETY
Alamance Comm Coll (NC)
Alvin Comm Coll (TX)
Asheville-Buncombe Tech Comm Coll (NC)
Bay de Noc Comm Coll (MI)
Blinn Coll (TX)
Blue Ridge Comm and Tech Coll (WV)
Bossier Parish Comm Coll (LA)
Bristol Comm Coll (MA)
Bucks County Comm Coll (PA)
Central Lakes Coll (MN)
Central Maine Comm Coll (ME)
Central Oregon Comm Coll (OR)
Century Coll (MN)
Chandler-Gilbert Comm Coll (AZ)
Cleveland Comm Coll (NC)
Collin County Comm Coll District (TX)
Craven Comm Coll (NC)
De Anza Coll (CA)
Dyersburg State Comm Coll (TN)
Fayetteville Tech Comm Coll (NC)
Fiorello H. LaGuardia Comm Coll of the City U of New York (NY)
Galveston Coll (TX)
Greenville Tech Coll (SC)
Halifax Comm Coll (NC)
Haywood Comm Coll (NC)
Iowa Central Comm Coll (IA)
James Sprunt Comm Coll (NC)
Kent State U at Tuscarawas (OH)
Kishwaukee Coll (IL)
Lackawanna Coll (PA)
Lenoir Comm Coll (NC)
Mayland Comm Coll (NC)
Minnesota State Comm and Tech Coll (MN)
Minnesota State Comm and Tech Coll–Moorhead (MN)
Mount Wachusett Comm Coll (MA)
Nassau Comm Coll (NY)
Northampton Comm Coll (PA)
Northeast State Comm Coll (TN)
Northwest State Comm Coll (OH)
Paris Jr Coll (TX)
Piedmont Comm Coll (NC)
Portland Comm Coll (OR)
Richmond Comm Coll (NC)
Southern Maine Comm Coll (ME)
South Suburban Coll (IL)
Southwestern Comm Coll (IA)
Southwestern Michigan Coll (MI)
Southwest Texas Jr Coll (TX)
Southwest Wisconsin Tech Coll (WI)
State U of New York Coll of Technology at Alfred (NY)
Truckee Meadows Comm Coll (NV)
Volunteer State Comm Coll (TN)
Walters State Comm Coll (TN)
Western Dakota Tech Inst (SD)
Westmoreland County Comm Coll (PA)

CRIMINOLOGY
Central Maine Comm Coll (ME)
Central Oregon Comm Coll (OR)
Paris Jr Coll (TX)
Westmoreland County Comm Coll (PA)

CRISIS/EMERGENCY/DISASTER MANAGEMENT
Austin Comm Coll District (TX)
Century Coll (MN)
Fayetteville Tech Comm Coll (NC)
Lenoir Comm Coll (NC)
Montgomery Coll (MD)
Raritan Valley Comm Coll (NJ)
Western Iowa Tech Comm Coll (IA)

CRITICAL INFRASTRUCTURE PROTECTION
Bucks County Comm Coll (PA)
Comm Coll of Allegheny County (PA)
Fox Valley Tech Coll (WI)

CROP PRODUCTION
Black Hawk Coll, Moline (IL)
Northeast Iowa Comm Coll (IA)
Ridgewater Coll (MN)
San Joaquin Delta Coll (CA)

CULINARY ARTS
Alamance Comm Coll (NC)
Alvin Comm Coll (TX)
Asheville-Buncombe Tech Comm Coll (NC)
Austin Comm Coll District (TX)
Bellingham Tech Coll (WA)
Blue Ridge Comm and Tech Coll (WV)
Bossier Parish Comm Coll (LA)
Bucks County Comm Coll (PA)
Cayuga County Comm Coll (NY)
Central Maine Comm Coll (ME)
Central Ohio Tech Coll (OH)
Central Oregon Comm Coll (OR)
Coll of DuPage (IL)
Coll of The Albemarle (NC)
Collin County Comm Coll District (TX)
Comm Coll of Allegheny County (PA)
Des Moines Area Comm Coll (IA)
Fayetteville Tech Comm Coll (NC)
Fox Valley Tech Coll (WI)
Galveston Coll (TX)
Grand Rapids Comm Coll (MI)
Greenville Tech Coll (SC)
Harrisburg Area Comm Coll (PA)
Houston Comm Coll (TX)
Kaskaskia Coll (IL)
Lackawanna Coll (PA)
Lenoir Comm Coll (NC)
Los Angeles Mission Coll (CA)
Luzerne County Comm Coll (PA)
Maysville Comm and Tech Coll, Maysville (KY)
Meridian Comm Coll (MS)
Miami Dade Coll (FL)
Montgomery County Comm Coll (PA)
Niagara County Comm Coll (NY)
Northampton Comm Coll (PA)
North Dakota State Coll of Science (ND)
North Idaho Coll (ID)
Piedmont Virginia Comm Coll (VA)
Rend Lake Coll (IL)
San Jacinto Coll (TX)
San Joaquin Delta Coll (CA)
Schoolcraft Coll (MI)
Somerset Comm Coll (KY)
Southern Maine Comm Coll (ME)
Southwestern Comm Coll (NC)
Southwest Wisconsin Tech Coll (WI)
State U of New York Coll of Technology at Alfred (NY)
Trident Tech Coll (SC)
Vincennes U (IN)
West Kentucky Comm and Tech Coll (KY)
Westmoreland County Comm Coll (PA)

CULINARY ARTS RELATED
Bristol Comm Coll (MA)
Oklahoma State U Inst of Technology (OK)

CUSTOMER SERVICE MANAGEMENT
Central Oregon Comm Coll (OR)

CUSTOMER SERVICE SUPPORT/ CALL CENTER/TELESERVICE OPERATION
Miami Dade Coll (FL)

CYBER/COMPUTER FORENSICS AND COUNTERTERRORISM
Century Coll (MN)
Columbia-Greene Comm Coll (NY)
Harper Coll (IL)
Paris Jr Coll (TX)
Pensacola State Coll (FL)
Union County Coll (NJ)

DAIRY HUSBANDRY AND PRODUCTION
Northeast Iowa Comm Coll (IA)
Ridgewater Coll (MN)

DAIRY SCIENCE
Mt. San Antonio Coll (CA)

DANCE
Austin Comm Coll District (TX)
Chandler-Gilbert Comm Coll (AZ)
Citrus Coll (CA)
Fullerton Coll (CA)
Miami Dade Coll (FL)
MiraCosta Coll (CA)
Montgomery County Comm Coll (PA)
Nassau Comm Coll (NY)
Queensborough Comm Coll of the City U of New York (NY)
Raritan Valley Comm Coll (NJ)
San Jacinto Coll (TX)
San Joaquin Delta Coll (CA)

DANCE RELATED
Citrus Coll (CA)

DATA ENTRY/ MICROCOMPUTER APPLICATIONS
Bellingham Tech Coll (WA)
Chandler-Gilbert Comm Coll (AZ)
Coll of The Albemarle (NC)
Luzerne County Comm Coll (PA)
MiraCosta Coll (CA)
Montgomery Coll (MD)
Northwest State Comm Coll (OH)
Sierra Coll (CA)

DATA ENTRY/ MICROCOMPUTER APPLICATIONS RELATED
Blue Ridge Comm and Tech Coll (WV)
Coll of DuPage (IL)

DATA MODELING/ WAREHOUSING AND DATABASE ADMINISTRATION
Chandler-Gilbert Comm Coll (AZ)
Quinsigamond Comm Coll (MA)

DATA PROCESSING AND DATA PROCESSING TECHNOLOGY
Anoka Tech Coll (MN)
Bristol Comm Coll (MA)
Cayuga County Comm Coll (NY)
Century Coll (MN)
Citrus Coll (CA)
Eastern Gateway Comm Coll (OH)
Greenville Tech Coll (SC)
Luzerne County Comm Coll (PA)
Morton Coll (IL)
Mt. San Antonio Coll (CA)
Nassau Comm Coll (NY)
Navarro Coll (TX)
Northern Essex Comm Coll (MA)
Queensborough Comm Coll of the City U of New York (NY)
San Juan Coll (NM)
Southwest Texas Jr Coll (TX)
Walters State Comm Coll (TN)

DEAF STUDIES
Comm Coll of Baltimore County (MD)
Quinsigamond Comm Coll (MA)
Western Nevada Coll (NV)

DENTAL ASSISTING
Camden County Coll (NJ)
Central Oregon Comm Coll (OR)
Century Coll (MN)
Citrus Coll (CA)
Delta Coll (MI)
Eastern Gateway Comm Coll (OH)
Grand Rapids Comm Coll (MI)
IBMC Coll, Fort Collins (CO)
Kaskaskia Coll (IL)
Lake Area Tech Inst (SD)
Lenoir Comm Coll (NC)
Minnesota State Comm and Tech Coll (MN)
Minnesota State Comm and Tech Coll–Moorhead (MN)
North Dakota State Coll of Science (ND)
Northern Essex Comm Coll (MA)
Truckee Meadows Comm Coll (NV)
Western Iowa Tech Comm Coll (IA)
Westmoreland County Comm Coll (PA)

DENTAL HYGIENE
Amarillo Coll (TX)
Asheville-Buncombe Tech Comm Coll (NC)
Austin Comm Coll District (TX)
Blinn Coll (TX)
Bristol Comm Coll (MA)
Camden County Coll (NJ)
Central Oregon Comm Coll (OR)
Century Coll (MN)
Coll of DuPage (IL)
Collin County Comm Coll District (TX)

Comm Coll of Baltimore County (MD)
Comm Coll of Denver (CO)
Daytona State Coll (FL)
Delta Coll (MI)
Des Moines Area Comm Coll (IA)
Fayetteville Tech Comm Coll (NC)
Florida SouthWestern State Coll (FL)
Fox Coll (IL)
Fox Valley Tech Coll (WI)
Grand Rapids Comm Coll (MI)
Great Falls Coll Montana State U (MT)
Greenville Tech Coll (SC)
Gulf Coast State Coll (FL)
Hagerstown Comm Coll (MD)
Halifax Comm Coll (NC)
Harper Coll (IL)
Harrisburg Area Comm Coll (PA)
Hawkeye Comm Coll (IA)
Hillsborough Comm Coll (FL)
Iowa Central Comm Coll (IA)
Lakeland Comm Coll (OH)
Lenoir Comm Coll (NC)
Luzerne County Comm Coll (PA)
Meridian Comm Coll (MS)
Miami Dade Coll (FL)
Middlesex County Coll (NJ)
Minnesota State Comm and Tech Coll (MN)
Minnesota State Comm and Tech Coll–Moorhead (MN)
Mississippi Delta Comm Coll (MS)
Montgomery County Comm Coll (PA)
Mount Wachusett Comm Coll (MA)
Northampton Comm Coll (PA)
North Dakota State Coll of Science (ND)
Northeast Wisconsin Tech Coll (WI)
Pensacola State Coll (FL)
Portland Comm Coll (OR)
Quinsigamond Comm Coll (MA)
Raritan Valley Comm Coll (NJ)
Rock Valley Coll (IL)
San Juan Coll (NM)
Springfield Tech Comm Coll (MA)
Stark State Coll (OH)
Tarrant County Coll District (TX)
Trident Tech Coll (SC)
Truckee Meadows Comm Coll (NV)
Westmoreland County Comm Coll (PA)

DENTAL LABORATORY TECHNOLOGY
Los Angeles City Coll (CA)
Portland Comm Coll (OR)

DENTAL SERVICES AND ALLIED PROFESSIONS RELATED
Quinsigamond Comm Coll (MA)

DESIGN AND APPLIED ARTS RELATED
Mississippi Delta Comm Coll (MS)
Niagara County Comm Coll (NY)
Raritan Valley Comm Coll (NJ)
Vincennes U (IN)
Westchester Comm Coll (NY)

DESIGN AND VISUAL COMMUNICATIONS
Adirondack Comm Coll (NY)
Austin Comm Coll District (TX)
Black Hawk Coll, Moline (IL)
Bristol Comm Coll (MA)
Coll of DuPage (IL)
Harrisburg Area Comm Coll (PA)
Hutchinson Comm Coll (KS)
Nassau Comm Coll (NY)
Northwest State Comm Coll (OH)

DESKTOP PUBLISHING AND DIGITAL IMAGING DESIGN
Alvin Comm Coll (TX)
Camden County Coll (NJ)
Coll of DuPage (IL)
Des Moines Area Comm Coll (IA)
Dunwoody Coll of Technology (MN)
Hawkeye Comm Coll (IA)
Houston Comm Coll (TX)
Iowa Central Comm Coll (IA)
Northeast Iowa Comm Coll (IA)
Northeast Wisconsin Tech Coll (WI)
Ridgewater Coll (MN)
Western Iowa Tech Comm Coll (IA)
Westmoreland County Comm Coll (PA)

DEVELOPMENTAL AND CHILD PSYCHOLOGY
Central Lakes Coll (MN)
De Anza Coll (CA)
Los Angeles Mission Coll (CA)
McLennan Comm Coll (TX)
Mississippi Delta Comm Coll (MS)
Navarro Coll (TX)
North Idaho Coll (ID)
Tarrant County Coll District (TX)

DEVELOPMENTAL SERVICES WORKER
Anoka Tech Coll (MN)

DIAGNOSTIC MEDICAL SONOGRAPHY AND ULTRASOUND TECHNOLOGY
Alvin Comm Coll (TX)
Asheville-Buncombe Tech Comm Coll (NC)
Austin Comm Coll District (TX)
Central Ohio Tech Coll (OH)
Comm Coll of Allegheny County (PA)
Delta Coll (MI)
Galveston Coll (TX)
Greenville Tech Coll (SC)
Gulf Coast State Coll (FL)
Harper Coll (IL)
Hillsborough Comm Coll (FL)
Lackawanna Coll (PA)
Lurleen B. Wallace Comm Coll (AL)
Miami Dade Coll (FL)
Montgomery Coll (MD)
Northampton Comm Coll (PA)
Northeast Wisconsin Tech Coll (WI)
Northwestern Coll–Chicago Campus (IL)
Northwest-Shoals Comm Coll (AL)
Pensacola State Coll (FL)
Piedmont Virginia Comm Coll (VA)
San Jacinto Coll (TX)
Southeastern Coll–West Palm Beach (FL)
Springfield Tech Comm Coll (MA)
State U of New York Coll of Technology at Alfred (NY)
Union County Coll (NJ)
Weatherford Coll (TX)
West Kentucky Comm and Tech Coll (KY)
Westmoreland County Comm Coll (PA)

DIESEL MECHANICS TECHNOLOGY
Alexandria Tech and Comm Coll (MN)
Asheville-Buncombe Tech Comm Coll (NC)
Bellingham Tech Coll (WA)
Central Lakes Coll (MN)
Citrus Coll (CA)
Coll of Eastern Idaho (ID)
Delta Coll (MI)
Des Moines Area Comm Coll (IA)
Eastern Arizona Coll (AZ)
Fox Valley Tech Coll (WI)
Gateway Comm and Tech Coll (KY)
Hawkeye Comm Coll (IA)
Iowa Central Comm Coll (IA)
Kishwaukee Coll (IL)
Lake Area Tech Inst (SD)
Lurleen B. Wallace Comm Coll (AL)
Minnesota State Comm and Tech Coll (MN)
Minnesota State Comm and Tech Coll–Moorhead (MN)
North Dakota State Coll of Science (ND)
Ohio Tech Coll (OH)
Oklahoma State U Inst of Technology (OK)
Owensboro Comm and Tech Coll (KY)
Portland Comm Coll (OR)
San Jacinto Coll (TX)
San Juan Coll (NM)
Southwest Texas Jr Coll (TX)
State U of New York Coll of Technology at Alfred (NY)
Truckee Meadows Comm Coll (NV)
Vincennes U (IN)

DIETETICS
Black River Tech Coll (AR)
Central Oregon Comm Coll (OR)
Harper Coll (IL)
Los Angeles City Coll (CA)
Miami Dade Coll (FL)
Pensacola State Coll (FL)
Tarrant County Coll District (TX)
Truckee Meadows Comm Coll (NV)
Vincennes U (IN)

DIETETIC TECHNOLOGY
Camden County Coll (NJ)
Chandler-Gilbert Comm Coll (AZ)
Fiorello H. LaGuardia Comm Coll of the City U of New York (NY)
Harper Coll (IL)
Hillsborough Comm Coll (FL)
Los Angeles City Coll (CA)
Miami Dade Coll (FL)
Northland Comm and Tech Coll (MN)
Southern Maine Comm Coll (ME)
Westmoreland County Comm Coll (PA)

DIETITIAN ASSISTANT
Chandler-Gilbert Comm Coll (AZ)
Middlesex County Coll (NJ)
Westchester Comm Coll (NY)

DIGITAL ARTS
Austin Comm Coll District (TX)
Fiorello H. LaGuardia Comm Coll of the City U of New York (NY)
Gulf Coast State Coll (FL)
Queensborough Comm Coll of the City U of New York (NY)
Volunteer State Comm Coll (TN)
Westchester Comm Coll (NY)

DIGITAL COMMUNICATION AND MEDIA/MULTIMEDIA
Chandler-Gilbert Comm Coll (AZ)
Clackamas Comm Coll (OR)
Daytona State Coll (FL)
Gulf Coast State Coll (FL)
Hawkeye Comm Coll (IA)
Hillsborough Comm Coll (FL)
Iowa Central Comm Coll (IA)
Ridgewater Coll (MN)
San Jacinto Coll (TX)
Sierra Coll (CA)
Southern Maine Comm Coll (ME)
Westchester Comm Coll (NY)

DIRECT ENTRY MIDWIFERY
Southwest Wisconsin Tech Coll (WI)

DIRECTING AND THEATRICAL PRODUCTION
Quinsigamond Comm Coll (MA)

DRAFTING AND DESIGN TECHNOLOGY
Alvin Comm Coll (TX)
Amarillo Coll (TX)
Austin Comm Coll District (TX)
Benjamin Franklin Inst of Technology (MA)
Bossier Parish Comm Coll (LA)
Camden County Coll (NJ)
Cayuga County Comm Coll (NY)
Central Oregon Comm Coll (OR)
Citrus Coll (CA)
Clackamas Comm Coll (OR)
Coll of DuPage (IL)
Collin County Comm Coll District (TX)
Comm Coll of Denver (CO)
Crowder Coll (MO)
Daytona State Coll (FL)
Eastern Arizona Coll (AZ)
Eastern Gateway Comm Coll (OH)
Florida SouthWestern State Coll (FL)
Fullerton Coll (CA)
Greenville Tech Coll (SC)
Houston Comm Coll (TX)
Luzerne County Comm Coll (PA)
Miami Dade Coll (FL)
MiraCosta Coll (CA)
Montgomery County Comm Coll (PA)
Morton Coll (IL)
Mt. San Antonio Coll (CA)
Navarro Coll (TX)
Niagara County Comm Coll (NY)
North Idaho Coll (ID)
Northwest-Shoals Comm Coll (AL)
Paris Jr Coll (TX)
Pensacola State Coll (FL)
St. Charles Comm Coll (MO)
San Jacinto Coll (TX)
San Juan Coll (NM)
Schoolcraft Coll (MI)
Southern Maine Comm Coll (ME)
State Tech Coll of Missouri (MO)
State U of New York Coll of Technology at Alfred (NY)
Tarrant County Coll District (TX)
Truckee Meadows Comm Coll (NV)
Westchester Comm Coll (NY)
Western Dakota Tech Inst (SD)

DRAFTING/DESIGN ENGINEERING TECHNOLOGIES RELATED
Asheville-Buncombe Tech Comm Coll (NC)
Coll of DuPage (IL)
Coll of The Albemarle (NC)
De Anza Coll (CA)
Luzerne County Comm Coll (PA)
Mt. San Antonio Coll (CA)
Niagara County Comm Coll (NY)
Rock Valley Coll (IL)

DRAMATIC/THEATER ARTS
Alvin Comm Coll (TX)
Amarillo Coll (TX)
Anoka-Ramsey Comm Coll (MN)
Austin Comm Coll District (TX)
Blinn Coll (TX)
Bossier Parish Comm Coll (LA)
Bristol Comm Coll (MA)
Century Coll (MN)
Chandler-Gilbert Comm Coll (AZ)
Citrus Coll (CA)
Coll of The Albemarle (NC)
Comm Coll of Allegheny County (PA)
Crowder Coll (MO)
De Anza Coll (CA)
Eastern Arizona Coll (AZ)
Edison State Comm Coll (OH)
Fiorello H. LaGuardia Comm Coll of the City U of New York (NY)
Fullerton Coll (CA)
Galveston Coll (TX)
Harrisburg Area Comm Coll (PA)
Los Angeles City Coll (CA)
Los Angeles Mission Coll (CA)
Manchester Comm Coll (CT)
Miami Dade Coll (FL)
Minnesota State Comm and Tech Coll–Moorhead (MN)
Mississippi Delta Comm Coll (MS)
Mount Wachusett Comm Coll (MA)
Nassau Comm Coll (NY)
Navarro Coll (TX)
Niagara County Comm Coll (NY)
Northeastern Jr Coll (CO)
North Idaho Coll (ID)
Owensboro Comm and Tech Coll (KY)
Paris Jr Coll (TX)
Pensacola State Coll (FL)
Queensborough Comm Coll of the City U of New York (NY)
San Jacinto Coll (TX)
San Joaquin Delta Coll (CA)
Vincennes U (IN)

DRAMATIC/THEATER ARTS AND STAGECRAFT RELATED
Lackawanna Coll (PA)

DRAWING
De Anza Coll (CA)
Luzerne County Comm Coll (PA)

EARLY CHILDHOOD EDUCATION
Alexandria Tech and Comm Coll (MN)
Alvin Comm Coll (TX)
Asheville-Buncombe Tech Comm Coll (NC)
Austin Comm Coll District (TX)
Black River Tech Coll (AR)
Bucks County Comm Coll (PA)
Camden County Coll (NJ)
Central Maine Comm Coll (ME)
Central Ohio Tech Coll (OH)
Central Oregon Comm Coll (OR)
Chesapeake Coll (MD)
Cleveland Comm Coll (NC)
Collin County Comm Coll District (TX)
Comm Coll of Baltimore County (MD)
Craven Comm Coll (NC)
Daytona State Coll (FL)
Eastern Arizona Coll (AZ)
Fayetteville Tech Comm Coll (NC)
Florida SouthWestern State Coll (FL)
Fox Valley Tech Coll (WI)
Front Range Comm Coll (CO)
Gulf Coast State Coll (FL)
Hagerstown Comm Coll (MD)
Halifax Comm Coll (NC)
Harper Coll (IL)
Harrisburg Area Comm Coll (PA)
Haywood Comm Coll (NC)
Houston Comm Coll (TX)
Iowa Central Comm Coll (IA)
James Sprunt Comm Coll (NC)
Lenoir Comm Coll (NC)
Luzerne County Comm Coll (PA)
Meridian Comm Coll (MS)
Miami Dade Coll (FL)
Minnesota State Comm and Tech Coll–Detroit Lakes (MN)
Montgomery Coll (MD)
Morton Coll (IL)
Northampton Comm Coll (PA)
Northeast Wisconsin Tech Coll (WI)
Paris Jr Coll (TX)
Pensacola State Coll (FL)
Piedmont Comm Coll (NC)
Quinsigamond Comm Coll (MA)
Richmond Comm Coll (NC)
South Arkansas Comm Coll (AR)
Southern Maine Comm Coll (ME)
Southwestern Michigan Coll (MI)
Southwest Wisconsin Tech Coll (WI)
Springfield Tech Comm Coll (MA)
Tohono O'odham Comm Coll (AZ)
U of Alaska Anchorage, Kenai Peninsula Coll (AK)
Vincennes U (IN)
Western Iowa Tech Comm Coll (IA)
Westmoreland County Comm Coll (PA)
Wor-Wic Comm Coll (MD)

E-COMMERCE
Century Coll (MN)
Lackawanna Coll (PA)

ECONOMICS
Austin Comm Coll District (TX)
Blinn Coll (TX)
Borough of Manhattan Comm Coll of the City U of New York (NY)
Chandler-Gilbert Comm Coll (AZ)
De Anza Coll (CA)
Edison State Comm Coll (OH)
Fullerton Coll (CA)
Miami Dade Coll (FL)
Mississippi Delta Comm Coll (MS)
Northeastern Jr Coll (CO)
San Joaquin Delta Coll (CA)

EDUCATION
Blinn Coll (TX)
Bossier Parish Comm Coll (LA)
Central Oregon Comm Coll (OR)
Century Coll (MN)
Chesapeake Coll (MD)
Cleveland State Comm Coll (TN)
Coll of The Albemarle (NC)
Comm Coll of Baltimore County (MD)
Crowder Coll (MO)
Dyersburg State Comm Coll (TN)
Edison State Comm Coll (OH)
Galveston Coll (TX)
Hagerstown Comm Coll (MD)
Hutchinson Comm Coll (KS)
Lackawanna Coll (PA)
Luzerne County Comm Coll (PA)
Miami Dade Coll (FL)
Mississippi Delta Comm Coll (MS)
Motlow State Comm Coll (TN)
Navarro Coll (TX)
Northeast State Comm Coll (TN)
Northern Essex Comm Coll (MA)
North Idaho Coll (ID)
Paris Jr Coll (TX)
Pensacola State Coll (FL)
Piedmont Virginia Comm Coll (VA)
Schoolcraft Coll (MI)
Southern Maine Comm Coll (ME)
Southwest Texas Jr Coll (TX)
Volunteer State Comm Coll (TN)
Walters State Comm Coll (TN)
Weatherford Coll (TX)
Wor-Wic Comm Coll (MD)

EDUCATIONAL/ INSTRUCTIONAL TECHNOLOGY
Bossier Parish Comm Coll (LA)
Tarrant County Coll District (TX)

EDUCATION (MULTIPLE LEVELS)
Camden County Coll (NJ)
Cayuga County Comm Coll (NY)
Houston Comm Coll (TX)
Kishwaukee Coll (IL)
Oklahoma State U Inst of Technology (OK)
Paris Jr Coll (TX)
South Arkansas Comm Coll (AR)

EDUCATION RELATED
Kent State U at Tuscarawas (OH)
Miami Dade Coll (FL)

EDUCATION (SPECIFIC LEVELS AND METHODS) RELATED
Miami Dade Coll (FL)
Pensacola State Coll (FL)

EDUCATION (SPECIFIC SUBJECT AREAS) RELATED
St. Charles Comm Coll (MO)

ELECTRICAL AND ELECTRONIC ENGINEERING TECHNOLOGIES RELATED
Benjamin Franklin Inst of Technology (MA)
Blue Ridge Comm and Tech Coll (WV)
Fox Valley Tech Coll (WI)
Kent State U at Tuscarawas (OH)
Lake Region State Coll (ND)
Miami Dade Coll (FL)
Minnesota State Comm and Tech Coll (MN)
North Dakota State Coll of Science (ND)
Northeast Wisconsin Tech Coll (WI)
Owensboro Comm and Tech Coll (KY)
Somerset Comm Coll (KY)

ELECTRICAL AND ELECTRONICS ENGINEERING
Comm Coll of Baltimore County (MD)
Fiorello H. LaGuardia Comm Coll of the City U of New York (NY)
Galveston Coll (TX)
Montgomery County Comm Coll (PA)

ELECTRICAL AND POWER TRANSMISSION INSTALLATION
Benjamin Franklin Inst of Technology (MA)
Chandler-Gilbert Comm Coll (AZ)
Clackamas Comm Coll (OR)
Comm Coll of Allegheny County (PA)
Galveston Coll (TX)
Oklahoma State U Inst of Technology (OK)
Piedmont Comm Coll (NC)
Richmond Comm Coll (NC)
San Jacinto Coll (TX)
State U of New York Coll of Technology at Alfred (NY)

ELECTRICAL AND POWER TRANSMISSION INSTALLATION RELATED
Minnesota State Comm and Tech Coll–Wadena (MN)

ELECTRICAL, ELECTRONIC AND COMMUNICATIONS ENGINEERING TECHNOLOGY
Adirondack Comm Coll (NY)
Alamance Comm Coll (NC)
Alvin Comm Coll (TX)
Amarillo Coll (TX)
Anoka Tech Coll (MN)
Asheville-Buncombe Tech Comm Coll (NC)
Austin Comm Coll District (TX)
Benjamin Franklin Inst of Technology (MA)
Bristol Comm Coll (MA)
Camden County Coll (NJ)
Cayuga County Comm Coll (NY)
Central Oregon Comm Coll (OR)
Citrus Coll (CA)
Clackamas Comm Coll (OR)
Cleveland Comm Coll (NC)
Cleveland State Comm Coll (TN)
Coll of DuPage (IL)
Collin County Comm Coll District (TX)
Comm Coll of Allegheny County (PA)
Craven Comm Coll (NC)
Crowder Coll (MO)
Daytona State Coll (FL)
Des Moines Area Comm Coll (IA)
Dunwoody Coll of Technology (MN)
Dutchess Comm Coll (NY)
Eastern Gateway Comm Coll (OH)
Edison State Comm Coll (OH)
Fayetteville Tech Comm Coll (NC)
Fox Valley Tech Coll (WI)
Front Range Comm Coll (CO)
Grand Rapids Comm Coll (MI)
Greenville Tech Coll (SC)
Gulf Coast State Coll (FL)
Hagerstown Comm Coll (MD)
Harper Coll (IL)
Harrisburg Area Comm Coll (PA)
Hawkeye Comm Coll (IA)
Haywood Comm Coll (NC)
Hillsborough Comm Coll (FL)
Hopkinsville Comm Coll (KY)
Kaskaskia Coll (IL)
Kirtland Comm Coll (MI)
Kishwaukee Coll (IL)
Lake Area Tech Inst (SD)
Lakeland Comm Coll (OH)
Luzerne County Comm Coll (PA)
Mayland Comm Coll (NC)
Meridian Comm Coll (MS)
Miami Dade Coll (FL)
Middlesex County Coll (NJ)
Minnesota State Comm and Tech Coll (MN)
Mississippi Delta Comm Coll (MS)
Montgomery County Comm Coll (PA)
Mt. San Antonio Coll (CA)
Northampton Comm Coll (PA)
Northeast Iowa Comm Coll (IA)
Northeast State Comm Coll (TN)
Northeast Wisconsin Tech Coll (WI)
Northern Essex Comm Coll (MA)
North Idaho Coll (ID)
Northwest State Comm Coll (OH)
Oakton Comm Coll (IL)
Paris Jr Coll (TX)
Penn State DuBois (PA)
Penn State Fayette, The Eberly Campus (PA)
Pensacola State Coll (FL)
Portland Comm Coll (OR)
Queensborough Comm Coll of the City U of New York (NY)
Quinsigamond Comm Coll (MA)
Richmond Comm Coll (NC)
Ridgewater Coll (MN)
Rock Valley Coll (IL)
San Jacinto Coll (TX)
San Joaquin Delta Coll (CA)
San Juan Coll (NM)
Schoolcraft Coll (MI)
Southern Maine Comm Coll (ME)
South Suburban Coll (IL)
Southwestern Comm Coll (NC)
Springfield Tech Comm Coll (MA)
State U of New York Coll of Technology at Alfred (NY)
Tarrant County Coll District (TX)
Trident Tech Coll (SC)
Vincennes U (IN)
Westchester Comm Coll (NY)
Westmoreland County Comm Coll (PA)

ELECTRICAL/ELECTRONICS DRAFTING AND CAD/CADD
Dunwoody Coll of Technology (MN)
Meridian Comm Coll (MS)

ELECTRICAL/ELECTRONICS EQUIPMENT INSTALLATION AND REPAIR
Coll of DuPage (IL)
Fullerton Coll (CA)
Hutchinson Comm Coll (KS)
Los Angeles City Coll (CA)
Mesabi Range Coll (MN)
Sierra Coll (CA)
State Tech Coll of Missouri (MO)

ELECTRICIAN
Asheville-Buncombe Tech Comm Coll (NC)
Bellingham Tech Coll (WA)
Bevill State Comm Coll (AL)
Cleveland Comm Coll (NC)
Coll of Eastern Idaho (ID)
Comm Coll of Allegheny County (PA)
Delta Coll (MI)
Dunwoody Coll of Technology (MN)
Fayetteville Tech Comm Coll (NC)
Gateway Comm and Tech Coll (KY)
Harrisburg Area Comm Coll (PA)
Haywood Comm Coll (NC)
Hutchinson Comm Coll (KS)
Luzerne County Comm Coll (PA)
Miami Dade Coll (FL)
Northampton Comm Coll (PA)
Northeast Iowa Comm Coll (IA)
Owensboro Comm and Tech Coll (KY)
Piedmont Comm Coll (NC)
Ridgewater Coll (MN)
Rock Valley Coll (IL)
Southwestern Comm Coll (IA)
State Tech Coll of Missouri (MO)
Tohono O'odham Comm Coll (AZ)
Western Dakota Tech Inst (SD)
West Kentucky Comm and Tech Coll (KY)

ELECTROMECHANICAL AND INSTRUMENTATION AND MAINTENANCE TECHNOLOGIES RELATED
Asheville-Buncombe Tech Comm Coll (NC)
Fayetteville Tech Comm Coll (NC)
Greenville Tech Coll (SC)
Halifax Comm Coll (NC)
Haywood Comm Coll (NC)
Lenoir Comm Coll (NC)
Northeast Wisconsin Tech Coll (WI)
Piedmont Comm Coll (NC)
Richmond Comm Coll (NC)

ELECTROMECHANICAL TECHNOLOGY
Bay de Noc Comm Coll (MI)
Bristol Comm Coll (MA)
Camden County Coll (NJ)
Central Maine Comm Coll (ME)
Chandler-Gilbert Comm Coll (AZ)
Cleveland State Comm Coll (TN)
Coll of DuPage (IL)
Craven Comm Coll (NC)
Edison State Comm Coll (OH)
Fox Valley Tech Coll (WI)
Galveston Coll (TX)
Kirtland Comm Coll (MI)
Maysville Comm and Tech Coll, Maysville (KY)
Motlow State Comm Coll (TN)
Northampton Comm Coll (PA)
Northeast Wisconsin Tech Coll (WI)
Paris Jr Coll (TX)
Richmond Comm Coll (NC)
Ridgewater Coll (MN)
Southwest Wisconsin Tech Coll (WI)
Springfield Tech Comm Coll (MA)
State U of New York Coll of Technology at Alfred (NY)
Tarrant County Coll District (TX)
Union County Coll (NJ)
Volunteer State Comm Coll (TN)

ELECTRONEURODIAGNOSTIC/ ELECTROENCEPHALOGRAPHIC TECHNOLOGY
Alvin Comm Coll (TX)
Collin County Comm Coll District (TX)
Comm Coll of Denver (CO)
Fox Valley Tech Coll (WI)
Lenoir Comm Coll (NC)

ELEMENTARY EDUCATION
Amarillo Coll (TX)
Anoka-Ramsey Comm Coll (MN)
Asheville-Buncombe Tech Comm Coll (NC)
Bristol Comm Coll (MA)
Century Coll (MN)
Chandler-Gilbert Comm Coll (AZ)
Chesapeake Coll (MD)
Cleveland Comm Coll (NC)
Comm Coll of Baltimore County (MD)
Craven Comm Coll (NC)
Crowder Coll (MO)
Eastern Arizona Coll (AZ)
Fayetteville Tech Comm Coll (NC)
Hagerstown Comm Coll (MD)
Harper Coll (IL)
Haywood Comm Coll (NC)
James Sprunt Comm Coll (NC)
Miami Dade Coll (FL)
Mississippi Delta Comm Coll (MS)
Montgomery Coll (MD)
Montgomery County Comm Coll (PA)
Mount Wachusett Comm Coll (MA)
Navarro Coll (TX)
Niagara County Comm Coll (NY)
Northeastern Jr Coll (CO)
Northern Essex Comm Coll (MA)
North Idaho Coll (ID)
Paris Jr Coll (TX)
Pensacola State Coll (FL)
Quinsigamond Comm Coll (MA)
San Juan Coll (NM)
Seminole State Coll (OK)
Springfield Tech Comm Coll (MA)
Tohono O'odham Comm Coll (AZ)
Truckee Meadows Comm Coll (NV)
Vincennes U (IN)
Western Iowa Tech Comm Coll (IA)
Wor-Wic Comm Coll (MD)

EMERGENCY MEDICAL TECHNOLOGY (EMT PARAMEDIC)
Alvin Comm Coll (TX)
Amarillo Coll (TX)
Arapahoe Comm Coll (CO)
Asheville-Buncombe Tech Comm Coll (NC)
Austin Comm Coll District (TX)
Bay de Noc Comm Coll (MI)
Bevill State Comm Coll (AL)
Black Hawk Coll, Moline (IL)
Black River Tech Coll (AR)
Blue Ridge Comm and Tech Coll (WV)
Borough of Manhattan Comm Coll of the City U of New York (NY)
Bossier Parish Comm Coll (LA)
Camden County Coll (NJ)
Central Ohio Tech Coll (OH)
Central Oregon Comm Coll (OR)
Century Coll (MN)
Chesapeake Coll (MD)
Clackamas Comm Coll (OR)
Cleveland Comm Coll (NC)
Cleveland State Comm Coll (TN)
Coll of DuPage (IL)
Collin County Comm Coll District (TX)
Comm Coll of Allegheny County (PA)
Comm Coll of Baltimore County (MD)
Crowder Coll (MO)
Daytona State Coll (FL)
Dutchess Comm Coll (NY)
Dyersburg State Comm Coll (TN)
Eastern Arizona Coll (AZ)
Eastern Gateway Comm Coll (OH)
Fayetteville Tech Comm Coll (NC)
Fiorello H. LaGuardia Comm Coll of the City U of New York (NY)
Florida SouthWestern State Coll (FL)
Galveston Coll (TX)
Gateway Comm and Tech Coll (KY)
Great Falls Coll Montana State U (MT)
Greenville Tech Coll (SC)
Gulf Coast State Coll (FL)
Hagerstown Comm Coll (MD)
Hawkeye Comm Coll (IA)
Hillsborough Comm Coll (FL)
Houston Comm Coll (TX)
Hutchinson Comm Coll (KS)
Iowa Central Comm Coll (IA)
Kaskaskia Coll (IL)
Kishwaukee Coll (IL)
Lackawanna Coll (PA)
Lake Area Tech Inst (SD)
Lenoir Comm Coll (NC)
Lurleen B. Wallace Comm Coll (AL)
Luzerne County Comm Coll (PA)
McHenry County Coll (IL)
Meridian Comm Coll (MS)
Miami Dade Coll (FL)
Motlow State Comm Coll (TN)
Mt. San Antonio Coll (CA)
North Dakota State Coll of Science (ND)
Northeastern Jr Coll (CO)
Northeast Iowa Comm Coll (IA)
Northeast State Comm Coll (TN)
Northeast Wisconsin Tech Coll (WI)
Northern Essex Comm Coll (MA)
Northland Comm and Tech Coll (MN)
Northwest-Shoals Comm Coll (AL)
Owensboro Comm and Tech Coll (KY)
Paris Jr Coll (TX)
Pensacola State Coll (FL)
Piedmont Virginia Comm Coll (VA)
Portland Comm Coll (OR)
Quinsigamond Comm Coll (MA)
Rend Lake Coll (IL)
St. Charles Comm Coll (MO)
San Jacinto Coll (TX)
San Juan Coll (NM)
Schoolcraft Coll (MI)
Somerset Comm Coll (KY)
South Arkansas Comm Coll (AR)
Southeastern Coll–West Palm Beach (FL)
Southern Maine Comm Coll (ME)
Southwestern Comm Coll (NC)
Southwest Texas Jr Coll (TX)
Tarrant County Coll District (TX)
Union County Coll (NJ)
U of Alaska Anchorage, Kenai Peninsula Coll (AK)
Weatherford Coll (TX)
Westchester Comm Coll (NY)
Western Dakota Tech Inst (SD)
Western Iowa Tech Comm Coll (IA)
West Kentucky Comm and Tech Coll (KY)
Wor-Wic Comm Coll (MD)

ENERGY MANAGEMENT AND SYSTEMS TECHNOLOGY
Century Coll (MN)
Crowder Coll (MO)
Danville Area Comm Coll (IL)
De Anza Coll (CA)
Delta Coll (MI)
Fiorello H. LaGuardia Comm Coll of the City U of New York (NY)
Front Range Comm Coll (CO)
Gateway Comm and Tech Coll (KY)
Great Falls Coll Montana State U (MT)
Houston Comm Coll (TX)
Lakeland Comm Coll (OH)
Middlesex County Coll (NJ)
Mount Wachusett Comm Coll (MA)
Northeast Iowa Comm Coll (IA)
Northeast Wisconsin Tech Coll (WI)
Northwest State Comm Coll (OH)
Quinsigamond Comm Coll (MA)
Raritan Valley Comm Coll (NJ)
Rock Valley Coll (IL)
Truckee Meadows Comm Coll (NV)
Walters State Comm Coll (TN)
Western Iowa Tech Comm Coll (IA)

ENGINEERING
Adirondack Comm Coll (NY)
Amarillo Coll (TX)
Austin Comm Coll District (TX)
Blinn Coll (TX)
Borough of Manhattan Comm Coll of the City U of New York (NY)
Bossier Parish Comm Coll (LA)
Bristol Comm Coll (MA)
Bucks County Comm Coll (PA)
Central Lakes Coll (MN)
Central Oregon Comm Coll (OR)
Citrus Coll (CA)
Coll of DuPage (IL)
Collin County Comm Coll District (TX)
Comm Coll of Baltimore County (MD)
Danville Area Comm Coll (IL)
De Anza Coll (CA)
Dutchess Comm Coll (NY)
Fullerton Coll (CA)
Hagerstown Comm Coll (MD)
Halifax Comm Coll (NC)
Harper Coll (IL)
Harrisburg Area Comm Coll (PA)
Hutchinson Comm Coll (KS)
Jamestown Comm Coll (NY)
Kaskaskia Coll (IL)
Kishwaukee Coll (IL)
Los Angeles City Coll (CA)
McHenry County Coll (IL)
Miami Dade Coll (FL)
Minnesota State Comm and Tech Coll–Moorhead (MN)
Montgomery Coll (MD)
Nassau Comm Coll (NY)
Navarro Coll (TX)
Northampton Comm Coll (PA)
North Idaho Coll (ID)
Oakton Comm Coll (IL)
Paris Jr Coll (TX)
Pensacola State Coll (FL)
Piedmont Virginia Comm Coll (VA)
Queensborough Comm Coll of the City U of New York (NY)
Rend Lake Coll (IL)
San Jacinto Coll (TX)
San Joaquin Delta Coll (CA)
San Juan Coll (NM)
Schoolcraft Coll (MI)
Seminole State Coll (OK)
Sierra Coll (CA)
Southern Maine Comm Coll (ME)
Southwest Texas Jr Coll (TX)
Springfield Tech Comm Coll (MA)
State U of New York Coll of Technology at Alfred (NY)
Truckee Meadows Comm Coll (NV)
Union County Coll (NJ)

ENGINEERING RELATED
Miami Dade Coll (FL)

Northwest State Comm Coll (OH)
San Joaquin Delta Coll (CA)

ENGINEERING-RELATED TECHNOLOGIES
Chesapeake Coll (MD)

ENGINEERING SCIENCE
Bristol Comm Coll (MA)
Camden County Coll (NJ)
Comm Coll of Allegheny County (PA)
Houston Comm Coll (TX)
Manchester Comm Coll (CT)
Middlesex Comm Coll (CT)
Middlesex County Coll (NJ)
Montgomery County Comm Coll (PA)
Northern Essex Comm Coll (MA)
Queensborough Comm Coll of the City U of New York (NY)
Raritan Valley Comm Coll (NJ)
Vincennes U (IN)

ENGINEERING TECHNOLOGIES AND ENGINEERING RELATED
Bristol Comm Coll (MA)
Camden County Coll (NJ)
Chesapeake Coll (MD)
Comm Coll of Baltimore County (MD)
Hagerstown Comm Coll (MD)
Harrisburg Area Comm Coll (PA)
Middlesex County Coll (NJ)
Montgomery County Comm Coll (PA)
Northwest State Comm Coll (OH)
Raritan Valley Comm Coll (NJ)
Truckee Meadows Comm Coll (NV)
Union County Coll (NJ)

ENGINEERING TECHNOLOGY
Benjamin Franklin Inst of Technology (MA)
Bucks County Comm Coll (PA)
Century Coll (MN)
Chandler-Gilbert Comm Coll (AZ)
Citrus Coll (CA)
Cleveland State Comm Coll (TN)
De Anza Coll (CA)
Gulf Coast State Coll (FL)
Hillsborough Comm Coll (FL)
Iowa Central Comm Coll (IA)
Luzerne County Comm Coll (PA)
Maysville Comm and Tech Coll, Maysville (KY)
Miami Dade Coll (FL)
Middlesex Comm Coll (CT)
Minnesota State Comm and Tech Coll–Detroit Lakes (MN)
Mt. San Antonio Coll (CA)
Oklahoma State U Inst of Technology (OK)
Pensacola State Coll (FL)
San Joaquin Delta Coll (CA)
San Juan Coll (NM)
Somerset Comm Coll (KY)
Southwestern Michigan Coll (MI)
Trident Tech Coll (SC)

ENGINE MACHINIST
Lake Area Tech Inst (SD)

ENGLISH
Amarillo Coll (TX)
Austin Comm Coll District (TX)
Blinn Coll (TX)
Borough of Manhattan Comm Coll of the City U of New York (NY)
Bucks County Comm Coll (PA)
Central Oregon Comm Coll (OR)
Citrus Coll (CA)
De Anza Coll (CA)
Edison State Comm Coll (OH)
Feather River Coll (CA)
Fiorello H. LaGuardia Comm Coll of the City U of New York (NY)
Fullerton Coll (CA)
Galveston Coll (TX)
Harper Coll (IL)
Houston Comm Coll (TX)
Hutchinson Comm Coll (KS)
Los Angeles City Coll (CA)
Los Angeles Mission Coll (CA)
Miami Dade Coll (FL)
Mississippi Delta Comm Coll (MS)
Navarro Coll (TX)
Northeastern Jr Coll (CO)
North Idaho Coll (ID)
Paris Jr Coll (TX)
Pensacola State Coll (FL)
Quinsigamond Comm Coll (MA)
Raritan Valley Comm Coll (NJ)
San Jacinto Coll (TX)
San Joaquin Delta Coll (CA)
Seminole State Coll (OK)
Sierra Coll (CA)
Truckee Meadows Comm Coll (NV)
Union County Coll (NJ)
Vincennes U (IN)
Western Iowa Tech Comm Coll (IA)

ENGLISH LANGUAGE AND LITERATURE RELATED
Citrus Coll (CA)
Mt. San Antonio Coll (CA)

ENGLISH/LANGUAGE ARTS TEACHER EDUCATION
Comm Coll of Baltimore County (MD)
Hagerstown Comm Coll (MD)
Montgomery Coll (MD)
Vincennes U (IN)

ENTREPRENEURIAL AND SMALL BUSINESS RELATED
Truckee Meadows Comm Coll (NV)

ENTREPRENEURSHIP
Austin Comm Coll District (TX)
Bristol Comm Coll (MA)
Central Oregon Comm Coll (OR)
Craven Comm Coll (NC)
Fayetteville Tech Comm Coll (NC)
Fox Valley Tech Coll (WI)
Haywood Comm Coll (NC)
Miami Dade Coll (FL)
Minnesota State Comm and Tech Coll–Detroit Lakes (MN)
Nassau Comm Coll (NY)
North Dakota State Coll of Science (ND)
Northeast Wisconsin Tech Coll (WI)
Northwest State Comm Coll (OH)

ENVIRONMENTAL BIOLOGY
Eastern Arizona Coll (AZ)

ENVIRONMENTAL CONTROL TECHNOLOGIES RELATED
Middlesex County Coll (NJ)
Northeast Wisconsin Tech Coll (WI)
Westchester Comm Coll (NY)
Western Dakota Tech Inst (SD)

ENVIRONMENTAL ENGINEERING TECHNOLOGY
Austin Comm Coll District (TX)
Bay de Noc Comm Coll (MI)
Bristol Comm Coll (MA)
Crowder Coll (MO)
Delta Coll (MI)
Miami Dade Coll (FL)
Northwest-Shoals Comm Coll (AL)
Schoolcraft Coll (MI)
State U of New York Coll of Technology at Alfred (NY)

ENVIRONMENTAL HEALTH
Amarillo Coll (TX)
North Idaho Coll (ID)
St. Charles Comm Coll (MO)

ENVIRONMENTAL SCIENCE
Anoka-Ramsey Comm Coll (MN)
Austin Comm Coll District (TX)
Bucks County Comm Coll (PA)
Cayuga County Comm Coll (NY)
Chesapeake Coll (MD)
Daytona State Coll (FL)
Fiorello H. LaGuardia Comm Coll of the City U of New York (NY)
Harrisburg Area Comm Coll (PA)
Hillsborough Comm Coll (FL)
Jamestown Comm Coll (NY)
Lackawanna Coll (PA)
Lake Area Tech Inst (SD)
Miami Dade Coll (FL)
Northampton Comm Coll (PA)
Queensborough Comm Coll of the City U of New York (NY)
Quinsigamond Comm Coll (MA)
San Jacinto Coll (TX)
Truckee Meadows Comm Coll (NV)
Westchester Comm Coll (NY)

ENVIRONMENTAL STUDIES
Bristol Comm Coll (MA)
Columbia-Greene Comm Coll (NY)
De Anza Coll (CA)
Feather River Coll (CA)
Fullerton Coll (CA)
Hagerstown Comm Coll (MD)
Harper Coll (IL)
Middlesex Comm Coll (CT)
Minnesota State Comm and Tech Coll (MN)
Minnesota State Comm and Tech Coll–Moorhead (MN)
Montgomery County Comm Coll (PA)
Mt. San Antonio Coll (CA)
Mount Wachusett Comm Coll (MA)
Vincennes U (IN)
Westchester Comm Coll (NY)

EQUESTRIAN STUDIES
Black Hawk Coll, Moline (IL)
Minnesota State Comm and Tech Coll (MN)
Northeastern Jr Coll (CO)
Sierra Coll (CA)

ETHNIC, CULTURAL MINORITY, GENDER, AND GROUP STUDIES RELATED
Borough of Manhattan Comm Coll of the City U of New York (NY)
Fullerton Coll (CA)

EXECUTIVE ASSISTANT/ EXECUTIVE SECRETARY
Alamance Comm Coll (NC)
Alvin Comm Coll (TX)
Bellingham Tech Coll (WA)
Crowder Coll (MO)
Danville Area Comm Coll (IL)
Edison State Comm Coll (OH)
Hopkinsville Comm Coll (KY)
Kaskaskia Coll (IL)
Luzerne County Comm Coll (PA)
Maysville Comm and Tech Coll, Maysville (KY)
Owensboro Comm and Tech Coll (KY)
Quinsigamond Comm Coll (MA)
Shawnee Comm Coll (IL)
Somerset Comm Coll (KY)
South Suburban Coll (IL)

FACILITIES PLANNING AND MANAGEMENT
Dunwoody Coll of Technology (MN)

FAMILY AND COMMUNITY SERVICES
Chandler-Gilbert Comm Coll (AZ)

FAMILY AND CONSUMER ECONOMICS RELATED
Los Angeles Mission Coll (CA)

FAMILY AND CONSUMER SCIENCES/HOME ECONOMICS TEACHER EDUCATION
Vincennes U (IN)

FAMILY AND CONSUMER SCIENCES/HUMAN SCIENCES
Hutchinson Comm Coll (KS)
Mississippi Delta Comm Coll (MS)
Mt. San Antonio Coll (CA)
San Joaquin Delta Coll (CA)
Vincennes U (IN)

FAMILY SYSTEMS
Maysville Comm and Tech Coll, Maysville (KY)

FARM AND RANCH MANAGEMENT
Crowder Coll (MO)
Hutchinson Comm Coll (KS)
Northeastern Jr Coll (CO)
Northeast Wisconsin Tech Coll (WI)
Southwest Texas Jr Coll (TX)

FASHION AND FABRIC CONSULTING
Coll of DuPage (IL)
Harper Coll (IL)

FASHION/APPAREL DESIGN
Austin Comm Coll District (TX)
Coll of DuPage (IL)
Fullerton Coll (CA)
Harper Coll (IL)
Houston Comm Coll (TX)
Nassau Comm Coll (NY)

FASHION MERCHANDISING
Alexandria Tech and Comm Coll (MN)
Coll of DuPage (IL)
Grand Rapids Comm Coll (MI)
Harper Coll (IL)
Houston Comm Coll (TX)
Minnesota State Comm and Tech Coll (MN)
Mt. San Antonio Coll (CA)
Nassau Comm Coll (NY)
San Joaquin Delta Coll (CA)
Tarrant County Coll District (TX)
Vincennes U (IN)

FIBER, TEXTILE AND WEAVING ARTS
Haywood Comm Coll (NC)

FILM/CINEMA/VIDEO STUDIES
De Anza Coll (CA)

FINANCE
Borough of Manhattan Comm Coll of the City U of New York (NY)
Harper Coll (IL)
Los Angeles City Coll (CA)
Los Angeles Mission Coll (CA)
McLennan Comm Coll (TX)
Miami Dade Coll (FL)
Morton Coll (IL)
Mt. San Antonio Coll (CA)
Stark State Coll (OH)
Western Iowa Tech Comm Coll (IA)

FINANCE AND FINANCIAL MANAGEMENT SERVICES RELATED
Bristol Comm Coll (MA)

FINANCIAL PLANNING AND SERVICES
Lackawanna Coll (PA)
Minnesota State Comm and Tech Coll (MN)

FINE ARTS RELATED
Schoolcraft Coll (MI)
Seminole State Coll (OK)
Truckee Meadows Comm Coll (NV)
Western Iowa Tech Comm Coll (IA)
Westmoreland County Comm Coll (PA)

FINE/STUDIO ARTS
Amarillo Coll (TX)
Anoka-Ramsey Comm Coll (MN)
Bay de Noc Comm Coll (MI)
Borough of Manhattan Comm Coll of the City U of New York (NY)
Bristol Comm Coll (MA)
Camden County Coll (NJ)
Cayuga County Comm Coll (NY)
Central Oregon Comm Coll (OR)
Chandler-Gilbert Comm Coll (AZ)
Columbia-Greene Comm Coll (NY)
Delta Coll (MI)
Eastern Arizona Coll (AZ)
Fiorello H. LaGuardia Comm Coll of the City U of New York (NY)
Grand Rapids Comm Coll (MI)
Harper Coll (IL)
Houston Comm Coll (TX)
Jamestown Comm Coll (NY)
Kishwaukee Coll (IL)
Manchester Comm Coll (CT)
McHenry County Coll (IL)
Middlesex Comm Coll (CT)
Morton Coll (IL)
Niagara County Comm Coll (NY)
Northampton Comm Coll (PA)
Northeastern Jr Coll (CO)
Owensboro Comm and Tech Coll (KY)
Raritan Valley Comm Coll (NJ)
Rend Lake Coll (IL)
South Suburban Coll (IL)
Springfield Tech Comm Coll (MA)
Tohono O'odham Comm Coll (AZ)
West Kentucky Comm and Tech Coll (KY)
Westmoreland County Comm Coll (PA)

FIRE PREVENTION AND SAFETY TECHNOLOGY
Austin Comm Coll District (TX)
Camden County Coll (NJ)
Cleveland Comm Coll (NC)
Collin County Comm Coll District (TX)
Comm Coll of Allegheny County (PA)
Daytona State Coll (FL)
Delta Coll (MI)
Des Moines Area Comm Coll (IA)
Fayetteville Tech Comm Coll (NC)
Florida SouthWestern State Coll (FL)
Gulf Coast State Coll (FL)
Hillsborough Comm Coll (FL)
Houston Comm Coll (TX)
Lakeland Comm Coll (OH)
Miami Dade Coll (FL)
Middlesex County Coll (NJ)
Montgomery Coll (MD)
Montgomery County Comm Coll (PA)
Mount Wachusett Comm Coll (MA)
Northland Comm and Tech Coll (MN)
Pensacola State Coll (FL)
Portland Comm Coll (OR)
Springfield Tech Comm Coll (MA)
Truckee Meadows Comm Coll (NV)
Union County Coll (NJ)

FIRE SCIENCE/FIREFIGHTING
Amarillo Coll (TX)
Black River Tech Coll (AR)
Blinn Coll (TX)
Bristol Comm Coll (MA)
Central Ohio Tech Coll (OH)
Central Oregon Comm Coll (OR)
Century Coll (MN)
Clackamas Comm Coll (OR)
Coll of DuPage (IL)
Coll of Eastern Idaho (ID)
Collin County Comm Coll District (TX)
Crowder Coll (MO)
Danville Area Comm Coll (IL)
Eastern Arizona Coll (AZ)
Fox Valley Tech Coll (WI)
Gateway Comm and Tech Coll (KY)
Harper Coll (IL)
Harrisburg Area Comm Coll (PA)
Hutchinson Comm Coll (KS)
Iowa Central Comm Coll (IA)
Luzerne County Comm Coll (PA)
McHenry County Coll (IL)
Meridian Comm Coll (MS)
Miami Dade Coll (FL)
Morton Coll (IL)
Mt. San Antonio Coll (CA)
Navarro Coll (TX)
Northampton Comm Coll (PA)
Northeast Iowa Comm Coll (IA)
Oakton Comm Coll (IL)
Owensboro Comm and Tech Coll (KY)
Rock Valley Coll (IL)
San Jacinto Coll (TX)
San Joaquin Delta Coll (CA)
San Juan Coll (NM)
Schoolcraft Coll (MI)
Sierra Coll (CA)
Southern Maine Comm Coll (ME)
Southwestern Michigan Coll (MI)
Tarrant County Coll District (TX)
Vincennes U (IN)
Volunteer State Comm Coll (TN)
Weatherford Coll (TX)
Western Dakota Tech Inst (SD)
Western Iowa Tech Comm Coll (IA)
West Kentucky Comm and Tech Coll (KY)

FIRE SERVICES ADMINISTRATION
Bucks County Comm Coll (PA)
Camden County Coll (NJ)
Central Oregon Comm Coll (OR)
Dutchess Comm Coll (NY)
Minnesota State Comm and Tech Coll (MN)
Northampton Comm Coll (PA)
Quinsigamond Comm Coll (MA)
Schoolcraft Coll (MI)

FIRE SYSTEMS TECHNOLOGY
Northeast Wisconsin Tech Coll (WI)

FISHING AND FISHERIES SCIENCES AND MANAGEMENT
Bellingham Tech Coll (WA)
North Idaho Coll (ID)

FLORICULTURE/FLORISTRY MANAGEMENT
Danville Area Comm Coll (IL)

FOODS AND NUTRITION RELATED
Schoolcraft Coll (MI)

FOOD SCIENCE
Chandler-Gilbert Comm Coll (AZ)
Miami Dade Coll (FL)

FOOD SERVICE AND DINING ROOM MANAGEMENT
Kaskaskia Coll (IL)
Montgomery County Comm Coll (PA)

FOOD SERVICE SYSTEMS ADMINISTRATION
Harper Coll (IL)
Pensacola State Coll (FL)
Westchester Comm Coll (NY)

FOODS, NUTRITION, AND WELLNESS
Bossier Parish Comm Coll (LA)
Fullerton Coll (CA)
Pensacola State Coll (FL)
Truckee Meadows Comm Coll (NV)

FOOD TECHNOLOGY AND PROCESSING
Luzerne County Comm Coll (PA)
Tarrant County Coll District (TX)

FOREIGN LANGUAGES AND LITERATURES
Borough of Manhattan Comm Coll of the City U of New York (NY)
Central Oregon Comm Coll (OR)
Eastern Arizona Coll (AZ)
Fullerton Coll (CA)
Hutchinson Comm Coll (KS)
Paris Jr Coll (TX)
San Jacinto Coll (TX)
Vincennes U (IN)

FORENSIC SCIENCE AND TECHNOLOGY
Black River Tech Coll (AR)
Borough of Manhattan Comm Coll of the City U of New York (NY)
Central Maine Comm Coll (ME)
Chandler-Gilbert Comm Coll (AZ)
Fayetteville Tech Comm Coll (NC)
Florida SouthWestern State Coll (FL)
Fox Valley Tech Coll (WI)
Gulf Coast State Coll (FL)
Kishwaukee Coll (IL)
Miami Dade Coll (FL)
Pensacola State Coll (FL)
Queensborough Comm Coll of the City U of New York (NY)
Shawnee Comm Coll (IL)

FOREST/FOREST RESOURCES MANAGEMENT
Central Oregon Comm Coll (OR)

FORESTRY
Central Oregon Comm Coll (OR)
Eastern Arizona Coll (AZ)
Miami Dade Coll (FL)
North Idaho Coll (ID)
Sierra Coll (CA)

FOREST TECHNOLOGY
Central Oregon Comm Coll (OR)
Haywood Comm Coll (NC)
Lurleen B. Wallace Comm Coll (AL)
Mt. San Antonio Coll (CA)
Penn State Mont Alto (PA)

FRENCH
Austin Comm Coll District (TX)
Blinn Coll (TX)
Citrus Coll (CA)
Los Angeles City Coll (CA)
Miami Dade Coll (FL)
North Idaho Coll (ID)

FUNERAL SERVICE AND MORTUARY SCIENCE
Amarillo Coll (TX)
American Acad McAllister Inst of Funeral Service (NY)
Arapahoe Comm Coll (CO)
Chandler-Gilbert Comm Coll (AZ)
Comm Coll of Baltimore County (MD)
Des Moines Area Comm Coll (IA)
Fayetteville Tech Comm Coll (NC)
Luzerne County Comm Coll (PA)
Miami Dade Coll (FL)
Nassau Comm Coll (NY)
Northampton Comm Coll (PA)
Vincennes U (IN)

GAME AND INTERACTIVE MEDIA DESIGN
Arapahoe Comm Coll (CO)
Cayuga County Comm Coll (NY)
Collin County Comm Coll District (TX)
Comm Coll of Allegheny County (PA)
Fayetteville Tech Comm Coll (NC)
Miami Dade Coll (FL)
Montgomery County Comm Coll (PA)
Quinsigamond Comm Coll (MA)
Raritan Valley Comm Coll (NJ)
State U of New York Coll of Technology at Alfred (NY)
Western Iowa Tech Comm Coll (IA)

GENERAL STUDIES
Alvin Comm Coll (TX)
Amarillo Coll (TX)
Arapahoe Comm Coll (CO)
Asheville-Buncombe Tech Comm Coll (NC)
Austin Comm Coll District (TX)
Bay de Noc Comm Coll (MI)
Bevill State Comm Coll (AL)
Black Hawk Coll, Moline (IL)
Blinn Coll (TX)
Blue Ridge Comm and Tech Coll (WV)
Borough of Manhattan Comm Coll of the City U of New York (NY)
Bossier Parish Comm Coll (LA)
Bristol Comm Coll (MA)
Bucks County Comm Coll (PA)
Central Maine Comm Coll (ME)
Central Oregon Comm Coll (OR)
Chandler-Gilbert Comm Coll (AZ)
Clackamas Comm Coll (OR)
Cleveland Comm Coll (NC)
Cleveland State Comm Coll (TN)
Columbia-Greene Comm Coll (NY)
Comm Coll of Allegheny County (PA)
Comm Coll of Denver (CO)
Craven Comm Coll (NC)
Crowder Coll (MO)
Danville Area Comm Coll (IL)
Delta Coll (MI)
Dutchess Comm Coll (NY)
Dyersburg State Comm Coll (TN)
Eastern Arizona Coll (AZ)
Front Range Comm Coll (CO)
Galveston Coll (TX)
Harrisburg Area Comm Coll (PA)
Hesston Coll (KS)
Houston Comm Coll (TX)
James Sprunt Comm Coll (NC)
Jamestown Comm Coll (NY)
Kaskaskia Coll (IL)
Kirtland Comm Coll (MI)
Lenoir Comm Coll (NC)
Lurleen B. Wallace Comm Coll (AL)
Luzerne County Comm Coll (PA)
Manchester Comm Coll (CT)
Marion Military Inst (AL)
Mayland Comm Coll (NC)
McHenry County Coll (IL)
Miami Dade Coll (FL)
Nassau Comm Coll (NY)
Niagara County Comm Coll (NY)
Northampton Comm Coll (PA)
Northeast State Comm Coll (TN)
Northern Essex Comm Coll (MA)
Northwest-Shoals Comm Coll (AL)
Paris Jr Coll (TX)
Piedmont Comm Coll (NC)
Piedmont Virginia Comm Coll (VA)
Portland Comm Coll (OR)
Quinsigamond Comm Coll (MA)
St. Charles Comm Coll (MO)
San Jacinto Coll (TX)
San Juan Coll (NM)
Seminole State Coll (OK)
Shawnee Comm Coll (IL)
Sierra Coll (CA)
South Arkansas Comm Coll (AR)
Southwestern Michigan Coll (MI)
Southwest Texas Jr Coll (TX)
State U of New York Coll of Technology at Alfred (NY)
Truckee Meadows Comm Coll (NV)
U of Alaska Anchorage, Kenai Peninsula Coll (AK)
Walters State Comm Coll (TN)
Western Nevada Coll (NV)

GEOGRAPHIC INFORMATION SCIENCE AND CARTOGRAPHY
Austin Comm Coll District (TX)
Borough of Manhattan Comm Coll of the City U of New York (NY)
Cayuga County Comm Coll (NY)
Central Oregon Comm Coll (OR)
Collin County Comm Coll District (TX)
Front Range Comm Coll (CO)
Harrisburg Area Comm Coll (PA)

GEOGRAPHY
Austin Comm Coll District (TX)
Blinn Coll (TX)
Central Oregon Comm Coll (OR)
Chandler-Gilbert Comm Coll (AZ)
Fullerton Coll (CA)
Los Angeles Mission Coll (CA)
Mississippi Delta Comm Coll (MS)
Montgomery Coll (MD)
Northeastern Jr Coll (CO)

GEOLOGY/EARTH SCIENCE
Amarillo Coll (TX)
Austin Comm Coll District (TX)
Blinn Coll (TX)
Central Oregon Comm Coll (OR)
Century Coll (MN)
Chandler-Gilbert Comm Coll (AZ)
Eastern Arizona Coll (AZ)
Edison State Comm Coll (OH)
Fullerton Coll (CA)
Miami Dade Coll (FL)
Middlesex County Coll (NJ)
Northeastern Jr Coll (CO)
North Idaho Coll (ID)
Pensacola State Coll (FL)
San Jacinto Coll (TX)
San Joaquin Delta Coll (CA)
Sierra Coll (CA)
Truckee Meadows Comm Coll (NV)

GERMAN
Austin Comm Coll District (TX)
Blinn Coll (TX)
Citrus Coll (CA)
Miami Dade Coll (FL)
North Idaho Coll (ID)

GERONTOLOGY
Borough of Manhattan Comm Coll of the City U of New York (NY)
Northeast Wisconsin Tech Coll (WI)
Portland Comm Coll (OR)

GOLF COURSE OPERATION AND GROUNDS MANAGEMENT
Anoka Tech Coll (MN)
Hawkeye Comm Coll (IA)
Southwest Wisconsin Tech Coll (WI)

GRAPHIC AND PRINTING EQUIPMENT OPERATION/PRODUCTION
Central Maine Comm Coll (ME)
Coll of DuPage (IL)
Fullerton Coll (CA)
Luzerne County Comm Coll (PA)
Mississippi Delta Comm Coll (MS)
Rock Valley Coll (IL)
Tarrant County Coll District (TX)

GRAPHIC COMMUNICATIONS
Central Maine Comm Coll (ME)
Hutchinson Comm Coll (KS)
Piedmont Comm Coll (NC)

GRAPHIC COMMUNICATIONS RELATED
Middlesex County Coll (NJ)

GRAPHIC DESIGN
Arapahoe Comm Coll (CO)
Bristol Comm Coll (MA)
Century Coll (MN)
Collin County Comm Coll District (TX)
Comm Coll of Allegheny County (PA)
Comm Coll of Denver (CO)
De Anza Coll (CA)
Dunwoody Coll of Technology (MN)
Eastern Arizona Coll (AZ)
Fullerton Coll (CA)
Harrisburg Area Comm Coll (PA)
Kirtland Comm Coll (MI)
Lenoir Comm Coll (NC)
Los Angeles City Coll (CA)
Luzerne County Comm Coll (PA)
Meridian Comm Coll (MS)
Minnesota State Comm and Tech Coll (MN)
Minnesota State Comm and Tech Coll–Moorhead (MN)
Northampton Comm Coll (PA)
Oakton Comm Coll (IL)
Oklahoma State U Inst of Technology (OK)
Pensacola State Coll (FL)
Rend Lake Coll (IL)
Sierra Coll (CA)
Southwestern Michigan Coll (MI)
State U of New York Coll of Technology at Alfred (NY)
Westmoreland County Comm Coll (PA)

GUNSMITHING
Fayetteville Tech Comm Coll (NC)
Lenoir Comm Coll (NC)

HAZARDOUS MATERIALS MANAGEMENT AND WASTE TECHNOLOGY
Fullerton Coll (CA)
Pensacola State Coll (FL)
Sierra Coll (CA)

HEALTH AND PHYSICAL EDUCATION/FITNESS
Alvin Comm Coll (TX)
Austin Comm Coll District (TX)
Blinn Coll (TX)
Central Oregon Comm Coll (OR)
Citrus Coll (CA)
Coll of The Albemarle (NC)
Comm Coll of Allegheny County (PA)
Eastern Arizona Coll (AZ)
Feather River Coll (CA)
Fullerton Coll (CA)
Galveston Coll (TX)
Harrisburg Area Comm Coll (PA)
Houston Comm Coll (TX)
Jamestown Comm Coll (NY)
Luzerne County Comm Coll (PA)
McHenry County Coll (IL)
Montgomery County Comm Coll (PA)
Mt. San Antonio Coll (CA)
Northern Essex Comm Coll (MA)
San Jacinto Coll (TX)
San Juan Coll (NM)
Sierra Coll (CA)
Vincennes U (IN)
Westchester Comm Coll (NY)

HEALTH AND PHYSICAL EDUCATION RELATED
Fayetteville Tech Comm Coll (NC)
Portland Comm Coll (OR)

HEALTH AND WELLNESS
Northeast Wisconsin Tech Coll (WI)

HEALTH/HEALTH-CARE ADMINISTRATION
Alvin Comm Coll (TX)
Coll of DuPage (IL)
Des Moines Area Comm Coll (IA)
Harrisburg Area Comm Coll (PA)
Iowa Central Comm Coll (IA)
Luzerne County Comm Coll (PA)
Northeast Wisconsin Tech Coll (WI)
North Idaho Coll (ID)
Pensacola State Coll (FL)
Quinsigamond Comm Coll (MA)
Schoolcraft Coll (MI)

HEALTH INFORMATION/MEDICAL RECORDS ADMINISTRATION
Amarillo Coll (TX)
Camden County Coll (NJ)
Coll of DuPage (IL)
The Coll of Westchester (NY)
Great Falls Coll Montana State U (MT)
McLennan Comm Coll (TX)
Meridian Comm Coll (MS)
Miami Dade Coll (FL)
Mississippi Delta Comm Coll (MS)
Northern Essex Comm Coll (MA)
Oakton Comm Coll (IL)
Pensacola State Coll (FL)
Portland Comm Coll (OR)
Southwestern Comm Coll (NC)
Stark State Coll (OH)
Tarrant County Coll District (TX)

HEALTH INFORMATION/MEDICAL RECORDS TECHNOLOGY
Anoka Tech Coll (MN)
Arapahoe Comm Coll (CO)
Austin Comm Coll District (TX)
Black Hawk Coll, Moline (IL)
Blinn Coll (TX)
Borough of Manhattan Comm Coll of the City U of New York (NY)
Bristol Comm Coll (MA)
Central Oregon Comm Coll (OR)
Coll of DuPage (IL)
Collin County Comm Coll District (TX)
Comm Coll of Allegheny County (PA)
Craven Comm Coll (NC)
Crowder Coll (MO)
Danville Area Comm Coll (IL)
Daytona State Coll (FL)
Dyersburg State Comm Coll (TN)
Florida SouthWestern State Coll (FL)
Fox Valley Tech Coll (WI)
Front Range Comm Coll (CO)
Gateway Comm and Tech Coll (KY)
Great Falls Coll Montana State U (MT)
Greenville Tech Coll (SC)
Houston Comm Coll (TX)
Hutchinson Comm Coll (KS)
Jamestown Comm Coll (NY)
Kaskaskia Coll (IL)
Kirtland Comm Coll (MI)
Lackawanna Coll (PA)
Miami Dade Coll (FL)
Minnesota State Comm and Tech Coll (MN)
Montgomery Coll (MD)
Morton Coll (IL)
North Dakota State Coll of Science (ND)
Northeast Iowa Comm Coll (IA)
Northeast Wisconsin Tech Coll (WI)
Northwestern Coll–Chicago Campus (IL)
Paris Jr Coll (TX)
Pensacola State Coll (FL)
Quinsigamond Comm Coll (MA)
Raritan Valley Comm Coll (NJ)
Rend Lake Coll (IL)
Richmond Comm Coll (NC)
Ridgewater Coll (MN)
St. Charles Comm Coll (MO)
San Jacinto Coll (TX)
San Juan Coll (NM)
Schoolcraft Coll (MI)
Southwestern Comm Coll (NC)
Southwestern Michigan Coll (MI)
Southwest Wisconsin Tech Coll (WI)
Springfield Tech Comm Coll (MA)
State U of New York Coll of Technology at Alfred (NY)
Vincennes U (IN)
Volunteer State Comm Coll (TN)
Walters State Comm Coll (TN)
Westchester Comm Coll (NY)

HEALTH/MEDICAL PREPARATORY PROGRAMS RELATED
Central Oregon Comm Coll (OR)
Edison State Comm Coll (OH)
Fullerton Coll (CA)
Miami Dade Coll (FL)

HEALTH PROFESSIONS RELATED
Bucks County Comm Coll (PA)
Cleveland State Comm Coll (TN)
Harrisburg Area Comm Coll (PA)
Lackawanna Coll (PA)
Lakeland Comm Coll (OH)
Miami Dade Coll (FL)
Middlesex County Coll (NJ)
Northeast State Comm Coll (TN)
Piedmont Comm Coll (NC)
Southeastern Coll–West Palm Beach (FL)
Volunteer State Comm Coll (TN)
Westchester Comm Coll (NY)

HEALTH SERVICES ADMINISTRATION
Harrisburg Area Comm Coll (PA)
Hillsborough Comm Coll (FL)

HEALTH SERVICES/ALLIED HEALTH/HEALTH SCIENCES
Alvin Comm Coll (TX)
Anoka-Ramsey Comm Coll (MN)
Borough of Manhattan Comm Coll of the City U of New York (NY)
Bucks County Comm Coll (PA)
Camden County Coll (NJ)
Cayuga County Comm Coll (NY)
Century Coll (MN)
Collin County Comm Coll District (TX)
Comm Coll of Baltimore County (MD)
Dyersburg State Comm Coll (TN)
Gateway Comm and Tech Coll (KY)
Gulf Coast State Coll (FL)
Houston Comm Coll (TX)
Miami Dade Coll (FL)
Middlesex County Coll (NJ)

Northland Comm and Tech Coll (MN)
Oklahoma State U Inst of Technology (OK)
Paris Jr Coll (TX)
Queensborough Comm Coll of the City U of New York (NY)
Quinsigamond Comm Coll (MA)
Raritan Valley Comm Coll (NJ)
Schoolcraft Coll (MI)
Southern Maine Comm Coll (ME)
Tohono O'odham Comm Coll (AZ)
Union County Coll (NJ)
Western Dakota Tech Inst (SD)
West Kentucky Comm and Tech Coll (KY)
Westmoreland County Comm Coll (PA)

HEALTH TEACHER EDUCATION
Harper Coll (IL)
Mississippi Delta Comm Coll (MS)
Vincennes U (IN)

HEATING, AIR CONDITIONING, VENTILATION AND REFRIGERATION MAINTENANCE TECHNOLOGY
Amarillo Coll (TX)
Asheville-Buncombe Tech Comm Coll (NC)
Bellingham Tech Coll (WA)
Central Maine Comm Coll (ME)
Century Coll (MN)
Coll of DuPage (IL)
Comm Coll of Allegheny County (PA)
Craven Comm Coll (NC)
Delta Coll (MI)
Des Moines Area Comm Coll (IA)
Dunwoody Coll of Technology (MN)
Eastern Arizona Coll (AZ)
Fayetteville Tech Comm Coll (NC)
Galveston Coll (TX)
Gateway Comm and Tech Coll (KY)
Grand Rapids Comm Coll (MI)
Harper Coll (IL)
Harrisburg Area Comm Coll (PA)
Kaskaskia Coll (IL)
Kirtland Comm Coll (MI)
Luzerne County Comm Coll (PA)
Miami Dade Coll (FL)
Morton Coll (IL)
Mt. San Antonio Coll (CA)
Northampton Comm Coll (PA)
North Dakota State Coll of Science (ND)
North Idaho Coll (ID)
Northland Comm and Tech Coll (MN)
Oklahoma State U Inst of Technology (OK)
Owensboro Comm and Tech Coll (KY)
Paris Jr Coll (TX)
Portland Comm Coll (OR)
Richmond Comm Coll (NC)
San Jacinto Coll (TX)
San Joaquin Delta Coll (CA)
Southern Maine Comm Coll (ME)
Southwest Texas Jr Coll (TX)
Springfield Tech Comm Coll (MA)
State Tech Coll of Missouri (MO)
State U of New York Coll of Technology at Alfred (NY)
Tarrant County Coll District (TX)
Truckee Meadows Comm Coll (NV)
Western Dakota Tech Inst (SD)
Westmoreland County Comm Coll (PA)

HEATING, VENTILATION, AIR CONDITIONING AND REFRIGERATION ENGINEERING TECHNOLOGY
Alamance Comm Coll (NC)
Austin Comm Coll District (TX)
Bevill State Comm Coll (AL)
Collin County Comm Coll District (TX)
Comm Coll of Baltimore County (MD)
Dunwoody Coll of Technology (MN)
Edison State Comm Coll (OH)
Front Range Comm Coll (CO)
Miami Dade Coll (FL)
Minnesota State Comm and Tech Coll (MN)
North Dakota State Coll of Science (ND)
Northeast Wisconsin Tech Coll (WI)
Oakton Comm Coll (IL)
Raritan Valley Comm Coll (NJ)

HEAVY EQUIPMENT MAINTENANCE TECHNOLOGY
Amarillo Coll (TX)
Northeast Wisconsin Tech Coll (WI)
North Idaho Coll (ID)
Rend Lake Coll (IL)
State Tech Coll of Missouri (MO)

HEAVY/INDUSTRIAL EQUIPMENT MAINTENANCE TECHNOLOGIES RELATED
Bellingham Tech Coll (WA)
State U of New York Coll of Technology at Alfred (NY)

HIGH PERFORMANCE AND CUSTOM ENGINE TECHNOLOGY
De Anza Coll (CA)
Ohio Tech Coll (OH)

HISPANIC-AMERICAN, PUERTO RICAN, AND MEXICAN-AMERICAN/CHICANO STUDIES
San Jacinto Coll (TX)

HISTOLOGIC TECHNICIAN
Houston Comm Coll (TX)
Miami Dade Coll (FL)

HISTOLOGIC TECHNOLOGY/ HISTOTECHNOLOGIST
Comm Coll of Baltimore County (MD)
Miami Dade Coll (FL)

HISTORIC PRESERVATION AND CONSERVATION
Piedmont Comm Coll (NC)

HISTORY
Alvin Comm Coll (TX)
Amarillo Coll (TX)
Austin Comm Coll District (TX)
Blinn Coll (TX)
Borough of Manhattan Comm Coll of the City U of New York (NY)
Bucks County Comm Coll (PA)
Central Oregon Comm Coll (OR)
Chandler-Gilbert Comm Coll (AZ)
Citrus Coll (CA)
De Anza Coll (CA)
Eastern Arizona Coll (AZ)
Edison State Comm Coll (OH)
Feather River Coll (CA)
Fullerton Coll (CA)
Galveston Coll (TX)
Harper Coll (IL)
Los Angeles Mission Coll (CA)
Miami Dade Coll (FL)
MiraCosta Coll (CA)
Mississippi Delta Comm Coll (MS)
Mount Wachusett Comm Coll (MA)
Northeastern Jr Coll (CO)
North Idaho Coll (ID)
Northwest State Comm Coll (OH)
Paris Jr Coll (TX)
Pensacola State Coll (FL)
Quinsigamond Comm Coll (MA)
San Jacinto Coll (TX)
San Joaquin Delta Coll (CA)
Truckee Meadows Comm Coll (NV)
Union County Coll (NJ)
Vincennes U (IN)

HISTORY TEACHER EDUCATION
Bucks County Comm Coll (PA)

HOLISTIC HEALTH
Anoka-Ramsey Comm Coll (MN)
Front Range Comm Coll (CO)

HOMELAND SECURITY
Harper Coll (IL)
Jamestown Comm Coll (NY)

HOMELAND SECURITY, LAW ENFORCEMENT, FIREFIGHTING AND PROTECTIVE SERVICES RELATED
Comm Coll of Allegheny County (PA)
Lakeland Comm Coll (OH)
Portland Comm Coll (OR)
Schoolcraft Coll (MI)
West Kentucky Comm and Tech Coll (KY)

HOMELAND SECURITY RELATED
Pensacola State Coll (FL)

HORSE HUSBANDRY/EQUINE SCIENCE AND MANAGEMENT
Black Hawk Coll, Moline (IL)
Feather River Coll (CA)
Minnesota State Comm and Tech Coll (MN)
Mt. San Antonio Coll (CA)

HORTICULTURAL SCIENCE
Central Lakes Coll (MN)
Century Coll (MN)
Miami Dade Coll (FL)
Mississippi Delta Comm Coll (MS)
Mt. San Antonio Coll (CA)
Tarrant County Coll District (TX)
Trident Tech Coll (SC)

HOSPITAL AND HEALTH-CARE FACILITIES ADMINISTRATION
Bossier Parish Comm Coll (LA)
Coll of DuPage (IL)

HOSPITALITY ADMINISTRATION
Adirondack Comm Coll (NY)
Austin Comm Coll District (TX)
Bristol Comm Coll (MA)
Bucks County Comm Coll (PA)
Camden County Coll (NJ)
Central Oregon Comm Coll (OR)
Chesapeake Coll (MD)
Coll of DuPage (IL)
Collin County Comm Coll District (TX)
Daytona State Coll (FL)
Des Moines Area Comm Coll (IA)
Fox Valley Tech Coll (WI)
Front Range Comm Coll (CO)
Gulf Coast State Coll (FL)
Harper Coll (IL)
Hawkeye Comm Coll (IA)
Hillsborough Comm Coll (FL)
Lackawanna Coll (PA)
Lakeland Comm Coll (OH)
Miami Dade Coll (FL)
MiraCosta Coll (CA)
Niagara County Comm Coll (NY)
Northeast Wisconsin Tech Coll (WI)
North Idaho Coll (ID)
Pensacola State Coll (FL)
Quinsigamond Comm Coll (MA)
Union County Coll (NJ)
Wor-Wic Comm Coll (MD)

HOSPITALITY ADMINISTRATION RELATED
Chesapeake Coll (MD)
Harrisburg Area Comm Coll (PA)

HOSPITALITY AND RECREATION MARKETING
Luzerne County Comm Coll (PA)
Montgomery County Comm Coll (PA)

HOTEL/MOTEL ADMINISTRATION
Austin Comm Coll District (TX)
Central Oregon Comm Coll (OR)
Coll of DuPage (IL)
Houston Comm Coll (TX)
Lackawanna Coll (PA)
Luzerne County Comm Coll (PA)
Manchester Comm Coll (CT)
Miami Dade Coll (FL)
Middlesex County Coll (NJ)
Montgomery Coll (MD)
Mt. San Antonio Coll (CA)
Nassau Comm Coll (NY)
Northampton Comm Coll (PA)
Northern Essex Comm Coll (MA)
Pensacola State Coll (FL)
Trident Tech Coll (SC)
Vincennes U (IN)
Westmoreland County Comm Coll (PA)

HOTEL, MOTEL, AND RESTAURANT MANAGEMENT
Craven Comm Coll (NC)
Fayetteville Tech Comm Coll (NC)
Meridian Comm Coll (MS)
Pensacola State Coll (FL)

HUMAN COMPUTER INTERACTION
Raritan Valley Comm Coll (NJ)

HUMAN DEVELOPMENT AND FAMILY STUDIES
Penn State DuBois (PA)
Penn State Fayette, The Eberly Campus (PA)
Penn State Mont Alto (PA)

HUMAN DEVELOPMENT AND FAMILY STUDIES RELATED
Northwest State Comm Coll (OH)

HUMANITIES
Bristol Comm Coll (MA)
Cayuga County Comm Coll (NY)
Central Oregon Comm Coll (OR)
Columbia-Greene Comm Coll (NY)
De Anza Coll (CA)
Dutchess Comm Coll (NY)
Feather River Coll (CA)
Fullerton Coll (CA)
Galveston Coll (TX)
Harper Coll (IL)
Housatonic Comm Coll (CT)
Jamestown Comm Coll (NY)
Los Angeles City Coll (CA)
Los Angeles Mission Coll (CA)
Luzerne County Comm Coll (PA)
Miami Dade Coll (FL)
Mt. San Antonio Coll (CA)
Niagara County Comm Coll (NY)
San Joaquin Delta Coll (CA)
Seminole State Coll (OK)
State U of New York Coll of Technology at Alfred (NY)
Westchester Comm Coll (NY)

HUMAN NUTRITION
Chandler-Gilbert Comm Coll (AZ)

HUMAN RESOURCES DEVELOPMENT
Minnesota State Comm and Tech Coll–Moorhead (MN)

HUMAN RESOURCES MANAGEMENT
Anoka-Ramsey Comm Coll (MN)
Asheville-Buncombe Tech Comm Coll (NC)
Comm Coll of Allegheny County (PA)
Edison State Comm Coll (OH)
Fox Valley Tech Coll (WI)
Hawkeye Comm Coll (IA)
Minnesota State Comm and Tech Coll (MN)
Minnesota State Comm and Tech Coll–Moorhead (MN)
Northeast Wisconsin Tech Coll (WI)
Northwest State Comm Coll (OH)
Western Iowa Tech Comm Coll (IA)
Westmoreland County Comm Coll (PA)

HUMAN SERVICES
Alexandria Tech and Comm Coll (MN)
Bay de Noc Comm Coll (MI)
Central Maine Comm Coll (ME)
Central Ohio Tech Coll (OH)
Century Coll (MN)
Coll of DuPage (IL)
Columbia-Greene Comm Coll (NY)
Comm Coll of Denver (CO)
Dutchess Comm Coll (NY)
Edison State Comm Coll (OH)
Gateway Comm and Tech Coll (KY)
Greenville Tech Coll (SC)
Halifax Comm Coll (NC)
Harper Coll (IL)
Harrisburg Area Comm Coll (PA)
Hopkinsville Comm Coll (KY)
Housatonic Comm Coll (CT)
Jamestown Comm Coll (NY)
Lackawanna Coll (PA)
Lake Area Tech Inst (SD)
Los Angeles City Coll (CA)
Luzerne County Comm Coll (PA)
Manchester Comm Coll (CT)
Mesabi Range Coll (MN)
Miami Dade Coll (FL)
Middlesex Comm Coll (CT)
Mount Wachusett Comm Coll (MA)
Niagara County Comm Coll (NY)
Northern Essex Comm Coll (MA)
North Idaho Coll (ID)
Quinsigamond Comm Coll (MA)
Raritan Valley Comm Coll (NJ)
Rock Valley Coll (IL)
St. Charles Comm Coll (MO)
Southern Maine Comm Coll (ME)
Stark State Coll (OH)
State U of New York Coll of Technology at Alfred (NY)
Trident Tech Coll (SC)
Union County Coll (NJ)
U of Alaska Anchorage, Kenai Peninsula Coll (AK)
Westmoreland County Comm Coll (PA)

HYDRAULICS AND FLUID POWER TECHNOLOGY
Comm Coll of Baltimore County (MD)

HYDROLOGY AND WATER RESOURCES SCIENCE
Citrus Coll (CA)

ILLUSTRATION
Collin County Comm Coll District (TX)

INDUSTRIAL AND PRODUCT DESIGN
Comm Coll of Allegheny County (PA)
Fiorello H. LaGuardia Comm Coll of the City U of New York (NY)
Luzerne County Comm Coll (PA)
Mt. San Antonio Coll (CA)
Rock Valley Coll (IL)

INDUSTRIAL ELECTRONICS TECHNOLOGY
Central Lakes Coll (MN)
Coll of DuPage (IL)
Danville Area Comm Coll (IL)
Des Moines Area Comm Coll (IA)
Dyersburg State Comm Coll (TN)
Eastern Arizona Coll (AZ)
Hagerstown Comm Coll (MD)
Iowa Central Comm Coll (IA)
Lurleen B. Wallace Comm Coll (AL)
Mayland Comm Coll (NC)
Northampton Comm Coll (PA)
Northwest-Shoals Comm Coll (AL)
Northwest State Comm Coll (OH)
Sierra Coll (CA)

INDUSTRIAL ENGINEERING
Central Lakes Coll (MN)
Clackamas Comm Coll (OR)
Manchester Comm Coll (CT)

INDUSTRIAL MECHANICS AND MAINTENANCE TECHNOLOGY
Bellingham Tech Coll (WA)
Bevill State Comm Coll (AL)
Black River Tech Coll (AR)
Bossier Parish Comm Coll (LA)
Danville Area Comm Coll (IL)
Delta Coll (MI)
Des Moines Area Comm Coll (IA)
Dyersburg State Comm Coll (TN)
Eastern Arizona Coll (AZ)
Gateway Comm and Tech Coll (KY)
Grand Rapids Comm Coll (MI)
Halifax Comm Coll (NC)
Kaskaskia Coll (IL)
Lackawanna Coll (PA)
Maysville Comm and Tech Coll, Maysville (KY)
Minnesota State Comm and Tech Coll (MN)
Minnesota State Comm and Tech Coll–Wadena (MN)
Northwest-Shoals Comm Coll (AL)
Northwest State Comm Coll (OH)
Oklahoma State U Inst of Technology (OK)
Owensboro Comm and Tech Coll (KY)
Rend Lake Coll (IL)
San Juan Coll (NM)
Somerset Comm Coll (KY)
Southwestern Comm Coll (IA)
Southwestern Michigan Coll (MI)
Western Iowa Tech Comm Coll (IA)
West Kentucky Comm and Tech Coll (KY)
Westmoreland County Comm Coll (PA)

INDUSTRIAL PRODUCTION TECHNOLOGIES RELATED
Camden County Coll (NJ)
Dawson Comm Coll (MT)
Middlesex County Coll (NJ)
North Dakota State Coll of Science (ND)
Northwest State Comm Coll (OH)

INDUSTRIAL RADIOLOGIC TECHNOLOGY
Amarillo Coll (TX)
Blinn Coll (TX)
Eastern Gateway Comm Coll (OH)
Los Angeles City Coll (CA)
McLennan Comm Coll (TX)
Middlesex Comm Coll (CT)
Mt. San Antonio Coll (CA)
Northern Essex Comm Coll (MA)
Tarrant County Coll District (TX)

INDUSTRIAL SAFETY TECHNOLOGY
Fox Valley Tech Coll (WI)

INDUSTRIAL TECHNOLOGY
Bossier Parish Comm Coll (LA)
Central Oregon Comm Coll (OR)
Clackamas Comm Coll (OR)
Cleveland State Comm Coll (TN)
Coll of DuPage (IL)
Crowder Coll (MO)
De Anza Coll (CA)
Eastern Gateway Comm Coll (OH)
Edison State Comm Coll (OH)
Gateway Comm and Tech Coll (KY)
Hopkinsville Comm Coll (KY)
Kent State U at Tuscarawas (OH)
Lackawanna Coll (PA)
Manchester Comm Coll (CT)
Miami Dade Coll (FL)
Navarro Coll (TX)
Northeast State Comm Coll (TN)
Piedmont Comm Coll (NC)
Rock Valley Coll (IL)
St. Charles Comm Coll (MO)
San Juan Coll (NM)
South Arkansas Comm Coll (AR)
Stark State Coll (OH)
Trident Tech Coll (SC)
Walters State Comm Coll (TN)
Western Nevada Coll (NV)

INFORMATION SCIENCE/ STUDIES
Alamance Comm Coll (NC)
Alexandria Tech and Comm Coll (MN)
Amarillo Coll (TX)
Asheville-Buncombe Tech Comm Coll (NC)
Bossier Parish Comm Coll (LA)
Bristol Comm Coll (MA)
Bucks County Comm Coll (PA)
Cayuga County Comm Coll (NY)
Coll of The Albemarle (NC)
De Anza Coll (CA)
Dutchess Comm Coll (NY)
Dyersburg State Comm Coll (TN)
Eastern Arizona Coll (AZ)
Jamestown Comm Coll (NY)
Manchester Comm Coll (CT)
McLennan Comm Coll (TX)
Miami Dade Coll (FL)
Niagara County Comm Coll (NY)
Paris Jr Coll (TX)
Penn State DuBois (PA)
Pensacola State Coll (FL)
Southwestern Comm Coll (NC)
State U of New York Coll of Technology at Alfred (NY)
Weatherford Coll (TX)
Westchester Comm Coll (NY)

INFORMATION TECHNOLOGY
Adirondack Comm Coll (NY)
Asheville-Buncombe Tech Comm Coll (NC)
Black Hawk Coll, Moline (IL)
Blue Ridge Comm and Tech Coll (WV)
Cayuga County Comm Coll (NY)
Chandler-Gilbert Comm Coll (AZ)
Cleveland Comm Coll (NC)
Cleveland State Comm Coll (TN)
Coll of The Albemarle (NC)
Columbia-Greene Comm Coll (NY)
Craven Comm Coll (NC)
Daytona State Coll (FL)
Des Moines Area Comm Coll (IA)
Dyersburg State Comm Coll (TN)
Fayetteville Tech Comm Coll (NC)
Florida SouthWestern State Coll (FL)
Fullerton Coll (CA)
Great Falls Coll Montana State U (MT)
Halifax Comm Coll (NC)
Haywood Comm Coll (NC)
Hillsborough Comm Coll (FL)
James Sprunt Comm Coll (NC)
Jamestown Comm Coll (NY)
Kishwaukee Coll (IL)
Lenoir Comm Coll (NC)
Los Angeles City Coll (CA)
McHenry County Coll (IL)
Mesabi Range Coll (MN)
Miami Dade Coll (FL)
Minnesota State Comm and Tech Coll (MN)
Minnesota State Comm and Tech Coll–Moorhead (MN)
Montgomery County Comm Coll (PA)
Morton Coll (IL)
Northeast State Comm Coll (TN)
Oakton Comm Coll (IL)
Oklahoma State U Inst of Technology (OK)
Pensacola State Coll (FL)
Piedmont Comm Coll (NC)
Piedmont Virginia Comm Coll (VA)
Queensborough Comm Coll of the City U of New York (NY)
Raritan Valley Comm Coll (NJ)
Richmond Comm Coll (NC)
Shawnee Comm Coll (IL)
Sierra Coll (CA)
Southeastern Coll–West Palm Beach (FL)
South Suburban Coll (IL)
Union County Coll (NJ)
Vincennes U (IN)
Volunteer State Comm Coll (TN)

INFORMATION TECHNOLOGY PROJECT MANAGEMENT
Hillsborough Comm Coll (FL)

INSTITUTIONAL FOOD WORKERS
James Sprunt Comm Coll (NC)

INSTRUMENTATION TECHNOLOGY
Amarillo Coll (TX)
Bellingham Tech Coll (WA)
Bevill State Comm Coll (AL)
Hagerstown Comm Coll (MD)
Houston Comm Coll (TX)
Lakeland Comm Coll (OH)
Mesabi Range Coll (MN)
Nassau Comm Coll (NY)
Ridgewater Coll (MN)
San Jacinto Coll (TX)
San Juan Coll (NM)
Southwest Wisconsin Tech Coll (WI)
U of Alaska Anchorage, Kenai Peninsula Coll (AK)
Westmoreland County Comm Coll (PA)

INSURANCE
Chandler-Gilbert Comm Coll (AZ)
Nassau Comm Coll (NY)

INTELLIGENCE
Fayetteville Tech Comm Coll (NC)

INTERCULTURAL/ MULTICULTURAL AND DIVERSITY STUDIES
De Anza Coll (CA)

INTERDISCIPLINARY STUDIES
Anoka-Ramsey Comm Coll (MN)
Gateway Comm and Tech Coll (KY)
Maysville Comm and Tech Coll, Maysville (KY)
Motlow State Comm Coll (TN)
Mount Wachusett Comm Coll (MA)
Northeast State Comm Coll (TN)
Northeast Wisconsin Tech Coll (WI)
Oklahoma State U Inst of Technology (OK)
Southwest Wisconsin Tech Coll (WI)
Tohono O'odham Comm Coll (AZ)
Western Dakota Tech Inst (SD)
Williamsburg Tech Coll (SC)

INTERIOR DESIGN
Alexandria Tech and Comm Coll (MN)
Amarillo Coll (TX)
Arapahoe Comm Coll (CO)
Century Coll (MN)
Coll of DuPage (IL)
Collin County Comm Coll District (TX)
Daytona State Coll (FL)
Fox Valley Tech Coll (WI)
Front Range Comm Coll (CO)
Fullerton Coll (CA)
Grand Rapids Comm Coll (MI)
Harper Coll (IL)
Houston Comm Coll (TX)
Miami Dade Coll (FL)
Montgomery Coll (MD)
Mt. San Antonio Coll (CA)
Nassau Comm Coll (NY)
Northampton Comm Coll (PA)
Portland Comm Coll (OR)
Raritan Valley Comm Coll (NJ)
San Jacinto Coll (TX)
State U of New York Coll of Technology at Alfred (NY)

INTERMEDIA/MULTIMEDIA
Bristol Comm Coll (MA)
Middlesex Comm Coll (CT)
Oklahoma State U Inst of Technology (OK)
Raritan Valley Comm Coll (NJ)

INTERNATIONAL BUSINESS/ TRADE/COMMERCE
Austin Comm Coll District (TX)
Fullerton Coll (CA)
Harper Coll (IL)
Houston Comm Coll (TX)
Luzerne County Comm Coll (PA)
Northwest State Comm Coll (OH)
San Jacinto Coll (TX)
Westchester Comm Coll (NY)

INTERNATIONAL/GLOBAL STUDIES
Jamestown Comm Coll (NY)
Northampton Comm Coll (PA)

INTERNATIONAL RELATIONS AND AFFAIRS
De Anza Coll (CA)
Harrisburg Area Comm Coll (PA)
Miami Dade Coll (FL)

ITALIAN
Austin Comm Coll District (TX)
Miami Dade Coll (FL)

JAPANESE
Austin Comm Coll District (TX)
Citrus Coll (CA)
Fiorello H. LaGuardia Comm Coll of the City U of New York (NY)
Los Angeles City Coll (CA)

JOURNALISM
Amarillo Coll (TX)
Arapahoe Comm Coll (CO)
Austin Comm Coll District (TX)
Bucks County Comm Coll (PA)
Citrus Coll (CA)
De Anza Coll (CA)
Delta Coll (MI)
Fullerton Coll (CA)
Los Angeles City Coll (CA)
Luzerne County Comm Coll (PA)
Manchester Comm Coll (CT)
Miami Dade Coll (FL)
Mt. San Antonio Coll (CA)
Northampton Comm Coll (PA)
Northeastern Jr Coll (CO)
Northern Essex Comm Coll (MA)
North Idaho Coll (ID)
Paris Jr Coll (TX)
Pensacola State Coll (FL)
San Jacinto Coll (TX)
San Joaquin Delta Coll (CA)
Vincennes U (IN)
Westchester Comm Coll (NY)

JUVENILE CORRECTIONS
Danville Area Comm Coll (IL)
Kaskaskia Coll (IL)

KINDERGARTEN/PRESCHOOL EDUCATION
Alamance Comm Coll (NC)
Bristol Comm Coll (MA)
Central Lakes Coll (MN)
Chandler-Gilbert Comm Coll (AZ)
Hesston Coll (KS)
Manchester Comm Coll (CT)
McLennan Comm Coll (TX)
Miami Dade Coll (FL)
Mt. San Antonio Coll (CA)
Nassau Comm Coll (NY)
Northern Essex Comm Coll (MA)
Northwest State Comm Coll (OH)
Raritan Valley Comm Coll (NJ)
Truckee Meadows Comm Coll (NV)

KINESIOLOGY AND EXERCISE SCIENCE
Anoka-Ramsey Comm Coll (MN)
Austin Comm Coll District (TX)
Bucks County Comm Coll (PA)
Central Oregon Comm Coll (OR)
Century Coll (MN)
Chandler-Gilbert Comm Coll (AZ)
De Anza Coll (CA)
Feather River Coll (CA)
Mount Wachusett Comm Coll (MA)
Paris Jr Coll (TX)
Raritan Valley Comm Coll (NJ)
South Suburban Coll (IL)

KNOWLEDGE MANAGEMENT
Fox Valley Tech Coll (WI)
Northeast Wisconsin Tech Coll (WI)

KOREAN
Los Angeles City Coll (CA)

LANDSCAPE ARCHITECTURE
Chesapeake Coll (MD)
Mt. San Antonio Coll (CA)
Truckee Meadows Comm Coll (NV)

LANDSCAPING AND GROUNDSKEEPING
Anoka Tech Coll (MN)
Clackamas Comm Coll (OR)
Coll of DuPage (IL)
Fullerton Coll (CA)
Grand Rapids Comm Coll (MI)
Hawkeye Comm Coll (IA)
Kishwaukee Coll (IL)
Miami Dade Coll (FL)
Northeast Wisconsin Tech Coll (WI)
Pensacola State Coll (FL)
Portland Comm Coll (OR)
Springfield Tech Comm Coll (MA)

LANGUAGE INTERPRETATION AND TRANSLATION
Des Moines Area Comm Coll (IA)
Lake Region State Coll (ND)

LASER AND OPTICAL TECHNOLOGY
Amarillo Coll (TX)
Quinsigamond Comm Coll (MA)
Springfield Tech Comm Coll (MA)

LATIN
Austin Comm Coll District (TX)

LATIN AMERICAN STUDIES
Miami Dade Coll (FL)

LEGAL ADMINISTRATIVE ASSISTANT/SECRETARY
Alamance Comm Coll (NC)
Alexandria Tech and Comm Coll (MN)
Alvin Comm Coll (TX)
Amarillo Coll (TX)
Anoka Tech Coll (MN)
Blinn Coll (TX)
Central Lakes Coll (MN)
Coll of DuPage (IL)
Craven Comm Coll (NC)
Crowder Coll (MO)
Eastern Gateway Comm Coll (OH)
Fullerton Coll (CA)
Harper Coll (IL)
Los Angeles City Coll (CA)
Manchester Comm Coll (CT)
McLennan Comm Coll (TX)
Miami Dade Coll (FL)
Minnesota State Comm and Tech Coll (MN)
Morton Coll (IL)
Mt. San Antonio Coll (CA)
Nassau Comm Coll (NY)
Navarro Coll (TX)
North Idaho Coll (ID)
Northwest State Comm Coll (OH)
Pensacola State Coll (FL)
Ridgewater Coll (MN)
Stark State Coll (OH)

LEGAL ASSISTANT/PARALEGAL
Alexandria Tech and Comm Coll (MN)
Alvin Comm Coll (TX)
Arapahoe Comm Coll (CO)
Austin Comm Coll District (TX)
Bellingham Tech Coll (WA)
Blue Ridge Comm and Tech Coll (WV)
Bristol Comm Coll (MA)
Camden County Coll (NJ)
Chesapeake Coll (MD)
Coll of Eastern Idaho (ID)
Collin County Comm Coll District (TX)
Comm Coll of Allegheny County (PA)
Comm Coll of Baltimore County (MD)
Comm Coll of Denver (CO)
Daytona State Coll (FL)
De Anza Coll (CA)
Delta Coll (MI)
Des Moines Area Comm Coll (IA)
Dutchess Comm Coll (NY)
Edison State Comm Coll (OH)
Fayetteville Tech Comm Coll (NC)
Fiorello H. LaGuardia Comm Coll of the City U of New York (NY)
Florida SouthWestern State Coll (FL)
Fox Valley Tech Coll (WI)
Front Range Comm Coll (CO)
Fullerton Coll (CA)
Greenville Tech Coll (SC)
Halifax Comm Coll (NC)
Harper Coll (IL)
Harrisburg Area Comm Coll (PA)
Hillsborough Comm Coll (FL)
Houston Comm Coll (TX)
Hutchinson Comm Coll (KS)
IBMC Coll, Fort Collins (CO)
Lackawanna Coll (PA)
Lakeland Comm Coll (OH)
Los Angeles City Coll (CA)
Luzerne County Comm Coll (PA)
Manchester Comm Coll (CT)
McLennan Comm Coll (TX)
Miami Dade Coll (FL)
Middlesex County Coll (NJ)
Minnesota State Comm and Tech Coll (MN)
Minnesota State Comm and Tech Coll–Detroit Lakes (MN)
Montgomery Coll (MD)
Mt. San Antonio Coll (CA)
Mount Wachusett Comm Coll (MA)
Nassau Comm Coll (NY)
Navarro Coll (TX)
Northampton Comm Coll (PA)
Northeast Wisconsin Tech Coll (WI)
North Idaho Coll (ID)
Northwestern Coll–Chicago Campus (IL)
Northwest State Comm Coll (OH)
Pensacola State Coll (FL)
Portland Comm Coll (OR)
Raritan Valley Comm Coll (NJ)
San Jacinto Coll (TX)
San Juan Coll (NM)
South Suburban Coll (IL)
Southwestern Comm Coll (NC)
Southwestern Michigan Coll (MI)
Tarrant County Coll District (TX)
Trident Tech Coll (SC)
Truckee Meadows Comm Coll (NV)
Union County Coll (NJ)
Vincennes U (IN)
Westchester Comm Coll (NY)
Western Iowa Tech Comm Coll (IA)
Westmoreland County Comm Coll (PA)

LEGAL PROFESSIONS AND STUDIES RELATED
Bristol Comm Coll (MA)
Bucks County Comm Coll (PA)

LEGAL STUDIES
Alvin Comm Coll (TX)
Navarro Coll (TX)
Trident Tech Coll (SC)

LIBERAL ARTS AND SCIENCES AND HUMANITIES RELATED
Arapahoe Comm Coll (CO)
Bossier Parish Comm Coll (LA)
Bristol Comm Coll (MA)
Bucks County Comm Coll (PA)
Cascadia Coll (WA)
Cayuga County Comm Coll (NY)
Chandler-Gilbert Comm Coll (AZ)
Chesapeake Coll (MD)
Cleveland Comm Coll (NC)
Comm Coll of Baltimore County (MD)
Craven Comm Coll (NC)
Dutchess Comm Coll (NY)
Fayetteville Tech Comm Coll (NC)
Front Range Comm Coll (CO)
Great Falls Coll Montana State U (MT)
Hagerstown Comm Coll (MD)
Halifax Comm Coll (NC)
Haywood Comm Coll (NC)
James Sprunt Comm Coll (NC)
Jamestown Comm Coll (NY)
Kent State U at Tuscarawas (OH)
Lackawanna Coll (PA)
Lenoir Comm Coll (NC)
Luzerne County Comm Coll (PA)

Montgomery Coll (MD)
Northampton Comm Coll (PA)
Piedmont Comm Coll (NC)
Piedmont Virginia Comm Coll (VA)
Ridgewater Coll (MN)
Southern Maine Comm Coll (ME)
State U of New York Coll of Technology at Alfred (NY)
Vincennes U (IN)
Westchester Comm Coll (NY)
Wor-Wic Comm Coll (MD)

LIBERAL ARTS AND SCIENCES/ LIBERAL STUDIES
Adirondack Comm Coll (NY)
Alamance Comm Coll (NC)
Alexandria Tech and Comm Coll (MN)
Alvin Comm Coll (TX)
Amarillo Coll (TX)
Anoka-Ramsey Comm Coll (MN)
Arapahoe Comm Coll (CO)
Asheville-Buncombe Tech Comm Coll (NC)
Bay de Noc Comm Coll (MI)
Bevill State Comm Coll (AL)
Black Hawk Coll, Moline (IL)
Black River Tech Coll (AR)
Blue Ridge Comm and Tech Coll (WV)
Borough of Manhattan Comm Coll of the City U of New York (NY)
Bossier Parish Comm Coll (LA)
Bristol Comm Coll (MA)
Bucks County Comm Coll (PA)
Camden County Coll (NJ)
Cascadia Coll (WA)
Cayuga County Comm Coll (NY)
Central Lakes Coll (MN)
Central Maine Comm Coll (ME)
Central Ohio Tech Coll (OH)
Central Oregon Comm Coll (OR)
Century Coll (MN)
Chandler-Gilbert Comm Coll (AZ)
Citrus Coll (CA)
Clackamas Comm Coll (OR)
Cleveland Comm Coll (NC)
Cleveland State Comm Coll (TN)
Coll of DuPage (IL)
Coll of Eastern Idaho (ID)
Coll of The Albemarle (NC)
Collin County Comm Coll District (TX)
Columbia-Greene Comm Coll (NY)
Comm Coll of Allegheny County (PA)
Comm Coll of Baltimore County (MD)
Comm Coll of Denver (CO)
Craven Comm Coll (NC)
Crowder Coll (MO)
Danville Area Comm Coll (IL)
Dawson Comm Coll (MT)
Daytona State Coll (FL)
De Anza Coll (CA)
Delta Coll (MI)
Des Moines Area Comm Coll (IA)
Donnelly Coll (KS)
Dutchess Comm Coll (NY)
Dyersburg State Comm Coll (TN)
Eastern Arizona Coll (AZ)
Edison State Comm Coll (OH)
Fayetteville Tech Comm Coll (NC)
Feather River Coll (CA)
Fiorello H. LaGuardia Comm Coll of the City U of New York (NY)
Florida SouthWestern State Coll (FL)
Front Range Comm Coll (CO)
Fullerton Coll (CA)
Galveston Coll (TX)
Gateway Comm and Tech Coll (KY)
Grand Rapids Comm Coll (MI)
Greenville Tech Coll (SC)
Gulf Coast State Coll (FL)
Hagerstown Comm Coll (MD)
Halifax Comm Coll (NC)
Harper Coll (IL)
Hawaii Tokai Intl Coll (HI)
Hawkeye Comm Coll (IA)
Haywood Comm Coll (NC)
Hesston Coll (KS)
Hillsborough Comm Coll (FL)
Hopkinsville Comm Coll (KY)
Housatonic Comm Coll (CT)
Hutchinson Comm Coll (KS)
Iowa Central Comm Coll (IA)
James Sprunt Comm Coll (NC)
Jamestown Comm Coll (NY)
Kaskaskia Coll (IL)
Kirtland Comm Coll (MI)
Kishwaukee Coll (IL)
Lackawanna Coll (PA)
Lakeland Comm Coll (OH)
Lake Region State Coll (ND)
Lenoir Comm Coll (NC)
Los Angeles City Coll (CA)
Los Angeles Mission Coll (CA)
Lurleen B. Wallace Comm Coll (AL)
Luzerne County Comm Coll (PA)
Manchester Comm Coll (CT)
Marion Military Inst (AL)
Mayland Comm Coll (NC)
Maysville Comm and Tech Coll, Maysville (KY)
McHenry County Coll (IL)
McLennan Comm Coll (TX)
Mesabi Range Coll (MN)
Miami Dade Coll (FL)
Middlesex Comm Coll (CT)
Middlesex County Coll (NJ)
Minnesota State Comm and Tech Coll (MN)
Minnesota State Comm and Tech Coll–Detroit Lakes (MN)
Minnesota State Comm and Tech Coll–Moorhead (MN)
Minnesota State Comm and Tech Coll–Wadena (MN)
MiraCosta Coll (CA)
Mississippi Delta Comm Coll (MS)
Montgomery Coll (MD)
Montgomery County Comm Coll (PA)
Morton Coll (IL)
Motlow State Comm Coll (TN)
Mount Wachusett Comm Coll (MA)
Nassau Comm Coll (NY)
Niagara County Comm Coll (NY)
Northampton Comm Coll (PA)
North Dakota State Coll of Science (ND)
Northeastern Jr Coll (CO)
Northeast Iowa Comm Coll (IA)
Northeast State Comm Coll (TN)
Northern Essex Comm Coll (MA)
North Idaho Coll (ID)
Northland Comm and Tech Coll (MN)
Northwest-Shoals Comm Coll (AL)
Northwest State Comm Coll (OH)
Oakton Comm Coll (IL)
Owensboro Comm and Tech Coll (KY)
Paris Jr Coll (TX)
Penn State DuBois (PA)
Penn State Fayette, The Eberly Campus (PA)
Penn State Mont Alto (PA)
Pensacola State Coll (FL)
Piedmont Comm Coll (NC)
Portland Comm Coll (OR)
Queensborough Comm Coll of the City U of New York (NY)
Quinsigamond Comm Coll (MA)
Raritan Valley Comm Coll (NJ)
Rend Lake Coll (IL)
Richmond Comm Coll (NC)
Ridgewater Coll (MN)
Rock Valley Coll (IL)
St. Charles Comm Coll (MO)
San Joaquin Delta Coll (CA)
San Juan Coll (NM)
Seminole State Coll (OK)
Sierra Coll (CA)
Somerset Comm Coll (KY)
Southern Maine Comm Coll (ME)
South Suburban Coll (IL)
Southwestern Comm Coll (IA)
Southwestern Comm Coll (NC)
Southwestern Michigan Coll (MI)
Southwest Texas Jr Coll (TX)
Springfield Tech Comm Coll (MA)
State U of New York Coll of Technology at Alfred (NY)
Tarrant County Coll District (TX)
Tohono O'odham Comm Coll (AZ)
Trident Tech Coll (SC)
Truckee Meadows Comm Coll (NV)
Union County Coll (NJ)
U of South Carolina Lancaster (SC)
Vincennes U (IN)
Volunteer State Comm Coll (TN)
Walters State Comm Coll (TN)
Weatherford Coll (TX)
Westchester Comm Coll (NY)
Western Iowa Tech Comm Coll (IA)
Western Nevada Coll (NV)
West Kentucky Comm and Tech Coll (KY)
Westmoreland County Comm Coll (PA)
Williamsburg Tech Coll (SC)

LIBRARY AND ARCHIVES ASSISTING
Citrus Coll (CA)
Coll of DuPage (IL)
Kaskaskia Coll (IL)
Western Dakota Tech Inst (SD)

LIBRARY AND INFORMATION SCIENCE
Citrus Coll (CA)
Coll of DuPage (IL)
Southwestern Comm Coll (IA)

LICENSED PRACTICAL/ VOCATIONAL NURSE TRAINING
Alvin Comm Coll (TX)
Amarillo Coll (TX)
Central Oregon Comm Coll (OR)
Chandler-Gilbert Comm Coll (AZ)
Citrus Coll (CA)
Coll of The Albemarle (NC)
Comm Coll of Denver (CO)
De Anza Coll (CA)
Des Moines Area Comm Coll (IA)
Eastern Gateway Comm Coll (OH)
Feather River Coll (CA)
Fiorello H. LaGuardia Comm Coll of the City U of New York (NY)
Iowa Central Comm Coll (IA)
Minnesota State Comm and Tech Coll (MN)
Minnesota State Comm and Tech Coll–Detroit Lakes (MN)
Minnesota State Comm and Tech Coll–Moorhead (MN)
Minnesota State Comm and Tech Coll–Wadena (MN)
MiraCosta Coll (CA)
Navarro Coll (TX)
North Dakota State Coll of Science (ND)
Northeastern Jr Coll (CO)
North Idaho Coll (ID)
San Joaquin Delta Coll (CA)
Sierra Coll (CA)
Western Dakota Tech Inst (SD)

LINEWORKER
Chandler-Gilbert Comm Coll (AZ)
Minnesota State Comm and Tech Coll (MN)
Minnesota State Comm and Tech Coll–Wadena (MN)
Oklahoma State U Inst of Technology (OK)
Raritan Valley Comm Coll (NJ)
State Tech Coll of Missouri (MO)

LINGUISTICS
Borough of Manhattan Comm Coll of the City U of New York (NY)

LITERATURE
Chandler-Gilbert Comm Coll (AZ)

LIVESTOCK MANAGEMENT
James Sprunt Comm Coll (NC)
North Dakota State Coll of Science (ND)

LOGISTICS, MATERIALS, AND SUPPLY CHAIN MANAGEMENT
Austin Comm Coll District (TX)
Collin County Comm Coll District (TX)
Edison State Comm Coll (OH)
Fayetteville Tech Comm Coll (NC)
Fox Valley Tech Coll (WI)
Gateway Comm and Tech Coll (KY)
Houston Comm Coll (TX)
Iowa Central Comm Coll (IA)
Miami Dade Coll (FL)
Northeast Wisconsin Tech Coll (WI)
Northern Essex Comm Coll (MA)
Northwest State Comm Coll (OH)
Shawnee Comm Coll (IL)
Union County Coll (NJ)
Vincennes U (IN)
West Kentucky Comm and Tech Coll (KY)

MACHINE SHOP TECHNOLOGY
Asheville-Buncombe Tech Comm Coll (NC)
Comm Coll of Denver (CO)
Craven Comm Coll (NC)
Delta Coll (MI)
Eastern Arizona Coll (AZ)
Fayetteville Tech Comm Coll (NC)
Gateway Comm and Tech Coll (KY)
Lenoir Comm Coll (NC)
Maysville Comm and Tech Coll, Maysville (KY)
Northeast Wisconsin Tech Coll (WI)
Owensboro Comm and Tech Coll (KY)
State U of New York Coll of Technology at Alfred (NY)
West Kentucky Comm and Tech Coll (KY)

MACHINE TOOL TECHNOLOGY
Alamance Comm Coll (NC)
Amarillo Coll (TX)
Bellingham Tech Coll (WA)
Central Lakes Coll (MN)
Central Maine Comm Coll (ME)
Clackamas Comm Coll (OR)
Coll of DuPage (IL)
De Anza Coll (CA)
Des Moines Area Comm Coll (IA)
Greenville Tech Coll (SC)
Hawkeye Comm Coll (IA)
Hutchinson Comm Coll (KS)
Iowa Central Comm Coll (IA)
Lake Area Tech Inst (SD)
Meridian Comm Coll (MS)
Mt. San Antonio Coll (CA)
North Dakota State Coll of Science (ND)
Northern Essex Comm Coll (MA)
North Idaho Coll (ID)
Northwest State Comm Coll (OH)
Portland Comm Coll (OR)
Ridgewater Coll (MN)
San Joaquin Delta Coll (CA)
Southern Maine Comm Coll (ME)
State Tech Coll of Missouri (MO)
Tarrant County Coll District (TX)
Trident Tech Coll (SC)
Western Dakota Tech Inst (SD)
Western Nevada Coll (NV)
Westmoreland County Comm Coll (PA)

MANAGEMENT INFORMATION SYSTEMS
Camden County Coll (NJ)
Central Oregon Comm Coll (OR)
Comm Coll of Allegheny County (PA)
Comm Coll of Baltimore County (MD)
Comm Coll of Denver (CO)
Florida SouthWestern State Coll (FL)
Gulf Coast State Coll (FL)
Hagerstown Comm Coll (MD)
Kirtland Comm Coll (MI)
Lackawanna Coll (PA)
Lakeland Comm Coll (OH)
Lake Region State Coll (ND)
Manchester Comm Coll (CT)
Mayland Comm Coll (NC)
Miami Dade Coll (FL)
Mississippi Delta Comm Coll (MS)
Nassau Comm Coll (NY)
Pensacola State Coll (FL)
Portland Comm Coll (OR)
Raritan Valley Comm Coll (NJ)
San Jacinto Coll (TX)
South Arkansas Comm Coll (AR)
Western Nevada Coll (NV)

MANAGEMENT INFORMATION SYSTEMS AND SERVICES RELATED
Pensacola State Coll (FL)
Seminole State Coll (OK)
Truckee Meadows Comm Coll (NV)

MANAGEMENT SCIENCE
Comm Coll of Allegheny County (PA)
Pensacola State Coll (FL)
Piedmont Virginia Comm Coll (VA)

MANUFACTURING ENGINEERING
Bristol Comm Coll (MA)
Penn State Fayette, The Eberly Campus (PA)

MANUFACTURING ENGINEERING TECHNOLOGY
Bevill State Comm Coll (AL)
Black Hawk Coll, Moline (IL)
Central Ohio Tech Coll (OH)
Central Oregon Comm Coll (OR)
Clackamas Comm Coll (OR)
Coll of DuPage (IL)
Comm Coll of Allegheny County (PA)
Crowder Coll (MO)
Danville Area Comm Coll (IL)
Delta Coll (MI)
Edison State Comm Coll (OH)
Fox Valley Tech Coll (WI)
Gateway Comm and Tech Coll (KY)
Grand Rapids Comm Coll (MI)
Gulf Coast State Coll (FL)
Houston Comm Coll (TX)
Hutchinson Comm Coll (KS)
Lake Area Tech Inst (SD)
Miami Dade Coll (FL)
Minnesota State Comm and Tech Coll (MN)
North Dakota State Coll of Science (ND)
Northeast Wisconsin Tech Coll (WI)
Northland Comm and Tech Coll (MN)
Oakton Comm Coll (IL)
Quinsigamond Comm Coll (MA)
Raritan Valley Comm Coll (NJ)
Rend Lake Coll (IL)
St. Charles Comm Coll (MO)
Schoolcraft Coll (MI)
Sierra Coll (CA)
State Tech Coll of Missouri (MO)
Truckee Meadows Comm Coll (NV)
Vincennes U (IN)
Western Nevada Coll (NV)
Westmoreland County Comm Coll (PA)

MARINE BIOLOGY AND BIOLOGICAL OCEANOGRAPHY
Southern Maine Comm Coll (ME)

MARINE MAINTENANCE AND SHIP REPAIR TECHNOLOGY
Minnesota State Comm and Tech Coll (MN)
Minnesota State Comm and Tech Coll–Detroit Lakes (MN)
North Idaho Coll (ID)
Northwest School of Wooden Boatbuilding (WA)

MARINE SCIENCE/MERCHANT MARINE OFFICER
San Jacinto Coll (TX)

MARINE TRANSPORTATION RELATED
West Kentucky Comm and Tech Coll (KY)

MARKETING/MARKETING MANAGEMENT
Adirondack Comm Coll (NY)
Alvin Comm Coll (TX)
Asheville-Buncombe Tech Comm Coll (NC)
Austin Comm Coll District (TX)
Bellingham Tech Coll (WA)
Bristol Comm Coll (MA)
Camden County Coll (NJ)
Central Lakes Coll (MN)
Central Oregon Comm Coll (OR)
Century Coll (MN)
Clackamas Comm Coll (OR)
Coll of DuPage (IL)
Coll of Eastern Idaho (ID)
Comm Coll of Allegheny County (PA)
De Anza Coll (CA)
Delta Coll (MI)
Des Moines Area Comm Coll (IA)
Edison State Comm Coll (OH)
Fox Valley Tech Coll (WI)
Harper Coll (IL)
Houston Comm Coll (TX)
Lake Area Tech Inst (SD)
Lakeland Comm Coll (OH)
Los Angeles City Coll (CA)
Manchester Comm Coll (CT)
Meridian Comm Coll (MS)
Miami Dade Coll (FL)
Middlesex Comm Coll (CT)
Middlesex County Coll (NJ)
Minnesota State Comm and Tech Coll (MN)
Minnesota State Comm and Tech Coll–Detroit Lakes (MN)
Morton Coll (IL)
Mt. San Antonio Coll (CA)
Nassau Comm Coll (NY)
Navarro Coll (TX)
Northampton Comm Coll (PA)
North Dakota State Coll of Science (ND)

Northeastern Jr Coll (CO)
Northeast Wisconsin Tech Coll (WI)
Northern Essex Comm Coll (MA)
Northwest State Comm Coll (OH)
Oakton Comm Coll (IL)
Ridgewater Coll (MN)
Rock Valley Coll (IL)
St. Charles Comm Coll (MO)
Schoolcraft Coll (MI)
Stark State Coll (OH)
Tarrant County Coll District (TX)
Trident Tech Coll (SC)
Union County Coll (NJ)

MARKETING RELATED
Northeast Wisconsin Tech Coll (WI)
Westchester Comm Coll (NY)

MARKETING RESEARCH
Chandler-Gilbert Comm Coll (AZ)

MASONRY
Mississippi Delta Comm Coll (MS)
State U of New York Coll of Technology at Alfred (NY)

MASSAGE THERAPY
Camden County Coll (NJ)
Central Oregon Comm Coll (OR)
Chandler-Gilbert Comm Coll (AZ)
Coll of DuPage (IL)
Comm Coll of Allegheny County (PA)
Comm Coll of Baltimore County (MD)
Gateway Comm and Tech Coll (KY)
Miami Dade Coll (FL)
Niagara County Comm Coll (NY)
Northwestern Coll–Chicago Campus (IL)
Queensborough Comm Coll of the City U of New York (NY)
Schoolcraft Coll (MI)
Southwestern Comm Coll (NC)

MASS COMMUNICATION/ MEDIA
Amarillo Coll (TX)
Blinn Coll (TX)
Borough of Manhattan Comm Coll of the City U of New York (NY)
Cayuga County Comm Coll (NY)
Crowder Coll (MO)
De Anza Coll (CA)
Fullerton Coll (CA)
Miami Dade Coll (FL)
Middlesex Comm Coll (CT)
Mount Wachusett Comm Coll (MA)
Nassau Comm Coll (NY)
Niagara County Comm Coll (NY)
North Idaho Coll (ID)
Quinsigamond Comm Coll (MA)
Union County Coll (NJ)

MATERIALS ENGINEERING
Southern Maine Comm Coll (ME)

MATERIALS SCIENCE
Mt. San Antonio Coll (CA)
Northern Essex Comm Coll (MA)

MATHEMATICS
Alvin Comm Coll (TX)
Amarillo Coll (TX)
Austin Comm Coll District (TX)
Blinn Coll (TX)
Borough of Manhattan Comm Coll of the City U of New York (NY)
Bucks County Comm Coll (PA)
Central Oregon Comm Coll (OR)
Chandler-Gilbert Comm Coll (AZ)
Citrus Coll (CA)
Comm Coll of Allegheny County (PA)
Crowder Coll (MO)
De Anza Coll (CA)
Eastern Arizona Coll (AZ)
Edison State Comm Coll (OH)
Feather River Coll (CA)
Fullerton Coll (CA)
Galveston Coll (TX)
Harper Coll (IL)
Harrisburg Area Comm Coll (PA)
Housatonic Comm Coll (CT)
Houston Comm Coll (TX)
Hutchinson Comm Coll (KS)
Iowa Central Comm Coll (IA)
Los Angeles City Coll (CA)
Los Angeles Mission Coll (CA)
Luzerne County Comm Coll (PA)
Miami Dade Coll (FL)
MiraCosta Coll (CA)
Mississippi Delta Comm Coll (MS)
Montgomery County Comm Coll (PA)
Mt. San Antonio Coll (CA)
Mount Wachusett Comm Coll (MA)
Nassau Comm Coll (NY)
Navarro Coll (TX)
Niagara County Comm Coll (NY)
Northampton Comm Coll (PA)
Northeastern Jr Coll (CO)
North Idaho Coll (ID)
Paris Jr Coll (TX)
Pensacola State Coll (FL)
San Jacinto Coll (TX)
San Joaquin Delta Coll (CA)
San Juan Coll (NM)
Seminole State Coll (OK)
Sierra Coll (CA)
Springfield Tech Comm Coll (MA)
Truckee Meadows Comm Coll (NV)
Union County Coll (NJ)
Western Iowa Tech Comm Coll (IA)
Westmoreland County Comm Coll (PA)

MATHEMATICS AND COMPUTER SCIENCE
Crowder Coll (MO)

MATHEMATICS AND STATISTICS RELATED
Bristol Comm Coll (MA)

MATHEMATICS TEACHER EDUCATION
Bucks County Comm Coll (PA)
Comm Coll of Baltimore County (MD)
Montgomery Coll (MD)
Vincennes U (IN)

MECHANICAL DRAFTING AND CAD/CADD
Alexandria Tech and Comm Coll (MN)
Anoka Tech Coll (MN)
Central Lakes Coll (MN)
Cleveland Comm Coll (NC)
Comm Coll of Allegheny County (PA)
Des Moines Area Comm Coll (IA)
Edison State Comm Coll (OH)
Fox Valley Tech Coll (WI)
Hutchinson Comm Coll (KS)
Minnesota State Comm and Tech Coll (MN)
Minnesota State Comm and Tech Coll–Moorhead (MN)
Northeast Wisconsin Tech Coll (WI)
Ridgewater Coll (MN)
Sierra Coll (CA)
Vincennes U (IN)
Western Iowa Tech Comm Coll (IA)
Westmoreland County Comm Coll (PA)

MECHANICAL ENGINEERING
Bristol Comm Coll (MA)
Fiorello H. LaGuardia Comm Coll of the City U of New York (NY)
Galveston Coll (TX)
Montgomery County Comm Coll (PA)
Northwest State Comm Coll (OH)

MECHANICAL ENGINEERING/ MECHANICAL TECHNOLOGY
Alamance Comm Coll (NC)
Arapahoe Comm Coll (CO)
Benjamin Franklin Inst of Technology (MA)
Bristol Comm Coll (MA)
Camden County Coll (NJ)
Cayuga County Comm Coll (NY)
Central Ohio Tech Coll (OH)
Citrus Coll (CA)
Comm Coll of Allegheny County (PA)
Craven Comm Coll (NC)
Delta Coll (MI)
Eastern Gateway Comm Coll (OH)
Fullerton Coll (CA)
Greenville Tech Coll (SC)
Hagerstown Comm Coll (MD)
Harrisburg Area Comm Coll (PA)
Jamestown Comm Coll (NY)
Kent State U at Tuscarawas (OH)
Lakeland Comm Coll (OH)
Lenoir Comm Coll (NC)
Middlesex County Coll (NJ)
Montgomery County Comm Coll (PA)
Northwest State Comm Coll (OH)
Oakton Comm Coll (IL)
Oklahoma State U Inst of Technology (OK)
Penn State DuBois (PA)
Portland Comm Coll (OR)
Queensborough Comm Coll of the City U of New York (NY)
Richmond Comm Coll (NC)
San Joaquin Delta Coll (CA)
Springfield Tech Comm Coll (MA)
Stark State Coll (OH)
State U of New York Coll of Technology at Alfred (NY)
Tarrant County Coll District (TX)
Trident Tech Coll (SC)
Westchester Comm Coll (NY)
Westmoreland County Comm Coll (PA)

MECHANICAL ENGINEERING TECHNOLOGIES RELATED
Asheville-Buncombe Tech Comm Coll (NC)
Camden County Coll (NJ)
Middlesex County Coll (NJ)

MECHANIC AND REPAIR TECHNOLOGIES RELATED
Chandler-Gilbert Comm Coll (AZ)
Greenville Tech Coll (SC)
Ohio Tech Coll (OH)
West Kentucky Comm and Tech Coll (KY)

MECHATRONICS, ROBOTICS, AND AUTOMATION ENGINEERING
Comm Coll of Allegheny County (PA)
Delta Coll (MI)
Harrisburg Area Comm Coll (PA)
Schoolcraft Coll (MI)
Southwestern Comm Coll (NC)

MEDICAL ADMINISTRATIVE ASSISTANT AND MEDICAL SECRETARY
Alamance Comm Coll (NC)
Alexandria Tech and Comm Coll (MN)
Alvin Comm Coll (TX)
Amarillo Coll (TX)
Anoka Tech Coll (MN)
Bay de Noc Comm Coll (MI)
Bristol Comm Coll (MA)
Central Lakes Coll (MN)
Century Coll (MN)
Coll of The Albemarle (NC)
Comm Coll of Baltimore County (MD)
Craven Comm Coll (NC)
Crowder Coll (MO)
Danville Area Comm Coll (IL)
Delta Coll (MI)
Des Moines Area Comm Coll (IA)
Eastern Gateway Comm Coll (OH)
Edison State Comm Coll (OH)
Galveston Coll (TX)
Gulf Coast State Coll (FL)
Halifax Comm Coll (NC)
Harper Coll (IL)
Hawkeye Comm Coll (IA)
IBMC Coll, Fort Collins (CO)
Lackawanna Coll (PA)
Los Angeles City Coll (CA)
Luzerne County Comm Coll (PA)
Manchester Comm Coll (CT)
Mayland Comm Coll (NC)
Maysville Comm and Tech Coll, Maysville (KY)
McLennan Comm Coll (TX)
Middlesex Comm Coll (CT)
Minnesota State Comm and Tech Coll (MN)
Minnesota State Comm and Tech Coll–Moorhead (MN)
Minnesota State Comm and Tech Coll–Wadena (MN)
Morton Coll (IL)
Mt. San Antonio Coll (CA)
Nassau Comm Coll (NY)
Northampton Comm Coll (PA)
Northern Essex Comm Coll (MA)
North Idaho Coll (ID)
Northland Comm and Tech Coll (MN)
Northwest State Comm Coll (OH)
Owensboro Comm and Tech Coll (KY)
Piedmont Comm Coll (NC)
Quinsigamond Comm Coll (MA)
Ridgewater Coll (MN)
Somerset Comm Coll (KY)
Springfield Tech Comm Coll (MA)
Trident Tech Coll (SC)
Westchester Comm Coll (NY)
West Kentucky Comm and Tech Coll (KY)
Westmoreland County Comm Coll (PA)

MEDICAL/CLINICAL ASSISTANT
Alamance Comm Coll (NC)
Anoka Tech Coll (MN)
Blue Ridge Comm and Tech Coll (WV)
Bossier Parish Comm Coll (LA)
Bucks County Comm Coll (PA)
Central Maine Comm Coll (ME)
Central Oregon Comm Coll (OR)
Cleveland Comm Coll (NC)
Cleveland State Comm Coll (TN)
Coll of Eastern Idaho (ID)
The Coll of Westchester (NY)
Columbia-Greene Comm Coll (NY)
Comm Coll of Allegheny County (PA)
Craven Comm Coll (NC)
De Anza Coll (CA)
Des Moines Area Comm Coll (IA)
Eastern Gateway Comm Coll (OH)
Edison State Comm Coll (OH)
Fox Coll (IL)
Gateway Comm and Tech Coll (KY)
Harper Coll (IL)
Haywood Comm Coll (NC)
IBMC Coll, Fort Collins (CO)
Iowa Central Comm Coll (IA)
Kirtland Comm Coll (MI)
Lake Area Tech Inst (SD)
Lenoir Comm Coll (NC)
Mayland Comm Coll (NC)
Miami Dade Coll (FL)
MiraCosta Coll (CA)
Mount Wachusett Comm Coll (MA)
Niagara County Comm Coll (NY)
Northwestern Coll–Chicago Campus (IL)
Northwest-Shoals Comm Coll (AL)
Northwest State Comm Coll (OH)
Owensboro Comm and Tech Coll (KY)
Piedmont Comm Coll (NC)
Queensborough Comm Coll of the City U of New York (NY)
Raritan Valley Comm Coll (NJ)
Rend Lake Coll (IL)
Richmond Comm Coll (NC)
Ridgewater Coll (MN)
San Jacinto Coll (TX)
Southeastern Coll–West Palm Beach (FL)
Southern Maine Comm Coll (ME)
Southwestern Michigan Coll (MI)
Springfield Tech Comm Coll (MA)
Stark State Coll (OH)
Volunteer State Comm Coll (TN)
Western Dakota Tech Inst (SD)

MEDICAL INFORMATICS
Cleveland State Comm Coll (TN)
Comm Coll of Baltimore County (MD)
Harrisburg Area Comm Coll (PA)

MEDICAL INSURANCE CODING
Bucks County Comm Coll (PA)
Central Maine Comm Coll (ME)
Collin County Comm Coll District (TX)
Hawkeye Comm Coll (IA)
Northland Comm and Tech Coll (MN)
Springfield Tech Comm Coll (MA)

MEDICAL INSURANCE/MEDICAL BILLING
Northeast Wisconsin Tech Coll (WI)

MEDICAL OFFICE ASSISTANT
Front Range Comm Coll (CO)
Meridian Comm Coll (MS)

MEDICAL OFFICE COMPUTER SPECIALIST
Mississippi Delta Comm Coll (MS)

MEDICAL OFFICE MANAGEMENT
Cleveland Comm Coll (NC)
Craven Comm Coll (NC)
Fayetteville Tech Comm Coll (NC)
Fox Valley Tech Coll (WI)
Halifax Comm Coll (NC)
Haywood Comm Coll (NC)
Lenoir Comm Coll (NC)
Meridian Comm Coll (MS)
Montgomery County Comm Coll (PA)
Paris Jr Coll (TX)
Piedmont Comm Coll (NC)
Quinsigamond Comm Coll (MA)
Richmond Comm Coll (NC)
Southwestern Comm Coll (NC)
Western Iowa Tech Comm Coll (IA)

MEDICAL RADIOLOGIC TECHNOLOGY
Bellingham Tech Coll (WA)
Coll of DuPage (IL)
Comm Coll of Allegheny County (PA)
Comm Coll of Baltimore County (MD)
Daytona State Coll (FL)
Delta Coll (MI)
Dunwoody Coll of Technology (MN)
Fiorello H. LaGuardia Comm Coll of the City U of New York (NY)
Florida SouthWestern State Coll (FL)
Galveston Coll (TX)
Greenville Tech Coll (SC)
Gulf Coast State Coll (FL)
Hagerstown Comm Coll (MD)
Hillsborough Comm Coll (FL)
Lakeland Comm Coll (OH)
Miami Dade Coll (FL)
Middlesex Comm Coll (CT)
Middlesex County Coll (NJ)
Mississippi Delta Comm Coll (MS)
Montgomery Coll (MD)
Nassau Comm Coll (NY)
Niagara County Comm Coll (NY)
Northeast Wisconsin Tech Coll (WI)
Northern Essex Comm Coll (MA)
Pensacola State Coll (FL)
Portland Comm Coll (OR)
Rend Lake Coll (IL)
Somerset Comm Coll (KY)
South Arkansas Comm Coll (AR)
Southwestern Comm Coll (NC)
Truckee Meadows Comm Coll (NV)
Volunteer State Comm Coll (TN)
Westchester Comm Coll (NY)
Wor-Wic Comm Coll (MD)

MEDICAL TRANSCRIPTION
Northern Essex Comm Coll (MA)
Western Dakota Tech Inst (SD)

MEDIUM/HEAVY VEHICLE AND TRUCK TECHNOLOGY
Edison State Comm Coll (OH)
James Sprunt Comm Coll (NC)
State Tech Coll of Missouri (MO)

MEETING AND EVENT PLANNING
Bucks County Comm Coll (PA)
Fox Valley Tech Coll (WI)
Northampton Comm Coll (PA)
Northeast Wisconsin Tech Coll (WI)
Raritan Valley Comm Coll (NJ)

MENTAL AND SOCIAL HEALTH SERVICES AND ALLIED PROFESSIONS RELATED
Chesapeake Coll (MD)
Halifax Comm Coll (NC)
Lackawanna Coll (PA)
Lenoir Comm Coll (NC)
Piedmont Comm Coll (NC)
Richmond Comm Coll (NC)

MENTAL HEALTH COUNSELING
Alvin Comm Coll (TX)
Austin Comm Coll District (TX)
Blinn Coll (TX)
Chandler-Gilbert Comm Coll (AZ)
McLennan Comm Coll (TX)
Middlesex Comm Coll (CT)
Mt. San Antonio Coll (CA)
Southwestern Comm Coll (NC)
Tarrant County Coll District (TX)
Truckee Meadows Comm Coll (NV)

MERCHANDISING
Coll of DuPage (IL)

MERCHANDISING, SALES, AND MARKETING OPERATIONS RELATED (GENERAL)
Lake Region State Coll (ND)
Minnesota State Comm and Tech Coll (MN)
Westchester Comm Coll (NY)

MERCHANDISING, SALES, AND MARKETING OPERATIONS RELATED (SPECIALIZED)
Middlesex County Coll (NJ)

METAL AND JEWELRY ARTS
Coll of The Albemarle (NC)
Haywood Comm Coll (NC)

METALLURGICAL TECHNOLOGY
Penn State DuBois (PA)
Penn State Fayette, The Eberly Campus (PA)
Schoolcraft Coll (MI)

METEOROLOGY
Chandler-Gilbert Comm Coll (AZ)

MICROBIOLOGY
Fullerton Coll (CA)

MIDDLE SCHOOL EDUCATION
Alvin Comm Coll (TX)
Austin Comm Coll District (TX)
Black River Tech Coll (AR)
Collin County Comm Coll District (TX)
Comm Coll of Allegheny County (PA)
Miami Dade Coll (FL)
Montgomery County Comm Coll (PA)
Northampton Comm Coll (PA)

MINING TECHNOLOGY
Eastern Arizona Coll (AZ)
Vincennes U (IN)

MODELING, VIRTUAL ENVIRONMENTS AND SIMULATION
Raritan Valley Comm Coll (NJ)

MODERN LANGUAGES
Amarillo Coll (TX)
Citrus Coll (CA)

MOTORCYCLE MAINTENANCE AND REPAIR TECHNOLOGY
Ohio Tech Coll (OH)
State U of New York Coll of Technology at Alfred (NY)

MULTI/INTERDISCIPLINARY STUDIES RELATED
Alexandria Tech and Comm Coll (MN)
Austin Comm Coll District (TX)
Black River Tech Coll (AR)
Blue Ridge Comm and Tech Coll (WV)
Bucks County Comm Coll (PA)
Central Maine Comm Coll (ME)
Century Coll (MN)
Cleveland State Comm Coll (TN)
Eastern Arizona Coll (AZ)
Fox Valley Tech Coll (WI)
Greenville Tech Coll (SC)
Hawkeye Comm Coll (IA)
Hopkinsville Comm Coll (KY)
Iowa Central Comm Coll (IA)
Lackawanna Coll (PA)
Minnesota State Comm and Tech Coll (MN)
Minnesota State Comm and Tech Coll–Detroit Lakes (MN)
Minnesota State Comm and Tech Coll–Moorhead (MN)
Minnesota State Comm and Tech Coll–Wadena (MN)
Northeast Wisconsin Tech Coll (WI)
Northwest-Shoals Comm Coll (AL)
Oklahoma State U Inst of Technology (OK)
Portland Comm Coll (OR)
Raritan Valley Comm Coll (NJ)
Somerset Comm Coll (KY)
South Arkansas Comm Coll (AR)
State Tech Coll of Missouri (MO)
Western Iowa Tech Comm Coll (IA)
West Kentucky Comm and Tech Coll (KY)

MUSEUM STUDIES
Queensborough Comm Coll of the City U of New York (NY)

MUSIC
Adirondack Comm Coll (NY)
Alvin Comm Coll (TX)
Amarillo Coll (TX)
Anoka-Ramsey Comm Coll (MN)
Austin Comm Coll District (TX)
Blinn Coll (TX)
Borough of Manhattan Comm Coll of the City U of New York (NY)
Bossier Parish Comm Coll (LA)
Bucks County Comm Coll (PA)
Central Oregon Comm Coll (OR)
Century Coll (MN)
Citrus Coll (CA)
Coll of The Albemarle (NC)
Collin County Comm Coll District (TX)
Comm Coll of Allegheny County (PA)
Crowder Coll (MO)
Dawson Comm Coll (MT)
De Anza Coll (CA)
Eastern Arizona Coll (AZ)
Fullerton Coll (CA)
Galveston Coll (TX)
Grand Rapids Comm Coll (MI)
Harper Coll (IL)
Jamestown Comm Coll (NY)
Kaskaskia Coll (IL)
Los Angeles City Coll (CA)
Los Angeles Mission Coll (CA)
Manchester Comm Coll (CT)
McHenry County Coll (IL)
McLennan Comm Coll (TX)
Miami Dade Coll (FL)
Minnesota State Comm and Tech Coll (MN)
MiraCosta Coll (CA)
Mississippi Delta Comm Coll (MS)
Morton Coll (IL)
Mt. San Antonio Coll (CA)
Navarro Coll (TX)
Niagara County Comm Coll (NY)
Northeastern Jr Coll (CO)
Northern Essex Comm Coll (MA)
North Idaho Coll (ID)
Oakton Comm Coll (IL)
Paris Jr Coll (TX)
Pensacola State Coll (FL)
Piedmont Virginia Comm Coll (VA)
Quinsigamond Comm Coll (MA)
Raritan Valley Comm Coll (NJ)
Rend Lake Coll (IL)
St. Charles Comm Coll (MO)
San Jacinto Coll (TX)
San Joaquin Delta Coll (CA)
Sierra Coll (CA)
Southwestern Comm Coll (IA)
Truckee Meadows Comm Coll (NV)
Vincennes U (IN)

MUSICAL INSTRUMENT FABRICATION AND REPAIR
Western Iowa Tech Comm Coll (IA)

MUSICAL THEATER
Chandler-Gilbert Comm Coll (AZ)

MUSIC HISTORY, LITERATURE, AND THEORY
Queensborough Comm Coll of the City U of New York (NY)

MUSIC MANAGEMENT
Austin Comm Coll District (TX)
Chandler-Gilbert Comm Coll (AZ)
Collin County Comm Coll District (TX)
Harrisburg Area Comm Coll (PA)
Houston Comm Coll (TX)
Jamestown Comm Coll (NY)

MUSIC PERFORMANCE
Adirondack Comm Coll (NY)
Chandler-Gilbert Comm Coll (AZ)
Cleveland State Comm Coll (TN)
Houston Comm Coll (TX)
Miami Dade Coll (FL)
Motlow State Comm Coll (TN)
Nassau Comm Coll (NY)
Truckee Meadows Comm Coll (NV)
Volunteer State Comm Coll (TN)
Walters State Comm Coll (TN)

MUSIC RELATED
Cayuga County Comm Coll (NY)
Chandler-Gilbert Comm Coll (AZ)

MUSIC TEACHER EDUCATION
Amarillo Coll (TX)
Grand Rapids Comm Coll (MI)
Miami Dade Coll (FL)
Mississippi Delta Comm Coll (MS)
Montgomery County Comm Coll (PA)
North Idaho Coll (ID)
Pensacola State Coll (FL)
St. Charles Comm Coll (MO)

MUSIC TECHNOLOGY
Arapahoe Comm Coll (CO)
Daytona State Coll (FL)
Gulf Coast State Coll (FL)
Miami Dade Coll (FL)

MUSIC THEORY AND COMPOSITION
Houston Comm Coll (TX)

NANOTECHNOLOGY
Comm Coll of Allegheny County (PA)
Harper Coll (IL)
Montgomery County Comm Coll (PA)

NATURAL RESOURCES/ CONSERVATION
Bay de Noc Comm Coll (MI)
Central Lakes Coll (MN)
Central Oregon Comm Coll (OR)
Feather River Coll (CA)
Fox Valley Tech Coll (WI)
Niagara County Comm Coll (NY)
Truckee Meadows Comm Coll (NV)
Vincennes U (IN)

NATURAL RESOURCES MANAGEMENT AND POLICY
Hawkeye Comm Coll (IA)
Hutchinson Comm Coll (KS)
Pensacola State Coll (FL)
San Joaquin Delta Coll (CA)

NATURAL SCIENCES
Amarillo Coll (TX)
Blinn Coll (TX)
Bossier Parish Comm Coll (LA)
Citrus Coll (CA)
Galveston Coll (TX)
Miami Dade Coll (FL)
Northeastern Jr Coll (CO)
San Joaquin Delta Coll (CA)

NAVAL ARCHITECTURE AND MARINE ENGINEERING
Northeast Wisconsin Tech Coll (WI)

NETWORK AND SYSTEM ADMINISTRATION
Bucks County Comm Coll (PA)
Central Maine Comm Coll (ME)
Chandler-Gilbert Comm Coll (AZ)
The Coll of Westchester (NY)
Collin County Comm Coll District (TX)
Daytona State Coll (FL)
De Anza Coll (CA)
Florida SouthWestern State Coll (FL)
Gulf Coast State Coll (FL)
Hillsborough Comm Coll (FL)
Houston Comm Coll (TX)
Kaskaskia Coll (IL)
Kishwaukee Coll (IL)
Miami Dade Coll (FL)
Minnesota State Comm and Tech Coll–Wadena (MN)
Montgomery County Comm Coll (PA)
Northwest State Comm Coll (OH)
Ridgewater Coll (MN)
Sierra Coll (CA)
Southern Maine Comm Coll (ME)

NEUROSCIENCE
Bucks County Comm Coll (PA)

NONPROFIT MANAGEMENT
Miami Dade Coll (FL)
Northwest State Comm Coll (OH)

NUCLEAR MEDICAL TECHNOLOGY
Amarillo Coll (TX)
Coll of DuPage (IL)
Comm Coll of Allegheny County (PA)
Galveston Coll (TX)
Gulf Coast State Coll (FL)
Hillsborough Comm Coll (FL)
Houston Comm Coll (TX)
Lakeland Comm Coll (OH)
Miami Dade Coll (FL)

NUCLEAR/NUCLEAR POWER TECHNOLOGY
Northeast Wisconsin Tech Coll (WI)
State Tech Coll of Missouri (MO)

NURSING ADMINISTRATION
Paris Jr Coll (TX)
South Suburban Coll (IL)

NURSING ASSISTANT/AIDE AND PATIENT CARE ASSISTANT/AIDE
Pensacola State Coll (FL)
Quinsigamond Comm Coll (MA)

NURSING PRACTICE
De Anza Coll (CA)
Minnesota State Comm and Tech Coll–Detroit Lakes (MN)
Minnesota State Comm and Tech Coll–Moorhead (MN)
Minnesota State Comm and Tech Coll–Wadena (MN)

NURSING SCIENCE
Pensacola State Coll (FL)
Piedmont Virginia Comm Coll (VA)

OCCUPATIONAL HEALTH AND INDUSTRIAL HYGIENE
Niagara County Comm Coll (NY)

OCCUPATIONAL SAFETY AND HEALTH TECHNOLOGY
Houston Comm Coll (TX)
Mt. San Antonio Coll (CA)
San Jacinto Coll (TX)
San Juan Coll (NM)

OCCUPATIONAL THERAPIST ASSISTANT
Anoka Tech Coll (MN)
Austin Comm Coll District (TX)
Bossier Parish Comm Coll (LA)
Bristol Comm Coll (MA)
Camden County Coll (NJ)
Cayuga County Comm Coll (NY)
Coll of DuPage (IL)
Comm Coll of Allegheny County (PA)
Crowder Coll (MO)
Daytona State Coll (FL)
Fiorello H. LaGuardia Comm Coll of the City U of New York (NY)
Fox Coll (IL)
Fox Valley Tech Coll (WI)
Greenville Tech Coll (SC)
Hawkeye Comm Coll (IA)
Houston Comm Coll (TX)
Jamestown Comm Coll (NY)
Kaskaskia Coll (IL)
Lake Area Tech Inst (SD)
Manchester Comm Coll (CT)
McHenry County Coll (IL)
North Dakota State Coll of Science (ND)
Northland Comm and Tech Coll (MN)
Penn State DuBois (PA)
Penn State Mont Alto (PA)
Quinsigamond Comm Coll (MA)
Raritan Valley Comm Coll (NJ)
St. Charles Comm Coll (MO)
San Juan Coll (NM)
Shawnee Comm Coll (IL)
South Arkansas Comm Coll (AR)
South Suburban Coll (IL)
Southwestern Comm Coll (NC)
Springfield Tech Comm Coll (MA)
Walters State Comm Coll (TN)
Weatherford Coll (TX)
Wor-Wic Comm Coll (MD)

OCCUPATIONAL THERAPY
Amarillo Coll (TX)
Coll of DuPage (IL)
Comm Coll of Baltimore County (MD)
Galveston Coll (TX)
Iowa Central Comm Coll (IA)
Navarro Coll (TX)
San Jacinto Coll (TX)
Stark State Coll (OH)
Trident Tech Coll (SC)
Vincennes U (IN)

OFFICE MANAGEMENT
Alexandria Tech and Comm Coll (MN)
Anoka Tech Coll (MN)
Asheville-Buncombe Tech Comm Coll (NC)
Clackamas Comm Coll (OR)
Cleveland Comm Coll (NC)
Coll of DuPage (IL)
Comm Coll of Denver (CO)
Craven Comm Coll (NC)
Daytona State Coll (FL)
De Anza Coll (CA)
Des Moines Area Comm Coll (IA)
Fayetteville Tech Comm Coll (NC)
Fox Valley Tech Coll (WI)
Gulf Coast State Coll (FL)
Halifax Comm Coll (NC)
Hillsborough Comm Coll (FL)
James Sprunt Comm Coll (NC)
Lenoir Comm Coll (NC)
Miami Dade Coll (FL)
Minnesota State Comm and Tech Coll (MN)
Minnesota State Comm and Tech Coll–Detroit Lakes (MN)
Minnesota State Comm and Tech Coll–Moorhead (MN)
Minnesota State Comm and Tech Coll–Wadena (MN)
MiraCosta Coll (CA)
Northeast Wisconsin Tech Coll (WI)
Northwest State Comm Coll (OH)
Pensacola State Coll (FL)
Piedmont Comm Coll (NC)
Portland Comm Coll (OR)
Richmond Comm Coll (NC)
St. Charles Comm Coll (MO)
South Suburban Coll (IL)
Southwestern Comm Coll (NC)
State Tech Coll of Missouri (MO)

OFFICE OCCUPATIONS AND CLERICAL SERVICES
Alamance Comm Coll (NC)
Alvin Comm Coll (TX)
IBMC Coll, Fort Collins (CO)
Paris Jr Coll (TX)

OPERATIONS MANAGEMENT
Blue Ridge Comm and Tech Coll (WV)
Clackamas Comm Coll (OR)
Daytona State Coll (FL)
Hillsborough Comm Coll (FL)
McHenry County Coll (IL)
Miami Dade Coll (FL)
Northeast Wisconsin Tech Coll (WI)
Oakton Comm Coll (IL)
Pensacola State Coll (FL)
Rend Lake Coll (IL)
Stark State Coll (OH)

OPHTHALMIC LABORATORY TECHNOLOGY
Middlesex Comm Coll (CT)

OPHTHALMIC TECHNOLOGY
Lakeland Comm Coll (OH)
Miami Dade Coll (FL)
Volunteer State Comm Coll (TN)

OPTICIANRY
Benjamin Franklin Inst of Technology (MA)
Camden County Coll (NJ)
Florida SouthWestern State Coll (FL)
Hillsborough Comm Coll (FL)
Miami Dade Coll (FL)
Raritan Valley Comm Coll (NJ)

OPTOMETRIC TECHNICIAN
Hillsborough Comm Coll (FL)
Portland Comm Coll (OR)
Raritan Valley Comm Coll (NJ)
San Jacinto Coll (TX)

ORGANIZATIONAL BEHAVIOR
Chandler-Gilbert Comm Coll (AZ)
Lackawanna Coll (PA)

ORGANIZATIONAL LEADERSHIP
Chandler-Gilbert Comm Coll (AZ)
Front Range Comm Coll (CO)

ORNAMENTAL HORTICULTURE
Clackamas Comm Coll (OR)
Coll of DuPage (IL)
Kishwaukee Coll (IL)
Miami Dade Coll (FL)
Mt. San Antonio Coll (CA)
Pensacola State Coll (FL)
San Joaquin Delta Coll (CA)
Walters State Comm Coll (TN)

ORTHOTICS/PROSTHETICS
Century Coll (MN)
Oklahoma State U Inst of Technology (OK)

OUTDOOR EDUCATION
Central Oregon Comm Coll (OR)

PAINTING
Luzerne County Comm Coll (PA)

PAINTING AND WALL COVERING
Tohono O'odham Comm Coll (AZ)

PARKS, RECREATION AND LEISURE
Feather River Coll (CA)
Fullerton Coll (CA)
Miami Dade Coll (FL)

Mt. San Antonio Coll (CA)
Niagara County Comm Coll (NY)
Northern Essex Comm Coll (MA)
San Juan Coll (NM)
Sierra Coll (CA)

PARKS, RECREATION AND LEISURE FACILITIES MANAGEMENT
Adirondack Comm Coll (NY)
Iowa Central Comm Coll (IA)
Mt. San Antonio Coll (CA)

PARKS, RECREATION, LEISURE, AND FITNESS STUDIES RELATED
Comm Coll of Baltimore County (MD)
Southwestern Comm Coll (NC)

PARTS, WAREHOUSING, AND INVENTORY MANAGEMENT
Central Maine Comm Coll (ME)

PASTORAL STUDIES/ COUNSELING
Hesston Coll (KS)

PEACE STUDIES AND CONFLICT RESOLUTION
Delta Coll (MI)

PETROLEUM TECHNOLOGY
Bossier Parish Comm Coll (LA)
Houston Comm Coll (TX)
Lackawanna Coll (PA)
Oklahoma State U Inst of Technology (OK)
U of Alaska Anchorage, Kenai Peninsula Coll (AK)

PHARMACY
Mount Wachusett Comm Coll (MA)
Navarro Coll (TX)

PHARMACY, PHARMACEUTICAL SCIENCES, AND ADMINISTRATION RELATED
Mount Wachusett Comm Coll (MA)

PHARMACY TECHNICIAN
Alvin Comm Coll (TX)
Anoka-Ramsey Comm Coll (MN)
Austin Comm Coll District (TX)
Bossier Parish Comm Coll (LA)
Comm Coll of Allegheny County (PA)
Eastern Arizona Coll (AZ)
Fayetteville Tech Comm Coll (NC)
Miami Dade Coll (FL)
Minnesota State Comm and Tech Coll (MN)
North Dakota State Coll of Science (ND)
Northland Comm and Tech Coll (MN)
Pensacola State Coll (FL)
San Jacinto Coll (TX)
Southeastern Coll–West Palm Beach (FL)
Vincennes U (IN)
Western Dakota Tech Inst (SD)

PHILOSOPHY
Austin Comm Coll District (TX)
Blinn Coll (TX)
Chandler-Gilbert Comm Coll (AZ)
De Anza Coll (CA)
Fiorello H. LaGuardia Comm Coll of the City U of New York (NY)
Fullerton Coll (CA)
Harper Coll (IL)
Harrisburg Area Comm Coll (PA)
Los Angeles Mission Coll (CA)
Miami Dade Coll (FL)
Northeastern Jr Coll (CO)
Pensacola State Coll (FL)
San Jacinto Coll (TX)
San Joaquin Delta Coll (CA)
Sierra Coll (CA)
Truckee Meadows Comm Coll (NV)
Vincennes U (IN)

PHILOSOPHY AND RELIGIOUS STUDIES RELATED
Edison State Comm Coll (OH)

PHLEBOTOMY TECHNOLOGY
Coll of The Albemarle (NC)
Miami Dade Coll (FL)

PHOTOGRAPHIC AND FILM/ VIDEO TECHNOLOGY
Austin Comm Coll District (TX)
Central Lakes Coll (MN)
Daytona State Coll (FL)
Eastern Arizona Coll (AZ)
Los Angeles City Coll (CA)
Miami Dade Coll (FL)
MiraCosta Coll (CA)
Westmoreland County Comm Coll (PA)

PHOTOGRAPHY
Amarillo Coll (TX)
Chandler-Gilbert Comm Coll (AZ)
Citrus Coll (CA)
Coll of DuPage (IL)
Daytona State Coll (FL)
De Anza Coll (CA)
Harrisburg Area Comm Coll (PA)
Luzerne County Comm Coll (PA)
Miami Dade Coll (FL)
Mt. San Antonio Coll (CA)
Nassau Comm Coll (NY)
Pensacola State Coll (FL)
San Joaquin Delta Coll (CA)

PHOTOJOURNALISM
Vincennes U (IN)

PHYSICAL EDUCATION TEACHING AND COACHING
Alvin Comm Coll (TX)
Amarillo Coll (TX)
Blinn Coll (TX)
Bucks County Comm Coll (PA)
Citrus Coll (CA)
Crowder Coll (MO)
De Anza Coll (CA)
Dutchess Comm Coll (NY)
Galveston Coll (TX)
Harper Coll (IL)
Luzerne County Comm Coll (PA)
McLennan Comm Coll (TX)
Miami Dade Coll (FL)
Mississippi Delta Comm Coll (MS)
Montgomery County Comm Coll (PA)
Navarro Coll (TX)
Niagara County Comm Coll (NY)
Northeastern Jr Coll (CO)
Northern Essex Comm Coll (MA)
San Joaquin Delta Coll (CA)
Seminole State Coll (OK)
Vincennes U (IN)

PHYSICAL FITNESS TECHNICIAN
Alexandria Tech and Comm Coll (MN)
Anoka-Ramsey Comm Coll (MN)
Austin Comm Coll District (TX)
Central Maine Comm Coll (ME)
Chandler-Gilbert Comm Coll (AZ)
Lake Region State Coll (ND)
Pensacola State Coll (FL)
Schoolcraft Coll (MI)

PHYSICAL SCIENCES
Alvin Comm Coll (TX)
Amarillo Coll (TX)
Borough of Manhattan Comm Coll of the City U of New York (NY)
Central Oregon Comm Coll (OR)
Chandler-Gilbert Comm Coll (AZ)
Citrus Coll (CA)
Crowder Coll (MO)
Feather River Coll (CA)
Harper Coll (IL)
Harrisburg Area Comm Coll (PA)
Hutchinson Comm Coll (KS)
Los Angeles Mission Coll (CA)
Miami Dade Coll (FL)
Middlesex County Coll (NJ)
Montgomery County Comm Coll (PA)
Mount Wachusett Comm Coll (MA)
Navarro Coll (TX)
Northeastern Jr Coll (CO)
North Idaho Coll (ID)
Paris Jr Coll (TX)
Queensborough Comm Coll of the City U of New York (NY)
San Jacinto Coll (TX)
San Joaquin Delta Coll (CA)
San Juan Coll (NM)
Seminole State Coll (OK)
Western Nevada Coll (NV)

PHYSICAL SCIENCES RELATED
Mt. San Antonio Coll (CA)

PHYSICAL SCIENCE TECHNOLOGIES RELATED
Northern Essex Comm Coll (MA)

PHYSICAL THERAPY
Amarillo Coll (TX)
Bossier Parish Comm Coll (LA)
Central Oregon Comm Coll (OR)
De Anza Coll (CA)
Housatonic Comm Coll (CT)
McLennan Comm Coll (TX)
Morton Coll (IL)
Stark State Coll (OH)
Tarrant County Coll District (TX)
Trident Tech Coll (SC)

PHYSICAL THERAPY TECHNOLOGY
Anoka-Ramsey Comm Coll (MN)
Arapahoe Comm Coll (CO)
Austin Comm Coll District (TX)
Black Hawk Coll, Moline (IL)
Blinn Coll (TX)
Blue Ridge Comm and Tech Coll (WV)
Bossier Parish Comm Coll (LA)
Chesapeake Coll (MD)
Coll of DuPage (IL)
Comm Coll of Allegheny County (PA)
Craven Comm Coll (NC)
Daytona State Coll (FL)
Delta Coll (MI)
Edison State Comm Coll (OH)
Fayetteville Tech Comm Coll (NC)
Fiorello H. LaGuardia Comm Coll of the City U of New York (NY)
Florida SouthWestern State Coll (FL)
Fox Coll (IL)
Great Falls Coll Montana State U (MT)
Greenville Tech Coll (SC)
Gulf Coast State Coll (FL)
Hawkeye Comm Coll (IA)
Houston Comm Coll (TX)
Hutchinson Comm Coll (KS)
Kaskaskia Coll (IL)
Lackawanna Coll (PA)
Lake Area Tech Inst (SD)
Manchester Comm Coll (CT)
Meridian Comm Coll (MS)
Miami Dade Coll (FL)
Montgomery Coll (MD)
Morton Coll (IL)
Mount Wachusett Comm Coll (MA)
Nassau Comm Coll (NY)
Niagara County Comm Coll (NY)
Northeast Wisconsin Tech Coll (WI)
Northland Comm and Tech Coll (MN)
Penn State DuBois (PA)
Penn State Mont Alto (PA)
Pensacola State Coll (FL)
San Jacinto Coll (TX)
San Juan Coll (NM)
Somerset Comm Coll (KY)
South Arkansas Comm Coll (AR)
Southwestern Comm Coll (NC)
Springfield Tech Comm Coll (MA)
State Tech Coll of Missouri (MO)
Union County Coll (NJ)
Vincennes U (IN)
Volunteer State Comm Coll (TN)
Walters State Comm Coll (TN)
Weatherford Coll (TX)
Western Iowa Tech Comm Coll (IA)
West Kentucky Comm and Tech Coll (KY)
Wor-Wic Comm Coll (MD)

PHYSICIAN ASSISTANT
Miami Dade Coll (FL)

PHYSICS
Amarillo Coll (TX)
Austin Comm Coll District (TX)
Blinn Coll (TX)
Central Oregon Comm Coll (OR)
Chandler-Gilbert Comm Coll (AZ)
Comm Coll of Allegheny County (PA)
De Anza Coll (CA)
Eastern Arizona Coll (AZ)
Fullerton Coll (CA)
Galveston Coll (TX)
Houston Comm Coll (TX)
Iowa Central Comm Coll (IA)
Los Angeles City Coll (CA)
Miami Dade Coll (FL)
Mount Wachusett Comm Coll (MA)
Navarro Coll (TX)
Northampton Comm Coll (PA)
North Idaho Coll (ID)
Paris Jr Coll (TX)
Pensacola State Coll (FL)
San Jacinto Coll (TX)
San Juan Coll (NM)
Sierra Coll (CA)
Springfield Tech Comm Coll (MA)
Truckee Meadows Comm Coll (NV)
Westmoreland County Comm Coll (PA)

PHYSICS TEACHER EDUCATION
Comm Coll of Baltimore County (MD)
Montgomery Coll (MD)

PIPEFITTING AND SPRINKLER FITTING
Delta Coll (MI)
Miami Dade Coll (FL)

PLANT NURSERY MANAGEMENT
Fullerton Coll (CA)
Miami Dade Coll (FL)
MiraCosta Coll (CA)

PLASTICS AND POLYMER ENGINEERING TECHNOLOGY
Coll of DuPage (IL)
Grand Rapids Comm Coll (MI)
Mount Wachusett Comm Coll (MA)
Northwest State Comm Coll (OH)
Schoolcraft Coll (MI)

PLUMBING TECHNOLOGY
Central Maine Comm Coll (ME)
Delta Coll (MI)
Luzerne County Comm Coll (PA)
Miami Dade Coll (FL)
Minnesota State Comm and Tech Coll (MN)
Minnesota State Comm and Tech Coll–Moorhead (MN)
Northeast Iowa Comm Coll (IA)
Southern Maine Comm Coll (ME)
Tohono O'odham Comm Coll (AZ)
Westmoreland County Comm Coll (PA)

POLITICAL SCIENCE AND GOVERNMENT
Austin Comm Coll District (TX)
Central Oregon Comm Coll (OR)
Chandler-Gilbert Comm Coll (AZ)
De Anza Coll (CA)
Eastern Arizona Coll (AZ)
Feather River Coll (CA)
Fullerton Coll (CA)
Galveston Coll (TX)
Los Angeles City Coll (CA)
Miami Dade Coll (FL)
Mississippi Delta Comm Coll (MS)
Northeastern Jr Coll (CO)
Northern Essex Comm Coll (MA)
North Idaho Coll (ID)
Paris Jr Coll (TX)
San Jacinto Coll (TX)
San Joaquin Delta Coll (CA)

POLYMER/PLASTICS ENGINEERING
Central Oregon Comm Coll (OR)

POLYSOMNOGRAPHY
Lenoir Comm Coll (NC)

PORTUGUESE
Miami Dade Coll (FL)

PRACTICAL NURSING, VOCATIONAL NURSING AND NURSING ASSISTANTS RELATED
Paris Jr Coll (TX)
U of Alaska Anchorage, Kenai Peninsula Coll (AK)
Westchester Comm Coll (NY)

PRE-CHIROPRACTIC
Eastern Arizona Coll (AZ)

PRECISION METAL WORKING RELATED
Delta Coll (MI)
Northwest State Comm Coll (OH)

PRECISION PRODUCTION RELATED
Delta Coll (MI)
St. Charles Comm Coll (MO)

PRECISION PRODUCTION TRADES
Coll of DuPage (IL)
Meridian Comm Coll (MS)

PRE-DENTISTRY STUDIES
Pensacola State Coll (FL)

PRE-ENGINEERING
Amarillo Coll (TX)
Anoka-Ramsey Comm Coll (MN)
Bay de Noc Comm Coll (MI)
Century Coll (MN)
Chandler-Gilbert Comm Coll (AZ)
Craven Comm Coll (NC)
Crowder Coll (MO)
De Anza Coll (CA)
Fayetteville Tech Comm Coll (NC)
Haywood Comm Coll (NC)
Lenoir Comm Coll (NC)
Mesabi Range Coll (MN)
Miami Dade Coll (FL)
Middlesex Comm Coll (CT)
Minnesota State Comm and Tech Coll (MN)
Minnesota State Comm and Tech Coll–Moorhead (MN)
Mt. San Antonio Coll (CA)
Navarro Coll (TX)
Northeastern Jr Coll (CO)
Quinsigamond Comm Coll (MA)
Richmond Comm Coll (NC)
Rock Valley Coll (IL)
St. Charles Comm Coll (MO)
Seminole State Coll (OK)

PRE-LAW STUDIES
Central Oregon Comm Coll (OR)
Paris Jr Coll (TX)
Pensacola State Coll (FL)
Vincennes U (IN)

PREMEDICAL STUDIES
Austin Comm Coll District (TX)
Bay de Noc Comm Coll (MI)
Central Oregon Comm Coll (OR)
Eastern Arizona Coll (AZ)
Paris Jr Coll (TX)
Pensacola State Coll (FL)
San Juan Coll (NM)
Springfield Tech Comm Coll (MA)

PRENURSING STUDIES
Edison State Comm Coll (OH)
James Sprunt Comm Coll (NC)
Lenoir Comm Coll (NC)
Paris Jr Coll (TX)
Pensacola State Coll (FL)

PRE-OPTOMETRY
Eastern Arizona Coll (AZ)

PRE-PHARMACY STUDIES
Amarillo Coll (TX)
Central Oregon Comm Coll (OR)
Eastern Arizona Coll (AZ)
Luzerne County Comm Coll (PA)
Paris Jr Coll (TX)
Pensacola State Coll (FL)
Quinsigamond Comm Coll (MA)
St. Charles Comm Coll (MO)
Schoolcraft Coll (MI)

PRE-PHYSICAL THERAPY
Eastern Arizona Coll (AZ)

PRE-VETERINARY STUDIES
Pensacola State Coll (FL)

PRINTMAKING
De Anza Coll (CA)

PROFESSIONAL, TECHNICAL, BUSINESS, AND SCIENTIFIC WRITING
Austin Comm Coll District (TX)
De Anza Coll (CA)
Fox Valley Tech Coll (WI)

PSYCHIATRIC/MENTAL HEALTH SERVICES TECHNOLOGY
Alvin Comm Coll (TX)
Comm Coll of Allegheny County (PA)
Fiorello H. LaGuardia Comm Coll of the City U of New York (NY)
Fox Valley Tech Coll (WI)
Hagerstown Comm Coll (MD)
Houston Comm Coll (TX)
Montgomery Coll (MD)
Montgomery County Comm Coll (PA)
Northeast Wisconsin Tech Coll (WI)
Northern Essex Comm Coll (MA)
San Jacinto Coll (TX)

PSYCHOLOGY
Alvin Comm Coll (TX)
Amarillo Coll (TX)
Austin Comm Coll District (TX)
Blinn Coll (TX)
Borough of Manhattan Comm Coll of the City U of New York (NY)
Bucks County Comm Coll (PA)

Chandler-Gilbert Comm Coll (AZ)
Citrus Coll (CA)
Comm Coll of Allegheny County (PA)
Crowder Coll (MO)
De Anza Coll (CA)
Eastern Arizona Coll (AZ)
Edison State Comm Coll (OH)
Fiorello H. LaGuardia Comm Coll of the City U of New York (NY)
Fullerton Coll (CA)
Galveston Coll (TX)
Harper Coll (IL)
Harrisburg Area Comm Coll (PA)
Hutchinson Comm Coll (KS)
Iowa Central Comm Coll (IA)
Lackawanna Coll (PA)
Los Angeles Mission Coll (CA)
Miami Dade Coll (FL)
MiraCosta Coll (CA)
Navarro Coll (TX)
Northampton Comm Coll (PA)
Northeastern Jr Coll (CO)
Northern Essex Comm Coll (MA)
North Idaho Coll (ID)
Paris Jr Coll (TX)
Pensacola State Coll (FL)
Queensborough Comm Coll of the City U of New York (NY)
Quinsigamond Comm Coll (MA)
San Jacinto Coll (TX)
San Joaquin Delta Coll (CA)
San Juan Coll (NM)
Sierra Coll (CA)
Truckee Meadows Comm Coll (NV)
Western Iowa Tech Comm Coll (IA)
Westmoreland County Comm Coll (PA)

PSYCHOLOGY RELATED
Lackawanna Coll (PA)
MiraCosta Coll (CA)
Seminole State Coll (OK)

PUBLIC ADMINISTRATION
Citrus Coll (CA)
Houston Comm Coll (TX)
Miami Dade Coll (FL)

PUBLIC ADMINISTRATION AND SOCIAL SERVICE PROFESSIONS RELATED
Cleveland State Comm Coll (TN)

PUBLIC HEALTH
Borough of Manhattan Comm Coll of the City U of New York (NY)
Central Oregon Comm Coll (OR)
Montgomery County Comm Coll (PA)
Northern Essex Comm Coll (MA)
Queensborough Comm Coll of the City U of New York (NY)

PUBLIC HEALTH EDUCATION AND PROMOTION
Borough of Manhattan Comm Coll of the City U of New York (NY)
Northampton Comm Coll (PA)

PUBLIC RELATIONS, ADVERTISING, AND APPLIED COMMUNICATION RELATED
Harper Coll (IL)

PUBLIC RELATIONS/IMAGE MANAGEMENT
Amarillo Coll (TX)
Crowder Coll (MO)
Vincennes U (IN)

PURCHASING, PROCUREMENT/ ACQUISITIONS AND CONTRACTS MANAGEMENT
De Anza Coll (CA)
Greenville Tech Coll (SC)

QUALITY CONTROL AND SAFETY TECHNOLOGIES RELATED
Comm Coll of Denver (CO)
Northeast Wisconsin Tech Coll (WI)

QUALITY CONTROL TECHNOLOGY
Grand Rapids Comm Coll (MI)
Lakeland Comm Coll (OH)
Mt. San Antonio Coll (CA)
Northampton Comm Coll (PA)
Northeast Wisconsin Tech Coll (WI)
Tarrant County Coll District (TX)

RADIATION PROTECTION/ HEALTH PHYSICS TECHNOLOGY
Northeast Wisconsin Tech Coll (WI)

RADIO AND TELEVISION
Alvin Comm Coll (TX)
Amarillo Coll (TX)
Austin Comm Coll District (TX)
De Anza Coll (CA)
Delta Coll (MI)
Fullerton Coll (CA)
Los Angeles City Coll (CA)
Miami Dade Coll (FL)
Mt. San Antonio Coll (CA)

RADIO AND TELEVISION BROADCASTING TECHNOLOGY
Adirondack Comm Coll (NY)
Borough of Manhattan Comm Coll of the City U of New York (NY)
Camden County Coll (NJ)
Cayuga County Comm Coll (NY)
Cleveland Comm Coll (NC)
Houston Comm Coll (TX)
Hutchinson Comm Coll (KS)
Iowa Central Comm Coll (IA)
Luzerne County Comm Coll (PA)
Miami Dade Coll (FL)
Mount Wachusett Comm Coll (MA)
Northampton Comm Coll (PA)
San Jacinto Coll (TX)
Schoolcraft Coll (MI)
Springfield Tech Comm Coll (MA)
Vincennes U (IN)

RADIOLOGIC TECHNOLOGY/ SCIENCE
Amarillo Coll (TX)
Asheville-Buncombe Tech Comm Coll (NC)
Austin Comm Coll District (TX)
Black Hawk Coll, Moline (IL)
Bucks County Comm Coll (PA)
Central Ohio Tech Coll (OH)
Central Oregon Comm Coll (OR)
Century Coll (MN)
Cleveland Comm Coll (NC)
Comm Coll of Denver (CO)
Danville Area Comm Coll (IL)
Fayetteville Tech Comm Coll (NC)
Galveston Coll (TX)
Harper Coll (IL)
Harrisburg Area Comm Coll (PA)
Houston Comm Coll (TX)
Hutchinson Comm Coll (KS)
Iowa Central Comm Coll (IA)
Kaskaskia Coll (IL)
Kishwaukee Coll (IL)
Lenoir Comm Coll (NC)
Los Angeles City Coll (CA)
Miami Dade Coll (FL)
Minnesota State Comm and Tech Coll (MN)
Minnesota State Comm and Tech Coll–Detroit Lakes (MN)
Montgomery County Comm Coll (PA)
Northampton Comm Coll (PA)
Northeast Iowa Comm Coll (IA)
Northern Essex Comm Coll (MA)
Northland Comm and Tech Coll (MN)
Northwestern Coll–Chicago Campus (IL)
Northwest-Shoals Comm Coll (AL)
Owensboro Comm and Tech Coll (KY)
Paris Jr Coll (TX)
Piedmont Virginia Comm Coll (VA)
Quinsigamond Comm Coll (MA)
Ridgewater Coll (MN)
St. Luke's Coll (IA)
San Jacinto Coll (TX)
Somerset Comm Coll (KY)
Southern Maine Comm Coll (ME)
South Suburban Coll (IL)
Southwest Texas Jr Coll (TX)
Springfield Tech Comm Coll (MA)
State Tech Coll of Missouri (MO)
State U of New York Coll of Technology at Alfred (NY)
Union County Coll (NJ)
Weatherford Coll (TX)
Westmoreland County Comm Coll (PA)

RADIO, TELEVISION, AND DIGITAL COMMUNICATION RELATED
Cayuga County Comm Coll (NY)
Fox Valley Tech Coll (WI)
Montgomery County Comm Coll (PA)
Northeast Wisconsin Tech Coll (WI)

REAL ESTATE
Amarillo Coll (TX)
Austin Comm Coll District (TX)
Blinn Coll (TX)
Bristol Comm Coll (MA)
Citrus Coll (CA)
Collin County Comm Coll District (TX)
De Anza Coll (CA)
Eastern Gateway Comm Coll (OH)
Fullerton Coll (CA)
Houston Comm Coll (TX)
Los Angeles City Coll (CA)
McLennan Comm Coll (TX)
Miami Dade Coll (FL)
MiraCosta Coll (CA)
Montgomery County Comm Coll (PA)
Mt. San Antonio Coll (CA)
Nassau Comm Coll (NY)
Oakton Comm Coll (IL)
San Jacinto Coll (TX)
Sierra Coll (CA)
Westmoreland County Comm Coll (PA)

RECEPTIONIST
Bristol Comm Coll (MA)

RECORDING ARTS TECHNOLOGY
Bossier Parish Comm Coll (LA)
Citrus Coll (CA)
Fiorello H. LaGuardia Comm Coll of the City U of New York (NY)
Front Range Comm Coll (CO)
Fullerton Coll (CA)
Miami Dade Coll (FL)
MiraCosta Coll (CA)
Montgomery County Comm Coll (PA)
Northeast State Comm Coll (TN)
Queensborough Comm Coll of the City U of New York (NY)
Ridgewater Coll (MN)
Schoolcraft Coll (MI)
Vincennes U (IN)
Western Iowa Tech Comm Coll (IA)

REGISTERED NURSING/ REGISTERED NURSE
Adirondack Comm Coll (NY)
Alamance Comm Coll (NC)
Alexandria Tech and Comm Coll (MN)
Alvin Comm Coll (TX)
Amarillo Coll (TX)
Anoka-Ramsey Comm Coll (MN)
Asheville-Buncombe Tech Comm Coll (NC)
Austin Comm Coll District (TX)
Bay de Noc Comm Coll (MI)
Bellingham Tech Coll (WA)
Bevill State Comm Coll (AL)
Black Hawk Coll, Moline (IL)
Black River Tech Coll (AR)
Blinn Coll (TX)
Blue Ridge Comm and Tech Coll (WV)
Borough of Manhattan Comm Coll of the City U of New York (NY)
Bossier Parish Comm Coll (LA)
Bristol Comm Coll (MA)
Bucks County Comm Coll (PA)
Camden County Coll (NJ)
Cayuga County Comm Coll (NY)
Central Lakes Coll (MN)
Central Maine Comm Coll (ME)
Central Ohio Tech Coll (OH)
Central Oregon Comm Coll (OR)
Century Coll (MN)
Chandler-Gilbert Comm Coll (AZ)
Chesapeake Coll (MD)
Citrus Coll (CA)
Clackamas Comm Coll (OR)
Cleveland Comm Coll (NC)
Cleveland State Comm Coll (TN)
Coll of DuPage (IL)
Coll of Eastern Idaho (ID)
Coll of The Albemarle (NC)
Collin County Comm Coll District (TX)
Columbia-Greene Comm Coll (NY)
Comm Coll of Allegheny County (PA)
Comm Coll of Baltimore County (MD)
Craven Comm Coll (NC)
Crowder Coll (MO)
Danville Area Comm Coll (IL)
Daytona State Coll (FL)
De Anza Coll (CA)
Delta Coll (MI)
Des Moines Area Comm Coll (IA)
Donnelly Coll (KS)
Dutchess Comm Coll (NY)
Dyersburg State Comm Coll (TN)
Eastern Arizona Coll (AZ)
Edison State Comm Coll (OH)
Fayetteville Tech Comm Coll (NC)
Fiorello H. LaGuardia Comm Coll of the City U of New York (NY)
Florida SouthWestern State Coll (FL)
Fox Valley Tech Coll (WI)
Front Range Comm Coll (CO)
Galveston Coll (TX)
Gateway Comm and Tech Coll (KY)
Grand Rapids Comm Coll (MI)
Great Falls Coll Montana State U (MT)
Greenville Tech Coll (SC)
Hagerstown Comm Coll (MD)
Halifax Comm Coll (NC)
Harper Coll (IL)
Harrisburg Area Comm Coll (PA)
Hawkeye Comm Coll (IA)
Haywood Comm Coll (NC)
Hesston Coll (KS)
Hillsborough Comm Coll (FL)
Hopkinsville Comm Coll (KY)
Houston Comm Coll (TX)
Hutchinson Comm Coll (KS)
James Sprunt Comm Coll (NC)
Jamestown Comm Coll (NY)
Kaskaskia Coll (IL)
Kent State U at Tuscarawas (OH)
Kirtland Comm Coll (MI)
Kishwaukee Coll (IL)
Lake Area Tech Inst (SD)
Lakeland Comm Coll (OH)
Lake Region State Coll (ND)
Lenoir Comm Coll (NC)
Los Angeles City Coll (CA)
Lurleen B. Wallace Comm Coll (AL)
Luzerne County Comm Coll (PA)
Mayland Comm Coll (NC)
Maysville Comm and Tech Coll, Maysville (KY)
McHenry County Coll (IL)
McLennan Comm Coll (TX)
Meridian Comm Coll (MS)
Miami Dade Coll (FL)
Middlesex County Coll (NJ)
Minnesota State Comm and Tech Coll (MN)
Minnesota State Comm and Tech Coll–Detroit Lakes (MN)
Minnesota State Comm and Tech Coll–Moorhead (MN)
Minnesota State Comm and Tech Coll–Wadena (MN)
MiraCosta Coll (CA)
Mississippi Delta Comm Coll (MS)
Montgomery Coll (MD)
Montgomery County Comm Coll (PA)
Morton Coll (IL)
Motlow State Comm Coll (TN)
Mt. San Antonio Coll (CA)
Mount Wachusett Comm Coll (MA)
Nassau Comm Coll (NY)
Navarro Coll (TX)
Niagara County Comm Coll (NY)
Northampton Comm Coll (PA)
North Dakota State Coll of Science (ND)
Northeastern Jr Coll (CO)
Northeast Iowa Comm Coll (IA)
Northeast State Comm Coll (TN)
Northeast Wisconsin Tech Coll (WI)
Northern Essex Comm Coll (MA)
North Idaho Coll (ID)
Northland Comm and Tech Coll (MN)
Northwestern Coll–Chicago Campus (IL)
Northwest-Shoals Comm Coll (AL)
Northwest State Comm Coll (OH)
Oakton Comm Coll (IL)
Oklahoma State U Inst of Technology (OK)
Owensboro Comm and Tech Coll (KY)
Paris Jr Coll (TX)
Penn State Fayette, The Eberly Campus (PA)
Penn State Mont Alto (PA)
Pensacola State Coll (FL)
Piedmont Comm Coll (NC)
Portland Comm Coll (OR)
Queensborough Comm Coll of the City U of New York (NY)
Quinsigamond Comm Coll (MA)
Raritan Valley Comm Coll (NJ)
Rend Lake Coll (IL)
Richmond Comm Coll (NC)
Ridgewater Coll (MN)
Rock Valley Coll (IL)
St. Charles Comm Coll (MO)
St. Luke's Coll (IA)
San Jacinto Coll (TX)
San Joaquin Delta Coll (CA)
San Juan Coll (NM)
Schoolcraft Coll (MI)
Seminole State Coll (OK)
Shawnee Comm Coll (IL)
Sierra Coll (CA)
Somerset Comm Coll (KY)
South Arkansas Comm Coll (AR)
Southeastern Coll–West Palm Beach (FL)
Southern Maine Comm Coll (ME)
Southwestern Comm Coll (IA)
Southwestern Comm Coll (NC)
Southwestern Michigan Coll (MI)
Southwest Texas Jr Coll (TX)
Southwest Wisconsin Tech Coll (WI)
Springfield Tech Comm Coll (MA)
Stark State Coll (OH)
State Tech Coll of Missouri (MO)
State U of New York Coll of Technology at Alfred (NY)
Tarrant County Coll District (TX)
Trident Tech Coll (SC)
Truckee Meadows Comm Coll (NV)
Union County Coll (NJ)
U of South Carolina Lancaster (SC)
Vincennes U (IN)
Volunteer State Comm Coll (TN)
Walters State Comm Coll (TN)
Weatherford Coll (TX)
Westchester Comm Coll (NY)
Western Iowa Tech Comm Coll (IA)
Western Nevada Coll (NV)
West Kentucky Comm and Tech Coll (KY)
Westmoreland County Comm Coll (PA)
Wor-Wic Comm Coll (MD)

REHABILITATION AND THERAPEUTIC PROFESSIONS RELATED
Camden County Coll (NJ)
Middlesex County Coll (NJ)
Nassau Comm Coll (NY)
Raritan Valley Comm Coll (NJ)
Union County Coll (NJ)

RELIGIOUS STUDIES
Amarillo Coll (TX)
Chandler-Gilbert Comm Coll (AZ)
Fullerton Coll (CA)
San Joaquin Delta Coll (CA)

RESPIRATORY CARE THERAPY
Alvin Comm Coll (TX)
Amarillo Coll (TX)
Bossier Parish Comm Coll (LA)
Coll of DuPage (IL)
Collin County Comm Coll District (TX)
Comm Coll of Allegheny County (PA)
Comm Coll of Baltimore County (MD)
Daytona State Coll (FL)
Delta Coll (MI)
Des Moines Area Comm Coll (IA)
Eastern Gateway Comm Coll (OH)
Fayetteville Tech Comm Coll (NC)
Florida SouthWestern State Coll (FL)
Greenville Tech Coll (SC)
Gulf Coast State Coll (FL)
Harrisburg Area Comm Coll (PA)
Hawkeye Comm Coll (IA)
Hillsborough Comm Coll (FL)
Houston Comm Coll (TX)
Hutchinson Comm Coll (KS)
Kaskaskia Coll (IL)
Lakeland Comm Coll (OH)
Luzerne County Comm Coll (PA)

Manchester Comm Coll (CT)
Maysville Comm and Tech Coll, Maysville (KY)
McLennan Comm Coll (TX)
Meridian Comm Coll (MS)
Miami Dade Coll (FL)
Middlesex County Coll (NJ)
Mt. San Antonio Coll (CA)
Nassau Comm Coll (NY)
Northeast Iowa Comm Coll (IA)
Northeast Wisconsin Tech Coll (WI)
Northern Essex Comm Coll (MA)
Northland Comm and Tech Coll (MN)
Quinsigamond Comm Coll (MA)
Raritan Valley Comm Coll (NJ)
Rock Valley Coll (IL)
St. Luke's Coll (IA)
San Jacinto Coll (TX)
San Juan Coll (NM)
Somerset Comm Coll (KY)
Southern Maine Comm Coll (ME)
Southwestern Comm Coll (NC)
Springfield Tech Comm Coll (MA)
Stark State Coll (OH)
Tarrant County Coll District (TX)
Trident Tech Coll (SC)
Union County Coll (NJ)
Volunteer State Comm Coll (TN)
Walters State Comm Coll (TN)
Weatherford Coll (TX)
Westchester Comm Coll (NY)

RESPIRATORY THERAPY TECHNICIAN
Borough of Manhattan Comm Coll of the City U of New York (NY)
Florida SouthWestern State Coll (FL)
Miami Dade Coll (FL)
Northern Essex Comm Coll (MA)

RESTAURANT, CULINARY, AND CATERING MANAGEMENT
Blue Ridge Comm and Tech Coll (WV)
Central Maine Comm Coll (ME)
Coll of DuPage (IL)
Daytona State Coll (FL)
Grand Rapids Comm Coll (MI)
Gulf Coast State Coll (FL)
Hillsborough Comm Coll (FL)
Lakeland Comm Coll (OH)
McHenry County Coll (IL)
Miami Dade Coll (FL)
MiraCosta Coll (CA)
Pensacola State Coll (FL)
Raritan Valley Comm Coll (NJ)
San Jacinto Coll (TX)
Southwest Wisconsin Tech Coll (WI)
Vincennes U (IN)
Westchester Comm Coll (NY)
Westmoreland County Comm Coll (PA)

RESTAURANT/FOOD SERVICES MANAGEMENT
Fiorello H. LaGuardia Comm Coll of the City U of New York (NY)
Hillsborough Comm Coll (FL)
Miami Dade Coll (FL)
Northampton Comm Coll (PA)
North Dakota State Coll of Science (ND)
Quinsigamond Comm Coll (MA)

RETAILING
Alamance Comm Coll (NC)
Arapahoe Comm Coll (CO)
Black Hawk Coll, Moline (IL)
Central Oregon Comm Coll (OR)
Clackamas Comm Coll (OR)
Coll of DuPage (IL)
Hutchinson Comm Coll (KS)
Nassau Comm Coll (NY)
Westchester Comm Coll (NY)

RETAIL MANAGEMENT
Chandler-Gilbert Comm Coll (AZ)
Collin County Comm Coll District (TX)

RHETORIC AND COMPOSITION
Amarillo Coll (TX)
Austin Comm Coll District (TX)
Blinn Coll (TX)
De Anza Coll (CA)
Galveston Coll (TX)
Navarro Coll (TX)
Paris Jr Coll (TX)
San Jacinto Coll (TX)
San Joaquin Delta Coll (CA)
Sierra Coll (CA)

ROBOTICS TECHNOLOGY
Central Lakes Coll (MN)
Coll of DuPage (IL)
Iowa Central Comm Coll (IA)
Kaskaskia Coll (IL)
Kirtland Comm Coll (MI)
Lake Area Tech Inst (SD)

RUSSIAN
Austin Comm Coll District (TX)

SALES, DISTRIBUTION, AND MARKETING OPERATIONS
Alexandria Tech and Comm Coll (MN)
Anoka-Ramsey Comm Coll (MN)
Coll of DuPage (IL)
Des Moines Area Comm Coll (IA)
Fullerton Coll (CA)
Greenville Tech Coll (SC)
Harper Coll (IL)
Hawkeye Comm Coll (IA)
Minnesota State Comm and Tech Coll (MN)
Minnesota State Comm and Tech Coll–Detroit Lakes (MN)
Minnesota State Comm and Tech Coll–Moorhead (MN)
MiraCosta Coll (CA)
Montgomery County Comm Coll (PA)
Northeast Iowa Comm Coll (IA)
Northland Comm and Tech Coll (MN)
Oakton Comm Coll (IL)
Ridgewater Coll (MN)
Sierra Coll (CA)
State U of New York Coll of Technology at Alfred (NY)
Westmoreland County Comm Coll (PA)

SALON/BEAUTY SALON MANAGEMENT
Delta Coll (MI)
Northwest-Shoals Comm Coll (AL)
Schoolcraft Coll (MI)

SCIENCE TEACHER EDUCATION
Mississippi Delta Comm Coll (MS)
San Jacinto Coll (TX)
Vincennes U (IN)

SCIENCE TECHNOLOGIES
Northern Essex Comm Coll (MA)

SCIENCE TECHNOLOGIES RELATED
Arapahoe Comm Coll (CO)
Blue Ridge Comm and Tech Coll (WV)
Cascadia Coll (WA)
Cleveland State Comm Coll (TN)
Comm Coll of Denver (CO)
Front Range Comm Coll (CO)
Montgomery County Comm Coll (PA)
Wor-Wic Comm Coll (MD)

SCIENCE, TECHNOLOGY AND SOCIETY
Truckee Meadows Comm Coll (NV)

SCULPTURE
De Anza Coll (CA)

SECONDARY EDUCATION
Alvin Comm Coll (TX)
Austin Comm Coll District (TX)
Blinn Coll (TX)
Chandler-Gilbert Comm Coll (AZ)
Collin County Comm Coll District (TX)
Eastern Arizona Coll (AZ)
Harrisburg Area Comm Coll (PA)
Houston Comm Coll (TX)
Iowa Central Comm Coll (IA)
Montgomery County Comm Coll (PA)
Northampton Comm Coll (PA)
Paris Jr Coll (TX)
San Jacinto Coll (TX)
San Juan Coll (NM)
Springfield Tech Comm Coll (MA)
Vincennes U (IN)
Western Iowa Tech Comm Coll (IA)

SECURITIES SERVICES ADMINISTRATION
Montgomery County Comm Coll (PA)

SECURITY AND LOSS PREVENTION
Citrus Coll (CA)
Delta Coll (MI)
Miami Dade Coll (FL)

SELLING SKILLS AND SALES
Coll of DuPage (IL)
Danville Area Comm Coll (IL)
McHenry County Coll (IL)
Ridgewater Coll (MN)

SHEET METAL TECHNOLOGY
Comm Coll of Allegheny County (PA)
Delta Coll (MI)
Miami Dade Coll (FL)
Rock Valley Coll (IL)
Shawnee Comm Coll (IL)

SIGNAL/GEOSPATIAL INTELLIGENCE
Northland Comm and Tech Coll (MN)

SIGN LANGUAGE INTERPRETATION AND TRANSLATION
Austin Comm Coll District (TX)
Camden County Coll (NJ)
Collin County Comm Coll District (TX)
Comm Coll of Allegheny County (PA)
Comm Coll of Baltimore County (MD)
Front Range Comm Coll (CO)
Houston Comm Coll (TX)
Lakeland Comm Coll (OH)
McLennan Comm Coll (TX)
Miami Dade Coll (FL)
Minnesota State Comm and Tech Coll (MN)
Minnesota State Comm and Tech Coll–Moorhead (MN)
Mt. San Antonio Coll (CA)
Northern Essex Comm Coll (MA)
Tarrant County Coll District (TX)

SMALL BUSINESS ADMINISTRATION
Bay de Noc Comm Coll (MI)
Black Hawk Coll, Moline (IL)
Borough of Manhattan Comm Coll of the City U of New York (NY)
Bristol Comm Coll (MA)
Bucks County Comm Coll (PA)
Delta Coll (MI)
Eastern Arizona Coll (AZ)
Fullerton Coll (CA)
Harper Coll (IL)
Hutchinson Comm Coll (KS)
Middlesex County Coll (NJ)
MiraCosta Coll (CA)
Raritan Valley Comm Coll (NJ)
Schoolcraft Coll (MI)
Sierra Coll (CA)
South Suburban Coll (IL)
Springfield Tech Comm Coll (MA)
Westchester Comm Coll (NY)
Westmoreland County Comm Coll (PA)

SMALL ENGINE MECHANICS AND REPAIR TECHNOLOGY
North Dakota State Coll of Science (ND)

SOCIAL SCIENCES
Amarillo Coll (TX)
Blinn Coll (TX)
Bristol Comm Coll (MA)
Bucks County Comm Coll (PA)
Central Oregon Comm Coll (OR)
Citrus Coll (CA)
De Anza Coll (CA)
Feather River Coll (CA)
Galveston Coll (TX)
Harrisburg Area Comm Coll (PA)
Hutchinson Comm Coll (KS)
Los Angeles Mission Coll (CA)
Luzerne County Comm Coll (PA)
Miami Dade Coll (FL)
Montgomery County Comm Coll (PA)
Mt. San Antonio Coll (CA)
Navarro Coll (TX)
Niagara County Comm Coll (NY)
Northeastern Jr Coll (CO)
North Idaho Coll (ID)
Paris Jr Coll (TX)
San Jacinto Coll (TX)
San Joaquin Delta Coll (CA)
Seminole State Coll (OK)
Sierra Coll (CA)
Tohono O'odham Comm Coll (AZ)

SOCIAL WORK
Amarillo Coll (TX)
Austin Comm Coll District (TX)
Bristol Comm Coll (MA)
Bucks County Comm Coll (PA)
Camden County Coll (NJ)
Chandler-Gilbert Comm Coll (AZ)
Clackamas Comm Coll (OR)
Edison State Comm Coll (OH)
Galveston Coll (TX)
Harrisburg Area Comm Coll (PA)
Hopkinsville Comm Coll (KY)
Iowa Central Comm Coll (IA)
Lakeland Comm Coll (OH)
Manchester Comm Coll (CT)
Miami Dade Coll (FL)
Mississippi Delta Comm Coll (MS)
Northampton Comm Coll (PA)
Northeast Iowa Comm Coll (IA)
Northwest State Comm Coll (OH)
Oakton Comm Coll (IL)
Paris Jr Coll (TX)
San Juan Coll (NM)
Shawnee Comm Coll (IL)
South Suburban Coll (IL)
Southwestern Michigan Coll (MI)
Vincennes U (IN)

SOCIOLOGY
Alvin Comm Coll (TX)
Austin Comm Coll District (TX)
Borough of Manhattan Comm Coll of the City U of New York (NY)
Chandler-Gilbert Comm Coll (AZ)
Citrus Coll (CA)
Comm Coll of Allegheny County (PA)
De Anza Coll (CA)
Eastern Arizona Coll (AZ)
Feather River Coll (CA)
Fullerton Coll (CA)
Galveston Coll (TX)
Iowa Central Comm Coll (IA)
Los Angeles Mission Coll (CA)
Miami Dade Coll (FL)
MiraCosta Coll (CA)
Navarro Coll (TX)
Northeastern Jr Coll (CO)
North Idaho Coll (ID)
Paris Jr Coll (TX)
Pensacola State Coll (FL)
Quinsigamond Comm Coll (MA)
San Jacinto Coll (TX)
San Joaquin Delta Coll (CA)
Western Iowa Tech Comm Coll (IA)

SOCIOLOGY AND ANTHROPOLOGY
Harper Coll (IL)

SOIL SCIENCE AND AGRONOMY
Northwest State Comm Coll (OH)

SOLAR ENERGY TECHNOLOGY
Crowder Coll (MO)

SPANISH
Austin Comm Coll District (TX)
Blinn Coll (TX)
Chandler-Gilbert Comm Coll (AZ)
Citrus Coll (CA)
De Anza Coll (CA)
Fiorello H. LaGuardia Comm Coll of the City U of New York (NY)
Los Angeles City Coll (CA)
Los Angeles Mission Coll (CA)
Miami Dade Coll (FL)
North Idaho Coll (ID)

SPANISH LANGUAGE TEACHER EDUCATION
Comm Coll of Baltimore County (MD)
Montgomery Coll (MD)

SPECIAL EDUCATION
Anoka-Ramsey Comm Coll (MN)
Century Coll (MN)
Craven Comm Coll (NC)
McHenry County Coll (IL)
Miami Dade Coll (FL)
Pensacola State Coll (FL)
Portland Comm Coll (OR)
San Juan Coll (NM)
Vincennes U (IN)

SPECIAL EDUCATION–INDIVIDUALS WITH HEARING IMPAIRMENTS
Miami Dade Coll (FL)

SPECIAL PRODUCTS MARKETING
Northland Comm and Tech Coll (MN)

SPEECH COMMUNICATION AND RHETORIC
Bristol Comm Coll (MA)
Bucks County Comm Coll (PA)
Central Oregon Comm Coll (OR)
Citrus Coll (CA)
Collin County Comm Coll District (TX)
Dutchess Comm Coll (NY)
Eastern Arizona Coll (AZ)
Edison State Comm Coll (OH)
Fiorello H. LaGuardia Comm Coll of the City U of New York (NY)
Fullerton Coll (CA)
Harper Coll (IL)
Houston Comm Coll (TX)
Hutchinson Comm Coll (KS)
Jamestown Comm Coll (NY)
Los Angeles City Coll (CA)
Manchester Comm Coll (CT)
Montgomery Coll (MD)
Montgomery County Comm Coll (PA)
Nassau Comm Coll (NY)
Northampton Comm Coll (PA)
Paris Jr Coll (TX)
Westchester Comm Coll (NY)

SPEECH-LANGUAGE PATHOLOGY
Coll of DuPage (IL)
Lake Region State Coll (ND)

SPEECH-LANGUAGE PATHOLOGY ASSISTANT
Alexandria Tech and Comm Coll (MN)
Fayetteville Tech Comm Coll (NC)

SPORT AND FITNESS ADMINISTRATION/ MANAGEMENT
Adirondack Comm Coll (NY)
Bucks County Comm Coll (PA)
Camden County Coll (NJ)
Cayuga County Comm Coll (NY)
Central Oregon Comm Coll (OR)
Delta Coll (MI)
Des Moines Area Comm Coll (IA)
Fullerton Coll (CA)
Hutchinson Comm Coll (KS)
Jamestown Comm Coll (NY)
Niagara County Comm Coll (NY)
Northampton Comm Coll (PA)
Paris Jr Coll (TX)
Rock Valley Coll (IL)
Southwestern Michigan Coll (MI)
State U of New York Coll of Technology at Alfred (NY)
Union County Coll (NJ)

STRUCTURAL ENGINEERING
Bristol Comm Coll (MA)
Harrisburg Area Comm Coll (PA)

SUBSTANCE ABUSE/ ADDICTION COUNSELING
Adirondack Comm Coll (NY)
Alvin Comm Coll (TX)
Amarillo Coll (TX)
Anoka-Ramsey Comm Coll (MN)
Austin Comm Coll District (TX)
Camden County Coll (NJ)
Central Oregon Comm Coll (OR)
Century Coll (MN)
Coll of DuPage (IL)
Comm Coll of Allegheny County (PA)
Comm Coll of Baltimore County (MD)
Dawson Comm Coll (MT)
Florida SouthWestern State Coll (FL)
Fox Valley Tech Coll (WI)
Jamestown Comm Coll (NY)
Los Angeles City Coll (CA)
Mesabi Range Coll (MN)
Miami Dade Coll (FL)
Middlesex Comm Coll (CT)
Montgomery County Comm Coll (PA)
Oakton Comm Coll (IL)
Portland Comm Coll (OR)
Richmond Comm Coll (NC)
Southwestern Comm Coll (NC)
Stark State Coll (OH)
Weatherford Coll (TX)
Westchester Comm Coll (NY)
Wor-Wic Comm Coll (MD)

SURGICAL TECHNOLOGY
Anoka Tech Coll (MN)
Asheville-Buncombe Tech Comm Coll (NC)
Austin Comm Coll District (TX)
Bellingham Tech Coll (WA)
Black Hawk Coll, Moline (IL)
Central Ohio Tech Coll (OH)
Coll of DuPage (IL)
Coll of Eastern Idaho (ID)

Collin County Comm Coll District (TX)
Comm Coll of Allegheny County (PA)
Delta Coll (MI)
Fayetteville Tech Comm Coll (NC)
Front Range Comm Coll (CO)
Galveston Coll (TX)
Great Falls Coll Montana State U (MT)
Gulf Coast State Coll (FL)
Harrisburg Area Comm Coll (PA)
Hutchinson Comm Coll (KS)
Kirtland Comm Coll (MI)
Lackawanna Coll (PA)
Lakeland Comm Coll (OH)
Luzerne County Comm Coll (PA)
Manchester Comm Coll (CT)
Minnesota State Comm and Tech Coll (MN)
Minnesota State Comm and Tech Coll–Moorhead (MN)
MiraCosta Coll (CA)
Montgomery Coll (MD)
Montgomery County Comm Coll (PA)
Nassau Comm Coll (NY)
Niagara County Comm Coll (NY)
Northeast State Comm Coll (TN)
Northland Comm and Tech Coll (MN)
Owensboro Comm and Tech Coll (KY)
Paris Jr Coll (TX)
Quinsigamond Comm Coll (MA)
Rock Valley Coll (IL)
San Jacinto Coll (TX)
San Juan Coll (NM)
Somerset Comm Coll (KY)
South Arkansas Comm Coll (AR)
Southern Maine Comm Coll (ME)
Springfield Tech Comm Coll (MA)
Stark State Coll (OH)
Tarrant County Coll District (TX)
Vincennes U (IN)
Walters State Comm Coll (TN)
Western Dakota Tech Inst (SD)
Western Iowa Tech Comm Coll (IA)
West Kentucky Comm and Tech Coll (KY)

SURVEYING ENGINEERING
Des Moines Area Comm Coll (IA)

SURVEYING TECHNOLOGY
Asheville-Buncombe Tech Comm Coll (NC)
Austin Comm Coll District (TX)
Bay de Noc Comm Coll (MI)
Bellingham Tech Coll (WA)
Clackamas Comm Coll (OR)
Fayetteville Tech Comm Coll (NC)
Middlesex County Coll (NJ)
Mt. San Antonio Coll (CA)
State U of New York Coll of Technology at Alfred (NY)
Vincennes U (IN)

SUSTAINABILITY STUDIES
Chandler-Gilbert Comm Coll (AZ)

SYSTEM, NETWORKING, AND LAN/WAN MANAGEMENT
Collin County Comm Coll District (TX)
Craven Comm Coll (NC)
Paris Jr Coll (TX)
Southwestern Comm Coll (NC)

TEACHER ASSISTANT/AIDE
Alamance Comm Coll (NC)
Borough of Manhattan Comm Coll of the City U of New York (NY)
Central Maine Comm Coll (ME)
Coll of The Albemarle (NC)
Comm Coll of Allegheny County (PA)
Danville Area Comm Coll (IL)
Fiorello H. LaGuardia Comm Coll of the City U of New York (NY)
Gateway Comm and Tech Coll (KY)
Jamestown Comm Coll (NY)
Kaskaskia Coll (IL)
Kishwaukee Coll (IL)
Manchester Comm Coll (CT)
Miami Dade Coll (FL)
Middlesex County Coll (NJ)
Minnesota State Comm and Tech Coll (MN)
Minnesota State Comm and Tech Coll–Detroit Lakes (MN)
Montgomery County Comm Coll (PA)
Northampton Comm Coll (PA)
Northeast Wisconsin Tech Coll (WI)
Northland Comm and Tech Coll (MN)
Northwest State Comm Coll (OH)
Portland Comm Coll (OR)
Ridgewater Coll (MN)
St. Charles Comm Coll (MO)
Somerset Comm Coll (KY)
Westchester Comm Coll (NY)

TECHNOLOGY/INDUSTRIAL ARTS TEACHER EDUCATION
Delta Coll (MI)
Fullerton Coll (CA)
Vincennes U (IN)

TELECOMMUNICATIONS TECHNOLOGY
Amarillo Coll (TX)
Arapahoe Comm Coll (CO)
Cayuga County Comm Coll (NY)
Collin County Comm Coll District (TX)
Meridian Comm Coll (MS)
Miami Dade Coll (FL)
Minnesota State Comm and Tech Coll (MN)
Northern Essex Comm Coll (MA)
Penn State DuBois (PA)
Penn State Fayette, The Eberly Campus (PA)
Pensacola State Coll (FL)
Queensborough Comm Coll of the City U of New York (NY)
Ridgewater Coll (MN)
Springfield Tech Comm Coll (MA)
Trident Tech Coll (SC)

THEATER DESIGN AND TECHNOLOGY
Austin Comm Coll District (TX)
Miami Dade Coll (FL)
MiraCosta Coll (CA)
Nassau Comm Coll (NY)
San Juan Coll (NM)

THEATER LITERATURE, HISTORY AND CRITICISM
Piedmont Virginia Comm Coll (VA)

THEATER/THEATER ARTS MANAGEMENT
Harper Coll (IL)

THERAPEUTIC RECREATION
Austin Comm Coll District (TX)
Comm Coll of Allegheny County (PA)
Ridgewater Coll (MN)

TOOL AND DIE TECHNOLOGY
Bevill State Comm Coll (AL)
Craven Comm Coll (NC)
Delta Coll (MI)
Des Moines Area Comm Coll (IA)
Ridgewater Coll (MN)
Rock Valley Coll (IL)
Vincennes U (IN)

TOURISM AND TRAVEL SERVICES MANAGEMENT
Adirondack Comm Coll (NY)
Amarillo Coll (TX)
Austin Comm Coll District (TX)
Coll of DuPage (IL)
Comm Coll of Allegheny County (PA)
Fiorello H. LaGuardia Comm Coll of the City U of New York (NY)
Houston Comm Coll (TX)
Lakeland Comm Coll (OH)
Miami Dade Coll (FL)
Niagara County Comm Coll (NY)

TOURISM AND TRAVEL SERVICES MARKETING
Coll of DuPage (IL)
Montgomery County Comm Coll (PA)

TOURISM PROMOTION
Coll of DuPage (IL)

TRADE AND INDUSTRIAL TEACHER EDUCATION
Lenoir Comm Coll (NC)

TRANSPORTATION AND MATERIALS MOVING RELATED
Coll of DuPage (IL)
Mt. San Antonio Coll (CA)
Nassau Comm Coll (NY)

TRANSPORTATION/MOBILITY MANAGEMENT
Comm Coll of Baltimore County (MD)
Gulf Coast State Coll (FL)
Hagerstown Comm Coll (MD)

TURF AND TURFGRASS MANAGEMENT
Danville Area Comm Coll (IL)
Florida SouthWestern State Coll (FL)
Houston Comm Coll (TX)
Iowa Central Comm Coll (IA)
State Tech Coll of Missouri (MO)

VEHICLE MAINTENANCE AND REPAIR TECHNOLOGIES
Bevill State Comm Coll (AL)
Ohio Tech Coll (OH)

VEHICLE MAINTENANCE AND REPAIR TECHNOLOGIES RELATED
Iowa Central Comm Coll (IA)
North Dakota State Coll of Science (ND)
State U of New York Coll of Technology at Alfred (NY)
Western Dakota Tech Inst (SD)

VETERINARY/ANIMAL HEALTH TECHNOLOGY
Asheville-Buncombe Tech Comm Coll (NC)
Austin Comm Coll District (TX)
Bel–Rea Inst of Animal Technology (CO)
Black Hawk Coll, Moline (IL)
Bristol Comm Coll (MA)
Camden County Coll (NJ)
Central Oregon Comm Coll (OR)
Comm Coll of Baltimore County (MD)
Comm Coll of Denver (CO)
Crowder Coll (MO)
Des Moines Area Comm Coll (IA)
Edison State Comm Coll (OH)
Fiorello H. LaGuardia Comm Coll of the City U of New York (NY)
Fox Coll (IL)
Fox Valley Tech Coll (WI)
Front Range Comm Coll (CO)
Hillsborough Comm Coll (FL)
Kaskaskia Coll (IL)
Kent State U at Tuscarawas (OH)
Miami Dade Coll (FL)
Middlesex Comm Coll (CT)
Mount Wachusett Comm Coll (MA)
Northampton Comm Coll (PA)
Owensboro Comm and Tech Coll (KY)
Pensacola State Coll (FL)
Portland Comm Coll (OR)
Ridgewater Coll (MN)
San Juan Coll (NM)
Shawnee Comm Coll (IL)
State U of New York Coll of Technology at Alfred (NY)
Trident Tech Coll (SC)
Truckee Meadows Comm Coll (NV)
Volunteer State Comm Coll (TN)
Weatherford Coll (TX)

VISUAL AND PERFORMING ARTS
Amarillo Coll (TX)
Anoka-Ramsey Comm Coll (MN)
Borough of Manhattan Comm Coll of the City U of New York (NY)
Bucks County Comm Coll (PA)
Chandler-Gilbert Comm Coll (AZ)
Citrus Coll (CA)
Comm Coll of Baltimore County (MD)
Dutchess Comm Coll (NY)
Feather River Coll (CA)
Fiorello H. LaGuardia Comm Coll of the City U of New York (NY)
Harrisburg Area Comm Coll (PA)
Hutchinson Comm Coll (KS)
Middlesex County Coll (NJ)
Mt. San Antonio Coll (CA)
Nassau Comm Coll (NY)
Sierra Coll (CA)
Westchester Comm Coll (NY)

VISUAL AND PERFORMING ARTS RELATED
Bossier Parish Comm Coll (LA)

VITICULTURE AND ENOLOGY
Northeast Wisconsin Tech Coll (WI)

VOICE AND OPERA
Alvin Comm Coll (TX)
Navarro Coll (TX)

WATCHMAKING AND JEWELRYMAKING
Austin Comm Coll District (TX)
Paris Jr Coll (TX)

WATER QUALITY AND WASTEWATER TREATMENT MANAGEMENT AND RECYCLING TECHNOLOGY
Bay de Noc Comm Coll (MI)
Citrus Coll (CA)
Clackamas Comm Coll (OR)
Delta Coll (MI)

WEB/MULTIMEDIA MANAGEMENT AND WEBMASTER
Clackamas Comm Coll (OR)
Delta Coll (MI)
Fox Valley Tech Coll (WI)
Kaskaskia Coll (IL)
MiraCosta Coll (CA)
Montgomery County Comm Coll (PA)
Morton Coll (IL)
Northeast Wisconsin Tech Coll (WI)
Northern Essex Comm Coll (MA)
Raritan Valley Comm Coll (NJ)
Trident Tech Coll (SC)

WEB PAGE, DIGITAL/MULTIMEDIA AND INFORMATION RESOURCES DESIGN
Borough of Manhattan Comm Coll of the City U of New York (NY)
Bucks County Comm Coll (PA)
Camden County Coll (NJ)
Central Ohio Tech Coll (OH)
Central Oregon Comm Coll (OR)
Century Coll (MN)
Chandler-Gilbert Comm Coll (AZ)
Coll of Eastern Idaho (ID)
The Coll of Westchester (NY)
Collin County Comm Coll District (TX)
Daytona State Coll (FL)
Dunwoody Coll of Technology (MN)
Edison State Comm Coll (OH)
Florida SouthWestern State Coll (FL)
Grand Rapids Comm Coll (MI)
Gulf Coast State Coll (FL)
Hagerstown Comm Coll (MD)
Harper Coll (IL)
Harrisburg Area Comm Coll (PA)
Hawkeye Comm Coll (IA)
Hillsborough Comm Coll (FL)
Hutchinson Comm Coll (KS)
Iowa Central Comm Coll (IA)
Mesabi Range Coll (MN)
Miami Dade Coll (FL)
Minnesota State Comm and Tech Coll (MN)
Montgomery Coll (MD)
Montgomery County Comm Coll (PA)
Motlow State Comm Coll (TN)
Mount Wachusett Comm Coll (MA)
Niagara County Comm Coll (NY)
Northampton Comm Coll (PA)
North Dakota State Coll of Science (ND)
Northeast Wisconsin Tech Coll (WI)
Northern Essex Comm Coll (MA)
Northwest State Comm Coll (OH)
Pensacola State Coll (FL)
Quinsigamond Comm Coll (MA)
Ridgewater Coll (MN)
Schoolcraft Coll (MI)
Sierra Coll (CA)
South Arkansas Comm Coll (AR)
Southwestern Comm Coll (IA)
Southwest Wisconsin Tech Coll (WI)
Stark State Coll (OH)
Trident Tech Coll (SC)
Walters State Comm Coll (TN)
Western Iowa Tech Comm Coll (IA)
Westmoreland County Comm Coll (PA)

WELDING ENGINEERING TECHNOLOGY
Central Oregon Comm Coll (OR)

WELDING TECHNOLOGY
Alamance Comm Coll (NC)
Anoka Tech Coll (MN)
Asheville-Buncombe Tech Comm Coll (NC)
Austin Comm Coll District (TX)
Bellingham Tech Coll (WA)
Blinn Coll (TX)
Central Lakes Coll (MN)
Clackamas Comm Coll (OR)
Coll of DuPage (IL)
Coll of Eastern Idaho (ID)
Collin County Comm Coll District (TX)
Comm Coll of Denver (CO)
Craven Comm Coll (NC)
Crowder Coll (MO)
Dawson Comm Coll (MT)
Delta Coll (MI)
Dunwoody Coll of Technology (MN)
Eastern Arizona Coll (AZ)
Fox Valley Tech Coll (WI)
Front Range Comm Coll (CO)
Galveston Coll (TX)
Gateway Comm and Tech Coll (KY)
Grand Rapids Comm Coll (MI)
Great Falls Coll Montana State U (MT)
Halifax Comm Coll (NC)
Hawkeye Comm Coll (IA)
Haywood Comm Coll (NC)
Hutchinson Comm Coll (KS)
Jamestown Comm Coll (NY)
Kaskaskia Coll (IL)
Kirtland Comm Coll (MI)
Lake Area Tech Inst (SD)
Lenoir Comm Coll (NC)
Meridian Comm Coll (MS)
Mt. San Antonio Coll (CA)
Northampton Comm Coll (PA)
North Dakota State Coll of Science (ND)
North Idaho Coll (ID)
Ohio Tech Coll (OH)
Owensboro Comm and Tech Coll (KY)
Paris Jr Coll (TX)
Portland Comm Coll (OR)
Rend Lake Coll (IL)
Ridgewater Coll (MN)
Rock Valley Coll (IL)
St. Charles Comm Coll (MO)
San Jacinto Coll (TX)
San Juan Coll (NM)
Schoolcraft Coll (MI)
Southwestern Comm Coll (IA)
State Tech Coll of Missouri (MO)
State U of New York Coll of Technology at Alfred (NY)
Tarrant County Coll District (TX)
Truckee Meadows Comm Coll (NV)
Vincennes U (IN)
Western Dakota Tech Inst (SD)
Western Iowa Tech Comm Coll (IA)
Western Nevada Coll (NV)
Westmoreland County Comm Coll (PA)

WILDLAND/FOREST FIREFIGHTING AND INVESTIGATION
Fox Valley Tech Coll (WI)

WILDLIFE BIOLOGY
Eastern Arizona Coll (AZ)
North Idaho Coll (ID)

WILDLIFE, FISH AND WILDLANDS SCIENCE AND MANAGEMENT
Feather River Coll (CA)
Front Range Comm Coll (CO)
Haywood Comm Coll (NC)
Mt. San Antonio Coll (CA)
North Idaho Coll (ID)
Penn State DuBois (PA)
Shawnee Comm Coll (IL)
Southwest Texas Jr Coll (TX)

WINE STEWARD/SOMMELIER
Cayuga County Comm Coll (NY)
Niagara County Comm Coll (NY)

WOMEN'S STUDIES
Borough of Manhattan Comm Coll of the City U of New York (NY)

Sierra Coll (CA)

WOOD SCIENCE AND WOOD PRODUCTS/PULP AND PAPER TECHNOLOGY
Kirtland Comm Coll (MI)

WRITING
Cayuga County Comm Coll (NY)
Eastern Arizona Coll (AZ)

YOUTH MINISTRY
Hesston Coll (KS)

ZOOLOGY/ANIMAL BIOLOGY
North Idaho Coll (ID)

Associate Degree Programs at Four-Year Colleges

ACCOUNTING
California U of Pennsylvania (PA)
Calumet Coll of Saint Joseph (IN)
Campbellsville U (KY)
Central Methodist U (MO)
Champlain Coll (VT)
Colegio Universitario de San Juan, San Juan (PR)
Davenport U, Grand Rapids (MI)
Husson U (ME)
Immaculata U (PA)
Inter American U of Puerto Rico, Aguadilla Campus (PR)
Inter American U of Puerto Rico, Barranquitas Campus (PR)
Inter American U of Puerto Rico, Bayamón Campus (PR)
Inter American U of Puerto Rico, Metropolitan Campus (PR)
Inter American U of Puerto Rico, San Germán Campus (PR)
Keiser U, Fort Lauderdale (FL)
Liberty U (VA)
Mount Aloysius Coll (PA)
Mount Marty Coll (SD)
Muhlenberg Coll (PA)
North Central U (MN)
Oakland City U (IN)
Rasmussen Coll Aurora (IL)
Rasmussen Coll Blaine (MN)
Rasmussen Coll Bloomington (MN)
Rasmussen Coll Brooklyn Park (MN)
Rasmussen Coll Eagan (MN)
Rasmussen Coll Fort Myers (FL)
Rasmussen Coll Green Bay (WI)
Rasmussen Coll Kansas City/ Overland Park (KS)
Rasmussen Coll Lake Elmo/ Woodbury (MN)
Rasmussen Coll Land O' Lakes (FL)
Rasmussen Coll Mankato (MN)
Rasmussen Coll Mokena/Tinley Park (IL)
Rasmussen Coll Moorhead (MN)
Rasmussen Coll New Port Richey (FL)
Rasmussen Coll Ocala (FL)
Rasmussen Coll Romeoville/Joliet (IL)
Rasmussen Coll St. Cloud (MN)
Rasmussen Coll Tampa/Brandon (FL)
Rasmussen Coll Topeka (KS)
Rasmussen Coll Wausau (WI)
Rogers State U (OK)
Saint Mary-of-the-Woods Coll (IN)
Siena Heights U (MI)
Trine U (IN)
The U of Findlay (OH)
Utah Valley U (UT)
Webber Intl U (FL)
Youngstown State U (OH)

ACCOUNTING AND BUSINESS/ MANAGEMENT
Kansas State U (KS)

ACCOUNTING AND FINANCE
Central Christian Coll of Kansas (KS)
Ohio Christian U (OH)

ACCOUNTING RELATED
Bayamón Central U (PR)
Florida National U (FL)

ACCOUNTING TECHNOLOGY AND BOOKKEEPING
American Public U System (WV)
Ferris State U (MI)
Florida National U (FL)
Lewis-Clark State Coll (ID)
Miami U Hamilton (OH)
Miami U Middletown (OH)
Montana Technological U (MT)
New York City Coll of Technology of the City U of New York (NY)
Polk State Coll (FL)
State U of New York Coll of Agriculture and Technology at Cobleskill (NY)
State U of New York Coll of Technology at Canton (NY)
State U of New York Coll of Technology at Delhi (NY)
Sullivan U (KY)
Trine U (IN)
The U of Akron (OH)
U of Alaska Fairbanks (AK)
U of Montana (MT)
The U of Toledo (OH)
Valencia Coll (FL)

ACTING
Academy of Art U (CA)
Central Christian Coll of Kansas (KS)
U of Hartford (CT)

ADMINISTRATIVE ASSISTANT AND SECRETARIAL SCIENCE
Arkansas Tech U (AR)
Ball State U (IN)
Bayamón Central U (PR)
Black Hills State U (SD)
Clarion U of Pennsylvania (PA)
Colegio Universitario de San Juan, San Juan (PR)
Dickinson State U (ND)
Eastern Kentucky U (KY)
EDP U of Puerto Rico–San Sebastian (PR)
Inter American U of Puerto Rico, San Germán Campus (PR)
Lewis-Clark State Coll (ID)
Miami U Hamilton (OH)
Miami U Middletown (OH)
Montana Technological U (MT)
Universidad Adventista de las Antillas (PR)
The U of Akron (OH)
U of Montana (MT)
U of Puerto Ricov at Ponce (PR)
Utah State U (UT)
Weber State U (UT)

ADULT DEVELOPMENT AND AGING
Madonna U (MI)

ADVERTISING
Academy of Art U (CA)
Fashion Inst of Technology (NY)

AERONAUTICAL/AEROSPACE ENGINEERING TECHNOLOGY
American Public U System (WV)

AERONAUTICS/AVIATION/ AEROSPACE SCIENCE AND TECHNOLOGY
LeTourneau U (TX)
Montana State U (MT)
Walla Walla U (WA)

AEROSPACE, AERONAUTICAL AND ASTRONAUTICAL/SPACE ENGINEERING
San Jose State U (CA)

AGRIBUSINESS
Southern Arkansas U–Magnolia (AR)
State U of New York Coll of Agriculture and Technology at Cobleskill (NY)
Vermont Tech Coll (VT)

AGRICULTURAL BUSINESS AND MANAGEMENT
State U of New York Coll of Agriculture and Technology at Cobleskill (NY)
U of New Hampshire (NH)

AGRICULTURAL BUSINESS AND MANAGEMENT RELATED
Penn State Abington (PA)
Penn State Altoona (PA)
Penn State Beaver (PA)
Penn State Berks (PA)
Penn State Brandywine (PA)
Penn State Erie, The Behrend Coll (PA)
Penn State Greater Allegheny (PA)
Penn State Hazleton (PA)
Penn State Lehigh Valley (PA)
Penn State New Kensington (PA)
Penn State Schuylkill (PA)
Penn State Shenango (PA)
Penn State Wilkes-Barre (PA)
Penn State York (PA)

AGRICULTURAL/FARM SUPPLIES RETAILING AND WHOLESALING
Dickinson State U (ND)

AGRICULTURAL MECHANIZATION
Utah State U (UT)

AGRICULTURAL PRODUCTION
Eastern New Mexico U (NM)
U of the Fraser Valley (BC, Canada)
Western Kentucky U (KY)

AGRICULTURE
South Dakota State U (SD)
State U of New York Coll of Agriculture and Technology at Cobleskill (NY)
Utah State U (UT)

AGRICULTURE AND AGRICULTURE OPERATIONS RELATED
Eastern Kentucky U (KY)
Murray State U (KY)

AGROECOLOGY AND SUSTAINABLE AGRICULTURE
Inter American U of Puerto Rico, Barranquitas Campus (PR)

AGRONOMY AND CROP SCIENCE
State U of New York Coll of Agriculture and Technology at Cobleskill (NY)

AIRCRAFT POWERPLANT TECHNOLOGY
Liberty U (VA)
Midland Coll (TX)
U of Alaska Fairbanks (AK)

AIRFRAME MECHANICS AND AIRCRAFT MAINTENANCE TECHNOLOGY
Lewis U (IL)
Midland Coll (TX)
St. Petersburg Coll (FL)

AIRLINE FLIGHT ATTENDANT
Liberty U (VA)

AIRLINE PILOT AND FLIGHT CREW
Central Christian Coll of Kansas (KS)
Edinboro U of Pennsylvania (PA)
Inter American U of Puerto Rico, Bayamón Campus (PR)
Lewis U (IL)
Polk State Coll (FL)
Southern Illinois U Carbondale (IL)
U of Alaska Fairbanks (AK)
Utah Valley U (UT)
Valparaiso U (IN)

AIR TRAFFIC CONTROL
Hampton U (VA)
Lewis U (IL)

ALLIED HEALTH AND MEDICAL ASSISTING SERVICES RELATED
Clarion U of Pennsylvania (PA)
Eastern U (PA)
Florida National U (FL)
Widener U (PA)

ALLIED HEALTH DIAGNOSTIC, INTERVENTION, AND TREATMENT PROFESSIONS RELATED
Ball State U (IN)
Cameron U (OK)

AMERICAN NATIVE/NATIVE AMERICAN LANGUAGES
U of Alaska Fairbanks (AK)

AMERICAN SIGN LANGUAGE (ASL)
Bethel U (IN)
Madonna U (MI)
North Central U (MN)
Weber State U (UT)

ANCIENT NEAR EASTERN AND BIBLICAL LANGUAGES
North Central U (MN)

ANIMAL/LIVESTOCK HUSBANDRY AND PRODUCTION
U of the Fraser Valley (BC, Canada)

ANIMAL SCIENCES
State U of New York Coll of Agriculture and Technology at Cobleskill (NY)
U of New Hampshire (NH)

ANIMAL TRAINING
Becker Coll (MA)

ANIMATION, INTERACTIVE TECHNOLOGY, VIDEO GRAPHICS AND SPECIAL EFFECTS
Academy of Art U (CA)
Ferris State U (MI)
New England Inst of Technology (RI)

APPAREL AND ACCESSORIES MARKETING
U of Montana (MT)

APPAREL AND TEXTILE MANUFACTURING
Academy of Art U (CA)
Fashion Inst of Technology (NY)
FIDM/Fashion Inst of Design & Merchandising, Los Angeles Campus (CA)

APPAREL AND TEXTILE MARKETING MANAGEMENT
Academy of Art U (CA)

APPAREL AND TEXTILES
Academy of Art U (CA)

APPLIED HORTICULTURE/ HORTICULTURAL BUSINESS SERVICES RELATED
U of Massachusetts Amherst (MA)

APPLIED HORTICULTURE/ HORTICULTURE OPERATIONS
State U of New York Coll of Technology at Delhi (NY)
U of Massachusetts Amherst (MA)
U of New Hampshire (NH)
U of the Fraser Valley (BC, Canada)

APPLIED LINGUISTICS
Johnson U Florida (FL)

APPLIED MATHEMATICS
Central Methodist U (MO)

ARCHEOLOGY
Weber State U (UT)

ARCHITECTURAL DRAFTING AND CAD/CADD
Academy of Art U (CA)
New York City Coll of Technology of the City U of New York (NY)

ARCHITECTURAL ENGINEERING TECHNOLOGY
Ferris State U (MI)
New England Inst of Technology (RI)
Purdue U Fort Wayne (IN)
State U of New York Coll of Technology at Delhi (NY)
Vermont Tech Coll (VT)

ARCHITECTURAL TECHNOLOGY
New York Inst of Technology (NY)

ARCHITECTURE
U of Detroit Mercy (MI)

ARCHITECTURE RELATED
Abilene Christian U (TX)

ART
Central Christian Coll of Kansas (KS)
Eastern New Mexico U (NM)
Oakland City U (IN)
State U of New York Empire State Coll (NY)
Weber State U (UT)

ART HISTORY, CRITICISM AND CONSERVATION
John Cabot U (Italy)

ART TEACHER EDUCATION
Central Christian Coll of Kansas (KS)

ATHLETIC TRAINING
Central Christian Coll of Kansas (KS)
Dean Coll (MA)
Limestone Coll (SC)
The U of Akron (OH)

AUTOBODY/COLLISION AND REPAIR TECHNOLOGY
Academy of Art U (CA)
Arkansas Tech U (AR)
Lewis-Clark State Coll (ID)
New England Inst of Technology (RI)
Utah Valley U (UT)

AUTOMATION ENGINEER TECHNOLOGY
ECPI U, Virginia Beach (VA)
Weber State U (UT)

AUTOMOBILE/AUTOMOTIVE MECHANICS TECHNOLOGY
Arkansas Tech U (AR)
Ferris State U (MI)
Lewis-Clark State Coll (ID)
Midland Coll (TX)
Montana Technological U (MT)
New England Inst of Technology (RI)
Pittsburg State U (KS)
State U of New York Coll of Technology at Canton (NY)
State U of New York Coll of Technology at Delhi (NY)
Utah State U (UT)
Utah Valley U (UT)
Walla Walla U (WA)
Weber State U (UT)

AUTOMOTIVE ENGINEERING TECHNOLOGY
Farmingdale State Coll (NY)
The U of West Alabama (AL)
Vermont Tech Coll (VT)

AVIATION/AIRWAY MANAGEMENT
Lynn U (FL)
Polk State Coll (FL)

AVIONICS MAINTENANCE TECHNOLOGY
Utah State U (UT)

BAKING AND PASTRY ARTS
The Culinary Inst of America (NY)
ECPI U, Virginia Beach (VA)
Keiser U, Fort Lauderdale (FL)
Sullivan U (KY)
Valencia Coll (FL)

BANKING AND FINANCIAL SUPPORT SERVICES
Arkansas Tech U (AR)
Northern State U (SD)
St. Petersburg Coll (FL)

BEHAVIORAL SCIENCES
Granite State Coll (NH)
Lewis-Clark State Coll (ID)
Loyola U Chicago (IL)
Lynn U (FL)

BIBLICAL STUDIES
Boise Bible Coll (ID)
Carolina Christian Coll (NC)
Carson-Newman U (TN)
Central Christian Coll of Kansas (KS)
Covenant Coll (GA)
Dallas Baptist U (TX)
Eastern Mennonite U (VA)
Ecclesia Coll (AR)
Emmaus Bible Coll (IA)
Johnson U (TN)
Johnson U Florida (FL)
Kentucky Mountain Bible Coll (KY)
Lancaster Bible Coll (PA)
North Central U (MN)
Nyack Coll (NY)
Trinity Coll of Florida (FL)

BIOCHEMISTRY
San Jose State U (CA)

BIOLOGICAL AND BIOMEDICAL SCIENCES RELATED
Roberts Wesleyan Coll (NY)

BIOLOGICAL AND PHYSICAL SCIENCES
Central Christian Coll of Kansas (KS)
Ferris State U (MI)
Penn State Altoona (PA)
Penn State Beaver (PA)
Penn State Greater Allegheny (PA)
Penn State New Kensington (PA)
Penn State Schuylkill (PA)
Penn State Shenango (PA)
Trine U (IN)
Valparaiso U (IN)

BIOLOGICAL/BIOSYSTEMS ENGINEERING
Utah State U (UT)

BIOLOGY/BIOLOGICAL SCIENCES
Bryn Athyn Coll of the New Church (PA)
Dallas Baptist U (TX)
Dean Coll (MA)
Immaculata U (PA)
New York U (NY)
Rogers State U (OK)
Siena Heights U (MI)
State U of New York Coll of Agriculture and Technology at Cobleskill (NY)
U of Puerto Ricov at Ponce (PR)
Utah Valley U (UT)
Wright State U (OH)
Wright State U–Lake Campus (OH)
York Coll of Pennsylvania (PA)

BIOLOGY/BIOTECHNOLOGY LABORATORY TECHNICIAN
State U of New York Coll of Agriculture and Technology at Cobleskill (NY)
Valencia Coll (FL)
Weber State U (UT)

BIOLOGY TEACHER EDUCATION
Central Christian Coll of Kansas (KS)

BIOMEDICAL SCIENCES
Eastern Mennonite U (VA)

BIOMEDICAL TECHNOLOGY
Indiana U-Purdue U Indianapolis (IN)
Penn State Altoona (PA)
Penn State Berks (PA)
Penn State Erie, The Behrend Coll (PA)
Penn State Hazleton (PA)
Penn State New Kensington (PA)
Penn State Schuylkill (PA)
Penn State Shenango (PA)
Penn State York (PA)

BIOTECHNOLOGY
Inter American U of Puerto Rico, Barranquitas Campus (PR)
Keiser U, Fort Lauderdale (FL)
Northern State U (SD)

BLOOD BANK TECHNOLOGY
Rasmussen Coll St. Cloud (MN)

BROADCAST JOURNALISM
Evangel U (MO)

BUILDING/CONSTRUCTION FINISHING, MANAGEMENT, AND INSPECTION RELATED
Pratt Inst (NY)
Utah State U (UT)

BUILDING/CONSTRUCTION SITE MANAGEMENT
State U of New York Coll of Technology at Canton (NY)
Wentworth Inst of Technology (MA)

BUILDING CONSTRUCTION TECHNOLOGY
Wentworth Inst of Technology (MA)

BUILDING/HOME/ CONSTRUCTION INSPECTION
Utah Valley U (UT)

BUILDING/PROPERTY MAINTENANCE
Utah Valley U (UT)

BUSINESS ADMINISTRATION AND MANAGEMENT
Anderson U (IN)
Arkansas Tech U (AR)
Austin Peay State U (TN)
Beacon Coll (FL)
Benedictine U (IL)
Bethel U (IN)
Bryan Coll (TN)
Calumet Coll of Saint Joseph (IN)
Cameron U (OK)
Campbellsville U (KY)
Chaminade U of Honolulu (HI)
Coll of Saint Mary (NE)
Dakota State U (SD)
Dallas Baptist U (TX)
Dallas Christian Coll (TX)
Dean Coll (MA)
Eastern Mennonite U (VA)
EDP U of Puerto Rico–San Sebastian (PR)
Endicott Coll (MA)
Excelsior Coll (NY)
Ferris State U (MI)
Fisher Coll (MA)
Florida National U (FL)
Geneva Coll (PA)
Granite State Coll (NH)
Gwynedd Mercy U (PA)
Hampton U (VA)
Husson U (ME)
Immaculata U (PA)
Inter American U of Puerto Rico, Aguadilla Campus (PR)
Inter American U of Puerto Rico, Barranquitas Campus (PR)
Inter American U of Puerto Rico, Bayamón Campus (PR)
Inter American U of Puerto Rico, Metropolitan Campus (PR)
Inter American U of Puerto Rico, San Germán Campus (PR)
John Cabot U (Italy)
Keiser U, Fort Lauderdale (FL)
Lancaster Bible Coll (PA)
Lock Haven U of Pennsylvania (PA)
Loyola U Chicago (IL)
Lynn U (FL)
Madonna U (MI)
Marian U (IN)
Marietta Coll (OH)
MidAmerica Nazarene U (KS)
Mount Aloysius Coll (PA)
Mount Marty Coll (SD)
Mount Saint Mary's U (CA)
Mount Vernon Nazarene U (OH)
Muhlenberg Coll (PA)
National U (CA)
New England Coll (NH)
New England Inst of Technology (RI)
Newman U (KS)
New Mexico Inst of Mining and Technology (NM)
New York Inst of Technology (NY)
Niagara U (NY)
North Central U (MN)
Northern State U (SD)
Nyack Coll (NY)
Oakland City U (IN)
Ohio Christian U (OH)
Ohio Dominican U (OH)
Peirce Coll (PA)
Providence Coll (RI)
Rasmussen Coll Aurora (IL)
Rasmussen Coll Blaine (MN)
Rasmussen Coll Bloomington (MN)
Rasmussen Coll Brooklyn Park (MN)
Rasmussen Coll Eagan (MN)
Rasmussen Coll Fort Myers (FL)
Rasmussen Coll Green Bay (WI)
Rasmussen Coll Kansas City/ Overland Park (KS)
Rasmussen Coll Lake Elmo/ Woodbury (MN)
Rasmussen Coll Land O' Lakes (FL)
Rasmussen Coll Mankato (MN)
Rasmussen Coll Mokena/Tinley Park (IL)
Rasmussen Coll Moorhead (MN)
Rasmussen Coll New Port Richey (FL)
Rasmussen Coll Ocala (FL)
Rasmussen Coll Romeoville/Joliet (IL)
Rasmussen Coll St. Cloud (MN)
Rasmussen Coll Tampa/Brandon (FL)
Rasmussen Coll Topeka (KS)
Rasmussen Coll Wausau (WI)
Regent U (VA)
Rogers State U (OK)
Saint Francis U (PA)
Saint Joseph's U (PA)
Saint Leo U (FL)
St. Petersburg Coll (FL)
Siena Heights U (MI)
Southern California Inst of Technology (CA)
Southwestern Oklahoma State U (OK)
State U of New York Coll of Agriculture and Technology at Cobleskill (NY)
State U of New York Coll of Technology at Delhi (NY)
Sullivan U (KY)
Toccoa Falls Coll (GA)
Trevecca Nazarene U (TN)
Universidad Adventista de las Antillas (PR)
The U of Akron (OH)
U of Alaska Fairbanks (AK)
U of Alaska Southeast (AK)
U of Cincinnati (OH)
U of Maine at Presque Isle (ME)
U of Management and Technology (VA)
U of New Haven (CT)
U of Pennsylvania (PA)
U of Pikeville (KY)
The U of Scranton (PA)
U of Southern Indiana (IN)
U of the Fraser Valley (BC, Canada)
U of the Incarnate Word (TX)
Upper Iowa U (IA)
Utah State U (UT)
Utah Valley U (UT)
Vermont Tech Coll (VT)
Walla Walla U (WA)
Wayland Baptist U (TX)
Webber Intl U (FL)
Western Kentucky U (KY)
Western New Mexico U (NM)
Wright State U (OH)
Wright State U–Lake Campus (OH)
Xavier U (OH)
Youngstown State U (OH)

BUSINESS ADMINISTRATION, MANAGEMENT AND OPERATIONS RELATED
Eastern Oregon U (OR)
San Jose State U (CA)

BUSINESS AUTOMATION/ TECHNOLOGY/DATA ENTRY
The U of Akron (OH)
Utah Valley U (UT)

BUSINESS/COMMERCE
Adams State U (CO)
American Public U System (WV)
Bayamón Central U (PR)
Bethel U (IN)
Bryn Athyn Coll of the New Church (PA)
Champlain Coll (VT)
Columbia Coll (MO)
Davenport U, Grand Rapids (MI)
Delaware Valley U (PA)
Gannon U (PA)
Glenville State Coll (WV)
Indiana U of Pennsylvania (PA)
Indiana U Southeast (IN)
Liberty U (VA)
Limestone Coll (SC)
Mayville State U (ND)
MidAmerica Nazarene U (KS)
Midland Coll (TX)
Midway U (KY)
Murray State U (KY)
New Charter U (UT)
New York U (NY)
Niagara U (NY)
Nichols Coll (MA)
Penn State Abington (PA)
Penn State Altoona (PA)
Penn State Beaver (PA)
Penn State Berks (PA)
Penn State Brandywine (PA)
Penn State Erie, The Behrend Coll (PA)
Penn State Greater Allegheny (PA)
Penn State Harrisburg (PA)
Penn State Hazleton (PA)
Penn State Lehigh Valley (PA)
Penn State New Kensington (PA)
Penn State Schuylkill (PA)
Penn State Shenango (PA)
Penn State Wilkes-Barre (PA)
Penn State York (PA)
Saint Mary-of-the-Woods Coll (IN)
Southeastern U (FL)
Southern Arkansas U–Magnolia (AR)
Southwest Baptist U (MO)
State U of New York Empire State Coll (NY)
Tabor Coll (KS)
Trine U (IN)
U of Massachusetts Lowell (MA)
U of Puerto Ricov at Ponce (PR)
The U of Toledo (OH)
Utah State U (UT)
Wright State U (OH)
Youngstown State U (OH)

BUSINESS/CORPORATE COMMUNICATIONS
Central Christian Coll of Kansas (KS)

BUSINESS, MANAGEMENT, AND MARKETING RELATED
Florida National U (FL)
North Central U (MN)
Tiffin U (OH)

BUSINESS/MANAGERIAL ECONOMICS
Central Christian Coll of Kansas (KS)
Niagara U (NY)
Weber State U (UT)

BUSINESS TEACHER EDUCATION
Central Christian Coll of Kansas (KS)

CABINETMAKING AND MILLWORK
Utah Valley U (UT)

CAD/CADD DRAFTING/DESIGN TECHNOLOGY
Academy of Art U (CA)
Ferris State U (MI)
Keiser U, Fort Lauderdale (FL)
Missouri Southern State U (MO)
Montana Technological U (MT)
State U of New York Coll of Technology at Delhi (NY)

CARDIOPULMONARY TECHNOLOGY
Inter American U of Puerto Rico, Barranquitas Campus (PR)

CARDIOVASCULAR TECHNOLOGY
Arkansas Tech U (AR)
Gwynedd Mercy U (PA)
Molloy Coll (NY)
New York U (NY)
Polk State Coll (FL)
Sentara Coll of Health Sciences (VA)
Valencia Coll (FL)

CARPENTRY
Montana Technological U (MT)
New England Inst of Technology (RI)
State U of New York Coll of Technology at Delhi (NY)
U of Alaska Fairbanks (AK)
U of Alaska Southeast (AK)

CELL BIOLOGY AND ANATOMICAL SCIENCES RELATED
National U (CA)

CHEMICAL ENGINEERING
Utah State U (UT)

CHEMICAL TECHNOLOGY
New York City Coll of Technology of the City U of New York (NY)
Purdue U Fort Wayne (IN)
State U of New York Coll of Agriculture and Technology at Cobleskill (NY)
U of South Dakota (SD)
Weber State U (UT)

CHEMISTRY
Central Methodist U (MO)
Ohio Dominican U (OH)
Siena Heights U (MI)
Southern Arkansas U–Magnolia (AR)
U of Saint Francis (IN)
Utah Valley U (UT)
Wright State U (OH)
Wright State U–Lake Campus (OH)
York Coll of Pennsylvania (PA)

CHEMISTRY TEACHER EDUCATION
Central Christian Coll of Kansas (KS)

CHILD-CARE AND SUPPORT SERVICES MANAGEMENT
Eastern New Mexico U (NM)

Ferris State U (MI)
Polk State Coll (FL)
Siena Heights U (MI)
Southeast Missouri State U (MO)
State U of New York Coll of Agriculture and Technology at Cobleskill (NY)
State U of New York Coll of Technology at Canton (NY)
U of the Fraser Valley (BC, Canada)
Youngstown State U (OH)

CHILD-CARE PROVISION
American Public U System (WV)
Eastern Kentucky U (KY)
Mayville State U (ND)

CHILD DEVELOPMENT
Arkansas Tech U (AR)
Evangel U (MO)
Lewis-Clark State Coll (ID)
Madonna U (MI)
Midland Coll (TX)
Polk State Coll (FL)
Youngstown State U (OH)

CHINESE
Weber State U (UT)

CHRISTIAN STUDIES
Messenger Coll (TX)
Oklahoma Baptist U (OK)
Regent U (VA)

CINEMATOGRAPHY AND FILM/ VIDEO PRODUCTION
Academy of Art U (CA)
Clayton State U (GA)
FIDM/Fashion Inst of Design & Merchandising, Los Angeles Campus (CA)
Keiser U, Fort Lauderdale (FL)
New England Inst of Technology (RI)
Valencia Coll (FL)

CIVIL ENGINEERING
Utah State U (UT)

CIVIL ENGINEERING TECHNOLOGY
Ferris State U (MI)
Montana Technological U (MT)
Murray State U (KY)
New England Inst of Technology (RI)
New York City Coll of Technology of the City U of New York (NY)
Purdue U Fort Wayne (IN)
State U of New York Coll of Technology at Canton (NY)
U of Massachusetts Lowell (MA)
U of New Hampshire (NH)
U of Puerto Ricov at Ponce (PR)
Valencia Coll (FL)
Vermont Tech Coll (VT)
Youngstown State U (OH)

CLASSICS AND CLASSICAL LANGUAGES
John Cabot U (Italy)

CLINICAL LABORATORY SCIENCE/MEDICAL TECHNOLOGY
U of Wisconsin–Parkside (WI)

CLINICAL/MEDICAL LABORATORY ASSISTANT
New England Inst of Technology (RI)
U of Alaska Fairbanks (AK)
U of Maine at Presque Isle (ME)

CLINICAL/MEDICAL LABORATORY SCIENCE AND ALLIED PROFESSIONS RELATED
State U of New York Coll of Agriculture and Technology at Cobleskill (NY)
Utah State U (UT)

CLINICAL/MEDICAL LABORATORY TECHNOLOGY
Eastern Kentucky U (KY)
Farmingdale State Coll (NY)
The George Washington U (DC)
Keiser U, Fort Lauderdale (FL)
Marshall U (WV)
Mount Aloysius Coll (PA)
Penn State Hazleton (PA)
Penn State Schuylkill (PA)
Rasmussen Coll Green Bay (WI)
Rasmussen Coll Lake Elmo/ Woodbury (MN)
Rasmussen Coll Mankato (MN)
Rasmussen Coll Moorhead (MN)
Rasmussen Coll St. Cloud (MN)
St. Petersburg Coll (FL)
Southwestern Oklahoma State U (OK)
Sullivan U (KY)
Tarleton State U (TX)
U of Maine at Presque Isle (ME)
U of Saint Francis (IN)
Weber State U (UT)
Youngstown State U (OH)

COMMERCIAL AND ADVERTISING ART
Academy of Art U (CA)
California U of Pennsylvania (PA)
Fashion Inst of Technology (NY)
Mount Saint Mary's U (CA)
New York City Coll of Technology of the City U of New York (NY)
Nossi Coll of Art (TN)
Pratt Inst (NY)
State U of New York Coll of Agriculture and Technology at Cobleskill (NY)
Western New Mexico U (NM)

COMMERCIAL PHOTOGRAPHY
Fashion Inst of Technology (NY)
Nossi Coll of Art (TN)

COMMUNICATION
John Cabot U (Italy)

COMMUNICATION AND JOURNALISM RELATED
Immaculata U (PA)
Madonna U (MI)
Valparaiso U (IN)

COMMUNICATION AND MEDIA RELATED
Cameron U (OK)

COMMUNICATION DISORDERS SCIENCES AND SERVICES RELATED
Granite State Coll (NH)

COMMUNITY HEALTH AND PREVENTIVE MEDICINE
Utah Valley U (UT)

COMMUNITY HEALTH SERVICES COUNSELING
Johnson U Florida (FL)
Sullivan U (KY)

COMMUNITY ORGANIZATION AND ADVOCACY
New York U (NY)
State U of New York Empire State Coll (NY)
The U of Akron (OH)
U of Alaska Fairbanks (AK)
Wright State U (OH)
Wright State U–Lake Campus (OH)

COMPARATIVE LITERATURE
North Central U (MN)

COMPUTER AND INFORMATION SCIENCES
Beacon Coll (FL)
Black Hills State U (SD)
Columbia Coll (MO)
Husson U (ME)
Lewis-Clark State Coll (ID)
Lincoln U (MO)
New England Inst of Technology (RI)
New York City Coll of Technology of the City U of New York (NY)
Penn State Schuylkill (PA)
Purdue U Fort Wayne (IN)
Rogers State U (OK)
State U of New York Coll of Agriculture and Technology at Cobleskill (NY)
Troy U (AL)
The U of Toledo (OH)
Utah Valley U (UT)
Webber Intl U (FL)
Youngstown State U (OH)

COMPUTER AND INFORMATION SCIENCES AND SUPPORT SERVICES RELATED
New Coll of Florida (FL)
New York U (NY)
Pace U, Pleasantville Campus (NY)

COMPUTER AND INFORMATION SCIENCES RELATED
Limestone Coll (SC)

COMPUTER AND INFORMATION SYSTEMS SECURITY
Arkansas Tech U (AR)
Davenport U, Grand Rapids (MI)
Ferris State U (MI)
MidAmerica Nazarene U (KS)
Montana Technological U (MT)
Saint Leo U (FL)
Sullivan U (KY)

COMPUTER ENGINEERING
The U of Scranton (PA)

COMPUTER ENGINEERING TECHNOLOGY
California U of Pennsylvania (PA)
Eastern Kentucky U (KY)
Penn State New Kensington (PA)
Polk State Coll (FL)
St. Petersburg Coll (FL)
Sullivan U (KY)
U of Hartford (CT)
Valencia Coll (FL)
Vermont Tech Coll (VT)

COMPUTER GRAPHICS
Academy of Art U (CA)
Sullivan U (KY)
Valencia Coll (FL)

COMPUTER/INFORMATION TECHNOLOGY SERVICES ADMINISTRATION RELATED
Limestone Coll (SC)
St. Petersburg Coll (FL)

COMPUTER INSTALLATION AND REPAIR TECHNOLOGY
Inter American U of Puerto Rico, Bayamón Campus (PR)
U of Alaska Fairbanks (AK)

COMPUTER PROGRAMMING
Bayamón Central U (PR)
Black Hills State U (SD)
Champlain Coll (VT)
Coll of Staten Island of the City U of New York (NY)
ECPI U, Virginia Beach (VA)
Limestone Coll (SC)
MidAmerica Nazarene U (KS)
Midland Coll (TX)
Missouri Southern State U (MO)
New England Inst of Technology (RI)
Polk State Coll (FL)
Rasmussen Coll Fargo (ND)
St. Petersburg Coll (FL)
U of Arkansas at Little Rock (AR)
U of the Fraser Valley (BC, Canada)
The U of Toledo (OH)
Walla Walla U (WA)
Youngstown State U (OH)

COMPUTER PROGRAMMING RELATED
Inter American U of Puerto Rico, Metropolitan Campus (PR)

COMPUTER PROGRAMMING (SPECIFIC APPLICATIONS)
Academy of Art U (CA)
Valencia Coll (FL)

COMPUTER SCIENCE
Black Hills State U (SD)
Central Christian Coll of Kansas (KS)
Central Methodist U (MO)
Creighton U (NE)
Endicott Coll (MA)
Florida National U (FL)
Inter American U of Puerto Rico, Aguadilla Campus (PR)
Inter American U of Puerto Rico, Barranquitas Campus (PR)
Inter American U of Puerto Rico, Bayamón Campus (PR)
Inter American U of Puerto Rico, San Germán Campus (PR)
Madonna U (MI)
New England Inst of Technology (RI)
New York City Coll of Technology of the City U of New York (NY)
Southern California Inst of Technology (CA)
Southwest Baptist U (MO)
Southwestern Oklahoma State U (OK)
Universidad Adventista de las Antillas (PR)
The U of Findlay (OH)
U of Management and Technology (VA)
U of the Virgin Islands (VI)
Utah Valley U (UT)
Weber State U (UT)
Western New Mexico U (NM)

COMPUTER SOFTWARE AND MEDIA APPLICATIONS RELATED
Academy of Art U (CA)
Champlain Coll (VT)
Pace U, Pleasantville Campus (NY)
Platt Coll San Diego (CA)
Polytechnic U of Puerto Rico (PR)
Tiffin U (OH)

COMPUTER SOFTWARE ENGINEERING
Rasmussen Coll Blaine (MN)
Rasmussen Coll Bloomington (MN)
Rasmussen Coll Brooklyn Park (MN)
Rasmussen Coll Eagan (MN)
Rasmussen Coll Fargo (ND)
Rasmussen Coll Fort Myers (FL)
Rasmussen Coll Green Bay (WI)
Rasmussen Coll Kansas City/ Overland Park (KS)
Rasmussen Coll Lake Elmo/ Woodbury (MN)
Rasmussen Coll Land O' Lakes (FL)
Rasmussen Coll Mankato (MN)
Rasmussen Coll Moorhead (MN)
Rasmussen Coll New Port Richey (FL)
Rasmussen Coll Ocala (FL)
Rasmussen Coll St. Cloud (MN)
Rasmussen Coll Tampa/Brandon (FL)
Rasmussen Coll Topeka (KS)
Rasmussen Coll Wausau (WI)
Vermont Tech Coll (VT)

COMPUTER SUPPORT SPECIALIST
Sullivan U (KY)
U of Alaska Fairbanks (AK)

COMPUTER SYSTEMS ANALYSIS
Davenport U, Grand Rapids (MI)
The U of Akron (OH)

COMPUTER SYSTEMS NETWORKING AND TELECOMMUNICATIONS
Davenport U, Grand Rapids (MI)
Inter American U of Puerto Rico, Aguadilla Campus (PR)
Montana Technological U (MT)
Pace U, Pleasantville Campus (NY)
The U of Akron (OH)
Weber State U (UT)

COMPUTER TEACHER EDUCATION
Central Christian Coll of Kansas (KS)

COMPUTER TECHNOLOGY/ COMPUTER SYSTEMS TECHNOLOGY
ECPI U, Virginia Beach (VA)
Excelsior Coll (NY)
New England Inst of Technology (RI)

CONSTRUCTION ENGINEERING TECHNOLOGY
Ferris State U (MI)
New York City Coll of Technology of the City U of New York (NY)
State U of New York Coll of Technology at Delhi (NY)
The U of Akron (OH)
U of Montana (MT)
Valencia Coll (FL)
Vermont Tech Coll (VT)

CONSTRUCTION MANAGEMENT
John Brown U (AR)
South Dakota State U (SD)
U of Alaska Fairbanks (AK)
Vermont Tech Coll (VT)
Weber State U (UT)
Wentworth Inst of Technology (MA)

CONSTRUCTION TRADES
Liberty U (VA)

CONSUMER MERCHANDISING/ RETAILING MANAGEMENT
Academy of Art U (CA)

CORRECTIONS
Mount Aloysius Coll (PA)
Xavier U (OH)
Youngstown State U (OH)

CORRECTIONS AND CRIMINAL JUSTICE RELATED
Cameron U (OK)
EDP U of Puerto Rico–San Sebastian (PR)
Inter American U of Puerto Rico, Aguadilla Campus (PR)
Inter American U of Puerto Rico, Metropolitan Campus (PR)
Rasmussen Coll Aurora (IL)
Rasmussen Coll Blaine (MN)
Rasmussen Coll Bloomington (MN)
Rasmussen Coll Brooklyn Park (MN)
Rasmussen Coll Eagan (MN)
Rasmussen Coll Fort Myers (FL)
Rasmussen Coll Green Bay (WI)
Rasmussen Coll Kansas City/ Overland Park (KS)
Rasmussen Coll Lake Elmo/ Woodbury (MN)
Rasmussen Coll Land O' Lakes (FL)
Rasmussen Coll Mankato (MN)
Rasmussen Coll Mokena/Tinley Park (IL)
Rasmussen Coll Moorhead (MN)
Rasmussen Coll New Port Richey (FL)
Rasmussen Coll Ocala (FL)
Rasmussen Coll Rockford (IL)
Rasmussen Coll Romeoville/Joliet (IL)
Rasmussen Coll St. Cloud (MN)
Rasmussen Coll Tampa/Brandon (FL)
Rasmussen Coll Topeka (KS)
Rasmussen Coll Wausau (WI)

COSMETOLOGY
Arkansas Tech U (AR)
Midland Coll (TX)
Utah State U (UT)

COSTUME DESIGN
FIDM/Fashion Inst of Design & Merchandising, Los Angeles Campus (CA)

CREATIVE WRITING
John Cabot U (Italy)
Liberty U (VA)
Trevecca Nazarene U (TN)

CRIMINALISTICS AND CRIMINAL SCIENCE
Keiser U, Fort Lauderdale (FL)

CRIMINAL JUSTICE/LAW ENFORCEMENT ADMINISTRATION
Anderson U (IN)
Arkansas Tech U (AR)
Bemidji State U (MN)
Campbellsville U (KY)
Central Christian Coll of Kansas (KS)
Clarion U of Pennsylvania (PA)
Columbia Coll (MO)
Excelsior Coll (NY)
Glenville State Coll (WV)
Husson U (ME)
Inter American U of Puerto Rico, Barranquitas Campus (PR)
Keiser U, Fort Lauderdale (FL)
Lincoln U (MO)
Lock Haven U of Pennsylvania (PA)
Mansfield U of Pennsylvania (PA)
Miami U Hamilton (OH)
Miami U Middletown (OH)
New England Coll (NH)
New England Inst of Technology (RI)
Peirce Coll (PA)
Polk State Coll (FL)
Regent U (VA)
Roger Williams U (RI)
St. Petersburg Coll (FL)
Salve Regina U (RI)
Southern Arkansas U–Magnolia (AR)
Tiffin U (OH)
Toccoa Falls Coll (GA)
Trevecca Nazarene U (TN)
Trine U (IN)

U of Maine at Presque Isle (ME)
U of Management and Technology (VA)
Utah Valley U (UT)
Valencia Coll (FL)
Webber Intl U (FL)
Western New Mexico U (NM)
York Coll of Pennsylvania (PA)
Youngstown State U (OH)

CRIMINAL JUSTICE/POLICE SCIENCE
Eastern Kentucky U (KY)
Farmingdale State Coll (NY)
Ferris State U (MI)
Inter American U of Puerto Rico, Barranquitas Campus (PR)
Inter American U of Puerto Rico, Bayamón Campus (PR)
Inter American U of Puerto Rico, Metropolitan Campus (PR)
Midland Coll (TX)
Missouri Southern State U (MO)
Rasmussen Coll Blaine (MN)
Rasmussen Coll Bloomington (MN)
Rasmussen Coll Brooklyn Park (MN)
Rasmussen Coll Eagan (MN)
Rasmussen Coll Lake Elmo/ Woodbury (MN)
Rasmussen Coll Mankato (MN)
Rasmussen Coll St. Cloud (MN)
Rogers State U (OK)
State U of New York Coll of Technology at Canton (NY)
Sullivan U (KY)
The U of Akron (OH)
U of Arkansas at Little Rock (AR)
U of New Haven (CT)
U of the Virgin Islands (VI)
Youngstown State U (OH)

CRIMINAL JUSTICE/SAFETY
American Public U System (WV)
Arkansas Tech U (AR)
Ball State U (IN)
Bethel U (IN)
Calumet Coll of Saint Joseph (IN)
Central Christian Coll of Kansas (KS)
Chaminade U of Honolulu (HI)
Colegio Universitario de San Juan, San Juan (PR)
Dean Coll (MA)
Edinboro U of Pennsylvania (PA)
Endicott Coll (MA)
Fisher Coll (MA)
Florida National U (FL)
Gannon U (PA)
Husson U (ME)
Inter American U of Puerto Rico, Aguadilla Campus (PR)
Inter American U of Puerto Rico, Metropolitan Campus (PR)
Keiser U, Fort Lauderdale (FL)
Liberty U (VA)
Madonna U (MI)
Mount Marty Coll (SD)
New Charter U (UT)
Northern State U (SD)
Oakland City U (IN)
Penn State Altoona (PA)
Rosemont Coll (PA)
Saint Leo U (FL)
Southwestern Oklahoma State U (OK)
State U of New York Coll of Technology at Delhi (NY)
U of Pikeville (KY)
U of Saint Francis (IN)
The U of Scranton (PA)
U of the Fraser Valley (BC, Canada)
Utah State U (UT)
Weber State U (UT)
Western New Mexico U (NM)
Xavier U (OH)
Youngstown State U (OH)

CRIMINOLOGY
LeTourneau U (TX)
Tiffin U (OH)

CRISIS/EMERGENCY/DISASTER MANAGEMENT
Eastern New Mexico U (NM)

CROP PRODUCTION
U of Massachusetts Amherst (MA)

CULINARY ARTS
The Culinary Inst of America (NY)
Eastern New Mexico U (NM)
ECPI U, Virginia Beach (VA)
Indiana U of Pennsylvania (PA)
Inter American U of Puerto Rico, Barranquitas Campus (PR)
Keiser U, Fort Lauderdale (FL)
State U of New York Coll of Agriculture and Technology at Cobleskill (NY)
State U of New York Coll of Technology at Delhi (NY)
Sullivan U (KY)
The U of Akron (OH)
U of Alaska Fairbanks (AK)
Utah Valley U (UT)
Valencia Coll (FL)

CULINARY ARTS RELATED
New York U (NY)
U of New Hampshire (NH)

CYBER/COMPUTER FORENSICS AND COUNTERTERRORISM
Sullivan U (KY)

CYBER/ELECTRONIC OPERATIONS AND WARFARE
LeTourneau U (TX)

DAIRY SCIENCE
Vermont Tech Coll (VT)

DANCE
Dean Coll (MA)
U of Saint Francis (IN)
Utah Valley U (UT)

DATA ENTRY/ MICROCOMPUTER APPLICATIONS
Davenport U, Grand Rapids (MI)

DATA MODELING/ WAREHOUSING AND DATABASE ADMINISTRATION
American Public U System (WV)
Limestone Coll (SC)

DATA PROCESSING AND DATA PROCESSING TECHNOLOGY
American Public U System (WV)
Campbellsville U (KY)
Miami U Hamilton (OH)
Miami U Middletown (OH)
Pace U, Pleasantville Campus (NY)
U of Puerto Ricov at Ponce (PR)
Youngstown State U (OH)

DEMOGRAPHY AND POPULATION
Tiffin U (OH)

DENTAL ASSISTING
ECPI U, Virginia Beach (VA)
New York U (NY)
U of Alaska Fairbanks (AK)
U of Southern Indiana (IN)

DENTAL HYGIENE
Farmingdale State Coll (NY)
Ferris State U (MI)
Florida National U (FL)
Indiana U-Purdue U Indianapolis (IN)
Missouri Southern State U (MO)
New York City Coll of Technology of the City U of New York (NY)
New York U (NY)
Purdue U Fort Wayne (IN)
Regis Coll (MA)
St. Petersburg Coll (FL)
U of Alaska Fairbanks (AK)
U of New Haven (CT)
Utah Valley U (UT)
Valencia Coll (FL)
Vermont Tech Coll (VT)
Weber State U (UT)
Western Kentucky U (KY)
West Liberty U (WV)

DENTAL LABORATORY TECHNOLOGY
Florida National U (FL)
Indiana U-Purdue U Indianapolis (IN)
Louisiana State U Health Sciences Center (LA)
New York City Coll of Technology of the City U of New York (NY)
Purdue U Fort Wayne (IN)

DENTAL SERVICES AND ALLIED PROFESSIONS RELATED
Valdosta State U (GA)

DESIGN AND APPLIED ARTS RELATED
U of Maine at Presque Isle (ME)

DESIGN AND VISUAL COMMUNICATIONS
FIDM/Fashion Inst of Design & Merchandising, Los Angeles Campus (CA)
Keiser U, Fort Lauderdale (FL)
U of Saint Francis (IN)
Utah Valley U (UT)

DESKTOP PUBLISHING AND DIGITAL IMAGING DESIGN
New England Inst of Technology (RI)
Platt Coll San Diego (CA)

DIAGNOSTIC MEDICAL SONOGRAPHY AND ULTRASOUND TECHNOLOGY
AdventHealth U (FL)
Concordia U, St. Paul (MN)
ECPI U, Virginia Beach (VA)
Ferris State U (MI)
Florida National U (FL)
Keiser U, Fort Lauderdale (FL)
Midland Coll (TX)
Nebraska Methodist Coll (NE)
Polk State Coll (FL)
St. Catherine U (MN)
The U of Findlay (OH)
Valencia Coll (FL)

DIESEL MECHANICS TECHNOLOGY
Lewis-Clark State Coll (ID)
Midland Coll (TX)
State U of New York Coll of Agriculture and Technology at Cobleskill (NY)
U of Montana (MT)
Utah State U (UT)
Utah Valley U (UT)
Vermont Tech Coll (VT)
Weber State U (UT)

DIETETICS
Northwest Missouri State U (MO)

DIETETIC TECHNOLOGY
Youngstown State U (OH)

DIETITIAN ASSISTANT
Youngstown State U (OH)

DIGITAL ARTS
Academy of Art U (CA)
Oakland City U (IN)

DIGITAL COMMUNICATION AND MEDIA/MULTIMEDIA
Eastern U (PA)
Lynn U (FL)
Platt Coll San Diego (CA)
Western New Mexico U (NM)

DISPUTE RESOLUTION
Life U (GA)

DIVINITY/MINISTRY
The Baptist Coll of Florida (FL)
Johnson U (TN)
Johnson U Florida (FL)
Messenger Coll (TX)
North Central U (MN)
Ohio Christian U (OH)
Southeastern U (FL)

DRAFTING AND DESIGN TECHNOLOGY
Academy of Art U (CA)
Black Hills State U (SD)
California U of Pennsylvania (PA)
Lewis-Clark State Coll (ID)
Lincoln U (MO)
Montana State U (MT)
The U of Akron (OH)
U of Alaska Fairbanks (AK)
U of Puerto Ricov at Ponce (PR)
Utah Valley U (UT)
Valencia Coll (FL)
Youngstown State U (OH)

DRAFTING/DESIGN ENGINEERING TECHNOLOGIES RELATED
Weber State U (UT)

DRAMA AND DANCE TEACHER EDUCATION
Central Christian Coll of Kansas (KS)

DRAMATIC/THEATER ARTS
Adams State U (CO)
Dean Coll (MA)
North Central U (MN)
U of the Fraser Valley (BC, Canada)
Utah Valley U (UT)

DRAWING
Pratt Inst (NY)

EARLY CHILDHOOD EDUCATION
Adams State U (CO)
Becker Coll (MA)
Bethel U (IN)
Boise Bible Coll (ID)
Chaminade U of Honolulu (HI)
Clarion U of Pennsylvania (PA)
Coll of Saint Mary (NE)
Dean Coll (MA)
Eastern U (PA)
Fisher Coll (MA)
Gannon U (PA)
Granite State Coll (NH)
Liberty U (VA)
Mount Aloysius Coll (PA)
Mount Saint Mary's U (CA)
Nova Southeastern U (FL)
Oakland City U (IN)
Rasmussen Coll Aurora (IL)
Rasmussen Coll Blaine (MN)
Rasmussen Coll Bloomington (MN)
Rasmussen Coll Brooklyn Park (MN)
Rasmussen Coll Eagan (MN)
Rasmussen Coll Fargo (ND)
Rasmussen Coll Fort Myers (FL)
Rasmussen Coll Green Bay (WI)
Rasmussen Coll Kansas City/ Overland Park (KS)
Rasmussen Coll Lake Elmo/ Woodbury (MN)
Rasmussen Coll Land O' Lakes (FL)
Rasmussen Coll Mankato (MN)
Rasmussen Coll Mokena/Tinley Park (IL)
Rasmussen Coll Moorhead (MN)
Rasmussen Coll New Port Richey (FL)
Rasmussen Coll Ocala (FL)
Rasmussen Coll Rockford (IL)
Rasmussen Coll Romeoville/Joliet (IL)
Rasmussen Coll St. Cloud (MN)
Rasmussen Coll Tampa/Brandon (FL)
Rasmussen Coll Topeka (KS)
Rasmussen Coll Wausau (WI)
St. Petersburg Coll (FL)
U of Alaska Fairbanks (AK)
U of Alaska Southeast (AK)
U of Cincinnati (OH)
U of Providence (MT)
U of the Virgin Islands (VI)
Utah Valley U (UT)
Wayland Baptist U (TX)
Western New Mexico U (NM)
Xavier U (OH)

E-COMMERCE
Western New Mexico U (NM)

ECONOMICS
Bethel U (IN)
Central Christian Coll of Kansas (KS)
John Cabot U (Italy)
U of Wisconsin–Parkside (WI)

EDUCATION
Eastern Oregon U (OR)
Florida National U (FL)
LeTourneau U (TX)
Ohio Christian U (OH)
Saint Francis U (PA)
Southwest Baptist U (MO)
State U of New York Empire State Coll (NY)
U of the Fraser Valley (BC, Canada)

EDUCATIONAL/ INSTRUCTIONAL TECHNOLOGY
Bayamón Central U (PR)

EDUCATIONAL LEADERSHIP AND ADMINISTRATION
U of the Fraser Valley (BC, Canada)

EDUCATION (MULTIPLE LEVELS)
Midland Coll (TX)
Western New Mexico U (NM)

EDUCATION RELATED
Liberty U (VA)
The U of Akron (OH)
Weber State U (UT)

EDUCATION (SPECIFIC LEVELS AND METHODS) RELATED
Immaculata U (PA)

EDUCATION (SPECIFIC SUBJECT AREAS) RELATED
Penn State U Park (PA)
U of New Hampshire (NH)

ELECTRICAL AND ELECTRONIC ENGINEERING TECHNOLOGIES RELATED
Colegio Universitario de San Juan, San Juan (PR)
Youngstown State U (OH)

ELECTRICAL AND ELECTRONICS ENGINEERING
New England Inst of Technology (RI)
Southern California Inst of Technology (CA)
The U of Scranton (PA)
Utah State U (UT)

ELECTRICAL AND POWER TRANSMISSION INSTALLATION
Edinboro U of Pennsylvania (PA)
Polk State Coll (FL)
State U of New York Coll of Technology at Delhi (NY)
U of Alaska Southeast (AK)

ELECTRICAL, ELECTRONIC AND COMMUNICATIONS ENGINEERING TECHNOLOGY
California U of Pennsylvania (PA)
Colegio Universitario de San Juan, San Juan (PR)
Coll of Staten Island of the City U of New York (NY)
Inter American U of Puerto Rico, Aguadilla Campus (PR)
Inter American U of Puerto Rico, San Germán Campus (PR)
New England Inst of Technology (RI)
New York City Coll of Technology of the City U of New York (NY)
Penn State Altoona (PA)
Penn State Berks (PA)
Penn State Brandywine (PA)
Penn State Erie, The Behrend Coll (PA)
Penn State Hazleton (PA)
Penn State New Kensington (PA)
Penn State Schuylkill (PA)
Penn State Shenango (PA)
Penn State Wilkes-Barre (PA)
Penn State York (PA)
Purdue U Fort Wayne (IN)
State U of New York Coll of Technology at Canton (NY)
State U of New York Coll of Technology at Delhi (NY)
The U of Akron (OH)
U of Arkansas at Little Rock (AR)
U of Hartford (CT)
U of Massachusetts Lowell (MA)
U of Montana (MT)
Utah State U (UT)
Vermont Tech Coll (VT)
Weber State U (UT)
Western New Mexico U (NM)
Youngstown State U (OH)

ELECTRICAL/ELECTRONICS EQUIPMENT INSTALLATION AND REPAIR
Colegio Universitario de San Juan, San Juan (PR)
Lewis-Clark State Coll (ID)
New England Inst of Technology (RI)
Pittsburg State U (KS)

ELECTRICAL/ELECTRONICS MAINTENANCE AND REPAIR TECHNOLOGY RELATED
Colegio Universitario de San Juan, San Juan (PR)
Western New Mexico U (NM)

ELECTRICIAN
Utah State U (UT)
Weber State U (UT)

ELECTROMECHANICAL AND INSTRUMENTATION AND MAINTENANCE TECHNOLOGIES RELATED
Excelsior Coll (NY)

ELECTROMECHANICAL TECHNOLOGY
Excelsior Coll (NY)
John Brown U (AR)
Midland Coll (TX)
New York City Coll of Technology of the City U of New York (NY)
State U of New York Coll of Technology at Delhi (NY)

ELECTRONEURODIAGNOSTIC/ ELECTROENCEPHALOGRAPHIC TECHNOLOGY
Baptist Coll of Health Sciences (TN)

ELEMENTARY EDUCATION
Adams State U (CO)
Brenau U (GA)
Bryn Athyn Coll of the New Church (PA)
Central Christian Coll of Kansas (KS)
Edinboro U of Pennsylvania (PA)
Ferris State U (MI)
LeTourneau U (TX)
Lynn U (FL)
New Mexico Highlands U (NM)
Rogers State U (OK)
Saint Mary-of-the-Woods Coll (IN)
U of Alaska Southeast (AK)
Vanguard U of Southern California (CA)

EMERGENCY MEDICAL TECHNOLOGY (EMT PARAMEDIC)
Arkansas Tech U (AR)
Creighton U (NE)
Eastern Kentucky U (KY)
ECPI U, Virginia Beach (VA)
EDP U of Puerto Rico–San Sebastian (PR)
Indiana U-Purdue U Indianapolis (IN)
Midland Coll (TX)
New England Inst of Technology (RI)
Polk State Coll (FL)
St. Petersburg Coll (FL)
Southwest Baptist U (MO)
State U of New York Coll of Agriculture and Technology at Cobleskill (NY)
The U of Akron (OH)
U of Alaska Fairbanks (AK)
U of New Haven (CT)
The U of West Alabama (AL)
Valencia Coll (FL)
Weber State U (UT)
Youngstown State U (OH)

ENERGY MANAGEMENT AND SYSTEMS TECHNOLOGY
U of Montana (MT)

ENGINEERING
Cameron U (OK)
Central Christian Coll of Kansas (KS)
Geneva Coll (PA)
San Jose State U (CA)
State U of New York Coll of Technology at Canton (NY)
State U of New York Coll of Technology at Delhi (NY)
Utah State U (UT)
Weber State U (UT)

ENGINEERING/INDUSTRIAL MANAGEMENT
U of Management and Technology (VA)

ENGINEERING RELATED
Eastern Kentucky U (KY)

ENGINEERING-RELATED TECHNOLOGIES
U of Alaska Southeast (AK)

ENGINEERING SCIENCE
Goucher Coll (MD)

ENGINEERING TECHNOLOGIES AND ENGINEERING RELATED
Missouri Southern State U (MO)
Rogers State U (OK)
State U of New York Coll of Agriculture and Technology at Cobleskill (NY)
State U of New York Coll of Technology at Canton (NY)
State U of New York Maritime Coll (NY)

ENGINEERING TECHNOLOGY
Austin Peay State U (TN)
Edinboro U of Pennsylvania (PA)
Kansas State U (KS)
Lawrence Technological U (MI)
Lincoln U (MO)
Miami U Hamilton (OH)
Miami U Middletown (OH)
Morehead State U (KY)
Northwestern State U of Louisiana (LA)
Polk State Coll (FL)
St. Petersburg Coll (FL)
Trine U (IN)
The U of Toledo (OH)
Wentworth Inst of Technology (MA)
Wright State U (OH)
Wright State U–Lake Campus (OH)
Youngstown State U (OH)

ENGLISH
Bryn Athyn Coll of the New Church (PA)
Calumet Coll of Saint Joseph (IN)
Central Methodist U (MO)
Dean Coll (MA)
Felician U (NJ)
Immaculata U (PA)
Madonna U (MI)
Utah Valley U (UT)
Xavier U (OH)

ENGLISH LANGUAGE AND LITERATURE RELATED
John Cabot U (Italy)
State U of New York Empire State Coll (NY)

ENTREPRENEURSHIP
Inter American U of Puerto Rico, Barranquitas Campus (PR)
John Cabot U (Italy)
Missouri Valley Coll (MO)
North Central U (MN)
The U of Findlay (OH)
Utah State U (UT)
Vermont Tech Coll (VT)

ENVIRONMENTAL ENGINEERING TECHNOLOGY
New York City Coll of Technology of the City U of New York (NY)

ENVIRONMENTAL/ ENVIRONMENTAL HEALTH ENGINEERING
Utah State U (UT)

ENVIRONMENTAL SCIENCE
Georgia Gwinnett Coll (GA)
Madonna U (MI)
U of Saint Francis (IN)

ENVIRONMENTAL STUDIES
Central Christian Coll of Kansas (KS)
Columbia Coll (MO)
State U of New York Coll of Agriculture and Technology at Cobleskill (NY)

EQUESTRIAN STUDIES
Delaware Valley U (PA)
Saint Mary-of-the-Woods Coll (IN)
The U of Findlay (OH)

EXPLOSIVE ORDINANCE/BOMB DISPOSAL
American Public U System (WV)

FAMILY AND COMMUNITY SERVICES
Central Christian Coll of Kansas (KS)

FAMILY AND CONSUMER SCIENCES/HUMAN SCIENCES
Eastern New Mexico U (NM)

FASHION/APPAREL DESIGN
Academy of Art U (CA)
EDP U of Puerto Rico–San Sebastian (PR)
Fashion Inst of Technology (NY)
FIDM/Fashion Inst of Design & Merchandising, Los Angeles Campus (CA)
Parsons School of Design (NY)

FASHION MERCHANDISING
Academy of Art U (CA)
Fashion Inst of Technology (NY)
FIDM/Fashion Inst of Design & Merchandising, Los Angeles Campus (CA)
Fisher Coll (MA)
Immaculata U (PA)
New York City Coll of Technology of the City U of New York (NY)
Parsons School of Design (NY)
The U of Akron (OH)

FASHION MODELING
Fashion Inst of Technology (NY)

FILM/CINEMA/VIDEO STUDIES
Fashion Inst of Technology (NY)
Los Angeles Film School (CA)
Southeastern U (FL)

FINANCE
Central Christian Coll of Kansas (KS)
Davenport U, Grand Rapids (MI)
The U of Findlay (OH)
Youngstown State U (OH)

FINE ARTS RELATED
Academy of Art U (CA)
Bryn Athyn Coll of the New Church (PA)

FINE/STUDIO ARTS
Academy of Art U (CA)
Adams State U (CO)
Beacon Coll (FL)
Bryn Athyn Coll of the New Church (PA)
Fashion Inst of Technology (NY)
Illinois State U (IL)
Pratt Inst (NY)
U of Saint Francis (IN)
York Coll of Pennsylvania (PA)

FIRE PREVENTION AND SAFETY TECHNOLOGY
Polk State Coll (FL)
The U of Akron (OH)
U of New Haven (CT)
Valencia Coll (FL)

FIRE SCIENCE/FIREFIGHTING
American Public U System (WV)
Keiser U, Fort Lauderdale (FL)
Lewis-Clark State Coll (ID)
Madonna U (MI)
Midland Coll (TX)
Polk State Coll (FL)
St. Petersburg Coll (FL)
Southwestern Oklahoma State U (OK)
U of Alaska Fairbanks (AK)
U of Cincinnati (OH)
Utah Valley U (UT)

FISHING AND FISHERIES SCIENCES AND MANAGEMENT
State U of New York Coll of Agriculture and Technology at Cobleskill (NY)
U of Alaska Southeast (AK)

FOOD SCIENCE
San Jose State U (CA)

FOOD SERVICE AND DINING ROOM MANAGEMENT
U of Montana (MT)

FOOD SERVICE SYSTEMS ADMINISTRATION
Inter American U of Puerto Rico, Aguadilla Campus (PR)
Wright State U (OH)
Wright State U–Lake Campus (OH)

FOODS, NUTRITION, AND WELLNESS
Madonna U (MI)
Youngstown State U (OH)

FOREIGN LANGUAGES AND LITERATURES
Bryn Athyn Coll of the New Church (PA)

FOREIGN LANGUAGES RELATED
U of Alaska Fairbanks (AK)

FORENSIC SCIENCE AND TECHNOLOGY
Keiser U, Fort Lauderdale (FL)
St. Petersburg Coll (FL)
Southern Arkansas U–Magnolia (AR)

FORESTRY
Vermont Tech Coll (VT)

FOREST TECHNOLOGY
Glenville State Coll (WV)
U of New Hampshire (NH)

FRENCH
Weber State U (UT)
Xavier U (OH)

FUNERAL SERVICE AND MORTUARY SCIENCE
Cincinnati Coll of Mortuary Science (OH)
St. Petersburg Coll (FL)

GAME AND INTERACTIVE MEDIA DESIGN
Academy of Art U (CA)
New England Inst of Technology (RI)

GENERAL STUDIES
AdventHealth U (FL)
Alverno Coll (WI)
American Public U System (WV)
Andrews U (MI)
Arkansas Tech U (AR)
Austin Peay State U (TN)
The Baptist Coll of Florida (FL)
Belhaven U (MS)
Bethel U (IN)
Black Hills State U (SD)
Brenau U (GA)
California Christian Coll (CA)
Cameron U (OK)
Carson-Newman U (TN)
Chaminade U of Honolulu (HI)
Clarion U of Pennsylvania (PA)
Columbia Coll (MO)
Concordia U, St. Paul (MN)
Dakota State U (SD)
Dean Coll (MA)
Eastern Kentucky U (KY)
Eastern Mennonite U (VA)
Ecclesia Coll (AR)
Ferris State U (MI)
Fisher Coll (MA)
Geneva Coll (PA)
Granite State Coll (NH)
Hampton U (VA)
Hope Intl U (CA)
Immaculata U (PA)
Inter American U of Puerto Rico, Bayamón Campus (PR)
John Brown U (AR)
King U (TN)
Lawrence Technological U (MI)
Lipscomb U (TN)
Louisiana Tech U (LA)
Loyola U Chicago (IL)
Madonna U (MI)
McNeese State U (LA)
Miami U Hamilton (OH)
Miami U Middletown (OH)
Midland Coll (TX)
Morehead State U (KY)
Mount Aloysius Coll (PA)
Mount Marty Coll (SD)
Mount Vernon Nazarene U (OH)
National U (CA)
New Mexico Inst of Mining and Technology (NM)
New York City Coll of Technology of the City U of New York (NY)
Northern State U (SD)
Northwest Christian U (OR)
Northwestern State U of Louisiana (LA)
Oakland City U (IN)
The Ohio State U at Lima (OH)
The Ohio State U at Mansfield (OH)
The Ohio State U at Marion (OH)
The Ohio State U at Newark (OH)
Pace U, Pleasantville Campus (NY)
Peirce Coll (PA)
Regent U (VA)
Sacred Heart U (CT)
Siena Heights U (MI)
South Dakota State U (SD)
Southeastern U (FL)
Southern Arkansas U–Magnolia (AR)
Southwest Baptist U (MO)
Southwestern Coll (KS)
Southwestern Oklahoma State U (OK)
State U of New York Coll of Technology at Canton (NY)
State U of New York Coll of Technology at Delhi (NY)
Suffolk U (MA)
Toccoa Falls Coll (GA)
Trevecca Nazarene U (TN)
U of Alaska Southeast (AK)
U of Arkansas at Little Rock (AR)
U of Central Arkansas (AR)
U of Hartford (CT)
U of La Verne (CA)
U of Louisiana at Monroe (LA)
U of Management and Technology (VA)
U of Montana (MT)
U of Saint Francis (IN)
U of the Fraser Valley (BC, Canada)
U of the Incarnate Word (TX)
The U of Toledo (OH)
U of Wisconsin–Superior (WI)
Utah State U (UT)
Utah Valley U (UT)
Wayland Baptist U (TX)
Weber State U (UT)
Western Kentucky U (KY)
Western New Mexico U (NM)
Widener U (PA)
York Coll of Pennsylvania (PA)

GEOGRAPHIC INFORMATION SCIENCE AND CARTOGRAPHY
The U of Akron (OH)

GEOGRAPHY
Wright State U (OH)
Wright State U–Lake Campus (OH)

GEOGRAPHY RELATED
Adams State U (CO)

GEOLOGY/EARTH SCIENCE
Wright State U (OH)
Wright State U–Lake Campus (OH)

GERMAN
Weber State U (UT)
Xavier U (OH)

GERONTOLOGY
Madonna U (MI)
Siena Heights U (MI)

GOLF COURSE OPERATION AND GROUNDS MANAGEMENT
Keiser U, Fort Lauderdale (FL)

GRAPHIC AND PRINTING EQUIPMENT OPERATION/ PRODUCTION
Lewis-Clark State Coll (ID)

GRAPHIC COMMUNICATIONS
Ferris State U (MI)
New England Inst of Technology (RI)
Walla Walla U (WA)

GRAPHIC COMMUNICATIONS RELATED
Rasmussen Coll Moorhead (MN)

GRAPHIC DESIGN
Academy of Art U (CA)
Creative Center (NE)
FIDM/Fashion Inst of Design & Merchandising, Los Angeles Campus (CA)
Inter American U of Puerto Rico, San Germán Campus (PR)
Lynn U (FL)
Madonna U (MI)
Northern State U (SD)
Parsons School of Design (NY)
Platt Coll San Diego (CA)
Pratt Inst (NY)
Southeastern U (FL)
State U of New York Coll of Agriculture and Technology at Cobleskill (NY)
U of South Dakota (SD)
U of the Fraser Valley (BC, Canada)
Western New Mexico U (NM)
Wright State U (OH)
Wright State U–Lake Campus (OH)

HEALTH AIDE
U of the Fraser Valley (BC, Canada)

HEALTH AND PHYSICAL EDUCATION/FITNESS
Central Christian Coll of Kansas (KS)
State U of New York Coll of Technology at Delhi (NY)
Tiffin U (OH)
Utah Valley U (UT)

HEALTH/HEALTH-CARE ADMINISTRATION
Mount Saint Mary's U (CA)
Regent U (VA)
The U of Scranton (PA)

HEALTH INFORMATION/ MEDICAL RECORDS ADMINISTRATION
Keiser U, Fort Lauderdale (FL)
St. Petersburg Coll (FL)
U of Alaska Southeast (AK)

HEALTH INFORMATION/ MEDICAL RECORDS TECHNOLOGY
Dakota State U (SD)
Davenport U, Grand Rapids (MI)
ECPI U, Virginia Beach (VA)
Ferris State U (MI)
Fisher Coll (MA)
Gwynedd Mercy U (PA)
Indiana U Northwest (IN)
Keiser U, Fort Lauderdale (FL)
Louisiana Tech U (LA)
Mercy Coll of Ohio (OH)
Midland Coll (TX)
New York U (NY)
Peirce Coll (PA)
Rasmussen Coll Aurora (IL)
Rasmussen Coll Blaine (MN)
Rasmussen Coll Bloomington (MN)
Rasmussen Coll Brooklyn Park (MN)
Rasmussen Coll Eagan (MN)
Rasmussen Coll Fort Myers (FL)
Rasmussen Coll Green Bay (WI)
Rasmussen Coll Kansas City/ Overland Park (KS)
Rasmussen Coll Lake Elmo/ Woodbury (MN)
Rasmussen Coll Land O' Lakes (FL)
Rasmussen Coll Mankato (MN)
Rasmussen Coll Mokena/Tinley Park (IL)
Rasmussen Coll Moorhead (MN)
Rasmussen Coll New Port Richey (FL)
Rasmussen Coll Ocala (FL)
Rasmussen Coll Rockford (IL)
Rasmussen Coll Romeoville/Joliet (IL)
Rasmussen Coll St. Cloud (MN)
Rasmussen Coll Tampa/Brandon (FL)
Rasmussen Coll Topeka (KS)
Rasmussen Coll Wausau (WI)
St. Catherine U (MN)
Sullivan U (KY)
Valencia Coll (FL)
Weber State U (UT)

HEALTH/MEDICAL PREPARATORY PROGRAMS RELATED
Baptist Coll of Health Sciences (TN)
Mount Saint Mary's U (CA)
Northwest U (WA)
Ohio Valley U (WV)

HEALTH PROFESSIONS RELATED
American Public U System (WV)
Ferris State U (MI)
Fisher Coll (MA)
Life U (GA)
Lock Haven U of Pennsylvania (PA)
Newman U (KS)
New York U (NY)
Northwest U (WA)
U of Alaska Southeast (AK)
U of Hartford (CT)

HEALTH SERVICES ADMINISTRATION
Florida National U (FL)
Keiser U, Fort Lauderdale (FL)

HEALTH SERVICES/ALLIED HEALTH/HEALTH SCIENCES
Aultman Coll of Nursing and Health Sciences (OH)
Cameron U (OK)
Colby-Sawyer Coll (NH)
Columbia Coll (MO)
Excelsior Coll (NY)
Fisher Coll (MA)
Mercy Coll of Ohio (OH)
Nebraska Methodist Coll (NE)
New York Coll of Health Professions (NY)
Ohio Dominican U (OH)
State U of New York Coll of Agriculture and Technology at Cobleskill (NY)
U of Hartford (CT)
U of the Incarnate Word (TX)
Weber State U (UT)

HEALTH TEACHER EDUCATION
Central Christian Coll of Kansas (KS)

HEATING, AIR CONDITIONING, VENTILATION AND REFRIGERATION MAINTENANCE TECHNOLOGY
Arkansas Tech U (AR)
Lewis-Clark State Coll (ID)
State U of New York Coll of Technology at Canton (NY)
State U of New York Coll of Technology at Delhi (NY)

HEATING, VENTILATION, AIR CONDITIONING AND REFRIGERATION ENGINEERING TECHNOLOGY
Ferris State U (MI)
Midland Coll (TX)
State U of New York Coll of Technology at Canton (NY)
Sullivan U (KY)

HEAVY EQUIPMENT MAINTENANCE TECHNOLOGY
Ferris State U (MI)

HEAVY/INDUSTRIAL EQUIPMENT MAINTENANCE TECHNOLOGIES RELATED
State U of New York Coll of Technology at Canton (NY)

HEBREW
Yeshiva U (NY)

HISTOLOGIC TECHNICIAN
Indiana U-Purdue U Indianapolis (IN)
Tarleton State U (TX)

HISTOLOGIC TECHNOLOGY/ HISTOTECHNOLOGIST
Keiser U, Fort Lauderdale (FL)

HISTORY
American Public U System (WV)
Bryn Athyn Coll of the New Church (PA)
Central Christian Coll of Kansas (KS)
Dean Coll (MA)
Immaculata U (PA)
John Cabot U (Italy)
Liberty U (VA)
Regent U (VA)
Rogers State U (OK)
State U of New York Empire State Coll (NY)
Utah Valley U (UT)
Wright State U (OH)
Wright State U–Lake Campus (OH)
Xavier U (OH)

HISTORY TEACHER EDUCATION
Central Christian Coll of Kansas (KS)

HOMELAND SECURITY
Keiser U, Fort Lauderdale (FL)
U of Management and Technology (VA)

HOMELAND SECURITY, LAW ENFORCEMENT, FIREFIGHTING AND PROTECTIVE SERVICES RELATED
St. Petersburg Coll (FL)

HORTICULTURAL SCIENCE
Andrews U (MI)
Temple U (PA)

HOSPITALITY ADMINISTRATION
Endicott Coll (MA)
Florida National U (FL)
Indiana U of Pennsylvania (PA)
Keiser U, Fort Lauderdale (FL)
Lewis-Clark State Coll (ID)
New York City Coll of Technology of the City U of New York (NY)
St. Petersburg Coll (FL)
The U of Akron (OH)
U of Montana (MT)
Utah Valley U (UT)
Valencia Coll (FL)
Webber Intl U (FL)
Youngstown State U (OH)

HOSPITALITY ADMINISTRATION RELATED
Penn State Beaver (PA)
Penn State Berks (PA)

HOTEL/MOTEL ADMINISTRATION
State U of New York Coll of Agriculture and Technology at Cobleskill (NY)
The U of Akron (OH)
Valencia Coll (FL)

HOTEL, MOTEL, AND RESTAURANT MANAGEMENT
Sullivan U (KY)

HUMAN DEVELOPMENT AND FAMILY STUDIES
Penn State Abington (PA)
Penn State Altoona (PA)
Penn State Berks (PA)
Penn State Brandywine (PA)
Penn State Erie, The Behrend Coll (PA)
Penn State New Kensington (PA)
Penn State Schuylkill (PA)
Penn State Shenango (PA)
Penn State York (PA)
South Dakota State U (SD)

HUMANITIES
Beacon Coll (FL)
Bryn Athyn Coll of the New Church (PA)
Fisher Coll (MA)
John Cabot U (Italy)
Michigan Technological U (MI)
Saint Mary-of-the-Woods Coll (IN)
State U of New York Coll of Agriculture and Technology at Cobleskill (NY)
State U of New York Coll of Technology at Delhi (NY)
U of Alaska Southeast (AK)
U of Cincinnati (OH)
Utah Valley U (UT)
Valparaiso U (IN)

HUMAN NUTRITION
Huntington U of Health Sciences (TN)

HUMAN RESOURCES MANAGEMENT
Central Christian Coll of Kansas (KS)
Madonna U (MI)
Rasmussen Coll Blaine (MN)
Rasmussen Coll Bloomington (MN)
Rasmussen Coll Brooklyn Park (MN)
Rasmussen Coll Eagan (MN)
Rasmussen Coll Fargo (ND)
Rasmussen Coll Fort Myers (FL)
Rasmussen Coll Green Bay (WI)
Rasmussen Coll Kansas City/ Overland Park (KS)
Rasmussen Coll Lake Elmo/ Woodbury (MN)
Rasmussen Coll Land O' Lakes (FL)
Rasmussen Coll Mankato (MN)
Rasmussen Coll Moorhead (MN)
Rasmussen Coll New Port Richey (FL)
Rasmussen Coll Ocala (FL)
Rasmussen Coll Tampa/Brandon (FL)
Rasmussen Coll Topeka (KS)
Rasmussen Coll Wausau (WI)
U of Cincinnati (OH)
The U of Findlay (OH)
U of Management and Technology (VA)
The U of Scranton (PA)

HUMAN RESOURCES MANAGEMENT AND SERVICES RELATED
Oakland City U (IN)

HUMAN SERVICES
Arkansas Tech U (AR)
Beacon Coll (FL)
Bethel U (IN)
Calumet Coll of Saint Joseph (IN)
The Catholic U of America (DC)
Columbia Coll (MO)
Geneva Coll (PA)
Mount Saint Mary's U (CA)
New York City Coll of Technology of the City U of New York (NY)
Ohio Christian U (OH)
Rasmussen Coll Blaine (MN)
Rasmussen Coll Bloomington (MN)
Rasmussen Coll Brooklyn Park (MN)
Rasmussen Coll Eagan (MN)
Rasmussen Coll Fargo (ND)
Rasmussen Coll Fort Myers (FL)
Rasmussen Coll Green Bay (WI)
Rasmussen Coll Kansas City/ Overland Park (KS)
Rasmussen Coll Lake Elmo/ Woodbury (MN)
Rasmussen Coll Land O' Lakes (FL)
Rasmussen Coll Mankato (MN)
Rasmussen Coll Moorhead (MN)
Rasmussen Coll New Port Richey (FL)
Rasmussen Coll Ocala (FL)
Rasmussen Coll St. Cloud (MN)
Rasmussen Coll Tampa/Brandon (FL)
Rasmussen Coll Topeka (KS)
Rasmussen Coll Wausau (WI)
The U of Scranton (PA)
Wayland Baptist U (TX)
Western New Mexico U (NM)

ILLUSTRATION
Academy of Art U (CA)
Fashion Inst of Technology (NY)
Pratt Inst (NY)

INDUSTRIAL AND PRODUCT DESIGN
Academy of Art U (CA)

INDUSTRIAL ELECTRONICS TECHNOLOGY
Ferris State U (MI)
Lewis-Clark State Coll (ID)

INDUSTRIAL MECHANICS AND MAINTENANCE TECHNOLOGY
The U of West Alabama (AL)

INDUSTRIAL PRODUCTION TECHNOLOGIES RELATED
California U of Pennsylvania (PA)
Clarion U of Pennsylvania (PA)
U of Alaska Fairbanks (AK)

INDUSTRIAL RADIOLOGIC TECHNOLOGY
The George Washington U (DC)
Widener U (PA)

INDUSTRIAL TECHNOLOGY
Arkansas Tech U (AR)
Eastern Kentucky U (KY)
Millersville U of Pennsylvania (PA)
Murray State U (KY)
Penn State York (PA)
Pittsburg State U (KS)
St. Petersburg Coll (FL)
Southeastern Louisiana U (LA)
Southern Arkansas U–Magnolia (AR)
U of Puerto Ricov at Ponce (PR)

INFORMATION RESOURCES MANAGEMENT
Rasmussen Coll Fort Myers (FL)
Rasmussen Coll Land O' Lakes (FL)
Rasmussen Coll New Port Richey (FL)
Rasmussen Coll Ocala (FL)
Rasmussen Coll Tampa/Brandon (FL)

INFORMATION SCIENCE/ STUDIES
Clayton State U (GA)
Colegio Universitario de San Juan, San Juan (PR)
Dakota State U (SD)
Immaculata U (PA)
Newman U (KS)
Penn State Abington (PA)
Penn State Altoona (PA)
Penn State Berks (PA)
Penn State Erie, The Behrend Coll (PA)
Penn State Hazleton (PA)
Penn State Lehigh Valley (PA)
Penn State New Kensington (PA)
Penn State Schuylkill (PA)
Penn State U Park (PA)
State U of New York Coll of Agriculture and Technology at Cobleskill (NY)
State U of New York Coll of Technology at Canton (NY)
State U of New York Coll of Technology at Delhi (NY)
U of Management and Technology (VA)
U of Massachusetts Lowell (MA)
U of Pittsburgh at Bradford (PA)
The U of Scranton (PA)
Utah State U (UT)

INFORMATION TECHNOLOGY
Arkansas Tech U (AR)
Cameron U (OK)
EDP U of Puerto Rico–San Sebastian (PR)
Ferris State U (MI)
Florida National U (FL)
Keiser U, Fort Lauderdale (FL)
Life U (GA)
Limestone Coll (SC)
Marian U (IN)
New England Inst of Technology (RI)
Peirce Coll (PA)
Regent U (VA)
Saint Leo U (FL)
Trevecca Nazarene U (TN)
U of Management and Technology (VA)
U of Montana (MT)
U of the Incarnate Word (TX)
Valencia Coll (FL)
Vermont Tech Coll (VT)
Youngstown State U (OH)

INSTITUTIONAL FOOD WORKERS
ECPI U, Virginia Beach (VA)

INSURANCE
Inter American U of Puerto Rico, Metropolitan Campus (PR)

INTERCULTURAL/ MULTICULTURAL AND DIVERSITY STUDIES
Nyack Coll (NY)

INTERDISCIPLINARY STUDIES
Central Methodist U (MO)
Doane U (NE)
Keiser U, Fort Lauderdale (FL)
Lesley U (MA)
North Central U (MN)
Ohio Christian U (OH)
Ohio Dominican U (OH)
U of North Florida (FL)

INTERIOR DESIGN
Academy of Art U (CA)
Chaminade U of Honolulu (HI)
EDP U of Puerto Rico–San Sebastian (PR)
Fashion Inst of Technology (NY)
FIDM/Fashion Inst of Design & Merchandising, Los Angeles Campus (CA)
Indiana U-Purdue U Indianapolis (IN)
Montana State U (MT)
New England Inst of Technology (RI)
Parsons School of Design (NY)
Weber State U (UT)

INTERMEDIA/MULTIMEDIA
Platt Coll San Diego (CA)

INTERNATIONAL BUSINESS/ TRADE/COMMERCE
John Cabot U (Italy)

INTERNATIONAL/GLOBAL STUDIES
Sacred Heart U (CT)

INTERNATIONAL RELATIONS AND AFFAIRS
John Cabot U (Italy)

ITALIAN STUDIES
John Cabot U (Italy)

JAPANESE
San Jose State U (CA)
Weber State U (UT)

JOURNALISM
Academy of Art U (CA)
North Central U (MN)

JOURNALISM RELATED
Adams State U (CO)

KINDERGARTEN/PRESCHOOL EDUCATION
California U of Pennsylvania (PA)
Central Christian Coll of Kansas (KS)
Fisher Coll (MA)
Miami U Hamilton (OH)
Miami U Middletown (OH)
Mount Saint Mary's U (CA)
U of Cincinnati (OH)

KINESIOLOGY AND EXERCISE SCIENCE
Central Christian Coll of Kansas (KS)
Dean Coll (MA)

LABOR AND INDUSTRIAL RELATIONS
Indiana U-Purdue U Indianapolis (IN)
State U of New York Empire State Coll (NY)

LABOR STUDIES
Indiana U Bloomington (IN)
Indiana U Northwest (IN)
Indiana U-Purdue U Indianapolis (IN)

LANDSCAPE ARCHITECTURE
Academy of Art U (CA)

LANDSCAPING AND GROUNDSKEEPING
State U of New York Coll of Technology at Delhi (NY)
U of Massachusetts Amherst (MA)
Valencia Coll (FL)
Vermont Tech Coll (VT)

LASER AND OPTICAL TECHNOLOGY
Colegio Universitario de San Juan, San Juan (PR)

LAY MINISTRY
Andrews U (MI)
Bethel U (IN)
U of Saint Francis (IN)

LEGAL ADMINISTRATIVE ASSISTANT/SECRETARY
Lewis-Clark State Coll (ID)

LEGAL ASSISTANT/PARALEGAL
American Public U System (WV)
Clayton State U (GA)
Coll of Saint Mary (NE)
Eastern Kentucky U (KY)
Elms Coll (MA)
Florida National U (FL)
Gannon U (PA)
Hampton U (VA)
Husson U (ME)
Keiser U, Fort Lauderdale (FL)
Lewis-Clark State Coll (ID)
Liberty U (VA)
Madonna U (MI)
Marian U (IN)
Midland Coll (TX)
Mount Aloysius Coll (PA)
National U (CA)
Newman U (KS)
New York City Coll of Technology of the City U of New York (NY)
Peirce Coll (PA)
Rasmussen Coll Aurora (IL)
Rasmussen Coll Blaine (MN)
Rasmussen Coll Bloomington (MN)
Rasmussen Coll Brooklyn Park (MN)
Rasmussen Coll Eagan (MN)
Rasmussen Coll Fargo (ND)
Rasmussen Coll Fort Myers (FL)
Rasmussen Coll Green Bay (WI)
Rasmussen Coll Kansas City/Overland Park (KS)
Rasmussen Coll Lake Elmo/Woodbury (MN)
Rasmussen Coll Land O' Lakes (FL)
Rasmussen Coll Mankato (MN)
Rasmussen Coll Mokena/Tinley Park (IL)
Rasmussen Coll Moorhead (MN)
Rasmussen Coll New Port Richey (FL)
Rasmussen Coll Ocala (FL)
Rasmussen Coll Rockford (IL)
Rasmussen Coll Romeoville/Joliet (IL)
Rasmussen Coll St. Cloud (MN)
Rasmussen Coll Tampa/Brandon (FL)
Rasmussen Coll Topeka (KS)
Rasmussen Coll Wausau (WI)
Saint Mary-of-the-Woods Coll (IN)
St. Petersburg Coll (FL)
Suffolk U (MA)
Sullivan U (KY)
The U of Akron (OH)
U of Alaska Fairbanks (AK)
U of Cincinnati (OH)
U of Hartford (CT)
U of Louisville (KY)
The U of Toledo (OH)
Utah Valley U (UT)
Valencia Coll (FL)
Western Kentucky U (KY)
Widener U (PA)

LEGAL STUDIES
Central Christian Coll of Kansas (KS)
U of Alaska Southeast (AK)
U of Montana (MT)
U of New Haven (CT)

LIBERAL ARTS AND SCIENCES AND HUMANITIES RELATED
Adams State U (CO)
Anderson U (IN)
Ball State U (IN)
Butler U (IN)
Coll of Saint Mary (NE)
Ferris State U (MI)
Florida National U (FL)
Marymount California U (CA)
Mount Aloysius Coll (PA)
New York U (NY)
Notre Dame Coll (OH)
State U of New York Coll of Technology at Delhi (NY)
Taylor U (IN)
Tiffin U (OH)
U of Maryland Global Campus (MD)
U of Wisconsin–Green Bay (WI)
U of Wisconsin–La Crosse (WI)
Utah State U (UT)
Wayland Baptist U (TX)
Wichita State U (KS)
William Penn U (IA)

LIBERAL ARTS AND SCIENCES/LIBERAL STUDIES
Adams State U (CO)
Alverno Coll (WI)
American U (DC)
Andrews U (MI)
Aquinas Coll (MI)
Arizona Christian U (AZ)
Averett U (VA)
Becker Coll (MA)
Bemidji State U (MN)
Bethel U (IN)
Bethel U (MN)
Boise State U (ID)
Brenau U (GA)
Bryan Coll (TN)
California U of Pennsylvania (PA)
Carson-Newman U (TN)
Charter Oak State Coll (CT)
Chestnut Hill Coll (PA)
Clayton State U (GA)
Colby-Sawyer Coll (NH)
Columbia Coll (MO)
Dickinson State U (ND)
Dominican Coll (NY)
Eastern New Mexico U (NM)
Eastern U (PA)
Emmanuel Coll (GA)
Endicott Coll (MA)
Excelsior Coll (NY)
Fairleigh Dickinson U (NJ)
Farmingdale State Coll (NY)
Felician U (NJ)
Fisher Coll (MA)
Florida Atlantic U (FL)
Gannon U (PA)
Georgia Southern U (GA)
Glenville State Coll (WV)
Holy Apostles Coll and Sem (CT)
Indiana U of Pennsylvania (PA)
Lewis-Clark State Coll (ID)
Limestone Coll (SC)
Loyola U Chicago (IL)
Mansfield U of Pennsylvania (PA)
Marian U (IN)
Marietta Coll (OH)
Marymount California U (CA)
Mercy Coll (NY)
Mid-America Christian U (OK)
MidAmerica Nazarene U (KS)
Minnesota State U Mankato (MN)
Missouri Valley Coll (MO)
Molloy Coll (NY)
Montana State U (MT)
Mount Aloysius Coll (PA)
Mount Marty Coll (SD)
Mount Saint Mary's U (CA)
Murray State U (KY)
National U (CA)
New England Coll (NH)
Newman U (KS)
New Saint Andrews Coll (ID)
New York City Coll of Technology of the City U of New York (NY)
New York U (NY)
Niagara U (NY)
Northern Kentucky U (KY)
Northwest U (WA)
Nyack Coll (NY)
The Ohio State U at Mansfield (OH)
The Ohio State U at Marion (OH)
The Ohio State U at Newark (OH)
Ohio Valley U (WV)
Penn State Abington (PA)
Penn State Altoona (PA)
Penn State Beaver (PA)
Penn State Berks (PA)
Penn State Brandywine (PA)
Penn State Erie, The Behrend Coll (PA)
Penn State Greater Allegheny (PA)
Penn State Harrisburg (PA)
Penn State Hazleton (PA)
Penn State Lehigh Valley (PA)
Penn State New Kensington (PA)
Penn State Schuylkill (PA)
Penn State Shenango (PA)
Penn State U Park (PA)
Penn State Wilkes-Barre (PA)
Penn State York (PA)
Polk State Coll (FL)
Providence Coll (RI)
Rochester U (MI)
Rocky Mountain Coll (MT)
Rogers State U (OK)
St. Catherine U (MN)
St. Cloud State U (MN)
Saint Joseph's U (PA)
Saint Leo U (FL)
St. Petersburg Coll (FL)
Salve Regina U (RI)
Schreiner U (TX)
Spring Arbor U (MI)
State U of New York Coll of Agriculture and Technology at Cobleskill (NY)
State U of New York Coll of Technology at Delhi (NY)
Suffolk U (MA)
Tabor Coll (KS)
Trine U (IN)
Troy U (AL)
The U of Akron (OH)
U of Alaska Fairbanks (AK)
U of Alaska Southeast (AK)
U of Dubuque (IA)
U of Hartford (CT)
U of Maine at Presque Isle (ME)
U of Northwestern–St. Paul (MN)
U of Pittsburgh at Bradford (PA)
U of Saint Francis (IN)
U of South Carolina Beaufort (SC)
U of South Dakota (SD)
U of South Florida, St. Petersburg (FL)
U of the Fraser Valley (BC, Canada)
U of the Incarnate Word (TX)
U of West Florida (FL)
U of Wisconsin–Eau Claire (WI)
U of Wisconsin–Parkside (WI)
U of Wisconsin–Superior (WI)
Upper Iowa U (IA)
Valdosta State U (GA)
Valencia Coll (FL)
Western Connecticut State U (CT)
Western New England U (MA)
Western New Mexico U (NM)
Xavier U (OH)
Youngstown State U (OH)

LIBRARY AND ARCHIVES ASSISTING
U of the Fraser Valley (BC, Canada)

LICENSED PRACTICAL/VOCATIONAL NURSE TRAINING
Arkansas Tech U (AR)
Central Christian Coll of Kansas (KS)
Dickinson State U (ND)
Inter American U of Puerto Rico, Aguadilla Campus (PR)
Inter American U of Puerto Rico, Barranquitas Campus (PR)
Inter American U of Puerto Rico, Bayamón Campus (PR)
Inter American U of Puerto Rico, Metropolitan Campus (PR)
Inter American U of Puerto Rico, San Germán Campus (PR)
Lewis-Clark State Coll (ID)
U of Montana (MT)
U of the Fraser Valley (BC, Canada)

LINGUISTIC AND COMPARATIVE LANGUAGE STUDIES RELATED
Northwest U (WA)

LITERATURE
North Central U (MN)

LOGISTICS, MATERIALS, AND SUPPLY CHAIN MANAGEMENT
American Public U System (WV)
Arkansas Tech U (AR)
FIDM/Fashion Inst of Design & Merchandising, Los Angeles Campus (CA)
Polytechnic U of Puerto Rico (PR)
Sullivan U (KY)

MACHINE SHOP TECHNOLOGY
Utah State U (UT)

MANAGEMENT INFORMATION SYSTEMS
Bayamón Central U (PR)
Liberty U (VA)
Morehead State U (KY)
U of Alaska Southeast (AK)
The U of Findlay (OH)
U of the Incarnate Word (TX)
Weber State U (UT)
Wright State U (OH)
Wright State U–Lake Campus (OH)

MANAGEMENT INFORMATION SYSTEMS AND SERVICES RELATED
Mount Aloysius Coll (PA)
Rasmussen Coll Aurora (IL)
Rasmussen Coll Blaine (MN)
Rasmussen Coll Bloomington (MN)
Rasmussen Coll Brooklyn Park (MN)
Rasmussen Coll Eagan (MN)
Rasmussen Coll Fargo (ND)
Rasmussen Coll Fort Myers (FL)
Rasmussen Coll Green Bay (WI)
Rasmussen Coll Kansas City/Overland Park (KS)
Rasmussen Coll Lake Elmo/Woodbury (MN)
Rasmussen Coll Land O' Lakes (FL)
Rasmussen Coll Mankato (MN)
Rasmussen Coll Mokena/Tinley Park (IL)
Rasmussen Coll Moorhead (MN)
Rasmussen Coll New Port Richey (FL)
Rasmussen Coll Ocala (FL)
Rasmussen Coll Rockford (IL)
Rasmussen Coll Romeoville/Joliet (IL)
Rasmussen Coll St. Cloud (MN)
Rasmussen Coll Tampa/Brandon (FL)
Rasmussen Coll Wausau (WI)

MANUFACTURING ENGINEERING
Penn State Greater Allegheny (PA)
Penn State Hazleton (PA)
Penn State Wilkes-Barre (PA)
Penn State York (PA)

MANUFACTURING ENGINEERING TECHNOLOGY
Edinboro U of Pennsylvania (PA)
Lawrence Technological U (MI)
Lewis-Clark State Coll (ID)
Missouri Southern State U (MO)
South Dakota State U (SD)
Sullivan U (KY)
The U of Akron (OH)
U of Cincinnati (OH)
Weber State U (UT)

MARINE MAINTENANCE AND SHIP REPAIR TECHNOLOGY
New England Inst of Technology (RI)

MARKETING/MARKETING MANAGEMENT
Central Christian Coll of Kansas (KS)
Ferris State U (MI)
FIDM/Fashion Inst of Design & Merchandising, Los Angeles Campus (CA)
John Cabot U (Italy)
Madonna U (MI)
Miami U Hamilton (OH)
Miami U Middletown (OH)
New York City Coll of Technology of the City U of New York (NY)
Rasmussen Coll Blaine (MN)
Rasmussen Coll Bloomington (MN)
Rasmussen Coll Brooklyn Park (MN)
Rasmussen Coll Eagan (MN)
Rasmussen Coll Fargo (ND)
Rasmussen Coll Fort Myers (FL)
Rasmussen Coll Green Bay (WI)
Rasmussen Coll Kansas City/Overland Park (KS)
Rasmussen Coll Lake Elmo/Woodbury (MN)
Rasmussen Coll Land O' Lakes (FL)
Rasmussen Coll Mankato (MN)
Rasmussen Coll Moorhead (MN)
Rasmussen Coll New Port Richey (FL)
Rasmussen Coll Ocala (FL)
Rasmussen Coll St. Cloud (MN)
Rasmussen Coll Tampa/Brandon (FL)
Rasmussen Coll Topeka (KS)
Rasmussen Coll Wausau (WI)
The U of Akron (OH)
Webber Intl U (FL)
Youngstown State U (OH)

MASSAGE THERAPY
ECPI U, Virginia Beach (VA)
Keiser U, Fort Lauderdale (FL)
New York Coll of Health Professions (NY)

MASS COMMUNICATION/MEDIA
Adams State U (CO)
Black Hills State U (SD)
Dean Coll (MA)
Johnson U Florida (FL)
North Central U (MN)
Wright State U–Lake Campus (OH)
York Coll of Pennsylvania (PA)

MATHEMATICS
Bryn Athyn Coll of the New Church (PA)
Central Christian Coll of Kansas (KS)
Creighton U (NE)
State U of New York Coll of Agriculture and Technology at Cobleskill (NY)
Taylor U (IN)
Tiffin U (OH)
Trevecca Nazarene U (TN)
The U of West Alabama (AL)
Utah Valley U (UT)
Weber State U (UT)
Western New Mexico U (NM)

MATHEMATICS TEACHER EDUCATION
Central Christian Coll of Kansas (KS)

MECHANICAL DRAFTING AND CAD/CADD
Midland Coll (TX)
New York City Coll of Technology of the City U of New York (NY)

MECHANICAL ENGINEERING
New England Inst of Technology (RI)
Utah State U (UT)

MECHANICAL ENGINEERING/MECHANICAL TECHNOLOGY
ECPI U, Virginia Beach (VA)
Farmingdale State Coll (NY)
Ferris State U (MI)

Miami U Hamilton (OH)
Miami U Middletown (OH)
New York City Coll of Technology of the City U of New York (NY)
Penn State Altoona (PA)
Penn State Berks (PA)
Penn State Erie, The Behrend Coll (PA)
Penn State Hazleton (PA)
Penn State New Kensington (PA)
Penn State Shenango (PA)
Penn State York (PA)
State U of New York Coll of Agriculture and Technology at Cobleskill (NY)
State U of New York Coll of Technology at Canton (NY)
The U of Akron (OH)
U of Arkansas at Little Rock (AR)
U of Cincinnati (OH)
Vermont Tech Coll (VT)
Weber State U (UT)
Youngstown State U (OH)

MECHANICAL ENGINEERING TECHNOLOGIES RELATED
Polytechnic U of Puerto Rico (PR)
U of Massachusetts Lowell (MA)

MECHANICS AND REPAIR
Lewis-Clark State Coll (ID)
Utah State U (UT)
Utah Valley U (UT)
Weber State U (UT)

MECHATRONICS, ROBOTICS, AND AUTOMATION ENGINEERING
U of the Fraser Valley (BC, Canada)
Utah Valley U (UT)

MEDICAL ADMINISTRATIVE ASSISTANT AND MEDICAL SECRETARY
Arkansas Tech U (AR)
Rasmussen Coll Aurora (IL)
Rasmussen Coll Blaine (MN)
Rasmussen Coll Bloomington (MN)
Rasmussen Coll Brooklyn Park (MN)
Rasmussen Coll Eagan (MN)
Rasmussen Coll Fargo (ND)
Rasmussen Coll Fort Myers (FL)
Rasmussen Coll Green Bay (WI)
Rasmussen Coll Kansas City/ Overland Park (KS)
Rasmussen Coll Lake Elmo/ Woodbury (MN)
Rasmussen Coll Land O' Lakes (FL)
Rasmussen Coll Mankato (MN)
Rasmussen Coll Mokena/Tinley Park (IL)
Rasmussen Coll Moorhead (MN)
Rasmussen Coll New Port Richey (FL)
Rasmussen Coll Ocala (FL)
Rasmussen Coll Rockford (IL)
Rasmussen Coll Romeoville/Joliet (IL)
Rasmussen Coll St. Cloud (MN)
Rasmussen Coll Tampa/Brandon (FL)
Rasmussen Coll Wausau (WI)
U of Montana (MT)

MEDICAL/CLINICAL ASSISTANT
Arkansas Tech U (AR)
Davenport U, Grand Rapids (MI)
ECPI U, Virginia Beach (VA)
Fisher Coll (MA)
Keiser U, Fort Lauderdale (FL)
Montana Technological U (MT)
Mount Aloysius Coll (PA)
New England Inst of Technology (RI)
New York U (NY)
Rasmussen Coll Aurora (IL)
Rasmussen Coll Blaine (MN)
Rasmussen Coll Bloomington (MN)
Rasmussen Coll Brooklyn Park (MN)
Rasmussen Coll Eagan (MN)
Rasmussen Coll Fort Myers (FL)
Rasmussen Coll Green Bay (WI)
Rasmussen Coll Kansas City/ Overland Park (KS)
Rasmussen Coll Lake Elmo/ Woodbury (MN)
Rasmussen Coll Land O' Lakes (FL)
Rasmussen Coll Mankato (MN)
Rasmussen Coll Mokena/Tinley Park (IL)
Rasmussen Coll Moorhead (MN)
Rasmussen Coll New Port Richey (FL)
Rasmussen Coll Ocala (FL)
Rasmussen Coll Rockford (IL)
Rasmussen Coll Romeoville/Joliet (IL)
Rasmussen Coll St. Cloud (MN)
Rasmussen Coll Tampa/Brandon (FL)
Rasmussen Coll Topeka (KS)
Rasmussen Coll Wausau (WI)
Sullivan U (KY)
The U of Akron (OH)
U of Alaska Fairbanks (AK)
Youngstown State U (OH)

MEDICAL/HEALTH MANAGEMENT AND CLINICAL ASSISTANT
Florida National U (FL)
Lewis-Clark State Coll (ID)

MEDICAL INFORMATICS
Montana Technological U (MT)

MEDICAL INSURANCE CODING
Davenport U, Grand Rapids (MI)
Fisher Coll (MA)
U of Montana (MT)

MEDICAL OFFICE ASSISTANT
Lewis-Clark State Coll (ID)
Liberty U (VA)

MEDICAL OFFICE MANAGEMENT
The U of Akron (OH)

MEDICAL RADIOLOGIC TECHNOLOGY
Ball State U (IN)
Cameron U (OK)
Drexel U (PA)
Fairleigh Dickinson U (NJ)
Ferris State U (MI)
Inter American U of Puerto Rico, San Germán Campus (PR)
Keiser U, Fort Lauderdale (FL)
La Roche U (PA)
Missouri Southern State U (MO)
Morehead State U (KY)
Mount Aloysius Coll (PA)
Newman U (KS)
New York City Coll of Technology of the City U of New York (NY)
New York U (NY)
Penn State New Kensington (PA)
Penn State Schuylkill (PA)
Polk State Coll (FL)
St. Catherine U (MN)
Southwestern Oklahoma State U (OK)
The U of Akron (OH)
U of Charleston (WV)

MEETING AND EVENT PLANNING
Sullivan U (KY)

MENTAL AND SOCIAL HEALTH SERVICES AND ALLIED PROFESSIONS RELATED
Clarion U of Pennsylvania (PA)
U of Alaska Fairbanks (AK)

MERCHANDISING
The U of Akron (OH)

MERCHANDISING, SALES, AND MARKETING OPERATIONS RELATED (GENERAL)
State U of New York Coll of Technology at Delhi (NY)

METAL AND JEWELRY ARTS
Academy of Art U (CA)
Fashion Inst of Technology (NY)
FIDM/Fashion Inst of Design & Merchandising, Los Angeles Campus (CA)

METALLURGICAL TECHNOLOGY
Penn State Altoona (PA)
Penn State Berks (PA)
Penn State Erie, The Behrend Coll (PA)
Penn State Hazleton (PA)
Penn State New Kensington (PA)
Penn State Schuylkill (PA)
Penn State Shenango (PA)
Penn State Wilkes-Barre (PA)
Penn State York (PA)

MICROBIOLOGY
Weber State U (UT)

MILITARY HISTORY
American Public U System (WV)

MILITARY TECHNOLOGIES AND APPLIED SCIENCES RELATED
Lynn U (FL)

MINING AND MINERAL ENGINEERING
Utah State U (UT)

MINING AND PETROLEUM TECHNOLOGIES RELATED
U of the Virgin Islands (VI)

MINING TECHNOLOGY
Utah State U (UT)

MISSIONARY STUDIES AND MISSIOLOGY
Boise Bible Coll (ID)
Central Christian Coll of Kansas (KS)
North Central U (MN)
Ohio Christian U (OH)
Southeastern U (FL)

MULTI/INTERDISCIPLINARY STUDIES RELATED
Arkansas Tech U (AR)
Dallas Baptist U (TX)
Dallas Christian Coll (TX)
John Brown U (AR)
Liberty U (VA)
Montana Technological U (MT)
State U of New York Empire State Coll (NY)
The U of Akron (OH)
U of Alaska Fairbanks (AK)
Utah Valley U (UT)
Wright State U (OH)
Wright State U–Lake Campus (OH)

MUSEUM STUDIES
U of Saint Francis (IN)

MUSIC
Central Christian Coll of Kansas (KS)
Los Angeles Film School (CA)
Marian U (IN)
Mount Vernon Nazarene U (OH)
North Central U (MN)
Nyack Coll (NY)
St. Petersburg Coll (FL)
Utah Valley U (UT)
York Coll of Pennsylvania (PA)

MUSICAL INSTRUMENT FABRICATION AND REPAIR
Indiana U Bloomington (IN)

MUSICAL THEATER
Dean Coll (MA)

MUSIC HISTORY, LITERATURE, AND THEORY
Central Christian Coll of Kansas (KS)

MUSIC MANAGEMENT
Inter American U of Puerto Rico, Metropolitan Campus (PR)

MUSIC PERFORMANCE
Central Christian Coll of Kansas (KS)
Inter American U of Puerto Rico, Metropolitan Campus (PR)
Trevecca Nazarene U (TN)

MUSIC RELATED
Academy of Art U (CA)
Trevecca Nazarene U (TN)

MUSIC TEACHER EDUCATION
Central Christian Coll of Kansas (KS)

MUSIC TECHNOLOGY
U of Saint Francis (IN)

NANOTECHNOLOGY
Lock Haven U of Pennsylvania (PA)

NATIONAL SECURITY POLICY
Tiffin U (OH)

NATURAL RESOURCE RECREATION AND TOURISM
State U of New York Coll of Technology at Delhi (NY)

NATURAL RESOURCES MANAGEMENT AND POLICY
U of Alaska Fairbanks (AK)

NATURAL SCIENCES
Alverno Coll (WI)
Central Christian Coll of Kansas (KS)
Chaminade U of Honolulu (HI)
Gwynedd Mercy U (PA)
Madonna U (MI)
Roberts Wesleyan Coll (NY)
St. Petersburg Coll (FL)
Saint Vincent Coll (PA)
U of Alaska Fairbanks (AK)

NETWORK AND SYSTEM ADMINISTRATION
ECPI U, Virginia Beach (VA)
Florida National U (FL)
Polk State Coll (FL)
Valencia Coll (FL)

NUCLEAR ENGINEERING TECHNOLOGY
Arkansas Tech U (AR)

NUCLEAR MEDICAL TECHNOLOGY
Ball State U (IN)
The George Washington U (DC)
Keiser U, Fort Lauderdale (FL)
Molloy Coll (NY)
The U of Findlay (OH)

NUCLEAR/NUCLEAR POWER TECHNOLOGY
Excelsior Coll (NY)

NURSING ASSISTANT/AIDE AND PATIENT CARE ASSISTANT/AIDE
Central Christian Coll of Kansas (KS)

NURSING PRACTICE
Alverno Coll (WI)

NURSING SCIENCE
EDP U of Puerto Rico–San Sebastian (PR)
Emmaus Bible Coll (IA)
Inter American U of Puerto Rico, Barranquitas Campus (PR)

NUTRITION SCIENCES
U of the Incarnate Word (TX)

OCCUPATIONAL THERAPIST ASSISTANT
AdventHealth U (FL)
Arkansas Tech U (AR)
Keiser U, Fort Lauderdale (FL)
Mercy Coll (NY)
New England Inst of Technology (RI)
Newman U (KS)
Penn State Berks (PA)
Polk State Coll (FL)
St. Catherine U (MN)
Southwestern Oklahoma State U (OK)
U of Charleston (WV)
U of Louisiana at Monroe (LA)
U of Southern Indiana (IN)

OFFICE MANAGEMENT
Emmanuel Coll (GA)
Inter American U of Puerto Rico, Aguadilla Campus (PR)
Inter American U of Puerto Rico, Barranquitas Campus (PR)
Inter American U of Puerto Rico, Bayamón Campus (PR)
Inter American U of Puerto Rico, Metropolitan Campus (PR)
Inter American U of Puerto Rico, San Germán Campus (PR)
Miami U Hamilton (OH)
Miami U Middletown (OH)
The U of Akron (OH)
Valencia Coll (FL)

OFFICE OCCUPATIONS AND CLERICAL SERVICES
Midland Coll (TX)

OPERATIONS MANAGEMENT
Polk State Coll (FL)

OPTICIANRY
New York City Coll of Technology of the City U of New York (NY)

OPTOMETRIC TECHNICIAN
Indiana U Bloomington (IN)

ORGANIZATIONAL BEHAVIOR
Concordia U Chicago (IL)
Johnson U Florida (FL)
Tiffin U (OH)

ORGANIZATIONAL COMMUNICATION
Creighton U (NE)

ORGANIZATIONAL LEADERSHIP
Southeastern U (FL)
Tiffin U (OH)

ORNAMENTAL HORTICULTURE
Farmingdale State Coll (NY)
State U of New York Coll of Agriculture and Technology at Cobleskill (NY)
U of the Fraser Valley (BC, Canada)
Utah State U (UT)

PAINTING
Pratt Inst (NY)

PALLIATIVE CARE NURSING
Madonna U (MI)

PARKS, RECREATION AND LEISURE
Dean Coll (MA)
Eastern New Mexico U (NM)
St. Petersburg Coll (FL)

PARKS, RECREATION AND LEISURE FACILITIES MANAGEMENT
State U of New York Coll of Technology at Delhi (NY)

PASTORAL STUDIES/ COUNSELING
Boise Bible Coll (ID)
Central Christian Coll of Kansas (KS)
Inter American U of Puerto Rico, Metropolitan Campus (PR)
North Central U (MN)

PETROLEUM TECHNOLOGY
Mansfield U of Pennsylvania (PA)
U of Pittsburgh at Bradford (PA)

PHARMACY, PHARMACEUTICAL SCIENCES, AND ADMINISTRATION RELATED
EDP U of Puerto Rico–San Sebastian (PR)

PHARMACY TECHNICIAN
Inter American U of Puerto Rico, Aguadilla Campus (PR)
Inter American U of Puerto Rico, Barranquitas Campus (PR)
Inter American U of Puerto Rico, Metropolitan Campus (PR)
Rasmussen Coll Aurora (IL)
Rasmussen Coll Blaine (MN)
Rasmussen Coll Bloomington (MN)
Rasmussen Coll Brooklyn Park (MN)
Rasmussen Coll Eagan (MN)
Rasmussen Coll Fort Myers (FL)
Rasmussen Coll Green Bay (WI)
Rasmussen Coll Kansas City/ Overland Park (KS)
Rasmussen Coll Lake Elmo/ Woodbury (MN)
Rasmussen Coll Land O' Lakes (FL)
Rasmussen Coll Mankato (MN)
Rasmussen Coll Mokena/Tinley Park (IL)
Rasmussen Coll Moorhead (MN)
Rasmussen Coll New Port Richey (FL)
Rasmussen Coll Ocala (FL)
Rasmussen Coll Rockford (IL)
Rasmussen Coll Romeoville/Joliet (IL)
Rasmussen Coll St. Cloud (MN)
Rasmussen Coll Tampa/Brandon (FL)
Rasmussen Coll Topeka (KS)
Rasmussen Coll Wausau (WI)

Sullivan U (KY)

PHILOSOPHY
John Cabot U (Italy)
Ramapo Coll of New Jersey (NJ)
Utah Valley U (UT)

PHILOSOPHY AND RELIGIOUS STUDIES
Bryn Athyn Coll of the New Church (PA)

PHILOSOPHY AND RELIGIOUS STUDIES RELATED
Andrews U (MI)

PHOTOGRAPHY
Andrews U (MI)
Central Christian Coll of Kansas (KS)
Inter American U of Puerto Rico, Bayamón Campus (PR)
Paier Coll of Art, Inc. (CT)
St. Petersburg Coll (FL)

PHYSICAL EDUCATION TEACHING AND COACHING
Central Christian Coll of Kansas (KS)

PHYSICAL FITNESS TECHNICIAN
The U of Findlay (OH)

PHYSICAL SCIENCES
New York City Coll of Technology of the City U of New York (NY)
Roberts Wesleyan Coll (NY)
U of the Fraser Valley (BC, Canada)
Utah Valley U (UT)

PHYSICAL SCIENCES RELATED
State U of New York Empire State Coll (NY)
U of Cincinnati (OH)

PHYSICAL THERAPY
Fairleigh Dickinson U (NJ)

PHYSICAL THERAPY TECHNOLOGY
Arkansas Tech U (AR)
California U of Pennsylvania (PA)
ECPI U, Virginia Beach (VA)
Florida National U (FL)
Keiser U, Fort Lauderdale (FL)
Mount Aloysius Coll (PA)
Nebraska Methodist Coll (NE)
New England Inst of Technology (RI)
New York U (NY)
Penn State Hazleton (PA)
Penn State Shenango (PA)
Polk State Coll (FL)
St. Catherine U (MN)
St. Petersburg Coll (FL)
Southern Illinois U Carbondale (IL)
Southwestern Oklahoma State U (OK)
State U of New York Coll of Technology at Canton (NY)
U of Cincinnati (OH)
U of Maine at Presque Isle (ME)
U of Puerto Ricov at Ponce (PR)
U of Saint Francis (IN)

PHYSICIAN ASSISTANT
Central Christian Coll of Kansas (KS)

PHYSICS
Rogers State U (OK)
U of the Virgin Islands (VI)
U of Wisconsin–Parkside (WI)
Utah Valley U (UT)
York Coll of Pennsylvania (PA)

PIPEFITTING AND SPRINKLER FITTING
New England Inst of Technology (RI)
State U of New York Coll of Technology at Delhi (NY)

PLANT SCIENCES
State U of New York Coll of Agriculture and Technology at Cobleskill (NY)

PLASTICS AND POLYMER ENGINEERING TECHNOLOGY
Ferris State U (MI)
Penn State Erie, The Behrend Coll (PA)

POLITICAL SCIENCE AND GOVERNMENT
John Cabot U (Italy)
Liberty U (VA)
Xavier U (OH)

POULTRY SCIENCE
State U of New York Coll of Agriculture and Technology at Cobleskill (NY)

PRACTICAL NURSING, VOCATIONAL NURSING AND NURSING ASSISTANTS RELATED
Rasmussen Coll Ocala School of Nursing (FL)

PRECISION METAL WORKING RELATED
Montana Technological U (MT)

PRE-DENTISTRY STUDIES
Concordia U Wisconsin (WI)

PRE-ENGINEERING
Columbia Coll (MO)
Newman U (KS)
Siena Heights U (MI)
Utah Valley U (UT)

PRE-LAW STUDIES
Central Christian Coll of Kansas (KS)
Florida National U (FL)
Wayland Baptist U (TX)

PREMEDICAL STUDIES
Concordia U Wisconsin (WI)

PRENURSING STUDIES
Columbia Coll (MO)
Concordia U Wisconsin (WI)
Dean Coll (MA)
Eastern New Mexico U (NM)

PRE-OCCUPATIONAL THERAPY
Webber Intl U (FL)

PRE-PHARMACY STUDIES
Ferris State U (MI)
Madonna U (MI)

PRE-THEOLOGY/PRE-MINISTERIAL STUDIES
Eastern Mennonite U (VA)
Nazarene Bible Coll (CO)
Tabor Coll (KS)

PSYCHOLOGY
Beacon Coll (FL)
Bryn Athyn Coll of the New Church (PA)
Calumet Coll of Saint Joseph (IN)
Central Christian Coll of Kansas (KS)
Central Methodist U (MO)
Dean Coll (MA)
Eastern New Mexico U (NM)
Ferris State U (MI)
Fisher Coll (MA)
Inter American U of Puerto Rico, Metropolitan Campus (PR)
John Cabot U (Italy)
Liberty U (VA)
Life U (GA)
Marian U (IN)
Muhlenberg Coll (PA)
New England Coll (NH)
North Central U (MN)
Regent U (VA)
Siena Heights U (MI)
State U of New York Empire State Coll (NY)
Utah Valley U (UT)
Wright State U (OH)
Wright State U–Lake Campus (OH)
Xavier U (OH)

PSYCHOLOGY TEACHER EDUCATION
Central Christian Coll of Kansas (KS)

PUBLIC ADMINISTRATION
Central Methodist U (MO)
Florida National U (FL)
U of Management and Technology (VA)

PUBLIC ADMINISTRATION AND SOCIAL SERVICE PROFESSIONS RELATED
Trevecca Nazarene U (TN)
The U of Akron (OH)

PUBLIC/APPLIED HISTORY
Tiffin U (OH)

PUBLIC HEALTH
American Public U System (WV)
U of Alaska Fairbanks (AK)
U of Alaska Southeast (AK)

PUBLIC RELATIONS, ADVERTISING, AND APPLIED COMMUNICATION
Lynn U (FL)

PUBLIC RELATIONS, ADVERTISING, AND APPLIED COMMUNICATION RELATED
U of Maine at Presque Isle (ME)

PUBLIC RELATIONS/IMAGE MANAGEMENT
Xavier U (OH)

PURCHASING, PROCUREMENT/ ACQUISITIONS AND CONTRACTS MANAGEMENT
Trevecca Nazarene U (TN)

QUALITY CONTROL AND SAFETY TECHNOLOGIES RELATED
Madonna U (MI)

QUALITY CONTROL TECHNOLOGY
San Jose State U (CA)

RADIATION BIOLOGY
Suffolk U (MA)

RADIATION PROTECTION/ HEALTH PHYSICS TECHNOLOGY
Keiser U, Fort Lauderdale (FL)

RADIO AND TELEVISION
Lawrence Technological U (MI)
U of Northwestern–St. Paul (MN)
Xavier U (OH)

RADIO AND TELEVISION BROADCASTING TECHNOLOGY
New England Inst of Technology (RI)

RADIOLOGIC TECHNOLOGY/ SCIENCE
AdventHealth U (FL)
Allen Coll (IA)
Aultman Coll of Nursing and Health Sciences (OH)
Charles R. Drew U of Medicine and Science (CA)
ECPI U, Virginia Beach (VA)
Fairleigh Dickinson U (NJ)
Florida National U (FL)
Gannon U (PA)
Indiana U Kokomo (IN)
Indiana U Northwest (IN)
Indiana U-Purdue U Indianapolis (IN)
Indiana U South Bend (IN)
Inter American U of Puerto Rico, Aguadilla Campus (PR)
Inter American U of Puerto Rico, Barranquitas Campus (PR)
Lewis-Clark State Coll (ID)
Mansfield U of Pennsylvania (PA)
Mercy Coll of Ohio (OH)
Montana Technological U (MT)
Nebraska Methodist Coll (NE)
Newman U (KS)
Regis Coll (MA)
Sacred Heart U (CT)
St. Petersburg Coll (FL)
Sullivan U (KY)
U of Montana (MT)
U of Saint Francis (IN)
Vermont Tech Coll (VT)
Weber State U (UT)
Widener U (PA)
Xavier U (OH)

RADIO, TELEVISION, AND DIGITAL COMMUNICATION RELATED
Madonna U (MI)

REAL ESTATE
American Public U System (WV)
Columbia Coll (MO)

RECORDING ARTS TECHNOLOGY
Academy of Art U (CA)
Indiana U Bloomington (IN)
Inter American U of Puerto Rico, Bayamón Campus (PR)
Los Angeles Film School (CA)
New England Inst of Technology (RI)

REGIONAL STUDIES
Arkansas Tech U (AR)

REGISTERED NURSING, NURSING ADMINISTRATION, NURSING RESEARCH AND CLINICAL NURSING RELATED
Rasmussen Coll Ocala School of Nursing (FL)

REGISTERED NURSING/ REGISTERED NURSE
Arkansas Tech U (AR)
Aultman Coll of Nursing and Health Sciences (OH)
Bayamón Central U (PR)
Becker Coll (MA)
Bethel U (IN)
California U of Pennsylvania (PA)
Campbellsville U (KY)
Central Christian Coll of Kansas (KS)
Clarion U of Pennsylvania (PA)
Colegio Universitario de San Juan, San Juan (PR)
Columbia Coll (MO)
Eastern Kentucky U (KY)
ECPI U, Virginia Beach (VA)
Excelsior Coll (NY)
Florida National U (FL)
Gwynedd Mercy U (PA)
Inter American U of Puerto Rico, Barranquitas Campus (PR)
Keiser U, Fort Lauderdale (FL)
La Roche U (PA)
Lincoln Memorial U (TN)
Lincoln U (MO)
Lock Haven U of Pennsylvania (PA)
Louisiana Tech U (LA)
Marshall U (WV)
Mercy Coll of Ohio (OH)
Midland Coll (TX)
Midway U (KY)
Morehead State U (KY)
Mount Aloysius Coll (PA)
Mount Saint Mary's U (CA)
New England Inst of Technology (RI)
New York City Coll of Technology of the City U of New York (NY)
Northwestern State U of Louisiana (LA)
Penn State Altoona (PA)
Penn State Berks (PA)
Penn State Erie, The Behrend Coll (PA)
Polk State Coll (FL)
Regis Coll (MA)
Sacred Heart U (CT)
St. Petersburg Coll (FL)
Southern Arkansas U–Magnolia (AR)
Southwest Baptist U (MO)
State U of New York Coll of Technology at Canton (NY)
State U of New York Coll of Technology at Delhi (NY)
Troy U (AL)
Universidad Adventista de las Antillas (PR)
U of Arkansas at Little Rock (AR)
U of Charleston (WV)
U of Montana (MT)
U of Pikeville (KY)
U of Pittsburgh at Bradford (PA)
U of Saint Francis (IN)
U of South Dakota (SD)
The U of West Alabama (AL)
Utah State U (UT)
Utah Valley U (UT)
Valencia Coll (FL)
Vermont Tech Coll (VT)
Weber State U (UT)
Western Kentucky U (KY)
Western New Mexico U (NM)

RELIGIOUS EDUCATION
Boise Bible Coll (ID)
Dallas Baptist U (TX)
Marian U (IN)
Nazarene Bible Coll (CO)

RELIGIOUS/SACRED MUSIC
The Baptist Coll of Florida (FL)
Boise Bible Coll (ID)
Central Christian Coll of Kansas (KS)
Mount Vernon Nazarene U (OH)
North Central U (MN)
Ohio Christian U (OH)
Southeastern U (FL)
Trevecca Nazarene U (TN)

RELIGIOUS STUDIES
Boise Bible Coll (ID)
Bryn Athyn Coll of the New Church (PA)
Campbellsville U (KY)
Central Christian Coll of Kansas (KS)
Holy Apostles Coll and Sem (CT)
Inter American U of Puerto Rico, Metropolitan Campus (PR)
Liberty U (VA)
Madonna U (MI)
Mount Marty Coll (SD)
Mount Vernon Nazarene U (OH)
Northwest U (WA)
Oakland City U (IN)
Xavier U (OH)

RESORT MANAGEMENT
State U of New York Coll of Technology at Delhi (NY)

RESPIRATORY CARE THERAPY
Clarion U of Pennsylvania (PA)
Dakota State U (SD)
Ferris State U (MI)
Florida National U (FL)
Gannon U (PA)
Gwynedd Mercy U (PA)
Keiser U, Fort Lauderdale (FL)
Mansfield U of Pennsylvania (PA)
Midland Coll (TX)
Missouri Southern State U (MO)
Molloy Coll (NY)
Morehead State U (KY)
Nebraska Methodist Coll (NE)
New England Inst of Technology (RI)
Newman U (KS)
New York U (NY)
Polk State Coll (FL)
St. Petersburg Coll (FL)
Sullivan U (KY)
Universidad Adventista de las Antillas (PR)
U of Montana (MT)
U of Southern Indiana (IN)
Valencia Coll (FL)
Vermont Tech Coll (VT)
Weber State U (UT)
York Coll of Pennsylvania (PA)

RESPIRATORY THERAPY TECHNICIAN
Florida National U (FL)
Keiser U, Fort Lauderdale (FL)
U of the Incarnate Word (TX)

RESTAURANT, CULINARY, AND CATERING MANAGEMENT
Ferris State U (MI)
St. Petersburg Coll (FL)
State U of New York Coll of Agriculture and Technology at Cobleskill (NY)
State U of New York Coll of Technology at Delhi (NY)

RESTAURANT/FOOD SERVICES MANAGEMENT
American Public U System (WV)
The U of Akron (OH)
Valencia Coll (FL)

RETAILING
American Public U System (WV)
The U of Findlay (OH)
Weber State U (UT)

RHETORIC AND COMPOSITION
Ferris State U (MI)

ROBOTICS TECHNOLOGY
New England Inst of Technology (RI)
Utah Valley U (UT)

SALES AND MARKETING/ MARKETING AND DISTRIBUTION TEACHER EDUCATION
Central Christian Coll of Kansas (KS)

SALES, DISTRIBUTION, AND MARKETING OPERATIONS
Inter American U of Puerto Rico, Aguadilla Campus (PR)
Sullivan U (KY)

SCIENCE TEACHER EDUCATION
Central Christian Coll of Kansas (KS)
Wright State U (OH)
Wright State U–Lake Campus (OH)

SCIENCE TECHNOLOGIES RELATED
Madonna U (MI)
Ohio Valley U (WV)
State U of New York Coll of Agriculture and Technology at Cobleskill (NY)
U of Alaska Fairbanks (AK)
U of Alaska Southeast (AK)

SECONDARY EDUCATION
Central Christian Coll of Kansas (KS)
Ferris State U (MI)
Rogers State U (OK)

SECURITIES SERVICES ADMINISTRATION
Dean Coll (MA)

SELLING SKILLS AND SALES
Inter American U of Puerto Rico, San Germán Campus (PR)
The U of Akron (OH)

SIGN LANGUAGE INTERPRETATION AND TRANSLATION
Mount Aloysius Coll (PA)
North Central U (MN)
St. Catherine U (MN)
U of Arkansas at Little Rock (AR)

SMALL BUSINESS ADMINISTRATION
Lewis-Clark State Coll (ID)
The U of Akron (OH)

SOCIAL PSYCHOLOGY
Central Christian Coll of Kansas (KS)

SOCIAL SCIENCES
Campbellsville U (KY)
Central Christian Coll of Kansas (KS)
Marymount Manhattan Coll (NY)
Rogers State U (OK)
State U of New York Empire State Coll (NY)
Trine U (IN)
U of Cincinnati (OH)
U of Puerto Ricov at Ponce (PR)
U of Southern Indiana (IN)
Valparaiso U (IN)
Wayland Baptist U (TX)

SOCIAL SCIENCES RELATED
U of Wisconsin–Parkside (WI)

SOCIAL SCIENCE TEACHER EDUCATION
Central Christian Coll of Kansas (KS)
Montana State U (MT)

SOCIAL STUDIES TEACHER EDUCATION
Central Christian Coll of Kansas (KS)

SOCIAL WORK
Central Christian Coll of Kansas (KS)
Ferris State U (MI)
State U of New York Coll of Agriculture and Technology at Cobleskill (NY)
U of the Fraser Valley (BC, Canada)
Youngstown State U (OH)

SOCIAL WORK RELATED
The U of Akron (OH)

SOCIOLOGY
Andrews U (MI)
Central Christian Coll of Kansas (KS)
Dean Coll (MA)
New England Coll (NH)
South Dakota State U (SD)
U of California, San Diego (CA)
The U of Scranton (PA)
Wright State U (OH)
Wright State U–Lake Campus (OH)
Xavier U (OH)

SPANISH
Weber State U (UT)
Xavier U (OH)

SPECIAL EDUCATION
U of Maine at Presque Isle (ME)

SPECIAL EDUCATION–INDIVIDUALS WHO ARE DEVELOPMENTALLY DELAYED
Saint Mary-of-the-Woods Coll (IN)

SPECIAL EDUCATION RELATED
Minot State U (ND)

SPEECH COMMUNICATION AND RHETORIC
American Public U System (WV)
Dean Coll (MA)
New Charter U (UT)
State U of New York Coll of Agriculture and Technology at Cobleskill (NY)
Taylor U (IN)
Tiffin U (OH)
Trevecca Nazarene U (TN)
Utah Valley U (UT)
Weber State U (UT)
Wright State U (OH)
Wright State U–Lake Campus (OH)

SPEECH-LANGUAGE PATHOLOGY
Elms Coll (MA)

SPEECH TEACHER EDUCATION
Central Christian Coll of Kansas (KS)

SPORT AND FITNESS ADMINISTRATION/ MANAGEMENT
Central Christian Coll of Kansas (KS)
Dean Coll (MA)
Keiser U, Fort Lauderdale (FL)
Mount Vernon Nazarene U (OH)
State U of New York Coll of Technology at Delhi (NY)
Webber Intl U (FL)
William Paterson U of New Jersey (NJ)

STATISTICS
South Dakota State U (SD)

STRATEGIC STUDIES
U of Wisconsin–Parkside (WI)

SUBSTANCE ABUSE/ ADDICTION COUNSELING
Midland Coll (TX)
National U (CA)
St. Petersburg Coll (FL)
U of Providence (MT)

SURGICAL TECHNOLOGY
ECPI U, Virginia Beach (VA)
Keiser U, Fort Lauderdale (FL)
Mount Aloysius Coll (PA)
Nebraska Methodist Coll (NE)
New England Inst of Technology (RI)
Rasmussen Coll Brooklyn Park (MN)
Rasmussen Coll St. Cloud (MN)
Sentara Coll of Health Sciences (VA)
Sullivan U (KY)
The U of Akron (OH)
U of Montana (MT)
U of Providence (MT)
U of Saint Francis (IN)
Utah State U (UT)

SURVEYING TECHNOLOGY
Glenville State Coll (WV)
Penn State Wilkes-Barre (PA)
Polytechnic U of Puerto Rico (PR)
The U of Akron (OH)
Utah Valley U (UT)

SUSTAINABILITY STUDIES
Lock Haven U of Pennsylvania (PA)

SYSTEM, NETWORKING, AND LAN/WAN MANAGEMENT
Dakota State U (SD)
Midland Coll (TX)

TEACHER ASSISTANT/AIDE
Alverno Coll (WI)
Eastern Mennonite U (VA)
Johnson U (TN)
New York U (NY)
Saint Mary-of-the-Woods Coll (IN)
State U of New York Coll of Agriculture and Technology at Cobleskill (NY)
U of Maine at Presque Isle (ME)
Valparaiso U (IN)

TELECOMMUNICATIONS TECHNOLOGY
New York City Coll of Technology of the City U of New York (NY)
Penn State Hazleton (PA)
Penn State New Kensington (PA)
Penn State Schuylkill (PA)
Penn State Shenango (PA)
Penn State Wilkes-Barre (PA)
Penn State York (PA)

TERRORISM AND COUNTERTERRORISM OPERATIONS
American Public U System (WV)

THEATER DESIGN AND TECHNOLOGY
Utah Valley U (UT)

THEOLOGICAL AND MINISTERIAL STUDIES RELATED
Boise Bible Coll (ID)
California Christian Coll (CA)
Northwest U (WA)

THEOLOGY
Central Christian Coll of Kansas (KS)
Creighton U (NE)
Holy Apostles Coll and Sem (CT)
Mid-America Baptist Theological Sem (TN)
Ohio Dominican U (OH)

THEOLOGY AND RELIGIOUS VOCATIONS RELATED
Boise Bible Coll (ID)
Trevecca Nazarene U (TN)

TOOL AND DIE TECHNOLOGY
Ferris State U (MI)

TOURISM AND TRAVEL SERVICES MANAGEMENT
Black Hills State U (SD)

TOURISM AND TRAVEL SERVICES MARKETING
State U of New York Coll of Agriculture and Technology at Cobleskill (NY)
State U of New York Coll of Technology at Delhi (NY)

TRADE AND INDUSTRIAL TEACHER EDUCATION
Eastern Kentucky U (KY)
Murray State U (KY)

TRANSPORTATION/MOBILITY MANAGEMENT
Polk State Coll (FL)

TURF AND TURFGRASS MANAGEMENT
State U of New York Coll of Technology at Delhi (NY)
U of Massachusetts Amherst (MA)

URBAN MINISTRY
Tabor Coll (KS)

VETERINARY/ANIMAL HEALTH TECHNOLOGY
Becker Coll (MA)
Lincoln Memorial U (TN)
Morehead State U (KY)
New England Inst of Technology (RI)
Northwestern State U of Louisiana (LA)
St. Petersburg Coll (FL)
State U of New York Coll of Technology at Canton (NY)
State U of New York Coll of Technology at Delhi (NY)
U of New Hampshire (NH)
Utah State U (UT)
Vermont Tech Coll (VT)

WEAPONS OF MASS DESTRUCTION
American Public U System (WV)

WEB/MULTIMEDIA MANAGEMENT AND WEBMASTER
American Public U System (WV)
Lewis-Clark State Coll (ID)
Montana Technological U (MT)
St. Petersburg Coll (FL)
Tiffin U (OH)

WEB PAGE, DIGITAL/ MULTIMEDIA AND INFORMATION RESOURCES DESIGN
Academy of Art U (CA)
Beacon Coll (FL)
Dakota State U (SD)
Florida National U (FL)
Limestone Coll (SC)
New England Inst of Technology (RI)
Polk State Coll (FL)
Rasmussen Coll Aurora (IL)
Rasmussen Coll Blaine (MN)
Rasmussen Coll Bloomington (MN)
Rasmussen Coll Brooklyn Park (MN)
Rasmussen Coll Eagan (MN)
Rasmussen Coll Fargo (ND)
Rasmussen Coll Fort Myers (FL)
Rasmussen Coll Green Bay (WI)
Rasmussen Coll Kansas City/ Overland Park (KS)
Rasmussen Coll Lake Elmo/ Woodbury (MN)
Rasmussen Coll Land O' Lakes (FL)
Rasmussen Coll Mankato (MN)
Rasmussen Coll Mokena/Tinley Park (IL)
Rasmussen Coll Moorhead (MN)
Rasmussen Coll New Port Richey (FL)
Rasmussen Coll Ocala (FL)
Rasmussen Coll Romeoville/Joliet (IL)
Rasmussen Coll St. Cloud (MN)
Rasmussen Coll Tampa/Brandon (FL)
Rasmussen Coll Topeka (KS)
Rasmussen Coll Wausau (WI)
St. Petersburg Coll (FL)
Sullivan U (KY)
Utah Valley U (UT)
Weber State U (UT)

WELDING ENGINEERING TECHNOLOGY
New England Inst of Technology (RI)

WELDING TECHNOLOGY
Arkansas Tech U (AR)
Ferris State U (MI)
Lewis-Clark State Coll (ID)
Midland Coll (TX)
State U of New York Coll of Technology at Delhi (NY)
U of Montana (MT)
Utah State U (UT)
Western New Mexico U (NM)

WILDLIFE BIOLOGY
Central Christian Coll of Kansas (KS)

WILDLIFE, FISH AND WILDLANDS SCIENCE AND MANAGEMENT
State U of New York Coll of Agriculture and Technology at Cobleskill (NY)

YOUTH MINISTRY
Central Christian Coll of Kansas (KS)
Johnson U Florida (FL)

ZOOLOGY/ANIMAL BIOLOGY
Central Christian Coll of Kansas (KS)

Alphabetical Listing of Two-Year Colleges

NOTES

NOTES

NOTES

NOTES

NOTES

NOTES

NOTES

NOTES